Everyday
ITALIAN
Dictionary

Everyday
ITALIAN
Dictionary

English-Italian
Italian-English

New York   Chicago   San Francisco   Lisbon   London   Madrid   Mexico City
Milan   New Delhi   San Juan   Seoul   Singapore   Sydney   Toronto

The *McGraw·Hill* Companies

Copyright © HarperCollins Publishers Ltd. 2009. All rights reserved. Printed in the United States of America. Except as permitted under the United States Copyright Act of 1976, no part of this publication may be reproduced or distributed in any form or by any means, or stored in a database or retrieval system, without the prior written permission of the publisher.

1 2 3 4 5 6 7 8 9 10 11 12 13 14 15   QFR/QFR   1 9 8 7 6 5 4 3 2 1

ISBN   978-0-07-176881-8
MHID   0-07-176881-5

Library of Congress Cataloging-in-Publication Data

Everyday Italian dictionary.
          p.   cm.
        ISBN 0-07-176881-5 (alk. paper)
        1. Italian language—Dictionaries—English.   I. HarperCollins (Firm).

    PC1640.E93   2011
    453'.21—dc22   2011015835

McGraw-Hill books are available at special quantity discounts to use as premiums and sales promotions or for use in corporate training programs. To contact a representative, please e-mail us at bulksales@mcgraw-hill.com.

This book is printed on acid-free paper.

INDICE

CONTENTS

I marchi registrati

I termini che a nostro parere costituiscono un marchio registrato sono stati designati come tali. In ogni caso, né la presenza né l'assenza di tale designazione implicano alcuna valutazione del loro reale stato giuridico.

Note on trademarks

Entered words that we have reason to believe constitute trademarks have been designated as such. However, neither the presence nor the absence of such designation should be regarded as affecting the legal status of any trademark.

ABBREVIAZIONI

ABBREVIATIONS

abbreviazione	*abbr*	abbreviation
aggettivo	*adj*	adjective
amministrazione	*Admin*	administration
avverbio	*adv*	adverb
aeronautica, viaggi aerei	*Aer*	flying, air travel
aggettivo	*ag*	adjective
agricoltura	*Agr*	agriculture
amministrazione	*Amm*	administration
anatomia	*Anat*	anatomy
architettura	*Archit*	architecture
articolo determinativo	*art def*	definite article
articolo indeterminativo	*art indef*	indefinite article
attributivo	*attrib*	attributive
ausiliare	*aus, aux*	auxiliary
automobile	*Aut*	motor car and motoring
avverbio	*av*	adverb
aeronautica, viaggi aerei	*Aviat*	flying, air travel
biologia	*Biol*	biology
botanica	*Bot*	botany
inglese britannico	*BRIT*	British English
consonante	C	consonant
chimica	*Chim, Chem*	chemistry
commercio, finanza	*Comm*	commerce, finance
comparativo	*compar*	comparative
informatica	*Comput*	computing
congiunzione	*cong, conj*	conjunction
edilizia	*Constr*	building
sostantivo usato come aggettivo, ma mai con funzione predicativa	*cpd*	compound element: noun used as adjective and which cannot follow the noun it qualifies
cucina	*Cuc, Culin*	cookery
davanti a	*dav*	before

ABBREVIAZIONI		ABBREVIATIONS
articolo determinativo	*def art*	definite article
determinativo; articolo, aggettivo dimostrativo o indefinito ecc	*det*	determiner: article, demonstrative etc
diminutivo	*dimin*	diminutive
diritto	*Dir*	law
economia	*Econ*	economics
edilizia	*Edil*	building
elettricità, elettronica	*Elettr, Elec*	electricity, electronics
esclamazione	*escl, excl*	exclamation
femminile	*f*	feminine
familiare (! da evitare)	*fam(!)*	colloquial usage (! particularly offensive)
ferrovia	*Ferr*	railways
senso figurato	*fig*	figurative use
fisiologia	*Fisiol*	physiology
fotografia	*Fot*	photography
verbo inglese la cui particella è inseparabile dal verbo	*fus*	(phrasal verb) where the particle cannot be separated from the main verb
nella maggior parte dei sensi; generalmente	*gen*	in most or all senses; generally
geografia, geologia	*Geo*	geography, geology
geometria	*Geom*	geometry
storia, storico	*Hist*	history, historical
impersonale	*impers*	impersonal
articolo indeterminativo	*indef art*	indefinite article
familiare (! da evitare)	*inf(!)*	colloquial usage (! particularly offensive)
infinito	*infin*	infinitive
informatica	*Inform*	computing

ABBREVIAZIONI		ABBREVIATIONS
insegnamento, sistema scolastico e universitario	*Ins*	schooling, schools and universities
invariabile	*inv*	invariable
irreqolare	*irreg*	irregular
grammatica, linguistica	*Ling*	grammar, linguistics
maschile	*m*	masculine
matematica	*Mat(h)*	mathematics
termine medico, medicina	*Med*	medical term, medicine
il tempo, meteorologia	*Meteor*	the weather, meteorology
maschile o femminile	*m/f*	masculine or feminine
esercito, linguaggio militare	*Mil*	military matters
musica	*Mus*	music
sostantivo	*n*	noun
nautica	*Naut*	sailing, navigation
numerale (aggettivo, sostantivo)	*num*	numeral adjective or noun
	o.s.	oneself
peggiorativo	*peg*, *pej*	derogatory, pejorative
fotografia	*Phot*	photography
fisiologia	*Physiol*	physiology
plurale	*pl*	plural
politica	*Pol*	politics
participio passato	*pp*	past participle
preposizione	*prep*	preposition
pronome	*pron*	pronoun
psicologia, psichiatria	*Psic*, *Psych*	psychology, psychiatry
tempo passato	*pt*	past tense
qualcosa	*qc*	
qualcuno	*qn*	
religione, liturgia	*Rel*	religions, church service
sostantivo	*s*	noun
	sb	somebody

ABBREVIAZIONI		ABBREVIATIONS
insegnamento, sistema scolastico e universitario	*Scol*	schooling, schools and universities
singolare	*sg*	singular
soggetto (grammaticale)	*sog*	(grammatical) subject
	sth	something
congiuntivo	*sub*	subjunctive
soggetto (grammaticale)	*subj*	(grammatical) subject
superlativo	*superl*	superlative
termine tecnico, tecnologia	*Tecn, Tech*	technical term, technology
telecomunicazioni	*Tel*	telecommunications
tipografia	*Tip*	typography, printing
televisione	*TV*	television
tipografia	*Typ*	typography, printing
università	*Univ*	university
inglese americano	*US*	American English
vocale	*V*	vowel
verbo	*vb*	verb
verbo o gruppo verbale con funzione intransitiva	*vi*	verb or phrasal verb used intransitively
verbo pronominale o riflessivo	*vpr*	pronominal or reflexive verb
verbo o gruppo verbale con funzione transitiva	*vt*	verb or phrasal verb used transitively
zoologia	*Zool*	zoology
marchio registrato	®	registered trademark
introduce un'equivalenza culturale	≈	introduces a cultural equivalent

TRASCRIZIONE FONETICA

Consonanti		Consonants
NB **p, b, t, d, k, g** sono seguite da un'aspirazione in inglese.		NB **p, b, t, d, k, g** are not aspirated in Italian.

padre	p	**p**uppy
bambino	b	**b**a**b**y
tu**tt**o	t	**t**en**t**
da**d**o	d	**d**a**dd**y
cane **ch**e	k	**c**ork **k**iss **ch**ord
gola **gh**iro	g	**g**a**g** **g**uess
sano	s	**s**o rice ki**ss**
svago e**s**ame	z	cou**s**in bu**zz**
scena	ʃ	**sh**eep **s**ugar
	ʒ	plea**s**ure bei**ge**
pe**c**e lan**ci**are	tʃ	**ch**urch
giro **gi**oco	dʒ	**j**u**dge** **g**eneral
a**f**a **f**aro	f	**f**arm ra**ff**le
vero bra**v**o	v	**v**ery re**v**
	θ	**th**in ma**th**s
	ð	**th**at o**th**er
le**tt**o a**l**a	l	**l**itt**l**e ball
gli	ʎ	mi**lli**on
rete a**r**co	r	**r**at **r**are
ramo ma**d**re	m	**m**u**mm**y co**mb**
no fuma**n**te	n	**n**o ra**n**
gnomo	ɲ	ca**ny**on
	ŋ	si**ng**i**ng** ba**n**k
	h	**h**at re**h**eat
bu**i**o p**i**acere	j	**y**et
uomo g**u**aio	w	**w**all be**w**ail
	x	lo**ch**

Varie		Miscellaneous
per l'inglese: la "r" finale viene pronunciata se seguita da una vocale	r	
precede la sillaba accentata	'	precedes the stressed syllable

PHONETIC TRANSCRIPTION

Vocali		Vowels
NB La messa in equivalenza di certi suoni indica solo una rassomiglianza approssimativa.		NB The pairing of some vowel sounds only indicates approximate equivalence.
vino idea	i iː	heel bead
	ɪ	hit pity
stella edera	e	
epoca eccetto	ɛ	set tent
mamma amore	a æ	bat apple
	ɑː	after car calm
	ɑ̃	fiancé
	ʌ	fun cousin
müsli	y	
	ə	over above
	əː	urn fern work
rosa occhio	ɔ	wash pot
	ɔː	born cork
ponte ognuno	o	
föhn	ø	
utile zucca	u	full soot
	uː	boon lewd

Dittonghi		Diphthongs
	ɪə	beer tier
	ɛə	tear fair there
	eɪ	date plaice day
	aɪ	life buy cry
	au	owl foul now
	əu	low no
	ɔɪ	boil boy oily
	uə	poor tour

ITALIAN PRONUNCIATION

Vowels

Where the vowel **e** or the vowel **o** appears in a stressed syllable it can be either open [ɛ], [ɔ] or closed [e], [o]. As the open or closed pronunciation of these vowels is subject to regional variation, the distinction is of little importance to the user of this dictionary. Phonetic transcription for headwords containing these vowels will therefore only appear where other pronunciation difficulties are present.

Consonants

c before "e" or "i" is pronounced like the "*tch*" in match.
ch is pronounced like the "*k*" in "kit".
g before "e" or "i" is pronounced like the "*j*" in "jet".
gh is pronounced like the "*g*" in "get".
gl before "e" or "i" is normally pronounced like the "*lli*" in "million", and in a few cases only like the "*gl*" in "glove".
gn is pronounced like the "*ny*" in "canyon"
sc before "e" or "i" is pronounced "*sh*".
z is pronounced like the "*ts*" in "stetson", or like the "*d's*" in "bird's-eye".

Headwords containing the above consonants and consonantal groups have been given full phonetic transcription in this dictionary.

NB All double written consonants in Italian are fully sounded: e.g. the *tt* in "tutto" is pronounced as in "hat trick".

ITALIAN VERB FORMS

1 Gerundio **2** Participio passato **3** Presente **4** Imperfetto **5** Passato remoto **6** Futuro **7** Condizionale **8** Congiuntivo presente **9** Congiuntivo passato **10** Imperativo

andare 3 vado, vai, va, andiamo, andate, vanno **6** andrò *ecc.* **8** vada **10** va'!, vada!, andate!, vadano!

apparire 2 apparso **3** appaio, appari *o* apparisci, appare *o* apparisce, appaiono *o* appariscono **5** apparvi *o* apparsi, apparisti, apparve *o* apparì *o* apparse, apparvero *o* apparirono *o* apparsero **8** appaia *o* apparisca

aprire 2 aperto **3** apro **5** aprii, apristi **8** apra

AVERE 3 ho, hai, ha, abbiamo, avete, hanno **5** ebbi, avesti, ebbe, avemmo, aveste, ebbero **6** avrò *ecc.* **8** abbia *ecc.* **10** abbi!, abbia!, abbiate!, abbiano!

bere 1 bevendo **2** bevuto **3** bevo *ecc.* **4** bevevo *ecc.* **5** bevvi *o* bevetti, bevesti **6** berrò *ecc.* **8** beva *ecc.* **9** bevessi *ecc.*

cadere 5 caddi, cadesti **6** cadrò *ecc.*

cogliere 2 colto **3** colgo, colgono **5** colsi, cogliesti **8** colga

correre 2 corso **5** corsi, corresti

cuocere 2 cotto **3** cuocio, cociamo, cuociono **5** cossi, cocesti

dare 3 do, dai, dà, diamo, date, danno **5** diedi *o* detti, desti **6** darò *ecc.* **8** dia *ecc.* **9** dessi *ecc.* **10** da'!, dai!, date!, diano!

dire 1 dicendo **2** detto **3** dico, dici, dice, diciamo, dite, dicono **4** dicevo *ecc.* **5** dissi, dicesti **6** dirò *ecc.* **8** dica, diciamo, diciate, dicano **9** dicessi *ecc.* **10** di'!, dica!, dite!, dicano!

dolere 3 dolgo, duoli, duole, dolgono **5** dolsi, dolesti **6** dorrò *ecc.* **8** dolga

dovere 3 devo *o* debbo, devi, deve, dobbiamo, dovete, devono *o* debbono **6** dovrò *ecc.* **8** debba, dobbiamo, dobbiate, devano *o* debbano

ESSERE 2 stato **3** sono, sei, è, siamo, siete, sono **4** ero, eri, era, eravamo, eravate, erano **5** fui, fosti, fu, fummo, foste, furono **6** sarò *ecc.* **8** sia *ecc.* **9** fossi, fossi, fosse, fossimo, foste, fossero **10** sii!, sia!, siate!, siano!

fare 1 facendo **2** fatto **3** faccio, fai, fa, facciamo, fate, fanno **4** facevo *ecc.* **5** feci, facesti **6** farò *ecc.* **8** faccia *ecc.* **9** facessi *ecc.* **10** fa'!, faccia!, fate!, facciano!

FINIRE 1 finendo **2** finito **3** finisco, finisci, finisce, finiamo, finite, finiscono **4** finivo, finivi, finiva, finivamo, finivate, finivano **5** finii, finisti, finì, finimmo, finiste, finirono **6** finirò, finirai, finirà, finiremo, finirete, finiranno **7** finirei, finiresti, finirebbe, finiremmo, finireste, finirebbero **8** finisca, finisca, finisca, finiamo, finiate, finiscano **9** finissi, finissi, finisse, finissimo, finiste, finissero **10** finisci!, finisca!, finite!, finiscano!

giungere 2 giunto **5** giunsi, giungesti

leggere 2 letto **5** lessi, leggesti

mettere 2 messo **5** misi, mettesti

morire 2 morto **3** muoio, muori, muore, moriamo, morite, muoiono **6** morirò *o* morrò *ecc.* **8** muoia

muovere 2 mosso **5** mossi, movesti

nascere 2 nato **5** nacqui, nascesti

nuocere 2 nuociuto **3** nuoccio, nuoci, nuoce, nociamo *o* nuociamo, nuocete, nuocciono **4** nuocevo *ecc.* **5** nocqui, nuocesti **6** nuocerò *ecc.* **7** nuoccia

offrire 2 offerto **3** offro **5** offersi *o* offrii, offristi **8** offra

parere 2 parso **3** paio, paiamo, paiono **5** parvi *o* parsi, paresti **6** parrò *ecc.* **8** paia, paiamo, paiate, paiano

PARLARE 1 parlando 2 parlato 3 parlo, parli, parla, parliamo, parlate, parlano 4 parlavo, parlavi, parlava, parlavamo, parlavate, parlavano 5 parlai, parlasti, parlò, parlammo, parlaste, parlarono 6 parlerò, parlerai, parlerà, parleremo, parlerete, parleranno 7 parlerei, parleresti, parlerebbe, parleremmo, parlereste, parlerebbero 8 parli, parli, parli, parliamo, parliate, parlino 9 parlassi, parlassi, parlasse, parlassimo, parlaste, parlassero 10 parla!, parli!, parlate!, parlino!

piacere 2 piaciuto 3 piaccio, piacciamo, piacciono 5 piacqui, piacesti 8 piacci ecc.

porre 1 ponendo 2 posto 3 pongo, poni, pone, poniamo, ponete, pongono 4 ponevo ecc. 5 posi, ponesti 6 porrò ecc. 8 ponga, poniamo, poniate, pongano 9 ponessi ecc.

potere 3 posso, puoi, può, possiamo, potete, possono 6 potrò ecc. 8 possa, possiamo, possiate, possano

prendere 2 preso 5 presi, prendesti

ridurre 1 riducendo 2 ridotto 3 riduco ecc. 4 riducevo ecc. 5 ridussi, riducesti 6 ridurrò ecc. 8 riduca ecc. 9 riducessi ecc.

riempire 1 riempiendo 3 riempio, riempi, riempie, riempiono

rimanere 2 rimasto 3 rimango, rimangono 5 rimasi, rimanesti 6 rimarrò ecc. 8 rimanga

rispondere 2 risposto 5 risposi, rispondesti

salire 3 salgo, sali, salgono 8 salga

sapere 3 so, sai, sa, sappiamo, sapete, sanno 5 seppi, sapesti 6 saprò ecc. 8 sappia ecc. 10 sappi!, sappia!, sappiate!, sappiano!

scrivere 2 scritto 5 scrissi, scrivesti

sedere 3 siedo, siedi, siede, siedono 8 sieda

spegnere 2 spento 3 spengo, spengono 5 spensi, spegnesti 8 spenga

stare 2 stato 3 sto, stai, sta, stiamo, state, stanno 5 stetti, stesti 6 starò ecc. 8 stia ecc. 9 stessi ecc. 10 sta'!, stia!, state!, stiano!

tacere 2 taciuto 3 taccio, tacciono 5 tacqui, tacesti 8 taccia

tenere 3 tengo, tieni, tiene, tengono 5 tenni, tenesti 6 terrò ecc. 8 tenga

trarre 1 traendo 2 tratto 3 traggo, trai, trae, traiamo, traete, traggono 4 traevo ecc. 5 trassi, traesti 6 trarrò ecc. 8 tragga 9 traessi ecc.

udire 3 odo, odi, ode, odono 8 oda

uscire 3 esco, esci, esce, escono 8 esca

valere 2 valso 3 valgo, valgono 5 valsi, valesti 6 varrò ecc. 8 valga

vedere 2 visto o veduto 5 vidi, vedesti 6 vedrò ecc.

VENDERE 1 vendendo 2 venduto 3 vendo, vendi, vende, vendiamo, vendete, vendono 4 vendevo, vendevi, vendeva, vendevamo, vendevate, vendevano 5 vendei o vendetti, vendesti, vendé o vendette, vendemmo, vendeste, venderono o vendettero 6 venderò, venderai, venderà, venderemo, venderete, venderanno 7 venderei, venderesti, venderebbe, venderemmo, vendereste, venderebbero 8 venda, venda, venda, vendiamo, vendiate, vendano 9 vendessi, vendessi, vendesse, vendessimo, vendeste, vendessero 10 vendi!, venda!, vendete!, vendano!

venire 2 venuto 3 vengo, vieni, viene, vengono 5 venni, venisti 6 verrò ecc. 8 venga

vivere 2 vissuto 5 vissi, vivesti

volere 3 voglio, vuoi, vuole, vogliamo, volete, vogliono 5 volli, volesti 6 vorrò ecc. 8 voglia ecc. 10 vogli!, voglia!, vogliate!, vogliano!

ENGLISH VERB FORMS

present	pt	pp
arise	arose	arisen
awake	awoke	awoken
be (am, is,	was, were	been
are; being)		
bear	bore	born(e)
beat	beat	beaten
become	became	become
begin	began	begun
bend	bent	bent
bet	bet,	bet,
	betted	betted
bid (at auction,	bid	bid
cards)		
bid (say)	bade	bidden
bind	bound	bound
bite	bit	bitten
bleed	bled	bled
blow	blew	blown
break	broke	broken
breed	bred	bred
bring	brought	brought
build	built	built
burn	burnt,	burnt,
	burned	burned
burst	burst	burst
buy	bought	bought
can	could	(been able)
cast	cast	cast
catch	caught	caught
choose	chose	chosen
cling	clung	clung
come	came	come
cost	cost	cost
cost (work	costed	costed
out price of)		
creep	crept	crept
cut	cut	cut
deal	dealt	dealt
dig	dug	dug
do (does)	did	done
draw	drew	drawn
dream	dreamed,	dreamed,
	dreamt	dreamt
drink	drank	drunk
drive	drove	driven
dwell	dwelt	dwelt
eat	ate	eaten
fall	fell	fallen

present	pt	pp
feed	fed	fed
feel	felt	felt
fight	fought	fought
find	found	found
flee	fled	fled
fling	flung	flung
fly	flew	flown
forbid	forbade	forbidden
forecast	forecast	forecast
forget	forgot	forgotten
forgive	forgave	forgiven
forsake	forsook	forsaken
freeze	froze	frozen
get	got	got, (US)
		gotten
give	gave	given
go (goes)	went	gone
grind	ground	ground
grow	grew	grown
hang	hung	hung
hang (execute)	hanged	hanged
have (has;	had	had
having)		
hear	heard	heard
hide	hid	hidden
hit	hit	hit
hold	held	held
hurt	hurt	hurt
keep	kept	kept
kneel	knelt,	knelt,
	kneeled	kneeled
know	knew	known
lay	laid	laid
lead	led	led
lean	leant,	leant,
	leaned	leaned
leap	leapt,	leapt,
	leaped	leaped
learn	learnt,	learnt,
	learned	learned
leave	left	left
lend	lent	lent
let	let	let
lie (lying)	lay	lain
light	lit,	lit,
	lighted	lighted
lose	lost	lost
make	made	made

present	pt	pp	present	pt	pp
may	might	—	spell	spelt,	spelt,
mean	meant	meant		spelled	spelled
meet	met	met	spend	spent	spent
mistake	mistook	mistaken	spill	spilt,	spilt,
mow	mowed	mown,		spilled	spilled
		mowed	spin	spun	spun
must	(had to)	(had to)	spit	spat	spat
pay	paid	paid	split	split	split
put	put	put	spoil	spoiled,	spoiled,
quit	quit,	quit,		spoilt	spoilt
	quitted	quitted	spread	spread	spread
read	read	read	spring	sprang	sprung
rid	rid	rid	stand	stood	stood
ride	rode	ridden	steal	stole	stolen
ring	rang	rung	stick	stuck	stuck
rise	rose	risen	sting	stung	stung
run	ran	run	stink	stank	stunk
saw	sawed	sawed,	stride	strode	stridden
		sawn	strike	struck	struck,
say	said	said			stricken
see	saw	seen	strive	strove	striven
seek	sought	sought	swear	swore	sworn
sell	sold	sold	sweep	swept	swept
send	sent	sent	swell	swelled	swollen,
set	set	set			swelled
sew	sewed	sewn	swim	swam	swum
shake	shook	shaken	swing	swung	swung
shear	sheared	shorn,	take	took	taken
		sheared	teach	taught	taught
shed	shed	shed	tear	tore	torn
shine	shone	shone	tell	told	told
shoot	shot	shot	think	thought	thought
show	showed	shown	throw	threw	thrown
shrink	shrank	shrunk	thrust	thrust	thrust
shut	shut	shut	tread	trod	trodden
sing	sang	sung	wake	woke,	woken,
sink	sank	sunk		waked	waked
sit	sat	sat	wear	wore	worn
slay	slew	slain	weave	wove,	woven,
sleep	slept	slept		weaved	weaved
slide	slid	slid	wed	wedded,	wedded,
sling	slung	slung		wed	wed
slit	slit	slit	weep	wept	wept
smell	smelt,	smelt,	win	won	won
	smelled	smelled	wind	wound	wound
sow	sowed	sown,	wring	wrung	wrung
		sowed	write	wrote	written
speak	spoke	spoken			
speed	sped,	sped,			
	speeded	speeded			

Everyday
ITALIAN
Dictionary

a

A *abbr* (= *autostrada*) ≈ M (*motorway*)

PAROLA CHIAVE

a (*a + il =* **al**, *a + lo =* **allo**, *a + l' =* **all'**, *a + la =* **alla**, *a + i =* **ai**, *a + gli =* **agli**, *a + le =* **alle**) *prep*
1 (*stato in luogo*) at; (*: in*) in; **essere alla stazione** to be at the station; **essere a casa/a scuola/a Roma** to be at home/at school/in Rome; **è a 10 km da qui** it's 10 km from here, it's 10 km away
2 (*moto a luogo*) to; **andare a casa/a scuola** to go home/to school
3 (*tempo*) at; (*epoca, stagione*) in; **alle cinque** at five (o'clock); **a mezzanotte/Natale** at midnight/Christmas; **al mattino** in the morning; **a maggio/primavera** in May/spring; **a cinquant'anni** at fifty (years of age); **a domani!** see you tomorrow!
4 (*complemento di termine*) to; **dare qc a qn** to give sth to sb
5 (*mezzo, modo*) with, by; **a piedi/cavallo** on foot/horseback; **fatto a mano** made by hand, handmade; **una barca a motore** a motorboat; **a uno a uno** one by one; **all'italiana** the Italian way, in the Italian fashion
6 (*rapporto*) a, per; (*: con prezzi*) at; **prendo 850 euro al mese** I get 850 euros a *o* per month; **pagato a ore** paid by the hour; **vendere qc a 2 euro il chilo** to sell sth at 2 euros a *o* per kilo

abbagli'ante [abbaʎ'ʎante] *ag* dazzling; **abbaglianti** *smpl* (*Aut*): **accendere gli abbaglianti** to put one's headlights on full (*BRIT*) *o* high (*US*) beam
abbagli'are [abbaʎ'ʎare] *vt* to dazzle; (*illudere*) to delude
abbai'are *vi* to bark
abbando'nare *vt* to leave, abandon, desert; (*trascurare*) to neglect; (*rinunciare a*) to abandon, give up; **abbandonarsi** *vpr* to let o.s. go; **abbandonarsi a** (*ricordi, vizio*) to give o.s. up to
abbas'sare *vt* to lower; (*radio*) to turn down; **abbassarsi** *vpr* (*chinarsi*) to stoop; (*livello, sole*) to go down; (*fig: umiliarsi*) to demean o.s.; **~ i fari** (*Aut*) to dip *o* dim (*US*) one's lights
ab'basso *escl* **~ il re!** down with the king!
abbas'tanza [abbas'tantsa] *av* (*a sufficienza*) enough; (*alquanto*) quite, rather, fairly; **non è ~ furbo** he's not shrewd enough; **un vino ~ dolce** quite a sweet wine; **averne ~ di qn/qc** to have had enough of sb/sth
ab'battere *vt* (*muro, casa*) to pull down; (*ostacolo*) to knock down; (*albero*) to fell; (*: vento*) to bring down; (*bestie da macello*) to slaughter; (*cane, cavallo*) to destroy, put down; (*selvaggina, aereo*) to shoot down; (*fig: malattia, disgrazia*) to lay low; **abbattersi** *vpr* (*avvilirsi*) to lose heart; **abbat'tuto, -a** *ag* (*fig*) depressed
abba'zia [abbat'tsia] *sf* abbey
'abbia *vb vedi* **avere**
abbi'ente *ag* well-to-do, well-off; **abbienti** *smpl* **gli abbienti** the well-to-do
abbiglia'mento [abbiʎʎa'mento] *sm* dress *no pl*; (*indumenti*) clothes *pl*; (*industria*) clothing industry
abbi'nare *vt* **~ (a)** to combine (with)
abboc'care *vi* (*pesce*) to bite; (*tubi*) to join; **~ (all'amo)** (*fig*) to swallow the bait
abbona'mento *sm* subscription; (*alle ferrovie ecc*) season ticket; **fare l'~** to take out a subscription (*o* season ticket)
abbo'narsi *vpr* **~ a un giornale** to take out a subscription to a newspaper; **~ al teatro/alle ferrovie** to take out a season ticket for the theatre/the train
abbon'dante *ag* abundant, plentiful; (*giacca*) roomy
abbon'danza [abbon'dantsa] *sf* abundance; plenty
abbor'dabile *ag* (*persona*) approachable; (*prezzo*) reasonable

abbotto'nare *vt* to button up, do up

abbracci'are [abbrat'tʃare] *vt* to embrace; (*persona*) to hug, embrace; (*professione*) to take up; (*contenere*) to include; **abbracciarsi** *vpr* to hug o embrace (one another); **ab'braccio** *sm* hug, embrace

abbrevi'are *vt* to shorten; (*parola*) to abbreviate

abbreviazi'one [abbrevjat'tsjone] *sf* abbreviation

abbron'zante [abbron'dzante] *ag* tanning, sun *cpd*

abbronzarsi *vpr* to tan, get a tan

abbron'zato, -a [abbron'dzato] *ag* (sun)tanned

abbrusto'lire *vt* (*pane*) to toast; (*caffè*) to roast; **abbrustolirsi** *vpr* to toast; (*fig: al sole*) to soak up the sun

abbuf'farsi *vpr* (*fam*): ~ **(di qc)** to stuff o.s. (with sth)

abdi'care *vi* to abdicate; ~ **a** to give up, renounce

a'bete *sm* fir (tree); **abete rosso** spruce

'abile *ag* (*idoneo*): ~ **(a qc/a fare qc)** fit (for sth/to do sth); (*capace*) able; (*astuto*) clever; (*accorto*) skilful; ~ **al servizio militare** fit for military service; **abilità** *sf inv* ability; cleverness; skill

a'bisso *sm* abyss, gulf

abi'tante *sm/f* inhabitant

abi'tare *vt* to live in, dwell in ▷ *vi* ~ **in campagna/a Roma** to live in the country/in Rome; **dove abita?** where do you live?; **abitazi'one** *sf* residence; house

'abito *sm* dress *no pl*; (*da uomo*) suit; (*da donna*) dress; (*abitudine, disposizione, Rel*) habit; **abiti** *smpl* (*vestiti*) clothes; **in ~ da sera** in evening dress

abitu'ale *ag* usual, habitual; (*cliente*) regular

abitual'mente *av* usually, normally

abitu'are *vt* ~ **qn a** to get sb used o accustomed to; **abituarsi a** to get used to, accustom o.s. to

abitudi'nario, -a *ag* of fixed habits ▷ *sm/f* regular customer

abi'tudine *sf* habit; **aver l'~ di fare qc** to be in the habit of doing sth; **d'~** usually; **per ~** from o out of habit

abo'lire *vt* to abolish; (*Dir*) to repeal

abor'tire *vi* (*Med*) to miscarry, have a miscarriage; (: *deliberatamente*) to have an abortion; (*fig*) to miscarry, fail; **a'borto** *sm* miscarriage; abortion

ABS [abıɛse] *sigla m* (= *Anti-Blockier System*) ABS

'abside *sf* apse

abu'sare *vi* ~ **di** to abuse, misuse; (*alcool*) to take to excess; (*approfittare, violare*) to take advantage of

abu'sivo, -a *ag* unauthorized, unlawful; **(occupante)** ~ (*di una casa*) squatter

▮ Attenzione! In inglese esiste la parola *abusive* che però vuol dire *ingiurioso*.

a.C. *av abbr* (= *avanti Cristo*) B.C.

a'cacia, -cie [a'katʃa] *sf* (*Bot*) acacia

ac'cadde *vb vedi* **accadere**

acca'demia *sf* (*società*) learned society; (*scuola: d'arte, militare*) academy

acca'dere *vb impers* to happen, occur

accal'dato *ag* hot

accalo'rarsi *vpr* (*fig*) to get excited

accampa'mento *sm* camp

accamparsi *vpr* to camp

acca'nirsi *vpr* (*infierire*) to rage; (*ostinarsi*) to persist; **acca'nito, -a** *ag* (*odio, gelosia*) fierce, bitter; (*lavoratore*) assiduous, dogged; (*fumatore*) inveterate

ac'canto *av* near, nearby; ~ **a** *prep* near, beside, close to

accanto'nare *vt* (*problema*) to shelve; (*somma*) to set aside

accappa'toio *sm* bathrobe

accarez'zare [akkaret'tsare] *vt* to caress, stroke, fondle; (*fig*) to toy with

acca'sarsi *vpr* to set up house; to get married

accasci'arsi [akkaʃ'ʃarsi] *vpr* to collapse; (*fig*) to lose heart

accat'tone, -a *sm/f* beggar

accaval'lare *vt* (*gambe*) to cross

acce'care [attʃe'kare] *vt* to blind ▷ *vi* to go blind

ac'cedere [at'tʃedere] *vi* ~ **a** to enter; (*richiesta*) to grant, accede to

accele'rare [attʃele'rare] *vt* to speed up ▷ *vi* (*Aut*) to accelerate; ~ **il passo** to quicken one's pace; **accelera'tore** *sm* (*Aut*) accelerator

ac'cendere [at'tʃɛndere] *vt* (*fuoco, sigaretta*) to light; (*luce, televisione*) to put on, switch on, turn on; (*Aut: motore*) to switch on; (*Comm: conto*) to open; (*fig: suscitare*) to inflame, stir up; **ha da ~?** have you got a light?; **non riesco ad ~ il riscaldamento** I can't turn the heating on; **accen'dino, accendi'sigaro** *sm* (cigarette) lighter

accen'nare [attʃen'nare] *vt* (*Mus*) to pick out the notes of; to hum ▷ *vi* ~ **a** (*fig: alludere a*) to hint at; (: *far atto di*) to make as if; ~ **un saluto** (*con la mano*) to make as if to wave; (*col capo*) to half nod; **accenna a piovere** it looks as if it's going to rain

ac'cenno [at'tʃenno] *sm* (*cenno*) sign; nod; (*allusione*) hint

accensi'one [attʃen'sjone] *sf* (*vedi verbo*) lighting; switching on; opening; (*Aut*) ignition

ac'cento [at'tʃɛnto] *sm* accent; (*Fonetica*, *fig*) stress; (*inflessione*) tone (of voice)

accentu'are [attʃentu'are] *vt* to stress, emphasize; **accentuarsi** *vpr* to become more noticeable

accerchi'are [attʃer'kjare] *vt* to surround, encircle

accerta'mento [attʃerta'mento] *sm* check; assessment

accer'tare [attʃer'tare] *vt* to ascertain; (*verificare*) to check; (*reddito*) to assess; **accertarsi** *vpr* **accertarsi (di)** to make sure (of)

ac'ceso, -a [at'tʃeso] *pp di* **accendere** ▷ *ag* lit; on; open; (*colore*) bright

acces'sibile [attʃes'sibile] *ag* (*luogo*) accessible; (*persona*) approachable; (*prezzo*) reasonable

ac'cesso [at'tʃɛsso] *sm* (*anche Inform*) access; (*Med*) attack, fit; (*impulso violento*) fit, outburst

accessori *smpl* accessories

ac'cetta [at'tʃetta] *sf* hatchet

accet'tabile [attʃet'tabile] *ag* acceptable

accet'tare [attʃet'tare] *vt* to accept; **accettate carte di credito?** do you accept credit cards?; ~ **di fare qc** to agree to do sth; **accettazi'one** *sf* acceptance; (*locale di servizio pubblico*) reception; **accettazione bagagli** (*Aer*) check-in (desk)

acchiap'pare [akkjap'pare] *vt* to catch

acciaie'ria [attʃaje'ria] *sf* steelworks *sg*

acci'aio [at'tʃajo] *sm* steel

acciden'tato, -a [attʃiden'tato, -a] *ag* (*terreno ecc*) uneven

accigli'ato, -a [attʃiʎ'ʎato] *ag* frowning

ac'cingersi [at'tʃindʒersi] *vpr* ~ **a fare qc** to be about to do sth

acciuf'fare [attʃuf'fare] *vt* to seize, catch

acci'uga, -ghe [at'tʃuga] *sf* anchovy

ac'cludere *vt* to enclose

accocco'larsi *vpr* to crouch

accogli'ente [akkoʎ'ʎɛnte] *ag* welcoming, friendly

ac'cogliere [ak'koʎʎere] *vt* (*ricevere*) to receive; (*dare il benvenuto*) to welcome; (*approvare*) to agree to, accept; (*contenere*) to hold, accommodate

ac'colgo *ecc vb vedi* **accogliere**

ac'colsi *ecc vb vedi* **accogliere**

accoltel'lare *vt* to knife, stab

accomoda'mento *sm* agreement, settlement

accomo'dante *ag* accommodating

accomodarsi *vpr* (*sedersi*) to sit down; (*entrare*) to come in; **s'accomodi!** (*venga avanti*) come in!; (*si sieda*) take a seat!

accompagna'mento [akkompaɲɲa'mento] *sm* (*Mus*) accompaniment

accompa'gnare [akkompaɲ'ɲare] *vt* to accompany, come *o* go with; (*Mus*) to accompany; (*unire*) to couple; ~ **la porta** to close the door gently

accompagna'tore, -trice *sm/f* companion; ~ **turistico** courier

acconcia'tura [akkontʃa'tura] *sf* hairstyle

accondiscen'dente [akkondiʃʃen'dɛnte] *ag* affable

acconsen'tire *vi* ~ **(a)** to agree *o* consent (to)

acconten'tare *vt* to satisfy; **accontentarsi** *vpr* **accontentarsi di** to be satisfied with, content *o.s.* with

ac'conto *sm* part payment; **pagare una somma in** ~ to pay a sum of money as a deposit

acco'rato, -a *ag* heartfelt

accorci'are [akkor'tʃare] *vt* to shorten; **accorciarsi** *vpr* to become shorter

accor'dare *vt* to reconcile; (*colori*) to match; (*Mus*) to tune; (*Ling*): ~ **qc con qc** to make sth agree with sth; (*Dir*) to grant; **accordarsi** *vpr* to agree, come to an agreement; (*colori*) to match

ac'cordo *sm* agreement; (*armonia*) harmony; (*Mus*) chord; **essere d'**~ to agree; **andare d'**~ to get on well together; **d'**~**!** all right!, agreed!; **accordo commerciale** trade agreement

ac'corgersi [ak'kordʒersi] *vpr* ~ **di** to notice; (*fig*) to realize

ac'correre *vi* to run up

ac'corto, -a *pp di* **accorgersi** ▷ *ag* shrewd; **stare** ~ to be on one's guard

accos'tare *vt* (*avvicinare*): ~ **qc a** to bring sth near to, put sth near to; (*avvicinarsi a*) to approach; (*socchiudere: imposte*) to half-close; (: *porta*) to leave ajar ▷ *vi* (*Naut*) to come alongside; **accostarsi** *vpr* **accostarsi a** to draw near, approach; (*fig*) to support

accredi'tare *vt* (*notizia*) to confirm the truth of; (*Comm*) to credit; (*diplomatico*) to accredit

ac'credito *sm* (*Comm: atto*) crediting; (: *effetto*) credit

accucci'arsi [akkut'tʃarsi] *vpr* (*cane*) to lie down

accu'dire *vt* (*anche: vi* ~ **a**) to attend to

accumu'lare *vt* to accumulate; **accumularsi** *vpr* to accumulate; (*Finanza*) to accrue

accu'rato, -a *ag* (*diligente*) careful; (*preciso*) accurate

ac'cusa *sf* accusation; (*Dir*) charge; **la pubblica ~** the prosecution

accu'sare *vt* **~ qn di qc** to accuse sb of sth; (*Dir*) to charge sb with sth; **~ ricevuta di** (*Comm*) to acknowledge receipt of

accusa'tore, -'trice *sm/f* accuser ▷ *sm* (*Dir*) prosecutor

a'cerbo, -a [a'tʃɛrbo] *ag* bitter; (*frutta*) sour, unripe; (*persona*) immature

'acero ['atʃero] *sm* maple

a'cerrimo, -a [a'tʃɛrrimo] *ag* very fierce

a'ceto [a'tʃeto] *sm* vinegar

ace'tone [atʃe'tone] *sm* nail varnish remover

A.C.I. ['atʃi] *sigla m* = **Automobile Club d'Italia**

'acido, -a ['atʃido] *ag* (*sapore*) acid, sour; (*Chim*) acid ▷ *sm* (*Chim*) acid

'acino ['atʃino] *sm* berry; **acino d'uva** grape

'acne *sf* acne

'acqua *sf* water; (*pioggia*) rain; **acque** *sfpl* (*di mare, fiume ecc*) waters; **fare ~** (*Naut*) to leak, take in water; **~ in bocca!** mum's the word!; **acqua corrente** running water; **acqua dolce/salata** fresh/salt water; **acqua minerale/potabile/tonica** mineral/drinking/tonic water; **acque termali** thermal waters

a'cquaio *sm* sink

acqua'ragia [akkwa'radʒa] *sf* turpentine

a'cquario *sm* aquarium; (*dello zodiaco*): **A~** Aquarius

acquascooter [akkwas'kuter] *sm inv* Jet Ski®

ac'quatico, -a, -ci, -che *ag* aquatic; (*Sport, Scienza*) water *cpd*

acqua'vite *sf* brandy

acquaz'zone [akkwat'tsone] *sm* cloudburst, heavy shower

acque'dotto *sm* aqueduct; waterworks *pl*, water system

acque'rello *sm* watercolour

acqui'rente *sm/f* purchaser, buyer

acquis'tare *vt* to purchase, buy; (*fig*) to gain; **a'cquisto** *sm* purchase; **fare acquisti** to go shopping

acquo'lina *sf* **far venire l'~ in bocca a qn** to make sb's mouth water

a'crobata, -i, -e *sm/f* acrobat

a'culeo *sm* (*Zool*) sting; (*Bot*) prickle

a'cume *sm* acumen, perspicacity

a'custico, -a, ci, che *ag* acoustic ▷ *sf* (*scienza*) acoustics *sg*; (*di una sala*) acoustics *pl*; **cornetto ~** ear trumpet; **apparecchio ~** hearing aid

a'cuto, -a *ag* (*appuntito*) sharp, pointed; (*suono, voce*) shrill, piercing; (*Mat, Ling, Med*) acute; (*Mus*) high-pitched; (*fig: dolore,*

desiderio) intense; (*: perspicace*) acute, keen

a'dagio [a'dadʒo] *av* slowly ▷ *sm* (*Mus*) adagio; (*proverbio*) adage, saying

adatta'mento *sm* adaptation

adat'tare *vt* to adapt; (*sistemare*) to fit; **adattarsi** *vpr* **adattarsi (a)** (*ambiente, tempi*) to adapt (to); (*essere adatto*) to be suitable (for)

a'datto, -a *ag* **~ (a)** suitable (for), right (for)

addebi'tare *vt* **~ qc a qn** to debit sb with sth

ad'debito *sm* (*Comm*) debit

adden'tare *vt* to bite into

adden'trarsi *vpr* **~ in** to penetrate, go into

addestra'mento *sm* training

addes'trare *vt* to train

ad'detto, -a *ag* **~ a** (*persona*) assigned to; (*oggetto*) intended for ▷ *sm* employee; (*funzionario*) attaché; **gli addetti ai lavori** authorized personnel; (*fig*) those in the know; **addetto commerciale** commercial attaché; **addetto stampa** press attaché

ad'dio *sm, escl* goodbye, farewell

addirit'tura *av* (*veramente*) really, absolutely; (*perfino*) even; (*direttamente*) directly, right away

addi'tare *vt* to point out; (*fig*) to expose

addi'tivo *sm* additive

addizi'one *sf* addition

addob'bare *vt* to decorate; **ad'dobbo** *sm* decoration

addolo'rare *vt* to pain, grieve; **addolorarsi (per)** to be distressed (by)

addolo'rato, -a *ag* distressed, upset; **l'Addolorata** (*Rel*) Our Lady of Sorrows

ad'dome *sm* abdomen

addomesti'care *vt* to tame

addomi'nale *ag* abdominal; **(muscoli** *mpl***) addominali** stomach muscles

addormen'tare *vt* to put to sleep; **addormentarsi** *vpr* to fall asleep, go to sleep

ad'dosso *av* on; **mettersi ~ il cappotto** to put one's coat on; **~ a** (*sopra*) on; (*molto vicino*) right next to; **stare ~ a qn** (*fig*) to breathe down sb's neck; **dare ~ a qn** (*fig*) to attack sb

adeguarsi *vpr* to adapt

adegu'ato, -a *ag* adequate; (*conveniente*) suitable; (*equo*) fair

a'dempiere *vt* to fulfil, carry out

ade'rente *ag* adhesive; (*vestito*) close-fitting ▷ *sm/f* follower

ade'rire *vi* (*stare attaccato*) to adhere, stick; **~ a** to adhere to, stick to; (*fig: società, partito*) to join; (*: opinione*) to support; (*richiesta*) to agree to

adesi'one *sf* adhesion; (*fig*) agreement,

acceptance; **ade'sivo, -a** *ag, sm* adhesive

a'desso *av* (*ora*) now; (*or ora, poco fa*) just now; (*tra poco*) any moment now

adia'cente [adja'tʃɛnte] *ag* adjacent

adi'bire *vt* (*usare*): **~ qc a** to turn sth into

adole'scente [adoleʃʃɛnte] *ag, sm/f* adolescent

adope'rare *vt* to use

ado'rare *vt* to adore; (*Rel*) to adore, worship

adot'tare *vt* to adopt; (*decisione, provvedimenti*) to pass; **adot'tivo, -a** *ag* (*genitori*) adoptive; (*figlio, patria*) adopted; **adozi'one** *sf* adoption; **adozione a distanza** child sponsorship

adri'atico, -a, -ci, -che *ag* Adriatic ▷ *sm* **l'A~, il mare A~** the Adriatic, the Adriatic Sea

adu'lare *vt* to adulate, flatter

a'dultero, -a *ag* adulterous ▷ *sm/f* adulterer (adulteress)

a'dulto, -a *ag* adult; (*fig*) mature ▷ *sm* adult, grown-up

a'ereo, -a *ag* air *cpd*; (*radice*) aerial ▷ *sm* aerial; (*aeroplano*) plane; **aereo da caccia** fighter (plane); **aereo di linea** airliner; **aereo a reazione** jet (plane); **ae'robica** *sf* aerobics *sg*; **aero'nautica** *sf* (*scienza*) aeronautics *sg*; **aeronautica militare** air force

aero'porto *sm* airport; **all'~ per favore** to the airport, please

aero'sol *sm inv* aerosol

'afa *sf* sultriness

af'fabile *ag* affable

affaccen'dato, -a [affattʃen'dato] *ag* (*persona*) busy

affacci'arsi [affat'tʃarsi] *vpr* **~ (a)** to appear (at)

affa'mato, -a *ag* starving; (*fig*): **~ (di)** eager (for)

affan'noso, -a *ag* (*respiro*) difficult; (*fig*) troubled, anxious

af'fare *sm* (*faccenda*) matter, affair; (*Comm*) piece of business, (business) deal; (*occasione*) bargain; (*Dir*) case; (*fam: cosa*) thing; **affari** *smpl* (*Comm*) business *sg*; **Ministro degli Affari esteri** Foreign Secretary (BRIT), Secretary of State (US)

affasci'nante [affaʃʃi'nante] *ag* fascinating

affasci'nare [affaʃʃi'nare] *vt* to bewitch; (*fig*) to charm, fascinate

affati'care *vt* to tire; **affaticarsi** *vpr* (*durar fatica*) to tire o.s. out; **affati'cato, -a** *ag* tired

af'fatto *av* completely; **non ... ~** not ... at all; **niente ~** not at all

affer'mare *vt* (*dichiarare*) to maintain,

affirm; **affermarsi** *vpr* to assert o.s., make one's name known; **affer'mato, -a** *ag* established, well-known; **affermazi'one** *sf* affirmation, assertion; (*successo*) achievement

affer'rare *vt* to seize, grasp; (*fig: idea*) to grasp; **afferrarsi** *vpr* **afferrarsi a** to cling to

affet'tare *vt* (*tagliare a fette*) to slice; (*ostentare*) to affect

affetta'trice [affetta'tritʃe] *sf* meat slicer

affet'tivo, -a *ag* emotional, affective

af'fetto *sm* affection; **affettu'oso, -a** *ag* affectionate

affezio'narsi [affettsjo'narsi] *vpr* **~ a** to grow fond of

affezio'nato, -a [affettsjo'nato] *ag* **~ a qn/qc** fond of sb/sth; (*attaccato*) attached to sb/sth

affia'tato, -a *ag* **essere molto affiatati** to get on very well

affibbi'are *vt* (*fig: dare*) to give

affi'dabile *ag* reliable

affida'mento *sm* (*Dir: di bambino*) custody; (*fiducia*): **fare ~ su qn** to rely on sb; **non dà nessun ~** he's not to be trusted

affi'dare *vt* **~ qc o qn a qn** to entrust sth o sb to sb; **affidarsi** *vpr* **affidarsi a** to place one's trust in

affi'lare *vt* to sharpen

affi'lato, -a *ag* (*gen*) sharp; (*volto, naso*) thin

affinché [affin'ke] *cong* in order that, so that

affit'tare *vt* (*dare in affitto*) to let, rent (out); (*prendere in affitto*) to rent; **af'fitto** *sm* rent; (*contratto*) lease

af'fliggere [af'fliddʒere] *vt* to torment; **affliggersi** *vpr* to grieve

af'flissi *ecc vb vedi* **affliggere**

afflosci'arsi [affloʃʃarsi] *vpr* to go limp

afflu'ente *sm* tributary

affo'gare *vt, vi* to drown

affol'lare *vt* to crowd; **affollarsi** *vpr* to crowd; **affol'lato, -a** *ag* crowded

affon'dare *vt* to sink

affran'care *vt* to free, liberate; (*Amm*) to redeem; (*lettera*) to stamp; (*: meccanicamente*) to frank (BRIT), meter (US)

af'fresco, -schi *sm* fresco

affrettarsi *vpr* to hurry; **~ a fare qc** to hurry o hasten to do sth

affret'tato, -a *ag* (*veloce: passo, ritmo*) quick, fast; (*frettoloso: decisione*) hurried, hasty; (*: lavoro*) rushed

affron'tare *vt* (*pericolo ecc*) to face; (*nemico*) to confront; **affrontarsi** *vpr* (*reciproco*) to come to blows

affumi'cato, -a *ag* (*prosciutto, aringa ecc*) smoked

affuso'lato, -a *ag* tapering

Af'ganistan *sm* **l'~** Afghanistan

a'foso, -a *ag* sultry, close

'Africa *sf* **l'~** Africa; **afri'cano, -a** *ag, sm/f* African

a'genda [a'dʒɛnda] *sf* diary

> Attenzione! In inglese esiste la parola *agenda* che però vuol dire *ordine del giorno*.

a'gente [a'dʒɛnte] *sm* agent; **agente di cambio** stockbroker; **agente di polizia** police officer; **agente segreto** secret agent; **agen'zia** *sf* agency; (*succursale*) branch; **agenzia immobiliare** estate agent's (office) (BRIT), real estate office (US); **agenzia di collocamento/stampa** employment/press agency; **agenzia viaggi** travel agency

agevo'lare [adʒevo'lare] *vt* to facilitate, make easy

agevolazi'one [adʒevolat'tsjone] *sf* (*facilitazione economica*) facility; **agevolazione di pagamento** payment on easy terms; **agevolazioni creditizie** credit facilities; **agevolazioni fiscali** tax concessions

a'gevole [a'dʒevole] *ag* easy; (*strada*) smooth

agganci'are [aggan'tʃare] *vt* to hook up; (*Ferr*) to couple

ag'geggio [ad'dʒeddʒo] *sm* gadget, contraption

agget'tivo [addʒet'tivo] *sm* adjective

agghiacci'ante [aggjat'tʃante] *ag* chilling

aggior'nare [addʒor'nare] *vt* (*opera, manuale*) to bring up-to-date; (*seduta ecc*) to postpone; **aggiornarsi** *vpr* to bring (o keep) o.s. up-to-date; **aggior'nato, -a** *ag* up-to-date

aggi'rare [addʒi'rare] *vt* to go round; (*fig: ingannare*) to trick; **aggirarsi** *vpr* to wander about; **il prezzo s'aggira sul milione** the price is around the million mark

aggi'ungere [ad'dʒundʒere] *vt* to add

aggi'unsi *ecc* [ad'dʒunsi] *vb vedi* **aggiungere**

aggius'tare [addʒus'tare] *vt* (*accomodare*) to mend, repair; (*riassettare*) to adjust; (*fig: lite*) to settle

aggrap'parsi *vpr* **~ a** to cling to

aggra'vare *vt* (*aumentare*) to increase; (*appesantire: anche fig*) to weigh down, make heavy; (*pena*) to make worse; **aggravarsi** *vpr* to worsen, become worse

aggre'dire *vt* to attack, assault

aggressi'one *sf* aggression; (*atto*) attack, assault

aggres'sivo, -a *ag* aggressive

aggres'sore *sm* aggressor, attacker

aggrot'tare *vt* **~ le sopracciglia** to frown

aggrovigliarsi *vpr* (*fig*) to become complicated

aggu'ato *sm* trap; (*imboscata*) ambush; **tendere un ~ a qn** to set a trap for sb

agguer'rito, -a *ag* fierce

agi'ato, -a [a'dʒato] *ag* (*vita*) easy; (*persona*) well-off, well-to-do

'agile ['adʒile] *ag* agile, nimble

'agio ['adʒo] *sm* ease, comfort; **mettersi a proprio ~** to make o.s. at home o comfortable; **agi** *smpl* comforts; **mettersi a proprio ~** to make o.s. at home o comfortable; **dare ~ a qn di fare qc** to give sb the chance of doing sth

a'gire [a'dʒire] *vi* to act; (*esercitare un'azione*) to take effect; (*Tecn*) to work, function; **~ contro qn** (*Dir*) to take action against sb

agi'tare [adʒi'tare] *vt* (*bottiglia*) to shake; (*mano, fazzoletto*) to wave; (*fig: turbare*) to disturb; (: *incitare*) to stir (up); (: *dibattere*) to discuss; **agitarsi** *vpr* (*mare*) to be rough; (*malato, dormitore*) to toss and turn; (*bambino*) to fidget; (*emozionarsi*) to get upset; (*Pol*) to agitate; **agi'tato, -a** *ag* rough; restless; fidgety; upset, perturbed

'aglio ['aʎʎo] *sm* garlic

a'gnello [aɲ'ɲɛllo] *sm* lamb

'ago (*pl* **'aghi**) *sm* needle

ago'nistico, -a, -ci, -che *ag* athletic; (*fig*) competitive

agopun'tura *sf* acupuncture

a'gosto *sm* August

a'grario, -a *ag* agrarian, agricultural; (*riforma*) land *cpd*

a'gricolo, -a *ag* agricultural, farm *cpd*; **agricol'tore** *sm* farmer; **agricol'tura** *sf* agriculture, farming

agri'foglio [agri'fɔʎʎo] *sm* holly

agritu'rismo *sm* farm holidays *pl*

agrodolce *ag* bittersweet; (*salsa*) sweet and sour

a'grume *sm* (*spesso al pl: pianta*) citrus; (: *frutto*) citrus fruit

a'guzzo, -a [a'guttso] *ag* sharp

'ahi *escl* (*dolore*) ouch!

'Aia *sf* **l'~** the Hague

'aids *abbr m* of Aids

airbag *sm inv* air bag

ai'rone *sm* heron

aiu'ola *sf* flower bed

aiu'tante *sm/f* assistant ▷ *sm* (*Mil*) adjutant; (*Naut*) master-at-arms; **aiutante di campo** aide-de-camp

aiu'tare *vt* to help; **~ qn (a fare)** to help sb

(to do); **aiutarsi** *vpr* to help each other; **~ qn in qc/a fare qc** to help sb with sth/to do sth; **può aiutarmi?** can you help me?

ai'uto *sm* help, assistance, aid; (*aiutante*) assistant; **venire in ~ di qn** to come to sb's aid; **aiuto chirurgo** assistant surgeon

'ala (*pl* **'ali**) *sf* wing; **fare ~** to fall back, make way; **ala destra/sinistra** (*Sport*) right/left wing

ala'bastro *sm* alabaster

a'lano *sm* Great Dane

'alba *sf* dawn

alba'nese *ag, sm/f, sm* Albanian

Alba'nia *sf* **l'~** Albania

albe'rato, -a *ag* (*viale, piazza*) lined with trees, tree-lined

al'bergo, -ghi *sm* hotel; **albergo della gioventù** youth hostel

'albero *sm* tree; (*Naut*) mast; (*Tecn*) shaft; **albero genealogico** family tree; **albero a gomiti** crankshaft; **albero maestro** mainmast; **albero di Natale** Christmas tree; **albero di trasmissione** transmission shaft

albi'cocca, -che *sf* apricot

'album *sm* album; **album da disegno** sketch book

al'bume *sm* albumen

'alce ['altʃe] *sm* elk

'alcol *sm inv* = **alcool**

al'colico, -a, -ci, -che *ag* alcoholic ▷ *sm* alcoholic drink

alcoliz'zato, -a [alkolid'dzato] *sm/f* alcoholic

'alcool *sm inv* alcohol

al'cuno, -a (*det: dav sm:* **alcun** + C, V, **alcuno** + *s impura, gn, pn, ps, x, z; dav sf:* **alcuna** + C, **alcun'** +V) *det* (*nessuno*): **non ... ~** no, not any; **alcuni, e** *det pl* some, a few; **non c'è alcuna fretta** there's no hurry, there isn't any hurry; **senza alcun riguardo** without any consideration ▷ *pron pl* **alcuni, e** some, a few

alfa'betico, -a, ci, che *ag* alphabetical

alfa'beto *sm* alphabet

'alga, -ghe *sf* seaweed *no pl*, alga

'algebra ['aldʒebra] *sf* algebra

Alge'ria [aldʒe'ria] *sf* **l'~** Algeria

alge'rino, -a [aldʒe'rino] *ag, sm/f* Algerian

ali'ante *sm* (*Aer*) glider

'alibi *sm inv* alibi

a'lice [a'litʃe] *sf* anchovy

ali'eno, -a *ag* (*avverso*): **~ (da)** opposed (to), averse (to) ▷ *sm/f* alien

alimen'tare *vt* to feed; (*Tecn*) to feed; to supply; (*fig*) to sustain ▷ *ag* food *cpd*; **alimentari** *smpl* foodstuffs; (*anche:*

negozio di alimentari) grocer's shop; **alimentazi'one** *sf* feeding; supplying; sustaining; (*gli alimenti*) diet

a'liquota *sf* share; (*d'imposta*) rate; **aliquota d'imposta** tax rate

alis'cafo *sm* hydrofoil

'alito *sm* breath

all. *abbr* (= *allegato*) encl.

allaccia'mento [allattʃa'mento] *sm* (*Tecn*) connection

allacci'are [allat'tʃare] *vt* (*scarpe*) to tie, lace (up); (*cintura*) to do up, fasten; (*luce, gas*) to connect; (*amicizia*) to form

allaccia'tura [allattʃa'tura] *sf* fastening

alla'gare *vt* to flood; **allagarsi** *vpr* to flood

allar'gare *vt* to widen; (*vestito*) to let out; (*aprire*) to open; (*fig: dilatare*) to extend; **allargarsi** *vpr* (*gen*) to widen; (*scarpe, pantaloni*) to stretch; (*fig: problema, fenomeno*) to spread

allar'mare *vt* to alarm

al'larme *sm* alarm; **allarme aereo** air-raid warning

allat'tare *vt* to feed

alle'anza [alle'antsa] *sf* alliance

alle'arsi *vpr* to form an alliance; **alle'ato, -a** *ag* allied ▷ *sm/f* ally

alle'gare *vt* (*accludere*) to enclose; (*Dir: citare*) to cite, adduce; (*denti*) to set on edge; **alle'gato, -a** *ag* enclosed ▷ *sm* enclosure; (*di e-mail*) attachment; **in allegato** enclosed

allegge'rire [alleddʒe'rire] *vt* to lighten, make lighter; (*fig: lavoro, tasse*) to reduce

alle'gria *sf* gaiety, cheerfulness

al'legro, -a *ag* cheerful, merry; (*un po' brillo*) merry, tipsy; (*vivace: colore*) bright ▷ *sm* (*Mus*) allegro

allena'mento *sm* training

alle'nare *vt* to train; **allenarsi** *vpr* to train; **allena'tore** *sm* (*Sport*) trainer, coach

allen'tare *vt* to slacken; (*disciplina*) to relax; **allentarsi** *vpr* to become slack; (*ingranaggio*) to work loose

aller'gia, -'gie [aller'dʒia] *sf* allergy; **al'lergico, -a, -ci, -che** *ag* allergic; **sono allergico alla penicillina** I'm allergic to penicillin

alles'tire *vt* (*cena*) to prepare; (*esercito, nave*) to equip, fit out; (*spettacolo*) to stage

allet'tante *ag* attractive, alluring

alle'vare *vt* (*animale*) to breed, rear; (*bambino*) to bring up

allevi'are *vt* to alleviate

alli'bito, -a *ag* astounded

alli'evo *sm* pupil; (*apprendista*) apprentice; (*Mil*) cadet

alliga'tore *sm* alligator

alline'are vt (persone, cose) to line up; (Tip) to align; (fig: economia, salari) to adjust, align; **allinearsi** vpr to line up; (fig: a idee): **allinearsi a** to come into line with

al'lodola sf (sky)lark

alloggi'are [allod'dʒare] vt to accommodate ▷ vi to live; **al'loggio** sm lodging, accommodation (BRIT), accommodations (US)

allonta'nare vt to send away, send off; (impiegato) to dismiss; (pericolo) to avert, remove; (estraniare) to alienate; **allontanarsi** vpr **allontanarsi (da)** to go away (from); (estraniarsi) to become estranged (from)

al'lora av (in quel momento) then ▷ cong (in questo caso) well then; (dunque) well then, so; **la gente d'~** people then o in those days; **da ~ in poi** from then on

al'loro sm laurel

'alluce ['allutʃe] sm big toe

alluci'nante [allutʃi'nante] ag awful; (fam) amazing

allucinazi'one [allutʃinat'tsjone] sf hallucination

al'ludere vi ~ **a** to allude to, hint at

allu'minio sm aluminium (BRIT), aluminum (US)

allun'gare vt to lengthen; (distendere) to prolong, extend; (diluire) to water down; **allungarsi** vpr to lengthen; (ragazzo) to stretch, grow taller; (sdraiarsi) to lie down, stretch out

al'lusi ecc vb vedi **alludere**

allusi'one sf hint, allusion

alluvi'one sf flood

al'meno av at least ▷ cong **(se)** ~ if only; **(se)** ~ **piovesse!** if only it would rain!

a'logeno, -a [a'lɔdʒeno] ag **lampada alogena** halogen lamp

a'lone sm halo

'Alpi sfpl **le** ~ the Alps

alpi'nismo sm mountaineering, climbing; **alpi'nista, -i, -e** sm/f mountaineer, climber

al'pino, -a ag Alpine; mountain cpd; **alpini** smpl (Mil) Italian Alpine troops

alt escl halt!, stop!

alta'lena sf (a funi) swing; (in bilico) seesaw

al'tare sm altar

alter'nare vt to alternate; **alternarsi** vpr to alternate; **alterna'tiva** sf alternative; **alterna'tivo, -a** ag alternative

al'terno, -a ag alternate; **a giorni alterni** on alternate days, every other day

al'tero, -a ag proud

al'tezza [al'tettsa] sf height; width, breadth; depth; pitch; (Geo) latitude; (titolo) highness; (fig: nobiltà) greatness; **essere all'~ di** to be on a level with; (fig) to be up to o equal to

al'ticcio, -a, -ci, -ce [al'tittʃo] ag tipsy

alti'tudine sf altitude

'alto, -a ag high; (persona) tall; (tessuto) wide, broad; (sonno, acque) deep; (suono) high(-pitched); (Geo) upper; (settentrionale) northern ▷ sm top (part) ▷ av high; (parlare) aloud, loudly; **il palazzo è ~ 20 metri** the building is 20 metres high; **ad alta voce** aloud; **a notte alta** in the dead of night; **in** ~ up, upwards; at the top; **dall'~ o al basso** up and down; **degli alti e bassi** (fig) ups and downs; **alta fedeltà** high fidelity, hi-fi; **alta finanza/società** high finance/society; **alta moda** haute couture

altopar'lante sm loudspeaker

altopi'ano (pl **altipi'ani**) sm plateau, upland plain

altret'tanto, -a ag, pron as much; (pl) as many ▷ av equally; **tanti auguri!** **— grazie, ~** all the best! — thank you, the same to you

altri'menti av otherwise

 PAROLA CHIAVE

'altro, -a det **1** (diverso) other, different; **questa è un'altra cosa** that's another o a different thing

2 (supplementare) other; **prendi un altro cioccolatino** have another chocolate; **hai avuto altre notizie?** have you had any more o any other news?

3 (nel tempo): **l'altro giorno** the other day; **l'altr'anno** last year; **l'altro ieri** the day before yesterday; **domani l'altro** the day after tomorrow; **quest'altro mese** next month

4: **d'altra parte** on the other hand ▷ pron **1** (persona, cosa diversa o supplementare): **un altro, un'altra** another (one); **lo farà un altro** someone else will do it; **altri, e** others; **gli altri** (la gente) others, other people; **l'uno e l'altro** both (of them); **aiutarsi l'un l'altro** to help one another; **da un giorno all'altro** from day to day; (nel giro di 24 ore) from one day to the next; (da un momento all'altro) any day now

2 (sostantivato: solo maschile) something else; (: in espressioni interrogative) anything else; **non ho altro da dire** I have nothing else o I don't have anything else to say; **più che altro** above all; **se non altro** at least; **tra l'altro** among other things; **ci mancherebbe altro!** that's all we need!; **non faccio altro che lavorare** I do nothing but work; **contento? — altro che!** are you pleased? — and how!; *vedi* **senza**; **noialtri**; **voialtri**; **tutto**

al'trove *av* elsewhere, somewhere else

altru'ista, -i, -e *ag* altruistic

a'lunno, -a *sm/f* pupil

alve'are *sm* hive

al'zare [al'tsare] *vt* to raise, lift; (*issare*) to hoist; (*costruire*) to build, erect; **alzarsi** *vpr* to rise; (*dal letto*) to get up; (*crescere*) to grow tall (*o* taller); **~ le spalle** to shrug one's shoulders; **alzarsi in piedi** to stand up, get to one's feet

a'maca, -che *sf* hammock

amalga'mare *vt* to amalgamate; **amalgamarsi** *vpr* to amalgamate

a'mante *ag* **~ di** (*musica ecc*) fond of ▷ *sm/f* lover/mistress

a'mare *vt* to love; (*amico, musica, sport*) to like; **amarsi** *vpr* to love each other

amareggi'ato, -a [amared'dʒato] *ag* upset, saddened

ama'rena *sf* sour black cherry

ama'rezza [ama'rettsa] *sf* bitterness

a'maro, -a *ag* bitter ▷ *sm* bitterness; (*liquore*) bitters *pl*

amaz'zonico, -a, ci, che [amad'dzɔniko] *ag* Amazonian; Amazon *cpd*

ambasci'ata [ambaʃʃata] *sf* embassy; (*messaggio*) message; **ambascia'tore, -'trice** *sm/f* ambassador/ambassadress

ambe'due *ag inv* **~ i ragazzi** both boys ▷ *pron inv* both

ambienta'lista, -i, e *ag* environmental ▷ *sm/f* environmentalist

ambien'tare *vt* to acclimatize; (*romanzo, film*) to set; **ambientarsi** *vpr* to get used to one's surroundings

ambi'ente *sm* environment; (*fig: insieme di persone*) milieu; (*stanza*) room

am'biguo, -a *ag* ambiguous

ambizi'one [ambit'tsjone] *sf* ambition; **ambizi'oso, -a** *ag* ambitious

'ambo *ag inv* both ▷ *sm* (*al gioco*) double

'ambra *sf* amber; **ambra grigia** ambergris

ambu'lante *ag* itinerant ▷ *sm* peddler

ambu'lanza [ambu'lantsa] *sf* ambulance; **chiamate un ~** call an ambulance

ambula'torio *sm* (*studio medico*) surgery

A'merica *sf* **l'~** America; **l'~ latina** Latin America; **ameri'cano, -a** *ag*, *sm/f* American

ami'anto *sm* asbestos

ami'chevole [ami'kevole] *ag* friendly

ami'cizia [ami'tʃittsja] *sf* friendship; **amicizie** *sfpl* (*amici*) friends

a'mico, -a, -ci, -che *sm/f* friend; (*fidanzato*) boyfriend/girlfriend; **amico del cuore** bosom friend

'amido *sm* starch

ammac'care *vt* (*pentola*) to dent; (*persona*) to bruise

ammacca'tura *sf* dent; bruise

ammaes'trare *vt* (*animale*) to train

ammai'nare *vt* to lower, haul down

amma'larsi *vpr* to fall ill; **amma'lato, -a** *ag* ill, sick ▷ *sm/f* sick person; (*paziente*) patient

ammanet'tare *vt* to handcuff

ammas'sare *vt* (*ammucchiare*) to amass; (*raccogliere*) to gather together; **ammassarsi** *vpr* to pile up; to gather

ammat'tire *vi* to go mad

ammaz'zare [ammat'tsare] *vt* to kill; **ammazzarsi** *vpr* (*uccidersi*) to kill o.s.; (*rimanere ucciso*) to be killed; **ammazzarsi di lavoro** to work o.s. to death

am'mettere *vt* to admit; (*riconoscere: fatto*) to acknowledge, admit; (*permettere*) to allow, accept; (*supporre*) to suppose

amminis'trare *vt* to run, manage; (*Rel, Dir*) to administer; **amministra'tore** *sm* administrator; (*di condominio*) flats manager; **amministratore delegato** managing director; **amministrazi'one** *sf* management; administration

ammi'raglio [ammi'raʎʎo] *sm* admiral

ammi'rare *vt* to admire; **ammirazi'one** *sf* admiration

am'misi *ecc vb vedi* **ammettere**

ammobili'ato, -a *ag* furnished

am'mollo *sm* **lasciare in ~** to leave to soak

ammo'niaca *sf* ammonia

ammo'nire *vt* (*avvertire*) to warn; (*rimproverare*) to admonish; (*Dir*) to caution

ammonizi'one [ammonit'tsjone] *sf* (*monito: anche Sport*) warning; (*rimprovero*) reprimand; (*Dir*) caution

ammon'tare *vi* **~ a** to amount to ▷ *sm* (*total*) amount

ammorbi'dente *sm* fabric conditioner

ammorbi'dire *vt* to soften

ammortizza'tore *sm* (*Aut, Tecn*) shock-absorber

ammucchi'are [ammuk'kjare] *vt* to pile up, accumulate

ammuf'fire *vi* to go mouldy (BRIT) *o* moldy (US)

ammuto'lire *vi* to be struck dumb

amne'sia *sf* amnesia

amnis'tia *sf* amnesty

'amo *sm* (*Pesca*) hook; (*fig*) bait

a'more *sm* love; **amori** *smpl* love affairs; **il tuo bambino è un ~** your baby's a darling; **fare l'~** *o* **all'~** to make love; **per ~ o per forza** by hook or by crook; **amor proprio**

self-esteem, pride

amo'roso, -a *ag (affettuoso)* loving, affectionate; *(d'amore: sguardo)* amorous; *(: poesia, relazione)* love *cpd*

'ampio, -a *ag* wide, broad; *(spazioso)* spacious; *(abbondante: vestito)* loose; *(: gonna)* full; *(: spiegazione)* ample, full

am'plesso *sm* intercourse

ampli'are *vt (ingrandire)* to enlarge; *(allargare)* to widen; **ampliarsi** *vpr* to grow, increase

amplifica'tore *sm (Tecn, Mus)* amplifier

ampu'tare *vt (Med)* to amputate

A.N. *sigla f (= Alleanza Nazionale)* Italian right-wing party

anabbaglianti *smpl* dipped (BRIT) *o* dimmed (US) headlights

anaboliz'zante *ag* anabolic ▷ *sm* anabolic steroid

anal'colico, -a, -ci, -che *ag* non-alcoholic ▷ *sm* soft drink

analfa'beta, -i, -e *ag, sm/f* illiterate

anal'gesico, -a, -ci, -che [anal'dʒɛziko] *ag, sm* analgesic

a'nalisi *sf inv* analysis; *(Med: esame)* test; **analisi del sangue** blood test *sg*

analiz'zare [analid'dzare] *vt* to analyse; *(Med)* to test

a'nalogo, -a, -ghi, -ghe *ag* analogous

'ananas *sm inv* pineapple

anar'chia [anar'kia] *sf* anarchy; **a'narchico, -a, -ci, -che** *ag* anarchic(al) ▷ *sm/f* anarchist

anarco-insurreziona'lista *ag* anarcho-revolutionary

'A.N.A.S. *sigla f (= Azienda Nazionale Autonoma delle Strade)* national roads department

anato'mia *sf* anatomy

'anatra *sf* duck

'anca, -che *sf (Anat)* hip

'anche ['anke] *cong (inoltre, pure)* also, too; *(perfino)* even; **vengo anch'io** I'm coming too; **~ se** even if

an'cora *av* still; *(di nuovo)* again; *(di più)* some more; *(persino)*: **~ più forte** even stronger; **non ~** not yet; **~ una volta** once more, once again; **~ un po'** a little more; *(di tempo)* a little longer

an'dare *sm* **a lungo ~** in the long run ▷ *vi* to go; *(essere adatto)*: **~ a** to suit; *(piacere)*: **il suo comportamento non mi va** I don't like the way he behaves; **ti va di ~ al cinema?** do you feel like going to the cinema?; **andarsene** to go away; **questa camicia va lavata** this shirt needs a wash *o* should be washed; **~ a cavallo** to ride; **~ in macchina/aereo** to go by car/plane; **~ a fare qc** to go and do sth; **~ a pescare/**

sciare to go fishing/skiing; **~ a male** to go bad; **come va?** *(lavoro, progetto)* how are things?; **come va? — bene, grazie!** how are you? — fine, thanks!; **va fatto entro oggi** it's got to be done today; **ne va della nostra vita** our lives are at stake; **an'data** *sf* going; *(viaggio)* outward journey; **biglietto di sola andata** single (BRIT) *o* one-way ticket; **biglietto di andata e ritorno** return (BRIT) *o* round-trip (US) ticket

andrò *ecc vb vedi* **andare**

a'neddoto *sm* anecdote

a'nello *sm* ring; *(di catena)* link; **anelli** *smpl (Ginnastica)* rings

a'nemico, -a, -ci, -che *ag* anaemic

aneste'sia *sf* anaesthesia

'angelo ['andʒelo] *sm* angel; **angelo custode** guardian angel

anghe'ria [ange'ria] *sf* vexation

angli'cano, -a *ag* Anglican

anglo'sassone *ag* Anglo-Saxon

'angolo *sm* corner; *(Mat)* angle; **angolo cottura** *(di appartamento ecc)* cooking area

an'goscia, -sce [an'gɔʃʃa] *sf* deep anxiety, anguish *no pl*

angu'illa *sf* eel

an'guria *sf* watermelon

'anice ['anitʃe] *sm (Cuc)* aniseed; *(Bot)* anise

'anima *sf* soul; *(abitante)* inhabitant; **non c'era ~ viva** there wasn't a living soul; **anima gemella** soul mate

ani'male *sm, ag* animal; **animale domestico** pet

anna'cquare *vt* to water down, dilute

annaffi'are *vt* to water; **annaffia'toio** *sm* watering can

an'nata *sf* year; *(importo annuo)* annual amount; **vino d'~** vintage wine

anne'gare *vt, vi* to drown

anne'rire *vt* to blacken ▷ *vi* to become black

annien'tare *vt* to annihilate, destroy

anniver'sario *sm* anniversary; **anniversario di matrimonio** wedding anniversary

'anno *sm* year; **ha 8 anni** he's 8 (years old)

anno'dare *vt* to knot, tie; *(fig: rapporto)* to form

annoi'are *vt* to bore; **annoiarsi** *vpr* to be bored

> Attenzione! In inglese esiste il verbo *to annoy* che però vuol dire *dare fastidio a*.

anno'tare *vt (registrare)* to note, note down; *(commentare)* to annotate

annu'ale *ag* annual

annu'ire *vi* to nod; *(acconsentire)* to agree

annul'lare *vt* to annihilate, destroy;

(*contratto, francobollo*) to cancel; (*matrimonio*) to annul; (*sentenza*) to quash; (*risultati*) to declare void

annunci'are [annun'tʃare] *vt* to announce; (*dar segni rivelatori*) to herald

an'nuncio [an'nuntʃo] *sm* announcement; (*fig*) sign; **annunci economici** classified advertisements, small ads; **annunci mortuari** (*colonna*) obituary column; **annuncio pubblicitario** advertisement

'annuo, -a *ag* annual, yearly

annu'sare *vt* to sniff, smell; **~ tabacco** to take snuff

a'nomalo, -a *ag* anomalous

a'nonimo, -a *ag* anonymous ▷ *sm* (*autore*) anonymous writer (*o painter ecc*); **società anonima** (*Comm*) joint stock company

ano'ressia *sf* anorexia

ano'ressico, -a, ci, che *ag* anorexic

anor'male *ag* abnormal ▷ *sm/f* subnormal person

ANSA *sigla f* (= *Agenzia Nazionale Stampa Associata*) *press agency*

'ansia *sf* anxiety

ansi'mare *vi* to pant

ansi'oso, -a *ag* anxious

'anta *sf* (*di finestra*) shutter; (*di armadio*) door

An'tartide *sf* **l'~** Antarctica

an'tenna *sf* (*Radio, TV*) aerial; (*Zool*) antenna, feeler; (*Naut*) yard; **antenna parabolica** satellite dish

ante'prima *sf* preview; **anteprima di stampa** (*Inform*) print preview

anteri'ore *ag* (*ruota, zampa*) front; (*fatti*) previous, preceding

antiade'rente *ag* non-stick

antibi'otico, -a, -ci, -che *ag, sm* antibiotic

anti'camera *sf* anteroom; **fare ~** to wait (for an audience)

antici'pare [antitʃi'pare] *vt* (*consegna, visita*) to bring forward, anticipate; (*somma di denaro*) to pay in advance; (*notizia*) to disclose ▷ *vi* to be ahead of time; **an'ticipo** *sm* anticipation; (*di denaro*) advance; **in anticipo** early, in advance; **occorre che prenoti in anticipo?** do I need to book in advance?

an'tico, -a, -chi, -che *ag* (*quadro, mobili*) antique; (*dell'antichità*) ancient; **all'antica** old-fashioned

anticoncezio'nale [antikontʃettsjo'nale] *sm* contraceptive

anticonfor'mista, -i, -e *ag, sm/f* nonconformist

anti'corpo *sm* antibody

antidolo'rifico, -ci *sm* painkiller

anti'doping *sm* drug testing ▷ *ag inv* **test ~ drugs** (*BRIT*) *o* **drug** (*US*) **test**

an'tifona *sf* (*Mus, Rel*) antiphon; **capire l'~** (*fig*) to take the hint

anti'forfora *ag inv* anti-dandruff

anti'furto *sm* anti-theft device

anti'gelo [anti'dʒɛlo] *ag inv* **(liquido) ~** (*per motore*) antifreeze; (*per cristalli*) de-icer

antiglobalizzazione [antiglobalidd zat'tsjone] *ag inv* **movimento ~** anti-globalization movement

An'tille *sfpl* **le ~** the West Indies

antin'cendio [antin'tʃɛndjo] *ag inv* fire *cpd*

anti'nebbia *sm inv* (*anche:* **faro ~**: *Aut*) fog lamp

antinfiamma'torio, -a *ag, sm* anti-inflammatory

antio'rario [antio'rarjo] *ag* **in senso ~** anticlockwise

anti'pasto *sm* hors d'œuvre

antipa'tia *sf* antipathy, dislike; **anti'patico, -a, -ci, -che** *ag* unpleasant, disagreeable

antiproi'ettile *ag inv* bulletproof

antiquari'ato *sm* antique trade; **un oggetto d'~** an antique

anti'quario *sm* antique dealer

anti'quato, -a *ag* antiquated, old-fashioned

anti'rughe *ag inv* (*crema, prodotto*) anti-wrinkle

antitraspi'rante *ag* antiperspirant

anti'vipera *ag inv* **siero ~** remedy for snake bites

antivirus [anti'virus] *sm inv* antivirus software *no pl* ▷ *ag inv* antivirus

antolo'gia, -'gie [antolo'dʒia] *sf* anthology

anu'lare *ag* ring *cpd* ▷ *sm* third finger

'anzi ['antsi] *av* (*invece*) on the contrary; (*o meglio*) or rather, or better still

anzi'ano, -a [an'tsjano] *ag* old; (*Amm*) senior ▷ *sm/f* old person; senior member

anziché [antsi'ke] *cong* rather than

a'patico, -a, -ci, -che *ag* apathetic

'ape *sf* bee

aperi'tivo *sm* apéritif

aperta'mente *av* openly

a'perto, -a *pp di* **aprire** ▷ *ag* open; **all'~** in the open (air); **è ~ al pubblico?** is it open to the public?; **quando è ~ il museo?** when is the museum open?

aper'tura *sf* opening; (*ampiezza*) width; (*Fot*) aperture; **apertura alare** wing span; **apertura mentale** open-mindedness

ap'nea *sf* **immergersi in ~** to dive without breathing apparatus

a'postrofo *sm* apostrophe

ap'paio ecc vb vedi **apparire**
ap'palto sm (Comm) contract; **dare/ prendere in ~ un lavoro** to let out/ undertake a job on contract
appannarsi vpr to mist over; to grow dim
apparecchi'are [apparek'kjare] vt to prepare; (tavola) to set ▷ vi to set the table
appa'recchio [appa'rekkjo] sm piece of apparatus, device; (aeroplano) aircraft inv; **apparecchio acustico** hearing aid; **apparecchio telefonico** telephone; **apparecchio televisivo** television set
appa'rente ag apparent
appa'rire vi to appear; (sembrare) to seem, appear
apparta'mento sm flat (BRIT), apartment (US)
appar'tarsi vpr to withdraw
apparte'nere vi ~ **a** to belong to
ap'parvi ecc vb vedi **apparire**
appassio'nare vt to thrill; (commuovere) to move; **appassionarsi** vpr **appassionarsi a qc** to take a great interest in sth; **appassio'nato, -a** ag passionate; (entusiasta): **appassionato (di)** keen (on)
appas'sire vi to wither
appas'sito, -a ag dead
ap'pello sm roll-call; (implorazione, Dir) appeal; **fare ~ a** to appeal to
ap'pena av (a stento) hardly, scarcely; (solamente, da poco) just ▷ cong as soon as; **(non) ~ furono arrivati ...** as soon as they had arrived ...; **~ ... che** o **quando** no sooner ... than
ap'pendere vt to hang (up)
appen'dice [appen'ditʃe] sf appendix; **romanzo d'~** popular serial
appendi'cite [appendi'tʃite] sf appendicitis
Appen'nini smpl **gli ~** the Apennines
appesan'tire vt to make heavy; **appesantirsi** vpr to grow stout
appe'tito sm appetite
appic'care vt ~ **il fuoco a** to set fire to, set on fire
appicci'care [appittʃi'kare] vt to stick; **appicciicarsi** vpr to stick; (fig: persona) to cling
appiso'larsi vpr to doze off
applau'dire vt, vi to applaud; **ap'plauso** sm applause
appli'care vt to apply; (regolamento) to enforce; **applicarsi** vpr to apply o.s.
appoggi'are [appod'dʒare] vt (mettere contro): ~ **qc a qc** to lean o rest sth against sth; (fig: sostenere) to support; **appoggiarsi** vpr **appoggiarsi a** to lean against; (fig) to rely upon; **ap'poggio** sm support

apposita'mente av specially; (apposta) on purpose
ap'posito, -a ag appropriate
ap'posta av on purpose, deliberately
appos'tarsi vpr to lie in wait
ap'prendere vt (imparare) to learn
appren'dista, -i, -e sm/f apprentice
apprensi'one sf apprehension
apprez'zare [appret'tsare] vt to appreciate
appro'dare vi (Naut) to land; (fig): **non ~ a nulla** to come to nothing
approfit'tare vi ~ **di** to make the most of; (peg) to take advantage of
approfon'dire vt to deepen; (fig) to study in depth
appropri'ato, -a ag appropriate
approssima'tivo, -a ag approximate, rough; (impreciso) inexact, imprecise
appro'vare vt (condotta, azione) to approve of; (candidato) to pass; (progetto di legge) to approve
appunta'mento sm appointment; (amoroso) date; **darsi ~** to arrange to meet (one another); **ho un ~ con...** I have an appointment with ...; **vorrei prendere un ~** I'd like to make an appointment
ap'punto sm note; (rimprovero) reproach ▷ av (proprio) exactly, just; **per l'~!, ~!** exactly!
apribot'tiglie [apribot'tiʎʎe] sm inv bottle opener
a'prile sm April
a'prire vt to open; (via, cadavere) to open up; (gas, luce, acqua) to turn on ▷ vi to open; **aprirsi** vpr to open; **aprirsi a qn** to confide in sb, open one's heart to sb; **a che ora aprite?** what time do you open?
apris'catole sm inv tin (BRIT) o can opener
APT sigla f (= Azienda di Promozione) ≈ tourist board
aquagym [akkwa'dʒim] sf aquaerobics
'aquila sf (Zool) eagle; (fig) genius
aqui'lone sm (giocattolo) kite; (vento) North wind
A/R abbr = **andata e ritorno** (biglietto) return ticket (BRIT), round-trip ticket (US)
A'rabia Sau'dita sf **l'~** Saudi Arabia
'arabo, -a ag, sm/f Arab ▷ sm (Ling) Arabic
a'rachide [a'rakide] sf peanut
ara'gosta sf crayfish; lobster
a'rancia, -ce [a'rantʃa] sf orange; **aranci'ata** sf orangeade; **aranci'one** ag inv **(color) arancione** bright orange
a'rare vt to plough (BRIT), plow (US)
a'ratro sm plough (BRIT), plow (US)
a'razzo [a'rattso] sm tapestry
arbi'trare vt (Sport) to referee; to umpire; (Dir) to arbitrate

arbi'trario, -a *ag* arbitrary

'arbitro *sm* arbiter, judge; (*Dir*) arbitrator; (*Sport*) referee; (: *Tennis, Cricket*) umpire

ar'busto *sm* shrub

archeolo'gia [arkeolo'dʒia] *sf* arch(a)eology; **arche'ologo, -a, -gi, -ghe** *sm/f* arch(a)eologist

architet'tare [arkitet'tare] *vt* (*fig: idearc*) to devise; (: *macchinare*) to plan, concoct

archi'tetto [arki'tetto] *sm* architect; **architet'tura** *sf* architecture

ar'chivio [ar'kivjo] *sm* archives *pl*; (*Inform*) file

'arco *sm* (*arma, Mus*) bow; (*Archit*) arch; (*Mat*) arc

arcoba'leno *sm* rainbow

arcu'ato, -a *ag* curved, bent

'ardere *vt, vi* to burn

ar'desia *sf* slate

'area *sf* area; (*Edil*) land, ground; **area di rigore** (*Sport*) penalty area; **area di servizio** (*Aut*) service area

a'rena *sf* arena; (*per corride*) bullring; (*sabbia*) sand

are'narsi *vpr* to run aground

argente'ria [ardʒente'ria] *sf* silverware, silver

Argen'tina [ardʒen'tina] *sf* **l'~** Argentina; **argen'tino, -a** *ag, sm/f* Argentinian

ar'gento [ar'dʒɛnto] *sm* silver; **argento vivo** quicksilver

ar'gilla [ar'dʒilla] *sf* clay

'argine ['ardʒine] *sm* embankment, bank; (*diga*) dyke, dike

argo'mento *sm* argument; (*motivo*) motive; (*materia, tema*) subject

'aria *sf* air; (*espressione, aspetto*) air, look; (*Mus: melodia*) tune; (*di opera*) aria; **mandare all'~** to ruin *o* upset sth; **all'~ aperta** in the open (air)

'arido, -a *ag* arid

arieggi'are [arjed'dʒare] *vt* (*cambiare aria*) to air; (*imitare*) to imitate

ari'ete *sm* ram; (*Mil*) battering ram; (*dello zodiaco*): **A~** Aries

a'ringa, -ghe *sf* herring *inv*

arit'metica *sf* arithmetic

'arma, -i *sf* weapon, arm; (*parte dell'esercito*) arm; **chiamare alle armi** to call up (BRIT), draft (US); **sotto le armi** in the army (*o* forces); **alle armi!** to arms!; **arma atomica/nucleare** atomic/nuclear weapon; **arma da fuoco** firearm; **armi di distruzione di massa** weapons of mass destruction

arma'dietto *sm* (*di medicinali*) medicine cabinet; (*in palestra ecc*) locker; (*in cucina*) (kitchen) cupboard

ar'madio *sm* cupboard; (*per abiti*) wardrobe; **armadio a muro** built-in cupboard

ar'mato, -a *ag* **~ (di)** (*anche fig*) armed (with) ▷ *sf* (*Mil*) army; (*Naut*) fleet; **rapina a mano armata** armed robbery

arma'tura *sf* (*struttura di sostegno*) framework; (*impalcatura*) scaffolding; (*Storia*) armour *no pl*, suit of armour

armis'tizio [armis'tittsjo] *sm* armistice

armo'nia *sf* harmony

ar'nese *sm* tool, implement; (*oggetto indeterminato*) thing, contraption; **male in ~** (*malvestito*) badly dressed; (*di salute malferma*) in poor health; (*povero*) down-at-heel

'arnia *sf* hive

a'roma, -i *sm* aroma; fragrance; **aromi** *smpl* (*Cuc*) herbs and spices; **aromatera'pia** *sf* aromatherapy

'arpa *sf* (*Mus*) harp

arrabbi'are *vi* (*cane*) to be affected with rabies; **arrabbiarsi** *vpr* (*essere preso dall'ira*) to get angry, fly into a rage; **arrabbi'ato, -a** *ag* rabid, with rabies; furious, angry

arrampi'carsi *vpr* to climb (up)

arrangiarsi *vpr* to manage, do the best one can

arreda'mento *sm* (*studio*) interior design; (*mobili ecc*) furnishings *pl*

arre'dare *vt* to furnish

ar'rendersi *vpr* to surrender

arres'tare *vt* (*fermare*) to stop, halt; (*catturare*) to arrest; **arrestarsi** *vpr* (*fermarsi*) to stop; **ar'resto** *sm* (*cessazione*) stopping; (*fermata*) stop; (*cattura, Med*) arrest; **subire un arresto** to come to a stop *o* standstill; **mettere agli arresti** to place under arrest; **arresti domiciliari** house arrest *sg*

arre'trare *vt, vi* to withdraw; **arre'trato, -a** *ag* (*lavoro*) behind schedule; (*paese, bambino*) backward; (*numero di giornale*) back *cpd*; **arretrati** *smpl* arrears

arric'chire [arrik'kire] *vt* to enrich; **arricchirsi** *vpr* to become rich

arri'vare *vi* to arrive; (*accadere*) to happen, occur; **~ a** (*livello, grado ecc*) to reach; **a che ora arriva il treno da Londra?** what time does the train from London arrive?; **non ci arrivo** I can't reach it; (*fig: non capisco*) I can't understand it

arrive'derci [arrive'dertʃi] *escl* goodbye!

arri'vista, -i, -e *sm/f* go-getter

ar'rivo *sm* arrival; (*Sport*) finish, finishing line

arro'gante *ag* arrogant

arros'sire *vi* (*per vergogna, timidezza*) to blush, flush; (*per gioia, rabbia*) to flush

arros'tire *vt* to roast; (*pane*) to toast; (*ai*

ferri) to grill

ar'rosto *sm, ag inv* roast

arroto'lare *vt* to roll up

arroton'dare *vt* (*forma, oggetto*) to round; (*stipendio*) to add to; (*somma*) to round off

arrugginito, -a [arruddʒin'nito] *ag* rusty

'arsi *vb vedi* **ardere**

'arte *sf* art; (*abilità*) skill

ar'teria *sf* artery; **arteria stradale** main road

'artico, -a, -ci, -che *ag* Arctic

articolazi'one *sf* articulation; (*Anat, Tecn*) joint

ar'ticolo *sm* article; **articolo di fondo** (*Stampa*) leader, leading article

artifici'ale [artifi'tʃale] *ag* artificial

artigia'nato [artidʒa'nato] *sm* craftsmanship; craftsmen *pl*

artigi'ano, -a [arti'dʒano] *sm/f* craftsman/woman

ar'tista, -i, -e *sm/f* artist; **ar'tistico, -a, -ci, -che** *ag* artistic

ar'trite *sf* (*Med*) arthritis

a'scella [aʃ'ʃella] *sf* (*Anat*) armpit

ascen'dente [aʃʃen'dɛnte] *sm* ancestor; (*fig*) ascendancy; (*Astr*) ascendant

ascen'sore [aʃʃen'sore] *sm* lift

a'scesso [aʃ'ʃesso] *sm* (*Med*) abscess

asciugaca'pelli [aʃʃugaka'pelli] *sm* hair-drier

asciuga'mano [aʃʃuga'mano] *sm* towel

asciu'gare [aʃʃu'gare] *vt* to dry; **asciugarsi** *vpr* to dry o.s.; (*diventare asciutto*) to dry

asci'utto, -a [aʃ'ʃutto] *ag* dry; (*fig: magro*) lean; (*: burbero*) curt; **restare a bocca asciutta** (*fig*) to be disappointed

ascol'tare *vt* to listen to

as'falto *sm* asphalt

'Asia *sf* l'**~** Asia; **asi'atico, -a, -ci, -che** *ag, sm/f* Asiatic, Asian

a'silo *sm* refuge, sanctuary; **~ (d'infanzia)** nursery(-school); **asilo nido** crèche; **asilo politico** political asylum

'asino *sm* donkey, ass

ASL *sigla f* (= *Azienda Sanitaria Locale*) local health centre

'asma *sf* asthma

as'parago, -gi *sm* asparagus *no pl*

aspet'tare *vt* to wait for; (*anche Comm*) to await; (*aspettarsi*) to expect ▷ *vi* to wait; **aspettami, per favore** wait for me, please

as'petto *sm* (*apparenza*) aspect, appearance, look; (*punto di vista*) point of view; **di bell'~** good-looking

aspira'polvere *sm inv* vacuum cleaner

aspi'rare *vt* (*respirare*) to breathe in, inhale; (*apparecchi*) to suck (up) ▷ *vi* **~ a** to

aspire to

aspi'rina *sf* aspirin

'aspro, -a *ag* (*sapore*) sour, tart; (*odore*) acrid, pungent; (*voce, clima, fig*) harsh; (*superficie*) rough; (*paesaggio*) rugged

assaggi'are [assad'dʒare] *vt* to taste; **posso assaggiarlo?** can I have a taste?; **assaggino** [assad'dʒino] *sm* **assaggini** (*Cuc*) selection of first courses; **solo un assaggino** just a little

as'sai *av* (*molto*) a lot, much; (: *con ag*) very; (*a sufficienza*) enough ▷ *ag inv* (*quantità*) a lot of, much; (*numero*) a lot of, many; **~ contento** very pleased

as'salgo *ecc vb vedi* **assalire**

assa'lire *vt* to attack, assail

assal'tare *vt* (*Mil*) to storm; (*banca*) to raid; (*treno, diligenza*) to hold up

as'salto *sm* attack, assault

assassi'nare *vt* to murder; to assassinate; (*fig*) to ruin; **assas'sino, -a** *ag* murderous ▷ *sm/f* murderer; assassin

'asse *sm* (*Tecn*) axle; (*Mat*) axis ▷ *sf* board; **asse** *sf* **da stiro** ironing board

assedi'are *vt* to besiege

asse'gnare [asseɲ'ɲare] *vt* to assign, allot; (*premio*) to award

as'segno [as'seɲɲo] *sm* allowance; (*anche:* **~ bancario**) cheque (*BRIT*), check (*US*); **contro ~** cash on delivery; **posso pagare con un ~?** can I pay by cheque?; **assegno circolare** bank draft; **assegni familiari** ≈ child benefit *no pl*; **assegno sbarrato** crossed cheque; **assegno di viaggio** traveller's cheque; **assegno a vuoto** dud cheque; **assegno di malattia/di invalidità** sick pay/disability benefit

assem'blea *sf* assembly

assen'tarsi *vpr* to go out

as'sente *ag* absent; (*fig*) faraway, vacant; **as'senza** *sf* absence

asse'tato, -a *ag* thirsty, parched

assicu'rare *vt* (*accertare*) to ensure; (*infondere certezza*) to assure; (*fermare, legare*) to make fast, secure; (*fare un contratto di assicurazione*) to insure; **assicurarsi** *vpr* (*accertarsi*): **assicurarsi (di)** to make sure (of); (*contro il furto ecc*): **assicurarsi (contro)** to insure o.s. (against); **assicurazi'one** *sf* assurance; insurance

assi'eme *av* (*insieme*) together; **~ a** (together) with

assil'lare *vt* to pester, torment

assis'tente *sm/f* assistant; **assistente sociale** social worker; **assistente di volo** (*Aer*) steward/stewardess

assis'tenza [assis'tɛntsa] *sf* assistance; **~ ospedaliera** free hospital treatment;

~ sociale welfare services *pl*; **assistenza sanitaria** health service

as'sistere *vt* (*aiutare*) to assist, help; (*curare*) to treat ▷ *vi* **~ (a qc)** (*essere presente*) to be present (at sth), to attend (sth)

'asso *sm* ace; **piantare qn in ~** to leave sb in the lurch

associ'are [asso'tʃare] *vt* to associate; **associarsi** *vpr* to enter into partnership; **associarsi a** to become a member of, join; (*dolori, gioie*) to share in; **~ qn alle carceri** to take sb to prison

associazi'one [assotʃat'tsjone] *sf* association; (*Comm*) association, society; **~ a delinquere** (*Dir*) criminal association

as'solsi *ecc vb vedi* **assolvere**

assoluta'mente *av* absolutely

asso'luto, -a *ag* absolute

assoluzi'one [assolut'tsjone] *sf* (*Dir*) acquittal; (*Rel*) absolution

as'solvere *vt* (*Dir*) to acquit; (*Rel*) to absolve; (*adempiere*) to carry out, perform

assomigli'are [assomiʎ'ʎare] *vi* **~ a** to resemble, look like; **assomigliarsi** *vpr* to look alike; (*nel carattere*) to be alike

asson'nato, -a *ag* sleepy

asso'pirsi *vpr* to doze off

assor'bente *ag* absorbent ▷ *sm*: **assorbente interno** tampon; **assorbente esterno/igienico** sanitary towel

assor'bire *vt* to absorb

assor'dare *vt* to deafen

assorti'mento *sm* assortment

assor'tito, -a *ag* assorted; matched, matching

assuefazi'one [assuefat'tsjone] *sf* (*Med*) addiction

as'sumere *vt* (*impiegato*) to take on, engage; (*responsabilità*) to assume, take upon o.s.; (*contegno, espressione*) to assume, put on; (*droga*) to consume

as'sunsi *ecc vb vedi* **assumere**

assurdità *sf inv* absurdity; **dire delle ~** to talk nonsense

as'surdo, -a *ag* absurd

'asta *sf* pole; (*vendita*) auction

as'temio, -a *ag* teetotal ▷ *sm/f* teetotaller

Attenzione! In inglese esiste la parola *abstemious* che però vuol dire *moderato*.

aste'nersi *vpr* **~ (da)** to abstain (from), refrain (from); (*Pol*) to abstain (from)

aste'risco, -schi *sm* asterisk

'astice ['astitʃe] *sm* lobster

astig'matico, -a, ci, che *ag* astigmatic

asti'nenza [asti'nɛntsa] *sf* abstinence; **essere in crisi di ~** to suffer from withdrawal symptoms

as'tratto, -a *ag* abstract

'astro... *prefisso*; **astrolo'gia** [astrolo'dʒia] *sf* astrology; **astro'nauta, -i, -e** *sm/f* astronaut; **astro'nave** *sf* space ship; **astrono'mia** *sf* astronomy; **astro'nomico, -a, -ci, -che** *ag* astronomic(al)

as'tuccio [as'tuttʃo] *sm* case, box, holder

as'tuto, -a *ag* astute, cunning, shrewd

A'tene *sf* Athens

'ateo, -a *ag, sm/f* atheist

at'lante *sm* atlas

at'lantico, -a, -ci, -che *ag* Atlantic ▷ *sm* **l'A~, l'Oceano A~** the Atlantic, the Atlantic Ocean

at'leta, -i, -e *sm/f* athlete; **at'letica** *sf* athletics *sg*; **atletica leggera** track and field events *pl*; **atletica pesante** weightlifting and wrestling

atmos'fera *sf* atmosphere

a'tomico, -a, -ci, -che *ag* atomic; (*nucleare*) atomic, atom *cpd*, nuclear

'atomo *sm* atom

'atrio *sm* entrance hall, lobby

a'troce [a'trotʃe] *ag* (*che provoca orrore*) dreadful; (*terribile*) atrocious

attac'cante *sm/f* (*Sport*) forward

attacca'panni *sm* hook, peg; (*mobile*) hall stand

attac'care *vt* (*unire*) to attach; (*cucendo*) to sew on; (*far aderire*) to stick (on); (*appendere*) to hang (up); (*assalire: anche fig*) to attack; (*iniziare*) to begin, start; (*fig: contagiare*) to pass on ▷ *vi* to stick, adhere; **attaccarsi** *vpr* to stick, adhere; (*trasmettersi per contagio*) to be contagious; (*afferrarsi*): **attaccarsi (a)** to cling to; (*fig: affezionarsi*): **attaccarsi (a)** to become attached (to); **~ discorso** to start a conversation; **at'tacco, -chi** *sm* (*azione offensiva: anche fig*) attack; (*Med*) attack, fit; (*Sci*) binding; (*Elettr*) socket

atteggia'mento [atteddʒa'mento] *sm* attitude

at'tendere *vt* to wait for, await ▷ *vi* **~ a** to attend to

atten'dibile *ag* (*storia*) credible; (*testimone*) reliable

atten'tato *sm* attack; **~ alla vita di qn** attempt on sb's life

at'tento, -a *ag* attentive; (*accurato*) careful, thorough; **stare ~ a qc** to pay attention to sth; **~! be careful!**

attenzi'one [atten'tsjone] *sf* attention; **~! watch out!, be careful!; attenzioni** *sfpl* (*premure*) attentions; **fare ~ a** to watch out for; **coprire qn di attenzioni** to lavish attentions on sb

atter'raggio [atter'raddʒo] *sm* landing

atter'rare *vt* to bring down ▷ *vi* to land

at'tesa *sf* waiting; (*tempo trascorso aspettando*) wait; **essere in ~ di qc** to be waiting for sth

at'tesi *ecc vb vedi* **attendere**

at'teso, -a *pp di* **attendere**

'attico, -ci *sm* attic

attil'lato, -a *ag* (*vestito*) close-fitting

'attimo *sm* moment; **in un ~** in a moment

atti'rare *vt* to attract

atti'tudine *sf* (*disposizione*) aptitude; (*atteggiamento*) attitude

attività *sf inv* activity; (*Comm*) assets *pl*

at'tivo, -a *ag* active; (*Comm*) profit-making, credit *cpd* ▷ *sm* (*Comm*) assets *pl*; **in ~** in credit

'atto *sm* act; (*azione, gesto*) action, act, deed; (*Dir: documento*) deed, document; **atti** *smpl* (*di congressi ecc*) proceedings; **mettere in ~** to put into action; **fare ~ di fare qc** to make as if to do sth; **atto di morte/di nascita** death/birth certificate

at'tore, -'trice *sm/f* actor/actress

at'torno *av* round, around, about; **~ a** round, around, about

attrac'care *vt, vi* (*Naut*) to dock, berth

at'tracco, -chi *sm* (*Naut*) docking *no pl*; berth

at'trae *ecc vb vedi* **attrarre**

attra'ente *ag* attractive

at'traggo *ecc vb vedi* **attrarre**

at'trarre *vt* to attract

at'trassi *ecc vb vedi* **attrarre**

attraver'sare *vt* to cross; (*città, bosco, fig: periodo*) to go through; (*fiume*) to run through

attra'verso *prep* through; (*da una parte all'altra*) across

attrazi'one [attrat'tsjone] *sf* attraction

at'trezzo *sm* tool, instrument; (*Sport*) piece of equipment

at'trice [at'tritʃe] *sf vedi* **attore**

attu'ale *ag* (*presente*) present; (*di attualità*) topical

▌ Attenzione! In inglese esiste la parola *actual* che però vuol dire *effettivo*.

attualità *sf inv* topicality; (*avvenimento*) current event

attual'mente *av* at the moment, at present

▌ Attenzione! In inglese esiste la parola *actually* che però vuol dire *effettivamente* oppure *veramente*.

attu'are *vt* to carry out

attu'tire *vt* to deaden, reduce

'audio *sm* (*TV, Radio, Cine*) sound

audiovi'sivo, -a *ag* audiovisual

audizi'one [audit'tsjone] *sf* hearing; (*Mus*) audition

augu'rare *vt* to wish; **augurarsi qc** to hope for sth

au'guri *smpl* best wishes; **fare gli ~ a qn** to give sb one's best wishes; **tanti ~!** best wishes!; (*per compleanno*) happy birthday!

'aula *sf* (*scolastica*) classroom; (*universitaria*) lecture theatre; (*di edificio pubblico*) hall

aumen'tare *vt, vi* to increase; **au'mento** *sm* increase

au'rora *sf* dawn

ausili'are *ag, sm, sm/f* auxiliary

Aus'tralia *sf* l'~ Australia; **australi'ano, -a** *ag, sm/f* Australian

'Austria *sf* l'~ Austria; **aus'triaco, -a, -ci, -che** *ag, sm/f* Austrian

au'tentico, -a, -ci, -che *ag* authentic, genuine

au'tista, -i *sm* driver

'auto *sf inv* car

autoabbron'zante *sm, ag* self-tan

autoade'sivo, -a *ag* self-adhesive ▷ *sm* sticker

autobio'grafico, -a, ci, che *ag* autobiographic(al)

'autobus *sm inv* bus

auto'carro *sm* lorry (BRIT), truck

autocertificazi'one [autotʃertifikat'tsjone] *sf* self-declaration

autodistrut'tivo, -a *ag* self-destructive

auto'gol *sm inv* own goal

au'tografo, -a *ag, sm* autograph

auto'grill® *sm inv* motorway restaurant

auto'matico, -a, -ci, -che *ag* automatic ▷ *sm* (*bottone*) snap fastener; (*fucile*) automatic

auto'mobile *sf* (motor) car

automobi'lista, -i, -e *sm/f* motorist

autono'leggio *sm* car hire

autono'mia *sf* autonomy; (*di volo*) range

au'tonomo, -a *ag* autonomous, independent

autop'sia *sf* post-mortem, autopsy

auto'radio *sf inv* (*apparecchio*) car radio; (*autoveicolo*) radio car

au'tore, -'trice *sm/f* author

autoreggente [autored'dʒɛnte] *ag* **calze autoreggenti** hold ups

auto'revole *ag* authoritative; (*persona*) influential

autoricari'cabile *ag* **scheda ~** top-up card

autori'messa *sf* garage

autorità *sf inv* authority

autoriz'zare [autorid'dzare] *vt* (*permettere*) to authorize; (*giustificare*) to allow, sanction

autos'contro *sm* dodgem car (BRIT), bumper car (US)

autoscu'ola *sf* driving school
autos'tima *sf* self-esteem
autos'top *sm* hitchhiking;
autostop'pista, -i, -e *sm/f* hitchhiker
autos'trada *sf* motorway (BRIT),
highway (US); **autostrada informatica**
information superhighway

● AUTOSTRADE
●
● You have to pay to use Italian
● motorways. They are indicated by an "A"
● followed by a number on a green sign.
● The speed limit on Italian motorways
● is 130 kph.

auto'velox® *sm inv* (police) speed camera
autovet'tura *sf* (motor) car
au'tunno *sm* autumn
avam'braccio [avam'brattʃo] (*pl (f)* **-cia**)
sm forearm
avangu'ardia *sf* vanguard
a'vanti *av* (*stato in luogo*) in front; (*moto: andare, venire*) forward; (*tempo: prima*)
before ▷ *prep* (*luogo*): **~ a** before, in front
of; (*tempo*): **~ Cristo** before Christ ▷ *escl*
(*entrate*) come (*o* go) in!; (*Mil*) forward!;
(*coraggio*) come on! ▷ *sm inv* (*Sport*)
forward; **~ e indietro** backwards and
forwards; **andare ~** to go forward;
(*continuare*) to go on; (*precedere*) to go
(on) ahead; (*orologio*) to be fast; **essere ~
negli studi** to be well advanced with one's
studies
avan'zare [avan'tsare] *vt* (*spostare
in avanti*) to move forward, advance;
(*domanda*) to put forward; (*promuovere*) to
promote; (*essere creditore*): **~ qc da qn** to be
owed sth by sb ▷ *vi* (*andare avanti*) to move
forward, advance; (*progredire*) to make
progress; (*essere d'avanzo*) to be left, remain
ava'ria *sf* (*guasto*) damage; (: *meccanico*)
breakdown
a'varo, -a *ag* avaricious, miserly ▷ *sm*
miser

◯ PAROLA CHIAVE

a'vere *sm* (*Comm*) credit; **gli averi** (*ricchezze*)
wealth *sg*
▷ *vt* **1** (*possedere*) to have; **ha due
bambini/una bella casa** she has (got)
two children/a lovely house; **ha i capelli
lunghi** he has (got) long hair; **non ho da
mangiare/bere** I've (got) nothing to eat/
drink, I don't have anything to eat/drink
2 (*indossare*) to wear, have on; **aveva una
maglietta rossa** he was wearing *o* he had
on a red tee-shirt; **ha gli occhiali** he wears

o has glasses
3 (*ricevere*) to get; **hai avuto l'assegno?**
did you get *o* have you had the cheque?
4 (*età, dimensione*) to be; **ha 9 anni** he
is 9 (years old); **la stanza ha 3 metri di
lunghezza** the room is 3 metres in length;
vedi **fame**; **paura** ecc
5 (*tempo*): **quanti ne abbiamo oggi?**
what's the date today?; **ne hai per molto?**
will you be long?
6 (*fraseologia*): **avercela con qn** to be
angry with sb; **cos'hai?** what's wrong *o*
what's the matter (with you)?; **non ha
niente a che vedere** *o* **fare con me** it's
got nothing to do with me
▷ *vb aus* **1** to have; **aver bevuto/
mangiato** to have drunk/eaten
2 (*i da + infinito*). **avere da fare qc** to have
to do sth; **non hai che da chiederlo** you
only have to ask him

aviazi'one [avjat'tsjone] *sf* aviation; (*Mil*)
air force
'avido, -a *ag* eager; (*peg*) greedy
avo'cado *sm* avocado
a'vorio *sm* ivory
Avv. *abbr* = **avvocato**
avvantaggi'are [avvantad'dʒare]
vt to favour; **avvantaggiarsi** *vpr*
**avvantaggiarsi negli affari/sui
concorrenti** to get ahead in business/of
one's competitors
avvele'nare *vt* to poison
av'vengo ecc *vb vedi* **avvenire**
avveni'mento *sm* event
avve'nire *vi, vb impers* to happen, occur
▷ *sm* future
av'venni ecc *vb vedi* **avvenire**
avven'tato, -a *ag* rash, reckless
avven'tura *sf* adventure; (*amorosa*) affair
avventu'rarsi *vpr* to venture
avventu'roso, -a *ag* adventurous
avve'rarsi *vpr* to come true
av'verbio *sm* adverb
avverrò ecc *vb vedi* **avvenire**
avver'sario, -a *ag* opposing ▷ *sm*
opponent, adversary
avver'tenza [avver'tɛntsa] *sf*
(*ammonimento*) warning; (*cautela*) care;
(*premessa*) foreword; **avvertenze** *sfpl*
(*istruzioni per l'uso*) instructions
avverti'mento *sm* warning
avver'tire *vt* (*avvisare*) to warn; (*rendere
consapevole*) to inform, notify; (*percepire*)
to feel
avvi'are *vt* (*mettere sul cammino*) to direct;
(*impresa, trattative*) to begin, start; (*motore*)
to start; **avviarsi** *vpr* to set off, set out
avvici'nare [avvitʃi'nare] *vt* to bring

near; (*trattare con: persona*) to approach;
avvicinarsi *vpr* **avvicinarsi (a qn/qc)** to
approach (sb/sth), draw near (to sb/sth)
avvi'lito, -a *ag* discouraged
avvin'cente *ag* captivating
avvi'sare *vt* (*far sapere*) to inform;
(*mettere in guardia*) to warn; **av'viso** *sm*
warning; (*annuncio*) announcement;
(: *affisso*) notice; (*inserzione pubblicitaria*)
advertisement; **a mio avviso** in my
opinion; **avviso di chiamata** (*servizio*)
call waiting; (*segnale*) call waiting signal;
avviso di garanzia (*Dir*) notification (*of
impending investigation and of the right to
name a defence lawyer*)

Attenzione! In inglese esiste la parola
advice che però vuol dire *consiglio*.

avvis'tare *vt* to sight
avvi'tare *vt* to screw down (*o* in)
avvo'cato, -'essa *sm/f* (*Dir*) barrister
(BRIT), lawyer; (*fig*) defender, advocate
av'volgere [av'vɔldʒere] *vt* to roll up;
(*avviluppare*) to wrap up; **avvolgersi** *vpr*
(*avvilupparsi*) to wrap o.s. up; **avvol'gibile**
sm roller blind (BRIT), blind
av'volsi *ecc vb vedi* **avvolgere**
avvol'toio *sm* vulture
aza'lea [addza'lɛa] *sf* azalea
azi'enda [ad'dzjɛnda] *sf* business, firm,
concern; **azienda agricola** farm
azi'one [at'tsjone] *sf* action; (*Comm*) share
a'zoto [ad'dzɔto] *sm* nitrogen
azzar'dare [addzar'dare] *vt* (*soldi, vita*) to
risk, hazard; (*domanda, ipotesi*) to hazard,
venture; **azzardarsi** *vpr* **azzardarsi a fare**
to dare (to) do
az'zardo [ad'dzardo] *sm* risk
azzec'care [attsek'kare] *vt* (*risposta ecc*)
to get right
azzuf'farsi [attsuf'farsi] *vpr* to come to
blows
az'zurro, -a [ad'dzurro] *ag* blue ▷ *sm*
(*colore*) blue; **gli azzurri** (*Sport*) the Italian
national team

'babbo *sm* (*fam*) dad, daddy; **Babbo
Natale** Father Christmas
baby'sitter ['beɪbɪsitəʳ] *sm/f inv* baby-
sitter
'bacca, -che *sf* berry
baccalà *sm* dried salted cod; (*fig: peg*)
dummy
bac'chetta [bak'ketta] *sf* (*verga*) stick, rod;
(*di direttore d'orchestra*) baton; (*di tamburo*)
drumstick; **~ magica** magic wand
ba'checa, -che [ba'kɛka] *sf* (*mobile*)
showcase, display case; (*Univ, in ufficio*)
notice board (BRIT), bulletin board (US)
baci'are [ba'tʃare] *vt* to kiss; **baciarsi** *vpr*
to kiss (one another)
baci'nella [batʃi'nɛlla] *sf* basin
ba'cino [ba'tʃino] *sm* basin; (*Mineralogia*)
field, bed; (*Anat*) pelvis; (*Naut*) dock
'bacio ['batʃo] *sm* kiss
'baco, -chi *sm* worm; **baco da seta**
silkworm
ba'dare *vi* (*fare attenzione*) to take care, be
careful; (*occuparsi di*): **~ a** to look after, take
care of; (*dar ascolto*): **~ a** to pay attention
to; **bada ai fatti tuoi!** mind your own
business!
'baffi *smpl* moustache *sg*; (*di animale*)
whiskers; **ridere sotto i ~** to laugh up
one's sleeve; **leccarsi i ~** to lick one's lips
bagagli'aio [bagaʎ'ʎajo] *sm* luggage van

(BRIT) o car (US); (Aut) boot (BRIT), trunk (US)

ba'gaglio [ba'gaʎʎo] sm luggage no pl, baggage no pl; **fare/disfare i bagagli** to pack/unpack; **i nostri bagagli non sono arrivati** our luggage has not arrived; **può mandare qualcuno a prendere i nostri bagagli?** could you send someone to collect our luggage?; **bagaglio a mano** hand luggage

bagli'ore [baʎ'ʎore] sm flash, dazzling light; **un ~ di speranza** a ray of hope

ba'gnante [baɲ'ɲante] sm/f bather

ba'gnare [baɲ'ɲare] vt to wet; (inzuppare) to soak; (innaffiare) to water; (fiume) to flow through; (: mare) to wash, bathe; **bagnarsi** vpr to get wet; (al mare) to go swimming o bathing; (in vasca) to have a bath

ba'gnato, -a [baɲ'ɲato] ag wet

ba'gnino [baɲ'ɲino] sm lifeguard

'bagno ['baɲɲo] sm bath; (stanza) bathroom; (toilette) toilet; **bagni** smpl (stabilimento) baths; **fare il ~** to have a bath; (nel mare) to go swimming o bathing; **dov'è il ~?** where's the toilet?; **fare il ~ a qn** to give sb a bath; **mettere a ~** to soak; **~ schiuma** bubble bath

bagnoma'ria [baɲɲoma'ria] sm **cuocere a ~** to cook in a double saucepan

bagnoschi'uma [baɲɲoskj'uma] sm inv bubble bath

'baia sf bay

balbet'tare vi to stutter, stammer; (bimbo) to babble ▷ vt to stammer out

bal'canico, -a, ci, che ag Balkan

bal'cone sm balcony; **avete una camera con ~?** do you have a room with a balcony?

bal'doria sf **fare ~** to have a riotous time

ba'lena sf whale

ba'leno sm flash of lightning; **in un ~** in a flash

bal'lare vt, vi to dance

balle'rina sf dancer; ballet dancer; (scarpa) ballet shoe

balle'rino sm dancer; ballet dancer

bal'letto sm ballet

'ballo sm dance; (azione) dancing no pl; **essere in ~** (fig: persona) to be involved; (: cosa) to be at stake

balne'are ag seaside cpd; (stagione) bathing

'balsamo sm (aroma) balsam; (lenimento, fig) balm

bal'zare [bal'tsare] vi to bounce; (lanciarsi) to jump, leap; **'balzo** sm bounce; jump, leap; (del terreno) crag

bam'bina ag, sf vedi **bambino**

bam'bino, -a sm/f child

'bambola sf doll

bambù sm bamboo

ba'nale ag banal, commonplace

ba'nana sf banana

'banca, -che sf bank; **banca dati** data bank

banca'rella sf stall

banca'rotta sf bankruptcy; **fare ~** to go bankrupt

ban'chetto [ban'ketto] sm banquet

banchi'ere [ban'kjɛre] sm banker

ban'china [ban'kina] sf (di porto) quay; (per pedoni, ciclisti) path; (di stazione) platform; **~ cedevole** (Aut) soft verge (BRIT) o shoulder (US)

'banco, -chi sm bench; (di negozio) counter; (di mercato) stall; (di officina) (work-)bench; (Geo, banca) bank; **banco di corallo** coral reef; **banco degli imputati** dock; **banco di prova** (fig) testing ground; **banco dei testimoni** witness box; **banco dei pegni** pawnshop; **banco di nebbia** bank of fog

'Bancomat® sm inv automated banking; (tessera) cash card

banco'nota sf banknote

'banda sf band; (di stoffa) band, stripe; (lato, parte) side; **~ perforata** punch tape

bandi'era sf flag, banner

ban'dito sm outlaw, bandit

'bando sm proclamation; (esilio) exile, banishment; **~ alle chiacchiere!** that's enough talk!; **bando di concorso** announcement of a competition

bar sm inv bar

'bara sf coffin

ba'racca, -che sf shed, hut; (peg) hovel; **mandare avanti la ~** to keep things going

ba'rare vi to cheat

'baratro sm abyss

ba'ratto sm barter

ba'rattolo sm (di latta) tin; (di vetro) jar; (di coccio) pot

'barba sf beard; **farsi la ~** to shave; **farla in ~ a qn** (fig) to do sth to sb's face; **che ~!** what a bore!

barbabi'etola sf beetroot (BRIT), beet (US); **barbabietola da zucchero** sugar beet

barbi'ere sm barber

bar'bone sm (cane) poodle; (vagabondo) tramp

'barca, -che sf boat; **barca a motore** motorboat; **barca a remi** rowing boat; **barca a vela** sail(ing) boat

barcol'lare vi to stagger

ba'rella sf (lettiga) stretcher

ba'rile sm barrel, cask

ba'rista, -i, -e sm/f barman/maid; (proprietario) bar owner

ba'rocco, -a, -chi, -che *ag, sm* baroque
ba'rometro *sm* barometer
ba'rone *sm* baron; **baro'nessa** *sf*
baroness
'barra *sf* bar; (*Naut*) helm; (*linea grafica*)
line, stroke
bar'rare *vt* to bar
barri'carsi *vpr* to barricade o.s.
barri'era *sf* barrier; (*Geo*) reef
ba'ruffa *sf* scuffle
barzel'letta [bardzel'letta] *sf* joke, funny
story
ba'sare *vt* to base, found; **basarsi** *vpr*
basarsi su (*fatti, prove*) to be based o
founded on; (: *persona*) to base one's
arguments on
'basco, -a, -schi, -sche *ag* Basque ▷ *sm*
(*copricapo*) beret
'base *sf* base; (*fig: fondamento*) basis; (*Pol*)
rank and file; **di ~** basic; **in ~ a** on the basis
of, according to; **a ~ di caffè** coffee-based
'baseball ['beisbɔːl] *sm* baseball
ba'sette *sfpl* sideburns
ba'silica, -che *sf* basilica
ba'silico *sm* basil
basket ['basket] *sm* basketball
bas'sista, -i, -e *sm/f* bass player
'basso, -a *ag* low; (*di statura*) short;
(*meridionale*) southern ▷ *sm* bottom, lower
part; (*Mus*) bass; **la bassa Italia** southern
Italy
bassorili'evo *sm* bas-relief
bas'sotto, -a *ag* squat ▷ *sm* (*cane*)
dachshund
'basta *escl* (that's) enough!, that will do!
bas'tardo, -a *ag* (*animale, pianta*) hybrid,
crossbreed; (*persona*) illegitimate, bastard;
(*peg*) ▷ *sm/f* illegitimate child, bastard
(*peg*)
bas'tare *vi, vb impers* to be enough, be
sufficient; **~ a qn** to be enough for sb;
basta chiedere *o* **che chieda a un**
vigile you have only to *o* need only ask
a policeman; **basta così, grazie** that's
enough, thanks
basto'nare *vt* to beat, thrash
baston'cino [baston'tʃino] *sm* (*Sci*) ski
pole; **bastoncini di pesce** fish fingers
bas'tone *sm* stick; **~ da passeggio**
walking stick
bat'taglia [bat'taʎʎa] *sf* battle; fight
bat'tello *sm* boat
bat'tente *sm* (*imposta: di porta*) wing, flap;
(: *di finestra*) shutter; (*batacchio: di porta*)
knocker; (: *di orologio*) hammer; **chiudere i**
battenti (*fig*) to shut up shop
'battere *vt* to beat; (*grano*) to thresh;
(*percorrere*) to scour ▷ *vi* (*bussare*) to knock;
(*urtare*): **~ contro** to hit *o* strike against;

(*pioggia, sole*) to beat down; (*cuore*) to beat;
(*Tennis*) to serve; **battersi** *vpr* to fight; **~**
le mani to clap; **~ i piedi** to stamp one's
feet; **~ a macchina** to type; **~ bandiera**
italiana to fly the Italian flag; **~ in testa**
(*Aut*) to knock; **in un batter d'occhio** in
the twinkling of an eye
batte'ria *sf* battery; (*Mus*) drums *pl*
bat'terio *sm* bacterium
batte'rista, -i, -e *sm/f* drummer
bat'tesimo *sm* (*rito*) baptism; christening
battez'zare [batted'dzare] *vt* to baptize;
to christen
batti'panni *sm inv* carpet-beater
battis'trada *sm inv* (*di pneumatico*) tread;
(*di gara*) pacemaker
'battito *sm* beat, throb; **battito cardiaco**
heartbeat
bat'tuta *sf* blow; (*di macchina da scrivere*)
stroke; (*Mus*) bar; beat; (*Teatro*) cue; (*frase*
spiritosa) witty remark; (*di caccia*) beating;
(*Polizia*) combing, scouring; (*Tennis*)
service
ba'tuffolo *sm* wad
ba'ule *sm* trunk; (*Aut*) boot (BRIT), trunk
(US)
'bava *sf* (*di animale*) slaver, slobber; (*di*
lumaca) slime; (*di vento*) breath
bava'glino [bavaʎ'ʎino] *sm* bib
ba'vaglio [ba'vaʎʎo] *sm* gag
'bavero *sm* collar
ba'zar [bad'dzar] *sm inv* bazaar
BCE *sigla f* (= *Banca centrale europea*) ECB
be'ato, -a *ag* blessed; (*fig*) happy; **~ te!**
lucky you!
bec'care *vt* to peck; (*fig: raffreddore*) to
catch; **beccarsi** *vpr* (*fig*) to squabble;
beccarsi qc to catch sth
beccherò *ecc* [bekke'rɔ] *vb vedi* **beccare**
'becco, -chi *sm* beak, bill; (*di caffettiera ecc*)
spout; lip
be'fana *sf* hag, witch; **la B~** old woman
who, according to legend, brings children
their presents at the Epiphany; (*Epifania*)
Epiphany

⬤ **BEFANA**
⬤
⬤ The **Befana** is a national holiday on the
⬤ feast of the Epiphany. It takes its name
⬤ from **la Befana**, the old woman who,
⬤ according to Italian legend comes down
⬤ the chimney during the night leaving
⬤ gifts for children who have been good,
⬤ and coal for those who have not.

bef'fardo, -a *ag* scornful, mocking
'begli ['beʎʎi] *ag vedi* **bello**
'bei *ag vedi* **bello**

beige [bɛʒ] *ag inv* beige
bel *ag vedi* **bello**
be'lare *vi* to bleat
'belga, -gi, -ghe *ag, sm/f* Belgian
'Belgio ['bɛldʒo] *sm* **il ~** Belgium
'bella *sf* (*Sport*) decider; *vedi anche* **bello**
bel'lezza [bel'lettsa] *sf* beauty

 PAROLA CHIAVE

'bello, -a (*ag: dav sm* **bel** + *C,* **bell'** + *V,*
bello + *s impura, gn, pn, ps, x, z, pl* **bei** +
C, **begli** + *s impura ecc o V*) *ag* **1** (*oggetto,
donna, paesaggio*) beautiful, lovely; (*uomo*)
handsome; (*tempo*) beautiful, fine, lovely;
le belle arti fine arts
2 (*quantità*): **una bella cifra** a considerable
sum of money; **un bel niente** absolutely
nothing
3 (*rafforzativo*): **è una truffa bella e
buona!** it's a real fraud!; **è bell'e finito** it's
already finished
▷ *sm* **1** (*bellezza*) beauty; (*tempo*) fine
weather
2: **adesso viene il bello** now comes the
best bit; **sul più bello** at the crucial point;
cosa fai di bello? are you doing anything
interesting?
▷ *av* **fa bello** the weather is fine, it's fine

'belva *sf* wild animal
belve'dere *sm inv* panoramic viewpoint
benché [ben'ke] *cong* although
'benda *sf* bandage; (*per gli occhi*) blindfold;
ben'dare *vt* to bandage; to blindfold
'bene *av* well; (*completamente, affatto*):
è ben difficile it's very difficult ▷ *ag inv*
gente ~ well-to-do people ▷ *sm* good;
beni *smpl* (*averi*) property *sg*, estate *sg*;
io sto ~/poco ~ I'm well/not very well;
va ~ all right; **volere un ~ dell'anima a
qn** to love sb very much; **un uomo per ~**
a respectable man; **fare ~** to do the right
thing; **fare ~ a** (*salute*) to be good for; **fare
del ~ a qn** to do sb a good turn; **beni di
consumo** consumer goods
bene'detto, -a *pp di* **benedire** ▷ *ag*
blessed, holy
bene'dire *vt* to bless; to consecrate
benedu'cato, -a *ag* well-mannered
benefi'cenza [benefi'tʃɛntsa] *sf* charity
bene'ficio [bene'fitʃo] *sm* benefit; **con ~
d'inventario** (*fig*) with reservations
be'nessere *sm* well-being
benes'tante *ag* well-to-do
be'nigno, -a [be'niɲɲo] *ag* kind, kindly;
(*critica ecc*) favourable; (*Med*) benign
benve'nuto, -a *ag, sm* welcome; **dare il ~
a qn** to welcome sb

ben'zina [ben'dzina] *sf* petrol (*BRIT*), gas
(*US*); **fare ~** to get petrol (*BRIT*) o gas (*US*);
sono rimasto senza ~ I have run out of
petrol (*BRIT*) o gas (*US*); **benzina verde**
unleaded (petrol); **benzi'naio** *sm* petrol
(*BRIT*) o gas (*US*) pump attendant
'bere *vt* to drink; **darla a ~ a qn** (*fig*) to fool
sb; **vuoi qualcosa da ~?** would you like
a drink?
ber'lina *sf* (*Aut*) saloon (car) (*BRIT*), sedan
(*US*)
Ber'lino *sf* Berlin
ber'muda *smpl* (*calzoncini*) Bermuda
shorts
ber'noccolo *sm* bump; (*inclinazione*) flair
ber'retto *sm* cap
berrò *ecc vb vedi* **bere**
ber'saglio [ber'saʎʎo] *sm* target
besciamella [beʃʃa'mɛlla] *sf* béchamel
sauce
bes'temmia *sf* curse; (*Rel*) blasphemy
bestemmi'are *vi* to curse, swear; to
blaspheme ▷ *vt* to curse, swear at; to
blaspheme
'bestia *sf* animal; **andare in ~** (*fig*) to fly
into a rage; **besti'ale** *ag* beastly; animal
cpd; (*fam*): **fa un freddo bestiale** it's
bitterly cold; **besti'ame** *sm* livestock;
(*bovino*) cattle *pl*
be'tulla *sf* birch
be'vanda *sf* drink, beverage
'bevo *ecc vb vedi* **bere**
be'vuto, -a *pp di* **bere**
'bevvi *ecc vb vedi* **bere**
bianche'ria [bjanke'ria] *sf* linen; **~
da donna** ladies' underwear, lingerie;
biancheria femminile lingerie;
biancheria intima underwear
bi'anco, -a, -chi, -che *ag* white; (*non
scritto*) blank ▷ *sm* white; (*intonaco*)
whitewash ▷ *sm/f* white, white man/
woman; **in ~** (*foglio, assegno*) blank; (*notte*)
sleepless; **in ~ e nero** (*TV, Fot*) black and
white; **mangiare in ~** to follow a bland
diet; **pesce in ~** boiled fish; **andare in
~** (*non riuscire*) to fail; **bianco dell'uovo**
egg-white
biasi'mare *vt* to disapprove of, censure
'Bibbia *sf* (*anche fig*) bible
bibe'ron *sm inv* feeding bottle
'bibita *sf* (soft) drink
biblio'teca, -che *sf* library; (*mobile*)
bookcase
bicarbo'nato *sm* **~ (di sodio)** bicarbonate
(of soda)
bicchi'ere [bik'kjɛre] *sm* glass
bici'cletta [bitʃi'kletta] *sf* bicycle; **andare
in ~** to cycle
bidè *sm inv* bidet

bi'dello, -a *sm/f (lns)* janitor

bi'done *sm* drum, can; *(anche:* **~ dell'immondizia)** (dust)bin; *(fam: truffa)* swindle; **fare un ~ a qn** *(fam)* to let sb down; to cheat sb

bien'nale *ag* biennial

● **BIENNALE DI VENEZIA**
●
● The **Biennale di Venezia** is an
● international contemporary art festival,
● which takes place every two years at
● Giardini in Venice. In its current form,
● it includes exhibits by artists from the
● many countries taking part, a thematic
● exhibition and a section for young
● artists.

bifamili'are *sf* ≈ semi-detached house

bifor'carsi *vpr* to fork

bigiotte'ria [bidʒotte'ria] *sf* costume jewellery; *(negozio)* jeweller's *(selling only costume jewellery)*

bigliet'taio, -a *sm/f (in treno)* ticket inspector; *(in autobus)* conductor

bigliette'ria [biʎʎette'ria] *sf (di stazione)* ticket office; booking office; *(di teatro)* box office

bigli'etto [biʎ'ʎetto] *sm (per viaggi, spettacoli ecc)* ticket; *(cartoncino)* card; *(anche:* **~ di banca)** (bank)note; **biglietto d'auguri** greetings card; **biglietto da visita** visiting card; **biglietto d'andata e ritorno** return (ticket), round-trip ticket (US); **biglietto di sola andata** single (ticket)

bignè [biɲ'ɲe] *sm inv* cream puff

bigo'dino *sm* roller, curler

bi'gotto, -a *ag* over-pious ▷ *sm/f* church fiend

bi'kini *sm inv* bikini

bi'lancia, -ce [bi'lantʃa] *sf (pesa)* scales *pl*; *(: di precisione)* balance; *(dello zodiaco):* **B~** Libra; **bilancia commerciale** balance of trade; **bilancia dei pagamenti** balance of payments

bi'lancio [bi'lantʃo] *sm (Comm)* balance(-sheet); *(statale)* budget; **fare il ~ di** *(fig)* to assess; **bilancio consuntivo** (final) balance; **bilancio preventivo** budget

bili'ardo *sm* billiards *sg*; billiard table

bi'lingue *ag* bilingual

bilo'cale *sm* two-room flat *(Brit)* o apartment *(US)*

bi'nario, -a *ag (sistema)* binary ▷ *sm* (railway) track o line; *(piattaforma)* platform; **da che ~ parte il treno per Londra?** which platform does the train for

London go from?; **binario morto** dead-end track

bi'nocolo *sm* binoculars *pl*

bio... *prefisso*; **biodegra'dabile** *ag* biodegradable; **biodi'namico, -a, -ci, -che** *ag* biodynamic; **biogra'fia** *sf* biography; **biolo'gia** *sf* biology

bio'logico, -a, -ci, -che *ag (scienze, fenomeni ecc)* biological; *(agricoltura, prodotti)* organic; **guerra biologica** biological warfare

bi'ondo, -a *ag* blond, fair

biotecnologia [bioteknolo'dʒia] *sf* biotechnology

biri'chino, -a [biri'kino] *ag* mischievous ▷ *sm/f* scamp, little rascal

bi'rillo *sm* skittle (BRIT), pin (US)

'biro® *sf inv* biro®

'birra *sf* beer; **a tutta ~** *(fig)* at top speed; **birra chiara/scura** ≈ lager/stout; **birre'ria** *sf* ≈ bierkeller

bis *escl, sm inv* encore

bis'betico, -a, -ci, -che *ag* ill-tempered, crabby

bisbigli'are [bisbiʎ'ʎare] *vt, vi* to whisper

'bisca, -sche *sf* gambling-house

'biscia, -sce ['biʃʃa] *sf* snake; **biscia d'acqua** grass snake

biscot'tato, -a *ag* crisp; **fette biscottate** rusks

bis'cotto *sm* biscuit

bisessu'ale *ag, sm/f* bisexual

bises'tile *ag* **anno ~** leap year

bis'nonno, -a *sm/f* great grandfather/grandmother

biso'gnare [bizoɲ'ɲare] *vb impers* **bisogna che tu parta/lo faccia** you'll have to go/do it; **bisogna parlargli** we'll *(o* I'll*)* have to talk to him

bi'sogno [bi'zoɲɲo] *sm* need; **ha ~ di qualcosa?** do you need anything?

bis'tecca, -che *sf* steak, beefsteak

bisticci'are [bistit'tʃare] *vi* to quarrel, bicker; **bisticciarsi** *vpr* to quarrel, bicker

'bisturi *sm* scalpel

'bivio *sm* fork; *(fig)* dilemma

biz'zarro, -a [bid'dzarro] *ag* bizarre, strange

blate'rare *vi* to chatter

blin'dato, -a *ag* armoured

bloc'care *vt* to block; *(isolare)* to isolate, cut off; *(porto)* to blockade; *(prezzi, beni)* to freeze; *(meccanismo)* to jam; **bloccarsi** *vpr (motore)* to stall; *(freni, porta)* to jam, stick; *(ascensore)* to stop, get stuck

bloccherò *ecc* [blokke'rɔ] *vb vedi* **bloccare**

bloc'chetto [blok'ketto] *sm* notebook; *(di biglietti)* book

'blocco, -chi *sm* block; (*Mil*) blockade; (*dei fitti*) restriction; (*quadernetto*) pad; (*fig: unione*) coalition; (*il bloccare*) blocking; isolating, cutting-off; blockading; freezing; jamming; **in ~** (*nell'insieme*) as a whole; (*Comm*) in bulk; **blocco cardiaco** cardiac arrest; **blocco stradale** road block

blu *ag inv, sm* dark blue

'blusa *sf* (*camiciotto*) smock; (*camicetta*) blouse

'boa *sm inv* (*Zool*) boa constrictor; (*sciarpa*) feather boa ▷ *sf* buoy

bo'ato *sm* rumble, roar

bob [bɔb] *sm inv* bobsleigh

'bocca, -che *sf* mouth; **in ~ al lupo!** good luck!

boc'caccia, -ce [bok'kattʃa] *sf* (*malalingua*) gossip; **fare le boccacce** to pull faces

boc'cale *sm* jug; **boccale da birra** tankard

boc'cetta [bot'tʃetta] *sf* small bottle

'boccia, -ce ['bottʃa] *sf* bottle; (*da vino*) decanter, carafe; (*palla*) bowl; **gioco delle bocce** bowls *sg*

bocci'are [bot'tʃare] *vt* (*proposta, progetto*) to reject; (*Ins*) to fail; (*Bocce*) to hit

bocci'olo [bot'tʃolo] *sm* bud

boc'cone *sm* mouthful, morsel

boicot'tare *vt* to boycott

'bolla *sf* bubble; (*Med*) blister; **bolla di consegna** (*Comm*) delivery note; **bolla papale** papal bull

bol'lente *ag* boiling; boiling hot

bol'letta *sf* bill; (*ricevuta*) receipt; **essere in ~** to be hard up

bollet'tino *sm* bulletin; (*Comm*) note; **bollettino meteorologico** weather report; **bollettino di spedizione** consignment note

bollicina [bolli'tʃina] *sf* bubble

bol'lire *vt, vi* to boil

bolli'tore *sm* (*Cuc*) kettle; (*per riscaldamento*) boiler

'bollo *sm* stamp; **bollo per patente** driving licence tax; **bollo postale** postmark

'bomba *sf* bomb; **bomba atomica** atom bomb; **bomba a mano** hand grenade; **bomba ad orologeria** time bomb

bombarda'mento *sm* bombardment; bombing

bombar'dare *vt* to bombard; (*da aereo*) to bomb

'bombola *sf* cylinder

bombo'letta *sf* aerosol

bomboni'era *sf* box of sweets (*as souvenir at weddings, first communions etc*)

bo'nifico, -ci *sm* (*riduzione, abbuono*) discount; (*versamento a terzi*) credit transfer

bontà *sf* goodness; (*cortesia*) kindness; **aver la ~ di fare qc** to be good *o* kind enough to do sth

borbot'tare *vi* to mumble

'borchia ['borkja] *sf* stud

bor'deaux [bor'do] *ag inv, sm inv* maroon

'bordo *sm* (*Naut*) ship's side; (*orlo*) edge; (*striscia di guarnizione*) border, trim; **a ~ di** (*nave, aereo*) aboard, on board; (*macchina*) in

bor'ghese [bor'geze] *ag* (*spesso peg*) middle-class; bourgeois; **abito ~** civilian dress

'borgo, -ghi *sm* (*paesino*) village; (*quartiere*) district; (*sobborgo*) suburb

boro'talco *sm* talcum powder

bor'raccia, -ce [bor'rattʃa] *sf* canteen, water-bottle

'borsa *sf* bag; (*anche:* **~ da signora**) handbag; (*Econ*): **la B~ (valori)** the Stock Exchange; **borsa dell'acqua calda** hot-water bottle; **borsa nera** black market; **borsa della spesa** shopping bag; **borsa di studio** grant; **borsel'lino** *sm* purse; **bor'setta** *sf* handbag

'bosco, -schi *sm* wood

bos'niaco, -a, ci, che *ag, sm/f* Bosnian

'Bosnia Erze'govina ['bɔsnja erdze'govina] *sf* **la ~** = Bosnia Herzegovina

Bot, bot *sigla m inv* (= *buono ordinario del Tesoro*) short-term Treasury bond

bo'tanica *sf* botany

bo'tanico, -a, -ci, -che *ag* botanical ▷ *sm* botanist

'botola *sf* trap door

'botta *sf* blow; (*rumore*) bang

'botte *sf* barrel, cask

bot'tega, -ghe *sf* shop; (*officina*) workshop

bot'tiglia [bot'tiʎʎa] *sf* bottle; **bottiglie'ria** *sf* wine shop

bot'tino *sm* (*di guerra*) booty; (*di rapina, furto*) loot

'botto *sm* bang; crash; **di ~** suddenly

bot'tone *sm* button; **attaccare ~ a qn** (*fig*) to buttonhole sb

bo'vino, -a *ag* bovine; **bovini** *smpl* cattle

box [bɔks] *sm inv* (*per cavalli*) horsebox; (*per macchina*) lock-up; (*per macchina da corsa*) pit; (*per bambini*) playpen

boxe [bɔks] *sf* boxing

'boxer ['bɔkser] *sm inv* (*cane*) boxer ▷ *smpl* (*mutande*): **un paio di ~** a pair of boxer shorts

BR *sigla fpl* = **Brigate Rosse**

brac'cetto [brat'tʃetto] *sm* **a ~** arm in arm

braccia'letto *sm* bracelet, bangle

bracci'ata [brat'tʃata] *sf* (*nel nuoto*) stroke

'**braccio** ['brattʃo] (*pl(f)* **braccia**) *sm* (*Anat*) arm; (*pl(m) bracci: di gru, fiume*) arm; (*: di edificio*) wing; **braccio di mare** sound; **bracci'olo** (*appoggio*) arm

'**bracco, -chi** *sm* hound

'**brace** ['bratʃe] *sf* embers *pl*

braci'ola [bra'tʃola] *sf* (*Cuc*) chop

'**branca, -che** *sf* branch

'**branchia** ['brankja] *sf* (*Zool*) gill

'**branco, -chi** *sm* (*di cani, lupi*) pack; (*di pecore*) flock; (*peg: di persone*) gang, pack

bran'dina *sf* camp bed (BRIT), cot (US)

'**brano** *sm* piece; (*di libro*) passage

Bra'sile *sm* **il ~** Brazil; **brasili'ano, -a** *ag*, *sm/f* Brazilian

'**bravo, -a** *ag* (*abile*) clever, capable, skilful; (*buono*) good, honest; (*: bambino*) good; (*coraggioso*) brave; **~!** well done!; (*a teatro*) bravo!

bra'vura *sf* cleverness, skill

Bre'tagna [bre'taɲɲa] *sf* **la ~** Brittany

bre'tella *sf* (*Aut*) link; **bretelle** *sfpl* (*di calzoni*) braces

bre'tone *ag*, *sm/f* Breton

'**breve** *ag* brief, short; **in ~** in short

brevet'tare *vt* to patent

bre'vetto *sm* patent; **brevetto di pilotaggio** pilot's licence (BRIT) o license (US)

'**bricco, -chi** *sm* jug; **bricco del caffè** coffeepot

'**briciola** ['britʃola] *sf* crumb

'**briciolo** ['britʃolo] *sm* (*specie fig*) bit

'**briga, -ghe** *sf* (*fastidio*) trouble, bother; **pigliarsi la ~ di fare qc** to take the trouble to do sth

bri'gata *sf* (*Mil*) brigade; (*gruppo*) group, party; **Brigate Rosse** (*Pol*) Red Brigades

'**briglia** ['briʎʎa] *sf* rein; **a ~ sciolta** at full gallop; (*fig*) at full speed

bril'lante *ag* bright; (*anche fig*) brilliant; (*che luccica*) shining ▷ *sm* diamond

bril'lare *vi* to shine; (*mina*) to blow up ▷ *vt* (*mina*) to set off

'**brillo, -a** *ag* merry, tipsy

'**brina** *sf* hoarfrost

brin'dare *vi* **~ a qn/qc** to drink to o toast sb/sth

'**brindisi** *sm inv* toast

bri'oche [bri'ɔʃ] *sf inv* brioche

bri'tannico, -a, -ci, -che *ag* British

'**brivido** *sm* shiver; (*di ribrezzo*) shudder; (*fig*) thrill

brizzo'lato, -a [brittso'lato] *ag* (*persona*) going grey; (*barba, capelli*) greying

'**brocca, -che** *sf* jug

'**broccoli** *smpl* broccoli *sg*

'**brodo** *sm* broth; (*per cucinare*) stock;

'**brodo ristretto** consommé

bron'chite [bron'kite] *sf* (*Med*) bronchitis

bronto'lare *vi* to grumble; (*tuono, stomaco*) to rumble

'**bronzo** ['brondzo] *sm* bronze

'**browser** ['brauzer] *sm inv* (*Inform*) browser

brucia'pelo [brutʃa'pelo]: **a ~** *av* point-blank

bruci'are [bru'tʃare] *vt* to burn; (*scottare*) to scald ▷ *vi* to burn; **bruciarsi** *vpr* to burn o.s.; (*fallire*) to ruin one's chances; **~ le tappe** (*fig*) to shoot ahead; **bruciarsi la carriera** to ruin one's career

'**bruco, -chi** *sm* caterpillar; grub

'**brufolo** *sm* pimple, spot

'**brullo, -a** *ag* bare, bleak

'**bruno, -a** *ag* brown, dark; (*persona*) dark(-haired)

'**brusco, -a, -schi, -sche** *ag* (*sapore*) sharp; (*modi, persona*) brusque, abrupt; (*movimento*) abrupt, sudden

bru'sio *sm* buzz, buzzing

bru'tale *ag* brutal

'**brutto, -a** *ag* ugly; (*cattivo*) bad; (*malattia, strada, affare*) nasty, bad; **~ tempo** bad weather

Bru'xelles [bry'sɛl] *sf* Brussels

BSE [biɛssɛ'e] *sigla f* (= *encefalopatia spongiforme bovina*) BSE

'**buca, -che** *sf* hole; (*avvallamento*) hollow; **buca delle lettere** letterbox

buca'neve *sm inv* snowdrop

bu'care *vt* (*forare*) to make a hole (o holes) in; (*pungere*) to pierce; (*biglietto*) to punch; **bucarsi** *vpr* (*di eroina*) to mainline; **~ una gomma** to have a puncture

bu'cato *sm* (*operazione*) washing; (*panni*) wash, washing

'**buccia, -ce** ['buttʃa] *sf* skin, peel

bucherò *ecc* [buke'rɔ] *vb vedi* **bucare**

'**buco, -chi** *sm* hole

bud'dismo *sm* Buddhism

bu'dino *sm* pudding

'**bue** *sm* ox; **carne di ~** beef

bu'fera *sf* storm

'**buffo, -a** *ag* funny; (*Teatro*) comic

bu'gia, -'gie [bu'dʒia] *sf* lie; **dire una ~** to tell a lie; **bugi'ardo, -a** *ag* lying, deceitful ▷ *sm/f* liar

'**buio, -a** *ag* dark ▷ *sm* dark, darkness

'**bulbo** *sm* (*Bot*) bulb; **bulbo oculare** eyeball

Bulga'ria *sf* **la ~** Bulgaria

'**bulgaro, -a** *ag*, *sm/f*, *sm* Bulgarian

buli'mia *sf* bulimia; **bu'limico, -a, -ci, -che** *ag* bulimic

bul'lone *sm* bolt

buona'notte *escl* good night! ▷ *sf* **dare la**

~ **a** to say good night to
buona'sera *escl* good evening!
buongi'orno [bwon'dʒorno] *escl* good morning (*o* afternoon)!
buongus'taio, -a *sm/f* gourmet

 PAROLA CHIAVE

bu'ono, -a (*ag: dav sm* **buon** + C *o* V, **buono** + *s impura, gn, pn, ps, x, z; dav sf* **buon'** + V) *ag*
1 (*gen*) good; **un buon pranzo/ristorante** a good lunch/restaurant; **(stai) buono!** behave!
2 (*benevolo*): **buono (con)** good (to), kind (to)
3 (*giusto, valido*) right; **al momento buono** at the right moment
4 (*adatto*): **buono a/da** fit for/to; **essere buono a nulla** to be no good o use at anything
5 (*auguri*): **buon anno!** happy New Year!; **buon appetito!** enjoy your meal!; **buon compleanno!** happy birthday!; **buon divertimento!** have a nice time!; **buona fortuna!** good luck!; **buon riposo!** sleep well!; **buon viaggio!** bon voyage!, have a good trip!
6: **a buon mercato** cheap; **di buon'ora** early; **buon senso** common sense; **alla buona** *ag* simple
▷ *av* in a simple way, without any fuss ▷ *sm*
1 (*bontà*) goodness, good
2 (*Comm*) voucher, coupon; **buono di cassa** cash voucher; **buono di consegna** delivery note; **buono del Tesoro** Treasury bill

buon'senso *sm* = **buon senso**
burat'tino *sm* puppet
'burbero, -a *ag* surly, gruff
buro'cratico, -a, ci, che *ag* bureaucratic
burocra'zia [burokrat'tsia] *sf* bureaucracy
bur'rasca, -sche *sf* storm
'burro *sm* butter
bur'rone *sm* ravine
bus'sare *vi* to knock
'bussola *sf* compass
'busta *sf* (*da lettera*) envelope; (*astuccio*) case; **in ~ aperta/chiusa** in an unsealed/sealed envelope; **busta paga** pay packet
busta'rella *sf* bribe, backhander
bus'tina *sf* (*piccola busta*) envelope; (*di cibi, farmaci*) sachet; (*Mil*) forage cap; **bustina di tè** tea bag
'busto *sm* bust; (*indumento*) corset, girdle; **a mezzo ~** (*foto*) half-length
but'tare *vt* to throw; (*anche: ~ **via**) to throw away; ~ **giù** (*scritto*) to scribble

down; (*cibo*) to gulp down; (*edificio*) to pull down, demolish; (*pasta, verdura*) to put into boiling water; **buttarsi** *vpr* (*saltare*) to jump; **buttarsi dalla finestra** to jump out of the window
byte ['bait] *sm inv* byte

to drop; (anche: **~ dal sonno**) to be falling asleep on one's feet; **~ dalle nuvole** (fig) to be taken aback

cadrò ecc vb vedi **cadere**

ca'duta sf fall; **la ~ dei capelli** hair loss

caffè sm inv coffee; (locale) café; **caffè corretto** espresso coffee with a shot of spirits; **caffè macchiato** coffee with a dash of milk; **caffè macinato** ground coffee

caffel'latte sm inv white coffee

caffetti'era sf coffeepot

'cagna ['kaɲɲa] sf (Zool, peg) bitch

CAI sigla m = **Club Alpino Italiano**

cala'brone sm hornet

cala'maro sm squid

cala'mita sf magnet

calamità sf inv calamity, disaster

ca'lare vt (far discendere) to lower; (Maglia) to decrease ▷ vi (discendere) to go (o come) down; (tramontare) to set, go down; **~ di peso** to lose weight

cal'cagno [kal'kaɲɲo] sm heel

cal'care sm (incrostazione) (lime)scale

'calce ['kaltʃe] sm **in ~** at the foot of the page ▷ sf lime; **calce viva** quicklime

calci'are [kal'tʃare] vt, vi to kick; **calcia'tore** sm footballer

'calcio ['kaltʃo] sm (pedata) kick; (sport) football, soccer; (di pistola, fucile) butt; (Chim) calcium; **calcio d'angolo** (Sport) corner (kick); **calcio di punizione** (Sport) free kick; **calcio di rigore** penalty

calco'lare vt to calculate, work out, reckon; (ponderare) to weigh (up); **calcola'tore, -'trice** ag calculating ▷ sm calculator; (fig) calculating person; **calcolatore elettronico** computer; **calco'latrice** sf calculator

'calcolo sm (anche Mat) calculation; (infinitesimale ecc) calculus; (Med) stone; **fare i propri calcoli** (fig) to weigh the pros and cons; **per ~** out of self-interest

cal'daia sf boiler

'caldo, -a ag warm; (molto caldo) hot; (fig: appassionato) keen; hearty ▷ sm heat; **ho ~** I'm warm; I'm hot; **fa ~** it's warm; it's hot

caleidos'copio sm kaleidoscope

calen'dario sm calendar

'calibro sm (di arma) calibre, bore; (Tecn) callipers pl; (fig) calibre; **di grosso ~** (fig) prominent

'calice ['kalitʃe] sm goblet; (Rel) chalice

Cali'fornia sf California

californi'ano, -a ag Californian

calligra'fia sf (scrittura) handwriting; (arte) calligraphy

'callo sm callus; (ai piedi) corn

'calma sf calm

ca'bina sf (di nave) cabin; (da spiaggia) beach hut; (di autocarro, treno) cab; (di aereo) cockpit; (di ascensore) cage; **cabi'nato** sm cabin cruiser; **cabina di pilotaggio** cockpit; **cabina telefonica** call o (tele)phone box

ca'cao sm cocoa

'caccia ['kattʃa] sf hunting; (con fucile) shooting; (inseguimento) chase; (cacciagione) game ▷ sm inv (aereo) fighter; (nave) destroyer; **caccia grossa** big-game hunting; **caccia all'uomo** manhunt

cacci'are [kat'tʃare] vt to hunt; (mandar via) to chase away; (ficcare) to shove, stick ▷ vi to hunt; **cacciarsi** vpr **dove s'è cacciata la mia borsa?** where has my bag got to?; **cacciarsi nei guai** to get into trouble; **~ fuori qc** to whip o pull sth out; **~ un urlo** to let out a yell; **caccia'tore** sm hunter; **cacciatore di frodo** poacher

caccia'vite [kattʃa'vite] sm inv screwdriver

'cactus sm inv cactus

ca'davere sm (dead) body, corpse

'caddi ecc vb vedi **cadere**

ca'denza [ka'dɛntsa] sf cadence; (ritmo) rhythm; (Mus) cadenza

ca'dere vi to fall; (denti, capelli) to fall out; (tetto) to fall in; **questa gonna cade bene** this skirt hangs well; **lasciar ~** (anche fig)

cal'mante sm tranquillizer
cal'mare vt to calm; (lenire) to soothe; **calmarsi** vpr to grow calm, calm down; (vento) to abate; (dolori) to ease
'calmo, -a ag calm, quiet
'calo sm (Comm: di prezzi) fall; (: di volume) shrinkage; (: di peso) loss
ca'lore sm warmth; heat; **in ~** (Zool) on heat
calo'ria sf calorie
calo'rifero sm radiator
calo'roso, -a ag warm
calpes'tare vt to tread on, trample on; **"è vietato ~ l'erba"** "keep off the grass"
ca'lunnia sf slander; (scritta) libel
cal'vizie [kal'vittsje] sf baldness
'calvo, -a ag bald
'calza ['kaltsa] sf (da donna) stocking; (da uomo) sock; **fare la ~** to knit; **calze di nailon** nylons, (nylon) stockings
calza'maglia [kaltsa'maʎʎa] sf tights pl; (per danza, ginnastica) leotard
calzet'tone [kaltset'tone] sm heavy knee-length sock
cal'zino [kal'tsino] sm sock
calzo'laio [kaltso'lajo] sm shoemaker; (che ripara scarpe) cobbler
calzon'cini [kaltson'tʃini] smpl shorts; **calzoncini da bagno** (swimming) trunks
cal'zone [kal'tsone] sm trouser leg; (Cuc) savoury turnover made with pizza dough; **calzoni** smpl (pantaloni) trousers (BRIT), pants (US)
camale'onte sm chameleon
cambia'mento sm change
cambi'are vt to change; (modificare) to alter, change; (barattare): **~ (qc con qn/qc)** to exchange (sth with sb/for sth) ▷ vi to change, alter; **cambiarsi** vpr (d'abito) to change; **~ casa** to move (house); **~ idea** to change one's mind; **~ treno** to change trains; **dove posso ~ dei soldi?** where can I change some money?; **ha da ~?** have you got any change?; **posso cambiarlo, per favore?** could I exchange this, please?
cambiava'lute sm inv exchange office
'cambio sm change; (modifica) alteration, change; (scambio, Comm) exchange; (corso dei cambi) rate (of exchange); (Tecn, Aut) gears pl; **in ~ di** in exchange for; **dare il ~ a qn** to take over from sb
'camera sf room; (anche: ~ da letto) bedroom; (Pol) chamber, house; **camera ardente** mortuary chapel; **camera d'aria** inner tube; (di pallone) bladder; **camera di commercio** Chamber of Commerce; **Camera dei Deputati** Chamber of Deputies, ≈ House of Commons (BRIT),

≈ House of Representatives (US); **camera a gas** gas chamber; **camera a un letto/due letti** single/twin-bedded room; **camera matrimoniale** double room; **camera oscura** (Fot) dark room

> Attenzione! In inglese esiste la parola *camera*, che però significa *macchina fotografica*.

came'rata, -i, -e sm/f companion, mate ▷ sf dormitory
cameri'era sf (domestica) maid; (che serve a tavola) waitress; (che fa le camere) chambermaid
cameri'ere sm (man)servant; (di ristorante) waiter
came'rino sm (Teatro) dressing room
'camice ['kamitʃe] sm (Rel) alb; (per medici ecc) white coat
cami'cetta [kami'tʃetta] sf blouse
ca'micia, -cie [ka'mitʃa] sf (da uomo) shirt; (da donna) blouse; **camicia di forza** straitjacket; **camicia da notte** (da donna) nightdress; (da uomo) nightshirt
cami'netto sm hearth, fireplace
ca'mino sm chimney; (focolare) fireplace, hearth
'camion sm inv lorry (BRIT), truck (US)
camio'nista, -i sm lorry driver (BRIT), truck driver (US)
cam'mello sm (Zool) camel; (tessuto) camel hair
cammi'nare vi to walk; (funzionare) to work, go
cam'mino sm walk; (sentiero) path; (itinerario, direzione, tragitto) way; **mettersi in ~** to set o start off
camo'milla sf camomile; (infuso) camomile tea
ca'moscio [ka'moʃʃo] sm chamois; **di ~** (scarpe, borsa) suede cpd
cam'pagna [kam'paɲɲa] sf country, countryside; (Pol, Comm, Mil) campaign; **in ~** in the country; **andare in ~** to go to the country; **fare una ~** to campaign; **campagna pubblicitaria** advertising campaign
cam'pana sf bell; (anche: ~ di vetro) bell jar; **campa'nello** sm (all'uscio, da tavola) bell
campa'nile sm bell tower, belfry
cam'peggio sm camping; (terreno) camp site; **fare (del) ~** to go camping
camper ['kamper] sm inv motor caravan (BRIT), motor home (US)
campio'nario, -a ag **fiera campionaria** trade fair ▷ sm collection of samples
campio'nato sm championship
campi'one, -'essa sm/f (Sport) champion ▷ sm (Comm) sample

'campo sm field; (Mil) field; (accampamento) camp; (spazio delimitato: sportivo ecc) ground; field; (di quadro) background; **i campi** (campagna) the countryside; **campo da aviazione** airfield; **campo di battaglia** (Mil, fig) battlefield; **campo di concentramento** concentration camp; **campo da golf** golf course; **campo profughi** refugee camp; **campo sportivo** sports ground; **campo da tennis** tennis court; **campo visivo** field of vision

'Canada sm **il ~** Canada; **cana'dese** ag, sm/f Canadian ▷ sf (anche: **tenda canadese**) ridge tent

ca'naglia [ka'naʎʎa] sf rabble, mob; (persona) scoundrel, rogue

ca'nale sm (anche fig) channel; (artificiale) canal

'canapa sf hemp; **canapa indiana** (droga) cannabis

cana'rino sm canary

cancel'lare [kantʃel'lare] vt (con la gomma) to rub out, erase; (con la penna) to strike out; (annullare) to annul, cancel; (disdire) to cancel

cancelle'ria [kantʃelle'ria] sf chancery; (materiale per scrivere) stationery

can'cello [kan'tʃello] sm gate

'cancro sm (Med) cancer; (dello zodiaco): **C~** Cancer

candeg'gina [kanded'dʒina] sf bleach

can'dela sf candle; **candela (di accensione)** (Aut) spark(ing) plug

cande'labro sm candelabra

candeli'ere sm candlestick

candi'dare vt to present as candidate; **candidarsi** vpr to present o.s. as candidate

candi'dato, -a sm/f candidate; (aspirante a una carica) applicant

'candido, -a ag white as snow; (puro) pure; (sincero) sincere, candid

can'dito, -a ag candied

'cane sm dog; (di pistola, fucile) cock; **fa un freddo ~** it's bitterly cold; **non c'era un ~** there wasn't a soul; **cane da caccia/da guardia** hunting/guard dog; **cane lupo** Alsatian; **cane pastore** sheepdog

ca'nestro sm basket

can'guro sm kangaroo

ca'nile sm kennel; (di allevamento) kennels pl; **canile municipale** dog pound

'canna sf (pianta) reed; (: indica, da zucchero) cane; (bastone) stick, cane; (di fucile) barrel; (di organo) pipe; (fam: droga) joint; **canna fumaria** chimney flue; **canna da pesca** (fishing) rod; **canna da zucchero** sugar cane

cannel'loni smpl pasta tubes stuffed with sauce and baked

cannocchi'ale [kannok'kjale] sm telescope

can'none sm (Mil) gun; (Storia) cannon; (tubo) pipe, tube; (piega) box pleat; (fig) ace

can'nuccia, -ce [kan'nuttʃa] sf (drinking) straw

ca'noa sf canoe

'canone sm canon, criterion; (mensile, annuo) rent; fee

canot'taggio [kanot'taddʒo] sm rowing

canotti'era sf vest

ca'notto sm small boat, dinghy; canoe

can'tante sm/f singer

can'tare vt, vi to sing; **cantau'tore, -'trice** sm/f singer-composer

canti'ere sm (Edil) (building) site; (cantiere navale) shipyard

can'tina sf cellar; (bottega) wine shop; **cantina sociale** cooperative winegrowers' association

◼ Attenzione! In inglese esiste la parola canteen, che però significa mensa.

'canto sm song; (arte) singing; (Rel) chant; chanting; (poesia) poem, lyric; (parte di una poesia) canto; (parte, lato): **da un ~** on the one hand; **d'altro ~** on the other hand

canzo'nare [kantso'nare] vt to tease

can'zone [kan'tsone] sf song; (Poesia) canzone

'caos sm inv chaos; **ca'otico, -a, -ci, -che** ag chaotic

CAP sigla m = **codice di avviamento postale**

ca'pace [ka'patʃe] ag able, capable; (ampio, vasto) large, capacious; **sei ~ di farlo?** can you o are you able to do it?; **capacità** sf inv ability; (Dir, di recipiente) capacity

ca'panna sf hut

capan'none sm (Agr) barn; (fabbricato industriale) (factory) shed

ca'parbio, -a ag stubborn

ca'parra sf deposit, down payment

ca'pello sm hair; **capelli** smpl (capigliatura) hair sg

ca'pezzolo [ka'pettsolo] sm nipple

ca'pire vt to understand; **non capisco I** don't understand

capi'tale ag (mortale) capital; (fondamentale) main, chief ▷ sf (città) capital ▷ sm (Econ) capital

capi'tano sm captain

capi'tare vi (giungere casualmente) to happen to go, find o.s.; (accadere) to happen; (presentarsi: cosa) to turn up, present itself ▷ vb impers to happen; **mi è capitato un guaio** I've had a spot of trouble

capi'tello sm (Archit) capital
ca'pitolo sm chapter
capi'tombolo sm headlong fall, tumble
'capo sm head; (persona) head, leader;
(: in ufficio) head, boss; (: in tribù) chief;
(di oggetti) head; top; end; (Geo) cape;
andare a ~ to start a new paragraph; **da ~**
over again; **capo di bestiame** head inv of
cattle; **capo di vestiario** item of clothing;
Capo'danno sm New Year; **capo'giro**
sm dizziness no pl; **capola'voro, -i** sm
masterpiece; **capo'linea** (pl **capi'linea**)
sm terminus; **capostazi'one** (pl
capistazi'one) sm station master
capo'tavola (pl(m) **capi'tavola**) pl(f) inv
sm/f (persona) head of the table; **sedere a**
~ to sit at the head of the table
capo'volgere [kapo'voldʒere] vt to
overturn; (fig) to reverse; **capovolgersi**
vpr to overturn; (barca) to capsize; (fig) to
be reversed
'cappa sf (mantello) cape, cloak; (del
camino) hood
cap'pella sf (Rel) chapel
cap'pello sm hat
'cappero sm caper
cap'pone sm capon
cap'potto sm (over)coat
cappuc'cino [kapput'tʃino] sm (frate)
Capuchin monk; (bevanda) cappuccino,
frothy white coffee
cap'puccio [kap'puttʃo] sm (copricapo)
hood; (della biro) cap
'capra sf (she-)goat
ca'priccio [ka'prittʃo] sm caprice, whim;
(bizza) tantrum; **fare i capricci** to be very
naughty; **capricci'oso, -a** ag capricious,
whimsical; naughty
Capri'corno sm Capricorn
capri'ola sf somersault
capri'olo sm roe deer
'capro sm **~ espiatorio** scapegoat
ca'prone sm billy-goat
'capsula sf capsule; (di arma, per bottiglie)
cap
cap'tare vt (Radio, TV) to pick up;
(cattivarsi) to gain, win
carabini'ere sm member of Italian military
police force

● **CARABINIERI**
●
● Originally part of the armed forces, the
● **carabinieri** are police who perform
● both military and civil duties. They
● include paratroopers and mounted
● divisions.

ca'raffa sf carafe

Ca'raibi smpl **il mar dei ~** the Caribbean
(Sea)
cara'mella sf sweet
ca'rattere sm character; (caratteristica)
characteristic, trait; **avere un buon**
~ to be good-natured; **carattere**
jolly wild card; **caratte'ristica, -che**
sf characteristic, trait, peculiarity;
caratte'ristico, -a, -ci, -che ag
characteristic
car'bone sm coal
carbu'rante sm (motor) fuel
carbura'tore sm carburettor
carce'rato, -a [kartʃe'rato] sm/f
prisoner
'carcere ['kartʃere] sm prison; (pena)
imprisonment
carci'ofo [kar'tʃɔfo] sm artichoke
cardel'lino sm goldfinch
car'diaco, -a, -ci, -che ag cardiac, heart
cpd
cardi'nale ag, sm cardinal
'cardine sm hinge
'cardo sm thistle
ca'rente ag **~ di** lacking in
cares'tia sf famine; (penuria) scarcity,
dearth
ca'rezza [ka'rettsa] sf caress
'carica, -che sf (mansione ufficiale) office,
position; (Mil, Tecn, Elettr) charge; **ha una**
forte ~ di simpatia he's very likeable; vedi
anche **carico**
caricabatte'ria sm inv battery charger
cari'care vt (merce, Inform) to load;
(orologio) to wind up; (batteria, Mil) to
charge
'carico, -a, -chi, -che ag (che porta un
peso): **~ di** loaded o laden with; (fucile)
loaded; (orologio) wound up; (batteria)
charged; (colore) deep; (caffè, tè) strong
▷ sm (il caricare) loading; (ciò che si carica)
load; (fig: peso) burden, weight; **persona a**
~ dependent; **essere a ~ di qn** (spese ecc) to
be charged to sb
'carie sf (dentaria) decay
ca'rino, -a ag (grazioso) lovely, pretty,
nice; (riferito a uomo, anche simpatico)
nice
carità sf charity; **per ~!** (escl di rifiuto) good
heavens, no!
carnagi'one [karna'dʒone] sf
complexion
'carne sf flesh; (bovina, ovina ecc) meat;
non mangio ~ I don't eat meat; **carne**
di maiale/manzo/pecora pork/beef/
mutton; **carne in scatola** tinned o canned
meat; **carne tritata** o **macinata** mince
(BRIT), hamburger meat (US), minced (BRIT)
o ground (US) meat

carne'vale *sm* carnival

● CARNEVALE
●
● **Carnevale** is the period between
● Epiphany (Jan. 6th) and the beginning
● of Lent. People wear fancy dress, and
● there are parties, processions of floats
● and bonfires. It culminates immediately
● before Lent in the festivities of **martedì**
● **grasso** (Shrove Tuesday).

'caro, -a *ag* (*amato*) dear; (*costoso*) dear,
expensive; **è troppo ~** it's too expensive
ca'rogna [ka'roɲɲa] *sf* carrion; (*anche:* **fig**:
fam) swine
ca'rota *sf* carrot
caro'vana *sf* caravan
car'poni *av* on all fours
car'rabile *ag* suitable for vehicles; **"passo**
~" "keep clear"
carreggi'ata [karred'dʒata] *sf*
carriageway (BRIT), (road)way
car'rello *sm* trolley; (*Aer*) undercarriage;
(*Cinema*) dolly; (*di macchina da scrivere*)
carriage
carri'era *sf* career; **fare ~** to get on; **a gran**
~ at full speed
carri'ola *sf* wheelbarrow
'carro *sm* cart, wagon; **carro armato**
tank; **carro attrezzi** breakdown van
car'rozza [kar'rottsa] *sf* carriage, coach
carrozze'ria [karrottse'ria] *sf* body,
coachwork (BRIT); (*officina*) coachbuilder's
workshop (BRIT), body shop
carroz'zina [karrot'tsina] *sf* pram (BRIT),
baby carriage (US)
'carta *sf* paper; (*al ristorante*) menu; (*Geo*)
map; plan; (*documento*) card; (*costituzione*)
charter; **carte** *sfpl* (*documenti*) papers,
documents; **alla ~** (*al ristorante*) à la
carte; **carta assegni** bank card; **carta**
assorbente blotting paper; **carta bollata**
o **da bollo** official stamped paper; **carta**
(da gioco) playing card; **carta di credito**
credit card; **carta (geografica)** map;
carta d'identità identity card; **carta**
igienica toilet paper; **carta d'imbarco**
(*Aer, Naut*) boarding card; **carta da lettere**
writing paper; **carta da pacchi** wrapping
paper; **carta da parati** wallpaper; **carta**
libera (*Amm*) unstamped paper; **carta**
stradale road map; **carta verde** (*Aut*)
green card; **carta vetrata** sandpaper;
carta da visita visiting card
car'taccia, -ce [kar'tattʃa] *sf* waste paper
carta'pesta *sf* papier-mâché
car'tella *sf* (*scheda*) card; (*Inform, custodia*:
di cartone) folder; (: *di uomo d'affari ecc*)

briefcase; (: *di scolaro*) schoolbag, satchel;
cartella clinica (*Med*) case sheet
cartel'lino *sm* (*etichetta*) label; (*su porta*)
notice; (*scheda*) card; **timbrare il ~**
(*all'entrata*) to clock in; (*all'uscita*) to clock
out; **cartellino di presenza** clock card,
timecard
car'tello *sm* sign; (*pubblicitario*) poster;
(*stradale*) sign, signpost; (*Econ*) cartel; (*in*
dimostrazioni) placard; **cartello stradale**
sign; **cartel'lone** *sm* (*della tombola*)
scoring frame; (*Teatro*) playbill; **tenere il**
cartellone (*spettacolo*) to have a long run;
cartellone pubblicitario advertising
poster
car'tina *sf* (*Aut, Geo*) map; **può**
indicarmelo sulla ~? can you show it to
me on the map?
car'toccio [kar'tɔttʃo] *sm* paper bag
cartole'ria *sf* stationer's (shop)
carto'lina *sf* postcard; **cartolina postale**
ready-stamped postcard
car'tone *sm* cardboard; (*Arte*) cartoon;
cartoni animati (*Cinema*) cartoons
car'tuccia, -ce [kar'tuttʃa] *sf* cartridge
'casa *sf* house; (*in senso astratto*) home;
(*Comm*) firm, house; **essere a ~** to be at
home; **vado a ~ mia/tua** I'm going home/
to your house; **vino della ~** house wine;
casa di cura nursing home; **casa editrice**
publishing house; **Casa delle Libertà**
centre-right coalition; **casa di riposo** (old
people's) home, care home; **case popolari**
≈ council houses (*o* flats) (BRIT), ≈ public
housing units (US); **casa dello studente**
student hostel
ca'sacca, -che *sf* military coat; (*di fantino*)
blouse
casa'linga, -ghe *sf* housewife
casa'lingo, -a, -ghi, -ghe *ag* household,
domestic; (*fatto a casa*) home-made;
(*semplice*) homely; (*amante della casa*)
home-loving
cas'care *vi* to fall; **cas'cata** *sf* fall;
(*d'acqua*) cascade, waterfall
cascherò [kaske'rɔ] *vb vedi* **cascare**
'casco, -schi *sm* helmet; (*del parrucchiere*)
hair-drier; (*di banane*) bunch; **casco blu**
(*Mil*) blue helmet (UN soldier)
casei'ficio [kazei'fitʃo] *sm* creamery
ca'sella *sf* pigeon-hole; **casella postale**
post office box
ca'sello *sm* (*di autostrada*) toll-house
ca'serma *sf* barracks pl
ca'sino (*fam*) *sm* brothel; (*confusione*) row,
racket
casinò *sm inv* casino
'caso *sm* chance; (*fatto, vicenda*) event,
incident; (*possibilità*) possibility; (*Med*,

Ling) case; **a ~** at random; **per ~** by chance, by accident; **in ogni ~, in tutti i casi** in any case, at any rate; **al ~** should the opportunity arise; **nel ~ che** in case; **~ mai** if by chance; **caso limite** borderline case

caso'lare *sm* cottage

'caspita *escl* (*di sorpresa*) good heavens!; (*di impazienza*) for goodness' sake!

'cassa *sf* case, crate, box; (*bara*) coffin; (*mobile*) chest; (*involucro: di orologio ecc*) case; (*macchina*) cash register, till; (*luogo di pagamento*) checkout (counter); (*fondo*) fund; (*istituto bancario*) bank; **cassa automatica prelievi** cash dispenser; **cassa continua** night safe; **cassa mutua** *o* **malattia** health insurance scheme; **cassa integrazione: mettere in cassa integrazione** ≈ to lay off; **cassa di risparmio** savings bank; **cassa toracica** (*Anat*) chest

cassa'forte (*pl* **casse'forti**) *sf* safe; **lo potrebbe mettere nella ~?** could you put this in the safe, please?

cassa'panca (*pl* **cassa'panche** *o* **casse'panche**) *sf* settle

casseru'ola *sf* saucepan

cas'setta *sf* box; (*per registratore*) cassette; (*Cinema, Teatro*) box-office takings *pl*; **film di ~** box-office draw; **cassetta di sicurezza** strongbox; **cassetta delle lettere** letterbox

cas'setto *sm* drawer

cassi'ere, -a *sm/f* cashier; (*di banca*) teller

casso'netto *sm* wheelie-bin

cas'tagna [kas'taɲɲa] *sf* chestnut

cas'tagno [kas'taɲɲo] *sm* chestnut (tree)

cas'tano, -a *ag* chestnut (brown)

cas'tello *sm* castle; (*Tecn*) scaffolding

casti'gare *vt* to punish; **cas'tigo, -ghi** *sm* punishment

cas'toro *sm* beaver

casu'ale *ag* chance *cpd*; (*Inform*) random *cpd*

cataliza'tore [kataliddza'tore] *sm* (*anche fig*) catalyst; (*Aut*) catalytic converter

ca'talogo, -ghi *sm* catalogue

catarifran'gente [katarifran'dʒɛnte] *sm* (*Aut*) reflector

ca'tarro *sm* catarrh

ca'tastrofe *sf* catastrophe, disaster

catego'ria *sf* category

ca'tena *sf* chain; **catena di montaggio** assembly line; **catene da neve** (*Aut*) snow chains; **cate'nina** *sf* (*gioiello*) (thin) chain

cate'ratta *sf* cataract; (*chiusa*) sluice-gate

ca'tino *sm* basin

ca'trame *sm* tar

'cattedra *sf* teacher's desk; (*di docente*) chair

catte'drale *sf* cathedral

catti'veria *sf* malice, spite; naughtiness; (*atto*) spiteful act; (*parole*) malicious *o* spiteful remark

cat'tivo, -a *ag* bad; (*malvagio*) bad, wicked; (*turbolento: bambino*) bad, naughty; (*: mare*) rough; (*odore, sapore*) nasty, bad

cat'tolico, -a, -ci, -che *ag, sm/f* (Roman) Catholic

cattu'rare *vt* to capture

'causa *sf* cause; (*Dir*) lawsuit, case, action; **a ~ di, per ~ di** because of; **fare** *o* **muovere ~ a qn** to take legal action against sb

cau'sare *vt* to cause

cau'tela *sf* caution, prudence

'cauto, -a *ag* cautious, prudent

cauzi'one [kaut'tsjone] *sf* security; (*Dir*) bail

'cava *sf* quarry

caval'care *vt* (*cavallo*) to ride; (*muro*) to sit astride; (*ponte*) to span; **caval'cata** *sf* ride; (*gruppo di persone*) riding party

cavalca'via *sm inv* flyover

cavalci'oni [kaval'tʃoni]: **a ~ di** *prep* astride

cavali'ere *sm* rider; (*feudale, titolo*) knight; (*soldato*) cavalryman; (*al ballo*) partner

caval'letta *sf* grasshopper

caval'letto *sm* (*Fot*) tripod; (*da pittore*) easel

ca'vallo *sm* horse; (*Scacchi*) knight; (*Aut: anche*: **~ vapore**) horsepower; (*dei pantaloni*) crotch; **a ~** on horseback; **a ~ di** astride, straddling; **cavallo di battaglia** (*fig*) hobby-horse; **cavallo da corsa** racehorse; **cavallo a dondolo** rocking horse

ca'vare *vt* (*togliere*) to draw out, extract, take out; (*: giacca, scarpe*) to take off; (*: fame, sete, voglia*) to satisfy; **cavarsela** to manage, get on all right; (*scamparla*) to get away with it

cava'tappi *sm inv* corkscrew

ca'verna *sf* cave

'cavia *sf* guinea pig

cavi'ale *sm* caviar

ca'viglia [ka'viʎʎa] *sf* ankle

'cavo, -a *ag* hollow ▷ *sm* (*Anat*) cavity; (*corda, Elettr, Tel*) cable

cavo'letto *sm* **~ di Bruxelles** Brussels sprout

cavolfi'ore *sm* cauliflower

'cavolo *sm* cabbage; (*fam*): **non m'importa un ~** I don't give a damn

'cazzo ['kattso] *sm* (*fam!: pene*) prick (!); **non gliene importa un ~** (*fig fam!*) he doesn't give a damn about it; **fatti i**

cazzi tuoi (*fig fam!*) mind your own damn business

C.C.D. *sigla m* (= *Centro Cristiano Democratico*) *Italian political party of the centre*

CD *sm inv* CD; (*lettore*) CD player

CD-Rom [tʃidi'rɔm] *sm inv* CD-ROM

C.D.U. *sigla m* (= *Cristiano Democratici Uniti*) *Italian centre-right political party*

ce [tʃe] *pron, av vedi* **ci**

Ce'cenia [tʃe'tʃenia] *sf* **la ~** Chechnya

ce'ceno, -a [tʃe'tʃeno] *sm/f, ag* Chechen

'ceco, -a, -chi, -che ['tʃeko] *ag, sm/f* Czech; **la Repubblica Ceca** the Czech Republic

'cedere ['tʃedere] *vt* (*concedere posto*) to give up; (*Dir*) to transfer, make over ▷ *vi* (*cadere*) to give way, subside; **~ (a)** to surrender (to), yield (to), give in (to)

'cedola ['tʃedola] *sf* (*Comm*) coupon; voucher

'ceffo ['tʃeffo] (*peg*) *sm* ugly mug

cef'fone [tʃef'fone] *sm* slap, smack

cele'brare [tʃele'brare] *vt* to celebrate

'celebre ['tʃelebre] *ag* famous, celebrated

ce'leste [tʃe'leste] *ag* celestial; heavenly; (*colore*) sky-blue

'celibe ['tʃelibe] *ag* single, unmarried

'cella ['tʃella] *sf* cell; **cella frigorifera** cold store

'cellula ['tʃellula] *sf* (*Biol, Elettr, Pol*) cell; **cellu'lare** *sm* cellphone

cellu'lite [tʃellu'lite] *sf* cellulite

cemen'tare [tʃemen'tare] *vt* (*anche fig*) to cement

ce'mento [tʃe'mento] *sm* cement; **cemento armato** reinforced concrete

'cena ['tʃena] *sf* dinner; (*leggera*) supper

ce'nare [tʃe'nare] *vi* to dine, have dinner

'cenere ['tʃenere] *sf* ash

'cenno ['tʃenno] *sm* (*segno*) sign, signal; (*gesto*) gesture; (*col capo*) nod; (*con la mano*) wave; (*allusione*) hint, mention; (*breve esposizione*) short account; **far ~ di sì/no** to nod (one's head)/shake one's head

censi'mento [tʃensi'mento] *sm* census

cen'sura [tʃen'sura] *sf* censorship; censor's office; (*fig*) censure

cente'nario, -a [tʃente'narjo] *ag* (*che ha cento anni*) hundred-year-old; (*che ricorre ogni cento anni*) centennial, centenary *cpd* ▷ *sm/f* centenarian ▷ *sm* centenary

cen'tesimo, -a [tʃen'tezimo] *ag, sm* hundredth; (*di euro, dollaro*) cent

cen'tigrado, -a [tʃen'tigrado] *ag* centigrade; **20 gradi centigradi** 20 degrees centigrade

cen'timetro [tʃen'timetro] *sm* centimetre

centi'naio [tʃenti'najo] (*pl(f)* **-aia**) *sm* **un ~**

(di) a hundred; about a hundred

'cento ['tʃento] *num* a hundred, one hundred

cento'mila [tʃento'mila] *num* a o one hundred thousand; **te l'ho detto ~ volte** (*fig*) I've told you a thousand times

cen'trale [tʃen'trale] *ag* central ▷ *sf*: **centrale telefonica** (telephone) exchange; **centrale elettrica** electric power station; **centrali'nista** *sm/f* operator; **centra'lino** *sm* (telephone) exchange; (*di albergo ecc*) switchboard; **centralizzato, -a** [tʃentralid'dzato] *ag* central

cen'trare [tʃen'trare] *vt* to hit the centre of; (*Tecn*) to centre

cen'trifuga [tʃen'trifuga] *sf* spin-drier

'centro ['tʃentro] *sm* centre; **centro civico** civic centre; **centro commerciale** shopping centre; (*città*) commercial centre

'ceppo ['tʃeppo] *sm* (*di albero*) stump; (*pezzo di legno*) log

'cera ['tʃera] *sf* wax; (*aspetto*) appearance

ce'ramica, -che [tʃe'ramika] *sf* ceramic; (*Arte*) ceramics *sg*

cerbi'atto [tʃer'bjatto] *sm* (*Zool*) fawn

cer'care [tʃer'kare] *vt* to look for, search for ▷ *vi* **~ di fare qc** to try to do sth; **stiamo cercando un albergo/ristorante** we're looking for a hotel/restaurant

cercherò *ecc* [tʃerke'rɔ] *vb vedi* **cercare**

'cerchia ['tʃerkja] *sf* circle

cerchietto [tʃer'kjetto] *sm* (*per capelli*) hairband

'cerchio ['tʃerkjo] *sm* circle; (*giocattolo, di botte*) hoop

cereali [tʃere'ali] *smpl* cereal *sg*

ceri'monia [tʃeri'mɔnja] *sf* ceremony

ce'rino [tʃe'rino] *sm* wax match

'cernia ['tʃernja] *sf* (*Zool*) stone bass

cerni'era [tʃer'njɛra] *sf* hinge; **cerniera lampo** zip (fastener) (*BRIT*), zipper (*US*)

'cero ['tʃero] *sm* (church) candle

ce'rotto [tʃe'rɔtto] *sm* sticking plaster

certa'mente [tʃerta'mente] *av* certainly

certifi'cato *sm* certificate; **certificato medico** medical certificate; **certificato di nascita/di morte** birth/death certificate

○ **PAROLA CHIAVE**

'certo, -a ['tʃerto] *ag* (*sicuro*): **certo (di/ che)** certain o sure (of/that)
▷ *det* **1** (*tale*) certain; **un certo signor Smith** a (certain) Mr Smith
2 (*qualche: con valore intensivo*) some; **dopo un certo tempo** after some time; **un fatto di una certa importanza** a matter of some importance; **di una certa età**

past one's prime, not so young ▷ *pron* **certi, e** *pl* some ▷ *av* (*certamente*) certainly; (*senz'altro*) of course; **di certo** certainly; **no (di) certo!, certo che no!** certainly not!; **sì certo** yes indeed, certainly

cer'vello, -i [tʃer'vɛllo] (Anat) (pl(f) **-a**) *sm* brain; **cervello elettronico** computer

'cervo, -a ['tʃɛrvo] *sm/f* stag/doe ▷ *sm* deer; **cervo volante** stag beetle

ces'puglio [tʃes'puʎʎo] *sm* bush

ces'sare [tʃes'sare] *vi, vt* to stop, cease; **~ di fare qc** to stop doing sth

ces'tino [tʃes'tino] *sm* basket; (*per la carta straccia*) wastepaper basket; **cestino da viaggio** (Ferr) packed lunch (o dinner)

'cesto ['tʃesto] *sm* basket

'ceto ['tʃeto] *sm* (social) class

cetrio'lino [tʃetrio'lino] *sm* gherkin

cetri'olo [tʃetri'ɔlo] *sm* cucumber

Cfr. *abbr* (= *confronta*) cf.

CGIL *sigla f* (= *Confederazione Generale Italiana del Lavoro*) trades union organization

chat line [tʃæt'laen] *sf inv* chat room

chattare [tʃat'tare] *vi* (Inform) to chat online

○ **PAROLA CHIAVE**

che [ke] *pron* **1** (*relativo: persona: soggetto*) who; (: *oggetto*) whom, that; (: *cosa, animale*) which, that; **il ragazzo che è venuto** the boy who came; **l'uomo che io vedo** the man (whom) I see; **il libro che è sul tavolo** the book which o that is on the table; **il libro che vedi** the book (which o that) you see; **la sera che ti ho visto** the evening I saw you

2 (*interrogativo, esclamativo*) what; **che (cosa) fai?** what are you doing?; **a che (cosa) pensi?** what are you thinking about?; **non sa che (cosa) fare** he doesn't know what to do; **ma che dici!** what are you saying!

3 (*indefinito*): **quell'uomo ha un che di losco** there's something suspicious about that man; **un certo non so che** an indefinable something

▷ *det* **1** (*interrogativo: tra tanti*) what; (: *tra pochi*) which; **che tipo di film preferisci?** what sort of film do you prefer?; **che vestito ti vuoi mettere?** what (o which) dress do you want to put on?

2 (*esclamativo: seguito da aggettivo*) how; (: *seguito da sostantivo*) what; **che buono!** how delicious!; **che bel vestito!** what a lovely dress!

▷ *cong* **1** (*con proposizioni subordinate*) that;

credo che verrà I think he'll come; **voglio che tu studi** I want you to study; **so che tu c'eri** I know (that) you were there; **non che, non che sia sbagliato, ma ...** not that it's wrong, but ...

2 (*finale*) so that; **vieni qua, che ti veda** come here, so (that) I can see you

3 (*temporale*): **arrivai che eri già partito** you had already left when I arrived; **sono anni che non lo vedo** I haven't seen him for years

4 (*in frasi imperative, concessive*): **che venga pure!** let him come by all means!; **che tu sia benedetto!** may God bless you!

5 (*comparativo: con più, meno*) than; *vedi anche* **più**; **meno**; **così** *ecc*

chemiotera'pia [kemjotera'pia] *sf* chemotherapy

chero'sene [kero'zɛne] *sm* kerosene

○ **PAROLA CHIAVE**

chi [ki] *pron* **1** (*interrogativo: soggetto*) who; (: *oggetto*) who, whom; **chi è?** who is it?; **di chi è questo libro?** whose book is this?, whose is this book?; **con chi parli?** who are you talking to?; **a chi pensi?** who are you thinking about?; **chi di voi?** which of you?; **non so a chi rivolgermi** I don't know who to ask

2 (*relativo*) whoever, anyone who; **dillo a chi vuoi** tell whoever you like

3 (*indefinito*): **chi ... chi ...** some ... others ...; **chi dice una cosa, chi dice un'altra** some say one thing, others say another

chiacchie'rare [kjakkje'rare] *vi* to chat; (*discorrere futilmente*) to chatter; (*far pettegolezzi*) to gossip; **chi'acchiere** *sfpl* **fare due** o **quattro chiacchiere** to have a chat

chia'mare [kja'mare] *vt* to call; (*rivolgersi a qn*) to call (in), send for; **chiamarsi** *vpr* (*aver nome*) to be called; **come ti chiami?** what's your name?; **mi chiamo Paolo** my name is Paolo, I'm called Paolo; **~ alle armi** to call up; **~ in giudizio** to summon; **chia'mata** *sf* (Tel) call; (Mil) call-up

chia'rezza [kja'rettsa] *sf* clearness; clarity

chia'rire [kja'rire] *vt* to make clear; (*fig: spiegare*) to clear up, explain

chi'aro, -a ['kjaro] *ag* clear; (*luminoso*) clear, bright; (*colore*) pale, light

chi'asso ['kjasso] *sm* uproar, row

chi'ave ['kjave] *sf* key ▷ *ag inv* key *cpd*; **posso avere la mia ~?** can I have my key?; **chiave d'accensione** (Aut) ignition key;

chiave di volta keystone; **chiave inglese** monkey wrench

chi'azza ['kjattsa] *sf* stain; splash

'chicco, -chi ['kikko] *sm* grain; (*di caffè*) bean; **chicco d'uva** grape

chi'edere ['kjɛdere] *vt* (*per sapere*) to ask; (*per avere*) to ask for ▷ *vi* **~ di qn** to ask after sb; (*al telefono*) to ask for o want sb; **~ qc a qn** to ask sb sth; to ask sb for sth; **chiedersi** *vpr* **chiedersi (se)** to wonder (whether)

chi'esa ['kjɛza] *sf* church

chi'esi *ecc* ['kjɛzi] *vb vedi* **chiedere**

'chiglia ['kiʎʎa] *sf* keel

'chilo ['kilo] *sm* kilo; **chi'lometro** *sm* kilometre

'chimica ['kimika] *sf* chemistry

'chimico, -a, -ci, -che ['kimiko] *ag* chemical ▷ *sm/f* chemist

chi'nare [ki'nare] *vt* to lower, bend; **chinarsi** *vpr* to stoop, bend

chi'occiola ['kjɔttʃola] *sf* snail; (*di indirizzo e-mail*) at sign, @; **scala a ~** spiral staircase

chi'odo ['kjɔdo] *sm* nail; (*fig*) obsession; **chiodo di garofano** (*Cuc*) clove

chi'osco, -schi ['kjɔsko] *sm* kiosk, stall

chi'ostro ['kjɔstro] *sm* cloister

chiro'mante [kiro'mante] *sm/f* palmist

chirur'gia [kirur'dʒia] *sf* surgery; **chirurgia estetica** cosmetic surgery; **chi'rurgo, -ghi** o **gi** *sm* surgeon

chissà [kis'sa] *av* who knows, I wonder

chi'tarra [ki'tarra] *sf* guitar

chitar'rista, -i, e [kitar'rista] *sm/f* guitarist, guitar player

chi'udere ['kjudere] *vt* to close, shut; (*luce, acqua*) to put off, turn off; (*definitivamente: fabbrica*) to close down, shut down; (*strada*) to close; (*recingere*) to enclose; (*porre termine a*) to end ▷ *vi* to close, shut; to close down, shut down; to end; **chiudersi** *vpr* to shut, close; (*ritirarsi: anche fig*) to shut o.s. away; (*ferita*) to close up; **a che ora chiudete?** what time do you close?

chi'unque [ki'unkwe] *pron* (*relativo*) whoever; (*indefinito*) anyone, anybody; **~ sia** whoever it is

'chiusi *ecc* ['kjusi] *vb vedi* **chiudere**

chi'uso, -a ['kjuso] *pp di* **chiudere** ▷ *sf* (*di corso d'acqua*) sluice, lock; (*recinto*) enclosure; (*di discorso ecc*) conclusion, ending; **chiu'sura** *sf* (*vedi* **chiudere**) closing; shutting; closing o shutting down; enclosing; putting o turning off; ending; (*dispositivo*) catch; fastening; fastener; **chiusura lampo®** zip (fastener) (BRIT), zipper (US)

C.I. *abbr* = **carta d'identità**

 PAROLA CHIAVE

ci [tʃi] (*dav lo, la, li, le, ne diventa* **ce**) *pron* **1** (*personale: complemento oggetto*) us; (: *a noi: complemento di termine*) (to) us; (: *riflessivo*) ourselves; (: *reciproco*) each other, one another; (*impersonale*): **ci si veste** we get dressed; **ci ha visti** he's seen us; **non ci ha dato niente** he gave us nothing; **ci vestiamo** we get dressed; **ci amiamo** we love one another o each other

2 (*dimostrativo: di ciò, su ciò, in ciò ecc*) about (*o* on *o* of) it; **non so cosa farci** I don't know what to do about it; **che c'entro io?** what have I got to do with it?
▷ *av* (*qui*) here; (*lì*) there; (*moto attraverso luogo*): **ci passa sopra un ponte** a bridge passes over it; **non ci passa più nessuno** nobody comes this way any more; **esserci** *vedi* **essere**

cia'batta [tʃa'batta] *sf* slipper; (*pane*) ciabatta

ciam'bella [tʃam'bɛlla] *sf* (*Cuc*) ring-shaped cake; (*salvagente*) rubber ring

ci'ao ['tʃao] *escl* (*all'arrivo*) hello!; (*alla partenza*) cheerio! (BRIT), bye!

cias'cuno, -a [tʃas'kuno] (*det: dav sm:* **ciascun** +C, V, **ciascuno** +*s impura, gn, pn, ps, x, z; dav sf:* **ciascuna** +C, **ciascun'** +V) *det* every, each; (*ogni*) every ▷ *pron* each (one); (*tutti*) everyone, everybody

ci'barie [tʃi'barje] *sfpl* foodstuffs

cibernauta, -i, -e [tʃiber'nauta] *sm/f* Internet surfer

ciberspazio [tʃiber'spattsjo] *sm* cyberspace

'cibo ['tʃibo] *sm* food

ci'cala [tʃi'kala] *sf* cicada

cica'trice [tʃika'tritʃe] *sf* scar

'cicca ['tʃikka] *sf* cigarette end

'ciccia ['tʃittʃa] (*fam*) *sf* fat

cicci'one, -a [tʃit'tʃone] *sm/f* (*fam*) fatty

cicla'mino [tʃikla'mino] *sm* cyclamen

ci'clismo [tʃi'klizmo] *sm* cycling; **ci'clista, -i, -e** *sm/f* cyclist

'ciclo ['tʃiklo] *sm* cycle; (*di malattia*) course

ciclomo'tore [tʃiklomo'tore] *sm* moped

ci'clone [tʃi'klone] *sm* cyclone

ci'cogna [tʃi'koɲɲa] *sf* stork

ci'eco, -a, -chi, -che ['tʃɛko] *ag* blind ▷ *sm/f* blind man/woman

ci'elo ['tʃɛlo] *sm* sky; (*Rel*) heaven

'cifra ['tʃifra] *sf* (*numero*) figure; numeral; (*somma di denaro*) sum, figure; (*monogramma*) monogram, initials *pl*; (*codice*) code, cipher

'ciglio, -i ['tʃiʎʎo] *(delle palpebre)* *(pl(f)* **ciglia)** *sm (margine)* edge, verge; (eye)lash; (eye)lid; *(sopracciglio)* eyebrow

'cigno ['tʃiɲɲo] *sm* swan

cigo'lare [tʃigo'lare] *vi* to squeak, creak

'Cile ['tʃile] *sm* **il ~** Chile

ci'leno, -a [tʃi'leno] *ag, sm/f* Chilean

cili'egia, -gie *o* **ge** [tʃi'ljedʒa] *sf* cherry

ciliegina [tʃilje'dʒina] *sf* glacé cherry

cilin'drata [tʃilin'drata] *sf (Aut)* (cubic) capacity; **una macchina di grossa ~ a** big-engined car

ci'lindro [tʃi'lindro] *sm* cylinder; *(cappello)* top hat

'cima ['tʃima] *sf (sommità)* top; *(di monte)* top, summit; *(estremità)* end; **in ~ a** at the top of; **da ~ a fondo** from top to bottom; *(fig)* from beginning to end

'cimice ['tʃimitʃe] *sf (Zool)* bug; *(puntina)* drawing pin (BRIT), thumbtack (US)

cimini'era [tʃimi'njɛra] *sf* chimney; *(di nave)* funnel

cimi'tero [tʃimi'tɛro] *sm* cemetery

'Cina ['tʃina] *sf* **la ~** China

cin'cin [tʃin'tʃin] *escl* cheers!

'cinema ['tʃinema] *sm inv* cinema

ci'nese [tʃi'nese] *ag, sm/f, sm* Chinese *inv*

'cinghia ['tʃingja] *sf* strap; *(cintura, Tecn)* belt

cinghi'ale [tʃin'gjale] *sm* wild boar

cinguet'tare [tʃingwet'tare] *vi* to twitter

'cinico, -a, -ci, -che ['tʃiniko] *ag* cynical ▷ *sm/f* cynic

cin'quanta [tʃin'kwanta] *num* fifty; **cinquan'tesimo, -a** *num* fiftieth

cinquan'tina [tʃinkwan'tina] *sf (serie)*: **una ~ (di)** about fifty; *(età)*: **essere sulla ~** to be about fifty

'cinque ['tʃinkwe] *num* five; **avere ~ anni** to be five (years old); **il ~ dicembre 1998** the fifth of December 1998; **alle ~ (ora)** at five (o'clock)

cinque'cento [tʃinkwe'tʃɛnto] *num* five hundred ▷ *sm* **il C~** the sixteenth century

cin'tura [tʃin'tura] *sf* belt; **cintura di salvataggio** lifebelt (BRIT), life preserver (US); **cintura di sicurezza** *(Aut, Aer)* safety *o* seat belt

cintu'rino [tʃintu'rino] *sm* strap; **~ dell'orologio** watch strap

ciò [tʃɔ] *pron* this; that; **~ che** what; **~ nonostante** *o* **nondimeno** nevertheless, in spite of that

ci'occa, -che ['tʃɔkka] *sf (di capelli)* lock

ciocco'lata [tʃokko'lata] *sf* chocolate; *(bevanda)* (hot) chocolate; **cioccola'tino** *sm* chocolate

cioè [tʃo'ɛ] *av* that is (to say)

ci'otola ['tʃɔtola] *sf* bowl

ci'ottolo ['tʃɔttolo] *sm* pebble; *(di strada)* cobble(stone)

ci'polla [tʃi'polla] *sf* onion; *(di tulipano ecc)* bulb

cipol'lina [tʃipol'lina] *sf* **cipolline sottaceto** pickled onions

ci'presso [tʃi'prɛsso] *sm* cypress (tree)

'cipria ['tʃiprja] *sf* (face) powder

'Cipro ['tʃipro] *sm* Cyprus

'circa ['tʃirka] *av* about, roughly ▷ *prep* about, concerning; **a mezzogiorno ~** about midday

'circo, -chi ['tʃirko] *sm* circus

circo'lare [tʃirko'lare] *vi* to circulate; *(Aut)* to drive (along), move (along) ▷ *ag* circular ▷ *sf (Amm)* circular; *(di autobus)* circle (line)

'circolo ['tʃirkolo] *sm* circle

circon'dare [tʃirkon'dare] *vt* to surround; **circondarsi** *vpr* **circondarsi di** to surround o.s. with

circonvallazi'one [tʃirkonvallat'tsjone] *sf* ring road (BRIT), beltway (US); *(per evitare una città)* by-pass

circos'petto, -a [tʃirkos'pɛtto] *ag* circumspect, cautious

circos'tante [tʃirkos'tante] *ag* surrounding, neighbouring

circos'tanza [tʃirkos'tantsa] *sf* circumstance; *(occasione)* occasion

cir'cuito [tʃir'kuito] *sm* circuit

CISL *sigla f (= Confederazione Italiana Sindacati Lavoratori)* trades union organization

cis'terna [tʃis'tɛrna] *sf* tank, cistern

'cisti ['tʃisti] *sf* cyst

cis'tite [tʃis'tite] *sf* cystitis

ci'tare [tʃi'tare] *vt (Dir)* to summon; *(autore)* to quote; *(a esempio, modello)* to cite

ci'tofono [tʃi'tɔfono] *sm* entry phone; *(in uffici)* intercom

città [tʃit'ta] *sf inv* town; *(importante)* city; **città universitaria** university campus

cittadi'nanza [tʃittadi'nantsa] *sf* citizens *pl*; *(Dir)* citizenship

citta'dino, -a [tʃitta'dino] *ag* town *cpd*; city *cpd* ▷ *sm/f (di uno Stato)* citizen; *(abitante di città)* townsman, city dweller

ci'uccio ['tʃuttʃo] *sm (fam)* comforter, dummy (BRIT), pacifier (US)

ci'uffo ['tʃuffo] *sm* tuft

ci'vetta [tʃi'vetta] *sf (Zool)* owl; *(fig: donna)* coquette, flirt ▷ *ag inv* **auto/nave ~** decoy car/ship

'civico, -a, -ci, -che ['tʃiviko] *ag* civic; *(museo)* municipal, town *cpd*

ci'vile [tʃi'vile] *ag* civil; *(non militare)* civilian; *(nazione)* civilized ▷ *sm* civilian

civiltà [tʃivil'ta] *sf* civilization; (*cortesia*) civility

'**clacson** *sm inv* (*Aut*) horn

clandes'tino, -a *ag* clandestine; (*Pol*) underground, clandestine; (*immigrato*) illegal ▷ *sm/f* stowaway; (*anche:* **immigrato ~**) illegal immigrant

'**classe** *sf* class; **di ~** (*fig*) with class; of excellent quality; **classe operaia** working class; **classe turistica** (*Aer*) economy class

'**classico, -a, -ci, -che** *ag* classical; (*tradizionale: moda*) classic(al) ▷ *sm* classic; classical author

clas'sifica *sf* classification; (*Sport*) placings *pl*

classifi'care *vt* to classify; (*candidato, compito*) to grade; **classificarsi** *vpr* to be placed

'**clausola** *sf* (*Dir*) clause

clavi'cembalo [klavi'tʃembalo] *sm* harpsichord

cla'vicola *sf* (*Anat*) collar bone

clic'care *vi* (*Inform*): **~ su** to click on

cli'ente *sm/f* customer, client

'**clima, -i** *sm* climate; **climatizzatore** *sm* air conditioning system

'**clinica, -che** *sf* (*scienza*) clinical medicine; (*casa di cura*) clinic, nursing home; (*settore d'ospedale*) clinic

clo'nare *vt* to clone; **clonazione** [klona'tsjone] *sf* cloning

'**cloro** *sm* chlorine

club *sm inv* club

c.m. *abbr* = **corrente mese**

cm *abbr* (= *centimetro*) cm

coalizi'one [koalit'tsjone] *sf* coalition

'**COBAS** *sigla mpl* (= *Comitati di base*) independent trades unions

'**coca** *sf* (*bibita*) Coke®; (*droga*) cocaine

coca'ina *sf* cocaine

cocci'nella [kottʃi'nɛlla] *sf* ladybird (*BRIT*), ladybug (*US*)

cocci'uto, -a [kot'tʃuto] *ag* stubborn, pigheaded

'**cocco, -chi** *sm* (*pianta*) coconut palm; (*frutto*): **noce di ~** coconut ▷ *sm/f* (*fam*) darling

cocco'drillo *sm* crocodile

cocco'lare *vt* to cuddle, fondle

cocerò *ecc* [kotʃe'rɔ] *vb vedi* **cuocere**

co'comero *sm* watermelon

'**coda** *sf* tail; (*fila di persone, auto*) queue (*BRIT*), line (*US*); (*di abiti*) train; **con la ~ dell'occhio** out of the corner of one's eye; **mettersi in ~** to queue (up) (*BRIT*), line up (*US*); to join the queue (*BRIT*) *o* line (*US*); **coda di cavallo** (*acconciatura*) ponytail

co'dardo, -a *ag* cowardly ▷ *sm/f* coward

'**codice** ['kɔditʃe] *sm* code; **codice di avviamento postale** postcode (*BRIT*), zip code (*US*); **codice a barre** bar code; **codice civile** civil code; **codice fiscale** tax code; **codice penale** penal code; **codice segreto** (*di tessera magnetica*) PIN (number); **codice della strada** highway code

coe'rente *ag* coherent

coe'taneo, -a *ag, sm/f* contemporary

'**cofano** *sm* (*Aut*) bonnet (*BRIT*), hood (*US*); (*forziere*) chest

'**cogliere** ['kɔʎʎere] *vt* (*fiore: frutto*) to pick, gather; (*sorprendere*) to catch, surprise; (*bersaglio*) to hit; (*fig: momento opportuno ecc*) to grasp, seize, take; (: *capire*) to grasp; **~ qn in flagrante** *o* **in fallo** to catch sb red-handed

co'gnato, -a [koɲ'ɲato] *sm/f* brother-/sister-in-law

co'gnome [koɲ'ɲome] *sm* surname

coinci'denza [kointʃi'dɛntsa] *sf* coincidence; (*Ferr, Aer, di autobus*) connection

coin'cidere [koin'tʃidere] *vi* to coincide

coin'volgere [koin'vɔldʒere] *vt* **~ in** to involve in

cola'pasta *sm inv* colander

co'lare *vt* (*liquido*) to strain; (*pasta*) to drain; (*oro fuso*) to pour ▷ *vi* (*sudore*) to drip; (*botte*) to leak; (*cera*) to melt; **~ a picco** *vt, vi* (*nave*) to sink

colazi'one [kolat'tsjone] *sf* breakfast; **fare ~** to have breakfast; **a che ora è servita la ~?** what time is breakfast?

co'lera *sm* (*Med*) cholera

'**colgo** *ecc vb vedi* **cogliere**

'**colica** *sf* (*Med*) colic

co'lino *sm* strainer

'**colla** *sf* glue; (*di farina*) paste

collabo'rare *vi* to collaborate; **~ a** to collaborate on; (*giornale*) to contribute to; **collabora'tore, -'trice** *sm/f* collaborator; contributor; **collaboratore esterno** freelance; **collaboratrice familiare** home help

col'lana *sf* necklace; (*collezione*) collection, series

col'lant [kɔ'lã] *sm inv* tights *pl*

col'lare *sm* collar

col'lasso *sm* (*Med*) collapse

collau'dare *vt* to test, try out

col'lega, -ghi, -ghe *sm/f* colleague

collega'mento *sm* connection; (*Mil*) liaison

colle'gare *vt* to connect, join, link; **collegarsi** *vpr* (*Radio, TV*) to link up; **collegarsi con** (*Tel*) to get through to

col'legio [kol'lɛdʒo] *sm* college; (*convitto*)

boarding school; **collegio elettorale** (Pol) constituency

'**collera** sf anger

col'lerico, -a, -ci, -che ag quick-tempered, irascible

col'letta sf collection

col'letto sm collar

collezio'nare [kollettsjo'nare] vt to collect

collezi'one [kollet'tsjone] sf collection

col'lina sf hill

col'lirio sm eyewash

'collo sm neck; (di abito) neck, collar; (pacco) parcel; **collo del piede** instep

colloca'mento sm (impiego) employment; (disposizione) placing, arrangement

collo'care vt (libri, mobili) to place; (Comm: merce) to find a market for

collocazi'one [kollokat'tsjone] sf placing; (di libro) classification

col'loquio sm conversation, talk; (ufficiale, per un lavoro) interview; (Ins) preliminary oral exam

col'mare vt ~ di (anche fig) to fill with; (dare in abbondanza) to load o overwhelm with

co'lombo, -a sm/f dove; pigeon

co'lonia sf colony; (per bambini) holiday camp; **(acqua di) ~** (eau de) cologne

co'lonna sf column; **colonna sonora** (Cinema) sound track; **colonna vertebrale** spine, spinal column

colon'nello sm colonel

colo'rante sm colouring

colo'rare vt to colour; (disegno) to colour in

co'lore sm colour; **a colori** in colour, colour cpd; **farne di tutti i colori** to get up to all sorts of mischief; **vorrei un ~ diverso** I'd like a different colour

colo'rito, -a ag coloured; (viso) rosy, pink; (linguaggio) colourful ▷ sm (tinta) colour; (carnagione) complexion

'colpa sf fault; (biasimo) blame; (colpevolezza) guilt; (azione colpevole) offence; (peccato) sin; **di chi è la ~?** whose fault is it?; **è ~ sua** it's his fault; **per ~ di** through, owing to; **col'pevole** ag guilty

col'pire vt to hit, strike; (fig) to strike; **rimanere colpito da qc** to be amazed o struck by sth

'colpo sm (urto) knock; (: affettivo) blow, shock; (: aggressivo) blow; (di pistola) shot; (Med) stroke; (rapina) raid; **di ~** suddenly; **fare ~** to make a strong impression; **colpo d'aria** chill; **colpo in banca** bank job o raid; **colpo basso** (Pugilato, fig) punch below the belt; **colpo di fulmine** love at first sight; **colpo di grazia** coup de grâce; **colpo di scena** (Teatro) coup de théâtre; (fig) dramatic turn of events; **colpo di sole** sunstroke; **colpo di Stato** coup d'état; **colpo di telefono** phone call; **colpo di testa** (sudden) impulse o whim; **colpo di vento** gust (of wind); **colpi di sole** (nei capelli) highlights

'colsi ecc vb vedi **cogliere**

coltel'lata sf stab

col'tello sm knife; **coltello a serramanico** clasp knife

colti'vare vt to cultivate; (verdura) to grow, cultivate

'colto, -a pp di **cogliere** ▷ ag (istruito) cultured, educated

'coma sm inv coma

comanda'mento sm (Rel) commandment

coman'dante sm (Mil) commander, commandant; (di reggimento) commanding officer; (Naut, Aer) captain

coman'dare vi to be in command ▷ vt to command; (imporre) to order, command; **~ a qn di fare** to order sb to do

combaci'are [komba'tʃare] vi to meet; (fig: coincidere) to coincide

com'battere vt, vi to fight

combi'nare vt to combine; (organizzare) to arrange; (fam: fare) to make, cause; **combinazi'one** sf combination; (caso fortuito) coincidence; **per combinazione** by chance

combus'tibile ag combustible ▷ sm fuel

⊙ **PAROLA CHIAVE**

'come av 1 (alla maniera di) like; **ti comporti come lui** you behave like him o like he does; **bianco come la neve** (as) white as snow; **come se** as if, as though

2 (in qualità di) as a; **lavora come autista** he works as a driver

3 (interrogativo) how; **come ti chiami?** what's your name?; **come sta?** how are you?; **com'è il tuo amico?** what's your friend like?; **come?** (prego) pardon?, sorry?; **come mai?** how come?; **come mai non ci hai avvertiti?** why on earth didn't you warn us?

4 (esclamativo): **come sei bravo!** how clever you are!; **come mi dispiace!** I'm terribly sorry!

▷ cong 1 (in che modo) how; **mi ha spiegato come l'ha conosciuto** he told me how he met him

2 (correlativo) as; (con comparativi di maggioranza) than; **non è bravo come pensavo** he isn't as clever as I thought; **è**

meglio di come pensassi it's better than I thought
3 (*appena che, quando*) as soon as; **come arrivò, iniziò a lavorare** as soon as he arrived, he set to work; *vedi* **così**; **tanto**

'comico, -a, -ci, -che *ag* (*Teatro*) comic; (*buffo*) comical ▷ *sm* (*attore*) comedian, comic actor
cominci'are [komin'tʃare] *vt, vi* to begin, start; **~ a fare/col fare** to begin to do/by doing; **a che ora comincia il film?** when does the film start?
comi'tato *sm* committee
comi'tiva *sf* party, group
co'mizio [ko'mittsjo] *sm* (*Pol*) meeting, assembly
com'media *sf* comedy; (*opera teatrale*) play; (: *che fa ridere*) comedy; (*fig*) playacting *no pl*
commemo'rare *vt* to commemorate
commen'tare *vt* to comment on; (*testo*) to annotate; (*Radio, TV*) to give a commentary on
commerci'ale [kommer'tʃale] *ag* commercial, trading; (*peg*) commercial
commercia'lista, -i, e [kommertʃa'lista] *sm/f* (*laureato*) graduate in economics and commerce; (*consulente*) business consultant
commerci'ante [kommer'tʃante] *sm/f* trader, dealer; (*negoziante*) shopkeeper
commerci'are [kommer'tʃare] *vt, vi* **~ in** to deal *o* trade in
com'mercio [kom'mertʃo] *sm* trade, commerce; **essere in ~** (*prodotto*) to be on the market *o* on sale; **essere nel ~** (*persona*) to be in business; **commercio al dettaglio/all'ingrosso** retail/wholesale trade; **commercio elettronico** e-commerce
com'messo, -a *pp di* **commettere** ▷ *sm/f* shop assistant (BRIT), sales clerk (US) ▷ *sm* (*impiegato*) clerk; **commesso viaggiatore** commercial traveller
commes'tibile *ag* edible
com'mettere *vt* to commit
com'misi *ecc vb vedi* **commettere**
commissari'ato *sm* (*Amm*) commissionership; (: *sede*) commissioner's office; **commissariato di polizia** police station
commis'sario *sm* commissioner; (*di pubblica sicurezza*) ≈ (police) superintendent (BRIT), ≈ (police) captain (US); (*Sport*) steward; (*membro di commissione*) member of a committee *o* board
commissi'one *sf* (*incarico*) errand;

(*comitato, percentuale*) commission; (*Comm: ordinazione*) order; **commissioni** *sfpl* (*acquisti*) shopping *sg*; **commissioni bancarie** bank charges; **commissione d'esame** examining board
com'mosso, -a *pp di* **commuovere**
commo'vente *ag* moving
commozi'one [kommot'tsjone] *sf* emotion, deep feeling; **commozione cerebrale** (*Med*) concussion
commu'overe *vt* to move, affect; **commuoversi** *vpr* to be moved
como'dino *sm* bedside table
comodità *sf inv* comfort; convenience
'comodo, -a *ag* comfortable; (*facile*) easy; (*conveniente*) convenient; (*utile*) useful, handy ▷ *sm* comfort; convenience; **con ~** at one's convenience *o* leisure; **fare il proprio ~** to do as one pleases; **far ~** to be useful *o* handy
compa'gnia [kompaɲ'ɲia] *sf* company; (*gruppo*) gathering
com'pagno, -a [kom'paɲɲo] *sm/f* (*di classe, gioco*) companion; (*Pol*) comrade
com'paio *ecc vb vedi* **comparire**
compa'rare *vt* to compare
compara'tivo, -a *ag, sm* comparative
compa'rire *vi* to appear
com'parvi *ecc vb vedi* **comparire**
compassi'one *sf* compassion, pity; **avere ~ di qn** to feel sorry for sb, to pity sb
com'passo *sm* (*pair of*) compasses *pl*; callipers *pl*
compa'tibile *ag* (*scusabile*) excusable; (*conciliabile, Inform*) compatible
compa'tire *vt* (*aver compassione di*) to sympathize with, feel sorry for; (*scusare*) to make allowances for
com'patto, -a *ag* compact; (*roccia*) solid; (*folla*) dense; (*fig: gruppo, partito*) united
compen'sare *vt* (*equilibrare*) to compensate for, make up for; **~ qn di** (*rimunerare*) to pay *o* remunerate sb for; (*risarcire*) to pay compensation to sb for; (*fig: fatiche, dolori*) to reward sb for; **com'penso** *sm* compensation payment, remuneration; reward; **in compenso** (*d'altra parte*) on the other hand
compe'rare *vt* = **comprare**
'compere *sfpl* **fare ~** to do the shopping
compe'tente *ag* competent; (*mancia*) apt, suitable
com'petere *vi* to compete, vie; (*Dir: spettare*): **~ a** to lie within the competence of; **competizi'one** *sf* competition
compi'angere [kom'pjandʒere] *vt* to sympathize with, feel sorry for
'compiere *vt* (*concludere*) to finish, complete; (*adempiere*) to carry out, fulfil;

compiersi *vpr* (*avverarsi*) to be fulfilled, come true; **~ gli anni** to have one's birthday

compi'lare *vt* (*modulo*) to fill in; (*dizionario, elenco*) to compile

'compito *sm* (*incarico*) task, duty; (*dovere*) duty; (*Ins*) exercise; (: *a casa*) piece of homework; **fare i compiti** to do one's homework

comple'anno *sm* birthday

complessità *sf* complexity

comples'sivo, -a *ag* (*globale*) comprehensive, overall; (*totale: cifra*) total

com'plesso, -a *ag* complex ▷ *ag* (*Psic, Edil*) complex; (*Mus: corale*) ensemble; (: *orchestrina*) band; (: *di musica pop*) group; **in** *o* **nel ~** on the whole; **complesso alberghiero** hotel complex; **complesso edilizio** building complex; **complesso vitaminico** vitamin complex

completa'mente *av* completely

comple'tare *vt* to complete

com'pleto, -a *ag* complete; (*teatro, autobus*) full ▷ *sm* suit; **al ~** full; (*tutti presenti*) all present; **completo da sci** ski suit

compli'care *vt* to complicate; **complicarsi** *vpr* to become complicated

'complice ['kɔmplitʃe] *sm/f* accomplice

complicità [komplitʃi'ta] *sf inv* complicity; **un sorriso/uno sguardo di ~** a knowing smile/look

complimen'tarsi *vpr* **~ con** to congratulate

compli'mento *sm* compliment; **complimenti** *smpl* (*cortesia eccessiva*) ceremony *sg*; (*ossequi*) regards, compliments; **complimenti!** congratulations!; **senza complimenti!** don't stand on ceremony!; make yourself at home!; help yourself!

complot'tare *vi* to plot, conspire

com'plotto *sm* plot, conspiracy

com'pone *ecc vb vedi* **comporre**

compo'nente *sm/f* member ▷ *sm* component

com'pongo *ecc vb vedi* **comporre**

componi'mento *sm* (*Dir*) settlement; (*Ins*) composition; (*poetico, teatrale*) work

com'porre *vt* (*musica, testo*) to compose; (*mettere in ordine*) to arrange; (*Dir: lite*) to settle; (*Tip*) to set; (*Tel*) to dial; **comporsi** *vpr* **comporsi di** to consist of, be composed of

comporta'mento *sm* behaviour

compor'tare *vt* (*implicare*) to involve; **comportarsi** *vpr* to behave

com'posi *ecc vb vedi* **comporre**

composi'tore, -'trice *sm/f* composer;

(*Tip*) compositor, typesetter

com'posto, -a *pp di* **comporre** ▷ *ag* (*persona*) composed, self-possessed; (: *decoroso*) dignified; (*formato da più elementi*) compound *cpd* ▷ *sm* compound

com'prare *vt* to buy; **dove posso ~ delle cartoline?** where can I buy some postcards?

com'prendere *vt* (*contenere*) to comprise, consist of; (*capire*) to understand

compren'sibile *ag* understandable

comprensi'one *sf* understanding

compren'sivo, -a *ag* (*prezzo*): **~ di** inclusive of; (*indulgente*) understanding

> Attenzione! In inglese esiste la parola *comprehensive*, che però in genere significa *completo*.

com'preso, -a *pp di* **comprendere** ▷ *ag* (*incluso*) included; **il servizio è ~?** is service included?

com'pressa *sf* (*Med: garza*) compress; (: *pastiglia*) tablet; *vedi anche* **compresso**

com'primere *vt* (*premere*) to press; (*Fisica*) to compress; (*fig*) to repress

compro'messo, -a *pp di* **compromettere** ▷ *sm* compromise

compro'mettere *vt* to compromise; **compromettersi** *vpr* to compromise o.s.

com'puter *sm inv* computer

comu'nale *ag* municipal, town *cpd*, ≈ borough *cpd*

co'mune *ag* common; (*consueto*) common, everyday; (*di livello medio*) average; (*ordinario*) ordinary ▷ *sm* (*Amm*) town council; (: *sede*) town hall ▷ *sf* (*di persone*) commune; **fuori del ~** out of the ordinary; **avere in ~** to have in common, share; **mettere in ~** to share

comuni'care *vt* (*notizia*) to pass on, convey; (*malattia*) to pass on; (*ansia ecc*) to communicate; (*trasmettere: calore ecc*) to transmit, communicate; (*Rel*) to administer communion to ▷ *vi* to communicate

comuni'cato *sm* communiqué; **comunicato stampa** press release

comunicazi'one [komunikat'tsjone] *sf* communication; (*annuncio*) announcement; (*Tel*): **dare la ~ a qn** to put sb through; **ottenere la ~** to get through; **comunicazione (telefonica)** (telephone) call

comuni'one *sf* communion; **comunione di beni** (*Dir*) joint ownership of property

comu'nismo *sm* communism

comunità *sf inv* community; **Comunità Europea** European Community

co'munque *cong* however, no matter how ▷ *av* (*in ogni modo*) in any case; (*tuttavia*) however, nevertheless

con prep with; **partire col treno** to leave by train; **~ mio grande stupore** to my great astonishment; **~ tutto ciò** for all that

con'cedere [kon'tʃedere] vt (accordare) to grant; (ammettere) to admit, concede; **concedersi qc** to treat o.s. to sth, to allow o.s. sth

concentrarsi vpr to concentrate

concentrazi'one sf concentration

conce'pire [kontʃe'pire] vt (bambino) to conceive; (progetto, idea) to conceive (of); (metodo, piano) to devise

con'certo [kon'tʃɛrto] sm (Mus) concert; (: componimento) concerto

con'cessi ecc [kon'tʃɛssi] vb vedi **concedere**

con'cetto [kon'tʃɛtto] sm (pensiero, idea) concept; (opinione) opinion

concezi'one [kontʃet'tsjone] sf conception

con'chiglia [kon'kiʎʎa] sf shell

conci'are [kon'tʃare] vt (pelli) to tan; (tabacco) to cure; (fig: ridurre in cattivo stato) to beat up; **conciarsi** vpr (sporcarsi) to get in a mess; (vestirsi male) to dress badly

concili'are [kontʃi'ljare] vt to reconcile; (contravvenzione) to pay on the spot; (sonno) to be conducive to, induce; **conciliarsi qc** to gain o win sth (for o.s.); **conciliarsi qn** to win sb over; **conciliarsi con** to be reconciled with

con'cime [kon'tʃime] sm manure; (chimico) fertilizer

con'ciso, -a [kon'tʃizo] ag concise, succinct

concitta'dino, -a [kontʃitta'dino] sm/f fellow citizen

con'cludere vt to conclude; (portare a compimento) to conclude, finish, bring to an end; (operare positivamente) to achieve ▷ vi (essere convincente) to be conclusive; **concludersi** vpr to come to an end, close

concor'dare vt (tregua, prezzo) to agree on; (Ling) to make agree ▷ vi to agree

con'corde ag (d'accordo) in agreement; (simultaneo) simultaneous

concor'rente sm/f competitor; (Ins) candidate; **concor'renza** sf competition

concorrenzi'ale [konkorren'tsjale] ag competitive

con'correre vi **~ (in)** (Mat) to converge o meet (in); **~ (a)** (competere) to compete (for); (: Ins: a una cattedra) to apply (for); (partecipare: a un'impresa) to take part (in), contribute (to); **con'corso, -a** pp di **concorrere** ▷ sm competition; (Ins) competitive examination; **concorso di colpa** (Dir) contributory negligence

con'creto, -a ag concrete

con'danna sf sentence; conviction; condemnation

condan'nare vt (Dir): **~ a** to sentence to; **~ per** to convict of; (disapprovare) to condemn

conden'sare vt to condense

condi'mento sm seasoning; dressing

con'dire vt to season; (insalata) to dress

condi'videre vt to share

condizio'nale [kondittsjo'nale] ag conditional ▷ sm (Ling) conditional ▷ sf (Dir) suspended sentence

condizio'nare [kondittsjo'nare] vt to condition; **ad aria condizionata** air-conditioned; **condiziona'tore** sm air conditioner

condizi'one [kondit'tsjone] sf condition

condogli'anze [kondoʎ'ʎantse] sfpl condolences

condo'minio sm joint ownership; (edificio) jointly-owned building

con'dotta sf (modo di comportarsi) conduct, behaviour; (di un affare ecc) handling; (di acqua) piping; (incarico sanitario) country medical practice controlled by a local authority

condu'cente [kondu'tʃɛnte] sm driver

con'duco ecc vb vedi **condurre**

con'durre vt to conduct; (azienda) to manage; (accompagnare: bambino) to take; (automobile) to drive; (trasportare: acqua, gas) to convey, conduct; (fig) to lead ▷ vi to lead

con'dussi ecc vb vedi **condurre**

confe'renza [konfe'rɛntsa] sf (discorso) lecture; (riunione) conference; **conferenza stampa** press conference

con'ferma sf confirmation

confer'mare vt to confirm

confes'sare vt to confess; **confessarsi** vpr to confess; **andare a confessarsi** (Rel) to go to confession

con'fetto sm sugared almond; (Med) pill

▮ Attenzione! In inglese esiste la parola confetti, che però significa coriandoli.

confet'tura sf (gen) jam; (di arance) marmalade

confezio'nare [konfettsjo'nare] vt (vestito) to make (up); (merci, pacchi) to package

confezi'one [konfet'tsjone] sf (di abiti: da uomo) tailoring; (: da donna) dressmaking; (imballaggio) packaging; **confezioni per signora** ladies' wear; **confezioni da uomo** menswear; **confezione regalo** gift pack

confic'care vt **~ qc in** to hammer o drive sth into; **conficcarsi** vpr to stick

confi'dare vi **~ in** to confide in, rely on ▷ vt to confide; **confidarsi con qn** to confide in sb

configu'rare vt (Inform) to set

configurazi'one [konfigurat'tsjone] sf configuration; (Inform) setting

confi'nare vi ~ **con** to border on ▷ vt (Pol) to intern; (fig) to confine

Confin'dustria sigla f (= Confederazione Generale dell'Industria Italiana) employers' association, ≈ CBI (BRIT)

con'fine sm boundary; (di paese) border, frontier

confis'care vt to confiscate

con'flitto sm conflict

conflu'enza [konflu'ɛntsa] sf (di fiumi) confluence; (di strade) junction

con'fondere vt to mix up, confuse; (imbarazzare) to embarrass; **confondersi** vpr (mescolarsi) to mingle; (turbarsi) to be confused; (sbagliare) to get mixed up

confor'tare vt to comfort, console

confron'tare vt to compare

con'fronto sm comparison; **in** o **a ~ di** in comparison with, compared to; **nei miei** (o **tuoi** ecc) **confronti** towards me (o you ecc)

con'fusi ecc vb vedi **confondere**

confusi'one sf confusion; (chiasso) racket, noise; (imbarazzo) embarrassment

con'fuso, -a pp di **confondere** ▷ ag (vedi confondere) confused; embarrassed

conge'dare [kondʒe'dare] vt to dismiss; (Mil) to demobilize; **congedarsi** vpr to take one's leave

con'gegno sm device, mechanism

conge'lare [kondʒe'lare] vt to freeze; **congelarsi** vpr to freeze; **congela'tore** sm freezer

congesti'one [kondʒes'tjone] sf congestion

conget'tura [kondʒet'tura] sf conjecture

con'giungere [kon'dʒundʒere] vt to join (together); **congiungersi** vpr to join (together)

congiunti'vite [kondʒunti'vite] sf conjunctivitis

congiun'tivo [kondʒun'tivo] sm (Ling) subjunctive

congi'unto, -a [kon'dʒunto] pp di **congiungere** ▷ ag (unito) joined ▷ sm/f relative

congiunzi'one [kondʒun'tsjone] sf (Ling) conjunction

congi'ura [kon'dʒura] sf conspiracy

congratu'larsi vpr ~ **con qn per qc** to congratulate sb on sth

congratulazi'oni [kongratulat'tsjoni] sfpl congratulations

con'gresso sm congress

C.O.N.I. sigla m (= Comitato Olimpico Nazionale Italiano) Italian Olympic Games Committee

coni'are vt to mint, coin; (fig) to coin

co'niglio [ko'niʎʎo] sm rabbit

coniu'gare vt (Ling) to conjugate; **coniugarsi** vpr to get married

'coniuge ['kɔnjudʒe] sm/f spouse

connazio'nale [konnattsjo'nale] sm/f fellow-countryman/woman

connessi'one sf connection

con'nettere vt to connect, join ▷ vi (fig) to think straight

'cono sm cone; **cono gelato** ice-cream cone

co'nobbi ecc vb vedi **conoscere**

cono'scente [konoʃ'ʃɛnte] sm/f acquaintance

cono'scenza [konoʃ'ʃɛntsa] sf (il sapere) knowledge no pl; (persona) acquaintance; (facoltà sensoriale) consciousness no pl; **perdere ~** to lose consciousness

co'noscere [ko'noʃʃere] vt to know; **ci siamo conosciuti a Firenze** we (first) met in Florence; **conoscersi** vpr to know o.s.; (reciproco) to know each other; (incontrarsi) to meet; **~ qn di vista** to know sb by sight; **farsi ~** (fig) to make a name for o.s.; **conosci'uto, -a** pp di **conoscere** ▷ ag well-known

con'quista sf conquest

conquis'tare vt to conquer; (fig) to gain, win

consa'pevole ag ~ **di** aware o conscious of

'conscio, -a, -sci, -sce ['kɔnʃo] ag ~ **di** aware o conscious of

consecu'tivo, -a ag consecutive; (successivo: giorno) following, next

con'segna [kon'seɲɲa] sf delivery; (merce consegnata) consignment; (custodia) care, custody; (Mil: ordine) orders pl; (: punizione) confinement to barracks; **pagamento alla ~** cash on delivery; **dare qc in ~ a qn** to entrust sth to sb

conse'gnare [konseɲ'ɲare] vt to deliver; (affidare) to entrust, hand over; (Mil) to confine to barracks

consegu'enza [konse'gwɛntsa] sf consequence; **per** o **di ~** consequently

con'senso sm approval, consent; **consenso informato** informed consent

consen'tire vi ~ **a** to consent o agree to ▷ vt to allow, permit

con'serva sf (Cuc) preserve; **conserva di frutta** jam; **conserva di pomodoro** tomato purée

conser'vante sm (per alimenti) preservative

conser'vare vt (Cuc) to preserve; (custodire) to keep; (: dalla distruzione ecc) to preserve, conserve

conserva'tore, -'trice *sm/f* (*Pol*) conservative

conserva'torio *sm* (*di musica*) conservatory

conservazi'one [konservat'tsjone] *sf* preservation; conservation

conside'rare *vt* to consider; (*reputare*) to consider, regard; **considerarsi** *vpr* to consider o.s.

consigli'are [konsiʎ'ʎare] *vt* (*persona*) to advise; (*metodo, azione*) to recommend, advise, suggest; **mi può ~ un buon ristorante?** can you recommend a good restaurant?; **con'siglio** *sm* (*suggerimento*) advice *no pl*, piece of advice; (*assemblea*) council; **consiglio d'amministrazione** board; **Consiglio d'Europa** Council of Europe; **Consiglio dei Ministri** (*Pol*): **il Consiglio dei Ministri** ≈ the Cabinet

consis'tente *ag* thick; solid; (*fig*) sound, valid

con'sistere *vi* **~ in** to consist of

conso'lare *ag* consular ▷ *vt* (*confortare*) to console, comfort; (*rallegrare*) to cheer up; **consolarsi** *vpr* to be comforted; to cheer up

conso'lato *sm* consulate

consolazi'one [konsolat'tsjone] *sf* consolation, comfort

'console *sm* consul

conso'nante *sf* consonant

'consono, -a *ag* **~ a** consistent with, consonant with

con'sorte *sm/f* consort

consta'tare *vt* to establish, verify

consu'eto, -a *ag* habitual, usual

consu'lente *sm/f* consultant

consul'tare *vt* to consult; **consultarsi** *vpr* **consultarsi con qn** to seek the advice of sb

consul'torio *sm* **~ familiare** family planning clinic

consu'mare *vt* (*logorare: abiti, scarpe*) to wear out; (*usare*) to consume, use up; (*mangiare, bere*) to consume; (*Dir*) to consummate; **consumarsi** *vpr* to wear out; to be used up; (*anche fig*) to be consumed; (*combustibile*) to burn out

con'tabile *ag* accounts *cpd*, accounting ▷ *sm/f* accountant

contachi'lometri [kontaki'lɔmetri] *sm inv* ≈ mileometer

conta'dino, -a *sm/f* countryman/ woman, farm worker; (*peg*) peasant

contagi'are [konta'dʒare] *vt* to infect

contagi'oso, -a *ag* infectious; contagious

conta'gocce [konta'gottʃe] *sm inv* (*Med*) dropper

contami'nare *vt* to contaminate

con'tante *sm* cash; **pagare in contanti** to pay cash; **non ho contanti** I haven't got any cash

con'tare *vt* to count; (*considerare*) to consider ▷ *vi* to count, be of importance; **~ su qn** to count o rely on sb; **~ di fare qc** to intend to do sth; **conta'tore** *sm* meter

contat'tare *vt* to contact

con'tatto *sm* contact

'conte *sm* count

conteggi'are [konted'dʒare] *vt* to charge, put on the bill

con'tegno [kon'teɲɲo] *sm* (*comportamento*) behaviour; (*atteggiamento*) attitude; **darsi un ~** to act nonchalant; to pull o.s. together

contemporanea'mente *av* simultaneously; at the same time

contempo'raneo, -a *ag*, *sm/f* contemporary

conten'dente *sm/f* opponent, adversary

conte'nere *vt* to contain; **conteni'tore** *sm* container

conten'tezza [konten'tettsa] *sf* contentment

con'tento, -a *ag* pleased, glad; **~ di** pleased with

conte'nuto *sm* contents *pl*; (*argomento*) content

con'tessa *sf* countess

contes'tare *vt* (*Dir*) to notify; (*fig*) to dispute

con'testo *sm* context

continen'tale *ag*, *sm/f* continental

conti'nente *ag* continent ▷ *sm* (*Geo*) continent; (: *terra ferma*) mainland

contin'gente [kontin'dʒɛnte] *ag* contingent ▷ *sm* (*Comm*) quota; (*Mil*) contingent

continua'mente *av* (*senza interruzione*) continuously, nonstop; (*ripetutamente*) continually

continu'are *vt* to continue (with), go on with ▷ *vi* to continue, go on; **~ a fare qc** to go on o continue doing sth

continuità *sf* continuity

con'tinuo, -a *ag* (*numerazione*) continuous; (*pioggia*) continual, constant; (*Elettr*): **corrente continua** direct current; **di ~** continually

'conto *sm* (*calcolo*) calculation; (*Comm, Econ*) account; (*di ristorante, albergo*) bill; (*fig: stima*) consideration, esteem; **il ~, per favore** can I have the bill, please?; **lo metta sul mio ~** put it on my bill; **fare i conti con qn** to settle one's account with sb; **fare ~ su qn/qc** to count o rely on sb; **rendere ~ a qn di qc** to be accountable to sb for sth; **tener ~ di qn/qc** to take sb/sth into account; **per ~ di** on behalf of; **per ~ mio** as far as I'm concerned; **a conti fatti, in fin dei conti** all things considered; **conto corrente** current account; **conto alla rovescia** countdown

con'torno sm (*linea*) outline, contour; (*ornamento*) border; (*Cuc*) vegetables *pl*

con'torto, -a *pp di* **contorcere**

contrabbandi'ere, -a sm/f smuggler

contrab'bando sm smuggling, contraband; **merce di ~** contraband, smuggled goods *pl*

contrab'basso sm (*Mus*) (double) bass

contraccambi'are vt (*favore ecc*) to return

contraccet'tivo, -a [kontrattʃet'tivo] *ag*, sm contraceptive

contrac'colpo sm rebound; (*di arma da fuoco*) recoil; (*fig*) repercussion

contrad'dire vt to contradict; **contraddirsi** vpr to contradict o.s.; (*uso reciproco: persone*) to contradict each other *o* one another; (: *testimonianze ecc*) to be contradictory

contraf'fare vt (*persona*) to mimic; (*alterare: voce*) to disguise; (*firma*) to forge, counterfeit

contraria'mente *av* **~ a** contrary to

contrari'are vt (*contrastare*) to thwart, oppose; (*irritare*) to annoy, bother

con'trario, -a *ag* opposite; (*sfavorevole*) unfavourable ▷ sm opposite; **essere ~ a qc** (*persona*) to be against sth; **in caso ~** otherwise; **avere qc in ~** to have some objection; **al ~** on the contrary

contrasse'gnare [kontrassɛɲ'ɲare] vt to mark

contras'tare vt (*avversare*) to oppose; (*impedire*) to bar; (*negare: diritto*) to contest, dispute ▷ vi **~ (con)** (*essere in disaccordo*) to contrast (with); (*lottare*) to struggle (with)

contrat'tacco sm counterattack

contrat'tare vt, vi to negotiate

contrat'tempo sm hitch

con'tratto, -a *pp di* **contrarre** ▷ sm contract

contravvenzi'one [kontravven'tsjone] sf contravention; (*ammenda*) fine

contrazi'one [kontrat'tsjone] sf contraction; (*di prezzi ecc*) reduction

contribu'ente sm/f taxpayer; ratepayer (ʙʀɪᴛ), property tax payer (ᴜs)

contribu'ire vi to contribute

'contro *prep* against; **~ di me/lui** against me/him; **pastiglie ~ la tosse** throat lozenges; **~ pagamento** (*Comm*) on payment ▷ *prefisso*: **controfi'gura** sf (*Cinema*) double

control'lare vt (*accertare*) to check;

(*sorvegliare*) to watch, control; (*tenere nel proprio potere, fig: dominare*) to control; **controllarsi** vpr to control o.s.; **con'trollo** sm check; watch; control; **controllo delle nascite** birth control; **control'lore** sm (*Ferr, Autobus*) (ticket) inspector

contro'luce [kontro'lutʃe] sf *inv* (*Fot*) backlit shot ▷ *av* **(in) ~** against the light; (*fotografare*) into the light

contro'mano *av* **guidare ~** to drive on the wrong side of the road; (*in un senso unico*) to drive the wrong way up a one-way street

controprodu'cente [kontroprodu'tʃɛnte] *ag* counterproductive

contro'senso sm (*contraddizione*) contradiction in terms; (*assurdità*) nonsense

controspio'naggio [kontrospio'naddʒo] sm counterespionage

contro'versia sf controversy; (*Dir*) dispute

contro'verso, -a *ag* controversial

contro'voglia [kontro'vɔʎʎa] *av* unwillingly

contusi'one sf (*Med*) bruise

convale'scente [konvaleʃ'ʃɛnte] *ag*, sm/f convalescent

convali'dare vt (*Amm*) to validate; (*fig: sospetto, dubbio*) to confirm

con'vegno [kon'veɲɲo] sm (*incontro*) meeting; (*congresso*) convention, congress; (*luogo*) meeting place

conve'nevoli sm*pl* civilities

conveni'ente *ag* suitable; (*vantaggioso*) profitable; (: *prezzo*) cheap

> Attenzione! In inglese esiste la parola *convenient*, che però significa *comodo*.

conve'nire vi (*riunirsi*) to gather, assemble; (*concordare*) to agree; (*tornare utile*) to be worthwhile ▷ vb *impers* **conviene fare questo** it is advisable to do this; **conviene andarsene** we should go; **ne convengo** I agree

con'vento sm (*di frati*) monastery; (*di suore*) convent

convenzio'nale [konventsjo'nale] *ag* conventional

convenzi'one [konven'tsjone] sf (*Dir*) agreement; (*nella società*) convention

conver'sare vi to have a conversation, converse

conversazi'one [konversat'tsjone] sf conversation; **fare ~** to chat, have a chat

conversi'one sf conversion; **conversione ad U** (*Aut*) U-turn

conver'tire vt (*trasformare*) to change; (*Pol, Rel*) to convert; **convertirsi** vpr **convertirsi (a)** to be converted (to)

con'vesso, -a *ag* convex

convin'cente [konvin'tʃɛnte] *ag* convincing

con'vincere [kon'vintʃere] *vt* to convince; **~ qn di qc** to convince sb of sth; **~ qn a fare qc** to persuade sb to do sth; **convincersi** *vpr* **convincersi (di qc)** to convince o.s. (of sth); **~ qn di qc** to convince sb of sth; **~ qn a fare qc** to convince sb to do sth

convi'vente *sm/f* common-law husband/wife

con'vivere *vi* to live together

convo'care *vt* to call, convene; (*Dir*) to summon

convulsi'one *sf* convulsion

coope'rare *vi* **~ (a)** to cooperate (in); **coopera'tiva** *sf* cooperative

coordi'nare *vt* to coordinate

co'perchio [ko'pɛrkjo] *sm* cover; (*di pentola*) lid

co'perta *sf* cover; (*di lana*) blanket; (*da viaggio*) rug; (*Naut*) deck

coper'tina *sf* (*Stampa*) cover, jacket

co'perto, -a *pp di* **coprire** ▷ *ag* covered; (*cielo*) overcast ▷ *sm* place setting; (*posto a tavola*) place; (*al ristorante*) cover charge; **~ di** covered in *o* with

coper'tone *sm* (*Aut*) rubber tyre

coper'tura *sf* (*anche Econ, Mil*) cover; (*di edificio*) roofing

'copia *sf* copy; **brutta/bella ~** rough/final copy

copi'are *vt* to copy

copi'one *sm* (*Cinema, Teatro*) script

'coppa *sf* (*bicchiere*) goblet; (*per frutta, gelato*) cup, (*trofeo*) cup, trophy; **coppa dell'olio** oil sump (BRIT) *o* pan (US)

'coppia *sf* (*di persone*) couple; (*di animali, Sport*) pair

coprifu'oco, -chi *sm* curfew

copri'letto *sm* bedspread

copripiu'mino *sm* duvet cover

co'prire *vt* to cover; (*occupare: carica, posto*) to hold; **coprirsi** *vpr* (*cielo*) to cloud over; (*vestirsi*) to wrap up, cover up; (*Econ*) to cover o.s.; **coprirsi di** (*macchie, muffa*) to become covered in

coque [kɔk] *sf* **uovo alla ~** boiled egg

co'raggio [ko'raddʒo] *sm* courage, bravery; **~!** (*forza!*) come on!; (*animo!*) cheer up!

co'rallo *sm* coral

Co'rano *sm* (*Rel*) Koran

co'razza [ko'rattsa] *sf* armour; (*di animali*) carapace, shell; (*Mil*) armour(-plating)

'corda *sf* cord; (*fune*) rope; (*spago, Mus*) string; **dare ~ a qn** to let sb have his (*o* her) way; **tenere sulla ~ qn** to keep sb on tenterhooks; **tagliare la ~** to slip away, sneak off; **corda vocale** vocal cords

cordi'ale *ag* cordial, warm ▷ *sm* (*bevanda*) cordial

'cordless ['kɔːdlɪs] *sm inv* cordless phone

cor'done *sm* cord, string; (*linea: di polizia*) cordon; **cordone ombelicale** umbilical cord

Co'rea *sf* **la ~** Korea

coreogra'fia *sf* choreography

cori'andolo *sm* (*Bot*) coriander; **coriandoli** *smpl* confetti *sg*

cor'nacchia [kor'nakkja] *sf* crow

corna'musa *sf* bagpipes *pl*

cor'netta *sf* (*Mus*) cornet; (*Tel*) receiver

cor'netto *sm* (*Cuc*) croissant; (*gelato*) cone

cor'nice [kor'nitʃe] *sf* frame; (*fig*) setting, background

cornici'one [korni'tʃone] *sm* (*di edificio*) ledge; (*Archit*) cornice

'corno (*pl(f)* **-a**) *sm* (*Zool*) horn; (*pl(m)* **-i**: *Mus*) horn; **fare le corna a qn** to be unfaithful to sb

Corno'vaglia [korno'vaʎʎa] *sf* **la ~** Cornwall

cor'nuto, -a *ag* (*con corna*) horned; (*fam!: marito*) cuckolded ▷ *sm* (*fam!*) cuckold; (: *insulto*) bastard (!)

'coro *sm* chorus; (*Rel*) choir

co'rona *sf* crown; (*di fiori*) wreath

'corpo *sm* body; (*militare, diplomatico*) corps *inv*; **prendere ~** to take shape; **a ~ a ~** hand-to-hand; **corpo di ballo** corps de ballet; **corpo insegnante** teaching staff

corpora'tura *sf* build, physique

cor'reggere [kor'reddʒere] *vt* to correct; (*compiti*) to correct, mark

cor'rente *ag* (*acqua: di fiume*) flowing; (: *di rubinetto*) running; (*moneta, prezzo*) current; (*comune*) everyday ▷ *sm* **essere al ~ (di)** to be well-informed (about); **mettere al ~ (di)** to inform (of) ▷ *sf* (*d'acqua*) current, stream; (*spiffero*) draught; (*Elettr, Meteor*) current; (*fig*) trend, tendency; **la vostra lettera del 5 ~ mese** (*Comm*) your letter of the 5th of this month; **corrente alternata/continua** alternate/direct current; **corrente'mente** *av* commonly; **parlare una lingua correntemente** to speak a language fluently

'correre *vi* to run; (*precipitarsi*) to rush; (*partecipare a una gara*) to race, run; (*fig: diffondersi*) to go round ▷ *vt* (*Sport: gara*) to compete in; (*rischio*) to run; (*pericolo*) to face; **~ dietro a qn** to run after sb; **corre voce che …** it is rumoured that …

cor'ressi *ecc vb vedi* **correggere**

correzi'one [korret'tsjone] *sf* correction; marking; **correzione di bozze** proofreading

corri'doio *sm* corridor; (*in aereo, al cinema*)

aisle; **vorrei un posto sul ~** I'd like an aisle seat

corri'dore *sm* (*Sport*) runner; (: *su veicolo*) racer

corri'era *sf* coach (BRIT), bus

corri'ere *sm* (*diplomatico, di guerra, postale*) courier; (*Comm*) carrier

corri'mano *sm* handrail

corrispon'dente *ag* corresponding ▷ *sm/f* correspondent

corrispon'denza [korrispon'dɛntsa] *sf* correspondence

corris'pondere *vi* (*equivalere*): **~ (a)** to correspond (to) ▷ *vt* (*stipendio*) to pay; (*fig: amore*) to return

cor'rodere *vt* to corrode

cor'rompere *vt* to corrupt; (*comprare*) to bribe

cor'roso, -a *pp di* corrodere

cor'rotto, -a *pp di* corrompere ▷ *ag* corrupt

corru'gare *vt* to wrinkle; **~ la fronte** to knit one's brows

cor'ruppi *ecc vb vedi* corrompere

corruzi'one [korrut'tsjone] *sf* corruption; bribery

'corsa *sf* running *no pl*; (*gara*) race; (*di autobus, taxi*) journey, trip; **fare una ~** to run, dash; (*Sport*) to run a race; **corsa campestre** cross-country race

'corsi *ecc vb vedi* correre

cor'sia *sf* (*Aut, Sport*) lane; (*di ospedale*) ward

'Corsica *sf* **la ~** Corsica

cor'sivo *sm* cursive (writing); (*Tip*) italics *pl*

'corso, -a *pp di* correre ▷ *ag* (*strada cittadina*) main street; (*di unità monetaria*) circulation; (*di titoli, valori*) rate, price; **in ~** in progress, under way; (*annata*) current; **corso d'acqua** river, stream; (*artificiale*) waterway; **corso d'aggiornamento** refresher course; **corso serale** evening class

'corte *sf* (court)yard; (*Dir, regale*) court; **fare la ~ a qn** to court sb; **corte marziale** court-martial

cor'teccia, -ce [kor'tettʃa] *sf* bark

corteggi'are [korted'dʒare] *vt* to court

cor'teo *sm* procession

cor'tese *ag* courteous; **corte'sia** *sf* courtesy; **per cortesia ...** excuse me, please ...

cor'tile *sm* (court)yard

cor'tina *sf* curtain; (*anche fig*) screen

'corto, -a *ag* short; **essere a ~ di qc** to be short of sth; **corto circuito** short-circuit

'corvo *sm* raven

'cosa *sf* thing; (*faccenda*) affair, matter, business *no pl*; **(che) ~?** what?; **(che)**

cos'è? what is it?; **a ~ pensi?** what are you thinking about?

'coscia, -sce ['kɔʃʃa] *sf* thigh; **coscia di pollo** (*Cuc*) chicken leg

cosci'ente [koʃʃɛnte] *ag* conscious; **~ di** conscious *o* aware of

 PAROLA CHIAVE

così *av* **1** (*in questo modo*) like this, (in) this way; (*in tal modo*) so; **le cose stanno così** this is the way things stand; **non ho detto così!** I didn't say that!; **come stai? — (e) così** how are you? — so-so; **e così via** and so on; **per così dire** so to speak

2 (*tanto*) so; **così lontano** so far away; **un ragazzo così intelligente** such an intelligent boy

▷ *ag inv* (*tale*): **non ho mai visto un film così** I've never seen such a film ▷ *cong* **1** (*perciò*) so, therefore

2: **così ... come** as ... as; **non è così bravo come te** he's not as good as you; **così ... che** so ... that

cosid'detto, -a *ag* so-called

cos'metico, -a, -ci, -che *ag, sm* cosmetic

cos'pargere [kos'pardʒere] *vt* **~ di** to sprinkle with

cos'picuo, -a *ag* considerable, large

cospi'rare *vi* to conspire

'cossi *ecc vb vedi* cuocere

'costa *sf* (*tra terra e mare*) coast(line); (*litorale*) shore; (*Anat*) rib; **la C~ Azzurra** the French Riviera

cos'tante *ag* constant; (*persona*) steadfast ▷ *sf* constant

cos'tare *vi, vt* to cost; **quanto costa?** how much does it cost?; **~ caro** to be expensive, cost a lot

cos'tata *sf* (*Cuc*) large chop

costeggi'are [kosted'dʒare] *vt* to be close to; to run alongside

costi'ero, -a *ag* coastal, coast *cpd*

costitu'ire *vt* (*comitato, gruppo*) to set up, form; (*elementi, parti: comporre*) to make up, constitute; (*rappresentare*) to constitute; (*Dir*) to appoint; **costituirsi** *vpr* **costituirsi alla polizia** to give o.s. up to the police

costituzi'one [kostitut'tsjone] *sf* setting up; building up; constitution

'costo *sm* cost; **a ogni** *o* **qualunque ~, a tutti i costi** at all costs

'costola *sf* (*Anat*) rib

cos'toso, -a *ag* expensive, costly

cos'tringere [kos'trindʒere] *vt* **~ qn a fare qc** to force sb to do sth

costru'ire *vt* to construct, build;

costruzi'one *sf* construction, building

cos'tume *sm* (*uso*) custom; (*foggia di vestire, indumento*) costume; **costume da bagno** bathing *o* swimming costume (BRIT), swimsuit; (*da uomo*) bathing *o* swimming trunks *pl*

co'tenna *sf* bacon rind

coto'letta *sf* (*di maiale, montone*) chop; (*di vitello, agnello*) cutlet

co'tone *sm* cotton; **cotone idrofilo** cotton wool (BRIT), absorbent cotton (US)

'cotta *sf* (*fam: innamoramento*) crush

'cottimo *sm* **lavorare a ~** to do piecework

'cotto, -a *pp di* **cuocere** ▷ *ag* cooked; (*fam: innamorato*) head-over-heels in love; **ben ~** (*carne*) well done

cot'tura *sf* cooking; (*in forno*) baking; (*in umido*) stewing

co'vare *vt* to hatch; (*fig: malattia*) to be sickening for; (: *odio, rancore*) to nurse ▷ *vi* (*fuoco, fig*) to smoulder

'covo *sm* den

co'vone *sm* sheaf

'cozza ['kɔttsa] *sf* mussel

coz'zare [kot'tsare] *vi* **~ contro** to bang into, collide with

'crampo *sm* cramp; **ho un ~ alla gamba** I've got cramp in my leg

'cranio *sm* skull

cra'tere *sm* crater

cra'vatta *sf* tie

cre'are *vt* to create

'crebbi *ecc vb vedi* **crescere**

cre'dente *sm/f* (*Rel*) believer

cre'denza [kre'dɛntsa] *sf* belief; (*armadio*) sideboard

'credere *vt* to believe ▷ *vi* **~ in, ~ a** to believe in; **~ qn onesto** to believe sb (to be) honest; **~ che** to believe *o* think that; **credersi furbo** to think one is clever

'credito *sm* (*anche Comm*) credit; (*reputazione*) esteem, repute; **comprare a ~** to buy on credit

'crema *sf* cream; (*con uova, zucchero ecc*) custard; **crema pasticciera** confectioner's custard; **crema solare** sun cream

cre'mare *vt* to cremate

'crepa *sf* crack

cre'paccio [kre'pattʃo] *sm* large crack, fissure; (*di ghiacciaio*) crevasse

crepacu'ore *sm* broken heart

cre'pare *vi* (*fam: morire*) to snuff it, kick the bucket; **~ dalle risa** to split one's sides laughing

crêpe [krɛp] *sf inv* pancake

cre'puscolo *sm* twilight, dusk

'crescere ['kreʃʃere] *vi* to grow ▷ *vt* (*figli*) to raise

'cresima *sf* (*Rel*) confirmation

'crespo, -a *ag* (*capelli*) frizzy; (*tessuto*) puckered ▷ *sm* crêpe

'cresta *sf* crest; (*di polli, uccelli*) crest, comb

'creta *sf* chalk; clay

creti'nata *sf* (*fam*): **dire/fare una ~** to say/do a stupid thing

cre'tino, -a *ag* stupid ▷ *sm/f* idiot, fool

CRI *sigla f* = **Croce Rossa Italiana**

cric *sm inv* (*Tecn*) jack

cri'ceto [kri'tʃeto] *sm* hamster

crimi'nale *ag, sm/f* criminal

criminalità *sf* crime; **criminalità organizzata** organized crime

'crimine *sm* (*Dir*) crime

crip'tare *vt* (*TV: programma*) to encrypt

crisan'temo *sm* chrysanthemum

'crisi *sf inv* crisis; (*Med*) attack, fit; **crisi di nervi** attack *o* fit of nerves

cris'tallo *sm* crystal; **cristalli liquidi** liquid crystals

cristia'nesimo *sm* Christianity

cristi'ano, -a *ag, sm/f* Christian

'Cristo *sm* Christ

cri'terio *sm* criterion; (*buon senso*) (common) sense

'critica, -che *sf* criticism; **la ~** (*attività*) criticism; (*persone*) the critics *pl*; *vedi anche* **critico**

criti'care *vt* to criticize

'critico, -a, -ci, -che *ag* critical ▷ *sm* critic

cro'ato, -a *ag, sm/f* Croatian, Croat

Croa'zia [kroa'ttsja] *sf* Croatia

croc'cante *ag* crisp, crunchy

'croce ['krotʃe] *sf* cross; **in ~** (*di traverso*) crosswise; (*fig*) on tenterhooks; **Croce Rossa** Red Cross

croci'ata [kro'tʃata] *sf* crusade

croci'era [kro'tʃɛra] *sf* (*viaggio*) cruise; (*Archit*) transept

croci'fisso, -a *pp di* **crocifiggere**

crol'lare *vi* to collapse; **'crollo** *sm* collapse; (*di prezzi*) slump, sudden fall; **crollo in Borsa** *slump in prices on the Stock Exchange*

cro'mato, -a *ag* chromium-plated

'cromo *sm* chrome, chromium

'cronaca, -che *sf* (*Stampa*) news *sg*; (: *rubrica*) column; (*TV, Radio*) commentary; **fatto** *o* **episodio di ~** news item; **cronaca nera** crime news *sg*; crime column

'cronico, -a, -ci, -che *ag* chronic

cro'nista, -i *sm* (*Stampa*) reporter

cro'nometro *sm* chronometer; (*a scatto*) stopwatch

'crosta *sf* crust

cros'tacei [kros'tatʃei] *smpl* shellfish

cros'tata *sf* (*Cuc*) tart

cros'tino *sm* (*Cuc*) crouton; (: *da antipasto*) canapé

cruci'ale [kru'tʃale] *ag* crucial
cruci'verba *sm inv* crossword (puzzle)
cru'dele *ag* cruel
'crudo, -a *ag* (*non cotto*) raw; (*aspro*) harsh, severe
cru'miro (*peg*) *sm* blackleg (BRIT), scab
'crusca *sf* bran
crus'cotto *sm* (*Aut*) dashboard
CSI *sigla f inv* (= *Comunità Stati Indipendenti*) CIS
CSM [tʃiɛsse'ɛmme] *sigla m* (= *consiglio superiore della magistratura*) Magistrates' Board of Supervisors
'Cuba *sf* Cuba
cu'bano, -a *ag, sm/f* Cuban
cu'betto *sm*; **cubetto di ghiaccio** ice cube
'cubico, -a, -ci, -che *ag* cubic
cu'bista, -i, -e *ag* (*Arte*) Cubist ▷ *sf* (*in discoteca*) podium dancer
'cubo, -a *ag* cubic ▷ *sm* cube; **elevare al ~** (*Mat*) to cube
cuc'cagna [kuk'kaɲɲa] *sf* **paese della ~** land of plenty; **albero della ~** greasy pole (*fig*)
cuc'cetta [kut'tʃetta] *sf* (*Ferr*) couchette; (*Naut*) berth
cucchiai'ata [kukja'jata] *sf* spoonful
cucchia'ino [kukkja'ino] *sm* teaspoon; coffee spoon
cucchi'aio [kuk'kjajo] *sm* spoon
'cuccia, -ce ['kuttʃa] *sf* dog's bed; **a ~!** down!
'cucciolo ['kuttʃolo] *sm* cub; (*di cane*) puppy
cu'cina [ku'tʃina] *sf* (*locale*) kitchen; (*arte culinaria*) cooking, cookery; (*le vivande*) food, cooking; (*apparecchio*) cooker; **cucina componibile** fitted kitchen; **cuci'nare** *vt* to cook
cu'cire [ku'tʃire] *vt* to sew, stitch; **cuci'trice** *sf* stapler
cucù *sm inv* cuckoo
'cuffia *sf* bonnet, cap; (*da infermiera*) cap; (*da bagno*) (bathing) cap; (*per ascoltare*) headphones *pl*, headset
cu'gino, -a [ku'dʒino] *sm/f* cousin

 PAROLA CHIAVE

'cui *pron* **1** (*nei complementi indiretti: persona*) whom; (: *oggetto, animale*) which; **la persona/le persone a cui accennavi** the person/people you were referring to *o* to whom you were referring; **i libri di cui parlavo** the books I was talking about *o* about which I was talking; **il quartiere in cui abito** the district where I live; **la ragione per cui** the reason why
2 (*inserito tra articolo e sostantivo*) whose;

la donna i cui figli sono scomparsi the woman whose children have disappeared; **il signore, dal cui figlio ho avuto il libro** the man from whose son I got the book

culi'naria *sf* cookery
'culla *sf* cradle
cul'lare *vt* to rock
'culmine *sm* top, summit
'culo (*fam!*) *sm* arse (BRIT!), ass (US!); (*fig: fortuna*): **aver ~** to have the luck of the devil
'culto *sm* (*religione*) religion; (*adorazione*) worship, adoration; (*venerazione: anche fig*) cult
cul'tura *sf* culture; education, learning; **cultu'rale** *ag* cultural
cultu'rismo *sm* body-building
cumula'tivo, -a *ag* cumulative; (*prezzo*) inclusive; (*biglietto*) group *cpd*
'cumulo *sm* (*mucchio*) pile, heap; (*Meteor*) cumulus
cu'netta *sf* (*avvallamento*) dip; (*di scolo*) gutter
cu'ocere ['kwɔtʃere] *vt* (*alimenti*) to cook; (*mattoni ecc*) to fire ▷ *vi* to cook; **~ al forno** (*pane*) to bake; (*arrosto*) to roast; **cu'oco, -a, -chi, -che** *sm/f* cook; (*di ristorante*) chef
cu'oio *sm* leather; **cuoio capelluto** scalp
cu'ore *sm* heart; **cuori** *smpl* (*Carte*) hearts; **avere buon ~** to be kind-hearted; **stare a ~ a qn** to be important to sb
'cupo, -a *ag* dark; (*suono*) dull; (*fig*) gloomy, dismal
'cupola *sf* dome; cupola
'cura *sf* care; (*Med: trattamento*) (course of) treatment; **aver ~ di** (*occuparsi di*) to look after; **a ~ di** (*libro*) edited by; **cura dimagrante** diet
cu'rare *vt* (*malato, malattia*) to treat; (: *guarire*) to cure; (*aver cura di*) to take care of; (*testo*) to edit; **curarsi** *vpr* to take care of o.s.; (*Med*) to follow a course of treatment; **curarsi di** to pay attention to
curio'sare *vi* to look round, wander round; (*tra libri*) to browse; **~ nei negozi** to look *o* wander round the shops
curiosità *sf inv* curiosity; (*cosa rara*) curio, curiosity
curi'oso, -a *ag* curious; **essere ~ di** to be curious about
cur'sore *sm* (*Inform*) cursor
'curva *sf* curve; (*stradale*) bend, curve
cur'vare *vt* to bend ▷ *vi* (*veicolo*) to take a bend; (*strada*) to bend, curve; **curvarsi** *vpr* to bend; (*legno*) to warp
'curvo, -a *ag* curved; (*piegato*) bent
cusci'netto [kuʃʃi'netto] *sm* pad; (*Tecn*) bearing ▷ *ag inv* **stato ~** buffer state; **cuscinetto a sfere** ball bearing

cu'scino [kuʃʃino] *sm* cushion; *(guanciale)* pillow

cus'tode *sm/f* keeper, custodian

cus'todia *sf* care; *(Dir)* custody; *(astuccio)* case, holder

custo'dire *vt (conservare)* to keep; *(assistere)* to look after, take care of; *(fare la guardia)* to guard

CV *abbr (= cavallo vapore)* h.p.

cybercaffè [tʃiberka'fe] *sm inv* cybercafé

cybernauta, -i, -e *sm/f* Internet surfer

cyberspazio *sm* cyberspace

 PAROLA CHIAVE

da (*da+il* = **dal**, *da+lo* = **dallo**, *da+l'* = **dall'**, *da+la* = **dalla**, *da+i* = **dai**, *da+gli* = **dagli**, *da+le* = **dalle**) *prep* **1** *(agente)* by; **dipinto da un grande artista** painted by a great artist

2 *(causa)* with; **tremare dalla paura** to tremble with fear

3 *(stato in luogo)* at; **abito da lui** I'm living at his house *o* with him; **sono dal giornalaio/da Francesco** I'm at the newsagent's/Francesco's (house)

4 *(moto a luogo)* to; *(moto per luogo)* through; **vado da Pietro/dal giornalaio** I'm going to Pietro's (house)/to the newsagent's; **sono passati dalla finestra** they came in through the window

5 *(provenienza, allontanamento)* from; **arrivare/partire da Milano** to arrive/depart from Milan; **scendere dal treno/dalla macchina** to get off the train/out of the car; **si trova a 5 km da qui** it's 5 km from here

6 *(tempo: durata)* for; *(: a partire da: nel passato)* since; *(: nel futuro)* from; **vivo qui da un anno** I've been living here for a year; **è dalle 3 che ti aspetto** I've been waiting for you since 3 (o'clock); **da oggi in poi** from today onwards; **da bambino** as a

child, when I (*o* he *ecc*) was a child
7 (*modo, maniera*) like; **comportarsi da uomo** to behave like a man; **l'ho fatto da me** I did it (by) myself
8 (*descrittivo*): **una macchina da corsa** a racing car; **una ragazza dai capelli biondi** a girl with blonde hair; **un vestito da 60 euro** a 60 euros dress

dà *vb vedi* **dare**
dac'capo *av* (*di nuovo*) (once) again; (*dal principio*) all over again, from the beginning
'dado *sm* (*da gioco*) dice *o* die; (*Cuc*) stock (BRIT) *o* bouillon (US) cube; (*Tecn*) (screw)nut; **dadi** *smpl* (game of) dice; **giocare a dadi** to play dice
'daino *sm* (*fallow*) deer *inv*; (*pelle*) buckskin
dal'tonico, -a, -ci, -che *ag* colour-blind
'dama *sf* lady; (*nei balli*) partner; (*gioco*) draughts *sg* (BRIT), checkers *sg* (US)
damigi'ana [dami'dʒana] *sf* demijohn
da'nese *ag* Danish ▷ *sm/f* Dane ▷ *sm* (*Ling*) Danish
Dani'marca *sf* **la ~** Denmark
dannazi'one *sf* damnation
danneggi'are [danned'dʒare] *vt* to damage; (*rovinare*) to spoil; (*nuocere*) to harm
'danno *sm* damage; (*a persona*) harm, injury; **danni** *smpl* (*Dir*) damages; **dan'noso, -a** *ag* **dannoso (a, per)** harmful (to), bad (for)
Da'nubio *sm* **il ~** the Danube
'danza ['dantsa] *sf* **la ~** dancing; **una ~** a dance
dan'zare [dan'tsare] *vt, vi* to dance
dapper'tutto *av* everywhere
dap'prima *av* at first
'dare *sm* (*Comm*) debit ▷ *vt* to give; (*produrre: frutti, suono*) to produce ▷ *vi* (*guardare*): **~ su** to look (out) onto; **darsi** *vpr* **darsi a** to dedicate o.s. to; **darsi al commercio** to go into business; **darsi al bere** to take to drink; **~ da mangiare a qn** to give sb sth to eat; **~ per certo qc** to consider sth certain; **~ per morto qn** to give sb up for dead; **darsi per vinto** to give in
'data *sf* date; **~ limite d'utilizzo** *or* **di consumo** best-before date; **data di nascita** date of birth; **data di scadenza** expiry date
'dato, -a *ag* (*stabilito*) given ▷ *sm* datum; **dati** *smpl* data *pl*; **un ~ che** given that; **un ~ di fatto** a fact; **dati sensibili** personal information
da'tore, -'trice *sm/f*; **datore di lavoro** employer
'dattero *sm* date

dattilogra'fia *sf* typing
datti'lografo, -a *sm/f* typist
da'vanti *av* in front; (*dirimpetto*) opposite ▷ *ag inv* front ▷ *sm* front; **~ a** in front of; facing, opposite; (*in presenza di*) before, in front of
davan'zale [davan'tsale] *sm* windowsill
dav'vero *av* really, indeed
d.C. *adv abbr* (= *dopo Cristo*) A.D.
'dea *sf* goddess
'debbo *ecc vb vedi* **dovere**
'debito, -a *ag* due, proper ▷ *sm* debt; (*Comm: dare*) debit; **a tempo ~** at the right time
'debole *ag* weak, feeble; (*suono*) faint; (*luce*) dim ▷ *sm* weakness; **debo'lezza** *sf* weakness
debut'tare *vi* to make one's debut
deca'denza [deka'dɛntsa] *sf* decline; (*Dir*) loss, forfeiture
decaffei'nato, -a *ag* decaffeinated
decapi'tare *vt* to decapitate, behead
decappot'tabile *ag*, *sf* convertible
de'cennio [de'tʃɛnnjo] *sm* decade
de'cente [de'tʃɛnte] *ag* decent, respectable, proper; (*accettabile*) satisfactory, decent
de'cesso [de'tʃɛsso] *sm* death
de'cidere [de'tʃidere] *vt* **~ qc** to decide on sth; (*questione, lite*) to settle sth; **~ di fare/che** to decide to do/that; **~ di qc** (*cosa*) to determine sth; **decidersi (a fare)** to decide (to do), make up one's mind (to do)
deci'frare [detʃi'frare] *vt* to decode; (*fig*) to decipher, make out
deci'male [detʃi'male] *ag* decimal
'decimo, -a ['dɛtʃimo] *num* tenth
de'cina [de'tʃina] *sf* ten; (*circa dieci*): **una ~ (di)** about ten
de'cisi *ecc* [de'tʃizi] *vb vedi* **decidere**
decisi'one [detʃi'zjone] *sf* decision; **prendere una ~** to make a decision
deci'sivo, -a [detʃi'zivo] *ag* (*gen*) decisive; (*fattore*) deciding
de'ciso, -a [de'tʃizo] *pp di* **decidere**
decli'nare *vi* (*pendio*) to slope down; (*fig: diminuire*) to decline ▷ *vt* to decline
declinazi'one *sf* (*Ling*) declension
de'clino *sm* decline
decodifica'tore *sm* (*Tel*) decoder
decol'lare *vi* (*Aer*) to take off; **de'collo** *sm* take-off
deco'rare *vt* to decorate; **decorazi'one** *sf* decoration
de'creto *sm* decree; **decreto legge** *decree with the force of law*
'dedica, -che *sf* dedication
dedi'care *vt* to dedicate, **dedicarsi** *vpr* **dedicarsi a** to devote o.s. to

dedicherò *ecc* [dedike'rɔ] *vb vedi* **dedicare**

'dedito, -a *ag* **~ a** (*studio ecc*) dedicated *o* devoted to; (*vizio*) addicted to

de'duco *ecc vb vedi* **dedurre**

de'durre *vt* (*concludere*) to deduce; (*defalcare*) to deduct

de'dussi *ecc vb vedi* **dedurre**

defici'ente [defi'tʃɛnte] *ag* (*mancante*): **~ di** deficient in; (*insufficiente*) insufficient ▷ *sm/f* mental defective; (*peg: cretino*) idiot

'deficit ['dɛfitʃit] *sm inv* (*Econ*) deficit

defi'nire *vt* to define; (*risolvere*) to settle; **defini'tiva** *sf* **in ~** (*dopotutto*) in the end; (*dunque*) hence; **defini'tivo, -a** *ag* definitive, final; **definizi'one** *sf* definition; settlement

defor'mare *vt* (*alterare*) to put out of shape; (*corpo*) to deform; (*pensiero, fatto*) to distort; **deformarsi** *vpr* to lose its shape

de'forme *ag* deformed; disfigured

de'funto, -a *ag* late *cpd* ▷ *sm/f* deceased

degene'rare [dedʒene'rare] *vi* to degenerate

de'gente [de'dʒɛnte] *sm/f* (*in ospedale*) in-patient

deglu'tire *vt* to swallow

de'gnare [deɲ'ɲare] *vt* **~ qn della propria presenza** to honour sb with one's presence; **degnarsi** *vpr* **degnarsi di fare qc** to deign *o* condescend to do sth

'degno, -a *ag* dignified; **~ di** worthy of; **~ di lode** praiseworthy

de'grado *sm*; **degrado urbano** urban decline

'delega, -ghe *sf* (*procura*) proxy

dele'terio, -a *ag* damaging; (*per salute ecc*) harmful

del'fino *sm* (*Zool*) dolphin; (*Storia*) dauphin; (*fig*) probable successor

deli'cato, -a *ag* delicate; (*salute*) delicate, frail; (*fig: gentile*) thoughtful, considerate; (: *che dimostra tatto*) tactful

delin'quente *sm/f* criminal, delinquent; **delinquente abituale** regular offender, habitual offender; **delin'quenza** *sf* criminality, delinquency; **delinquenza minorile** juvenile delinquency

deli'rare *vi* to be delirious, rave; (*fig*) to rave

de'lirio *sm* delirium; (*ragionamento insensato*) raving; (*fig*): **andare/mandare in ~** to go/send into a frenzy

de'litto *sm* crime

delizi'oso, -a *ag* delightful; (*cibi*) delicious

delta'plano *sm* hang-glider; **volo col ~** hang-gliding

delu'dente *ag* disappointing

de'ludere *vt* to disappoint; **delusi'one** *sf* disappointment; **de'luso, -a** *pp di* **deludere**

'demmo *vb vedi* **dare**

demo'cratico, -a, -ci, -che *ag* democratic

democra'zia [demokrat'tsia] *sf* democracy

demo'lire *vt* to demolish

de'monio *sm* demon, devil; **il D~** the Devil

de'naro *sm* money

densità *sf inv* density

'denso, -a *ag* thick, dense

den'tale *ag* dental

'dente *sm* tooth; (*di forchetta*) prong; **al ~** (*Cuc: pasta*) al dente; **denti del giudizio** wisdom teeth; **denti da latte** milk teeth; **denti'era** *sf* (set of) false teeth *pl*

denti'fricio [denti'fritʃo] *sm* toothpaste

den'tista, -i, -e *sm/f* dentist

'dentro *av* inside; (*in casa*) indoors; (*fig: nell'intimo*) inwardly ▷ *prep* **~ (a)** in; **piegato in ~** folded over; **qui/là ~** in here/there; **~ di sé** (*pensare, brontolare*) to oneself

de'nuncia, -ce *o* **cie** [de'nuntʃa] *sf* denunciation; declaration; **denuncia dei redditi** (*income*) tax return

denunci'are [denun'tʃare] *vt* to denounce; (*dichiarare*) to declare; (*persona, smarrimento ecc*) report; **vorrei ~ un furto** I'd like to report a theft

denu'trito, -a *ag* undernourished

denutrizi'one [denutrit'tsjone] *sf* malnutrition

deodo'rante *sm* deodorant

depe'rire *vi* to waste away

depi'larsi *vpr* **~ (le gambe)** (*con rasoio*) to shave (one's legs); (*con ceretta*) to wax (one's legs)

depila'torio, -a *ag* hair-removing *cpd*, depilatory

dépli'ant [depli'ã] *sm inv* leaflet; (*opuscolo*) brochure

deplo'revole *ag* deplorable

de'pone, de'pongo *ecc vb vedi* **deporre**

de'porre *vt* (*depositare*) to put down; (*rimuovere: da una carica*) to remove; (: *re*) to depose; (*Dir*) to testify

depor'tare *vt* to deport

de'posi *ecc vb vedi* **deporre**

deposi'tare *vt* (*gen, Geo, Econ*) to deposit; (*lasciare*) to leave; (*merci*) to store; **depositarsi** *vpr* (*sabbia, polvere*) to settle

de'posito *sm* deposit; (*luogo*) warehouse; depot; (: *Mil*) depot; **deposito bagagli** left-luggage office

deposizi'one [depozit'tsjone] *sf* deposition; (*da una carica*) removal

depra'vato, -a *ag* depraved ▷ *sm/f* degenerate

depre'dare *vt* to rob, plunder

depressi'one *sf* depression

de'presso, -a *pp di* **deprimere** ▷ *ag* depressed

deprez'zare [depret'tsare] *vt* (*Econ*) to depreciate

depri'mente *ag* depressing

de'primere *vt* to depress

depu'rare *vt* to purify

depu'tato *sm* (*Pol*) deputy, ≈ Member of Parliament (BRIT), ≈ Member of Congress (US)

deragli'are [deraʎ'ʎare] *vi* to be derailed; **far ~** to derail

de'ridere *vt* to mock, deride

de'risi *ecc vb vedi* **deridere**

de'riva *sf* (*Naut, Aer*) drift; **andare alla ~** (*anche fig*) to drift

deri'vare *vi* **~ da** to derive from ▷ *vt* to derive; (*corso d'acqua*) to divert

derma'tologo, -a, -gi, -ghe *sm/f* dermatologist

deru'bare *vt* to rob

des'crivere *vt* to describe; **descrizi'one** *sf* description

de'serto, -a *ag* deserted ▷ *sm* (*Geo*) desert; **isola deserta** desert island

deside'rare *vt* to want, wish for; (*sessualmente*) to desire; **~ fare/che qn faccia** to want o wish to do/sb to do; **desidera fare una passeggiata?** would you like to go for a walk?

desi'derio *sm* wish; (*più intenso, carnale*) desire

deside'roso, -a *ag* **~ di** longing o eager for

desi'nenza [dezi'nɛntsa] *sf* (*Ling*) ending, inflexion

de'sistere *vi* **~ da** to give up, desist from

deso'lato, -a *ag* (*paesaggio*) desolate; (*persona: spiacente*) sorry

'dessi *ecc vb vedi* **dare**

'deste *ecc vb vedi* **dare**

desti'nare *vt* to destine; (*assegnare*) to appoint, assign; (*indirizzare*) to address; **~ qc a qn** to intend to give sth to sb, intend sb to have sth; **destina'tario, -a** *sm/f* (*di lettera*) addressee

destinazi'one [destinat'tsjone] *sf* destination; (*uso*) purpose

des'tino *sm* destiny, fate

destitu'ire *vt* to dismiss, remove

'destra *sf* (*mano*) right hand; (*parte*) right (side); (*Pol*): **la ~** the Right; **a ~** (*essere*) on the right; (*andare*) to the right

destreggi'arsi [destred'dʒarsi] *vpr* to manoeuvre (BRIT), maneuver (US)

des'trezza [des'trettsa] *sf* skill, dexterity

'destro, -a *ag* right, right-hand

dete'nuto, -a *sm/f* prisoner

deter'gente [deter'dʒɛnte] *ag* (*crema, latte*) cleansing ▷ *sm* cleanser

 Attenzione! In inglese esiste la parola *detergent* che però significa *detersivo*.

determi'nare *vt* to determine

determina'tivo, -a *ag* determining; **articolo ~** (*Ling*) definite article

determi'nato, -a *ag* (*gen*) certain; (*particolare*) specific; (*risoluto*) determined, resolute

deter'sivo *sm* detergent

detes'tare *vt* to detest, hate

de'trae, de'traggo *ecc vb vedi* **detrarre**

de'trarre *vt* **~ (da)** to deduct (from), take away (from)

de'trassi *ecc vb vedi* **detrarre**

'detta *sf* **a ~ di** according to

det'taglio [det'taʎʎo] *sm* detail, (*Comm*): **il ~** retail; **al ~** (*Comm*) retail; separately

det'tare *vt* to dictate; **~ legge** (*fig*) to lay down the law; **det'tato** *sm* dictation

'detto, -a *pp di* **dire** ▷ *ag* (*soprannominato*) called, known as; (*già nominato*) above-mentioned ▷ *sm* saying; **~ fatto** no sooner said than done

devas'tare *vt* to devastate; (*fig*) to ravage

devi'are *vi* **~ (da)** to turn off (from) ▷ *vt* to divert; **deviazi'one** *sf* (*anche Aut*) diversion

'devo *ecc vb vedi* **dovere**

de'volvere *vt* (*Dir*) to transfer, devolve

de'voto, -a *ag* (*Rel*) devout, pious; (*affezionato*) devoted

devozi'one [devot'tsjone] *sf* devoutness; (*anche Rel*) devotion

---

O **PAROLA CHIAVE**

di (*di+il* = **del**, *di+lo* = **dello**, *di+l'* = **dell'**, *di+la* = **della**, *di+i* = **dei**, *di+gli* = **degli**, *di+le* = **delle**) *prep* **1** (*possesso, specificazione*) of; (*composto da, scritto da*) by; **la macchina di Paolo/mio fratello** Paolo's/my brother's car; **un amico di mio fratello** a friend of my brother's, one of my brother's friends; **un quadro di Botticelli** a painting by Botticelli

2 (*caratterizzazione, misura*) of; **una casa di mattoni** a brick house, a house made of bricks; **un orologio d'oro** a gold watch; **un bimbo di 3 anni** a child of 3, a 3-year-old child

3 (*causa, mezzo, modo*) with; **tremare di paura** to tremble with fear; **morire di cancro** to die of cancer; **spalmare di burro** to spread with butter

4 (*argomento*) about, of; **discutere di sport** to talk about sport

5 (*luogo: provenienza*) from; out of; **essere**

di Roma to be from Rome; **uscire di casa** to come out of o leave the house **6** (*tempo*) in; **d'estate/d'inverno** in (the) summer/winter; **di notte** by night, at night; **di mattina/sera** in the morning/ evening; **di lunedì** on Mondays ▷ *det* (*una certa quantità di*) some; (: *negativo*) any; (*interrogativo*) any; some; **del pane** (some) bread; **delle caramelle** (some) sweets; **degli amici miei** some friends of mine; **vuoi del vino?** do you want some o any wine?

dia'bete *sm* diabetes *sg*
dia'betico, -a, ci, che *ag, sm/f* diabetic
dia'framma, -i *sm* (*divisione*) screen; (*Anat, Fot, contraccettivo*) diaphragm
di'agnosi [di'aɲɲozi] *sf* diagnosis *sg*
diago'nale *ag, sf* diagonal
dia'gramma, -i *sm* diagram
dia'letto *sm* dialect
di'alisi *sf* dialysis *sg*
di'alogo, -ghi *sm* dialogue
dia'mante *sm* diamond
di'ametro *sm* diameter
diaposi'tiva *sf* transparency, slide
di'ario *sm* diary
diar'rea *sf* diarrhoea
di'avolo *sm* devil
di'battito *sm* debate, discussion
'dice ['ditʃe] *vb vedi* **dire**
di'cembre [di'tʃɛmbre] *sm* December
dice'ria [ditʃe'ria] *sf* rumour, piece of gossip
dichia'rare [dikja'rare] *vt* to declare; **dichiararsi** *vpr* to declare o.s.; (*innamorato*) to declare one's love; **dichiararsi vinto** to acknowledge defeat; **dichiarazi'one** *sf* declaration; **dichiarazione dei redditi** statement of income; (*modulo*) tax return
dician'nove [ditʃan'nɔve] *num* nineteen
dicias'sette [ditʃas'sɛtte] *num* seventeen
dici'otto [di'tʃɔtto] *num* eighteen
dici'tura [ditʃi'tura] *sf* words *pl*, wording
'dico *ecc vb vedi* **dire**
didasca'lia *sf* (*di illustrazione*) caption; (*Cine*) subtitle; (*Teatro*) stage directions *pl*
di'eci ['djɛtʃi] *num* ten
di'edi *ecc vb vedi* **dare**
'diesel ['dizəl] *sm inv* diesel engine
dies'sino, -a *sm/f* member of the DS political party
di'eta *sf* diet; **essere a ~** to be on a diet
di'etro *av* behind; (*in fondo*) at the back ▷ *prep* behind; (*tempo: dopo*) after ▷ *sm* back, rear ▷ *ag inv* back *cpd*; **le zampe di ~** the hind legs; **~ richiesta** on demand; (*scritta*) on application

di'fendere *vt* to defend; **difendersi** *vpr* (*cavarsela*) to get by; **difendersi da/contro** to defend o.s. from/against; **difendersi dal freddo** to protect o.s. from the cold; **difen'sore, -a** *sm/f* defender; **avvocato difensore** counsel for the defence; **di'fesa** *sf* defence
di'fesi *ecc vb vedi* **difendere**
di'fetto *sm* (*mancanza*) **~ di** lack of; shortage of; (*di fabbricazione*) fault, flaw, defect; (*morale*) fault, failing, defect; (*fisico*) defect; **far ~** to be lacking; **in ~** at fault; in the wrong; **difet'toso, -a** *ag* defective, faulty
diffe'rente *ag* different
diffe'renza [diffe'rɛntsa] *sf* difference; **a ~ di** unlike
diffe'rire *vt* to postpone, defer ▷ *vi* to be different
diffe'rita *sf* **in ~** (*trasmettere*) prerecorded
dif'ficile [dif'fitʃile] *ag* difficult; (*persona*) hard to please, difficult (to please); (*poco probabile*): **è ~ che sia libero** it is unlikely that he'll be free ▷ *sm* difficult part; difficulty; **difficoltà** *sf inv* difficulty
diffi'dente *ag* suspicious, distrustful
diffi'denza *sf* suspicion, distrust
dif'fondere *vt* (*luce, calore*) to diffuse; (*notizie*) to spread, circulate; **diffondersi** *vpr* to spread
dif'fusi *ecc vb vedi* **diffondere**
dif'fuso, -a *pp di* **diffondere** ▷ *ag* (*malattia, fenomeno*) widespread
'diga, -ghe *sf* dam; (*portuale*) breakwater
dige'rente [didʒe'rɛnte] *ag* (*apparato*) digestive
dige'rire [didʒe'rire] *vt* to digest; **digesti'one** *sf* digestion; **diges'tivo, -a** *ag* digestive ▷ *sm* (after-dinner) liqueur
digi'tale [didʒi'tale] *ag* (*delle dita*) finger *cpd*, digital ▷ *sf* (*Bot*) foxglove
digi'tare [didʒi'tare] *vt, vi* (*Inform*) to key (in)
digiu'nare [didʒu'nare] *vi* to starve o.s.; (*Rel*) to fast; **digi'uno, -a** *ag* **essere digiuno** not to have eaten ▷ *sm* fast; **a digiuno** on an empty stomach
dignità [diɲɲi'ta] *sf inv* dignity
'DIGOS ['digɔs] *sigla f* (= *Divisione Investigazioni Generali e Operazioni Speciali*) *police department dealing with political security*
digri'gnare [digriɲ'ɲare] *vt* **~ i denti** to grind one's teeth
dilapi'dare *vt* to squander, waste
dila'tare *vt* to dilate; (*gas*) to cause to expand; (*passaggio, cavità*) to open (up); **dilatarsi** *vpr* to dilate; (*Fisica*) to expand
dilazio'nare [dilattsjo'nare] *vt* to delay,

defer

di'lemma, -i sm dilemma

dilet'tante sm/f dilettante; (anche Sport) amateur

dili'gente [dili'dʒɛnte] ag (scrupoloso) diligent; (accurato) careful, accurate

dilu'ire vt to dilute

dilun'garsi vpr (fig): ~ **su** to talk at length on o about

diluvi'are vb impers to pour (down)

di'luvio sm downpour; (inondazione, fig) flood

dima'grante ag slimming cpd

dima'grire vi to get thinner, lose weight

dime'nare vt to wave, shake; **dimenarsi** vpr to toss and turn; (fig) to struggle; ~ **la coda** (cane) to wag its tail

dimensi'one sf dimension; (grandezza) size

dimenti'canza [dimenti'kantsa] sf forgetfulness; (errore) oversight, slip; **per ~** inadvertently

dimenti'care vt to forget; **ho dimenticato la chiave/il passaporto** I forgot the key/my passport; **dimenticarsi** vpr **dimenticarsi di qc** to forget sth

dimesti'chezza [dimesti'kettsa] sf familiarity

di'mettere vt ~ **qn da** to dismiss sb from; (dall'ospedale) to discharge sb from; **dimettersi** vpr **dimettersi (da)** to resign (from)

dimez'zare [dimed'dzare] vt to halve

diminu'ire vt to reduce, diminish; (prezzi) to bring down, reduce ▷ vi to decrease, diminish; (rumore) to die down, die away; (prezzi) to fall, go down

diminu'tivo, -a ag, sm diminutive

diminuzi'one sf decreasing, diminishing

di'misi ecc vb vedi **dimettere**

dimissi'oni sfpl resignation sg; **dare** o **presentare le ~** to resign, hand in one's resignation

dimos'trare vt to demonstrate, show; (provare) to prove, demonstrate; **dimostrarsi** vpr **dimostrarsi molto abile** to show o.s. o prove to be very clever; **dimostra 30 anni** he looks about 30 (years old); **dimostrazi'one** sf demonstration; proof

di'namica sf dynamics sg

di'namico, -a, -ci, -che ag dynamic

dina'mite sf dynamite

'dinamo sf inv dynamo

dino'sauro sm dinosaur

dintorni smpl outskirts; **nei ~ di** in the vicinity o neighbourhood of

'dio (pl **'dei**) sm god; **D~** God; **gli dei** the gods; **D~ mio!** my goodness!, my God!

diparti'mento sm department

dipen'dente ag dependent ▷ sm/f employee; **dipendente statale** state employee

di'pendere vi ~ **da** to depend on; (finanziariamente) to be dependent on; (derivare) to come from, be due to

di'pesi ecc vb vedi **dipendere**

di'pingere [di'pindʒere] vt to paint

di'pinsi ecc vb vedi **dipingere**

di'pinto, -a pp di **dipingere** ▷ sm painting

di'ploma, -i sm diploma

diplo'matico, -a, -ci, -che ag diplomatic ▷ sm diplomat

diploma'zia [diplomat'tsia] sf diplomacy

di'porto: imbarcazione da ~ sf pleasure craft

dira'dare vt to thin (out), (visite) to reduce, make less frequent; **diradarsi** vpr to disperse; (nebbia) to clear (up)

'dire vt to say; (segreto, fatto) to tell; ~ **qc a qn** to tell sb sth; ~ **a qn di fare qc** to tell sb to do sth; ~ **di sì/no** to say yes/no; **si dice che ...** they say that ...; **si ~bbe che ...** it looks (o sounds) as though ...; **dica, signora?** (in un negozio) yes, Madam, can I help you?; **come si dice in inglese...?** what's the English (word) for ...?

di'ressi ecc vb vedi **dirigere**

di'retta sf vedi **diretto**

di'retto, -a pp di **dirigere** ▷ ag direct ▷ sm (Ferr) through train

diret'tore, -'trice sm/f (di azienda) director: manager/ess; (di scuola elementare) head (teacher) (BRIT), principal (US); **direttore d'orchestra** conductor; **direttore vendite** sales director o manager

direzi'one [diret'tsjone] sf board of directors; management; (senso di movimento) direction; **in ~ di** in the direction of, towards

diri'gente [diri'dʒɛnte] sm/f executive; (Pol) leader ▷ ag **classe** ~ ruling class

di'rigere [di'ridʒere] vt to direct; (impresa) to run, manage; (Mus) to conduct; **dirigersi** vpr **dirigersi verso** o **a** to make o head for

dirim'petto av opposite; ~ **a** opposite, facing

di'ritto, -a ag straight; (onesto) straight, upright ▷ av straight, directly; **andare ~** to go straight on ▷ sm right side; (Tennis) forehand; (Maglia) plain stitch; (prerogativa) right; (leggi, scienza): **il ~** law; **diritti** smpl (tasse) duty sg; **stare ~** to stand up straight; **aver ~ a qc** to be entitled to sth; **diritti d'autore** royalties

dirotta'mento sm; **dirottamento**

(aereo) hijack

dirot'tare *vt* (*nave, aereo*) to change the course of; (*aereo sotto minaccia*) to hijack; (*traffico*) to divert ▷ *vi* (*nave, aereo*) to change course; **dirotta'tore, -'trice** *sm/f* hijacker

di'rotto, -a *ag* (*pioggia*) torrential; (*pianto*) unrestrained; **piovere a ~** to pour; **piangere a ~** to cry one's heart out

di'rupo *sm* crag, precipice

di'sabile *sm/f* disabled person ▷ *ag* disabled; **i disabili** the disabled

disabi'tato, -a *ag* uninhabited

disabitu'arsi *vpr* **~ a** to get out of the habit of

disac'cordo *sm* disagreement

disadat'tato, -a *ag* (*Psic*) maladjusted

disa'dorno, -a *ag* plain, unadorned

disagi'ato, -a [diza'dʒato] *ag* poor, needy; (*vita*) hard

di'sagio [di'zadʒo] *sm* discomfort; (*disturbo*) inconvenience; (*fig: imbarazzo*) embarrassment; **essere a ~** to be ill at ease

disappro'vare *vt* to disapprove of; **disapprovazi'one** *sf* disapproval

disap'punto *sm* disappointment

disar'mare *vt, vi* to disarm; **di'sarmo** *sm* (*Mil*) disarmament

di'sastro *sm* disaster

disas'troso, -a *ag* disastrous

disat'tento, -a *ag* inattentive; **disattenzi'one** *sf* carelessness, lack of attention

disavven'tura *sf* misadventure, mishap

dis'capito *sm* **a ~ di** to the detriment of

dis'carica, -che *sf* (*di rifiuti*) rubbish tip *o* dump

di'scendere [diʃ'ʃɛndere] *vt* to go (*o* come) down ▷ *vi* to go (*o* come) down; (*strada*) to go down; (*smontare*) to get off; **~ da** (*famiglia*) to be descended from; **~ dalla macchina/dal treno** to get out of the car/out of *o* off the train; **~ da cavallo** to dismount, get off one's horse

di'scesa [diʃ'ʃesa] *sf* descent; (*pendio*) slope; **in ~** (*strada*) downhill *cpd*, sloping; **discesa libera** (*Sci*) downhill (race)

disci'plina [diʃʃi'plina] *sf* discipline

'disco, -schi *sm* disc; (*Sport*) discus; (*fonografico*) record; (*Inform*) disk; **disco orario** (*Aut*) parking disc; **disco rigido** (*Inform*) hard disk; **disco volante** flying saucer

disco'grafico, -a, ci, che *ag* record *cpd*, recording *cpd* ▷ *sm* record producer; **casa discografica** record(ing) company

dis'correre *vi* **~ (di)** to talk (about)

dis'corso, -a *pp di* **discorrere** ▷ *sm* speech; (*conversazione*) conversation, talk

disco'teca, -che *sf* (*raccolta*) record library; (*locale*) disco

discre'panza [diskre'pantsa] *sf* disagreement

dis'creto, -a *ag* discreet; (*abbastanza buono*) reasonable, fair

discriminazi'one [diskriminat'tsjone] *sf* discrimination

dis'cussi *ecc vb vedi* **discutere**

discussi'one *sf* discussion; (*litigio*) argument; **fuori ~** out of the question

dis'cutere *vt* to discuss, debate; (*contestare*) to question ▷ *vi* (*conversare*): **~ (di)** to discuss; (*litigare*) to argue

dis'detta *sf* (*di prenotazione ecc*) cancellation; (*sfortuna*) bad luck

dis'dire *vt* (*prenotazione*) to cancel; (*Dir*): **~ un contratto d'affitto** to give notice (to quit); **vorrei ~ la mia prenotazione** I want to cancel my booking

dise'gnare [disen'nare] *vt* to draw; (*progettare*) to design; (*fig*) to outline

disegna'tore, -'trice *sm/f* designer

di'segno [di'senno] *sm* drawing; design; outline; **disegno di legge** (*Dir*) bill

diser'bante *sm* weed-killer

diser'tare *vt, vi* to desert

dis'fare *vt* to undo; (*valigie*) to unpack; (*meccanismo*) to take to pieces; (*neve*) to melt; **disfarsi** *vpr* to come undone; (*neve*) to melt; **~ il letto** to strip the bed; **disfarsi di qn** (*liberarsi*) to get rid of sb; **dis'fatto, -a** *pp di* **disfare**

dis'gelo [diz'dʒɛlo] *sm* thaw

dis'grazia [diz'grattsja] *sf* (*sventura*) misfortune; (*incidente*) accident, mishap

disgu'ido *sm* hitch; **disguido postale** error in postal delivery

disgus'tare *vt* to disgust

dis'gusto *sm* disgust; **disgus'toso, -a** *ag* disgusting

disidra'tare *vt* to dehydrate

disimpa'rare *vt* to forget

disinfet'tante *ag, sm* disinfectant

disinfet'tare *vt* to disinfect

disini'bito, -a *ag* uninhibited

disinstal'lare *vt* (*software*) to uninstall

disinte'grare *vt, vi* to disintegrate; **disintegrarsi** *vpr* to disintegrate

disinteres'sarsi *vpr* **~ di** to take no interest in

disinte'resse *sm* indifference; (*generosità*) unselfishness

disintossicarsi *vpr* to clear out one's system; (*alcolizzato, drogato*) to be treated for alcoholism (*o* drug addiction)

disin'volto, -a *ag* casual, free and easy

dismi'sura *sf* excess; **a ~** to excess, excessively

disoccu'pato, -a *ag* unemployed ▷ *sm/f* unemployed person; **disoccupazi'one** *sf* unemployment

diso'nesto, -a *ag* dishonest

disordi'nato, -a *ag* untidy; (*privo di misura*) irregular, wild

di'sordine *sm* (*confusione*) disorder, confusion; (*sregolatezza*) debauchery; **disordini** *smpl* (*Pol ecc*) disorder *sg*; (*tumulti*) riots

disorien'tare *vt* to disorientate

disorien'tato, -a *ag* disorientated

'dispari *ag inv* odd, uneven

dis'parte: **in ~** *av* (*da lato*) aside, apart; **tenersi** *o* **starsene in ~** to keep to o.s., hold o.s. aloof

dispendi'oso, -a *ag* expensive

dis'pensa *sf* pantry, larder; (*mobile*) sideboard; (*Dir*) exemption; (*Rel*) dispensation; (*fascicolo*) number, issue

dispe'rato, -a *ag* (*persona*) in despair; (*caso, tentativo*) desperate

disperazi'one *sf* despair

dis'perdere *vt* (*disseminare*) to disperse; (*Mil*) to scatter, rout; (*fig: consumare*) to waste, squander; **disperdersi** *vpr* to disperse; to scatter; **dis'perso, -a** *pp di* **disperdere** ▷ *sm/f* missing person

dis'petto *sm* spite *no pl*, spitefulness *no pl*; **fare un ~ a qn** to play a (nasty) trick on sb; **a ~ di** in spite of; **dispet'toso, -a** *ag* spiteful

dispia'cere [dispja'tʃere] *sm* (*rammarico*) regret, sorrow; (*dolore*) grief; **dispiaceri** *smpl* (*preoccupazioni*) troubles, worries *vi* **~ a** to displease *vb impers* **mi dispiace (che)** I am sorry (that); **le dispiace se…?** do you mind if …?

dis'pone, dis'pongo *ecc vb vedi* **disporre**

dispo'nibile *ag* available

dis'porre *vt* (*sistemare*) to arrange; (*preparare*) to prepare; (*Dir*) to order; (*persuadere*): **~ qn a** to incline *o* dispose sb towards ▷ *vi* (*decidere*) to decide; (*usufruire*): **~ di** to use, have at one's disposal; (*essere dotato*): **~ di** to have

dis'posi *ecc vb vedi* **disporre**

disposi'tivo *sm* (*meccanismo*) device

disposizi'one [dispozit'tsjone] *sf* arrangement, layout; (*stato d'animo*) mood; (*tendenza*) bent, inclination; (*comando*) order; (*Dir*) provision, regulation; **a ~ di qn** at sb's disposal

dis'posto, -a *pp di* **disporre**

disprez'zare [dispret'tsare] *vt* to despise

dis'prezzo [dis'prettso] *sm* contempt

'disputa *sf* dispute, quarrel

dispu'tare *vt* (*contendere*) to dispute, contest; (*gara*) to take part in ▷ *vi* to quarrel; **~ di** to discuss; **disputarsi qc** to fight for sth

'disse *vb vedi* **dire**

dissente'ria *sf* dysentery

dissen'tire *vi* **~ (da)** to disagree (with)

disse'tante *ag* refreshing

'dissi *vb vedi* **dire**

dissimu'lare *vt* (*fingere*) to dissemble; (*nascondere*) to conceal

dissi'pare *vt* to dissipate; (*scialacquare*) to squander, waste

dissu'adere *vt* **~ qn da** to dissuade sb from

distac'care *vt* to detach, separate; (*Sport*) to leave behind; **distaccarsi** *vpr* to be detached; (*fig*) to stand out; **distaccarsi da** (*fig: allontanarsi*) to grow away from

dis'tacco, -chi *sm* (*separazione*) separation; (*fig: indifferenza*) detachment; (*Sport*): **vincere con un ~ di …** to win by a distance of …

dis'tante *av* far away ▷ *ag* **~ (da)** distant (from), far away (from)

dis'tanza [dis'tantsa] *sf* distance

distanzi'are [distan'tsjare] *vt* to space out, place at intervals; (*Sport*) to outdistance; (*fig: superare*) to outstrip, surpass

dis'tare *vi* **distiamo pochi chilometri da Roma** we are only a few kilometres (away) from Rome; **quanto dista il centro da qui?** how far is the town centre?

dis'tendere *vt* (*coperta*) to spread out; (*gambe*) to stretch (out); (*mettere a giacere*) to lay; (*rilassare: muscoli, nervi*) to relax; **distendersi** *vpr* (*rilassarsi*) to relax; (*sdraiarsi*) to lie down

dis'tesa *sf* expanse, stretch

dis'teso, -a *pp di* **distendere**

distil'lare *vt* to distil

distille'ria *sf* distillery

dis'tinguere *vt* to distinguish; **distinguersi** *vpr* (*essere riconoscibile*) to be distinguished; (*emergere*) to stand out, be conspicuous, distinguish o.s.

dis'tinta *sf* (*nota*) note; (*elenco*) list; **distinta di versamento** pay-in slip

distin'tivo *ag* distinctive; distinguishing ▷ *sm* badge

dis'tinto, -a *pp di* **distinguere** ▷ *ag* (*dignitoso ed elegante*) distinguished; **"distinti saluti"** (*in lettera*) yours faithfully

distinzi'one [distin'tsjone] *sf* distinction

dis'togliere [dis'tɔʎʎere] *vt* **~ da** to take away from; (*fig*) to dissuade from

distorsi'one *sf* (*Med*) sprain; (*Fisica, Ottica*) distortion

dis'trarre *vt* to distract; (*divertire*) to entertain, amuse; **distrarsi** *vpr* (*non* *fare attenzione*) to be distracted, let one's mind wander; (*svagarsi*) to amuse o enjoy o.s.; **dis'tratto, -a** *pp di* **distrarre** ▷ *ag* absent-minded; (*disattento*) inattentive; **distrazi'one** *sf* absent-mindedness; inattention; (*svago*) distraction, entertainment

dis'tretto *sm* district

distribu'ire *vt* to distribute; (*Carte*) to deal (out); (*posta*) to deliver; (*lavoro*) to allocate, assign; (*ripartire*) to share out; **distribu'tore** *sm* (*di benzina*) petrol (BRIT) o gas (US) pump; (*Aut, Elettr*) distributor; **distributore automatico** vending machine

distri'care *vt* to disentangle, unravel; **districarsi** *vpr* (*tirarsi fuori*): **districarsi da** to get out of, disentangle o.s. from

dis'truggere [dis'truddʒere] *vt* to destroy; **distruzi'one** *sf* destruction

distur'bare *vt* to disturb, trouble; (*sonno, lezioni*) to disturb, interrupt; **disturbarsi** *vpr* to put o.s. out

dis'turbo *sm* trouble, bother, inconvenience; (*indisposizione*) (slight) disorder, ailment; **scusi il ~** I'm sorry to trouble you

disubbidi'ente *ag* disobedient

disubbi'dire *vi* **~ (a qn)** to disobey (sb)

disu'mano, -a *ag* inhuman

di'tale *sm* thimble

'dito (*pl(f)* **'dita**) *sm* finger; (*misura*) finger, finger's breadth; **dito (del piede)** toe

'ditta *sf* firm, business

ditta'tore *sm* dictator

ditta'tura *sf* dictatorship

dit'tongo, -ghi *sm* diphthong

di'urno, -a *ag* day *cpd*, daytime *cpd*

'diva *sf vedi* **divo**

di'vano *sm* sofa; divan; **divano letto** bed settee, sofa bed

divari'care *vt* to open wide

di'vario *sm* difference

diven'tare *vi* to become; **~ famoso/ professore** to become famous/a teacher

diversifi'care *vt* to diversify, vary; to differentiate; **diversificarsi** *vpr* **diversificarsi (per)** to differ (in)

diversità *sf inv* difference, diversity; (*varietà*) variety

diver'sivo *sm* diversion, distraction

di'verso, -a *ag* (*differente*): **~ (da)** different (from); **diversi, -e** *det pl* several, various; (*Comm*) sundry *pron pl* several (people), many (people)

diver'tente *ag* amusing

diverti'mento *sm* amusement, pleasure; (*passatempo*) pastime, recreation

diver'tire *vt* to amuse, entertain;

divertirsi *vpr* to amuse o enjoy o.s.

di'videre *vt* (*anche Mat*) to divide; (*distribuire, ripartire*) to divide (up), split (up); **dividersi** *vpr* (*separarsi*) to separate; (*strade*) to fork

divi'eto *sm* prohibition; **"~ di sosta"** (*Aut*) "no parking"

divinco'larsi *vpr* to wriggle, writhe

di'vino, -a *ag* divine

di'visa *sf* (*Mil ecc*) uniform; (*Comm*) foreign currency

di'visi *ecc vb vedi* **dividere**

divisi'one *sf* division

'divo, -a *sm/f* star

divo'rare *vt* to devour

divorzi'are [divor'tsjare] *vi* **~ (da qn)** to divorce (sb)

di'vorzio [di'vɔrtsjo] *sm* divorce

divul'gare *vt* to divulge, disclose; (*rendere comprensibile*) to popularize

dizio'nario [ditsjo'narjo] *sm* dictionary

DJ [di'dʒei] *sigla m/f* (= *Disk Jockey*) DJ

do *sm* (*Mus*) C; (*: solfeggiando*) do(h)

dobbi'amo *vb vedi* **dovere**

D.O.C. [dɔk] *abbr* (= *denominazione di origine controllata*) *label guaranteeing the quality of wine*

'doccia, -ce ['dottʃa] *sf* (*bagno*) shower; **fare la ~** to have a shower

do'cente [do'tʃɛnte] *ag* teaching ▷ *sm/f* teacher; (*di università*) lecturer

'docile ['dɔtʃile] *ag* docile

documen'tario *sm* documentary

documentarsi *vpr* **~ (su)** to gather information o material (about)

docu'mento *sm* document; **documenti** *smpl* (*d'identità ecc*) papers

dodi'cesimo, -a [dodi'tʃɛzimo] *num* twelfth

'dodici ['doditʃi] *num* twelve

do'gana *sf* (*ufficio*) customs *pl*; (*tassa*) (customs) duty; **passare la ~** to go through customs; **dogani'ere** *sm* customs officer

'doglie ['dɔʎʎe] *sfpl* (*Med*) labour *sg*, labour pains

'dolce ['doltʃe] *ag* sweet; (*carattere, persona*) gentle, mild; (*fig: mite: clima*) mild; (*non ripido: pendio*) gentle ▷ *sm* (*sapore dolce*) sweetness, sweet taste; (*Cuc: portata*) sweet, dessert; (*: torta*) cake; **dolcifi'cante** *sm* sweetener

'dollaro *sm* dollar

Dolo'miti *sfpl* **le ~** the Dolomites

do'lore *sm* (*fisico*) pain; (*morale*) sorrow, grief; **dolo'roso, -a** *ag* painful; sorrowful, sad

do'manda *sf* (*interrogazione*) question; (*richiesta*) demand; (*: cortese*) request;

(*Dir: richiesta scritta*) application; (*Econ*): **la ~** demand; **fare una ~ a qn** to ask sb a question; **fare ~ (per un lavoro)** to apply (for a job)

doman'dare *vt* (*per avere*) to ask for; (*per sapere*) to ask; (*esigere*) to demand; **domandarsi** *vpr* to wonder; to ask o.s.; **~ qc a qn** to ask sb for sth; to ask sb sth

do'mani *av* tomorrow ▷ *sm* **il ~** (*il futuro*) the future; (*il giorno successivo*) the next day; **~ l'altro** the day after tomorrow

do'mare *vt* to tame

doma'tore, -'trice *sm/f* (*gen*) tamer; **domatore di cavalli** horsebreaker; **domatore di leoni** lion tamer

domat'tina *av* tomorrow morning

do'menica, -che *sf* Sunday; **di** *o* **la ~** on Sundays

do'mestico, -a, -ci, -che *ag* domestic ▷ *sm/f* servant, domestic

domi'cilio [domi't∫iljo] *sm* (*Dir*) domicile, place of residence

domi'nare *vt* to dominate; (*fig: sentimenti*) to control, master ▷ *vi* to be in the dominant position

do'nare *vt* to give, present; (*per beneficenza ecc*) to donate ▷ *vi* (*fig*): **~ a** to suit, become; **~ sangue** to give blood; **dona'tore, -'trice** *sm/f* donor; **donatore di sangue/di organi** blood/organ donor

dondo'lare *vt* (*cullare*) to rock; **dondolarsi** *vpr* to swing, sway; **'dondolo** *sm* **sedia/cavallo a dondolo** rocking chair/horse

'donna *sf* woman; **donna di casa** housewife; home-loving woman; **donna di servizio** maid

donnai'olo *sm* ladykiller

'donnola *sf* weasel

'dono *sm* gift

doping ['dɔpiŋ] *sm* doping

'dopo *av* (*tempo*) afterwards; (*più tardi*) later; (*luogo*) after, next ▷ *prep* after ▷ *cong* (*temporale*): **~ aver studiato** after having studied; **~ mangiato va a dormire** after having eaten *o* after a meal he goes for a sleep ▷ *ag inv* **il giorno ~** the following day; **un anno ~** a year later; **~ di me/lui** after me/him; **~, a ~!** see you later!

dopo'barba *sm inv* after-shave

dopodo'mani *av* the day after tomorrow

doposci [dopo'∫∫i] *sm inv* après-ski outfit

dopo'sole *sm inv* aftersun (lotion)

dopo'tutto *av* (*tutto considerato*) after all

doppi'aggio [dop'pjaddʒo] *sm* (*Cinema*) dubbing

doppi'are *vt* (*Naut*) to round; (*Sport*) to lap; (*Cinema*) to dub

'doppio, -a *ag* double; (*fig: falso*) double-dealing, deceitful ▷ *sm* (*quantità*): **il ~**

(**di**) twice as much (*o* many), double the amount (*o* number) of; (*Sport*) doubles *pl* ▷ *av* double

doppi'one *sm* duplicate (copy)

doppio'petto *sm* double-breasted jacket

dormicchi'are [dormik'kjare] *vi* to doze

dormigli'one, -a [dormiʎ'ʎone] *sm/f* sleepyhead

dor'mire *vt, vi* to sleep; **andare a ~** to go to bed; **dor'mita** *sf* **farsi una dormita** to have a good sleep

dormi'torio *sm* dormitory

dormi'veglia [dormi'veʎʎa] *sm* drowsiness

'dorso *sm* back; (*di montagna*) ridge, crest; (*di libro*) spine; **a ~ di cavallo** on horseback

do'sare *vt* to measure out; (*Med*) to dose

'dose *sf* quantity, amount; (*Med*) dose

do'tato, -a *ag* **~ di** (*attrezzature*) equipped with; (*bellezza, intelligenza*) endowed with; **un uomo ~** a gifted man

'dote *sf* (*di sposa*) dowry; (*assegnata a un ente*) endowment; (*fig*) gift, talent

Dott. *abbr* (= *dottore*) Dr.

dotto'rato *sm* degree; **dottorato di ricerca** doctorate, doctor's degree

dot'tore, -essa *sm/f* doctor; **chiamate un ~** call a doctor

---

● **DOTTORE**
●
● In Italy, anyone who has a degree in any
● subject can use the title **dottore**. Thus
● a person who is addressed as **dottore** is
● not necessarily a doctor of medicine.

---

dot'trina *sf* doctrine

Dott.ssa *abbr* (= *dottoressa*) Dr.

'dove *av* (*gen*) where; (*in cui*) where, in which; (*dovunque*) wherever ▷ *cong* (*mentre, laddove*) whereas; **~ sei?/vai?** where are you?/are you going?; **dimmi dov'è** tell me where it is; **di ~ sei?** where are you from?; **per ~ si passa?** which way should we go?; **la città ~ abito** the town where *o* in which I live; **siediti ~ vuoi** sit wherever you like

do'vere *sm* (*obbligo*) duty ▷ *vt* (*essere debitore*): **~ qc (a qn)** to owe (sb) sth ▷ *vi* (*seguito dall'infinito: obbligo*) to have to; **rivolgersi a chi di ~** to apply to the appropriate authority *o* person; **lui deve farlo** he has to do it, he must do it; **quanto le devo?** how much do I owe you?; **è dovuto partire** he had to leave; **ha dovuto pagare** he had to pay; (: *intenzione*): **devo partire domani** I'm (due) to leave tomorrow; (: *probabilità*): **dev'essere tardi** it must be late; **come**

si deve (*lavorare, comportarsi*) properly; **una persona come si deve** a respectable person

dove'roso, -a *ag* (right and) proper

dovrò *ecc vb vedi* **dovere**

do'vunque *av* (*in qualunque luogo*) wherever; (*dappertutto*) everywhere; **~ io vada** wherever I go

do'vuto, -a *ag* (*causato*): **~ a** due to

doz'zina [dod'dzina] *sf* dozen; **una ~ di uova** a dozen eggs

dozzi'nale [doddzi'nale] *ag* cheap, second-rate

'drago, -ghi *sm* dragon

'dramma, -i *sm* drama; **dram'matico, -a, -ci, -che** *ag* dramatic

'drastico, -a, -ci, -che *ag* drastic

'dritto, -a *ag, av* = **diritto**

'droga, -ghe *sf* (*sostanza aromatica*) spice; (*stupefacente*) drug; **droghe leggere/pesanti** soft/hard drugs

drogarsi *vpr* to take drugs

dro'gato, -a *sm/f* drug addict

droghe'ria [droge'ria] *sf* grocer's shop (*BRIT*), grocery (store) (*US*)

drome'dario *sm* dromedary

DS [di'ɛsse] *sigla mpl* (= *Democratici di Sinistra*) Italian left-wing party

'dubbio, -a *ag* (*incerto*) doubtful, dubious; (*ambiguo*) dubious ▷ *sm* (*incertezza*) doubt; **avere il ~ che** to be afraid that, suspect that; **mettere in ~ qc** to question sth

dubi'tare *vi* **~ di** to doubt; (*risultato*) to be doubtful of

Dub'lino *sf* Dublin

'duca, -chi *sm* duke

du'chessa [du'kessa] *sf* duchess

'due *num* two

due'cento [due'tʃɛnto] *num* two hundred ▷ *sm* **il D~** the thirteenth century

due'pezzi [due'pɛttsi] *sm* (*costume da bagno*) two-piece swimsuit; (*abito femminile*) two-piece suit

'dunque *cong* (*perciò*) so, therefore; (*riprendendo il discorso*) well (then) ▷ *sm inv* **venire al ~** to come to the point

du'omo *sm* cathedral

▨ Attenzione! In inglese esiste la parola *dome*, che però significa *cupola*.

dupli'cato *sm* duplicate

'duplice ['duplitʃe] *ag* double, twofold; **in ~ copia** in duplicate

du'rante *prep* during

du'rare *vi* to last; **~ fatica a** to have difficulty in

du'rezza [du'rettsa] *sf* hardness; stubbornness; harshness; toughness

'duro, -a *ag* (*pietra, lavoro, materasso, problema*) hard; (*persona: ostinato*) stubborn, obstinate; (*severo*) harsh, hard; (*voce*) harsh; (*carne*) tough ▷ *sm* hardness; (*difficoltà*) hard part; (*persona*) tough guy; **tener ~** to stand firm, hold out; **~ d'orecchi** hard of hearing

DVD [divu'di] *sigla m* (= *digital versatile (or) video disc*) DVD; (*lettore*) DVD player

e (davV spesso **ed**) cong and; **e lui?** what about him?; **e compralo!** well buy it then!

E abbr (= est) E

è vb vedi **essere**

eb'bene cong well (then)

'ebbi ecc vb vedi **avere**

e'braico, -a, -ci, -che ag Hebrew, Hebraic ▷ sm (Ling) Hebrew

e'breo, -a ag Jewish ▷ sm/f Jew/ess

EC abbr (= Eurocity) fast train connecting Western European cities

ecc. av abbr (= eccetera) etc

eccel'lente [ettʃel'lɛnte] ag excellent

ec'centrico, -a, -ci, -che [et'tʃɛntriko] ag eccentric

ecces'sivo, -a [ettʃes'sivo] ag excessive

ec'cesso [et'tʃɛsso] sm excess; **all'~** (gentile, generoso) to excess, excessively; **eccesso di velocità** (Aut) speeding

ec'cetera [et'tʃɛtera] av et cetera, and so on

ec'cetto [et'tʃɛtto] prep except, with the exception of; **~ che** except, other than; **~ che (non)** unless

eccezio'nale [ettʃetsjo'nale] ag exceptional

eccezi'one [ettʃet'tsjone] sf exception; (Dir) objection; **a ~ di** with the exception of, except for; **d'~** exceptional

ecci'tare [ettʃi'tare] vt (curiosità, interesse)

to excite, arouse; (folla) to incite; **eccitarsi** vpr to get excited; (sessualmente) to become aroused

'ecco av (per dimostrare): **~ il treno!** here's o here comes the train!; (dav pron): **~mi!** here I am!; **~ne uno!** here's one (of them)!; (dav pp): **~ fatto!** there, that's it done!

ec'come av rather; **ti piace? — ~!** do you like it? — I'll say! o and how! o rather! (BRIT)

e'clisse sf eclipse

'eco (pl(m) **'echi**) sm o f echo

ecogra'fia sf (Med) scan

ecolo'gia [ekolo'dʒia] sf ecology

eco'logico, -a, ci, che [eko'lɔdʒiko] ag ecological

econo'mia sf economy; (scienza) economics sg; (risparmio: azione) saving; **fare ~** to economize, make economies; **eco'nomico, -a, -ci, -che** ag economic; (poco costoso) economical

ecstasy ['ekstazi] sf Ecstasy

'edera sf ivy

e'dicola sf newspaper kiosk o stand (US)

edi'ficio [edi'fitʃo] sm building

e'dile ag building cpd

Edim'burgo sf Edinburgh

edi'tore, -'trice ag publishing cpd ▷ sm/f publisher

> Attenzione! In inglese esiste la parola *editor*, che però significa *redattore*.

edizi'one [edit'tsjone] sf edition; (tiratura) printing; **edizione straordinaria** special edition

edu'care vt to educate; (gusto, mente) to train; **~ qn a fare** to train sb to do; **edu'cato, -a** ag polite, well-mannered; **educazi'one** sf education; (familiare) upbringing; (comportamento) (good) manners pl; **educazione fisica** (Ins) physical training o education

> Attenzione! In inglese esiste la parola *educated*, che però significa *istruito*.

educherò ecc [eduke'rɔ] vb vedi **educare**

effemi'nato, -a ag effeminate

efferve'scente [efferveʃ'ʃɛnte] ag effervescent

effet'tivo, -a ag (reale) real, actual; (impiegato, professore) permanent; (Mil) regular ▷ sm (Mil) strength; (di patrimonio ecc) sum total

ef'fetto sm effect; (Comm: cambiale) bill; (fig: impressione) impression; **in effetti** in fact, actually; **effetto serra** greenhouse effect; **effetti personali** personal effects, personal belongings

effi'cace [effi'katʃe] ag effective

effici'ente [effi'tʃɛnte] ag efficient

E'geo [e'dʒɛo] sm **l'~, il mare ~** the Aegean (Sea)

E'gitto [e'dʒitto] *sm* **l'~** Egypt

egizi'ano, -a [edʒit'tsjano] *ag, sm/f* Egyptian

'egli ['eʎʎi] *pron* he; **~ stesso** he himself

ego'ismo *sm* selfishness, egoism; **ego'ista, -i, -e** *ag* selfish, egoistic ▷ *sm/f* egoist

Egr. *abbr* = **egregio**

e'gregio, -a, -gi, -gie [e'grɛdʒo] *ag* (*nelle lettere*): **E~ Signore** Dear Sir

E.I. *abbr* = **Esercito Italiano**

elabo'rare *vt* (*progetto*) to work out, elaborate; (*dati*) to process

elasticiz'zato, -a [elastitʃid'dzato] *ag* stretch *cpd*

e'lastico, -a, -ci, -che *ag* elastic; (*fig: andatura*) springy; (: *decisione, vedute*) flexible ▷ *sm* (*di gomma*) rubber band; (*per il cucito*) elastic *no pl*

ele'fante *sm* elephant

ele'gante *ag* elegant

e'leggere [e'lɛddʒere] *vt* to elect

elemen'tare *ag* elementary; **le (scuole) elementari** *sfpl* primary (BRIT) o grade (US) school

ele'mento *sm* element; (*parte componente*) element, component, part; **elementi** *smpl* (*della scienza ecc*) elements, rudiments

ele'mosina *sf* charity, alms *pl*; **chiedere l'~** to beg

elen'care *vt* to list

elencherò *ecc* [elenke'rɔ] *vb vedi* **elencare**

e'lenco, -chi *sm* list; **elenco telefonico** telephone directory

e'lessi *ecc vb vedi* **eleggere**

eletto'rale *ag* electoral, election *cpd*

elet'tore, -'trice *sm/f* voter, elector

elet'trauto *sm inv* workshop for car electrical repairs; (*tecnico*) car electrician

elettri'cista, -i [elettri'tʃista] *sm* electrician

elettricità [elettritʃi'ta] *sf* electricity

e'lettrico, -a, -ci, -che *ag* electric(al)

elettriz'zante [elettrid'dzante] *ag* (*fig*) electrifying, thrilling

elettriz'zare [elettrid'dzare] *vt* to electrify; **elettrizzarsi** *vpr* to become charged with electricity

e'lettro... *prefisso*; **elettrodo'mestico, -a, -ci, -che** *ag* **apparecchi elettrodomestici** domestic (electrical) appliances; **elet'tronico, -a, -ci, -che** *ag* electronic

elezi'one [elet'tsjone] *sf* election; **elezioni** *sfpl* (*Pol*) election(s)

'elica, -che *sf* propeller

eli'cottero *sm* helicopter

elimi'nare *vt* to eliminate

elisoc'corso *sm* helicopter ambulance

el'metto *sm* helmet

elogi'are [elo'dʒare] *vt* to praise

elo'quente *ag* eloquent

e'ludere *vt* to evade

e'lusi *ecc vb vedi* **eludere**

e-mail [i'mɛil] *sf inv* (*messaggio, sistema*) e-mail ▷ *ag inv* (*indirizzo*) e-mail

emargi'nato, -a [emardʒi'nato] *sm/f* outcast; **emarginazione** [emardʒinat'tsjone] *sf* marginalization

embri'one *sm* embryo

emenda'mento *sm* amendment

emer'genza [emer'dʒɛntsa] *sf* emergency; **in caso di ~** in an emergency

e'mergere [e'mɛrdʒere] *vi* to emerge; (*sommergibile*) to surface; (*fig: distinguersi*) to stand out

e'mersi *ecc vb vedi* **emergere**

e'mettere *vt* (*suono, luce*) to give out, emit; (*onde radio*) to send out; (*assegno, francobollo, ordine*) to issue

emi'crania *sf* migraine

emi'grare *vi* to emigrate

emis'fero *sm* hemisphere; **emisfero australe** southern hemisphere; **emisfero boreale** northern hemisphere

e'misi *ecc vb vedi* **emettere**

emit'tente *ag* (*banca*) issuing; (*Radio*) broadcasting, transmitting ▷ *sf* (*Radio*) transmitter

emorra'gia, -'gie [emorra'dʒia] *sf* haemorrhage

emor'roidi *sfpl* haemorrhoids *pl* (BRIT), hemorrhoids *pl* (US)

emo'tivo, -a *ag* emotional

emozio'nante [emottsjo'nante] *ag* exciting, thrilling

emozionare [emottsjo'nare] *vt* (*commuovere*) to move; (*agitare*) to make nervous; (*elettrizzare*) to excite; **emozionarsi** *vpr* to be moved; to be nervous; to be excited; **emozionato, -a** [emottsjo'nato] *ag* (*commosso*) moved; (*agitato*) nervous; (*elettrizzato*) excited

emozi'one [emot'tsjone] *sf* emotion; (*agitazione*) excitement

enciclope'dia [entʃiklope'dia] *sf* encyclopaedia

endove'noso, -a *ag* (*Med*) intravenous

'E.N.E.L. ['enel] *sigla m* (= *Ente Nazionale per l'Energia Elettrica*) national electricity company

ener'getico, -a, ci, che [ener'dʒɛtiko] *ag* (*risorse, crisi*) energy *cpd*; (*sostanza, alimento*) energy-giving

ener'gia, -'gie [ener'dʒia] *sf* (*Fisica*) energy; (*fig*) energy, strength, vigour; **energia eolica** wind power; **energia solare** solar energy, solar power;

e'nergico, -a, -ci, -che *ag* energetic, vigorous

'enfasi *sf* emphasis; (*peg*) bombast, pomposity

en'nesimo, -a *ag* (*Mat, fig*) nth; **per l'ennesima volta** for the umpteenth time

e'norme *ag* enormous, huge

'ente *sm* (*istituzione*) body, board, corporation; (*Filosofia*) being; **enti pubblici** public bodies; **ente di ricerca** research organization

en'trambi, -e *pron pl* both (of them) ▷ *ag pl* **~ i ragazzi** both boys, both of the boys

en'trare *vi* to go (*o* come) in; **~ in** (*luogo*) to enter, go (*o* come) into; (*trovar posto, poter stare*) to fit into; (*essere ammesso a: club ecc*) to join, become a member of; **~ in automobile** to get into the car; **far ~ qn** (*visitatore ecc*) to show sb in; **questo non c'entra** (*fig*) that's got nothing to do with it; **en'trata** *sf* entrance, entry; **dov'è l'entrata?** where's the entrance?; **entrate** *sfpl* (*Comm*) receipts, takings; (*Econ*) income *sg*

'entro *prep* (*temporale*) within

entusias'mare *vt* to excite, fill with enthusiasm; **entusiasmarsi** *vpr* **entusiasmarsi (per qc/qn)** to become enthusiastic (about sth/sb); **entusi'asmo** *sm* enthusiasm; **entusi'asta, -i, -e** *ag* enthusiastic ▷ *sm/f* enthusiast

epa'tite *sf* hepatitis

epide'mia *sf* epidemic

epiles'sia *sf* epilepsy

epi'lettico, -a, ci, che *ag, sm/f* epileptic

epi'sodio *sm* episode

'epoca, -che *sf* (*periodo storico*) age, era; (*tempo*) time; (*Geo*) age

ep'pure *cong* and yet, nevertheless

EPT *sigla m* (= *Ente Provinciale per il Turismo*) district tourist bureau

equa'tore *sm* equator

equazi'one [ekwat'tsjone] *sf* (*Mat*) equation

e'questre *ag* equestrian

equi'librio *sm* balance, equilibrium; **perdere l'equilibrare** to lose one's balance

e'quino, -a *ag* horse *cpd*, equine

equipaggia'mento [ekwipaddʒa'mento] *sm* (*operazione: di nave*) equipping, fitting out; (: *di spedizione, esercito*) equipping, kitting out; (*attrezzatura*) equipment

equipaggi'are [ekwipad'dʒare] *vt* (*di persone*) to man; (*di mezzi*) to equip; **equipaggiarsi** *vpr* to equip o.s.; **equi'paggio** *sm* crew

equitazi'one [ekwitat'tsjone] *sf* (horse-)riding

equiva'lente *ag, sm* equivalent

e'quivoco, -a, -ci, -che *ag* equivocal, ambiguous; (*sospetto*) dubious ▷ *sm* misunderstanding; **a scanso di equivoci** to avoid any misunderstanding; **giocare sull'~** to equivocate

'equo, -a *ag* fair, just

'era *sf* era

'era *ecc vb vedi* **essere**

'erba *sf* grass; **in ~** (*fig*) budding; **erbe aromatiche** herbs; **erba medica** lucerne; **er'baccia, -ce** *sf* weed

erboriste'ria *sf* (*scienza*) study of medicinal herbs; (*negozio*) herbalist's (shop)

e'rede *sm/f* heir; **eredità** *sf* (*Dir*) inheritance; (*Biol*) heredity; **lasciare qc in eredità a qn** to leave *o* bequeath sth to sb; **eredi'tare** *vt* to inherit; **eredi'tario, -a** *ag* hereditary

ere'mita, -i *sm* hermit

er'gastolo *sm* (*Dir: pena*) life imprisonment

'erica *sf* heather

er'metico, -a, -ci, -che *ag* hermetic

'ernia *sf* (*Med*) hernia

'ero *vb vedi* **essere**

e'roe *sm* hero

ero'gare *vt* (*somme*) to distribute; (*gas, servizi*) to supply

e'roico, -a, -ci, -che *ag* heroic

ero'ina *sf* heroine; (*droga*) heroin

erosi'one *sf* erosion

e'rotico, -a, -ci, -che *ag* erotic

er'rato, -a *ag* wrong

er'rore *sm* error, mistake; (*morale*) error; **per ~** by mistake; **ci dev'essere un ~** there must be some mistake; **errore giudiziario** miscarriage of justice

eruzi'one [erut'tsjone] *sf* eruption

esacer'bare [ezatʃer'bare] *vt* to exacerbate

esage'rare [ezadʒe'rare] *vt* to exaggerate ▷ *vi* to exaggerate; (*eccedere*) to go too far

esal'tare *vt* to exalt; (*entusiasmare*) to excite, stir

e'same *sm* examination; (*Ins*) exam, examination; **fare** *o* **dare un ~** to sit *o* take an exam; **esame di guida** driving test; **esame del sangue** blood test

esami'nare *vt* to examine

esaspe'rare *vt* to exasperate; to exacerbate

esatta'mente *av* exactly; accurately, precisely

esat'tezza [ezat'tettsa] *sf* exactitude, accuracy, precision

e'satto, -a *pp di* **esigere** ▷ *ag* (*calcolo, ora*) correct, right, exact; (*preciso*) accurate,

precise; (*puntuale*) punctual
esau'dire *vt* to grant, fulfil
esauri'ente *ag* exhaustive
esauri'mento *sm* exhaustion;
  esaurimento nervoso nervous
  breakdown
esau'rire *vt* (*stancare*) to exhaust, wear
  out; (*provviste, miniera*) to exhaust;
  esaurirsi *vpr* to exhaust o.s., wear o.s.
  out; (*provviste*) to run out; **esau'rito, -a**
  ag exhausted; (*merci*) sold out; **registrare**
  il tutto esaurito (*Teatro*) to have a full
  house; **e'sausto, -a** *ag* exhausted
'esca (*pl* **'esche**) *sf* bait
'esce ['ɛʃʃe] *vb vedi* **uscire**
eschi'mese [eski'mese] *ag, sm/f* Eskimo
'esci ['ɛʃʃi] *vb vedi* **uscire**
escla'mare *vi* to exclaim, cry out
esclama'tivo, -a *ag* **punto ~** exclamation
  mark
esclamazi'one *sf* exclamation
es'cludere *vt* to exclude
es'clusi *ecc vb vedi* **escludere**
esclusi'one *sf* exclusion; **a ~ di, fatta**
  ~ per except (for), apart from; **senza ~**
  (alcuna) without exception; **procedere**
  per ~ to follow a process of elimination;
  senza ~ di colpi (*fig*) with no holds barred;
  esclusione sociale social exclusion
esclu'siva *sf* (*Dir, Comm*) exclusive *o* sole
  rights *pl*
esclusiva'mente *av* exclusively, solely
esclu'sivo, -a *ag* exclusive
es'cluso, -a *pp di* **escludere**
'esco *vb vedi* **uscire**
escogi'tare [eskodʒi'tare] *vt* to devise,
  think up
'escono *vb vedi* **uscire**
escursi'one *sf* (*gita*) excursion, trip;
  (: *a piedi*) hike, walk; (*Meteor*) range;
  escursione termica temperature range
esecuzi'one [ezekut'tsjone] *sf* execution,
  carrying out; (*Mus*) performance;
  esecuzione capitale execution
esegu'ire *vt* to carry out, execute; (*Mus*) to
  perform, execute
e'sempio *sm* example; **per ~** for example,
  for instance; **fare un ~** to give an example;
  esem'plare *ag* exemplary ▷ *sm* example;
  (*copia*) copy
eserci'tare [ezertʃi'tare] *vt* (*professione*)
  to practise (*BRIT*), practice (*US*); (*allenare:*
  corpo, mente) to exercise, train; (*diritto*)
  to exercise; (*influenza, pressione*) to exert;
  esercitarsi *vpr* to practise; **esercitarsi**
  alla lotta to practise fighting
e'sercito [e'zɛrtʃito] *sm* army
eser'cizio [ezer'tʃittsjo] *sm* practice;
  exercising; (*fisico: di matematica*) exercise;

(*Econ*) financial year; (*azienda*) business,
  concern; **in ~** (*medico ecc*) practising;
  esercizio pubblico (*Comm*) commercial
  concern
esi'bire *vt* to exhibit, display; (*documenti*)
  to produce, present; **esibirsi** *vpr* (*attore*)
  to perform; (*fig*) to show off; **esibizi'one**
  sf exhibition; (*di documento*) presentation;
  (*spettacolo*) show, performance
esi'gente [ezi'dʒɛnte] *ag* demanding
e'sigere [e'zidʒere] *vt* (*pretendere*) to
  demand; (*richiedere*) to demand, require;
  (*imposte*) to collect
'esile *ag* (*persona*) slender, slim; (*stelo*) thin;
  (*voce*) faint
esili'are *vt* to exile; **e'silio** *sm* exile
esis'tenza [ezis'tɛntsa] *sf* existence
e'sistere *vi* to exist
esi'tare *vi* to hesitate
'esito *sm* result, outcome
'esodo *sm* exodus
esone'rare *vt* to exempt
e'sordio *sm* debut
esor'tare *vt* **~ qn a fare** to urge sb to do
e'sotico, -a, -ci, -che *ag* exotic
es'pandere *vt* to expand; (*confini*) to
  extend; (*influenza*) to extend, spread;
  espandersi *vpr* to expand; **espansi'one**
  sf expansion; **espansione di memoria**
  (*Inform*) memory upgrade; **espan'sivo, -a**
  ag expansive, communicative
espatri'are *vi* to leave one's country
espedi'ente *sm* expedient
es'pellere *vt* to expel
esperi'enza [espe'rjɛntsa] *sf* experience
esperi'mento *sm* experiment
es'perto, -a *ag, sm* expert
espi'rare *vt, vi* to breathe out
es'plicito, -a [es'plitʃito] *ag* explicit
es'plodere *vi* (*anche fig*) to explode ▷ *vt*
  to fire
esplo'rare *vt* to explore
esplosi'one *sf* explosion
es'pone *ecc vb vedi* **esporre**
es'pongo, es'poni *ecc vb vedi* **esporre**
es'porre *vt* (*merci*) to display; (*quadro*)
  to exhibit, show; (*fatti, idee*) to explain,
  set out; (*porre in pericolo, Fot*) to expose:
  esporsi *vpr* **esporsi a** (*sole, pericolo*) to
  expose o.s. to; (*critiche*) to lay o.s. open to
espor'tare *vt* to export
es'pose *ecc vb vedi* **esporre**
esposizi'one [espozit'tsjone] *sf*
  displaying; exhibiting; setting out;
  (*anche Fot*) exposure; (*mostra*) exhibition;
  (*narrazione*) explanation, exposition
es'posto, -a *pp di* **esporre** ▷ *ag* **~ a nord**
  facing north ▷ *sm* (*Amm*) statement,
  account; (: *petizione*) petition

espressi'one *sf* expression

espres'sivo, -a *ag* expressive

es'presso, -a *pp di* **esprimere** ▷ *ag* express ▷ *sm* (*lettera*) express letter; (*anche*: **treno ~**) express train; (*anche*: **caffè ~**) espresso

es'primere *vt* to express; **esprimersi** *vpr* to express o.s.

es'pulsi *ecc vb vedi* **espellere**

espulsi'one *sf* expulsion

es'senza [es'sɛntsa] *sf* essence; **essenzi'ale** *ag* essential; **l'essenziale** the main *o* most important thing

 PAROLA CHIAVE

'essere *sm* being; **essere umano** human being

▷ *vb copulativo* **1** (*con attributo, sostantivo*) to be; **sei giovane/simpatico** you are *o* you're young/nice; **è medico** he is *o* he's a doctor

2 (+ *di*: *appartenere*) to be; **di chi è la penna?** whose pen is it?; **è di Carla** it is *o* it's Carla's, it belongs to Carla

3 (+ *di*: *provenire*) to be; **è di Venezia** he is *o* he's from Venice

4 (*data, ora*): **è il 15 agosto/lunedì** it is *o* it's the 15th of August/Monday; **che ora è?, che ore sono?** what time is it?; **è l'una** it is *o* it's one o'clock; **sono le due** it is *o* it's two o'clock

5 (*costare*): **quant'è?** how much is it?; **sono 10 euro** it's 10 euros

▷ *vb aus* **1** (*attivo*): **essere arrivato/venuto** to have arrived/come; **è già partita** she has already left

2 (*passivo*) to be; **essere fatto da** to be made by; **è stata uccisa** she has been killed

3 (*riflessivo*): **si sono lavati** they washed, they got washed

4 (+ *da* + *infinito*): **è da farsi subito** it must be *o* is to be done immediately

▷ *vi* **1** (*esistere, trovarsi*) to be; **sono a casa** I'm at home; **essere in piedi/seduto** to be standing/sitting

2: **esserci**: **c'è** there is; **ci sono** there are; **che c'è?** what's the matter?, what is it?; **ci sono!** (*fig*: *ho capito*) I get it!; *vedi anche* **ci**

▷ *vb impers*: **è tardi/Pasqua** it's late/Easter; **è possibile che venga** he may come; **è così** that's the way it is

'essi *pron mpl vedi* **esso**

'esso, -a *pron* it; (*riferito a persona: soggetto*) he/she; (*: complemento*) him/her

est *sm* east

es'tate *sf* summer

esteri'ore *ag* outward, external

es'terno, -a *ag* (*porta, muro*) outer, outside; (*scala*) outside; (*alunno, impressione*) external ▷ *sm* outside, exterior ▷ *sm/f* (*allievo*) day pupil; **all'~** outside; **per uso ~** for external use only; **esterni** *smpl* (*Cinema*) location shots

'estero, -a *ag* foreign ▷ *sm* **all'~** abroad

es'teso, -a *pp di* **estendere** ▷ *ag* extensive, large; **scrivere per ~** to write in full

es'tetico, -a, -ci, -che *ag* aesthetic ▷ *sf* (*disciplina*) aesthetics *sg*; (*bellezza*) attractiveness; **este'tista, -i, -e** *sm/f* beautician

es'tinguere *vt* to extinguish, put out; (*debito*) to pay off; **estinguersi** *vpr* to go out; (*specie*) to become extinct

es'tinsi *ecc vb vedi* **estinguere**

estin'tore *sm* (*fire*) extinguisher

estinzi'one *sf* putting out; (*di specie*) extinction

estir'pare *vt* (*pianta*) to uproot, pull up; (*fig*: *vizio*) to eradicate

es'tivo, -a *ag* summer *cpd*

es'torcere [es'tɔrtʃere] *vt* **~ qc (a qn)** to extort sth (from sb)

estradizi'one [estradit'tsjone] *sf* extradition

es'trae, es'traggo *ecc vb vedi* **estrarre**

es'traneo, -a *ag* foreign ▷ *sm/f* stranger; **rimanere ~ a qc** to take no part in sth

es'trarre *vt* to extract; (*minerali*) to mine; (*sorteggiare*) to draw

es'trassi *ecc vb vedi* **estrarre**

estrema'mente *av* extremely

estre'mista, -i, e *sm/f* extremist

estremità *sf inv* extremity, end ▷ *sf pl* (*Anat*) extremities

es'tremo, -a *ag* extreme; (*ultimo*: *ora, tentativo*) final, last ▷ *sm* extreme; (*di pazienza, forze*) limit, end; **estremi** *smpl* (*Amm*: *dati essenziali*) details, particulars; **l'~ Oriente** the Far East

estro'verso, -a *ag, sm* extrovert

età *sf inv* age; **all'~ di 8 anni** at the age of 8, at 8 years of age; **ha la mia ~** he (*o* she) is the same age as me *o* as I am; **raggiungere la maggiore ~** to come of age; **essere in ~ minore** to be under age

'etere *sm* ether

eternità *sf* eternity

e'terno, -a *ag* eternal

etero'geneo, -a [etero'dʒɛneo] *ag* heterogeneous

eterosessu'ale *ag, sm/f* heterosexual

'etica *sf* ethics *sg*; *vedi anche* **etico**

eti'chetta [eti'ketta] *sf* label; (*cerimoniale*): **l'~** etiquette

'etico, -a, -ci, -che *ag* ethical

eti'lometro *sm* Breathalyzer®

etimolo'gia, -'gie [etimolo'dʒia] *sf*
etymology

Eti'opia *sf* l'~ Ethiopia

'etnico, -a, -ci, -che *ag* ethnic

e'trusco, -a, -schi, -sche *ag, sm/f*
Etruscan

'ettaro *sm* hectare (= 10,000 m²)

'etto *sm abbr* (= *ettogrammo*) 100 grams

'euro *sm inv* (*divisa*) euro

Eu'ropa *sf* l'~ Europe

europarlamen'tare *sm/f* Member of the
European Parliament, MEP

euro'peo, -a *ag, sm/f* European

eutana'sia *sf* euthanasia

evacu'are *vt* to evacuate

e'vadere *vi* (*fuggire*): ~ **da** to escape from
▷ *vt* (*sbrigare*) to deal with, dispatch; (*tasse*)
to evade

evapo'rare *vi* to evaporate

e'vasi *ecc vb vedi* **evadere**

evasi'one *sf* (*vedi evadere*) escape;
dispatch; **evasione fiscale** tax evasion

eva'sivo, -a *ag* evasive

e'vaso, -a *pp di* **evadere** ▷ *sm* escapee

e'vento *sm* event

eventu'ale *ag* possible

Attenzione! In inglese esiste la parola
eventual, che però significa *finale*.

eventual'mente *av* if necessary

Attenzione! In inglese esiste la
parola *eventually*, che però significa
alla fine.

evi'dente *ag* evident, obvious

evidente'mente *av* evidently;
(*palesemente*) obviously, evidently

evi'tare *vt* to avoid; ~ **di** fare to avoid
doing; ~ **qc a qn** to spare sb sth

evoluzi'one [evolut'tsjone] *sf* evolution

e'volversi *vpr* to evolve

ev'viva *escl* hurrah!; ~ **il re!** long live the
king!, hurrah for the king!

ex *prefisso* ex, former

'extra *ag inv* first-rate; top-quality ▷ *sm
inv* extra; **extracomuni'tario, -a** *ag* from
outside the EC ▷ *sm/f* non-EC citizen

extrater'restre *ag, sm/f* extraterrestrial

fa *vb vedi* **fare** ▷ *sm inv* (*Mus*) F;
(: *solfeggiando la scala*) fa ▷ *av* **10 anni fa** 10
years ago

'fabbrica *sf* factory; **fabbri'care** *vt* to
build; (*produrre*) to manufacture, make;
(*fig*) to fabricate, invent

Attenzione! In inglese esiste la parola
fabric, che però significa *stoffa*.

fac'cenda [fat'tʃɛnda] *sf* matter, affair;
(*cosa da fare*) task, chore

fac'chino [fak'kino] *sm* porter

'faccia, -ce ['fattʃa] *sf* face; (*di moneta,
medaglia*) side; **faccia a faccia** face to face

facci'ata [fat'tʃata] *sf* façade; (*di pagina*)
side

'faccio ['fattʃo] *vb vedi* **fare**

fa'cessi *ecc* [fa'tʃessi] *vb vedi* **fare**

fa'cevo *ecc* [fa'tʃevo] *vb vedi* **fare**

'facile ['fatʃile] *ag* easy; (*disposto*): ~ **a**
inclined to, prone to; (*probabile*): **è** ~ **che
piova** it's likely to rain

facoltà *sf inv* faculty; (*autorità*) power

facolta'tivo, -a *ag* optional; (*fermata
d'autobus*) request *cpd*

'faggio ['faddʒo] *sm* beech

fagi'ano [fa'dʒano] *sm* pheasant

fagio'lino [fadʒo'lino] *sm* French (BRIT) o
string bean

fagi'olo [fa'dʒɔlo] *sm* bean

'fai *vb vedi* **fare**

'fai-da-'te *sm inv* DIY, do-it-yourself

'falce ['faltʃe] *sf* scythe; **falci'are** *vt* to cut; (*fig*) to mow down

falcia'trice [faltʃa'tritʃe] *sf* (*per fieno*) reaping machine; (*per erba*) mowing machine

'falco, -chi *sm* hawk

'falda *sf* layer, stratum; (*di cappello*) brim; (*di cappotto*) tails *pl*; (*di monte*) lower slope; (*di tetto*) pitch

fale'gname [faleɲ'ɲame] *sm* joiner

falli'mento *sm* failure; bankruptcy

fal'lire *vi* (*non riuscire*) **~ (in)** to fail (in); (*Dir*) to go bankrupt ▷ *vt* (*colpo, bersaglio*) to miss

'fallo *sm* error, mistake; (*imperfezione*) defect, flaw; (*Sport*) foul; fault; **senza ~** without fail

falò *sm inv* bonfire

falsifi'care *vt* to forge; (*monete*) to forge, counterfeit

'falso, -a *ag* false; (*errato*) wrong; (*falsificato*) forged; fake; (: *oro, gioielli*) imitation *cpd* ▷ *sm* forgery; **giurare il ~** to commit perjury

'fama *sf* fame; (*reputazione*) reputation, name

'fame *sf* hunger; **aver ~** to be hungry

fa'miglia [fa'miʎʎa] *sf* family

famili'are *ag* (*della famiglia*) family *cpd*; (*ben noto*) familiar; (*rapporti, atmosfera*) friendly; (*Ling*) informal, colloquial ▷ *sm/f* relative, relation

fa'moso, -a *ag* famous, well-known

fa'nale *sm* (*Aut*) light, lamp (BRIT); (*luce stradale, Naut*) light; (*di faro*) beacon

fa'natico, -a, -ci, -che *ag* fanatical; (*del teatro, calcio ecc*): **~ di** *o* **per** mad *o* crazy about ▷ *sm/f* fanatic; (*tifoso*) fan

'fango, -ghi *sm* mud

'fanno *vb vedi* **fare**

fannul'lone, -a *sm/f* idler, loafer

fantasci'enza [fantaʃ'ʃɛntsa] *sf* science fiction

fanta'sia *sf* fantasy, imagination; (*capriccio*) whim, caprice ▷ *ag inv* **vestito ~** patterned dress

fan'tasma, -i *sm* ghost, phantom

fan'tastico, -a, -ci, -che *ag* fantastic; (*potenza, ingegno*) imaginative

fan'tino *sm* jockey

fara'butto *sm* crook

fard *sm inv* blusher

○ **PAROLA CHIAVE**

'fare *sm* **1** (*modo di fare*): **con fare distratto** absent-mindedly; **ha un fare simpatico** he has a pleasant manner

2: **sul far del giorno/della notte** at daybreak/nightfall

▷ *vt* **1** (*fabbricare, creare*) to make; (: *casa*) to build; (: *assegno*) to make out; **fare un pasto/una promessa/un film** to make a meal/a promise/a film; **fare rumore** to make a noise

2 (*effettuare: lavoro, attività, studi*) to do; (: *sport*) to play; **cosa fa?** (*adesso*) what are you doing?; (*di professione*) what do you do?; **fare psicologia/italiano** (*Ins*) to do psychology/Italian; **fare un viaggio** to go on a trip *o* journey; **fare una passeggiata** to go for a walk; **fare la spesa** to do the shopping

3 (*funzione*) to be; (*Teatro*) to play, be; **fare il medico** to be a doctor; **fare il malato** (*fingere*) to act the invalid

4 (*suscitare: sentimenti*): **fare paura a qn** to frighten sb; **(non) fa niente** (*non importa*) it doesn't matter

5 (*ammontare*): **3 più 3 fa 6** 3 and 3 are *o* make 6; **fanno 3 euro** that's 3 euros; **Roma fa 2.000.000 di abitanti** Rome has 2,000,000 inhabitants; **che ora fai?** what time do you make it?

6 (+ *infinito*): **far fare qc a qn** (*obbligare*) to make sb do sth; (*permettere*) to let sb do sth; **fammi vedere** let me see; **far partire il motore** to start (up) the engine; **far riparare la macchina/costruire una casa** to get *o* have the car repaired/a house built

7: **farsi: farsi una gonna** to make o.s. a skirt; **farsi un nome** to make a name for o.s.; **farsi la permanente** to get a perm; **farsi tagliare i capelli** to get one's hair cut; **farsi operare** to have an operation

8 (*fraseologia*): **farcela** to succeed, manage; **non ce la faccio più** I can't go on; **ce la faremo** we'll make it; **me l'hanno fatta!** (*imbrogliare*) I've been done!; **lo facevo più giovane** I thought he was younger; **fare sì/no con la testa** to nod/shake one's head

▷ *vi* **1** (*agire*) to act, do; **fate come volete** do as you like; **fare presto** to be quick; **fare da** to act as; **non c'è niente da fare** it's no use; **saperci fare con qn/qc** to know how to deal with sb/sth; **faccia pure!** go ahead!

2 (*dire*) to say; **"davvero?" fece** "really?" he said

3: **fare per** (*essere adatto*) to be suitable for; **fare per fare qc** to be about to do sth; **fece per andarsene** he made as if to leave

4: **farsi: si fa così** you do it like this, this is the way it's done; **non si fa così!** (*rimprovero*) that's no way to behave!; **la festa non si fa** the party is off

5: **fare a gara con qn** to compete o vie with sb; **fare a pugni** to come to blows; **fare in tempo a fare** to be in time to do ▷ *vb impers* **fa bel tempo** the weather is fine; **fa caldo/freddo** it's hot/cold; **fa notte** it's getting dark ▷ *vpr* **farsi 1** (*diventare*) to become; **farsi prete** to become a priest; **farsi grande/vecchio** to grow tall/old

2 (*spostarsi*): **farsi avanti/indietro** to move forward/back

3 (*fam*: *drogarsi*) to be a junkie

far'falla *sf* butterfly

fa'rina *sf* flour

farma'cia, -'cie [farma'tʃia] *sf* pharmacy; (*negozio*) chemist's (shop) (BRIT), pharmacy; **farma'cista, -i, -e** *sm/f* chemist (BRIT), pharmacist

'farmaco, -ci o **chi** *sm* drug, medicine

'faro *sm* (*Naut*) lighthouse; (*Aer*) beacon; (*Aut*) headlight

'fascia, -sce ['faʃʃa] *sf* band, strip; (*Med*) bandage; (*di sindaco, ufficiale*) sash; (*parte di territorio*) strip, belt; (*di contribuenti ecc*) group, band; **essere in fasce** (*anche fig*) to be in one's infancy; **fascia oraria** time band

fasci'are [faʃʃare] *vt* to bind; (*Med*) to bandage

fa'scicolo [faʃʃikolo] *sm* (*di documenti*) file, dossier; (*di rivista*) issue, number; (*opuscolo*) booklet, pamphlet

'fascino ['faʃʃino] *sm* charm, fascination

fa'scismo [faʃʃizmo] *sm* fascism

'fase *sf* phase; (*Tecn*) stroke; **fuori ~** (*motore*) rough

fas'tidio *sm* bother, trouble; **dare ~ a qn** to bother o annoy sb; **sento ~ allo stomaco** my stomach's upset; **avere fastidi con la polizia** to have trouble o bother with the police; **fastidi'oso, -a** *ag* annoying, tiresome

▪ Attenzione! In inglese esiste la parola *fastidious*, che però significa *pignolo*.

'fata *sf* fairy

fa'tale *ag* fatal; (*inevitabile*) inevitable; (*fig*) irresistible

fa'tica, -che *sf* hard work, toil; (*sforzo*) effort; (*di metalli*) fatigue; **a ~** with difficulty; **fare ~ a fare qc** to have a job doing sth; **fati'coso, -a** *ag* tiring, exhausting; (*lavoro*) laborious

'fatto, -a *pp di* **fare** ▷ *ag* **un uomo ~** a grown man; **~ a mano/in casa** hand-/home-made ▷ *sm* fact; (*azione*) deed; (*avvenimento*) event, occurrence; (*di romanzo, film*) action, story; **cogliere qn sul ~** to catch sb red-handed; **il ~ sta** o **è**

che the fact remains o is that; **in ~ di** as for, as far as … is concerned

fat'tore *sm* (*Agr*) farm manager; (*Mat, elemento costitutivo*) factor; **fattore di protezione** (*di lozione solare*) factor; **vorrei una crema solare con ~ di protezione 15** I'd like a factor 15 suntan cream

fatto'ria *sf* farm; farmhouse

▪ Attenzione! In inglese esiste la parola *factory*, che però significa *fabbrica*.

fatto'rino *sm* errand-boy; (*di ufficio*) office-boy; (*d'albergo*) porter

fat'tura *sf* (*Comm*) invoice; (*di abito*) tailoring; (*malia*) spell

fattu'rato *sm* (*Comm*) turnover

'fauna *sf* fauna

'fava *sf* broad bean

'favola *sf* (*fiaba*) fairy tale; (*d'intento morale*) fable; (*fandonia*) yarn; **favo'loso, -a** *ag* fabulous; (*incredibile*) incredible

fa'vore *sm* favour; **per ~** please; **fare un ~ a qn** to do sb a favour

favo'rire *vt* to favour; (*il commercio, l'industria, le arti*) to promote, encourage; **vuole ~?** won't you help yourself?; **favorisca in salotto** please come into the sitting room

fax *sm inv* fax; **mandare qc via ~** to fax sth

fazzo'letto [fattso'letto] *sm* handkerchief; (*per la testa*) (head)scarf; **fazzoletto di carta** tissue

feb'braio *sm* February

'febbre *sf* fever; **aver la ~** to have a high temperature; **febbre da fieno** hay fever

'feci *ecc* ['fetʃi] *vb vedi* **fare**

fecondazi'one [fekondat'tsjone] *sf* fertilization; **fecondazione artificiale** artificial insemination

fe'condo, -a *ag* fertile

'fede *sf* (*credenza*) belief, faith; (*Rel*) faith; (*fiducia*) faith, trust; (*fedeltà*) loyalty; (*anello*) wedding ring; (*attestato*) certificate; **aver ~ in qn** to have faith in sb; **in buona/cattiva ~** in good/bad faith; **"in ~"** (*Dir*) "in witness whereof"; **fe'dele** *ag* **fedele (a)** faithful (to) ▷ *sm/f* follower; **i fedeli** (*Rel*) the faithful

'federa *sf* pillowslip, pillowcase

fede'rale *ag* federal

'fegato *sm* liver; (*fig*) guts *pl*, nerve

'felce ['feltʃe] *sf* fern

fe'lice [fe'litʃe] *ag* happy; (*fortunato*) lucky; **felicità** *sf* happiness

felici'tarsi [felitʃi'tarsi] *vpr* (*congratularsi*): **~ con qn per qc** to congratulate sb on sth

fe'lino, -a *ag, sm* feline

'felpa *sf* sweatshirt

'femmina *sf* (*Zool, Tecn*) female; (*figlia*) girl, daughter; (*spesso peg*) woman;

femmi'nile *ag* feminine; (*sesso*) female; (*lavoro, giornale, moda*) woman's ▷ *sm* (*Ling*) feminine

'femore *sm* thighbone, femur

fe'nomeno *sm* phenomenon

feri'ale *ag* giorno ~ weekday

'ferie *sfpl* holidays (BRIT), vacation *sg* (US); **andare in ~** to go on holiday *o* vacation

fe'rire *vt* to injure; (*deliberatamente: Mil ecc*) to wound; (*colpire*) to hurt; **ferirsi** *vpr* to hurt o.s., injure o.s; **fe'rita** *sf* injury, wound; **fe'rito, -a** *sm/f* wounded *o* injured man/woman

fer'maglio [fer'maλλo] *sm* clasp; (*per documenti*) clip

fer'mare *vt* to stop, halt; (*Polizia*) to detain, hold ▷ *vi* to stop; **fermarsi** *vpr* to stop, halt; **fermarsi a fare qc** to stop to do sth; **può fermarsi qui/all'angolo?** could you stop here/at the corner?

fer'mata *sf* stop; **fermata dell'autobus** bus stop

fer'menti *smpl* ~ **lattici** probiotic bacteria

fer'mezza [fer'mettsa] *sf* (*fig*) firmness, steadfastness

'fermo, -a *ag* still, motionless; (*veicolo*) stationary; (*orologio*) not working; (*saldo: anche fig*) firm; (*voce, mano*) steady ▷ *escl* stop!; keep still! ▷ *sm* (*chiusura*) catch, lock; (*Dir*): **fermo di polizia** police detention

fe'roce [fe'rɔtʃe] *ag* (*animale*) fierce, ferocious; (*persona*) cruel, fierce; (*fame, dolore*) raging; **le bestie feroci** wild animals

ferra'gosto *sm* (*festa*) feast of the Assumption; (*periodo*) August holidays *pl*

⚬ **FERRAGOSTO**

⚬
⚬
⚬ **Ferragosto**, August 15th, is a national
⚬ holiday. Marking the Feast of the
⚬ Assumption, its origins are religious
⚬ but in recent years it has simply become
⚬ the most important public holiday of
⚬ the summer season. Most people take
⚬ some extra time off work and head out
⚬ of town to the holiday resorts.

ferra'menta *sfpl* **negozio di ~** ironmonger's (BRIT), hardware shop *o* store (US)

'ferro *sm* iron; **una bistecca ai ferri** a grilled steak; **ferro battuto** wrought iron; **ferro da calza** knitting needle; **ferro di cavallo** horseshoe; **ferro da stiro** iron

ferro'via *sf* railway (BRIT), railroad (US); **ferrovi'ario, -a** *ag* railway *cpd* (BRIT), railroad *cpd* (US); **ferrovi'ere** *sm*

railwayman (BRIT), railroad man (US)

'fertile *ag* fertile

'fesso, -a *pp di* **fendere** ▷ *ag* (*fam: sciocco*) crazy, cracked

fes'sura *sf* crack, split; (*per gettone, moneta*) slot

'festa *sf* (*religiosa*) feast; (*pubblica*) holiday; (*compleanno*) birthday; (*onomastico*) name day; (*ricevimento*) celebration, party; **far ~** to have a holiday; to live it up; **far ~ a qn** to give sb a warm welcome

festeggi'are [fested'dʒare] *vt* to celebrate; (*persona*) to have a celebration for

fes'tivo, -a *ag* (*atmosfera*) festive; **giorno ~** holiday

'feto *sm* foetus (BRIT), fetus (US)

'fetta *sf* slice

fettuc'cine [fettut'tʃine] *sfpl* (*Cuc*) ribbon-shaped pasta

FF.SS. *abbr* = **Ferrovie dello Stato**

FI *sigla* = **Firenze** ▷ *abbr* (= Forza Italia) *Italian centre-right political party*

fi'aba *sf* fairy tale

fi'acca *sf* weariness; (*svogliatezza*) listlessness

fi'acco, -a, -chi, -che *ag* (*stanco*) tired, weary; (*svogliato*) listless; (*debole*) weak; (*mercato*) slack

fi'accola *sf* torch

fi'ala *sf* phial

fi'amma *sf* flame

fiam'mante *ag* (*colore*) flaming; **nuovo ~** brand new

fiam'mifero *sm* match

fiam'mingo, -a, -ghi, -ghe *ag* Flemish ▷ *sm/f* Fleming ▷ *sm* (*Ling*) Flemish; **i Fiamminghi** the Flemish

fi'anco, -chi *sm* side; (*Mil*) flank; **di ~** sideways, from the side; **a ~ a ~** side by side

fi'asco, -schi *sm* flask; (*fig*) fiasco; **fare ~** to fail

fia'tare *vi* (*fig: parlare*): **senza ~** without saying a word

fi'ato *sm* breath; (*resistenza*) stamina; **avere il ~ grosso** to be out of breath; **prendere ~** to catch one's breath

'fibbia *sf* buckle

'fibra *sf* fibre; (*fig*) constitution

fic'care *vt* to push, thrust, drive; **ficcarsi** *vpr* (*andare a finire*) to get to

ficcherò *ecc* [fikke'rɔ] *vb vedi* **ficcare**

'fico, -chi *sm* (*pianta*) fig tree; (*frutto*) fig; **fico d'India** prickly pear; **fico secco** dried fig

fidanza'mento [fidantsa'mento] *sm* engagement

fidan'zarsi [fidan'tsarsi] *vpr* to get engaged; **fidan'zato, -a** *sm/f* fiancé/

fiancée

fi'darsi *vpr* ~ **di** to trust; **fi'dato, -a** *ag* reliable, trustworthy

fi'ducia [fi'dutʃa] *sf* confidence, trust; **incarico di** ~ position of trust, responsible position; **persona di** ~ reliable person

fie'nile *sm* barn; hayloft

fi'eno *sm* hay

fi'era *sf* fair

fi'ero, -a *ag* proud; (*audace*) bold

'fifa (*fam*) *sf* **aver** ~ to have the jitters

fig. *abbr* (= *figura*) fig.

'figlia ['fiʎʎa] *sf* daughter

figli'astro, -a [fiʎ'ʎastro] *sm/f* stepson/daughter

'figlio ['fiʎʎo] *sm* son; (*senza distinzione di sesso*) child; **figlio di papà** spoilt, wealthy young man; **figlio unico** only child

fi'gura *sf* figure; (*forma, aspetto esterno*) form, shape; (*illustrazione*) picture, illustration; **far** ~ to look smart; **fare una brutta** ~ to make a bad impression

figu'rina *sf* figurine; (*cartoncino*) picture card

'fila *sf* row, line; (*coda*) queue; (*serie*) series, string; **di** ~ in succession; **fare la** ~ to queue; **in** ~ **indiana** in single file

fi'lare *vt* to spin ▷ *vi* (*baco, ragno*) to spin; (*formaggio fuso*) to go stringy; (*discorso*) to hang together; (*fam: amoreggiare*) to go steady; (*muoversi a forte velocità*) to go at full speed; ~ **diritto** (*fig*) to toe the line; ~ **via** to dash off

filas'trocca, -che *sf* nursery rhyme

filate'lia *sf* philately, stamp collecting

fi'letto *sm* (*di vite*) thread; (*di carne*) fillet

fili'ale *ag* filial ▷ *sf* (*di impresa*) branch

film *sm inv* film

'filo *sm* (*anche fig*) thread; (*filato*) yarn; (*metallico*) wire; (*di lama, rasoio*) edge; **per** ~ **e per segno** in detail; **con un** ~ **di voce** in a whisper; **filo d'erba** blade of grass; **filo interdentale** dental floss; **filo di perle** string of pearls; **filo spinato** barbed wire

fi'lone *sm* (*di minerali*) seam, vein; (*pane*) ≈ Vienna loaf; (*fig*) trend

filoso'fia *sf* philosophy; **fi'losofo, -a** *sm/f* philosopher

fil'trare *vt, vi* to filter

'filtro *sm* filter; **filtro dell'olio** (*Aut*) oil filter

fi'nale *ag* final ▷ *sm* (*di opera*) end, ending; (: *Mus*) finale ▷ *sf* (*Sport*) final; **final'mente** *av* finally, at last

fi'nanza [fi'nantsa] *sf* finance; **finanze** *sfpl* (*di individuo, Stato*) finances

finché [fin'ke] *cong* (*per tutto il tempo che*) as long as; (*fino al momento in cui*) until; **aspetta** ~ **io (non) sia ritornato** wait until I get back

'fine *ag* (*lamina, carta*) thin; (*capelli, polvere*) fine; (*vista, udito*) keen, sharp; (*persona: raffinata*) refined, distinguished; (*osservazione*) subtle ▷ *sf* end ▷ *sm* aim, purpose; (*esito*) result, outcome; **secondo** ~ ulterior motive; **in** *o* **alla** ~ in the end, finally

fi'nestra *sf* window; **fines'trino** *sm* window; **vorrei un posto vicino al finestrino** I'd like a window seat

'fingere ['findʒere] *vt* to feign; (*supporre*) to imagine, suppose; **fingersi** *vpr* **fingersi ubriaco/pazzo** to pretend to be drunk/mad; ~ **di fare** to pretend to do

fi'nire *vt* to finish ▷ *vi* to finish, end; **quando finisce lo spettacolo?** when does the show finish?; ~ **di fare** (*compiere*) to finish doing; (*smettere*) to stop doing; ~ **in galera** to end up *o* finish up in prison

finlan'dese *ag, sm* (*Ling*) Finnish ▷ *sm/f* Finn

Fin'landia *sf* **la** ~ Finland

'fino, -a *ag* (*capelli, seta*) fine; (*oro*) pure; (*fig: acuto*) shrewd ▷ *av* (*spesso troncato in* **fin**: *pure, anche*) even ▷ *prep* (*spesso troncato in* **fin**: *tempo*): **fin quando?** till when?; (: *luogo*): **fin qui** as far as here; ~ **a** (*tempo*) until, till; (*luogo*) as far as, (up) to; **fin da domani** from tomorrow onwards; **fin da ieri** since yesterday; **fin dalla nascita** from *o* since birth

fi'nocchio [fi'nɔkkjo] *sm* fennel; (*fam: peg: omosessuale*) queer

fi'nora *av* up till now

'finsi *ecc vb vedi* **fingere**

'finta *sf* pretence, sham; (*Sport*) feint; **far** ~ **(di fare)** to pretend (to do)

'finto, -a *pp di* **fingere** ▷ *ag* false; artificial

finzi'one [fin'tsjone] *sf* pretence, sham

fi'occo, -chi *sm* (*di nastro*) bow; (*di stoffa, lana*) flock; (*di neve*) flake; (*Naut*) jib; **coi fiocchi** (*fig*) first-rate; **fiocchi di avena** oatflakes; **fiocchi di granturco** cornflakes

fi'ocina ['fjɔtʃina] *sf* harpoon

fi'oco, -a, -chi, -che *ag* faint, dim

fi'onda *sf* catapult

fio'raio, -a *sm/f* florist

fi'ore *sm* flower; **fiori** *smpl* (*Carte*) clubs; **a fior d'acqua** on the surface of the water; **avere i nervi a fior di pelle** to be on edge; **fior di latte** cream; **fiori di campo** wild flowers

fioren'tino, -a *ag* Florentine

fio'retto *sm* (*Scherma*) foil

fio'rire *vi* (*rosa*) to flower; (*albero*) to blossom; (*fig*) to flourish

Fi'renze [fi'rɛntse] *sf* Florence

'firma sf signature

Attenzione! In inglese esiste la parola firm, che però significa ditta.

fir'mare vt to sign; **un abito firmato** a designer suit; **dove devo ~?** where do I sign?

fisar'monica, -che sf accordion

fis'cale ag fiscal, tax cpd; **medico ~** doctor employed by Social Security to verify cases of sick leave

fischi'are [fis'kjare] vi to whistle ▷ vt to whistle; (attore) to boo, hiss

fischi'etto [fis'kjetto] sm (strumento) whistle

'fischio ['fiskjo] sm whistle

'fisco sm tax authorities pl, ≈ Inland Revenue (BRIT), ≈ Internal Revenue Service (US)

'fisica sf physics sg

'fisico, -a, -ci, -che ag physical ▷ sm/f physicist ▷ sm physique

fisiotera'pia sf physiotherapy

fisiotera'pista sm/f physiotherapist

fis'sare vt to fix, fasten; (guardare intensamente) to stare at; (data, condizioni) to fix, establish, set; (prenotare) to book; **fissarsi** vpr **fissarsi su** (sguardo, attenzione) to focus on; (fig: idea) to become obsessed with

'fisso, -a ag fixed; (stipendio, impiego) regular ▷ av **guardare ~ qc/qn** to stare at sth/sb

'fitta sf sharp pain; vedi anche **fitto**

fit'tizio, -a ag fictitious, imaginary

'fitto, -a ag thick, dense; (pioggia) heavy ▷ sm depths pl, middle; (affitto, pigione) rent

fi'ume sm river

fiu'tare vt to smell, sniff; (animale) to scent; (fig: inganno) to get wind of, smell; **~ tabacco/cocaina** to take snuff/cocaine

fla'grante ag **cogliere qn in ~** to catch sb red-handed

fla'nella sf flannel

flash [flaʃ] sm inv (Fot) flash; (giornalistico) newsflash

'flauto sm flute

fles'sibile ag pliable; (fig: che si adatta) flexible

flessibili'tà sf (anche fig) flexibility

flessi'one sf (gen) bending; (Ginnastica: a terra) sit-up; (: in piedi) forward bend; (: sulle gambe) knee-bend; (diminuzione) slight drop, slight fall; (Ling) inflection; **fare una ~** to bend; **una ~ economica** a downward trend in the economy

'flettere vt to bend

'flipper sm inv pinball machine

F.lli abbr (= fratelli) Bros.

'flora sf flora

'florido, -a ag flourishing; (fig) glowing with health

'floscio, -a, -sci, -sce ['flɔʃʃo] ag (cappello) floppy, soft; (muscoli) flabby

'flotta sf fleet

'fluido, -a ag, sm fluid

flu'oro sm fluorine

'flusso sm flow; (Fisica, Med) flux; **~ e ri~** ebb and flow

fluvi'ale ag river cpd, fluvial

FMI sigla m (= Fondo Monetario Internazionale) IMF

'foca, -che sf (Zool) seal

fo'caccia, -ce [fo'kattʃa] sf kind of pizza; (dolce) bun

'foce ['fotʃe] sf (Geo) mouth

foco'laio sm (Med) centre of infection; (fig) hotbed

foco'lare sm hearth, fireside; (Tecn) furnace

'fodera sf (di vestito) lining; (di libro, poltrona) cover

'fodero sm (di spada) scabbard; (di pugnale) sheath; (di pistola) holster

'foga sf enthusiasm, ardour

'foglia ['fɔʎʎa] sf leaf; **foglia d'argento/ d'oro** silver/gold leaf

'foglio ['fɔʎʎo] sm (di carta) sheet (of paper); (di metallo) sheet; **foglio di calcolo** (Inform) spreadsheet; **foglio rosa** (Aut) provisional licence; **foglio di via** (Dir) expulsion order; **foglio volante** pamphlet

'fogna ['foɲɲa] sf drain, sewer

föhn [føːn] sm inv hair dryer

'folla sf crowd, throng

'folle ag mad, insane; (Tecn) idle; **in ~** (Aut) in neutral

fol'lia sf folly, foolishness; foolish act; (pazzia) madness, lunacy

'folto, -a ag thick

fon sm inv hair dryer

fondamen'tale ag fundamental, basic

fonda'mento sm foundation; **fondamenta** sfpl (Edil) foundations

fon'dare vt to found; (fig: dar base): **~ qc su** to base sth on

fon'dente ag **cioccolato ~** plain o dark chocolate

'fondere vt (neve) to melt; (metallo) to fuse, melt; (fig: colori) to merge, blend; (: imprese, gruppi) to merge ▷ vi to melt; **fondersi** vpr to melt; (fig: partiti, correnti) to unite, merge

'fondo, -a ag deep ▷ sm (di recipiente, pozzo) bottom; (di stanza) back; (quantità di liquido che resta, deposito) dregs pl; (sfondo) background; (unità immobiliare) property, estate; (somma di denaro) fund; (Sport) long-distance race; **fondi** *smpl* (*denaro*) funds; **a notte fonda** at dead of night; **in ~ a** at the bottom of; at the back of; (*strada*) at the end of; **andare a ~** (*nave*) to sink; **conoscere a ~** to know inside out; **dar ~ a** (*fig: provviste, soldi*) to use up; **in ~** (*fig*) after all, all things considered; **andare fino in ~ a** (*fig*) to examine thoroughly; **a ~ perduto** (*Comm*) without security; **fondi di magazzino** old *o* unsold stock *sg*; **fondi di caffè** coffee grounds; **fondo comune di investimento** investment trust

fondo'tinta *sm inv* (*cosmetico*) foundation

fo'netica *sf* phonetics *sg*

fon'tana *sf* fountain

'fonte *sf* spring, source; (*fig*) source ▷ *sm*: **fonte battesimale** (*Rel*) font; **fonte energetica** source of energy

fo'raggio [fo'raddʒo] *sm* fodder, forage

fo'rare *vt* to pierce, make a hole in; (*pallone*) to burst; (*biglietto*) to punch; **~ una gomma** to burst a tyre (*BRIT*) *o* tire (*US*)

'forbici ['fɔrbitʃi] *sfpl* scissors

'forca, -che *sf* (*Agr*) fork, pitchfork; (*patibolo*) gallows *sg*

for'chetta [for'ketta] *sf* fork

for'cina [for'tʃina] *sf* hairpin

fo'resta *sf* forest

foresti'ero, -a *ag* foreign ▷ *sm/f* foreigner

'forfora *sf* dandruff

'forma *sf* form; (*aspetto esteriore*) form, shape; (*Dir: procedura*) procedure; (*per calzature*) last; (*stampo da cucina*) mould

formag'gino [formad'dʒino] *sm* processed cheese

for'maggio [for'maddʒo] *sm* cheese

for'male *ag* formal

for'mare *vt* to form, shape, make; (*numero di telefono*) to dial; (*fig: carattere*) to form, mould; **formarsi** *vpr* to form, take shape; **for'mato** *sm* format, size; **formazi'one** *sf* formation; (*fig: educazione*) training; **formazione professionale** vocational training

for'mica¹, -che *sf* ant

formica®² ['fɔrmika] *sf* (*materiale*) Formica®

formi'dabile *ag* powerful, formidable; (*straordinario*) remarkable

'formula *sf* formula; **formula di cortesia** courtesy form

formu'lare *vt* to formulate; to express

for'naio *sm* baker

for'nello *sm* (*elettrico, a gas*) ring; (*di pipa*) bowl

for'nire *vt* **~ qn di qc, ~ qc a qn** to provide *o* supply sb with sth, supply sth to sb

'forno *sm* (*di cucina*) oven; (*panetteria*) bakery; (*Tecn: per calce ecc*) kiln; (: *per metalli*) furnace; **forno a microonde** microwave oven

'foro *sm* (*buco*) hole; (*Storia*) forum; (*tribunale*) (law) court

'forse *av* perhaps, maybe; (*circa*) about; **essere in ~** to be in doubt

'forte *ag* strong; (*suono*) loud; (*spesa*) considerable, great; (*passione, dolore*) great, deep ▷ *av* strongly; (*velocemente*) fast; (*a voce alta*) loud(ly); (*violentemente*) hard ▷ *sm* (*edificio*) fort; (*specialità*) forte, strong point; **essere ~ in qc** to be good at sth

for'tezza [for'tettsa] *sf* (*morale*) strength; (*luogo fortificato*) fortress

for'tuito, -a *ag* fortuitous, chance

for'tuna *sf* (*destino*) fortune, luck; (*buona sorte*) success, fortune; (*eredità, averi*) fortune; **per ~** luckily, fortunately; **di ~** makeshift, improvised; **atterraggio di ~** emergency landing; **fortu'nato, -a** *ag* lucky, fortunate; (*coronato da successo*) successful

'forza ['fɔrtsa] *sf* strength; (*potere*) power; (*Fisica*) force; **forze** *sfpl* (*fisiche*) strength *sg*; (*Mil*) forces *escl* come on!; **per ~** against one's will; (*naturalmente*) of course; **a viva ~** by force; **a ~ di** by dint of; **~ maggiore** circumstances beyond one's control; **la ~ pubblica** the police *pl*; **forze armate** armed forces; **forze dell'ordine** the forces of law and order; **Forza Italia** *Italian centre-right political party*; **forza di pace** peacekeeping force

for'zare [for'tsare] *vt* to force; **~ qn a fare** to force sb to do

for'zista, -i, e [for'tsista] *ag* of Forza Italia ▷ *sm/f* member (*o* supporter) of Forza Italia

fos'chia [fos'kia] *sf* mist, haze

'fosco, -a, -schi, -sche *ag* dark, gloomy

'fosforo *sm* phosphorous

'fossa *sf* pit; (*di cimitero*) grave; **fossa biologica** septic tank

fos'sato *sm* ditch; (*di fortezza*) moat

fos'setta *sf* dimple

'fossi *ecc vb vedi* **essere**

'fossile *ag, sm* fossil

'fosso *sm* ditch; (*Mil*) trench

'foste *ecc vb vedi* **essere**

'foto *sf* photo; **può farci una ~, per favore?** would you take a picture of us, please? ▷ *prefisso:* **foto ricordo** souvenir photo; **foto tessera** passport(-type) photo; **foto'camera** *sf* **fotocamera digitale** digital camera; **foto'copia** *sf* photocopy; **fotocopi'are** *vt* to photocopy; **fotocopia'trice** [fotokopja'tritʃe] *sf* photocopier; **fotogra'fare** *vt* to photograph; **fotogra'fia** *sf* (*procedimento*) photography; (*immagine*) photograph; **fare una fotografia** to take a photograph; **una fotografia a colori/in bianco e nero** a colour/black and white photograph; **foto'grafico, -a, ci, che** *ag* photographic; **macchina fotografica** camera; **fo'tografo, -a** *sm/f* photographer; **fotoro'manzo** *sm* romantic picture story

fou'lard [fu'lar] *sm inv* scarf

fra *prep* = **tra**

'fradicio, -a, -ci, -ce ['fraditʃo] *ag* (*molto bagnato*) soaking (wet); **ubriaco ~** blind drunk

'fragile ['fradʒile] *ag* fragile; (*fig: salute*) delicate

'fragola *sf* strawberry

fra'grante *ag* fragrant

frain'tendere *vt* to misunderstand

fram'mento *sm* fragment

'frana *sf* landslide; (*fig: persona*): **essere una ~** to be useless

fran'cese [fran'tʃeze] *ag* French ▷ *sm/f* Frenchman/woman ▷ *sm* (*Ling*) French; **i Francesi** the French

'Francia ['frantʃa] *sf* **la ~** France

'franco, -a, -chi, -che *ag* (*Comm*) free; (*sincero*) frank, open, sincere ▷ *sm* (*moneta*) franc; **farla franca** (*fig*) to get off scot-free; **prezzo ~ fabbrica** ex-works price; **franco di dogana** duty-free

franco'bollo *sm* (postage) stamp

'frangia, -ge ['frandʒa] *sf* fringe

frap'pé *sm* milk shake

'frase *sf* (*Ling*) sentence; (*locuzione, espressione, Mus*) phrase; **frase fatta** set phrase

'frassino *sm* ash (tree)

frastagli'ato, -a [frastaʎ'ʎato] *ag* (*costa*) indented, jagged

frastor'nare *vt* to daze; to befuddle

frastu'ono *sm* hubbub, din

'frate *sm* friar, monk

fratel'lastro *sm* stepbrother; (*con genitore in comune*) half-brother

fra'tello *sm* brother; **fratelli** *smpl* brothers; (*nel senso di fratelli e sorelle*) brothers and sisters

fra'terno, -a *ag* fraternal, brotherly

frat'tempo *sm* **nel ~** in the meantime, meanwhile

frat'tura *sf* fracture; (*fig*) split, break

frazi'one [frat'tsjone] *sf* fraction; (*di comune*) small town

'freccia, -ce ['frettʃa] *sf* arrow; **freccia di direzione** (*Aut*) indicator

fred'dezza [fred'dettsa] *sf* coldness

'freddo, -a *ag, sm* cold; **fa ~** it's cold;

aver ~ to be cold; **a ~** (*fig*) deliberately; **freddo'loso, -a** *ag* sensitive to the cold

fre'gare *vt* to rub; (*fam: truffare*) to take in, cheat; (: *rubare*) to swipe, pinch; **fregarsene** (*fam!*): **chi se ne frega?** who gives a damn (about it)?

fregherò *ecc* [frege'rɔ] *vb vedi* **fregare**

fre'nare *vt* (*veicolo*) to slow down; (*cavallo*) to rein in; (*lacrime*) to restrain, hold back ▷ *vi* to brake; **frenarsi** *vpr* (*fig*) to restrain o.s., control o.s.

'freno *sm* brake; (*morso*) bit; **tenere a ~** to restrain; **freno a disco** disc brake; **freno a mano** handbrake

frequen'tare *vt* (*scuola, corso*) to attend; (*locale, bar*) to go to, frequent; (*persone*) to see (often)

frequen'tato, -a *ag* (*locale*) busy

fre'quente *ag* frequent; **di ~** frequently

fres'chezza [fres'kettsa] *sf* freshness

'fresco, -a, -schi, -sche *ag* fresh; (*temperatura*) cool; (*notizia*) recent, fresh ▷ *sm* **godere il ~** to enjoy the cool air; **stare ~** (*fig*) to be in for it; **mettere al ~** to put in a cool place

'fretta *sf* hurry, haste; **in ~** in a hurry; **in ~ e furia** in a mad rush; **aver ~** to be in a hurry

'friggere ['friddʒere] *vt* to fry ▷ *vi* (*olio ecc*) to sizzle

'frigido, -a ['fridʒido] *ag* (*Med*) frigid

'frigo *sm* fridge

frigo'bar *sm inv* minibar

frigo'rifero, -a *ag* refrigerating ▷ *sm* refrigerator

fringu'ello *sm* chaffinch

'frissi *ecc vb vedi* **friggere**

frit'tata *sf* omelette; **fare una ~** (*fig*) to make a mess of things

frit'tella *sf* (*Cuc*) fritter

'fritto, -a *pp di* **friggere** ▷ *ag* fried ▷ *sm* fried food; **fritto misto** mixed fry

frit'tura *sf* (*Cuc*): **frittura di pesce** mixed fried fish

'frivolo, -a *ag* frivolous

frizi'one [frit'tsjone] *sf* friction; (*sulla pelle*) rub, rub-down; (*Aut*) clutch

friz'zante [frid'dzante] *ag* (*anche fig*) sparkling

fro'dare *vt* to defraud, cheat

'frode *sf* fraud; **frode fiscale** tax evasion

'fronda *sf* (leafy) branch; (*di partito politico*) internal opposition; **fronde** *sfpl* (*di albero*) foliage *sg*

fron'tale *ag* frontal; (*scontro*) head-on

'fronte *sf* (*Anat*) forehead; (*di edificio*) front, façade ▷ *sm* (*Mil, Pol, Meteor*) front; **a ~, di ~** facing, opposite; **di ~ a** (*posizione*) opposite, facing, in front of; (*a paragone di*) compared with

fronti'era *sf* border, frontier

'frottola *sf* fib

fru'gare *vi* to rummage ▷ *vt* to search

frugherò *ecc* [fruge'rɔ] *vb vedi* **frugare**

frul'lare *vt* (*Cuc*) to whisk ▷ *vi* (*uccelli*) to flutter; **frul'lato** *sm* milk shake; fruit drink; **frulla'tore** *sm* electric mixer

fru'mento *sm* wheat

fru'scio [fruʃʃio] *sm* rustle; rustling; (*di acque*) murmur

'frusta *sf* whip; (*Cuc*) whisk

frus'tare *vt* to whip

frus'trato, -a *ag* frustrated

'frutta *sf* fruit; (*portata*) dessert; **frutta candita** candied fruit; **frutta secca** dried fruit

frut'tare *vi* to bear dividends, give a return

frut'teto *sm* orchard

frutti'vendolo, -a *sm/f* greengrocer (*BRIT*), produce dealer (*US*)

'frutto *sm* fruit; (*fig: risultato*) result(s); (*Econ: interesse*) interest; (: *reddito*) income; **frutti di bosco** berries; **frutti di mare** seafood *sg*

FS *abbr* = **Ferrovie dello Stato**

fu *vb vedi* **essere** ▷ *ag inv* **il fu Paolo Bianchi** the late Paolo Bianchi

fuci'lare [futʃi'lare] *vt* to shoot

fu'cile [fu'tʃile] *sm* rifle, gun; (*da caccia*) shotgun, gun

'fucsia *sf* fuchsia

'fuga *sf* escape, flight; (*di gas, liquidi*) leak; (*Mus*) fugue; **fuga di cervelli** brain drain

fug'gire [fud'dʒire] *vi* to flee, run away; (*fig: passar veloce*) to fly ▷ *vt* to avoid

'fui *vb vedi* **essere**

fu'liggine [fu'liddʒine] *sf* soot

'fulmine *sm* thunderbolt; lightning *no pl*

fu'mare *vi* to smoke; (*emettere vapore*) to steam ▷ *vt* to smoke; **le dà fastidio se fumo?** do you mind if I smoke?; **fuma'tore, -'trice** *sm/f* smoker

fu'metto *sm* comic strip; **giornale** *sm*, **a fumetti** comic

'fummo *vb vedi* **essere**

'fumo *sm* smoke; (*vapore*) steam; (*il fumare tabacco*) smoking; **fumi** *smpl* (*industriali ecc*) fumes; **i fumi dell'alcool** the after-effects of drink; **vendere ~** to deceive, cheat; **fumo passivo** passive smoking

'fune *sf* rope, cord; (*più grossa*) cable

'funebre *ag* (*rito*) funeral; (*aspetto*) gloomy, funereal

fune'rale *sm* funeral

'fungere ['fundʒere] *vi* **~ da** to act as

'fungo, -ghi *sm* fungus; (*commestibile*) mushroom; **fungo velenoso** toadstool

funico'lare *sf* funicular railway

funi'via *sf* cable railway

'funsi *ecc vb vedi* **fungere**

funzio'nare [funtsjo'nare] *vi* to work, function; (*fungere*): **~ da** to act as; **come funziona?** how does this work?; **la TV non funziona** the TV isn't working

funzio'nario [funtsjo'narjo] *sm* official; **funzionario statale** civil servant

funzi'one [fun'tsjone] *sf* function; (*carica*) post, position; (*Rel*) service; **in ~** (*meccanismo*) in operation; **in ~ di** (*come*) as; **fare la ~ di qn** (*farne le veci*) to take sb's place

fu'oco, -chi *sm* fire; (*fornello*) ring; (*Fot, Fisica*) focus; **dare ~ a qc** to set fire to sth; **far ~** (*sparare*) to fire; **al ~!** fire!; **fuoco d'artificio** firework

fuorché [fwor'ke] *cong, prep* except

fu'ori *av* outside; (*all'aperto*) outdoors, outside; (*fuori di casa, Sport*) out; (*esclamativo*) get out! ▷ *prep* **~ (di)** out of, outside ▷ *sm* outside; **lasciar ~ qc/qn** to leave sth/sb out; **far ~ qn** (*fam*) to kill sb, do sb in; **essere ~ di sé** to be beside o.s.; **~ luogo** (*inopportuno*) out of place, uncalled for; **~ mano** out of the way, remote; **~ pericolo** out of danger; **~ uso** old-fashioned; obsolete; **fuorigi'oco** *sm* offside; **fuori'strada** *sm* (*Aut*) cross-country vehicle

'furbo, -a *ag* clever, smart; (*peg*) cunning

fu'rente *ag* **~ (contro)** furious (with)

fur'fante *sm* rascal, scoundrel

fur'gone *sm* van

'furia *sf* (*ira*) fury, rage; (*fig: impeto*) fury, violence; (*fretta*) rush; **a ~ di** by dint of; **andare su tutte le furie** to get into a towering rage; **furi'bondo, -a** *ag* furious

furi'oso, -a *ag* furious

'furono *vb vedi* **essere**

fur'tivo, -a *ag* furtive

'furto *sm* theft; **vorrei denunciare un ~** I'd like to report a theft; **furto con scasso** burglary

'fusa *sfpl* **fare le ~** to purr

fu'seaux *smpl inv* leggings

'fusi *ecc vb vedi* **fondere**

fu'sibile *sm* (*Elettr*) fuse

fusi'one *sf* (*di metalli*) fusion, melting; (*colata*) casting; (*Comm*) merger; (*fig*) merging

'fuso, -a *pp di* **fondere** ▷ *sm* (*Filatura*) spindle; **fuso orario** time zone

fus'tino *sm* (*di detersivo*) tub

'fusto *sm* stem; (*Anat, di albero*) trunk; (*recipiente*) drum, can

fu'turo, -a *ag, sm* future

g

'gabbia sf cage; (da imballaggio) crate; **gabbia dell'ascensore** lift (BRIT) o elevator (US) shaft; **gabbia toracica** (Anat) rib cage

gabbi'ano sm (sea)gull

gabi'netto sm (Med ecc) consulting room; (Pol) ministry; (WC) toilet, lavatory; (Ins: di fisica ecc) laboratory

'gaffe [gaf] sf inv blunder

ga'lante ag gallant, courteous; (avventura) amorous

ga'lassia sf galaxy

ga'lera sf (Naut) galley; (prigione) prison

'galla sf **a ~** afloat; **venire a ~** to surface, come to the surface; (fig: verità) to come out

galleggi'are [galled'dʒare] vi to float

galle'ria sf (traforo) tunnel; (Archit, d'arte) gallery; (Teatro) circle; (strada coperta con negozi) arcade

'Galles sm **il ~** Wales

gal'lina sf hen

'gallo sm cock

galop'pare vi to gallop

ga'loppo sm gallop; **al** o **di ~** at a gallop

'gamba sf leg; (asta: di lettera) stem; **in ~** (in buona salute) well; (bravo, sveglio) bright, smart; **prendere qc sotto ~** (fig) to treat sth too lightly

gambe'retto sm shrimp

'gambero sm (di acqua dolce) crayfish; (di mare) prawn

'gambo sm stem; (di frutta) stalk

'gamma sf (Mus) scale; (di colori, fig) range

'gancio ['gantʃo] sm hook

'gara sf competition; (Sport) competition; contest; match; (: corsa) race; **fare a ~** to compete, vie

ga'rage [ga'raʒ] sm inv garage

garan'tire vt to guarantee; (debito) to stand surety for; (dare per certo) to assure

garan'zia [garan'tsia] sf guarantee; (pegno) security

gar'bato, -a ag courteous, polite

gareggi'are [gared'dʒare] vi to compete

garga'rismo sm gargle; **fare i gargarismi** to gargle

ga'rofano sm carnation; **chiodo di ~** clove

'garza ['gardza] sf (per bende) gauze

gar'zone [gar'dzone] sm (di negozio) boy

gas sm inv gas; **sento odore di ~** I can smell gas; **a tutto ~** at full speed; **dare ~** (Aut) to accelerate

ga'solio sm diesel (oil)

gas'sato, -a ag fizzy

gast'rite sf gastritis

gastrono'mia sf gastronomy

gat'tino sm kitten

'gatto, -a sm/f cat, tomcat/she-cat; **gatto delle nevi** (Aut, Sci) snowcat; **gatto selvatico** wildcat

'gazza ['gaddza] sf magpie

gel [dʒɛl] sm inv gel

ge'lare [dʒe'lare] vt, vi, vb impers to freeze

gelate'ria [dʒelate'ria] sf ice-cream shop

gela'tina [dʒela'tina] sf gelatine; **gelatina esplosiva** dynamite; **gelatina di frutta** fruit jelly

ge'lato, -a [dʒe'lato] ag frozen ▷ sm ice cream

'gelido, -a ['dʒɛlido] ag icy, ice-cold

'gelo ['dʒɛlo] sm (temperatura) intense cold; (brina) frost; (fig) chill

gelo'sia [dʒelo'sia] sf jealousy

ge'loso, -a [dʒe'loso] ag jealous

'gelso ['dʒɛlso] sm mulberry (tree)

gelso'mino [dʒelso'mino] sm jasmine

ge'mello, -a [dʒe'mɛllo] ag, sm/f twin; **gemelli** smpl (di camicia) cufflinks; (dello zodiaco): **Gemelli** Gemini sg

'gemere ['dʒɛmere] vi to moan, groan; (cigolare) to creak

'gemma ['dʒɛmma] sf (Bot) bud; (pietra preziosa) gem

gene'rale [dʒene'rale] ag, sm general; **in ~** (per sommi capi) in general terms; (di solito) usually, in general

gene'rare [dʒene'rare] vt (dar vita) to give birth to; (produrre) to produce; (causare) to arouse; (*Tecn*) to produce, generate; **generazi'one** *sf* generation

'genere ['dʒɛnere] *sm* kind, type, sort; (*Biol*) genus; (*merce*) article, product; (*Ling*) gender; (*Arte, Letteratura*) genre; **in ~** generally, as a rule; **genere umano** mankind; **generi alimentari** foodstuffs

ge'nerico, -a, -ci, -che [dʒe'nɛriko] *ag* generic; (*vago*) vague, imprecise

'genero ['dʒɛnero] *sm* son-in-law

gene'roso, -a [dʒene'roso] *ag* generous

ge'netica [dʒe'nɛtika] *sf* genetics *sg*

ge'netico, -a, -ci, -che [dʒe'nɛtiko] *ag* genetic

gen'giva [dʒen'dʒiva] *sf* (*Anat*) gum

geni'ale [dʒen'jale] *ag* (*persona*) of genius; (*idea*) ingenious, brilliant

'genio ['dʒɛnjo] *sm* genius; **andare a ~ a qn** to be to sb's liking, appeal to sb

geni'tore [dʒeni'tore] *sm* parent, father *o* mother; **i miei genitori** my parents, my father and mother

gen'naio [dʒen'najo] *sm* January

'Genova ['dʒɛnova] *sf* Genoa

'gente ['dʒɛnte] *sf* people *pl*

gen'tile [dʒen'tile] *ag* (*persona, atto*) kind; (: *garbato*) courteous, polite; (*nelle lettere*): **G~ Signore** Dear Sir; (: *sulla busta*): **G~ Signor Fernando Villa** Mr Fernando Villa

genu'ino, -a [dʒenu'ino] *ag* (*prodotto*) natural; (*persona, sentimento*) genuine, sincere

geogra'fia [dʒeogra'fia] *sf* geography

geolo'gia [dʒeolo'dʒia] *sf* geology

ge'ometra, -i, -e [dʒe'ɔmetra] *sm/f* (*professionista*) surveyor

geome'tria [dʒeome'tria] *sf* geometry

ge'ranio [dʒe'ranjo] *sm* geranium

gerar'chia [dʒerar'kia] *sf* hierarchy

'gergo, -ghi ['dʒɛrgo] *sm* jargon; slang

geria'tria [dʒerja'tria] *sf* geriatrics *sg*

Ger'mania [dʒer'manja] *sf* **la ~** Germany; **la ~ occidentale/orientale** West/East Germany

'germe ['dʒɛrme] *sm* germ; (*fig*) seed

germogli'are [dʒermoʎ'ʎare] *vi* to sprout; to germinate

gero'glifico, -ci [dʒero'glifiko] *sm* hieroglyphic

ge'rundio [dʒe'rundjo] *sm* gerund

'gesso ['dʒɛsso] *sm* chalk; (*Scultura, Med, Edil*) plaster; (*statua*) plaster figure; (*minerale*) gypsum

gesti'one [dʒes'tjone] *sf* management

ges'tire [dʒes'tire] *vt* to run, manage

'gesto ['dʒɛsto] *sm* gesture

Gesù [dʒe'zu] *sm* Jesus

gesu'ita, -i [dʒezu'ita] *sm* Jesuit

get'tare [dʒet'tare] *vt* to throw; (*anche:* **~ via**) to throw away *o* out; (*Scultura*) to cast; (*Edil*) to lay; (*acqua*) to spout; (*grido*) to utter; **gettarsi** *vpr* **gettarsi in** (*fiume*) to flow into; **~ uno sguardo su** to take a quick look at

'getto ['dʒɛtto] *sm* (*di gas, liquido, Aer*) jet; **a ~ continuo** uninterruptedly; **di ~** (*fig*) straight off, in one go

get'tone [dʒet'tone] *sm* token; (*per giochi*) counter; (: *roulette ecc*) chip; **gettone telefonico** telephone token

ghiacci'aio [gjat'tʃajo] *sm* glacier

ghiacci'ato, -a *ag* frozen; (*bevanda*) ice-cold

ghi'accio ['gjattʃo] *sm* ice

ghiacci'olo [gjat'tʃolo] *sm* icicle; (*tipo di gelato*) ice lolly (BRIT), Popsicle® (US)

ghi'aia ['gjaja] *sf* gravel

ghi'anda ['gjanda] *sf* (*Bot*) acorn

ghi'andola ['gjandola] *sf* gland

ghi'otto, -a ['gjotto] *ag* greedy; (*cibo*) delicious, appetizing

ghir'landa [gir'landa] *sf* garland, wreath

'ghiro ['giro] *sm* dormouse

'ghisa ['giza] *sf* cast iron

già [dʒa] *av* already; (*ex, in precedenza*) formerly ▷ *escl* of course!, yes indeed!

gi'acca, -che ['dʒakka] *sf* jacket; **giacca a vento** windcheater (BRIT), windbreaker (US)

giacché [dʒak'ke] *cong* since, as

giac'cone [dʒak'kone] *sm* heavy jacket

gi'ada ['dʒada] *sf* jade

giagu'aro [dʒa'gwaro] *sm* jaguar

gi'allo ['dʒallo] *ag* yellow; (*carnagione*) sallow ▷ *sm* yellow; (*anche:* **romanzo ~**) detective novel; (*anche:* **film ~**) detective film; **giallo dell'uovo** yolk

Giamaica [dʒa'maika] *sf* **la ~** Jamaica

Giap'pone [dʒap'pone] *sm* Japan; **giappo'nese** *ag, sm/f, sm* Japanese *inv*

giardi'naggio [dʒardi'naddʒo] *sm* gardening

giardini'ere, -a [dʒardi'njɛre] *sm/f* gardener

giar'dino [dʒar'dino] *sm* garden; **giardino d'infanzia** nursery school; **giardino pubblico** public gardens *pl*, (public) park; **giardino zoologico** zoo

giavel'lotto [dʒavel'lɔtto] *sm* javelin

gigabyte [dʒiga'bait] *sm inv* gigabyte

gi'gante, -'essa [dʒi'gante] *sm/f* giant ▷ *ag* giant, gigantic; (*Comm*) giant-size

'giglio ['dʒiʎʎo] *sm* lily

gilè [dʒi'lɛ] *sm inv* waistcoat

gin [dʒin] *sm inv* gin

gine'cologo, -a, -gi, -ghe [dʒine'kɔlogo] *sm/f* gynaecologist

gi'nepro [dʒi'nepro] *sm* juniper

gi'nestra [dʒi'nɛstra] *sf* (*Bot*) broom
Gi'nevra [dʒi'nevra] *sf* Geneva
gin'nastica *sf* gymnastics *sg*; (*esercizio fisico*) keep-fit exercises; (*Ins*) physical education
gi'nocchio [dʒi'nɔkkjo] (*pl(m)* **gi'nocchi**, *o pl(f)* **gi'nocchia**) *sm* knee; **stare in ~** to kneel, be on one's knees; **mettersi in ~** to kneel (down)
gio'care [dʒo'kare] *vt* to play; (*scommettere*) to stake, wager, bet; (*ingannare*) to take in ▷ *vi* to play; (*a roulette ecc*) to gamble; (*fig*) to play a part, be important; **~ a** (*gioco, sport*) to play; (*cavalli*) to bet on; **giocarsi la carriera** to put one's career at risk; **gioca'tore, -'trice** *sm/f* player; gambler
gio'cattolo [dʒo'kattolo] *sm* toy
giocherò ecc [dʒoke'rɔ] *vb vedi* **giocare**
gi'oco, -chi ['dʒɔko] *sm* game; (*divertimento, Tecn*) play; (*al casinò*) gambling; (*Carte*) hand; (*insieme di pezzi ecc necessari per un gioco*) set; **per ~** for fun; **fare il doppio ~ con qn** to double-cross sb; **i Giochi Olimpici** the Olympic Games; **gioco d'azzardo** game of chance; **gioco degli scacchi** chess set
giocoli'ere [dʒoko'ljɛre] *sm* juggler
gi'oia ['dʒɔja] *sf* joy, delight; (*pietra preziosa*) jewel, precious stone
gioielle'ria [dʒojelle'ria] *sf* jeweller's craft; jeweller's (shop)
gioielli'ere, -a [dʒojel'ljɛre] *sm/f* jeweller
gioi'ello [dʒo'jɛllo] *sm* jewel, piece of jewellery; **i miei gioielli** my jewels *o* jewellery; **gioielli** *smpl* (*anelli, collane ecc*) jewellery; **i gioielli della Corona** the crown jewels
Gior'dania [dʒor'danja] *sf* **la ~** Jordan
giorna'laio, -a [dʒorna'lajo] *sm/f* newsagent (*BRIT*), newsdealer (*US*)
gior'nale [dʒor'nale] *sm* (news)paper; (*diario*) journal, diary; (*Comm*) journal; **giornale di bordo** log; **giornale radio** radio news *sg*
giornali'ero, -a [dʒorna'ljɛro] *ag* daily; (*che varia: umore*) changeable ▷ *sm* day labourer
giorna'lismo [dʒorna'lizmo] *sm* journalism
giorna'lista, -i, -e [dʒorna'lista] *sm/f* journalist
gior'nata [dʒor'nata] *sf* day; **giornata lavorativa** working day
gi'orno ['dʒorno] *sm* day; (*opposto alla notte*) day, daytime; (*anche: **luce del ~***) daylight; **al ~** per day; **di ~** by day; **al ~ d'oggi** nowadays
gi'ostra ['dʒɔstra] *sf* (*per bimbi*) merry-go-round; (*torneo storico*) joust

gi'ovane ['dʒovane] *ag* young; (*aspetto*) youthful ▷ *sm/f* youth/girl, young man/woman; **i giovani** young people
gio'vare [dʒo'vare] *vi* **~ a** (*essere utile*) to be useful to; (*far bene*) to be good for ▷ *vb impers* (*essere bene, utile*) to be useful; **giovarsi di qc** to make use of sth
giovedì [dʒove'di] *sm inv* Thursday; **di** *o* **il ~** on Thursdays
gioventù [dʒoven'tu] *sf* (*periodo*) youth; (*i giovani*) young people *pl*, youth
G.I.P. [dʒip] *sigla m inv* (= Giudice per le Indagini Preliminari) judge for preliminary enquiries
gira'dischi [dʒira'diski] *sm inv* record player
gi'raffa [dʒi'raffa] *sf* giraffe
gi'rare [dʒi'rare] *vt* (*far ruotare*) to turn; (*percorrere, visitare*) to go round; (*Cinema*) to shoot; to make; (*Comm*) to endorse ▷ *vi* to turn; (*più veloce*) to spin; (*andare in giro*) to wander, go around; **girarsi** *vpr* to turn; **~ attorno a** to go round; to revolve round; **al prossimo incrocio giri a destra/sinistra** turn right/left at the next junction; **far ~ la testa a qn** to make sb dizzy; (*fig*) to turn sb's head
girar'rosto [dʒirar'rɔsto] *sm* (*Cuc*) spit
gira'sole [dʒira'sole] *sm* sunflower
gi'revole [dʒi'revole] *ag* revolving, turning
gi'rino [dʒi'rino] *sm* tadpole
'giro ['dʒiro] *sm* (*circuito, cerchio*) circle; (*di chiave, manovella*) turn; (*viaggio*) tour, excursion; (*passeggiata*) stroll, walk; (*in macchina*) drive; (*in bicicletta*) ride; (*Sport: della pista*) lap; (*di denaro*) circulation; (*Carte*) hand; (*Tecn*) revolution; **prendere in ~ qn** (*fig*) to pull sb's leg; **fare un ~** to go for a walk (*o* a drive *o* a ride); **andare in ~** to go about, walk around; **a stretto ~ di posta** by return of post; **nel ~ di un mese** in a month's time; **essere nel ~** (*fig*) to belong to a circle (of friends); **giro d'affari** (*Comm*) turnover; **giro di parole** circumlocution; **giro di prova** (*Aut*) test drive; **giro turistico** sightseeing tour; **giro collo** *sm* **a girocollo** crew-neck *cpd*
gironzo'lare [dʒirondzo'lare] *vi* to stroll about
'gita ['dʒita] *sf* excursion, trip; **fare una ~** to go for a trip, go on an outing
gi'tano, -a [dʒi'tano] *sm/f* gipsy
giù [dʒu] *av* down; (*dabbasso*) downstairs; **in ~** downwards, down; **~ di lì** (*pressappoco*) thereabouts; **bambini dai 6 anni in ~** children aged 6 and under; **~ per, cadere ~ per le scale** to fall down the stairs; **essere ~** (*fig: di salute*) to be run down; (: *di spirito*)

to be depressed

giub'botto [dʒub'bɔtto] *sm* jerkin; **giubbotto antiproiettile** bulletproof vest; **giubbotto salvagente** life jacket

giudi'care [dʒudi'kare] *vt* to judge; *(accusato)* to try; *(lite)* to arbitrate in; **~ qn/qc bello** to consider sb/sth (to be) beautiful

gi'udice ['dʒuditʃe] *sm* judge; **giudice conciliatore** justice of the peace; **giudice istruttore** examining (*BRIT*) *o* committing (*US*) magistrate; **giudice popolare** member of a jury

giu'dizio [dʒu'dittsjo] *sm* judgment; *(opinione)* opinion; *(Dir)* judgment, sentence; *(: processo)* trial; *(: verdetto)* verdict; **aver ~** to be wise *o* prudent; **citare in ~** to summons

gi'ugno ['dʒuɲɲo] *sm* June

gi'ungere ['dʒundʒere] *vi* to arrive ▷ *vt* *(mani ecc)* to join; **~ a** to arrive at, reach

gi'ungla ['dʒungla] *sf* jungle

gi'unsi *ecc* ['dʒunsi] *vb vedi* **giungere**

giura'mento [dʒura'mento] *sm* oath; **giuramento falso** perjury

giu'rare [dʒu'rare] *vt* to swear ▷ *vi* to swear, take an oath

giu'ria [dʒu'ria] *sf* jury

giu'ridico, -a, -ci, -che [dʒu'ridiko] *ag* legal

giustifi'care [dʒustifi'kare] *vt* to justify; **giustificazi'one** *sf* justification; *(Ins)* (note of) excuse

gius'tizia [dʒus'tittsja] *sf* justice; **giustizi'are** *vt* to execute, put to death

gi'usto, -a ['dʒusto] *ag* *(equo)* fair, just; *(vero)* true, correct; *(adatto)* right, suitable; *(preciso)* exact, correct ▷ *av* *(esattamente)* exactly, precisely; *(per l'appunto, appena)* just; **arrivare ~** to arrive just in time; **ho ~ bisogno di te** you're just the person I need

glaci'ale [gla'tʃale] *ag* glacial

gli [ʎi] *(davV, s impura, gn, pn, ps, x, z)* *det mpl* the ▷ *pron* *(a lui)* to him; *(a esso)* to it; *(in coppia con lo, la, li, le, ne: a lui, a lei, a loro ecc)*: **~ele do** I'm giving them to him (*o* her *o* them); *vedi anche* **il**

glo'bale *ag* overall

'globo *sm* globe

'globulo *sm* *(Anat)*: **globulo rosso/bianco** red/white corpuscle

'gloria *sf* glory

'gnocchi ['ɲɔkki] *smpl* *(Cuc)* small dumplings made of semolina pasta or potato

'gobba *sf* *(Anat)* hump; *(protuberanza)* bump

'gobbo, -a *ag* hunchbacked; *(ricurvo)* round-shouldered ▷ *sm/f* hunchback

'goccia, -ce ['gottʃa] *sf* drop; **goccio'lare**

vi, vt to drip

go'dere *vi* *(compiacersi)*: **~ (di)** to be delighted (at), rejoice (at); *(trarre vantaggio)*: **~ di** benefit from ▷ *vt* to enjoy; **godersi la vita** to enjoy life; **godersela** to have a good time, enjoy o.s.

godrò *ecc vb vedi* **godere**

'goffo, -a *ag* clumsy, awkward

'gola *sf* *(Anat)* throat; *(golosità)* gluttony, greed; *(di camino)* flue; *(di monte)* gorge; **fare ~** *(anche fig)* to tempt

golf *sm inv* *(Sport)* golf; *(maglia)* cardigan

'golfo *sm* gulf

go'loso, -a *ag* greedy

gomi'tata *sf* **dare una ~ a qn** to elbow sb; **farsi avanti a (forza** *o* **furia di) gomitate** to elbow one's way through; **fare a gomitate per qc** to fight to get sth

'gomito *sm* elbow; *(di strada ecc)* sharp bend

go'mitolo *sm* ball

'gomma *sf* rubber; *(per cancellare)* rubber, eraser; *(di veicolo)* tyre (*BRIT*), tire (*US*); **gomma americana** *o* **da masticare** chewing gum; **gomma a terra** flat tyre (*BRIT*) *o* tire (*US*); **ho una ~ a terra** I've got a flat tyre; **gom'mone** *sm* rubber dinghy

gonfi'are *vt* *(pallone)* to blow up, inflate; *(dilatare, ingrossare)* to swell; *(fig: notizia)* to exaggerate; **gonfiarsi** *vpr* to swell; *(fiume)* to rise; **'gonfio, -a** *ag* swollen; *(stomaco)* bloated; *(vela)* full; **gonfi'ore** *sm* swelling

'gonna *sf* skirt; **gonna pantalone** culottes *pl*

'gorgo, -ghi *sm* whirlpool

gorgogli'are [gorgoʎ'ʎare] *vi* to gurgle

go'rilla *sm inv* gorilla; *(guardia del corpo)* bodyguard

'gotico, -a, ci, che *ag, sm* Gothic

'gotta *sf* gout

gover'nare *vt* *(stato)* to govern, rule; *(pilotare, guidare)* to steer; *(bestiame)* to tend, look after

go'verno *sm* government

GPL *sigla m* (= *Gas di Petrolio Liquefatto*) LPG

GPS *sigla m* (= *Global Positioning System*) GPS

graci'dare [gratʃi'dare] *vi* to croak

'gracile ['gratʃile] *ag* frail, delicate

gradazi'one [gradat'tsjone] *sf* *(sfumatura)* gradation; **gradazione alcolica** alcoholic content, strength

gra'devole *ag* pleasant, agreeable

gradi'nata *sf* flight of steps; *(in teatro, stadio)* tiers *pl*

gra'dino *sm* step; *(Alpinismo)* foothold

gra'dire *vt* *(accettare con piacere)* to accept; *(desiderare)* to wish, like; **gradisce una tazza di tè?** would you like a cup of tea?

'grado *sm* *(Mat, Fisica ecc)* degree; *(stadio)*

degree, level; (Mil, sociale) rank; **essere in ~ di fare** to be in a position to do

gradu'ale ag gradual

graf'fetta sf paper clip

graffi'are vt to scratch; **graffiarsi** vpr to get scratched; (con unghie) to scratch o.s.

'graffio sm scratch

gra'fia sf spelling; (scrittura) handwriting

'grafico, -a, -ci, -che ag graphic ▷ sm graph; (persona) graphic designer

gram'matica, -che sf grammar

'grammo sm gram(me)

'grana sf (granello, di minerali, corpi spezzati) grain; (fam: seccatura) trouble; (: soldi) cash ▷ sm inv Parmesan (cheese)

gra'naio sm granary, barn

gra'nata sf (proiettile) grenade

Gran Bre'tagna [-bre'taɲɲa] sf **la ~** Great Britain

'granchio ['grankjo] sm crab; (fig) blunder; **prendere un ~** (fig) to blunder

'grande (qualche volta **gran** + C, **grand'** + V) ag (grosso, largo, vasto) big, large; (alto) tall; (lungo) long; (in sensi astratti) great ▷ sm/f (persona adulta) adult, grown-up; (chi ha ingegno e potenza) great man/woman; **fare le cose in ~** to do things in style; **una gran bella donna** a very beautiful woman; **non è una gran cosa** o **un gran che** it's nothing special; **non ne so gran che** I don't know very much about it

gran'dezza [gran'dettsa] sf (dimensione) size; magnitude; (fig) greatness; **in ~ naturale** life-size(d)

grandi'nare vb impers to hail

'grandine sf hail

gra'nello sm (di cereali, uva) seed; (di frutta) pip; (di sabbia, sale ecc) grain

gra'nito sm granite

'grano sm (in quasi tutti i sensi) grain; (frumento) wheat; (di rosario, collana) bead; **grano di pepe** peppercorn

gran'turco sm maize

'grappa sf rough, strong brandy

'grappolo sm bunch, cluster

gras'setto sm (Tip) bold (type)

'grasso, -a ag fat; (cibo) fatty; (pelle) greasy; (terreno) rich; (fig: guadagno, annata) plentiful ▷ sm (di persona, animale) fat; (sostanza che unge) grease

'grata sf grating

gra'ticola sf grill

'gratis av free, for nothing

grati'tudine sf gratitude

'grato, -a ag grateful; (gradito) pleasant, agreeable

gratta'capo sm worry, headache

grattaci'elo [gratta'tʃɛlo] sm skyscraper

gratta e vinci ['gratta e 'vintʃi] sm inv (biglietto) scratchcard; (lotteria) scratchcard lottery

grat'tare vt (pelle) to scratch; (raschiare) to scrape; (pane, formaggio, carote) to grate; (fam: rubare) to pinch ▷ vi (stridere) to grate; (Aut) to grind; **grattarsi** vpr to scratch o.s.; **grattarsi la pancia** (fig) to twiddle one's thumbs

grat'tugia, -gie [grat'tudʒa] sf grater; **grattugi'are** vt to grate; **pane grattugiato** breadcrumbs pl

gra'tuito, -a ag free; (fig) gratuitous

'grave ag (danno, pericolo, peccato ecc) grave, serious; (responsabilità) heavy, grave; (contegno) grave, solemn; (voce, suono) deep, low-pitched; (Ling): **accento ~** grave accent; **un malato ~** a person who is seriously ill

grave'mente av (ammalato, ferito) seriously

gravi'danza [gravi'dantsa] sf pregnancy

gravità sf seriousness; (anche Fisica) gravity

gra'voso, -a ag heavy, onerous

'grazia ['grattsja] sf grace; (favore) favour; (Dir) pardon

'grazie ['grattsje] escl thank you!; **~ mille!** o **tante!** o **infinite!** thank you very much!; **~ a** thanks to

grazi'oso, -a [grat'tsjoso] ag charming, delightful; (gentile) gracious

'Grecia ['grɛtʃa] sf **la ~** Greece; **'greco, -a, -ci, -che** ag, sm/f, sm Greek

'gregge ['greddʒe] (pl(f) **-i**) sm flock

grembi'ule sm apron; (sopravveste) overall

'grembo sm lap; (ventre della madre) womb

'grezzo, -a ['greddzo] ag raw, unrefined; (diamante) rough, uncut; (tessuto) unbleached

gri'dare vi (per chiamare) to shout, cry (out); (strillare) to scream, yell ▷ vt to shout (out), yell (out); **~ aiuto** to cry o shout for help

'grido (pl(m) **-i**, o pl(f) **-a**) sm shout, cry; scream, yell; (di animale) cry; **di ~** famous

'grigio, -a, -gi, -gie ['gridʒo] ag, sm grey

'griglia ['griʎʎa] sf (per arrostire) grill; (Elettr) grid; (inferriata) grating; **alla ~** (Cuc) grilled

gril'letto sm trigger

'grillo sm (Zool) cricket; (fig) whim

'grinta sf grim expression; (Sport) fighting spirit

gris'sino sm bread-stick

Groen'landia sf **la ~** Greenland

gron'daia sf gutter

gron'dare vi to pour; (essere bagnato): **~ di** to be dripping with ▷ vt to drip with

'groppa sf (di animale) back, rump; (fam:

dell'uomo) back, shoulders *pl*

gros'sezza [gros'settsa] *sf* size; thickness

gros'sista, -i, -e *sm/f (Comm)* wholesaler

'grosso, -a *ag* big, large; (*di spessore*) thick; (*grossolano: anche fig*) coarse; (*grave, insopportabile*) serious, great; (*tempo, mare*) rough ▷ *sm* **il ~ di** the bulk of; **un pezzo ~** (*fig*) a VIP, a bigwig; **farla grossa** to do something very stupid; **dirle grosse** to tell tall stories; **sbagliarsi di ~** to be completely wrong

'grotta *sf* cave; grotto

grot'tesco, -a, -schi, -sche *ag* grotesque

gro'viglio [gro'viʎʎo] *sm* tangle; (*fig*) muddle

gru *sf inv* crane

'gruccia, -ce ['gruttʃa] *sf* (*per camminare*) crutch; (*per abiti*) coat-hanger

'grumo *sm* (*di sangue*) clot; (*di farina ecc*) lump

'gruppo *sm* group; **gruppo sanguigno** blood group

GSM *sigla m* (= *Global System for Mobile Communication*) GSM

guada'gnare [gwadaɲ'ɲare] *vt* (*ottenere*) to gain; (*soldi, stipendio*) to earn; (*vincere*) to win; (*raggiungere*) to reach

gua'dagno [gwa'daɲɲo] *sm* earnings *pl*; (*Comm*) profit; (*vantaggio, utile*) advantage, gain; **guadagno lordo/netto** gross/net earnings *pl*

gu'ado *sm* ford; **passare a ~** to ford

gu'ai *escl* **~ a te** (*o lui ecc*)! woe betide you (*o him ecc*)!

gu'aio *sm* trouble, mishap; (*inconveniente*) trouble, snag

gua'ire *vi* to whine, yelp

gu'ancia, -ce ['gwantʃa] *sf* cheek

guanci'ale [gwan'tʃale] *sm* pillow

gu'anto *sm* glove

guarda'linee *sm inv* (*Sport*) linesman

guar'dare *vt* (*con lo sguardo: osservare*) to look at; (*film, televisione*) to watch; (*custodire*) to look after, take care of ▷ *vi* to look; (*badare*): **~ a** to pay attention to; (*luoghi: esser orientato*): **~ a** to face; **guardarsi** *vpr* to look at o.s.; **guardarsi da** (*astenersi*) to refrain from; (*stare in guardia*) to beware of; **guardarsi dal fare** to take care not to do; **guarda di non sbagliare** try not to make a mistake; **~ a vista qn** to keep a close watch on sb

guarda'roba *sm inv* wardrobe; (*locale*) cloakroom

gu'ardia *sf* (*individuo, corpo*) guard; (*sorveglianza*) watch; **fare la ~ a qc/qn** to guard sth/sb; **stare in ~** (*fig*) to be on one's guard; **di ~** (*medico*) on call; **guardia carceraria** (prison) warder; **guardia del**

corpo bodyguard; **Guardia di finanza** (*corpo*) customs *pl*; (*persona*) customs officer; **guardia medica** emergency doctor service

● **GUARDIA DI FINANZA**
●
● The **Guardia di Finanza** is a military
● body which deals with infringements
● of the laws governing income tax and
● monopolies. It reports to the Ministers
● of Finance, Justice or Agriculture,
● depending on the function it is
● performing.

guardi'ano, -a *sm/f* (*di carcere*) warder; (*di villa ecc*) caretaker; (*di museo*) custodian; (*di zoo*) keeper; **guardiano notturno** night watchman

guarigi'one [gwari'dʒone] *sf* recovery

gua'rire *vt* (*persona, malattia*) to cure; (*ferita*) to heal ▷ *vi* to recover, be cured; to heal (up)

guar'nire *vt* (*ornare: abiti*) to trim; (*Cuc*) to garnish

guasta'feste *sm/f inv* spoilsport

guastarsi *vpr* (*cibo*) to go bad; (*meccanismo*) to break down; (*tempo*) to change for the worse

gu'asto, -a *ag* (*non funzionante*) broken; (: *telefono ecc*) out of order; (*andato a male*) bad, rotten; (: *dente*) decayed, bad; (*fig: corrotto*) depraved ▷ *sm* breakdown; (*avaria*) failure; **guasto al motore** engine failure

gu'erra *sf* war; (*tecnica: atomica, chimica ecc*) warfare; **fare la ~ (a)** to wage war (against); **guerra mondiale** world war; **guerra preventiva** preventive war

'gufo *sm* owl

gu'ida *sf* (*libro*) guidebook; (*persona*) guide; (*comando, direzione*) guidance, direction; (*Aut*) driving; (*tappeto: di tenda, cassetto*) runner; **avete una ~ in italiano?** do you have a guidebook in Italian?; **c'è una ~ che parla italiano?** is there an Italian-speaking guide?; **guida a destra/a sinistra** (*Aut*) right-/left-hand drive; **guida telefonica** telephone directory; **guida turistica** tourist guide

gui'dare *vt* to guide; (*squadra, rivolta*) to lead; (*auto*) to drive; (*aereo, nave*) to pilot; **sai ~?** can you drive?; **guida'tore, -trice** *sm/f* (*conducente*) driver

guin'zaglio [gwin'tsaʎʎo] *sm* leash, lead

'guscio ['guʃʃo] *sm* shell

gus'tare *vt* (*cibi*) to taste; (: *assaporare con piacere*) to enjoy, savour; (*fig*) to enjoy, appreciate ▷ *vi* **~ a** to please; **non mi**

gusta affatto I don't like it at all
'gusto sm taste; (*sapore*) flavour;
(*godimento*) enjoyment; **che gusti avete?**
which flavours do you have?; **al ~ di
fragola** strawberry-flavoured; **mangiare
di ~** to eat heartily; **prenderci ~: ci ha
preso ~** he's acquired a taste for it, he's
got to like it; **gus'toso, -a** ag tasty; (*fig*)
agreeable

H, h ['akka] sf o m inv (*lettera*) H, h ▷ abbr
(= *ora*) hr; (= *etto, altezza*) h; **H come hotel**
≈ H for Harry (*BRIT*), H for How (*US*)
ha, 'hai [a, ai] vb vedi **avere**
ha'cker [hæ'kəʳ] sm inv hacker
hall [hɔl] sf inv hall, foyer
hamburger [am'burger] sm inv (*carne*)
hamburger; (*panino*) burger
'handicap ['handikap] sm inv handicap;
handicap'pato, -a ag handicapped ▷ sm/
f handicapped person, disabled person
'hanno ['anno] vb vedi **avere**
hard discount [ardi'kaunt] sm inv
discount supermarket
hard disk [ar'disk] sm inv hard disk
hardware ['ardwer] sm inv hardware
hascisch [aʃʃiʃ] sm hashish
Hawaii [a'vai] sfpl **le ~** Hawaii sg
help [ɛlp] sm inv (*Inform*) help
'herpes ['ɛrpes] sm (*Med*) herpes sg; **herpes
zoster** shingles sg
'hi-fi ['haifai] sm inv, ag inv hi-fi
ho [ɔ] vb vedi **avere**
'hobby ['hɔbi] sm inv hobby
'hockey ['hɔki] sm hockey; **hockey su
ghiaccio** ice hockey
home page ['houm'pɛidʒ] sf inv home
page
Hong Kong ['ɔkɔg] sf Hong Kong
'hostess ['houstis] sf inv air hostess (*BRIT*)

o stewardess
hot dog ['hɔtdɔg] *sm inv* hot dog
ho'tel *sm inv* hotel
humour ['hjuːmə] *sm inv* (sense of)
humour
'humus *sm* humus
husky ['aski] *sm inv* (*cane*) husky *m inv*

i *det mpl* the
IC *abbr* (= *Intercity*) Intercity
ICI ['itʃi] *sigla f* (= *Imposta Comunale sugli
Immobili*) ≈ Council Tax
i'cona *sf* (*Rel, Inform, fig*) icon
i'dea *sf* idea; (*opinione*) opinion, view;
(*ideale*) ideal; **dare l'~ di** to seem, look like;
neanche *o* **neppure per ~!** certainly not!;
idea fissa obsession
ide'ale *ag, sm* ideal
ide'are *vt* (*immaginare*) to think up,
conceive; (*progettare*) to plan
i'dentico, -a, -ci, -che *ag* identical
identifi'care *vt* to identify; **identificarsi**
vpr **identificarsi (con)** to identify o.s.
(with)
identità *sf inv* identity
ideolo'gia, -'gie [ideolo'dʒia] *sf* ideology
idio'matico, -a, -ci, -che *ag* idiomatic;
frase idiomatica idiom
idi'ota, -i, -e *ag* idiotic ▷ *sm/f* idiot
'idolo *sm* idol
idoneità *sf* suitability
i'doneo, -a *ag* **~ a** suitable for, fit for; (*Mil*)
fit for; (*qualificato*) qualified for
i'drante *sm* hydrant
idra'tante *ag* moisturizing ▷ *sm*
moisturizer
i'draulico, -a, -ci, -che *ag* hydraulic ▷ *sm*
plumber

idroe'lettrico, -a, -ci, -che *ag* hydroelectric

i'drofilo, -a *ag vedi* **cotone**

i'drogeno [i'drɔdʒeno] *sm* hydrogen

idrovo'lante *sm* seaplane

i'ena *sf* hyena

i'eri *av, sm* yesterday; **il giornale di ~** yesterday's paper; **~ l'altro** the day before yesterday; **~ sera** yesterday evening

igi'ene [i'dʒɛne] *sf* hygiene; **igiene pubblica** public health; **igi'enico, -a, -ci, -he** *ag* hygienic; (*salubre*) healthy

i'gnaro, -a [iɲ'ɲaro] *ag* **~ di** unaware of, ignorant of

i'gnobile [iɲ'ɲɔbile] *ag* despicable, vile

igno'rante [iɲɲo'rante] *ag* ignorant

igno'rare [iɲɲo'rare] *vt* (*non sapere, conoscere*) to be ignorant o unaware of, not to know; (*fingere di non vedere, sentire*) to ignore

i'gnoto, -a [iɲ'ɲɔto] *ag* unknown

 PAROLA CHIAVE

il (*pl(m)* **i**; *diventa* **lo** (*pl* **gli**) *davanti a s impura, gn, pn, ps, x, z; f* **la** (*pl* **le**)) *det m* **1** the; **il libro/lo studente/l'acqua** the book/the student/the water; **gli scolari** the pupils
2 (*astrazione*): **il coraggio/l'amore/la giovinezza** courage/love/youth
3 (*tempo*): **il mattino/la sera** in the morning/evening; **il venerdì** *ecc* (*abitualmente*) on Fridays *ecc*; (*quel giorno*) on (the) Friday *ecc*; **la settimana prossima** next week
4 (*distributivo*) a, an; **2 euro il chilo/paio** 2 euros a o per kilo/pair
5 (*partitivo*) some, any; **hai messo lo zucchero?** have you added sugar?; **hai comprato il latte?** did you buy (some o any) milk?
6 (*possesso*): **aprire gli occhi** to open one's eyes; **rompersi la gamba** to break one's leg; **avere i capelli neri/il naso rosso** to have dark hair/a red nose
7 (*con nomi propri*): **il Petrarca** Petrarch; **il Presidente Bush** President Bush; **dov'è la Francesca?** where's Francesca?
8 (*con nomi geografici*): **il Tevere** the Tiber; **l'Italia** Italy; **il Regno Unito** the United Kingdom; **l'Everest** Everest

ille'gale *ag* illegal

illeg'gibile [illed'dʒibile] *ag* illegible

ille'gittimo, -a [ille'dʒittimo] *ag* illegitimate

il'leso, -a *ag* unhurt, unharmed

illimi'tato, -a *ag* boundless; unlimited

ill.mo *abbr* = **illustrissimo**

il'ludere *vt* to deceive, delude; **illudersi** *vpr* to deceive o.s., delude o.s.

illumi'nare *vt* to light up, illuminate; (*fig*) to enlighten; **illuminarsi** *vpr* to light up; **~ a giorno** to floodlight; **illuminazi'one** *sf* lighting; illumination; floodlighting; (*fig*) flash of inspiration

il'lusi *ecc vb vedi* **illudere**

illusi'one *sf* illusion; **farsi delle illusioni** to delude o.s.; **illusione ottica** optical illusion

il'luso, -a *pp di* **illudere**

illus'trare *vt* to illustrate; **illustrazi'one** *sf* illustration

il'lustre *ag* eminent, renowned; **illus'trissimo, -a** *ag* (*negli indirizzi*) very revered

imbal'laggio [imbal'laddʒo] *sm* packing *no pl*

imbal'lare *vt* to pack; (*Aut*) to race

imbalsa'mare *vt* to embalm

imbambo'lato, -a *ag* (*sguardo*) vacant, blank

imbaraz'zante [imbarat'tsante] *ag* embarrassing, awkward

imbaraz'zare [imbarat'tsare] *vt* (*mettere a disagio*) to embarrass; (*ostacolare movimenti*) to hamper

imbaraz'zato, -a [imbarat'tsato] *ag* embarrassed; **avere lo stomaco ~** to have an upset stomach

imba'razzo [imba'rattso] *sm* (*disagio*) embarrassment; (*perplessità*) puzzlement, bewilderment; **imbarazzo di stomaco** indigestion

imbar'care *vt* (*passeggeri*) to embark; (*merci*) to load; **imbarcarsi** *vpr* **imbarcarsi su** to board; **imbarcarsi per l'America** to sail for America; **imbarcarsi in** (*fig: affare ecc*) to embark on

imbarcazi'one [imbarkat'tsjone] *sf* (small) boat, (small) craft *inv*; **imbarcazione di salvataggio** lifeboat

im'barco, -chi *sm* embarkation; loading; boarding; (*banchina*) landing stage

imbas'tire *vt* (*cucire*) to tack; (*fig: abbozzare*) to sketch, outline

im'battersi *vpr* **~ in** (*incontrare*) to bump o run into

imbat'tibile *ag* unbeatable, invincible

imbavagli'are [imbavaʎ'ʎare] *vt* to gag

imbe'cille [imbe'tʃille] *ag* idiotic ▷ *sm/f* idiot; (*Med*) imbecile

imbian'care *vt* to whiten; (*muro*) to whitewash ▷ *vi* to become o turn white

imbian'chino [imbjan'kino] *sm* (house) painter, painter and decorator

imboc'care *vt* (*bambino*) to feed; (*entrare: strada*) to enter, turn into

imbocca'tura *sf* mouth; (*di strada, porto*) entrance; (*Mus, del morso*) mouthpiece

imbos'cata *sf* ambush

imbottigli'are [imbottiʎ'ʎare] *vt* to bottle; (*Naut*) to blockade; (*Mil*) to hem in; **imbottigliarsi** *vpr* to be stuck in a traffic jam

imbot'tire *vt* to stuff; (*giacca*) to pad; **imbottirsi** *vpr* **imbottirsi di** (*rimpinzarsi*) to stuff o.s. with; **imbot'tito, -a** *ag* stuffed; (*giacca*) padded; **panino imbottito** filled roll

imbra'nato, -a *ag* clumsy, awkward ▷ *sm/f* clumsy person

imbrogli'are [imbroʎ'ʎare] *vt* to mix up; (*fig: raggirare*) to deceive, cheat; (: *confondere*) to confuse, mix up; **imbrogli'one, -a** *sm/f* cheat, swindler

imbronci'ato, -a *ag* sulky

imbu'care *vt* to post; **dove posso ~ queste cartoline?** where can I post these cards?

imbur'rare *vt* to butter

im'buto *sm* funnel

imi'tare *vt* to imitate; (*riprodurre*) to copy; (*assomigliare*) to look like

immagazzi'nare [immagaddzi'nare] *vt* to store

immagi'nare [immadʒi'nare] *vt* to imagine; (*supporre*) to suppose; (*inventare*) to invent; **s'immagini!** don't mention it!, not at all!; **immaginazi'one** *sf* imagination; (*cosa immaginata*) fancy

im'magine [im'madʒine] *sf* image; (*rappresentazione grafica, mentale*) picture

imman'cabile *ag* certain; unfailing

im'mane *ag* (*smisurato*) enormous; (*spaventoso*) terrible

immangi'abile [imman'dʒabile] *ag* inedible

immatrico'lare *vt* to register; **immatricolarsi** *vpr* (*Ins*) to matriculate, enrol

imma'turo, -a *ag* (*frutto*) unripe; (*persona*) immature; (*prematuro*) premature

immedesi'marsi *vpr* ~ **in** to identify with

immediata'mente *av* immediately, at once

immedi'ato, -a *ag* immediate

im'menso, -a *ag* immense

im'mergere [im'mɛrdʒere] *vt* to immerse, plunge; **immergersi** *vpr* to plunge; (*sommergibile*) to dive, submerge; (*dedicarsi a*): **immergersi in** to immerse o.s. in

immeri'tato, -a *ag* undeserved

immersi'one *sf* immersion; (*di sommergibile*) submersion, dive; (*di palombaro*) dive

im'mettere *vt* ~ **(in)** to introduce (into); ~ **dati in un computer** to enter data on a computer

immi'grato, -a *sm/f* immigrant

immi'nente *ag* imminent

immischiarsi *vpr* ~ **in** to interfere o meddle in

im'mobile *ag* motionless, still; **immobili'are** *ag* (*Dir*) property *cpd*

immon'dizia [immon'dittsja] *sf* dirt, filth; (*spesso al pl: spazzatura, rifiuti*) rubbish *no pl*, refuse *no pl*

immo'rale *ag* immoral

immor'tale *ag* immortal

im'mune *ag* (*esente*) exempt; (*Med, Dir*) immune

immu'tabile *ag* immutable; unchanging

impacchet'tare [impakket'tare] *vt* to pack up

impacci'ato, -a *ag* awkward, clumsy; (*imbarazzato*) embarrassed

im'pacco, -chi *sm* (*Med*) compress

impadro'nirsi *vpr* ~ **di** to seize, take possession of; (*fig: apprendere a fondo*) to master

impa'gabile *ag* priceless

impa'lato, -a *ag* (*fig*) stiff as a board

impalca'tura *sf* scaffolding

impalli'dire *vi* to turn pale; (*fig*) to fade

impa'nato, -a *ag* (*Cuc*) coated in breadcrumbs

impanta'narsi *vpr* to sink (in the mud); (*fig*) to get bogged down

impappi'narsi *vpr* to stammer, falter

impa'rare *vt* to learn

impar'tire *vt* to bestow, give

imparzi'ale [impar'tsjale] *ag* impartial, unbiased

impas'sibile *ag* impassive

impas'tare *vt* (*pasta*) to knead

impastic'carsi *vpr* to pop pills

im'pasto *sm* (*l'impastare: di pane*) kneading; (: *di cemento*) mixing; (*pasta*) dough; (*anche fig*) mixture

im'patto *sm* impact

impau'rire *vt* to scare, frighten ▷ *vi* (*anche*: **impaurirsi**) to become scared o frightened

impazi'ente [impat'tsjɛnte] *ag* impatient

impaz'zata [impat'tsata] *sf* **all'~** (*precipitosamente*) at breakneck speed

impaz'zire [impat'tsire] *vi* to go mad; ~ **per qn/qc** to be crazy about sb/sth

impec'cabile *ag* impeccable

impedi'mento *sm* obstacle, hindrance

impe'dire *vt* (*vietare*): ~ **a qn di fare** to prevent sb from doing; (*ostruire*) to obstruct; (*impacciare*) to hamper, hinder

impegnarsi *vpr* (*vincolarsi*): ~ **a fare** to undertake to do; (*mettersi risolutamente*): ~ **in qc** to devote o.s. to sth; ~ **con qn** (*accordarsi*) to come to an agreement with sb

impegna'tivo, -a *ag* binding; (*lavoro*) demanding, exacting

impe'gnato, -a *ag* (*occupato*) busy; (*fig: romanzo, autore*) committed, engagé

im'pegno [im'peɲɲo] *sm* (*obbligo*) obligation; (*promessa*) promise, pledge; (*zelo*) diligence, zeal; (*compito, d'autore*) commitment

impel'lente *ag* pressing, urgent

impen'narsi *vpr* (*cavallo*) to rear up; (*Aer*) to nose up; (*fig*) to bridle

impensie'rire *vt* to worry; **impensierirsi** *vpr* to worry

impera'tivo, -a *ag, sm* imperative

impera'tore, -'trice *sm/f* emperor/ empress

imperdo'nabile *ag* unforgivable, unpardonable

imper'fetto, -a *ag* imperfect ▷ *sm* (*Ling*) imperfect (tense)

imperi'ale *ag* imperial

imperi'oso, -a *ag* (*persona*) imperious; (*motivo, esigenza*) urgent, pressing

imperme'abile *ag* waterproof ▷ *sm* raincoat

im'pero *sm* empire; (*forza, autorità*) rule, control

imperso'nale *ag* impersonal

imperso'nare *vt* to personify; (*Teatro*) to play, act (the part of)

imperter'rito, -a *ag* fearless, undaunted; impassive

imperti'nente *ag* impertinent

'impeto *sm* (*moto, forza*) force, impetus; (*assalto*) onslaught; (*fig: impulso*) impulse; (: *slancio*) transport; **con ~** energetically; vehemently

impet'tito, -a *ag* stiff, erect

impetu'oso, -a *ag* (*vento*) strong, raging; (*persona*) impetuous

impi'anto *sm* (*installazione*) installation; (*apparecchiature*) plant; (*sistema*) system; **impianto elettrico** wiring; **impianto di risalita** (*Sci*) ski lift; **impianto di riscaldamento** heating system; **impianto sportivo** sports complex

impic'care *vt* to hang; **impiccarsi** *vpr* to hang o.s.

impicciarsi [impit'tʃarsi] *vpr* (*immischiarsi*): ~ **(in)** to meddle (in); **impicciati degli affari tuoi!** mind your own business!

impicci'one, -a [impit'tʃone] *sm/f*

busybody

impie'gare *vt* (*usare*) to use, employ; (*spendere: denaro, tempo*) to spend; (*investire*) to invest; **impie'gato, -a** *sm/f* employee

impi'ego, -ghi *sm* (*uso*) use; (*occupazione*) employment; (*posto di lavoro*) (regular) job, post; (*Econ*) investment

impieto'sire *vt* to move to pity; **impietosirsi** *vpr* to be moved to pity

impigli'arsi *vpr* to get caught up *o* entangled

impi'grirsi *vpr* to grow lazy

impli'care *vt* to imply; (*coinvolgere*) to involve

im'plicito, -a [im'plitʃito] *ag* implicit

implo'rare *vt* to implore; (*pietà ecc*) to beg for

impolve'rarsi *vpr* to get dusty

im'pone *ecc vb vedi* **imporre**

impo'nente *ag* imposing, impressive

im'pongo *ecc vb vedi* **imporre**

impo'nibile *ag* taxable ▷ *sm* taxable income

impopo'lare *ag* unpopular

im'porre *vt* to impose; (*costringere*) to force, make; (*far valere*) to impose, enforce; **imporsi** *vpr* (*persona*) to assert o.s.; (*cosa: rendersi necessario*) to become necessary; (*aver successo: moda, attore*) to become popular; ~ **a qn di fare** to force sb to do, make sb do

impor'tante *ag* important; **impor'tanza** *sf* importance; **dare importanza a qc** to attach importance to sth; **darsi importanza** to give o.s. airs

impor'tare *vt* (*introdurre dall'estero*) to import ▷ *vi* to matter, be important ▷ *vb impers* (*essere necessario*) to be necessary; (*interessare*) to matter; **non importa!** it doesn't matter!; **non me ne importa!** I don't care!

im'porto *sm* (*total*) amount

importu'nare *vt* to bother

im'posi *ecc vb vedi* **imporre**

imposizi'one [impozit'tsjone] *sf* imposition; order, command; (*onere, imposta*) tax

imposses'sarsi *vpr* ~ **di** to seize, take possession of

impos'sibile *ag* impossible; **fare l'~** to do one's utmost, do all one can

im'posta *sf* (*di finestra*) shutter; (*tassa*) tax; **imposta sul reddito** income tax; **imposta sul valore aggiunto** value added tax (BRIT), sales tax (US)

impos'tare *vt* (*imbucare*) to post; (*preparare*) to plan, set out; (*avviare*) to begin, start off; (*voce*) to pitch

impostazi'one [impostat'tsjone] *sf*
(*di lettera*) posting (BRIT), mailing (US);
(*di problema, questione*) formulation,
statement; (*di lavoro*) organization,
planning; (*di attività*) setting up; (*Mus:
di voce*) pitch; **impostazioni** *sfpl* (*di
computer*) settings

impo'tente *ag* weak, powerless; (*anche
Med*) impotent

imprati'cabile *ag* (*strada*) impassable;
(*campo da gioco*) unplayable

impre'care *vi* to curse, swear; **~ contro** to
hurl abuse at

imprecazi'one [imprekat'tsjone] *sf*
abuse, curse

impre'gnare [impreɲ'ɲare] *vt* **~ (di)**
(*imbevere*) to soak *o* impregnate (with);
(*riempire*) to fill (with)

imprendi'tore *sm* (*industriale*)
entrepreneur; (*appaltatore*) contractor;
piccolo ~ small businessman

im'presa *sf* (*iniziativa*) enterprise; (*azione*)
exploit; (*azienda*) firm, concern

impressio'nante *ag* impressive;
upsetting

impressio'nare *vt* to impress; (*turbare*) to
upset; (*Fot*) to expose; **impressionarsi** *vpr*
to be easily upset

impressi'one *sf* impression; (*fig:
sensazione*) sensation, feeling; (*stampa*)
printing; **fare ~** (*colpire*) to impress;
(*turbare*) to frighten, upset; **fare
buona/cattiva ~ a** to make a good/bad
impression on

impreve'dibile *ag* unforeseeable;
(*persona*) unpredictable

impre'visto, -a *ag* unexpected,
unforeseen ▷ *sm* unforeseen event; **salvo
imprevisti** unless anything unexpected
happens

imprigio'nare [impridʒo'nare] *vt* to
imprison

impro'babile *ag* improbable, unlikely

im'pronta *sf* imprint, impression, sign;
(*di piede, mano*) print; (*fig*) mark, stamp;
impronta digitale fingerprint

improvvisa'mente *av* suddenly;
unexpectedly

improvvi'sare *vt* to improvise

improv'viso, -a *ag* (*imprevisto*)
unexpected; (*subitaneo*) sudden; **all'~**
unexpectedly; suddenly

impru'dente *ag* unwise, rash

impu'gnare [impuɲ'ɲare] *vt* to grasp,
grip; (*Dir*) to contest

impul'sivo, -a *ag* impulsive

im'pulso *sm* impulse

impun'tarsi *vpr* to stop dead, refuse to
budge; (*fig*) to be obstinate

impu'tato, -a *sm/f* (*Dir*) accused,
defendant

 PAROLA CHIAVE

in (*in + il* = **nel**, *in + lo* = **nello**, *in + l'* = **nell'**, *in
+ la* = **nella**, *in + i* = **nei**, *in + gli* = **negli**, *in + le*
= **nelle**) *prep* **1** (*stato in luogo*) in; **vivere in
Italia/città** to live in Italy/town; **essere in
casa/ufficio** to be at home/the office; **se
fossi in te** if I were you

2 (*moto a luogo*) to; (: *dentro*) into; **andare
in Germania/città** to go to Germany/
town; **andare in ufficio** to go to the office;
entrare in macchina/casa to get into the
car/go into the house

3 (*tempo*) in; **nel 1989** in 1989; **in giugno/
estate** in June/summer

4 (*modo, maniera*) in; **in silenzio** in silence;
in abito da sera in evening dress; **in
guerra** at war; **in vacanza** on holiday;
Maria Bianchi in Rossi Maria Rossi née
Bianchi

5 (*mezzo*) by; **viaggiare in autobus/treno**
to travel by bus/train

6 (*materia*) made of; **in marmo** made of
marble, marble *cpd*; **una collana in oro** a
gold necklace

7 (*misura*) in; **siamo in quattro** there are
four of us; **in tutto** in all

8 (*fine*): **dare in dono** to give as a gift;
spende tutto in alcool he spends all his
money on drink; **in onore di** in honour of

inabi'tabile *ag* uninhabitable

inacces'sibile [inattʃes'sibile] *ag* (*luogo*)
inaccessible; (*persona*) unapproachable

inaccet'tabile [inattʃet'tabile] *ag*
unacceptable

ina'datto, -a *ag* **~ (a)** unsuitable *o* unfit
(for)

inadegu'ato, -a *ag* inadequate

inaffi'dabile *ag* unreliable

inami'dato, -a *ag* starched

inar'care *vt* (*schiena*) to arch; (*sopracciglia*)
to raise

inaspet'tato, -a *ag* unexpected

inas'prire *vt* (*disciplina*) to tighten up,
make harsher; (*carattere*) to embitter;
inasprirsi *vpr* to become harsher; to
become bitter; to become worse

inattac'cabile *ag* (*anche fig*) unassailable;
(*alibi*) cast-iron

inatten'dibile *ag* unreliable

inat'teso, -a *ag* unexpected

inattu'abile *ag* impracticable

inau'dito, -a *ag* unheard of

inaugu'rare *vt* to inaugurate, open;
(*monumento*) to unveil

inaugurazi'one [inaugurat'tsjone] *sf* inauguration; unveiling

incal'lito, -a *ag* calloused; (*fig*) hardened, inveterate; (: *insensibile*) hard

incande'scente [inkandeʃʃɛnte] *ag* incandescent, white-hot

incan'tare *vt* to enchant, bewitch; **incantarsi** *vpr* (*rimanere intontito*) to be spellbound; to be in a daze; (*meccanismo*: *bloccarsi*) to jam; **incan'tevole** *ag* charming, enchanting

in'canto *sm* spell, charm, enchantment; (*asta*) auction; **come per ~** as if by magic; **mettere all'~** to put up for auction

inca'pace [inka'patʃe] *ag* incapable

incarce'rare [inkartʃe'rare] *vt* to imprison

incari'care *vt* **~ qn di fare** to give sb the responsibility of doing; **incaricarsi di** to take care o charge of

in'carico, -chi *sm* task, job

incarta'mento *sm* dossier, file

incar'tare *vt* to wrap (in paper)

incas'sare *vt* (*merce*) to pack (in cases); (*gemma*: *incastonare*) to set; (*Econ*: *riscuotere*) to collect; (*Pugilato*: *colpi*) to take, stand up to; **in'casso** *sm* cashing, encashment; (*introito*) takings *pl*

incas'trare *vt* to fit in, insert; (*fig*: *intrappolare*) to catch; **incastrarsi** *vpr* (*combaciare*) to fit together; (*restare bloccato*) to become stuck

incate'nare *vt* to chain up

in'cauto, -a *ag* imprudent, rash

inca'vato, -a *ag* hollow; (*occhi*) sunken

incendi'are [intʃen'djare] *vt* to set fire to; **incendiarsi** *vpr* to catch fire, burst into flames

in'cendio [in'tʃɛndjo] *sm* fire

inceneri'tore [intʃeneri'tore] *sm* incinerator

in'censo [in'tʃɛnso] *sm* incense

incensu'rato, -a [intʃensu'rato] *ag* (*Dir*): **essere ~** to have a clean record

incenti'vare [intʃenti'vare] *vt* (*produzione, vendite*) to boost; (*persona*) to motivate

incen'tivo [intʃen'tivo] *sm* incentive

incepparsi *vpr* to jam

incer'tezza [intʃer'tettsa] *sf* uncertainty

in'certo, -a [in'tʃɛrto] *ag* uncertain; (*irresoluto*) undecided, hesitating ▷ *sm* uncertainty

in'cetta [in'tʃetta] *sf* buying up; **fare ~ di qc** to buy up sth

inchi'esta [in'kjɛsta] *sf* investigation, inquiry

inchinarsi *vpr* to bend down; (*per riverenza*) to bow; (: *donna*) to curtsy

inchio'dare [inkjo'dare] *vt* to nail (down); **~ la macchina** (*Aut*) to jam on the brakes

inchi'ostro [in'kjɔstro] *sm* ink; **inchiostro simpatico** invisible ink

inciam'pare [intʃam'pare] *vi* to trip, stumble

inci'dente [intʃi'dɛnte] *sm* accident; **ho avuto un ~** I've had an accident; **incidente automobilistico** o **d'auto** car accident; **incidente diplomatico** diplomatic incident

in'cidere [in'tʃidere] *vi* **~ su** to bear upon, affect ▷ *vt* (*tagliare incavando*) to cut into; (*Arte*) to engrave; to etch; (*canzone*) to record

in'cinta [in'tʃinta] *ag f* pregnant

incipri'are [intʃi'prjare] *vt* to powder **incipriarsi** ▷ *vpr* to powder one's face

in'circa [in'tʃirka] *av* **all'~** more or less, very nearly

in'cisi *ecc* [in'tʃizi] *vb vedi* **incidere**

incisi'one [intʃi'zjone] *sf* cut; (*disegno*) engraving; etching; (*registrazione*) recording; (*Med*) incision

in'ciso, -a [in'tʃizo] *pp di* **incidere** ▷ *sm* **per ~** incidentally, by the way

inci'tare [intʃi'tare] *vt* to incite

inci'vile [intʃi'vile] *ag* uncivilized; (*villano*) impolite

incl. *abbr* (= *incluso*) encl.

incli'nare *vt* to tilt; **inclinarsi** *vpr* (*barca*) to list; (*aereo*) to bank

in'cludere *vt* to include; (*accludere*) to enclose; **in'cluso, -a** *pp di* **includere** ▷ *ag* included; enclosed

incoe'rente *ag* incoherent; (*contraddittorio*) inconsistent

in'cognita [in'koɲɲita] *sf* (*Mat, fig*) unknown quantity

in'cognito, -a [in'koɲɲito] *ag* unknown ▷ *sm* **in ~** incognito

incol'lare *vt* to glue, gum; (*unire con colla*) to stick together

inco'lore *ag* colourless

incol'pare *vt* **~ qn di** to charge sb with

in'colto, -a *ag* (*terreno*) uncultivated; (*trascurato*: *capelli*) neglected; (*persona*) uneducated

in'colume *ag* safe and sound, unhurt

incom'benza [inkom'bɛntsa] *sf* duty, task

in'combere *vi* (*sovrastare minacciando*): **~ su** to threaten, hang over

incominci'are [inkomin'tʃare] *vi, vt* to begin, start

incompe'tente *ag* incompetent

incompi'uto, -a *ag* unfinished, incomplete

incom'pleto, -a *ag* incomplete

incompren'sibile *ag* incomprehensible

inconce'pibile [inkontʃe'pibile] *ag*

inconceivable

inconcili'abile [inkontʃi'ljabile] *ag* irreconcilable

inconclu'dente *ag* inconclusive; (*persona*) ineffectual

incondizio'nato, -a [inkondittsjo'nato] *ag* unconditional

inconfon'dibile *ag* unmistakable

inconsa'pevole *ag* ~ **di** unaware of, ignorant of

in'conscio, -a, -sci, -sce [in'kɔnʃo] *ag* unconscious ▷ *sm* (*Psic*): **l'**~ the unconscious

inconsis'tente *ag* insubstantial; unfounded

inconsu'eto, -a *ag* unusual

incon'trare *vt* to meet; (*difficoltà*) to meet with; **incontrarsi** *vpr* to meet

in'contro *av* ~ **a** (*verso*) towards ▷ *sm* meeting; (*Sport*) match; meeting; **incontro di calcio** football match

inconveni'ente *sm* drawback, snag

incoraggia'mento [inkoraddʒa'mento] *sm* encouragement

incoraggi'are [inkorad'dʒare] *vt* to encourage

incornici'are [inkorni'tʃare] *vt* to frame

incoro'nare *vt* to crown

in'correre *vi* ~ **in** to meet with, run into

incosci'ente [inkoʃ'ʃɛnte] *ag* (*inconscio*) unconscious; (*irresponsabile*) reckless, thoughtless

incre'dibile *ag* incredible, unbelievable

in'credulo, -a *ag* incredulous, disbelieving

incremen'tare *vt* to increase; (*dar sviluppo a*) to promote

incre'mento *sm* (*sviluppo*) development; (*aumento numerico*) increase, growth

incresci'oso, -a [inkreʃ'ʃoso] *ag* (*incidente ecc*) regrettable

incrimi'nare *vt* (*Dir*) to charge

incri'nare *vt* to crack; (*fig: rapporti, amicizia*) to cause to deteriorate; **incrinarsi** *vpr* to crack; to deteriorate

incroci'are [inkro'tʃare] *vt* to cross; (*incontrare*) to meet ▷ *vi* (*Naut, Aer*) to cruise; **incrociarsi** *vpr* (*strade*) to cross, intersect; (*persone, veicoli*) to pass each other; ~ **le braccia/le gambe** to fold one's arms/cross one's legs

in'crocio [in'krotʃo] *sm* (*anche Ferr*) crossing; (*di strade*) crossroads

incuba'trice [inkuba'tritʃe] *sf* incubator

'incubo *sm* nightmare

incu'rabile *ag* incurable

incu'rante *ag* ~ (**di**) heedless (of), careless (of)

incurio'sire *vt* to make curious; **incuriosirsi** *vpr* to become curious

incursi'one *sf* raid

incur'vare *vt* to bend, curve; **incurvarsi** *vpr* to bend, curve

incusto'dito, -a *ag* unguarded, unattended

in'cutere *vt* ~ **timore/rispetto a qn** to strike fear into sb/command sb's respect

'indaco *sm* indigo

indaffa'rato, -a *ag* busy

inda'gare *vt* to investigate

in'dagine [in'dadʒine] *sf* investigation, inquiry; (*ricerca*) research, study; **indagine di mercato** market survey

indebi'tarsi *vpr* to run o get into debt

indebo'lire *vt, vi* (*anche:* **indebolirsi**) to weaken

inde'cente [inde'tʃɛnte] *ag* indecent

inde'ciso, -a [inde'tʃizo] *ag* indecisive; (*irresoluto*) undecided

indefi'nito, -a *ag* (*anche Ling*) indefinite; (*impreciso, non determinato*) undefined

in'degno, -a [in'deɲɲo] *ag* (*atto*) shameful; (*persona*) unworthy

indemoni'ato, -a *ag* possessed (by the devil)

in'denne *ag* unhurt, uninjured

indenniz'zare [indennid'dzare] *vt* to compensate

indetermina'tivo, -a *ag* (*Ling*) indefinite

'India *sf* **l'**~ India; **indi'ano, -a** *ag* Indian ▷ *sm/f* (*d'India*) Indian; (*d'America*) Native American, (American) Indian

indi'care *vt* (*mostrare*) to show, indicate; (: *col dito*) to point to, point out; (*consigliare*) to suggest, recommend; **indica'tivo, -a** *ag* indicative ▷ *sm* (*Ling*) indicative (mood); **indicazi'one** *sf* indication; (*informazione*) piece of information

'indice ['inditʃe] *sm* index; (*fig*) sign; (*dito*) index finger, forefinger; **indice di gradimento** (*Radio, TV*) popularity rating

indicherò *ecc* [indike'rɔ] *vb vedi* **indicare**

indi'cibile [indi'tʃibile] *ag* inexpressible

indietreggi'are [indietred'dʒare] *vi* to draw back, retreat

indi'etro *av* back; (*guardare*) behind, back; (*andare, cadere: anche:* **all'**~) backwards; **rimanere** ~ to be left behind; **essere** ~ (*col lavoro*) to be behind; (*orologio*) to be slow; **rimandare qc** ~ to send sth back

indi'feso, -a *ag* (*città ecc*) undefended; (*persona*) defenceless

indiffe'rente *ag* indifferent

in'digeno, -a [in'didʒeno] *ag* indigenous, native ▷ *sm/f* native

indigesti'one [indidʒes'tjone] *sf* indigestion

indi'gesto, -a [indi'dʒɛsto] *ag* indigestible

indi'gnare [indiɲ'ɲare] *vt* to fill with indignation; **indignarsi** *vpr* to get indignant

indimenti'cabile *ag* unforgettable

indipen'dente *ag* independent

in'dire *vt* (*concorso*) to announce; (*elezioni*) to call

indi'retto, -a *ag* indirect

indiriz'zare [indirit'tsare] *vt* (*dirigere*) to direct; (*mandare*) to send; (*lettera*) to address

indi'rizzo [indi'rittso] *sm* address; (*direzione*) direction; (*avvio*) trend, course; **il mio - è...** my address is ...

indis'creto, -a *ag* indiscreet

indis'cusso, -a *ag* unquestioned

indispen'sabile *ag* indispensable, essential

indispet'tire *vt* to irritate, annoy ▷ *vi* (*anche:* **indispettirsi**) to get irritated *o* annoyed

individu'ale *ag* individual

individu'are *vt* (*dar forma distinta a*) to characterize; (*determinare*) to locate; (*riconoscere*) to single out

indi'viduo *sm* individual

indizi'ato, -a *ag* suspected ▷ *sm/f* suspect

in'dizio [in'dittsjo] *sm* (*segno*) sign, indication; (*Polizia*) clue; (*Dir*) piece of evidence

'indole *sf* nature, character

indolen'zito, -a [indolen'tsito] *ag* stiff, aching; (*intorpidito*) numb

indo'lore *ag* painless

indo'mani *sm* **l'~** the next day, the following day

Indo'nesia *sf* **l'~** Indonesia

indos'sare *vt* (*mettere indosso*) to put on; (*avere indosso*) to have on; **indossa'tore, -'trice** *sm/f* model

indottri'nare *vt* to indoctrinate

indovi'nare *vt* (*scoprire*) to guess; (*immaginare*) to imagine, guess; (*il futuro*) to foretell; **indovi'nello** *sm* riddle

indubbia'mente *av* undoubtedly

in'dubbio, -a *ag* certain, undoubted

in'duco *ecc vb vedi* **indurre**

indugi'are [indu'dʒare] *vi* to take one's time, delay

in'dugio [in'dudʒo] *sm* (*ritardo*) delay; **senza -** without delay

indul'gente [indul'dʒɛnte] *ag* indulgent; (*giudice*) lenient

indu'mento *sm* article of clothing, garment

indu'rire *vt* to harden ▷ *vi* (*anche:* **indurirsi**) to harden, become hard

in'durre *vt* **~ qn a fare qc** to induce *o* persuade sb to do sth; **~ qn in errore** to mislead sb

in'dussi *ecc vb vedi* **indurre**

in'dustria *sf* industry; **industri'ale** *ag* industrial ▷ *sm* industrialist

inecce'pibile [inettʃe'pibile] *ag* unexceptionable

i'nedito, -a *ag* unpublished

ine'rente *ag* **~ a** concerning, regarding

i'nerme *ag* unarmed; defenceless

inerpi'carsi *vpr* **~ (su)** to clamber (up)

i'nerte *ag* inert; (*inattivo*) indolent, sluggish

ine'satto, -a *ag* (*impreciso*) inexact; (*erroneo*) incorrect; (*Amm: non riscosso*) uncollected

inesis'tente *ag* non-existent

inesperi'enza [inɛspe'rjɛntsa] *sf* inexperience

ines'perto, -a *ag* inexperienced

inevi'tabile *ag* inevitable

i'nezia [i'nɛttsja] *sf* trifle, thing of no importance

infagot'tare *vt* to bundle up, wrap up; **infagottarsi** *vpr* to wrap up

infal'libile *ag* infallible

infa'mante *ag* defamatory

in'fame *ag* infamous; (*fig: cosa, compito*) awful, dreadful

infan'gare *vt* to cover with mud; (*fig: reputazione*) to sully; **infangarsi** *vpr* to get covered in mud; to be sullied

infan'tile *ag* child *cpd*; childlike; (*adulto, azione*) childish; **letteratura ~** children's books *pl*

in'fanzia [in'fantsja] *sf* childhood; (*bambini*) children *pl*; **prima ~** babyhood, infancy

infari'nare *vt* to cover with (*o sprinkle with o dip in*) flour; **infarina'tura** *sf* (*fig*) smattering

in'farto *sm* (*Med*) heart attack

infasti'dire *vt* to annoy, irritate; **infastidirsi** *vpr* to get annoyed *o* irritated

infati'cabile *ag* tireless, untiring

in'fatti *cong* actually, as a matter of fact

> Attenzione! In inglese esiste l'espressione *in fact* che però vuol dire *in effetti*.

infatu'arsi *vpr* **~ di** to become infatuated with, fall for

infe'dele *ag* unfaithful

infe'lice [infe'litʃe] *ag* unhappy; (*sfortunato*) unlucky, unfortunate; (*inopportuno*) inopportune, ill-timed; (*mal riuscito: lavoro*) bad, poor

inferi'ore *ag* lower; (*per intelligenza, qualità*) inferior ▷ *sm/f* inferior; **~ a** (*numero, quantità*) less *o* smaller than;

(*meno buono*) inferior to; **~ alla media** below average; **inferiorità** *sf* inferiority

inferme'ria *sf* infirmary; (*di scuola, nave*) sick bay

infermi'ere, -a *sm/f* nurse

infermità *sf inv* illness; infirmity; **infermità mentale** mental illness; (*Dir*) insanity

in'fermo, -a *ag* (*ammalato*) ill; (*debole*) infirm

infer'nale *ag* infernal; (*proposito, complotto*) diabolical

in'ferno *sm* hell

inferri'ata *sf* grating

infes'tare *vt* to infest

infet'tare *vt* to infect; **infettarsi** *vpr* to become infected; **infezi'one** *sf* infection

infiam'mabile *ag* inflammable

infiam'mare *vt* to set alight; (*fig, Med*) to inflame; **infiammarsi** *vpr* to catch fire; (*Med*) to become inflamed; **infiammazi'one** *sf* (*Med*) inflammation

infie'rire *vi* **~ su** (*fisicamente*) to attack furiously; (*verbalmente*) to rage at

infi'lare *vt* (*ago*) to thread; (*mettere: chiave*) to insert; (: *anello, vestito*) to slip *o* put on; (*strada*) to turn into, take; **infilarsi** *vpr* **infilarsi in** to slip into; (*indossare*) to slip on; **~ l'uscio** to slip in; to slip out

infil'trarsi *vpr* to penetrate, seep through; (*Mil*) to infiltrate

infil'zare [infil'tsare] *vt* (*infilare*) to string together; (*trafiggere*) to pierce

'infimo, -a *ag* lowest

in'fine *av* finally; (*insomma*) in short

infinità *sf* infinity; (*in quantità*): **un'~ di** an infinite number of

infi'nito, -a *ag* infinite; (*Ling*) infinitive ▷ *sm* infinity; (*Ling*) infinitive; **all'~** (*senza fine*) endlessly

infinocchi'are [infinok'kjare] (*fam*) *vt* to hoodwink

infischi'arsi [infis'kjarsi] *vpr* **~ di** not to care about

in'fisso, -a (*pp*) *di* **infiggere** *sm* fixture; (*di porta, finestra*) frame

inflazi'one [inflat'tsjone] *sf* inflation

in'fliggere [in'fliddʒere] *vt* to inflict

in'flissi *ecc vb vedi* **infliggere**

influ'ente *ag* influential; **influ'enza** *sf* influence; (*Med*) influenza, flu

influen'zare [influen'tsare] *vt* to influence, have an influence on

influ'ire *vi* **~ su** to influence

in'flusso *sm* influence

infon'dato, -a *ag* unfounded, groundless

in'fondere *vt* **~ qc in qn** to instill sth in sb

infor'mare *vt* to inform, tell; **informarsi**

vpr **informarsi (di** *o* **su)** to inquire (about)

infor'matica *sf* computer science

informa'tivo, -a *ag* informative

infor'mato, -a *ag* informed; **tenersi ~** to keep o.s. (well-)informed

informa'tore *sm* informer

informazi'one [informat'tsjone] *sf* piece of information; **prendere informazioni sul conto di qn** to get information about sb; **chiedere un'~** to ask for (some) information

in'forme *ag* shapeless

informico'larsi *vpr* to have pins and needles

infortu'nato, -a *ag* injured, hurt ▷ *sm/f* injured person

infor'tunio *sm* accident; **infortunio sul lavoro** industrial accident, accident at work

infra'dito *sm inv* (*calzatura*) flip flop (BRIT), thong (US)

infrazi'one [infrat'tsjone] *sf* **~ a** breaking of, violation of

infredda'tura *sf* slight cold

infreddo'lito, -a *ag* cold, chilled

infu'ori *av* out; **all'~** outwards; **all'~ di** (*eccetto*) except, with the exception of

infuri'arsi *vpr* to fly into a rage

infusi'one *sf* infusion

in'fuso, -a *pp di* **infondere** ▷ *sm* infusion

Ing. *abbr* = **ingegnere**

ingaggi'are [ingad'dʒare] *vt* (*assumere con compenso*) to take on, hire; (*Sport*) to sign on; (*Mil*) to engage

ingan'nare *vt* to deceive; (*fisco*) to cheat; (*eludere*) to dodge, elude; (*fig: tempo*) to while away ▷ *vi* (*apparenza*) to be deceptive; **ingannarsi** *vpr* to be mistaken, be wrong

in'ganno *sm* deceit, deception; (*azione*) trick; (*menzogna, frode*) cheat, swindle; (*illusione*) illusion

inge'gnarsi [indʒeɲ'ɲarsi] *vpr* to do one's best, try hard; **~ per vivere** to live by one's wits

inge'gnere [indʒeɲ'ɲɛre] *sm* engineer; **~ civile/navale** civil/naval engineer; **ingegne'ria** *sf* engineering; **ingegnere genetica** genetic engineering

in'gegno [in'dʒeɲɲo] *sm* (*intelligenza*) intelligence, brains *pl*; (*capacità creativa*) ingenuity; (*disposizione*) talent; **inge'gnoso, -a** *ag* ingenious, clever

ingelo'sire [indʒelo'zire] *vt* to make jealous ▷ *vi* (*anche*: **ingelosirsi**) to become jealous

in'gente [in'dʒɛnte] *ag* huge, enormous

ingenuità [indʒenui'ta] *sf* ingenuousness

in'genuo, -a [in'dʒɛnuo] *ag* naïve
Attenzione! In inglese esiste la parola *ingenious*, che però significa *ingegnoso*.

inge'rire [indʒe'rire] *vt* to ingest

inges'sare [indʒes'sare] *vt* (*Med*) to put in plaster; **ingessa'tura** *sf* plaster

Inghil'terra [ingil'tɛrra] *sf* **l'~** England

inghiot'tire [ingjot'tire] *vt* to swallow

ingial'lire [indʒal'lire] *vi* to go yellow

inginocchi'arsi [indʒinok'kjarsi] *vpr* to kneel (down)

ingiù [in'dʒu] *av* down, downwards

ingi'uria [in'dʒurja] *sf* insult; (*fig: danno*) damage

ingius'tizia [indʒus'tittsja] *sf* injustice

ingi'usto, -a [in'dʒusto] *ag* unjust, unfair

in'glese *ag* English ▷ *sm/f* Englishman/woman ▷ *sm* (*Ling*) English; **gli Inglesi** the English; **andarsene** o **filare all'~** to take French leave

ingoi'are *vt* to gulp (down); (*fig*) to swallow (up)

ingol'farsi *vpr* to flood

ingom'brante *ag* cumbersome

ingom'brare *vt* (*strada*) to block; (*stanza*) to clutter up

in'gordo, -a *ag* **~ di** greedy for; (*fig*) greedy o avid for

in'gorgo, -ghi *sm* blockage, obstruction; (*anche:* **~ stradale**) traffic jam

ingoz'zarsi *vpr* **~ (di)** to stuff o.s. (with)

ingra'naggio [ingra'naddʒo] *sm* (*Tecn*) gear; (*di orologio*) mechanism; **gli ingranaggi della burocrazia** the bureaucratic machinery

ingra'nare *vi* to mesh, engage ▷ *vt* to engage; **~ la marcia** to get into gear

ingrandi'mento *sm* enlargement; extension

ingran'dire *vt* (*anche Fot*) to enlarge; (*estendere*) to extend; (*Ottica, fig*) to magnify ▷ *vi* (*anche:* **ingrandirsi**) to become larger o bigger; (*aumentare*) to grow, increase; (*espandersi*) to expand

ingras'sare *vt* to make fat; (*animali*) to fatten; (*lubrificare*) to oil, lubricate ▷ *vi* (*anche:* **ingrassarsi**) to get fat, put on weight

in'grato, -a *ag* ungrateful; (*lavoro*) thankless, unrewarding

ingredi'ente *sm* ingredient

in'gresso *sm* (*porta*) entrance; (*atrio*) hall; (*l'entrare*) entrance, entry; (*facoltà di entrare*) admission; **ingresso libero** admission free

ingros'sare *vt* to increase; (*folla, livello*) to swell ▷ *vi* (*anche:* **ingrossarsi**) to increase; to swell

in'grosso *av* **all'~** (*Comm*) wholesale;

(*all'incirca*) roughly, about

ingua'ribile *ag* incurable

'inguine *sm* (*Anat*) groin

ini'bire *vt* to forbid, prohibit; (*Psic*) to inhibit; **inibirsi** *vpr* to restrain o.s.

ini'bito, -a *ag* inhibited ▷ *sm/f* inhibited person

iniet'tare *vt* to inject; **iniezi'one** *sf* injection

ininterrotta'mente *av* non-stop, continuously

ininter'rotto, -a *ag* unbroken; uninterrupted

inizi'ale [init'tsjale] *ag, sf* initial

inizi'are [init'tsjare] *vi, vt* to begin, start; **a che ora inizia il film?** when does the film start?; **~ qn a** to initiate sb into; (*pittura ecc*) to introduce sb to; **~ a fare qc** to start doing sth

inizia'tiva [inittsja'tiva] *sf* initiative; **iniziativa privata** private enterprise

i'nizio [i'nittsjo] *sm* beginning; **all'~** at the beginning, at the start; **dare ~ a qc** to start sth, get sth going

innaffi'are *ecc* = **annaffiare** *ecc*

innamo'rarsi *vpr* **~ (di qn)** to fall in love (with sb); **innamo'rato, -a** *ag* (*che nutre amore*): **innamorato (di)** in love (with); (*appassionato*): **innamorato di** very fond of ▷ *sm/f* lover; sweetheart

innanzi'tutto *av* first of all

in'nato, -a *ag* innate

innatu'rale *ag* unnatural

inne'gabile *ag* undeniable

innervo'sire *vt* **~ qn** to get on sb's nerves; **innervosirsi** *vpr* to get irritated o upset

innes'care *vt* to prime

'inno *sm* hymn; **inno nazionale** national anthem

inno'cente [inno'tʃɛnte] *ag* innocent

in'nocuo, -a *ag* innocuous, harmless

innova'tivo, -a *ag* innovative

innume'revole *ag* innumerable

inol'trare *vt* (*Amm*) to pass on, forward

i'noltre *av* besides, moreover

inon'dare *vt* to flood

inoppor'tuno, -a *ag* untimely, ill-timed; (*inappropriato*) inappropriate; (*momento*) inopportune

inorri'dire *vt* to horrify ▷ *vi* to be horrified

inosser'vato, -a *ag* (*non notato*) unobserved; (*non rispettato*) not observed, not kept

inossi'dabile *ag* stainless

INPS *sigla m* (= *Istituto Nazionale Previdenza Sociale*) social security service

inqua'drare *vt* (*foto, immagine*) to frame; (*fig*) to situate, set

inqui'eto, -a *ag* restless; (*preoccupato*) worried, anxious

inqui'lino, -a *sm/f* tenant
inquina'mento *sm* pollution
inqui'nare *vt* to pollute
insabbi'are *vt* (*fig: pratica*) to shelve; **insabbiarsi** *vpr* (*arenarsi: barca*) to run aground; (*fig: pratica*) to be shelved
insac'cati *smpl* (*Cuc*) sausages
insa'lata *sf* salad; **insalata mista** mixed salad; **insalata russa** (*Cuc*) Russian salad (*comprised of cold diced cooked vegetables in mayonnaise*); **insalati'era** *sf* salad bowl
insa'nabile *ag* (*piaga*) which cannot be healed; (*situazione*) irremediable; (*odio*) implacable
insa'puta *sf* **all'~ di qn** without sb knowing
inse'diarsi *vpr* to take up office; (*popolo, colonia*) to settle
in'segna [in'seɲɲa] *sf* sign; (*emblema*) sign, emblem; (*bandiera*) flag, banner
insegna'mento [inseɲɲa'mento] *sm* teaching
inse'gnante [inseɲ'ɲante] *ag* teaching ▷ *sm/f* teacher
inse'gnare [inseɲ'ɲare] *vt, vi* to teach; **~ a qn qc** to teach sb sth; **~ a qn a fare qc** to teach sb (how) to do sth
insegui'mento *sm* pursuit, chase
insegu'ire *vt* to pursue, chase
insena'tura *sf* inlet, creek
insen'sato, -a *ag* senseless, stupid
insen'sibile *ag* (*nervo*) insensible; (*persona*) indifferent
inse'rire *vt* to insert; (*Elettr*) to connect; (*allegare*) to enclose; (*annuncio*) to put in, place; **inserirsi** *vpr* (*fig*): **inserirsi in** to become part of
inservi'ente *sm/f* attendant
inserzi'one [inser'tsjone] *sf* insertion; (*avviso*) advertisement; **fare un'~ sul giornale** to put an advertisement in the paper
insetti'cida, -i [insetti'tʃida] *sm* insecticide
in'setto *sm* insect
insi'curo, -a *ag* insecure
insi'eme *av* together ▷ *prep* **~ a** *o* **con** together with ▷ *sm* whole; (*Mat, servizio, assortimento*) set; (*Moda*) ensemble, outfit; **tutti ~** all together; **tutto ~** all together; (*in una volta*) at one go; **nell'~** on the whole; **d'~** (*veduta ecc*) overall
in'signe [in'siɲɲe] *ag* (*persona*) famous, distinguished; (*città, monumento*) notable
insignifi'cante [insiɲɲifi'kante] *ag* insignificant
insinu'are *vt* (*introdurre*): **~ qc in** to slip *o* slide sth into; (*fig*) to insinuate, imply; **insinuarsi** *vpr* **insinuarsi in** to seep into;

(*fig*) to creep into; to worm one's way into
in'sipido, -a *ag* insipid
insis'tente *ag* insistent; persistent
in'sistere *vi* **~ su qc** to insist on sth; **~ in qc/a fare** (*perseverare*) to persist in sth/in doing
insoddis'fatto, -a *ag* dissatisfied
insoffe'rente *ag* intolerant
insolazi'one [insolat'tsjone] *sf* (*Med*) sunstroke
inso'lente *ag* insolent
in'solito, -a *ag* unusual, out of the ordinary
inso'luto, -a *ag* (*non risolto*) unsolved
in'somma *av* (*in conclusione*) in short; (*dunque*) well ▷ *escl* for heaven's sake!
in'sonne *ag* sleepless; **in'sonnia** *sf* insomnia, sleeplessness
insonno'lito, -a *ag* sleepy, drowsy
insoppor'tabile *ag* unbearable
in'sorgere [in'sordʒere] *vi* (*ribellarsi*) to rise up, rebel; (*apparire*) to come up, arise
in'sorsi *ecc vb vedi* **insorgere**
insospet'tire *vt* to make suspicious ▷ *vi* (*anche*: **insospettirsi**) to become suspicious
inspi'rare *vt* to breathe in, inhale
in'stabile *ag* (*carico, indole*) unstable; (*tempo*) unsettled; (*equilibrio*) unsteady
instal'lare *vt* to install
instan'cabile *ag* untiring, indefatigable
instau'rare *vt* to introduce, institute
insuc'cesso [insut'tʃɛsso] *sm* failure, flop
insuffici'ente [insuffi'tʃɛnte] *ag* insufficient; (*compito, allievo*) inadequate; **insuffici'enza** *sf* insufficiency; inadequacy; (*Ins*) fail; **insufficienza di prove** (*Dir*) lack of evidence; **insufficienza renale** renal insufficiency
insu'lina *sf* insulin
in'sulso, -a *ag* (*sciocco*) inane, silly; (*persona*) dull, insipid
insul'tare *vt* to insult, affront
in'sulto *sm* insult, affront
intac'care *vt* (*fare tacche*) to cut into; (*corrodere*) to corrode; (*fig: cominciare ad usare: risparmi*) to break into; (: *ledere*) to damage
intagli'are [intaʎ'ʎare] *vt* to carve
in'tanto *av* (*nel frattempo*) meanwhile, in the meantime; (*per cominciare*) just to begin with; **~ che** while
inta'sare *vt* to choke (up), block (up); (*Aut*) to obstruct, block; **intasarsi** *vpr* to become choked *o* blocked
intas'care *vt* to pocket
in'tatto, -a *ag* intact; (*puro*) unsullied
intavo'lare *vt* to start, enter into
inte'grale *ag* complete; (*pane, farina*)

wholemeal (BRIT), whole-wheat (US);
(Mat): **calcolo ~** integral calculus
inte'grante ag **parte ~** integral part
inte'grare vt to complete; (Mat) to
integrate; **integrarsi** vpr (persona) to
become integrated
integra'tore sm **integratori alimentari**
nutritional supplements
integrità sf integrity
'integro, -a ag (intatto, intero) complete,
whole; (retto) upright
intelaia'tura sf frame; (fig) structure,
framework
intel'letto sm intellect; **intellettu'ale** ag,
sm/f intellectual
intelli'gente [intelli'dʒɛnte] ag
intelligent
intem'perie sfpl bad weather sg
in'tendere vt (avere intenzione): **~ fare qc**
to intend o mean to do sth; (comprendere)
to understand; (udire) to hear; (significare)
to mean; **intendersi** vpr (conoscere):
intendersi di to know a lot about, be
a connoisseur of; (accordarsi) to get on
(well); **intendersela con qn** (avere una
relazione amorosa) to have an affair with sb;
intendi'tore, -'trice sm/f connoisseur,
expert
inten'sivo, -a ag intensive
in'tenso, -a ag intense
in'tento, -a ag (teso, assorto): **~ (a)** intent
(on), absorbed (in) ▷ sm aim, purpose
intenzio'nale [intentsjo'nale] ag
intentional
intenzi'one [inten'tsjone] sf intention;
(Dir) intent; **avere ~ di fare qc** to intend to
do sth, have the intention of doing sth
interat'tivo, -a ag interactive
intercet'tare [intertʃet'tare] vt to
intercept
intercity [intǝsi'ti] sm inv (Ferr) ≈ intercity
(train)
inter'detto, -a pp di **interdire** ▷ ag
forbidden, prohibited; (sconcertato)
dumbfounded ▷ sm (Rel) interdict
interes'sante ag interesting; **essere in
stato ~** to be expecting (a baby)
interes'sare vt to interest; (concernere) to
concern, be of interest to; (far intervenire):
~ qn a to draw sb's attention to ▷ vi **~ a**
to interest, matter to; **interessarsi** vpr
(mostrare interesse): **interessarsi a** to take
an interest in, be interested in; (occuparsi):
interessarsi di to take care of
inte'resse sm (anche Comm) interest
inter'faccia, -ce [inter'fattʃa] sf (Inform)
interface
interfe'renza [interfe'rɛntsa] sf
interference

interfe'rire vi to interfere
interiezi'one [interjet'tsjone] sf
exclamation, interjection
interi'ora sfpl entrails
interi'ore ag interior, inner, inside,
internal; (fig) inner
inter'medio, -a ag intermediate
inter'nare vt (arrestare) to intern; (Med) to
commit (to a mental institution)
inter'nauta sm/f Internet user
internazio'nale [internattsjo'nale] ag
international
'Internet ['internet] sf Internet; **in ~** on
the Internet
in'terno, -a ag (di dentro) internal,
interior, inner; (: mare) inland; (nazionale)
domestic; (allievo) boarding ▷ sm inside,
interior; (di paese) interior; (fodera) lining;
(di appartamento) flat (number); (Tel)
extension ▷ sm/f (Ins) boarder; **interni**
smpl (Cinema) interior shots; **all'~** inside;
Ministero degli Interni Ministry of the
Interior, ≈ Home Office (BRIT), Department
of the Interior (US)
in'tero, -a ag (integro, intatto) whole,
entire; (completo, totale) complete;
(numero) whole; (non ridotto: biglietto) full;
(latte) full-cream
interpel'lare vt to consult
interpre'tare vt to interpret; **in'terprete**
sm/f interpreter; (Teatro) actor/actress,
performer; (Mus) performer; **ci potrebbe
fare da interprete?** could you act as an
interpreter for us?
interregio'nale [interredʒo'nale] sm
train that travels between two or more regions
of Italy, stopping frequently
interro'gare vt to question; (Ins) to test;
interrogazi'one sf questioning no pl; (Ins)
oral test
inter'rompere vt to interrupt; (studi,
trattative) to break off, interrupt;
interrompersi vpr to break off, stop
interrut'tore sm switch
interruzi'one [interrut'tsjone] sf
interruption; break
interur'bana sf trunk o long-distance call
inter'vallo sm interval; (spazio) space, gap
interve'nire vi (partecipare): **~ a** to
take part in; (intromettersi: anche Pol)
to intervene; (Med: operare) to operate;
inter'vento sm participation;
(intromissione) intervention; (Med)
operation; **fare un intervento nel corso
di** (dibattito, programma) to take part in
inter'vista sf interview; **intervis'tare** vt
to interview
intes'tare vt (lettera) to address;
(proprietà): **~ a** to register in the name of;

~ un assegno a qn to make out a cheque to sb

intestato, -a *ag (proprietà, casa, conto)* in the name of; *(assegno)* made out to; **carta intestata** headed paper

intes'tino *sm (Anat)* intestine

intimidazi'one [intimidat'tsjone] *sf* intimidation

intimi'dire *vt* to intimidate ▷ *vi (intimidirsi)* to grow shy

intimità *sf* intimacy; privacy; *(familiarità)* familiarity

'intimo, -a *ag* intimate; *(affetti, vita)* private; *(fig: profondo)* inmost ▷ *sm (persona)* intimate o close friend; *(dell'animo)* bottom, depths *pl*; **parti intime** *(Anat)* private parts

in'tingolo *sm* sauce; *(pietanza)* stew

intito'lare *vt* to give a title to; *(dedicare)* to dedicate; **intitolarsi** *vpr (libro, film)* to be called

intolle'rabile *ag* intolerable

intolle'rante *ag* intolerant

in'tonaco, -ci *o* **chi** *sm* plaster

into'nare *vt (canto)* to start to sing; *(armonizzare)* to match; **intonarsi** *vpr (colori)* to go together; **intonarsi a** *(carnagione)* to suit; *(abito)* to go with, match

inton'tito, -a *ag* stunned, dazed; **~ dal sonno** stupid with sleep

in'toppo *sm* stumbling block, obstacle

in'torno *av* around; **~ a** *(attorno a)* around; *(riguardo, circa)* about

intossi'care *vt* to poison; **intossicazi'one** *sf* poisoning

intralci'are [intral'tʃare] *vt* to hamper, hold up

intransi'tivo, -a *ag, sm* intransitive

intrapren'dente *ag* enterprising, go-ahead

intra'prendere *vt* to undertake

intrat'tabile *ag* intractable

intratte'nere *vt* to entertain; to engage in conversation; **intrattenersi** *vpr* to linger; **intrattenersi su qc** to dwell on sth

intrave'dere *vt* to catch a glimpse of; *(fig)* to foresee

intrecci'are [intret'tʃare] *vt (capelli)* to plait, braid; *(intessere: anche fig)* to weave, interweave, intertwine

intri'gante *ag* scheming ▷ *sm/f* schemer, intriguer

in'trinseco, -a, -ci, -che *ag* intrinsic

in'triso, -a *ag* **~ (di)** soaked (in)

intro'durre *vt* to introduce; *(chiave ecc):* **~ qc in** to insert sth into; *(persone: far entrare)* to show in; **introdursi** *vpr (moda, tecniche)* to be introduced; **introdursi in** *(persona:*

penetrare) to enter; *(: entrare furtivamente)* to steal *o* slip into; **introduzi'one** *sf* introduction

in'troito *sm* income, revenue

intro'mettersi *vpr* to interfere, meddle; *(interporsi)* to intervene

in'truglio [in'truʎʎo] *sm* concoction

intrusi'one *sf* intrusion; interference

in'truso, -a *sm/f* intruder

intu'ire *vt* to perceive by intuition; *(rendersi conto)* to realize; **in'tuito** *sm* intuition; *(perspicacia)* perspicacity

inu'mano, -a *ag* inhuman

inumi'dire *vt* to dampen, moisten; **inumidirsi** *vpr* to become damp *o* wet

i'nutile *ag* useless; *(superfluo)* pointless, unnecessary

inutil'mente *av* unnecessarily; *(senza risultato)* in vain

inva'dente *ag (fig)* interfering, nosey

in'vadere *vt* to invade; *(affollare)* to swarm into, overrun; *(acque)* to flood

inva'ghirsi [inva'girsi] *vpr* **~ di** to take a fancy to

invalidità *sf* infirmity; disability; *(Dir)* invalidity

in'valido, -a *ag (infermo)* infirm, invalid; *(al lavoro)* disabled; *(Dir: nullo)* invalid ▷ *sm/f* invalid; disabled person

in'vano *av* in vain

invasi'one *sf* invasion

inva'sore, invadi'trice [invadi'tritʃe] *ag* invading ▷ *sm* invader

invecchi'are [invek'kjare] *vi (persona)* to grow old; *(vino, popolazione)* to age; *(moda)* to become dated ▷ *vt* to age; *(far apparire più vecchio)* to make look older

in'vece [in'vetʃe] *av* instead; *(al contrario)* on the contrary; **~ di** instead of

inve'ire *vi* **~ contro** to rail against

inven'tare *vt* to invent; *(pericoli, pettegolezzi)* to make up, invent

inven'tario *sm* inventory; *(Comm)* stocktaking *no pl*

inven'tore *sm* inventor

invenzi'one [inven'tsjone] *sf* invention; *(bugia)* lie, story

inver'nale *ag* winter *cpd*; *(simile all'inverno)* wintry

in'verno *sm* winter

invero'simile *ag* unlikely

inversi'one *sf* inversion; reversal; **"divieto d'~"** *(Aut)* "no U-turns"

in'verso, -a *ag* opposite; *(Mat)* inverse ▷ *sm* contrary, opposite; **in senso ~** in the opposite direction; **in ordine ~** in reverse order

inver'tire *vt* to invert, reverse; **~ la marcia** *(Aut)* to do a U-turn

investi'gare vt, vi to investigate; **investiga'tore, -'trice** sm/f investigator, detective; **investigatore privato** private investigator

investi'mento sm (Econ) investment

inves'tire vt (denaro) to invest; (veicolo: pedone) to knock down; (: altro veicolo) to crash into; (apostrofare) to assail; (incaricare): **~ qn di** to invest sb with

invi'are vt to send; **invi'ato, -a** sm/f envoy; (Stampa) correspondent; **inviato speciale** (Pol) special envoy; (di giornale) special correspondent

in'vidia sf envy; **invidi'are** vt invidiare qn (per qc) to envy sb for sth; **invidiare qc a qn** to envy sb sth; **invidi'oso, -a** ag envious

in'vio, -'vii sm sending; (insieme di merci) consignment; (tasto) Return (key), Enter (key)

invipe'rito, -a ag furious

invi'sibile ag invisible

invi'tare vt to invite; **~ qn a fare** to invite sb to do; **invi'tato, -a** sm/f guest; **in'vito** sm invitation

invo'care vt (chiedere: aiuto, pace) to cry out for; (appellarsi: la legge, Dio) to appeal to, invoke

invogli'are [invoʎ'ʎare] vt **~ qn a fare** to tempt sb to do, induce sb to do

involon'tario, -a ag (errore) unintentional; (gesto) involuntary

invol'tino sm (Cuc) roulade

in'volto sm (pacco) parcel; (fagotto) bundle

in'volucro sm cover, wrapping

inzup'pare [intsup'pare] vt to soak; **inzupparsi** vpr to get soaked

'io pron I ▷ sm inv **l'~** the ego, the self; **~ stesso(a)** I myself

i'odio sm iodine

l'onio sm **lo ~, il mar ~** the Ionian (Sea)

ipermer'cato sm hypermarket

ipertensi'one sf high blood pressure, hypertension

iper'testo sm hypertext

ip'nosi sf hypnosis; **ipnotiz'zare** vt to hypnotize

ipocri'sia sf hypocrisy

i'pocrita, -i, -e ag hypocritical ▷ sm/f hypocrite

ipo'teca, -che sf mortgage

i'potesi sf inv hypothesis

'ippica sf horseracing

'ippico, -a, -ci, -che ag horse cpd

ippocas'tano sm horse chestnut

ip'podromo sm racecourse

ippo'potamo sm hippopotamus

'ipsilon sf o m inv (lettera) Y, y; (: dell'alfabeto greco) epsilon

IR abbr (= Interregionale) long distance train which stops frequently

ira'cheno, -a [ira'kɛno] ag, sm/f Iraqi

l'ran sm **l'~** Iran

irani'ano, -a ag, sm/f Iranian

l'raq sm **l'~** Iraq

'iride sf (arcobaleno) rainbow; (Anat, Bot) iris

'iris sm inv iris

Ir'landa sf **l'~** Ireland; **l'~ del Nord** Northern Ireland, Ulster; **la Repubblica d'~** Eire, the Republic of Ireland; **irlan'dese** ag Irish ▷ sm/f Irishman/woman; **gli Irlandesi** the Irish

iro'nia sf irony; **i'ronico, -a, -ci, -che** ag ironic(al)

irragio'nevole [irradʒo'nevole] ag irrational; unreasonable

irrazio'nale [irrattsjo'nale] ag irrational

irre'ale ag unreal

irrego'lare ag irregular; (terreno) uneven

irremo'vibile ag (fig) unshakeable, unyielding

irrequi'eto, -a ag restless

irresis'tibile ag irresistible

irrespon'sabile ag irresponsible

irri'gare vt (annaffiare) to irrigate; (fiume ecc) to flow through

irrigi'dire [irridʒi'dire] vt to stiffen; **irrigidirsi** vpr to stiffen

irri'sorio, -a ag derisory

irri'tare vt (mettere di malumore) to irritate, annoy; (Med) to irritate; **irritarsi** vpr (stizzirsi) to become irritated o annoyed; (Med) to become irritated

ir'rompere vi **~ in** to burst into

irru'ente ag (fig) impetuous, violent

ir'ruppi ecc vb vedi **irrompere**

irruzi'one [irrut'tsjone] sf **fare ~ in** to burst into; (polizia) to raid

is'crissi ecc vb vedi **iscrivere**

is'critto, -a pp di **iscrivere** ▷ sm/f member; **per o in ~** in writing

is'crivere vt to register, enter; (persona): **~ (a)** to register (in), enrol (in); **iscriversi** vpr **iscriversi (a)** (club, partito) to join; (università) to register o enrol (at); (esame, concorso) to register o enter (for); **iscrizi'one** sf (epigrafe ecc) inscription; (a scuola, società) enrolment, registration; (registrazione) registration

Is'lam sm **l'~** Islam

Is'landa sf **l'~** Iceland

islan'dese ag Icelandic ▷ sm/f Icelander ▷ sm (Ling) Icelandic

'isola sf island; **isola pedonale** (Aut) pedestrian precinct

isola'mento sm isolation; (Tecn) insulation

iso'lante ag insulating ▷ sm insulator

iso'lare *vt* to isolate; (*Tecn*) to insulate; (: *acusticamente*) to soundproof; **isolarsi** *vpr* to isolate o.s.; **iso'lato, -a** *ag* isolated; insulated ▷ *sm* (*gruppo di edifici*) block

ispet'tore *sm* inspector

ispezio'nare [ispettsjo'nare] *vt* to inspect

'ispido, -a *ag* bristly, shaggy

ispi'rare *vt* to inspire

Isra'ele *sm* l'~ Israel; **israeli'ano, -a** *ag*, *sm/f* Israeli

is'sare *vt* to hoist

istan'taneo, -a *ag* instantaneous ▷ *sf* (*Fot*) snapshot

is'tante *sm* instant, moment; **all'~, sull'~** instantly, immediately

is'terico, -a, -ci, -che *ag* hysterical

isti'gare *vt* to incite

is'tinto *sm* instinct

istitu'ire *vt* (*fondare*) to institute, found; (*porre: confronto*) to establish; (*intraprendere: inchiesta*) to set up

isti'tuto *sm* institute; (*di università*) department; (*ente, Dir*) institution; **istituto di bellezza** beauty salon; **istituto di credito** bank, banking institution; **istituto di ricerca** research institute

istituzi'one [istitut'tsjone] *sf* institution

'istmo *sm* (*Geo*) isthmus

'istrice ['istritʃe] *sm* porcupine

istru'ito, -a *ag* educated

istrut'tore, -'trice *sm/f* instructor ▷ *ag* **giudice ~** *vedi* **giudice**

istruzi'one *sf* education; training; (*direttiva*) instruction; **istruzioni** *sfpl* (*norme*) instructions; **istruzioni per l'uso** instructions for use; **~ obbligatoria** (*Scol*) compulsory education

l'talia *sf* l'~ Italy

itali'ano, -a *ag* Italian ▷ *sm/f* Italian ▷ *sm* (*Ling*) Italian; **gli italiani** the Italians

itine'rario *sm* itinerary

'ittico, -a, -ci, -che *ag* fish *cpd*; fishing *cpd*

Iugos'lavia = **Jugoslavia**

IVA ['iva] *sigla f* (= *imposta sul valore aggiunto*) VAT

jazz [dʒaz] *sm* jazz

jeans [dʒinz] *smpl* jeans

jeep® [dʒip] *sm inv* jeep

'jogging ['dʒɔgiŋ] *sm* jogging; **fare ~** to go jogging

'jolly ['dʒɔli] *sm inv* joker

joystick [dʒɔis'tik] *sm inv* joystick

ju'do [dʒu'dɔ] *sm* judo

Jugos'lavia [jugoz'lavja] *sf* (*Storia*): **la ~** Yugoslavia; **la ex-~** former Yugoslavia; **jugos'lavo, -a** *ag, sm/f* (*Storia*) Yugoslav(ian)

K l

K, k ['kappa] *sf o m inv (lettera)* K, k ▷ *abbr* (= *kilo-, chilo-*) k; (*Inform*) K; **K come Kursaal** ≈ K for King

kamikaze [kami'kaddze] *sm inv* kamikaze

karaoke [ka'raokɛ] *sm inv* karaoke

karatè *sm* karate

ka'yak [ka'jak] *sm inv* kayak

Kenia ['kɛnja] *sm* **il ~** Kenya

kg *abbr* (= *chilogrammo*) kg

'killer *sm inv* gunman, hired gun

kitsch [kitʃ] *sm* kitsch

'kiwi ['kiwi] *sm inv* kiwi fruit

km *abbr* (= *chilometro*) km

K.O. [kappa'o] *sm inv* knockout

ko'ala [ko'ala] *sm inv* koala (bear)

koso'varo, -a [koso'varo] *ag, sm/f* Kosovan

Ko'sovo *sm* Kosovo

'krapfen *sm inv* (*Cuc*) doughnut

Kuwait [ku'vait] *sm* **il ~** Kuwait

l' *det vedi* **la; lo; il**

la (*dav V* **l'**) *det f* the ▷ *pron (oggetto: persona)* her; (: *cosa*) it; (: *forma di cortesia*) you; *vedi anche* **il**

là *av* there; **di là** (*da quel luogo*) from there; (*in quel luogo*) in there; (*dall'altra parte*) over there; **di là di** beyond; **per di là** that way; **più in là** further on; (*tempo*) later on; **fatti in là** move up; **là dentro/sopra/sotto** in/up (*o* on)/under there; *vedi anche* **quello**

'labbro (*pl(f)* **labbra**) (*solo nel senso Anat*) *sm* lip

labi'rinto *sm* labyrinth, maze

labora'torio *sm* (*di ricerca*) laboratory; (*di arti, mestieri*) workshop; **laboratorio linguistico** language laboratory

labori'oso, -a *ag* (*faticoso*) laborious; (*attivo*) hard-working

'lacca, -che *sf* lacquer

'laccio ['lattʃo] *sm* noose; (*legaccio, tirante*) lasso; (*di scarpa*) lace; **laccio emostatico** tourniquet

lace'rare [latʃe'rare] *vt* to tear to shreds, lacerate; **lacerarsi** *vpr* to tear

'lacrima *sf* tear; **in lacrime** in tears; **lacri'mogeno, -a** *ag* **gas lacrimogeno** tear gas

la'cuna *sf* (*fig*) gap

'ladro *sm* thief

laggiù [lad'dʒu] *av* down there; (*di là*) over there

la'gnarsi [laɲ'ɲarsi] *vpr* ~ **(di)** to complain (about)

'lago, -ghi *sm* lake

la'guna *sf* lagoon

'laico, -a, -ci, -che *ag* (*apostolato*) lay; (*vita*) secular; (*scuola*) non-denominational ▷ *sm/f* layman/woman

'lama *sm inv* (*Zool*) llama; (*Rel*) lama ▷ *sf* blade

lamentarsi *vpr* (*emettere lamenti*) to moan, groan; (*rammaricarsi*): ~ **(di)** to complain (about)

lamen'tela *sf* complaining *no pl*

la'metta *sf* razor blade

'lamina *sf* (*lastra sottile*) thin sheet (*o* layer *o* plate); **lamina d'oro** gold leaf; gold foil

'lampada *sf* lamp; **lampada a gas** gas lamp; **lampada da tavolo** table lamp

lampa'dario *sm* chandelier

lampa'dina *sf* light bulb; **lampadina tascabile** pocket torch (*BRIT*) *o* flashlight (*US*)

lam'pante *ag* (*fig: evidente*) crystal clear, evident

lampeggi'are [lamped'dʒare] *vi* (*luce, fari*) to flash ▷ *vb impers* **lampeggia** there's lightning; **lampeggia'tore** *sm* (*Aut*) indicator

lampi'one *sm* street light *o* lamp (*BRIT*)

'lampo *sm* (*Meteor*) flash of lightning; (*di luce: fig*) flash

lam'pone *sm* raspberry

'lana *sf* wool; **pura ~ vergine** pure new wool; **lana d'acciaio** steel wool; **lana di vetro** glass wool

lan'cetta [lan'tʃetta] *sf* (*indice*) pointer, needle; (*di orologio*) hand

'lancia ['lantʃa] *sf* (*arma*) lance; (: *picca*) spear; (*di pompa antincendio*) nozzle; (*imbarcazione*) launch; **lancia di salvataggio** lifeboat

lanciafi'amme [lantʃa'fjamme] *sm inv* flamethrower

lanci'are [lan'tʃare] *vt* to throw, hurl, fling; (*Sport*) to throw; (*far partire: automobile*) to get up to full speed; (*bombe*) to drop; (*razzo, prodotto, moda*) to launch; **lanciarsi** *vpr* **lanciarsi contro/su** to throw *o* hurl *o* fling o.s. against/on; **lanciarsi in** (*fig*) to embark on

lanci'nante [lantʃi'nante] *ag* (*dolore*) shooting, throbbing; (*grido*) piercing

'lancio ['lantʃo] *sm* throwing *no pl*; throw; dropping *no pl*; drop; launching *no pl*; launch; **lancio del disco** (*Sport*) throwing the discus; **lancio del peso** putting the shot

'languido, -a *ag* (*fiacco*) languid, weak; (*tenero, malinconico*) languishing

lan'terna *sf* lantern; (*faro*) lighthouse

'lapide *sf* (*di sepolcro*) tombstone; (*commemorativa*) plaque

'lapsus *sm inv* slip

'lardo *sm* bacon fat, lard

lar'ghezza [lar'gettsa] *sf* width; breadth; looseness; generosity; **larghezza di vedute** broad-mindedness

'largo, -a, -ghi, -ghe *ag* wide; broad; (*maniche*) wide; (*abito: troppo ampio*) loose; (*fig*) generous ▷ *sm* width; breadth; (*mare aperto*): **il ~** the open sea ▷ *sf* **stare** *o* **tenersi alla larga (da qn/qc)** to keep one's distance (from sb/sth), keep away (from sb/sth); **~ due metri** two metres wide; **~ di spalle** broad-shouldered; **di larghe vedute** broad-minded; **su larga scala** on a large scale; **di manica larga** generous, open-handed; **al ~ di Genova** off (the coast of) Genoa; **farsi ~ tra la folla** to push one's way through the crowd

'larice ['laritʃe] *sm* (*Bot*) larch

larin'gite [larin'dʒite] *sf* laryngitis

'larva *sf* larva; (*fig*) shadow

la'sagne [la'zaɲɲe] *sfpl* lasagna *sg*

lasci'are [laʃʃare] *vt* to leave; (*abbandonare*) to leave, abandon, give up; (*cessare di tenere*) to let go of ▷ *vb aus* ~ **fare qn** to let sb do; ~ **andare** *o* **correre** *o* **perdere** to let things go their own way; ~ **stare qc/qn** to leave sth/sb alone; **lasciarsi** *vpr* (*persone*) to part; (*coppia*) to split up; **lasciarsi andare** to let o.s. go

'laser ['lazer] *ag, sm inv* (*raggio*) ~ laser (beam)

lassa'tivo, -a *ag, sm* laxative

'lasso *sm*; **lasso di tempo** interval, lapse of time

lassù *av* up there

'lastra *sf* (*di pietra*) slab; (*di metallo, Fot*) plate; (*di ghiaccio, vetro*) sheet; (*radiografica*) X-ray (plate)

lastri'cato *sm* paving

late'rale *ag* lateral, side *cpd*; (*uscita, ingresso ecc*) side *cpd* ▷ *sm* (*Calcio*) half-back

la'tino, -a *ag, sm* Latin

lati'tante *sm/f* fugitive (from justice)

lati'tudine *sf* latitude

'lato, -a *ag* (*fig*) wide, broad ▷ *sm* side; (*fig*) aspect, point of view; **in senso ~** broadly speaking

'latta *sf* tin (plate); (*recipiente*) tin, can

lat'tante *ag* unweaned

'latte *sm* milk; **latte detergente** cleansing milk *o* lotion; **latte intero** full-cream milk;

latte a lunga conservazione UHT milk, long-life milk; **latte magro** o **scremato** skimmed milk; **latte in polvere** dried o powdered milk; **latte solare** suntan lotion; **latti'cini** smpl dairy products
lat'tina sf (di birra ecc) can
lat'tuga, -ghe sf lettuce
'laurea sf degree; **laurea in ingegneria** engineering degree; **laurea in lettere** ≈ arts degree

● **LAUREA**
●
● The **laurea** is awarded to students
● who successfully complete their
● degree courses. Traditionally,
● this takes between four and six
● years; a major element of the final
● examinations is the presentation
● and discussion of a dissertation. A
● shorter, more vocational course of
● study, taking from two to three years,
● is also available; at the end of this time
● students receive a diploma called the
● **laurea breve**.

laure'arsi vpr to graduate
laure'ato, -a ag, sm/f graduate
'lauro sm laurel
'lauto, -a ag (pranzo, mancia) lavish
'lava sf lava
la'vabo sm washbasin
la'vaggio [la'vaddʒo] sm washing no pl; **lavaggio del cervello** brainwashing no pl; **lavaggio a secco** dry-cleaning
la'vagna [la'vaɲɲa] sf (Geo) slate; (di scuola) blackboard
la'vanda sf (anche Med) wash; (Bot) lavender; **lavande'ria** sf laundry; **lavanderia automatica** launderette; **lavanderia a secco** dry-cleaner's; **lavan'dino** sm sink
lavapi'atti sm/f dishwasher
la'vare vt to wash; **lavarsi** vpr to wash, have a wash; **~ a secco** to dry-clean; **lavarsi le mani/i denti** to wash one's hands/clean one's teeth
lava'secco sm o f inv dry cleaner's
lavasto'viglie [lavasto'viʎʎe] sm o f inv (macchina) dishwasher
lava'trice [lava'tritʃe] sf washing machine
lavo'rare vi to work; (fig: bar, studio ecc) to do good business ▷ vt to work; **lavorarsi qn** (persuaderlo) to work on sb; **~ a** to work on; **~ a maglia** to knit; **lavora'tivo, -a** ag working; **lavora'tore, -'trice** sm/f worker ▷ ag working

la'voro sm work; (occupazione) job, work no pl; (opera) piece of work, job; (Econ) labour; **che ~ fa?** what do you do?; **lavori forzati** hard labour sg; **lavoro interinale** o **in affitto** temporary work
le det fpl the ▷ pron (oggetto) them; (: a lei, a essa) (to) her; (: forma di cortesia) (to) you; vedi anche **il**
le'ale ag loyal; (sincero) sincere; (onesto) fair
'lecca 'lecca sm inv lollipop
leccapi'edi (peg) sm/f inv toady, bootlicker
lec'care vt to lick; (gatto: latte ecc) to lick o lap up; (fig) to flatter; **leccarsi i baffi** to lick one's lips
leccherò ecc [lekke'rɔ] vb vedi **leccare**
'leccio ['lettʃo] sm holm oak, ilex
leccor'nia sf titbit, delicacy
'lecito, -a ['lɛtʃito] ag permitted, allowed
'lega, -ghe sf league; (di metalli) alloy
le'gaccio [le'gattʃo] sm string, lace
le'gale ag legal ▷ sm lawyer; **legaliz'zare** vt to authenticate; (regolarizzare) to legalize
le'game sm (corda, fig: affettivo) tie, bond; (nesso logico) link, connection
le'gare vt (prigioniero, capelli, cane) to tie (up); (libro) to bind; (Chim) to alloy; (fig: collegare) to bind, join ▷ vi (far lega) to unite; (fig) to get on well
le'genda [le'dʒɛnda] sf (di carta geografica ecc) = **leggenda**
'legge ['leddʒe] sf law
leg'genda [led'dʒɛnda] sf (narrazione) legend; (di carta geografica ecc) key, legend
'leggere ['leddʒere] vt, vi to read
legge'rezza [leddʒe'rettsa] sf lightness; thoughtlessness; fickleness
leg'gero, -a [led'dʒɛro] ag light; (agile, snello) nimble, agile, light; (tè, caffè) weak; (fig: non grave, piccolo) slight; (: spensierato) thoughtless; (: incostante) fickle; free and easy; **alla leggera** thoughtlessly
leg'gio, -'gii [led'dʒio] sm lectern; (Mus) music stand
legherò ecc [lege'rɔ] vb vedi **legare**
legisla'tivo, -a [ledʒizla'tivo] ag legislative
legisla'tura [ledʒizla'tura] sf legislature
le'gittimo, -a [le'dʒittimo] ag legitimate; (fig: giustificato, lecito) justified, legitimate; **legittima difesa** (Dir) self-defence
'legna ['leɲɲa] sf firewood
'legno ['leɲɲo] sm wood; (pezzo di legno) piece of wood; **di ~** wooden; **legno compensato** plywood
'lei pron (soggetto) she; (oggetto: per dare rilievo, con preposizione) her; (forma di cortesia: anche: **L~**) you ▷ sm **dare del ~**

a qn to address sb as "lei"; **~ stessa** she herself; you yourself

lenta'mente *av* slowly
'lente *sf* (*Ottica*) lens *sg*; **lenti a contatto** *o* **corneali** contact lenses; **lenti (a contatto) morbide/rigide** soft/hard contact lenses; **lente d'ingrandimento** magnifying glass; **lenti** *sfpl* (*occhiali*) lenses
len'tezza [len'tettsa] *sf* slowness
len'ticchia [len'tikkja] *sf* (*Bot*) lentil
len'tiggine [len'tiddʒine] *sf* freckle
'lento, -a *ag* slow; (*molle: fune*) slack; (*non stretto: vite, abito*) loose ▷ *sm* (*ballo*) slow dance
'lenza ['lɛntsa] *sf* fishing-line
lenzu'olo [len'tswɔlo] *sm* sheet
le'one *sm* lion; (*dello zodiaco*): **L~** Leo
lepo'rino, -a *ag* **labbro ~** harelip
'lepre *sf* hare
'lercio, -a, -ci, -cie ['lɛrtʃo] *ag* filthy
lesi'one *sf* (*Med*) lesion; (*Dir*) injury, damage; (*Edil*) crack
les'sare *vt* (*Cuc*) to boil
'lessi *ecc vb vedi* **leggere**
'lessico, -ci *sm* vocabulary; lexicon
'lesso, -a *ag* boiled ▷ *sm* boiled meat
le'tale *ag* lethal; fatal
leta'maio *sm* dunghill
le'tame *sm* manure, dung
le'targo, -ghi *sm* lethargy; (*Zool*) hibernation
'lettera *sf* letter; **lettere** *sfpl* (*letteratura*) literature *sg*; (*studi umanistici*) arts (subjects); **alla ~** literally; **in lettere** in words, in full
letteral'mente *av* literally
lette'rario, -a *ag* literary
lette'rato, -a *ag* well-read, scholarly
lettera'tura *sf* literature
let'tiga, -ghe *sf* (*barella*) stretcher
let'tino *sm* cot (*BRIT*), crib (*US*); **lettino solare** sunbed
'letto, -a *pp di* **leggere** ▷ *sm* bed; **andare a ~** to go to bed; **letto a castello** bunk beds *pl*; **letto a una piazza** single; **letto a due piazze** *o* **matrimoniale** double bed
let'tore, -'trice *sm/f* reader; (*Ins*) (foreign language) assistant (*BRIT*), (foreign) teaching assistant (*US*) ▷ *sm* (*Tecn*): **~ ottico** optical character reader; **lettore**

CD CD player; **lettore DVD** DVD player
let'tura *sf* reading

leuce'mia [leutʃe'mia] *sf* leukaemia
'leva *sf* lever; (*Mil*) conscription; **far ~ su qn** to work on sb; **leva del cambio** (*Aut*) gear lever
le'vante *sm* east; (*vento*) East wind; **il L~** the Levant
le'vare *vt* (*occhi, braccio*) to raise; (*sollevare, togliere: tassa, divieto*) to lift; (*indumenti*) to take off, remove; (*rimuovere*) to take away; (: *dal di sopra*) to take off; (: *dal di dentro*) to take out
leva'toio, -a *ag* **ponte ~** drawbridge
lezi'one [let'tsjone] *sf* lesson; (*Univ*) lecture; **fare ~** to teach; to lecture; **dare una ~ a qn** to teach sb a lesson; **lezioni private** private lessons
li *pron pl* (*oggetto*) them
lì *av* there; **di** *o* **da lì** from there; **per di lì** that way; **di lì a pochi giorni** a few days later; **lì per lì** there and then; at first; **essere lì (lì) per fare** to be on the point of doing, be about to do; **lì dentro** in there; **lì sotto** under there; **lì sopra** on there; up there; *vedi anche* **quello**
liba'nese *ag, sm/f* Lebanese *inv*
Li'bano *sm* **il ~** the Lebanon
'libbra *sf* (*peso*) pound
li'beccio [li'bettʃo] *sm* south-west wind
li'bellula *sf* dragonfly
libe'rale *ag, sm/f* liberal
liberaliz'zare [liberalid'dzare] *vt* to liberalize
libe'rare *vt* (*rendere libero: prigioniero*) to release; (: *popolo*) to free, liberate; (*sgombrare: passaggio*) to clear; (: *stanza*) to vacate; (*produrre: energia*) to release; **liberarsi** *vpr* **liberarsi di qc/qn** to get rid of sth/sb; **liberazi'one** *sf* liberation, freeing; release; rescuing

'libero, -a *ag* free; (*strada*) clear; (*non occupato: posto ecc*) vacant; free; not taken; empty; not engaged; **~ di fare qc** free to do sth; **~ da** free from; **è ~ questo posto?** is this seat free?; **~ arbitrio** free will; **~ professionista** self-employed professional person; **~ scambio** free trade;

libertà *sf inv* freedom; *(tempo disponibile)* free time ▷ *sfpl (licenza)* liberties; **in libertà provvisoria/vigilata** released without bail/on probation

'Libia *sf* **la ~** Libya; **'libico, -a, -ci, -che** *ag, sm/f* Libyan

li'bidine *sf* lust

li'braio *sm* bookseller

li'brarsi *vpr* to hover

libre'ria *sf (bottega)* bookshop; *(mobile)* bookcase

▎ Attenzione! In inglese esiste la parola *library*, che però significa *biblioteca*.

li'bretto *sm* booklet; *(taccuino)* notebook; *(Mus)* libretto; **libretto degli assegni** cheque book; **libretto di circolazione** *(Aut)* logbook; **libretto di risparmio** *(savings)* bank-book, passbook; **libretto universitario** student's report book

'libro *sm* book; **libro di cassa** cash book; **libro mastro** ledger; **libro paga** payroll; **libro di testo** textbook

li'cenza [li'tʃɛntsa] *sf (permesso)* permission, leave; *(di pesca, caccia, circolazione)* permit, licence; *(Mil)* leave; *(Ins)* school leaving certificate; *(libertà)* liberty; licence; licentiousness; **andare in ~** *(Mil)* to go on leave

licenzia'mento [litʃentsja'mento] *sm* dismissal

licenzi'are [litʃen'tsjare] *vt (impiegato)* to dismiss; *(Comm: per eccesso di personale)* to make redundant; *(Ins)* to award a certificate to; **licenziarsi** *vpr (impiegato)* to resign, hand in one's notice; *(Ins)* to obtain one's school-leaving certificate

li'ceo [li'tʃɛo] *sm (Ins)* secondary *(BRIT)* o high *(US)* school *(for 14- to 19-year-olds)*

'lido *sm* beach, shore

Liechtenstein ['liktənstain] *sm* **il ~** Liechtenstein

li'eto, -a *ag* happy, glad; **"molto ~"** *(nelle presentazioni)* "pleased to meet you"

li'eve *ag* light; *(di poco valore)* slight; *(sommesso: voce)* faint, soft

lievi'tare *vi (anche fig)* to rise ▷ *vt* to leaven

li'evito *sm* yeast; **lievito di birra** brewer's yeast

'ligio, -a, -gi, -gie ['lidʒo] *ag* faithful, loyal

'lilla *sm inv* lilac

'lillà *sm inv* lilac

'lima *sf* file; **lima da unghie** nail file

limacci'oso, -a [limat'tʃoso] *ag* slimy; muddy

li'mare *vt* to file (down); *(fig)* to polish

limi'tare *vt* to limit, restrict; *(circoscrivere)* to bound, surround; **limitarsi** *vpr* **limitarsi nel mangiare** to limit one's

eating; **limitarsi a qc/a fare qc** to limit o.s. to sth/to doing sth

'limite *sm* limit; *(confine)* border, boundary; **limite di velocità** speed limit

limo'nata *sf* lemonade *(BRIT)*, (lemon) soda *(US)*; lemon squash *(BRIT)*, lemonade *(US)*

li'mone *sm (pianta)* lemon tree; *(frutto)* lemon

'limpido, -a *ag* clear; *(acqua)* limpid, clear

'lince ['lintʃe] *sf* lynx

linci'are *vt* to lynch

'linea *sf* line; *(di mezzi pubblici di trasporto: itinerario)* route; *(: servizio)* service; **a grandi linee** in outline; **mantenere la ~** to look after one's figure; **aereo di ~** airliner; **nave di ~** liner; **volo di ~** scheduled flight; **linea aerea** airline; **linea di partenza/ d'arrivo** *(Sport)* starting/finishing line; **linea di tiro** line of fire

linea'menti *smpl* features; *(fig)* outlines

line'are *ag* linear; *(fig)* coherent, logical

line'etta *sf (trattino)* dash; *(d'unione)* hyphen

lin'gotto *sm* ingot, bar

'lingua *sf (Anat, Cuc)* tongue; *(idioma)* language; **mostrare la ~** to stick out one's tongue; **di ~ italiana** Italian-speaking; **che lingue parla?** what languages do you speak?; **una ~ di terra** a spit of land; **lingua madre** mother tongue

lingu'aggio [lin'gwaddʒo] *sm* language

lingu'etta *sf (di strumento)* reed; *(di scarpa, Tecn)* tongue; *(di busta)* flap

'lino *sm (pianta)* flax; *(tessuto)* linen

li'noleum *sm inv* linoleum, lino

liposuzi'one [liposut'tsjone] *sf* liposuction

lique'fatto, -a *pp* di **liquefare**

liqui'dare *vt (società, beni: persona: uccidere)* to liquidate; *(persona: sbarazzarsene)* to get rid of; *(conto, problema)* to settle; *(Comm: merce)* to sell off, clear; **liquidazi'one** *sf* liquidation; settlement; clearance sale

liquidità *sf* liquidity

'liquido, -a *ag, sm* liquid; **liquido per freni** brake fluid

liqui'rizia [likwi'rittsja] *sf* liquorice

li'quore *sm* liqueur

'lira *sf (Storia: unità monetaria)* lira; *(Mus)* lyre; **lira sterlina** pound sterling

'lirico, -a, -ci, -che *ag* lyric(al); *(Mus)* lyric; **cantante/teatro ~** opera singer/house

Lis'bona *sf* Lisbon

'lisca, -sche *sf (di pesce)* fishbone

lisci'are [liʃʃare] *vt* to smooth; *(fig)* to flatter

'liscio, -a, -sci, -sce ['liʃʃo] *ag* smooth;

(capelli) straight; (mobile) plain; (bevanda alcolica) neat; (fig) straightforward, simple ▷ av **andare ~** to go smoothly; **passarla liscia** to get away with it

'liso, -a ag worn out, threadbare

'lista sf (elenco) list; **lista elettorale** electoral roll; **lista delle spese** shopping list; **lista dei vini** wine list; **lista delle vivande** menu

lis'tino sm list; **listino dei cambi** (foreign) exchange rate; **listino dei prezzi** price list

'lite sf quarrel, argument; (Dir) lawsuit

liti'gare vi to quarrel; (Dir) to litigate

li'tigio [li'tidʒo] sm quarrel

lito'rale ag coastal, coast cpd ▷ sm coast

'litro sm litre

livel'lare vt to level, make level

li'vello sm level; (fig) level, standard; **ad alto ~** (fig) high-level; **livello del mare** sea level

'livido, -a ag livid; (per percosse) bruised, black and blue; (cielo) leaden ▷ sm bruise

Li'vorno sf Livorno, Leghorn

'lizza ['littsa] sf lists pl; **scendere in ~** to enter the lists

lo (dav s impura, gn, pn, ps, x, z; dav V **l'**) det m the ▷ pron (oggetto: persona) him; (: cosa) it; **lo sapevo** I knew it; **lo so** I know; **sii buono, anche se lui non lo è** be good, even if he isn't; vedi anche **il**

lo'cale ag local ▷ sm room; (luogo pubblico) premises pl; **locale notturno** nightclub; **località** sf inv locality

lo'canda sf inn

locomo'tiva sf locomotive

locuzi'one [lokut'tsjone] sf phrase, expression

lo'dare vt to praise

'lode sf praise; (Ins): **laurearsi con 110 e ~** ≈ to graduate with a first-class honours degree (BRIT), graduate summa cum laude (US)

'loden sm inv (stoffa) loden; (cappotto) loden overcoat

lo'devole ag praiseworthy

loga'ritmo sm logarithm

'loggia, -ge ['lɔddʒa] sf (Archit) loggia; (circolo massonico) lodge; **loggi'one** sm (di teatro): **il loggione** the Gods sg

'logico, -a, -ci, -che ['lɔdʒiko] ag logical

logo'rare vt to wear out; (sciupare) to waste; **logorarsi** vpr to wear out; (fig) to wear o.s. out

'logoro, -a ag (stoffa) worn out, threadbare; (persona) worn out

Lombar'dia sf **la ~** Lombardy

lom'bata sf (taglio di carne) loin

lom'brico, -chi sm earthworm

londi'nese ag London cpd ▷ sm/f Londoner

'Londra sf London

lon'gevo, -a [lon'dʒevo] ag long-lived

longi'tudine [londʒi'tudine] sf longitude

lonta'nanza [lonta'nantsa] sf distance; absence

lon'tano, -a ag (distante) distant, faraway; (assente) absent; (vago: sospetto) slight, remote; (tempo: remoto) far-off, distant; (parente) distant, remote ▷ av far; **è lontana la casa?** is it far to the house?, is the house far from here?; **è ~ un chilometro** it's a kilometre away o a kilometre from here; **più ~** farther; **da** o **di ~** from a distance; **~ da** a long way from; **è molto ~ da qui?** is it far from here?; **alla lontana** slightly, vaguely

lo'quace [lo'kwatʃe] ag talkative, loquacious; (fig: gesto ecc) eloquent

'lordo, -a ag dirty, filthy; (peso, stipendio) gross

'loro pron pl (oggetto, con preposizione) them; (complemento di termine) to them; (soggetto) they; (forma di cortesia: anche: **L~**) you; to you; **il(la) ~, i(le) ~** det their; (forma di cortesia: anche: **L~**) your ▷ pron theirs; (forma di cortesia: anche: **L~**) yours; **~ stessi(e)** they themselves; you yourselves

'losco, -a, -schi, -sche ag (fig) shady, suspicious

'lotta sf struggle, fight; (Sport) wrestling; **lotta libera** all-in wrestling; **lot'tare** vi to fight, struggle; to wrestle

lotte'ria sf lottery; (di gara ippica) sweepstake

'lotto sm (gioco) (state) lottery; (parte) lot; (Edil) site

● **LOTTO**
●
● The **Lotto** is an official lottery run by the
● Italian Finance Ministry. It consists of
● a weekly draw of numbers and is very
● popular.

lozi'one [lot'tsjone] sf lotion

lubrifi'cante sm lubricant

lubrifi'care vt to lubricate

luc'chetto [luk'ketto] sm padlock

lucci'care [luttʃi'kare] vi to sparkle, glitter, twinkle

'luccio ['luttʃo] sm (Zool) pike

'lucciola ['luttʃola] sf (Zool) firefly; glowworm

'luce ['lutʃe] sf light; (finestra) window; **alla ~ di** by the light of; **fare ~ su qc** (fig) to shed o throw light on sth; **~ del sole/della luna**

sun/moonlight
lucer'nario [lutʃer'narjo] *sm* skylight
lu'certola [lu'tʃertola] *sf* lizard
luci'dare [lutʃi'dare] *vt* to polish
lucida'trice [lutʃida'tritʃe] *sf* floor
  polisher
'lucido, -a ['lutʃido] *ag* shining, bright;
  (*lucidato*) polished; (*fig*) lucid ▷ *sm* shine,
  lustre; (*disegno*) tracing; **lucido per scarpe**
  shoe polish
'lucro *sm* profit, gain
'luglio ['luʎʎo] *sm* July
'lugubre *ag* gloomy
'lui *pron* (*soggetto*) he; (*oggetto: per dare
  rilievo, con preposizione*) him; **~ stesso** he
  himself
lu'maca, -che *sf* slug; (*chiocciola*) snail
lumi'noso, -a *ag* (*che emette luce*)
  luminous; (*cielo, colore, stanza*) bright;
  (*sorgente*) of light, light *cpd*; (*fig: sorriso*)
  bright, radiant
'luna *sf* moon; **luna nuova/piena** new/
  full moon; **luna di miele** honeymoon;
  siamo in ~ di miele we're on honeymoon
'luna park *sm inv* amusement park,
  funfair
lu'nare *ag* lunar, moon *cpd*
lu'nario *sm* almanac; **sbarcare il ~** to
  make ends meet
lu'natico, -a, -ci, -che *ag* whimsical,
  temperamental
lunedì *sm inv* Monday; **di** *o* **il ~** on
  Mondays
lun'ghezza [lun'gettsa] *sf* length;
  lunghezza d'onda (*Fisica*) wavelength
'lungo, -a, -ghi, -ghe *ag* long; (*lento:
  persona*) slow; (*diluito: caffè, brodo*) weak,
  watery, thin ▷ *sm* length ▷ *prep* along; **~
  3 metri** 3 metres long; **a ~** for a long time;
  a ~ andare in the long run; **di gran lunga**
  (*molto*) by far; **andare in ~** *o* **per le lunghe**
  to drag on; **saperla lunga** to know what's
  what; **in ~ e in largo** far and wide, all
  over; **~ il corso dei secoli** throughout the
  centuries
lungo'mare *sm* promenade
lu'notto *sm* (*Aut*) rear *o* back window;
  lunotto termico heated rear window
lu'ogo, -ghi *sm* place; (*posto: di incidente
  ecc*) scene, site; (*punto, passo di libro*)
  passage; **in ~ di** instead of; **in primo ~**
  in the first place; **aver ~** to take place;
  dar ~ a to give rise to; **luogo di nascita**
  birthplace; (*Amm*) place of birth; **luogo
  di provenienza** place of origin; **luogo
  comune** commonplace
'lupo, -a *sm/f* wolf
'luppolo *sm* (*Bot*) hop
'lurido, -a *ag* filthy

lusin'gare *vt* to flatter
Lussem'burgo *sm* (*stato*): **il ~**
  Luxembourg ▷ *sf* (*città*) Luxembourg
'lusso *sm* luxury; **di ~** luxury *cpd*;
  lussu'oso, -a *ag* luxurious
lus'suria *sf* lust
lus'trino *sm* sequin
'lutto *sm* mourning; **essere in/portare il
  ~** to be in/wear mourning

m

m. *abbr* = **mese**; **metro**; **miglia**; **monte**

ma *cong* but; **ma insomma!** for goodness sake!; **ma no!** of course not!

'macabro, -a *ag* gruesome, macabre

macché [mak'ke] *escl* not at all!, certainly not!

macche'roni [makke'roni] *smpl* macaroni *sg*

'macchia ['makkja] *sf* stain, spot; (*chiazza di diverso colore*) spot, splash, patch; (*tipo di boscaglia*) scrub; **alla ~** (*fig*) in hiding; **macchi'are** *vt* (*sporcare*) to stain, mark; **macchiarsi** *vpr* (*persona*) to get o.s. dirty; (*stoffa*) to stain; to get stained o marked

macchi'ato, -a [mak'kjato] *ag* (*pelle, pelo*) spotted; **~ di** stained with; **caffè ~** coffee with a dash of milk

'macchina ['makkina] *sf* machine; (*motore, locomotiva*) engine; (*automobile*) car; (*fig: meccanismo*) machinery; **andare in ~** (*Aut*) to go by car; (*Stampa*) to go to press; **macchina da cucire** sewing machine; **macchina fotografica** camera; **macchina da presa** cine o movie camera; **macchina da scrivere** typewriter; **macchina a vapore** steam engine

macchi'nario [makki'narjo] *sm* machinery

macchi'nista, -i [makki'nista] *sm* (*di treno*) engine-driver; (*di nave*) engineer

Macedonia [matʃe'dɔnja] *sf* **la ~** Macedonia

mace'donia [matʃe'dɔnja] *sf* fruit salad

macel'laio [matʃel'lajo] *sm* butcher

macelle'ria *sf* butcher's (shop)

ma'cerie [ma'tʃɛrje] *sfpl* rubble *sg*, debris *sg*

ma'cigno [ma'tʃiɲɲo] *sm* (*masso*) rock, boulder

maci'nare [matʃi'nare] *vt* to grind; (*carne*) to mince (BRIT), grind (US)

macrobi'otico, -a *ag* macrobiotic ▷ *sf* macrobiotics *sg*

Ma'donna *sf* (*Rel*) Our Lady

mador'nale *ag* enormous, huge

'madre *sf* mother; (*matrice di bolletta*) counterfoil ▷ *ag inv* mother *cpd*; **ragazza ~** unmarried mother; **scena ~** (*Teatro*) principal scene; (*fig*) terrible scene

madre'lingua *sf* mother tongue, native language

madre'perla *sf* mother-of-pearl

ma'drina *sf* godmother

maestà *sf inv* majesty

ma'estra *sf vedi* **maestro**

maes'trale *sm* north-west wind, mistral

ma'estro, -a *sm/f* (*Ins: anche:* **~ di scuola o elementare**) primary (BRIT) o grade school (US) teacher; (*esperto*) expert ▷ *sm* (*artigiano, fig: guida*) master; (*Mus*) maestro ▷ *ag* (*principale*) main; (*di grande abilità*) masterly, skilful; **maestra d'asilo** nursery teacher; **~ di cerimonie** master of ceremonies

'mafia *sf* Mafia

'maga *sf* sorceress

ma'gari *escl* (*esprime desiderio*): **~ fosse vero!** if only it were true!; **ti piacerebbe andare in Scozia? — ~!** would you like to go to Scotland? — and how! ▷ *av* (*anche*) even; (*forse*) perhaps

magaz'zino [magad'dzino] *sm* warehouse; **grande ~** department store

Attenzione! In inglese esiste la parola *magazine* che però significa *rivista*.

'maggio ['maddʒo] *sm* May

maggio'rana [maddʒo'rana] *sf* (*Bot*) (sweet) marjoram

maggio'ranza [maddʒo'rantsa] *sf* majority

maggior'domo [maddʒor'dɔmo] *sm* butler

maggi'ore [mad'dʒore] *ag* (*comparativo: più grande*) bigger, larger; taller; greater; (: *più vecchio: sorella, fratello*) older, elder; (: *di grado superiore*) senior; (: *più importante: Mil, Mus*) major; (*superlativo*) biggest, largest; tallest; greatest; oldest, eldest ▷ *sm/f* (*di grado*) superior; (*di età*) elder;

(*Mil*) major; (: *Aer*) squadron leader; **la maggior parte** the majority; **andare per la ~** (*cantante ecc*) to be very popular; **maggio'renne** *ag* of age ▷ *sm/f* person who has come of age

ma'gia [ma'dʒia] *sf* magic; **'magico, -a, -ci, -che** *ag* magic; (*fig*) fascinating, charming, magical

magis'trato [madʒis'trato] *sm* magistrate

'maglia ['maʎʎa] *sf* stitch; (*lavoro ai ferri*) knitting *no pl*; (*tessuto, Sport*) jersey; (*maglione*) jersey, sweater; (*di catena*) link; (*di rete*) mesh; **maglia diritta/rovescia** plain/purl; **magli'etta** *sf* (*canottiera*) vest; (*tipo camicia*) T-shirt

magli'one *sm* sweater, jumper

ma'gnetico, -a, -ci, -che *ag* magnetic

ma'gnifico, -a, -ci, -che [maɲ'ɲifiko] *ag* magnificent, splendid; (*ospite*) generous

ma'gnolia [maɲ'ɲɔlja] *sf* magnolia

'mago, -ghi *sm* (*stregone*) magician, wizard; (*illusionista*) magician

ma'grezza [ma'grettsa] *sf* thinness

'magro, -a *ag* (*very*) thin, skinny; (*carne*) lean; (*formaggio*) low-fat; (*fig: scarso, misero*) meagre, poor; (: *meschino: scusa*) poor, lame; **mangiare di ~** not to eat meat

'mai *av* (*nessuna volta*) never; (*talvolta*) ever; **non ... ~** never; **~ più** never again; **non sono ~ stato in Spagna** I've never been to Spain; **come ~?** why (*o* how) on earth?; **chi/dove/quando ~?** whoever/wherever/whenever?

mai'ale *sm* (*Zool*) pig; (*carne*) pork

maio'nese *sf* mayonnaise

'mais *sm inv* maize

mai'uscolo, -a *ag* (*lettera*) capital; (*fig*) enormous, huge

mala'fede *sf* bad faith

malan'dato, -a *ag* (*persona: di salute*) in poor health; (: *di condizioni finanziarie*) badly off; (*trascurato*) shabby

ma'lanno *sm* (*disgrazia*) misfortune; (*malattia*) ailment

mala'pena *sf* **a ~** hardly, scarcely

ma'laria *sf* (*Med*) malaria

ma'lato, -a *ag* ill, sick; (*gamba*) bad; (*pianta*) diseased ▷ *sm/f* sick person; (*in ospedale*) patient; **malat'tia** *sf* (*infettiva ecc*) illness, disease; (*cattiva salute*) illness, sickness; (*di pianta*) disease

mala'vita *sf* underworld

mala'voglia [mala'vɔʎʎa] *sf* **di ~** unwillingly, reluctantly

Mala'ysia *sf* Malaysia

mal'concio, -a, -ci, -ce [mal'kontʃo] *ag* in a sorry state

malcon'tento *sm* discontent

malcos'tume *sm* immorality

mal'destro, -a *ag* (*inabile*) inexpert, inexperienced; (*goffo*) awkward

'male *av* badly ▷ *sm* (*ciò che è ingiusto, disonesto*) evil; (*danno, svantaggio*) harm; (*sventura*) misfortune; (*dolore fisico, morale*) pain, ache; **di ~ in peggio** from bad to worse; **sentirsi ~** to feel ill; **far ~** (*dolere*) to hurt; **far ~ alla salute** to be bad for one's health; **far del ~ a qn** to hurt *o* harm sb; **restare** *o* **rimanere ~** to be sorry; to be disappointed; to be hurt; **andare a ~** to go bad; **come va? — non c'è ~** how are you? — not bad; **avere male di gola/testa** to have a sore throat/a headache; **aver ~ ai piedi** to have sore feet; **mal d'auto** carsickness; **mal di cuore** heart trouble; **male di dente** toothache; **mal di mare** seasickness

male'detto, -a *pp di* **maledire** ▷ *ag* cursed, damned; (*fig: fam*) damned, blasted

male'dire *vt* to curse; **maledizi'one** *sf* curse; **maledizione!** damn it!

maledu'cato, -a *ag* rude, ill-mannered

maleducazi'one [maledukat'tsjone] *sf* rudeness

ma'lefico, -a, -ci, -che *ag* (*influsso, azione*) evil

ma'lessere *sm* indisposition, slight illness; (*fig*) uneasiness

malfa'mato, -a *ag* notorious

malfat'tore, -'trice *sm/f* wrongdoer

mal'fermo, -a *ag* unsteady, shaky; (*salute*) poor, delicate

mal'grado *prep* in spite of, despite ▷ *cong* although; **mio (*o* tuo *ecc*) ~** against my (*o* your *ecc*) will

ma'ligno, -a [ma'liɲɲo] *ag* (*malvagio*) malicious, malignant; (*Med*) malignant

malinco'nia *sf* melancholy, gloom; **malin'conico, -a, -ci, -che** *ag* melancholy

malincu'ore: **a ~** *av* reluctantly, unwillingly

malin'teso, -a *ag* misunderstood; (*riguardo, senso del dovere*) mistaken, wrong ▷ *sm* misunderstanding; **c'è stato un ~** there's been a misunderstanding

ma'lizia [ma'littsja] *sf* (*malignità*) malice; (*furbizia*) cunning; (*espediente*) trick; **malizi'oso, -a** *ag* malicious; cunning; (*vivace, birichino*) mischievous

malme'nare *vt* to beat up

ma'locchio [ma'lɔkkjo] *sm* evil eye

ma'lora *sf* **andare in ~** to go to the dogs

ma'lore *sm* (*sudden*) illness

mal'sano, -a *ag* unhealthy

'malta *sf* (*Edil*) mortar

mal'tempo *sm* bad weather

'malto *sm* malt

maltrat'tare *vt* to ill-treat

malu'more *sm* bad mood; (*irritabilità*) bad temper; (*discordia*) ill feeling; **di ~** in a bad mood

'malva *sf* (*Bot*) mallow ▷ *ag*, *sm inv* mauve

mal'vagio, -a, -gi, -gie [mal'vadʒo] *ag* wicked, evil

malvi'vente *sm* criminal

malvolenti'eri *av* unwillingly, reluctantly

'mamma *sf* mummy, mum; **~ mia!** my goodness!

mam'mella *sf* (*Anat*) breast; (*di vacca, capra ecc*) udder

mam'mifero *sm* mammal

ma'nata *sf* (*colpo*) slap; (*quantità*) handful

man'canza [man'kantsa] *sf* lack; (*carenza*) shortage, scarcity; (*fallo*) fault; (*imperfezione*) failing, shortcoming; **per ~ di tempo** through lack of time; **in ~ di meglio** for lack of anything better

man'care *vi* (*essere insufficiente*) to be lacking; (*venir meno*) to fail; (*sbagliare*) to be wrong, make a mistake; (*non esserci*) to be missing, not to be there; (*essere lontano*): **~ (da)** to be away (from) ▷ *vt* to miss; **~ di** to lack; **~ a** (*promessa*) to fail to keep; **tu mi manchi** I miss you; **mancò poco che morisse** he very nearly died; **mancano ancora 10 sterline** we're still £10 short; **manca un quarto alle 6** it's a quarter to 6

mancherò *ecc* [manke'rɔ] *vb vedi* **mancare**

'mancia, -ce ['mantʃa] *sf* tip; **quanto devo lasciare di ~?** how much should I tip?; **~ competente** reward

manci'ata [man'tʃata] *sf* handful

man'cino, -a [man'tʃino] *ag* (*braccio*) left; (*persona*) left-handed; (*fig*) underhand

manda'rancio [manda'rantʃo] *sm* clementine

man'dare *vt* to send; (*far funzionare: macchina*) to drive; (*emettere*) to send out; (: *grido*) to give, utter, let out; **~ a chiamare qn** to send for sb; **~ avanti** (*fig: famiglia*) to provide for; (: *fabbrica*) to run, look after; **~ giù** to send down; (*anche fig*) to swallow; **~ via** to send away; (*licenziare*) to fire

manda'rino *sm* mandarin (orange); (*cinese*) mandarin

man'data *sf* (*quantità*) lot, batch; (*di chiave*) turn; **chiudere a doppia ~** to double-lock

man'dato *sm* (*incarico*) commission; (*Dir: provvedimento*) warrant; (*di deputato ecc*) mandate; (*ordine di pagamento*) postal *o* money order; **mandato d'arresto** warrant for arrest

man'dibola *sf* mandible, jaw

'mandorla *sf* almond; **'mandorlo** *sm* almond tree

'mandria *sf* herd

maneggi'are [maned'dʒare] *vt* (*creta, cera*) to mould, work, fashion; (*arnesi, utensili*) to handle; (: *adoperare*) to use; (*fig: persone, denaro*) to handle, deal with; **ma'neggio** *sm* moulding; handling; use; (*intrigo*) plot, scheme; (*per cavalli*) riding school

ma'nesco, -a, -schi, -sche *ag* free with one's fists

ma'nette *sfpl* handcuffs

manga'nello *sm* club

mangi'are [man'dʒare] *vt* to eat; (*intaccare*) to eat into *o* away; (*Carte, Scacchi ecc*) to take ▷ *vi* to eat ▷ *sm* eating; (*cibo*) food; (*cucina*) cooking; **possiamo ~ qualcosa?** can we have something to eat?; **mangiarsi le parole** to mumble; **mangiarsi le unghie** to bite one's nails

man'gime [man'dʒime] *sm* fodder

'mango, -ghi *sm* mango

ma'nia *sf* (*Psic*) mania; (*fig*) obsession, craze; **ma'niaco, -a, -ci, -che** *ag* suffering from a mania; **maniaco (di)** obsessed (by), crazy (about)

'manica *sf* sleeve; (*fig: gruppo*) gang, bunch; (*Geo*): **la M~, il Canale della M~** the (English) Channel; **essere di ~ larga/ stretta** to be easy-going/strict; **manica a vento** (*Aer*) wind sock

mani'chino [mani'kino] *sm* (*di sarto, vetrina*) dummy

'manico, -ci *sm* handle; (*Mus*) neck

mani'comio *sm* mental hospital; (*fig*) madhouse

mani'cure *sm o f inv* manicure ▷ *sf inv* manicurist

mani'era *sf* way, manner; (*stile*) style, manner; **maniere** *sfpl* (*comportamento*) manners; **in ~ che** so that; **in ~ da** so as to; **in tutte le maniere** at all costs

manifes'tare *vt* to show, display; (*esprimere*) to express; (*rivelare*) to reveal, disclose ▷ *vi* to demonstrate; **manifestazi'one** *sf* show, display; expression; (*sintomo*) sign, symptom; (*dimostrazione pubblica*) demonstration; (*cerimonia*) event

mani'festo, -a *ag* obvious, evident ▷ *sm* poster, bill; (*scritto ideologico*) manifesto

ma'niglia [ma'niʎʎa] *sf* handle; (*sostegno: negli autobus ecc*) strap

manipo'lare *vt* to manipulate; (*alterare: vino*) to adulterate

man'naro: **lupo ~** *sm* werewolf

'mano, -i *sf* hand; (*strato: di vernice ecc*) coat; **di prima ~** (*notizia*) first-hand; **di**

seconda ~ second-hand; **man ~** little by little, gradually; **man ~ che** as; **darsi o stringersi la ~** to shake hands; **mettere le mani avanti** (*fig*) to safeguard o.s.; **restare a mani vuote** to be left empty-handed; **venire alle mani** to come to blows; **a ~** by hand; **mani in alto!** hands up!

mano'dopera *sf* labour

ma'nometro *sm* gauge, manometer

mano'mettere *vt* (*alterare*) to tamper with; (*aprire indebitamente*) to break open illegally

ma'nopola *sf* (*dell'armatura*) gauntlet; (*guanto*) mitt; (*di impugnatura*) hand-grip; (*pomello*) knob

manos'critto, -a *ag* handwritten ▷ *sm* manuscript

mano'vale *sm* labourer

mano'vella *sf* handle; (*Tecn*) crank

ma'novra *sf* manoeuvre (BRIT), maneuver (US); (*Ferr*) shunting

man'sarda *sf* attic

mansi'one *sf* task, duty, job

mansu'eto, -a *ag* gentle, docile

man'tello *sm* cloak; (*fig: di neve ecc*) blanket, mantle; (*Zool*) coat

mante'nere *vt* to maintain; (*adempiere: promesse*) to keep, abide by; (*provvedere a*) to support, maintain; **mantenersi** *vpr* **mantenersi calmo/giovane** to stay calm/young

'Mantova *sf* Mantua

manu'ale *ag* manual ▷ *sm* (*testo*) manual, handbook

ma'nubrio *sm* handle; (*di bicicletta ecc*) handlebars *pl*; (*Sport*) dumbbell

manutenzi'one [manuten'tsjone] *sf* maintenance, upkeep; (*d'impianti*) maintenance, servicing

'manzo ['mandzo] *sm* (*Zool*) steer; (*carne*) beef

'mappa *sf* (*Geo*) map; **mappa'mondo** *sm* map of the world; (*globo girevole*) globe

mara'tona *sf* marathon

'marca, -che *sf* (*Comm: di prodotti*) brand; (*contrassegno, scontrino*) ticket, check; **prodotto di ~** (*di buona qualità*) high-class product; **marca da bollo** official stamp

mar'care *vt* (*munire di contrassegno*) to mark; (*a fuoco*) to brand; (*Sport: gol*) to score; (*: avversario*) to mark; (*accentuare*) to stress; **~ visita** (*Mil*) to report sick

marcherò *ecc* [marke'rɔ] *vb vedi* **marcare**

mar'chese, -a [mar'keze] *sm/f* marquis o marquess/marchioness

marchi'are [mar'kjare] *vt* to brand

'marcia, -ce ['martʃa] *sf* (*anche Mus, Mil*) march; (*funzionamento*) running; (*il*

camminare) walking; (*Aut*) gear; **mettere in ~** to start; **mettersi in ~** to get moving; **far ~ indietro** (*Aut*) to reverse; (*fig*) to back-pedal

marciapi'ede [martʃa'pjɛde] *sm* (*di strada*) pavement (BRIT), sidewalk (US); (*Ferr*) platform

marci'are [mar'tʃare] *vi* to march; (*andare: treno, macchina*) to go; (*funzionare*) to run, work

'marcio, -a, -ci, -ce ['martʃo] *ag* (*frutta, legno*) rotten, bad; (*Med*) festering; (*fig*) corrupt, rotten

mar'cire [mar'tʃire] *vi* (*andare a male*) to go bad, rot; (*suppurare*) to fester; (*fig*) to rot, waste away

'marco, -chi *sm* (*unità monetaria*) mark

'mare *sm* sea; **in ~** at sea; **andare al ~** (*in vacanza ecc*) to go to the seaside; **il M~ del Nord** the North Sea

ma'rea *sf* tide; **alta/bassa ~** high/low tide

mareggi'ata [mared'dʒata] *sf* heavy sea

mare'moto *sm* seaquake

maresci'allo [mareʃ'ʃallo] *sm* (*Mil*) marshal; (*: sottufficiale*) warrant officer

marga'rina *sf* margarine

marghe'rita [marge'rita] *sf* (*ox-eye*) daisy, marguerite; (*di stampante*) daisy wheel

'margine ['mardʒine] *sm* margin; (*di bosco, via*) edge, border

mariju'ana [mæri'wa:nə] *sf* marijuana

ma'rina *sf* navy; (*costa*) coast; (*quadro*) seascape; **marina mercantile/militare** navy/merchant navy (BRIT) o marine (US)

mari'naio *sm* sailor

mari'nare *vt* (*Cuc*) to marinate; **~ la scuola** to play truant

ma'rino, -a *ag* sea *cpd*, marine

mario'netta *sf* puppet

ma'rito *sm* husband

ma'rittimo, -a *ag* maritime, sea *cpd*

marmel'lata *sf* jam; (*di agrumi*) marmalade

mar'mitta *sf* (*recipiente*) pot; (*Aut*) silencer; **marmitta catalitica** catalytic converter

'marmo *sm* marble

mar'motta *sf* (*Zool*) marmot

maroc'chino, -a [marok'kino] *ag, sm/f* Moroccan

Ma'rocco *sm* **il ~** Morocco

mar'rone *ag inv* brown ▷ *sm* (*Bot*) chestnut

> Attenzione! In inglese esiste la parola *maroon*, che però indica un altro colore, il rosso bordeaux.

mar'supio *sm* pouch; (*per denaro*) bum bag; (*per neonato*) sling

martedì *sm inv* Tuesday; **di o il ~** on

Tuesdays; **martedì grasso** Shrove Tuesday

martel'lare vt to hammer ▷ vi (pulsare) to throb; (: cuore) to thump

mar'tello sm hammer; (: di uscio) knocker; **martello pneumatico** pneumatic drill

'martire sm/f martyr

mar'xista, -i, -e ag, sm/f Marxist

marza'pane [martsa'pane] sm marzipan

'marzo ['martso] sm March

mascal'zone [maskal'tsone] sm rascal, scoundrel

mas'cara sm inv mascara

ma'scella [maʃʃɛlla] sf (Anat) jaw

'maschera ['maskera] sf mask; (travestimento) disguise; (: per un ballo ecc) fancy dress; (Teatro, Cinema) usher/usherette; (personaggio del teatro) stock character; **masche'rare** vt to mask; (travestire) to disguise; to dress up; (fig: celare) to hide, conceal; (Mil) to camouflage; **mascherarsi da** to disguise o.s. as; to dress up as; (fig) to masquerade as

mas'chile [mas'kile] ag masculine; (sesso, popolazione) male; (abiti) men's; (per ragazzi: scuola) boys'

mas'chilista, -i, -e ag, sm/f (uomo) (male) chauvinist, sexist; (donna) sexist

'maschio, -a ['maskjo] ag (Biol) male; (virile) manly ▷ sm (anche Zool, Tecn) male; (uomo) man; (ragazzo) boy; (figlio) son

masco'lino, -a ag masculine

'massa sf mass; (di errori ecc): **una ~ di** heaps of, masses of; (di gente) mass, multitude; (Elettr) earth; **in ~** (Comm) in bulk; (tutti insieme) en masse; **adunata in ~** mass meeting; **di ~** (cultura, manifestazione) mass cpd

mas'sacro sm massacre, slaughter; (fig) mess, disaster

massaggi'are [massad'dʒare] vt to massage

mas'saggio [mas'saddʒo] sm massage; **massaggio cardiaco** cardiac massage

mas'saia sf housewife

masse'rizie [masse'rittsje] sfpl (household) furnishings

mas'siccio, -a, -ci, -ce [mas'sittʃo] ag (oro, legno) solid; (palazzo) massive; (corporatura) stout ▷ sm (Geo) massif

'massima sf (sentenza, regola) maxim; (Meteor) maximum temperature; **in linea di ~** generally speaking; vedi **massimo**

massi'male sm maximum

'massimo, -a ag, sm maximum; **al ~** at (the) most

'masso sm rock, boulder

masteriz'zare [masterid'dzare] vt (CD, DVD) to burn

masterizza'tore [masteriddza'tore] sm CD burner o writer

masti'care vt to chew

'mastice ['mastitʃe] sm mastic; (per vetri) putty

mas'tino sm mastiff

ma'tassa sf skein

mate'matica sf mathematics sg

mate'matico, -a, -ci, -che ag mathematical ▷ sm/f mathematician

materas'sino sm mat; **materassino gonfiabile** air bed

mate'rasso sm mattress; **materasso a molle** spring o interior-sprung mattress

ma'teria sf (Fisica) matter; (Tecn, Comm) material, matter no pl; (disciplina) subject; (argomento) subject matter, material; **in ~ di** (per quanto concerne) on the subject of; **materie prime** raw materials

materi'ale ag material; (fig: grossolano) rough, rude ▷ sm material; (insieme di strumenti ecc) equipment no pl, materials pl

maternità sf motherhood, maternity; (reparto) maternity ward

ma'terno, -a ag (amore, cura ecc) maternal, motherly; (nonno) maternal; (lingua, terra) mother cpd

ma'tita sf pencil; **matite colorate** coloured pencils; **matita per gli occhi** eyeliner (pencil)

ma'tricola sf (registro) register; (numero) registration number; (nell'università) freshman, fresher

ma'trigna [ma'triɲɲa] sf stepmother

matrimoni'ale ag matrimonial, marriage cpd

matri'monio sm marriage, matrimony; (durata) marriage, married life; (cerimonia) wedding

mat'tina sf morning

'matto, -a ag mad, crazy; (fig: falso) false, imitation ▷ sm/f madman/woman; **avere una voglia matta di qc** to be dying for sth

mat'tone sm brick; (fig): **questo libro/ film è un ~** this book/film is heavy going

matto'nella sf tile

matu'rare vi (anche: **maturarsi**: frutta, grano) to ripen; (ascesso) to come to a head; (fig: persona, idea, Econ) to mature ▷ vt to ripen, to (make) mature

maturità sf maturity; (di frutta) ripeness, maturity; (Ins) school-leaving examination, ≈ GCE A-levels (BRIT)

ma'turo, -a ag mature; (frutto) ripe, mature

max. abbr (= massimo) max

maxischermo [maxis'kermo] sm giant screen

'mazza ['mattsa] sf (bastone) club;

(*martello*) sledge-hammer; (*Sport: da golf*) club; (: *da baseball, cricket*) bat

maz'zata [mat'tsata] *sf* (*anche fig*) heavy blow

'mazzo ['mattso] *sm* (*di fiori, chiavi ecc*) bunch; (*di carte da gioco*) pack

me *pron* me; **me stesso(a)** myself; **sei bravo quanto me** you are as clever as I (am) о as me

mec'canico, -a, -ci, -che *ag* mechanical ▷ *sm* mechanic; **può mandare un ~?** can you send a mechanic?

mecca'nismo *sm* mechanism

me'daglia [me'daʎʎa] *sf* medal

me'desimo, -a *ag* same; (*in persona*): **io ~ I** myself

'media *sf* average; (*Mat*) mean; (*Ins: voto*) end-of-term average; **le medie** *sfpl* = **scuola media**; **in ~** on average; *vedi anche* **medio**

medi'ante *prep* by means of

media'tore, -'trice *sm/f* mediator; (*Comm*) middle man, agent

medi'care *vt* to treat; (*ferita*) to dress

medi'cina [medi'tʃina] *sf* medicine; **medicina legale** forensic medicine

'medico, -a, -ci, -che *ag* medical ▷ *sm* doctor; **chiamate un ~** call a doctor; **medico generico** general practitioner, GP

medie'vale *ag* medieval

'medio, -a *ag* average; (*punto, ceto*) middle; (*altezza, statura*) medium ▷ *sm* (*dito*) middle finger; **licenza media** *leaving certificate awarded at the end of 3 years of secondary education*; **scuola media** *first 3 years of secondary school*

medi'ocre *ag* mediocre, poor

medi'tare *vt* to ponder over, meditate on; (*progettare*) to plan, think out ▷ *vi* to meditate

mediter'raneo, -a *ag* Mediterranean; **il (mare) M~** the Mediterranean (Sea)

me'dusa *sf* (*Zool*) jellyfish

mega'byte *sm inv* (*Comput*) megabyte

me'gafono *sm* megaphone

'meglio ['mɛʎʎo] *av, ag inv* better; (*con senso superlativo*) best ▷ *sm* (*la cosa migliore*): **il ~** the best (thing); **faresti ~ ad andartene** you had better leave; **alla ~** as best one can; **andar di bene in ~** to get better and better; **fare del proprio ~** to do one's best; **per il ~** for the best; **aver la ~ su qn** to get the better of sb

'mela *sf* apple; **mela cotogna** quince

mela'grana *sf* pomegranate

melan'zana [melan'dzana] *sf* aubergine (BRIT), eggplant (US)

melato'nina *sf* melatonin

'melma *sf* mud, mire

'melo *sm* apple tree

melo'dia *sf* melody

me'lone *sm* (musk)melon

'membro *sm* member (*pl(f)* **membra**) (*arto*) limb

memo'randum *sm inv* memorandum

me'moria *sf* memory; **memorie** *sfpl* (*opera autobiografica*) memoirs; **a ~** (*imparare, sapere*) by heart; **a ~ d'uomo** within living memory

mendi'cante *sm/f* beggar

 PAROLA CHIAVE

'meno *av* **1** (*in minore misura*) less; **dovresti mangiare meno** you should eat less, you shouldn't eat so much

2 (*comparativo*): **meno ... di** not as ... as, less ... than; **sono meno alto di te** I'm not as tall as you (are), I'm less tall than you (are); **meno ... che** not as ... as, less ... than; **meno che mai** less than ever; **è meno intelligente che ricco** he's more rich than intelligent; **meno fumo più mangio** the less I smoke the more I eat

3 (*superlativo*) least; **il meno dotato degli studenti** the least gifted of the students; **è quello che compro meno spesso** it's the one I buy least often

4 (*Mat*) minus; **8 meno 5** 8 minus 5, 8 take away 5; **sono le 8 meno un quarto** it's a quarter to 8; **meno 5 gradi** 5 degrees below zero, minus 5 degrees; **1 euro in meno** 1 euro less

5 (*fraseologia*): **quanto meno poteva telefonare** he could at least have phoned; **non so se accettare o meno** I don't know whether to accept or not; **fare a meno di qc/qn** to do without sth/sb; **non potevo fare a meno di ridere** I couldn't help laughing; **meno male!** thank goodness!; **meno male che sei arrivato** it's a good job that you've come

▷ *ag inv* (*tempo, denaro*) less; (*errori, persone*) fewer; **ha fatto meno errori di tutti** he made fewer mistakes than anyone, he made the fewest mistakes of all ▷ *sm inv* **1**: **il meno** (*il minimo*) the least; **parlare del più e del meno** to talk about this and that **2** (*Mat*) minus

▷ *prep* (*eccetto*) except (for), apart from; **a meno che, a meno di** unless; **a meno che non piova** unless it rains; **non posso, a meno di prendere ferie** I can't, unless I take some leave

meno'pausa *sf* menopause

'mensa *sf* (*locale*) canteen; (: *Mil*) mess; (: *nelle università*) refectory

m

men'sile *ag* monthly ▷ *sm* (*periodico*) monthly (magazine); (*stipendio*) monthly salary

'mensola *sf* bracket; (*ripiano*) shelf; (*Archit*) corbel

'menta *sf* mint; (*anche*: **~ piperita**) peppermint; (*bibita*) peppermint cordial; (*caramella*) mint, peppermint

men'tale *ag* mental; **mentalità** *sf inv* mentality

'mente *sf* mind; **imparare/sapere qc a ~** to learn/know sth by heart; **avere in ~ qc** to have sth in mind; **passare di ~ a qn** to slip sb's mind

men'tire *vi* to lie

'mento *sm* chin

'mentre *cong* (*temporale*) while; (*avversativo*) whereas

menù *sm inv* menu; **ci può portare il ~?** could we see the menu?; **menù turistico** set menu

menzio'nare [mentsjo'nare] *vt* to mention

men'zogna [men'tsɔɲɲa] *sf* lie

mera'viglia [mera'viʎʎa] *sf* amazement, wonder; (*persona, cosa*) marvel, wonder; **a ~** perfectly, wonderfully; **meravigli'are** *vt* to amaze, astonish; **meravigliarsi (di)** to marvel (at); (*stupirsi*) to be amazed (at), be astonished (at); **meravigli'oso, -a** *ag* wonderful, marvellous

mer'cante *sm* merchant; **mercante d'arte** art dealer

merca'tino *sm* (*rionale*) local street market; (*Econ*) unofficial stock market

mer'cato *sm* market; **mercato dei cambi** exchange market; **mercato nero** black market

'merce ['mɛrtʃe] *sf* goods *pl*, merchandise

mercé [mer'tʃe] *sf* mercy

merce'ria [mertʃe'ria] *sf* (*articoli*) haberdashery (*BRIT*), notions *pl* (*US*); (*bottega*) haberdasher's shop (*BRIT*), notions store (*US*)

mercoledì *sm inv* Wednesday; **di** *o* **il ~** on Wednesdays; **mercoledì delle Ceneri** Ash Wednesday

mer'curio *sm* mercury

'merda (*fam!*) *sf* shit (*!*)

me'renda *sf* afternoon snack

meren'dina *sf* snack

meridi'ana *sf* (*orologio*) sundial

meridi'ano, -a *ag* meridian; midday *cpd*, noonday ▷ *sm* meridian

meridio'nale *ag* southern ▷ *sm/f* southerner

meridi'one *sm* south

me'ringa, -ghe *sf* (*Cuc*) meringue

meri'tare *vt* to deserve, merit ▷ *vb impers*

merita andare it's worth going

meri'tevole *ag* worthy

'merito *sm* merit; (*valore*) worth; **in ~ a** as regards, with regard to; **dare ~ a qn di** to give sb credit for; **finire a pari ~** to finish joint first (*o* second *ecc*); to tie

mer'letto *sm* lace

'merlo *sm* (*Zool*) blackbird; (*Archit*) battlement

mer'luzzo [mer'luttso] *sm* (*Zool*) cod

mes'chino, -a [mes'kino] *ag* wretched; (*scarso*) scanty, poor; (*persona: gretta*) mean; (: *limitata*) narrow-minded, petty

mesco'lare *vt* to mix; (*vini, colori*) to blend; (*mettere in disordine*) to mix up, muddle up; (*carte*) to shuffle

'mese *sm* month

'messa *sf* (*Rel*) mass; (*il mettere*): **messa in moto** starting; **messa in piega** set; **messa a punto** (*Tecn*) adjustment; (*Aut*) tuning; (*fig*) clarification; **messa in scena** = **messinscena**

messag'gero [messad'dʒɛro] *sm* messenger

messaggino [messad'dʒino] *sm* (*di telefonino*) text (message)

mes'saggio [mes'saddʒo] *sm* message; **posso lasciare un ~?** can I leave a message?; **ci sono messaggi per me?** are there any messages for me?; **messaggio di posta elettronica** e-mail message

messag'gistica [messad'dʒistica] *sf* **~ immediata** (*Inform*) instant messaging; **programma di ~ immediata** instant messenger

mes'sale *sm* (*Rel*) missal

messi'cano, -a *ag, sm/f* Mexican

'Messico *sm* **il ~** Mexico

messin'scena [messin'ʃɛna] *sf* (*Teatro*) production

'messo, -a *pp di* **mettere** ▷ *sm* messenger

mesti'ere *sm* (*professione*) job; (: *manuale*) trade; (: *artigianale*) craft; (*fig: abilità nel lavoro*) skill, technique; **essere del ~** to know the tricks of the trade

'mestolo *sm* (*Cuc*) ladle

mestruazi'one [mestruat'tsjone] *sf* menstruation

'meta *sf* destination; (*fig*) aim, goal

metà *sf inv* half; (*punto di mezzo*) middle; **dividere qc a** *o* **per ~** to divide sth in half, halve sth; **fare a ~ (di qc con qn)** to go halves (with sb in sth); **a ~ prezzo** at half price; **a ~ strada** halfway

meta'done *sm* methadone

me'tafora *sf* metaphor

me'tallico, -a, -ci, -che *ag* (*di metallo*) metal *cpd*; (*splendore, rumore ecc*) metallic

me'tallo *sm* metal

metalmec'canico, -a, -ci, -che *ag*
engineering *cpd* ▷ *sm* engineering worker
me'tano *sm* methane
me'ticcio, -a, -ci, -ce [me'tittʃo] *sm/f*
half-caste, half-breed
me'todico, -a, -ci, -che *ag* methodical
'metodo *sm* method
'metro *sm* metre; (*nastro*) tape measure;
(*asta*) (metre) rule
metropoli'tana *sf* underground, subway
'mettere *vt* to put; (*abito*) to put on;
(: *portare*) to wear; (*installare: telefono*) to
put in; (*fig: provocare*): **~ fame/allegria a
qn** to make sb hungry/happy; (*supporre*):
mettiamo che ... let's suppose *o* say
that ...; **mettersi** *vpr* (*persona*) to put
o.s.; (*oggetto*) to go; (*disporsi: faccenda*) to
turn out; **mettersi a sedere** to sit down;
mettersi a letto to get into bed; (*per
malattia*) to take to one's bed; **mettersi il
cappello** to put on one's hat; **mettersi a**
(*cominciare*) to begin to, start to; **mettersi
al lavoro** to set to work; **mettersi con qn**
(*in società*) to team up with sb; (*in coppia*)
to start going out with sb; **metterci:
metterci molta cura/molto tempo** to
take a lot of care/a lot of time; **ci ho messo
3 ore per venire** it's taken me 3 hours to
get here; **mettercela tutta** to do one's
best; **~ a tacere qn/qc** to keep sb/sth
quiet; **~ su casa** to set up house; **~ su un
negozio** to start a shop; **~ via** to put away
mezza'notte [meddza'nɔtte] *sf* midnight
'mezzo, -a ['mɛddzo] *ag* half; **un ~ litro/
panino** half a litre/roll ▷ *av* half-; **~ morto**
half-dead ▷ *sm* (*metà*) half; (*parte centrale:
di strada ecc*) middle; (*per raggiungere un fine*)
means *sg*; (*veicolo*) vehicle; (*nell'indicare
l'ora*): **le nove e ~** half past nine; **~ giorno e
~** half past twelve; **mezzi** *smpl* (*possibilità
economiche*) means; **di mezza età** middle-
aged; **un soprabito di mezza stagione**
a spring (*o* autumn) coat; **di ~** middle, in
the middle; **andarci di ~** (*patir danno*) to
suffer; **levarsi** *o* **togliersi di ~** to get out of
the way; **in ~ a** in the middle of; **per** *o* **a ~
di** by means of; **mezzi di comunicazione
di massa** mass media *pl*; **mezzi pubblici**
public transport *sg*; **mezzi di trasporto**
means of transport
mezzogi'orno [meddzo'dʒorno] *sm*
midday, noon; **a ~** at 12 (o'clock) *o* midday *o*
noon; **il ~ d'Italia** southern Italy
mi (*dav lo, la, li, le, ne diventa* **me**) *pron*
(*oggetto*) me; (*complemento di termine*)
to me; (*riflessivo*) myself ▷ *sm* (*Mus*) E;
(: *solfeggiando la scala*) mi
miago'lare *vi* to miaow, mew
'mica *av* (*fam*): **non ... ~** not ... at all; **non**

sono ~ stanco I'm not a bit tired; **non sarà
~ partito?** he wouldn't have left, would
he?; **~ male** not bad
'miccia, -ce ['mittʃa] *sf* fuse
micidi'ale [mitʃi'djale] *ag* fatal;
(*dannosissimo*) deadly
micro'fibra *sf* microfibre
mi'crofono *sm* microphone
micros'copio *sm* microscope
mi'dollo (*pl(f)* **midolla**) *sm* (*Anat*) marrow;
midollo osseo bone marrow
mi'ele *sm* honey
'miglia ['miʎʎa] *sfpl di* **miglio**
migli'aio [miʎ'ʎajo] (*(pl)f* **migliaia**) *sm*
thousand; **un ~ (di)** about a thousand; **a
migliaia** by the thousand, in thousands
'miglio ['miʎʎo] *sm* (*Bot*) millet (*pl(f)*
miglia) (*unità di misura*) mile; **~ marino** *o*
nautico nautical mile
migliora'mento [miʎʎora'mento] *sm*
improvement
miglio'rare [miʎʎo'rare] *vt, vi* to improve
migli'ore [miʎ'ʎore] *ag* (*comparativo*)
better; (*superlativo*) best ▷ *sm* **il ~** the best
(thing) ▷ *sm/f* **il(la) ~** the best (person); **il
miglior vino di questa regione** the best
wine in this area
'mignolo ['miɲɲolo] *sm* (*Anat*) little finger,
pinkie; (: *dito del piede*) little toe
Mi'lano *sf* Milan
miliar'dario, -a *sm/f* millionaire
mili'ardo *sm* thousand million, billion (*us*)
mili'one *sm* million; **mille euro** one
thousand euros
mili'tante *ag, sm/f* militant
mili'tare *vi* (*Mil*) to be a soldier, serve; (*fig:
in un partito*) to be a militant ▷ *ag* military
▷ *sm* serviceman; **fare il ~** to do one's
military service
'mille (*pl* **mila**) *num* a *o* one thousand; **dieci
mila** ten thousand
mil'lennio *sm* millennium
millepi'edi *sm inv* centipede
mil'lesimo, -a *ag, sm* thousandth
milli'grammo *sm* milligram(me)
mil'limetro *sm* millimetre
'milza ['miltsa] *sf* (*Anat*) spleen
mimetiz'zare [mimetid'dzare] *vt* to
camouflage; **mimetizzarsi** *vpr* to
camouflage o.s.
'mimo *sm* (*attore, componimento*) mime
mi'mosa *sf* mimosa
min. *abbr* (= *minuto, minimo*) min.
'mina *sf* (*esplosiva*) mine; (*di matita*) lead
mi'naccia, -ce [mi'nattʃa] *sf* threat;
minacciare *vt* to threaten; **minacciare
qn di morte** to threaten to kill sb;
minacciare di fare qc to threaten to do
sth

m

mi'nare vt (Mil) to mine; (fig) to undermine

mina'tore sm miner

mine'rale ag, sm mineral

mine'rario, -a ag (delle miniere) mining; (dei minerali) ore cpd

mi'nestra sf soup; **minestra in brodo** noodle soup; **minestra di verdure** vegetable soup

minia'tura sf miniature

mini'bar sm inv minibar

mini'era sf mine

mini'gonna sf miniskirt

'minimo, -a ag minimum, least, slightest; (piccolissimo) very small, slight; (il più basso) lowest, minimum ▷ sm minimum; **al ~** at least; **girare al ~** (Aut) to idle

minis'tero sm (Pol, Rel) ministry; (governo) government; **M~ delle Finanze** Ministry of Finance, ≈ Treasury

mi'nistro sm (Pol, Rel) minister

mino'ranza [mino'rantsa] sf minority

mi'nore ag (comparativo) less; (più piccolo) smaller; (numero) lower; (inferiore) lower, inferior; (meno importante) minor; (più giovane) younger; (superlativo) least; smallest; lowest; youngest ▷ sm/f = **minorenne**

mino'renne ag under age ▷ sm/f minor, person under age

mi'nuscolo, -a ag (scrittura, carattere) small; (piccolissimo) tiny ▷ sf small letter

mi'nuto, -a ag tiny, minute; (pioggia) fine; (corporatura) delicate, fine ▷ sm (unità di misura) minute; **al ~** (Comm) retail

'mio (f 'mia, pl mi'ei or 'mie) det **il ~, la mia** ecc my ▷ pron **il ~, la mia** ecc mine; **i miei** my family; **un ~ amico** a friend of mine

'miope ag short-sighted

'mira sf (anche fig) aim; **prendere la ~** to take aim; **prendere di ~ qn** (fig) to pick on sb

mi'racolo sm miracle

mi'raggio [mi'raddʒo] sm mirage

mi'rare vi **~ a** to aim at

mi'rino sm (Tecn) sight; (Fot) viewer, viewfinder

mir'tillo sm bilberry (BRIT), blueberry (US), whortleberry

mi'scela [miʃʃela] sf mixture; (di caffè) blend

'mischia ['miskja] sf scuffle; (Rugby) scrum, scrummage

mis'cuglio [mis'kuʎʎo] sm mixture, hotchpotch, jumble

'mise vb vedi **mettere**

mise'rabile ag (infelice) miserable, wretched; (povero) poverty-stricken; (di scarso valore) miserable

mi'seria sf extreme poverty; (infelicità) misery

miseri'cordia sf mercy, pity

'misero, -a ag miserable, wretched; (povero) poverty-stricken; (insufficiente) miserable

'misi vb vedi **mettere**

mi'sogino [mi'zɔdʒino] sm misogynist

'missile sm missile

missio'nario, -a ag, sm/f missionary

missi'one sf mission

misteri'oso, -a ag mysterious

mis'tero sm mystery

'misto, -a ag mixed; (scuola) mixed, coeducational ▷ sm mixture

mis'tura sf mixture

mi'sura sf measure; (misurazione, dimensione) measurement; (taglia) size; (provvedimento) measure, step; (moderazione) moderation; (Mus) time; (: divisione) bar; (fig: limite) bounds pl, limit; **nella ~ in cui** inasmuch as, insofar as; **(fatto) su ~** made to measure

misu'rare vt (ambiente, stoffa) to measure; (terreno) to survey; (abito) to try on; (pesare) to weigh; (fig: parole ecc) to weigh up; (: spese, cibo) to limit ▷ vi to measure; **misurarsi** vpr **misurarsi con qn** to have a confrontation with sb; to compete with sb

'mite ag mild

'mitico, -a, ci, che ag mythical

'mito sm myth; **mitolo'gia, -'gie** sf mythology

'mitra sf (Rel) mitre ▷ sm inv (arma) sub-machine gun

mit'tente sm/f sender

mm abbr (= millimetro) mm

'mobile ag mobile; (parte di macchina) moving; (Dir: bene) movable, personal ▷ sm (arredamento) piece of furniture; **mobili** smpl (mobilia) furniture sg

mocas'sino sm moccasin

'moda sf fashion; **alla ~, di ~** fashionable, in fashion

modalità sf inv formality

mo'della sf model

mo'dello sm model; (stampo) mould ▷ ag inv model cpd

'modem sm inv modem

modera'tore, -'trice sm/f moderator

mo'derno, -a ag modern

mo'desto, -a ag modest

'modico, -a, -ci, -che ag reasonable, moderate

mo'difica, -che sf modification

modifi'care vt to modify, alter

'modo sm way, manner; (mezzo) means, way; (occasione) opportunity; (Ling) mood; (Mus) mode; **modi** smpl (comportamento) manners; **a suo ~, a ~ suo** in his own way;

ad *o* **in ogni ~** anyway; **di** *o* **in ~ che** so that; **in ~ da** so as to; **in tutti i modi** at all costs; (*comunque sia*) anyway; (*in ogni caso*) in any case; **in qualche ~** somehow or other; **per ~ di dire** so to speak; **modo di dire** turn of phrase

'**modulo** *sm* (*modello*) form; (*Archit, lunare, di comando*) module

'**mogano** *sm* mahogany

'**mogio, -a, -gi, -gie** ['mɔdʒo] *ag* down in the dumps, dejected

'**moglie** ['moʎʎe] *sf* wife

mo'ine *sfpl* cajolery *sg*; (*leziosità*) affectation *sg*

mo'lare *sm* (*dente*) molar

'**mole** *sf* mass; (*dimensioni*) size; (*edificio grandioso*) massive structure

moles'tare *vt* to bother, annoy; **mo'lestia** *sf* annoyance, bother; **recar molestia a qn** to bother sb; **molestie sessuali** sexual harassment *sg*

'**molla** *sf* spring; **molle** *sfpl* (*per camino*) tongs

mol'lare *vt* to release, let go; (*Naut*) to ease; (*fig: ceffone*) to give ▷ *vi* (*cedere*) to give in

'**molle** *ag* soft; (*muscoli*) flabby

mol'letta *sf* (*per capelli*) hairgrip; (*per panni stesi*) clothes peg

'**mollica, -che** *sf* crumb, soft part

mol'lusco, -schi *sm* mollusc

'**molo** *sm* mole, breakwater; jetty

moltipli'care *vt* to multiply; **moltiplicarsi** *vpr* to multiply; to increase in number; **moltiplicazi'one** *sf* multiplication

⬤ **PAROLA CHIAVE**

'**molto, -a** *det* (*quantità*) a lot of, much; (*numero*) a lot of, many; **molto pane/ carbone** a lot of bread/coal; **molta gente** a lot of people, many people; **molti libri** a lot of books, many books; **non ho molto tempo** I haven't got much time; **per molto (tempo)** for a long time
▷ *av* **1** a lot, (very) much; **viaggia molto** he travels a lot; **non viaggia molto** he doesn't travel much *o* a lot
2 (*intensivo: con aggettivi, avverbi*) very; (: *con participio passato*) (very) much; **molto buono** very good; **molto migliore, molto meglio** much *o* a lot better
▷ *pron* much, a lot

momentanea'mente *av* at the moment, at present

momen'taneo, -a *ag* momentary, fleeting

mo'mento *sm* moment; **da un ~ all'altro**
at any moment; (*all'improvviso*) suddenly; **al ~ di fare** just as I was (*o* you were *o* he was *ecc*) doing; **per il ~** for the time being; **dal ~ che** ever since; (*dato che*) since; **a momenti** (*da un momento all'altro*) any time *o* moment now; (*quasi*) nearly

'**monaca, -che** *sf* nun

'**Monaco** *sf* Monaco; **Monaco (di Baviera)** Munich

'**monaco, -ci** *sm* monk

monar'chia *sf* monarchy

monas'tero *sm* (*di monaci*) monastery; (*di monache*) convent

mon'dano, -a *ag* (*anche fig*) worldly; (*anche:* **dell'alta società**) society *cpd*; fashionable

mondi'ale *ag* (*campionato, popolazione*) world *cpd*; (*influenza*) world-wide

'**mondo** *sm* world; (*grande quantità*): **un ~ di** lots of, a host of; **il bel ~** high society

mo'nello, -a *sm/f* street urchin; (*ragazzo vivace*) scamp, imp

mo'neta *sf* coin; (*Econ: valuta*) currency; (*denaro spicciolo*) (small) change; **moneta estera** foreign currency; **moneta legale** legal tender

mongol'fiera *sf* hot-air balloon

'**monitor** *sm inv* (*Tecn, TV*) monitor

monolo'cale *sm* studio flat

mono'polio *sm* monopoly

mo'notono, -a *ag* monotonous

monovo'lume *ag inv, sf inv* (**automobile**) **~** people carrier, MPV

mon'sone *sm* monsoon

monta'carichi [monta'kariki] *sm inv* hoist, goods lift

mon'taggio [mon'taddʒo] *sm* (*Tecn*) assembly; (*Cinema*) editing

mon'tagna [mon'taɲɲa] *sf* mountain; (*zona montuosa*): **la ~** the mountains *pl*; **andare in ~** to go to the mountains; **montagne russe** roller coaster *sg*, big dipper *sg* (BRIT)

monta'naro, -a *ag* mountain *cpd* ▷ *sm/f* mountain dweller

mon'tano, -a *ag* mountain *cpd*; alpine

mon'tare *vt* to go (*o* come) up; (*cavallo*) to ride; (*apparecchiatura*) to set up, assemble; (*Cuc*) to whip; (*Zool*) to cover; (*incastonare*) to mount, set; (*Cinema*) to edit; (*Fot*) to mount ▷ *vi* to go (*o* come) up; (*a cavallo*): **~ bene/male** to ride well/badly; (*aumentare di livello, volume*) to rise

monta'tura *sf* assembling *no pl*; (*di occhiali*) frames *pl*; (*di gioiello*) mounting, setting; (*fig*): **montatura pubblicitaria** publicity stunt

'**monte** *sm* mountain; **a ~** upstream; **mandare a ~ qc** to upset sth, cause sth to fail; **il M~ Bianco** Mont Blanc; **monte di pietà** pawnshop; **monte premi** prize

mon'tone *sm* (*Zool*) ram; **carne di ~** mutton

montu'oso, -a *ag* mountainous

monu'mento *sm* monument

mo'quette [mɔ'kɛt] *sf inv* fitted carpet

'mora *sf* (*del rovo*) blackberry; (*del gelso*) mulberry; (*Dir*) delay; (: *somma*) arrears *pl*

mo'rale *ag* moral ▷ *sf* (*scienza*) ethics *sg*, moral philosophy; (*complesso di norme*) moral standards *pl*, morality; (*condotta*) morals *pl*; (*insegnamento morale*) moral ▷ *sm* morale; **essere giù di ~** to be feeling down

'morbido, -a *ag* soft; (*pelle*) soft, smooth

Attenzione! In inglese esiste la parola *morbid*, che però significa *morboso*.

mor'billo *sm* (*Med*) measles *sg*

'morbo *sm* disease

mor'boso, -a *ag* (*fig*) morbid

'mordere *vt* to bite; (*addentare*) to bite into

mori'bondo, -a *ag* dying, moribund

mo'rire *vi* to die; (*abitudine, civiltà*) to die out; **~ di fame** to die of hunger; (*fig*) to be starving; **~ di noia/paura** to be bored/scared to death; **fa un caldo da ~** it's terribly hot

mormo'rare *vi* to murmur; (*brontolare*) to grumble

'moro, -a *ag* dark(-haired), dark(-complexioned)

'morsa *sf* (*Tecn*) vice; (*fig*: *stretta*) grip

morsi'care *vt* to nibble (at), gnaw (at); (*insetto*) to bite

'morso, -a *pp di* **mordere** ▷ *sm* bite; (*di insetto*) sting; (*parte della briglia*) bit; **morsi della fame** pangs of hunger

morta'della *sf* (*Cuc*) mortadella (*type of salted pork meat*)

mor'taio *sm* mortar

mor'tale *ag, sm* mortal

'morte *sf* death

'morto, -a *pp di* **morire** ▷ *ag* dead ▷ *sm/f* dead man/woman; **i morti** the dead; **fare il ~** (*nell'acqua*) to float on one's back; **il Mar M~** the Dead Sea

mo'saico, -ci *sm* mosaic

'Mosca *sf* Moscow

'mosca, -sche *sf* fly; **mosca cieca** blind-man's-buff

mosce'rino [moʃʃe'rino] *sm* midge, gnat

mos'chea [mos'kɛa] *sf* mosque

'moscio, -a, -sci, -sce ['mɔʃʃo] *ag* (*fig*) lifeless

mos'cone *sm* (*Zool*) bluebottle; (*barca*) pedalo; (: *a remi*) kind of pedalo with oars

'mossa *sf* movement; (*nel gioco*) move

'mossi *ecc vb vedi* **muovere**

'mosso, -a *pp di* **muovere** ▷ *ag* (*mare*) rough; (*capelli*) wavy; (*Fot*) blurred

mos'tarda *sf* mustard; **mostarda di Cremona** pickled fruit with mustard

'mostra *sf* exhibition, show; (*ostentazione*) show; **in ~** on show; **far ~ di** (*fingere*) to pretend; **far ~ di sé** to show off

mos'trare *vt* to show; **può mostrarmi dov'è, per favore?** can you show me where it is, please?

'mostro *sm* monster; **mostru'oso, -a** *ag* monstrous

mo'tel *sm inv* motel

moti'vare *vt* (*causare*) to cause; (*giustificare*) to justify, account for

mo'tivo *sm* (*causa*) reason, cause; (*movente*) motive; (*letterario*) (central) theme; (*disegno*) motif, design, pattern; (*Mus*) motif; **per quale ~?** why?, for what reason?

'moto *sm* (*anche Fisica*) motion; (*movimento, gesto*) movement; (*esercizio fisico*) exercise; (*sommossa*) rising, revolt; (*commozione*) feeling, impulse ▷ *sf inv* (*motocicletta*) motorbike; **mettere in ~** to set in motion; (*Aut*) to start up

motoci'clista, -i, -e *sm/f* motorcyclist

mo'tore, -'trice *ag* motor; (*Tecn*) driving ▷ *sm* engine, motor; **a ~** motor *cpd*, power-driven; **~ a combustione interna/a reazione** internal combustion/jet engine; **motore di ricerca** (*Inform*) search engine; **moto'rino** *sm* moped; **motorino di avviamento** (*Aut*) starter

motos'cafo *sm* motorboat

'motto *sm* (*battuta scherzosa*) witty remark; (*frase emblematica*) motto, maxim

'mouse ['maus] *sm inv* (*Inform*) mouse

mo'vente *sm* motive

movi'mento *sm* movement; (*fig*) activity, hustle and bustle; (*Mus*) tempo, movement

mozi'one [mot'tsjone] *sf* (*Pol*) motion

mozza'rella [mottsa'rɛlla] *sf* mozzarella, *a moist Neapolitan curd cheese*

mozzi'cone [mottsi'kone] *sm* stub, butt, end; (*anche*: **~ di sigaretta**) cigarette end

'mucca, -che *sf* cow; **mucca pazza** mad cow disease

'mucchio ['mukkjo] *sm* pile, heap; (*fig*): **un ~ di** lots of, heaps of

'muco, -chi *sm* mucus

'muffa *sf* mould, mildew

mug'gire [mud'dʒire] *vi* (*vacca*) to low, moo; (*toro*) to bellow; (*fig*) to roar

mu'ghetto [mu'getto] *sm* lily of the valley

mu'lino *sm* mill; **mulino a vento** windmill

'mulo *sm* mule

'multa *sf* fine

multi'etnico, -a, -ci, -che *ag* multiethnic
multirazziale [multirat'tsjale] *ag* multiracial
multi'sala *ag inv* multiscreen
multivitami'nico, -a, -ci, -che *ag* **complesso ~** multivitamin
'mummia *sf* mummy
'mungere ['mundʒere] *vt (anche fig)* to milk
munici'pale [munitʃi'pale] *ag* municipal; town *cpd*
muni'cipio [muni'tʃipjo] *sm* town council, corporation; *(edificio)* town hall
munizi'oni [munit'tsjoni] *sfpl (Mil)* ammunition *sg*
'munsi *ecc vb vedi* **mungere**
mu'oio *ecc vb vedi* **morire**
mu'overe *vt* to move; *(ruota, macchina)* to drive; *(sollevare: questione, obiezione)* to raise, bring up; *(: accusa)* to make, bring forward; **muoversi** *vpr* to move; **muoviti!** hurry up!, get a move on!
'mura *sfpl vedi* **muro**
mu'rale *ag* wall *cpd*; mural
mura'tore *sm* mason; bricklayer
'muro *sm* wall
'muschio ['muskjo] *sm (Zool)* musk; *(Bot)* moss
musco'lare *ag* muscular, muscle *cpd*
'muscolo *sm (Anat)* muscle
mu'seo *sm* museum
museru'ola *sf* muzzle
'musica *sf* music; **musica da ballo/ camera** dance/chamber music; **musi'cale** *ag* musical; **musi'cista, -i, -e** *sm/f* musician
'müsli ['mysli] *sm* muesli
'muso *sm* muzzle; *(di auto, aereo)* nose; **tenere il ~** to sulk
mussul'mano, -a *ag, sm/f* Muslim, Moslem
'muta *sf (di animali)* moulting; *(di serpenti)* sloughing; *(per immersioni subacquee)* diving suit; *(gruppo di cani)* pack
mu'tande *sfpl (da uomo)* (under)pants
'muto, -a *ag (Med)* dumb; *(emozione, dolore, Cinema)* silent; *(Ling)* silent, mute; *(carta geografica)* blank; **~ per lo stupore** *ecc* speechless with amazement *ecc*
'mutuo, -a *ag (reciproco)* mutual ▷ *sm (Econ)* (long-term) loan

N *abbr (= nord)* N
n. *abbr (= numero)* no.
'nafta *sf* naphtha; *(per motori diesel)* diesel oil
nafta'lina *sf (Chim)* naphthalene; *(tarmicida)* mothballs *pl*
'naia *sf (Mil) slang term for national service*
na'if [na'if] *ag inv* naïve
'nanna *sf (linguaggio infantile):* **andare a ~** to go to beddy-byes
'nano, -a *ag, sm/f* dwarf
napole'tano, -a *ag, sm/f* Neapolitan
'Napoli *sf* Naples
nar'ciso [nar'tʃizo] *sm* narcissus
nar'cotico, -ci *sm* narcotic
na'rice [na'ritʃe] *sf* nostril
nar'rare *vt* to tell the story of, recount; **narra'tiva** *sf (branca letteraria)* fiction
na'sale *ag* nasal
'nascere ['naʃʃere] *vi (bambino)* to be born; *(pianta)* to come o spring up; *(fiume)* to rise, have its source; *(sole)* to rise; *(dente)* to come through; *(fig: derivare, conseguire):* **~ da** to arise from, be born out of; **è nata nel 1952** she was born in 1952; **'nascita** *sf* birth
nas'condere *vt* to hide, conceal; **nascondersi** *vpr* to hide; **nascon'diglio** *sm* hiding place; **nascon'dino** *sm (gioco)* hide-and-seek; **nas'cosi** *ecc vb*

vedi **nascondere**; **nas'costo, -a** *pp di*
nascondere ▷ *ag* hidden; **di nascosto**
secretly
na'sello *sm* (*Zool*) hake
'naso *sm* nose
'nastro *sm* ribbon; (*magnetico, isolante,*
Sport) tape; **nastro adesivo** adhesive
tape; **nastro trasportatore** conveyor belt
nas'turzio [nas'turtsjo] *sm* nasturtium
na'tale *ag* of one's birth ▷ *sm* (*Rel*): **N~**
Christmas; (*giorno della nascita*) birthday;
nata'lizio, -a *ag* (*del Natale*) Christmas *cpd*
'natica, -che *sf* (*Anat*) buttock
'nato, -a *pp di* **nascere** ▷ *ag* **un attore ~** a
born actor; **nata Pieri** née Pieri
na'tura *sf* nature; **pagare in ~** to pay in
kind; **natura morta** still life
natu'rale *ag* natural
natural'mente *av* naturally; (*certamente,*
sì) of course
natu'rista, -i, e *ag, sm/f* naturist, nudist
naufra'gare *vi* (*nave*) to be wrecked;
(*persona*) to be shipwrecked; (*fig*) to fall
through; **'naufrago, -ghi** *sm* castaway,
shipwreck victim
'nausea *sf* nausea; **nause'ante** *ag* (*odore*)
nauseating; (*sapore*) disgusting; (*fig*)
sickening
'nautico, -a, -ci, -che *ag* nautical
na'vale *ag* naval
na'vata *sf* (*anche:* **~ centrale**) nave; (*anche:*
~ laterale) aisle
'nave *sf* ship, vessel; **nave cisterna**
tanker; **nave da guerra** warship; **nave**
passeggeri passenger ship
na'vetta *sf* shuttle; (*servizio di*
collegamento) shuttle (service)
navi'cella [navi'tʃɛlla] *sf* (*di aerostato*)
gondola; **navicella spaziale** spaceship
navi'gare *vi* to sail; **~ in Internet** to surf
the Net; **navigazi'one** *sf* navigation
nazio'nale [nattsjo'nale] *ag* national ▷ *sf*
(*Sport*) national team; **nazionalità** *sf inv*
nationality
nazi'one [nat'tsjone] *sf* nation
naziskin ['nɑ:tsiskin] *sm inv* Nazi
skinhead
NB *abbr* (= *nota bene*) NB

🔘 **PAROLA CHIAVE**

ne *pron* **1** (*di lui, lei, loro*) of him/her/them;
about him/her/them; **ne riconosco la**
voce I recognize his (*o* her) voice
2 (*di questa, quella cosa*) of it; about it; **ne**
voglio ancora I want some more (of it *o*
them); **non parliamone più!** let's not talk
about it any more!
3 (*con valore partitivo*): **hai dei libri? — sì,**

ne ho have you any books? — yes, I have
(some); **hai del pane? — no, non ne ho**
have you any bread? — no, I haven't any;
quanti anni hai? — ne ho 17 how old are
you? — I'm 17
▷ *av* (*moto da luogo: da lì*) from there; **ne**
vengo ora I've just come from there

né *cong* **né ... né** neither ... nor; **né l'uno**
né l'altro lo vuole neither of them wants
it; **non parla né l'italiano né il tedesco**
he speaks neither Italian nor German, he
doesn't speak either Italian or German;
non piove né nevica it isn't raining or
snowing
ne'anche [ne'anke] *av, cong* not even;
non ... ~ not even; **~ se volesse**
potrebbe venire he couldn't come even
if he wanted to; **non l'ho visto — ~ io**
I didn't see him — neither did I *o* I didn't
either; **~ per idea** *o* **sogno!** not on your
life!
'nebbia *sf* fog; (*foschia*) mist
necessaria'mente [netʃessarjamɛnte]
av necessarily
neces'sario, -a [netʃes'sarjo] *ag*
necessary
necessità [netʃessi'ta] *sf inv* necessity;
(*povertà*) need, poverty
necro'logio [nekro'lɔdʒo] *sm* obituary
notice
ne'gare *vt* to deny; (*rifiutare*) to deny,
refuse; **~ di aver fatto/che** to deny
having done/that; **nega'tivo, -a** *ag, sf, sm*
negative
negherò *ecc* [nege'rɔ] *vb vedi* **negare**
negli'gente [negli'dʒɛnte] *ag* negligent,
careless
negozi'ante [negot'tsjante] *sm/f* trader,
dealer; (*bottegaio*) shopkeeper (BRIT),
storekeeper (US)
negozi'are [negot'tsjare] *vt* to negotiate
▷ *vi* **~ in** to trade *o* deal in; **negozi'ato** *sm*
negotiation
ne'gozio [ne'gɔttsjo] *sm* (*locale*) shop
(BRIT), store (US)
'negro, -a *ag, sm/f* Negro
ne'mico, -a, -ci, -che *ag* hostile; (*Mil*)
enemy *cpd* ▷ *sm/f* enemy; **essere ~ di** to be
strongly averse *o* opposed to
nem'meno *av, cong* = **neanche**
'neo *sm* mole; (*fig*) (slight) flaw
'neon *sm* (*Chim*) neon
neo'nato, -a *ag* newborn ▷ *sm/f* newborn
baby
neozelan'dese [neoddzelan'dese] *ag*
New Zealand *cpd* ▷ *sm/f* New Zealander
'Nepal *sm* **il ~** Nepal
nep'pure *av, cong* = **neanche**

'nero, -a *ag* black; (*scuro*) dark ▷ *sm* black; **il Mar N~** the Black Sea

'nervo *sm* (*Anat*) nerve; (*Bot*) vein; **avere i nervi** to be on edge; **dare sui nervi a qn** to get on sb's nerves; **ner'voso, -a** *ag* nervous; (*irritabile*) irritable ▷ *sm* (*fam*): **far venire il nervoso a qn** to get on sb's nerves

'nespola *sf* (*Bot*) medlar; (*fig*) blow, punch

'nesso *sm* connection, link

 PAROLA CHIAVE

nes'suno, -a (*det: dav sm* **nessun** +C, V, **nessuno** +*s impura*, *gn*, *pn*, *ps*, *x*, *z*; *dav sf* **nessuna** +C, **nessun'** +V) *det* **1** (*non uno*) no; (, *espressione negativa* +) any; **non c'è nessun libro** there isn't any book, there is no book; **nessun altro** no one else, nobody else; **nessun'altra cosa** nothing else; **in nessun luogo** nowhere

2 (*qualche*) any; **hai nessuna obiezione?** do you have any objections?

▷ *pron* **1** (*non uno*) no one, nobody; (, *espressione negativa* +) any(one); (: *cosa*) none; (, *espressione negativa* +) any; **nessuno è venuto, non è venuto nessuno** nobody came

2 (*qualcuno*) anyone, anybody; **ha telefonato nessuno?** did anyone phone?

net'tare *vt* to clean

net'tezza [net'tettsa] *sf* cleanness, cleanliness; **nettezza urbana** cleansing department

'netto, -a *ag* (*pulito*) clean; (*chiaro*) clear, clear-cut; (*deciso*) definite; (*Econ*) net

nettur'bino *sm* dustman (BRIT), garbage collector (US)

neu'trale *ag* neutral

'neutro, -a *ag* neutral; (*Ling*) neuter ▷ *sm* (*Ling*) neuter

'neve *sf* snow; **nevi'care** *vb impers* to snow; **nevi'cata** *sf* snowfall

ne'vischio [ne'viskjo] *sm* sleet

ne'voso, -a *ag* snowy; snow-covered

nevral'gia [nevral'dʒia] *sf* neuralgia

nevras'tenico, -a, -ci, -che *ag* (*Med*) neurasthenic; (*fig*) hot-tempered

ne'vrosi *sf* neurosis

ne'vrotico, -a, ci, che *ag*, *sm/f* (*anche fig*) neurotic

'nicchia ['nikkja] *sf* niche; (*naturale*) cavity, hollow; **nicchia di mercato** (*Comm*) niche market

nicchi'are [nik'kjare] *vi* to shilly-shally, hesitate

'nichel ['nikel] *sm* nickel

nico'tina *sf* nicotine

'nido *sm* nest; **a ~ d'ape** (*tessuto ecc*) honeycomb *cpd*

 PAROLA CHIAVE

ni'ente *pron* **1** (*nessuna cosa*) nothing; **niente può fermarlo** nothing can stop him; **niente di niente** absolutely nothing; **nient'altro** nothing else; **nient'altro che** nothing but, just, only; **niente affatto** not at all, not in the least; **come se niente fosse** as if nothing had happened; **cose da niente** trivial matters; **per niente** (*gratis, invano*) for nothing

2 (*qualcosa*): **hai bisogno di niente?** do you need anything?

3: **non ... niente** nothing; (*espressione negativa* +) anything; **non ho visto niente** I saw nothing, I didn't see anything; **non ho niente da dire** I have nothing o haven't anything to say

▷ *sm* nothing; **un bel niente** absolutely nothing; **basta un niente per farla piangere** the slightest thing is enough to make her cry ▷ *av* (*in nessuna misura*): **non ... niente** not ... at all; **non è (per) niente buono** it isn't good at all

Ni'geria [ni'dʒɛrja] *sf* **la ~** Nigeria

'ninfa *sf* nymph

nin'fea *sf* water lily

ninna-'nanna *sf* lullaby

'ninnolo *sm* (*gingillo*) knick-knack

ni'pote *sm/f* (*di zii*) nephew/niece; (*di nonni*) grandson/daughter, grandchild

'nitido, -a *ag* clear; (*specchio*) bright

ni'trire *vi* to neigh

ni'trito *sm* (*di cavallo*) neighing *no pl*; neigh; (*Chim*) nitrite

nitroglice'rina [nitroglitʃe'rina] *sf* nitroglycerine

no *av* (*risposta*) no; **vieni o no?** are you coming or not?; **perché no?** why not?; **lo conosciamo? — tu no ma io sì** do we know him? — you don't but I do; **verrai, no?** you'll come, won't you?

'nobile *ag* noble ▷ *sm/f* noble, nobleman/woman

'nocca, -che *sf* (*Anat*) knuckle

'noccio *ecc* ['nɔttʃo] *vb vedi* **nuocere**

nocci'ola [not'tʃɔla] *ag inv* (*colore*) hazel, light brown ▷ *sf* hazelnut

noccio'lina [nottʃo'lina] *sf*; **nocciolina americana** peanut

'nocciolo ['nɔttʃolo] *sm* (*di frutto*) stone; (*fig*) heart, core

'noce ['notʃe] *sm* (*albero*) walnut tree ▷ *sf* (*frutto*) walnut; **noce di cocco** coconut; **noce moscata** nutmeg

no'cevo *ecc* [no'tʃevo] *vb vedi* **nuocere**

no'civo, -a [no'tʃivo] *ag* harmful, noxious

'nocqui *ecc vb vedi* **nuocere**

'nodo *sm* (*di cravatta, legname, Naut*) knot; (*Aut, Ferr*) junction; (*Med, Astr, Bot*) node; (*fig: legame*) bond, tie; (: *punto centrale*) heart, crux; **avere un ~ alla gola** to have a lump in one's throat

no-'global *sm/f* anti-globalization protester ▷ *ag* (*movimento, manifestante*) anti-globalization

'noi *pron* (*soggetto*) we; (*oggetto: per dare rilievo, con preposizione*) us; **~ stessi(e)** we ourselves; (*oggetto*) ourselves

'noia *sf* boredom; (*disturbo, impaccio*) bother *no pl*, trouble *no pl*; **avere qn/qc a ~** not to like sb/sth; **mi è venuto a ~** I'm tired of it; **dare ~ a** to annoy; **avere delle noie con qn** to have trouble with sb

noi'oso, -a *ag* boring; (*fastidioso*) annoying, troublesome

Attenzione! In inglese esiste la parola *noisy*, che però significa *rumoroso*.

noleggi'are [noled'dʒare] *vt* (*prendere a noleggio*) to hire (BRIT), rent; (*dare a noleggio*) to hire out (BRIT), rent (out); (*aereo, nave*) to charter; **vorrei ~ una macchina** I'd like to hire a car; **no'leggio** *sm* hire (BRIT), rental; charter

'nomade *ag* nomadic ▷ *sm/f* nomad

'nome *sm* name; (*Ling*) noun; **in/a ~ di** in the name of; **di o per ~** (*chiamato*) called, named; **conoscere qn di ~** to know sb by name; **nome d'arte** stage name; **nome di battesimo** Christian name; **nome di famiglia** surname

no'mignolo [no'miɲɲolo] *sm* nickname

'nomina *sf* appointment

nomi'nale *ag* nominal; (*Ling*) noun *cpd*

nomi'nare *vt* to name; (*eleggere*) to appoint; (*citare*) to mention

nomina'tivo, -a *ag* (*Ling*) nominative; (*Econ*) registered ▷ *sm* (*Ling: anche:* **caso ~**) nominative (case); (*Amm*) name

non *av* not ▷ *prefisso* non-; *vedi* **affatto**; **appena** *ecc*

nonché [non'ke] *cong* (*tanto più, tanto meno*) let alone; (*e inoltre*) as well as

noncu'rante *ag* **~ (di)** careless (of), indifferent (to)

'nonno, -a *sm/f* grandfather/mother; (*in senso più familiare*) grandma/grandpa; **i nonni** *smpl* the grandparents

non'nulla *sm inv* **un ~** nothing, a trifle

'nono, -a *ag, sm* ninth

nonos'tante *prep* in spite of, notwithstanding ▷ *cong* although, even though

nontiscordardimé *sm inv* (*Bot*) forget-me-not

nord *sm* North ▷ *ag inv* north; northern; **il Mare del N~** the North Sea; **nor'dest** *sm* north-east; **nor'dovest** *sm* north-west

'norma *sf* (*principio*) norm; (*regola*) regulation, rule; (*consuetudine*) custom, rule; **a ~ di legge** according to law, as laid down by law; **norme per l'uso** instructions for use; **norme di sicurezza** safety regulations

nor'male *ag* normal; standard *cpd*

normal'mente *av* normally

norve'gese [norve'dʒese] *ag, sm/f, sm* Norwegian

Nor'vegia [nor'vedʒa] *sf* **la ~** Norway

nostal'gia [nostal'dʒia] *sf* (*di casa, paese*) homesickness; (*del passato*) nostalgia

nos'trano, -a *ag* local; national; home-produced

'nostro, -a *det* **il (la) ~(-a)** *ecc* our ▷ *pron* **il (la) ~(-a)** *ecc* ours ▷ *sm* **il ~** our money; our belongings; **i nostri** our family; our own people; **è dei nostri** he's one of us

'nota *sf* (*segno*) mark; (*comunicazione scritta, Mus*) note; (*fattura*) bill; (*elenco*) list; **degno di ~** noteworthy, worthy of note

no'taio *sm* notary

no'tare *vt* (*segnare: errori*) to mark; (*registrare*) to note (down), write down; (*rilevare, osservare*) to note, notice; **farsi ~** to get o.s. noticed

no'tevole *ag* (*talento*) notable, remarkable; (*peso*) considerable

no'tifica, -che *sf* notification

no'tizia [no'tittsja] *sf* (*piece of*) news *sg*; (*informazione*) piece of information; **notizi'ario** *sm* (*Radio, TV, Stampa*) news *sg*

'noto, -a *ag* (well-)known

notorietà *sf* fame; notoriety

no'torio, -a *ag* well-known; (*peg*) notorious

not'tambulo, -a *sm/f* night-bird; (*fig*)

not'tata *sf* night

'notte *sf* night; **di ~** at night; (*durante la notte*) in the night, during the night; **notte bianca** sleepless night

not'turno, -a *ag* nocturnal; (*servizio, guardiano*) night *cpd*

no'vanta *num* ninety; **novan'tesimo, -a** *num* ninetieth

'nove *num* nine

nove'cento [nove'tʃento] *num* nine hundred ▷ *sm* **il N~** the twentieth century

no'vella *sf* (*Letteratura*) short story

no'vello, -a *ag* (*piante, patate*) new; (*insalata, verdura*) early; (*sposo*) newly-married

no'vembre *sm* November

novità *sf inv* novelty; (*innovazione*)

innovation; (*cosa originale, insolita*)
something new; (*notizia*) (piece of) news
sg; **le ~ della moda** the latest fashions
nozi'one [not'tsjone] *sf* notion, idea
'nozze ['nɔttse] *sfpl* wedding *sg*, marriage
sg; **nozze d'argento/d'oro** silver/golden
wedding *sg*
'nubile *ag* (*donna*) unmarried, single
'nuca *sf* nape of the neck
nucle'are *ag* nuclear
'nucleo *sm* nucleus; (*gruppo*) team,
unit, group; (*Mil, Polizia*) squad; **nucleo
familiare** family unit
nu'dista, -i, -e *sm/f* nudist
'nudo, -a *ag* (*persona*) bare, naked, nude;
(*membra*) bare, naked; (*montagna*) bare
▷ *sm* (*Arte*) nude
'nulla *pron, av* = **niente** ▷ *sm* = **il nulla**
nothing
nullità *sf inv* nullity; (*persona*) nonentity
'nullo, -a *ag* useless, worthless; (*Dir*) null
(and void); (*Sport*): **incontro ~** draw
nume'rale *ag, sm* numeral
nume'rare *vt* to number
nu'merico, -a, -ci, -che *ag* numerical
'numero *sm* number; (*romano, arabo*)
numeral; (*di spettacolo*) act, turn; **numero
civico** house number; **numero di scarpe**
shoe size; **numero di telefono** telephone
number; **nume'roso, -a** *ag* numerous,
many; (*con sostantivo sg*) large
nu'occio *ecc* ['nwɔttʃo] *vb vedi* **nuocere**
nu'ocere ['nwɔtʃere] *vi* **~ a** to harm,
damage
nu'ora *sf* daughter-in-law
nuo'tare *vi* to swim; (*galleggiare: oggetti*) to
float; **nuota'tore, -'trice** *sm/f* swimmer;
nu'oto *sm* swimming
nu'ova *sf* (*notizia*) (piece of) news *sg*; *vedi
anche* **nuovo**
nuova'mente *av* again
Nu'ova Ze'landa [-dze'landa] *sf* **la ~** New
Zealand
nu'ovo, -a *ag* new; **di ~** again; **~
fiammante** *o* **di zecca** brand-new
nutri'ente *ag* nutritious, nourishing
nutri'mento *sm* food, nourishment
nu'trire *vt* to feed; (*fig: sentimenti*) to
harbour, nurse; **nutrirsi** *vpr* **nutrirsi di** to
feed on, to eat
'nuvola *sf* cloud; **nuvo'loso, -a** *ag* cloudy
nuzi'ale [nut'tsjale] *ag* nuptial; wedding
cpd
'nylon ['nailən] *sm* nylon

o (*davV spesso* **od**) *cong* or; **o ... o** either ...
or; **o l'uno o l'altro** either (of them)
O *abbr* (= *ovest*) W
'oasi *sf inv* oasis
obbedi'ente *ecc* = **ubbidiente** *ecc*
obbli'gare *vt* (*costringere*): **~ qn a fare**
to force *o* oblige sb to do; (*Dir*) to bind;
obbliga'torio, -a *ag* compulsory,
obligatory; **'obbligo, -ghi** *sm* obligation;
(*dovere*) duty; **avere l'obbligo di fare** to be
obliged to do; **essere d'obbligo** (*discorso,
applauso*) to be called for
o'beso, -a *ag* obese
obiet'tare *vt* **~ che** to object that; **~
su qc** to object to sth, raise objections
concerning sth
obiet'tivo, -a *ag* objective ▷ *sm* (*Ottica,
Fot*) lens *sg*, objective; (*Mil, fig*) objective
obiet'tore *sm* objector; **obiettore di
coscienza** conscientious objector
obiezi'one [objet'tsjone] *sf* objection
obi'torio *sm* morgue, mortuary
o'bliquo, -a *ag* oblique; (*inclinato*)
slanting; (*fig*) devious, underhand
oblite'rare *vt* (*biglietto*) to stamp;
(*francobollo*) to cancel
oblò *sm inv* porthole
'oboe *sm* (*Mus*) oboe
'oca (*pl* **'oche**) *sf* goose
occasi'one *sf* (*caso favorevole*) opportunity;

(*causa, motivo, circostanza*) occasion; (*Comm*) bargain; **d'~** (*a buon prezzo*) bargain *cpd*; (*usato*) secondhand

occhi'aia [ok'kjaja] *sf* **avere le occhiaie** to have shadows under one's eyes

occhi'ali [ok'kjali] *smpl* glasses, spectacles; **occhiali da sole/da vista** sunglasses/(prescription) glasses

occhi'ata [ok'kjata] *sf* look, glance; **dare un'~ a** to have a look at

occhi'ello [ok'kjɛllo] *sm* buttonhole; (*asola*) eyelet

'occhio ['ɔkkjo] *sm* eye; **~!** careful!, watch out!; **a ~ nudo** with the naked eye; **a quattr'occhi** privately, tête-à-tête; **dare all'~** *o* **nell'~ a qn** to catch sb's eye; **fare l'~ a qc** to get used to sth; **tenere d'~ qn** to keep an eye on sb; **vedere di buon/mal ~ qc** to look favourably/unfavourably on sth

occhio'lino [okkjo'lino] *sm* **fare l'~ a qn** to wink at sb

occiden'tale [ottʃiden'tale] *ag* western ▷ *sm/f* Westerner

occi'dente [ottʃi'dɛnte] *sm* west; (*Pol*): **l'O~** the West; **a ~** in the west

occor'rente *ag* necessary ▷ *sm* all that is necessary

occor'renza [okkor'rɛntsa] *sf* necessity, need; **all'~** in case of need

oc'correre *vi* to be needed, be required ▷ *vb impers* **occorre farlo** it must be done; **occorre che tu parta** you must leave, you'll have to leave; **mi occorrono i soldi** I need the money

Attenzione! In inglese esiste il verbo *to occur*, che però significa *succedere*.

oc'culto, -a *ag* hidden, concealed; (*scienze, forze*) occult

occu'pare *vt* to occupy; (*manodopera*) to employ; (*ingombrare*) to occupy, take up; **occuparsi** *vpr* to occupy o.s., keep o.s. busy; (*impiegarsi*) to get a job; **occuparsi di** (*interessarsi*) to take an interest in; (*prendersi cura di*) to look after, take care of; **occu'pato, -a** *ag* (*Mil, Pol*) occupied; (*persona: affaccendato*) busy; (*posto, sedia*) taken; (*toilette, Tel*) engaged; **la linea è occupata** the line's engaged; **è occupato questo posto?** is this seat taken?; **occupazi'one** *sf* occupation; (*impiego, lavoro*) job; (*Econ*) employment

o'ceano [o'tʃeano] *sm* ocean

'ocra *sf* ochre

'OCSE *sigla f* (= *Organizzazione per la Cooperazione e lo Sviluppo Economico*) OECD (*Organization for Economic Cooperation and Development*)

ocu'lare *ag* ocular, eye *cpd*; **testimone ~** eye witness

ocu'lato, -a *ag* (*attento*) cautious, prudent; (*accorto*) shrewd

ocu'lista, -i, -e *sm/f* eye specialist, oculist

odi'are *vt* to hate, detest

odi'erno, -a *ag* today's, of today; (*attuale*) present

'odio *sm* hatred; **avere in ~ qc/qn** to hate *o* detest sth/sb; **odi'oso, -a** *ag* hateful, odious

odo'rare *vt* (*annusare*) to smell; (*profumare*) to perfume, scent ▷ *vi* **~ (di)** to smell (of)

o'dore *sm* smell; **odori** *smpl* (*Cuc*) (aromatic) herbs

of'fendere *vt* to offend; (*violare*) to break, violate; (*insultare*) to insult; (*ferire*) to hurt; **offendersi** *vpr* (*con senso reciproco*) to insult one another; (*risentirsi*): **offendersi (di)** to take offence (at), be offended (by)

offe'rente *sm* (*in aste*): **al maggior ~** to the highest bidder

of'ferta *sf* offer; (*donazione, anche Rel*) offering; (*in gara d'appalto*) tender; (*in aste*) bid; (*Econ*) supply; **fare un'~** to make an offer; to tender; to bid; **"offerte d'impiego"** "situations vacant"; **offerta speciale** special offer

of'fesa *sf* insult, affront; (*Mil*) attack; (*Dir*) offence; *vedi anche* **offeso**

of'feso, -a *pp di* **offendere** ▷ *ag* offended; (*fisicamente*) hurt, injured ▷ *sm/f* offended party; **essere ~ con qn** to be annoyed with sb; **parte offesa** (*Dir*) plaintiff

offi'cina [offi'tʃina] *sf* workshop

of'frire *vt* to offer; **offrirsi** *vpr* (*proporsi*) to offer (o.s.), volunteer; (*occasione*) to present itself; (*esporsi*): **offrirsi a** to expose o.s. to; **ti offro da bere** I'll buy you a drink

offus'care *vt* to obscure, darken; (*fig: intelletto*) to dim, cloud; (: *fama*) to obscure, overshadow; **offuscarsi** *vpr* to grow dark; to cloud, grow dim; to be obscured

ogget'tivo, -a [oddʒet'tivo] *ag* objective

og'getto [od'dʒetto] *sm* object; (*materia, argomento*) subject (matter); **oggetti smarriti** lost property *sg*

'oggi ['ɔddʒi] *av, sm* today; **~ a otto** a week today; **oggigi'orno** *av* nowadays

OGM *sigla m* (= *organismo geneticamente modificato*) GMO

'ogni ['oɲɲi] *det* every, each; (*tutti*) all; (*con valore distributivo*) every; **~ uomo è mortale** all men are mortal; **viene ~ due giorni** he comes every two days; **~ cosa** everything; **ad ~ costo** at all costs, at any price; **in ~ luogo** everywhere; **~ tanto** every so often; **~ volta che** every time that

Ognis'santi [oɲɲis'santi] *sm* All Saints' Day

o'gnuno [oɲ'ɲuno] *pron* everyone,

everybody

O'landa *sf* **l'~** Holland; **olan'dese** *ag* Dutch ▷ *sm* (*Ling*) Dutch ▷ *sm/f* Dutchman/woman; **gli Olandesi** the Dutch

ole'andro *sm* oleander

oleo'dotto *sm* oil pipeline

ole'oso, -a *ag* oily; (*che contiene olio*) oil-yielding

ol'fatto *sm* sense of smell

oli'are *vt* to oil

oli'era *sf* oil cruet

Olim'piadi *sfpl* Olympic games; **o'limpico, -a, -ci, -che** *ag* Olympic

'olio *sm* oil; **sott'~** (*Cuc*) in oil; **~ di fegato di merluzzo** cod liver oil; **olio d'oliva** olive oil; **olio di semi** vegetable oil

o'liva *sf* olive; **o'livo** *sm* olive tree

'olmo *sm* elm

OLP *sigla f* (= *Organizzazione per la Liberazione della Palestina*) PLO

ol'traggio [ol'traddʒo] *sm* outrage; offence, insult; **~ a pubblico ufficiale** (*Dir*) insulting a public official; **oltraggio al pudore** (*Dir*) indecent behaviour

ol'tranza [ol'trantsa] *sf* **a ~** to the last, to the bitter end

'oltre *av* (*più in là*) further; (*di più: aspettare*) longer, more ▷ *prep* (*di là da*) beyond, over, on the other side of; (*più di*) more than, over; (*in aggiunta a*) besides; (*eccetto*): **~ a** except, apart from; **oltrepas'sare** *vt* to go beyond, exceed

o'maggio [o'maddʒo] *sm* (*dono*) gift; (*segno di rispetto*) homage, tribute; **omaggi** *smpl* (*complimenti*) respects; **rendere ~ a** to pay homage *o* tribute to; **in ~** (*copia, biglietto*) complimentary

ombe'lico, -chi *sm* navel

'ombra *sf* (*zona non assolata, fantasma*) shade; (*sagoma scura*) shadow; **sedere all'~** to sit in the shade; **restare nell'~** (*fig*) to remain in obscurity

om'brello *sm* umbrella; **ombrel'lone** *sm* beach umbrella

om'bretto *sm* eye shadow

O.M.C. *sigla f* (= *Organizzazione Mondiale del Commercio*) WTO

ome'lette [ɔmə'lɛt] *sf inv* omelet(te)

ome'lia *sf* (*Rel*) homily, sermon

omeopa'tia *sf* homoeopathy

omertà *sf* conspiracy of silence

o'mettere *vt* to omit, leave out; **~ di fare** to omit *o* fail to do

omi'cida, -i, -e [omi'tʃida] *ag* homicidal, murderous ▷ *sm/f* murderer/eress

omi'cidio [omi'tʃidjo] *sm* murder; **omicidio colposo** culpable homicide

o'misi *ecc vb vedi* **omettere**

omissi'one *sf* omission; **omissione di soccorso** (*Dir*) failure to stop and give assistance

omogeneiz'zato [omodʒeneid'dzato] *sm* baby food

omo'geneo, -a [omo'dʒɛneo] *ag* homogeneous

o'monimo, -a *sm/f* namesake ▷ *sm* (*Ling*) homonym

omosessu'ale *ag, sm/f* homosexual

O.M.S. *sigla f* (= *Organizzazione Mondiale della Sanità*) WHO

On. *abbr* (*Pol*) = **onorevole**

'onda *sf* wave; **mettere** *o* **mandare in ~** (*Radio, TV*) to broadcast; **andare in ~** (*Radio, TV*) to go on the air; **onde corte/lunghe/medie** short/long/medium wave

'onere *sm* burden; **oneri fiscali** taxes

onestà *sf* honesty

o'nesto, -a *ag* (*probo, retto*) honest; (*giusto*) fair; (*casto*) chaste, virtuous

ONG *sigla f inv* **Organizzazione Non Governativa** NGO

onnipo'tente *ag* omnipotent

ono'mastico, -ci *sm* name-day

ono'rare *vt* to honour; (*far onore a*) to do credit to

ono'rario, -a *ag* honorary ▷ *sm* fee

o'nore *sm* honour; **in ~ di** in honour of; **fare gli onori di casa** to play host (*o* hostess); **fare ~ a** to honour; (*pranzo*) to do justice to; (*famiglia*) to be a credit to; **farsi ~** to distinguish o.s.; **ono'revole** *ag* honourable ▷ *sm/f* (*Pol*) ≈ Member of Parliament (*BRIT*), ≈ Congressman/woman (*US*)

on'tano *sm* (*Bot*) alder

'O.N.U. ['ɔnu] *sigla f* (= *Organizzazione delle Nazioni Unite*) UN, UNO

o'paco, -a, -chi, -che *ag* (*vetro*) opaque; (*metallo*) dull, matt

o'pale *sm o f* opal

'opera *sf* work; (*azione rilevante*) action, deed, work; (*Mus*) work; opus; (: *melodramma*) opera; (: *teatro*) opera house; (*ente*) institution, organization; **opere pubbliche** public works; **opera d'arte** work of art; **opera lirica** (grand) opera

ope'raio, -a *ag* working-class; workers' ▷ *sm/f* worker; **classe operaia** working class

ope'rare *vt* to carry out, make; (*Med*) to operate on ▷ *vi* to operate, work; (*rimedio*) to act, work; (*Med*) to operate; **operarsi** *vpr* (*Med*) to have an operation; **operarsi d'appendicite** to have one's appendix out; **operazi'one** *sf* operation

ope'retta *sf* (*Mus*) operetta, light opera

opini'one *sf* opinion; **opinione pubblica** public opinion

'oppio *sm* opium

op'pongo *ecc vb vedi* **opporre**

op'porre *vt* to oppose; **opporsi** *vpr* **opporsi (a qc)** to oppose (sth); to object (to sth); **~ resistenza/un rifiuto** to offer resistance/refuse

opportu'nista, -i, -e *sm/f* opportunist

opportunità *sf inv* opportunity; (*convenienza*) opportuneness, timeliness

oppor'tuno, -a *ag* timely, opportune

op'posi *ecc vb vedi* **opporre**

opposizi'one [oppozit'tsjone] *sf* opposition; (*Dir*) objection

op'posto, -a *pp di* **opporre** ▷ *ag* opposite; (*opinioni*) conflicting ▷ *sm* opposite, contrary; **all'~** on the contrary

oppressi'one *sf* oppression

oppri'mente *ag* (*caldo, noia*) oppressive; (*persona*) tiresome; (*deprimente*) depressing

op'primere *vt* (*premere, gravare*) to weigh down; (*estenuare: caldo*) to suffocate, oppress; (*tiranneggiare: popolo*) to oppress

op'pure *cong* or (else)

op'tare *vi* **~ per** to opt for

o'puscolo *sm* booklet, pamphlet

opzi'one [op'tsjone] *sf* option

'ora *sf* (*60 minuti*) hour; (*momento*) time; **che ~ è?, che ore sono?** what time is it?; **a che ~ apre il museo/negozio?** what time does the museum/shop open?; **non veder l'~ di fare** to long to do, look forward to doing; **di buon'~** early; **alla buon'~!** at last!; **~ legale** *o* **estiva** summer time (BRIT), daylight saving time (US); **ora di cena** dinner time; **ora locale** local time; **ora di pranzo** lunchtime; **ora di punta** (*Aut*) rush hour

o'racolo *sm* oracle

o'rale *ag, sm* oral

o'rario, -a *ag* hourly; (*fuso, segnale*) time *cpd*; (*velocità*) per hour ▷ *sm* timetable, schedule; (*di ufficio, visite ecc*) hours *pl*, time(s *pl*); **in ~** on time

o'rata *sf* (*Zool*) sea bream

ora'tore, -'trice *sm/f* speaker; orator

'orbita *sf* (*Astr, Fisica*) orbit; (*Anat*) (eye-)socket

or'chestra [or'kɛstra] *sf* orchestra

orchi'dea [orki'dɛa] *sf* orchid

or'digno [or'diɲɲo] *sm* (*esplosivo*) explosive device

ordi'nale *ag, sm* ordinal

ordi'nare *vt* (*mettere in ordine*) to arrange, organize; (*Comm*) to order; (*prescrivere: medicina*) to prescribe; (*comandare*): **posso ~ per favore?** can I order now please?; **~ a qn di fare qc** to order *o* command sb to do

sth; (*Rel*) to ordain

ordi'nario, -a *ag* (*comune*) ordinary; everyday; standard; (*grossolano*) coarse, common ▷ *sm* ordinary; (*Ins: di università*) full professor

ordi'nato, -a *ag* tidy, orderly

ordinazi'one [ordinat'tsjone] *sf* (*Comm*) order; (*Rel*) ordination; **eseguire qc su ~** to make sth to order

'ordine *sm* order; (*carattere*): **d'~ pratico** of a practical nature; **all'~** (*Comm: assegno*) to order; **di prim'~** first-class; **fino a nuovo ~** until further notice; **essere in ~** (*documenti*) to be in order; (*stanza, persona*) to be tidy; **mettere in ~** to put in order, tidy (up); **l'~ pubblico** law and order; **ordini (sacri)** (*Rel*) holy orders; **ordine del giorno** (*di seduta*) agenda; (*Mil*) order of the day; **ordine di pagamento** (*Comm*) order for payment

orec'chino [orek'kino] *sm* earring

o'recchio [o'rekkjo] (*pl(f)* **o'recchie**) *sm* (*Anat*) ear

orecchi'oni [orek'kjoni] *smpl* (*Med*) mumps *sg*

o'refice [o'rɛfitʃe] *sm* goldsmith; jeweller; **orefice'ria** (*arte*) goldsmith's art; (*negozio*) jeweller's (shop)

'orfano, -a *ag* orphan(ed) ▷ *sm/f* orphan; **~ di padre/madre** fatherless/motherless

orga'netto *sm* barrel organ; (*fam: armonica a bocca*) mouth organ; (: *fisarmonica*) accordion

or'ganico, -a, -ci, -che *ag* organic ▷ *sm* personnel, staff

organi'gramma, -i *sm* organization chart

orga'nismo *sm* (*Biol*) organism; (*corpo umano*) body; (*Amm*) body, organism

organiz'zare [organid'dzare] *vt* to organize; **organizzarsi** *vpr* to get organized; **organizzazi'one** *sf* organization

'organo *sm* organ; (*di congegno*) part; (*portavoce*) spokesman, mouthpiece

'orgia, -ge ['ɔrdʒa] *sf* orgy

or'goglio [or'ɡɔʎʎo] *sm* pride; **orgogli'oso, -a** *ag* proud

orien'tale *ag* oriental; eastern; east

orienta'mento *sm* positioning; orientation; direction; **senso di ~** sense of direction; **perdere l'~** to lose one's bearings; **orientamento professionale** careers guidance

orientarsi *vpr* to find one's bearings; (*fig: tendere*) to tend, lean; (: *indirizzarsi*): **~ verso** to take up, go in for

ori'ente *sm* east; **l'O~** the East, the Orient; **a ~** in the east

o'rigano sm oregano

origi'nale [oridʒi'nale] ag original; (bizzarro) eccentric ▷ sm original

origi'nario, -a [oridʒi'narjo] ag original; **essere ~ di** to be a native of; (provenire da) to originate from; to be native to

o'rigine [o'ridʒine] sf origin; **all'~** originally; **d'~ inglese** of English origin; **dare ~ a** to give rise to

origli'are [oriʎ'ʎare] vi **~ (a)** to eavesdrop (on)

o'rina sf urine

ori'nare vi to urinate ▷ vt to pass

orizzon'tale [oriddzon'tale] ag horizontal

oriz'zonte [orid'dzonte] sm horizon

'orlo sm edge, border; (di recipiente) rim, brim; (di vestito ecc) hem

'orma sf (di persona) footprint; (di animale) track; (impronta, traccia) mark, trace

or'mai av by now, by this time; (adesso) now; (quasi) almost, nearly

ormeggi'are [ormed'dʒare] vt (Naut) to moor

or'mone sm hormone

ornamen'tale ag ornamental, decorative

or'nare vt to adorn, decorate; **ornarsi** vpr **ornarsi (di)** to deck o.s. (out) (with)

ornitolo'gia [ornitolo'dʒia] sf ornithology

'oro sm gold; **d'~, in ~** gold cpd; **d'~** (colore, occasione) golden; (persona) marvellous

oro'logio [oro'lɔdʒo] sm clock; (da tasca, da polso) watch; **orologio al quarzo** quartz watch; **orologio da polso** wristwatch

o'roscopo sm horoscope

or'rendo, -a ag (spaventoso) horrible, awful; (bruttissimo) hideous

or'ribile ag horrible

or'rore sm horror; **avere in ~ qn/qc** to loathe o detest sb/sth; **mi fanno ~** I loathe o detest them

orsacchi'otto [orsak'kjɔtto] sm teddy bear

'orso sm bear; **orso bruno/bianco** brown/polar bear

or'taggio [or'taddʒo] sm vegetable

or'tensia sf hydrangea

or'tica, -che sf (stinging) nettle

orti'caria sf nettle rash

'orto sm vegetable garden, kitchen garden; (Agr) market garden (BRIT), truck farm (US); **orto botanico** botanical garden(s) (pl)

orto'dosso, -a ag orthodox

ortogra'fia sf spelling

orto'pedico, -a, -ci, -che ag orthopaedic ▷ sm orthopaedic specialist

orzai'olo [ordza'jɔlo] sm (Med) stye

'orzo ['ordzo] sm barley

o'sare vt, vi to dare; **~ fare** to dare (to) do

oscenità [oʃʃeni'ta] sf inv obscenity

o'sceno, -a [oʃ'ʃeno] ag obscene; (ripugnante) ghastly

oscil'lare [oʃʃil'lare] vi (pendolo) to swing; (dondolare: al vento ecc) to rock; (variare) to fluctuate; (Tecn) to oscillate; (fig): **~ fra** to waver o hesitate between

oscu'rare vt to darken, obscure; (fig) to obscure, **oscurarsi** vpr (cielo) to darken, cloud over; (persona): **si oscurò in volto** his face clouded over

oscurità sf (vedi ag) darkness; obscurity

os'curo, -a ag dark; (fig) obscure; humble, lowly ▷ sm **all'~** in the dark; **tenere qn all'~ di qc** to keep sb in the dark about sth

ospe'dale sm hospital; **dov'è l'~ più vicino?** where's the nearest hospital?

ospi'tale ag hospitable

ospi'tare vt to give hospitality to; (albergo) to accommodate

'ospite sm/f (persona che ospita) host/hostess; (persona ospitata) guest

os'pizio [os'pittsjo] sm (per vecchi ecc) home

osser'vare vt to observe, watch; (esaminare) to examine; (notare, rilevare) to notice, observe; (Dir: la legge) to observe, respect; (mantenere: silenzio) to keep, observe; **far ~ qc a qn** to point sth out to sb; **osservazi'one** sf observation; (di legge ecc) observance; (considerazione critica) observation, remark; (rimprovero) reproof; **in osservazione** under observation

ossessio'nare vt to obsess, haunt; (tormentare) to torment, harass

ossessi'one sf obsession

os'sia cong that is, to be precise

'ossido sm oxide; **ossido di carbonio** carbon monoxide

ossige'nare [ossidʒe'nare] vt to oxygenate; (decolorare) to bleach; **acqua ossigenata** hydrogen peroxide

os'sigeno sm oxygen

'osso (pl(f) **ossa**) (nel senso Anat) sm bone; **d'~** (bottone ecc) of bone, bone cpd; **osso di seppia** cuttlebone

ostaco'lare vt to block, obstruct

os'tacolo sm obstacle; (Equitazione) hurdle, jump

os'taggio [os'taddʒo] sm hostage

os'tello sm; **ostello della gioventù** youth hostel

osten'tare vt to make a show of, flaunt

oste'ria sf inn

os'tetrico, -a, -ci, -che ag obstetric ▷ sm obstetrician

'ostia sf (Rel) host; (per medicinali) wafer

'ostico, -a, -ci, -che ag (fig) harsh; hard, difficult; unpleasant

os'tile ag hostile

osti'narsi *vpr* to insist, dig one's heels in;
  ~ a fare to persist (obstinately) in doing;
  osti'nato, -a *ag* (*caparbio*) obstinate;
  (*tenace*) persistent, determined
'ostrica, -che *sf* oyster

   Attenzione! In inglese esiste la parola
  ostrich, che però significa *struzzo*.

ostru'ire *vt* to obstruct, block
o'tite *sf* ear infection
ot'tanta *num* eighty
ot'tavo, -a *num* eighth
otte'nere *vt* to obtain, get; (*risultato*) to
  achieve, obtain
'ottica *sf* (*scienza*) optics *sg*; (*Fot: lenti,
  prismi ecc*) optics *pl*
'ottico, -a, -ci, -che *ag* (*della vista: nervo*)
  optic; (*dell'ottica*) optical ▷ *sm* optician
ottima'mente *av* excellently, very well
otti'mismo *sm* optimism; **otti'mista, -i,
  -e** *sm/f* optimist
'ottimo, -a *ag* excellent, very good
'otto *num* eight
ot'tobre *sm* October
otto'cento [otto'tʃɛnto] *num* eight
  hundred ▷ *sm* **l'O~** the nineteenth century
ot'tone *sm* brass; **gli ottoni** (*Mus*) the
  brass
ottu'rare *vt* to close (up); (*dente*) to fill; **il
  lavandino è otturato** the sink is blocked;
  otturarsi *vpr* to become o get blocked up;
  otturazi'one *sf* closing (up); (*dentaria*)
  filling
ot'tuso, -a *ag* (*Mat, fig*) obtuse; (*suono*) dull
o'vaia *sf* (*Anat*) ovary
o'vale *ag, sm* oval
o'vatta *sf* cotton wool; (*per imbottire*)
  padding, wadding
'ovest *sm* west
o'vile *sm* pen, enclosure
ovulazi'one [ovulat'tsjone] *sf* ovulation
'ovulo *sm* (*Fisiol*) ovum
o'vunque *av* = **dovunque**
ovvi'are *vi* **~ a** to obviate
'ovvio, -a *ag* obvious
ozi'are [ot'tsjare] *vi* to laze, idle
'ozio ['ɔttsjo] *sm* idleness; (*tempo libero*)
  leisure; **ore d'~** leisure time; **stare in ~** to
  be idle
o'zono [o'dzɔno] *sm* ozone

P

P *abbr* (= *parcheggio*) P; (*Aut:* = *principiante*) L
p. *abbr* (= *pagina*) p.
pac'chetto [pak'ketto] *sm* packet;
  pacchetto azionario (*Comm*)
  shareholding
'pacco, -chi *sm* parcel; (*involto*) bundle;
  pacco postale parcel
'pace ['patʃe] *sf* peace; **darsi ~** to resign
  o.s.; **fare la ~ con** to make it up with
pa'cifico, -a, -ci, -che [pa'tʃiːfiko] *ag*
  (*persona*) peaceable; (*vita*) peaceful; (*fig:
  indiscusso*) indisputable; (: *ovvio*) obvious,
  clear ▷ *sm* **il P~, l'Oceano P~** the Pacific
  (Ocean)
paci'fista, -i, -e [patʃi'fista] *sm/f*
  pacifist
pa'della *sf* frying pan; (*per infermi*)
  bedpan
padigli'one [padiʎ'ʎone] *sm* pavilion
'Padova *sf* Padua
'padre *sm* father
pa'drino *sm* godfather
padro'nanza [padro'nantsa] *sf*
  command, mastery
pa'drone, -a *sm/f* master/mistress;
  (*proprietario*) owner; (*datore di lavoro*)
  employer; **essere ~ di sé** to be in control
  of o.s.; **padrone(a) di casa** master/
  mistress of the house; (*per gli inquilini*)
  landlord/lady

pae'saggio [pae'zaddʒo] sm landscape

pa'ese sm (nazione) country, nation; (terra) country, land; (villaggio) village, (small) town; **i Paesi Bassi** the Netherlands; **paese di provenienza** country of origin

'paga, -ghe sf pay, wages pl

paga'mento sm payment

pa'gare vt to pay; (acquisto, fig: colpa) to pay for; (contraccambiare) to repay, pay back ▷ vi to pay; **quanto l'hai pagato?** how much did you pay for it?; **posso ~ con la carta di credito?** can I pay by credit card?; **~ in contanti** to pay cash

pa'gella [pa'dʒɛlla] sf (Ins) report card

pagherò [page'rɔ] sm inv acknowledgement of a debt, IOU

'pagina ['padʒina] sf page; **pagine bianche** phone book, telephone directory; **pagine gialle** Yellow Pages

'paglia ['paʎʎa] sf straw

pagli'accio [paʎ'ʎattʃo] sm clown

pagli'etta [paʎ'ʎetta] sf (cappello per uomo) (straw) boater; (per tegami ecc) steel wool

pa'gnotta [paɲ'ɲɔtta] sf round loaf

'paio (pl(f) **'paia**) sm pair; **un ~ di** (alcuni) a couple of

'Pakistan sm **il ~** Pakistan

'pala sf shovel; (di remo, ventilatore, elica) blade; (di ruota) paddle

pa'lato sm palate

pa'lazzo [pa'lattso] sm (reggia) palace; (edificio) building; **palazzo di giustizia** courthouse; **palazzo dello sport** sports stadium

'palco, -chi sm (Teatro) box; (tavolato) platform, stand; (ripiano) layer

palco'scenico, -ci [palkoʃʃɛniko] sm (Teatro) stage

pa'lese ag clear, evident

Pales'tina sf **la ~** Palestine

palesti'nese ag, sm/f Palestinian

pa'lestra sf gymnasium; (esercizio atletico) exercise, training; (fig) training ground, school

pa'letta sf spade; (per il focolare) shovel; (del capostazione) signalling disc

pa'letto sm stake, peg; (spranga) bolt

'palio sm (gara): **il P~** horse race run at Siena; **mettere qc in ~** to offer sth as a prize

⬤ **PALIO**
⬤
⬤ The **palio** is a horse race which takes
⬤ place in a number of Italian towns, the
⬤ most famous being the one in Siena.
⬤ This is usually held twice a year on July
⬤ 2nd and August 16th in the Piazza del
⬤ Campo in Siena. 10 of the 17 **contrade** or

⬤ districts take part, each represented by
⬤ a horse and rider. The winner is the first
⬤ horse to complete the course, whether
⬤ it has a rider or not.

'palla sf ball; (pallottola) bullet; **palla di neve** snowball; **palla ovale** rugby ball; **pallaca'nestro** sf basketball; **palla'mano** sf handball; **pallanu'oto** sf water polo; **palla'volo** sf volleyball

palleggi'are [palled'dʒare] vi (Calcio) to practise with the ball; (Tennis) to knock up

pallia'tivo sm palliative; (fig) stopgap measure

'pallido, -a ag pale

pal'lina sf (bilia) marble

pallon'cino [pallon'tʃino] sm balloon; (lampioncino) Chinese lantern

pal'lone sm (palla) ball; (Calcio) football; (aerostato) balloon; **gioco del ~** football

pal'lottola sf pellet; (proiettile) bullet

'palma sf (Anat) = **palmo**; (Bot, simbolo) palm; **palma da datteri** date palm

'palmo sm (Anat) palm; **restare con un ~ di naso** to be badly disappointed

'palo sm (legno appuntito) stake; (sostegno) pole; **fare da o il ~** (fig) to act as look-out

palom'baro sm diver

pal'pare vt to feel, finger

'palpebra sf eyelid

pa'lude sf marsh, swamp

pan'cetta [pan'tʃetta] sf (Cuc) bacon

pan'china [pan'kina] sf garden seat; (di giardino pubblico) (park) bench

'pancia, -ce ['pantʃa] sf belly, stomach; **mettere o fare ~** to be getting a paunch; **avere mal di ~** to have stomachache o a sore stomach

panci'otto [pan'tʃotto] sm waistcoat

'pancreas sm inv pancreas

panda sm inv panda

'pane sm bread; (pagnotta) loaf (of bread); (forma): **un ~ di burro** a pat of butter; **guadagnarsi il ~** to earn one's living; **pane a cassetta** sliced bread; **pane di Spagna** sponge cake; **pane integrale** wholemeal bread; **pane tostato** toast

panette'ria sf (forno) bakery; (negozio) baker's (shop), bakery

panetti'ere, -a sm/f baker

panet'tone sm a kind of spiced brioche with sultanas, eaten at Christmas

pangrat'tato sm breadcrumbs pl

'panico, -a, -ci, -che ag, sm panic

pani'ere sm basket

pani'ficio [pani'fitʃo] sm (forno) bakery; (negozio) baker's (shop), bakery

pa'nino sm roll; **panino caldo** toasted sandwich; **panino imbottito** filled roll;

sandwich

'panna sf (Cuc) cream; (Tecn) = **panne**; **panna da cucina** cooking cream; **panna montata** whipped cream

'panne sf inv **essere in ~** (Aut) to have broken down

pan'nello sm panel; **pannello solare** solar panel

'panno sm cloth; **panni** smpl (abiti) clothes; **mettiti nei miei panni** (fig) put yourself in my shoes

pan'nocchia [pan'nɔkkja] sf (di mais ecc) ear

panno'lino sm (per bambini) nappy (BRIT), diaper (US)

pano'rama, -i sm panorama

panta'loni smpl trousers (BRIT), pants (US), pair sg, of trousers o pants

pan'tano sm bog

pan'tera sf panther

pan'tofola sf slipper

'Papa, -i sm pope

papà sm inv dad(dy)

pa'pavero sm poppy

'pappa sf baby cereal; **pappa reale** royal jelly

pappa'gallo sm parrot; (fig: uomo) Romeo, wolf

pa'rabola sf (Mat) parabola; (Rel) parable

para'bolico, -a, ci, che ag (Mat) parabolic; vedi anche **antenna**

para'brezza [para'breddza] sm inv (Aut) windscreen (BRIT), windshield (US)

paraca'dute sm inv parachute

para'diso sm paradise

parados'sale ag paradoxical

para'fulmine sm lightning conductor

pa'raggi [pa'raddʒi] smpl **nei ~** in the vicinity, in the neighbourhood

parago'nare vt **~ con/a** to compare with/to

para'gone sm comparison; (esempio analogo) analogy, parallel; **reggere al ~** to stand comparison

pa'ragrafo sm paragraph

pa'ralisi sf paralysis

paral'lelo, -a ag parallel ▷ sm (Geo) parallel; (comparazione): **fare un ~ tra** to draw a parallel between

para'lume sm lampshade

pa'rametro sm parameter

para'noia sf paranoia; **para'noico, -a, -ci, -che** ag, sm/f paranoid

para'occhi [para'ɔkki] smpl blinkers

para'petto sm balustrade

pa'rare vt (addobbare) to adorn, deck; (proteggere) to shield, protect; (scansare: colpo) to parry; (Calcio) to save ▷ vi **dove**

vuole andare a ~? what are you driving at?

pa'rata sf (Sport) save; (Mil) review, parade

para'urti sm inv (Aut) bumper

para'vento sm folding screen; **fare da ~ a qn** (fig) to shield sb

par'cella [par'tʃɛlla] sf account, fee (of lawyer etc)

parcheggi'are [parked'dʒare] vt to park; **posso ~ qui?** can I park here?; **parcheggiatore, -trice** [parkeddʒa'tore] sm/f (Aut) parking attendant

par'cheggio sm parking no pl; (luogo) car park; (singolo posto) parking space

par'chimetro [par'kimetro] sm parking meter

'parco, -chi sm park; (spazio per deposito) depot; (complesso di veicoli) fleet

par'cometro sm (pay-and-display) ticket machine

pa'recchio, -a [pa'rekkjo] det quite a lot of; (tempo) quite a lot of, a long

pareggi'are [pared'dʒare] vt to make equal; (terreno) to level, make level; (bilancio, conti) to balance ▷ vi (Sport) to draw; **pa'reggio** sm (Econ) balance; (Sport) draw

pa'rente sm/f relative, relation

Attenzione! In inglese esiste la parola parent, che però significa genitore.

paren'tela sf (vincolo di sangue, fig) relationship

pa'rentesi sf (segno grafico) bracket, parenthesis; (frase incisa) parenthesis; (digressione) parenthesis, digression

pa'rere sm (opinione) opinion; (consiglio) advice, opinion; **a mio ~** in my opinion ▷ vi to seem, appear ▷ vb impers **pare che** it seems o appears that, they say that; **mi pare che** it seems to me that; **mi pare di sì** I think so; **fai come ti pare** do as you like; **che ti pare del mio libro?** what do you think of my book?

pa'rete sf wall

'pari ag inv (uguale) equal, same; (in giochi) equal; drawn, tied; (Mat) even ▷ sm inv (Pol: di Gran Bretagna) peer ▷ sm/f inv peer, equal; **copiato ~ ~** copied word for word; **alla ~** on the same level; **ragazza alla ~** au pair girl; **mettersi alla ~ con** to place o.s. on the same level as; **mettersi in ~ con** to catch up with; **andare di ~ passo con qn** to keep pace with sb

Pa'rigi [pa'ridʒi] sf Paris

pari'gino, -a [pari'dʒino] ag, sm/f Parisian

parità sf parity, equality; (Sport) draw, tie

parlamen'tare ag parliamentary ▷ sm/f ≈ Member of Parliament (BRIT), ≈ Congressman/woman (US) ▷ vi to

negotiate, parley
parla'mento *sm* parliament

parlan'tina (*fam*) *sf* talkativeness; **avere ~**
to have the gift of the gab
par'lare *vi* to speak, talk; (*confidare cose
segrete*) to talk ▷ *vt* to speak; **~ (a qn) di** to
speak *o* talk (to sb) about; **posso ~ con...?**
can I speak to ...?; **parla italiano?** do you
speak Italian?; **non parlo inglese** I don't
speak English
parmigi'ano [parmi'dʒano] *sm* (*grana*)
Parmesan (cheese)
pa'rola *sf* word; (*facoltà*) speech; **parole**
sfpl (*chiacchiere*) talk *sg*; **chiedere la ~** to
ask permission to speak; **prendere la ~**
to take the floor; **parola d'onore** word of
honour; **parola d'ordine** (*Mil*) password;
parole incrociate crossword (puzzle) *sg*;
paro'laccia, -ce *sf* bad word, swearword
parrò *ecc vb vedi* **parere**
par'rocchia [par'rɔkkja] *sf* parish; parish
church
par'rucca, -che *sf* wig
parrucchi'ere, -a [parruk'kjɛre] *sm/f*
hairdresser ▷ *sm* barber
'parte *sf* part; (*lato*) side; (*quota spettante a
ciascuno*) share; (*direzione*) direction; (*Pol*)
party; faction; (*Dir*) party; **a ~** *ag* separate
▷ *av* separately; **scherzi a ~** joking aside;
a ~ ciò apart from that; **da ~** (*in disparte*)
to one side, aside; **d'altra ~** on the other
hand; **da ~ di** (*per conto di*) on behalf of; **da
~ mia** as far as I'm concerned, as for me;
da ~ a ~ right through; **da ogni ~** on all
sides, everywhere; (*moto da luogo*) from all
sides; **da nessuna ~** nowhere; **da questa
~** (*in questa direzione*) this way; **prendere
~ a qc** to take part in sth; **mettere da ~**
to put aside; **mettere qn a ~ di** to inform
sb of
parteci'pare [partetʃi'pare] *vi* **~ a** to take
part in, participate in; (*utili ecc*) to share in;
(*spese ecc*) to contribute to; (*dolore, successo
di qn*) to share (in)
parteggi'are [parted'dʒare] *vi* **~ per** to
side with, be on the side of
par'tenza [par'tɛntsa] *sf* departure;
(*Sport*) start; **essere in ~** to be about to
leave, be leaving
parti'cipio [parti'tʃipjo] *sm* participle

partico'lare *ag* (*specifico*) particular;
(*proprio*) personal, private; (*speciale*)
special, particular; (*caratteristico*)
distinctive, characteristic; (*fuori dal
comune*) peculiar ▷ *sm* detail, particular; **in
~** in particular, particularly
par'tire *vi* to go, leave; (*allontanarsi*) to go
(*o drive ecc*) away *o* off; (*petardo, colpo*) to
go off; (*fig: avere inizio, Sport*) to start; **sono
partita da Roma alle 7** I left Rome at 7; **a
che ora parte il treno/l'autobus?** what
time does the train/bus leave?; **il volo
parte da Ciampino** the flight leaves from
Ciampino; **a ~ da** from
par'tita *sf* (*Comm*) lot, consignment; (*Econ:
registrazione*) entry, item; (*Carte, Sport:
gioco*) game; (: *competizione*) match, game;
partita di caccia hunting party; **partita
IVA** VAT registration number
par'tito *sm* (*Pol*) party; (*decisione*) decision,
resolution; (*persona da maritare*) match
'parto *sm* (*Med*) delivery, (child)birth;
labour
'parvi *ecc vb vedi* **parere**
parzi'ale [par'tsjale] *ag* (*limitato*) partial;
(*non obiettivo*) biased, partial
pasco'lare *vt, vi* to graze
'pascolo *sm* pasture
'Pasqua *sf* Easter; **Pas'quetta** *sf* Easter
Monday
pas'sabile *ag* fairly good, passable
pas'saggio [pas'saddʒo] *sm* passing *no
pl*, passage; (*traversata*) crossing *no pl*,
passage; (*luogo, prezzo della traversata,
brano di libro ecc*) passage; (*su veicolo altrui*)
lift (BRIT), ride; (*Sport*) pass; **di ~** (*persona*)
passing through; **può darmi un ~ fino
alla stazione?** can you give me a lift to the
station?; **passaggio a livello** level (BRIT) *o*
grade (US) crossing; **passaggio pedonale**
pedestrian crossing
passamon'tagna [passamon'taɲɲa] *sm
inv* balaclava
pas'sante *sm/f* passer-by ▷ *sm* loop
passa'porto *sm* passport
pas'sare *vi* (*andare*) to go; (*veicolo, pedone*)
to pass (by), go by; (*fare una breve sosta:
postino ecc*) to come, call; (: *amico: per fare
una visita*) to call *o* drop in; (*sole, aria, luce*)
to get through; (*trascorrere: giorni, tempo*)
to pass, go by; (*fig: proposta di legge*) to
be passed; (: *dolore*) to pass, go away;
(*Carte*) to pass ▷ *vt* (*attraversare*) to cross;
(*trasmettere: messaggio*): **~ qc a qn** to pass
sth on to sb; (*dare*): **~ qc a qn** to pass sth to
sb, give sb sth; (*trascorrere: tempo*) to spend;
(*superare: esame*) to pass; (*triturare: verdura*)
to strain; (*approvare*) to pass, approve;
(*oltrepassare, sorpassare: anche fig*) to go

beyond, pass; (fig: subire) to go through; **mi passa il sale/l'olio per favore?** could you pass the salt/oil please?; **~ da ... a** to pass from ... to; **~ di padre in figlio** to be handed down o to pass from father to son; **~ per** (anche fig) to go through; **~ per stupido/un genio** to be taken for a fool/a genius; **~ sopra** (anche fig) to pass over; **~ attraverso** (anche fig) to go through; **~ alla storia** to pass into history; **~ a un esame** to go up (to the next class) after an exam; **~ inosservato** to go unnoticed; **~ di moda** to go out of fashion; **le passo il Signor X** (al telefono) here is Mr X; I'm putting you through to Mr X; **lasciar ~ qn/qc** to let sb/sth through; **come te la passi?** how are you getting on o along?

passa'tempo sm pastime, hobby

pas'sato, -a ag past; (sfiorito) faded ▷ sm past; (Ling) past (tense); **passato prossimo/remoto** (Ling) present perfect/past historic; **passato di verdura** (Cuc) vegetable purée

passeg'gero, -a [passed'dʒero] ag passing ▷ sm/f passenger

passeggi'are [passed'dʒare] vi to go for a walk; (in veicolo) to go for a drive; **passeggi'ata** sf walk; drive; (luogo) promenade; **fare una passeggiata** to go for a walk (o drive); **passeg'gino** sm pushchair (BRIT), stroller (US)

passe'rella sf footbridge; (di nave, aereo) gangway; (pedana) catwalk

'passero sm sparrow

passi'one sf passion

pas'sivo, -a ag passive ▷ sm (Ling) passive; (Econ) debit; (: complesso dei debiti) liabilities pl

'passo sm step; (andatura) pace; (rumore) (foot)step; (orma) footprint; (passaggio, fig: brano) passage; (valico) pass; **a ~ d'uomo** at walking pace; **~ (a) ~** step by step; **fare due o quattro passi** to go for a walk o a stroll; **di questo ~** at this rate; **"passo carraio"** "vehicle entrance — keep clear"

'pasta sf (Cuc) dough; (: impasto per dolce) pastry; (: anche: **~ alimentare**) pasta; (massa molle di materia) paste; (fig: indole) nature; **paste** sfpl (pasticcini) pastries; **pasta in brodo** noodle soup; **pasta sfoglia** puff pastry o paste (US)

pastasci'utta [pastaʃ'ʃutta] sf pasta

pas'tella sf batter

pas'tello sm pastel

pasticce'ria [pastittʃe'ria] sf (pasticcini) pastries pl, cakes pl; (negozio) cake shop; (arte) confectionery

pasticci'ere, -a [pastit'tʃere] sm/f pastrycook; confectioner

pastic'cino [pastit'tʃino] sm petit four

pas'ticcio [pas'tittʃo] sm (Cuc) pie; (lavoro disordinato, imbroglio) mess; **trovarsi nei pasticci** to get into trouble

pas'tiglia [pas'tiʎʎa] sf pastille, lozenge

pas'tina sf small pasta shapes used in soup

'pasto sm meal

pas'tore sm shepherd; (Rel) pastor, minister; (anche: **cane ~**) sheepdog; **pastore tedesco** (Zool) Alsatian, German shepherd

pa'tata sf potato; **patate fritte** chips (BRIT), French fries; **pata'tine** sfpl (potato) crisps; **patatine fritte** chips

pa'tente sf licence; **patente di guida** driving licence (BRIT), driver's license (US); **patente a punti** driving licence with penalty points

> Attenzione! In inglese esiste la parola patent, che però significa brevetto.

paternità sf paternity, fatherhood

pa'tetico, -a, -ci, -che ag pathetic; (commovente) moving, touching

pa'tibolo sm gallows sg, scaffold

'patina sf (su rame ecc) patina; (sulla lingua) fur, coating

pa'tire vt, vi to suffer

pa'tito, -a sm/f enthusiast, fan, lover

patolo'gia [patolo'dʒia] sf pathology

'patria sf homeland

pa'trigno [pa'triɲɲo] sm stepfather

patri'monio sm estate, property; (fig) heritage

pa'trono sm (Rel) patron saint; (socio di patronato) patron; (Dir) counsel

patteggi'are [patted'dʒare] vt, vi to negotiate; (Dir) to plea-bargain

patti'naggio [patti'naddʒo] sm skating; **pattinaggio a rotelle/sul ghiaccio** roller-/ice-skating

patti'nare vi to skate; **~ sul ghiaccio** to ice-skate; **pattina'tore, -'trice** sm/f skater; **'pattino** sm skate; (di slitta) runner; (Aer) skid; (Tecn) sliding block; **pattini in linea** Rollerblades®; **pattini da ghiaccio/a rotelle** ice/roller skates

'patto sm (accordo) pact, agreement; (condizione) term, condition; **a ~ che** on condition that

pat'tuglia [pat'tuʎʎa] sf (Mil) patrol

pattu'ire vt to reach an agreement on

pattumi'era sf (dust)bin (BRIT), ashcan (US)

pa'ura sf fear; **aver ~ di/di fare/che** to be frightened o afraid of/of doing/that; **far ~ a** to frighten; **per ~ di/che** for fear of/that; **pau'roso, -a** ag (che fa paura) frightening; (che ha paura) fearful, timorous

'pausa sf (sosta) break; (nel parlare, Mus) pause

pavi'mento sm floor

Attenzione! In inglese esiste la parola pavement, che però significa marciapiede.

pa'vone sm peacock

pazien'tare [pattsjen'tare] vi to be patient

pazi'ente [pat'tsjɛnte] ag, sm/f patient; **pazi'enza** sf patience

paz'zesco, -a, -schi, -sche [pat'tsesko] ag mad, crazy

paz'zia [pat'tsia] sf (Med) madness, insanity; (azione) folly; (di azione, decisione) madness, folly

'pazzo, -a ['pattso] ag (Med) mad, insane; (strano) wild, mad ▷ sm/f madman/ woman; **~ di** (gioia, amore ecc) mad o crazy with; **~ per qc/qn** mad o crazy about sth/sb

PC [pit'tʃi] sigla m inv (= personal computer) PC; **PC portatile** laptop

pec'care vi to sin; (fig) to err

pec'cato sm sin; **è un ~ che** it's a pity that; **che ~!** what a shame o pity!

peccherò ecc [pekke'rɔ] vb vedi **peccare**

'pece ['petʃe] sf pitch

Pe'chino [pe'kino] sf Beijing

'pecora sf sheep; **peco'rino** sm sheep's milk cheese

pe'daggio [pe'daddʒo] sm toll

pedago'gia [pedago'dʒia] sf pedagogy, educational methods pl

peda'lare vi to pedal; (andare in bicicletta) to cycle

pe'dale sm pedal

pe'dana sf footboard; (Sport: nel salto) springboard; (: nella scherma) piste

pe'dante ag pedantic ▷ sm/f pedant

pe'data sf (impronta) footprint; (colpo) kick; **prendere a pedate qn/qc** to kick sb/sth

pedi'atra, -i, -e sm/f paediatrician

pedi'cure sm/f inv chiropodist

pe'dina sf (della dama) draughtsman (BRIT), draftsman (US); (fig) pawn

pedi'nare vt to shadow, tail

pe'dofilo, -a ag, sm/f paedophile

pedo'nale ag pedestrian

pe'done, -a sm/f pedestrian ▷ sm (Scacchi) pawn

'peggio ['pɛddʒo] av, ag inv worse ▷ sm o f **il** o **la ~** the worst; **alla ~** at worst, if the worst comes to the worst; **peggio'rare** vt to make worse, worsen ▷ vi to grow worse, worsen; **peggi'ore** ag (comparativo) worse; (superlativo) worst ▷ sm/f **il(la) peggiore** the worst (person)

'pegno ['peɲɲo] sm (Dir) security, pledge; (nei giochi di società) forfeit; (fig) pledge, token; **dare in ~ qc** to pawn sth

pe'lare vt (spennare) to pluck; (spellare) to skin; (sbucciare) to peel; (fig) to make pay through the nose

pe'lato, -a ag **pomodori pelati** tinned tomatoes

'pelle sf skin; (di animale) skin, hide; (cuoio) leather; **avere la ~ d'oca** to have goose pimples o goose flesh

pellegri'naggio [pellegri'naddʒo] sm pilgrimage

pelle'rossa (pl **pelli'rosse**) sm/f Red Indian

pelli'cano sm pelican

pel'liccia, -ce [pel'littʃa] sf (mantello di animale) coat, fur; (indumento) fur coat; **pelliccia ecologica** fake fur

pel'licola sf (membrana sottile) film, layer; (Fot, Cinema) film

'pelo sm hair; (pelame) coat, hair; (pelliccia) fur; (di tappeto) pile; (di liquido) surface; **per un ~: per un ~ non ho perduto il treno** I very nearly missed the train; **c'è mancato un ~ che affogasse** he escaped drowning by the skin of his teeth; **pe'loso, -a** ag hairy

'peltro sm pewter

pe'luche [pə'lyʃ] sm plush; **giocattoli di ~** soft toys

pe'luria sf down

'pena sf (Dir) sentence; (punizione) punishment; (sofferenza) sadness no pl, sorrow; (fatica) trouble no pl, effort; (difficoltà) difficulty; **far ~** to be pitiful; **mi fai ~** I feel sorry for you; **prendersi** o **darsi la ~ di fare** to go to the trouble of doing; **pena di morte** death sentence; **pena pecuniaria** fine; **pe'nale** ag penal

pen'dente ag hanging; leaning ▷ sm (ciondolo) pendant; (orecchino) drop earring

'pendere vi (essere appeso): **~ da** to hang from; (essere inclinato) to lean; (fig: incombere): **~ su** to hang over

pen'dio, -'dii sm slope, slant; (luogo in pendenza) slope

'pendola sf pendulum clock

pendo'lare sm/f commuter

pendo'lino sm high-speed train

pene'trante ag piercing, penetrating

pene'trare vi to come o get in ▷ vt to penetrate; **~ in** to enter; (proiettile) to penetrate; (: acqua, aria) to go o come into

penicil'lina [penitʃil'lina] sf penicillin

pe'nisola sf peninsula

penitenzi'ario [peniten'tsjarjo] sm prison

P

'penna *sf* (*di uccello*) feather; (*per scrivere*) pen; **penne** *sfpl* (*Cuc*) quills (*type of pasta*); **penna a sfera** ballpoint pen; **penna stilografica** fountain pen

penna'rello *sm* felt(-tip) pen

pen'nello *sm* brush; (*per dipingere*) (paint)brush; **a ~** (*perfettamente*) to perfection, perfectly; **pennello per la barba** shaving brush

pe'nombra *sf* half-light, dim light

pen'sare *vi* to think ▷ *vt* to think; (*inventare, escogitare*) to think out; **~ a** to think of; (*amico, vacanze*) to think of o about; (*problema*) to think about; **~ di fare qc** to think of doing sth; **ci penso io** I'll see to o take care of it

pensi'ero *sm* thought; (*modo di pensare, dottrina*) thinking *no pl*; (*preoccupazione*) worry, care, trouble; **stare in ~ per qn** to be worried about sb; **pensie'roso, -a** *ag* thoughtful

'pensile *ag* hanging

pensio'nato, -a *sm/f* pensioner

pensi'one *sf* (*al prestatore di lavoro*) pension; (*vitto e alloggio*) board and lodging; (*albergo*) boarding house; **andare in ~** to retire; **mezza ~** half board; **pensione completa** full board

pen'tirsi *vpr* **~ di** to repent of; (*rammaricarsi*) to regret, be sorry for

'pentola *sf* pot; **pentola a pressione** pressure cooker

pe'nultimo, -a *ag* last but one (BRIT), next to last, penultimate

penzo'lare [pendzo'lare] *vi* to dangle, hang loosely

'pepe *sm* pepper; **pepe in grani/ macinato** whole/ground pepper

peperon'cino [peperon'tʃino] *sm* chilli pepper

pepe'rone *sm* pepper, capsicum; (*piccante*) chili

pe'pita *sf* nugget

 PAROLA CHIAVE

per *prep* **1** (*moto attraverso luogo*) through; **i ladri sono passati per la finestra** the thieves got in (o out) through the window; **l'ho cercato per tutta la casa** I've searched the whole house o all over the house for it

2 (*moto a luogo*) for, to; **partire per la Germania/il mare** to leave for Germany/ the sea; **il treno per Roma** the Rome train, the train for o to Rome

3 (*stato in luogo*): **seduto/sdraiato per terra** sitting/lying on the ground

4 (*tempo*) for; **per anni/lungo tempo**

for years/a long time; **per tutta l'estate** throughout the summer, all summer long; **lo rividi per Natale** I saw him again at Christmas; **lo faccio per lunedì** I'll do it for Monday

5 (*mezzo, maniera*) by; **per lettera/via aerea/ferrovia** by letter/airmail/rail; **prendere qn per un braccio** to take sb by the arm

6 (*causa, scopo*) for; **assente per malattia** absent because of o through o owing to illness; **ottimo per il mal di gola** excellent for sore throats

7 (*limitazione*) for; **è troppo difficile per lui** it's too difficult for him; **per quel che mi riguarda** as far as I'm concerned; **per poco che sia** however little it may be; **per questa volta ti perdono** I'll forgive you this time

8 (*prezzo, misura*) for; (*distributivo*) a, per; **venduto per 3 milioni** sold for 3 million; **1 euro per persona** 1 euro a o per person; **uno per volta** one at a time; **uno per uno** one by one; **5 per cento** 5 per cent; **3 per 4 fa 12** 3 times 4 equals 12; **dividere/ moltiplicare 12 per 4** to divide/multiply 12 by 4

9 (*in qualità di*) as; (*al posto di*) for; **avere qn per professore** to have sb as a teacher; **ti ho preso per Mario** I mistook you for Mario, I thought you were Mario; **dare per morto qn** to give sb up for dead

10 (*seguito da vb: finale*): **per fare qc** so as to do sth, in order to do sth; (: *causale*): **per aver fatto qc** for having done sth; (: *consecutivo*): **è abbastanza grande per andarci da solo** he's big enough to go on his own

'pera *sf* pear

per'bene *ag inv* respectable, decent ▷ *av* (*con cura*) properly, well

percentu'ale [pertʃentu'ale] *sf* percentage

perce'pire [pertʃe'pire] *vt* (*sentire*) to perceive; (*ricevere*) to receive

 PAROLA CHIAVE

perché [per'ke] *av* why; **perché no?** why not?; **perché non vuoi andarci?** why don't you want to go?; **spiegami perché l'hai fatto** tell me why you did it

▷ *cong* **1** (*causale*) because; **non posso uscire perché ho da fare** I can't go out because o as I've a lot to do

2 (*finale*) in order that, so that; **te lo do perché tu lo legga** I'm giving it to you so (that) you can read it

3 (*consecutivo*): **è troppo forte perché si possa batterlo** he's too strong to be beaten
▷ *sm inv* reason; **il perché di** the reason for

perciò [per'tʃɔ] *cong* so, for this (*o* that) reason

per'correre *vt* (*luogo*) to go all over; (: *paese*) to travel up and down, go all over; (*distanza*) to travel

per'corso, -a *pp di* **percorrere** ▷ *sm* (*tragitto*) journey; (*tratto*) route

percu'otere *vt* to hit, strike

percussi'one *sf* percussion; **strumenti a ~** (*Mus*) percussion instruments

'perdere *vt* to lose; (*lasciarsi sfuggire*) to miss; (*sprecare: tempo, denaro*) to waste ▷ *vi* to lose; (*serbatoio ecc*) to leak; **perdersi** *vpr* (*smarrirsi*) to get lost; (*svanire*) to disappear, vanish; **mi sono perso** I'm lost; **ho perso il portafoglio/passaporto** I've lost my wallet/passport; **abbiamo perso il treno** we missed our train; **saper ~** to be a good loser; **lascia ~!** forget it!, never mind!

perdigi'orno [perdi'dʒorno] *sm/f inv* idler, waster

'perdita *sf* loss; (*spreco*) waste; (*fuoriuscita*) leak; **siamo in ~** (*Comm*) we are running at a loss; **a ~ d'occhio** as far as the eye can see

perdo'nare *vt* to pardon, forgive; (*scusare*) to excuse, pardon

per'dono *sm* forgiveness; (*Dir*) pardon

perduta'mente *av* desperately, passionately

pe'renne *ag* eternal, perpetual, perennial; (*Bot*) perennial

perfetta'mente *av* perfectly; **sai ~ che ...** you know perfectly well that ...

per'fetto, -a *ag* perfect ▷ *sm* (*Ling*) perfect (tense)

perfeziona'mento [perfettsjona'mento] *sm* **~ (di)** improvement (in), perfection (of); **corso di ~** proficiency course

perfezio'nare [perfettsjo'nare] *vt* to improve, perfect; **perfezionarsi** *vpr* to improve

perfezi'one [perfet'tsjone] *sf* perfection

per'fino *av* even

perfo'rare *vt* to perforate, to punch a hole (*o* holes) in; (*banda, schede*) to punch; (*trivellare*) to drill

perga'mena *sf* parchment

perico'lante *ag* precarious

pe'ricolo *sm* danger; **mettere in ~** to endanger, put in danger; **perico'loso, -a** *ag* dangerous

perife'ria *sf* (*di città*) outskirts *pl*

pe'rifrasi *sf* circumlocution

pe'rimetro *sm* perimeter

peri'odico, -a, -ci, -che *ag* periodic(al); (*Mat*) recurring ▷ *sm* periodical

pe'riodo *sm* period

peripe'zie [peripet'tsie] *sfpl* ups and downs, vicissitudes

pe'rito, -a *ag* expert, skilled ▷ *sm/f* expert; (*agronomo, navale*) surveyor; **perito chimico** qualified chemist

peri'zoma, -i [peri'dzoma] *sm* G-string

'perla *sf* pearl; **per'lina** *sf* bead

perlus'trare *vt* to patrol

perma'loso, -a *ag* touchy

perma'nente *ag* permanent ▷ *sf* permanent wave, perm; **perma'nenza** *sf* permanence; (*soggiorno*) stay

perme'are *vt* to permeate

per'messo, -a *pp di* **permettere** ▷ *sm* (*autorizzazione*) permission, leave; (*dato a militare, impiegato*) leave; (*licenza*) licence, permit; (*Mil: foglio*) pass; **~?, è ~?** (*posso entrare?*) may I come in?; (*posso passare?*) excuse me; **permesso di lavoro/pesca** work/fishing permit; **permesso di soggiorno** residence permit

per'mettere *vt* to allow, permit; **~ a qn qc/di fare qc** to allow sb sth/to do sth; **permettersi qc/di fare qc** to allow o.s. sth/to do sth; (*avere la possibilità*) to afford sth/to do sth

per'misi *ecc vb vedi* **permettere**

per'nacchia [per'nakkja] (*fam*) *sf* **fare una ~** to blow a raspberry

per'nice [per'nitʃe] *sf* partridge

'perno *sm* pivot

pernot'tare *vi* to spend the night, stay overnight

'pero *sm* pear tree

però *cong* (*ma*) but; (*tuttavia*) however, nevertheless

perpendico'lare *ag, sf* perpendicular

per'plesso, -a *ag* perplexed; uncertain, undecided

perqui'sire *vt* to search; **perquisizi'one** *sf* (police) search

'perse *ecc vb vedi* **perdere**

persecuzi'one [persekut'tsjone] *sf* persecution

persegui'tare *vt* to persecute

perseve'rante *ag* persevering

'persi *ecc vb vedi* **perdere**

persi'ana *sf* shutter; **persiana avvolgibile** roller shutter

per'sino *av* = **perfino**

persis'tente *ag* persistent

'perso, -a *pp di* **perdere**

per'sona *sf* person; (*qualcuno*): **una ~** someone, somebody; (*espressione interrogativa +*) anyone *o* anybody

perso'naggio [perso'naddʒo] *sm* (*persona*

ragguardevole) personality, figure; *(tipo)* character, individual; *(Letteratura)* character

perso'nale *ag* personal ▷ *sm* staff; personnel; *(figura fisica)* build

personalità *sf inv* personality

perspi'cace [perspi'katʃe] *ag* shrewd, discerning

persu'adere *vt* ~ **qn (di qc/a fare)** to persuade sb (of sth/to do)

per'tanto *cong (quindi)* so, therefore

'pertica, -che *sf* pole

perti'nente *ag* ~ **(a)** relevant (to), pertinent (to)

per'tosse *sf* whooping cough

perturbazi'one [perturbat'tsjone] *sf* disruption; perturbation; **perturbazione atmosferica** atmospheric disturbance

per'vadere *vt* to pervade

per'verso, -a *ag* depraved; perverse

perver'tito, -a *sm/f* pervert

p.es. *abbr* (= *per esempio*) e.g.

pe'sante *ag* heavy; **è troppo ~** it's too heavy

pe'sare *vt* to weigh ▷ *vi (avere un peso)* to weigh; *(essere pesante)* to be heavy; *(fig)* to carry weight; **~ su** *(fig)* to lie heavy on; to influence; to bear upon; **pesarsi** *vpr* to weigh o.s.; **~ le parole** to weigh one's words; **~ sulla coscienza** to weigh on sb's conscience; **mi pesa ammetterlo** I don't like admitting it; **tutta la responsabilità pesa su di lui** all the responsibility rests on him; **è una situazione che mi pesa** I find the situation difficult; **il suo parere pesa molto** his opinion counts for a lot

'pesca *(pl* **pesche)** (: *frutto)* *sf* peach; *(il pescare)* fishing; **andare a ~** to go fishing; **~ con la lenza** angling; **pesca di beneficenza** *(lotteria)* lucky dip

pes'care *vt* to fish for; to catch; *(qc nell'acqua)* to fish out; *(fig: trovare)* to get hold of, find; **andare a ~** to go fishing

pesca'tore *sm* fisherman; angler

'pesce ['peʃʃe] *sm* fish *gen inv*; **Pesci** *(dello zodiaco)* Pisces; **pesce d'aprile!** April Fool!; **pesce rosso** goldfish; **pesce spada** swordfish; **pesce'cane** *sm* shark

pesche'reccio [peske'rettʃo] *sm* fishing boat

pesche'ria [peske'ria] *sf* fishmonger's (shop) (BRIT), fish store (US)

pescherò *ecc* [peske'rɔ] *vb vedi* **pescare**

'peso *sm* weight; *(Sport)* shot; **rubare sul ~** to give short weight; **essere di ~ a qn** *(fig)* to be a burden to sb; **peso lordo/netto** gross/net weight; **peso massimo/medio** *(Pugilato)* heavy/middleweight

pessi'mismo *sm* pessimism; **pessi'mista,**

-i, -e *ag* pessimistic ▷ *sm/f* pessimist

'pessimo, -a *ag* very bad, awful

pes'tare *vt* to tread on, trample on; *(sale, pepe)* to grind; *(uva, aglio)* to crush; *(fig: picchiare)*: **~ qn** to beat sb up

'peste *sf* plague; *(persona)* nuisance, pest

pes'tello *sm* pestle

'petalo *sm (Bot)* petal

pe'tardo *sm* firecracker, banger (BRIT)

petizi'one [petit'tsjone] *sf* petition

petroli'era *sf (nave)* oil tanker

pe'trolio *sm* oil, petroleum; *(per lampada, fornello)* paraffin

▮ Attenzione! In inglese esiste la parola *petrol* che però significa *benzina*.

pettego'lare *vi* to gossip

pettego'lezzo [pettego'leddzo] *sm* gossip *no pl*; **fare pettegolezzi** to gossip

pet'tegolo, -a *ag* gossipy ▷ *sm/f* gossip

petti'nare *vt* to comb (the hair of); **pettinarsi** *vpr* to comb one's hair; **pettina'tura** *sf (acconciatura)* hairstyle

'pettine *sm* comb; *(Zool)* scallop

petti'rosso *sm* robin

'petto *sm* chest; *(seno)* breast, bust; *(Cuc: di carne bovina)* brisket; (: *di pollo ecc)* breast; **a doppio ~** *(abito)* double-breasted

petu'lante *ag* insolent

'pezza ['pettsa] *sf* piece of cloth; *(toppa)* patch; *(cencio)* rag, cloth

pez'zente [pet'tsɛnte] *sm/f* beggar

'pezzo ['pettso] *sm (gen)* piece; *(brandello, frammento)* piece, bit; *(di macchina, arnese ecc)* part; *(Stampa)* article; *(di tempo)*: **aspettare un ~** to wait quite a while *o* some time; **in** *o* **a pezzi** in pieces; **andare in pezzi** to break into pieces; **un bel ~ d'uomo** a fine figure of a man; **abito a due pezzi** two-piece suit; **pezzo di cronaca** *(Stampa)* report; **pezzo grosso** *(fig)* bigwig; **pezzo di ricambio** spare part

pi'accio *ecc* ['pjattʃo] *vb vedi* **piacere**

pia'cente [pja'tʃɛnte] *ag* attractive

pia'cere [pja'tʃere] *vi* to please; **una ragazza che piace** a likeable girl; an attractive girl; **~ a: mi piace** I like it; **quei ragazzi non mi piacciono** I don't like those boys; **gli ~bbe andare al cinema** he would like to go to the cinema ▷ *sm* pleasure; *(favore)* favour; **"~!"** *(nelle presentazioni)* "pleased to meet you!"; **~ (di conoscerla)** nice to meet you; **con ~** certainly, with pleasure; **per ~!** please; **fare un ~ a qn** to do sb a favour; **pia'cevole** *ag* pleasant, agreeable

pi'acqui *ecc* *vb vedi* **piacere**

pi'aga, -ghe *sf (lesione)* sore; *(ferita: anche fig)* wound; *(fig: flagello)* scourge, curse; (: *persona)* pest, nuisance

piagnuco'lare [pjaɲɲuko'lare] *vi* to whimper

pianeggi'ante [pjaned'dʒante] *ag* flat, level

piane'rottolo *sm* landing

pia'neta *sm* (*Astr*) planet

pi'angere ['pjandʒere] *vi* to cry, weep; (*occhi*) to water ▷ *vt* to cry, weep; (*lamentare*) to bewail, lament; **~ la morte di qn** to mourn sb's death

pianifi'care *vt* to plan

pia'nista, -i, -e *sm/f* pianist

pi'ano, -a *ag* (*piatto*) flat, level; (*Mat*) plane; (*chiaro*) clear, plain ▷ *av* (*adagio*) slowly; (*a bassa voce*) softly; (*con cautela*) slowly, carefully ▷ *sm* (*Mat*) plane; (*Geo*) plain; (*livello*) level, plane; (*di edificio*) floor; (*programma*) plan; (*Mus*) piano; **a che ~ si trova?** what floor is it on?; **pian ~** very slowly; (*poco a poco*) little by little; **in primo/secondo ~** in the foreground/ background; **di primo ~** (*fig*) prominent, high-ranking

piano'forte *sm* piano, pianoforte

piano'terra *sm inv* ground floor

pi'ansi *ecc vb vedi* **piangere**

pi'anta *sf* (*Bot*) plant; (*Anat: anche*: **~ del piede**) sole (of the foot); (*grafico*) plan; (*topografica*) map; **in ~ stabile** on the permanent staff; **pian'tare** *vt* to plant; (*conficcare*) to drive o hammer in; (*tenda*) to put up, pitch; (*fig*: *lasciare*) to leave, desert; **piantarsi** *vpr* **piantarsi davanti a qn** to plant o.s. in front of sb; **piantala!** (*fam*) cut it out!

pianter'reno *sm* = **pianoterra**

pia'nura *sf* plain

pi'astra *sf* plate; (*di pietra*) slab; (*di fornello*) hotplate; **panino alla ~** ≈ toasted sandwich; **piastra di registrazione** tape deck

pias'trella *sf* tile

pias'trina *sf* (*Mil*) identity disc

piatta'forma *sf* (*anche fig*) platform

piat'tino *sm* saucer

pi'atto, -a *ag* flat; (*fig: scialbo*) dull ▷ *sm* (*recipiente, vivanda*) dish; (*portata*) course; (*parte piana*) flat (part); **piatti** *smpl* (*Mus*) cymbals; **piatto fondo** soup dish; **piatto forte** main course; **piatto del giorno** dish of the day, plat du jour; **piatto del giradischi** turntable; **piatto piano** dinner plate

pi'azza ['pjattsa] *sf* square; (*Comm*) market; **far ~ pulita** to make a clean sweep; **piazza d'armi** (*Mil*) parade ground; **piaz'zale** *sm* (large) square

piaz'zola [pjat'tsɔla] *sf* (*Aut*) lay-by; (*di tenda*) pitch

pic'cante *ag* hot, pungent; (*fig*) racy; biting

pic'chetto [pik'ketto] *sm* (*Mil, di scioperanti*) picket; (*di tenda*) peg

picchi'are [pik'kjare] *vt* (*persona: colpire*) to hit, strike; (: *prendere a botte*) to beat (up); (*battere*) to beat; (*sbattere*) to bang ▷ *vi* (*bussare*) to knock; (: *con forza*) to bang; (*colpire*) to hit, strike; (*sole*) to beat down; **picchi'ata** *sf* (*Aer*) dive

'picchio ['pikkjo] *sm* woodpecker

pic'cino, -a [pit'tʃino] *ag* tiny, very small

picci'one [pit'tʃone] *sm* pigeon

'picco, -chi *sm* peak; **a ~** vertically

'piccolo, -a *ag* small; (*oggetto, mano, di età: bambino*) small, little; (*dav sostantivo: di breve durata: viaggio*) short; (*fig*) mean, petty ▷ *sm/f* child, little one

pic'cone *sm* pick(-axe)

pic'cozza [pik'kɔttsa] *sf* ice-axe

pic'nic *sm inv* picnic

pi'docchio [pi'dɔkkjo] *sm* louse

pi'ede *sm* foot; (*di mobile*) leg; **in piedi** standing; **a piedi** on foot; **a piedi nudi** barefoot; **su due piedi** (*fig*) at once; **prendere ~** (*fig*) to gain ground, catch on; **sul ~ di guerra** (*Mil*) ready for action; **piede di porco** crowbar

pi'ega, -ghe *sf* (*piegatura, Geo*) fold; (*di gonna*) pleat; (*di pantaloni*) crease; (*grinza*) wrinkle, crease; **prendere una brutta ~** (*fig*) to take a turn for the worse

pie'gare *vt* to fold; (*braccia, gambe, testa*) to bend ▷ *vi* to bend; **piegarsi** *vpr* to bend; (*fig*): **piegarsi (a)** to yield (to), submit (to)

pieghe'rò *ecc* [pjege'rɔ] *vb vedi* **piegare**

pie'ghevole *ag* pliable, flexible; (*porta*) folding

Pie'monte *sm* **il ~** Piedmont

pi'ena *sf* (*di fiume*) flood, spate

pi'eno, -a *ag* full; (*muro, mattone*) solid ▷ *sm* (*colmo*) height, peak; (*carico*) full load; **~ di** full of; **in ~ giorno** in broad daylight; **il ~, per favore** (*Aut*) fill it up, please

piercing ['pirsing] *sm* piercing; **farsi il ~ all'ombelico** to have one's navel pierced

pietà *sf* pity; (*Rel*) piety; **senza ~** pitiless, merciless; **avere ~ di** (*compassione*) to pity, feel sorry for; (*misericordia*) to have pity o mercy on

pie'tanza [pje'tantsa] *sf* dish, course

pie'toso, -a *ag* (*compassionevole*) pitying, compassionate; (*che desta pietà*) pitiful

pi'etra *sf* stone; **pietra preziosa** precious stone, gem

'piffero *sm* (*Mus*) pipe

pigi'ama, -i [pi'dʒama] *sm* pyjamas *pl*

pigli'are [piʎ'ʎare] *vt* to take, grab; (*afferrare*) to catch

'pigna ['piɲɲa] *sf* pine cone
pi'gnolo, -a [piɲ'ɲɔlo] *ag* pernickety
pi'grizia [pi'grittsja] *sf* laziness
'pigro, -a *ag* lazy
PIL *sigla m* (= *prodotto interno lordo*) GDP
'pila *sf* (*catasta, di ponte*) pile; (*Elettr*)
battery; (*torcia*) torch (BRIT), flashlight
pi'lastro *sm* pillar
'pile ['pail] *sm inv* fleece
'pillola *sf* pill; **prendere la ~** to be on the
pill
pi'lone *sm* (*di ponte*) pier; (*di linea elettrica*)
pylon
pi'lota, -i, -e *sm/f* pilot; (*Aut*) driver
▷ *ag inv* pilot *cpd*; **pilota automatico**
automatic pilot
pinaco'teca, -che *sf* art gallery
pi'neta *sf* pinewood
ping-'pong [piŋ'pɔŋ] *sm* table tennis
pingu'ino *sm* (*Zool*) penguin
'pinna *sf* (*di pesce*) fin; (*di cetaceo, per
nuotare*) flipper
'pino *sm* pine (tree); **pi'nolo** *sm* pine
kernel
'pinza ['pintsa] *sf* pliers *pl*; (*Med*) forceps *pl*;
(*Zool*) pincer
pinzette [pin'tsette] *sfpl* tweezers
pi'oggia, -ge ['pjɔddʒa] *sf* rain; **pioggia
acida** acid rain
pi'olo *sm* peg; (*di scala*) rung
piom'bare *vi* to fall heavily; (*gettarsi con
impeto*) **~ su** to fall upon, assail ▷ *vt* (*dente*)
to fill; **piomba'tura** *sf* (*di dente*) filling
piom'bino *sm* (*sigillo*) (lead) seal; (*del filo a
piombo*) plummet; (*Pesca*) sinker
pi'ombo *sm* (*Chim*) lead; **a ~** (*cadere*)
straight down; **senza ~** (*benzina*) unleaded
pioni'ere, -a *sm/f* pioneer
pi'oppo *sm* poplar
pi'overe *vb impers* to rain ▷ *vi* (*fig: scendere
dall'alto*) to rain down; (*lettere, regali*) to
pour into; **piovig'ginare** *vb impers* to
drizzle; **pio'voso, -a** *ag* rainy
pi'ovra *sf* octopus
pi'ovve *ecc vb vedi* **piovere**
'pipa *sf* pipe
pipì (*fam*) *sf* **fare ~** to have a wee (wee)
pipis'trello *sm* (*Zool*) bat
pi'ramide *sf* pyramid
pi'rata, -i *sm* pirate; **pirata della strada**
hit-and-run driver; **pirata informatica**
hacker
Pire'nei *smpl* **i ~** the Pyrenees
pi'romane *sm/f* pyromaniac; arsonist
pi'roscafo *sm* steamer, steamship
pisci'are [piʃ'ʃare] (*fam!*) *vi* to piss (!), pee (!)
pi'scina [piʃ'ʃina] *sf* (swimming) pool;
(*stabilimento*) (swimming) baths *pl*
pi'sello *sm* pea

piso'lino *sm* nap
'pista *sf* (*traccia*) track, trail; (*di stadio*)
track; (*di pattinaggio*) rink; (*da sci*) run;
(*Aer*) runway; (*di circo*) ring; **pista da ballo**
dance floor
pis'tacchio [pis'takkjo] *sm* pistachio
(tree); pistachio (nut)
pis'tola *sf* pistol, gun
pis'tone *sm* piston
pi'tone *sm* python
pit'tore, -'trice *sm/f* painter;
pitto'resco, -a, -schi, -sche *ag*
picturesque
pit'tura *sf* painting; **pittu'rare** *vt* to
paint

 PAROLA CHIAVE

più *av* **1** (*in maggiore quantità*) more; **più
del solito** more than usual; **in più, di più**
more; **ne voglio di più** I want some more;
ci sono 3 persone in o di più there are 3
more *o* extra people; **più o meno** more
or less; **per di più** (*inoltre*) what's more,
moreover
2 (*comparativo*) more; (*aggettivo corto +*)
...er; **più ... di/che** more ... than; **lavoro
più di te/Paola** I work harder than you/
Paola; **è più intelligente che ricco** he's
more intelligent than rich
3 (*superlativo*) most; (*aggettivo corto +*)
...est; **il più grande/intelligente** the
biggest/most intelligent; **è quello che
compro più spesso** that's the one I buy
most often; **al più presto** as soon as
possible; **al più tardi** at the latest
4 (*negazione*): **non ... più** no more, no
longer; **non ho più soldi** I've got no more
money, I don't have any more money; **non
lavoro più** I'm no longer working, I don't
work any more; **a più non posso** (*gridare*)
at the top of one's voice; (*correre*) as fast
as one can
5 (*Mat*) plus; **4 più 5 fa 9** 4 plus 5 equals 9;
più 5 gradi 5 degrees above freezing, plus 5
▷ *prep* plus ▷ *ag inv* **1**: **più ... (di)** more
... (than); **più denaro/tempo** more
money/time; **più persone di quante
ci aspettassimo** more people than we
expected
2 (*numerosi, diversi*) several; **l'aspettai per
più giorni** I waited for it for several days
▷ *sm* **1** (*la maggior parte*): **il più è fatto**
most of it is done
2 (*Mat*) plus (sign)
3: **i più** the majority

pi'uma *sf* feather; **piu'mino** *sm*
(eider)down; (*per letto*) eiderdown; (: *tipo*

danese) duvet, continental quilt; (*giacca*) quilted jacket (*with goose-feather padding*); (*per cipria*) powder puff; (*per spolverare*) feather duster

piut'tosto *av* rather; **~ che** (*anziché*) rather than

'pizza ['pittsa] *sf* pizza; **pizze'ria** *sf* place *where pizzas are made, sold or eaten*

pizzi'care [pittsi'kare] *vt* (*stringere*) to nip, pinch; (*pungere*) to sting; to bite; (*Mus*) to pluck ▷ *vi* (*prudere*) to itch, be itchy; (*cibo*) to be hot *o* spicy

'pizzico, -chi ['pittsiko] *sm* (*pizzicotto*) pinch, nip; (*piccola quantità*) pinch, dash; (*d'insetto*) sting; bite

pizzi'cotto [pittsi'kɔtto] *sm* pinch, nip

'pizzo ['pittso] *sm* (*merletto*) lace; (*barbetta*) goatee beard

plagi'are [pla'dʒare] *vt* (*copiare*) to plagiarize

plaid [plɛd] *sm inv* (*travelling*) rug (*BRIT*), lap robe (*US*)

pla'nare *vi* (*Aer*) to glide

'plasma *sm* plasma

plas'mare *vt* to mould, shape

'plastica, -che *sf* (*arte*) plastic arts *pl*; (*Med*) plastic surgery; (*sostanza*) plastic; **plastica facciale** face lift

'platano *sm* plane tree

pla'tea *sf* (*Teatro*) stalls *pl*

'platino *sm* platinum

plau'sibile *ag* plausible

pleni'lunio *sm* full moon

'plettro *sm* plectrum

pleu'rite *sf* pleurisy

'plico, -chi *sm* (*pacco*) parcel; **in ~ a parte** (*Comm*) under separate cover

plo'tone *sm* (*Mil*) platoon; **plotone d'esecuzione** firing squad

plu'rale *ag, sm* plural

PM *abbr* (*Pol*) = **Pubblico Ministero**; (= *Polizia Militare*) MP (*Military Police*)

pneu'matico, -a, -ci, -che *ag* inflatable; pneumatic ▷ *sm* (*Aut*) tyre (*BRIT*), tire (*US*)

po' *av, sm vedi* **poco**

⬤ **PAROLA CHIAVE**

'poco, -a, -chi, -che *ag* (*quantità*) little, not much; (*numero*) few, not many; **poco pane/denaro/spazio** little *o* not much bread/money/space; **poche persone/ idee** few *o* not many people/ideas; **ci vediamo tra poco** (*sottinteso: tempo*) see you soon

▷ *av* **1** (*in piccola quantità*) little, not much; (*numero limitato*) few, not many; **guadagna poco** he doesn't earn much, he earns little

2 (*con ag, av*) (a) little, not very; **sta poco bene** he isn't very well; **è poco più vecchia di lui** she's a little *o* slightly older than him

3 (*tempo*): **poco dopo/prima** shortly afterwards/before; **il film dura poco** the film doesn't last very long; **ci vediamo molto poco** we don't see each other very often, we hardly ever see each other

4: **un po'** a little, a bit; **è un po' corto** it's a little *o* a bit short; **arriverà fra un po'** he'll arrive shortly *o* in a little while

5: **a dir poco** to say the least; **a poco a poco** little by little; **per poco non cadevo** I nearly fell; **è una cosa da poco** it's nothing, it's of no importance; **una persona da poco** a worthless person

▷ *pron* (a) little

po'dere *sm* (*Agr*) farm

'podio *sm* dais, platform; (*Mus*) podium

po'dismo *sm* (*Sport*) track events *pl*

poe'sia *sf* (*arte*) poetry; (*componimento*) poem

po'eta, -'essa *sm/f* poet/poetess

poggi'are [pod'dʒare] *vt* to lean, rest; (*posare*) to lay, place; **poggia'testa** *sm inv* (*Aut*) headrest

'poggio ['pɔddʒo] *sm* hillock, knoll

'poi *av* then; (*alla fine*) finally, at last; **e ~** (*inoltre*) and besides; **questa ~ (è bella)!** (*ironico*) that's a good one!

poiché [poi'ke] *cong* since, as

'poker *sm* poker

po'lacco, -a, -chi, -che *ag* Polish ▷ *sm/f* Pole

po'lare *ag* polar

po'lemica, -che *sf* controversy

po'lemico, -a, -ci, -che *ag* polemic(al), controversial

po'lenta *sf* (*Cuc*) sort of thick porridge made with maize flour

'polio(mie'lite) *sf* polio(myelitis)

'polipo *sm* polyp

polisti'rolo *sm* polystyrene

po'litica, -che *sf* politics *sg*; (*linea di condotta*) policy; (*anche*: **politico**); **politica'mente** *av* politically; **politicamente corretto** politically correct

po'litico, -a, -ci, -che *ag* political ▷ *sm/f* politician

poli'zia [polit'tsia] *sf* police; **polizia giudiziaria** ≈ Criminal Investigation Department (*BRIT*), ≈ Federal Bureau of Investigation (*US*); **polizia stradale** traffic police; **polizi'esco, -a, -schi, -sche** *ag* police *cpd*; (*film, romanzo*) detective *cpd*; **polizi'otto** *sm* policeman; **cane poliziotto** police dog; **donna poliziotto**

policewoman; **poliziotto di quartiere** local police officer

'polizza ['pɔlittsa] *sf* (*Comm*) bill; **~ di assicurazione** insurance policy; **polizza di carico** bill of lading
pol'laio *sm* henhouse
'pollice ['pɔllitʃe] *sm* thumb
'polline *sm* pollen
'pollo *sm* chicken
pol'mone *sm* lung; **polmone d'acciaio** (*Med*) iron lung; **polmo'nite** *sf* pneumonia; **polmonite atipica** SARS
'polo *sm* (*Geo, Fisica*) pole; (*gioco*) polo; **polo nord/sud** North/South Pole
Po'lonia *sf* **la ~** Poland
'polpa *sf* flesh, pulp; (*carne*) lean meat
pol'paccio [pol'pattʃo] *sm* (*Anat*) calf
polpas'trello *sm* fingertip
pol'petta *sf* (*Cuc*) meatball
'polpo *sm* octopus
pol'sino *sm* cuff
'polso *sm* (*Anat*) wrist; (*pulsazione*) pulse; (*fig: forza*) drive, vigour
pol'trire *vi* to laze about
pol'trona *sf* armchair; (*Teatro: posto*) seat in the front stalls (*BRIT*) *o* orchestra (*US*)
'polvere *sf* dust; (*sostanza ridotta minutissima*) powder, dust; **latte in ~** dried *o* powdered milk; **caffè in ~** instant coffee; **sapone in ~** soap powder; **polvere da sparo/pirica** gunpowder
po'mata *sf* ointment, cream
po'mello *sm* knob
pome'riggio [pome'riddʒo] *sm* afternoon
'pomice ['pɔmitʃe] *sf* pumice
'pomo *sm* (*mela*) apple; (*ornamentale*) knob; (*di sella*) pommel; **pomo d'Adamo** (*Anat*) Adam's apple
pomo'doro *sm* tomato; **pomodori pelati** skinned tomatoes
'pompa *sf* pump; (*sfarzo*) pomp (and ceremony); **pompe funebri** funeral parlour *sg* (*BRIT*), undertaker's *sg*; **pompa di benzina** petrol (*BRIT*) *o* gas (*US*) pump; (*distributore*) filling *o* gas (*US*) station; **pom'pare** *vt* to pump; (*trarre*) to pump out; (*gonfiare d'aria*) to pump up
pom'pelmo *sm* grapefruit
pompi'ere *sm* fireman

po'nente *sm* west
pongo, poni *ecc vb vedi* **porre**
'ponte *sm* bridge; (*di nave*) deck; (~ *anche:* ~ **di comando**) bridge; (*impalcatura*) scaffold; **fare il ~** (*fig*) to take the extra day off (*between 2 public holidays*); **governo ~** interim government; **ponte aereo** airlift; **ponte levatoio** drawbridge; **ponte sospeso** suspension bridge
pon'tefice [pon'tɛfitʃe] *sm* (*Rel*) pontiff
'popcorn ['pɔpkɔːn] *sm inv* popcorn
popo'lare *ag* popular; (*quartiere, clientela*) working-class ▷ *vt* (*rendere abitato*) to populate; **popolarsi** *vpr* to fill with people, get crowded; **popolazi'one** *sf* population
'popolo *sm* people
'poppa *sf* (*di nave*) stern; (*seno*) breast
porcel'lana [portʃel'lana] *sf* porcelain, china; piece of china
porcel'lino, -a [portʃel'lino] *sm/f* piglet; **porcellino d'India** guinea pig
porche'ria [porke'ria] *sf* filth, muck; (*fig: oscenità*) obscenity; (~ *azione disonesta*) dirty trick; (~ *cosa mal fatta*) rubbish
por'cile [por'tʃile] *sm* pigsty
por'cino, -a [por'tʃino] *ag* of pigs, pork *cpd* ▷ *sm* (*fungo*) type of edible mushroom
'porco, -ci *sm* pig; (*carne*) pork
porcos'pino *sm* porcupine
'porgere ['pɔrdʒere] *vt* to hand, give; (*tendere*) to hold out
pornogra'fia *sf* pornography; **porno'grafico, -a, -ci, -che** *ag* pornographic
'poro *sm* pore
'porpora *sf* purple
'porre *vt* (*mettere*) to put; (*collocare*) to place; (*posare*) to lay (down), put (down); (*fig: supporre*): **poniamo (il caso) che ...** let's suppose that ...
'porro *sm* (*Bot*) leek; (*Med*) wart
'porsi *ecc vb vedi* **porgere**
'porta *sf* door; (*Sport*) goal; **portaba'gagli** *sm inv* (*facchino*) porter; (*Aut, Ferr*) luggage rack; **porta-CD** [portatʃi'di] *sm inv* (*mobile*) CD rack; (*astuccio*) CD holder; **porta'cenere** *sm inv* ashtray; **portachi'avi** *sm inv* keyring; **porta'erei** *sf inv* (*nave*) aircraft carrier; **portafi'nestra** (*pl* **portefi'nestre**) *sf* French window; **porta'foglio** *sm* wallet; (*Pol, Borsa*) portfolio; **non trovo il portafoglio** I can't find my wallet; **portafor'tuna** *sm inv* lucky charm; mascot
por'tale *sm* (*di chiesa, Inform*) portal
porta'mento *sm* carriage, bearing
portamo'nete *sm inv* purse

por'tante ag (muro ecc) supporting, load-bearing

portan'tina sf sedan chair; (per ammalati) stretcher

portaom'brelli sm inv umbrella stand

porta'pacchi [porta'pakki] sm inv (di moto, bicicletta) luggage rack

por'tare vt (sostenere, sorreggere: peso, bambino, pacco) to carry; (indossare: abito, occhiali) to wear; (: capelli lunghi) (avere: nome, titolo) to have, bear; (recare): ~ qc a qn to take (o bring) sth to sb; (fig: sentimenti) to bear

portasiga'rette sm inv cigarette case

por'tata sf (vivanda) course; (Aut) carrying (o loading) capacity; (di arma) range; (volume d'acqua) (rate of) flow; (fig: limite) scope, capability; (: importanza) impact, import; **alla ~ di tutti** (conoscenza) within everybody's capabilities; (prezzo) within everybody's means; **a/fuori ~ (di)** within/out of reach (of); **a ~ di mano** within (arm's) reach

por'tatile ag portable

por'tato, -a ag (incline): ~ **a** inclined o apt to

portau'ovo sm inv eggcup

porta'voce [porta'votʃe] sm/f inv spokesman/woman

por'tento sm wonder, marvel

porti'era sf (Aut) door

porti'ere sm (portinaio) concierge, caretaker; (di hotel) porter; (nel calcio) goalkeeper

porti'naio, -a sm/f concierge, caretaker

portine'ria sf caretaker's lodge

'porto, -a pp di **porgere** ▷ sm (Naut) harbour, port ▷ sm inv port (wine); **porto d'armi** (documento) gun licence

Porto'gallo sm **il ~** Portugal; **porto'ghese** ag, sm/f, sm Portuguese inv

por'tone sm main entrance, main door

portu'ale ag harbour cpd, port cpd ▷ sm dock worker

porzi'one [por'tsjone] sf portion, share; (di cibo) portion, helping

'posa sf (Fot) exposure; (atteggiamento, di modello) pose

po'sare vt to put (down), lay (down) ▷ vi (ponte, edificio, teoria): ~ **su** to rest on; (Fot: atteggiarsi) to pose; **posarsi** vpr (aereo) to land; (uccello) to alight; (sguardo) to settle

po'sata sf piece of cutlery

pos'critto sm postscript

'posi ecc vb vedi **porre**

posi'tivo, -a ag positive

posizi'one [pozit'tsjone] sf position; **prendere ~** (fig) to take a stand; **luci di ~** (Aut) sidelights

pos'porre vt to place after; (differire) to postpone, defer

posse'dere vt to own, possess; (qualità, virtù) to have, possess

posses'sivo, -a ag possessive

pos'sesso sm ownership no pl; possession

posses'sore sm owner

pos'sibile ag possible ▷ sm **fare tutto il ~** to do everything possible; **nei limiti del ~** as far as possible; **al più tardi ~** as late as possible; **possibilità** sf inv possibility ▷ sfpl (mezzi) means; **aver la possibilità di fare** to be in a position to do; to have the opportunity to do

possi'dente sm/f landowner

possi'edo ecc vb vedi **possedere**

'posso ecc vb vedi **potere**

'posta sf (servizio) post, postal service; (corrispondenza) post, mail; (ufficio postale) post office; (nei giochi d'azzardo) stake; **Poste** sfpl (amministrazione) post office; **c'è ~ per me?** are there any letters for me?; **ministro delle Poste e Telecomunicazioni** Postmaster General; **posta aerea** airmail; **posta elettronica** E-mail, e-mail, electronic mail; **posta ordinaria** ≈ second-class mail; **posta prioritaria** ≈ first-class post; **pos'tale** ag postal, post office cpd

posteggi'are [posted'dʒare] vt, vi to park; **pos'teggio** sm car park (BRIT), parking lot (US); (di taxi) rank (BRIT), stand (US)

'poster sm inv poster

posteri'ore ag (dietro) back; (dopo) later ▷ sm (fam: sedere) behind

postici'pare [postitʃi'pare] vt to defer, postpone

pos'tino sm postman (BRIT), mailman (US)

'posto, -a pp di **porre** ▷ sm (sito, posizione) place; (impiego) job; (spazio libero) room, space; (di parcheggio) space; (sedile: al teatro, in treno ecc) seat; (Mil) post; **a ~** (in ordine) in place, tidy; (fig) settled; (: persona) reliable; **vorrei prenotare due posti** I'd like to book two seats; **al ~ di** in place of; **sul ~** on the spot; **mettere a ~** to tidy (up), put in order; (faccende) to straighten out; **posto di blocco** roadblock; **posto di lavoro** job; **posti in piedi** (in teatro, in autobus) standing room; **posto di polizia** police station

po'tabile ag drinkable; **acqua ~** drinking water

po'tare vt to prune

po'tassio sm potassium

po'tente ag (nazione) strong, powerful; (veleno, farmaco) potent, strong; **po'tenza** sf power; (forza) strength

potenzi'ale [poten'tsjale] *ag, sm*
potential

 PAROLA CHIAVE

po'tere *sm* power; **al potere** (*partito ecc*)
in power; **potere d'acquisto** purchasing
power
▷ *vb aus* **1** (*essere in grado di*) can, be able
to; **non ha potuto ripararlo** he couldn't
o he wasn't able to repair it; **non è potuto
venire** he couldn't *o* he wasn't able to
come; **spiacente di non poter aiutare**
sorry not to be able to help
2 (*avere il permesso*) can, may, be allowed
to; **posso entrare?** can *o* may I come in?;
si può sapere dove sei stato? where on
earth have you been?
3 (*eventualità*) may, might, could;
potrebbe essere vero it might *o* could be
true; **può aver avuto un incidente** he
may *o* might *o* could have had an accident;
può darsi perhaps; **può darsi** *o* **essere
che non venga** he may *o* might not come
4 (*augurio*): **potessi almeno parlargli!** if
only I could speak to him!
5 (*suggerimento*): **potresti almeno
scusarti!** you could at least apologize!
▷ *vt* can, be able to; **può molto per noi** he
can do a lot for us; **non ne posso più** (*per
stanchezza*) I'm exhausted; (*per rabbia*) I
can't take any more

potrò *ecc vb vedi* **potere**
'povero, -a *ag* poor; (*disadorno*) plain, bare
▷ *sm/f* poor man/woman; **i poveri** the
poor; **~ di** lacking in, having little; **povertà**
sf poverty
poz'zanghera [pot'tsangera] *sf* puddle
'pozzo ['pottso] *sm* well; (*cava: di carbone*)
pit; (*di miniera*) shaft; **pozzo petrolifero**
oil well
P.R.A. [pra] *sigla m* (= *Pubblico Registro
Automobilistico*) ≈ DVLA
pran'zare [pran'dzare] *vi* to dine, have
dinner; to lunch, have lunch
'pranzo ['prandzo] *sm* dinner; (*a
mezzogiorno*) lunch
'prassi *sf* usual procedure
'pratica, -che *sf* practice; (*esperienza*)
experience; (*conoscenza*) knowledge,
familiarity; (*tirocinio*) training, practice;
(*Amm: affare*) matter, case; (: *incartamento*)
file, dossier; **in ~** (*praticamente*) in practice;
mettere in ~ to put into practice
prati'cabile *ag* (*progetto*) practicable,
feasible; (*luogo*) passable, practicable
pratica'mente *av* (*in modo pratico*)
in a practical way, practically; (*quasi*)

practically, almost
prati'care *vt* to practise; (*Sport: tennis ecc*)
to play; (: *nuoto, scherma ecc*) to go in for;
(*eseguire: apertura, buco*) to make; **~ uno
sconto** to give a discount
'pratico, -a, -ci, -che *ag* practical; **~ di**
(*esperto*) experienced *o* skilled in; (*familiare*)
familiar with
'prato *sm* meadow; (*di giardino*) lawn
preav'viso *sm* notice; **telefonata con ~**
personal *o* person to person call
pre'cario, -a *ag* precarious; (*Ins*)
temporary
precauzi'one [prekaut'tsjone] *sf* caution,
care; (*misura*) precaution
prece'dente [pretʃe'dɛnte] *ag* previous
▷ *sm* precedent; **il discorso/film ~** the
previous *o* preceding speech/film; **senza
precedenti** unprecedented; **precedenti
penali** criminal record *sg*; **prece'denza** *sf*
priority, precedence; (*Aut*) right of way
pre'cedere [pre'tʃedere] *vt* to precede, go
(*o* come) before
precipi'tare [pretʃipi'tare] *vi* (*cadere*) to
fall headlong; (*fig: situazione*) to get out
of control ▷ *vt* (*gettare dall'alto in basso*)
to hurl, fling; (*fig: affrettare*) to rush;
precipitarsi *vpr* (*gettarsi*) to hurl *o* fling
o.s.; (*affrettarsi*) to rush; **precipi'toso, -a**
ag (*caduta, fuga*) headlong; (*fig: avventato*)
rash, reckless; (: *affrettato*) hasty, rushed
preci'pizio [pretʃi'pittsjo] *sm* precipice; **a
~** (*fig: correre*) headlong
precisa'mente [pretʃiza'mente] *av* (*gen*)
precisely; (*con esattezza*) exactly
preci'sare [pretʃi'zare] *vt* to state, specify;
(*spiegare*) to explain (in detail)
precisi'one [pretʃi'zjone] *sf* precision;
accuracy
pre'ciso, -a [pre'tʃizo] *ag* (*esatto*) precise;
(*accurato*) accurate, precise; (*deciso: idee*)
precise, definite; (*uguale*): **2 vestiti precisi**
2 dresses exactly the same; **sono le 9
precise** it's exactly 9 o'clock
pre'cludere *vt* to block, obstruct
pre'coce [pre'kotʃe] *ag* early; (*bambino*)
precocious; (*vecchiaia*) premature
precon'cetto [prekon'tʃetto] *sm*
preconceived idea, prejudice
precur'sore *sm* forerunner, precursor
'preda *sf* (*bottino*) booty; (*animale, fig*) prey;
essere ~ di to fall prey to; **essere in ~ a** to
be prey to
'predica, -che *sf* sermon; (*fig*) lecture,
talking-to
predi'care *vt, vi* to preach
predi'cato *sm* (*Ling*) predicate
predi'letto, -a *pp di* **prediligere** ▷ *ag, sm/f*
favourite

predi'ligere [predi'lidʒere] *vt* to prefer, have a preference for

pre'dire *vt* to foretell, predict

predis'porre *vt* to get ready, prepare; **~ qn a qc** to predispose sb to sth

predizi'one [predit'tsjone] *sf* prediction

prefazi'one [prefat'tsjone] *sf* preface, foreword

prefe'renza [prefe'rentsa] *sf* preference

prefe'rire *vt* to prefer, like better; **~ il caffè al tè** to prefer coffee to tea, like coffee better than tea

pre'figgersi [pre'fiddʒersi] *vpr* **~ uno scopo** to set o.s. a goal

pre'fisso, -a *pp di* **prefiggere** ▷ *sm* (*Ling*) prefix; (*Tel*) dialling (BRIT) o dial (US) code; **qual è il ~ telefonico di Londra?** what is the dialling code for London?

pre'gare *vi* to pray ▷ *vt* (*Rel*) to pray to; (*implorare*) to beg; (*chiedere*): **~ qn di fare** to ask sb to do; **farsi ~** to need coaxing o persuading

pre'gevole [pre'dʒevole] *ag* valuable

pregherò *ecc* [prege'rɔ] *vb vedi* **pregare**

preghi'era [pre'gjɛra] *sf* (*Rel*) prayer; (*domanda*) request

pregi'ato, -a [pre'dʒato] *ag* (*di valore*) valuable; **vino ~** vintage wine

'pregio ['prɛdʒo] *sm* (*stima*) esteem, regard; (*qualità*) (good) quality, merit; (*valore*) value, worth

pregiudi'care [predʒudi'kare] *vt* to prejudice, harm, be detrimental to

pregiu'dizio [predʒu'dittsjo] *sm* (*idea errata*) prejudice; (*danno*) harm *no pl*

'prego *escl* (*a chi ringrazia*) don't mention it!; (*invitando qn ad accomodarsi*) please sit down!; (*invitando qn ad andare prima*) after you!

pregus'tare *vt* to look forward to

prele'vare *vt* (*denaro*) to withdraw; (*campione*) to take; (*polizia*) to take, capture

preli'evo *sm* (*di denaro*) withdrawal; (*Med*): **fare un ~ (di)** to take a sample (of); **prelievo di sangue; fare un ~ di sangue** to take a blood sample

prelimi'nare *ag* preliminary

'premere *vt* to press ▷ *vi* **~ su** to press down on; (*fig*) to put pressure on; **~ a** (*fig: importare*) to matter to

pre'mettere *vt* to put before; (*dire prima*) to start by saying, state first

premi'are *vt* to give a prize to; (*fig: merito, onestà*) to reward

premiazi'one [premjat'tsjone] *sf* prize giving

'premio *sm* prize; (*ricompensa*) reward; (*Comm*) premium; (*Amm: indennità*) bonus

pre'misi *ecc vb vedi* **premettere**

premu'nirsi *vpr* **~ di** to provide o.s. with; **~ contro** to protect o.s. from, guard o.s. against

pre'mura *sf* (*fretta*) haste, hurry; (*riguardo*) attention, care; **premure** *sfpl* (*attenzioni, cure*) care *sg*; **aver ~** to be in a hurry; **far ~ a qn** to hurry sb; **usare ogni ~ nei riguardi di qn** to be very attentive to sb; **premu'roso, -a** *ag* thoughtful, considerate

'prendere *vt* to take; (*andare a prendere*) to get, fetch; (*ottenere*) to get; (*guadagnare*) to get, earn; (*catturare: ladro, pesce*) to catch; (*collaboratore, dipendente*) to take on; (*passeggero*) to pick up; (*chiedere: somma, prezzo*) to charge, ask; (*trattare: persona*) to handle ▷ *vi* (*colla, cemento*) to set; (*pianta*) to take; (*fuoco: nel camino*) to catch; (*voltare*): **~ a destra** to turn (to the) right; **prendersi** *vpr* (*azzuffarsi*): **prendersi a pugni** to come to blows; **dove si prende il traghetto per...** where do we get the ferry to ...; **prendi qualcosa?** (*da bere, da mangiare*) would you like something to eat (o drink)?; **prendo un caffè** I'll have a coffee; **~ qn/qc per** (*scambiare*) to take sb/sth for; **~ fuoco** to catch fire; **~ parte a** to take part in; **prendersi cura di qn/qc** to look after sb/sth; **prendersela** (*adirarsi*) to get annoyed; (*preoccuparsi*) to get upset, worry

preno'tare *vt* to book, reserve; **vorrei ~ una camera doppia** I'd like to book a double room; **ho prenotato un tavolo al nome di ...** I booked a table in the name of ...; **prenotazi'one** *sf* booking, reservation; **ho confermato la prenotazione per fax/e-mail** I confirmed my booking by fax/e-mail

preoccu'pare *vt* to worry; to preoccupy; **preoccuparsi** *vpr* **preoccuparsi di qn/qc** to worry about sb/sth; **preoccuparsi per qn** to be anxious for sb; **preoccupazi'one** *sf* worry, anxiety

prepa'rare *vt* to prepare; (*esame, concorso*) to prepare for; **prepararsi** *vpr* (*vestirsi*) to get ready; **prepararsi a qc/a fare** to get ready o prepare (o.s.) for sth/to do; **~ da mangiare** to prepare a meal; **prepara'tivi** *smpl* preparations

preposizi'one [prepozit'tsjone] *sf* (*Ling*) preposition

prepo'tente *ag* (*persona*) domineering, arrogant; (*bisogno, desiderio*) overwhelming, pressing ▷ *sm/f* bully

'presa *sf* taking *no pl*; catching *no pl*; (*di città*) capture; (*indurimento: di cemento*) setting; (*appiglio, Sport*) hold; (*di acqua, gas*) (supply) point; (*piccola quantità: di sale* *ecc*) pinch; (*Carte*) trick; **far ~** (*colla*) to set; **far ~ sul pubblico** to catch the public's imagination; **essere alle prese con** (*fig*) to be struggling with; **presa d'aria** air inlet; **presa (di corrente)** (*Elettr*) socket; (: *al muro*) point

pre'sagio [pre'zadʒo] *sm* omen

'presbite *ag* long-sighted

pres'crivere *vt* to prescribe

'prese *ecc vb vedi* **prendere**

presen'tare *vt* to present; (*far conoscere*): **~ qn (a)** to introduce sb (to); (*Amm: inoltrare*) to submit; **presentarsi** *vpr* (*recarsi, farsi vedere*) to present o.s., appear; (*farsi conoscere*) to introduce o.s.; (*occasione*) to arise; **presentarsi come candidato** (*Pol*) to stand as a candidate; **presentarsi bene/male** to have a good/poor appearance

pre'sente *ag* present; (*questo*) this ▷ *sm* present; **i presenti** those present; **aver ~ qc/qn** to remember sth/sb; **presenti** (*persone*) people present; **aver ~ qc/qn** to remember sth/sb; **tenere ~ qn/qc** to keep sth/sb in mind

presenti'mento *sm* premonition

pre'senza [pre'zɛntsa] *sf* presence; (*aspetto esteriore*) appearance; **presenza di spirito** presence of mind

pre'sepio, pre'sepe *sm* crib

preser'vare *vt* to protect; to save; **preserva'tivo** *sm* sheath, condom

'presi *ecc vb vedi* **prendere**

'preside *sm/f* (*Ins*) head (teacher) (*BRIT*), principal (*US*); (*di facoltà universitaria*) dean; **preside di facoltà** (*Univ*) dean of faculty

presi'dente *sm* (*Pol*) president; (*di assemblea, Comm*) chairman; **presidente del consiglio** prime minister

presi'edere *vt* to preside over ▷ *vi* **~ a** to direct, be in charge of

pressap'poco *av* about, roughly

pres'sare *vt* to press

pressi'one *sf* pressure; **far ~ su qn** to put pressure on sb; **pressione sanguigna** blood pressure; **pressione atmosferica** atmospheric pressure

'presso *av* (*vicino*) nearby, close at hand ▷ *prep* (*vicino a*) near; (*accanto a*) beside, next to; (*in casa di*): **~ qn** at sb's home; (*nelle lettere*) care of, c/o; (*alle dipendenze di*): **lavora ~ di noi** he works for o with us ▷ *smpl* **nei pressi di** near, in the vicinity of

pres'tante *ag* good-looking

pres'tare *vt* **~ (qc a qn)** to lend (sb sth o sth to sb); **prestarsi** *vpr* (*offrirsi*): **prestarsi a fare** to offer to do; (*essere adatto*): **prestarsi a** to lend itself to, be suitable for; **mi può ~ dei soldi?** can you

lend me some money?; **~ aiuto** to lend a hand; **~ attenzione** to pay attention; **~ fede a qc/qn** to give credence to sth/sb; **~ orecchio** to listen; **prestazi'one** *sf* (*Tecn, Sport*) performance

prestigia'tore, -'trice [prestidʒa'tore] *sm/f* conjurer

pres'tigio [pres'tidʒo] *sm* (*fama*) prestige; (*illusione*): **gioco di ~** conjuring trick

'prestito *sm* lending *no pl*; loan; **dar in ~** to lend; **prendere in ~** to borrow

'presto *av* (*tra poco*) soon; (*in fretta*) quickly; (*di buon'ora*) early; **a ~** see you soon; **fare ~ a fare qc** to hurry up and do sth; (*non costare fatica*) to have no trouble doing sth; **si fa ~ a criticare** it's easy to criticize

pre'sumere *vt* to presume, assume

pre'sunsi *ecc vb vedi* **presumere**

presuntu'oso, -a *ag* presumptuous

presunzi'one [prezun'tsjone] *sf* presumption

'prete *sm* priest

preten'dente *sm/f* pretender ▷ *sm* (*corteggiatore*) suitor

pre'tendere *vt* (*esigere*) to demand, require; (*sostenere*): **~ che** to claim that; **pretende di aver sempre ragione** he thinks he's always right

> ■ Attenzione! In inglese esiste il verbo *to pretend*, che però significa *far finta*.

pre'tesa *sf* (*esigenza*) claim, demand; (*presunzione, sfarzo*) pretentiousness; **senza pretese** unpretentious

pre'testo *sm* pretext, excuse

preva'lere *vi* to prevail

preve'dere *vt* (*indovinare*) to foresee; (*presagire*) to foretell; (*considerare*) to make provision for

preve'nire *vt* (*anticipare*) to forestall; to anticipate; (*evitare*) to avoid, prevent

preven'tivo, -a *ag* preventive ▷ *sm* (*Comm*) estimate

prevenzi'one [preven'tsjone] *sf* prevention; (*preconcetto*) prejudice

previ'dente *ag* showing foresight; prudent; **previ'denza** *sf* foresight; **istituto di previdenza** provident institution; **previdenza sociale** social security (*BRIT*), welfare (*US*)

pre'vidi *ecc vb vedi* **prevedere**

previsi'one *sf* forecast, prediction; **previsioni meteorologiche** weather forecast *sg*; **previsioni del tempo** weather forecast *sg*

pre'visto, -a *pp di* **prevedere** ▷ *sm* **più/ meno del ~** more/less than expected

prezi'oso, -a [pret'tsjoso] *ag* precious; invaluable ▷ *sm* jewel; valuable

prez'zemolo [pret'tsemolo] *sm* parsley

'**prezzo** ['prɛttso] *sm* price; **prezzo d'acquisto/di vendita** buying/selling price

prigi'one [pri'dʒone] *sf* prison; **prigioni'ero, -a** *ag* captive ▷ *sm/f* prisoner

'**prima** *sf* (*Teatro*) first night; (*Cinema*) première; (*Aut*) first gear; *vedi anche* **primo** ▷ *av* before; (*in anticipo*) in advance, beforehand; (*per l'addietro*) at one time, formerly; (*più presto*) sooner, earlier; (*in primo luogo*) first ▷ *cong* ~ **di fare/che parta** before doing/he leaves; ~ **di** before; ~ **o poi** sooner or later

pri'mario, -a *ag* primary; (*principale*) chief, leading, primary ▷ *sm* (*Med*) chief physician

prima'tista, -i, e *sm/f* (*Sport*) record holder

pri'mato *sm* supremacy; (*Sport*) record

prima'vera *sf* spring

primi'tivo, -a *ag* primitive; original

pri'mizie [pri'mittsje] *sfpl* early produce *sg*

'**primo, -a** *ag* first; (*fig*) initial; basic; prime ▷ *sm/f* first (one) ▷ *sm* (*Cuc*) first course; (*in date*): **il ~ luglio** the first of July; **le prime ore del mattino** the early hours of the morning; **ai primi di maggio** at the beginning of May; **viaggiare in prima** to travel first-class; **in ~ luogo** first of all, in the first place; **di prim'ordine** o **prima qualità** first-class, first-rate; **in un ~ tempo** at first; **prima donna** leading lady; (*di opera lirica*) prima donna

primordi'ale *ag* primordial

'**primula** *sf* primrose

princi'pale [printʃi'pale] *ag* main, principal ▷ *sm* manager, boss

principal'mente [printʃipal'mente] *av* mainly, principally

'**principe** ['printʃipe] *sm* prince; **principe ereditario** crown prince; **princi'pessa** *sf* princess

principi'ante [printʃi'pjante] *sm/f* beginner

prin'cipio [prin'tʃipjo] *sm* (*inizio*) beginning, start; (*origine*) origin, cause; (*concetto, norma*) principle; **al** o **in ~** at first; **per ~** on principle; **principi** *smpl* (*concetti fondamentali*) principles; **una questione di ~** a matter of principle

priorità *sf* priority

priori'tario, -a *ag* having priority, of utmost importance

pri'vare *vt* ~ **qn di** to deprive sb of; **privarsi di** to go o do without

pri'vato, -a *ag* private ▷ *sm/f* private citizen; **in ~** in private

privilegi'are [privile'dʒare] *vt* to grant a privilege to

privilegi'ato, -a [privile'dʒato] *ag* (*individuo, classe*) privileged; (*trattamento, Comm: credito*) preferential; **azioni ~e** preference shares (BRIT), preferred stock (US)

privi'legio [privi'lɛdʒo] *sm* privilege

'**privo, -a** *ag* ~ **di** without, lacking

pro *prep* for, on behalf of ▷ *sm inv* (*utilità*) advantage, benefit; **a che ~?** what's the use?; **il ~ e il contro** the pros and cons

pro'babile *ag* probable, likely; **probabilità** *sf inv* probability

probabil'mente *av* probably

pro'blema, -i *sm* problem

pro'boscide [pro'bɔʃʃide] *sf* (*di elefante*) trunk

pro'cedere [pro'tʃɛdere] *vi* to proceed; (*comportarsi*) to behave; (*iniziare*): ~ **a** to start; ~ **contro** (*Dir*) to start legal proceedings against; **proce'dura** *sf* (*Dir*) procedure

proces'sare [protʃes'sare] *vt* (*Dir*) to try

processi'one [protʃes'sjone] *sf* procession

pro'cesso [pro'tʃɛsso] *sm* (*Dir*) trial; proceedings *pl*; (*metodo*) process

pro'cinto [pro'tʃinto] *sm* **in ~ di fare** about to do, on the point of doing

procla'mare *vt* to proclaim

procre'are *vt* to procreate

procu'rare *vt* ~ **qc a qn** (*fornire*) to get o obtain sth for sb; (*causare: noie ecc*) to bring o give sb sth

pro'digio [pro'didʒo] *sm* marvel, wonder; (*persona*) prodigy

pro'dotto, -a *pp di* **produrre** ▷ *sm* product; **prodotti agricoli** farm produce *sg*

pro'duco *ecc vb vedi* **produrre**

pro'durre *vt* to produce

pro'dussi *ecc vb vedi* **produrre**

produzi'one *sf* production; (*rendimento*) output

Prof. *abbr* (= *professore*) Prof.

profa'nare *vt* to desecrate

profes'sare *vt* to profess; (*medicina ecc*) to practise

professio'nale *ag* professional

professi'one *sf* profession; **professio'nista, -i, -e** *sm/f* professional

profes'sore, -'essa *sm/f* (*Ins*) teacher; (: *di università*) lecturer; (: *titolare di cattedra*) professor

pro'filo *sm* profile; (*breve descrizione*) sketch, outline; **di ~** in profile

pro'fitto *sm* advantage, profit, benefit; (*fig: progresso*) progress; (*Comm*) profit

profondità *sf inv* depth

pro'fondo, -a *ag* deep; (*rancore,*

meditazione) profound ▷ *sm* depth(s *pl*),
bottom; **quanto è profonda l'acqua?**
how deep is the water?; **~ 8 metri** 8 metres
deep

ˈ**profugo, -a, -ghi, -ghe** *sm/f* refugee
profuˈmare *vt* to perfume ▷ *vi* to be
fragrant; **profumarsi** *vpr* to put on
perfume *o* scent
profuˈmato, -a *ag* (*fiore, aria*) fragrant;
(*fazzoletto, saponetta*) scented; (*pelle*)
sweet-smelling; (*persona*) with perfume on
profumeˈria *sf* perfumery; (*negozio*)
perfume shop
proˈfumo *sm* (*prodotto*) perfume, scent;
(*fragranza*) scent, fragrance
progetˈtare [prodʒetˈtare] *vt* to plan;
(*edificio*) to plan, design; **proˈgetto** *sm*
plan; (*idea*) plan, project; **progetto di
legge** bill
proˈgramma, -i *sm* programme; (*TV,
Radio*) programmes *pl*; (*Ins*) syllabus,
curriculum; (*Inform*) program;
programˈmare *vt* (*TV, Radio*) to put
on; (*Inform*) to program; (*Econ*) to plan;
programmaˈtore, -ˈtrice *sm/f* (*Inform*)
computer programmer
progreˈdire *vi* to progress, make progress
proˈgresso *sm* progress *no pl*; **fare
progressi** to make progress
proiˈbire *vt* to forbid, prohibit
proietˈtare *vt* (*gen, Geom, Cinema*) to
project; (: *presentare*) to show, screen; (*luce,
ombra*) to throw, cast, project; **proiˈettile**
sm projectile, bullet (*o* shell *ecc*);
proietˈtore *sm* (*Cinema*) projector; (*Aut*)
headlamp; (*Mil*) searchlight; **proieziˈone**
sf (*Cinema*) projection; showing
prolifeˈrare *vi* (*fig*) to proliferate
proˈlunga, -ghe *sf* (*di cavo ecc*) extension
prolunˈgare *vt* (*discorso, attesa*) to
prolong; (*linea, termine*) to extend
promeˈmoria *sm inv* memorandum
proˈmessa *sf* promise
proˈmettere *vt* to promise ▷ *vi* to be *o*
look promising; **~ a qn di fare** to promise
sb that one will do
promiˈnente *ag* prominent
proˈmisi *ecc vb vedi* **promettere**
promonˈtorio *sm* promontory, headland
promoziˈone [promotˈtsjone] *sf*
promotion
promuˈovere *vt* to promote
proniˈpote *sm/f* (*di nonni*) great-
grandchild, great-grandson/
granddaughter; (*di zii*) great-nephew/
niece
proˈnome *sm* (*Ling*) pronoun
pronˈtezza [pronˈtettsa] *sf* readiness;
quickness, promptness

ˈ**pronto, -a** *ag* ready; (*rapido*) fast, quick,
prompt; **quando saranno pronte le mie
foto?** when will my photos be ready?;
~! (*Tel*) hello!; **~ all'ira** quick-tempered;
pronto soccorso (*cure*) first aid; (*reparto*)
A&E (*BRIT*), ER (*US*)
prontuˈario *sm* manual, handbook
proˈnuncia [proˈnuntʃa] *sf* pronunciation
pronunciˈare [pronunˈtʃare] *vt* (*parola,
sentenza*) to pronounce; (*dire*) to utter;
(*discorso*) to deliver; **come si pronuncia?**
how do you pronounce it?
propaˈganda *sf* propaganda
proˈpendere *vi* **~ per** to favour, lean
towards
propiˈnare *vt* to administer
proˈporre *vt* (*suggerire*) **~ qc (a qn)** to
suggest sth (to sb); (*candidato*) to put
forward; (*legge, brindisi*) to propose; **~ di
fare** to suggest *o* propose doing; **proporsi
di fare** to propose *o* intend to do; **proporsi
una meta** to set o.s. a goal
proporzioˈnale [proportsjoˈnale] *ag*
proportional
proporziˈone [proporˈtsjone] *sf*
proportion; **in ~ a** in proportion to;
proporzioni *sfpl* (*dimensioni*) proportions;
di vaste proporzioni huge
proˈposito *sm* (*intenzione*) intention,
aim; (*argomento*) subject, matter; **a ~ di**
regarding, with regard to; **di ~** (*apposta*)
deliberately, on purpose; **a ~** by the way;
capitare a ~ (*cosa, persona*) to turn up at
the right time
proposiziˈone [propozitˈtsjone] *sf* (*Ling*)
clause; (: *periodo*) sentence
proˈposta *sf* proposal; (*suggerimento*)
suggestion; **proposta di legge** bill
proprietà *sf inv* (*ciò che si possiede*) property
gen no pl, estate; (*caratteristica*) property;
(*correttezza*) correctness; **proprietà
privata** private property; **propieˈtario,
-a** *sm/f* owner; (*di albergo ecc*) proprietor,
owner; (*per l'inquilino*) landlord/lady
ˈ**proprio, -a** *ag* (*possessivo*) own;
(: *impersonale*) one's; (*esatto*) exact,
correct, proper; (*senso, significato*)
literal; (*Ling: nome*) proper; (*particolare*):
~ di characteristic of, peculiar to ▷ *av*
(*precisamente*) just, exactly; (*davvero*) really;
(*affatto*): **non ... ~** not ... at all; **l'ha visto
con i (suoi) propri occhi** he saw it with
his own eyes
proroˈgare *vt* to extend; (*differire*) to
postpone, defer
ˈ**prosa** *sf* prose
proˈsciogliere [proʃˈʃɔʎʎere] *vt* to release;
(*Dir*) to acquit
prosciuˈgare [proʃʃuˈgare] *vt* (*terreni*) to

drain, reclaim; **prosciugarsi** *vpr* to dry up

prosci'utto [proʃʃutto] *sm* ham;
prosciutto cotto/crudo cooked/cured ham

prosegui'mento *sm* continuation; **buon ~!** all the best!; (*a chi viaggia*) enjoy the rest of your journey!

prosegu'ire *vt* to carry on with, continue ▷ *vi* to carry on, go on

prospe'rare *vi* to thrive

prospet'tare *vt* (*esporre*) to point out, show; **prospettarsi** *vpr* to look, appear

prospet'tiva *sf* (*Arte*) perspective; (*veduta*) view; (*fig: previsione, possibilità*) prospect

pros'petto *sm* (*Disegno*) elevation; (*veduta*) view, prospect; (*facciata*) façade, front; (*tabella*) table; (*sommario*) summary; **prospetto informativo** prospectus

prossimità *sf* nearness, proximity; **in ~ di** near (to), close to

'prossimo, -a *ag* (*vicino*): **~ a** near (to), close to; (*che viene subito dopo*) next; (*parente*) close ▷ *sm* neighbour, fellow man

prostitu'irsi *vpr* to prostitute o.s.

prosti'tuta *sf* prostitute

protago'nista, -i, -e *sm/f* protagonist

pro'teggere [pro'tɛddʒere] *vt* to protect

prote'ina *sf* protein

pro'tendere *vt* to stretch out

pro'testa *sf* protest

protes'tante *ag, sm/f* Protestant

protes'tare *vt, vi* to protest

pro'tetto, -a *pp di* **proteggere**

protezi'one [protet'tsjone] *sf* protection; (*patrocinio*) patronage

pro'totipo *sm* prototype

pro'trarre *vt* (*prolungare*) to prolong; **protrarsi** *vpr* to go on, continue

protube'ranza [protube'rantsa] *sf* protuberance, bulge

'prova *sf* (*esperimento, cimento*) test, trial; (*tentativo*) attempt, try; (*Mat, testimonianza, documento ecc*) proof; (*Dir*) evidence *no pl*, proof; (*Ins*) exam, test; (*Teatro*) rehearsal; (*di abito*) fitting; **a ~ di** (*in testimonianza di*) as proof of; **a ~ di fuoco** fireproof; **fino a ~ contraria** until it is proved otherwise; **mettere alla ~** to put to the test; **giro di ~** test *o* trial run; **prova generale** (*Teatro*) dress rehearsal

pro'vare *vt* (*sperimentare*) to test; (*tentare*) to try, attempt; (*assaggiare*) to try, taste; (*sperimentare in sé*) to experience; (*sentire*) to feel; (*cimentare*) to put to the test; (*dimostrare*) to prove; (*abito*) to try on; **~ a fare** to try *o* attempt to do

proveni'enza [prove'njentsa] *sf* origin, source

prove'nire *vi* **~ da** to come from

pro'venti *smpl* revenue *sg*

pro'verbio *sm* proverb

pro'vetta *sf* test tube; **bambino in ~** test-tube baby

pro'vider [pro'vaider] *sm inv* (*Inform*) service provider

pro'vincia, -ce *o* **cie** [pro'vintʃa] *sf* province

pro'vino *sm* (*Cinema*) screen test; (*campione*) specimen

provo'cante *ag* (*attraente*) provocative

provo'care *vt* (*causare*) to cause, bring about; (*eccitare: riso, pietà*) to arouse; (*irritare, sfidare*) to provoke; **provocazi'one** *sf* provocation

provve'dere *vi* (*disporre*): **~ (a)** to provide (for); (*prendere un provvedimento*) to take steps, act; **provvedi'mento** *sm* measure; (*di previdenza*) precaution

provvi'denza [provvi'dentsa] *sf* **la ~** providence

provvigi'one [provvi'dʒone] *sf* (*Comm*) commission

provvi'sorio, -a *ag* temporary

prov'viste *sfpl* supplies

'prua *sf* (*Naut*) bow(s) (*pl*), prow

pru'dente *ag* cautious, prudent; (*assennato*) sensible, wise; **pru'denza** *sf* prudence, caution; wisdom

'prudere *vi* to itch, be itchy

'prugna ['pruɲɲa] *sf* plum; **prugna secca** prune

pru'rito *sm* itchiness *no pl*; itch

P.S. *abbr* (= *postscriptum*) P.S.; (*Polizia*) = **Pubblica Sicurezza**

pseu'donimo *sm* pseudonym

psica'nalisi *sf* psychoanalysis

psicana'lista, -i, -e *sm/f* psychoanalyst

'psiche ['psike] *sf* (*Psic*) psyche

psichi'atra, -i, -e [psi'kjatra] *sm/f* psychiatrist; **psichi'atrico, -a, -ci, -che** *ag* psychiatric

psicolo'gia [psikolo'dʒia] *sf* psychology; **psico'logico, -a, -ci, -che** *ag* psychological; **psi'cologo, -a, -gi, -ghe** *sm/f* psychologist

psico'patico, -a, -ci, -che *ag* psychopathic ▷ *sm/f* psychopath

pubbli'care *vt* to publish

pubblicazi'one [pubblikat'tsjone] *sf* publication

pubblicità [pubblitʃi'ta] *sf* (*diffusione*) publicity; (*attività*) advertising; (*annunci nei giornali*) advertisements *pl*

'pubblico, -a, -ci, -che *ag* public; (*statale: scuola ecc*) state *cpd* ▷ *sm* public; (*spettatori*) audience; **in ~** in public; **P~ Ministero** Public Prosecutor's Office; **la Pubblica Sicurezza** the police; **pubblico**

funzionario civil servant

'pube sm (Anat) pubis

pubertà sf puberty

'pudico, -a, -ci, -che ag modest

pu'dore sm modesty

pue'rile ag childish

pugi'lato [pudʒi'lato] sm boxing

'pugile ['pudʒile] sm boxer

pugna'lare [puɲɲa'lare] vt to stab

pu'gnale [puɲ'ɲale] sm dagger

'pugno ['puɲɲo] sm fist; (colpo) punch; (quantità) fistful

'pulce ['pultʃe] sf flea

pul'cino [pul'tʃino] sm chick

pu'lire vt to clean; (lucidare) to polish; **pu'lito, -a** ag (anche fig) clean; (ordinato) neat, tidy; **puli'tura** sf cleaning; **pulitura a secco** dry cleaning; **puli'zia** sf cleaning; cleanness; **fare le pulizie** to do the cleaning o the housework; **pulizia etnica** ethnic cleansing

'pullman sm inv coach

pul'lover sm inv pullover, jumper

pullu'lare vi to swarm, teem

pul'mino sm minibus

'pulpito sm pulpit

pul'sante sm (push-)button

pul'sare vi to pulsate, beat

pul'viscolo sm fine dust; **pulviscolo atmosferico** specks pl of dust

'puma sm inv puma

pun'gente [pun'dʒɛnte] ag prickly; stinging; (anche fig) biting

'pungere ['pundʒere] vt to prick; (insetto, ortica) to sting; (: freddo) to bite

pungigli'one [pundʒiʎ'ʎone] sm sting

pu'nire vt to punish; **punizi'one** sf punishment; (Sport) penalty

'punsi ecc vb vedi **pungere**

'punta sf point; (parte terminale) tip, end; (di monte) peak; (di costa) promontory; (minima parte) touch, trace; **in ~ di piedi** on tip-toe; **ore di ~** peak hours; **uomo di ~** front-rank o leading man

pun'tare vt (piedi a terra, gomiti sul tavolo) to plant; (dirigere: pistola) to point; (scommettere) to bet ▷ vi (mirare): **~ a** to aim at; **~ su** (dirigersi) to head o make for; (fig: contare) to count o rely on

pun'tata sf (gita) short trip; (scommessa) bet; (parte di opera) instalment; **romanzo a puntate** serial

punteggia'tura [punteddʒa'tura] sf (Ling) punctuation

pun'teggio [pun'teddʒo] sm score

puntel'lare vt to support

pun'tello sm prop, support

pun'tina sf; **puntina da disegno** drawing pin

pun'tino sm dot; **fare qc a ~** to do sth properly

'punto, -a pp di **pungere** ▷ sm (segno, macchiolina) dot; (Ling) full stop; (di indirizzo e-mail) dot; (Mat, momento, di punteggio: fig: argomento) point; (posto) spot; (a scuola) mark; (nel cucire, nella maglia, Med) stitch ▷ av **non ... ~** not at all; **punto cardinale** point of the compass, cardinal point; **punto debole** weak point; **punto esclamativo** exclamation mark; **punto interrogativo** question mark; **punto nero** (comedone) blackhead; **punto di partenza** (anche fig) starting point; **punto di riferimento** landmark; (fig) point of reference; **punto (di) vendita** retail outlet; **punto e virgola** semicolon; **punto di vista** (fig) point of view

puntu'ale ag punctual

pun'tura sf (di ago) prick; (Med) puncture; (: iniezione) injection; (dolore) sharp pain; **puntura d'insetto** sting, bite

Attenzione! In inglese esiste la parola puncture, che si usa per indicare la foratura di una gomma.

punzecchi'are [puntsek'kjare] vt to prick; (fig) to tease

può ecc, **-puo'oi** vb vedi **potere**

pu'pazzo [pu'pattso] sm puppet

pu'pilla sf (Anat) pupil

purché [pur'ke] cong provided that, on condition that

'pure cong (tuttavia) and yet, nevertheless; (anche se) even if ▷ av (anche) too, also; **pur di** (al fine di) just to; **faccia ~!** go ahead!, please do!

purè sm (Cuc) purée; (: di patate) mashed potatoes

pu'rezza [pu'rettsa] sf purity

pur'gante sm (Med) purgative, purge

purga'torio sm purgatory

purifi'care vt to purify; (metallo) to refine

'puro, -a ag pure; (acqua) clear, limpid; (vino) undiluted; **puro'sangue** sm/f inv thoroughbred

pur'troppo av unfortunately

pus sm pus

'pustola sf pimple

puti'ferio sm rumpus, row

putre'fatto, -a pp di **putrefare**

put'tana (fam!) sf whore (!)

puz'zare [put'tsare] vi to stink

'puzzo ['puttso] sm stink, foul smell

'puzzola ['puttsola] sf polecat

puzzo'lente [puttso'lɛnte] ag stinking

pvc [pivi'tʃi] sigla m (= polyvinyl chloride) PVC

q *abbr* (= *quintale*) q.

qua *av* here; **in ~** (*verso questa parte*) this way; **da un anno in ~** for a year now; **da ~ndo in ~?** since when?; **per di ~** (*passare*) this way; **al di ~ di** (*fiume, strada*) on this side of; **~ dentro/fuori** *ecc* in/out here *ecc*; *vedi anche* **questo**

qua'derno *sm* notebook; (*per scuola*) exercise book

qua'drante *sm* quadrant; (*di orologio*) face

qua'drare *vi* (*bilancio*) to balance, tally; (*descrizione*) to correspond ▷ *vt* (*Mat*) to square; **non mi quadra** I don't like it; **qua'drato, -a** *ag* square; (*fig: equilibrato*) level-headed, sensible; (: *peg*) square ▷ *sm* (*Mat*) square; (*Pugilato*) ring; **5 al quadrato** 5 squared

quadri'foglio [kwadri'fɔʎʎo] *sm* four-leaf clover

quadri'mestre *sm* (*periodo*) four-month period; (*Ins*) term

'quadro *sm* (*pittura*) painting, picture; (*quadrato*) square; (*tabella*) table, chart; (*Tecn*) board, panel; (*Teatro*) scene; (*fig: scena, spettacolo*) sight; (: *descrizione*) outline, description; **quadri** *smpl* (*Pol*) party organizers; (*Mil*) cadres; (*Comm*) managerial staff; (*Carte*) diamonds

'quadruplo, -a *ag, sm* quadruple

quaggiù [kwad'dʒu] *av* down here

'quaglia ['kwaʎʎa] *sf* quail

 PAROLA CHIAVE

'qualche ['kwalke] *det* **1** some, a few; (*in interrogative*) any; **ho comprato qualche libro** I've bought some *o* a few books; **qualche volta** sometimes; **hai qualche sigaretta?** have you any cigarettes?
2 (*uno*): **c'è qualche medico?** is there a doctor?; **in qualche modo** somehow
3 (*un certo, parecchio*) some; **un personaggio di qualche rilievo** a figure of some importance
4: **qualche cosa = qualcosa**

qual'cosa *pron* something; (*in espressioni interrogative*) anything; **qualcos'altro** something else; anything else; **~ di nuovo** something new; anything new; **~ da mangiare** something to eat; anything to eat; **c'è ~ che non va?** is there something *o* anything wrong?

qual'cuno *pron* (*persona*) someone, somebody; (: *in espressioni interrogative*) anyone, anybody; (*alcuni*) some; **~ è favorevole a noi** some are on our side; **qualcun altro** someone *o* somebody else; anyone *o* anybody else

 PAROLA CHIAVE

'quale (*spesso troncato in* qual) *det* **1** (*interrogativo*) what; (: *scegliendo tra due o più cose o persone*) which; **quale uomo/ denaro?** what man/money?, which man/ money?; **quali sono i tuoi programmi?** what are your plans?; **quale stanza preferisci?** which room do you prefer?
2 (*relativo: come*): **il risultato fu quale ci si aspettava** the result was as expected
3 (*esclamativo*) what; **quale disgrazia!** what bad luck!
▷ *pron* **1** (*interrogativo*) which; **quale dei due scegli?** which of the two do you want?
2 (*relativo*): **il (la) quale** (*persona: soggetto*) who; (: *oggetto, con preposizione*) whom; (*cosa*) which; (*possessivo*) whose; **suo padre, il quale è avvocato, ...** his father, who is a lawyer, ...; **il signore con il quale parlavo** the gentleman to whom I was speaking; **l'albergo al quale ci siamo fermati** the hotel where we stayed *o* which we stayed at; **la signora della quale ammiriamo la bellezza** the lady whose beauty we admire
3 (*relativo: in elenchi*) such as, like; **piante**

quali l'edera plants like o such as ivy;
quale sindaco di questa città as mayor
of this town

qua'lifica, -che *sf* qualification; (*titolo*)
title
qualifi'cato, -a *ag* (*dotato di qualifica*)
qualified; (*esperto, abile*) skilled; **non mi
ritengo ~ per questo lavoro** I don't think
I'm qualified for this job; **è un medico
molto ~** he is a very distinguished doctor
qualificazi'one *sf* **gara di ~** (*Sport*)
qualifying event
qualità *sf inv* quality; **in ~ di** in one's
capacity as
qua'lora *cong* in case, if
qual'siasi *det inv* = **qualunque**
qua'lunque *det inv* any; (*quale che sia*)
whatever; (*discriminativo*) whichever;
(*posposto: mediocre*) poor, indifferent;
ordinary; **mettiti un vestito ~** put on any
old dress; **~ cosa** anything; **~ cosa accada**
whatever happens; **a ~ costo** at any cost,
whatever the cost; **l'uomo ~** the man in
the street; **~ persona** anyone, anybody
'quando *cong, av* when; **~ sarò ricco** when
I'm rich; **da ~** (*dacché*) since; (*interrogativo*):
da ~ sei qui? how long have you been
here?; **quand'anche** even if
quantità *sf inv* quantity; (*gran numero*):
una ~ di a great deal of; a lot of; **in grande
~** in large quantities

PAROLA CHIAVE

'quanto, -a *det* **1** (*interrogativo: quantità*)
how much; (: *numero*) how many; **quanto
pane/denaro?** how much bread/money?;
quanti libri/ragazzi? how many books/
boys?; **quanto tempo?** how long?; **quanti
anni hai?** how old are you?
2 (*esclamativo*): **quante storie!** what a lot
of nonsense!; **quanto tempo sprecato!**
what a waste of time!
3 (*relativo: quantità*) as much … as;
(: *numero*) as many … as; **ho quanto
denaro mi occorre** I have as much money
as I need; **prendi quanti libri vuoi** take as
many books as you like
▷ *pron* **1** (*interrogativo: quantità*) how much;
(: *numero*) how many; (: *tempo*) how long;
quanto mi dai? how much will you give
me?; **quanti me ne hai portati?** how
many did you bring me?; **da quanto sei
qui?** how long have you been here?; **quanti
ne abbiamo oggi?** what's the date today?
2 (*relativo: quantità*) as much as; (: *numero*)
as many as; **farò quanto posso** I'll do as
much as I can; **possono venire quanti**

sono stati invitati all those who have
been invited can come
▷ *av* **1** (*interrogativo: con ag, av*) how;
(: *con vb*) how much; **quanto stanco ti
sembrava?** how tired did he seem to you?;
quanto corre la tua moto? how fast can
your motorbike go?; **quanto costa?** how
much does it cost?; **quant'è?** how much
is it?
2 (*esclamativo: con ag, av*) how; (: *con vb*)
how much; **quanto sono felice!** how
happy I am!; **sapessi quanto abbiamo
camminato!** if you knew how far we've
walked!; **studierò quanto posso** I'll study
as much as o all I can; **quanto prima** as
soon as possible
3: **in quanto** (*in qualità di*) as; (*perché, per il
fatto che*) as, since; **(in) quanto a** (*per ciò
che riguarda*) as for, as regards
4: **per quanto** (*nonostante, anche se*)
however; **per quanto si sforzi, non ce
la farà** try as he may, he won't manage
it; **per quanto sia brava, fa degli errori**
however good she may be, she makes
mistakes; **per quanto io sappia** as far as
I know

qua'ranta *num* forty
quaran'tena *sf* quarantine
quaran'tesimo, -a *num* fortieth
quaran'tina *sf* **una ~ (di)** about forty
'quarta *sf* (*Aut*) fourth (gear); *vedi anche*
quarto
quar'tetto *sm* quartet(te)
quarti'ere *sm* district, area; (*Mil*) quarters
pl; **quartier generale** headquarters *pl*
'quarto, -a *ag* fourth ▷ *sm* fourth; (*quarta
parte*) quarter; **le 6 e un ~** a quarter past
six; **quarti di finale** quarter final; **quarto
d'ora** quarter of an hour
'quarzo ['kwartso] *sm* quartz
'quasi *av* almost, nearly ▷ *cong* (*anche*: **~
che**) as if; **(non) … ~ mai** hardly ever; **~ ~
me ne andrei** I've half a mind to leave
quassù *av* up here
quat'tordici [kwat'torditʃi] *num* fourteen
quat'trini *smpl* money *sg*, cash *sg*
'quattro *num* four; **in ~ e quattr'otto** in
less than no time; **quattro'cento** *num*
four hundred ▷ *sm* **il Quattrocento** the
fifteenth century

PAROLA CHIAVE

'quello, -a (*dav sm* **quel** + *C*, **quell'** + *V*,
quello + *s impura, gn, pn, ps, x, z; pl* **quei** +
C, **quegli** + *V o s impura, gn, pn, ps, x, z; dav sf*
quella + *C*, **quell'** + *V; pl* **quelle**) *det* that;
those *pl*; **quella casa** that house; **quegli**

uomini those men; **voglio quella camicia (lì** o **là)** I want that shirt
▷ pron **1** (dimostrativo) that (one), those (ones) pl; (ciò) that; **conosci quella?** do you know that woman?; **prendo quello bianco** I'll take the white one; **chi è quello?** who's that?; **prendi quello (lì** o **là)** take that one (there)
2 (relativo): **quello(a) che** (persona) the one (who); (cosa) the one (which), the one (that); **quelli(e) che** (persone) those who; (cose) those which; **è lui quello che non voleva venire** he's the one who didn't want to come; **ho fatto quello che potevo** I did what I could

'quercia, -ce ['kwɛrtʃa] sf oak (tree); (legno) oak
que'rela sf (Dir) (legal) action
que'sito sm question, query; problem
questio'nario sm questionnaire
questi'one sf problem, question; (controversia) issue; (litigio) quarrel; **in ~** in question; **è ~ di tempo** it's a matter o question of time

⬤ **PAROLA CHIAVE**

'questo, -a det **1** (dimostrativo) this; these pl; **questo libro (qui** o **qua)** this book; **io prendo questo cappotto, tu quello** I'll take this coat, you take that one; **quest'oggi** today; **questa sera** this evening
2 (enfatico): **non fatemi più prendere di queste paure** don't frighten me like that again
▷ pron (dimostrativo) this (one); these (ones) pl; (ciò) this; **prendo questo (qui** o **qua)** I'll take this one; **preferisci questi o quelli?** do you prefer these (ones) or those (ones)?; **questo intendevo io** this is what I meant; **vengono Paolo e Luca: questo da Roma, quello da Palermo** Paolo and Luca are coming: the former from Palermo, the latter from Rome

ques'tura sf police headquarters pl
qui av here; **da** o **di ~** from here; **di ~ in avanti** from now on; **di ~ a poco/una settimana** in a little while/a week's time; **~ dentro/sopra/vicino** in/up/near here; vedi anche **questo**
quie'tanza [kwje'tantsa] sf receipt
qui'ete sf quiet, quietness; calmness; stillness; peace
qui'eto, -a ag quiet; (notte) calm, still; (mare) calm
'quindi av then ▷ cong therefore, so

'quindici ['kwinditʃi] num fifteen; **~ giorni** a fortnight (BRIT), two weeks
quindi'cina [kwindi'tʃina] sf (serie): **una ~ (di)** about fifteen; **fra una ~ di giorni** in a fortnight
quinta sf vedi **quinto**
quin'tale sm quintal (100 kg)
'quinto, -a num fifth
quiz [kwidz] sm inv (domanda) question; (anche): **gioco a ~** quiz game
'quota sf (parte) quota, share; (Aer) height, altitude; (Ippica) odds pl; **prendere/ perdere ~** (Aer) to gain/lose height o altitude; **quota d'iscrizione** enrolment fee; (a club) membership fee
quotidi'ano, -a ag daily; (banale) everyday ▷ sm (giornale) daily (paper)
quozi'ente [kwot'tsjɛnte] sm (Mat) quotient; **quoziente d'intelligenza** intelligence quotient, IQ

q

R, r ['ɛrre] *sf o m* (*lettera*) R, r; **R come Roma**
≈ R for Robert (BRIT), R for Roger (US)
'rabbia *sf* (*ira*) anger, rage; (*accanimento,
furia*) fury; (*Med: idrofobia*) rabies *sg*
rab'bino *sm* rabbi
rabbi'oso, -a *ag* angry, furious; (*facile
all'ira*) quick-tempered; (*forze, acqua ecc*)
furious, raging; (*Med*) rabid, mad
rabbo'nire *vt* to calm down
rabbrivi'dire *vi* to shudder, shiver
raccapez'zarsi [rakkapet'tsarsi] *vpr* **non
~** to be at a loss
raccapricci'ante [rakkaprit'tʃante] *ag*
horrifying
raccatta'palle *sm inv* (*Sport*) ballboy
raccat'tare *vt* to pick up
rac'chetta [rak'ketta] *sf* (*per tennis*)
racket; (*per ping-pong*) bat; **racchetta da
neve** snowshoe; **racchetta da sci** ski stick
racchi'udere [rak'kjudere] *vt* to contain
rac'cogliere [rak'kɔʎʎere] *vt* to collect;
(*raccattare*) to pick up; (*frutti, fiori*) to pick,
pluck; (*Agr*) to harvest; (*approvazione, voti*)
to win
rac'colta *sf* collecting *no pl*; collection;
(*Agr*) harvesting *no pl*, gathering *no pl*;
harvest, crop; (*adunata*) gathering;
raccolta differenziata (*dei rifiuti*) *separate
collection of different kinds of household waste*
rac'colto, -a *pp di* **raccogliere** ▷ *ag*
(*persona: pensoso*) thoughtful; (*luogo:
appartato*) secluded, quiet ▷ *sm* (*Agr*) crop,
harvest
raccoman'dabile *ag* (highly)
commendable; **è un tipo poco ~** he is not
to be trusted
raccoman'dare *vt* to recommend;
(*affidare*) to entrust; (*esortare*): **~ a qn
di non fare** to tell *o* warn sb not to do;
raccoman'data *sf* (*anche: lettera
raccomandata*) recorded-delivery letter
raccon'tare *vt* **~ (a qn)** (*dire*) to tell (sb);
(*narrare*) to relate (to sb), tell (sb) about;
rac'conto *sm* telling *no pl*, relating *no pl*;
(*fatto raccontato*) story, tale; **racconti per
bambini** children's stories
rac'cordo *sm* (*Tecn: giunto*) connection,
joint; (*Aut*): **raccordo anulare** (*Aut*)
ring road (BRIT), beltway (US); **raccordo
autostradale** slip road (BRIT), entrance
(*o* exit) ramp (US); **raccordo ferroviario**
siding; **raccordo stradale** link road
racimo'lare [ratʃimo'lare] *vt* (*fig*) to
scrape together, glean
'rada *sf* (natural) harbour
'radar *sm* radar
raddoppi'are *vt, vi* to double
raddriz'zare [raddrit'tsare] *vt* to
straighten; (*fig: correggere*) to put straight,
correct
'radere *vt* (*barba*) to shave off; (*mento*) to
shave; (*fig: rasentare*) to graze; to skim;
radersi *vpr* to shave (o.s.); **~ al suolo** to
raze to the ground
radi'are *vt* to strike off
radia'tore *sm* radiator
radiazi'one [radjat'tsjone] *sf* (*Fisica*)
radiation; (*cancellazione*) striking off
radi'cale *ag* radical ▷ *sm* (*Ling*) root
ra'dicchio [ra'dikkjo] *sm* chicory
ra'dice [ra'ditʃe] *sf* root
'radio *sf inv* radio ▷ *sm* (*Chim*) radium;
radioat'tivo, -a *ag* radioactive;
radio'cronaca, -che *sf* radio
commentary; **radiogra'fia** *sf*
radiography; (*foto*) X-ray photograph
radi'oso, -a *ag* radiant
radios'veglia [radjoz'veʎʎa] *sf* radio
alarm
'rado, -a *ag* (*capelli*) sparse, thin; (*visite*)
infrequent; **di ~** rarely
radu'nare *vt* to gather, assemble;
radunarsi *vpr* to gather, assemble
ra'dura *sf* clearing
raf'fermo, -a *ag* stale
'raffica, -che *sf* (*Meteor*) gust (of wind); (*di
colpi: scarica*) burst of gunfire
raffigu'rare *vt* to represent
raffi'nato, -a *ag* refined

raffor'zare [raffor'tsare] *vt* to reinforce
raffredda'mento *sm* cooling
raffred'dare *vt* to cool; (*fig*) to dampen, have a cooling effect on; **raffreddarsi** *vpr* to grow cool *o* cold; (*prendere un raffreddore*) to catch a cold; (*fig*) to cool (off)
raffred'dato, -a *ag* (*Med*): **essere ~** to have a cold
raffred'dore *sm* (*Med*) cold
raf'fronto *sm* comparison
'rafia *sf* (*fibra*) raffia
rafting ['rafting] *sm* white-water rafting
ra'gazza [ra'gattsa] *sf* girl; (*fam: fidanzato*) girlfriend; **nome da ~** maiden name; **ragazza madre** unmarried mother
ra'gazzo [ra'gattso] *sm* boy; (*fam: fidanzato*) boyfriend; **ragazzi** *smpl* (*figli*) kids; **ciao ragazzi!** (*gruppo*) hi guys!
raggi'ante [radd'ʒante] *ag* radiant, shining
'raggio ['raddʒo] *sm* (*di sole ecc*) ray; (*Mat, distanza*) radius; (*di ruota ecc*) spoke; **raggio d'azione** range; **raggi X** X-rays
raggi'rare [raddʒi'rare] *vt* to take in, trick
raggi'ungere [rad'dʒundʒere] *vt* to reach; (*persona: riprendere*) to catch up (with); (*bersaglio*) to hit; (*fig: meta*) to achieve
raggomito'larsi *vpr* to curl up
raggranel'lare *vt* to scrape together
raggrup'pare *vt* to group (together)
ragiona'mento [radʒona'mento] *sm* reasoning *no pl*; arguing *no pl*; argument
ragio'nare [radʒo'nare] *vi* to reason; **~ di** (*discorrere*) to talk about
ragi'one [ra'dʒone] *sf* reason; (*dimostrazione, prova*) argument, reason; (*diritto*) right; **aver ~** to be right; **aver ~ di qn** to get the better of sb; **dare ~ a qn** to agree with sb; to prove sb right; **perdere la ~** to become insane; (*fig*) to take leave of one's senses; **in ~ di** at the rate of; to the amount of; according to; **a** *o* **con ~** rightly, justly; **a ragion veduta** after due consideration; **ragione sociale** (*Comm*) corporate name
ragione'ria [radʒone'ria] *sf* accountancy; accounts department
ragio'nevole [radʒo'nevole] *ag* reasonable
ragioni'ere, -a [radʒo'njɛre] *sm/f* accountant
ragli'are [raʎ'ʎare] *vi* to bray
ragna'tela [raɲɲa'tela] *sf* cobweb, spider's web
'ragno ['raɲɲo] *sm* spider
ragù *sm inv* (*Cuc*) meat sauce; stew
RAI-TV [raiti'vu] *sigla f* = **Radio televisione italiana**
ralle'grare *vt* to cheer up; **rallegrarsi** *vpr*

to cheer up; (*provare allegrezza*) to rejoice; **rallegrarsi con qn** to congratulate sb
rallen'tare *vt* to slow down; (*fig*) to lessen, slacken ▷ *vi* to slow down
rallenta'tore *sm* (*Cinema*) slow-motion camera; **al ~** (*anche fig*) in slow motion
raman'zina [raman'dzina] *sf* lecture, telling-off
'rame *sm* (*Chim*) copper
rammari'carsi *vpr* **~ (di)** (*rincrescersi*) to be sorry (about), regret; (*lamentarsi*) to complain (about)
rammen'dare *vt* to mend; (*calza*) to darn
'ramo *sm* branch
ramo'scello [ramoʃ'ʃello] *sm* twig
'rampa *sf* flight (of stairs); **rampa di lancio** launching pad
rampi'cante *ag* (*Bot*) climbing
'rana *sf* frog
'rancido, -a ['rantʃido] *ag* rancid
ran'core *sm* rancour, resentment
ran'dagio, -a, -gi, -gie *o* **ge** [ran'dadʒo] *ag* (*gatto, cane*) stray
ran'dello *sm* club, cudgel
'rango, -ghi *sm* (*condizione sociale, Mil, riga*) rank
rannicchi'arsi [rannik'kjarsi] *vpr* to crouch, huddle
rannuvo'larsi *vpr* to cloud over, become overcast
'rapa *sf* (*Bot*) turnip
ra'pace [ra'patʃe] *ag* (*animale*) predatory; (*fig*) rapacious, grasping ▷ *sm* bird of prey
ra'pare *vt* (*capelli*) to crop, cut very short
rapida'mente *av* quickly, rapidly
rapidità *sf* speed
'rapido, -a *ag* fast; (*esame, occhiata*) quick, rapid ▷ *sm* (*Ferr*) express (train)
rapi'mento *sm* kidnapping; (*fig*) rapture
ra'pina *sf* robbery; **rapina in banca** bank robbery; **rapina a mano armata** armed robbery; **rapi'nare** *vt* to rob; **rapina'tore, -'trice** *sm/f* robber
ra'pire *vt* (*cose*) to steal; (*persone*) to kidnap; (*fig*) to enrapture, delight; **rapi'tore, -'trice** *sm/f* kidnapper
rap'porto *sm* (*resoconto*) report; (*legame*) relationship; (*Mat, Tecn*) ratio; **rapporti sessuali** sexual intercourse *sg*
rappre'saglia [rappre'saʎʎa] *sf* reprisal, retaliation
rappresen'tante *sm/f* representative
rappresen'tare *vt* to represent; (*Teatro*) to perform; **rappresentazi'one** *sf* representation; performing *no pl*; (*spettacolo*) performance
rara'mente *av* seldom, rarely
rare'fatto, -a *ag* rarefied
'raro, -a *ag* rare

r

ra'sare vt (barba ecc) to shave off; (siepi, erba) to trim, cut; **rasarsi** vpr to shave (o.s.)

raschi'are [ras'kjare] vt to scrape; (macchia, fango) to scrape off ▷ vi to clear one's throat

ra'sente prep **~ (a)** close to, very near

'raso, -a pp di **radere** ▷ ag (barba) shaved; (capelli) cropped; (con misure di capacità) level; (pieno: bicchiere) full to the brim ▷ sm (tessuto) satin; **un cucchiaio ~** a level spoonful; **raso terra** close to the ground

ra'soio sm razor; **rasoio elettrico** electric shaver o razor

ras'segna [ras'seɲɲa] sf (Mil) inspection, review; (esame) inspection; (resoconto) review, survey; (pubblicazione letteraria ecc) review; (mostra) exhibition, show; **passare in ~** (Mil, fig) to review

rassegnarsi vpr (accettare): **~ (a qc/a fare)** to resign o.s. (to sth/to doing)

rassicu'rare vt to reassure

rasso'dare vt to harden, stiffen; **rassodarsi** vpr to harden, to strengthen

rassomigli'anza [rassomiʎ'ʎantsa] sf resemblance

rassomigli'are [rassomiʎ'ʎare] vi **~ a** to resemble, look like

rastrel'lare vt to rake; (fig: perlustrare) to comb

ras'trello sm rake

'rata sf (quota) instalment; **pagare a rate** to pay by instalments o on hire purchase (BRIT)

ratifi'care vt (Dir) to ratify

'ratto sm (Dir) abduction; (Zool) rat

rattop'pare vt to patch

rattris'tare vt to sadden; **rattristarsi** vpr to become sad

'rauco, -a, -chi, -che ag hoarse

rava'nello sm radish

ravi'oli smpl ravioli sg

ravvi'vare vt to revive; (fig) to brighten up, enliven

razio'nale [rattsjo'nale] ag rational

razio'nare [rattsjo'nare] vt to ration

razi'one [rat'tsjone] sf ration; (porzione) portion, share

'razza ['rattsa] sf race; (Zool) breed; (discendenza, stirpe) stock, race; (sorta) sort, kind

razzi'ale [rat'tsjale] ag racial

raz'zismo [rat'tsizmo] sm racism, racialism

raz'zista, -i, -e [rat'tsista] ag, sm/f racist, racialist

'razzo ['raddzo] sm rocket

R.C. sigla m (= partito della Rifondazione Comunista) left-wing Italian political party

re sm inv king; (Mus) D; (: solfeggiando) re

rea'gire [rea'dʒire] vi to react

re'ale ag real; (di, da re) royal ▷ sm **il ~** reality

realiz'zare [realid'dzare] vt (progetto ecc) to realize, carry out; (sogno, desiderio) to realize, fulfil; (scopo) to achieve; (Comm: titoli ecc) to realize; (Calcio ecc) to score; **realizzarsi** vpr to be realized

real'mente av really, actually

realtà sf inv reality

re'ato sm offence

reat'tore sm (Fisica) reactor; (Aer: aereo) jet; (: motore) jet engine

reazio'nario, -a [reattsjo'narjo] ag (Pol) reactionary

reazi'one [reat'tsjone] sf reaction

'rebus sm inv rebus; (fig) puzzle; enigma

recapi'tare vt to deliver

re'capito sm (indirizzo) address; (consegna) delivery; **recapito a domicilio** home delivery (service); **recapito telefonico** phone number

re'cedere [re'tʃɛdere] vi to withdraw

recensi'one [retʃen'sjone] sf review

re'cente [re'tʃɛnte] ag recent; **di ~** recently; **recente'mente** av recently

re'cidere [re'tʃidere] vt to cut off, chop off

recin'tare [retʃin'tare] vt to enclose, fence off

re'cinto [re'tʃinto] sm enclosure; (ciò che recinge) fence; surrounding wall

recipi'ente [retʃi'pjɛnte] sm container

re'ciproco, -a, -ci, -che [re'tʃiproko] ag reciprocal

'recita ['rɛtʃita] sf performance

reci'tare [retʃi'tare] vt (poesia, lezione) to recite; (dramma) to perform; (ruolo) to play o act (the part of)

recla'mare vi to complain ▷ vt (richiedere) to demand

re'clamo sm complaint

recli'nabile ag (sedile) reclining

reclusi'one sf (Dir) imprisonment

re'cluta sf recruit

re'condito, -a ag secluded; (fig) secret, hidden

'record ag inv record cpd ▷ sm inv record; **in tempo ~, a tempo di ~** in record time; **detenere il ~ di** to hold the record for; **record mondiale** world record

recriminazi'one [rekriminat'tsjone] sf recrimination

recupe'rare vt (rientrare in possesso di) to recover, get back; (tempo perduto) to make up for; (Naut) to salvage; (: naufraghi) to rescue; (delinquente) to rehabilitate; **~ lo svantaggio** (Sport) to close the gap

redargu'ire vt to rebuke

re'dassi *ecc vb vedi* **redigere**
reddi'tizio, -a [reddi'tittsjo] *ag* profitable
'reddito *sm* income; (*dello Stato*) revenue;
(*di un capitale*) yield
re'digere [re'didʒere] *vt* to write;
(*contratto*) to draw up
'redini *sfpl* reins
'reduce ['rɛdutʃe] *ag* ~ **da** returning from,
back from ▷ *sm/f* survivor
refe'rendum *sm inv* referendum
referenze [refe'rɛntse] *sfpl* references
re'ferto *sm* medical report
rega'lare *vt* to give (as a present), make a
present of
re'galo *sm* gift, present
re'gata *sf* regatta
'reggere ['rɛddʒere] *vt* (*tenere*) to hold;
(*sostenere*) to support, bear, hold up;
(*portare*) to carry, bear; (*resistere*) to
withstand; (*dirigere: impresa*) to manage,
run; (*governare*) to rule, govern; (*Ling*) to
take, be followed by ▷ *vi* (*resistere*): ~ **a** to
stand up to, hold out against; (*sopportare*):
~ **a** to stand; (*durare*) to last; (*fig: teoria ecc*)
to hold water; **reggersi** *vpr* (*stare ritto*)
to stand
'reggia, -ge ['rɛddʒa] *sf* royal palace
reggi'calze [reddʒi'kaltse] *sm inv*
suspender belt
reggi'mento [reddʒi'mento] *sm* (*Mil*)
regiment
reggi'seno [reddʒi'seno] *sm* bra
re'gia, -'gie [re'dʒia] *sf* (*TV, Cinema ecc*)
direction
re'gime [re'dʒime] *sm* (*Pol*) regime; (*Dir:
aureo, patrimoniale ecc*) system; (*Med*) diet;
(*Tecn*) (engine) speed
re'gina [re'dʒina] *sf* queen
regio'nale [redʒo'nale] *ag* regional ▷ *sm*
local train (*stopping frequently*)
regi'one [re'dʒone] *sf* region; (*territorio*)
region, district, area
re'gista, -i, -e [re'dʒista] *sm/f* (*TV, Cinema
ecc*) director
regis'trare [redʒis'trare] *vt* (*Amm*) to
register; (*Comm*) to enter; (*notare*) to note,
take note of; (*canzone, conversazione:
strumento di misura*) to record; (*mettere
a punto*) to adjust, regulate; (*bagagli*) to
check in; **registra'tore** *sm* (*strumento*)
recorder, register; (*magnetofono*) tape
recorder; **registratore di cassa** cash
register; **registratore a cassette** cassette
recorder
re'gistro [re'dʒistro] *sm* (*libro, Mus, Tech*)
register; ledger; logbook; (*Dir*) registry
re'gnare [reɲ'ɲare] *vi* to reign, rule
'regno ['reɲɲo] *sm* kingdom; (*periodo*)
reign; (*fig*) realm; **il R~ Unito** the United

Kingdom; **regno animale/vegetale**
animal/vegetable kingdom
'regola *sf* rule; **a ~ d'arte** duly; perfectly;
in ~ in order
rego'labile *ag* adjustable
regola'mento *sm* (*complesso di norme*)
regulations *pl*; (*di debito*) settlement;
regolamento di conti (*fig*) settling of
scores
rego'lare *ag* regular; (*in regola: domanda*)
in order, lawful ▷ *vt* to regulate, control;
(*apparecchio*) to adjust, regulate; (*questione,
conto, debito*) to settle; **regolarsi** *vpr*
(*moderarsi*): **regolarsi nel bere/nello
spendere** to control one's drinking/
spending; (*comportarsi*) to behave, act
rela'tivo, -a *ag* relative
relazi'one [relat'sjone] *sf* (*fra cose,
persone*) relation(ship); (*resoconto*) report,
account
rele'gare *vt* to banish; (*fig*) to relegate
religi'one [reli'dʒone] *sf* religion
re'liquia *sf* relic
re'litto *sm* wreck; (*fig*) down-and-out
re'mare *vi* to row
remini'scenze [reminiʃ'ʃentse] *sfpl*
reminiscences
remis'sivo, -a *ag* submissive, compliant
'remo *sm* oar
re'moto, -a *ag* remote
'rendere *vt* (*ridare*) to return, give back;
(: *saluto ecc*) to return; (*produrre*) to yield,
bring in; (*esprimere, tradurre*) to render; ~ **qc
possibile** to make sth possible; **rendersi**
vpr **rendersi utile** to make o.s. useful;
rendersi conto di qc to realize sth; ~ **qc
possibile** to make sth possible; ~ **grazie
a qn** give thanks to sb; ~ **omaggio a qn**
to pay homage to sb; ~ **un servizio a qn**
to do sb a service; ~ **una testimonianza**
to give evidence; **non so se rendo l'idea** I
don't know if I'm making myself clear
rendi'mento *sm* (*reddito*) yield; (*di
manodopera, Tecn*) efficiency; (*capacità di
produrre*) output; (*di studenti*) performance
'rendita *sf* (*di individuo*) private *o* unearned
income; (*Comm*) revenue; **rendita annua**
annuity
'rene *sm* kidney
'renna *sf* reindeer *inv*
re'parto *sm* department, section; (*Mil*)
detachment
repel'lente *ag* repulsive
repen'taglio [repen'taʎʎo] *sm* **mettere a
~** to jeopardize, risk
repen'tino, -a *ag* sudden, unexpected
reper'torio *sm* (*Teatro*) repertory; (*elenco*)
index, (alphabetical) list
'replica, -che *sf* repetition; reply, answer;

replicare | 150

(*obiezione*) objection; (*Teatro, Cinema*) repeat performance; (*copia*) replica

repli'care *vt* (*ripetere*) to repeat; (*rispondere*) to answer, reply

repressi'one *sf* repression

re'presso, -a *pp di* **reprimere**

re'primere *vt* to suppress, repress

re'pubblica, -che *sf* republic

reputazi'one [reputat'tsjone] *sf* reputation

requi'sire *vt* to requisition

requi'sito *sm* requirement

'resa *sf* (*l'arrendersi*) surrender; (*restituzione, rendimento*) return; **resa dei conti** rendering of accounts; (*fig*) day of reckoning

'resi *ecc vb vedi* **rendere**

resi'dente *ag* resident; **residenzi'ale** *ag* residential

re'siduo, -a *ag* residual, remaining ▷ *sm* remainder; (*Chim*) residue

'resina *sf* resin

resis'tente *ag* (*che resiste*): **~ a** resistant to; (*forte*) strong; (*duraturo*) long-lasting, durable; **~ al caldo** heat-resistant; **resis'tenza** *sf* resistance; (*di persona: fisica*) stamina, endurance; (*: mentale*) endurance, resistance

● **RESISTENZA**
●
● The **Resistenza** in Italy fought against
● the Nazis and the Fascists during the
● Second World War. Members of the
● **Resistenza** spanned a wide political
● spectrum and played a vital role in the
● Liberation and in the formation of the
● new democratic government at the end
● of the war.

re'sistere *vi* to resist; **~ a** (*assalto, tentazioni*) to resist; (*dolore: pianta*) to withstand; (*non patir danno*) to be resistant to

reso'conto *sm* report, account

res'pingere [res'pindʒere] *vt* to drive back, repel; (*rifiutare*) to reject; (*Ins: bocciare*) to fail

respi'rare *vi* to breathe; (*fig*) to get one's breath; to breathe again ▷ *vt* to breathe (in), inhale; **respirazi'one** *sf* breathing; **respirazione artificiale** artificial respiration; **res'piro** *sm* breathing *no pl*; (*singolo atto*) breath; (*fig*) respite, rest; **mandare un respiro di sollievo** to give a sigh of relief

respon'sabile *ag* responsible ▷ *sm/f* person responsible; (*capo*) person in charge; **~ di** responsible for; (*Dir*) liable

for; **responsabilità** *sf inv* responsibility; (*legale*) liability

res'ponso *sm* answer

'ressa *sf* crowd, throng

'ressi *ecc vb vedi* **reggere**

res'tare *vi* (*rimanere*) to remain, stay; (*avanzare*) to be left, remain; **~ orfano/cieco** to become o be left an orphan/become blind; **~ d'accordo** to agree; **non resta più niente** there's nothing left; **restano pochi giorni** there are only a few days left

restau'rare *vt* to restore

res'tio, -a, -'tii, -'tie *ag* **~ a** reluctant to

restitu'ire *vt* to return, give back; (*energie, forze*) to restore

'resto *sm* remainder, rest; (*denaro*) change; (*Mat*) remainder; **resti** *smpl* (*di cibo*) leftovers; (*di città*) remains; **del ~** moreover, besides; **tenga pure il ~** keep the change; **resti mortali** (mortal) remains

res'tringere [res'trindʒere] *vt* to reduce; (*vestito*) to take in; (*stoffa*) to shrink; (*fig*) to restrict, limit; **restringersi** *vpr* (*strada*) to narrow; (*stoffa*) to shrink

'rete *sf* net; (*fig*) trap, snare; (*di recinzione*) wire netting; (*Aut, Ferr, di spionaggio ecc*) network; **segnare una ~** (*Calcio*) to score a goal; **la R~** the Web; **rete ferroviaria** railway network; **rete del letto** (sprung) bed base; **rete stradale** road network; **rete (televisiva)** (*sistema*) network; (*canale*) channel

reti'cente [reti'tʃɛnte] *ag* reticent

retico'lato *sm* grid; (*rete*) wire netting; (*di filo spinato*) barbed wire (fence)

'retina *sf* (*Anat*) retina

re'torico, -a, -ci, -che *ag* rhetorical

retribu'ire *vt* to pay

'retro *sm inv* back ▷ *av* (*dietro*): **vedi ~** see over(leaf)

retro'cedere [retro'tʃɛdere] *vi* to withdraw ▷ *vt* (*Calcio*) to relegate; (*Mil*) to degrade

re'trogrado, -a *ag* (*fig*) reactionary, backward-looking

retro'marcia [retro'martʃa] *sf* (*Aut*) reverse; (*: dispositivo*) reverse gear

retro'scena [retroʃ'ʃena] *sm inv* (*Teatro*) backstage; **i ~** (*fig*) the behind-the-scenes activities

retrovi'sore *sm* (*Aut*) (rear-view) mirror

'retta *sf* (*Mat*) straight line; (*di convitto*) charge for bed and board; (*fig: ascolto*): **dar ~ a** to listen to, pay attention to

rettango'lare *ag* rectangular

ret'tangolo, -a *ag* right-angled ▷ *sm* rectangle

ret'tifica, -che *sf* rectification, correction
'rettile *sm* reptile
retti'lineo, -a *ag* rectilinear
'retto, -a *pp di* **reggere** ▷ *ag* straight;
(*Mat*): **angolo ~** right angle; (*onesto*)
honest, upright; (*giusto, esatto*) correct,
proper, right
ret'tore *sm* (*Rel*) rector; (*di università*)
≈ chancellor
reuma'tismo *sm* rheumatism
revisi'one *sf* auditing *no pl*; audit;
servicing *no pl*; overhaul; review; revision;
revisione di bozze proofreading
revi'sore *sm*; **revisore di bozze**
proofreader; **revisore di conti** auditor
revival [ri'vaivəl] *sm inv* revival
'revoca *sf* revocation
revo'care *vt* to revoke
re'volver *sm inv* revolver
ri'abbia *ecc vb vedi* **riavere**
riabili'tare *vt* to rehabilitate
rianimazi'one [rianimat'tsjone] *sf* (*Med*)
resuscitation; **centro di ~** intensive care
unit
ria'prire *vt* to reopen, open again;
riaprirsi *vpr* to reopen, open again
ri'armo *sm* (*Mil*) rearmament
rias'sumere *vt* (*riprendere*) to resume;
(*impiegare di nuovo*) to re-employ;
(*sintetizzare*) to summarize; **rias'sunto, -a**
pp di **riassumere** ▷ *sm* summary
riattac'care *vt* (*attaccare di nuovo*): **~ (a)**
(*manifesto, francobollo*) to stick back (on);
(*bottone*) to sew back (on); (*quadro, chiavi*)
to hang back up (on); **~ (il telefono** *o* **il
ricevitore)** to hang up (the receiver)
ria'vere *vt* to have again; (*avere indietro*) to
get back; (*riacquistare*) to recover; **riaversi**
vpr to recover
riba'dire *vt* (*fig*) to confirm
ri'balta *sf* flap; (*Teatro: proscenio*) front
of the stage; (*fig*) limelight; **luci della ~**
footlights *pl*
ribal'tabile *ag* (*sedile*) tip-up
ribal'tare *vt, vi* (*anche:* **ribaltarsi**) to turn
over, tip over
ribas'sare *vt* to lower, bring down ▷ *vi* to
come down, fall
ri'battere *vt* to return, hit back; (*confutare*)
to refute; **~ che** to retort that
ribel'larsi *vpr* **~ (a)** to rebel (against);
ri'belle *ag* (*soldati*) rebel; (*ragazzo*)
rebellious ▷ *sm/f* rebel
'ribes *sm inv* currant; **ribes nero**
blackcurrant; **ribes rosso** redcurrant
ri'brezzo [ri'breddzo] *sm* disgust,
loathing; **far ~ a** to disgust
ribut'tante *ag* disgusting, revolting
rica'dere *vi* to fall again; (*scendere a terra:*

fig: nel peccato ecc) to fall back; (*vestiti,
capelli ecc*) to hang (down); (*riversarsi:
fatiche, colpe*): **~ su** to fall on; **rica'duta** *sf*
(*Med*) relapse
rica'mare *vt* to embroider
ricambi'are *vt* to change again;
(*contraccambiare*) to repay, return;
ri'cambio *sm* exchange, return; (*Fisiol*)
metabolism
ri'camo *sm* embroidery
ricapito'lare *vt* to recapitulate, sum up
ricari'care *vt* (*arma, macchina fotografica*)
to reload; (*pipa*) to refill; (*orologio*) to
rewind; (*batteria*) to recharge
ricat'tare *vt* to blackmail; **ri'catto** *sm*
blackmail
rica'vare *vt* (*estrarre*) to draw out, extract;
(*ottenere*) to obtain, gain
ric'chezza [rik'kettsa] *sf* wealth; (*fig*)
richness
'riccio, -a ['rittʃo] *ag* curly ▷ *sm* (*Zool*)
hedgehog; **riccio di mare** sea urchin;
'ricciolo *sm* curl
'ricco, -a, -chi, -che *ag* rich; (*persona,
paese*) rich, wealthy ▷ *sm/f* rich man/
woman; **i ricchi** the rich; **~ di** full of; rich in
ri'cerca, -che [ri'tʃerka] *sf* search;
(*indagine*) investigation, inquiry; (*studio*):
la ~ research; **una ~** piece of research;
ricerca di mercato market research
ricer'care [ritʃer'kare] *vt* (*motivi, cause*)
to look for, try to determine; (*successo,
piacere*) to pursue; (*onore, gloria*) to seek;
ricer'cato, -a *ag* (*apprezzato*) much
sought-after; (*affettato*) studied, affected
▷ *sm/f* (*Polizia*) wanted man/woman
ricerca'tore, -'trice [ritʃerka'tore] *sm/f*
(*Ins*) researcher
ri'cetta [ri'tʃetta] *sf* (*Med*) prescription;
(*Cuc*) recipe; **mi può fare una ~ medica?**
could you write me a prescription?
ricettazi'one [ritʃettat'tsjone] *sf* (*Dir*)
receiving (stolen goods)
ri'cevere [ri'tʃevere] *vt* to receive;
(*stipendio, lettera*) to get, receive;
(*accogliere: ospite*) to welcome; (*vedere:
cliente, rappresentante ecc*) to see;
ricevi'mento *sm* receiving *no pl*; (*festa*)
reception; **ricevi'tore** *sm* (*Tecn*) receiver;
rice'vuta *sf* receipt; **posso avere una
ricevuta, per favore?** can I have a receipt,
please?; **ricevuta fiscale** receipt for tax
purposes; **ricevuta di ritorno** (*Posta*)
advice of receipt
richia'mare [rikja'mare] *vt* (*chiamare
indietro, ritelefonare*) to call back;
(*ambasciatore, truppe*) to recall;
(*rimproverare*) to reprimand; (*attirare*) to
attract, draw; **può ~ più tardi?** can you

call back later?; **richiamarsi a** (*riferirsi a*) to refer to

richi'edere [ri'kjɛdere] *vt* to ask again for; (*chiedere indietro*): **~ qc** to ask for sth back; (*chiedere: per sapere*) to ask; (: *per avere*) to ask for; (*Amm: documenti*) to apply for; (*esigere*) to need, require; **richi'esta** *sf* (*domanda*) request; (*Amm*) application, request; (*esigenza*) demand, request; **a richiesta** on request

rici'clare [ritʃi'klare] *vt* to recycle

'ricino ['ritʃino] *sm* **olio di ~** castor oil

ricognizi'one [rikoɲɲi'tsjone] *sf* (*Mil*) reconnaissance; (*Dir*) recognition, acknowledgement

ricominci'are [rikomin'tʃare] *vt*, *vi* to start again, begin again

ricom'pensa *sf* reward

ricompen'sare *vt* to reward

riconciliarsi *vpr* to be reconciled

ricono'scente [rikonoʃ'ʃɛnte] *ag* grateful

rico'noscere [riko'noʃʃere] *vt* to recognize; (*Dir: figlio, debito*) to acknowledge; (*ammettere: errore*) to admit, acknowledge

rico'perto, -a *pp di* **ricoprire**

ricopi'are *vt* to copy

rico'prire *vt* (*coprire*) to cover; (*occupare: carica*) to hold

ricor'dare *vt* to remember, recall; (*richiamare alla memoria*): **~ qc a qn** to remind sb of sth; **ricordarsi** *vpr* **ricordarsi (di)** to remember; **ricordarsi di qc/di aver fatto** to remember sth/having done

ri'cordo *sm* memory; (*regalo*) keepsake, souvenir; (*di viaggio*) souvenir

ricor'rente *ag* recurrent, recurring; **ricor'renza** *sf* recurrence; (*festività*) anniversary

ri'correre *vi* (*ripetersi*) to recur; **~ a** (*rivolgersi*) to turn to; (: *Dir*) to appeal to; (*servirsi di*) to have recourse to

ricostitu'ente *ag* (*Med*): **cura ~** tonic

ricostru'ire *vt* (*casa*) to rebuild; (*fatti*) to reconstruct

ri'cotta *sf soft white unsalted cheese made from sheep's milk*

ricove'rare *vt* to give shelter to; **~ qn in ospedale** to admit sb to hospital

ri'covero *sm* shelter, refuge; (*Mil*) shelter; (*Med*) admission (to hospital)

ricreazi'one [rikreat'tsjone] *sf* recreation, entertainment; (*Ins*) break

ri'credersi *vpr* to change one's mind

ridacchi'are [ridak'kjare] *vi* to snigger

ri'dare *vt* to return, give back

'ridere *vi* to laugh; (*deridere, beffare*): **~ di** to laugh at, make fun of

ri'dicolo, -a *ag* ridiculous, absurd

ridimensio'nare *vt* to reorganize; (*fig*) to see in the right perspective

ri'dire *vt* to repeat; (*criticare*) to find fault with; to object to; **trova sempre qualcosa da ~** he always manages to find fault

ridon'dante *ag* redundant

ri'dotto, -a *pp di* **ridurre** ▷ *ag* (*biglietto*) reduced; (*formato*) small

ri'duco *ecc vb vedi* **ridurre**

ri'durre *vt* (*anche Chim, Mat*) to reduce; (*prezzo, spese*) to cut, reduce; (*accorciare: opera letteraria*) to abridge; (: *Radio, TV*) to adapt; **ridursi** *vpr* (*diminuirsi*) to be reduced, shrink; **ridursi a** to be reduced to; **ridursi pelle e ossa** to be reduced to skin and bone; **ri'dussi** *ecc vb vedi* **ridurre**; **ridut'tore** *sm* (*Elec*) adaptor; **riduzi'one** *sf* reduction; abridgement; adaptation; **ci sono riduzioni per i bambini/gli studenti?** is there a reduction for children/students?

ri'ebbi *ecc vb vedi* **riavere**

riem'pire *vt* to fill (up); (*modulo*) to fill in o out; **riempirsi** *vpr* to fill (up); **~ qc di** to fill sth (up) with

rien'tranza [rien'trantsa] *sf* recess; indentation

rien'trare *vi* (*entrare di nuovo*) to go (o come) back in; (*tornare*) to return; (*fare una rientranza*) to go in, curve inwards; to be indented; (*riguardare*) **~ in** to be included among, form part of

riepilo'gare *vt* to summarize ▷ *vi* to recapitulate

ri'esco *ecc vb vedi* **riuscire**

ri'fare *vt* to do again; (*ricostruire*) to make again; (*nodo*) to tie again, do up again; (*imitare*) to imitate, copy; **rifarsi** *vpr* (*risarcirsi*): **rifarsi di** to make up for; (*vendicarsi*): **rifarsi di qc su qn** to get one's own back on sb for sth; (*riferirsi*): **rifarsi a** to go back to; to follow; **~ il letto** to make the bed; **rifarsi una vita** to make a new life for o.s.

riferi'mento *sm* reference; **in** o **con ~ a** with reference to

rife'rire *vt* (*riportare*) to report ▷ *vi* to do a report; **riferirsi** *vpr* **riferirsi a** to refer to

rifi'nire *vt* to finish off, put the finishing touches to

rifiu'tare *vt* to refuse; **~ di fare** to refuse to do; **rifi'uto** *sm* refusal; **rifiuti** *smpl* (*spazzatura*) rubbish *sg*, refuse *sg*

riflessi'one *sf* (*Fisica, meditazione*) reflection; (*il pensare*) thought, reflection; (*osservazione*) remark

rifles'sivo, -a *ag* (*persona*) thoughtful, reflective; (*Ling*) reflexive

ri'flesso, -a *pp di* **riflettere** ▷ *sm* (*di luce, allo specchio*) reflection; (*Fisiol*) reflex; **di o per ~** indirectly

riflessologia [riflessolo'dʒia] *sf* reflexology

ri'flettere *vt* to reflect ▷ *vi* to think; **riflettersi** *vpr* to be reflected; **~ su** to think over

riflet'tore *sm* reflector; (*proiettore*) floodlight; searchlight

ri'flusso *sm* flowing back; (*della marea*) ebb; **un'epoca di ~** an era of nostalgia

ri'forma *sf* reform; **la R~** (*Rel*) the Reformation

riforma'torio *sm* (*Dir*) community home (*BRIT*), reformatory (*US*)

riforni'mento *sm* supplying, providing; restocking; **rifornimenti** *smpl* (*provviste*) supplies, provisions

rifor'nire *vt* (*provvedere*): **~ di** to supply o provide with; (*fornire di nuovo: casa ecc*) to restock; **rifornirsi** *vpr* **rifornirsi di qc** to stock up on sth

rifugi'arsi [rifu'dʒarsi] *vpr* to take refuge; **rifugi'ato, -a** *sm/f* refugee

ri'fugio [ri'fudʒo] *sm* refuge, shelter; (*in montagna*) shelter; **rifugio antiaereo** air-raid shelter

'riga, -ghe *sf* line; (*striscia*) stripe; (*di persone, cose*) line, row; (*regolo*) ruler; (*scriminatura*) parting; **mettersi in ~** to line up; **a righe** (*foglio*) lined; (*vestito*) striped

ri'gare *vt* (*foglio*) to rule ▷ *vi* **~ diritto** (*fig*) to toe the line

rigatti'ere *sm* junk dealer

righerò *ecc* [rige'rɔ] *vb vedi* **rigare**

'rigido, -a ['ridʒido] *ag* rigid, stiff; (*membra ecc: indurite*) stiff; (*Meteor*) harsh, severe; (*fig*) strict

rigogli'oso, -a [rigoʎ'ʎoso] *ag* (*pianta*) luxuriant; (*fig: commercio, sviluppo*) thriving

ri'gore *sm* (*Meteor*) harshness, rigours *pl*; (*fig*) severity, strictness; (*anche: **calcio di ~***) penalty; **di ~** compulsory; **a rigor di termini** strictly speaking

riguar'dare *vt* to look at again; (*considerare*) to regard, consider; (*concernere*) to regard, concern; **riguardarsi** *vpr* (*aver cura di sé*) to look after o.s.

rigu'ardo *sm* (*attenzione*) care; (*considerazione*) regard, respect; **~ a** concerning, with regard to; **non aver riguardi nell'agire/nel parlare** to act/speak freely

rilasci'are [rilaʃ'ʃare] *vt* (*rimettere in libertà*) to release; (*Amm: documenti*) to issue

rilassarsi *vpr* to relax; (*fig: disciplina*) to become slack

rile'gare *vt* (*libro*) to bind

ri'leggere [ri'lɛddʒere] *vt* to reread, read again; (*rivedere*) to read over

ri'lento: a ~ *av* slowly

rile'vante *ag* considerable; important

rile'vare *vt* (*ricavare*) to find; (*notare*) to notice; (*mettere in evidenza*) to point out; (*venire a conoscere: notizia*) to learn; (*raccogliere: dati*) to gather, collect; (*Topografia*) to survey; (*Mil*) to relieve; (*Comm*) to take over

rili'evo *sm* (*Arte, Geo*) relief; (*fig: rilevanza*) importance; (*Topografia*) survey; **dar ~ a** o **mettere in ~ qc** (*fig*) to bring sth out, highlight sth

rilut'tante *ag* reluctant

'rima *sf* rhyme; (*verso*) verse

riman'dare *vt* to send again; (*restituire, rinviare*) to send back, return; (*differire*): **~ qc (a)** to postpone sth o put sth off (till); (*fare riferimento*): **~ qn a** to refer sb to; **essere rimandato** (*Ins*) to have to repeat one's exams

ri'mando *sm* (*rinvio*) return; (*dilazione*) postponement; (*riferimento*) cross-reference

rima'nente *ag* remaining ▷ *sm* rest, remainder; **i rimanenti** (*persone*) the rest of them, the others

rima'nere *vi* (*restare*) to remain, stay; (*avanzare*) to be left, remain; (*restare stupito*) to be amazed; (*restare, mancare*): **rimangono poche settimane a Pasqua** there are only a few weeks left till Easter; **rimane da vedere se** it remains to be seen whether; (*diventare*): **~ vedovo** to be left a widower; (*trovarsi*): **~ sorpreso** to be surprised

rimangi'are [riman'dʒare] *vt* to eat again; **~rsi la parola/una promessa** (*fig*) to go back on one's word/one's promise

ri'mango *ecc vb vedi* **rimanere**

rimargi'narsi *vpr* to heal

rimbal'zare [rimbal'tsare] *vi* to bounce back, rebound; (*proiettile*) to ricochet

rimbam'bito, -a *ag* senile, in one's dotage

rimboc'care *vt* (*coperta*) to tuck in; (*maniche, pantaloni*) to turn o roll up

rimbom'bare *vi* to resound

rimbor'sare *vt* to pay back, repay

rimedi'are *vi* **~ a** to remedy ▷ *vt* (*fam: procurarsi*) to get o scrape together

ri'medio *sm* (*medicina*) medicine; (*cura, fig*) remedy, cure

ri'mettere *vt* (*mettere di nuovo*) to put back; (*indossare di nuovo*): **~ qc** to put sth back on, put sth on again; (*affidare*) to entrust; (*: decisione*) to refer; (*condonare*) to remit; (*Comm: merci*) to deliver; (*: denaro*)

r

to remit; (*vomitare*) to bring up; (*perdere: anche*: **rimetterci**) to lose; **rimettersi al bello** (*tempo*) to clear up; **rimettersi in salute** to get better, recover one's health

ri'misi *ecc vb vedi* **rimettere**

'rimmel® *sm inv* mascara

rimoder'nare *vt* to modernize

rimorchi'are [rimor'kjare] *vt* to tow; (*fig: ragazza*) to pick up

ri'morchio [ri'mɔrkjo] *sm* tow; (*veicolo*) trailer

ri'morso *sm* remorse

rimozi'one [rimot'tsjone] *sf* removal; (*da un impiego*) dismissal; (*Psic*) repression

rimpatri'are *vi* to return home ▷ *vt* to repatriate

rimpi'angere [rim'pjandʒere] *vt* to regret; (*persona*) to miss; **rimpi'anto, -a** *pp di* **rimpiangere** ▷ *sm* regret

rimpiaz'zare [rimpjat'tsare] *vt* to replace

rimpiccio'lire [rimpittʃo'lire] *vt* to make smaller ▷ *vi* (*anche*: **rimpicciolirsi**) to become smaller

rimpinzarsi [rimpin'tsarsi] *vpr* ~ **(di qc)** to stuff o.s. (with sth)

rimprove'rare *vt* to rebuke, reprimand

rimu'overe *vt* to remove; (*destituire*) to dismiss

Rinasci'mento [rinaʃʃi'mento] *sm* **il** ~ the Renaissance

ri'nascita [ri'naʃʃita] *sf* rebirth, revival

rinca'rare *vt* to increase the price of ▷ *vi* to go up, become more expensive

rinca'sare *vi* to go home

rinchi'udere [rin'kjudere] *vt* to shut (*o* lock) up; **rinchiudersi** *vpr* **rinchiudersi in** to shut o.s. up in; **rinchiudersi in se stesso** to withdraw into o.s.

rin'correre *vt* to chase, run after; **rin'corsa** *sf* short run

rin'crescere [rin'kreʃʃere] *vb impers* **mi rincresce che/di non poter fare** I'm sorry that/I can't do, I regret that/being unable to do

rinfacci'are [rinfat'tʃare] *vt* (*fig*): ~ **qc a qn** to throw sth in sb's face

rinfor'zare [rinfor'tsare] *vt* to reinforce, strengthen ▷ *vi* (*anche*: **rinforzarsi**) to grow stronger

rinfres'care *vt* (*atmosfera, temperatura*) to cool (down); (*abito, pareti*) to freshen up ▷ *vi* (*tempo*) to grow cooler; **rinfrescarsi** *vpr* (*ristorarsi*) to refresh o.s.; (*lavarsi*) to freshen up; **rin'fresco, -schi** *sm* (*festa*) party; **rinfreschi** *smpl* refreshments

rin'fusa *sf* **alla** ~ in confusion, higgledy-piggledy

ringhi'are [rin'gjare] *vi* to growl, snarl

ringhi'era [rin'gjɛra] *sf* railing; (*delle scale*) banister(s) (*pl*)

ringiova'nire [rindʒova'nire] *vt* (*vestito, acconciatura ecc*): ~ **qn** to make sb look younger; (: *vacanze ecc*) to rejuvenate ▷ *vi* (*anche*: **ringiovanirsi**) to become (*o* look) younger

ringrazia'mento [ringrattsja'mento] *sm* thanks *pl*

ringrazi'are [ringrat'tsjare] *vt* to thank; ~ **qn di qc** to thank sb for sth

rinne'gare *vt* (*fede*) to renounce; (*figlio*) to disown, repudiate

rinnova'mento *sm* renewal; (*economico*) revival

rinno'vare *vt* to renew; (*ripetere*) to repeat, renew

rinoce'ronte [rinotʃe'ronte] *sm* rhinoceros

rino'mato, -a *ag* renowned, celebrated

rintracci'are [rintrat'tʃare] *vt* to track down

rintro'nare *vi* to boom, roar ▷ *vt* (*assordare*) to deafen; (*stordire*) to stun

rinunci'are [rinun'tʃare] *vi* ~ **a** to give up, renounce; ~ **a fare qc** to give up doing sth

rinvi'are *vt* (*rimandare indietro*) to send back, return; (*differire*): ~ **qc (a)** to postpone sth *o* put sth off (till); to adjourn sth (till); (*fare un rimando*): ~ **qn a** to refer sb to

rin'vio, -'vii *sm* (*rimando*) return; (*differimento*) postponement; (: *di seduta*) adjournment; (*in un testo*) cross-reference; **rinvio a giudizio** (*Dir*) indictment

riò *ecc vb vedi* **riavere**

ri'one *sm* district, quarter

riordi'nare *vt* (*rimettere in ordine*) to tidy; (*riorganizzare*) to reorganize

riorganiz'zare [riorganid'dzare] *vt* to reorganize

ripa'gare *vt* to repay

ripa'rare *vt* (*proteggere*) to protect, defend; (*correggere: male, torto*) to make up for; (: *errore*) to put right; (*aggiustare*) to repair ▷ *vi* (*mettere rimedio*): ~ **a** to make up for; **ripararsi** *vpr* (*rifugiarsi*) to take refuge *o* shelter; **dove lo posso far ~?** where can I get this repaired?; **riparazi'one** *sf* (*di un torto*) reparation; (*di guasto, scarpe*) repairing *no pl*; repair; (*risarcimento*) compensation

ri'paro *sm* (*protezione*) shelter, protection; (*rimedio*) remedy

ripar'tire *vt* (*dividere*) to divide up; (*distribuire*) to share out ▷ *vi* to set off again; to leave again

ripas'sare *vi* to come (*o* go) back ▷ *vt* (*scritto, lezione*) to go over (again)

ripen'sare *vi* to think; (*cambiare pensiero*)

to change one's mind; (*tornare col pensiero*): **~ a** to recall

ripercu'otersi *vpr* **~ su** (*fig*) to have repercussions on

ripercussi'one *sf* (*fig*): **avere una ~ o delle ripercussioni su** to have repercussions on

ripes'care *vt* (*pesce*) to catch again; (*persona, cosa*) to fish out; (*fig: ritrovare*) to dig out

ri'petere *vt* to repeat; (*ripassare*) to go over; **può ~ per favore?** can you repeat that please?; **ripetizi'one** *sf* repetition; (*di lezione*) revision; **ripetizioni** *sfpl* (*Ins*) private tutoring *o* coaching *sg*

ripi'ano *sm* (*di mobile*) shelf

ri'picca *sf* **per ~** out of spite

'ripido, -a *ag* steep

ripie'gare *vt* to refold, (*piegare più volte*) to fold (up) ▷ *vi* (*Mil*) to retreat, fall back; (*fig: accontentarsi*): **~ su** to make do with

ripi'eno, -a *ag* full; (*Cuc*) stuffed; (: *panino*) filled ▷ *sm* (*Cuc*) stuffing

ri'pone, ri'pongo *ecc vb vedi* **riporre**

ri'porre *vt* (*porre al suo posto*) to put back, replace; (*mettere via*) to put away; (*fiducia, speranza*): **~ qc in qn** to place *o* put sth in sb

ripor'tare *vt* (*portare indietro*) to bring (*o* take) back; (*riferire*) to report; (*citare*) to quote; (*vittoria*) to gain; (*successo*) to have; (*Mat*) to carry; **riportarsi a** (*anche fig*) to go back to; (*riferirsi a*) to refer to; **~ danni** to suffer damage

ripo'sare *vt, vi* to rest; **riposarsi** *vpr* to rest

ri'posi *ecc vb vedi* **riporre**

ri'poso *sm* rest; (*Mil*): **~!** at ease!; **a ~** (*in pensione*) retired; **giorno di ~** day off

ripos'tiglio [ripos'tiʎʎo] *sm* lumber-room

ri'prendere *vt* (*prigioniero, fortezza*) to recapture; (*prendere indietro*) to take back; (*ricominciare: lavoro*) to resume; (*andare a prendere*) to fetch, come back for; (*riassumere: impiegati*) to take on again, re-employ; (*rimproverare*) to tell off; (*restringere: abito*) to take in; (*Cinema*) to shoot; **riprendersi** *vpr* to recover; (*correggersi*) to correct o.s.; **ri'presa** *sf* recapture; resumption; (*economica, da malattia, emozione*) recovery; (*Aut*) acceleration *no pl*; (*Teatro, Cinema*) rerun; (*Cinema: presa*) shooting *no pl*; shot; (*Sport*) second half; (: *Pugilato*) round; **a più riprese** on several occasions, several times; **ripresa cinematografica** shot

ripristi'nare *vt* to restore

ripro'durre *vt* to reproduce; **riprodursi** *vpr* (*Biol*) to reproduce; (*riformarsi*) to form again

ripro'vare *vt* (*provare di nuovo: gen*) to try

again; (*vestito*) to try on again; (: *sensazione*) to experience again ▷ *vi* (*tentare*): **~ (a fare qc)** to try (to do sth) again; **riproverò più tardi** I'll try again later

ripudi'are *vt* to repudiate, disown

ripu'gnante [ripuɲ'ɲante] *ag* disgusting, repulsive

ri'quadro *sm* square; (*Archit*) panel

ri'saia *sf* paddy field

risa'lire *vi* (*ritornare in su*) to go back up; **~ a** (*ritornare con la mente*) to go back to; (*datare da*) to date back to, go back to

risal'tare *vi* (*fig: distinguersi*) to stand out; (*Archit*) to project, jut out

risa'puto, -a *ag* **è ~ che ...** everyone knows that ..., it is common knowledge that ...

risarci'mento [risartʃi'mento] *sm* **~ (di)** compensation (for); **risarcimento danni** damages

risar'cire [risar'tʃire] *vt* (*cose*) to pay compensation for; (*persona*): **~ qn di qc** to compensate sb for sth

ri'sata *sf* laugh

riscalda'mento *sm* heating; **riscaldamento centrale** central heating

riscal'dare *vt* (*scaldare*) to heat; (: *mani, persona*) to warm; (*minestra*) to reheat; **riscaldarsi** *vpr* to warm up

ris'catto *sm* ransom; redemption

rischia'rare [riskja'rare] *vt* (*illuminare*) to light up; (*colore*) to make lighter; **rischiararsi** *vpr* (*tempo*) to clear up; (*cielo*) to clear; (*fig: volto*) to brighten up; **rischiararsi la voce** to clear one's throat

rischi'are [ris'kjare] *vt* to risk ▷ *vi* **~ di fare qc** to risk *o* run the risk of doing sth

'rischio ['riskjo] *sm* risk; **rischi'oso, -a** *ag* risky, dangerous

riscia'cquare [riʃʃa'kware] *vt* to rinse

riscon'trare *vt* (*rilevare*) to find

ris'cuotere *vt* (*ritirare: somma*) to collect; (: *stipendio*) to draw, collect; (*assegno*) to cash; (*fig: successo ecc*) to win, earn

'rise *ecc vb vedi* **ridere**

risenti'mento *sm* resentment

risen'tire *vt* to hear again; (*provare*) to feel ▷ *vi* **~ di** to feel (*o* show) the effects of; **risentirsi** *vpr* **risentirsi di** *o* **per** to take offence at, resent; **risen'tito, -a** *ag* resentful

ri'serbo *sm* reserve

ri'serva *sf* reserve; (*di caccia, pesca*) preserve; (*restrizione, di indigeni*) reservation; **di ~** (*provviste ecc*) in reserve

riser'vare *vt* (*tenere in serbo*) to keep, put aside; (*prenotare*) to book, reserve; **ho riservato un tavolo a nome...** I booked a table in the name of ...; **riser'vato,**

-a *ag* (*prenotato: fig: persona*) reserved; (*confidenziale*) confidential

'risi *ecc vb vedi* **ridere**

risi'edere *vi* **~ a** *o* **in** to reside in

'risma *sf* (*di carta*) ream; (*fig*) kind, sort

'riso (*pl(f)* **risa**) (*: il ridere*) *sm* **il ~** laughter; (*pianta*) rice ▷ *pp di* **ridere**

riso'lino *sm* snigger

ri'solsi *ecc vb vedi* **risolvere**

ri'solto, -a *pp di* **risolvere**

riso'luto, -a *ag* determined, resolute

risoluzi'one [risolut'tsjone] *sf* solving *no pl*; (*Mat*) solution; (*decisione, di schermo, immagine*) resolution

ri'solvere *vt* (*difficoltà, controversia*) to resolve; (*problema*) to solve; (*decidere*): **~ di fare** to resolve to do; **risolversi** *vpr* (*decidersi*): **risolversi a fare** to make up one's mind to do; (*andare a finire*): **risolversi in** to end up, turn out; **risolversi in nulla** to come to nothing

riso'nanza [riso'nantsa] *sf* resonance; **aver vasta ~** (*fig: fatto ecc*) to be known far and wide

ri'sorgere [ri'sordʒere] *vi* to rise again; **risorgi'mento** *sm* revival; **il Risorgimento** (*Storia*) the Risorgimento

● **RISORGIMENTO**
●
● The **Risorgimento** was the political
● movement which led to the
● proclamation of the Kingdom of Italy
● in 1861, and eventually to unification
● in 1871.

ri'sorsa *sf* expedient, resort; **risorse umane** human resources

ri'sorsi *ecc vb vedi* **risorgere**

ri'sotto *sm* (*Cuc*) risotto

risparmi'are *vt* to save; (*non uccidere*) to spare ▷ *vi* to save; **~ qc a qn** to spare sb sth

ris'parmio *sm* saving *no pl*; (*denaro*) savings *pl*; **risparmi** *smpl* (*denaro*) savings

rispec'chiare [rispek'kjare] *vt* to reflect

rispet'tabile *ag* respectable

rispet'tare *vt* to respect; **farsi ~** to command respect

rispet'tivo, -a *ag* respective

ris'petto *sm* respect; **rispetti** *smpl* (*saluti*) respects, regards; **~ a** (*in paragone a*) compared to; (*in relazione a*) as regards, as for

ris'pondere *vi* to answer, reply; (*freni*) to respond; **~ a** (*domanda*) to answer, reply to; (*persona*) to answer; (*invito*) to reply to; (*provocazione: veicolo, apparecchio*) to respond to; (*corrispondere a*) to correspond to; (*: speranze, bisogno*) to answer; **~ di** to

answer for; **ris'posta** *sf* answer, reply; **in risposta a** in reply to

'rissa *sf* brawl

ris'tampa *sf* reprinting *no pl*; reprint

risto'rante *sm* restaurant; **mi può consigliare un buon ~?** can you recommend a good restaurant?

ris'tretto, -a *pp di* **restringere** ▷ *ag* (*racchiuso*) enclosed, hemmed in; (*angusto*) narrow; (*limitato*): **~ (a)** restricted *o* limited (to); (*Cuc: brodo*) thick; (*: caffè*) extra strong

ristruttu'rare *vt* (*azienda*) to reorganize; (*edificio*) to restore; (*appartamento*) to alter; (*crema, balsamo*) to repair

risucchi'are [risuk'kjare] *vt* to suck in

risul'tare *vi* (*dimostrarsi*) to prove (to be), turn out (to be); (*riuscire*): **~ vincitore** to emerge as the winner; **~ da** (*provenire*) to result from, be the result of; **mi risulta che ...** I understand that ...; **non mi risulta** not as far as I know; **risul'tato** *sm* result

risuo'nare *vi* (*rimbombare*) to resound

risurrezi'one [risurret'tsjone] *sf* (*Rel*) resurrection

risusci'tare [risuʃʃi'tare] *vt* to resuscitate, restore to life; (*fig*) to revive, bring back ▷ *vi* to rise (from the dead)

ris'veglio [riz'veʎʎo] *sm* waking up; (*fig*) revival

ris'volto *sm* (*di giacca*) lapel; (*di pantaloni*) turn-up; (*di manica*) cuff; (*di tasca*) flap; (*di libro*) inside flap; (*fig*) implication

ritagli'are [ritaʎ'ʎare] *vt* (*tagliar via*) to cut out

ritar'dare *vi* (*persona, treno*) to be late; (*orologio*) to be slow ▷ *vt* (*rallentare*) to slow down; (*impedire*) to delay, hold up; (*differire*) to postpone, delay

ri'tardo *sm* delay; (*di persona aspettata*) lateness *no pl*; (*fig: mentale*) backwardness; **in ~** late; **il volo ha due ore di ~** the flight is two hours late; **scusi il ~** sorry I'm late

ri'tegno [ri'teɲɲo] *sm* restraint

rite'nere *vt* (*trattenere*) to hold back; (*: somma*) to deduct; (*giudicare*) to consider, believe

ri'tengo, ri'tenni *ecc vb vedi* **ritenere**

riterrò, ritiene *ecc vb vedi* **ritenere**

riti'rare *vt* to withdraw; (*Pol: richiamare*) to recall; (*andare a prendere: pacco ecc*) to collect, pick up; **ritirarsi** *vpr* to withdraw; (*da un'attività*) to retire; (*stoffa*) to shrink; (*marea*) to recede

'ritmo *sm* rhythm; (*fig*) rate; (*: della vita*) pace, tempo

'rito *sm* rite; **di ~** usual, customary

ritoc'care *vt* (*disegno, fotografia*) to touch up; (*testo*) to alter

ritor'nare *vi* to return, go (*o come*)

back, to get back; (*ripresentarsi*) to recur; (*ridiventare*): **~ ricco** to become rich again ▷ *vt* (*restituire*) to return, give back; **quando ritorniamo?** when do we get back?

ritor'nello *sm* refrain

ri'torno *sm* return; **essere di ~** to be back; **avere un ~ di fiamma** (*Aut*) to backfire; (*fig: persona*) to be back in love again

ri'trarre *vt* (*trarre indietro, via*) to withdraw; (*distogliere: sguardo*) to turn away; (*rappresentare*) to portray, depict; (*ricavare*) to get, obtain

ritrat'tare *vt* (*disdire*) to retract, take back; (*trattare nuovamente*) to deal with again

ri'tratto, -a *pp di* **ritrarre** ▷ *sm* portrait

ritro'vare *vt* to find; (*salute*) to regain; (*persona*) to find; to meet again; **ritrovarsi** *vpr* (*essere, capitare*) to find o.s.; (*raccapezzarsi*) to find one's way; (*con senso reciproco*) to meet (again)

'ritto, -a *ag* (*in piedi*) standing, on one's feet; (*levato in alto*) erect, raised; (*: capelli*) standing on end; (*posto verticalmente*) upright

ritu'ale *ag, sm* ritual

riuni'one *sf* (*adunanza*) meeting; (*riconciliazione*) reunion

riu'nire *vt* (*ricongiungere*) to join (together); (*riconciliare*) to reunite, bring together (again); **riunirsi** *vpr* (*adunarsi*) to meet; (*tornare insieme*) to be reunited

riu'scire [riuʃʃire] *vi* (*uscire di nuovo*) to go out again, go back out; (*aver esito: fatti, azioni*) to go, turn out; (*aver successo*) to succeed, be successful; (*essere, apparire*) to be, prove; (*raggiungere il fine*) to manage, succeed; **~ a fare qc** to manage to do *o* succeed in doing *o* be able to do sth

'riva *sf* (*di fiume*) bank; (*di lago, mare*) shore

ri'vale *sm/f* rival; **rivalità** *sf* rivalry

rivalu'tare *vt* (*Econ*) to revalue

rive'dere *vt* to see again; (*ripassare*) to revise; (*verificare*) to check

rivedrò *ecc vb vedi* **rivedere**

rive'lare *vt* to reveal; (*divulgare*) to reveal, disclose; (*dare indizio*) to reveal, show; **rivelarsi** *vpr* (*manifestarsi*) to be revealed; **rivelarsi onesto** *ecc* to prove to be honest *ecc*; **rivelazi'one** *sf* revelation

rivendi'care *vt* to claim, demand

rivendi'tore, -'trice *sm/f* retailer; **rivenditore autorizzato** (*Comm*) authorized dealer

ri'verbero *sm* (*di luce, calore*) reflection; (*di suono*) reverberation

rivesti'mento *sm* covering; coating

rives'tire *vt* to dress again; (*ricoprire*) to cover; to coat; (*fig: carica*) to hold

ri'vidi *ecc vb vedi* **rivedere**

ri'vincita [ri'vintʃita] *sf* (*Sport*) return match; (*fig*) revenge

ri'vista *sf* review; (*periodico*) magazine, review; (*Teatro*) revue; variety show

ri'volgere [ri'vɔldʒere] *vt* (*attenzione, sguardo*) to turn, direct; (*parole*) to address; **rivolgersi** *vpr* to turn round; (*fig: dirigersi per informazioni*): **rivolgersi a** to go and see, go and speak to; (*: ufficio*) to enquire at

ri'volsi *ecc vb vedi* **rivolgere**

ri'volta *sf* revolt, rebellion

rivol'tella *sf* revolver

rivoluzio'nare [rivoluttsjo'nare] *vt* to revolutionize

rivoluzio'nario, -a [rivoluttsjo'narjo] *ag, sm/f* revolutionary

rivoluzi'one [rivolut'tsjone] *sf* revolution

riz'zare [rit'tsare] *vt* to raise, erect; **rizzarsi** *vpr* to stand up; (*capelli*) to stand on end

'roba *sf* stuff, things *pl*; (*possessi, beni*) belongings *pl*, things *pl*, possessions *pl*; **~ da mangiare** things *pl* to eat, food; **~ da matti** sheer madness *o* lunacy

'robot *sm inv* robot

ro'busto, -a *ag* robust, sturdy; (*solido: catena*) strong

roc'chetto [rok'ketto] *sm* reel, spool

'roccia, -ce ['rɔttʃa] *sf* rock; **fare ~** (*Sport*) to go rock climbing

'roco, -a, chi, che *ag* hoarse

ro'daggio [ro'daddʒo] *sm* running (*BRIT*) *o* breaking (*US*) in; **in ~** running (*BRIT*) *o* breaking (*US*) in

rodi'tore *sm* (*Zool*) rodent

rodo'dendro *sm* rhododendron

ro'gnone [roɲ'ɲone] *sm* (*Cuc*) kidney

'rogo, -ghi *sm* (*per cadaveri*) (funeral) pyre; (*supplizio*): **il ~** the stake

rol'lio *sm* roll(ing)

'Roma *sf* Rome

Roma'nia *sf* **la ~** Romania

ro'manico, -a, -ci, -che *ag* Romanesque

ro'mano, -a *ag, sm/f* Roman

ro'mantico, -a, -ci, -che *ag* romantic

romanzi'ere [roman'dzjere] *sm* novelist

ro'manzo, -a [ro'mandzo] *ag* (*Ling*) romance *cpd* ▷ *sm* novel; **romanzo d'appendice** serial (story); **romanzo giallo/poliziesco** detective story; **romanzo rosa** romantic novel

'rombo *sm* rumble, thunder, roar; (*Mat*) rhombus; (*Zool*) turbot; brill

'rompere *vt* to break; (*fidanzamento*) to break off ▷ *vi* to break; **rompersi** *vpr* to break; **mi rompe le scatole** (*fam*) he (*o* she) is a pain in the neck; **rompersi un braccio** to break an arm; **mi si è rotta**

la macchina my car has broken down;
rompis'catole (fam) sm/f inv pest, pain
in the neck

'rondine sf (Zool) swallow

ron'zare [ron'dzare] vi to buzz, hum

ron'zio [ron'dzio] sm buzzing

'rosa sf rose ▷ ag inv, sm pink; **ro'sato, -a**
ag pink, rosy ▷ sm (vino) rosé (wine)

rosicchi'are [rosik'kjare] vt to gnaw (at);
(mangiucchiare) to nibble (at)

rosma'rino sm rosemary

roso'lare vt (Cuc) to brown

roso'lia sf (Med) German measles sg,
rubella

ro'sone sm rosette; (vetrata) rose window

'rospo sm (Zool) toad

ros'setto sm (per labbra) lipstick

'rosso, -a ag, sm, sm/f red; **il mar R~** the
Red Sea; **rosso d'uovo** egg yolk

rosticce'ria [rostitʃe'ria] sf shop selling
roast meat and other cooked food

ro'taia sf rut, track; (Ferr) rail

ro'tella sf small wheel; (di mobile) castor

roto'lare vt, vi to roll; **rotolarsi** vpr to roll
(about)

'rotolo sm roll; **andare a rotoli** (fig) to go
to rack and ruin

ro'tondo, -a ag round

'rotta sf (Aer, Naut) course, route; (Mil)
rout; **a ~ di collo** at breakneck speed;
essere in ~ con qn to be on bad terms
with sb

rotta'mare vt to scrap

rottamazione [rottama'tsjone] sf (come
incentivo) the scrapping of old vehicles in
return for incentives

rot'tame sm fragment, scrap, broken bit;
rottami smpl (di nave, aereo ecc) wreckage
sg

'rotto, -a pp di **rompere** ▷ ag broken;
(calzoni) torn, split; **per il ~ della cuffia** by
the skin of one's teeth

rot'tura sf breaking no pl; break; breaking
off; (Med) fracture, break

rou'lotte [ru'lɔt] sf caravan

ro'vente ag red-hot

'rovere sm oak

ro'vescia [ro'veʃʃa] sf **alla ~** upside-down;
inside-out; **oggi mi va tutto alla ~**
everything is going wrong (for me) today

rovesci'are [roveʃ'ʃare] vt (versare in
giù) to pour; (: accidentalmente) to spill;
(capovolgere) to turn upside down; (gettare
a terra) to knock down; (: fig: governo)
to overthrow; (piegare all'indietro: testa)
to throw back; **rovesciarsi** vpr (sedia,
macchina) to overturn; (barca) to capsize;
(liquido) to spill; (fig: situazione) to be
reversed

ro'vescio, -sci [ro'veʃʃo] sm other side,
wrong side; (della mano) back; (di moneta)
reverse; (pioggia) sudden downpour; (fig)
setback; (Maglia: anche: **punto ~**) purl
(stitch); (Tennis) backhand (stroke); **a ~**
upside-down; inside-out; **capire qc a ~** to
misunderstand sth

ro'vina sf ruin; **andare in ~** (andare a pezzi)
to collapse; (fig) to go to rack and ruin;
rovine sfpl (ruderi) ruins; **mandare in ~**
to ruin

rovi'nare vi to collapse, fall down ▷ vt
(danneggiare: fig) to ruin; **rovinarsi** vpr
(persona) to ruin o.s.; (oggetto, vestito) to
be ruined

rovis'tare vt (casa) to ransack; (tasche) to
rummage in (o through)

'rovo sm (Bot) blackberry bush, bramble
bush

'rozzo, -a ['roddzo] ag rough, coarse

ru'bare vt to steal; **~ qc a qn** to steal sth
from sb; **mi hanno rubato il portafoglio**
my wallet has been stolen

rubi'netto sm tap, faucet (US)

ru'bino sm ruby

ru'brica, -che sf (Stampa) column;
(quadernetto) index book; address book;
rubrica d'indirizzi address book; **rubrica
telefonica** list of telephone numbers

'rudere sm (rovina) ruins pl

rudimen'tale ag rudimentary, basic

rudi'menti smpl rudiments; basic
principles; basic knowledge sg

ruffi'ano sm pimp

'ruga, -ghe sf wrinkle

'ruggine ['ruddʒine] sf rust

rug'gire [rud'dʒire] vi to roar

rugi'ada [ru'dʒada] sf dew

ru'goso, -a ag wrinkled

rul'lino sm (Fot) spool; (: pellicola) film;
vorrei un ~ da 36 pose I'd like a 36-
exposure film

'rullo sm (di tamburi) roll; (arnese cilindrico,
Tip) roller; **rullo compressore** steam
roller; **rullo di pellicola** roll of film

rum sm rum

ru'meno, -a ag, sm/f, sm Romanian

rumi'nare vt (Zool) to ruminate

ru'more sm **un ~** a noise, a sound; **il ~**
noise; **non riesco a dormire a causa del
~** I can't sleep for the noise; **rumo'roso,
-a** ag noisy

▌ Attenzione! In inglese esiste la
parola rumour, che però significa voce
nel senso diceria.

ru'olo sm (Teatro: fig) role, part; (elenco)
roll, register, list; **di ~** permanent, on the
permanent staff

ru'ota sf wheel; **ruota anteriore/**

posteriore front/back wheel; **ruota di scorta** spare wheel
ruo'tare *vt, vi* to rotate
'rupe *sf* cliff
'ruppi *ecc vb vedi* **rompere**
ru'rale *ag* rural, country *cpd*
ru'scello [ruʃʃɛllo] *sm* stream
'ruspa *sf* excavator
rus'sare *vi* to snore
'Russia *sf* **la ~** Russia; **'russo, -a** *ag, sm/f, sm* Russian
'rustico, -a, -ci, -che *ag* rustic; (*fig*) rough, unrefined
rut'tare *vi* to belch; **'rutto** *sm* belch
'ruvido, -a *ag* rough, coarse

S

S. *abbr* (= *sud*) S; (= *santo*) St
sa *vb vedi* **sapere**
'sabato *sm* Saturday; **di** *o* **il ~** on Saturdays
'sabbia *sf* sand; **sabbie mobili** quicksand(s); **sabbi'oso, -a** *ag* sandy
'sacca, -che *sf* bag; (*bisaccia*) haversack; **sacca da viaggio** travelling bag
sacca'rina *sf* saccharin(e)
saccheggi'are [sakked'dʒare] *vt* to sack, plunder
sac'chetto [sak'ketto] *sm* (small) bag, (small) sack; **sacchetto di carta/di plastica** paper/plastic bag
'sacco, -chi *sm* bag; (*per carbone ecc*) sack; (*Anat, Biol*) sac; (*tela*) sacking; (*saccheggio*) sack(ing); (*fig: grande quantità*): **un ~ di** lots of, heaps of; **sacco a pelo** sleeping bag; **sacco per i rifiuti** bin bag
sacer'dote [satʃer'dɔte] *sm* priest
sacrifi'care *vt* to sacrifice; **sacrificarsi** *vpr* to sacrifice o.s.; (*privarsi di qc*) to make sacrifices
sacri'ficio [sakri'fitʃo] *sm* sacrifice
'sacro, -a *ag* sacred
'sadico, -a, -ci, -che *ag* sadistic ▷ *sm/f* sadist
sa'etta *sf* arrow; (*fulmine*) thunderbolt; flash of lightning
sa'fari *sm inv* safari
sag'gezza [sad'dʒettsa] *sf* wisdom

s

'saggio, -a, -gi, -ge ['saddʒo] *ag* wise
▷ *sm* (*persona*) sage; (*esperimento*) test; (*fig:
prova*) proof; (*campione*) sample; (*scritto*)
essay

Sagit'tario [sadʒit'tarjo] *sm* Sagittarius

'sagoma *sf* (*profilo*) outline, profile; (*forma*)
form, shape; (*Tecn*) template; (*bersaglio*)
target; (*fig: persona*) character

'sagra *sf* festival

sagres'tano *sm* sacristan; sexton

sagres'tia *sf* sacristy

Sa'hara [sa'ara] *sm* **il (deserto del) ~** the
Sahara (Desert)

'sai *vb vedi* **sapere**

'sala *sf* hall; (*stanza*) room; (*Cinema: Yyy: di
proiezione*) cinema; **sala d'aspetto** waiting
room; **sala da ballo** ballroom; **sala giochi**
amusement arcade; **sala operatoria**
operating theatre; **sala da pranzo** dining
room; **sala per concerti** concert hall

sa'lame *sm* salami *no pl*, salami sausage

sala'moia *sf* (*Cuc*) brine

sa'lato, -a *ag* (*sapore*) salty; (*Cuc*) salted,
salt *cpd*; (*fig: prezzo*) steep, stiff

sal'dare *vt* (*congiungere*) to join, bind;
(*parti metalliche*) to solder; (: *con saldatura
autogena*) to weld; (*conto*) to settle, pay

'saldo, -a *ag* (*resistente, forte*) strong,
firm; (*fermo*) firm, steady, stable; (*fig*) firm,
steadfast ▷ *sm* (*svendita*) sale; (*di conto*)
settlement; (*Econ*) balance; **saldi** *smpl*
(*Comm*) sales; **essere ~ nella propria fede**
(*fig*) to stick to one's guns

'sale *sm* salt; (*fig*): **ha poco ~ in zucca** he
doesn't have much sense; **sale fino** table
salt; **sale grosso** cooking salt

'salgo *ecc vb vedi* **salire**

'salice ['salitʃe] *sm* willow; **salice
piangente** weeping willow

sali'ente *ag* (*fig*) salient, main

sali'era *sf* salt cellar

sa'lire *vi* to go (*o come*) up; (*aereo ecc*)
to climb, go up; (*passeggero*) to get on;
(*sentiero, prezzi, livello*) to go up, rise ▷ *vt*
(*scale, gradini*) to go (*o come*) up; **~ su** to
climb (up); **~ sul treno/sull'autobus** to
board the train/the bus; **~ in macchina** to
get into the car; **sa'lita** *sf* climb, ascent;
(*erta*) hill, slope; **in salita** *ag, av* uphill

sa'liva *sf* saliva

'salma *sf* corpse

'salmo *sm* psalm

sal'mone *sm* salmon

sa'lone *sm* (*stanza*) sitting room, lounge;
(*in albergo*) lounge; (*su nave*) lounge,
saloon; (*mostra*) show, exhibition; **salone
di bellezza** beauty salon

sa'lotto *sm* lounge, sitting room; (*mobilio*)
lounge suite

sal'pare *vi* (*Naut*) to set sail; (*anche:* **~
l'ancora**) to weigh anchor

'salsa *sf* (*Cuc*) sauce; **salsa di pomodoro**
tomato sauce

sal'siccia, -ce [sal'sittʃa] *sf* pork sausage

sal'tare *vi* to jump, leap; (*esplodere*) to blow
up, explode; (: *valvola*) to blow; (*venir via*)
to pop off; (*non aver luogo: corso ecc*) to be
cancelled ▷ *vt* to jump (over), leap (over);
(*fig: pranzo, capitolo*) to skip, miss (out);
(*Cuc*) to sauté; **far ~** to blow up; to burst
open; **~ fuori** (*fig: apparire all'improvviso*)
to turn up

saltel'lare *vi* to skip; to hop

'salto *sm* jump; (*Sport*) jumping; **fare un ~**
to jump, leap; **fare un ~ da qn** to pop over
to sb's (place); **salto in alto/lungo** high/
long jump; **salto con l'asta** pole vaulting;
salto mortale somersault

saltu'ario, -a *ag* occasional, irregular

sa'lubre *ag* healthy, salubrious

salume'ria *sf* delicatessen

sa'lumi *smpl* salted pork meats

salu'tare *ag* healthy; (*fig*) salutary,
beneficial ▷ *vt* (*incontrandosi*) to greet;
(*congedandosi*) to say goodbye to; (*Mil*) to
salute

sa'lute *sf* health; **~!** (*a chi starnutisce*) bless
you!; (*nei brindisi*) cheers!; **bere alla ~ di qn**
to drink (to) sb's health

sa'luto *sm* (*gesto*) wave; (*parola*) greeting;
(*Mil*) salute

salvada'naio *sm* money box, piggy bank

salva'gente [salva'dʒɛnte] *sm* (*Naut*)
lifebuoy; (*ciambella*) life belt; (*giubbotto*) life
jacket; (*stradale*) traffic island

salvaguar'dare *vt* to safeguard

sal'vare *vt* to save; (*trarre da un pericolo*) to
rescue; (*proteggere*) to protect; **salvarsi**
vpr to save o.s.; to escape; **salvaschermo**
[salvas'kermo] *sm* (*Inform*) screen saver;
salvaslip [salva'zlip] *sm inv* panty liner;
salva'taggio *sm* rescue

'salve (*fam*) *escl* hi!

'salvia *sf* (*Bot*) sage

salvi'etta *sf* napkin; **salvietta
umidificata** baby wipe

'salvo, -a *ag* safe, unhurt, unharmed;
(*fuori pericolo*) safe, out of danger ▷ *sm* **in
~** safe ▷ *prep* (*eccetto*) except; **mettere qc
in ~** to put sth in a safe place; **~ che** (*a meno
che*) unless; (*eccetto che*) except (that); **~
imprevisti** barring accidents

sam'buco *sm* elder (tree)

'sandalo *sm* (*Bot*) sandalwood; (*calzatura*)
sandal

'sangue *sm* blood; **farsi cattivo ~** to
fret, get in a state; **sangue freddo** (*fig*)
sang-froid, calm; **a ~ freddo** in cold blood;

sangui'nare *vi* to bleed

sanità *sf* health; (*salubrità*) healthiness; **Ministero della S~** Department of Health; **sanità mentale** sanity

sani'tario, -a *ag* health *cpd*; (*condizioni*) sanitary ▷ *sm* (*Amm*) doctor; **sanitari** *smpl* (*impianti*) bathroom *o* sanitary fittings

'sanno *vb vedi* **sapere**

'sano, -a *ag* healthy; (*denti, costituzione*) healthy, sound; (*integro*) whole, unbroken; (*fig: politica, consigli*) sound; **~ di mente** sane; **di sana pianta** completely, entirely; **~ e salvo** safe and sound

'santo, -a *ag* holy; (*fig*) saintly; (*seguito da nome proprio*) saint ▷ *sm/f* saint; **la Santa Sede** the Holy See

santu'ario *sm* sanctuary

sanzi'one [san'tsjone] *sf* sanction; (*penale, civile*) sanction, penalty

sa'pere *vt* to know; (*essere capace di*): **so nuotare** I know how to swim, I can swim ▷ *vi* **~ di** (*aver sapore*) to taste of; (*aver odore*) to smell of ▷ *sm* knowledge; **far ~ qc a qn** to inform sb about sth, let sb know sth; **mi sa che non sia vero** I don't think that's true; **non lo so** I don't know; **non so l'inglese** I don't speak English; **sa dove posso...?** do you know where I can ...?

sa'pone *sm* soap; **sapone da bucato** washing soap

sa'pore *sm* taste, flavour; **sapo'rito, -a** *ag* tasty

sappi'amo *vb vedi* **sapere**

saprò *ecc vb vedi* **sapere**

sarà *ecc vb vedi* **essere**

saraci'nesca [saratʃi'neska] *sf* (*serranda*) rolling shutter

sar'castico, -a, ci, che *ag* sarcastic

Sar'degna [sar'deɲɲa] *sf* **la ~** Sardinia

sar'dina *sf* sardine

sa'rei *ecc vb vedi* **essere**

SARS *sigla f* (*Med*: = *severe acute respiratory syndrome*) SARS

'sarta *sf vedi* **sarto**

'sarto, -a *sm/f* tailor/dressmaker

'sasso *sm* stone; (*ciottolo*) pebble; (*masso*) rock

sas'sofono *sm* saxophone

sas'soso, -a *ag* stony; pebbly

'Satana *sm* Satan

sa'tellite *sm, ag* satellite

'satira *sf* satire

'sauna *sf* sauna

sazi'are [sat'tsjare] *vt* to satisfy, satiate; **saziarsi** *vpr* **saziarsi (di)** to eat one's fill (of); (*fig*): **saziarsi di** to grow tired *o* weary of

'sazio, -a ['sattsjo] *ag* **~ (di)** sated (with), full (of); (*fig: stufo*) fed up (with), sick (of);

sono ~ I'm full (up)

sba'dato, -a *ag* careless, inattentive

sbadigli'are [zbadiʎ'ʎare] *vi* to yawn; **sba'diglio** *sm* yawn

sbagli'are [zbaʎ'ʎare] *vt* to make a mistake in, get wrong ▷ *vi* to make a mistake, be mistaken, be wrong; (*operare in modo non giusto*) to err; **sbagliarsi** *vpr* to make a mistake, be mistaken, be wrong; **~ strada/la mira** to take the wrong road/ miss one's aim

sbagli'ato, -a [zbaʎ'ʎato] *ag* (*gen*) wrong; (*compito*) full of mistakes; (*conclusione*) erroneous

'sbaglio *sm* mistake, error; (*morale*) error; **fare uno ~** to make a mistake

sbalor'dire *vt* to stun, amaze ▷ *vi* to be stunned, be amazed

sbal'zare [zbal'tsare] *vt* to throw, hurl ▷ *vi* (*balzare*) to bounce; (*saltare*) to leap, bound

sban'dare *vi* (*Naut*) to list; (*Aer*) to bank; (*Aut*) to skid

sba'raglio [zba'raʎʎo] *sm* rout; defeat; **gettarsi allo ~** to risk everything

sbaraz'zarsi [zbarat'tsarsi] *vpr* **~ di** to get rid of, rid o.s. of

sbar'care *vt* (*passeggeri*) to disembark; (*merci*) to unload ▷ *vi* to disembark

'sbarra *sf* bar; (*di passaggio a livello*) barrier; (*Dir*): **presentarsi alla ~** to appear before the court

sbar'rare *vt* (*strada ecc*) to block, bar; (*assegno*) to cross; **~ il passo** to bar the way; **~ gli occhi** to open one's eyes wide

'sbattere *vt* (*porta*) to slam, bang; (*tappeti, ali, Cuc*) to beat; (*urtare*) to knock, hit ▷ *vi* (*porta, finestra*) to bang; (*agitarsi: ali, vele ecc*) to flap; **me ne sbatto!** (*fam*) I don't give a damn!

sba'vare *vi* to dribble; (*colore*) to smear, smudge

'sberla *sf* slap

sbia'dire *vi, vt* to fade; **sbia'dito, -a** *ag* faded; (*fig*) colourless, dull

sbian'care *vt* to whiten; (*tessuto*) to bleach ▷ *vi* (*impallidire*) to grow pale *o* white

sbirci'ata [zbir'tʃata] *sf* **dare una ~ a qc** to glance at sth, have a look at sth

sbloc'care *vt* to unblock, free; (*freno*) to release; (*prezzi, affitti*) to decontrol; **sbloccarsi** *vpr* (*gen*) to become unblocked; (*passaggio, strada*) to clear, become unblocked

sboc'care *vi* **~ in** (*fiume*) to flow into; (*strada*) to lead into; (*persona*) to come (out) into; (*fig: concludersi*) to end (up) in

sboc'cato, -a *ag* (*persona*) foul-mouthed; (*linguaggio*) foul

sbocci'are [zbot'tʃare] *vi* (*fiore*) to bloom,

S

open (out)

sbol'lire *vi* (*fig*) to cool down, calm down

'sbornia (*fam*) *sf* **prendersi una ~** to get plastered

sbor'sare *vt* (*denaro*) to pay out

sbot'tare *vi* **~ in una risata/per la collera** to burst out laughing/explode with anger

sbotto'nare *vt* to unbutton, undo

sbrai'tare *vi* to yell, bawl

sbra'nare *vt* to tear to pieces

sbricio'lare [zbritʃo'lare] *vt* to crumble; **sbriciolarsi** *vpr* to crumble

sbri'gare *vt* to deal with; **sbrigarsi** *vpr* to hurry (up)

'sbronza ['zbrontsa] (*fam*) *sf* (*ubriaco*): **prendersi una ~** to get plastered

sbron'zarsi [zbron'tsarsi] *vpr* (*fam*) to get sozzled

'sbronzo, -a ['zbrontso] (*fam*) *ag* plastered

sbruf'fone, -a *sm/f* boaster

sbu'care *vi* to come out, emerge; (*improvvisamente*) to pop out (*o* up)

sbucci'are [zbut'tʃare] *vt* (*arancia, patata*) to peel; (*piselli*) to shell; **sbucciarsi un ginocchio** to graze one's knee

sbucherò *ecc* [zbuke'rɔ] *vb vedi* **sbucare**

sbuf'fare *vi* (*persona, cavallo*) to snort; (*ansimare*) to puff, pant; (*treno*) to puff

sca'broso, -a *ag* (*fig: difficile*) difficult, thorny; (*: imbarazzante*) embarrassing; (*: sconcio*) indecent

scacchi *smpl* (*gioco*) chess *sg*; **a ~** (*tessuto*) check(ed)

scacchi'era [skak'kjɛra] *sf* chessboard

scacci'are [skat'tʃare] *vt* to chase away *o* out, drive away *o* out

'scaddi *ecc vb vedi* **scadere**

sca'dente *ag* shoddy, of poor quality

sca'denza [ska'dɛntsa] *sf* (*di cambiale, contratto*) maturity; (*di passaporto*) expiry date; **a breve/lunga ~** short-/long-term; **data di ~** expiry date

sca'dere *vi* (*contratto ecc*) to expire; (*debito*) to fall due; (*valore, forze, peso*) to decline, go down

sca'fandro *sm* (*di palombaro*) diving suit; (*di astronauta*) space-suit

scaf'fale *sm* shelf; (*mobile*) set of shelves

'scafo *sm* (*Naut, Aer*) hull

scagio'nare [skadʒo'nare] *vt* to exonerate, free from blame

'scaglia ['skaʎʎa] *sf* (*Zool*) scale; (*scheggia*) chip, flake

scagli'are [skaʎ'ʎare] *vt* (*lanciare: anche fig*) to hurl, fling; **scagliarsi** (*anche:* **vr**): **scagliarsi su** *o* **contro** to hurl *o* fling o.s. at; (*fig*) to rail at

'scala *sf* (*a gradini ecc*) staircase, stairs *pl*;

(*a pioli, di corda*) ladder; (*Mus, Geo, di colori, valori, fig*) scale; **scale** *sfpl* (*scalinata*) stairs; **su vasta ~/~ ridotta** on a large/small scale; **~ mobile (dei salari)** index-linked pay scale; **scala a libretto** stepladder; **scala mobile** escalator; (*Econ*) sliding scale

🌑 **Scala**
🌑
🌑 Milan's world-famous **la Scala** theatre
🌑 first opened its doors in 1778 with a
🌑 performance of Salieri's opera, "L'Europa
🌑 riconosciuta". It suffered serious
🌑 damage in the bombing of Milan in 1943
🌑 and reopened in 1946 with a concert
🌑 conducted by Toscanini. It also has a
🌑 famous classical dance school.

sca'lare *vt* (*Alpinismo, muro*) to climb, scale; (*debito*) to scale down, reduce

scalda'bagno [skalda'baɲɲo] *sm* water-heater

scal'dare *vt* to heat; **scaldarsi** *vpr* to warm up, heat up; (*al fuoco, al sole*) to warm o.s.; (*fig*) to get excited

scal'fire *vt* to scratch

scali'nata *sf* staircase

sca'lino *sm* (*anche fig*) step; (*di scala a pioli*) rung

'scalo *sm* (*Naut*) slipway; (*: porto d'approdo*) port of call; (*Aer*) stopover; **fare ~ (a)** (*Naut*) to call (at), put in (at); (*Aer*) to land (at), make a stop (at); **scalo merci** (*Ferr*) goods (BRIT) *o* freight yard

scalop'pina *sf* (*Cuc*) escalope

scal'pello *sm* chisel

scal'pore *sm* noise, row; **far ~** (*notizia*) to cause a sensation *o* a stir

'scaltro, -a *ag* cunning, shrewd

'scalzo, -a ['skaltso] *ag* barefoot

scambi'are *vt* to exchange; (*confondere*): **~ qn/qc per** to take *o* mistake sb/sth for; **mi hanno scambiato il cappello** they've given me the wrong hat; **scambiarsi** *vpr* (*auguri, confidenze, visite*) to exchange; **~ qn/qc per** (*confondere*) to mistake sth/sb for

'scambio *sm* exchange; (*Ferr*) points *pl*; **fare (uno) ~** to make a swap

scampa'gnata [skampaɲ'ɲata] *sf* trip to the country

scam'pare *vt* (*salvare*) to rescue, save; (*evitare: morte, prigione*) to escape ▷ *vi* **~ (a qc)** to survive (sth), escape (sth); **scamparla bella** to have a narrow escape

'scampo *sm* (*salvezza*) escape; (*Zool*) prawn; **cercare ~ nella fuga** to seek safety in flight

'scampolo *sm* remnant

scanala'tura sf (incavo) channel, groove

scandagli'are [skandaʎ'ʎare] vt (Naut) to sound; (fig) to sound out; to probe

scandaliz'zare [skandalid'dzare] vt to shock, scandalize; **scandalizzarsi** vpr to be shocked

'scandalo sm scandal

Scandi'navia sf la ~ Scandinavia; **scandi'navo, -a** ag, sm/f Scandinavian

scanner ['skanner] sm inv (Inform) scanner

scansafa'tiche [skansafa'tike] sm/f inv idler, loafer

scan'sare vt (rimuovere) to move (aside), shift; (schivare: schiaffo) to dodge; (sfuggire) to avoid; **scansarsi** vpr to move aside

scan'sia sf shelves pl; (per libri) bookcase

'scanso sm a ~ di in order to avoid, as a precaution against

scanti'nato sm basement

scapacci'one [skapat'tʃone] sm clout

scapes'trato, -a ag dissolute

'scapola sf shoulder blade

'scapolo sm bachelor

scappa'mento sm (Aut) exhaust

scap'pare vi (fuggire) to escape; (andare via in fretta) to rush off; **lasciarsi ~ un'occasione** to let an opportunity go by; **~ di prigione** to escape from prison; **~ di mano** (oggetto) to slip out of one's hands; **~ di mente a qn** to slip sb's mind; **mi scappò detto** I let it slip; **scappa'toia** sf way out

scara'beo sm beetle

scarabocchi'are [skarabok'kjare] vt to scribble, scrawl; **scara'bocchio** sm scribble, scrawl

scara'faggio [skara'faddʒo] sm cockroach

scaraman'zia [skaraman'tsia] sf per ~ for luck

scaraven'tare vt to fling, hurl; **scaraventarsi** vpr to fling o.s.

scarce'rare [skartʃe'rare] vt to release (from prison)

scardi'nare vt ~ **una porta** to take a door off its hinges

scari'care vt (merci, camion ecc) to unload; (passeggeri) to set down, put off; (arma) to unload; (: sparare, Elettr) to discharge; (corso d'acqua) to empty, pour; (fig: liberare da un peso) to unburden, relieve; (da Internet) to download; **scaricarsi** vpr (orologio) to run o wind down; (batteria, accumulatore) to go flat o dead; (fig: rilassarsi) to unwind; (: sfogarsi) to let off steam

'scarico, -a, -chi, -che ag unloaded; (orologio) run down; (accumulatore) dead, flat ▷ sm (di merci, materiali) unloading; (di immondizie) dumping, tipping (BRIT); (Tecn: deflusso) draining; (: dispositivo) drain; (Aut) exhaust

scarlat'tina sf scarlet fever

scar'latto, -a ag scarlet

'scarpa sf shoe; **scarpe da ginnastica/ tennis** gym/tennis shoes

scar'pata sf escarpment

scarpi'era sf shoe rack

scar'pone sm boot; **scarponi da montagna** climbing boots; **scarponi da sci** ski-boots

scarseggi'are [skarsed'dʒare] vi to be scarce; **~ di** to be short of, lack

'scarso, -a ag (insufficiente) insufficient, meagre; (povero: annata) poor, lean; (Ins: voto) poor; **~ di** lacking in; **3 chili scarsi** just under 3 kilos, barely 3 kilos

scar'tare vt (pacco) to unwrap; (idea) to reject; (Mil) to declare unfit for military service; (carte da gioco) to discard; (Calcio) to dodge (past) ▷ vi to swerve

'scarto sm (cosa scartata: anche Comm) reject; (di veicolo) swerve of, (differenza) gap, difference

scassi'nare vt to break, force

scate'nare vt (fig) to incite, stir up; **scatenarsi** vpr (temporale) to break; (rivolta) to break out; (persona: infuriarsi) to rage

'scatola sf box; (di latta) tin (BRIT), can; **cibi in ~** tinned (BRIT) o canned foods; **scatola cranica** cranium; **scato'lone** sm (big) box

scat'tare vt (fotografia) to take ▷ vi (congegno, molla ecc) to be released; (balzare) to spring up; (Sport) to put on a spurt; (fig: per l'ira) to fly into a rage; **~ in piedi** to spring to one's feet

'scatto sm (dispositivo) release; (: di arma da fuoco) trigger mechanism; (rumore) click; (balzo) jump, start; (Sport) spurt; (fig: di ira ecc) fit; (: di stipendio) increment; **di ~** suddenly

scaval'care vt (ostacolo) to pass (o climb) over; (fig) to get ahead of, overtake

sca'vare vt (terreno) to dig; (legno) to hollow out; (pozzo, galleria) to bore; (città sepolta ecc) to excavate

'scavo sm excavating no pl; excavation

'scegliere ['ʃeʎʎere] vt to choose, select

sce'icco, -chi [ʃe'ikko] sm sheik

'scelgo ecc ['ʃelgo] vb vedi **scegliere**

scel'lino [ʃel'lino] sm shilling

'scelta ['ʃelta] sf choice; selection; **di prima ~** top grade o quality; **frutta o formaggi a ~** choice of fruit or cheese

'scelto, -a ['ʃelto] pp di **scegliere** ▷ ag (gruppo) carefully selected; (frutta, verdura) choice, top quality; (Mil: specializzato) crack cpd, highly skilled

'scemo, -a ['ʃemo] *ag* stupid, silly
'scena ['ʃɛna] *sf* (*gen*) scene; (*palcoscenico*) stage; **le scene** (*fig: teatro*) the stage; **fare una ~** to make a scene; **andare in ~** to be staged *o* put on *o* performed; **mettere in ~** to stage
sce'nario [ʃe'narjo] *sm* scenery; (*di film*) scenario
sce'nata [ʃe'nata] *sf* row, scene
'scendere ['ʃendere] *vi* to go (*o come*) down; (*strada, sole*) to go down; (*notte*) to fall; (*passeggero: fermarsi*) to get out, alight; (*fig: temperatura, prezzi*) to go *o* come down, fall, drop ▷ *vt* (*scale, pendio*) to go (*o come*) down; **~ dalle scale** to go (*o come*) down the stairs; **~ dal treno** to get off *o* out of the train; **dove devo ~?** where do I get off?; **~ dalla macchina** to get out of the car; **~ da cavallo** to dismount, get off one's horse
scenegg'iato [ʃened'dʒato] *sm* television drama
'scettico, -a, -ci, -che ['ʃettiko] *ag* sceptical
'scettro ['ʃettro] *sm* sceptre
'scheda ['skɛda] *sf* (index) card; **scheda elettorale** ballot paper; **scheda ricaricabile** (*Tel*) top-up card; **scheda telefonica** phone card; **sche'dario** *sm* file; (*mobile*) filing cabinet
sche'dina [ske'dina] *sf* ≈ pools coupon (BRIT)
'scheggia, -ge ['skeddʒa] *sf* splinter, sliver
'scheletro ['skɛletro] *sm* skeleton
'schema, -i ['skɛma] *sm* (*diagramma*) diagram, sketch; (*progetto, abbozzo*) outline, plan
'scherma ['skɛrma] *sf* fencing
scher'maglia [sker'maʎʎa] *sf* (*fig*) skirmish
'schermo ['skɛrmo] *sm* shield, screen; (*Cinema, TV*) screen
scher'nire [sker'nire] *vt* to mock, sneer at
scher'zare [sker'tsare] *vi* to joke
'scherzo ['skɛrtso] *sm* joke; (*tiro*) trick; (*Mus*) scherzo; **è uno ~!** (*una cosa facile*) it's child's play!, it's easy!; **per ~** in jest; for a joke *o* a laugh; **fare un brutto ~ a qn** to play a nasty trick on sb
schiaccia'noci [skjattʃa'notʃi] *sm inv* nutcracker
schiacci'are [skjat'tʃare] *vt* (*dito*) to crush; (*noci*) to crack; **~ un pisolino** to have a nap; **schiacciarsi** *vpr* (*appiattirsi*) to get squashed; (*frantumarsi*) to get crushed
schiaffeggi'are [skjaffed'dʒare] *vt* to slap
schi'affo ['skjaffo] *sm* slap
schiantarsi *vpr* to break (up), shatter
schia'rire [skja'rire] *vt* to lighten, make

lighter; **schiarirsi** *vpr* to grow lighter; (*tornar sereno*) to clear, brighten up; **schiarirsi la voce** to clear one's throat
schiavitù [skjavi'tu] *sf* slavery
schi'avo, -a ['skjavo] *sm/f* slave
schi'ena ['skjɛna] *sf* (*Anat*) back; **schie'nale** *sm* (*di sedia*) back
schi'era ['skjɛra] *sf* (*Mil*) rank; (*gruppo*) group, band
schiera'mento [skjera'mento] *sm* (*Mil, Sport*) formation; (*fig*) alliance
schie'rare [skje'rare] *vt* (*esercito*) to line up, draw up, marshal; **schierarsi** *vpr* to line up; (*fig*): **schierarsi con** *o* **dalla parte di/contro qn** to side with/oppose sb
'schifo ['skifo] *sm* disgust; **fare ~** (*essere fatto male, dare pessimi risultati*) to be awful; **mi fa ~** it makes me sick, it's disgusting; **quel libro è uno ~** that book's rotten; **schi'foso, -a** *ag* disgusting, revolting; (*molto scadente*) rotten, lousy
schioc'care [skjɔk'kare] *vt* (*frusta*) to crack; (*dita*) to snap; (*lingua*) to click; **~ le labbra** to smack one's lips
schiudersi *vpr* to open
schi'uma ['skjuma] *sf* foam; (*di sapone*) lather; (*di latte*) froth; (*fig: feccia*) scum
schi'vare [ski'vare] *vt* to dodge, avoid
'schivo, -a ['skivo] *ag* (*ritroso*) stand-offish, reserved; (*timido*) shy
schiz'zare [skit'tsare] *vt* (*spruzzare*) to spurt, squirt; (*sporcare*) to splash, spatter; (*fig: abbozzare*) to sketch ▷ *vi* to spurt, squirt; (*saltar fuori*) to dart up (*o off ecc*)
schizzi'noso, -a [skittsi'noso] *ag* fussy, finicky
'schizzo ['skittso] *sm* (*di liquido*) spurt; splash, spatter; (*abbozzo*) sketch
sci [ʃi] *sm* (*attrezzo*) ski; (*attività*) skiing; **sci d'acqua** water-skiing; **sci di fondo** cross-country skiing, ski touring (US); **sci nautico** water-skiing
'scia ['ʃia] (*pl* **scie**) *sf* (*di imbarcazione*) wake; (*di profumo*) trail
scià [ʃa] *sm inv* shah
sci'abola ['ʃabola] *sf* sabre
scia'callo [ʃa'kallo] *sm* jackal
sciac'quare [ʃak'kware] *vt* to rinse
scia'gura [ʃa'gura] *sf* disaster, calamity; misfortune
scialac'quare [ʃalak'kware] *vt* to squander
sci'albo, -a ['ʃalbo] *ag* pale, dull; (*fig*) dull, colourless
sci'alle ['ʃalle] *sm* shawl
scia'luppa [ʃa'luppa] *sf*; **scialuppa di salvataggio** lifeboat
sci'ame ['ʃame] *sm* swarm
sci'are [ʃi'are] *vi* to ski

sci'arpa [ˈʃarpa] *sf* scarf; (*fascia*) sash
scia'tore, -'trice [ʃiaˈtore] *sm/f* skier
sci'atto, -a [ˈʃatto] *ag* (*persona*) slovenly, unkempt
scien'tifico, -a, -ci, -che [ʃenˈtifiko] *ag* scientific
sci'enza [ˈʃɛntsa] *sf* science; (*sapere*) knowledge; **scienze** *sfpl* (*Ins*) science *sg*; **scienze naturali** natural sciences; **scienzi'ato, -a** *sm/f* scientist
'scimmia [ˈʃimmja] *sf* monkey
scimpanzé [ʃimpanˈtse] *sm inv* chimpanzee
scin'tilla [ʃinˈtilla] *sf* spark; **scintil'lare** *vi* to spark; (*acqua, occhi*) to sparkle
scioc'chezza [ʃokˈkettsa] *sf* stupidity *no pl*; stupid *o* foolish thing; **dire sciocchezze** to talk nonsense
sci'occo, -a, -chi, -che [ˈʃɔkko] *ag* stupid, foolish
sci'ogliere [ˈʃɔʎʎere] *vt* (*nodo*) to untie; (*capelli*) to loosen; (*persona, animale*) to untie, release; (*fig: persona*) to release from; (*neve*) to melt; (*nell'acqua: zucchero ecc*) to dissolve; (*fig: mistero*) to solve; (*porre fine a: contratto*) to cancel; (: *società, matrimonio*) to dissolve; (: *riunione*) to bring to an end; **sciogliersi** *vpr* to loosen, come untied; to melt; to dissolve; (*assemblea ecc*) to break up; **~ i muscoli** to limber up; **scioglilingua** [ʃoʎʎiˈlingwa] *sm inv* tongue-twister
sci'olgo *ecc* [ˈʃɔlgo] *vb vedi* **sciogliere**
sci'olto, -a [ˈʃɔlto] *pp di* **sciogliere** ▷ *ag* loose; (*agile*) agile, nimble; supple; (*disinvolto*) free and easy; **versi sciolti** (*Poesia*) blank verse
sciope'rare [ʃopeˈrare] *vi* to strike, go on strike
sci'opero [ˈʃɔpero] *sm* strike; **fare ~** to strike; **sciopero bianco** work-to-rule (*BRIT*), slowdown (*US*); **sciopero selvaggio** wildcat strike; **sciopero a singhiozzo** on-off strike
scio'via [ʃioˈvia] *sf* ski lift
scip'pare [ʃipˈpare] *vt* **~ qn** to snatch sb's bag; **mi hanno scippato** they snatched my bag
sci'rocco [ʃiˈrɔkko] *sm* sirocco
sci'roppo [ʃiˈrɔppo] *sm* syrup
'scisma, -i [ˈʃizma] *sm* (*Rel*) schism
scissi'one [ʃisˈsjone] *sf* (*anche fig*) split, division; (*Fisica*) fission
sciu'pare [ʃuˈpare] *vt* (*abito, libro, appetito*) to spoil, ruin; (*tempo, denaro*) to waste
scivo'lare [ʃivoˈlare] *vi* to slide *o* glide along; (*involontariamente*) to slip, slide; **'scivolo** *sm* slide; (*Tecn*) chute; **scivo'loso, -a** *ag* slippery

scle'rosi *sf* sclerosis
scoc'care *vt* (*freccia*) to shoot ▷ *vi* (*guizzare*) to shoot up; (*battere: ora*) to strike
scoccherò *ecc* [skokkeˈrɔ] *vb vedi* **scoccare**
scocci'are [skotˈtʃare] (*fam*) *vt* to bother, annoy; **scocciarsi** *vpr* to be bothered *o* annoyed
sco'della *sf* bowl
scodinzo'lare [skodintsoˈlare] *vi* to wag its tail
scogli'era [skoʎˈʎɛra] *sf* reef; cliff
'scoglio [ˈskɔʎʎo] *sm* (*al mare*) rock
scoi'attolo *sm* squirrel
scola'pasta *sm inv* colander
scolapi'atti *sm inv* drainer (*for plates*)
sco'lare *ag* **età scolare** school age ▷ *vt* to drain ▷ *vi* to drip
scola'resca *sf* schoolchildren *pl*, pupils *pl*
sco'laro, -a *sm/f* pupil, schoolboy/girl
> Attenzione! In inglese esiste la parola *scholar*, che però significa *studioso*.
sco'lastico, -a, -ci, -che *ag* school *cpd*; scholastic
scol'lato, -a *ag* (*vestito*) low-cut, low-necked; (*donna*) wearing a low-cut dress (*o* blouse *ecc*)
scolla'tura *sf* neckline
scolle'gare *vt* (*fili, apparecchi*) to disconnect
'scolo *sm* drainage
scolo'rire *vt* to fade; to discolour; **scolorirsi** *vpr* to become discoloured; (*impallidire*) to turn pale
scol'pire *vt* to carve, sculpt
scombusso'lare *vt* to upset
scom'messa *sf* bet, wager
scom'mettere *vt, vi* to bet
scomo'dare *vt* to trouble, bother; to disturb; **scomodarsi** *vpr* to put o.s. out; **scomodarsi a fare** to go to the bother *o* trouble of doing
'scomodo, -a *ag* uncomfortable; (*sistemazione, posto*) awkward, inconvenient
scompa'rire *vi* (*sparire*) to disappear, vanish; (*fig*) to be insignificant
scomparti'mento *sm* compartment; **uno ~ per non-fumatori** a non-smoking compartment
scompigli'are [skompiʎˈʎare] *vt* (*cassetto, capelli*) to mess up, disarrange; (*fig: piani*) to upset
scomuni'care *vt* to excommunicate
'sconcio, -a, -ci, -ce [ˈskontʃo] *ag* (*osceno*) indecent, obscene ▷ *sm* disgrace
scon'figgere [skonˈfiddʒere] *vt* to defeat, overcome
sconfi'nare *vi* to cross the border; (*in proprietà privata*) to trespass; (*fig*): **~ da** to

stray o digress from

scon'fitta sf defeat

scon'forto sm despondency

sconge'lare [skondʒe'lare] vt to defrost

scongiu'rare [skondʒu'rare] vt (implorare) to entreat, beseech, implore; (eludere: pericolo) to ward off, avert; **scongi'uro** sm entreaty; (esorcismo) exorcism; **fare gli scongiuri** to touch wood (BRIT), knock on wood (US)

scon'nesso, -a ag incoherent

sconosci'uto, -a [skonoʃʃuto] ag unknown; new, strange ▷ sm/f stranger; unknown person

sconsigli'are [skonsiʎ'ʎare] vt ~ **qc a qn** to advise sb against sth; ~ **qn dal fare qc** to advise sb not to do o against doing sth

sconso'lato, -a ag inconsolable; desolate

scon'tare vt (Comm: detrarre) to deduct; (: debito) to pay off; (: cambiale) to discount; (pena) to serve; (colpa, errori) to pay for, suffer for

scon'tato, -a ag (previsto) foreseen, taken for granted; **dare per ~ che** to take it for granted that

scon'tento, -a ag ~ **(di)** dissatisfied (with) ▷ sm dissatisfaction

'sconto sm discount; **fare uno ~** to give a discount; **ci sono sconti per studenti?** are there discounts for students?

scon'trarsi vpr (treni ecc) to crash, collide; (venire ad uno scontro, fig) to clash; ~ **con** to crash into, collide with

scon'trino sm ticket; (di cassa) receipt; **potrei avere lo ~ per favore?** can I have a receipt, please?

'scontro sm clash, encounter; crash, collision

scon'troso, -a ag sullen, surly; (permaloso) touchy

sconveni'ente ag unseemly, improper

scon'volgere [skon'vɔldʒere] vt to throw into confusion, upset; (turbare) to shake, disturb, upset; **scon'volto, -a** pp di **sconvolgere**

scooter ['skuter] sm inv scooter

'scopa sf broom; (Carte) Italian card game; **sco'pare** vt to sweep

sco'perta sf discovery

sco'perto, -a pp di **scoprire** ▷ ag uncovered; (capo) uncovered, bare; (macchina) open; (Mil) exposed, without cover; (conto) overdrawn

'scopo sm aim, purpose; **a che ~?** what for?

scoppi'are vi (spaccarsi) to burst; (esplodere) to explode; (fig) to break out; ~ **in pianto** o **a piangere** to burst out crying;

~ **dalle risa** o **dal ridere** to split one's sides laughing

scoppiet'tare vi to crackle

'scoppio sm explosion; (di tuono, arma ecc) crash, bang; (fig: di risa, ira) fit, outburst; (: di guerra) outbreak; **a ~ ritardato** delayed-action

sco'prire vt to discover; (liberare da ciò che copre) to uncover; (: monumento) to unveil; **scoprirsi** vpr to put on lighter clothes; (fig) to give o.s. away

scoraggi'are [skorad'dʒare] vt to discourage; **scoraggiarsi** vpr to become discouraged, lose heart

scorcia'toia [skortʃa'toja] sf short cut

'scorcio ['skortʃo] sm (Arte) foreshortening; (di secolo, periodo) end, close; **scorcio panoramico** vista

scor'dare vt to forget; **scordarsi** vpr **scordarsi di qc/di fare** to forget sth/to do

'scorgere ['skɔrdʒere] vt to make out, distinguish, see

scorpacci'ata [skorpat'tʃata] sf **fare una ~ (di)** to stuff o.s. (with), eat one's fill (of)

scorpi'one sm scorpion; (dello zodiaco): **S~** Scorpio

'scorrere vt (giornale, lettera) to run o skim through ▷ vi (liquido, fiume) to run, flow; (fune) to run; (cassetto, porta) to slide easily; (tempo) to pass (by)

scor'retto, -a ag incorrect; (sgarbato) impolite; (sconveniente) improper

scor'revole ag (porta) sliding; (fig: stile) fluent, flowing

'scorsi ecc vb vedi **scorgere**

'scorso, -a pp di **scorrere** ▷ ag last

scor'soio, -a ag **nodo ~** noose

'scorta sf (di personalità, convoglio) escort; (provvista) supply, stock

scor'tese ag discourteous, rude

'scorza ['skɔrdza] sf (di albero) bark; (di agrumi) peel, skin

sco'sceso, -a [skoʃʃeso] ag steep

'scossa sf jerk, jolt, shake; (Elettr: fig) shock; **scossa di terremoto** earth tremor

'scosso, -a pp di **scuotere** ▷ ag (turbato) shaken, upset

scos'tante ag (fig) off-putting (BRIT), unpleasant

scotch [skɔtʃ] sm inv (whisky) Scotch; (nastro adesivo) Scotch tape®, Sellotape®

scot'tare vt (ustionare) to burn; (: con liquido bollente) to scald ▷ vi to burn; (caffè) to be too hot; **scottarsi** vpr to burn/scald o.s.; (fig) to have one's fingers burnt; **scotta'tura** sf burn; scald

'scotto, -a ag overcooked ▷ sm (fig):

pagare lo ~ (di) to pay the penalty (for)
sco'vare vt to drive out, flush out; (fig) to discover
'Scozia ['skɔttsia] sf **la ~** Scotland; **scoz'zese** ag Scottish ▷ sm/f Scot
scredi'tare vt to discredit
screen saver ['skriin'seivər] sm inv (Inform) screen saver
scre'mato, -a ag skimmed; **parzialmente ~** semi-skimmed
screpo'lato, -a ag (labbra) chapped; (muro) cracked
'screzio ['skrɛttsjo] sm disagreement
scricchio'lare [skrikkjo'lare] vi to creak, squeak
'scrigno ['skriɲɲo] sm casket
scrimina'tura sf parting
'scrissi ecc vb vedi **scrivere**
'scritta sf Inscription
'scritto, -a pp di **scrivere** ▷ ag written ▷ sm writing; (lettera) letter, note
scrit'toio sm writing desk
scrit'tore, -'trice sm/f writer
scrit'tura sf writing; (Comm) entry; (contratto) contract; (Rel): **la Sacra S~** the Scriptures pl
scrittu'rare vt (Teatro, Cinema) to sign up, engage; (Comm) to enter
scriva'nia sf desk
'scrivere vt to write; **come si scrive?** how is it spelt?, how do you write it?
scroc'cone, -a sm/f scrounger
'scrofa sf (Zool) sow
scrol'lare vt to shake; **scrollarsi** vpr (anche fig) to give o.s. a shake; (anche: ~ **le spalle/il capo**) to shrug one's shoulders/ shake one's head
'scrupolo sm scruple; (meticolosità) care, conscientiousness
scrupo'loso, -a ag scrupulous; conscientious
scru'tare vt to scrutinize; (intenzioni, causa) to examine, scrutinize
scu'cire [sku'tʃire] vt (orlo ecc) to unpick, undo; **scucirsi** vpr to come unstitched
scude'ria sf stable
scu'detto sm (Sport) (championship) shield; (distintivo) badge
'scudo sm shield
sculacci'are [skulat'tʃare] vt to spank
scul'tore, -'trice sm/f sculptor
scul'tura sf sculpture
scu'ola sf school; **scuola elementare/ materna** primary (BRIT) o grade (US) /nursery school; **scuola guida** driving school; **scuola media** secondary (BRIT) o high (US) school; **scuola dell'obbligo** compulsory education; **scuola tecnica** technical college; **scuole serali** evening classes, night school sg

scu'otere vt to shake
'scure sf axe
'scuro, -a ag dark; (fig: espressione) grim ▷ sm darkness; dark colour; (imposta) (window) shutter; **verde/rosso** ecc ~ dark green/red ecc
'scusa sf apology; (pretesto) excuse; **chiedere ~ a qn (per)** to apologize to sb (for); **chiedo ~** I'm sorry; (disturbando ecc) excuse me
scu'sare vt to excuse; **scusarsi** vpr **scusarsi (di)** to apologize (for); **(mi) scusi** I'm sorry; (per richiamare l'attenzione) excuse me
sde'gnato, -a [zdeɲ'ɲato] ag indignant, angry
'sdegno ['zdeɲɲo] sm scorn, disdain
sdolci'nato, -a [zdoltʃi'nato] ag mawkish, oversentimental
sdrai'arsi vpr to stretch out, lie down
'sdraio sm **sedia a ~** deck chair
sdruccio'levole [zdruttʃo'levole] ag slippery

◯ **PAROLA CHIAVE**

se pron vedi **si**
▷ cong 1 (condizionale, ipotetica) if; **se nevica non vengo** I won't come if it snows; **sarei rimasto se me l'avessero chiesto** I would have stayed if they'd asked me; **non puoi fare altro se non telefonare** all you can do is phone; **se mai** if, if ever; **siamo noi se mai che le siamo grati** it is we who should be grateful to you; **se no** (altrimenti) or (else), otherwise
2 (in frasi dubitative, interrogative indirette) if, whether; **non so se scrivere o telefonare** I don't know whether o if I should write or phone

sé pron (gen) oneself; (esso, essa, lui, lei, loro) itself; himself; herself; themselves; **sé stesso(a)** pron oneself; itself; himself; herself
seb'bene cong although, though
sec. abbr (= secolo) c.
'secca sf (del mare) shallows pl; vedi anche **secco**
sec'care vt to dry; (prosciugare) to dry up; (fig: importunare) to annoy, bother ▷ vi to dry; to dry up; **seccarsi** vpr to dry; to dry up; (fig) to grow annoyed
sec'cato, -a ag (fig: infastidito) bothered, annoyed; (: stufo) fed up
secca'tura sf (fig) bother no pl, trouble no pl
seccherò ecc [sekke'rɔ] vb vedi **seccare**

secchi'ello *sm* bucket; **secchiello del ghiaccio** ice bucket

'secchio ['sekkjo] *sm* bucket, pail

'secco, -a, -chi, -che *ag* dry; (*fichi, pesce*) dried; (*foglie, ramo*) withered; (*magro: persona*) thin, skinny; (*fig: risposta, modo di fare*) curt, abrupt; (*: colpo*) clean, sharp ▷ *sm* (*siccità*) drought; **restarci ~** (*fig: morire sul colpo*) to drop dead; **mettere in ~** (*barca*) to beach; **rimanere a ~** (*fig*) to be left in the lurch

seco'lare *ag* age-old, centuries-old; (*laico, mondano*) secular

'secolo *sm* century; (*epoca*) age

se'conda *sf* (*Aut*) second (gear); **viaggiare in ~** to travel second-class; *vedi anche* **secondo**; **seconda colazione** lunch

secon'dario, -a *ag* secondary

se'condo, -a *ag* second ▷ *sm* second; (*di pranzo*) main course ▷ *prep* according to; (*nel modo prescritto*) in accordance with; **~ me** in my opinion, to my mind; **di seconda mano** second-hand; **a seconda di** according to; in accordance with; **seconda classe** second-class

'sedano *sm* celery

seda'tivo, -a *ag, sm* sedative

'sede *sf* seat; (*di ditta*) head office; (*di organizzazione*) headquarters *pl*; **sede centrale** head office; **sede sociale** registered office

seden'tario, -a *ag* sedentary

se'dere *vi* to sit, be seated

'sedia *sf* chair; **sedia elettrica** electric chair; **sedia a rotelle** wheelchair

'sedici ['seditʃi] *num* sixteen

se'dile *sm* seat; (*panchina*) bench

sedu'cente [sedu'tʃɛnte] *ag* seductive; (*proposta*) very attractive

se'durre *vt* to seduce

se'duta *sf* session, sitting; (*riunione*) meeting; **seduta spiritica** séance; **seduta stante** (*fig*) immediately

seduzi'one [sedut'tsjone] *sf* seduction; (*fascino*) charm, appeal

SEeO *abbr* (= *salvo errori e omissioni*) E and OE

'sega, -ghe *sf* saw

'segale *sf* rye

se'gare *vt* to saw; (*recidere*) to saw off

'seggio ['sɛddʒo] *sm* seat; **seggio elettorale** polling station

'seggiola ['sɛddʒola] *sf* chair; **seggio'lone** *sm* (*per bambini*) highchair

seggio'via [sɛddʒo'via] *sf* chairlift

segherò *ecc* [sege'rɔ] *vb vedi* **segare**

segna'lare [seɲɲa'lare] *vt* (*manovra ecc*) to signal; to indicate; (*annunciare*) to announce; to report; (*fig: far conoscere*) to point out; (*: persona*) to single out

se'gnale [seɲ'ɲale] *sm* signal; (*cartello*): **segnale acustico** acoustic o sound signal; **segnale d'allarme** alarm; (*Ferr*) communication cord; **segnale orario** (*Radio*) time signal; **segnale stradale** road sign

segna'libro [seɲɲa'libro] *sm* (*anche Inform*) bookmark

se'gnare [seɲ'ɲare] *vt* to mark; (*prendere nota*) to note; (*indicare*) to indicate, mark; (*Sport: goal*) to score

'segno ['seɲɲo] *sm* sign; (*impronta, contrassegno*) mark; (*limite*) limit, bounds *pl*; (*bersaglio*) target; **fare ~ di sì/no** to nod (one's head)/shake one's head; **fare ~ a qn di fermarsi** to motion (to) sb to stop; **cogliere** o **colpire nel ~** (*fig*) to hit the mark; **segno zodiacale** star sign

segre'tario, -a *sm/f* secretary; **segretario comunale** town clerk; **Segretario di Stato** Secretary of State

segrete'ria *sf* (*di ditta, scuola*) (secretary's) office; (*d'organizzazione internazionale*) secretariat; (*Pol ecc: carica*) office of Secretary; **segreteria telefonica** answering service

se'greto, -a *ag* secret ▷ *sm* secret; secrecy *no pl*; **in ~** in secret, secretly

segu'ace [se'gwatʃe] *sm/f* follower, disciple

segu'ente *ag* following, next

segu'ire *vt* to follow; (*frequentare: corso*) to attend ▷ *vi* to follow; (*continuare: testo*) to continue

segui'tare *vt* to continue, carry on with ▷ *vi* to continue, carry on

'seguito *sm* (*scorta*) suite, retinue; (*discepoli*) followers *pl*; (*favore*) following; (*continuazione*) continuation; (*conseguenza*) result; **di ~** at a stretch, on end; **in ~** later on; **in ~ a, a ~ di** following; (*a causa di*) as a result of, owing to

'sei *vb vedi* **essere** ▷ *num* six

sei'cento [sei'tʃɛnto] *num* six hundred ▷ *sm* **il S~** the seventeenth century

selci'ato [sel'tʃato] *sm* cobbled surface

selezio'nare [selettsjo'nare] *vt* to select

selezi'one [selet'tsjone] *sf* selection

'sella *sf* saddle

sel'lino *sm* saddle

selvag'gina [selvad'dʒina] *sf* (*animali*) game

sel'vaggio, -a, -gi, -ge [sel'vaddʒo] *ag* wild; (*tribù*) savage, uncivilized; (*fig*) savage, brutal ▷ *sm/f* savage

sel'vatico, -a, -ci, -che *ag* wild

se'maforo *sm* (*Aut*) traffic lights *pl*

sem'brare vi to seem ▷ vb impers **sembra che** it seems that; **mi sembra che** it seems to me that, I think (that); **~ di essere** to seem to be

'seme sm seed; (sperma) semen; (Carte) suit

se'mestre sm half-year, six-month period

semifi'nale sf semifinal

semi'freddo sm ice-cream cake

semi'nare vt to sow

semi'nario sm seminar; (Rel) seminary

seminter'rato sm basement; (appartamento) basement flat

'semola sf; **semola di grano duro** durum wheat

semo'lino sm semolina

'semplice ['semplitʃe] ag simple; (di un solo elemento) single

'sempre av always; (ancora) still; **posso ~ tentare** I can always o still try; **da ~** always; **per ~** forever; **una volta per ~** once and for all; **~ che** provided (that); **~ più** more and more; **~ meno** less and less

sempre'verde ag, sm o f (Bot) evergreen

'senape sf (Cuc) mustard

se'nato sm senate; **sena'tore, -'trice** sm/f senator

'senno sm judgment, (common) sense; **col ~ di poi** with hindsight

'seno sm (Anat: petto, mammella) breast; (: grembo, fig) womb; (: cavità) sinus

sen'sato, -a ag sensible

sensazio'nale [sensattsjo'nale] ag sensational

sensazi'one [sensat'tsjone] sf feeling, sensation; **avere la ~ che** to have a feeling that; **fare ~** to cause a sensation, create a stir

sen'sibile ag sensitive; (ai sensi) perceptible; (rilevante, notevole) appreciable, noticeable; **~ a** sensitive to

Attenzione! In inglese esiste la parola sensible, che però significa ragionevole.

'senso sm (Fisiol, istinto) sense; (impressione, sensazione) feeling, sensation; (significato) meaning, sense; (direzione) direction; **sensi** smpl (coscienza) consciousness sg; (sensualità) senses; **ciò non ha ~** that doesn't make sense; **fare ~ a** (ripugnare) to disgust, repel; **in ~ orario/antiorario** clockwise/anticlockwise; **senso di colpa** sense of guilt; **senso comune** common sense; **senso unico** (strada) one-way; **senso vietato** (Aut) no entry

sensu'ale ag sensual; sensuous

sen'tenza [sen'tentsa] sf (Dir) sentence; (massima) maxim

senti'ero sm path

sentimen'tale ag sentimental; (vita, avventura) love cpd

senti'mento sm feeling

senti'nella sf sentry

sen'tire vt (percepire al tatto, fig) to feel; (udire) to hear; (ascoltare) to listen to; (odore) to smell; (avvertire con il gusto, assaggiare) to taste ▷ vi **~ di** (avere sapore) to taste of; (avere odore) to smell of;

sentirsi vpr (uso reciproco) to be in touch; **sentirsi bene/male** to feel well/unwell o ill; **non mi sento bene** I don't feel well; **sentirsi di fare qc** (essere disposto) to feel like doing sth

sen'tito, -a ag (sincero) sincere, warm; **per ~ dire** by hearsay

'senza ['sɛntsa] prep, cong without; **~ dir nulla** without saying a word; **fare ~ qc** to do without sth; **~ di me** without me; **~ che io lo sapessi** without me o my knowing; **senz'altro** of course, certainly; **~ dubbio** no doubt; **~ scrupoli** unscrupulous; **~ amici** friendless

sepa'rare vt to separate; (dividere) to divide; (tenere distinto) to distinguish; **separarsi** vpr (coniugi) to separate, part; (amici) to part, leave each other; **separarsi da** (coniuge) to separate o part from; (amico, socio) to part company with; (oggetto) to part with; **sepa'rato, -a** ag (letti, conto ecc) separate; (coniugi) separated

seppel'lire vt to bury

'seppi ecc vb vedi **sapere**

'seppia sf cuttlefish ▷ ag inv sepia

se'quenza [se'kwentsa] sf sequence

seques'trare vt (Dir) to impound; (rapire) to kidnap; **se'questro** sm (Dir) impoundment; **sequestro di persona** kidnapping

'sera sf evening; **di ~** in the evening; **domani ~** tomorrow evening, tomorrow night; **se'rale** ag evening cpd; **se'rata** sf evening; (ricevimento) party

ser'bare vt to keep; (mettere da parte) to put aside; **~ rancore/odio verso qn** to bear sb a grudge/hate sb

serba'toio sm tank; (cisterna) cistern

'Serbia sf **la ~** Serbia

'serbo ag Serbian ▷ sm/f Serbian, Serb ▷ sm (Ling) Serbian; (il serbare): **mettere/tenere o avere in ~ qc** to put/keep sth aside

se'reno, -a ag (tempo, cielo) clear; (fig) serene, calm

ser'gente [ser'dʒente] sm (Mil) sergeant

'serie sf inv (successione) series inv; (gruppo, collezione) set; (Sport) division; league; (Comm): **modello di ~/fuori ~** standard/

custom-built model; **in ~** in quick succession; (*Comm*) mass *cpd*
serietà *sf* seriousness; reliability
'serio, -a *ag* serious; (*impiegato*) responsible, reliable; (*ditta, cliente*) reliable, dependable; **sul ~** (*davvero*) really, truly; (*seriamente*) seriously, in earnest
ser'pente *sm* snake; **serpente a sonagli** rattlesnake
'serra *sf* greenhouse; hothouse
ser'randa *sf* roller shutter
serra'tura *sf* lock
server ['sɛrvɛr] *sm inv* (*Inform*) server
ser'vire *vt* to serve; (*clienti: al ristorante*) to wait on; (: *al negozio*) to serve, attend to; (*fig: giovare*) to aid, help; (*Carte*) to deal ▷ *vi* (*Tennis*) to serve; (*essere utile*): **~ a qn** to be of use to sb; **~ a qc/a fare** (*utensile ecc*) to be used for sth/for doing; **~ (a qn) da** to serve as (for sb); **servirsi** *vpr* (*usare*): **servirsi di** to use; (*prendere: cibo*): **servirsi (di)** to help o.s. (to); **serviti pure!** help yourself!; (*essere cliente abituale*): **servirsi da** to be a regular customer at, go to
servizi'evole [servit'tsjevole] *ag* obliging, willing to help
ser'vizio [ser'vittsjo] *sm* service; (*al ristorante: sul conto*) service (charge); (*Stampa, TV, Radio*) report; (*da tè, caffè ecc*) set, service; **servizi** *smpl* (*di casa*) kitchen and bathroom; (*Econ*) services; **essere di ~** to be on duty; **fuori ~** (*telefono ecc*) out of order; **~ compreso** service included; **servizio militare** military service; **servizio di posate** set of cutlery; **servizi segreti** secret service *sg*; **servizio da tè** tea set
ses'santa *num* sixty; **sessan'tesimo, -a** *num* sixtieth
sessi'one *sf* session
'sesso *sm* sex; **sessu'ale** *ag* sexual, sex *cpd*
ses'tante *sm* sextant
'sesto, -a *ag, sm* sixth
'seta *sf* silk
'sete *sf* thirst; **avere ~** to be thirsty
'setola *sf* bristle
'setta *sf* sect
set'tanta *num* seventy; **settan'tesimo, -a** *num* seventieth
set'tare *vt* (*Inform*) to set up
'sette *num* seven
sette'cento [sette'tʃɛnto] *num* seven hundred ▷ *sm* **il S~** the eighteenth century
set'tembre *sm* September
settentrio'nale *ag* northern
settentri'one *sm* north

setti'mana *sf* week; **settima'nale** *ag, sm* weekly

'settimo, -a *ag, sm* seventh
set'tore *sm* sector
severità *sf* severity
se'vero, -a *ag* severe
sevizi'are [sevit'tsjare] *vt* to torture
sezio'nare [settsjo'nare] *vt* to divide into sections; (*Med*) to dissect
sezi'one [set'tsjone] *sf* section
sfacchi'nata [sfakki'nata] *sf* (*fam*) chore, drudgery *no pl*
sfacci'ato, -a [sfat'tʃato] *ag* (*maleducato*) cheeky, impudent; (*vistoso*) gaudy
sfa'mare *vt* to feed; (*cibo*) to fill; **sfamarsi** *vpr* to satisfy one's hunger, fill o.s. up
sfasci'are [sfaʃ'ʃare] *vt* (*ferita*) to unbandage; (*distruggere*) to smash, shatter; **sfasciarsi** *vpr* (*rompersi*) to smash, shatter
sfavo'revole *ag* unfavourable
'sfera *sf* sphere
sfer'rare *vt* (*fig: colpo*) to land, deal; (: *attacco*) to launch
'sfida *sf* challenge
sfi'dare *vt* to challenge; (*fig*) to defy, brave
sfi'ducia [sfi'dutʃa] *sf* distrust, mistrust
sfi'gato, -a (*fam*) *ag* (*sfortunato*) unlucky
sfigu'rare *vt* (*persona*) to disfigure; (*quadro, statua*) to deface ▷ *vi* (*far cattiva figura*) to make a bad impression
sfi'lare *vt* (*ago*) to unthread; (*abito, scarpe*) to slip off ▷ *vi* (*truppe*) to march past; (*atleti*) to parade; **sfilarsi** *vpr* (*perle ecc*) to come unstrung; (*orlo, tessuto*) to fray; (*calza*) to run, ladder; **sfi'lata** *sf* march past; parade; **sfilata di moda** fashion show
'sfinge ['sfindʒe] *sf* sphinx
sfi'nito, -a *ag* exhausted
sfio'rare *vt* to brush (against); (*argomento*) to touch upon
sfio'rire *vi* to wither, fade
sfo'cato, -a *ag* (*Fot*) out of focus
sfoci'are [sfo'tʃare] *vi* **~ in** to flow into; (*fig: malcontento*) to develop into
sfode'rato, -a *ag* (*vestito*) unlined
sfogarsi *vpr* (*sfogare la propria rabbia*) to give vent to one's anger; (*confidarsi*): **~ (con)** to pour out one's feelings (to); **non**

sfogarti su di me! don't take your bad temper out on me!

sfoggi'are [sfod'dʒare] *vt, vi* to show off

'sfoglia ['sfoʎʎa] *sf* sheet of pasta dough; **pasta ~** (*Cuc*) puff pastry

sfogli'are [sfoʎ'ʎare] *vt* (*libro*) to leaf through

'sfogo, -ghi *sm* (*eruzione cutanea*) rash; (*fig*) outburst; **dare ~ a** (*fig*) to give vent to

sfon'dare *vt* (*porta*) to break down; (*scarpe*) to wear a hole in; (*cesto, scatola*) to burst, knock the bottom out of; (*Mil*) to break through ▷ *vi* (*riuscire*) to make a name for o.s.

'sfondo *sm* background

sfor'mato *sm* (*Cuc*) type of soufflé

sfor'tuna *sf* misfortune, ill luck *no pl*; **avere ~** to be unlucky; **sfortu'nato, -a** *ag* unlucky; (*impresa, film*) unsuccessful

sforzarsi *vpr* **~ di** *o* **a** *o* **per fare** to try hard to do

'sforzo ['sfɔrtso] *sm* effort; (*tensione eccessiva, Tecn*) strain; **fare uno ~** to make an effort

sfrat'tare *vt* to evict; **'sfratto** *sm* eviction

sfrecci'are [sfret'tʃare] *vi* to shoot *o* flash past

sfre'gare *vt* (*strofinare*) to rub; (*graffiare*) to scratch; **sfregarsi le mani** to rub one's hands; **~ un fiammifero** to strike a match

sfregi'are [sfre'dʒare] *vt* to slash, gash; (*persona*) to disfigure; (*quadro*) to deface

sfre'nato, -a *ag* (*fig*) unrestrained, unbridled

sfron'tato, -a *ag* shameless

sfrutta'mento *sm* exploitation

sfrut'tare *vt* (*terreno*) to overwork, exhaust; (*miniera*) to exploit, work; (*fig: operai, occasione, potere*) to exploit

sfug'gire [sfud'dʒire] *vi* to escape; **~ a** (*custode*) to escape (from); (*morte*) to escape; **~ a qn** (*dettaglio, nome*) to escape sb; **~ di mano a qn** to slip out of sb's hand (*o* hands)

sfu'mare *vt* (*colori, contorni*) to soften, shade off ▷ *vi* to shade (off), fade; (*fig: svanire*) to vanish, disappear; (: *speranze*) to come to nothing

sfuma'tura *sf* shading off *no pl*; (*tonalità*) shade, tone; (*fig*) touch, hint

sfuri'ata *sf* (*scatto di collera*) fit of anger; (*rimprovero*) sharp rebuke

sga'bello *sm* stool

sgabuz'zino [sgabud'dzino] *sm* lumber room

sgambet'tare *vi* to kick one's legs about

sgam'betto *sm* **far lo ~ a qn** to trip sb up; (*fig*) to oust sb

sganci'are [zgan'tʃare] *vt* to unhook; (*Ferr*) to uncouple; (*bombe: da aereo*) to release, drop; (*fig: fam: soldi*) to fork out; **sganciarsi** *vpr* (*fig*): **sganciarsi (da)** to get away (from)

sganghe'rato, -a [zgange'rato] *ag* (*porta*) off its hinges; (*auto*) ramshackle; (*risata*) wild, boisterous

sgar'bato, -a *ag* rude, impolite

'sgarbo *sm* **fare uno ~ a qn** to be rude to sb

sgargi'ante [zgar'dʒante] *ag* gaudy, showy

sgattaio'lare *vi* to sneak away *o* off

sge'lare [zdʒe'lare] *vi, vt* to thaw

sghignaz'zare [zgiɲɲat'tsare] *vi* to laugh scornfully

sgob'bare (*fam*) *vi* (*scolaro*) to swot; (*operaio*) to slog

sgombe'rare *vt* (*tavolo, stanza*) to clear; (*piazza, città*) to evacuate ▷ *vi* to move

'sgombro, -a *ag* **~ (di)** clear (of), free (from) ▷ *sm* (*Zool*) mackerel; (*anche:* **sgombero**) clearing; vacating; evacuation; (: *trasloco*) removal

sgonfi'are *vt* to let down, deflate; **sgonfiarsi** *vpr* to go down

'sgonfio, -a *ag* (*pneumatico, pallone*) flat

'sgorbio *sm* blot; scribble

sgra'devole *ag* unpleasant, disagreeable

sgra'dito, -a *ag* unpleasant, unwelcome

sgra'nare *vt* (*piselli*) to shell; **~ gli occhi** to open one's eyes wide

sgranchire [zgran'kire] *vt* (*anche:* **sgranchirsi**) to stretch; **~ le gambe** to stretch one's legs

sgranocchi'are [zgranok'kjare] *vt* to munch

'sgravio *sm* **~ fiscale** tax relief

sgrazi'ato, -a [zgrat'tsjato] *ag* clumsy, ungainly

sgri'dare *vt* to scold

sgual'cire [zgwal'tʃire] *vt* to crumple (up), crease

sgual'drina (*peg*) *sf* slut

sgu'ardo *sm* (*occhiata*) look, glance; (*espressione*) look (in one's eye)

sguaz'zare [zgwat'tsare] *vi* (*nell'acqua*) to splash about; (*nella melma*) to wallow; **~ nell'oro** to be rolling in money

sguinzagli'are [zgwintsaʎ'ʎare] *vt* to let off the leash; (*fig: persona*): **~ qn dietro a qn** to set sb on sb

sgusci'are [zguʃ'ʃare] *vt* to shell ▷ *vi* (*sfuggire di mano*) to slip; **~ via** to slip *o* slink away

'shampoo ['ʃampo] *sm inv* shampoo

shiatzu [ʃi'atstsu] *sm inv* shiatsu

shock [ʃɔk] *sm inv* shock

○ **PAROLA CHIAVE**

si (*dav* lo, la, li, le, ne *diventa* **se**) *pron* **1**
(*riflessivo: maschile*) himself; (: *femminile*)
herself; (: *neutro*) itself; (: *impersonale*)
oneself; (: *pl*) themselves; **lavarsi** to wash
(oneself); **si è tagliato** he has cut himself;
si credono importanti they think a lot of
themselves
2 (*riflessivo: con complemento oggetto*):
lavarsi le mani to wash one's hands; **si
sta lavando i capelli** he (*o* she) is washing
his (*o* her) hair
3 (*reciproco*) one another, each other; **si
amano** they love one another *o* each other
4 (*passivo*): **si ripara facilmente** it is easily
repaired
5 (*impersonale*): **si dice che ...** they *o*
people say that ...; **si vede che è vecchio**
one *o* you can see that it's old
6 (*noi*) we; **tra poco si parte** we're leaving
soon

sì *av* yes; **un giorno sì e uno no** every
other day
'sia *cong* ~ ... ~ (*o* ... *o*): ~ **che lavori**, ~ **che
non lavori** whether he works or not;
(*tanto ... quanto*): **verranno ~ Luigi ~ suo
fratello** both Luigi and his brother will be
coming
si'amo *vb vedi* **essere**
si'cario *sm* hired killer
sicché [sik'ke] *cong* (*perciò*) so (that),
therefore; (*e quindi*) (and) so
siccità [sittʃi'ta] *sf* drought
sic'come *cong* since, as
Si'cilia [si'tʃilja] *sf* **la ~** Sicily
si'cura *sf* safety catch; (*Aut*) safety lock
sicu'rezza [siku'rettsa] *sf* safety; security;
(*fiducia*) confidence; (*certezza*) certainty; **di
~** safety *cpd*; **la ~ stradale** road safety
si'curo, -a *ag* safe; (*ben difeso*) secure;
(*fiducioso*) confident; (*certo*) sure, certain;
(*notizia, amico*) reliable; (*esperto*) skilled
▷ *av* (*anche:* **di ~**) certainly; **essere/
mettere al ~** to be safe/put in a safe place;
~ di sé self-confident, sure of o.s.; **sentirsi
~** to feel safe *o* secure
si'edo *ecc vb vedi* **sedere**
si'epe *sf* hedge
si'ero *sm* (*Med*) serum; **sieronega'tivo,
-a** *ag* HIV-negative; **sieroposi'tivo, -a** *ag*
HIV-positive
si'ete *vb vedi* **essere**
si'filide *sf* syphilis
Sig. *abbr* (= *signore*) Mr
siga'retta *sf* cigarette

'sigaro *sm* cigar
Sigg. *abbr* (= *signori*) Messrs
sigil'lare [sidʒil'lare] *vt* to seal
si'gillo [si'dʒillo] *sm* seal
'sigla *sf* initials *pl*; acronym, abbreviation;
sigla automobilistica *abbreviation of
province on vehicle number plate*; **sigla
musicale** signature tune
Sig.na *abbr* (= *signorina*) Miss
signifi'care [siɲɲifi'kare] *vt* to mean;
signifi'cato *sm* meaning
si'gnora [siɲ'ɲora] *sf* lady; **la ~ X** Mrs X;
buon giorno S~/Signore/Signorina
good morning; (*deferente*) good morning
Madam/Sir/Madam; (*quando si conosce
il nome*) good morning Mrs/Mr/Miss X;
Gentile S~/Signore/Signorina (*in una
lettera*) Dear Madam/Sir/Madam; **il signor
Rossi e ~** Mr Rossi and his wife; **signore e
signori** ladies and gentlemen
si'gnore [siɲ'ɲore] *sm* gentleman;
(*padrone*) lord, master; (*Rel*): **il S~** the Lord;
il signor X Mr X; **i signori Bianchi** (*coniugi*)
Mr and Mrs Bianchi; *vedi anche* **signora**
signo'rile [siɲɲo'rile] *ag* refined
signo'rina [siɲɲo'rina] *sf* young lady; **la ~
X** Miss X; *vedi anche* **signora**
Sig.ra *abbr* (= *signora*) Mrs
silenzia'tore [silentsja'tore] *sm* silencer
si'lenzio [si'lɛntsjo] *sm* silence; **fare ~** to
be quiet, stop talking; **silenzi'oso, -a** *ag*
silent, quiet
si'licio [si'litʃo] *sm* silicon
sili'cone *sm* silicone
'sillaba *sf* syllable
si'luro *sm* torpedo
simboleggi'are [simboled'dʒare] *vt* to
symbolize
'simbolo *sm* symbol
'simile *ag* (*analogo*) similar; (*di questo tipo*):
un uomo ~ such a man, a man like this;
libri simili such books; **~ a** similar to; **i suoi
simili** one's fellow men; one's peers
simme'tria *sf* symmetry
simpa'tia *sf* (*qualità*) pleasantness;
(*inclinazione*) liking; **avere ~ per qn** to like
sb, have a liking for sb; **sim'patico, -a, -ci,
-che** *ag* (*persona*) nice, pleasant, likeable;
(*casa, albergo ecc*) nice, pleasant
▌ Attenzione! In inglese esiste la
parola *sympathetic*, che però significa
comprensivo.

simpatiz'zare [simpatid'dzare] *vi* ~ **con**
to take a liking to
simu'lare *vt* to sham, simulate; (*Tecn*) to
simulate
simul'taneo, -a *ag* simultaneous
sina'goga, -ghe *sf* synagogue
sincerità [sintʃeri'ta] *sf* sincerity

sin'cero, -a [sin'tʃero] *ag* sincere; genuine; heartfelt

sinda'cale *ag* (trade-)union *cpd*

sinda'cato *sm* (*di lavoratori*) (trade) union; (*Amm, Econ, Dir*) syndicate, trust, pool

'sindaco, -ci *sm* mayor

sinfo'nia *sf* (*Mus*) symphony

singhioz'zare [singjot'tsare] *vi* to sob; to hiccup

singhi'ozzo [sin'gjottso] *sm* sob; (*Med*) hiccup; **avere il ~** to have the hiccups; **a ~** (*fig*) by fits and starts

single ['singol] *ag inv, sm/f inv* single

singo'lare *ag* (*insolito*) remarkable, singular; (*Ling*) singular ▷ *sm* (*Ling*) singular; (*Tennis*): **~ maschile/femminile** men's/women's singles

'singolo, -a *ag* single, individual ▷ *sm* (*persona*) individual; (*Tennis*) = **singolare**

si'nistra *sf* (*Pol*) left (wing); **a ~** on the left; (*direzione*) to the left

si'nistro, -a *ag* left, left-hand; (*fig*) sinister ▷ *sm* (*incidente*) accident

si'nonimo *sm* synonym; **~ di** synonymous with

sin'tassi *sf* syntax

'sintesi *sf* synthesis; (*riassunto*) summary, résumé

sin'tetico, -a, -ci, -che *ag* synthetic

sintetiz'zare [sintetid'dzare] *vt* to synthesize; (*riassumere*) to summarize

sinto'matico, -a, -ci, -che *ag* symptomatic

'sintomo *sm* symptom

sintonizzarsi *vpr* **~ su** to tune in to

si'pario *sm* (*Teatro*) curtain

si'rena *sf* (*apparecchio*) siren; (*nella mitologia, fig*) siren, mermaid

'Siria *sf* **la ~** Syria

si'ringa, -ghe *sf* syringe

'sismico, -a, -ci, -che *ag* seismic

sis'tema, -i *sm* system; method, way; **sistema nervoso** nervous system; **sistema operativo** (*Inform*) operating system; **sistema solare** solar system

siste'mare *vt* (*mettere a posto*) to tidy, put in order; (*risolvere: questione*) to sort out, settle; (*procurare un lavoro a*) to find a job for; (*dare un alloggio a*) to settle, find accommodation for; **sistemarsi** *vpr* (*problema*) to be settled; (*persona: trovare alloggio*) to find accommodation (BRIT) o accommodations (US); (: *trovarsi un lavoro*) to get fixed up with a job; **ti sistemo io!** I'll soon sort you out!

siste'matico, -a, -ci, -che *ag* systematic

sistemazi'one [sistemat'tsjone] *sf* arrangement, order; settlement; employment; accommodation (BRIT),

accommodations (US)

'sito *sm* **~ Internet** website

situazi'one [situat'tsjone] *sf* situation

ski-lift ['ski:lift] *sm inv* ski tow

slacci'are [zlat'tʃare] *vt* to undo, unfasten

slanci'ato, -a [zlan'tʃato] *ag* slender

'slancio *sm* dash, leap; (*fig*) surge; **di ~** impetuously

'slavo, -a *ag* Slav(onic), Slavic

sle'ale *ag* disloyal; (*concorrenza ecc*) unfair

sle'gare *vt* to untie

slip [zlip] *sm inv* briefs *pl*

'slitta *sf* sledge; (*trainata*) sleigh

slit'tare *vi* to slip, slide; (*Aut*) to skid

s.l.m. *abbr* (= *sul livello del mare*) a.s.l.

slo'gare *vt* (*Med*) to dislocate

sloggi'are [zlod'dʒare] *vt* (*inquilino*) to turn out ▷ *vi* to move out

Slo'vacchia [zlo'vakkja] *sf* Slovakia

slo'vacco, -a, -chi, -che *ag, sm/f* Slovak

Slovenia [zlo'vɛnja] *sf* Slovenia

slo'veno, -a *ag, sm/f* Slovene, Slovenian ▷ *sm* (*Ling*) Slovene

smacchi'are [zmak'kjare] *vt* to remove stains from; **smacchia'tore** *sm* stain remover

'smacco, -chi *sm* humiliating defeat

smagli'ante [zmaʎ'ʎante] *ag* brilliant, dazzling

smaglia'tura [zmaʎʎa'tura] *sf* (*su maglia, calza*) ladder; (*della pelle*) stretch mark

smalizi'ato, -a [zmalit'tsjato] *ag* shrewd, cunning

smalti'mento *sm* (*di rifiuti*) disposal

smal'tire *vt* (*merce*) to sell off; (*rifiuti*) to dispose of; (*cibo*) to digest; (*peso*) to lose; (*rabbia*) to get over; **~ la sbornia** to sober up

'smalto *sm* (*anche: **di denti***) enamel; (*per ceramica*) glaze; **smalto per unghie** nail varnish

smantel'lare *vt* to dismantle

smarri'mento *sm* loss; (*fig*) bewilderment; dismay

smar'rire *vt* to lose; (*non riuscire a trovare*) to mislay; **smarrirsi** *vpr* (*perdersi*) to lose one's way, get lost; (: *oggetto*) to go astray

smasche'rare [zmaske'rare] *vt* to unmask

SME *sigla m* (= *Sistema Monetario Europeo*) EMS (*European Monetary System*)

smen'tire *vt* (*negare*) to deny; (*testimonianza*) to refute; **smentirsi** *vpr* to be inconsistent

sme'raldo *sm* emerald

'smesso, -a *pp di* **smettere**

'smettere *vt* to stop; (*vestiti*) to stop wearing ▷ *vi* to stop, cease; **~ di fare** to stop doing

'smilzo, -a ['zmiltso] *ag* thin, lean
sminu'ire *vt* to diminish, lessen; (*fig*) to
belittle
sminuz'zare [zminut'tsare] *vt* to break
into small pieces; to crumble
'smisi *ecc vb vedi* **smettere**
smis'tare *vt* (*pacchi ecc*) to sort; (*Ferr*) to
shunt
smisu'rato, -a *ag* boundless,
immeasurable; (*grandissimo*) immense,
enormous
smoking ['sməukıŋ] *sm inv* dinner jacket
smon'tare *vt* (*mobile, macchina ecc*) to
take to pieces, dismantle; (*fig: scoraggiare*)
to dishearten ▷ *vi* (*scendere: da cavallo*) to
dismount; (: *da treno*) to get off; (*terminare
il lavoro*) to stop (work); **smontarsi** *vpr* to
lose heart; to lose one's enthusiasm
'smorfia *sf* grimace; (*atteggiamento lezioso*)
simpering; **fare smorfie** to make faces;
to simper
'smorto, -a *ag* (*viso*) pale, wan; (*colore*) dull
smor'zare [zmor'tsare] *vt* (*suoni*) to
deaden; (*colori*) to tone down; (*luce*) to dim;
(*sete*) to quench; (*entusiasmo*) to dampen;
smorzarsi *vpr* (*suono, luce*) to fade;
(*entusiasmo*) to dampen
SMS *sigla m inv* (= *short message service*) text
(message)
smu'overe *vt* to move, shift; (*fig:
commuovere*) to move; (: *dall'inerzia*) to
rouse, stir
snatu'rato, -a *ag* inhuman, heartless
'snello, -a *ag* (*agile*) agile; (*svelto*) slender,
slim
sner'vante *ag* (*attesa, lavoro*) exasperating
snob'bare *vt* to snub
sno'dare *vt* (*rendere agile, mobile*) to loosen;
snodarsi *vpr* to come loose; (*articolarsi*) to
bend; (*strada, fiume*) to wind
sno'dato, -a *ag* (*articolazione, persona*)
flexible; (*fune ecc*) undone
so *vb vedi* **sapere**
sobbar'carsi *vpr* ~ **a** to take on, undertake
'sobrio, -a *ag* sober
socchi'udere [sok'kjudere] *vt* (*porta*) to
leave ajar; (*occhi*) to half-close; **socchi'uso,
-a** *pp di* **socchiudere**
soc'correre *vt* to help, assist
soccorri'tore, -'trice *sm/f* rescuer
soc'corso, -a *pp di* **soccorrere** ▷ *sm*
help, aid, assistance; **soccorso stradale**
breakdown service
soci'ale [so'tʃale] *ag* social; (*di associazione*)
club *cpd*, association *cpd*
socia'lismo [sotʃa'lizmo] *sm* socialism;
socia'lista, -i, -e *ag, sm/f* socialist
società [sotʃe'ta] *sf inv* society; (*sportiva*)
club; (*Comm*) company; ~ **a responsabilità**

limitata *type of limited liability company*;
società per azioni limited (BRIT) o
incorporated (US) company
soci'evole [so'tʃevole] *ag* sociable
'socio ['sɔtʃo] *sm* (*Dir, Comm*) partner;
(*membro di associazione*) member
'soda *sf* (*Chim*) soda; (*bibita*) soda (water)
soddisfa'cente [soddisfa'tʃente] *ag*
satisfactory
soddis'fare *vt, vi* ~ **a** to satisfy; (*impegno*)
to fulfil; (*debito*) to pay off; (*richiesta*) to
meet, comply with; **soddis'fatto, -a** *pp
di* **soddisfare** ▷ *ag* satisfied; **soddisfatto
di** happy o satisfied with; pleased with;
soddisfazi'one *sf* satisfaction
'sodo, -a *ag* firm, hard; (*uovo*) hard-boiled
▷ *av* (*picchiare, lavorare*) hard; (*dormire*)
soundly
sofà *sm inv* sofa
soffe'renza [soffe'rɛntsa] *sf* suffering
sof'ferto, -a *pp di* **soffrire**
soffi'are *vt* to blow; (*notizia, segreto*) to
whisper ▷ *vi* to blow; (*sbuffare*) to puff (and
blow); **soffiarsi il naso** to blow one's nose;
~ **qc/qn a qn** (*fig*) to pinch o steal sth/sb
from sb; ~ **via qc** to blow sth away
soffi'ata *sf* (*fam*) tip-off; **fare una** ~ **alla
polizia** to tip off the police
'soffice ['sɔffitʃe] *ag* soft
'soffio *sm* (*di vento*) breath; **soffio al cuore**
heart murmur
sof'fitta *sf* attic
sof'fitto *sm* ceiling
soffo'cante *ag* suffocating, stifling
soffo'care *vi* (*anche:* **soffocarsi**) to
suffocate, choke ▷ *vt* to suffocate, choke;
(*fig*) to stifle, suppress
sof'frire *vt* to suffer, endure; (*sopportare*)
to bear, stand ▷ *vi* to suffer; to be in pain; ~
(**di**) **qc** (*Med*) to suffer from sth
sof'fritto, -a *pp di* **soffriggere** ▷ *sm* (*Cuc*)
fried mixture of herbs, bacon and onions
sofisti'cato, -a *ag* sophisticated; (*vino*)
adulterated
'software ['sɔftwɛa] *sm* ~ **applicativo**
applications package
sogget'tivo, -a [soddʒet'tivo] *ag*
subjective
sog'getto, -a [sod'dʒɛtto] *ag* ~ **a**
(*sottomesso*) subject to; (*esposto: a
variazioni, danni ecc*) subject o liable to ▷ *sm*
subject
soggezi'one [soddʒet'tsjone] *sf*
subjection; (*timidezza*) awe; **avere** ~ **di qn**
to stand in awe of sb; to be ill at ease in sb's
presence
soggi'orno *sm* (*invernale, marino*) stay;
(*stanza*) living room
'soglia ['sɔʎʎa] *sf* doorstep; (*anche fig*)

threshold
'sogliola ['sɔʎʎola] *sf* (*Zool*) sole
so'gnare [soɲ'ɲare] *vt, vi* to dream; **~ a occhi aperti** to daydream
'sogno ['soɲɲo] *sm* dream
'soia *sf* (*Bot*) soya
sol *sm* (*Mus*) G; (: *solfeggiando*) so(h)
so'laio *sm* (*soffitta*) attic
sola'mente *av* only, just
so'lare *ag* solar, sun *cpd*
'solco, -chi *sm* (*scavo, fig: ruga*) furrow; (*incavo*) rut, track; (*di disco*) groove
sol'dato *sm* soldier; **soldato semplice** private
soldi *smpl* (*denaro*) money *sg*; **non ho ~ I** haven't got any money
'sole *sm* sun; (*luce*) sun(light); (*tempo assolato*) sun(shine); **prendere il ~** to sunbathe
soleggi'ato, -a [soled'dʒato] *ag* sunny
so'lenne *ag* solemn
soli'dale *ag* **essere ~ (con)** to be in agreement (with)
solidarietà *sf* solidarity
'solido, -a *ag* solid; (*forte, robusto*) sturdy, solid; (*fig: ditta*) sound, solid ▷ *sm* (*Mat*) solid
so'lista, -i, -e *ag* solo ▷ *sm/f* soloist
solita'mente *av* usually, as a rule
soli'tario, -a *ag* (*senza compagnia*) solitary, lonely; (*solo, isolato*) solitary, lone; (*deserto*) lonely ▷ *sm* (*gioiello, gioco*) solitaire
'solito, -a *ag* usual; **essere ~ fare** to be in the habit of doing; **di ~** usually; **più tardi del ~** later than usual; **come al ~** as usual
soli'tudine *sf* solitude
sol'letico *sm* tickling; **soffrire il ~** to be ticklish
solleva'mento *sm* raising; lifting; revolt; **sollevamento pesi** (*Sport*) weight-lifting
solle'vare *vt* to lift, raise; (*fig: persona: alleggerire*): **~ (da)** to relieve (of); (: *dar conforto*) to comfort, relieve; (: *questione*) to raise; (: *far insorgere*) to stir (to revolt); **sollevarsi** *vpr* to rise; (*fig: riprendersi*) to recover; (: *ribellarsi*) to rise up
solli'evo *sm* relief; (*conforto*) comfort
'solo, -a *ag* alone; (*in senso spirituale: isolato*) lonely; (*unico*) **un ~ libro** only one book, a single book; (*con ag numerale*): **veniamo noi tre soli** just *o* only the three of us are coming ▷ *av* (*soltanto*) only, just; **non ~ ... ma anche** not only ... but also; **fare qc da ~** to do sth (all) by oneself
sol'tanto *av* only
so'lubile *ag* (*sostanza*) soluble
soluzi'one [solut'tsjone] *sf* solution
sol'vente *ag, sm* solvent
so'maro *sm* ass, donkey

somigli'anza [somiʎ'ʎantsa] *sf* resemblance
somigli'are [somiʎ'ʎare] *vi* **~ a** to be like, resemble; (*nell'aspetto fisico*) to look like; **somigliarsi** *vpr* to be (*o* look) alike
'somma *sf* (*Mat*) sum; (*di denaro*) sum (of money)
som'mare *vt* to add up; (*aggiungere*) to add; **tutto sommato** all things considered
som'mario, -a *ag* (*racconto, indagine*) brief; (*giustizia*) summary ▷ *sm* summary
sommer'gibile [sommer'dʒibile] *sm* submarine
som'merso, -a *pp di* **sommergere**
sommità *sf inv* summit, top; (*fig*) height
som'mossa *sf* uprising
'sonda *sf* (*Med, Meteor, Aer*) probe; (*Mineralogia*) drill ▷ *ag inv* **pallone m ~** weather balloon
son'daggio [son'daddʒo] *sm* sounding; probe; boring, drilling; (*indagine*) survey; **sondaggio d'opinioni** opinion poll
son'dare *vt* (*Naut*) to sound; (*atmosfera, piaga*) to probe; (*Mineralogia*) to bore, drill; (*fig: opinione ecc*) to survey, poll
so'netto *sm* sonnet
son'nambulo, -a *sm/f* sleepwalker
sonnel'lino *sm* nap
son'nifero *sm* sleeping drug (*o* pill)
'sonno *sm* sleep; **prendere ~** to fall asleep; **aver ~** to be sleepy
'sono *vb vedi* **essere**
so'noro, -a *ag* (*ambiente*) resonant; (*voce*) sonorous, ringing; (*onde, film*) sound *cpd*
sontu'oso, -a *ag* sumptuous; lavish
sop'palco, -chi *sm* mezzanine
soppor'tare *vt* (*subire: perdita, spese*) to bear, sustain; (*soffrire: dolore*) to bear, endure; (*cosa: freddo*) to withstand; (*persona: freddo, vino*) to take; (*tollerare*) to put up with, tolerate

> ▮ Attenzione! In inglese esiste il verbo *to support*, che però non significa *sopportare*.

sop'primere *vt* (*carica, privilegi, testimone*) to do away with; (*pubblicazione*) to suppress; (*parola, frase*) to delete
'sopra *prep* (*gen*) on; (*al di sopra di, più in alto di*) above; over; (*riguardo a*) on, about ▷ *av* on top; (*attaccato, scritto*) on it; (*al di sopra*) above; (*al piano superiore*) upstairs; **donne ~ i 30 anni** women over 30 (years of age); **abito di ~** I live upstairs; **dormirci ~** (*fig*) to sleep on it
so'prabito *sm* overcoat
soprac'ciglio [soprat'tʃiʎʎo] (*pl(f)* **sopracciglia**) *sm* eyebrow
sopraf'fare *vt* to overcome, overwhelm
sopral'luogo, -ghi *sm* (*di esperti*)

inspection; (*di polizia*) on-the-spot investigation

sopram'mobile *sm* ornament

soprannatu'rale *ag* supernatural

sopran'nome *sm* nickname

so'prano, -a *sm/f* (*persona*) soprano ▷ *sm* (*voce*) soprano

soprappensi'ero *av* lost in thought

sopras'salto *sm* **di ~** with a start; suddenly

soprasse'dere *vi* **~ a** to delay, put off

soprat'tutto *av* (*anzitutto*) above all; (*specialmente*) especially

sopravvalu'tare *vt* to overestimate

soprav'vento *sm* **avere/prendere il ~ su** to have/get the upper hand over

sopravvis'suto, -a *pp di* **sopravvivere**

soprav'vivere *vi* to survive; (*continuare a vivere*): **~ (in)** to live on (in); **~ a** (*incidente ecc*) to survive; (*persona*) to outlive

so'pruso *sm* abuse of power; **subire un ~** to be abused

soq'quadro *sm* **mettere a ~** to turn upside-down

sor'betto *sm* sorbet, water ice

sor'dina *sf* **in ~** softly; (*fig*) on the sly

'sordo, -a *ag* deaf; (*rumore*) muffled; (*dolore*) dull; (*odio, rancore*) veiled ▷ *sm/f* deaf person; **sordo'muto, -a** *ag* deaf-and-dumb ▷ *sm/f* deaf-mute

so'rella *sf* sister; **sorel'lastra** *sf* stepsister; (*con genitore in comune*) half-sister

sor'gente [sor'dʒɛnte] *sf* (*d'acqua*) spring; (*di fiume, Fisica, fig*) source

'sorgere ['sordʒere] *vi* to rise; (*scaturire*) to spring, rise; (*fig: difficoltà*) to arise

sorni'one, -a *ag* sly

sorpas'sare *vt* (*Aut*) to overtake; (*fig*) to surpass; (: *eccedere*) to exceed, go beyond; **~ in altezza** to be higher than; (*persona*) to be taller than

sorpren'dente *ag* surprising

sor'prendere *vt* (*cogliere: in flagrante ecc*) to catch; (*stupire*) to surprise; **sorprendersi** *vpr* **sorprendersi (di)** to be surprised (at); **sor'presa** *sf* surprise; **fare una sorpresa a qn** to give sb a surprise; **sor'preso, -a** *pp di* **sorprendere**

sor'reggere [sor'rɛddʒere] *vt* to support, hold up; (*fig*) to sustain; **sorreggersi** *vpr* (*tenersi ritto*) to stay upright

sor'ridere *vi* to smile; **sor'riso, -a** *pp di* **sorridere** ▷ *sm* smile

'sorsi *ecc vb vedi* **sorgere**

'sorso *sm* sip

'sorta *sf* sort, kind; **di ~** whatever, of any kind, at all

'sorte *sf* (*fato*) fate, destiny; (*evento fortuito*) chance; **tirare a ~** to draw lots

sor'teggio [sor'tɛddʒo] *sm* draw

sorvegli'ante [sorveʎ'ʎante] *sm/f* (*di carcere*) guard, warder (BRIT); (*di fabbrica ecc*) supervisor

sorvegli'anza [sorveʎ'ʎantsa] *sf* watch; supervision; (*Polizia, Mil*) surveillance

sorvegli'are [sorveʎ'ʎare] *vt* (*bambino, bagagli, prigioniero*) to watch, keep an eye on; (*malato*) to watch over; (*territorio, casa*) to watch *o* keep watch over; (*lavori*) to supervise

sorvo'lare *vt* (*territorio*) to fly over ▷ *vi* **~ su** (*fig*) to skim over

S.O.S. *sigla m* mayday, SOS

'sosia *sm inv* double

sos'pendere *vt* (*appendere*) to hang (up); (*interrompere, privare di una carica*) to suspend; (*rimandare*) to defer; (*appendere*) to hang

sospet'tare *vt* to suspect ▷ *vi* **~ di** to suspect; (*diffidare*) to be suspicious of

sos'petto, -a *ag* suspicious ▷ *sm* suspicion; **sospet'toso, -a** *ag* suspicious

sospi'rare *vi* to sigh ▷ *vt* to long for, yearn for; **sos'piro** *sm* sigh

'sosta *sf* (*fermata*) stop, halt; (*pausa*) pause, break; **senza ~** non-stop, without a break

sostan'tivo *sm* noun, substantive

sos'tanza [sos'tantsa] *sf* substance; **sostanze** *sfpl* (*ricchezze*) wealth *sg*, possessions; **in ~** in short, to sum up

sos'tare *vi* (*fermarsi*) to stop (for a while), stay; (*fare una pausa*) to take a break

sos'tegno [sos'teɲɲo] *sm* support

soste'nere *vt* to support; (*prendere su di sé*) to take on, bear; (*resistere*) to withstand, stand up to; (*affermare*): **~ che** to maintain that; **sostenersi** *vpr* to hold o.s. up, support o.s.; (*fig*) to keep up one's strength; **~ gli esami** to sit exams

sostenta'mento *sm* maintenance, support

sostitu'ire *vt* (*mettere al posto di*): **~ qn/qc a** to substitute sb/sth for; (*prendere il posto di: persona*) to substitute for; (: *cosa*) to take the place of

sosti'tuto, -a *sm/f* substitute

sostituzi'one [sostitut'tsjone] *sf* substitution; **in ~ di** as a substitute for, in place of

sotta'ceti [sotta'tʃeti] *smpl* pickles

sot'tana *sf* (*sottoveste*) underskirt; (*gonna*) skirt; (*Rel*) soutane, cassock

sotter'fugio [sotter'fudʒo] *sm* subterfuge

sotter'raneo, -a *ag* underground ▷ *sm* cellar

sotter'rare *vt* to bury

sot'tile *ag* thin; (*figura, caviglia*) thin, slim,

slender; (*fine: polvere, capelli*) fine; (*fig: leggero*) light; (: *vista*) sharp, keen; (: *olfatto*) fine, discriminating; (: *mente*) subtle; shrewd ▷ *sm* **non andare per il ~** not to mince matters

sottin'teso, -a *pp di* **sottintendere** ▷ *sm* allusion; **parlare senza sottintesi** to speak plainly

'sotto *prep* (*gen*) under; (*più in basso di*) below ▷ *av* underneath, beneath; below; **(al piano) di ~** downstairs; **~ forma di** in the form of; **~ il monte** at the foot of the mountain; **siamo ~ Natale** it's nearly Christmas; **~ la pioggia/il sole** in the rain/sun(shine); **~ terra** underground; **chiuso ~ vuoto** vacuum-packed

sotto'fondo *sm* background; **sottofondo musicale** background music

sottoline'are *vt* to underline; (*fig*) to emphasize, stress

sottoma'rino, -a *ag* (*flora*) submarine; (*cavo, navigazione*) underwater ▷ *sm* (*Naut*) submarine

sottopas'saggio [sottopas'saddʒo] *sm* (*Aut*) underpass; (*pedonale*) subway, underpass

sotto'porre *vt* (*costringere*) to subject; (*fig: presentare*) to submit; **sottoporsi** *vpr* to submit; **sottoporsi a** (*subire*) to undergo

sottos'critto, -a *pp di* **sottoscrivere**

sotto'sopra *av* upside-down

sotto'terra *av* underground

sotto'titolo *sm* subtitle

sottovalu'tare *vt* to underestimate

sotto'veste *sf* underskirt

sotto'voce [sotto'votʃe] *av* in a low voice

sottovu'oto *av* **confezionare ~** to vacuum-pack ▷ *ag* **confezione** *f* **~** vacuum packed

sot'trarre *vt* (*Mat*) to subtract, take away; **~ qn/qc a** (*togliere*) to remove sb/sth from; (*salvare*) to save o rescue sb/sth from; **~ qc a qn** (*rubare*) to steal sth from sb; **sottrarsi** *vpr* **sottrarsi a** (*sfuggire*) to escape; (*evitare*) to avoid; **sottrazi'one** *sf* subtraction; removal

souve'nir [suv(ə)'nir] *sm inv* souvenir

sovi'etico, -a, -ci, -che *ag* Soviet ▷ *sm/f* Soviet citizen

sovrac'carico, -a, chi, che *ag* **~ (di)** overloaded (with) ▷ *sm* excess load; **~ di lavoro** extra work

sovraffol'lato, -a *ag* overcrowded

sovrannatu'rale *ag* = **soprannatu'rale**

so'vrano, -a *ag* sovereign; (*fig: sommo*) supreme ▷ *sm/f* sovereign, monarch

sovrap'porre *vt* to place on top of, put on top of

sovvenzi'one [sovven'tsjone] *sf* subsidy, grant

'sozzo, -a ['sottso] *ag* filthy, dirty

S.P.A. *abbr* = **società per azioni**

spac'care *vt* to split, break; (*legna*) to chop; **spaccarsi** *vpr* to split, break; **spacca'tura** *sf* split

spacchè rò *ecc* [spakke'rɔ] *vb vedi* **spaccare**

spacci'are [spat'tʃare] *vt* (*vendere*) to sell (off); (*mettere in circolazione*) to circulate; (*droga*) to peddle, push; **spacciarsi** *vpr* **spacciarsi per** (*farsi credere*) to pass o.s. off as, pretend to be; **spaccia'tore, -'trice** *sm/f* (*di droga*) pusher; (*di denaro falso*) dealer; **'spaccio** *sm* (*di merce rubata, droga*): **spaccio (di)** trafficking (in); **spaccio (di)** passing (of); (*vendita*) sale; (*bottega*) shop

'spacco, -chi *sm* (*fenditura*) split, crack; (*strappo*) tear; (*di gonna*) slit

spac'cone *sm/f* boaster, braggart

'spada *sf* sword

spae'sato, -a *ag* disorientated, lost

spa'ghetti [spa'getti] *smpl* (*Cuc*) spaghetti *sg*

'Spagna ['spaɲɲa] *sf* **la ~** Spain; **spa'gnolo, -a** *ag* Spanish ▷ *sm/f* Spaniard ▷ *sm* (*Ling*) Spanish; **gli Spagnoli** the Spanish

'spago, -ghi *sm* string, twine

spai'ato, -a *ag* (*calza, guanto*) odd

spalan'care *vt* to open wide; **spalancarsi** *vpr* to open wide

spa'lare *vt* to shovel

'spalla *sf* shoulder; (*fig: Teatro*) stooge; **spalle** *sfpl* (*dorso*) back

spalli'era *sf* (*di sedia ecc*) back; (*di letto: da capo*) head(board); (: *da piedi*) foot(board); (*Ginnastica*) wall bars *pl*

spal'lina *sf* (*bretella*) strap; (*imbottitura*) shoulder pad

spal'mare *vt* to spread

'spalti *smpl* (*di stadio*) terracing

'spandere *vt* to spread; (*versare*) to pour (out)

spa'rare *vt* to fire ▷ *vi* (*far fuoco*) to fire; (*tirare*) to shoot; **spara'toria** *sf* exchange of shots

sparecchi'are [sparek'kjare] *vt* **~ (la tavola)** to clear the table

spa'reggio [spa'reddʒo] *sm* (*Sport*) play-off

'spargere ['spardʒere] *vt* (*sparpagliare*) to scatter; (*versare: vino*) to spill; (: *lacrime, sangue*) to shed; (*diffondere*) to spread; (*emanare*) to give off (*o* out); **spargersi** *vpr* to spread

spa'rire *vi* to disappear, vanish

spar'lare *vi* **~ di** to run down, speak ill of

'sparo *sm* shot

spar'tire *vt (eredità, bottino)* to share out; *(avversari)* to separate

spar'tito *sm (Mus)* score

sparti'traffico *sm inv (Aut)* central reservation *(BRIT)*, median (strip) *(US)*

sparvi'ero *sm (Zool)* sparrowhawk

spasi'mante *sm* suitor

spassio'nato, -a *ag* dispassionate, impartial

'spasso *sm (divertimento)* amusement, enjoyment; **andare a ~** to go out for a walk; **essere a ~** *(fig)* to be out of work; **mandare qn a ~** *(fig)* to give sb the sack

'spatola *sf* spatula; *(di muratore)* trowel

spa'valdo, -a *ag* arrogant, bold

spaventa'passeri *sm inv* scarecrow

spaven'tare *vt* to frighten, scare; **spaventarsi** *vpr* to be frightened, be scared; to get a fright; **spa'vento** *sm* fear, fright; **far spavento a qn** to give sb a fright; **spaven'toso, -a** *ag* frightening, terrible; *(fig: fam)* tremendous, fantastic

spazientirsi [spattsjen'tirsi] *vpr* to lose one's patience

'spazio ['spattsjo] *sm* space; **spazio aereo** airspace; **spazi'oso, -a** *ag* spacious

spazzaca'mino [spattsaka'mino] *sm* chimney sweep

spazza'neve [spattsa'neve] *sm inv* snowplough

spaz'zare [spat'tsare] *vt* to sweep; *(foglie ecc)* to sweep up; *(cacciare)* to sweep away; **spazza'tura** *sf* sweepings *pl*; *(immondizia)* rubbish; **spaz'zino** *sm* street sweeper

'spazzola ['spattsola] *sf* brush; **spazzola da capelli** hairbrush; **spazzola per abiti** clothesbrush; **spazzo'lare** *vt* to brush; **spazzo'lino** *sm* (small) brush; **spazzolino da denti** toothbrush

specchi'arsi [spek'kjarsi] *vpr* to look at o.s. in a mirror; *(riflettersi)* to be mirrored, be reflected

specchi'etto [spek'kjetto] *sm (tabella)* table, chart; **specchietto da borsetta** pocket mirror; **specchietto retrovisore** *(Aut)* rear-view mirror

'specchio ['spɛkkjo] *sm* mirror

speci'ale [spe'tʃale] *ag* special; **specia'lista, -i, -e** *sm/f* specialist; **specialità** *sf inv* speciality; *(branca di studio)* special field, speciality; **vorrei assaggiare una specialità del posto** I'd like to try a local speciality; **special'mente** *av* especially, particularly

'specie ['spɛtʃe] *sf inv (Biol, Bot, Zool)* species *inv*; *(tipo)* kind, sort ▷ *av* especially, particularly; **una ~ di** a kind of; **fare ~ a qn** to surprise sb; **la ~ umana** mankind

specifi'care [spetʃifi'kare] *vt* to specify, state

spe'cifico, -a, -ci, -che [spe'tʃifiko] *ag* specific

specu'lare *vi* **~ su** *(Comm)* to speculate in; *(sfruttare)* to exploit; *(meditare)* to speculate on; **speculazi'one** *sf* speculation

spe'dire *vt* to send

'spegnere ['spɛɲɲere] *vt (fuoco, sigaretta)* to put out, extinguish; *(apparecchio elettrico)* to turn o switch off; *(gas)* to turn off; *(fig: suoni, passioni)* to stifle; *(debito)* to extinguish; **spegnersi** *vpr* to go out; to go off; *(morire)* to pass away; **puoi ~ la luce?** could you switch off the light?; **non riesco a ~ il riscaldamento** I can't turn the heating off

spellarsi *vpr* to peel

'spendere *vt* to spend

'spengo *ecc vb vedi* **spegnere**

'spensi *ecc vb vedi* **spegnere**

spensie'rato, -a *ag* carefree

'spento, -a *pp di* **spegnere** ▷ *ag (suono)* muffled; *(colore)* dull; *(sigaretta)* out; *(civiltà, vulcano)* extinct

spe'ranza [spe'rantsa] *sf* hope

spe'rare *vt* to hope for ▷ *vi* **~ in** to trust in; **~ che/di fare** to hope that/to do; **lo spero, spero di sì** I hope so

sper'duto, -a *ag (isolato)* out-of-the-way; *(persona: smarrita, a disagio)* lost

sperimen'tale *ag* experimental

sperimen'tare *vt* to experiment with, test; *(fig)* to test, put to the test

'sperma, -i *sm* sperm

spe'rone *sm* spur

sperpe'rare *vt* to squander

'spesa *sf (somma di denaro)* expense; *(costo)* cost; *(acquisto)* purchase; *(fam: acquisto del cibo quotidiano)* shopping; **spese postali** postage *sg*; **spese di viaggio** travelling expenses

'spesso, -a *ag (fitto)* thick; *(frequente)* frequent ▷ *av* often; **spesse volte** frequently, often

spes'sore *sm* thickness

Spett. *abbr vedi* **spettabile**

spet'tabile *(abbr: Spett.: in lettere) ag* **~ Ditta X** Messrs X and Co.

spet'tacolo *sm (rappresentazione)* performance, show; *(vista, scena)* sight; **dare ~ di sé** to make an exhibition o a spectacle of o.s.

spet'tare *vi* **~ a** *(decisione)* to be up to; *(stipendio)* to be due to; **spetta a te decidere** it's up to you to decide

spetta'tore, -'trice *sm/f (Cinema, Teatro)* member of the audience; *(di avvenimento)* onlooker, witness

spettego'lare *vi* to gossip

spetti'nato, -a *ag* dishevelled

'spettro *sm* (*fantasma*) spectre; (*Fisica*) spectrum

'spezie ['spɛttsje] *sfpl* (*Cuc*) spices

spez'zare [spet'tsare] *vt* (*rompere*) to break; (*fig: interrompere*) to break up; **spezzarsi** *vpr* to break

spezza'tino [spettsa'tino] *sm* (*Cuc*) stew

spezzet'tare [spettset'tare] *vt* to break up (*o chop*) into small pieces

'spia *sf* spy; (*confidente della polizia*) informer; (*Elettr*) indicating light; warning light; (*fessura*) peep-hole; (*fig: sintomo*) sign, indication

spia'cente [spja'tʃɛnte] *ag* sorry; **essere ~ di qc/di fare qc** to be sorry about sth/for doing sth

spia'cevole [spja'tʃevole] *ag* unpleasant

spi'aggia, -ge ['spjaddʒa] *sf* beach; **spiaggia libera** public beach

spia'nare *vt* (*terreno*) to level, make level; (*edificio*) to raze to the ground; (*pasta*) to roll out; (*rendere liscio*) to smooth (out)

spi'are *vt* to spy on

spi'azzo ['spjattso] *sm* open space; (*radura*) clearing

'spicchio ['spikkjo] *sm* (*di agrumi*) segment; (*di aglio*) clove; (*parte*) piece, slice

spicciarsi *vpr* to hurry up

spiccioli *smpl* (small) change; **mi dispiace, non ho ~** sorry, I don't have any change

'spicco, -chi *sm* **di ~** outstanding; (*tema*) main, principal; **fare ~** to stand out

spie'dino *sm* (*utensile*) skewer; (*pietanza*) kebab

spi'edo *sm* (*Cuc*) spit

spie'gare *vt* (*far capire*) to explain; (*tovaglia*) to unfold; (*vele*) to unfurl; **spiegarsi** *vpr* to explain o.s., make o.s. clear; **~ qc a qn** to explain sth to sb; **spiegazi'one** *sf* explanation

spiegherò *ecc* [spjege'rɔ] *vb vedi* **spiegare**

spie'tato, -a *ag* ruthless, pitiless

spiffe'rare (*fam*) *vt* to blurt out, blab

'spiffero *sm* draught (BRIT), draft (US)

'spiga, -ghe *sf* (*Bot*) ear

spigli'ato, -a [spiʎ'ʎato] *ag* self-possessed, self-confident

'spigolo *sm* corner; (*Mat*) edge

'spilla *sf* brooch; (*da cravatta, cappello*) pin; **~ di sicurezza** *o* **da balia** safety pin

'spillo *sm* pin; **spillo da balia** *o* **di sicurezza** safety pin

spi'lorcio, -a, -ci, -ce [spi'lortʃo] *ag* mean, stingy

'spina *sf* (*Bot*) thorn; (*Zool*) spine, prickle; (*di pesce*) bone; (*Elettr*) plug; (*di botte*) bunghole; **birra alla ~** draught beer; **spina dorsale** (*Anat*) backbone

spinaci [spi'natʃi] *smpl* spinach *sg*

spi'nello *sm* (*Droga: gergo*) joint

'spingere ['spindʒere] *vt* to push; (*condurre: anche fig*) to drive; (*stimolare*): **~ qn a fare** to urge *o* press sb to do

spi'noso, -a *ag* thorny, prickly

'spinsi *ecc vb vedi* **spingere**

'spinta *sf* (*urto*) push; (*Fisica*) thrust; (*fig: stimolo*) incentive, spur; (*: appoggio*) string-pulling *no pl*; **dare una ~ a qn** (*fig*) to pull strings for sb

'spinto, -a *pp di* **spingere**

spio'naggio [spio'naddʒo] *sm* espionage, spying

spion'cino [spion'tʃino] *sm* peephole

spi'raglio [spi'raʎʎo] *sm* (*fessura*) chink, narrow opening; (*raggio di luce, fig*) glimmer, gleam

spi'rale *sf* spiral; (*contraccettivo*) coil; **a ~** spiral(-shaped)

spiri'tato, -a *ag* possessed; (*fig: persona, espressione*) wild

spiri'tismo *sm* spiritualism

'spirito *sm* (*Rel, Chim, disposizione d'animo, di legge ecc, fantasma*) spirit; (*pensieri, intelletto*) mind; (*arguzia*) wit; (*umorismo*) humour, wit; **lo S~ Santo** the Holy Spirit *o* Ghost

spirito'saggine [spirito'saddʒine] *sf* witticism; (*peg*) wisecrack

spiri'toso, -a *ag* witty

spiritu'ale *ag* spiritual

'splendere *vi* to shine

'splendido, -a *ag* splendid; (*splendente*) shining; (*sfarzoso*) magnificent, splendid

splen'dore *sm* splendour; (*luce intensa*) brilliance, brightness

spogli'are [spoʎ'ʎare] *vt* (*svestire*) to undress; (*privare, fig: depredare*): **~ qn di qc** to deprive sb of sth; (*togliere ornamenti: anche fig*): **~ qn/qc di** to strip sb/sth of; **spogliarsi** *vpr* to undress, strip; **spogliarsi di** (*ricchezze ecc*) to deprive o.s. of, give up; (*pregiudizi*) to rid o.s. of; **spoglia'rello** [spoʎʎa'rɛllo] *sm* striptease; **spoglia'toio** *sm* dressing room; (*di scuola ecc*) cloakroom; (*Sport*) changing room

'spola *sf* (*bobina di filo*) cop; **fare la ~ (fra)** to go to and fro *o* shuttle (between)

spolve'rare *vt* (*anche Cuc*) to dust; (*con spazzola*) to brush; (*con battipanni*) to beat; (*fig*) to polish off ▷ *vi* to dust

spon'taneo, -a *ag* spontaneous; (*persona*) unaffected, natural

spor'care *vt* to dirty, make dirty; (*fig*) to sully, soil; **sporcarsi** *vpr* to get dirty

spor'cizia [spor'tʃittsja] *sf* (*stato*) dirtiness; (*sudiciume*) dirt, filth; (*cosa* *sporca*) dirt *no pl*, something dirty

'**sporco, -a, -chi, -che** *ag* dirty, filthy

spor'genza [spor'dʒɛntsa] *sf* projection

'**sporgere** ['spordʒere] *vt* to put out, stretch out ▷ *vi* (*venire in fuori*) to stick out; **sporgersi** *vpr* to lean out; ~ **querela contro qn** (*Dir*) to take legal action against sb

'**sporsi** *ecc vb vedi* **sporgere**

sport *sm inv* sport

spor'tello *sm* (*di treno, auto ecc*) door; (*di banca, ufficio*) window, counter; **sportello automatico** (*Banca*) cash dispenser, automated telling machine

spor'tivo, -a *ag* (*gara, giornale, centro*) sports *cpd*; (*persona*) sporty; (*abito*) casual; (*spirito, atteggiamento*) sporting

'**sposa** *sf* bride; (*moglie*) wife

sposa'lizio [spoza'littsjo] *sm* wedding

spo'sare *vt* to marry; (*fig: idea, fede*) to espouse; **sposarsi** *vpr* to get married, marry; **sposarsi con qn** to marry sb, get married to sb; **spo'sato, -a** *ag* married

'**sposo** *sm* (*bride*)groom; (*marito*) husband

spos'sato, -a *ag* exhausted, weary

spos'tare *vt* to move, shift; (*cambiare: orario*) to change; **spostarsi** *vpr* to move; **può ~ la macchina, per favore?** can you move your car please?

'**spranga, -ghe** *sf* (*sbarra*) bar

spre'care *vt* to waste

spre'gevole [spre'dʒevole] *ag* contemptible, despicable

'**spremere** *vt* to squeeze

spremia'grumi *sm inv* lemon squeezer

spre'muta *sf* fresh juice; **spremuta d'arancia** fresh orange juice

sprez'zante [spret'tsante] *ag* scornful, contemptuous

sprofon'dare *vi* to sink; (*casa*) to collapse; (*suolo*) to give way, subside

spro'nare *vt* to spur (on)

sproporzio'nato, -a [sproportsjo'nato] *ag* disproportionate, out of all proportion

sproporzi'one [spropor'tsjone] *sf* disproportion

spro'posito *sm* blunder; **a ~** at the wrong time; (*rispondere, parlare*) irrelevantly

sprovve'duto, -a *ag* inexperienced, naïve

sprov'visto, -a *ag* (*mancante*): **~ di** lacking in, without; **alla sprovvista** unawares

spruz'zare [sprut'tsare] *vt* (*a nebulizzazione*) to spray; (*aspergere*) to sprinkle; (*inzaccherare*) to splash

'**spugna** ['spuɲɲa] *sf* (*Zool*) sponge; (*tessuto*) towelling

'**spuma** *sf* (*schiuma*) foam; (*bibita*) fizzy drink

spu'mante *sm* sparkling wine

spun'tare *vt* (*coltello*) to break the point of; (*capelli*) to trim ▷ *vi* (*uscire: germogli*) to sprout; (: *capelli*) to begin to grow; (: *denti*) to come through; (*apparire*) to appear (suddenly)

spun'tino *sm* snack

'**spunto** *sm* (*Teatro, Mus*) cue; (*fig*) starting point; **dare lo ~ a** (*fig*) to give rise to

spu'tare *vt* to spit out; (*fig*) to belch (out) ▷ *vi* to spit

'**squadra** *sf* (*strumento*) (set) square; (*gruppo*) team, squad; (*di operai*) gang, squad; (*Mil*) squad; (: *Aer, Naut*) squadron; (*Sport*) team; **lavoro a squadre** teamwork

squagli'arsi [skwaʎ'ʎarsi] *vpr* to melt; (*fig*) to sneak off

squa'lifica *sf* disqualification

squalifi'care *vt* to disqualify

'**squallido, -a** *ag* wretched, bleak

'**squalo** *sm* shark

'**squama** *sf* scale

squarcia'gola [skwartʃa'gola]: **a ~** *av* at the top of one's voice

squattri'nato, -a *ag* penniless

squili'brato, -a *ag* (*Psic*) unbalanced

squil'lante *ag* shrill, sharp

squil'lare *vi* (*campanello, telefono*) to ring (out); (*tromba*) to blare; '**squillo** *sm* ring, ringing *no pl*; blare; **ragazza *f* squillo** *inv* call girl

squi'sito, -a *ag* exquisite; (*cibo*) delicious; (*persona*) delightful

squit'tire *vi* (*uccello*) to squawk; (*topo*) to squeak

sradi'care *vt* to uproot; (*fig*) to eradicate

srego'lato, -a *ag* (*senza ordine: vita*) disorderly; (*smodato*) immoderate; (*dissoluto*) dissolute

S.r.l. *abbr* = **società a responsabilità limitata**

sroto'lare *vt*, **srotolarsi** ▷ *vpr* to unroll

SS *sigla* = **strada statale**

S.S.N. *abbr* (= *Servizio Sanitario Nazionale*) ≈ NHS

sta *ecc vb vedi* **stare**

'**stabile** *ag* stable, steady; (*tempo: non variabile*) settled; (*Teatro: compagnia*) resident ▷ *sm* (*edificio*) building

stabili'mento *sm* (*edificio*) establishment; (*fabbrica*) plant, factory

stabi'lire *vt* to establish; (*fissare: prezzi, data*) to fix; (*decidere*) to decide; **stabilirsi** *vpr* (*prendere dimora*) to settle

stac'care *vt* (*levare*) to detach, remove; (*separare: anche fig*) to separate, divide; (*strappare*) to tear off (o out); (*scandire: parole*) to pronounce clearly; (*Sport*) to leave behind; **staccarsi** *vpr* (*bottone ecc*) to come off; (*scostarsi*): **staccarsi (da)**

to move away (from); (*fig: separarsi*):
staccarsi da to leave; **non ~ gli occhi da
qn** not to take one's eyes off sb

'stadio *sm* (*Sport*) stadium; (*periodo, fase*)
phase, stage

'staffa *sf* (*di sella, Tecn*) stirrup; **perdere le
staffe** (*fig*) to fly off the handle

staf'fetta *sf* (*messo*) dispatch rider; (*Sport*)
relay race

stagio'nale [stadʒo'nale] *ag* seasonal

stagio'nato, -a [stadʒo'nato] *ag* (*vedi vb*)
seasoned; matured; (*scherzoso: attempato*)
getting on in years

stagi'one [sta'dʒone] *sf* season; **alta/
bassa ~** high/low season

stagista, -i, -e [sta'd[gh]ista] *sm/f*
trainee, intern (*us*)

'stagno, -a ['staɲɲo] *ag* watertight; (*a
tenuta d'aria*) airtight ▷ *sm* (*acquitrino*)
pond; (*Chim*) tin

sta'gnola [staɲ'ɲɔla] *sf* tinfoil

'stalla *sf* (*per bovini*) cowshed; (*per cavalli*)
stable

stal'lone *sm* stallion

stamat'tina *av* this morning

stam'becco, -chi *sm* ibex

'stampa *sf* (*Tip, Fot: tecnica*) printing;
(*impressione, copia fotografica*) print;
(*insieme di quotidiani, giornalisti ecc*) press

stam'pante *sf* (*Inform*) printer

stam'pare *vt* to print; (*pubblicare*) to
publish; (*coniare*) to strike, coin; (*imprimere:
anche fig*) to impress

stampa'tello *sm* block letters *pl*

stam'pella *sf* crutch

'stampo *sm* mould; (*fig: indole*) type, kind,
sort

sta'nare *vt* to drive out

stan'care *vt* to tire, make tired; (*annoiare*)
to bore; (*infastidire*) to annoy; **stancarsi**
vpr to get tired, tire o.s. out; **stancarsi (di)**
to grow weary (of), grow tired (of)

stan'chezza [stan'kettsa] *sf* tiredness,
fatigue

'stanco, -a, -chi, -che *ag* tired; **~ di** tired
of, fed up with

stan'ghetta [stan'getta] *sf* (*di occhiali*) leg;
(*Mus, di scrittura*) bar

'stanno *vb vedi* **stare**

sta'notte *av* tonight; (*notte passata*) last
night

'stante *prep* **a sé ~** (*appartamento, casa*)
independent, separate

stan'tio, -a, -'tii, -'tie *ag* stale; (*burro*)
rancid; (*fig*) old

stan'tuffo *sm* piston

'stanza ['stantsa] *sf* room; (*Poesia*) stanza;
stanza da bagno bathroom; **stanza da
letto** bedroom

stap'pare *vt* to uncork; to uncap

'stare *vi* (*restare in un luogo*) to stay, remain;
(*abitare*) to stay, live; (*essere situato*) to be,
be situated; (*anche: ~ in piedi*) to be, stand;
(*essere, trovarsi*) to be; (*dipendere*): **se stesse
in me** if it were up to me, if it depended on
me; (*seguito da gerundio*): **sta studiando**
he's studying; **starci** (*esserci spazio*): **nel
baule non ci sta più niente** there's no
more room in the boot; (*accettare*) to
accept; **ci stai?** is that okay with you?; **~
a** (*attenersi a*) to follow, stick to; (*seguito
dall'infinito*): **stiamo a discutere** we're
talking; (*toccare a*): **sta a te giocare** it's
your turn to play; **~ per fare qc** to be about
to do sth; **come sta?** how are you?; **io sto
bene/male** I'm very well/not very well; **~
a qn** (*abiti ecc*) to fit sb; **queste scarpe mi
stanno strette** these shoes are tight for
me; **il rosso ti sta bene** red suits you

starnu'tire *vi* to sneeze; **star'nuto** *sm*
sneeze

sta'sera *av* this evening, tonight

sta'tale *ag* state *cpd*; government *cpd*
▷ *sm/f* state employee, local authority
employee; (*nell'amministrazione*) ≈ civil
servant; **strada statale** ≈ trunk (*Brit*) o
main road

sta'tista, -i *sm* statesman

sta'tistica *sf* statistics *sg*

'stato, -a *pp di* **essere**; **stare** ▷ *sm*
(*condizione*) state, condition; (*Pol*) state;
(*Dir*) status; **essere in ~ d'accusa** (*Dir*)
to be committed for trial; **~ d'assedio/
d'emergenza** state of siege/emergency;
~ civile (*Amm*) marital status; **gli Stati
Uniti (d'America)** the United States (of
America); **stato d'animo** mood; **stato
maggiore** (*Mil*) staff

'statua *sf* statue

statuni'tense *ag* United States *cpd*, of the
United States

sta'tura *sf* (*Anat*) height, stature; (*fig*)
stature

sta'tuto *sm* (*Dir*) statute; constitution

sta'volta *av* this time

stazio'nario, -a [stattsjo'narjo] *ag*
stationary; (*fig*) unchanged

stazi'one [stat'tsjone] *sf* station;
(*balneare, termale*) resort; **stazione degli
autobus** bus station; **stazione balneare**
seaside resort; **stazione ferroviaria**
railway (*BRIT*) o railroad (*US*) station;
stazione invernale winter sports resort;
stazione di polizia police station (*in small
town*); **stazione di servizio** service o petrol
(*BRIT*) o filling station

'stecca, -che *sf* stick; (*di ombrello*) rib; (*di
sigarette*) carton; (*Med*) splint; (*stonatura*):

fare una ~ to sing (o play) a wrong note
stec'cato _sm_ fence
'stella _sf_ star; **stella alpina** (_Bot_)
edelweiss; **stella cadente** shooting star;
stella di mare (_Zool_) starfish
'stelo _sm_ stem; (_asta_) rod; **lampada a ~**
standard lamp
'stemma, -i _sm_ coat of arms
'stemmo _vb vedi_ **stare**
stempi'ato, -a _ag_ with a receding hairline
'stendere _vt_ (_braccia, gambe_) to stretch
(out); (_tovaglia_) to spread (out); (_bucato_)
to hang out; (_mettere a giacere_) to lay
(down); (_spalmare: colore_) to spread;
(_mettere per iscritto_) to draw up; **stendersi**
vpr (_coricarsi_) to stretch out, lie down;
(_estendersi_) to extend, stretch
stenogra'fia _sf_ shorthand
sten'tare _vi_ **~ a fare** to find it hard to do,
have difficulty doing
'stento _sm_ (_fatica_) difficulty; **stenti** _smpl_
(_privazioni_) hardship _sg_, privation _sg_; **a ~**
with difficulty, barely
'sterco _sm_ dung
stereo ['stɛreo] _ag inv_ stereo ▷ _sm inv_
(_impianto_) stereo
'sterile _ag_ sterile; (_terra_) barren; (_fig_) futile,
fruitless
steriliz'zare [sterilid'dzare] _vt_ to sterilize
ster'lina _sf_ pound (sterling)
stermi'nare _vt_ to exterminate, wipe out
stermi'nato, -a _ag_ immense; endless
ster'minio _sm_ extermination, destruction
'sterno _sm_ (_Anat_) breastbone
ste'roide _sm_ steroid
ster'zare [ster'tsare] _vt, vi_ (_Aut_) to steer;
'sterzo _sm_ steering; (_volante_) steering
wheel
'stessi _ecc vb vedi_ **stare**
'stesso, -a _ag_ same; (_rafforzativo: in
persona, proprio_): **il re ~** the king himself _o_ in
person ▷ _pron_ **lo(la) ~(a)** the same (one); **i
suoi stessi avversari lo ammirano** even
his enemies admire him; **fa lo ~** it doesn't
matter; **per me è lo ~** it's all the same to
me, it doesn't matter to me; _vedi_ **io; tu** _ecc_
ste'sura _sf_ drafting _no pl_, drawing up _no
pl_; draft
'stetti _ecc vb vedi_ **stare**
'stia _ecc vb vedi_ **stare**
sti'lare _vt_ to draw up, draft
'stile _sm_ style; **stile libero** freestyle;
sti'lista, -i _sm_ designer
stilo'grafica, -che _sf_ (_anche:_ **penna ~**)
fountain pen
'stima _sf_ esteem; valuation; assessment,
estimate
sti'mare _vt_ (_persona_) to esteem, hold in
high regard; (_terreno, casa ecc_) to value;

(_stabilire in misura approssimativa_) to
estimate, assess; (_ritenere_): **~ che** to
consider that; **stimarsi fortunato** to
consider o.s. (to be) lucky
stimo'lare _vt_ to stimulate; (_incitare_): **~ qn
(a fare)** to spur sb on (to do)
'stimolo _sm_ (_anche fig_) stimulus
'stingere ['stindʒere] _vt, vi_ (_anche:_
stingersi) to fade; **'stinto, -a** _pp di_
stingere
sti'pare _vt_ to cram, pack; **stiparsi** _vpr_
(_accalcarsi_) to crowd, throng
sti'pendio _sm_ salary
'stipite _sm_ (_di porta, finestra_) jamb
stipu'lare _vt_ (_redigere_) to draw up
sti'rare _vt_ (_abito_) to iron; (_distendere_) to
stretch; (_strappare: muscolo_) to strain;
stirarsi _vpr_ to stretch (o.s.)
stiti'chezza [stiti'kettsa] _sf_ constipation
'stitico, -a, -ci, -che _ag_ constipated
'stiva _sf_ (_di nave_) hold
sti'vale _sm_ boot
'stizza ['stittsa] _sf_ anger, vexation
'stoffa _sf_ material, fabric; (_fig_): **aver la ~ di**
to have the makings of
'stomaco, -chi _sm_ stomach; **dare di ~** to
vomit, be sick
sto'nato, -a _ag_ (_persona_) off-key;
(_strumento_) off-key, out of tune
stop _sm inv_ (_Tel_) stop; (_Aut: cartello_) stop
sign; (: _fanalino d'arresto_) brake-light
'storcere ['stɔrtʃere] _vt_ to twist; **storcersi**
vpr to writhe, twist; **~ il naso** (_fig_) to turn
up one's nose; **storcersi la caviglia** to
twist one's ankle
stor'dire _vt_ (_intontire_) to stun, daze;
stor'dito, -a _ag_ stunned
'storia _sf_ (_scienza, avvenimenti_) history;
(_racconto, bugia_) story; (_faccenda, questione_)
business _no pl_; (_pretesto_) excuse, pretext;
storie _sfpl_ (_smancerie_) fuss _sg_; **'storico, -a,
-ci, -che** _ag_ historic(al) ▷ _sm_ historian
stori'one _sm_ (_Zool_) sturgeon
'stormo _sm_ (_di uccelli_) flock
'storpio, -a _ag_ crippled, maimed
'storsi _ecc vb vedi_ **storcere**
'storta _sf_ (_distorsione_) sprain, twist
'storto, -a _pp di_ **storcere** ▷ _ag_ (_chiodo_)
twisted, bent; (_gamba, quadro_) crooked
sto'viglie [sto'viʎʎe] _sfpl_ dishes _pl_,
crockery
'strabico, -a, -ci, -che _ag_ squint-eyed;
(_occhi_) squint
strac'chino [strak'kino] _sm_ type of soft
cheese
stracci'are [strat'tʃare] _vt_ to tear;
stracciarsi _vpr_ to tear
'straccio, -a, -ci, -ce ['strattʃo] _ag_ **carta
straccia** waste paper ▷ _sm_ rag; (_per pulire_)

cloth, duster; **stracci** smpl (peg: indumenti) rags; **si è ridotto a uno ~** he's worn himself out; **non ha uno ~ di lavoro** he's not got a job of any sort

'strada sf road; (di città) street; (cammino, via, fig) way; **che ~ devo prendere per andare a …?** which road do I take for …?; **farsi ~** (fig) to do well for o.s.; **essere fuori ~** (fig) to be on the wrong track; **~ facendo** on the way; **strada senza uscita** dead end; **stra'dale** ag road cpd

strafalci'one [strafal'tʃone] sm blunder, howler

stra'fare vi to overdo it

strafot'tente ag **è ~** he doesn't give a damn, he couldn't care less

'strage ['stradʒe] sf massacre, slaughter

stralu'nato, -a ag (occhi) rolling; (persona) beside o.s., very upset

'strambo, -a ag strange, queer

strampa'lato, -a ag odd, eccentric

stra'nezza [stra'nettsa] sf strangeness

strango'lare vt to strangle

strani'ero, -a ag foreign ▷ sm/f foreigner

> Attenzione! In inglese esiste la parola stranger, che però significa sconosciuto oppure estraneo.

'strano, -a ag strange, odd

straordi'nario, -a ag extraordinary; (treno ecc) special ▷ sm (lavoro) overtime

strapi'ombo sm overhanging rock; **a ~** overhanging

strap'pare vt (gen) to tear, rip; (pagina ecc) to tear off, tear out; (sradicare) to pull up; (togliere): **~ qc a qn** to snatch sth from sb; (fig) to wrest sth from sb; **strapparsi** vpr (lacerarsi) to rip, tear; (rompersi) to break; **strapparsi un muscolo** to tear a muscle; **'strappo** sm pull, tug; tear, rip; **fare uno strappo alla regola** to make an exception to the rule; **strappo muscolare** torn muscle

strari'pare vi to overflow

'strascico, -chi ['straʃʃiko] sm (di abito) train; (conseguenza) after-effect

strata'gemma, -i [strata'dʒemma] sm stratagem

strate'gia, -'gie [strate'dʒia] sf strategy; **stra'tegico, -a, -ci, -che** ag strategic

'strato sm layer; (rivestimento) coat, coating; (Geo, fig) stratum; (Meteor) stratus; **strato d'ozono** ozone layer

strat'tone sm tug, jerk; **dare uno ~ a qc** to tug o jerk sth, give sth a tug o jerk

strava'gante ag odd, eccentric

stra'volto, -a pp di **stravolgere**

'strazio sm torture; (fig: cosa fatta male): **essere uno ~** to be appalling

'strega, -ghe sf witch

stre'gare vt to bewitch

stre'gone sm (mago) wizard; (di tribù) witch doctor

strepi'toso, -a ag clamorous, deafening; (fig: successo) resounding

stres'sante ag stressful

stres'sato, -a ag under stress

stretch [stretʃ] ag inv stretch

'stretta sf (di mano) grasp; (finanziaria) squeeze; (fig: dolore, turbamento) pang; **una ~ di mano** a handshake; **essere alle strette** to have one's back to the wall; vedi anche **stretto**

stretta'mente av tightly; (rigorosamente) strictly

'stretto, -a pp di **stringere** ▷ ag (corridoio, limiti) narrow; (gonna, scarpe, nodo, curva) tight; (intimo: parente, amico) close, (rigoroso: osservanza) strict; (preciso: significato) precise, exact ▷ sm (braccio di mare) strait; **a denti stretti** with clenched teeth; **lo ~ necessario** the bare minimum; **stret'toia** sf bottleneck; (fig) tricky situation

stri'ato, -a ag streaked

'stridulo, -a ag shrill

stril'lare vt, vi to scream, shriek; **'strillo** sm scream, shriek

strimin'zito, -a [strimin'tsito] ag (misero) shabby; (molto magro) skinny

strimpel'lare vt (Mus) to strum

'stringa, -ghe sf lace

strin'gato, -a ag (fig) concise

'stringere ['strindʒere] vt (avvicinare due cose) to press (together), squeeze (together); (tenere stretto) to hold tight, clasp, clutch; (pugno, mascella, denti) to clench; (labbra) to compress; (avvitare) to tighten; (abito) to take in; (scarpe) to pinch, be tight for; (fig: concludere: patto) to make; (: accelerare: passo, tempo) to quicken ▷ vi (essere stretto) to be tight; (tempo: incalzare) to be pressing

'strinsi ecc vb vedi **stringere**

'striscia, -sce ['striʃʃa] sf (di carta, tessuto ecc) strip; (riga) stripe; **strisce (pedonali)** zebra crossing sg

strisci'are [striʃʃare] vt (piedi) to drag; (muro, macchina) to graze ▷ vi to crawl, creep

'striscio ['striʃʃo] sm graze; (Med) smear; **colpire di ~** to graze

strisci'one [striʃʃone] sm banner

strito'lare vt to grind

striz'zare [strit'tsare] vt (panni) to wring (out); **~ l'occhio** to wink

'strofa sf strophe

strofi'naccio [strofi'nattʃo] sm duster, cloth; (per piatti) dishcloth; (per pavimenti)

floorcloth

strofi'nare vt to rub

stron'care vt to break off; (fig: ribellione) to suppress, put down; (: film, libro) to tear to pieces

'stronzo ['strontso] sm (sterco) turd; (fig fam!: persona) shit (!)

stroz'zare [strot'tsare] vt (soffocare) to choke, strangle

struccarsi vpr to remove one's make-up

strumen'tale ag (Mus) instrumental

strumentaliz'zare [strumentalid'dzare] vt to exploit, use to one's own ends

stru'mento sm (arnese, fig) instrument, tool; (Mus) instrument; **~ a corda** o **ad arco/a fiato** stringed/wind instrument

'strutto sm lard

strut'tura sf structure

'struzzo ['struttso] sm ostrich

stuc'care vt (muro) to plaster; (vetro) to putty; (decorare con stucchi) to stucco

'stucco, -chi sm plaster; (da vetri) putty; (ornamentale) stucco; **rimanere di ~** (fig) to be dumbfounded

stu'dente, -'essa sm/f student; (scolaro) pupil, schoolboy/girl

studi'are vt to study

'studio sm studying; (ricerca, saggio, stanza) study; (di professionista) office; (di artista, Cinema, TV, Radio) studio; **studi** smpl (Ins) studies; **studio medico** doctor's surgery (BRIT) o office (US)

studi'oso, -a ag studious, hard-working ▷ sm/f scholar

'stufa sf stove; **stufa elettrica** electric fire o heater

stu'fare vt (Cuc) to stew; (fig: fam) to bore; **stufarsi** vpr (fam): **stufarsi (di)** (fig) to get fed up (with); **'stufo, -a** (fam) ag **essere stufo di** to be fed up with, be sick and tired of

stu'oia sf mat

stupefa'cente [stupefa'tʃɛnte] ag stunning, astounding ▷ sm drug, narcotic

stupe'fatto, -a pp di **stupefare**

stu'pendo, -a ag marvellous, wonderful

stupi'daggine [stupi'daddʒine] sf stupid thing (to do o say)

stupidità sf stupidity

'stupido, -a ag stupid

stu'pire vt to amaze, stun ▷ vi **stupirsi**; **~ (di)** to be amazed (at), be stunned (by)

stu'pore sm amazement, astonishment

stu'prare vt to rape

'stupro sm rape

stu'rare vt (lavandino) to clear

stuzzica'denti [stuttsika'dɛnti] sm toothpick

stuzzi'care [stuttsi'kare] vt (ferita ecc)

to poke (at), prod (at); (fig) to tease; (: appetito) to whet; (: curiosità) to stimulate; **~ i denti** to pick one's teeth

 PAROLA CHIAVE

su (su +il = **sul**, su +lo = **sullo**, su +l' = **sull'**, su +la = **sulla**, su +i = **sui**, su +gli = **sugli**, su +le = **sulle**) prep **1** (gen) on; (moto) on(to); (in cima a) on (top of); **mettilo sul tavolo** put it on the table; **un paesino sul mare** a village by the sea

2 (argomento) about, on; **un libro su Cesare** a book on o about Caesar

3 (circa) about; **costerà sui 3 milioni** it will cost about 3 million; **una ragazza sui 17 anni** a girl of about 17 (years of age)

4: **su misura** made to measure; **su richiesta** on request; **3 casi su dieci** 3 cases out of 10

▷ av **1** (in alto, verso l'alto) up; **vieni su** come on up; **guarda su** look up; **su le mani!** hands up!; **in su** (verso l'alto) up(wards); (in poi) onwards; **dai 20 anni in su** from the age of 20 onwards

2 (addosso) on; **cos'hai su?** what have you got on?

▷ escl come on!; **su coraggio!** come on, cheer up!

su'bacqueo, -a ag underwater ▷ sm skin-diver

sub'buglio [sub'buʎʎo] sm confusion, turmoil

'subdolo, -a ag underhand, sneaky

suben'trare vi **~ a qn in qc** to take over sth from sb

su'bire vt to suffer, endure

'subito av immediately, at once, straight away

subodo'rare vt (insidia ecc) to smell, suspect

subordi'nato, -a ag subordinate; (dipendente): **~ a** dependent on, subject to

suc'cedere [sut'tʃedere] vi (prendere il posto di qn): **~ a** to succeed; (venire dopo): **~ a** to follow; (accadere) to happen; **cos'è successo?** what happened?; **succes'sivo, -a** ag successive; **suc'cesso, -a** pp di **succedere** ▷ sm (esito) outcome; (buona riuscita) success; **di successo** (libro, personaggio) successful

succhi'are [suk'kjare] vt to suck (up); **succhi'otto** sm (per bambino) dummy

succhi'otto [suk'kjɔtto] sm dummy (BRIT), pacifier (US), comforter (US)

suc'cinto, -a [sut'tʃinto] ag (discorso) succinct; (abito) brief

'succo, -chi sm juice; (fig) essence, gist;

succo di frutta/pomodoro fruit/tomato juice

succur'sale *sf* branch (office)

sud *sm* south ▷ *ag inv* south; (*lato*) south, southern

Su'dafrica *sm* **il ~** South Africa; **sudafri'cano, -a** *ag, sm/f* South African

Suda'merica *sm* **il ~** South America

su'dare *vi* to perspire, sweat; **~ freddo** to come out in a cold sweat

su'dato, -a *ag* (*persona, mani*) sweaty; (*fig: denaro*) hard-earned ▷ *sf* (*anche fig*) sweat; **una vittoria sudata** a hard-won victory; **ho fatto una bella sudata per finirlo in tempo** it was a real sweat to get it finished in time

suddi'videre *vt* to subdivide

su'dest *sm* south-east

'sudicio, -a, -ci, -ce ['sudit∫u] *ag* dirty, filthy

su'dore *sm* perspiration, sweat

su'dovest *sm* south-west

suffici'ente [suffi't∫ɛnte] *ag* enough, sufficient; (*borioso*) self-important; (*Ins*) satisfactory; **suffici'enza** *sf* self-importance; pass mark; **a sufficienza** enough; **ne ho avuto a sufficienza!** I've had enough of this!

suf'fisso *sm* (*Ling*) suffix

suggeri'mento [suddʒeri'mento] *sm* suggestion; (*consiglio*) piece of advice, advice *no pl*

sugge'rire [suddʒe'rire] *vt* (*risposta*) to tell; (*consigliare*) to advise; (*proporre*) to suggest; (*Teatro*) to prompt

suggestio'nare [suddʒestjo'nare] *vt* to influence

sugges'tivo, -a [suddʒes'tivo] *ag* (*paesaggio*) evocative; (*teoria*) interesting, attractive

'sughero ['sugero] *sm* cork

'sugo, -ghi *sm* (*succo*) juice; (*di carne*) gravy; (*condimento*) sauce; (*fig*) gist, essence

sui'cida, -i, -e [sui't∫ida] *ag* suicidal ▷ *sm/f* suicide

suici'darsi [suit∫i'darsi] *vpr* to commit suicide

sui'cidio [sui't∫idjo] *sm* suicide

su'ino, -a *ag* **carne suina** pork ▷ *sm* pig

sul'tano, -a *sm/f* sultan/sultana

'suo (*f* **'sua**, *pl* **'sue, su'oi**) *det* **il ~, la sua** *ecc* (*di lui*) his; (*di lei*) her; (*di esso*) its; (*con valore indefinito*) one's, his/her; (*anche:* **S~**: *forma di cortesia*) your ▷ *pron* **il ~, la sua** *ecc* his; hers; yours; **i ~i** his (*o* her *o* one's *o* your) family

su'ocero, -a ['swɔt∫ero] *sm/f* father/mother-in-law

su'ola *sf* (*di scarpa*) sole

su'olo *sm* (*terreno*) ground; (*terra*) soil

suo'nare *vt* (*Mus*) to play; (*campana*) to ring; (*ore*) to strike; (*clacson, allarme*) to sound ▷ *vi* to play; (*telefono, campana*) to ring; (*ore*) to strike; (*clacson, fig: parole*) to sound

suone'ria *sf* alarm

su'ono *sm* sound

su'ora *sf* (*Rel*) sister

'super *sf* (*anche:* **benzina ~**) ≈ four-star (petrol) (BRIT), premium (US)

supe'rare *vt* (*oltrepassare: limite*) to exceed, surpass; (*percorrere*) to cover; (*attraversare: fiume*) to cross; (*sorpassare: veicolo*) to overtake; (*fig: essere più bravo di*) to surpass, outdo; (*: difficoltà*) to overcome; (*: esame*) to get through; **~ qn in altezza/peso** to be taller/heavier than sb; **ha superato la cinquantina** he's over fifty (years of age)

su'perbia *sf* pride; **su'perbo, -a** *ag* proud; (*fig*) magnificent, superb

superfici'ale [superfi't∫ale] *ag* superficial

super'ficie, -ci [super'fit∫e] *sf* surface

su'perfluo, -a *ag* superfluous

superi'ore *ag* (*piano, arto, classi*) upper; (*più elevato: temperatura, livello*): **~ (a)** higher (than); (*migliore*): **~ (a)** superior (to)

superla'tivo, -a *ag, sm* superlative

supermer'cato *sm* supermarket

su'perstite *ag* surviving ▷ *sm/f* survivor

superstizi'one [superstit'tsjone] *sf* superstition; **superstizi'oso, -a** *ag* superstitious

super'strada *sf* ≈ (toll-free) motorway

su'pino, -a *ag* supine

supplemen'tare *ag* extra; (*treno*) relief *cpd*; (*entrate*) additional

supple'mento *sm* supplement

sup'plente *sm/f* temporary member of staff, supply (*o* substitute) teacher

'supplica, -che *sf* (*preghiera*) plea; (*domanda scritta*) petition, request

suppli'care *vt* to implore, beseech

sup'plizio [sup'plittsjo] *sm* torture

sup'pongo, sup'poni *ecc vb vedi* **supporre**

sup'porre *vt* to suppose

sup'porto *sm* (*sostegno*) support

sup'posta *sf* (*Med*) suppository

su'premo, -a *ag* supreme

surge'lare [surdʒe'lare] *vt* to (deep-)freeze

surge'lato, -a [surdʒe'lato] *ag* (deep-)frozen ▷ *smpl* **i surgelati** frozen food *sg*

sur'plus *sm inv* (*Econ*) surplus

surriscal'dare *vt* to overheat

suscet'tibile [suʃʃet'tibile] *ag* (*sensibile*) touchy, sensitive

susci'tare [suʃʃi'tare] *vt* to provoke,

arouse
su'sina *sf* plum
susseguirsi *vpr* to follow one another
sus'sidio *sm* subsidy; **sussidi didattici** teaching aids
sussul'tare *vi* to shudder
sussur'rare *vt, vi* to whisper, murmur; **sus'surro** *sm* whisper, murmur
svagarsi *vpr* to amuse o.s.; to enjoy o.s.
'svago, -ghi *sm* (*riposo*) relaxation; (*ricreazione*) amusement; (*passatempo*) pastime
svaligi'are [zvali'dʒare] *vt* to rob, burgle (BRIT), burglarize (US)
svalutarsi *vpr* (Econ) to be devalued
svalutazi'one *sf* devaluation
sva'nire *vi* to disappear, vanish
svantaggi'ato, -a [zvantad'dʒato] *ag* at a disadvantage
svan'taggio [zvan'taddʒo] *sm* disadvantage; (*inconveniente*) drawback, disadvantage
svari'ato, -a *ag* varied; various
'svastica *sf* swastika
sve'dese *ag* Swedish ▷ *sm/f* Swede ▷ *sm* (Ling) Swedish
'sveglia ['zveʎʎa] *sf* waking up; (*orologio*) alarm (clock); **sveglia telefonica** alarm call
svegli'are [zveʎ'ʎare] *vt* to wake up; (*fig*) to awaken, arouse; **svegliarsi** *vpr* to wake up; (*fig*) to be revived, reawaken; **vorrei essere svegliato alle 7, per favore** could I have an alarm call at 7 am, please?
'sveglio, -a ['zveʎʎo] *ag* awake; (*fig*) quick-witted
sve'lare *vt* to reveal
'svelto, -a *ag* (*passo*) quick; (*mente*) quick, alert; **alla svelta** quickly
'svendere *vt* to sell off, clear
'svendita *sf* (Comm) (clearance) sale
'svengo *ecc vb vedi* **svenire**
sveni'mento *sm* fainting fit, faint
sve'nire *vi* to faint
sven'tare *vt* to foil, thwart
sven'tato, -a *ag* (*distratto*) scatterbrained; (*imprudente*) rash
svento'lare *vt, vi* to wave, flutter
sven'tura *sf* misfortune
sverrò *ecc vb vedi* **svenire**
sves'tire *vt* to undress; **svestirsi** *vpr* to get undressed
'Svezia ['zvɛttsja] *sf* **la ~** Sweden
svi'are *vt* to divert; (*fig*) to lead astray
svi'gnarsela [zviɲ'ɲarsela] *vpr* to slip away, sneak off
svilup'pare *vt* to develop; **svilupparsi** *vpr* to develop; **può ~ questo rullino?** can you develop this film?
svi'luppo *sm* development
'svincolo *sm* (*stradale*) motorway (BRIT) o expressway (US) intersection
'svista *sf* oversight
svi'tare *vt* to unscrew
'Svizzera ['zvittsera] *sf* **la ~** Switzerland
'svizzero, -a ['zvittsero] *ag, sm/f* Swiss
svogli'ato, -a [zvoʎ'ʎato] *ag* listless; (*pigro*) lazy
'svolgere ['zvɔldʒere] *vt* to unwind; (*srotolare*) to unroll; (*fig: argomento*) to develop; (*: piano, programma*) to carry out; **svolgersi** *vpr* to unwind; to unroll; (*fig: aver luogo*) to take place; (*: procedere*) to go on
'svolsi *ecc vb vedi* **svolgere**
'svolta *sf* (*atto*) turning *no pl*; (*curva*) turn, bend; (*fig*) turning-point
svol'tare *vi* to turn
svuo'tare *vt* to empty (out)

T, t [ti] *sf o m inv* (*lettera*) T, t; **T come Taranto** ≈ T for Tommy

t *abbr* = **tonnellata**

tabacche'ria [tabakke'ria] *sf* tobacconist's (shop)

ta'bacco, -chi *sm* tobacco

ta'bella *sf* (*tavola*) table; (*elenco*) list

tabel'lone *sm* (*pubblicitario*) billboard; (*con orario*) timetable board

TAC *sigla f* (*Med*: = *Tomografia Assiale Computerizzata*) CAT

tac'chino [tak'kino] *sm* turkey

'tacco, -chi *sm* heel; **tacchi a spillo** stiletto heels

taccu'ino *sm* notebook

ta'cere [ta'tʃere] *vi* to be silent *o* quiet; (*smettere di parlare*) to fall silent ▷ *vt* to keep to oneself, say nothing about; **far ~ qn** to make sb be quiet; (*fig*) to silence sb

ta'chimetro [ta'kimetro] *sm* speedometer

'tacqui *ecc vb vedi* **tacere**

ta'fano *sm* horsefly

'taglia ['taʎʎa] *sf* (*statura*) height; (*misura*) size; (*riscatto*) ransom; (*ricompensa*) reward; **taglia forte** (*di abito*) large size

taglia'carte [taʎʎa'karte] *sm inv* paperknife

tagli'ando [taʎ'ʎando] *sm* coupon

tagli'are [taʎ'ʎare] *vt* to cut; (*recidere, interrompere*) to cut off; (*intersecare*) to cut across, intersect; (*carne*) to carve; (*vini*) to blend ▷ *vi* to cut; (*prendere una scorciatoia*) to take a short-cut; **tagliarsi** *vpr* to cut o.s.; **mi sono tagliato** I've cut myself; **~ corto** (*fig*) to cut short; **~ la corda** (*fig*) to sneak off; **~ i ponti (con)** (*fig*) to break off relations (with); **~ la strada a qn** to cut across sb; **mi sono tagliato** I've cut myself

taglia'telle [taʎʎa'tɛlle] *sfpl* tagliatelle *pl*

taglia'unghie [taʎʎa'ungje] *sm inv* nail clippers *pl*

tagli'ente [taʎ'ʎɛnte] *ag* sharp

'taglio ['taʎʎo] *sm* cutting *no pl*; cut; (*parte tagliente*) cutting edge; (*di abito*) cut, style; (*di stoffa: lunghezza*) length; (*di vini*) blending; **di ~** on edge, edgeways; **banconote di piccolo/grosso ~** notes of small/large denomination; **taglio cesareo** Caesarean section

tailan'dese *ag, sm/f, sm* Thai

Tai'landia *sf* **la ~** Thailand

'talco *sm* talcum powder

  PAROLA CHIAVE

'tale *det* **1** (*simile, così grande*) such; **un(a) tale …** such (a) …; **non accetto tali discorsi** I won't allow such talk; **è di una tale arroganza** he is so arrogant; **fa una tale confusione!** he makes such a mess!

2 (*persona o cosa indeterminata*) such-and-such; **il giorno tale all'ora tale** on such-and-such a day at such-and-such a time; **la tal persona** that person; **ha telefonato una tale Giovanna** somebody called Giovanna phoned

3 (*nelle similitudini*): **tale … tale** like … like; **tale padre tale figlio** like father, like son; **hai il vestito tale quale il mio** your dress is just *o* exactly like mine

▷ *pron* (*indefinito: persona*): **un(a) tale** someone; **quel** (*o* **quella**) **tale** that person, that man (*o* woman); **il tal dei tali** what's-his-name

tale'bano *sm* Taliban

ta'lento *sm* talent

talis'mano *sm* talisman

tallon'cino [tallon'tʃino] *sm* counterfoil
tal'lone *sm* heel
tal'mente *av* so
'talpa *sf* (*Zool*) mole
tal'volta *av* sometimes, at times
tambu'rello *sm* tambourine
tam'buro *sm* drum
Ta'migi [ta'midʒi] *sm* **il ~** the Thames
tampo'nare *vt* (*otturare*) to plug; (*urtare:
macchina*) to crash o ram into
tam'pone *sm* (*Med*) wad, pad; (*per timbri*)
ink-pad; (*respingente*) buffer; **tampone
assorbente** tampon
'tana *sf* lair, den
'tanga *sm inv* G-string
tan'gente [tan'dʒɛnte] *ag* (*Mat*): **~ a**
tangential to ▷ *sf* tangent; (*quota*) share
tangenzi'ale [tandʒen'tsjale] *sf* (*Aut*)
bypass
'tanica *sf* (*contenitore*) jerry can

 PAROLA CHIAVE

'tanto, -a *det* **1** (*molto: quantità*) a lot of,
much; (: *numero*) a lot of, many; (*così tanto:
quantità*) so much, such a lot of; (: *numero*)
so many, such a lot of; **tante volte** so
many times, so often; **tanti auguri!** all
the best!; **tante grazie** many thanks;
tanto tempo so long, such a long time;
ogni tanti chilometri every so many
kilometres
2: **tanto ... quanto** (*quantità*) as much
... as; (*numero*) as many ... as; **ho tanta
pazienza quanta ne hai tu** I have as
much patience as you have o as you; **ha
tanti amici quanti nemici** he has as
many friends as he has enemies
3 (*rafforzativo*) such; **ho aspettato per
tanto tempo** I waited so long o for such a
long time
▷ *pron* **1** (*molto*) much, a lot; (*così tanto*)
so much, such a lot; **tanti, e** many, a lot;
so many, such a lot; **credevo ce ne fosse
tanto** I thought there was (such) a lot, I
thought there was plenty
2: **tanto quanto** (*denaro*) as much as;
(*cioccolatini*) as many as; **ne ho tanto
quanto basta** I have as much as I need;
due volte tanto twice as much
3 (*indeterminato*) so much; **tanto per
l'affitto, tanto per il gas** so much for the
rent, so much for the gas; **costa un tanto
al metro** it costs so much per metre;
di tanto in tanto, ogni tanto every so
often; **tanto vale che ...** I (*o we ecc*) may
as well ...; **tanto meglio!** so much the
better!; **tanto peggio per lui!** so much the
worse for him!

▷ *av* **1** (*molto*) very; **vengo tanto
volentieri** I'd be very glad to come; **non
ci vuole tanto a capirlo** it doesn't take
much to understand it
2 (*così tanto: con ag, av*) so; (: *con vb*) so
much, such a lot; **è tanto bella!** she's so
beautiful!; **non urlare tanto** don't shout
so much; **sto tanto meglio adesso** I'm
so much better now; **tanto ... che** so ...
(that); **tanto ... da** so ... as
3: **tanto ... quanto** as ... as; **conosco
tanto Carlo quanto suo padre** I know
both Carlo and his father; **non è poi tanto
complicato quanto sembri** it's not as
difficult as it seems; **tanto più insisti,
tanto più non mollerà** the more you
insist, the more stubborn he'll be; **quanto
più ... tanto meno** the more ... the less
4 (*solamente*) just; **tanto per cambiare/
scherzare** just for a change/a joke; **una
volta tanto** for once
5 (*a lungo*) (for) long
▷ *cong* after all

'tappa *sf* (*luogo di sosta, fermata*) stop, halt;
(*parte di un percorso*) stage, leg; (*Sport*) lap; **a
tappe** in stages
tap'pare *vt* to plug, stop up; (*bottiglia*) to
cork; **tapparsi** *vpr* **tapparsi in casa** to
shut o.s. up at home; **tapparsi la bocca**
to shut up; **tapparsi le orecchie** to turn
a deaf ear
tappa'rella *sf* rolling shutter
tappe'tino *sm* (*per auto*) car mat;
tappetino antiscivolo (*da bagno*) non-slip
mat
tap'peto *sm* carpet; (*anche*: **tappetino**)
rug; (*Sport*): **andare al ~** to go down for the
count; **mettere sul ~** (*fig*) to bring up for
discussion
tappez'zare [tappet'tsare] *vt* (*con carta*)
to paper; (*rivestire*): **~ qc (di)** to cover
sth (with); **tappezze'ria** *sf* (*tessuto*)
tapestry; (*carta da parati*) wallpaper; (*arte*)
upholstery; **far da tappezzeria** (*fig*) to be
a wallflower
'tappo *sm* stopper; (*in sughero*) cork
tar'dare *vi* to be late ▷ *vt* to delay; **~ a fare**
to delay doing
'tardi *av* late; **più ~** later (on); **ai più ~** at
the latest; **sul ~** (*verso sera*) late in the day;
far ~ to be late; (*restare alzato*) to stay up
late; **è troppo ~** it's too late
'targa, -ghe *sf* plate; (*Aut*) number (BRIT)
o license (US) plate; **tar'ghetta** *sf* (*su
bagaglio*) name tag; (*su porta*) nameplate
ta'riffa *sf* (*gen*) rate, tariff; (*di trasporti*)
fare; (*elenco*) price list; tariff
'tarlo *sm* woodworm

'**tarma** sf moth
tarocchi smpl (gioco) tarot sg
tarta'ruga, -ghe sf tortoise; (di mare)
turtle; (materiale) tortoiseshell
tar'tina sf canapé
tar'tufo sm (Bot) truffle
'**tasca, -sche** sf pocket; **tas'cabile** ag
(libro) pocket cpd
'**tassa** sf (imposta) tax; (doganale) duty;
(per iscrizione: a scuola ecc) fee; **tassa di
circolazione** road tax; **tassa di soggiorno**
tourist tax
tas'sare vt to tax; to levy a duty on
tas'sello sm plug; wedge
tassì sm inv = **taxi; tas'sista, -i, -e** sm/f
taxi driver
'**tasso** sm (di natalità, d'interesse ecc) rate;
(Bot) yew; (Zool) badger; **tasso di cambio/
d'interesse** rate of exchange/interest
tas'tare vt to feel; ~ **il terreno** (fig) to see
how the land lies
tasti'era sf keyboard
'**tasto** sm key; (tatto) touch, feel
tas'toni av **procedere (a)** ~ to grope one's
way forward
'**tatto** sm (senso) touch; (fig) tact; **duro al
~** hard to the touch; **aver ~** to be tactful,
have tact
tatu'aggio [tatu'addʒo] sm tattooing;
(disegno) tattoo
tatu'are vt to tattoo
'**tavola** sf table; (asse) plank, board;
(lastra) tablet; (quadro) panel (painting);
(illustrazione) plate; **tavola calda** snack
bar; **tavola rotonda** (fig) round table;
tavola a vela windsurfer
tavo'letta sf tablet, bar; **a** ~ (Aut) flat out
tavo'lino sm small table; (scrivania) desk
'**tavolo** sm table; **un** ~ **per 4 per favore** a
table for 4, please
'**taxi** sm inv taxi; **può chiamarmi un** ~ **per
favore?** can you call me a taxi, please?
'**tazza** ['tattsa] sf cup; **una** ~ **di caffè/tè**
a cup of coffee/tea; **tazza da tè/caffè**
tea/coffee cup
TBC abbr f (= tubercolosi) TB
te pron (soggetto: in forme comparative,
oggetto) you
tè sm inv tea; (trattenimento) tea party
tea'trale ag theatrical
te'atro sm theatre
techno ['tɛkno] ag inv (musica) techno
'**tecnica, -che** sf technique; (tecnologia)
technology
'**tecnico, -a, -ci, -che** ag technical ▷ sm/f
technician
tecnolo'gia [teknolo'dʒia] sf technology
te'desco, -a, -schi, -sche ag, sm/f, sm
German

te'game sm (Cuc) pan
'**tegola** sf tile
tei'era sf teapot
tel. abbr (= telefono) tel.
'**tela** sf (tessuto) cloth; (per vele, quadri)
canvas; (dipinto) canvas, painting; **di** ~
(calzoni) (heavy) cotton cpd; (scarpe, borsa)
canvas cpd; **tela cerata** oilcloth
te'laio sm (apparecchio) loom; (struttura)
frame
tele'camera sf television camera
teleco'mando sm remote control
tele'cronaca sf television report
telefo'nare vi to telephone, ring; to make
a phone call ▷ vt to telephone; ~ **a** to
phone up, ring up, call up
telefo'nata sf (telephone) call; ~ **a carico
del destinatario** reverse charge (BRIT) o
collect (US) call
tele'fonico, -a, -ci, -che ag (tele)phone
cpd
telefon'ino sm mobile phone
te'lefono sm telephone; **telefono a
gettoni** ≈ pay phone
telegior'nale [teledʒor'nale] sm
television news (programme)
tele'gramma, -i sm telegram
telela'voro sm teleworking
Tele'pass® sm inv automatic payment card
for use on Italian motorways
telepa'tia sf telepathy
teles'copio sm telescope
teleselezi'one [teleselet'tsjone] sf direct
dialling
telespetta'tore, -'trice sm/f (television)
viewer
tele'vendita sf teleshopping
televisi'one sf television
televi'sore sm television set
'**tema, -i** sm theme; (Ins) essay,
composition
te'mere vt to fear, be afraid of; (essere
sensibile a: freddo, calore) to be sensitive to
▷ vi to be afraid; (essere preoccupato): ~ **per**
to worry about, fear for; ~ **di/che** to be
afraid of/that
temperama'tite sm inv pencil sharpener
tempera'mento sm temperament
tempera'tura sf temperature
tempe'rino sm penknife
tem'pesta sf storm; **tempesta di sabbia/
neve** sand/snowstorm
'**tempia** sf (Anat) temple
'**tempio** sm (edificio) temple
'**tempo** sm (Meteor) weather; (cronologico)
time; (epoca) time, times pl; (di film, gioco:
parte) part; (Mus) time; (: battuta) beat;
(Ling) tense; **che** ~ **fa?** what's the weather
like?; **un** ~ once; ~ **fa** some time ago; **al** ~

stesso o **a un ~** at the same time; **per ~** early; **ha fatto il suo ~** it has had its day; **primo/secondo ~** (*Teatro*) first/second part; (*Sport*) first/second half; **in ~ utile** in due time o course; **a ~ pieno** full-time; **tempo libero** free time

tempo'rale *ag* temporal ▷ *sm* (*Meteor*) (thunder)storm

tempo'raneo, -a *ag* temporary

te'nace [te'natʃe] *ag* strong, tough; (*fig*) tenacious

te'naglie [te'naʎʎe] *sfpl* pincers *pl*

'tenda *sf* (*riparo*) awning; (*di finestra*) curtain; (*per campeggio ecc*) tent

ten'denza [ten'dentsa] *sf* tendency; (*orientamento*) trend; **avere ~ a** o **per qc** to have a bent for sth

'tendere *vt* (*allungare al massimo*) to stretch, draw tight; (*porgere: mano*) to hold out; (*fig: trappola*) to lay, set ▷ *vi* **~ a qc/a fare** to tend towards sth/to do; **~ l'orecchio** to prick up one's ears; **il tempo tende al caldo** the weather is getting hot; **un blu che tende al verde** a greenish blue

'tendine *sm* tendon, sinew

ten'done *sm* (*da circo*) tent

'tenebre *sfpl* darkness *sg*

te'nente *sm* lieutenant

te'nere *vt* to hold; (*conservare, mantenere*) to keep; (*ritenere, considerare*) to consider; (*spazio: occupare*) to take up, occupy; (*seguire: strada*) to keep to ▷ *vi* to hold; (*colori*) to be fast; (*dare importanza*): **~ a** to care about; **~ a fare** to want to do, be keen to do; **tenersi** *vpr* (*stare in una determinata posizione*) to stand; (*stimarsi*) to consider o.s.; (*aggrapparsi*): **tenersi a** to hold on to; (*attenersi*): **tenersi a** to stick to; **~ una conferenza** to give a lecture; **~ conto di qc** to take sth into consideration; **~ presente qc** to bear sth in mind

'tenero, -a *ag* tender; (*pietra, cera, colore*) soft; (*fig*) tender, loving

'tengo *ecc vb vedi* **tenere**

'tenni *ecc vb vedi* **tenere**

'tennis *sm* tennis

ten'nista, -i, e *sm/f* tennis player

te'nore *sm* (*tono*) tone; (*Mus*) tenor; **tenore di vita** (*livello*) standard of living

tensi'one *sf* tension

ten'tare *vt* (*indurre*) to tempt; (*provare*): **~ qc/di fare** to attempt o try sth/to do; **tenta'tivo** *sm* attempt; **tentazi'one** *sf* temptation

tenten'nare *vi* to shake, be unsteady; (*fig*) to hesitate, waver

ten'toni *av* **andare a ~** (*anche fig*) to grope one's way

'tenue *ag* (*sottile*) fine; (*colore*) soft; (*fig*) slender, slight

te'nuta *sf* (*capacità*) capacity; (*divisa*) uniform; (*abito*) dress; (*Agr*) estate; **a ~ d'aria** airtight; **tenuta di strada** roadholding power

teolo'gia [teolo'dʒia] *sf* theology

teo'ria *sf* theory

te'pore *sm* warmth

tep'pista, -i *sm* hooligan

tera'pia *sf* therapy; **terapia intensiva** intensive care

tergicris'tallo [terdʒikris'tallo] *sm* windscreen (*BRIT*) o windshield (*US*) wiper

tergiver'sare [terdʒiver'sare] *vi* to shilly-shally

ter'male *ag* thermal; **stazione** *sf* **~** spa

'terme *sfpl* thermal baths

termi'nale *ag, sm* terminal

termi'nare *vt* to end; (*lavoro*) to finish ▷ *vi* to end

'termine *sm* term; (*fine, estremità*) end; (*di territorio*) boundary, limit; **contratto a ~** (*Comm*) forward contract; **a breve/lungo ~** short-/long-term; **parlare senza mezzi termini** to talk frankly, not to mince one's words

ter'mometro *sm* thermometer

'termos *sm inv* = **thermos®**

termosi'fone *sm* radiator

ter'mostato *sm* thermostat

'terra *sf* (*gen, Elettr*) earth; (*sostanza*) soil, earth; (*opposto al mare*) land *no pl*; (*regione, paese*) land; (*argilla*) clay; **terre** *sfpl* (*possedimento*) lands, land *sg*; **a** o **per ~** (*stato*) on the ground (o floor); (*moto*) to the ground, down; **mettere a ~** (*Elettr*) to earth

terra'cotta *sf* terracotta; **vasellame** *sm* **di ~** earthenware

terra'ferma *sf* dry land, terra firma; (*continente*) mainland

ter'razza [ter'rattsa] *sf* terrace

ter'razzo [ter'rattso] *sm* = **terrazza**

terre'moto *sm* earthquake

ter'reno, -a *ag* (*vita, beni*) earthly ▷ *sm* (*suolo, fig*) ground; (*Comm*) land *no pl*, plot (of land); site; (*Sport, Mil*) field

ter'restre *ag* (*superficie*) of the earth, earth's; (*di terra: battaglia, animale*) land *cpd*; (*Rel*) earthly, worldly

ter'ribile *ag* terrible, dreadful

terrifi'cante *ag* terrifying

ter'rina *sf* tureen

territori'ale *ag* territorial

terri'torio *sm* territory

ter'rore *sm* terror; **terro'rismo** *sm* terrorism; **terro'rista, -i, -e** *sm/f* terrorist

terroriz'zare [terrorid'dzare] *vt* to terrorize

terza ['tɛrtsa] sf (Scol: elementare) ≈ third year at primary school; (: media) ≈ second year at secondary school; (: superiore) ≈ fifth year at secondary school; (Aut) third gear

ter'zino [ter'tsino] sm (Calcio) fullback, back

'terzo, -a ['tɛrtso] ag third ▷ sm (frazione) third; (Dir) third party; **terza pagina** (Stampa) Arts page; **terzi** smpl (altri) others, other people

'teschio ['tɛskjo] sm skull

'tesi¹ sf thesis; **tesi di laurea** degree thesis

'tesi ecc² vb vedi **tendere**

'teso, -a pp di **tendere** ▷ ag (tirato) taut, tight; (fig) tense

te'soro sm treasure; **il Ministero del T~** the Treasury

'tessera sf (documento) card

tes'suto sm fabric, material; (Biol) tissue

test ['tɛst] sm inv test

'testa sf head; (di cose: estremità, parte anteriore) head, front; **di ~** (vettura ecc) front; **tenere ~ a qn** (nemico ecc) to stand up to sb; **fare di ~ propria** to go one's own way; **in ~** (Sport) in the lead; **~ o croce?** heads or tails?; **avere la ~ dura** to be stubborn; **testa d'aglio** bulb of garlic; **testa di serie** (Tennis) seed, seeded player

testa'mento sm (atto) will; **l'Antico/il Nuovo T~** (Rel) the Old/New Testament

tes'tardo, -a ag stubborn, pig-headed

tes'tata sf (parte anteriore) head; (intestazione) heading

tes'ticolo sm testicle

testi'mone sm/f (Dir) witness; **testimone oculare** eye witness

testimoni'are vt to testify; (fig) to bear witness to, testify to ▷ vi to give evidence, testify

'testo sm text; **fare ~** (opera, autore) to be authoritative; **questo libro non fa ~** this book is not essential reading

tes'tuggine [tes'tuddʒine] sf tortoise; (di mare) turtle

'tetano sm (Med) tetanus

'tetto sm roof; **tet'toia** sf roofing; canopy

tettuccio [tet'tuttʃo] sm **~ apribile** (Aut) sunroof

'Tevere sm **il ~** the Tiber

TG, Tg abbr = **telegiornale**

'thermos® ['tɛrmos] sm inv vacuum o Thermos® flask

ti pron (dav lo, la, li, le, ne diventa **te**) ▷ pron (oggetto) you; (complemento di termine) (to) you; (riflessivo) yourself

'Tibet sm **il ~** Tibet

'tibia sf tibia, shinbone

tic sm inv tic, (nervous) twitch; (fig) mannerism

ticchet'tio [tikket'tio] sm (di macchina da scrivere) clatter; (di orologio) ticking; (della pioggia) patter

'ticket sm inv (su farmaci) prescription charge

ti'ene ecc vb vedi **tenere**

ti'epido, -a ag lukewarm, tepid

'tifo sm (Med) typhus; (fig): **fare il ~ per** to be a fan of

ti'fone sm typhoon

ti'foso, -a sm/f (Sport ecc) fan

tigì [ti'dʒi] sm inv TV news

'tiglio ['tiʎʎo] sm lime (tree), linden (tree)

'tigre sf tiger

tim'brare vt to stamp; (annullare: francobolli) to postmark; **~ il cartellino** to clock in

'timbro sm stamp; (Mus) timbre, tone

'timido, -a ag shy; timid

'timo sm thyme

ti'mone sm (Naut) rudder

ti'more sm (paura) fear; (rispetto) awe

'timpano sm (Anat) eardrum; (Mus)

'tingere ['tindʒere] vt to dye

'tinsi ecc vb vedi **tingere**

'tinta sf (materia colorante) dye; (colore) colour, shade

tintin'nare vi to tinkle

tinto'ria sf (lavasecco) dry cleaner's (shop)

tin'tura sf (operazione) dyeing; (colorante) dye; **tintura di iodio** tincture of iodine

'tipico, -a, -ci, -che ag typical

'tipo sm type; (genere) kind, type; (fam) chap, fellow; **che ~ di...?** what kind of ...?

tipogra'fia sf typography; (procedimento) letterpress (printing); (officina) printing house

TIR sigla m (= Transports Internationaux Routiers) International Heavy Goods Vehicle

ti'rare vt (gen) to pull; (estrarre): **~ qc da** to take o pull sth out of; to get sth out of; to extract sth from; (chiudere: tenda ecc) to draw, pull; (tracciare: disegnare) to draw, trace; (lanciare: sasso, palla) to throw; (stampare) to print; (pistola, freccia) to fire ▷ vi (pipa, camino) to draw; (vento) to blow; (abito) to be tight; (fare fuoco) to fire; (fare del tiro, Calcio) to shoot; **~ avanti** vi to struggle on ▷ vt to keep going; **~ fuori** (estrarre) to take out, pull out; **~ giù** (abbassare) to bring down, to lower; (da scaffale ecc.) to take down; **~ su** to pull up; (capelli) to put up; (fig: bambino) to bring up; **tirarsi** vpr **tirarsi indietro** to draw back; (fig) to back out; **~ a indovinare** to take a guess; **~ sul prezzo** to bargain; **tirar dritto** to keep right on going; **tirati su!** (fig) cheer up!; **~ via** (togliere) to take off

tira'tura *sf* (*azione*) printing; (*di libro*) (print) run; (*di giornale*) circulation

'tirchio, -a ['tirkjo] *ag* mean, stingy

'tiro *sm* shooting *no pl*, firing *no pl*; (*colpo, sparo*) shot; (*di palla: lancio*) throwing *no pl*; throw; (*fig*) trick; **cavallo da ~** draught (BRIT) *o* draft (US) horse; **tiro a segno** target shooting; (*luogo*) shooting range; **tiro con l'arco** archery

tiro'cinio [tiro'tʃinjo] *sm* apprenticeship; (*professionale*) training

ti'roide *sf* thyroid (gland)

Tir'reno *sm* **il (mar) ~** the Tyrrhenian Sea

ti'sana *sf* herb tea

tito'lare *sm/f* incumbent; (*proprietario*) owner; (*Calcio*) regular player

'titolo *sm* title; (*di giornale*) headline; (*diploma*) qualification; (*Comm*) security; (*: azione*) share; **a che ~?** for what reason?; **a ~ di amicizia** out of friendship; **a ~ di premio** as a prize; **titolo di credito** share; **titoli di stato** government securities; **titoli di testa** (*Cinema*) credits

titu'bante *ag* hesitant, irresolute

toast [toust] *sm inv* toasted sandwich (*generally with ham and cheese*)

toc'cante *ag* touching

toc'care *vt* to touch; (*tastare*) to feel; (*fig: riguardare*) to concern; (*: commuovere*) to touch, move; (*: pungere*) to hurt, wound; (*: far cenno a: argomento*) to touch on, mention ▷ *vi* **~ a** (*accadere*) to happen to; (*spettare*) to be up to; **~ (il fondo)** (*in acqua*) to touch the bottom; **tocca a te difenderci** it's up to you to defend us; **a chi tocca?** whose turn is it?; **mi toccò pagare** I had to pay

toccherò *ecc* [tokke'rɔ] *vb vedi* **toccare**

'togliere ['tɔʎʎere] *vt* (*rimuovere*) to take away (*o* off), remove; (*riprendere, non concedere più*) to take away, remove; (*Mat*) to take away, subtract; **~ qc a qn** to take sth (away) from sb; **ciò non toglie che** nevertheless, be that as it may; **togliersi il cappello** to take off one's hat

toi'lette [twa'lɛt] *sf inv* toilet; (*mobile*) dressing table; **dov'è la ~?** where's the toilet?

'Tokyo *sf* Tokyo

'tolgo *ecc* *vb vedi* **togliere**

tolle'rare *vt* to tolerate

'tolsi *ecc* *vb vedi* **togliere**

'tomba *sf* tomb

tom'bino *sm* manhole cover

'tombola *sf* (*gioco*) tombola; (*ruzzolone*) tumble

'tondo, -a *ag* round

'tonfo *sm* splash; (*rumore sordo*) thud; (*caduta*): **fare un ~** to take a tumble

tonifi'care *vt* (*muscoli, pelle*) to tone up; (*irrobustire*) to invigorate, brace

tonnel'lata *sf* ton

'tonno *sm* tuna (fish)

'tono *sm* (*gen*) tone; (*Mus: di pezzo*) key; (*di colore*) shade, tone

ton'silla *sf* tonsil

'tonto, -a *ag* dull, stupid

to'pazio [to'pattsjo] *sm* topaz

'topo *sm* mouse

'toppa *sf* (*serratura*) keyhole; (*pezza*) patch

to'race [to'ratʃe] *sm* chest

'torba *sf* peat

'torcere ['tɔrtʃere] *vt* to twist; **torcersi** *vpr* to twist, writhe

'torcia, -ce ['tɔrtʃa] *sf* torch; **torcia elettrica** torch (BRIT), flashlight (US)

torci'collo [tortʃi'kɔllo] *sm* stiff neck

'tordo *sm* thrush

To'rino *sf* Turin

tor'menta *sf* snowstorm

tormen'tare *vt* to torment; **tormentarsi** *vpr* to fret, worry o.s.

tor'nado *sm* tornado

tor'nante *sm* hairpin bend

tor'nare *vi* to return, go (*o* come) back; (*ridiventare: anche fig*) to become (again); (*riuscire giusto, esatto: conto*) to work out; (*risultare*) to turn out (to be), prove (to be); **~ utile** to prove *o* turn out (to be) useful; **~ a casa** to go (*o* come) home; **torno a casa martedì** I'm going home on Tuesday

tor'neo *sm* tournament

'tornio *sm* lathe

'toro *sm* bull; (*dello zodiaco*): **T~** Taurus

'torre *sf* tower; (*Scacchi*) rook, castle; **torre di controllo** (*Aer*) control tower

tor'rente *sm* torrent

torri'one *sm* keep

tor'rone *sm* nougat

'torsi *ecc* *vb vedi* **torcere**

torsi'one *sf* twisting; torsion

'torso *sm* torso, trunk; (*Arte*) torso

'torsolo *sm* (*di cavolo ecc*) stump; (*di frutta*) core

'torta *sf* cake

tortel'lini *smpl* (*Cuc*) tortellini

'torto, -a *pp di* **torcere** ▷ *ag* (*ritorto*) twisted; (*storto*) twisted, crooked ▷ *sm* (*ingiustizia*) wrong; (*colpa*) fault; **a ~** wrongly; **aver ~** to be wrong

'tortora *sf* turtle dove

tor'tura *sf* torture; **tortu'rare** *vt* to torture

to'sare *vt* (*pecora*) to shear; (*siepe*) to clip

Tos'cana *sf* **la ~** Tuscany

'tosse *sf* cough; **ho la ~** I've got a cough

'tossico, -a, -ci, -che *ag* toxic

tossicodipen'dente *sm/f* drug addict

tos'sire *vi* to cough

tosta'pane *sm inv* toaster

to'tale *ag, sm* total

toto'calcio [toto'kaltʃo] *sm gambling pool betting on football results*, ≈ (football) pools *pl* (BRIT)

to'vaglia [to'vaʎʎa] *sf* tablecloth; **tovagli'olo** *sm* napkin

tra *prep* (*di due persone, cose*) between; (*di più persone, cose*) among(st); (*tempo: entro*) within, in; ~ **5 giorni** in 5 days' time; **sia detto ~ noi ...** between you and me ...; **litigano ~ (di) loro** they're fighting amongst themselves; ~ **breve** soon; ~ **sé e sé** (*parlare ecc*) to oneself

traboc'care *vi* to overflow

traboc'chetto [trabok'ketto] *sm* (*fig*) trap

'traccia, -ce ['trattʃa] *sf* (*segno, striscia*) trail, track; (*orma*) tracks *pl*: (*residuo, testimonianza*) trace, sign; (*abbozzo*) outline

tracci'are [trat'tʃare] *vt* to trace, mark (out); (*disegnare*) to draw; (*fig: abbozzare*) to outline

tra'chea [tra'kɛa] *sf* windpipe, trachea

tra'colla *sf* shoulder strap; **borsa a ~** shoulder bag

tradi'mento *sm* betrayal; (*Dir, Mil*) treason

tra'dire *vt* to betray; (*coniuge*) to be unfaithful to; (*doveri: mancare*) to fail in; (*rivelare*) to give away, reveal; **tradirsi** *vpr* to give o.s. away

tradizio'nale [tradittsjo'nale] *ag* traditional

tradizi'one [tradit'tsjone] *sf* tradition

tra'durre *vt* to translate; (*spiegare*) to render, convey; **me lo può ~?** can you translate this for me?; **traduzi'one** *sf* translation

'trae *vb vedi* **trarre**

traffi'cante *sm/f* dealer; (*peg*) trafficker

traffi'care *vi* (*commerciare*): ~ **(in)** to trade (in), deal (in); (*affaccendarsi*) to busy o.s. ▷ *vt* (*peg*) to traffic in

'traffico, -ci *sm* traffic; (*commercio*) trade, traffic; **traffico di armi/droga** arms/drug trafficking

tra'gedia [tra'dʒɛdja] *sf* tragedy

'traggo *ecc vb vedi* **trarre**

tra'ghetto [tra'getto] *sm* ferry(boat)

'tragico, -a, -ci, -che ['tradʒiko] *ag* tragic

tra'gitto [tra'dʒitto] *sm* (*passaggio*) crossing; (*viaggio*) journey

tragu'ardo *sm* (*Sport*) finishing line; (*fig*) goal, aim

'trai *ecc vb vedi* **trarre**

traiet'toria *sf* trajectory

trai'nare *vt* to drag, haul; (*rimorchiare*) to tow

tralasci'are [tralaʃ'ʃare] *vt* (*studi*) to

neglect; (*dettagli*) to leave out, omit

tra'liccio [tra'littʃo] *sm* (*Elettr*) pylon

tram *sm inv* tram

'trama *sf* (*filo*) weft, woof; (*fig: argomento, maneggio*) plot

traman'dare *vt* to pass on, hand down

tram'busto *sm* turmoil

tramez'zino [tramed'dzino] *sm* sandwich

'tramite *prep* through

tramon'tare *vi* to set, go down; **tra'monto** *sm* setting; (*del sole*) sunset

trampo'lino *sm* (*per tuffi*) springboard, diving board; (*per lo sci*) ski-jump

tra'nello *sm* trap

'tranne *prep* except (for), but (for); ~ **che** unless

tranquil'lante *sm* (*Med*) tranquillizer

tranquillità *sf* calm, stillness; quietness; peace of mind

tranquilliz'zare [trankwillid'dzare] *vt* to reassure

Attenzione! In inglese esiste il verbo *to tranquillize*, che però significa "calmare con un tranquillante".

tran'quillo, -a *ag* calm, quiet; (*bambino, scolaro*) quiet; (*sereno*) with one's mind at rest; **sta' ~** don't worry

transazi'one [transat'tsjone] *sf* compromise; (*Dir*) settlement; (*Comm*) transaction, deal

tran'senna *sf* barrier

transgenico, -a, -ci, -che [trans'dʒɛniko] *ag* genetically modified

tran'sigere [tran'sidʒere] *vi* (*venire a patti*) to compromise, come to an agreement

transi'tabile *ag* passable

transi'tare *vi* to pass

transi'tivo, -a *ag* transitive

'transito *sm* transit; **di ~** (*merci*) in transit; (*stazione*) transit *cpd*; **"divieto di ~"** "no entry"

'trapano *sm* (*utensile*) drill; (*Med*) trepan

trape'lare *vi* to leak, drip; (*fig*) to leak out

tra'pezio [tra'pɛttsjo] *sm* (*Mat*) trapezium; (*attrezzo ginnico*) trapeze

trapian'tare *vt* to transplant; **trapi'anto** *sm* transplanting; (*Med*) transplant; **trapianto cardiaco** heart transplant

'trappola *sf* trap

tra'punta *sf* quilt

'trarre *vt* to draw, pull; (*portare*) to take; (*prendere, tirare fuori*) to take (out), draw; (*derivare*) to obtain; ~ **origine da qc** to have its origins o originate in sth

trasa'lire *vi* to start, jump

trasan'dato, -a *ag* shabby

trasci'nare [traʃʃi'nare] *vt* to drag; **trascinarsi** *vpr* to drag o.s. along; (*fig*) to drag on

tras'correre vt (tempo) to spend, pass ▷ vi to pass

tras'crivere vt to transcribe

trascu'rare vt to neglect; (non considerare) to disregard

trasferi'mento sm transfer; (trasloco) removal, move; **trasferimento di chiamata** (Tel) call forwarding

trasfe'rire vt to transfer; **trasferirsi** vpr to move; **tras'ferta** sf transfer; (indennità) travelling expenses pl; (Sport) away game

trasfor'mare vt to transform, change; **trasformarsi** vpr to be transformed; **trasformarsi in qc** to turn into sth; **trasforma'tore** sm (Elec) transformer

trasfusi'one sf (Med) transfusion

trasgre'dire vt to disobey, contravene

traslo'care vt to move, transfer; **tras'loco, -chi** sm removal

tras'mettere vt (passare): ~ qc a qn to pass sth on to sb; (mandare) to send; (Tecn, Tel, Med) to transmit; (TV, Radio) to broadcast; **trasmissi'one** sf (gen, Fisica, Tecn) transmission; (passaggio) transmission, passing on; (TV, Radio) broadcast

traspa'rente ag transparent

traspor'tare vt to carry, move; (merce) to transport, convey; **lasciarsi ~ (da qc)** (fig) to let o.s. be carried away (by sth); **tras'porto** sm transport

'trassi ecc vb vedi **trarre**

trasver'sale ag transverse, cross(-); running at right angles

'tratta sf (Econ) draft; (di persone): **la ~ delle bianche** the white slave trade

tratta'mento sm treatment; (servizio) service

trat'tare vt (gen) to treat; (commerciare) to deal in; (svolgere: argomento) to discuss, deal with; (negoziare) to negotiate ▷ vi ~ **di** to deal with; ~ **con** (persona) to deal with; **si tratta di ...** it's about ...

tratte'nere vt (far rimanere: persona) to detain; (intrattenere: ospiti) to entertain; (tenere, frenare, reprimere) to hold back, keep back; (astenersi dal consegnare) to hold, keep; (detrarre: somma) to deduct; **trattenersi** vpr (astenersi) to restrain o.s., stop o.s.; (soffermarsi) to stay, remain

trat'tino sm dash; (in parole composte) hyphen

'tratto, -a pp di **trarre** ▷ sm (di penna, matita) stroke; (parte) part, piece; (di strada) stretch; (di mare, cielo) expanse; (di tempo) period (of time)

trat'tore sm tractor

tratto'ria sf restaurant

'trauma, -i sm trauma

tra'vaglio [tra'vaʎʎo] sm (angoscia) pain, suffering; (Med) pains pl

trava'sare vt to decant

tra'versa sf (trave) crosspiece; (via) side street; (Ferr) sleeper (BRIT), (railroad) tie (US); (Calcio) crossbar

traver'sata sf crossing; (Aer) flight, trip; **quanto dura la ~?** how long does the crossing take?

traver'sie sfpl mishaps, misfortunes

tra'verso, -a ag oblique; **di ~** ag askew ▷ av sideways; **andare di ~** (cibo) to go down the wrong way; **guardare di ~** to look askance at

travesti'mento sm disguise

travestirsi vpr to disguise o.s.

tra'volgere [tra'vɔldʒere] vt to sweep away, carry away; (fig) to overwhelm

tre num three

'treccia, -ce ['trettʃa] sf plait, braid

tre'cento [tre'tʃɛnto] num three hundred ▷ sm **il T~** the fourteenth century

'tredici ['treditʃi] num thirteen

'tregua sf truce; (fig) respite

tre'mare vi ~ **di** (freddo ecc) to shiver o tremble with; (paura, rabbia) to shake o tremble with

tre'mendo, -a ag terrible, awful

> Attenzione! In inglese esiste la parola tremendous, che però significa enorme oppure fantastico, strepitoso.

'tremito sm trembling no pl; shaking no pl; shivering no pl

'treno sm train; **è questo il ~ per...?** is this the train for ...?; **treno di gomme** set of tyres (BRIT) o tires (US); **treno merci** goods (BRIT) o freight train; **treno viaggiatori** passenger train

● **TRENI**
●
● There are various types of train in
● Italy. For short journeys there are
● the "Regionali" (R), which generally
● operate within a particular region,
● and the "Interregionali" (IR), which
● operate beyond regional boundaries.
● Medium- and long-distance passenger
● journeys are carried out by "Intercity" (I)
● and "Eurocity" (EC) trains. The "Eurostar"
● service (ES) offers fast connections
● between the major Italian cities. Night
● services are operated by "Intercity
● Notte" (ICN), "Euronight" (EN) and by
● "Espressi" (EXP).

'trenta num thirty; **tren'tesimo, -a** num thirtieth; **tren'tina** sf **una trentina (di)** thirty or so, about thirty

'trepidante *ag* anxious
tri'angolo *sm* triangle
tribù *sf inv* tribe
tri'buna *sf* (*podio*) platform; (*in aule ecc*)
gallery; (*di stadio*) stand
tribu'nale *sm* court
tri'ciclo [tri'tʃiklo] *sm* tricycle
tri'foglio [tri'fɔʎʎo] *sm* clover
'triglia ['triʎʎa] *sf* red mullet
tri'mestre *sm* period of three months;
(*Ins*) term, quarter (*Us*); (*Comm*) quarter
trin'cea [trin'tʃea] *sf* trench
trion'fare *vi* to triumph, win; **~ su** to
triumph over, overcome; **tri'onfo** *sm*
triumph
tripli'care *vt* to triple
'triplo, -a *ag* triple; treble ▷ *sm* **il ~ (di)**
three times as much (as); **la spesa è tripla**
it costs three times as much
'trippa *sf* (*Cuc*) tripe
'triste *ag* sad; (*luogo*) dreary, gloomy
tri'tare *vt* to mince, grind (*Us*)
trivi'ale *ag* vulgar, low
tro'feo *sm* trophy
'tromba *sf* (*Mus*) trumpet; (*Aut*) horn;
tromba d'aria whirlwind; **tromba delle
scale** stairwell
trom'bone *sm* trombone
trom'bosi *sf* thrombosis
tron'care *vt* to cut off; (*spezzare*) to break
off
'tronco, -a, -chi, -che *ag* cut off; broken
off; (*Ling*) truncated; (*fig*) cut short ▷ *sm*
(*Bot, Anat*) trunk; (*fig: tratto*) section;
licenziare qn in ~ to fire sb on the spot
'trono *sm* throne
tropi'cale *ag* tropical

 PAROLA CHIAVE

'troppo, -a *det* (*in eccesso: quantità*) too
much; (: *numero*) too many; **c'era troppa
gente** there were too many people; **fa
troppo caldo** it's too hot
▷ *pron* (*in eccesso: quantità*) too much;
(: *numero*) too many; **ne hai messo troppo**
you've put in too much; **meglio troppi
che pochi** better too many than too few
▷ *av* (*eccessivamente: con ag, av*) too; (: *con
vb*) too much; **troppo amaro/tardi** too
bitter/late; **lavora troppo** he works too
much; **costa troppo** it costs too much;
di troppo too much; too many; **qualche
tazza di troppo** a few cups too many; **2
euro di troppo** 2 euros too much; **essere
di troppo** to be in the way

'trota *sf* trout
'trottola *sf* spinning top

tro'vare *vt* to find; (*giudicare*): **trovo che**
I find o think that; **trovarsi** *vpr* (*reciproco:
incontrarsi*) to meet; (*essere, stare*) to be;
(*arrivare, capitare*) to find o.s.; **non trovo
più il portafoglio** I can't find my wallet;
andare a ~ qn to go and see sb; **~ qn
colpevole** to find sb guilty; **trovarsi bene**
(*in un luogo, con qn*) to get on well
truc'care *vt* (*falsare*) to fake; (*attore ecc*) to
make up; (*travestire*) to disguise; (*Sport*) to
fix; (*Aut*) to soup up; **truccarsi** *vpr* to make
up (one's face)
'trucco, -chi *sm* trick; (*cosmesi*) make-up
'truffa *sf* fraud, swindle; **truf'fare** *vt* to
swindle, cheat
truffa'tore, -'trice *sm/f* swindler, cheat
'truppa *sf* troop
tu *pron* you; **tu stesso(a)** you yourself;
dare del tu a qn to address sb as "tu"
'tubo *sm* tube; pipe; **tubo digerente**
(*Anat*) alimentary canal, digestive tract;
tubo di scappamento (*Aut*) exhaust
pipe
tuffarsi *vpr* to plunge, dive
'tuffo *sm* dive; (*breve bagno*) dip
tuli'pano *sm* tulip
tu'more *sm* (*Med*) tumour
Tuni'sia *sf* **la ~** Tunisia
'tuo (*f* **'tua**, *pl* **tu'oi**, **'tue**) *det* **il ~**, **la tua** *ecc*
your ▷ *pron* **il ~**, **la tua** *ecc* yours
tuo'nare *vi* to thunder; **tuona** it is
thundering, there's some thunder
tu'ono *sm* thunder
tu'orlo *sm* yolk
tur'bante *sm* turban
tur'bare *vt* to disturb, trouble
tur'bato, -a *ag* upset; (*preoccupato,
ansioso*) anxious
turbo'lenza [turbo'lɛntsa] *sf*
turbulence
tur'chese [tur'kese] *sf* turquoise
Tur'chia [tur'kia] *sf* **la ~** Turkey
'turco, -a, -chi, -che *ag* Turkish
▷ *sm/f* Turk/Turkish woman ▷ *sm* (*Ling*)
Turkish; **parlare ~** (*fig*) to talk double-
dutch
tu'rismo *sm* tourism; tourist industry;
tu'rista, -i, -e *sm/f* tourist; **turismo
sessuale** sex tourism; **tu'ristico, -a, -ci,
-che** *ag* tourist *cpd*
'turno *sm* turn; (*di lavoro*) shift; **di ~**
(*soldato, medico, custode*) on duty; **a ~**
(*rispondere*) in turn; (*lavorare*) in shifts; **fare
a ~ a fare qc** to take turns to do sth; **è il
suo ~** it's your (*o* his *ecc*) turn)
'turpe *ag* filthy, vile
'tuta *sf* overalls *pl*; (*Sport*) tracksuit
tu'tela *sf* (*Dir: di minore*) guardianship;
(: *protezione*) protection; (*difesa*) defence

tutta'via *cong* nevertheless, yet

'tutto, -a *det* **1** (*intero*) all; **tutto il latte**
all the milk; **tutta la notte** all night, the
whole night; **tutto il libro** the whole book;
tutta una bottiglia a whole bottle
  2 (*pl, collettivo*) all; every; **tutti i libri** all the
books; **tutte le notti** every night; **tutti i
venerdì** every Friday; **tutti gli uomini** all
the men; (*collettivo*) all men; **tutto l'anno**
all year long; **tutti e due** both *o* each of us
(*o* them *o* you); **tutti e cinque** all five of us
(*o* them *o* you)
  3 (*completamente*): **era tutta sporca**
she was all dirty; **tremava tutto** he was
trembling all over; **è tutta sua madre**
she's just *o* exactly like her mother
  4: **a tutt'oggi** so far, up till now; **a tutta
velocità** at full *o* top speed
  ▷ *pron* **1** (*ogni cosa*) everything, all;
(*qualsiasi cosa*) anything; **ha mangiato
tutto** he's eaten everything; **tutto
considerato** all things considered; **in
tutto: 5 euro in tutto** 5 euros in all; **in
tutto eravamo 50** there were 50 of us
in all
  2: **tutti, e** (*ognuno*) all, everybody;
vengono tutti they are all coming,
everybody's coming; **tutti quanti** all and
sundry
  ▷ *av* (*completamente*) entirely, quite; **è
tutto il contrario** it's quite *o* exactly the
opposite; **tutt'al più: saranno stati
tutt'al più una cinquantina** there were
about fifty of them at (the very) most;
tutt'al più possiamo prendere un treno
if the worst comes to the worst we can
take a train; **tutt'altro** on the contrary;
è tutt'altro che felice he's anything but
happy; **tutt'a un tratto** suddenly ▷ *sm* **il
tutto** the whole lot, all of it

tut'tora *av* still
TV [ti'vu] *sf inv* (= *televisione*) TV ▷ *sigla*
= **Treviso**

ubbidi'ente *ag* obedient
ubbi'dire *vi* to obey; **~ a** to obey; (*veicolo,
macchina*) to respond to
ubria'care *vt* **~ qn** to get sb drunk; (*alcool*)
to make sb drunk; (*fig*) to make sb's head
spin *o* reel; **ubriacarsi** *vpr* to get drunk;
ubriacarsi di (*fig*) to become intoxicated
with
ubri'aco, -a, -chi, -che *ag, sm/f* drunk
uc'cello [ut'tʃɛllo] *sm* bird
uc'cidere [ut'tʃidere] *vt* to kill; **uccidersi**
vpr (*suicidarsi*) to kill o.s.; (*perdere la vita*) to
be killed
u'dito *sm* (sense of) hearing
UE *sigla f* (= *Unione Europea*) EU
UEM *sigla f* (= *Unione economica e monetaria*)
EMU
'uffa *escl* tut!
uffici'ale [uffi'tʃale] *ag* official ▷ *sm* (*Amm*)
official, officer; (*Mil*) officer; **~ di stato
civile** registrar
uf'ficio [uf'fitʃo] *sm* (*gen*) office; (*dovere*)
duty; (*mansione*) task, function, job;
(*agenzia*) agency, bureau; (*Rel*) service; **d'~**
ag office *cpd*; official ▷ *av* officially; **ufficio
di collocamento** employment office;
ufficio informazioni information bureau;
ufficio oggetti smarriti lost property
office (*BRIT*), lost and found (*US*); **ufficio
(del) personale** personnel department;

ufficio postale post office

uffici'oso, -a [uffi'tʃoso] *ag* unofficial

uguagli'anza [ugwaʎ'ʎantsa] *sf* equality

uguagli'are [ugwaʎ'ʎare] *vt* to make equal; (*essere uguale*) to equal, be equal to; (*livellare*) to level; **uguagliarsi a** *o* **con qn** (*paragonarsi*) to compare o.s. to sb

ugu'ale *ag* equal; (*identico*) identical, the same; (*uniforme*) level, even ▷ *av* **costano ~** they cost the same; **sono bravi ~** they're equally good

UIL *sigla f* (= *Unione Italiana del Lavoro*) trade union federation

'ulcera ['ultʃera] *sf* ulcer

U'livo *sm* **l'~** *centre-left Italian political grouping*

u'livo = **olivo**

ulteri'ore *ag* further

ultima'mente *av* lately, of late

ulti'mare *vt* to finish, complete

'ultimo, -a *ag* (*finale*) last; (*estremo*) farthest, utmost; (*recente: notizia, moda*) latest; (*fig: sommo, fondamentale*) ultimate ▷ *sm/f* last (one); **fino all'~** to the last, until the end; **da ~, in ~** in the end; **abitare all'~ piano** to live on the top floor; **per ~** (*entrare, arrivare*) last

ulu'lare *vi* to howl

umanità *sf* humanity

u'mano, -a *ag* human; (*comprensivo*) humane

umidità *sf* dampness; humidity

'umido, -a *ag* damp; (*mano, occhi*) moist; (*clima*) humid ▷ *sm* dampness, damp; **carne in ~** stew

'umile *ag* humble

umili'are *vt* to humiliate; **umiliarsi** *vpr* to humble o.s.

u'more *sm* (*disposizione d'animo*) mood; (*carattere*) temper; **di buon/cattivo ~** in a good/bad mood

umo'rismo *sm* humour; **avere il senso dell'~** to have a sense of humour; **umo'ristico, -a, -ci, -che** *ag* humorous, funny

u'nanime *ag* unanimous

unci'netto [untʃi'netto] *sm* crochet hook

un'cino [un'tʃino] *sm* hook

undi'cenne [undi'tʃenne] *ag, sm/f* eleven-year-old

undi'cesimo, -a [undi'tʃɛzimo] *num* eleventh

'undici ['unditʃi] *num* eleven

'ungere ['undʒere] *vt* to grease, oil; (*Rel*) to anoint; (*fig*) to flatter, butter up

unghe'rese [unge'rese] *ag, sm/f, sm* Hungarian

Unghe'ria [unge'ria] *sf* **l'~** Hungary

'unghia ['ungja] *sf* (*Anat*) nail; (*di animale*)

claw; (*di rapace*) talon; (*di cavallo*) hoof

ungu'ento *sm* ointment

'unico, -a, -ci, -che *ag* (*solo*) only; (*ineguagliabile*) unique; (*singolo: binario*) single; **figlio(a) ~(a)** only son/daughter, only child

unifi'care *vt* to unite, unify; (*sistemi*) to standardize; **unificazi'one** *sf* uniting; unification; standardization

uni'forme *ag* uniform; (*superficie*) even ▷ *sf* (*divisa*) uniform

uni'one *sf* union; (*fig: concordia*) unity, harmony; **Unione europea** European Union; **ex Unione Sovietica** former Soviet Union

u'nire *vt* to unite; (*congiungere*) to join, connect; (: *ingredienti, colori*) to combine; (*in matrimonio*) to unite, join together; **unirsi** *vpr* to unite; (*in matrimonio*) to be joined together; **~ qc a** to unite sth with; to join *o* connect sth with; to combine sth with; **unirsi a** (*gruppo, società*) to join

unità *sf inv* (*unione, concordia*) unity; (*Mat, Mil, Comm, di misura*) unit; **unità di misura** unit of measurement

u'nito, -a *ag* (*paese*) united; (*amici, famiglia*) close; **in tinta unita** plain, self-coloured

univer'sale *ag* universal; general

università *sf inv* university

uni'verso *sm* universe

 PAROLA CHIAVE

'uno, -a (*dav sm* **un** + *C, V,* **uno** + *s impura, gn, pn, ps, x, z; dav sf* **un'** +*V,* **una** + *C*) *art indef* **1** a; (*dav vocale*) an; **un bambino** a child; **una strada** a street; **uno zingaro** a gypsy

2 (*intensivo*): **ho avuto una paura!** I got such a fright!

▷ *pron* **1** one; **prendine uno** take one (of them); **l'uno o l'altro** either (of them); **l'uno e l'altro** both (of them); **aiutarsi l'un l'altro** to help one another *o* each other; **sono entrati l'uno dopo l'altro** they came in one after the other

2 (*un tale*) someone, somebody

3 (*con valore impersonale*) one, you; **se uno vuole** if one wants, if you want

▷ *num* one; **una mela e due pere** one apple and two pears; **uno più uno fa due** one plus one equals two, one and one are two ▷ *sf* **è l'una** it's one (o'clock)

'unsi *ecc vb vedi* **ungere**

'unto, -a *pp di* **ungere** ▷ *ag* greasy, oily ▷ *sm* grease

u'omo (*pl* **u'omini**) *sm* man; **da ~** (*abito, scarpe*) men's, for men; **uomo d'affari** businessman; **uomo di paglia** stooge;

uomo politico politician; **uomo rana** frogman

u'ovo (*pl(f)* **u'ova**) *sm* egg; **uovo affogato/alla coque** poached/boiled egg; **uovo bazzotto/sodo** soft-/hard-boiled egg; **uovo di Pasqua** Easter egg; **uovo in camicia** poached egg; **uova strapazzate/al tegame** scrambled/fried eggs

ura'gano *sm* hurricane

urba'nistica *sf* town planning

ur'bano, -a *ag* urban, city *cpd*, town *cpd*; (*Tel: chiamata*) local; (*fig*) urbane

ur'gente [urˈdʒɛnte] *ag* urgent; **ur'genza** *sf* urgency; **in caso d'urgenza** in (case of) an emergency; **d'urgenza** *ag* emergency ▷ *av* urgently, as a matter of urgency

ur'lare *vi* (*persona*) to scream, yell; (*animale, vento*) to howl ▷ *vt* to scream, yell

'urlo (*pl(m)* **'urli**, *pl(f)* **'urla**) *sm* scream, yell; howl

urrà *escl* hurrah!

U.R.S.S. *abbr f* **l'U.R.S.S.** the USSR

ur'tare *vt* to bump into, knock against; (*fig: irritare*) to annoy ▷ *vi* **~ contro** *o* **in** to bump into, knock against, crash into; (*fig: imbattersi*) to come up against; **urtarsi** *vpr* (*reciproco: scontrarsi*) to collide; (: *fig*) to clash; (*irritarsi*) to get annoyed

'U.S.A. ['uza] *smpl* **gli U.S.A.** the USA

u'sanza [uˈzantsa] *sf* custom; (*moda*) fashion

u'sare *vt* to use, employ ▷ *vi* (*servirsi*): **~ di** to use; (: *diritto*) to exercise; (*essere di moda*) to be fashionable; (*essere solito*): **~ fare** to be in the habit of doing, be accustomed to doing ▷ *vb impers* **qui usa così** it's the custom round here; **u'sato, -a** *ag* used; (*consumato*) worn; (*di seconda mano*) used, second-hand ▷ *sm* second-hand goods *pl*

u'scire [uˈʃʃire] *vi* (*gen*) to come out; (*partire, andare a passeggio, a uno spettacolo ecc*) to go out; (*essere sorteggiato: numero*) to come up; **~ da** (*gen*) to leave; (*posto*) to go (*o* come) out of, leave; (*solco, vasca ecc*) to come out of; (*muro*) to stick out of; (*competenza ecc*) to be outside; (*infanzia, adolescenza*) to leave behind; (*famiglia nobile ecc*) to come from; **~ da** *o* **di casa** to go out; (*fig*) to leave home; **~ in automobile** to go out in the car, go for a drive; **~ di strada** (*Aut*) to go off *o* leave the road

u'scita [uˈʃʃita] *sf* (*passaggio, varco*) exit, way out; (*per divertimento*) outing; (*Econ: somma*) expenditure; (*Teatro*) entrance; (*fig: battuta*) witty remark; **dov'è l'~?** where's the exit?; **uscita di sicurezza** emergency exit

usi'gnolo [uziɲˈɲɔlo] *sm* nightingale

'uso *sm* (*utilizzazione*) use; (*esercizio*) practice; (*abitudine*) custom; **a ~ di** for (the use of); **d'~** (*corrente*) in use; **fuori ~** out of use; **uso esterno**; **per ~ esterno** for external use only

usti'one *sf* burn

usu'ale *ag* common, everyday

u'sura *sf* usury; (*logoramento*) wear (and tear)

uten'sile *sm* tool, implement; **utensili da cucina** kitchen utensils

u'tente *sm/f* user

'utero *sm* uterus

'utile *ag* useful ▷ *sm* (*vantaggio*) advantage, benefit; (*Econ: profitto*) profit

utiliz'zare [utilidˈdzare] *vt* to use, make use of, utilize

'uva *sf* grapes *pl*; **uva passa** raisins *pl*; **uva spina** gooseberry

UVA *abbr* (= *ultravioletto prossimo*) UVA

UVB *abbr* (= *ultravioletto remoto*) UVB

V

v. *abbr* (= *vedi*) v

va, va' *vb vedi* **andare**

va'cante *ag* vacant

va'canza [va'kantsa] *sf* (*riposo, ferie*) holiday(s) *pl* (BRIT), vacation (US); (*giorno di permesso*) day off, holiday; **vacanze** *sfpl* (*periodo di ferie*) holiday(s) *pl* (BRIT), vacation *sg* (US); **essere/andare in ~** to be/go on holiday *o* vacation; **sono qui in ~** I'm on holiday here; **vacanze estive** summer holiday(s) *o* vacation; **vacanze natalizie** Christmas holidays *o* vacation

> Attenzione! In inglese esiste la parola *vacancy* che però indica un posto vacante *o* una camera disponibile.

'vacca, -che *sf* cow

vacci'nare [vattʃi'nare] *vt* to vaccinate

vac'cino [vat'tʃino] *sm* (*Med*) vaccine

vacil'lare [vatʃil'lare] *vi* to sway, wobble; (*luce*) to flicker; (*fig: memoria, coraggio*) to be failing, falter

'vacuo, -a *ag* (*fig*) empty, vacuous

'vado *ecc vb vedi* **andare**

vaga'bondo, -a *sm/f* tramp, vagrant

va'gare *vi* to wander

vagherò *ecc* [vage'rɔ] *vb vedi* **vagare**

va'gina [va'dʒina] *sf* vagina

'vaglia ['vaʎʎa] *sm inv* money order; **vaglia postale** postal order

vagli'are [vaʎ'ʎare] *vt* to sift; (*fig*) to weigh up

'vago, -a, -ghi, -ghe *ag* vague

va'gone *sm* (*Ferr: per passeggeri*) coach; (: *per merci*) truck, wagon; **vagone letto** sleeper, sleeping car; **vagone ristorante** dining *o* restaurant car

'vai *vb vedi* **andare**

vai'olo *sm* smallpox

va'langa, -ghe *sf* avalanche

va'lere *vi* (*avere forza, potenza*) to have influence; (*essere valido*) to be valid; (*avere vigore, autorità*) to hold, apply; (*essere capace: poeta, studente*) to be good, be able ▷ *vt* (*prezzo, sforzo*) to be worth; (*corrispondere*) to correspond to; (*procurare*): **~ qc a qn** to earn sb sth; **valersi di** to make use of, take advantage of; **far ~** (*autorità ecc*) to assert; **vale a dire** that is to say; **~ la pena** to be worth the effort *o* worth it

'valgo *ecc vb vedi* **valere**

vali'care *vt* to cross

'valico, -chi *sm* (*passo*) pass

'valido, -a *ag* valid; (*rimedio*) effective; (*aiuto*) real; (*persona*) worthwhile

vali'getta [vali'dʒetta] *sf* briefcase; **valigetta ventiquattrore** overnight bag *o* case

va'ligia, -gie *o* **ge** [va'lidʒa] *sf* (suit)case; **fare le valigie** to pack (up)

'valle *sf* valley; **a ~** (*di fiume*) downstream; **scendere a ~** to go downhill

va'lore *sm* (*gen*) value; (*merito*) merit, worth; (*coraggio*) valour, courage; (*Comm: titolo*) security; **valori** *smpl* (*oggetti preziosi*) valuables

valoriz'zare [valorid'dzare] *vt* (*terreno*) to develop; (*fig*) to make the most of

va'luta *sf* currency, money; (*Banca*): **~ 15 gennaio** interest to run from January 15th

valu'tare *vt* (*casa, gioiello, fig*) to value; (*stabilire: peso, entrate, fig*) to estimate

'valvola *sf* (*Tecn, Anat*) valve; (*Elettr*) fuse

'valzer ['valtser] *sm inv* waltz

vam'pata *sf* (*di fiamma*) blaze; (*di calore*) blast; (: *al viso*) flush

vam'piro *sm* vampire

vanda'lismo *sm* vandalism

'vandalo *sm* vandal

vaneggi'are [vaned'dʒare] *vi* to rave

'vanga, -ghe *sf* spade

van'gelo [van'dʒɛlo] *sm* gospel

va'niglia [va'niʎʎa] *sf* vanilla

vanità *sf* vanity; (*di promessa*) emptiness; (*di sforzo*) futility; **vani'toso, -a** *ag* vain, conceited

'vanno *vb vedi* **andare**

'vano, -a *ag* vain ▷ *sm* (*spazio*) space; (*apertura*) opening; (*stanza*) room

V

van'taggio [van'taddʒo] *sm* advantage;
essere/portarsi in ~ *(Sport)* to be
in/take the lead; **vantaggi'oso, -a** *ag*
advantageous; favourable

vantarsi *vpr* **~ (di/di aver fatto)** to boast
o brag (about/about having done)

'vanvera *sf* **a ~** haphazardly; **parlare a ~**
to talk nonsense

va'pore *sm* vapour; *(anche: ~* **acqueo)**
steam; *(nave)* steamer; **a ~** *(turbina ecc)*
steam *cpd;* **al ~** *(Cuc)* steamed

va'rare *vt (Naut, fig)* to launch; *(Dir)* to pass

var'care *vt* to cross

'varco, -chi *sm* passage; **aprirsi un ~ tra
la folla** to push one's way through the
crowd

vare'china [vare'kina] *sf* bleach

vari'abile *ag* variable; *(tempo, umore)*
changeable, variable ▷ *sf (Mat)* variable

vari'cella [vari'tʃɛlla] *sf* chickenpox

vari'coso, -a *ag* varicose

varietà *sf inv* variety ▷ *sm inv* variety show

'vario, -a *ag* varied; *(parecchi: col sostantivo
al pl)* various; *(mutevole: umore)* changeable

'varo *sm (Naut: fig)* launch; *(di leggi)* passing

varrò *ecc vb vedi* **valere**

Var'savia *sf* Warsaw

va'saio *sm* potter

'vasca, -sche *sf* basin; **vasca da bagno**
bathtub, bath

vas'chetta [vas'ketta] *sf (per gelato)* tub;
(per sviluppare fotografie) dish

vase'lina *sf* Vaseline®

'vaso *sm (recipiente)* pot; *(: barattolo)* jar;
(: decorativo) vase; *(Anat)* vessel; **vaso da
fiori** vase; *(per piante)* flowerpot

vas'soio *sm* tray

'vasto, -a *ag* vast, immense

Vati'cano *sm* **il ~** the Vatican

ve *pron, av vedi* **vi**

vecchi'aia [vek'kjaja] *sf* old age

'vecchio, -a ['vɛkkjo] *ag* old ▷ *sm/f* old
man/woman; **i vecchii** the old

ve'dere *vt, vi* to see; **vedersi** *vpr* to meet,
see one another; **avere a che ~ con** to
have something to do with; **far ~ qc a qn**
to show sb sth; **farsi ~** to show o.s.; *(farsi
vivo)* to show one's face; **vedi di non farlo**
make sure you don't do it; **non (ci) si
vede** *(è buio ecc)* you can't see a thing; **non
lo posso ~** *(fig)* I can't stand him

ve'detta *sf (sentinella, posto)* look-out;
(Naut) patrol boat

'vedovo, -a *sm/f* widower/widow

vedrò *ecc vb vedi* **vedere**

ve'duta *sf* view; **vedute** *sfpl (fig: opinioni)*
views; **di larghe** *o* **ampie vedute** broad-
minded; **di vedute limitate** narrow-
minded

vege'tale [vedʒe'tale] *ag, sm* vegetable

vegetari'ano, -a [vedʒeta'rjano] *ag, sm/f*
vegetarian; **avete piatti vegetariani?** do
you have any vegetarian dishes?

vegetazi'one [vedʒetat'tsjone] *sf*
vegetation

'vegeto, -a ['vɛdʒeto] *ag (pianta)* thriving;
(persona) strong, vigorous

'veglia ['veʎʎa] *sf* wakefulness;
(sorveglianza) watch; *(trattenimento)*
evening gathering; **fare la ~ a un malato**
to watch over a sick person

vegli'one [veʎ'ʎone] *sm* ball, dance;
veglione di Capodanno New Year's Eve
party

ve'icolo *sm* vehicle

'vela *sf (Naut: tela)* sail; *(Sport)* sailing

ve'leno *sm* poison; **vele'noso, -a** *ag*
poisonous

veli'ero *sm* sailing ship

vel'luto *sm* velvet; **velluto a coste** cord

'velo *sm* veil; *(tessuto)* voile

ve'loce [ve'lotʃe] *ag* fast, quick ▷ *av*
fast, quickly; **velocità** *sf* speed; **a forte
velocità** at high speed; **velocità di
crociera** cruising speed

'vena *sf (gen)* vein; *(filone)* vein, seam; *(fig:
ispirazione)* inspiration; *(: umore)* mood;
essere in ~ di qc to be in the mood for sth

ve'nale *ag (prezzo, valore)* market *cpd; (fig)*
venal; mercenary

ven'demmia *sf (raccolta)* grape harvest;
(quantità d'uva) grape crop, grapes *pl; (vino
ottenuto)* vintage

'vendere *vt* to sell; **"vendesi"** "for sale"

ven'detta *sf* revenge

vendicarsi *vpr* **~ (di)** to avenge o.s. (for);
(per rancore) to take one's revenge (for); **~
su qn** to revenge o.s. on sb

'vendita *sf* sale; **la ~** *(attività)* selling;
(smercio) sales *pl;* **in ~** on sale; **vendita
all'asta** sale by auction; **vendita per
telefono** telesales *sg*

vene'rare *vt* to venerate

venerdì *sm inv* Friday; **di** *o* **il ~** on Fridays;
V~ Santo Good Friday

ve'nereo, -a *ag* venereal

Ve'nezia [ve'nɛttsja] *sf* Venice

'vengo *ecc vb vedi* **venire**

veni'ale *ag* venial

ve'nire *vi* to come; *(riuscire: dolce,
fotografia)* to turn out; *(come ausiliare:
essere)*: **viene ammirato da tutti** he is
admired by everyone; **~ da** to come from;
quanto viene? how much does it cost?;
far ~ *(mandare a chiamare)* to send for; **~ giù**
to come down; **~ meno** *(svenire)* to faint;
~ meno a qc not to fulfil sth; **~ su** to come
up; **~ a trovare qn** to come and see sb; **~**

via to come away
'**venni** *ecc vb vedi* **venire**
ven'taglio [ven'taʎʎo] *sm* fan
ven'tata *sf* gust (of wind)
ven'tenne *ag* **una ragazza ~** a twenty-year-old girl, a girl of twenty
ven'tesimo, -a *num* twentieth
'**venti** *num* twenty
venti'lare *vt* (*stanza*) to air, ventilate; (*fig: idea, proposta*) to air; **ventila'tore** *sm* ventilator, fan
ven'tina *sf* **una ~ (di)** around twenty, twenty or so
'**vento** *sm* wind
'**ventola** *sf* (*Aut, Tecn*) fan
ven'tosa *sf* (*Zool*) sucker; (*di gomma*) suction pad
ven'toso, -a *ag* windy
'**ventre** *sm* stomach
'**vera** *sf* wedding ring
vera'mente *av* really
ve'randa *sf* veranda(h)
ver'bale *ag* verbal ▷ *sm* (*di riunione*) minutes *pl*
'**verbo** *sm* (*Ling*) verb; (*parola*) word; (*Rel*): **il V~** the Word
'**verde** *ag, sm* green; **essere al ~** to be broke; **verde bottiglia/oliva** bottle/olive green
ver'detto *sm* verdict
ver'dura *sf* vegetables *pl*
'**vergine** ['verdʒine] *sf* virgin; (*dello zodiaco*): **V~** Virgo ▷ *ag* virgin; (*ragazza*): **essere ~** to be a virgin
ver'gogna [ver'ɡoɲɲa] *sf* shame; (*timidezza*) shyness, embarrassment; **vergo'gnarsi** *vpr* **vergognarsi (di)** to be *o* feel ashamed (of); to be shy (about), be embarrassed (about); **vergo'gnoso, -a** *ag* ashamed; (*timido*) shy, embarrassed; (*causa di vergogna: azione*) shameful
ve'rifica, -che *sf* checking *no pl*, check
verifi'care *vt* (*controllare*) to check; (*confermare*) to confirm, bear out
verità *sf inv* truth
'**verme** *sm* worm
ver'miglio [ver'miʎʎo] *sm* vermilion, scarlet
ver'nice [ver'nitʃe] *sf* (*colorazione*) paint; (*trasparente*) varnish; (*pelle*) patent leather; "**~ fresca**" "wet paint"; **vernici'are** *vt* to paint; to varnish
'**vero, -a** *ag* (*veridico: fatti, testimonianza*) true; (*autentico*) real ▷ *sm* (*verità*) truth; (*realtà*) (real) life; **un ~ e proprio delinquente** a real criminal, an out-and-out criminal
vero'simile *ag* likely, probable
verrò *ecc vb vedi* **venire**

ver'ruca, -che *sf* wart
versa'mento *sm* (*pagamento*) payment; (*deposito di denaro*) deposit
ver'sante *sm* slopes *pl*, side
ver'sare *vt* (*fare uscire: vino, farina*) to pour (out); (*spargere: lacrime, sangue*) to shed; (*rovesciare*) to spill; (*Econ*) to pay; (: *depositare*) to deposit, pay in
versa'tile *ag* versatile
versi'one *sf* version; (*traduzione*) translation
'**verso** *sm* (*di poesia*) verse, line; (*di animale, uccello*) cry; (*direzione*) direction; (*modo*) way; (*di foglio di carta*) verso; (*di moneta*) reverse; **versi** *smpl* (*poesia*) verse *sg*; **non c'è ~ di persuaderlo** there's no way of persuading him, he can't be persuaded *prep* (*in direzione di*) toward(s); (*nei pressi di*) near, around (about); (*in senso temporale*) about, around; (*nei confronti di*) for; **~ di me** towards me; **~ sera** towards evening
'**vertebra** *sf* vertebra
verte'brale *ag* vertebral; **colonna ~** spinal column, spine
verti'cale *ag, sf* vertical
'**vertice** ['vertitʃe] *sm* summit, top; (*Mat*) vertex; **conferenza al ~** (*Pol*) summit conference
ver'tigine [ver'tidʒine] *sf* dizziness *no pl*; dizzy spell; (*Med*) vertigo; **avere le vertigini** to feel dizzy
ve'scica, -che [veʃʃika] *sf* (*Anat*) bladder; (*Med*) blister
'**vescovo** *sm* bishop
'**vespa** *sf* wasp
ves'taglia [ves'taʎʎa] *sf* dressing gown
ves'tire *vt* (*bambino, malato*) to dress; (*avere indosso*) to have on, wear; **vestirsi** *vpr* to dress, get dressed; **ves'tito, -a** *ag* dressed ▷ *sm* garment; (*da donna*) dress; (*da uomo*) suit; **vestiti** *smpl* (*indumenti*) clothes; **vestito di bianco** dressed in white
veteri'nario, -a *ag* veterinary ▷ *sm* veterinary surgeon (BRIT), veterinarian (US), vet
'**veto** *sm inv* veto
ve'traio *sm* glassmaker; glazier
ve'trata *sf* glass door (*o* window); (*di chiesa*) stained glass window
ve'trato, -a *ag* (*porta, finestra*) glazed; (*che contiene vetro*) glass *cpd* ▷ *sf* glass door (*o* window); (*di chiesa*) stained glass window; **carta vetrata** sandpaper
ve'trina *sf* (*di negozio*) (shop) window; (*armadio*) display cabinet; **vetri'nista, -i, -e** *sm/f* window dresser
'**vetro** *sm* glass; (*per finestra, porta*) pane (of glass)
'**vetta** *sf* peak, summit, top

vet'tura *sf* (*carrozza*) carriage; (*Ferr*) carriage (*BRIT*), car (*US*); (*auto*) car (*BRIT*), automobile (*US*)

vezzeggia'tivo [vettseddʒa'tivo] *sm* (*Ling*) term of endearment

vi (*dav lo, la, li, le, ne diventa* **ve**) *pron* (*oggetto*) you; (*complemento di termine*) (to) you; (*riflessivo*) yourselves; (*reciproco*) each other ▷ *av* (*lì*) there; (*qui*) here; (*per questo/quel luogo*) through here/there; **vi è/sono** there is/are

'via *sf* (*gen*) way; (*strada*) street; (*sentiero, pista*) path, track; (*Amm: procedimento*) channels *pl* ▷ *prep* (*passando per*) via, by way of ▷ *av* away ▷ *escl* go away!; (*suvvia*) come on!; (*Sport*) go! ▷ *sm* (*Sport*) starting signal; **in ~ di guarigione** on the road to recovery; **per ~ di** (*a causa di*) because of, on account of; **in o per ~** on the way; **per ~ aerea** by air; (*lettere*) by airmail; **andare/essere ~** to go/be away; **~ ~ che** (*a mano a mano*) as; **dare il ~** (*Sport*) to give the starting signal; **dare il ~ a** (*fig*) to start; **in ~ provvisoria** provisionally; **Via lattea** (*Astr*) Milky Way; **via di mezzo** middle course; **via d'uscita** (*fig*) way out

via'dotto *sm* viaduct

viaggi'are [viad'dʒare] *vi* to travel; **viaggia'tore, -'trice** *ag* travelling ▷ *sm* traveller; (*passeggero*) passenger

vi'aggio ['vjaddʒo] *sm* travel(ling); (*tragitto*) journey, trip; **buon ~!** have a good trip!; **com'è andato il ~?** how was your journey?; **il ~ dura due ore** the journey takes two hours; **viaggio di nozze** honeymoon; **siamo in ~ di nozze** we're on honeymoon

vi'ale *sm* avenue

via'vai *sm* coming and going, bustle

vi'brare *vi* to vibrate

'vice ['vitʃe] *sm/f* deputy

vi'cenda [vi'tʃɛnda] *sf* event; **a ~** in turn

vice'versa [vitʃe'vɛrsa] *av* vice versa; **da Roma a Pisa e ~** from Rome to Pisa and back

vici'nanza [vitʃi'nantsa] *sf* nearness, closeness

vi'cino, -a [vi'tʃino] *ag* (*gen*) near; (*nello spazio*) near, nearby; (*accanto*) next; (*nel tempo*) near, close at hand ▷ *sm/f* neighbour ▷ *av* near, close; **da ~** (*guardare*) close up; (*esaminare, seguire*) closely; (*conoscere*) well, intimately; **~ a** near (to), close to; (*accanto a*) beside; **c'è una banca qui ~?** is there a bank nearby?; **~ di casa** neighbour

'vicolo *sm* alley; **vicolo cieco** blind alley

'video *sm inv* (*TV: schermo*) screen; **video'camera** *sf* camcorder;

videocas'setta *sf* videocassette; **videoclip** [video'klip] *sm inv* videoclip; **videogi'oco, -chi** [video'dʒɔko] *sm* video game; **videoregistra'tore** *sm* video (recorder); **videote'lefono** *sm* videophone

'vidi *ecc vb vedi* **vedere**

vie'tare *vt* to forbid; (*Amm*) to prohibit; **~ a qn di fare** to forbid sb to do; to prohibit sb from doing; **"vietato fumare/l'ingresso"** "no smoking/admittance"

vie'tato, -a *ag* (*vedi vb*) forbidden; prohibited; banned; **"~ fumare/ l'ingresso"** "no smoking/admittance"; **~ ai minori di 14/18 anni** prohibited to children under 14/18; **"senso ~"** (*Aut*) "no entry"; **"sosta vietata"** (*Aut*) "no parking"

Viet'nam *sm* **il ~** Vietnam; **vietna'mita, -i, -e** *ag, sm/f, sm* Vietnamese *inv*

vi'gente [vi'dʒɛnte] *ag* in force

'vigile ['vidʒile] *ag* watchful ▷ *sm* (*anche:* **~ urbano**) policeman (*in towns*); **vigile del fuoco** fireman

vi'gilia [vi'dʒilja] *sf* (*giorno antecedente*) eve; **la ~ di Natale** Christmas Eve

vigli'acco, -a, -chi, -che [viʎ'ʎakko] *ag* cowardly ▷ *sm/f* coward

vi'gneto [viɲ'ɲeto] *sm* vineyard

vi'gnetta [viɲ'ɲetta] *sf* cartoon

vi'gore *sm* vigour; (*Dir*): **essere/entrare in ~** to be in/come into force

'vile *ag* (*spregevole*) low, mean, base; (*codardo*) cowardly

'villa *sf* villa

vil'laggio [vil'laddʒo] *sm* village; **villaggio turistico** holiday village

vil'lano, -a *ag* rude, ill-mannered

villeggia'tura [villeddʒa'tura] *sf* holiday(s) *pl* (*BRIT*), vacation (*US*)

vil'letta *sf*, **vil'lino** ▷ *sm* small house (with a garden), cottage

'vimini *smpl* **di ~** wicker

'vincere ['vintʃere] *vt* (*in guerra, al gioco, a una gara*) to defeat, beat; (*premio, guerra, partita*) to win; (*fig*) to overcome, conquer ▷ *vi* to win; **~ qn in bellezza** to be better-looking than sb; **vinci'tore** *sm* winner; (*Mil*) victor

vi'nicolo, -a *ag* wine *cpd*

'vino *sm* wine; **vino bianco/rosato/rosso** white/rosé/red wine; **vino da pasto** table wine

'vinsi *ecc vb vedi* **vincere**

vi'ola *sf* (*Bot*) violet; (*Mus*) viola ▷ *ag, sm inv* (*colore*) purple

vio'lare *vt* (*chiesa*) to desecrate, violate; (*giuramento, legge*) to violate

violen'tare *vt* to use violence on; (*donna*) to rape

vio'lento, -a *ag* violent; **vio'lenza** *sf* violence; **violenza carnale** rape

vio'letta *sf* (*Bot*) violet

vio'letto, -a *ag*, *sm* (*colore*) violet

violi'nista, -i, -e *sm/f* violinist

vio'lino *sm* violin

violon'cello [violon't∫εllo] *sm* cello

vi'ottolo *sm* path, track

vip [vip] *sigla m* (= *very important person*) VIP

'vipera *sf* viper, adder

vi'rare *vi* (*Naut, Aer*) to turn; (*Fot*) to tone; **~ di bordo** (*Naut*) to tack

'virgola *sf* (*Ling*) comma; (*Mat*) point; **virgo'lette** *sfpl* inverted commas, quotation marks

vi'rile *ag* (*proprio dell'uomo*) masculine; (*non puerile, da uomo*) manly, virile

virtù *sf inv* virtue; **in o per ~ di** by virtue of, by

virtu'ale *ag* virtual

'virus *sm inv* (*anche Inform*) virus

'viscere ['vi∫∫ere] *sfpl* (*di animale*) entrails *pl*; (*fig*) bowels *pl*

'vischio ['viskjo] *sm* (*Bot*) mistletoe; (*pania*) birdlime

'viscido, -a ['vi∫∫ido] *ag* slimy

vi'sibile *ag* visible

visibilità *sf* visibility

visi'era *sf* (*di elmo*) visor; (*di berretto*) peak

visi'one *sf* vision; **prendere ~ di qc** to examine sth, look sth over; **prima/seconda ~** (*Cinema*) first/second showing

'visita *sf* visit; (*Med*) visit, call; (*: esame*) examination; **visita guidata** guided tour; **a che ora comincia la ~ guidata?** what time does the guided tour start?; **visita medica** medical examination; **visi'tare** *vt* to visit; (*Med*) to visit, call on; (*: esaminare*) to examine; **visita'tore, -'trice** *sm/f* visitor

vi'sivo, -a *ag* visual

'viso *sm* face

vi'sone *sm* mink

'vispo, -a *ag* quick, lively

'vissi *ecc vb vedi* **vivere**

'vista *sf* (*facoltà*) (eye)sight; (*fatto di vedere*): **la ~ di** the sight of; (*veduta*) view; **sparare a ~** to shoot on sight; **in ~** in sight; **perdere qn di ~** to lose sight of sb; (*fig*) to lose touch with sb; **a ~ d'occhio** as far as the eye can see; (*fig*) before one's very eyes; **far ~ di fare** to pretend to do

'visto, -a *pp di* **vedere** ▷ *sm* visa; **~ che** seeing (that)

vis'toso, -a *ag* gaudy, garish; (*ingente*) considerable

visu'ale *ag* visual

'vita *sf* life; (*Anat*) waist; **a ~** for life

vi'tale *ag* vital

vita'mina *sf* vitamin

'vite *sf* (*Bot*) vine; (*Tecn*) screw

vi'tello *sm* (*Zool*) calf; (*carne*) veal; (*pelle*) calfskin

'vittima *sf* victim

'vitto *sm* food; (*in un albergo ecc*) board; **vitto e alloggio** board and lodging

vit'toria *sf* victory

'viva *escl* **~ il re!** long live the king!

vi'vace [vi'vat∫e] *ag* (*vivo, animato*) lively; (*: mente*) lively, sharp; (*colore*) bright

vi'vaio *sm* (*di pesci*) hatchery; (*Agr*) nursery

vivavoce [viva'vot∫e] *sm inv* (*dispositivo*) loudspeaker; **mettere il ~** to switch on the loudspeaker

vi'vente *ag* living, alive; **i viventi** the living

'vivere *vi* to live ▷ *vt* to live; (*passare: brutto momento*) to live through, go through; (*sentire: gioie, pene di qn*) to share ▷ *sm* life; (*anche: modo di ~*) way of life; **viveri** *smpl* (*cibo*) food *sg*, provisions; **~ di** to live on

'vivido, -a *ag* (*colore*) vivid, bright

vivisezi'one [viviset'tsjone] *sf* vivisection

'vivo, -a *ag* (*vivente*) alive, living; (*: animale*) live; (*fig*) lively; (*: colore*) bright, brilliant; **i vivi** the living; **~ e vegeto** hale and hearty; **farsi ~** to show one's face; to be heard from; **ritrarre dal ~** to paint from life; **pungere qn nel ~** (*fig*) to cut sb to the quick

vivrò *ecc vb vedi* **vivere**

vizi'are [vit'tsjare] *vt* (*bambino*) to spoil; (*corrompere moralmente*) to corrupt; **vizi'ato, -a** *ag* spoilt; (*aria, acqua*) polluted

'vizio ['vittsjo] *sm* (*morale*) vice; (*cattiva abitudine*) bad habit; (*imperfezione*) flaw, defect; (*errore*) fault, mistake

V.le *abbr* = **viale**

vocabo'lario *sm* (*dizionario*) dictionary; (*lessico*) vocabulary

vo'cabolo *sm* word

vo'cale *ag* vocal ▷ *sf* vowel

vocazi'one [vokat'tsjone] *sf* vocation; (*fig*) natural bent

'voce ['vot∫e] *sf* voice; (*diceria*) rumour; (*di un elenco, in bilancio*) item; **aver ~ in capitolo** (*fig*) to have a say in the matter

'voga *sf* (*Naut*) rowing; (*usanza*): **essere in ~** to be in fashion o in vogue

vo'gare *vi* to row

voghe'rò *ecc* [voge'rɔ] *vb vedi* **vogare**

'voglia ['vɔʎʎa] *sf* desire, wish; (*macchia*) birthmark; **aver ~ di qc/di fare** to feel like sth/like doing; (*più forte*) to want sth/to do

'voglio *ecc* ['vɔʎʎo] *vb vedi* **volere**

'voi *pron* you; **voi'altri** *pron* you

vo'lante *ag* flying ▷ *sm* (steering) wheel

volan'tino *sm* leaflet

vo'lare *vi* (*uccello, aereo, fig*) to fly; (*cappello*) to blow away *o* off, fly away *o* off; **~ via** to fly away *o* off

vo'latile *ag* (*Chim*) volatile ▷ *sm* (*Zool*) bird

volente'roso, -a *ag* willing

volenti'eri *av* willingly; **"~"** "with pleasure", "I'd be glad to"

 PAROLA CHIAVE

vo'lere *sm* will, wish(es); **contro il volere di** against the wishes of; **per volere di qn** in obedience to sb's will *o* wishes
▷ *vt* **1** (*esigere, desiderare*) to want; **voler fare/che qn faccia** to want to do/sb to do; **volete del caffè?** would you like *o* do you want some coffee?; **vorrei questo/fare** I would *o* I'd like this/to do; **come vuoi** as you like; **senza volere** (*inavvertitamente*) without meaning to, unintentionally
2 (*consentire*): **vogliate attendere, per piacere** please wait; **vogliamo andare?** shall we go?; **vuole essere così gentile da …?** would you be so kind as to …?; **non ha voluto ricevermi** he wouldn't see me
3: **volerci** (*essere necessario: materiale, attenzione*) to need; (: *tempo*) to take; **quanta farina ci vuole per questa torta?** how much flour do you need for this cake?; **ci vuole un'ora per arrivare a Venezia** it takes an hour to get to Venice
4: **voler bene a qn** (*amore*) to love sb; (*affetto*) to be fond of sb, like sb very much; **voler male a qn** to dislike sb; **volerne a qn** to bear sb a grudge; **voler dire** to mean

vol'gare *ag* vulgar

voli'era *sf* aviary

voli'tivo, -a *ag* strong-willed

'volli *ecc vb vedi* **volere**

'volo *sm* flight; **al ~: colpire qc al ~** to hit sth as it flies past; **capire al ~** to understand straight away; **volo charter** charter flight; **volo di linea** scheduled flight

volontà *sf* will; **a ~** (*mangiare, bere*) as much as one likes; **buona/cattiva ~** goodwill/lack of goodwill

volon'tario, -a *ag* voluntary ▷ *sm* (*Mil*) volunteer

'volpe *sf* fox

'volta *sf* (*momento, circostanza*) time; (*turno, giro*) turn; (*curva*) turn, bend; (*Archit*) vault; (*direzione*): **partire alla ~ di** to set off for; **a mia (o tua ecc) ~** in turn; **una ~** once; **una ~ sola** only once; **due volte** twice; **una cosa per ~** one thing at a time; **una ~ per tutte** once and for all; **a volte** at times, sometimes; **una ~ che** (*temporale*) once;

(*causale*) since; **3 volte 4** 3 times 4

volta'faccia [volta'fattʃa] *sm inv* (*fig*) volte-face

vol'taggio [vol'taddʒo] *sm* (*Elettr*) voltage

vol'tare *vt* to turn; (*girare: moneta*) to turn over; (*rigirare*) to turn round ▷ *vi* to turn; **voltarsi** *vpr* to turn; to turn over; to turn round

voltas'tomaco *sm* nausea; (*fig*) disgust

'volto, -a *pp di* **volgere** ▷ *sm* face

vo'lubile *ag* changeable, fickle

vo'lume *sm* volume

vomi'tare *vt, vi* to vomit; **'vomito** *sm* vomiting *no pl*; vomit

'vongola *sf* clam

vo'race [vo'ratʃe] *ag* voracious, greedy

vo'ragine [vo'radʒine] *sf* abyss, chasm

vorrò *ecc vb vedi* **volere**

'vortice ['vɔrtitʃe] *sm* whirlwind; whirlpool; (*fig*) whirl

'vostro, -a *det* **il(la) ~(a)** *ecc* your ▷ *pron* **il(la) ~(a)** *ecc* yours

vo'tante *sm/f* voter

vo'tare *vi* to vote ▷ *vt* (*sottoporre a votazione*) to take a vote on; (*approvare*) to vote for; (*Rel*): **~ qc a** to dedicate sth to

'voto *sm* (*Pol*) vote; (*Ins*) mark; (*Rel*) vow; (: *offerta*) votive offering; **aver voti belli/brutti** (*Ins*) to get good/bad marks

vs. *abbr* (*Comm*) = **vostro**

vul'cano *sm* volcano

vulne'rabile *ag* vulnerable

vu'oi, vu'ole *vb vedi* **volere**

vuo'tare *vt* to empty; **vuotarsi** *vpr* to empty

vu'oto, -a *ag* empty; (*fig: privo*): **~ di** (*senso ecc*) devoid of ▷ *sm* empty space, gap; (*spazio in bianco*) blank; (*Fisica*) vacuum; (*fig: mancanza*) gap, void; **a mani vuote** empty-handed; **vuoto d'aria** air pocket; **vuoto a rendere** returnable bottle

W X

'wafer ['vafer] *sm inv* (*Cuc, Elettr*) wafer
'water ['wɔːtəʳ] *sm inv* toilet
watt [vat] *sm inv* watt
W.C. *sm inv* WC
web [ueb] *sm* **il ~** the Web; **cercare nel ~**
    to search the Web ▷ *ag inv* **pagina ~** web
    page
'weekend ['wiːkend] *sm inv* weekend
'western ['wɛstern] *ag* (*Cinema*) cowboy
    cpd ▷ *sm inv* western, cowboy film;
    western all'italiana spaghetti western
'whisky ['wiski] *sm inv* whisky
'windsurf ['windsəːf] *sm inv* (*tavola*)
    windsurfer; (*sport*) windsurfing
'würstel ['vyrstəl] *sm inv* frankfurter

xe'nofobo, -a [kse'nɔfobo] *ag* xenophobic
    ▷ *sm/f* xenophobe
xi'lofono [ksi'lɔfono] *sm* xylophone

Y   Z

yacht [jɔt] *sm inv* yacht
'yoga [ˈjɔga] *ag inv, sm* yoga (*cpd*)
yogurt [ˈjɔgurt] *sm inv* yog(h)urt

zabai'one [dzabaˈjone] *sm dessert made of egg yolks, sugar and marsala*
zaf'fata [tsafˈfata] *sf* (*tanfo*) stench
zaffe'rano [dzaffeˈrano] *sm* saffron
zaf'firo [dzafˈfiro] *sm* sapphire
'zaino [ˈdzaino] *sm* rucksack
'zampa [ˈtsampa] *sf* (*di animale: gamba*) leg; (: *piede*) paw; **a quattro zampe** on all fours
zampil'lare [tsampilˈlare] *vi* to gush, spurt
zan'zara [dzanˈdzara] *sf* mosquito; **zanzari'era** *sf* mosquito net
'zappa [ˈtsappa] *sf* hoe
'zapping [ˈtsapiŋ] *sm* (*TV*) channel-hopping
zar, za'rina [tsar, tsaˈrina] *sm/f* tsar/tsarina
'zattera [ˈdzattera] *sf* raft
'zebra [ˈdzɛbra] *sf* zebra; **zebre** *sfpl* (*Aut*) zebra crossing *sg* (*BRIT*), crosswalk *sg* (*US*)
'zecca, -che [ˈtsekka] *sf* (*Zool*) tick; (*officina di monete*) mint
'zelo [ˈdzɛlo] *sm* zeal
'zenzero [ˈdzendzero] *sm* ginger
'zeppa [ˈtseppa] *sf* wedge
'zeppo, -a [ˈtseppo] *ag* ~ **di** crammed *o* packed with
zer'bino [dzerˈbino] *sm* doormat
'zero [ˈdzɛro] *sm* zero, nought; **vincere per**

tre a ~ (Sport) to win three-nil
'zia ['tsia] sf aunt
zibel'lino [dzibel'lino] sm sable
'zigomo ['dzigomo] sm cheekbone
zig'zag [dzig'dzag] sm inv zigzag; **andare a ~** to zigzag
Zimbabwe [tsim'babwe] sm **lo ~** Zimbabwe
'zinco ['dzinko] sm zinc
'zingaro, -a ['dzingaro] sm/f gipsy
'zio ['tsio] (pl **'zii**) sm uncle
zip'pare vt (Inform: file) to zip
zi'tella [dzi'tella] sf spinster; (peg) old maid
'zitto, -a ['tsitto] ag quiet, silent; **sta' ~!** be quiet!
'zoccolo ['tsɔkkolo] sm (calzatura) clog; (di cavallo ecc) hoof; (basamento) base; plinth
zodia'cale [dzodia'kale] ag zodiac cpd; **segno ~** sign of the zodiac
zo'diaco [dzo'diako] sm zodiac
'zolfo ['tsolfo] sm sulphur
'zolla ['dzɔlla] sf clod (of earth)
zol'letta [dzol'letta] sf sugar lump
'zona ['dzɔna] sf zone, area; **zona di depressione** (Meteor) trough of low pressure; **zona disco** (Aut) ≈ meter zone; **zona industriale** industrial estate; **zona pedonale** pedestrian precinct; **zona verde** (di abitato) green area
'zonzo ['dzondzo]: **a ~** av, **andare a ~** to wander about, stroll about
zoo ['dzoo] sm inv zoo
zoolo'gia [dzoolo'dʒia] sf zoology
zoppi'care [tsoppi'kare] vi to limp; to be shaky, rickety
'zoppo, -a ['tsɔppo] ag lame; (fig: mobile) shaky, rickety
Z.T.L. sigla f (= Zona a Traffico Limitato) controlled traffic zone
'zucca, -che ['tsukka] sf (Bot) marrow; pumpkin
zucche'rare [tsukke'rare] vt to put sugar in; **zucche'rato, -a** ag sweet, sweetened
zuccheri'era [tsukke'rjera] sf sugar bowl
'zucchero ['tsukkero] sm sugar; **zucchero di canna** cane sugar; **zucchero filato** candy floss, cotton candy (us)
zuc'china [tsuk'kina] sf courgette (BRIT), zucchini (us)
'zuffa ['tsuffa] sf brawl
'zuppa ['tsuppa] sf soup; (fig) mixture, muddle; **zuppa inglese** (Cuc) dessert made with sponge cake, custard and chocolate, ≈ trifle (BRIT)
'zuppo, -a ['tsuppo] ag ~ **(di)** drenched (with), soaked (with)

A [eɪ] *n* (*Mus*) la *m*

 KEYWORD

a [ə] (*before vowel or silent h* **an**) *indef art* **1** un (uno + *s impure, gn, pn, ps, x, z*), una *f* (un' + *vowel*); **a book** un libro; **a mirror** uno specchio; **an apple** una mela; **she's a doctor** è medico
2 (*instead of the number "one"*) un(o), *f* una; **a year ago** un anno fa; **a hundred/ thousand** *etc* **pounds** cento/mille *etc* sterline
3 (*in expressing ratios, prices etc*) a, per; **3 a day/week** 3 al giorno/alla settimana; **10 km an hour** 10 km all'ora; **£5 a person** 5 sterline a persona *or* per persona

A.A. *n abbr* (= *Alcoholics Anonymous*) AA; (*BRIT*: = *Automobile Association*) ≈ A.C.I. *m*
A.A.A. (*US*) *n abbr* (= *American Automobile Association*) ≈ A.C.I. *m*
aback [ə'bæk] *adv* **to be taken ~** essere sbalordito(-a)
abandon [ə'bændən] *vt* abbandonare ▷ *n* **with ~** sfrenatamente, spensieratamente
abattoir ['æbətwɑːʳ] (*BRIT*) *n* mattatoio
abbey ['æbɪ] *n* abbazia, badia
abbreviation [əbriːvɪ'eɪʃən] *n* abbreviazione *f*

abdomen ['æbdəmən] *n* addome *m*
abduct [æb'dʌkt] *vt* rapire
abide [ə'baɪd] *vt* **I can't ~ it/him** non lo posso soffrire *or* sopportare; **abide by** *vt fus* conformarsi a
ability [ə'bɪlɪtɪ] *n* abilità *f inv*
able ['eɪbl] *adj* capace; **to be ~ to do sth** essere capace di fare qc, poter fare qc
abnormal [æb'nɔːməl] *adj* anormale
aboard [ə'bɔːd] *adv* a bordo ▷ *prep* a bordo di
abolish [ə'bɔlɪʃ] *vt* abolire
abolition [æbəu'lɪʃən] *n* abolizione *f*
abort [ə'bɔːt] *vt* abortire; **abortion** [ə'bɔːʃən] *n* aborto; **to have an abortion** abortire

 KEYWORD

about [ə'baut] *adv* **1** (*approximately*) circa, quasi; **about a hundred/thousand** *etc* un centinaio/migliaio *etc*, circa cento/mille *etc*; **it takes about 10 hours** ci vogliono circa 10 ore; **at about 2 o'clock** verso le 2; **I've just about finished** ho quasi finito
2 (*referring to place*) qua e là, in giro; **to leave things lying about** lasciare delle cose in giro; **to run about** correre qua e là; **to walk about** camminare
3: **to be about to do sth** stare per fare qc ▷ *prep* **1** (*relating to*) su, di; **a book about London** un libro su Londra; **what is it about?** di che si tratta?; (*book, film etc*) di cosa tratta?; **we talked about it** ne abbiamo parlato; **what** *or* **how about doing this?** che ne dici di fare questo?
2 (*referring to place*): **to walk about the town** camminare per la città; **her clothes were scattered about the room** i suoi vestiti erano sparsi *or* in giro per tutta la stanza

above [ə'bʌv] *adv, prep* sopra; **mentioned ~** suddetto; **~ all** soprattutto
abroad [ə'brɔːd] *adv* all'estero
abrupt [ə'brʌpt] *adj* (*sudden*) improvviso(-a); (*gruff, blunt*) brusco(-a)
abscess ['æbsɪs] *n* ascesso
absence ['æbsəns] *n* assenza
absent ['æbsənt] *adj* assente; **absent-minded** *adj* distratto(-a)
absolute ['æbsəluːt] *adj* assoluto(-a); **absolutely** [-'luːtlɪ] *adv* assolutamente
absorb [əb'zɔːb] *vt* assorbire; **to be ~ed in a book** essere immerso in un libro; **absorbent cotton** [əb'zɔːbənt-] (*US*) *n* cotone *m* idrofilo; **absorbing** *adj* avvincente, molto interessante
abstain [əb'steɪn] *vi* **to ~ (from)**

astenersi (da)

abstract ['æbstrækt] *adj* astratto(-a)

absurd [əb'sə:d] *adj* assurdo(-a)

abundance [ə'bʌndəns] *n* abbondanza

abundant [ə'bʌndənt] *adj* abbondante

abuse [*n* ə'bju:s, *vb* a'bju:z] *n* abuso; (*insults*) ingiurie *fpl* ▷ *vt* abusare di; **abusive** *adj* ingiurioso(-a)

abysmal [ə'bɪzməl] *adj* spaventoso(-a)

academic [ækə'dɛmɪk] *adj* accademico(-a); (*pej: issue*) puramente formale ▷ *n* universitario(-a); **academic year** *n* anno accademico

academy [ə'kædəmɪ] *n* (*learned body*) accademia; (*school*) scuola privata; **academy of music** *n* conservatorio

accelerate [æk'sɛləreɪt] *vt, vi* accelerare; **acceleration** *n* accelerazione *f*; **accelerator** *n* acceleratore *m*

accent ['æksɛnt] *n* accento

accept [ək'sɛpt] *vt* accettare; **acceptable** *adj* accettabile; **acceptance** *n* accettazione *f*

access ['æksɛs] *n* accesso; **accessible** [æk'sɛsəbl] *adj* accessibile

accessory [æk'sɛsərɪ] *n* accessorio; (*Law*): **~ to** complice *m/f* di

accident ['æksɪdənt] *n* incidente *m*; (*chance*) caso; **I've had an ~** ho avuto un incidente; **by ~** per caso; **accidental** [-'dɛntl] *adj* accidentale; **accidentally** [-'dɛntəlɪ] *adv* per caso; **Accident and Emergency Department** *n* (BRIT) pronto soccorso; **accident insurance** *n* assicurazione *f* contro gli infortuni

acclaim [ə'kleɪm] *n* acclamazione *f*

accommodate [ə'kɔmədeɪt] *vt* alloggiare; (*oblige, help*) favorire

accommodation [əkɔmə'deɪʃən] (US **accommodations**) *n* alloggio

accompaniment [ə'kʌmpənɪmənt] *n* accompagnamento

accompany [ə'kʌmpənɪ] *vt* accompagnare

accomplice [ə'kʌmplɪs] *n* complice *m/f*

accomplish [ə'kʌmplɪʃ] *vt* compiere; (*goal*) raggiungere; **accomplishment** *n* compimento; realizzazione *f*

accord [ə'kɔ:d] *n* accordo ▷ *vt* accordare; **of his own ~** di propria iniziativa; **accordance** *n* **in accordance with** in conformità con; **according**: **according to** *prep* secondo; **accordingly** *adv* in conformità

account [ə'kaunt] *n* (*Comm*) conto; (*report*) descrizione *f*; **~s** *npl* (*Comm*) conti *mpl*; **of no ~** di nessuna importanza; **on ~** in acconto; **on no ~** per nessun motivo; **on ~ of** a causa di; **to take into ~, take**

~ of tener conto di; **account for** *vt fus* spiegare; giustificare; **accountable** *adj* **accountable (to)** responsabile (verso); **accountant** [ə'kauntənt] *n* ragioniere(-a); **account number** *n* numero di conto

accumulate [ə'kju:mjuleɪt] *vt* accumulare ▷ *vi* accumularsi

accuracy ['ækjurəsɪ] *n* precisione *f*

accurate ['ækjurɪt] *adj* preciso(-a); **accurately** *adv* precisamente

accusation [ækju'zeɪʃən] *n* accusa

accuse [ə'kju:z] *vt* accusare; **accused** *n* accusato(-a)

accustomed [ə'kʌstəmd] *adj* **~ to** abituato(-a) a

ace [eɪs] *n* asso

ache [eɪk] *n* male *m*, dolore *m* ▷ *vi* (*be sore*) far male, dolere; **my head ~s** mi fa male la testa

achieve [ə'tʃi:v] *vt* (*aim*) raggiungere; (*victory, success*) ottenere; **achievement** *n* compimento; successo

acid ['æsɪd] *adj* acido(-a) ▷ *n* acido

acknowledge [ək'nɔlɪdʒ] *vt* (*letter: also:* **~ receipt of**) confermare la ricevuta di; (*fact*) riconoscere; **acknowledgement** *n* conferma; riconoscimento

acne ['æknɪ] *n* acne *f*

acorn ['eɪkɔ:n] *n* ghianda

acoustic [ə'ku:stɪk] *adj* acustico(-a)

acquaintance [ə'kweɪntəns] *n* conoscenza; (*person*) conoscente *m/f*

acquire [ə'kwaɪə'] *vt* acquistare; **acquisition** [ækwɪ'zɪʃən] *n* acquisto

acquit [ə'kwɪt] *vt* assolvere; **to ~ o.s. well** comportarsi bene

acre ['eɪkə'] *n* acro, ≈ 4047 m²

acronym ['ækrənɪm] *n* acronimo

across [ə'krɔs] *prep* (*on the other side*) dall'altra parte di; (*crosswise*) attraverso ▷ *adv* dall'altra parte; in larghezza; **to run/ swim ~** attraversare di corsa/a nuoto; **~ from** di fronte a

acrylic [ə'krɪlɪk] *adj* acrilico(-a)

act [ækt] *n* atto; (*in music-hall etc*) numero; (*Law*) decreto ▷ *vi* agire; (*Theatre*) recitare; (*pretend*) fingere ▷ *vt* (*part*) recitare; **to ~ as** agire da; **act up** (*inf*) *vi* (*person*) comportarsi male; (*knee, back, injury*) fare male; (*machine*) non funzionare; **acting** *adj* che fa le funzioni di ▷ *n* (*of actor*) recitazione *f*; (*activity*): **to do some acting** fare del teatro (*or* del cinema)

action ['ækʃən] *n* azione *f*; (*Mil*) combattimento; (*Law*) processo; **out of ~** fuori combattimento; fuori servizio; **to take ~** agire; **action replay** *n* (TV) replay *m inv*

activate ['æktɪveɪt] vt (mechanism) attivare

active ['æktɪv] adj attivo(-a); **actively** adv (participate) attivamente; (discourage, dislike) vivamente

activist ['æktɪvɪst] n attivista m/f

activity [æk'tɪvɪtɪ] n attività f inv; **activity holiday** n vacanza organizzata con attività ricreative per ragazzi

actor ['æktə'] n attore m

actress ['æktrɪs] n attrice f

actual ['æktjʊəl] adj reale, effettivo(-a).
> Be careful not to translate **actual** by the Italian word **attuale**.

actually ['æktjʊəlɪ] adv veramente; (even) addirittura
> Be careful not to translate **actually** by the Italian word **attualmente**.

acupuncture ['ækjʊpʌŋktfə'] n agopuntura

acute [ə'kjuːt] adj acuto(-a); (mind, person) perspicace

ad [æd] n abbr = **advertisement**

A.D. adv abbr (= Anno Domini) d.C.

adamant ['ædəmənt] adj irremovibile

adapt [ə'dæpt] vt adattare ▷ vi **to ~ (to)** adattarsi (a); **adapter, adaptor** n (Elec) adattatore m

add [æd] vt aggiungere ▷ vi **to ~ to** (increase) aumentare; **add up** vt (figures) addizionare ▷ vi (fig): **it doesn't ~ up** non ha senso; **add up to** vt fus (Math) ammontare a; (fig: mean) significare; **it doesn't ~ up to much** non è un granché

addict ['ædɪkt] n tossicomane m/f; (fig) fanatico(-a); **addicted** [ə'dɪktɪd] adj **to be addicted to** (drink etc) essere dedito(-a) a; (fig: football etc) essere tifoso(-a) di; **addiction** [ə'dɪkʃən] n (Med) tossicodipendenza; **addictive** [ə'dɪktɪv] adj che dà assuefazione

addition [ə'dɪʃən] n addizione f; (thing added) aggiunta; **in ~** inoltre; **in ~ to** oltre; **additional** adj supplementare

additive ['ædɪtɪv] n additivo

address [ə'drɛs] n indirizzo; (talk) discorso ▷ vt indirizzare; (speak to) fare un discorso a; (issue) affrontare; **my ~ is ...** il mio indirizzo è...; **address book** n rubrica

adequate ['ædɪkwɪt] adj adeguato(-a), sufficiente

adhere [əd'hɪə'] vi **to ~ to** aderire a; (fig: rule, decision) seguire

adhesive [əd'hiːzɪv] n adesivo; **adhesive tape** n (BRIT: for parcels etc) nastro adesivo; (US Med) cerotto adesivo

adjacent [ə'dʒeɪsənt] adj adiacente; **~ to** accanto a

adjective ['ædʒɛktɪv] n aggettivo

adjoining [ə'dʒɔɪnɪŋ] adj accanto inv, adiacente

adjourn [ə'dʒəːn] vt rimandare ▷ vi essere aggiornato(-a)

adjust [ə'dʒʌst] vt aggiustare; (change) rettificare ▷ vi **to ~ (to)** adattarsi (a); **adjustable** adj regolabile; **adjustment** n (Psych) adattamento; (of machine) regolazione f; (of prices, wages) modifica

administer [əd'mɪnɪstə'] vt amministrare; (justice, drug) somministrare; **administration** [ədmɪnɪs'treɪʃən] n amministrazione f; **administrative** [əd'mɪnɪstrətɪv] adj amministrativo(-a)

administrator [əd'mɪnɪstreɪtə'] n amministratore(-trice)

admiral ['ædmərəl] n ammiraglio

admiration [ædmə'reɪʃən] n ammirazione f

admire [əd'maɪə'] vt ammirare; **admirer** n ammiratore(-trice)

admission [əd'mɪʃən] n ammissione f; (to exhibition, nightclub etc) ingresso; (confession) confessione f

admit [əd'mɪt] vt ammettere; far entrare; (agree) riconoscere; **admit to** vt fus riconoscere; **admittance** n ingresso; **admittedly** adv bisogna pur riconoscere (che)

adolescent [ædəʊ'lɛsnt] adj, n adolescente m/f

adopt [ə'dɔpt] vt adottare; **adopted** adj adottivo(-a); **adoption** [ə'dɔpʃən] n adozione f

adore [ə'dɔː'] vt adorare

adorn [ə'dɔːn] vt ornare

Adriatic [eɪdrɪ'ætɪk] n **the ~ (Sea)** il mare Adriatico, l'Adriatico

adrift [ə'drɪft] adv alla deriva

adult ['ædʌlt] adj adulto(-a); (work, education) per adulti ▷ n adulto(-a); **adult education** n scuola per adulti

adultery [ə'dʌltərɪ] n adulterio

advance [əd'vɑːns] n avanzamento; (money) anticipo ▷ adj (booking etc) in anticipo ▷ vt (money) anticipare ▷ vi avanzare; **in ~** in anticipo; **do I need to book in ~?** occorre che prenoti in anticipo?; **advanced** adj avanzato(-a); (Scol: studies) superiore

advantage [əd'vɑːntɪdʒ] n (also Tennis) vantaggio; **to take ~ of** approfittarsi di

advent ['ædvənt] n avvento; (Rel): **A~** Avvento

adventure [əd'vɛntʃə'] n avventura; **adventurous** [əd'vɛntʃərəs] adj avventuroso(-a)

adverb ['ædvəːb] n avverbio

adversary ['ædvəsərɪ] n avversario(-a)

adverse ['ædvə:s] adj avverso(-a)

advert ['ædvə:t] (BRIT) n abbr
= **advertisement**

advertise ['ædvətaɪz] vi, vt fare pubblicità
or réclame (a); fare un'inserzione (per
vendere); **to ~ for** (staff) mettere un
annuncio sul giornale per trovare;
advertisement [əd'və:tɪsmənt] n
(Comm) réclame f inv, pubblicità f inv; (in
classified ads) inserzione f; **advertiser** n
azienda che reclamizza un prodotto; (in
newspaper) inserzionista m/f; **advertising**
['ædvətaɪzɪŋ] n pubblicità

advice [əd'vaɪs] n consigli mpl; **piece of ~**
consiglio; **to take legal ~** consultare un
avvocato

advisable [əd'vaɪzəbl] adj consigliabile

advise [əd'vaɪz] vt consigliare; **to ~ sb of**
sth informare qn di qc; **to ~ sb against**
sth/doing sth sconsigliare qc a qn/a qn
di fare qc; **adviser** n consigliere(-a); (in
business) consulente m/f, consigliere(-a);
advisory [-ərɪ] adj consultivo(-a)

advocate [n 'ædvəkɪt, vb 'ædvəkeɪt]
n (upholder) sostenitore(-trice); (Law)
avvocato (difensore) ▷ vt propugnare

Aegean [ɪ'dʒɪ:ən] n **the ~ (Sea)** il mar
Egeo, l'Egeo

aerial ['ɛərɪəl] n antenna ▷ adj aereo(-a)

aerobics [ɛə'rəubɪks] n aerobica

aeroplane ['ɛərəpleɪn] (BRIT) n aeroplano

aerosol ['ɛərəsɔl] (BRIT) n aerosol m inv

affair [ə'fɛər] n affare m; (also: **love ~**)
relazione f amorosa; **~s** (business) affari

affect [ə'fɛkt] vt toccare; (influence)
influire su, incidere su; (feign) fingere;
affected adj affettato(-a); **affection**
[ə'fɛkʃən] n affezione f; **affectionate** adj
affettuoso(-a)

afflict [ə'flɪkt] vt affliggere

affluent ['æfluənt] adj ricco(-a); **the ~**
society la società del benessere

afford [ə'fɔ:d] vt permettersi; (provide)
fornire; **affordable** adj (che ha un prezzo)
abbordabile

Afghanistan [æf'gænɪstɑ:n] n Afganistan
m

afraid [ə'freɪd] adj impaurito(-a); **to be ~**
of or **to/that** aver paura di/che; **I am ~**
so/not ho paura di sì/no

Africa ['æfrɪkə] n Africa; **African** adj, n
africano(-a); **African-American** adj, n
afroamericano(-a)

after ['ɑ:ftər] prep, adv dopo ▷ conj dopo
che; **what/who are you ~?** che/chi
cerca?; **~ he left/having done** dopo
che se ne fu andato/dopo aver fatto; **to**
name sb ~ sb dare a qn il nome di qn; **it's**

twenty ~ eight (US) sono le otto e venti;
to ask ~ sb chiedere di qn; **~ all** dopo
tutto; **~ you!** dopo di lei!; **after-effects**
npl conseguenze fpl; (of illness) postumi
mpl; **aftermath** n conseguenze fpl; **in**
the aftermath of nel periodo dopo;
afternoon n pomeriggio; **after-shave**
(lotion) ['ɑ:ftəʃeɪv-] n dopobarba m inv;
aftersun (lotion/cream) n doposole m
inv; **afterwards** (US **afterward**) adv dopo

again [ə'gɛn] adv di nuovo; **to begin/see ~**
ricominciare/rivedere; **not ... ~** non ... più;
~ and ~ ripetutamente

against [ə'gɛnst] prep contro

age [eɪdʒ] n età f inv ▷ vt, vi invecchiare;
it's been ~s since sono secoli che; **he is**
20 years of ~ ha 20 anni; **to come of ~**
diventare maggiorenne; **~d 10** di 10 anni;
the ~d ['eɪdʒɪd] gli anziani; **age group** n
generazione f; **age limit** n limite m d'età

agency ['eɪdʒənsɪ] n agenzia

agenda [ə'dʒɛndə] n ordine m del giorno

agent ['eɪdʒənt] n agente m

aggravate ['ægrəveɪt] vt aggravare;
(person) irritare

aggression [ə'grɛʃən] n aggressione f

aggressive [ə'grɛsɪv] adj aggressivo(-a)

agile ['ædʒaɪl] adj agile

agitated ['ædʒɪteɪtɪd] adj agitato(-a),
turbato(-a)

AGM n abbr = **annual general meeting**

ago [ə'gəu] adv **2 days ~** 2 giorni fa; **not**
long ~ poco tempo fa; **how long ~?**
quanto tempo fa?

agony ['ægənɪ] n dolore m atroce; **to be in**
~ avere dolori atroci

agree [ə'gri:] vt (price) pattuire ▷ vi **to**
~ (with) essere d'accordo (con); (Ling)
concordare (con); **to ~ to sth/to do sth**
accettare qc/di fare qc; **to ~ that** (admit)
ammettere che; **to ~ on sth** accordarsi su
qc; **garlic doesn't ~ with me** l'aglio non
mi va; **agreeable** adj gradevole; (willing)
disposto(-a); **agreed** adj (time, place)
stabilito(-a); **agreement** n accordo; **in**
agreement d'accordo

agricultural [ægrɪ'kʌltʃərəl] adj
agricolo(-a)

agriculture ['ægrɪkʌltʃər] n agricoltura

ahead [ə'hɛd] adv avanti; davanti; **~ of**
davanti a; (fig: schedule etc) in anticipo su;
~ of time in anticipo; **go right** or **straight**
~ tiri diritto

aid [eɪd] n aiuto ▷ vt aiutare; **in ~ of** a
favore di

aide [eɪd] n (person) aiutante m/f

AIDS [eɪdz] n abbr (= acquired immune
deficiency syndrome) AIDS f

ailing ['eɪlɪŋ] adj sofferente; (fig: economy,

industry etc) in difficoltà

ailment ['eɪlmənt] *n* indisposizione *f*

aim [eɪm] *vt* **to ~ sth at** (*such as gun*) mirare qc a, puntare qc a; (*camera*) rivolgere qc a; (*missile*) lanciare qc contro ▷ *vi* (*also:* **to take ~**) prendere la mira ▷ *n* mira; **to ~ at** mirare; **to ~ to do** aver l'intenzione di fare

ain't [eɪnt] (*inf*) = **am not**; **aren't**; **isn't**

air [ɛəʳ] *n* aria ▷ *vt* (*room*) arieggiare; (*clothes*) far prendere aria a; (*grievances, ideas*) esprimere pubblicamente ▷ *cpd* (*currents*) d'aria; (*attack*) aereo(-a); **to throw sth into the ~** lanciare qc in aria; **by ~** (*travel*) in aereo; **on the ~** (*Radio, TV*) in onda; **airbag** *n* airbag *m inv*; **airbed** (*BRIT*) *n* materassino; **airborne** ['ɛəbɔːn] *adj* (*plane*) in volo; (*troops*) aerotrasportato(-a); **as soon as the plane was airborne** appena l'aereo ebbe decollato; **air-conditioned** *adj* con or ad aria condizionata; **air conditioning** *n* condizionamento d'aria; **aircraft** *n inv* apparecchio; **airfield** *n* campo d'aviazione; **Air Force** *n* aviazione *f* militare; **air hostess** (*BRIT*) *n* hostess *f inv*; **airing cupboard** ['ɛərɪŋ-] *n* armadio riscaldato per asciugare panni.; **airlift** *n* ponte *m* aereo; **airline** *n* linea aerea; **airliner** *n* aereo di linea; **airmail** *n* **by airmail** per via aerea; **airplane** (*US*) *n* aeroplano; **airport** *n* aeroporto; **air raid** *n* incursione *f* aerea; **airsick** *adj* **to be airsick** soffrire di mal d'aria; **airspace** *n* spazio aereo; **airstrip** *n* pista d'atterraggio; **air terminal** *n* air-terminal *m inv*; **airtight** *adj* ermetico(-a); **air-traffic controller** *n* controllore *m* del traffico aereo; **airy** *adj* arioso(-a); (*manners*) noncurante

aisle [aɪl] *n* (*of church*) navata laterale; navata centrale; (*of plane*) corridoio; **aisle seat** *n* (*on plane*) posto sul corridoio

ajar [ə'dʒɑːʳ] *adj* socchiuso(-a)

à la carte [ɑ:lɑ:'kɑ:t] *adv* alla carta

alarm [ə'lɑ:m] *n* allarme *m* ▷ *vt* allarmare; **alarm call** *n* (*in hotel etc*) sveglia; **could I have an alarm call at 7 am, please?** vorrei essere svegliato alle 7, per favore; **alarm clock** *n* sveglia; **alarmed** *adj* (*person*) allarmato(-a); (*house, car etc*) dotato(-a) di allarme; **alarming** *adj* allarmante, preoccupante

Albania [æl'beɪnɪə] *n* Albania

albeit [ɔːl'biːɪt] *conj* sebbene + *sub*, benché + *sub*

album ['ælbəm] *n* album *m inv*

alcohol ['ælkəhɔl] *n* alcool *m*; **alcohol-free** *adj* analcolico(-a); **alcoholic** [-'hɔlɪk] *adj* alcolico(-a) ▷ *n* alcolizzato(-a)

alcove ['ælkəuv] *n* alcova

ale [eɪl] *n* birra

alert [ə'ləːt] *adj* vigile ▷ *n* allarme *m* ▷ *vt* avvertire; mettere in guardia; **on the ~** all'erta

algebra ['ældʒɪbrə] *n* algebra

Algeria [æl'dʒɪərɪə] *n* Algeria

alias ['eɪlɪəs] *adv* alias ▷ *n* pseudonimo, falso nome *m*

alibi ['ælɪbaɪ] *n* alibi *m inv*

alien ['eɪlɪən] *n* straniero(-a); (*extraterrestrial*) alieno(-a) ▷ *adj* **~ (to)** estraneo(-a) (a); **alienate** *vt* alienare

alight [ə'laɪt] *adj* acceso(-a) ▷ *vi* scendere; (*bird*) posarsi

align [ə'laɪn] *vt* allineare

alike [ə'laɪk] *adj* simile ▷ *adv* sia … sia; **to look ~** assomigliarsi

alive [ə'laɪv] *adj* vivo(-a); (*lively*) vivace

 KEYWORD

all [ɔːl] *adj* tutto(-a); **all day** tutto il giorno; **all night** tutta la notte; **all men** tutti gli uomini; **all five came** sono venuti tutti e cinque; **all the books** tutti i libri; **all the food** tutto il cibo; **all the time** sempre; tutto il tempo; **all his life** tutta la vita

▷ *pron* **1** tutto(-a); **I ate it all, I ate all of it** l'ho mangiato tutto; **all of us went** tutti noi siamo andati; **all of the boys went** tutti i ragazzi sono andati

2 (*in phrases*): **above all** soprattutto; **after all** dopotutto; **at all: not at all** (*in answer to question*) niente affatto; (*in answer to thanks*) prego!, di niente!, s'immagini!; **I'm not at all tired** non sono affatto stanco(-a); **anything at all will do** andrà bene qualsiasi cosa; **all in all** tutto sommato

▷ *adv* **all alone** tutto(-a) solo(-a); **it's not as hard as all that** non è poi così difficile; **all the more/the better** tanto più/meglio; **all but** quasi; **the score is two all** il punteggio è di due a due

Allah ['ælə] *n* Allah *m*

allegation [ælɪ'geɪʃən] *n* asserzione *f*

alleged [ə'lɛdʒd] *adj* presunto(-a); **allegedly** [ə'lɛdʒɪdlɪ] *adv* secondo quanto si asserisce

allegiance [ə'liːdʒəns] *n* fedeltà

allergic [ə'ləːdʒɪk] *adj* **~ to** allergico(-a) a; **I'm ~ to penicillin** sono allergico alla penicillina

allergy ['ælədʒɪ] *n* allergia

alleviate [ə'liːvɪeɪt] *vt* sollevare

alley ['ælɪ] *n* vicolo

alliance [ə'laɪəns] *n* alleanza

allied ['ælaɪd] adj alleato(-a)

alligator ['ælɪgeɪtə^r] n alligatore m

all-in ['ɔːlɪn] adj (BRIT: also adv: charge) tutto compreso

allocate ['æləkeɪt] vt assegnare

allot [ə'lɔt] vt assegnare

all-out ['ɔːlaut] adj (effort etc) totale ▷ adv **to go all out for** mettercela tutta per

allow [ə'lau] vt (practice, behaviour) permettere; (sum, time estimated) dare; (concede): **to ~ that** ammettere che; **to ~ sb to do** permettere a qn di fare; **he is ~ed to** lo può fare; **allow for** vt fus tener conto di; **allowance** n (money received) assegno; indennità f inv; (Tax) detrazione f di imposta; **to make allowances for** tener conto di

all right adv (feel, work) bene; (as answer) va bene

ally ['ælaɪ] n alleato

almighty [ɔːl'maɪtɪ] adj onnipotente; (row etc) colossale

almond ['ɑːmənd] n mandorla

almost ['ɔːlməust] adv quasi

alone [ə'ləun] adj, adv solo(-a); **to leave sb ~** lasciare qn in pace; **to leave sth ~** lasciare stare qc; **let ~ ...** figuriamoci poi ..., tanto meno ...

along [ə'lɔŋ] prep lungo ▷ adv **is he coming ~?** viene con noi?; **he was limping ~** veniva zoppicando; **~ with** insieme con; **all ~** (all the time) sempre, fin dall'inizio; **alongside** prep accanto a; lungo ▷ adv accanto

aloof [ə'luːf] adj distaccato(-a) ▷ adv **to stand ~** tenersi a distanza or in disparte

aloud [ə'laud] adv ad alta voce

alphabet ['ælfəbɛt] n alfabeto

Alps [ælps] npl **the ~** le Alpi

already [ɔːl'rɛdɪ] adv già

alright ['ɔːl'raɪt] (BRIT) adv = **all right**

also ['ɔːlsəu] adv anche

altar ['ɔltə^r] n altare m

alter ['ɔltə^r] vt, vi alterare; **alteration** [ɔltə'reɪʃən] n modificazione f, alterazione f; **alterations** (Sewing, Archit) modifiche fpl; **timetable subject to alteration** orario soggetto a variazioni

alternate [adj ɔl'təːnɪt, vb 'ɔltəːneɪt] adj alterno(-a); (US: plan etc) alternativo(-a) ▷ vi **to ~ (with)** alternarsi (a); **on ~ days** ogni due giorni

alternative [ɔl'təːnətɪv] adj alternativo(-a) ▷ n (choice) alternativa; **alternatively** adv **alternatively one could ...** come alternativa si potrebbe ...

although [ɔːl'ðəu] conj benché + sub, sebbene + sub

altitude ['æltɪtjuːd] n altitudine f

altogether [ɔːltə'gɛðə^r] adv del tutto, completamente; (on the whole) tutto considerato; (in all) in tutto

aluminium [ælju'mɪnɪəm] (BRIT), **aluminum** [ə'luːmɪnəm] (US) n alluminio

always ['ɔːlweɪz] adv sempre

Alzheimer's (disease) ['æltshaɪməz-] n (malattia di) Alzheimer

am [æm] vb see **be**

amalgamate [ə'mælgəmeɪt] vt amalgamare ▷ vi amalgamarsi

amass [ə'mæs] vt ammassare

amateur ['æmətə^r] n dilettante m/f ▷ adj (Sport) dilettante

amaze [ə'meɪz] vt stupire; **amazed** adj sbalordito(-a); **to be amazed (at)** essere sbalordito (da); **amazement** n stupore m; **amazing** adj sorprendente, sbalorditivo(-a)

Amazon ['æməzən] n (Mythology) Amazzone f; (river): **the ~** il Rio delle Amazzoni ▷ cpd (basin, jungle) amazzonico(-a)

ambassador [æm'bæsədə^r] n ambasciatore(-trice)

amber ['æmbə^r] n ambra; **at ~** (BRIT Aut) giallo

ambiguous [æm'bɪgjuəs] adj ambiguo(-a)

ambition [æm'bɪʃən] n ambizione f; **ambitious** [æm'bɪʃəs] adj ambizioso(-a)

ambulance ['æmbjuləns] n ambulanza; **call an ~!** chiamate un'ambulanza!

ambush ['æmbuʃ] n imboscata

amen ['ɑː'mɛn] excl così sia, amen

amend [ə'mɛnd] vt (law) emendare; (text) correggere; **to make ~s** fare ammenda; **amendment** n emendamento; correzione f

amenities [ə'miːnɪtɪz] npl attrezzature fpl ricreative e culturali

America [ə'mɛrɪkə] n America; **American** adj, n americano(-a); **American football** n (BRIT) football m americano

amicable ['æmɪkəbl] adj amichevole

amid(st) [ə'mɪd(st)] prep in mezzo a

ammunition [æmju'nɪʃən] n munizioni fpl

amnesty ['æmnɪstɪ] n amnistia; **to grant an ~ to** concedere l'amnistia a, amnistiare

among(st) [ə'mʌŋ(st)] prep fra, tra, in mezzo a

amount [ə'maunt] n somma; ammontare m; quantità f inv ▷ vi **to ~ to** (total) ammontare a; (be same as) essere come

amp(ère) ['æmp(ɛə^r)] n ampère m inv

ample ['æmpl] adj ampio(-a); spazioso(-a); (enough): **this is ~** questo è più che sufficiente

amplifier ['æmplɪfaɪə'] *n* amplificatore *m*

amputate ['æmpjuteɪt] *vt* amputare

Amtrak ['æmtræk] (*US*) *n* società ferroviaria americana

amuse [ə'mju:z] *vt* divertire; **amusement** *n* divertimento; **amusement arcade** *n* sala giochi; **amusement park** *n* luna park *m inv*

amusing [ə'mju:zɪŋ] *adj* divertente

an [æn] *indef art see* **a**

anaemia [ə'ni:mɪə] (*US* **anemia**) *n* anemia

anaemic [ə'ni:mɪk] (*US* **anemic**) *adj* anemico(-a)

anaesthetic [ænɪs'θɛtɪk] (*US* **anesthetic**) *adj* anestetico(-a) ▷ *n* anestetico

analog(ue) ['ænəlɔg] *adj* (*watch, computer*) analogico(-a)

analogy [ə'nælədʒɪ] *n* analogia; **to draw an ~ between** farc un'analogia tra

analyse ['ænəlaɪz] (*US* **analyze**) *vt* analizzare; **analysis** [ə'næləsɪs] (*pl* **analyses**) *n* analisi *f inv*; **analyst** ['ænəlɪst] *n* (*Pol etc*) analista *m/f*; (*US*) (psic)analista *m/f*

analyze ['ænəlaɪz] (*US*) *vt* = **analyse**

anarchy ['ænəkɪ] *n* anarchia

anatomy [ə'nætəmɪ] *n* anatomia

ancestor ['ænsɪstə'] *n* antenato(-a)

anchor ['æŋkə'] *n* ancora ▷ *vi* (*also*: **to drop ~**) gettare l'ancora ▷ *vt* ancorare; **to weigh ~** salpare *or* levare l'ancora

anchovy ['æntʃəvɪ] *n* acciuga

ancient ['eɪnʃənt] *adj* antico(-a); (*person, car*) vecchissimo(-a)

and [ænd] *conj* e; (*often ed before vowel*): **~ so on** e così via; **try ~ come** cerca di venire; **he talked ~ talked** non la finiva di parlare; **better ~ better** sempre meglio

Andes ['ændi:z] *npl* **the ~** le Ande

anemia *etc* [ə'ni:mɪə] (*US*) = **anaemia** *etc*

anesthetic [ænɪs'θɛtɪk] (*US*) *adj, n* = **anaesthetic**

angel ['eɪndʒəl] *n* angelo

anger ['æŋgə'] *n* rabbia

angina [æn'dʒaɪnə] *n* angina pectoris

angle ['æŋgl] *n* angolo; **from their ~** dal loro punto di vista

angler ['æŋglə'] *n* pescatore *m* con la lenza

Anglican ['æŋglɪkən] *adj, n* anglicano(-a)

angling ['æŋglɪŋ] *n* pesca con la lenza

angrily ['æŋgrɪlɪ] *adv* con rabbia

angry ['æŋgrɪ] *adj* arrabbiato(-a), furioso(-a); (*wound*) infiammato(-a); **to be ~ with sb/at sth** essere in collera con qn/per qc; **to get ~** arrabbiarsi; **to make sb ~** fare arrabbiare qn

anguish ['æŋgwɪʃ] *n* angoscia

animal ['ænɪməl] *adj* animale ▷ *n* animale *m*

animated ['ænɪmeɪtɪd] *adj* animato(-a)

animation [ænɪ'meɪʃən] *n* animazione *f*

aniseed ['ænɪsi:d] *n* semi *mpl* di anice

ankle ['æŋkl] *n* caviglia

annex [*n* 'ænɛks, *vb* ə'nɛks] *n* (*BRIT: also:* **~e**) (edificio) annesso ▷ *vt* annettere

anniversary [ænɪ'və:sərɪ] *n* anniversario

announce [ə'nauns] *vt* annunciare; **announcement** *n* annuncio; (*letter, card*) partecipazione *f*; **announcer** *n* (*Radio, TV*: *between programmes*) annunciatore(-trice); (: *in a programme*) presentatore(-trice)

annoy [ə'nɔɪ] *vt* dare fastidio a; **don't get ~ed!** non irritarti!; **annoying** *adj* noioso(-a)

annual ['ænjuəl] *adj* annuale ▷ *n* (*Bot*) pianta annua; (*book*) annuario; **annually** *adv* annualmente

annum ['ænəm] *n see* **per**

anonymous [ə'nɔnɪməs] *adj* anonimo(-a)

anorak ['ænəræk] *n* giacca a vento

anorexia [ænə'rɛksɪə] *n* (*Med: also:* **~ nervosa**) anoressia

anorexic [ænə'rɛksɪk] *adj, n* anoressico(-a)

another [ə'nʌðə'] *adj* **~ book** (*one more*) un altro libro, ancora un libro; (*a different one*) un altro libro ▷ *pron* un altro(un'altra), ancora uno(-a); *see also* **one**

answer ['ɑ:nsə'] *n* risposta; soluzione *f* ▷ *vi* rispondere ▷ *vt* (*reply to*) rispondere a; (*problem*) risolvere; (*prayer*) esaudire; **in ~ to your letter** in risposta alla sua lettera; **to ~ the phone** rispondere (al telefono); **to ~ the bell** rispondere al campanello; **to ~ the door** aprire la porta; **answer back** *vi* ribattere; **answerphone** *n* (*esp BRIT*) segreteria telefonica

ant [ænt] *n* formica

Antarctic [ænt'ɑ:ktɪk] *n* **the ~** l'Antartide *f*

antelope ['æntɪləup] *n* antilope *f*

antenatal ['æntɪ'neɪtl] *adj* prenatale

antenna [æn'tɛnə, -ni:] (*pl* **antennae**) *n* antenna

anthem ['ænθəm] *n* **national ~** inno nazionale

anthology [æn'θɔlədʒɪ] *n* antologia

anthrax ['ænθræks] *n* antrace *m*

anthropology [ænθrə'pɔlədʒɪ] *n* antropologia

anti [æntɪ] *prefix* anti; **antibiotic** ['æntɪbaɪ'ɔtɪk] *n* antibiotico; **antibody** ['æntɪbɔdɪ] *n* anticorpo

anticipate [æn'tɪsɪpeɪt] *vt* prevedere; pregustare; (*wishes, request*) prevenire; **anticipation** [æntɪsɪ'peɪʃən] *n* anticipazione *f*; (*expectation*) aspettative *fpl*

anticlimax ['æntɪ'klaɪmæks] *n* **it was an ~** fu una completa delusione

anticlockwise ['æntɪ'klɔkwaɪz] *adj, adv* in senso antiorario

antics ['æntɪks] *npl* buffonerie *fpl*

anti: **antidote** ['æntɪdəut] *n* antidoto; **antifreeze** ['æntɪ'fri:z] *n* anticongelante *m*; **anti-globalization** [æntɪgləubəlaɪ'zeɪʃən] *n* antiglobalizzazione *f*; **antihistamine** [æntɪ'hɪstəmɪn] *n* antistaminico; **antiperspirant** ['æntɪ'pə:spərənt] *adj* antitraspirante

antique [æn'ti:k] *n* antichità *f inv* ▷ *adj* antico(-a); **antique shop** *n* negozio d'antichità

antiseptic [æntɪ'sɛptɪk] *n* antisettico

antisocial ['æntɪ'səuʃəl] *adj* asociale

antlers ['æntləz] *npl* palchi *mpl*

anxiety [æŋ'zaɪətɪ] *n* ansia; (*keenness*): ~ **to do** smania di fare

anxious ['æŋkʃəs] *adj* ansioso(-a), inquieto(-a); (*worrying*) angosciante; (*keen*): ~ **to do/that** impaziente di fare/che + *sub*

 KEYWORD

any ['ɛnɪ] *adj* **1** (*in questions etc*): **have you any butter?** hai del burro?, hai un po' di burro?; **have you any children?** hai bambini?; **if there are any tickets left** se ci sono ancora (dei) biglietti, se c'è ancora qualche biglietto
2 (*with negative*): **I haven't any money/books** non ho soldi/libri
3 (*no matter which*) qualsiasi, qualunque; **choose any book you like** scegli un libro qualsiasi
4 (*in phrases*): **in any case** in ogni caso; **any day now** da un giorno all'altro; **at any moment** in qualsiasi momento, da un momento all'altro; **at any rate** ad ogni modo
▷ *pron* **1** (*in questions, with negative*): **have you got any?** ne hai?; **can any of you sing?** qualcuno di voi sa cantare?; **I haven't any (of them)** non ne ho
2 (*no matter which one(s)*): **take any of those books (you like)** prendi uno qualsiasi di quei libri
▷ *adv* **1** (*in questions etc*): **do you want any more soup/sandwiches?** vuoi ancora un po' di minestra/degli altri panini?; **are you feeling any better?** ti senti meglio?
2 (*with negative*): **I can't hear him any more** non lo sento più; **don't wait any longer** non aspettare più

any: **anybody** ['ɛnɪbɔdɪ] *pron* (*in questions etc*) qualcuno, nessuno; (*with negative*) nessuno; (*no matter who*) chiunque; **can you see anybody?** vedi qualcuno *or* nessuno?; **if anybody should phone ...** se telefona qualcuno ...; **I can't see anybody** non vedo nessuno; **anybody could do it** chiunque potrebbe farlo; **anyhow** ['ɛnɪhau] *adv* (*at any rate*) ad ogni modo, comunque; (*haphazard*): **do it anyhow you like** fallo come ti pare; **I shall go anyhow** ci andrò lo stesso *or* comunque; **she leaves things just anyhow** lascia tutto come capita; **anyone** ['ɛnɪwʌn] *pron* = **anybody**; **anything** ['ɛnɪθɪŋ] *pron* (*in question etc*) qualcosa, niente; (*with negative*) niente; (*no matter what*): **you can say anything you like** puoi dire quello che ti pare; **can you see anything?** vedi niente *or* qualcosa?; **if anything happens to me ...** se mi dovesse succedere qualcosa ...; **I can't see anything** non vedo niente; **anything will do** va bene qualsiasi cosa *or* tutto; **anytime** *adv* in qualunque momento; quando vuole; **anyway** ['ɛnɪweɪ] *adv* (*at any rate*) ad ogni modo, comunque; (*besides*) ad ogni modo; **anywhere** ['ɛnɪwɛəʳ] *adv* (*in questions etc*) da qualche parte; (*with negative*) da nessuna parte; (*no matter where*) da qualsiasi *or* qualunque parte, dovunque; **can you see him anywhere?** lo vedi da qualche parte?; **I can't see him anywhere** non lo vedo da nessuna parte; **anywhere in the world** dovunque nel mondo

apart [ə'pɑ:t] *adv* (*to one side*) a parte; (*separately*) separatamente; **with one's legs ~** con le gambe divaricate; **10 miles ~** a 10 miglia di distanza (l'uno dall'altro); **to take ~** smontare; **~ from** a parte, eccetto

apartment [ə'pɑ:tmənt] (*us*) *n* appartamento; (*room*) locale *m*; **apartment building** (*us*) *n* stabile *m*, caseggiato

apathy ['æpəθɪ] *n* apatia

ape [eɪp] *n* scimmia ▷ *vt* scimmiottare

aperitif [ə'pɛrɪti:f] *n* aperitivo

aperture ['æpətʃuəʳ] *n* apertura

APEX *n abbr* (= *advance purchase excursion*) APEX *m inv*

apologize [ə'pɔlədʒaɪz] *vi* **to ~ (for sth to sb)** scusarsi (di qc a qn), chiedere scusa (a qn per qc)

apology [ə'pɔlədʒɪ] *n* scuse *fpl*

apostrophe [ə'pɔstrəfɪ] *n* (*sign*) apostrofo

appal [ə'pɔ:l] (*us* **appall**) *vt* scioccare; **appalling** *adj* spaventoso(-a)

apparatus [æpə'reɪtəs] *n* apparato; (*in gymnasium*) attrezzatura

apparent [ə'pærənt] *adj* evidente; **apparently** *adv* evidentemente

appeal [ə'piːl] *vi* (*Law*) appellarsi alla legge ▷ *n* (*Law*) appello; (*request*) richiesta; (*charm*) attrattiva; **to ~ for** chiedere (con insistenza); **to ~ to** (*person*) appellarsi a; (*thing*) piacere a; **it doesn't ~ to me** mi dice poco; **appealing** *adj* (*nice*) attraente

appear [ə'pɪə'] *vi* apparire; (*Law*) comparire; (*publication*) essere pubblicato(-a); (*seem*) sembrare; **it would ~ that** sembra che; **appearance** *n* apparizione *f*; apparenza; (*look, aspect*) aspetto

appendicitis [əpɛndɪ'saɪtɪs] *n* appendicite *f*

appendix [ə'pɛndɪks] (*pl* **appendices**) *n* appendice *f*

appetite ['æpɪtaɪt] *n* appetito

appetizer ['æpɪtaɪzə'] *n* stuzzichino

applaud [ə'plɔːd] *vt, vi* applaudire

applause [ə'plɔːz] *n* applauso

apple ['æpl] *n* mela; **apple pie** *n* torta di mele

appliance [ə'plaɪəns] *n* apparecchio

applicable [ə'plɪkəbl] *adj* applicabile; **to be ~ to** essere valido per; **the law is ~ from January** la legge entrerà in vigore in gennaio

applicant ['æplɪkənt] *n* candidato(-a)

application [æplɪ'keɪʃən] *n* applicazione *f*; (*for a job, a grant etc*) domanda; **application form** *n* modulo per la domanda

apply [ə'plaɪ] *vt* **to ~ (to)** (*paint, ointment*) dare (a); (*theory, technique*) applicare (a) ▷ *vi* **to ~ to** (*ask*) rivolgersi a; (*be suitable for, relevant to*) riguardare, riferirsi a; **to ~ (for)** (*permit, grant, job*) fare domanda (per); **to ~ o.s. to** dedicarsi a

appoint [ə'pɔɪnt] *vt* nominare; **appointment** *n* nomina; (*arrangement to meet*) appuntamento; **I have an appointment (with)** ... ho un appuntamento (con) ...; **I'd like to make an appointment (with)** vorrei prendere un appuntamento (con)

appraisal [ə'preɪzl] *n* valutazione *f*

appreciate [ə'priːʃɪeɪt] *vt* (*like*) apprezzare; (*be grateful for*) essere riconoscente di; (*be aware of*) rendersi conto di ▷ *vi* (*Finance*) aumentare; **I'd ~ your help** ti sono grato per l'aiuto; **appreciation** [əpriːʃɪ'eɪʃən] *n* apprezzamento; (*Finance*) aumento del valore

apprehension [æprɪ'hɛnʃən] *n* (*fear*) inquietudine *f*

apprehensive [æprɪ'hɛnsɪv] *adj* apprensivo(-a)

apprentice [ə'prɛntɪs] *n* apprendista *m/f*

approach [ə'prəʊtʃ] *vi* avvicinarsi ▷ *vt* (*come near*) avvicinarsi a; (*ask, apply to*) rivolgersi a; (*subject, passer-by*) avvicinare ▷ *n* approccio; accesso; (*to problem*) modo di affrontare

appropriate [*adj* ə'prəʊprɪɪt, *vb* ə'prəʊprɪeɪt] *adj* appropriato(-a), adatto(-a) ▷ *vt* (*take*) appropriarsi

approval [ə'pruːvəl] *n* approvazione *f*; **on ~** (*Comm*) in prova, in esame

approve [ə'pruːv] *vt, vi* approvare; **approve of** *vt fus* approvare

approximate [ə'prɒksɪmɪt] *adj* approssimativo(-a); **approximately** *adv* circa

Apr. *abbr* (= *April*) apr.

apricot ['eɪprɪkɒt] *n* albicocca

April ['eɪprəl] *n* aprile *m*; **~ fool!** pesce d'aprile!; **April Fools' Day** *n* vedi nota nel riquadro

⬤ **APRIL FOOLS' DAY**
⬤
⬤ **April Fool's Day** è il primo aprile, il
⬤ giorno degli scherzi e delle burle. Il nome
⬤ deriva dal fatto che, se una persona
⬤ cade nella trappola che gli è stata tesa,
⬤ fa la figura del "fool", cioè dello sciocco.
⬤ Tradizionalmente, gli scherzi vengono
⬤ fatti entro mezzogiorno.

apron ['eɪprən] *n* grembiule *m*

apt [æpt] *adj* (*suitable*) adatto(-a); (*able*) capace; (*likely*): **to be ~ to do** avere tendenza a fare

aquarium [ə'kwɛərɪəm] *n* acquario

Aquarius [ə'kwɛərɪəs] *n* Acquario

Arab ['ærəb] *adj, n* arabo(-a)

Arabia [ə'reɪbɪə] *n* Arabia; **Arabian** [ə'reɪbɪən] *adj* arabo(-a); **Arabic** ['ærəbɪk] *adj* arabico(-a), arabo(-a) ▷ *n* arabo; **Arabic numerals** *n* numeri *mpl* arabi, numerazione *f* araba

arbitrary ['ɑːbɪtrərɪ] *adj* arbitrario(-a)

arbitration [ɑːbɪ'treɪʃən] *n* (*Law*) arbitrato; (*Industry*) arbitraggio

arc [ɑːk] *n* arco

arcade [ɑː'keɪd] *n* portico; (*passage with shops*) galleria

arch [ɑːtʃ] *n* arco; (*of foot*) arco plantare ▷ *vt* inarcare

archaeology [ɑːkɪ'ɒlədʒɪ] (*US* **archeology**) *n* archeologia

archbishop [ɑːtʃ'bɪʃəp] *n* arcivescovo

archeology *etc* [ɑːkɪ'ɒlədʒɪ] (*US*) = **archaeology** *etc*

architect ['ɑːkɪtɛkt] *n* architetto; **architectural** [ɑːkɪ'tɛktʃərəl] *adj* architettonico(-a); **architecture** ['ɑːkɪtɛktʃə'] *n* architettura

archive ['ɑːkaɪv] n (often pl: also Comput) archivio

Arctic ['ɑːktɪk] adj artico(-a) ▷ n **the ~** l'Artico

are [ɑːʳ] vb see **be**

area ['ɛərɪə] n (Geom) area; (zone) zona; (: smaller) settore m; **area code** (US) n (Tel) prefisso

arena [əˈriːnə] n arena

aren't [ɑːnt] = **are not**

Argentina [ɑːdʒənˈtiːnə] n Argentina; **Argentinian** [-ˈtɪnɪən] adj, n argentino(-a)

arguably ['ɑːgjuəblɪ] adv **it is ~ ...** si può sostenere che sia ...

argue ['ɑːgjuː] vi (quarrel) litigare; (reason) ragionare; **to ~ that** sostenere che

argument ['ɑːgjumənt] n (reasons) argomento; (quarrel) lite f

Aries ['ɛərɪz] n Ariete m

arise [əˈraɪz] (pt **arose**, pp **arisen**) vi (opportunity, problem) presentarsi

arithmetic [əˈrɪθmətɪk] n aritmetica

arm [ɑːm] n braccio ▷ vt armare; **~s** npl (weapons) armi fpl; **~ in ~** a braccetto; **armchair** n poltrona

armed [ɑːmd] adj armato(-a); **armed robbery** n rapina a mano armata

armour ['ɑːməʳ] (US **armor**) n armatura; (Mil: tanks) mezzi mpl blindati

armpit ['ɑːmpɪt] n ascella

armrest ['ɑːmrɛst] n bracciolo

army ['ɑːmɪ] n esercito

A road n strada statale

aroma [əˈrəumə] n aroma; **aromatherapy** n aromaterapia

arose [əˈrəuz] pt of **arise**

around [əˈraund] adv attorno, intorno ▷ prep intorno a; (fig: about): **~ £5/3 o'clock** circa 5 sterline/le 3; **is he ~?** è in giro?

arouse [əˈrauz] vt (sleeper) svegliare; (curiosity, passions) suscitare

arrange [əˈreɪndʒ] vt sistemare; (programme) preparare; **to ~ to do sth** mettersi d'accordo per fare qc; **arrangement** n sistemazione f; (agreement) accordo; **arrangements** npl (plans) progetti mpl, piani mpl

array [əˈreɪ] n **~ of** fila di

arrears [əˈrɪəz] npl arretrati mpl; **to be in ~ with one's rent** essere in arretrato con l'affitto

arrest [əˈrɛst] vt arrestare; (sb's attention) attirare ▷ n arresto; **under ~** in arresto

arrival [əˈraɪvəl] n arrivo; (person) arrivato(-a); **a new ~** un nuovo venuto; (baby) un neonato

arrive [əˈraɪv] vi arrivare; **what time does the train from Rome ~?** a che ora arriva il treno da Roma?; **arrive at** vt fus arrivare a

arrogance ['ærəgəns] n arroganza

arrogant ['ærəgənt] adj arrogante

arrow ['ærəu] n freccia

arse [ɑːs] (inf!) n culo (!)

arson ['ɑːsn] n incendio doloso

art [ɑːt] n arte f; (craft) mestiere m; **art college** n scuola di belle arti

artery ['ɑːtərɪ] n arteria

art gallery n galleria d'arte

arthritis [ɑːˈθraɪtɪs] n artrite f

artichoke ['ɑːtɪtʃəuk] n carciofo; **Jerusalem ~** topinambur m inv

article ['ɑːtɪkl] n articolo

articulate [adj ɑːˈtɪkjulɪt, vb ɑːˈtɪkjuleɪt] adj (person) che si esprime forbitamente; (speech) articolato(-a) ▷ vi articolare

artificial [ɑːtɪˈfɪʃəl] adj artificiale

artist ['ɑːtɪst] n artista m/f; **artistic** [ɑːˈtɪstɪk] adj artistico(-a)

art school n scuola d'arte

 KEYWORD

as [æz] conj **1** (referring to time) mentre; **as the years went by** col passare degli anni; **he came in as I was leaving** arrivò mentre stavo uscendo; **as from tomorrow** da domani

2 (in comparisons): **as big as** grande come; **twice as big as** due volte più grande di; **as much/many as** tanto quanto/tanti quanti; **as soon as possible** prima possibile

3 (since, because) dal momento che, siccome

4 (referring to manner, way) come; **do as you wish** fa' come vuoi; **as she said** come ha detto lei

5 (concerning): **as for** or **to that** per quanto riguarda or quanto a quello

6: **as if** or **as though** come se; **he looked as if he was ill** sembrava stare male; see also **long**; **such**; **well**

▷ prep **he works as a driver** fa l'autista; **as chairman of the company he ...** come presidente della compagnia lui ...; **he gave me it as a present** me lo ha regalato

a.s.a.p. abbr = **as soon as possible**

asbestos [æzˈbɛstəs] n asbesto, amianto

ascent [əˈsɛnt] n salita

ash [æʃ] n (dust) cenere f; (wood, tree) frassino

ashamed [əˈʃeɪmd] adj vergognoso(-a); **to be ~ of** vergognarsi di

ashore [əˈʃɔːʳ] adv a terra

ashtray ['æʃtreɪ] n portacenere m

Ash Wednesday n mercoledì m inv delle

Ceneri

Asia ['eɪʃə] n Asia; **Asian** adj, n asiatico(-a)

aside [ə'saɪd] adv da parte ▷ n a parte m

ask [ɑːsk] vt (question) domandare; (invite) invitare; **to ~ sb sth/sb to do sth** chiedere qc a qn/a qn di fare qc; **to ~ sb about sth** chiedere a qn di qc; **to ~ (sb) a question** fare una domanda (a qn); **to ~ sb out to dinner** invitare qn a mangiare fuori; **ask for** vt fus chiedere; (trouble etc) cercare

asleep [ə'sliːp] adj addormentato(-a); **to be ~** dormire; **to fall ~** addormentarsi

asparagus [əs'pærəgəs] n asparagi mpl

aspect ['æspɛkt] n aspetto

aspirations [æspə'reɪʃənz] npl aspirazioni fpl

aspire [əs'paɪər] vi **to ~ to** aspirare a

aspirin ['æsprɪn] n aspirina

ass [æs] n asino; (inf) scemo(-a); (US: inf!) culo (!)

assassin [ə'sæsɪn] n assassino; **assassinate** [ə'sæsɪneɪt] vt assassinare

assault [ə'sɔːlt] n (Mil) assalto; (gen: attack) aggressione f ▷ vt assaltare; aggredire; (sexually) violentare

assemble [ə'sɛmbl] vt riunire; (Tech) montare ▷ vi riunirsi

assembly [ə'sɛmblɪ] n (meeting) assemblea; (construction) montaggio

assert [ə'səːt] vt asserire; (insist on) far valere; **assertion** [ə'səːʃən] n asserzione f

assess [ə'sɛs] vt valutare; **assessment** n valutazione f

asset ['æsɛt] n vantaggio; **~s** npl (Finance: of individual) beni mpl; (: of company) attivo

assign [ə'saɪn] vt **to ~ (to)** (task) assegnare (a); (resources) riservare (a); (cause, meaning) attribuire (a); **to ~ a date to sth** fissare la data di qc; **assignment** n compito

assist [ə'sɪst] vt assistere, aiutare; **assistance** n assistenza, aiuto; **assistant** n assistente m/f; (BRIT: also: **shop assistant**) commesso(-a)

associate [adj, n ə'səuʃɪɪt, vb ə'səuʃɪeɪt] adj associato(-a); (member) aggiunto(-a) ▷ n collega m/f ▷ vt associare ▷ vi **to ~ with sb** frequentare qn

association [əsəusɪ'eɪʃən] n associazione f

assorted [ə'sɔːtɪd] adj assortito(-a)

assortment [ə'sɔːtmənt] n assortimento

assume [ə'sjuːm] vt supporre; (responsibilities etc) assumere; (attitude, name) prendere

assumption [ə'sʌmpʃən] n supposizione f, ipotesi f inv; (of power) assunzione f

assurance [ə'ʃuərəns] n assicurazione f; (self-confidence) fiducia in se stesso

assure [ə'ʃuər] vt assicurare

asterisk ['æstərɪsk] n asterisco

asthma ['æsmə] n asma

astonish [ə'stɔnɪʃ] vt stupire; **astonished** adj stupito(-a), sorpreso(-a); **to be astonished (at)** essere stupito(-a) (da); **astonishing** adj sorprendente, stupefacente; **I find it astonishing that ...** mi stupisce che ...; **astonishment** n stupore m

astound [ə'staund] vt sbalordire

astray [ə'streɪ] adv **to go ~** smarrirsi; **to lead ~** portare sulla cattiva strada

astrology [əs'trɔlədʒɪ] n astrologia

astronaut ['æstrənɔːt] n astronauta m/f

astronomer [əs'trɔnəmər] n astronomo(-a)

astronomical [æstrə'nɔmɪkl] adj astronomico(-a)

astronomy [əs'trɔnəmɪ] n astronomia

astute [əs'tjuːt] adj astuto(-a)

asylum [ə'saɪləm] n (politico) asilo; (per malati) manicomio

○ **KEYWORD**

at [æt] prep **1** (referring to position, direction) a; **at the top** in cima; **at the desk** al banco, alla scrivania; **at home/school** a casa/scuola; **at the baker's** dal panettiere; **to look at sth** guardare qc; **to throw sth at sb** lanciare qc a qn

2 (referring to time) a; **at 4 o'clock** alle 4; **at night** di notte; **at Christmas** a Natale; **at times** a volte

3 (referring to rates, speed etc) a; **at £1 a kilo** a 1 sterlina al chilo; **two at a time** due alla volta, due per volta; **at 50 km/h** a 50 km/h

4 (referring to manner): **at a stroke** d'un solo colpo; **at peace** in pace

5 (referring to activity): **to be at work** essere al lavoro; **to play at cowboys** giocare ai cowboy; **to be good at sth/doing sth** essere bravo in qc/fare qc

6 (referring to cause): **shocked/surprised/annoyed at sth** colpito da/sorpreso da/arrabbiato per qc; **I went at his suggestion** ci sono andato dietro suo consiglio

ate [eɪt] pt of **eat**

atheist ['eɪθɪɪst] n ateo(-a)

Athens ['æθɪnz] n Atene f

athlete ['æθliːt] n atleta m/f

athletic [æθ'lɛtɪk] adj atletico(-a); **athletics** n atletica

Atlantic [ət'læntɪk] adj atlantico(-a) ▷ n **the ~ (Ocean)** l'Atlantico, l'Oceano Atlantico

atlas ['ætləs] n atlante m

A.T.M. *n abbr* (= *automated telling machine*) cassa automatica prelievi, sportello automatico

atmosphere ['ætməsfɪə'] *n* atmosfera

atom ['ætəm] *n* atomo; **atomic** [ə'tɒmɪk] *adj* atomico(-a); **atom(ic) bomb** *n* bomba atomica

A to Z® *n* (*map*) stradario

atrocity [ə'trɒsɪtɪ] *n* atrocità *f inv*

attach [ə'tætʃ] *vt* attaccare; (*document, letter*) allegare; (*importance etc*) attribuire; **to be ~ed to sb/sth** (*to like*) essere affezionato(-a) a qn/qc; **attachment** [ə'tætʃmənt] *n* (*tool*) accessorio; (*love*): **attachment (to)** affetto (per)

attack [ə'tæk] *vt* attaccare; (*person*) aggredire; (*task etc*) iniziare; (*problem*) affrontare ▷ *n* attacco; **heart ~** infarto; **attacker** *n* aggressore *m*

attain [ə'teɪn] *vt* (*also:* **to ~ to**) arrivare a, raggiungere

attempt [ə'tɛmpt] *n* tentativo ▷ *vt* tentare; **to make an ~ on sb's life** attentare alla vita di qn

attend [ə'tɛnd] *vt* frequentare; (*meeting, talk*) andare a; (*patient*) assistere; **attend to** *vt fus* (*needs, affairs etc*) prendersi cura di; (*customer*) occuparsi di; **attendance** *n* (*being present*) presenza; (*people present*) gente *f* presente; **attendant** *n* custode *m/f*; persona di servizio ▷ *adj* concomitante

> Be careful not to translate *attend* by the Italian word *attendere*.

attention [ə'tɛnʃən] *n* attenzione *f* ▷ *excl* (*Mil*) attenti!; **for the ~ of** (*Admin*) per l'attenzione di

attic ['ætɪk] *n* soffitta

attitude ['ætɪtjuːd] *n* atteggiamento; posa

attorney [ə'təːnɪ] *n* (*lawyer*) avvocato; (*having proxy*) mandatario; **Attorney General** *n* (*BRIT*) Procuratore *m* Generale; (*US*) Ministro della Giustizia

attract [ə'trækt] *vt* attirare; **attraction** [ə'trækʃən] *n* (*gen pl: pleasant things*) attrattiva; (*Physics, fig: towards sth*) attrazione *f*; **attractive** *adj* attraente

attribute [*n* 'ætrɪbjuːt, *vb* ə'trɪbjuːt] *n* attributo ▷ *vt* **to ~ sth to** attribuire qc a

aubergine ['əubəʒiːn] *n* melanzana

auburn ['ɔːbən] *adj* tizianesco(-a)

auction ['ɔːkʃən] *n* (*also:* **sale by ~**) asta ▷ *vt* (*also:* **to sell by ~**) vendere all'asta; (*also:* **to put up for ~**) mettere all'asta

audible ['ɔːdɪbl] *adj* udibile

audience ['ɔːdɪəns] *n* (*people*) pubblico; spettatori *mpl*; ascoltatori *mpl*; (*interview*) udienza

audit ['ɔːdɪt] *vt* rivedere, verificare

audition [ɔː'dɪʃən] *n* audizione *f*

auditor ['ɔːdɪtə'] *n* revisore *m*

auditorium [ɔːdɪ'tɔːrɪəm] *n* sala, auditorio

Aug. *abbr* (= *August*) ago., ag.

August ['ɔːgəst] *n* agosto

aunt [ɑːnt] *n* zia; **auntie** *n* zietta; **aunty** *n* zietta

au pair ['əu'pɛə'] *n* (*also:* **~ girl**) (ragazza *f*) alla pari *inv*

aura ['ɔːrə] *n* aura

austerity [ɒs'tɛrɪtɪ] *n* austerità *f inv*

Australia [ɒs'treɪlɪə] *n* Australia; **Australian** *adj*, *n* australiano(-a)

Austria ['ɒstrɪə] *n* Austria; **Austrian** *adj*, *n* austriaco(-a)

authentic [ɔː'θɛntɪk] *adj* autentico(-a)

author ['ɔːθə'] *n* autore(-trice)

authority [ɔː'θɒrɪtɪ] *n* autorità *f inv*; (*permission*) autorizzazione *f*; **the authorities** *npl* (*government etc*) le autorità

authorize ['ɔːθəraɪz] *vt* autorizzare

auto ['ɔːtəu] (*US*) *n* auto *f inv*; **autobiography** [ɔːtəbaɪ'ɒgrəfɪ] *n* autobiografia; **autograph** ['ɔːtəgrɑːf] *n* autografo ▷ *vt* firmare; **automatic** [ɔː tə'mætɪk] *adj* automatico(-a) ▷ *n* (*gun*) arma automatica; (*washing machine*) lavatrice *f* automatica; (*car*) automobile *f* con cambio automatico; **automatically** *adv* automaticamente; **automobile** ['ɔːtə məbiːl] (*US*) *n* automobile *f*; **autonomous** [ɔː'tɒnəməs] *adj* autonomo(-a); **autonomy** [ɔː'tɒnəmɪ] *n* autonomia

autumn ['ɔːtəm] *n* autunno

auxiliary [ɔːg'zɪlɪərɪ] *adj* ausiliario(-a) ▷ *n* ausiliare *m/f*

avail [ə'veɪl] *vt* **to ~ o.s. of** servirsi di; approfittarsi di ▷ *n* **to no ~** inutilmente

availability [əveɪlə'bɪlɪtɪ] *n* disponibilità

available [ə'veɪləbl] *adj* disponibile

avalanche ['ævəlɑːnʃ] *n* valanga

Ave. *abbr* = **avenue**

avenue ['ævənjuː] *n* viale *m*; (*fig*) strada, via

average ['ævərɪdʒ] *n* media ▷ *adj* medio(-a) ▷ *vt* (*a certain figure*) fare di *or* in media; **on ~** in media

avert [ə'vəːt] *vt* evitare, prevenire; (*one's eyes*) distogliere

avid ['ævɪd] *adj* (*supporter etc*) accanito(-a)

avocado [ævə'kɑːdəu] *n* (*BRIT: also:* **~ pear**) avocado *m inv*

avoid [ə'vɔɪd] *vt* evitare

await [ə'weɪt] *vt* aspettare

awake [ə'weɪk] (*pt* **awoke**, *pp* **awoken**, **awaked**) *adj* sveglio(-a) ▷ *vt* svegliare ▷ *vi* svegliarsi

award [ə'wɔːd] *n* premio; (*Law*)
risarcimento ▷ *vt* assegnare; (*Law:*
damages) accordare

aware [ə'wɛə^r] *adj* ~ **of** (*conscious*)
conscio(-a) di; (*informed*) informato(-a) di;
to become ~ of accorgersi di; **awareness**
n consapevolezza

away [ə'weɪ] *adj, adv* via; lontano(-a); **two
kilometres ~** a due chilometri di distanza;
two hours ~ by car a due ore di distanza
in macchina; **the holiday was two weeks
~** mancavano due settimane alle vacanze;
he's ~ for a week è andato via per una
settimana; **to take ~** togliere; **he was
working/pedalling** *etc* ~ (*la particella
indica la continuità e l'energia dell'azione*)
lavorava/pedalava *etc* più che poteva; **to
fade/wither** *etc* ~ (*la particella rinforza
l'idea della diminuzione*)

awe [ɔː] *n* timore *m*; **awesome** *adj*
imponente

awful ['ɔːfəl] *adj* terribile; **an ~ lot of**
un mucchio di; **awfully** *adv* (*very*)
terribilmente

awkward ['ɔːkwəd] *adj* (*clumsy*) goffo(-a);
(*inconvenient*) scomodo(-a); (*embarrassing*)
imbarazzante

awoke [ə'wəuk] *pt of* **awake**

awoken [ə'wəukn] *pp of* **awake**

axe [æks] (*US* **ax**) *n* scure *f* ▷ *vt* (*project etc*)
abolire; (*jobs*) sopprimere

axle ['æksl] *n* (*also:* **~-tree**) asse *m*

ay(e) [aɪ] *excl* (*yes*) sì

azalea [ə'zeɪlɪə] *n* azalea

b

B [biː] *n* (*Mus*) si *m*

B.A. *n abbr* = **Bachelor of Arts**

baby ['beɪbɪ] *n* bambino(-a); **baby
carriage** (*US*) *n* carrozzina; **baby-sit** *vi*
fare il (*or* la) baby-sitter; **baby-sitter** *n*
baby-sitter *m/f inv*; **baby wipe** *n* salvietta
umidificata

bachelor ['bætʃələ^r] *n* scapolo; **B~ of Arts/
Science** ≈ laureato(-a) in lettere/scienze

back [bæk] *n* (*of person, horse*) dorso,
schiena; (*as opposed to front*) dietro; (*of
hand*) dorso; (*of train*) coda; (*of chair*)
schienale *m*; (*of page*) rovescio; (*of book*)
retro; (*Football*) difensore *m* ▷ *vt* (*candidate*)
appoggiare; (*horse: at races*) puntare
su; (*car*) guidare a marcia indietro ▷ *vi*
indietreggiare; (*car etc*) fare marcia
indietro ▷ *cpd* posteriore, di dietro; (*Aut:
seat, wheels*) posteriore ▷ *adv* (*not forward*)
indietro; (*returned*): **he's ~** è tornato; **he
ran ~** tornò indietro di corsa; (*restitution*):
throw the ball ~ ritira la palla; **can I have
it ~?** posso riaverlo?; (*again*): **he called
~** ha richiamato; **back down** *vi* fare
marcia indietro; **back out** *vi* (*of promise*)
tirarsi indietro; **back up** *vt* (*support*)
appoggiare, sostenere; (*Comput*) fare una
copia di riserva di; **backache** *n* mal *m* di
schiena; **backbencher** (*BRIT*) *n* membro
del Parlamento senza potere amministrativo;

backbone n spina dorsale; **back door** n
porta sul retro; **backfire** vi (Aut) dar ritorni
di fiamma; (plans) fallire; **backgammon**
n tavola reale; **background** n sfondo; (of
events) background m inv; (basic knowledge)
base f; (experience) esperienza; **family
background** ambiente m familiare;
backing n (fig) appoggio; **backlog**
n **backlog of work** lavoro arretrato;
backpack n zaino; **backpacker** n chi
viaggia con zaino e sacco a pelo; **backslash**
n backslash m inv, barra obliqua
inversa; **backstage** adv nel retroscena;
backstroke n nuoto sul dorso; **backup**
adj (train, plane) supplementare; (Comput)
di riserva ▷ n (support) appoggio,
sostegno; (also: **backup file**) file m inv
di riserva; **backward** adj (movement)
indietro inv; (person) tardivo(-a); (country)
arretrato(-a); **backwards** adv indietro;
(fall, walk) all'indietro; **backyard** n cortile
m dietro la casa
bacon ['beɪkən] n pancetta
bacteria [bæk'tɪərɪə] npl batteri mpl
bad [bæd] adj cattivo(-a); (accident, injury)
brutto(-a); (meat, food) andato(-a) a male;
his ~ leg la sua gamba malata; **to go ~**
andare a male
badge [bædʒ] n insegna; (of policeman)
stemma m
badger ['bædʒər] n tasso
badly ['bædlɪ] adv (work, dress etc) male; **~
wounded** gravemente ferito; **he needs it
~** ne ha un gran bisogno
bad-mannered [bæd'mænəd] adj
maleducato(-a), sgarbato(-a)
badminton ['bædmɪntən] n badminton m
bad-tempered ['bæd'tɛmpəd] adj
irritabile; di malumore
bag [bæg] n sacco; (handbag etc) borsa;
~s of (inf: lots of) un sacco di; **baggage**
n bagagli mpl; **baggage allowance**
n franchigia f bagaglio inv; **baggage
reclaim** n ritiro m bagaglio inv; **baggy**
adj largo(-a), sformato(-a); **bagpipes** npl
cornamusa
bail [beɪl] n cauzione f ▷ vt (prisoner:
also: **grant ~ to**) concedere la libertà
provvisoria su cauzione a; (boat: also: **~
out**) aggottare; **on ~** in libertà provvisoria
su cauzione
bait [beɪt] n esca ▷ vt (hook) innescare;
(trap) munire di esca; (fig) tormentare
bake [beɪk] vt cuocere al forno ▷ vi
cuocersi al forno; **baked beans** [-biːnz]
npl fagioli mpl in salsa di pomodoro;
baked potato n patata cotta al forno
con la buccia; **baker** n fornaio(-a),
panettiere(-a); **bakery** n panetteria;

baking n cottura (al forno); **baking
powder** n lievito in polvere
balance ['bæləns] n equilibrio; (Comm:
sum) bilancio; (remainder) resto; (scales)
bilancia ▷ vt tenere in equilibrio; (budget)
far quadrare; (account) pareggiare;
(compensate) contrappesare; **~ of trade/
payments** bilancia commerciale/dei
pagamenti; **balanced** adj (personality, diet)
equilibrato(-a); **balance sheet** n bilancio
balcony ['bælkənɪ] n balcone m; (in
theatre) balconata; **do you have a room
with a ~?** avete una camera con balcone?
bald [bɔːld] adj calvo(-a); (tyre) liscio(-a)
Balearics [bælɪ'ærɪks] npl **the ~** le Baleari
fpl
ball [bɔːl] n palla; (football) pallone m; (for
golf) pallina; (of wool, string) gomitolo;
(dance) ballo; **to play ~** (fig) stare al gioco
ballerina [bælə'riːnə] n ballerina
ballet ['bæleɪ] n balletto; **ballet dancer** n
ballerino(-a) classico(-a)
balloon [bə'luːn] n pallone m
ballot ['bælət] n scrutinio
ballpoint (pen) ['bɔːlpɔɪnt(-)] n penna
a sfera
ballroom ['bɔːlrum] n sala da ballo
Baltic ['bɔːltɪk] adj, n **the ~ Sea** il (mar)
Baltico
bamboo [bæm'buː] n bambù m
ban [bæn] n interdizione f ▷ vt interdire
banana [bə'nɑːnə] n banana
band [bænd] n banda; (at a dance)
orchestra; (Mil) fanfara
bandage ['bændɪdʒ] n benda, fascia
Band-Aid® ['bændeɪd] (US) n cerotto
B. & B. n abbr = **bed and breakfast**
bandit ['bændɪt] n bandito
bang [bæŋ] n (of door) lo sbattere; (of gun,
blow) colpo ▷ vt battere (violentemente);
(door) sbattere ▷ vi scoppiare; sbattere
Bangladesh [bɑːŋglə'dɛʃ] n Bangladesh m
bangle ['bæŋgl] n braccialetto
bangs [bæŋz] (US) npl (fringe) frangia,
frangetta
banish ['bænɪʃ] vt bandire
banister(s) ['bænɪstə(z)] n(pl) ringhiera
banjo ['bændʒəu] (pl **banjoes** or **banjos**) n
banjo m inv
bank [bæŋk] n banca, banco; (of river, lake)
riva, sponda; (of earth) banco ▷ vi (Aviat)
inclinarsi in virata; **bank on** vt fus contare
su; **bank account** n conto in banca;
bank balance n saldo; **a healthy bank
balance** un solido conto in banca; **bank
card** n carta f assegni inv; **bank charges**
npl (BRIT) spese fpl bancarie; **banker** n
banchiere m; **bank holiday** (BRIT) n giorno
di festa; vedi nota nel riquadro; **banking**

n attività bancaria; professione *f* di banchiere; **bank manager** *n* direttore *m* di banca; **banknote** *n* banconota

⬤ **BANK HOLIDAY**
⬤
⬤ Una **bank holiday**, in Gran Bretagna,
⬤ è una giornata in cui banche e molti
⬤ negozi sono chiusi. Generalmente le
⬤ **bank holidays** cadono di lunedì e molti
⬤ ne approfittano per fare una breve
⬤ vacanza fuori città.

bankrupt ['bæŋkrʌpt] *adj* fallito(-a); **to go ~** fallire; **bankruptcy** *n* fallimento
bank statement *n* estratto conto
banner ['bænəʳ] *n* striscione *m*
bannister(s) ['bænɪstə(z)] *n(pl) see* **banister(s)**
banquet ['bæŋkwɪt] *n* banchetto
baptism ['bæptɪzəm] *n* battesimo
baptize [bæp'taɪz] *vt* battezzare
bar [bɑːʳ] *n* (*place*) bar *m inv*; (*counter*) banco; (*rod*) barra; (*of window etc*) sbarra; (*of chocolate*) tavoletta; (*fig*) ostacolo; restrizione *f*; (*Mus*) battuta ▷ *vt* (*road, window*) sbarrare; (*person*) escludere; (*activity*) interdire; **~ of soap** saponetta; **the B~** (*Law*) l'Ordine *m* degli avvocati; **behind ~s** (*prisoner*) dietro le sbarre; **~ none** senza eccezione
barbaric [bɑː'bærɪk] *adj* barbarico(-a)
barbecue ['bɑːbɪkjuː] *n* barbecue *m inv*
barbed wire ['bɑːbd-] *n* filo spinato
barber ['bɑːbəʳ] *n* barbiere *m*; **barber's (shop)** (*US* **barber (shop)**) *n* barbiere *m*
bar code *n* (*on goods*) codice *m* a barre
bare [bɛəʳ] *adj* nudo(-a) ▷ *vt* scoprire, denudare; (*teeth*) mostrare; **the ~ necessities** lo stretto necessario; **barefoot** *adj, adv* scalzo(-a); **barely** *adv* appena
bargain ['bɑːgɪn] *n* (*transaction*) contratto; (*good buy*) affare *m* ▷ *vi* trattare; **into the ~** per giunta; **bargain for** *vt fus* **he got more than he ~ed for** gli è andata peggio di quel che si aspettasse
barge [bɑːdʒ] *n* chiatta; **barge in** *vi* (*walk in*) piombare dentro; (*interrupt talk*) intromettersi a sproposito
bark [bɑːk] *n* (*of tree*) corteccia; (*of dog*) abbaio ▷ *vi* abbaiare
barley ['bɑːlɪ] *n* orzo
barmaid ['bɑːmeɪd] *n* cameriera al banco
barman ['bɑːmən] (*irreg*) *n* barista *m*
barn [bɑːn] *n* granaio
barometer [bə'rɔmɪtəʳ] *n* barometro
baron ['bærən] *n* barone *m*; **baroness** *n* baronessa

barracks ['bærəks] *npl* caserma
barrage ['bærɑːʒ] *n* (*Mil, dam*) sbarramento; (*fig*) fiume *m*
barrel ['bærəl] *n* barile *m*; (*of gun*) canna
barren ['bærən] *adj* sterile; (*soil*) arido(-a)
barrette [bə'rɛt] (*US*) *n* fermaglio per capelli
barricade [bærɪ'keɪd] *n* barricata
barrier ['bærɪəʳ] *n* barriera
barring ['bɑːrɪŋ] *prep* salvo
barrister ['bærɪstəʳ] (*BRIT*) *n* avvocato(-essa) (*con diritto di parlare davanti a tutte le corti*)
barrow ['bærəu] *n* (*cart*) carriola
bartender ['bɑːtɛndəʳ] (*US*) *n* barista *m*
base [beɪs] *n* base *f* ▷ *vt* **to ~ sth on** basare qc su ▷ *adj* vile
baseball ['beɪsbɔːl] *n* baseball *m*; **baseball cap** *n* berretto da baseball
basement ['beɪsmənt] *n* seminterrato; (*of shop*) interrato
bases¹ ['beɪsiːz] *npl of* **basis**
bases² ['beɪsɪz] *npl of* **base**
bash [bæʃ] (*inf*) *vt* picchiare
basic ['beɪsɪk] *adj* rudimentale; essenziale; **basically** [-lɪ] *adv* fondamentalmente; sostanzialmente; **basics** *npl* **the basics** l'essenziale *m*
basil ['bæzl] *n* basilico
basin ['beɪsn] *n* (*vessel: also Geo*) bacino; (*also:* **wash~**) lavabo
basis ['beɪsɪs] (*pl* **bases**) *n* base *f*; **on a part-time ~** part-time; **on a trial ~** in prova
basket ['bɑːskɪt] *n* cesta; (*smaller*) cestino; (*with handle*) paniere *m*; **basketball** *n* pallacanestro *f*
bass [beɪs] *n* (*Mus*) basso
bastard ['bɑːstəd] *n* bastardo(-a); (*inf!*) stronzo (!)
bat [bæt] *n* pipistrello; (*for baseball etc*) mazza; (*BRIT: for table tennis*) racchetta ▷ *vt* **he didn't ~ an eyelid** non battè ciglio
batch [bætʃ] *n* (*of bread*) infornata; (*of papers*) cumulo
bath [bɑːθ] *n* bagno; (*bathtub*) vasca da bagno ▷ *vt* far fare il bagno a; **to have a ~** fare un bagno; *see also* **baths** ▷ *vt*
bathe [beɪð] *vi* fare il bagno ▷ *vt* (*wound*) lavare
bathing ['beɪðɪŋ] *n* bagni *mpl*; **bathing costume** (*US* **bathing suit**) *n* costume *m* da bagno
bath: **bathrobe** ['bɑːθrəub] *n* accappatoio; **bathroom** ['bɑːθrum] *n* stanza da bagno; **baths** [bɑːðz] *npl* bagni *mpl* pubblici; **bath towel** *n* asciugamano da bagno; **bathtub** *n* (*vasca da*) bagno
baton ['bætən] *n* (*Mus*) bacchetta;

(*Athletics*) testimone *m*; (*club*) manganello

batter ['bætə'] *vt* battere ▷ *n* pastetta;
  battered *adj* (*hat*) sformato(-a); (*pan*)
  ammaccato(-a)

battery ['bætərɪ] *n* batteria; (*of torch*) pila;
  battery farming *n* allevamento in batteria

battle ['bætl] *n* battaglia ▷ *vi* battagliare,
  lottare; **battlefield** *n* campo di battaglia

bay [beɪ] *n* (*of sea*) baia; **to hold sb at ~**
  tenere qn a bada

bazaar [bə'zɑ:'] *n* bazar *m inv*; vendita di
  beneficenza

BBC *n abbr* (= British Broadcasting
  Corporation) rete nazionale di radiotelevisione
  in Gran Bretagna

B.C. *adv abbr* (= *before Christ*) a.C.

 KEYWORD

be [bi:] (*pt* **was, were**, *pp* **been**) *aux vb* **1**
  (*with present participle: forming continuous
  tenses*): **what are you doing?** che fa?, che
  sta facendo?; **they're coming tomorrow**
  vengono domani; **I've been waiting for
  her for hours** sono ore che l'aspetto
  2 (*with pp: forming passives*) essere; **to be
  killed** essere *or* venire ucciso(-a); **the box
  had been opened** la scatola era stata
  aperta; **the thief was nowhere to be
  seen** il ladro non si trovava da nessuna
  parte
  3 (*in tag questions*): **it was fun, wasn't it?** è
  stato divertente, no?; **he's good-looking,
  isn't he?** è un bell'uomo, vero?; **she's
  back, is she?** così è tornata, eh?
  4 (+ *to* + *infinitive*): **the house is
  to be sold** abbiamo *or* hanno *etc*
  intenzione di vendere casa; **you're to
  be congratulated for all your work**
  dovremo farvi i complimenti per tutto il
  vostro lavoro; **he's not to open it** non
  deve aprirlo
  ▷ *vb* + *complement* **1** (*gen*) essere; **I'm
  English** sono inglese; **I'm tired** sono

stanco(-a); **I'm hot/cold** ho caldo/freddo;
he's a doctor è medico; **2 and 2 are 4** 2
più 2 fa 4; **be careful!** sta attento(-a)!; **be
good** sii buono(-a)
  2 (*of health*) stare; **how are you?** come
sta?; **he's very ill** sta molto male
  3 (*of age*): **how old are you?** quanti anni
hai?; **I'm sixteen (years old)** ho sedici
anni
  4 (*cost*) costare; **how much was the
meal?** quant'era *or* quanto costava il
pranzo?; **that'll be £5, please** (fa) 5
sterline, per favore
  ▷ *vi* **1** (*exist, occur etc*) essere, esistere; **the
best singer that ever was** il migliore
cantante mai esistito *or* di tutti i tempi; **be
that as it may** comunque sia, sia come
sia; **so be it** sia pure, e sia
  2 (*referring to place*) essere, trovarsi; **I won't
be here tomorrow** non ci sarò domani;
Edinburgh is in Scotland Edimburgo si
trova in Scozia
  3 (*referring to movement*): **where have you
been?** dov'è stato?; **I've been to China**
sono stato in Cina
  ▷ *impers vb* **1** (*referring to time, distance*)
essere; **it's 5 o'clock** sono le 5; **it's the
28th of April** è il 28 aprile; **it's 10 km to
the village** di qui al paese sono 10 km
  2 (*referring to the weather*) fare; **it's too
hot/cold** fa troppo caldo/freddo; **it's
windy** c'è vento
  3 (*emphatic*): **it's me** sono io; **it was Maria
who paid the bill** è stata Maria che ha
pagato il conto

beach [bi:tʃ] *n* spiaggia ▷ *vt* tirare in secco

beacon ['bi:kən] *n* (*lighthouse*) faro;
  (*marker*) segnale *m*

bead [bi:d] *n* perlina; **~s** *npl* (*necklace*)
  collana

beak [bi:k] *n* becco

beam [bi:m] *n* trave *f*; (*of light*) raggio ▷ *vi*
  brillare

bean [bi:n] *n* fagiolo; (*of coffee*) chicco;
  runner ~ fagiolino; **beansprouts** *npl*
  germogli *mpl* di soia

bear [bɛə'] (*pt* **bore**, *pp* **borne**) *n* orso ▷ *vt*
  portare; (*endure*) sopportare; (*produce*)
  generare ▷ *vi* **to ~ right/left** piegare a
  destra/sinistra

beard [bɪəd] *n* barba

bearer ['bɛərə'] *n* portatore *m*

bearing ['bɛərɪŋ] *n* portamento;
  (*connection*) rapporto

beast [bi:st] *n* bestia

beat [bi:t] (*pt* **beat**, *pp* **beaten**) *n* colpo;
  (*of heart*) battito; (*Mus*) tempo; battuta;
  (*of policeman*) giro ▷ *vt* battere; (*eggs,*

b

cream) sbattere ▷ *vi* battere; **off the ~en track** fuori mano; **~ it!** (*inf*) fila!, fuori dai piedi!; **beat up** *vt* (*person*) picchiare; (*eggs*) sbattere; **beating** *n* bastonata

beautiful ['bjuːtɪful] *adj* bello(-a); **beautifully** *adv* splendidamente

beauty ['bjuːtɪ] *n* bellezza; **beauty parlour** [-'pɑːlə'] (*us* **beauty parlor**) *n* salone *m* di bellezza; **beauty salon** *n* istituto di bellezza; **beauty spot** (*BRIT*) *n* (*Tourism*) luogo pittoresco

beaver ['biːvə'] *n* castoro

became [bɪ'keɪm] *pt of* **become**

because [bɪ'kɔz] *conj* perché; **~ of** a causa di

beckon ['bɛkən] *vt* (*also:* **~ to**) chiamare con un cenno

become [bɪ'kʌm] (*irreg: like* **come**) *vt* diventare; **to ~ fat/thin** ingrassarsi/dimagrire

bed [bɛd] *n* letto; (*of flowers*) aiuola; (*of coal, clay*) strato; **single/double ~** letto a una piazza/a due piazze *or* matrimoniale; **bed and breakfast** *n* (*place*) ≈ pensione *f* familiare; (*terms*) camera con colazione; *vedi nota nel riquadro*; **bedclothes** ['bɛdklə uðz] *npl* biancheria e coperte *fpl* da letto; **bedding** *n* coperte e lenzuola *fpl*; **bed linen** *n* biancheria da letto; **bedroom** *n* camera da letto; **bedside** *n* **at sb's bedside** al capezzale di qn; **bedside lamp** *n* lampada da comodino; **bedside table** *n* comodino; **bedsit(ter)** (*BRIT*) *n* monolocale *m*; **bedspread** *n* copriletto; **bedtime** *n* **it's bedtime** è ora di andare a letto

⬤ **BED AND BREAKFAST**
⬤
⬤ I **bed and breakfasts**, anche **B & Bs**,
⬤ sono piccole pensioni a conduzione
⬤ familiare, più economiche rispetto agli
⬤ alberghi, dove al mattino viene servita
⬤ la tradizionale colazione all'inglese.

bee [biː] *n* ape *f*

beech [biːtʃ] *n* faggio

beef [biːf] *n* manzo; **roast ~** arrosto di manzo; **beefburger** *n* hamburger *m inv*; **Beefeater** *n* guardia della Torre di Londra

been [biːn] *pp of* **be**

beer [bɪə'] *n* birra; **beer garden** *n* (*BRIT*) giardino (*di pub*)

beet [biːt] (*us*) *n* (*also:* **red ~**) barbabietola rossa

beetle ['biːtl] *n* scarafaggio; coleottero

beetroot ['biːtruːt] (*BRIT*) *n* barbabietola

before [bɪ'fɔː'] *prep* (*in time*) prima di; (*in space*) davanti a ▷ *conj* prima che + *sub*;

prima di ▷ *adv* prima; **~ going** prima di andare; **~ she goes** prima che vada; **the week ~** la settimana prima; **I've seen it ~** l'ho già visto; **I've never seen it ~** è la prima volta che lo vedo; **beforehand** *adv* in anticipo

beg [bɛg] *vi* chiedere l'elemosina ▷ *vt* (*also:* **~ for**) chiedere in elemosina; (*favour*) chiedere; **to ~ sb to do** pregare qn di fare

began [bɪ'gæn] *pt of* **begin**

beggar ['bɛgə'] *n* mendicante *m/f*

begin [bɪ'gɪn] (*pt* **began**, *pp* **begun**) *vt*, *vi* cominciare; **to ~ doing** *or* **to do sth** incominciare *or* iniziare a fare qc; **beginner** *n* principiante *m/f*; **beginning** *n* inizio, principio

begun [bɪ'gʌn] *pp of* **begin**

behalf [bɪ'hɑːf] *n* **on ~ of** per conto di, a nome di

behave [bɪ'heɪv] *vi* comportarsi; (*well: also:* **~ o.s.**) comportarsi bene; **behaviour** [bɪ'heɪvjə'] (*us* **behavior**) *n* comportamento, condotta

behind [bɪ'haɪnd] *prep* dietro; (*followed by pronoun*) dietro di; (*time*) in ritardo con ▷ *adv* dietro; (*leave, stay*) indietro ▷ *n* dietro; **to be ~ (schedule)** essere in ritardo rispetto al programma; **~ the scenes** (*fig*) dietro le quinte

beige [beɪʒ] *adj* beige *inv*

Beijing ['beɪ'dʒɪŋ] *n* Pechino *f*

being ['biːɪŋ] *n* essere *m*

belated [bɪ'leɪtɪd] *adj* tardo(-a)

belch [bɛltʃ] *vi* ruttare ▷ *vt* (*gen: belch out: smoke etc*) eruttare

Belgian ['bɛldʒən] *adj, n* belga *m/f*

Belgium ['bɛldʒəm] *n* Belgio

belief [bɪ'liːf] *n* (*opinion*) opinione *f*, convinzione *f*; (*trust, faith*) fede *f*

believe [bɪ'liːv] *vt, vi* credere; **to ~ in** (*God*) credere in; (*ghosts*) credere a; (*method*) avere fiducia in; **believer** *n* (*Rel*) credente *m/f*; (*in idea, activity*): **to be a believer in** credere in

bell [bɛl] *n* campana; (*small, on door, electric*) campanello

bellboy ['bɛlbɔɪ, (*us* **bellhop**) 'bɛlhɔp] *n* ragazzo d'albergo, fattorino d'albergo

bellow ['bɛləu] *vi* muggire

bell pepper (*esp us*) *n* peperone *m*

belly ['bɛlɪ] *n* pancia; **belly button** *n* ombelico

belong [bɪ'lɔŋ] *vi* **to ~ to** appartenere a; (*club etc*) essere socio di; **this book ~s here** questo libro va qui; **belongings** *npl* cose *fpl*, roba

beloved [bɪ'lʌvɪd] *adj* adorato(-a)

below [bɪ'ləu] *prep* sotto, al di sotto di ▷ *adv* sotto, di sotto; giù; **see ~** vedi sotto *or* oltre

belt [bɛlt] *n* cintura; (*Tech*) cinghia ▷ *vt*
(*thrash*) picchiare ▷ *vi* (*inf*) filarsela;
beltway (*US*) *n* (*Aut*: *ring road*)
circonvallazione *f*; (: *motorway*) autostrada

bemused [bɪˈmjuːzd] *adj* perplesso(-a),
stupito(-a)

bench [bɛntʃ] *n* panca; (*in workshop, Pol*)
banco; **the B~** (*Law*) la Corte

bend [bɛnd] (*pt, pp* **bent**) *vt* curvare; (*leg,
arm*) piegare ▷ *vi* curvarsi; piegarsi ▷ *n*
(*BRIT*: *in road*) curva; (*in pipe, river*) gomito;
bend down *vi* chinarsi; **bend over** *vi*
piegarsi

beneath [bɪˈniːθ] *prep* sotto, al di sotto di;
(*unworthy of*) indegno(-a) di ▷ *adv* sotto,
di sotto

beneficial [bɛnɪˈfɪʃəl] *adj* che fa bene;
vantaggioso(-a)

benefit [ˈbɛnɪfɪt] *n* beneficio, vantaggio;
(*allowance of money*) indennità *f inv* ▷ *vt*
far bene a ▷ *vi* **he'll ~ from it** ne trarrà
beneficio *or* profitto

benign [bɪˈnaɪn] *adj* (*person, smile*)
benevolo(-a); (*Med*) benigno(-a)

bent [bɛnt] *pt, pp of* **bend** ▷ *n* inclinazione
f ▷ *adj* (*inf: dishonest*) losco(-a); **to be ~ on**
essere deciso(-a) a

bereaved [bɪˈriːvd] *n* **the ~** i familiari in
lutto

beret [ˈbɛreɪ] *n* berretto

Berlin [bəːˈlɪn] *n* Berlino *f*

Bermuda [bəːˈmjuːdə] *n* le Bermude

berry [ˈbɛrɪ] *n* bacca

berth [bəːθ] *n* (*bed*) cuccetta; (*for ship*)
ormeggio ▷ *vi* (*in harbour*) entrare in porto;
(*at anchor*) gettare l'ancora

beside [bɪˈsaɪd] *prep* accanto a; **to be ~
o.s. (with anger)** essere fuori di sé (dalla
rabbia); **that's ~ the point** non c'entra;
besides [bɪˈsaɪdz] *adv* inoltre, per di più
▷ *prep* oltre a; a parte

best [bɛst] *adj* migliore ▷ *adv* meglio; **the
~ part of** (*quantity*) la maggior parte di; **at
~** tutt'al più; **to make the ~ of sth** cavare
il meglio possibile da qc; **to do one's ~**
fare del proprio meglio; **to the ~ of my
knowledge** per quel che ne so; **to the ~ of
my ability** al massimo delle mie capacità;
best-before date *n* scadenza; **best
man** (*irreg*) *n* testimone *m* dello sposo;
bestseller *n* bestseller *m inv*

bet [bɛt] (*pt, pp* **bet** *or* **betted**) *n*
scommessa ▷ *vt, vi* scommettere; **to ~ sb
sth** scommettere qc con qn

betray [bɪˈtreɪ] *vt* tradire

better [ˈbɛtəʳ] *adj* migliore ▷ *adv* meglio
▷ *vt* migliorare ▷ *n* **to get the ~ of** avere la
meglio su; **you had ~ do it** è meglio che lo

faccia; **he thought ~ of it** cambiò idea; **to
get ~** migliorare

betting [ˈbɛtɪŋ] *n* scommesse *fpl*; **betting
shop** (*BRIT*) *n* ufficio dell'allibratore

between [bɪˈtwiːn] *prep* tra ▷ *adv* in
mezzo, nel mezzo

beverage [ˈbɛvərɪdʒ] *n* bevanda

beware [bɪˈwɛəʳ] *vt, vi* **to ~ (of)** stare
attento(-a) (a); **"~ of the dog"** "attenti
al cane"

bewildered [bɪˈwɪldəd] *adj*
sconcertato(-a), confuso(-a)

beyond [bɪˈjɔnd] *prep* (*in space*) oltre;
(*exceeding*) al di sopra di ▷ *adv* di là; **~
doubt** senza dubbio; **~ repair** irreparabile

bias [ˈbaɪəs] *n* (*prejudice*) pregiudizio;
(*preference*) preferenza; **bias(s)ed** *adj*
parziale

bib [bɪb] *n* bavaglino

Bible [ˈbaɪbl] *n* Bibbia

bicarbonate of soda [baɪˈkɑːbənɪt-] *n*
bicarbonato (di sodio)

biceps [ˈbaɪsɛps] *n* bicipite *m*

bicycle [ˈbaɪsɪkl] *n* bicicletta; **bicycle
pump** *n* pompa della bicicletta

bid [bɪd] (*pt* **bade** *or* **bid**, *pp* **bidden** *or* **bid**)
n offerta; (*attempt*) tentativo ▷ *vi* fare
un'offerta ▷ *vt* fare un'offerta di; **to ~ sb
good day** dire buon giorno a qn; **bidder** *n*
the highest bidder il maggior offerente

bidet [ˈbiːdeɪ] *n* bidè *m inv*

big [bɪg] *adj* grande; grosso(-a); **Big
Apple** *n* vedi nota nel riquadro; **bigheaded**
[ˈbɪgˈhɛdɪd] *adj* presuntuoso(-a); **big toe**
n alluce *m*

● **BIG APPLE**
●
● Tutti sanno che **The Big Apple**, la
● Grande Mela, è New York ("apple"
● in gergo significa grande città), ma
● sicuramente i soprannomi di altre città
● americane non sono così conosciuti.
● Chicago è soprannominata "the Windy
● City" perché è ventosa, New Orleans
● si chiama "the Big Easy" per il modo di
● vivere tranquillo e rilassato dei suoi
● abitanti, e l'industria automobilistica
● ha fatto sì che Detroit fosse
● soprannominata "Motown".

bike [baɪk] *n* bici *f inv*; **bike lane** *n* pista
ciclabile

bikini [bɪˈkiːnɪ] *n* bikini *m inv*

bilateral [baɪˈlætərl] *adj* bilaterale

bilingual [baɪˈlɪŋgwəl] *adj* bilingue

bill [bɪl] *n* conto; (*Pol*) atto; (*US: banknote*)
banconota; (*of bird*) becco; (*of show*)
locandina; **can I have the ~, please** il

conto, per favore; **put it on my ~** lo metta
sul mio conto; **"post no ~s"** "divieto di
affissione"; **to fit** or **fill the ~** (fig) fare al
caso; **billboard** n tabellone m; **billfold**
['bɪlfəʊld] (US) n portafoglio
billiards ['bɪljədz] n biliardo
billion ['bɪljən] num (BRIT) bilione m; (US)
miliardo
bin [bɪn] n (for coal, rubbish) bidone m; (for
bread) cassetta; (dustbin) pattumiera; (litter
bin) cestino
bind [baɪnd] (pt, pp **bound**) vt legare;
(oblige) obbligare ▷ n (inf) scocciatura
binge [bɪndʒ] (inf) n **to go on a ~** fare
baldoria
bingo ['bɪŋɡəʊ] n gioco simile alla tombola
binoculars [bɪ'nɔkjuləz] npl binocolo
bio... [baɪə'...] prefix: **biochemistry**
n biochimica; **biodegradable** adj
biodegradabile; **biography** [baɪ'ɔɡrəfɪ]
n biografia; **biological** adj biologico(-a);
biology [baɪ'ɔlədʒɪ] n biologia
birch [bəːtʃ] n betulla
bird [bəːd] n uccello; (BRIT: inf: girl)
bambola; **bird of prey** n (uccello) rapace
m; **birdwatching** n birdwatching m
Biro® ['baɪrəʊ] n biro® f inv
birth [bəːθ] n nascita; **to give ~ to**
partorire; **birth certificate** n certificato
di nascita; **birth control** n controllo
delle nascite; contraccezione f; **birthday**
n compleanno ▷ cpd di compleanno;
birthmark n voglia; **birthplace** n luogo
di nascita
biscuit ['bɪskɪt] (BRIT) n biscotto
bishop ['bɪʃəp] n vescovo
bistro ['biːstrəʊ] n bistrò m inv
bit [bɪt] pt of **bite** ▷ n pezzo; (Comput) bit
m inv; (of horse) morso; **a ~ of** un po' di; **a ~
mad** un po' matto; **~ by ~** a poco a poco
bitch [bɪtʃ] n (dog) cagna; (inf!) vacca
bite [baɪt] (pt, pp **bit, bitten**) vt, vi mordere;
(insect) pungere ▷ n morso; (insect bite)
puntura; (mouthful) boccone m; **let's have
a ~ to eat** mangiamo un boccone; **to ~
one's nails** mangiarsi le unghie
bitten ['bɪtn] pp of **bite**
bitter ['bɪtəʳ] adj amaro(-a); (wind, criticism)
pungente ▷ n (BRIT: beer) birra amara
bizarre [bɪ'zɑːʳ] adj bizzarro(-a)
black [blæk] adj nero(-a) ▷ n nero;
(person): **B~** negro(-a) ▷ vt (BRIT Industry)
boicottare; **to give sb a ~ eye** fare un
occhio nero a qn; **in the ~** (bank account)
in attivo; **black out** vi (faint) svenire;
blackberry n mora; **blackbird** n merlo;
blackboard n lavagna; **black coffee** n
caffè m inv nero; **blackcurrant** n ribes
m inv; **black ice** n strato trasparente

di ghiaccio; **blackmail** n ricatto ▷ vt
ricattare; **black market** n mercato nero;
blackout n oscuramento; (TV, Radio)
interruzione f delle trasmissioni; (fainting)
svenimento; **black pepper** n pepe m nero;
black pudding n sanguinaccio; **Black
Sea** n **the Black Sea** il Mar Nero
bladder ['blædəʳ] n vescica
blade [bleɪd] n lama; (of oar) pala; **~ of
grass** filo d'erba
blame [bleɪm] n colpa ▷ vt **to ~ sb/sth for
sth** dare la colpa di qc a qn/qc; **who's to ~?**
chi è colpevole?
bland [blænd] adj mite; (taste) blando(-a)
blank [blæŋk] adj bianco(-a); (look)
distratto(-a) ▷ n spazio vuoto; (cartridge)
cartuccia a salve
blanket ['blæŋkɪt] n coperta
blast [blɑːst] n (of wind) raffica; (of bomb
etc) esplosione f ▷ vt far saltare
blatant ['bleɪtənt] adj flagrante
blaze [bleɪz] n (fire) incendio; (fig)
vampata; splendore m ▷ vi (fire) ardere,
fiammeggiare; (guns) sparare senza sosta;
(fig: eyes) ardere ▷ vt **to ~ a trail** (fig)
tracciare una via nuova; **in a ~ of publicity**
circondato da grande pubblicità
blazer ['bleɪzəʳ] n blazer m inv
bleach [bliːtʃ] n (also: **household ~**)
varechina ▷ vt (material) candeggiare;
bleachers (US) npl (Sport) posti mpl di
gradinata
bleak [bliːk] adj tetro(-a)
bled [blɛd] pt, pp of **bleed**
bleed [bliːd] (pt, pp **bled**) vi sanguinare;
my nose is ~ing mi viene fuori sangue
dal naso
blemish ['blɛmɪʃ] n macchia
blend [blɛnd] n miscela ▷ vt mescolare
▷ vi (colours etc: also: **~ in**) armonizzare;
blender n (Culin) frullatore m
bless [blɛs] (pt, pp **blessed** or **blest**) vt
benedire; **~ you!** (after sneeze) salute!;
blessing n benedizione f; fortuna
blew [bluː] pt of **blow**
blight [blaɪt] vt (hopes etc) deludere; (life)
rovinare
blind [blaɪnd] adj cieco(-a) ▷ n (for window)
avvolgibile m; (Venetian blind) veneziana
▷ vt accecare; **the ~** npl i ciechi; **blind
alley** n vicolo cieco; **blindfold** n benda
▷ adj, adv bendato(-a) ▷ vt bendare gli
occhi a
blink [blɪŋk] vi battere gli occhi; (light)
lampeggiare
bliss [blɪs] n estasi f
blister ['blɪstəʳ] n (on skin) vescica; (on
paintwork) bolla ▷ vi (paint) coprirsi di bolle
blizzard ['blɪzəd] n bufera di neve

bloated ['bləʊtɪd] *adj* gonfio(-a)

blob [blɔb] *n* (*drop*) goccia; (*stain, spot*) macchia

block [blɔk] *n* blocco; (*in pipes*) ingombro; (*toy*) cubo; (*of buildings*) isolato ▷ *vt* bloccare; **the sink is ~ed** il lavandino è otturato; **block up** *vt* bloccare; (*pipe*) ingorgare, intasare; **blockade** [-'keɪd] *n* blocco; **blockage** *n* ostacolo; **blockbuster** *n* (*film, book*) grande successo; **block capitals** *npl* stampatello; **block letters** *npl* stampatello

bloke [bləʊk] (*BRIT: inf*) *n* tizio

blond(e) [blɔnd] *adj, n* biondo(-a)

blood [blʌd] *n* sangue *m*; **blood donor** *n* donatore(-trice) di sangue; **blood group** *n* gruppo sanguigno; **blood poisoning** *n* setticemia; **blood pressure** *n* pressione *f* sanguigna; **bloodshed** *n* spargimento di sangue; **bloodshot** *adj* **bloodshot eyes** occhi iniettati di sangue; **bloodstream** *n* flusso del sangue; **blood test** *n* analisi *f inv* del sangue; **blood transfusion** *n* trasfusione *f* di sangue; **blood type** *n* gruppo sanguigno; **blood vessel** *n* vaso sanguigno; **bloody** *adj* (*fight*) sanguinoso(-a); (*nose*) sanguinante; (*BRIT: inf!*): **this bloody ...** questo maledetto ...; **bloody awful/good** (*inf!*) veramente terribile/forte

bloom [bluːm] *n* fiore *m* ▷ *vi* (*tree*) essere in fiore; (*flower*) aprirsi

blossom ['blɔsəm] *n* fiore *m*; (*with pl sense*) fiori *mpl* ▷ *vi* essere in fiore

blot [blɔt] *n* macchia ▷ *vt* macchiare

blouse [blauz] *n* (*feminine garment*) camicetta

blow [bləʊ] (*pt* **blew**, *pp* **blown**) *n* colpo ▷ *vi* soffiare ▷ *vt* (*fuse*) far saltare; (*wind*) spingere; (*instrument*) suonare; **to ~ one's nose** soffiarsi il naso; **to ~ a whistle** fischiare; **blow away** *vt* portare via; **blow out** *vi* scoppiare; **blow up** *vi* saltare in aria ▷ *vt* far saltare in aria; (*tyre*) gonfiare; (*Phot*) ingrandire; **blow-dry** *n* messa in piega a föhn

blown [bləʊn] *pp of* **blow**

blue [bluː] *adj* azzurro(-a); (*depressed*) giù *inv*; **~ film/joke** film/barzelletta pornografico(-a); **out of the ~** (*fig*) all'improvviso; **bluebell** *n* giacinto dei boschi; **blueberry** *n* mirtillo; **blue cheese** *n* formaggio tipo gorgonzola; **blues** *npl* **the blues** (*Mus*) il blues; **to have the blues** (*inf: feeling*) essere a terra; **bluetit** *n* cinciarella

bluff [blʌf] *vi* bluffare ▷ *n* bluff *m inv* ▷ *adj* (*person*) brusco(-a); **to call sb's ~** mettere alla prova il bluff di qn

blunder ['blʌndə'] *n* abbaglio ▷ *vi* prendere un abbaglio

blunt [blʌnt] *adj* smussato(-a); spuntato(-a); (*person*) brusco(-a)

blur [blə:'] *n* forma indistinta ▷ *vt* offuscare; **blurred** *adj* (*photo*) mosso(-a); (*TV*) sfuocato(-a)

blush [blʌʃ] *vi* arrossire ▷ *n* rossore *m*; **blusher** *n* fard *m inv*

board [bɔːd] *n* tavola; (*on wall*) tabellone *m*; (*committee*) consiglio, comitato; (*in firm*) consiglio d'amministrazione; (*Naut, Aviat*): **on ~** a bordo ▷ *vt* (*ship*) salire a bordo di; (*train*) salire su; **full ~** (*BRIT*) pensione completa; **half ~** (*BRIT*) mezza pensione; **~ and lodging** vitto e alloggio; **which goes by the ~** (*fig*) che viene abbandonato; **board game** *n* gioco da tavolo; **boarding card** *n* = **boarding pass; boarding pass** *n* (*Aviat, Naut*) carta d'imbarco; **boarding school** *n* collegio; **board room** *n* sala del consiglio

boast [bəust] *vi* **to ~ (about** *or* **of)** vantarsi (di)

boat [bəut] *n* nave *f*; (*small*) barca

bob [bɔb] *vi* (*boat, cork on water: also:* **~ up and down**) andare su e giù

bobby pin ['bɔbɪ-] (*us*) *n* fermaglio per capelli

body ['bɔdɪ] *n* corpo; (*of car*) carrozzeria; (*of plane*) fusoliera; (*fig: group*) gruppo; (*: organization*) organizzazione *f*; (*: quantity*) quantità *f inv*; **body-building** *n* culturismo; **bodyguard** *n* guardia del corpo; **bodywork** *n* carrozzeria

bog [bɔg] *n* palude *f* ▷ *vt* **to get ~ged down** (*fig*) impantanarsi

bogus ['bəugəs] *adj* falso(-a); finto(-a)

boil [bɔɪl] *vt, vi* bollire ▷ *n* (*Med*) foruncolo; **to come to the** (*BRIT*) *or* **a** (*US*) **~** raggiungere l'ebollizione; **boil over** *vi* traboccare (bollendo); **boiled egg** *n* uovo alla coque; **boiled potatoes** *npl* patate *fpl* bollite *or* lesse; **boiler** *n* caldaia; **boiling** *adj* bollente; **I'm boiling (hot)** (*inf*) sto morendo di caldo; **boiling point** *n* punto di ebollizione

bold [bəuld] *adj* audace; (*child*) impudente; (*colour*) deciso(-a)

Bolivia [bə'lɪvɪə] *n* Bolivia

Bolivian [bə'lɪvɪən] *adj, n* boliviano(-a)

bollard ['bɔləd] (*BRIT*) *n* (*Aut*) colonnina luminosa

bolt [bəult] *n* chiavistello; (*with nut*) bullone *m* ▷ *adv* **~ upright** diritto(-a) come un fuso ▷ *vt* serrare; (*also:* **~ together**) imbullonare; (*food*) mangiare in fretta ▷ *vi* scappare via

bomb [bɔm] *n* bomba ▷ *vt* bombardare;

bombard [bɔmˈbɑːd] *vt* bombardare;
bomber *n* (*Aviat*) bombardiere *m*; **bomb
scare** *n* stato di allarme (*per sospetta
presenza di una bomba*)
bond [bɔnd] *n* legame *m*; (*binding promise,
Finance*) obbligazione *f*; (*Comm*): **in ~** in
attesa di sdoganamento
bone [bəun] *n* osso; (*of fish*) spina, lisca ▷ *vt*
disossare; togliere le spine a
bonfire [ˈbɔnfaɪəʳ] *n* falò *m inv*
bonnet [ˈbɔnɪt] *n* cuffia; (*BRIT: of car*)
cofano
bonus [ˈbəunəs] *n* premio; (*fig*) sovrappiù
m inv
boo [buː] *excl* ba! ▷ *vt* fischiare
book [buk] *n* libro; (*of stamps etc*)
blocchetto ▷ *vt* (*ticket, seat, room*)
prenotare; (*driver*) multare; (*football
player*) ammonire; **~s** *npl* (*Comm*) conti
mpl; **I'd like to ~ a double room** vorrei
prenotare una camera doppia; **I ~ed a
table in the name of ...** ho prenotato un
tavolo al nome di...; **book in** *vi* (*BRIT: at
hotel*) prendere una camera; **book up** *vt*
riservare, prenotare; **the hotel is ~ed up**
l'albergo è al completo; **all seats are ~ed
up** è tutto esaurito; **bookcase** *n* scaffale
m; **booking** *n* (*BRIT*) prenotazione *f*; **I
confirmed my booking by fax/e-mail**
ho prenotato la mia prenotazione
tramite fax/e-mail; **booking office** (*BRIT*)
n (*Rail*) biglietteria; (*Theatre*) botteghino;
book-keeping *n* contabilità; **booklet**
n libricino; **bookmaker** *n* allibratore *m*;
bookmark (*also Comput*) *n* segnalibro
▷ *vt* (*Comput*) mettere un segnalibro a;
(*Internet Explorer*) aggiungere a "Preferiti";
bookseller *n* libraio; **bookshelf** *n*
mensola (per libri); **bookshop, bookstore**
n libreria
boom [buːm] *n* (*noise*) rimbombo; (*in prices
etc*) boom *m inv* ▷ *vi* rimbombare; andare
a gonfie vele
boost [buːst] *n* spinta ▷ *vt* spingere
boot [buːt] *n* stivale *m*; (*for hiking*) scarpone
m da montagna; (*for football etc*) scarpa;
(*BRIT: of car*) portabagagli *m inv* ▷ *vt*
(*Comput*) inizializzare; **to ~** (*in addition*) per
giunta, in più
booth [buːð] *n* cabina; (*at fair*) baraccone
m
booze [buːz] (*inf*) *n* alcool *m*
border [ˈbɔːdəʳ] *n* orlo; margine *m*; (*of
a country*) frontiera; (*for flowers*) aiuola
(laterale) ▷ *vt* (*road*) costeggiare; (*another
country: also:* **~ on**) confinare con; **the B~s**
la zona di confine tra l'Inghilterra e la Scozia;
borderline *n* (*fig*): **on the borderline**
incerto(-a)

bore [bɔːʳ] *pt of* **bear** ▷ *vt* (*hole etc*)
scavare; (*person*) annoiare ▷ *n* (*person*)
seccatore(-trice); (*of gun*) calibro; **bored**
adj annoiato(-a); **to be bored** annoiarsi;
he's bored to tears *or* **to death** *or* **stiff** è
annoiato a morte; **boredom** *n* noia
boring [ˈbɔːrɪŋ] *adj* noioso(-a)
born [bɔːn] *adj* **to be ~** nascere; **I was ~ in
1960** sono nato nel 1960
borne [bɔːn] *pp of* **bear**
borough [ˈbʌrə] *n* comune *m*
borrow [ˈbɔrəu] *vt* **to ~ sth (from sb)**
prendere in prestito qc (da qn)
Bosnia(-Herzegovina) [ˈbɔznɪə(hɜrzəˈgə
uviːnə)] *n* Bosnia-Erzegovina; **Bosnian**
[ˈbɔznɪən] *n, adj* bosniaco(-a) *m/f*
bosom [ˈbuzəm] *n* petto; (*fig*) seno
boss [bɔs] *n* capo ▷ *vt* comandare; **bossy**
adj prepotente
both [bəuθ] *adj* entrambi(-e), tutt'e due
▷ *pron* **~ of them** entrambi(-e); **~ of us
went, we ~ went** ci siamo andati tutt'e
due ▷ *adv* **they sell ~ meat and poultry**
vendono insieme la carne ed il pollame
bother [ˈbɔðəʳ] *vt* (*worry*) preoccupare;
(*annoy*) infastidire ▷ *vi* (*also:* **~ o.s.**)
preoccuparsi ▷ *n* **it is a ~ to have to do** è
una seccatura dover fare; **it was no ~** non
c'era problema; **to ~ doing sth** darsi la
pena di fare qc
bottle [ˈbɔtl] *n* bottiglia; (*baby's*) biberon
m inv ▷ *vt* imbottigliare; **bottle bank** *n*
contenitore *m* per la raccolta del vetro;
bottle-opener *n* apribottiglie *m inv*
bottom [ˈbɔtəm] *n* fondo; (*buttocks*) sedere
m ▷ *adj* più basso(-a); ultimo(-a); **at the ~
of** in fondo a
bought [bɔːt] *pt, pp of* **buy**
boulder [ˈbəuldəʳ] *n* masso (tondeggiante)
bounce [bauns] *vi* (*ball*) rimbalzare;
(*cheque*) essere restituito(-a) ▷ *vt* far
rimbalzare ▷ *n* (*rebound*) rimbalzo;
bouncer (*inf*) *n* buttafuori *m inv*
bound [baund] *pt, pp of* **bind** ▷ *n* (*gen pl*)
limite *m*; (*leap*) salto ▷ *vi* saltare ▷ *vt* (*limit*)
delimitare ▷ *adj* **~ by law** obbligato(-a) per
legge; **to be ~ to do sth** (*obliged*) essere
costretto(-a) a fare qc; **he's ~ to fail** (*likely*)
fallirà di certo; **~ for** diretto(-a) a; **out of ~s**
il cui accesso è vietato
boundary [ˈbaundrɪ] *n* confine *m*
bouquet [ˈbukeɪ] *n* bouquet *m inv*
bourbon [ˈbuəbən] (*US*) *n* (*also:* **~ whiskey**)
bourbon *m inv*
bout [baut] *n* periodo; (*of malaria etc*)
attacco; (*Boxing etc*) incontro
boutique [buːˈtiːk] *n* boutique *f inv*
bow¹ [bəu] *n* nodo; (*weapon*) arco; (*Mus*)
archetto

bow² [bau] n (with body) inchino; (Naut: also: ~s) prua ▷ vi inchinarsi; (yield): **to ~ to** or **before** sottomettersi a

bowels ['bauəlz] npl intestini mpl; (fig) viscere fpl

bowl [bəul] n (for eating) scodella; (for washing) bacino; (ball) boccia ▷ vi (Cricket) servire (la palla); **bowler** ['bəulə'] n (Cricket, Baseball) lanciatore m; (BRIT: also: **bowler hat**) bombetta; **bowling** ['bə ulɪŋ] n (game) gioco delle bocce; **bowling alley** n pista da bowling; **bowling green** n campo di bocce; **bowls** [bəulz] n gioco delle bocce

bow tie n cravatta a farfalla

box [bɒks] n scatola; (also: **cardboard ~**) cartone m; (Theatre) palco ▷ vt inscatolare ▷ vi fare del pugilato; **boxer** n (person) pugile m; **boxer shorts** ['bɒksəfɔːts] pl n boxer; **a pair of boxer shorts** un paio di boxer; **boxing** n (Sport) pugilato; **Boxing Day** (BRIT) n ≈ Santo Stefano; vedi nota nel riquadro; **boxing gloves** npl guantoni mpl da pugile; **boxing ring** n ring m inv; **box office** n biglietteria

boy [bɔɪ] n ragazzo

boycott ['bɔɪkɔt] n boicottaggio ▷ vt boicottare

boyfriend ['bɔɪfrɛnd] n ragazzo

bra [brɑː] n reggipetto, reggiseno

brace [breɪs] n (on teeth) apparecchio correttore; (tool) trapano ▷ vt rinforzare, sostenere; **~s** (BRIT) npl (Dress) bretelle fpl; **to ~ o.s.** (also fig) tenersi forte

bracelet ['breɪslɪt] n braccialetto

bracket ['brækɪt] n (Tech) mensola; (group) gruppo; (Typ) parentesi f inv ▷ vt mettere fra parentesi

brag [bræg] vi vantarsi

braid [breɪd] n (trimming) passamano; (of hair) treccia

brain [breɪn] n cervello; **~s** npl (intelligence) cervella fpl; **he's got ~s** è intelligente

braise [breɪz] vt brasare

brake [breɪk] n (on vehicle) freno ▷ vi frenare; **brake light** n (fanalino dello) stop m inv

bran [bræn] n crusca

branch [brɑːntʃ] n ramo; (Comm)

succursale f; **branch off** vi diramarsi; **branch out** vi (fig) intraprendere una nuova attività

brand [brænd] n marca; (fig) tipo ▷ vt (cattle) marcare (a ferro rovente); **brand name** n marca; **brand-new** adj nuovo(-a) di zecca

brandy ['brændɪ] n brandy m inv

brash [bræʃ] adj sfacciato(-a)

brass [brɑːs] n ottone m; **the ~** (Mus) gli ottoni; **brass band** n fanfara

brat [bræt] (pej) n marmocchio, monello(-a)

brave [breɪv] adj coraggioso(-a) ▷ vt affrontare; **bravery** n coraggio

brawl [brɔːl] n rissa

Brazil [brə'zɪl] n Brasile m; **Brazilian** adj, n brasiliano(-a)

breach [briːtʃ] vt aprire una breccia in ▷ n (gap) breccia, varco; (breaking): **~ of contract** rottura di contratto; **~ of the peace** violazione f dell'ordine pubblico

bread [brɛd] n pane m; **breadbin** n cassetta f portapane inv; **breadbox** (US) n cassetta f portapane inv; **breadcrumbs** npl briciole fpl; (Culin) pangrattato

breadth [brɛtθ] n larghezza; (fig: of knowledge etc) ampiezza

break [breɪk] (pt **broke**, pp **broken**) vt rompere; (law) violare; (record) battere ▷ vi rompersi; (storm) scoppiare; (weather) cambiare; (dawn) spuntare; (news) saltare fuori ▷ n (gap) breccia; (fracture) rottura; (rest, also Scol) intervallo; (: short) pausa; (chance) possibilità f inv; **to ~ one's leg** etc rompersi la gamba ecc; **to ~ the news to sb** comunicare per primo la notizia a qn; **to ~ even** coprire le spese; **to ~ free** or **loose** spezzare i legami; **to ~ open** (door etc) sfondare; **break down** vt (figures, data) analizzare ▷ vi (person) avere un esaurimento (nervoso); (Aut) guastarsi; **my car has broken down** mi si è rotta la macchina; **break in** vt (horse etc) domare ▷ vi (burglar) fare irruzione; (interrupt) interrompere; **break into** vt fus (house) fare irruzione in; **break off** vi (speaker) interrompersi; (branch) troncarsi; **break out** vi evadere; (war, fight) scoppiare; **to ~ out in spots** coprirsi di macchie; **break up** vi (ship) sfondarsi; (meeting) sciogliersi; (crowd) disperdersi; (marriage) andare a pezzi; (Scol) chiudere ▷ vt fare a pezzi, spaccare; (fight etc) interrompere, far cessare; **breakdown** n (Aut) guasto; (in communications) interruzione f; (of marriage) rottura; (Med: also: **nervous breakdown**) esaurimento nervoso; (of statistics) resoconto; **breakdown truck,**

breakdown van n carro m attrezzi inv
breakfast ['brɛkfəst] n colazione f; **what time is ~?** a che ora è servita la colazione?
break: **break-in** n irruzione f; **breakthrough** n (fig) passo avanti
breast [brɛst] n (of woman) seno; (chest, Culin) petto; **breast-feed** (irreg: like **feed**) vt, vi allattare (al seno); **breast-stroke** n nuoto a rana
breath [brɛθ] n respiro; **out of ~** senza fiato
Breathalyser® ['brɛθəlaɪzər] (BRIT) n alcoltest m inv
breathe [briːð] vt, vi respirare; **breathe in** vt respirare ▷ vi inspirare; **breathe out** vt, vi espirare; **breathing** n respiro, respirazione f
breath: **breathless** ['brɛθlɪs] adj senza fiato; **breathtaking** ['brɛθteɪkɪŋ] adj mozzafiato inv; **breath test** n ≈ prova del palloncino
bred [brɛd] pt, pp of **breed**
breed [briːd] (pt, pp **bred**) vt allevare ▷ vi riprodursi ▷ n razza; (type, class) varietà f inv
breeze [briːz] n brezza
breezy ['briːzɪ] adj allegro(-a), ventilato(-a)
brew [bruː] vt (tea) fare un infuso di; (beer) fare ▷ vi (storm, fig: trouble etc) prepararsi; **brewery** n fabbrica di birra
bribe [braɪb] n bustarella ▷ vt comprare; **bribery** n corruzione f
bric-a-brac ['brɪkəbræk] n bric-a-brac m
brick [brɪk] n mattone m; **bricklayer** n muratore m
bride [braɪd] n sposa; **bridegroom** n sposo; **bridesmaid** n damigella d'onore
bridge [brɪdʒ] n ponte m; (Naut) ponte di comando; (of nose) dorso; (Cards) bridge m inv ▷ vt (fig: gap) colmare
bridle ['braɪdl] n briglia
brief [briːf] adj breve ▷ n (Law) comparsa; (gen) istruzioni fpl ▷ vt mettere al corrente; **~s** npl (underwear) mutande fpl; **briefcase** n cartella; **briefing** n briefing m inv; **briefly** adv (glance) di sfuggita; (explain, say) brevemente
brigadier [brɪgə'dɪər] n generale m di brigata
bright [braɪt] adj luminoso(-a); (clever) sveglio(-a); (lively) vivace
brilliant ['brɪljənt] adj brillante; (light, smile) radioso(-a); (inf) splendido(-a)
brim [brɪm] n orlo
brine [braɪn] n (Culin) salamoia
bring [brɪŋ] (pt, pp **brought**) vt portare; **bring about** vt causare; **bring back** vt riportare; **bring down** vt portare giù; abbattere; **bring in** vt (person)

fare entrare; (object) portare; (Pol: bill) presentare; (: legislation) introdurre; (Law: verdict) emettere; (produce: income) rendere; **bring on** vt (illness, attack) causare, provocare; (player, substitute) far scendere in campo; **bring out** vt tirar fuori; (meaning) mettere in evidenza; (book, album) far uscire; **bring up** vt (carry up) portare su; (child) allevare; (question) introdurre; (food: vomit) rimettere, rigurgitare
brink [brɪŋk] n orlo
brisk [brɪsk] adj (manner) spiccio(-a); (trade) vivace; (pace) svelto(-a)
bristle ['brɪsl] n setola ▷ vi rizzarsi; **bristling with** irto(-a) di
Brit [brɪt] n abbr (inf: = British person) britannico(-a)
Britain ['brɪtən] n (also: **Great ~**) Gran Bretagna
British ['brɪtɪʃ] adj britannico(-a); **British Isles** npl Isole Britanniche
Briton ['brɪtən] n britannico(-a)
brittle ['brɪtl] adj fragile
broad [brɔːd] adj largo(-a); (distinction) generale; (accent) spiccato(-a); **in ~ daylight** in pieno giorno; **broadband** adj (Comput) a banda larga ▷ n banda larga; **broad bean** n fava; **broadcast** (pt, pp **broadcast**) n trasmissione f ▷ vt trasmettere per radio (or per televisione) ▷ vi fare una trasmissione; **broaden** vt allargare ▷ vi allargarsi; **broadly** adv (fig) in generale; **broad-minded** adj di mente aperta
broccoli ['brɔkəlɪ] n broccoli mpl
brochure ['brəʊʃjuər] n dépliant m inv
broil [brɔɪl] vt cuocere a fuoco vivo
broiler ['brɔɪlər] (US) n (grill) griglia
broke [brəʊk] pt of **break** ▷ adj (inf) squattrinato(-a)
broken ['brəʊkn] pp of **break** ▷ adj rotto(-a); **a ~ leg** una gamba rotta; **in ~ English** in un inglese stentato
broker ['brəʊkər] n agente m
bronchitis [brɔŋ'kaɪtɪs] n bronchite f
bronze [brɔnz] n bronzo
brooch [brəʊtʃ] n spilla
brood [bruːd] n covata ▷ vi (person) rimuginare
broom [brum] n scopa; (Bot) ginestra
Bros. abbr (= Brothers) F.lli
broth [brɔθ] n brodo
brothel ['brɔθl] n bordello
brother ['brʌðər] n fratello; **brother-in-law** n cognato
brought [brɔːt] pt, pp of **bring**
brow [braʊ] n fronte f; (rare, gen: eyebrow) sopracciglio; (of hill) cima

brown [braun] *adj* bruno(-a), marrone; (*tanned*) abbronzato(-a) ▷ *n* (*colour*) color *m* bruno *or* marrone ▷ *vt* (*Culin*) rosolare; **brown bread** *n* pane *m* integrale, pane nero

Brownie ['braunɪ] *n* giovane esploratrice *f*

brown rice *n* riso greggio

brown sugar *n* zucchero greggio

browse [brauz] *vi* (*among books*) curiosare fra i libri; **to ~ through a book** sfogliare un libro; **browser** *n* (*Comput*) browser *m inv*

bruise [bru:z] *n* (*on person*) livido ▷ *vt* farsi un livido a

brunette [bru:'nɛt] *n* bruna

brush [brʌʃ] *n* spazzola; (*for painting, shaving*) pennello; (*quarrel*) schermaglia ▷ *vt* spazzolare; (*also:* **~ against**) sfiorare

Brussels ['brʌslz] *n* Bruxelles *f*

Brussels sprout [spraut] *n* cavolo di Bruxelles

brutal ['bru:tl] *adj* brutale

B.Sc. *n abbr* (*Univ*) = **Bachelor of Science**

BSE *n abbr* (= *bovine spongiform encephalopathy*) encefalite *f* bovina spongiforme

bubble ['bʌbl] *n* bolla ▷ *vi* ribollire; (*sparkle: fig*) essere effervescente; **bubble bath** *n* bagnoschiuma *m inv*; **bubble gum** *n* gomma americana

buck [bʌk] *n* maschio (*di camoscio, caprone, coniglio ecc*); (*us: inf*) dollaro ▷ *vi* sgroppare; **to pass the ~ to sb** scaricare (su di qn) la propria responsabilità

bucket ['bʌkɪt] *n* secchio

buckle ['bʌkl] *n* fibbia ▷ *vt* allacciare ▷ *vi* (*wheel etc*) piegarsi

bud [bʌd] *n* gemma; (*of flower*) bocciolo ▷ *vi* germogliare; (*flower*) sbocciare

Buddhism ['budɪzəm] *n* buddismo

Buddhist ['budɪst] *adj*, *n* buddista (*m/f*)

buddy ['bʌdɪ] (*us*) *n* compagno

budge [bʌdʒ] *vt* scostare; (*fig*) smuovere ▷ *vi* spostarsi; smuoversi

budgerigar ['bʌdʒərɪgɑ:ʳ] *n* pappagallino

budget ['bʌdʒɪt] *n* bilancio preventivo ▷ *vi* **to ~ for sth** fare il bilancio per qc

budgie ['bʌdʒɪ] *n* = **budgerigar**

buff [bʌf] *adj* color camoscio ▷ *n* (*inf: enthusiast*) appassionato(-a)

buffalo ['bʌfələu] (*pl* **buffalo** *or* **buffaloes**) *n* bufalo; (*us*) bisonte *m*

buffer ['bʌfəʳ] *n* respingente *m*; (*Comput*) memoria tampone, buffer *m inv*

buffet¹ ['bʌfɪt] *vt* sferzare

buffet² ['bufeɪ] *n* (*food, BRIT: bar*) buffet *m inv*; **buffet car** (*BRIT*) *n* (*Rail*) ≈ servizio ristoro

bug [bʌg] *n* (*esp us: insect*) insetto; (*Comput, fig: germ*) virus *m inv*; (*spy device*) microfono spia ▷ *vt* mettere sotto controllo; (*inf: annoy*) scocciare

buggy ['bʌgɪ] *n* (*baby buggy*) passeggino

build [bɪld] (*pt, pp* **built**) *n* (*of person*) corporatura ▷ *vt* costruire; **build up** *vt* accumulare; aumentare; **builder** *n* costruttore *m*; **building** *n* costruzione *f*; edificio; (*industry*) edilizia; **building site** *n* cantiere *m* di costruzione; **building society** (*BRIT*) *n* società *f inv* immobiliare

built [bɪlt] *pt, pp of* **build**; **built-in** *adj* (*cupboard*) a muro; (*device*) incorporato(-a); **built-up** *adj* **built-up area** abitato

bulb [bʌlb] *n* (*Bot*) bulbo; (*Elec*) lampadina

Bulgaria [bʌl'geərɪə] *n* Bulgaria; **Bulgarian** *adj* bulgaro(-a) ▷ *n* bulgaro(-a); (*Ling*) bulgaro

bulge [bʌldʒ] *n* rigonfiamento ▷ *vi* essere protuberante *or* rigonfio(-a); **to be bulging with** essere pieno(-a) *or* zeppo(-a) di

bulimia [bə'lɪmɪə] *n* bulimia

bulimic [bju:'lɪmɪk] *adj*, *n* bulimico(-a)

bulk [bʌlk] *n* massa, volume *m*; **in ~** a pacchi *or* cassette *etc*; (*Comm*) all'ingrosso; **the ~ of** il grosso di; **bulky** *adj* grosso(-a), voluminoso(-a)

bull [bul] *n* toro; (*male elephant, whale*) maschio

bulldozer ['buldəuzəʳ] *n* bulldozer *m inv*

bullet ['bulɪt] *n* pallottola

bulletin ['bulɪtɪn] *n* bollettino; **bulletin board** *n* (*Comput*) bulletin board *m inv*

bullfight ['bulfaɪt] *n* corrida; **bullfighter** *n* torero; **bullfighting** *n* tauromachia

bully ['bulɪ] *n* prepotente *m* ▷ *vt* angariare; (*frighten*) intimidire

bum [bʌm] (*inf*) *n* (*backside*) culo; (*tramp*) vagabondo(-a)

bumblebee ['bʌmblbi:] *n* bombo

bump [bʌmp] *n* (*in car*) piccolo tamponamento; (*jolt*) scossa; (*on road etc*) protuberanza; (*on head*) bernoccolo ▷ *vt* battere; **bump into** *vt fus* scontrarsi con; (*person*) imbattersi in; **bumper** *n* paraurti *m inv* ▷ *adj* **bumper harvest** raccolto eccezionale; **bumpy** ['bʌmpɪ] *adj* (*road*) dissestato(-a)

bun [bʌn] *n* focaccia; (*of hair*) crocchia

bunch [bʌntʃ] *n* (*of flowers, keys*) mazzo; (*of bananas*) casco; (*of people*) gruppo; **~ of grapes** grappolo d'uva; **~es** *npl* (*in hair*) codine *fpl*

bundle ['bʌndl] *n* fascio ▷ *vt* (*also:* **~ up**) legare in un fascio; (*put*): **to ~ sth/sb into** spingere qc/qn in

bungalow ['bʌŋgələu] *n* bungalow *m inv*

bungee jumping ['bʌndʒiː'dʒʌmpɪŋ] *n*
salto nel vuoto da ponti, grattacieli etc con un
cavo fissato alla caviglia

bunion ['bʌnjən] *n* callo (al piede)

bunk [bʌŋk] *n* cuccetta; **bunk beds** *npl*
letti *mpl* a castello

bunker ['bʌŋkə'] *n* (*coal store*) ripostiglio
per il carbone; (*Mil, Golf*) bunker *m inv*

bunny ['bʌnɪ] *n* (*also*: **~ rabbit**)
coniglietto

buoy [bɔɪ] *n* boa; **buoyant** *adj*
galleggiante; (*fig*) vivace

burden ['bəːdn] *n* carico, fardello ▷ *vt* **to ~**
sb with caricare qn di

bureau [bjuə'rəu] (*pl* **bureaux**) *n* (BRIT:
writing desk) scrivania; (US: *chest of drawers*)
cassettone *m*; (*office*) ufficio, agenzia

bureaucracy [bjuə'rɔkrəsɪ] *n* burocrazia

bureaucrat ['bjuərokræt] *n* burocrate *m/f*

bureau de change [-də'ʃɑ̃ʒ] (*pl* **bureaux**
de change) *n* cambiavalute *m inv*

bureaux [bjuə'rəuz] *npl of* **bureau**

burger ['bəːgə'] *n* hamburger *m inv*

burglar ['bəːglə'] *n* scassinatore *m*;
burglar alarm *n* campanello antifurto;
burglary *n* furto con scasso

burial ['bɛrɪəl] *n* sepoltura

burn [bəːn] (*pt, pp* **burned** *or* **burnt**) *vt, vi*
bruciare ▷ *n* bruciatura, scottatura; **burn**
down *vt* distruggere col fuoco; **burn**
out *vt* (*writer etc*): **to ~ o.s. out** esaurirsi;
burning *adj* in fiamme; (*sand*) che scotta;
(*ambition*) bruciante

Burns Night *n vedi nota nel riquadro*

burnt [bəːnt] *pt, pp of* **burn**

burp [bəːp] (*inf*) *n* rutto ▷ *vi* ruttare

burrow ['bʌrəu] *n* tana ▷ *vt* scavare

burst [bəːst] (*pt, pp* **burst**) *vt* far
scoppiare ▷ *vi* esplodere; (*tyre*) scoppiare
▷ *n* scoppio; (*also*: **~ pipe**) rottura nel
tubo, perdita; **a ~ of speed** uno scatto
di velocità; **to ~ into flames/tears**
scoppiare in fiamme/lacrime; **to ~ out**
laughing scoppiare a ridere; **to be ~ing**
with scoppiare di; **burst into** *vt fus* (*room*
etc) irrompere in

bury ['bɛrɪ] *vt* seppellire

bus [bʌs] (*pl* **buses**) *n* autobus *m inv*; **bus**
conductor *n* autista *m/f* (dell'autobus)

bush [buʃ] *n* cespuglio; (*scrub land*)
macchia; **to beat about the ~** menare il
cane per l'aia

business ['bɪznɪs] *n* (*matter*) affare *m*;
(*trading*) affari *mpl*; (*firm*) azienda; (*job,*
duty) lavoro; **to be away on ~** essere
andato via per affari; **it's none of my ~**
questo non mi riguarda; **he means ~** non
scherza; **business class** *n* (*Aer*) business
class *f*; **businesslike** *adj* serio(-a),
efficiente; **businessman** (*irreg*) *n* uomo
d'affari; **business trip** *n* viaggio d'affari;
businesswoman (*irreg*) *n* donna d'affari

busker ['bʌskə'] (BRIT) *n* suonatore(-trice)
ambulante

bus: **bus pass** *n* tessera dell'autobus;
bus shelter *n* pensilina (*alla fermata*
dell'autobus); **bus station** *n* stazione *f*
delle corriere, autostazione *f*; **bus-stop** *n*
fermata d'autobus

bust [bʌst] *n* busto; (*Anat*) seno ▷ *adj* (*inf*:
broken) rotto(-a); **to go ~** fallire

bustling ['bʌslɪŋ] *adj* movimentato(-a)

busy ['bɪzɪ] *adj* occupato(-a); (*shop, street*)
molto frequentato(-a) ▷ *vt* **to ~ o.s.** darsi
da fare; **busy signal** (US) *n* (*Tel*) segnale *m*
di occupato

O KEYWORD

but [bʌt] *conj* ma; **I'd love to come, but**
I'm busy vorrei tanto venire, ma ho da fare
▷ *prep* (*apart from, except*) eccetto, tranne,
meno; **he was nothing but trouble** non
dava altro che guai; **no-one but him can**
do it nessuno può farlo tranne lui; **but for**
you/your help se non fosse per te/per il
tuo aiuto; **anything but that** tutto ma
non questo
▷ *adv* (*just, only*) solo, soltanto; **she's but**
a child è solo una bambina; **had I but**
known se solo avessi saputo; **I can but**
try tentar non nuoce; **all but finished**
quasi finito

butcher ['butʃə'] *n* macellaio ▷ *vt*
macellare; **butcher's (shop)** *n*
macelleria

butler ['bʌtlə'] *n* maggiordomo

butt [bʌt] *n* (*cask*) grossa botte *f*; (*of gun*)
calcio; (*of cigarette*) mozzicone *m*; (BRIT: *fig*:
target) oggetto ▷ *vt* cozzare

butter ['bʌtə'] *n* burro ▷ *vt* imburrare;
buttercup *n* ranuncolo

butterfly ['bʌtəflaɪ] *n* farfalla; (*Swimming*:
also: **~ stroke**) (nuoto a) farfalla

buttocks ['bʌtəks] *npl* natiche *fpl*

button ['bʌtn] *n* bottone *m*; (US: *badge*)

distintivo ▷ vt (also: **~ up**) abbottonare ▷ vi abbottonarsi

buy [baɪ] (pt, pp **bought**) vt comprare ▷ n acquisto; **where can I ~ some postcards?** dove posso comprare delle cartoline?; **to ~ sb sth/sth from sb** comprare qc per qn/qc da qn; **to ~ sb a drink** offrire da bere a qn; **buy out** vt (business) rilevare; **buy up** vt accaparrare; **buyer** n compratore(-trice)

buzz [bʌz] n ronzio; (inf: phone call) colpo di telefono ▷ vi ronzare; **buzzer** ['bʌzər] n cicalino

 KEYWORD

by [baɪ] prep **1** (referring to cause, agent) da; **killed by lightning** ucciso da un fulmine; **surrounded by a fence** circondato da uno steccato; **a painting by Picasso** un quadro di Picasso

2 (referring to method, manner, means): **by bus/car/train** in autobus/macchina/treno, con l'autobus/la macchina/il treno; **to pay by cheque** pagare con (un) assegno; **by moonlight** al chiaro di luna; **by saving hard, he ...** risparmiando molto, lui ...

3 (via, through) per; **we came by Dover** siamo venuti via Dover

4 (close to, past) accanto a; **the house by the river** la casa sul fiume; **a holiday by the sea** una vacanza al mare; **she sat by his bed** si sedette accanto al suo letto; **she rushed by me** mi è passata accanto correndo; **I go by the post office every day** passo davanti all'ufficio postale ogni giorno

5 (not later than) per, entro; **by 4 o'clock** per or entro le 4; **by this time tomorrow** domani a quest'ora; **by the time I got here it was too late** quando sono arrivato era ormai troppo tardi

6 (during): **by day/night** di giorno/notte

7 (amount) a; **by the kilo/metre** a chili/metri; **paid by the hour** pagato all'ora; **one by one** uno per uno; **little by little** a poco a poco

8 (Math, measure): **to divide/multiply by 3** dividere/moltiplicare per 3; **it's broader by a metre** è un metro più largo, è più largo di un metro

9 (according to) per; **to play by the rules** attenersi alle regole; **it's all right by me** per me va bene

10: **(all) by oneself** etc (tutto(-a)) solo(-a); **he did it (all) by himself** lo ha fatto (tutto) da solo

11: **by the way** a proposito; **this wasn't**

my idea by the way tra l'altro l'idea non è stata mia

▷ adv **1** see **go**; **pass** etc

2: **by and by** (in past) poco dopo; (in future) fra breve; **by and large** nel complesso

bye(-bye) ['baɪ('baɪ)] excl ciao!, arrivederci!

by-election ['baɪɪlɛkʃən] (BRIT) n elezione f straordinaria

bypass ['baɪpɑːs] n circonvallazione f; (Med) by-pass m inv ▷ vt fare una deviazione intorno a

byte [baɪt] n (Comput) byte m inv, bicarattere m

C

C [siː] n (Mus) do

cab [kæb] n taxi m inv; (of train, truck) cabina

cabaret ['kæbəreɪ] n cabaret m inv

cabbage ['kæbɪdʒ] n cavolo

cabin ['kæbɪn] n capanna; (on ship) cabina; **cabin crew** n equipaggio

cabinet ['kæbɪnɪt] n (Pol) consiglio dei ministri; (furniture) armadietto; (also: **display ~**) vetrinetta; **cabinet minister** n ministro (membro del Consiglio)

cable ['keɪbl] n cavo; fune f; (Tel) cablogramma m ▷ vt telegrafare; **cable car** n funivia; **cable television** n televisione f via cavo

cactus ['kæktəs] (pl **cacti**) n cactus m inv

café ['kæfeɪ] n caffè m inv

cafeteria [kæfɪ'tɪərɪə] n self-service m inv

caffein(e) ['kæfiːn] n caffeina

cage [keɪdʒ] n gabbia

cagoule [kə'guːl] n K-way® m inv

cake [keɪk] n (large) torta; (small) pasticcino; **cake of soap** n saponetta

calcium ['kælsɪəm] n calcio

calculate ['kælkjuleɪt] vt calcolare; **calculation** [-'leɪʃən] n calcolo; **calculator** n calcolatrice f

calendar ['kæləndər] n calendario

calf [kɑːf] (pl **calves**) n (of cow) vitello; (of other animals) piccolo; (also: **~skin**) (pelle f di) vitello; (Anat) polpaccio

calibre ['kælɪbər] (US **caliber**) n calibro

call [kɔːl] vt (gen: also Tel) chiamare; (meeting) indire ▷ vi chiamare; (visit: also: **~ in, ~ round**) passare ▷ n (shout) grido, urlo; (Tel) telefonata; **to be ~ed** (person, object) chiamarsi; **can you ~ back later?** può richiamare più tardi?; **can I make a ~ from here?** posso telefonare da qui?; **to be on ~** essere a disposizione; **call back** vi (return) ritornare; (Tel) ritelefonare, richiamare; **call for** vt fus richiedere; (fetch) passare a prendere; **call in** vt (doctor, expert, police) chiamare, far venire; **call off** vt disdire; **call on** vt fus (visit) passare da; (appeal to) chiedere a; **call out** vi (in pain) urlare; (to person) chiamare; **call up** vt (Mil) richiamare; (Tel) telefonare a; **callbox** (BRIT) n cabina telefonica; **call centre** (US **call center**) n centro informazioni telefoniche; **caller** n persona che chiama, visitatore(-trice)

callous ['kæləs] adj indurito(-a), insensibile

calm [kɑːm] adj calmo(-a) ▷ n calma ▷ vt calmare; **calm down** vi calmarsi ▷ vt calmare; **calmly** adv con calma

Calor gas® ['kælər-] n butano

calorie ['kælərɪ] n caloria

calves [kɑːvz] npl of **calf**

camcorder ['kæmkɔːdər] n camcorder f inv

came [keɪm] pt of **come**

camel ['kæməl] n cammello

camera ['kæmərə] n macchina fotografica; (Cinema, TV) cinepresa; **in ~** a porte chiuse; **cameraman** (irreg) n cameraman m inv

camouflage ['kæməflɑːʒ] n (Mil, Zool) mimetizzazione f ▷ vt mimetizzare

camp [kæmp] n campeggio; (Mil) campo ▷ vi accamparsi ▷ adj effeminato(-a)

campaign [kæm'peɪn] n (Mil, Pol etc) campagna ▷ vi (also fig) fare una campagna; **campaigner** n **campaigner for** fautore(-trice) di; **campaigner against** oppositore(-trice) di

camp: **campbed** n (BRIT) brandina; **camper** ['kæmpər] n campeggiatore(-trice); (vehicle) camper m inv; **campground** (US) n campeggio; **camping** ['kæmpɪŋ] n campeggio; **to go camping** andare in campeggio; **campsite** ['kæmpsaɪt] n campeggio

campus ['kæmpəs] n campus m inv

can¹ [kæn] n (of milk) scatola; (of oil) bidone m; (of water) tanica; (tin) scatola ▷ vt

mettere in scatola

 KEYWORD

can² [kæn] (negative **cannot, can't**, conditional and pt **could**) aux vb **1** (be able to) potere; **I can't go any further** non posso andare oltre; **you can do it if you try** sei in grado di farlo — basta provarci; **I'll help you all I can** ti aiuterò come potrò; **I can't see you** non ti vedo
2 (know how to) sapere, essere capace di; **I can swim** so nuotare; **can you speak French?** parla francese?
3 (may) potere; **could I have a word with you?** posso parlarle un momento?
4 (expressing disbelief, puzzlement etc): **it can't be true!** non può essere vero!; **what CAN he want?** cosa può mai volere?
5 (expressing possibility, suggestion etc): **he could be in the library** può darsi che sia in biblioteca; **she could have been delayed** può aver avuto un contrattempo

Canada ['kænədə] n Canada m; **Canadian** [kə'neɪdɪən] adj, n canadese m/f
canal [kə'næl] n canale m
canary [kə'nɛərɪ] n canarino
Canary Islands, Canaries [kə'nɛərɪz] npl **the ~** le (isole) Canarie
cancel ['kænsəl] vt annullare; (train) sopprimere; (cross out) cancellare; **I want to ~ my booking** vorrei disdire la mia prenotazione; **cancellation** [-'leɪʃən] n annullamento; soppressione f; cancellazione f; (Tourism) prenotazione f annullata
cancer ['kænsər] n cancro
Cancer ['kænsər] n (sign) Cancro
candidate ['kændɪdeɪt] n candidato(-a)
candle ['kændl] n candela; (in church) cero; **candlestick** n bugia; (bigger, ornate) candeliere m
candy ['kændɪ] n zucchero candito; (US) caramella; caramelle fpl; **candy bar** (US) n lungo biscotto, in genere ricoperto di cioccolata; **candyfloss** ['kændɪflɒs] n (BRIT) zucchero filato
cane [keɪn] n canna; (for furniture) bambù m; (stick) verga ▷ vt (BRIT Scol) punire a colpi di verga
canister ['kænɪstər] n scatola metallica
cannabis ['kænəbɪs] n canapa indiana
canned ['kænd] adj (food) in scatola
cannon ['kænən] (pl **cannon** or **cannons**) n (gun) cannone m
cannot ['kænɒt] = **can not**

canoe [kə'nuː] n canoa; **canoeing** n canottaggio
canon ['kænən] n (clergyman) canonico; (standard) canone m
can-opener ['kænəupnər] n apriscatole m inv
can't [kænt] = **can not**
canteen [kæn'tiːn] n mensa; (BRIT: of cutlery) portaposate m inv

Be careful not to translate **canteen** by the Italian word **cantina**.

canter ['kæntər] vi andare al piccolo galoppo
canvas ['kænvəs] n tela
canvass ['kænvəs] vi (Pol): **to ~ for** raccogliere voti per ▷ vt fare un sondaggio di
canyon ['kænjən] n canyon m inv
cap [kæp] n (hat) berretto; (of pen) coperchio; (of bottle, toy gun) tappo; (contraceptive) diaframma m ▷ vt (outdo) superare; (limit) fissare un tetto a(d)
capability [keɪpə'bɪlɪtɪ] n capacità f inv, abilità f inv
capable ['keɪpəbl] adj capace
capacity [kə'pæsɪtɪ] n capacità f inv; (of lift etc) capienza
cape [keɪp] n (garment) cappa; (Geo) capo
caper ['keɪpər] n (Culin) cappero; (prank) scherzetto
capital ['kæpɪtl] n (also: **~ city**) capitale f; (money) capitale m; (also: **~ letter**) (lettera) maiuscola; **capitalism** n capitalismo; **capitalist** adj, n capitalista m/f; **capital punishment** n pena capitale
Capitol ['kæpɪtl] n **the ~** il Campidoglio
Capricorn ['kæprɪkɔːn] n Capricorno
capsize [kæp'saɪz] vt capovolgere ▷ vi capovolgersi
capsule ['kæpsjuːl] n capsula
captain ['kæptɪn] n capitano
caption ['kæpʃən] n leggenda
captivity [kæp'tɪvɪtɪ] n cattività
capture ['kæptʃər] vt catturare; (Comput) registrare ▷ n cattura; (data) registrazione f or rilevazione f di dati
car [kɑːr] n (Aut) macchina, automobile f; (Rail) vagone m
carafe [kə'ræf] n caraffa
caramel ['kærəməl] n caramello
carat ['kærət] n carato; **18 ~ gold** oro a 18 carati
caravan ['kærəvæn] n (BRIT) roulotte f inv; (of camels) carovana; **caravan site** (BRIT) n campeggio per roulotte
carbohydrate [kɑːbəu'haɪdreɪt] n carboidrato
carbon ['kɑːbən] n carbonio; **carbon dioxide** [-daɪ'ɒksaɪd] n diossido di

carbonio; **carbon monoxide** [-mɔ'nɔksaɪd] n monossido di carbonio

car boot sale n vedi nota nel riquadro

● **CAR BOOT SALE**

Il **car boot sale** è un mercatino dell'usato molto popolare in Gran Bretagna. Normalmente ha luogo in un parcheggio o in un grande spiazzo, e la merce viene in genere esposta nei bagagliai, in inglese appunto "boots", aperti delle macchine.

carburettor [kɑ:bju'rɛtəʳ] (us **carburetor**) n carburatore m

card [kɑ:d] n carta; (visiting card etc) biglietto; (Christmas card etc) cartolina; **cardboard** n cartone m; **card game** n gioco di carte

cardigan ['kɑ:dɪgən] n cardigan m inv

cardinal ['kɑ:dɪnl] adj cardinale ▷ n cardinale m

cardphone ['kɑ:dfəun] n telefono a scheda

care [kɛəʳ] n cura, attenzione f; (worry) preoccupazione f ▷ vi **to ~ about** curarsi di; (thing, idea) interessarsi di; **~ of** presso; **in sb's ~** alle cure di qn; **to take ~ (to do)** fare attenzione (a fare); **to take ~ of** curarsi di; (bill, problem) occuparsi di; **I don't ~** non me ne importa; **I couldn't ~ less** non m'interessa affatto; **care for** vt fus aver cura di; (like) volere bene a

career [kə'rɪəʳ] n carriera ▷ vi (also: **~ along**) andare di (gran) carriera

care: carefree ['kɛəfri:] adj sgombro(-a) di preoccupazioni; **careful** ['kɛəful] adj attento(-a); (cautious) cauto(-a); **(be) careful!** attenzione!; **carefully** adv con cura; cautamente; **caregiver** (us) n (professional) badante m/f; (unpaid) persona che si prende cura di un parente malato o anziano; **careless** ['kɛəlɪs] adj negligente; (heedless) spensierato(-a); **carelessness** n negligenza; mancanza di tatto; **carer** ['kɛərəʳ] n assistente m/f (di persone malata o handicappata); **caretaker** ['kɛəteɪkəʳ] n custode m

car-ferry ['kɑ:fɛrɪ] n traghetto

cargo ['kɑ:gəu] (pl **cargoes**) n carico

car hire n autonoleggio

Caribbean [kærɪ'bi:ən] adj **the ~ Sea** il Mar dei Caraibi

caring ['kɛərɪŋ] adj (person) premuroso(-a); (society, organization) umanitario(-a)

carnation [kɑ:'neɪʃən] n garofano

carnival ['kɑ:nɪvəl] n (public celebration) carnevale m; (us: funfair) luna park m inv

carol ['kærəl] n **Christmas ~** canto di Natale

carousel [kærə'sɛl] (us) n giostra

car park (BRIT) n parcheggio

carpenter ['kɑ:pɪntəʳ] n carpentiere m

carpet ['kɑ:pɪt] n tappeto ▷ vt coprire con tappeto

car rental (us) n autonoleggio

carriage ['kærɪdʒ] n vettura; (of goods) trasporto; **carriageway** (BRIT) n (part of road) carreggiata

carrier ['kærɪəʳ] n (of disease) portatore(-trice); (Comm) impresa di trasporti; **carrier bag** (BRIT) n sacchetto

carrot ['kærət] n carota

carry ['kærɪ] vt (person) portare; (: vehicle) trasportare; (involve: responsibilities etc) comportare; (Med) essere portatore(trice) di ▷ vi (sound) farsi sentire; **to be** or **get carried away** (fig) entusiasmarsi; **carry on** vi **to ~ on with sth/doing** continuare qc/a fare ▷ vt mandare avanti; **carry out** vt (orders) eseguire; (investigation) svolgere

cart [kɑ:t] n carro ▷ vt (inf) trascinare

carton ['kɑ:tən] n (box) scatola di cartone; (of yogurt) cartone m; (of cigarettes) stecca

cartoon [kɑ:'tu:n] n (Press) disegno umoristico; (comic strip) fumetto; (Cinema) disegno animato

cartridge ['kɑ:trɪdʒ] n (for gun, pen) cartuccia; (music tape) cassetta

carve [kɑ:v] vt (meat) trinciare; (wood, stone) intagliare; **carving** n (in wood etc) scultura

car wash n lavaggio auto

case [keɪs] n caso; (Law) causa, processo; (box) scatola; (BRIT: also: **suit~**) valigia; **in ~ of** in caso di; **in ~ he** caso mai lui; **in any ~** in ogni caso; **just in ~** in caso di bisogno

cash [kæʃ] n denaro; (coins, notes) denaro liquido ▷ vt incassare; **I haven't got any ~** non ho contanti; **to pay (in) ~** pagare in contanti; **~ on delivery** pagamento alla consegna; **cashback** n (discount) sconto; (at supermarket etc) anticipo di contanti ottenuto presso la cassa di un negozio tramite una carta di debito; **cash card** (BRIT) n tesserino di prelievo; **cash desk** (BRIT) n cassa; **cash dispenser** (BRIT) n sportello automatico

cashew [kæ'ʃu:] n (also: **~ nut**) anacardio

cashier [kæ'ʃɪəʳ] n cassiere(-a)

cashmere ['kæʃmɪəʳ] n cachemire m

cash point n sportello bancario automatico, Bancomat® m inv

cash register n registratore m di cassa

casino [kə'si:nəu] n casinò m inv

casket ['kɑ:skɪt] n cofanetto; (us: coffin) bara

casserole ['kæsərəʊl] n casseruola; (food):
chicken ~ pollo in casseruola
cassette [kæ'sɛt] n cassetta; **cassette**
player n riproduttore m a cassette
cast [kɑːst] (pt, pp **cast**) vt (throw) gettare;
(metal) gettare, fondere; (Theatre): **to ~**
sb as Hamlet scegliere qn per la parte
di Amleto ▷ n (Theatre) cast m inv; (also:
plaster ~) ingessatura; **to ~ one's vote**
votare, dare il voto; **cast off** vi (Naut)
salpare; (Knitting) calare
castanets [kæstə'nɛts] npl castagnette fpl
caster sugar ['kɑːstəʳ-] (BRIT) n zucchero
semolato
cast-iron ['kɑːstaɪən] adj (lit) di ghisa; (fig:
case) di ferro
castle ['kɑːsl] n castello
casual ['kæʒjul] adj (chance) casuale,
fortuito(-a); (: work etc) avventizio(-a);
(unconcerned) noncurante, indifferente; **~**
wear casual m
casualty ['kæʒjultɪ] n ferito(-a); (dead)
morto(-a), vittima; (Med: department)
pronto soccorso
cat [kæt] n gatto
catalogue ['kætəlɔg] (US **catalog**) n
catalogo ▷ vt catalogare
catalytic converter [kætəlɪtɪk-] n
marmitta catalitica, catalizzatore m
cataract ['kætərækt] n (also Med)
cateratta
catarrh [kə'tɑːʳ] n catarro
catastrophe [kə'tæstrəfɪ] n catastrofe f
catch [kætʃ] (pt, pp **caught**) vt prendere;
(ball) afferrare; (surprise: person)
sorprendere; (attention) attirare; (comment,
whisper) cogliere; (person) raggiungere
▷ vi (fire) prendere ▷ n (fish etc caught)
retata; (of ball) presa; (trick) inganno;
(Tech) gancio; (game) catch m inv; **to ~ fire**
prendere fuoco; **to ~ sight of** scorgere;
catch up vi mettersi in pari ▷ vt (also: **~**
up with) raggiungere; **catching** ['kætʃɪŋ]
adj (Med) contagioso(-a)
category ['kætɪgərɪ] n categoria
cater ['keɪtəʳ] vi **~ for** (BRIT: needs)
provvedere a; (: readers, consumers)
incontrare i gusti di; (Comm: provide food)
provvedere alla ristorazione di
caterpillar ['kætəpɪləʳ] n bruco
cathedral [kə'θiːdrəl] n cattedrale f,
duomo
Catholic ['kæθəlɪk] adj, n (Rel) cattolico(-a)
Catseye® ['kætsaɪ] (BRIT) n (Aut)
catarifrangente m
cattle ['kætl] npl bestiame m, bestie fpl
catwalk ['kætwɔːk] n passerella
caught [kɔːt] pt, pp of **catch**
cauliflower ['kɔlɪflauəʳ] n cavolfiore m

cause [kɔːz] n causa ▷ vt causare
caution ['kɔːʃən] n prudenza; (warning)
avvertimento ▷ vt avvertire; ammonire;
cautious ['kɔːʃəs] adj cauto(-a), prudente
cave [keɪv] n caverna, grotta; **cave in** vi
(roof etc) crollare
caviar(e) ['kævɪɑːʳ] n caviale m
cavity ['kævɪtɪ] n cavità f inv
cc abbr =**cubic centimetres**; **carbon copy**
CCTV n abbr (= closed-circuit television)
televisione f a circuito chiuso
CD abbr (disc) CD m inv; (player) lettore m CD
inv; **CD player** n lettore m CD; **CD-ROM**
[-rɔm] n abbr CD-ROM m inv
cease [siːs] vt, vi cessare; **ceasefire** n
cessate il fuoco m inv
cedar ['siːdəʳ] n cedro
ceilidh ['keɪlɪ] n festa con musiche e danze
popolari scozzesi o irlandesi
ceiling ['siːlɪŋ] n soffitto; (on wages etc)
tetto
celebrate ['sɛlɪbreɪt] vt, vi celebrare;
celebration [-'breɪʃən] n celebrazione f
celebrity [sɪ'lɛbrɪtɪ] n celebrità f inv
celery ['sɛlərɪ] n sedano
cell [sɛl] n cella; (of revolutionaries, Biol)
cellula; (Elec) elemento (di batteria)
cellar ['sɛləʳ] n sottosuolo; cantina
cello ['tʃɛləu] n violoncello
Cellophane® ['sɛləfeɪn] n cellophane® m
cellphone ['sɛləfeɪn] n cellulare m
Celsius ['sɛlsɪəs] adj Celsius inv
Celtic ['kɛltɪk, 'sɛltɪk] adj celtico(-a)
cement [sə'mɛnt] n cemento
cemetery ['sɛmɪtrɪ] n cimitero
censor ['sɛnsəʳ] n censore m ▷ vt
censurare; **censorship** n censura
census ['sɛnsəs] n censimento
cent [sɛnt] n (US: coin) centesimo (= 1.100
di un dollaro); (unit of euro) centesimo; see
also **per**
centenary [sɛn'tiːnərɪ] n centenario
centennial [sɛn'tɛnɪəl] (US) n centenario
center ['sɛntəʳ] (US) n, vt =**centre**
centi... [sɛntɪ] prefix: **centigrade**
['sɛntɪgreɪd] adj centigrado(-a);
centimetre ['sɛntɪmiːtəʳ] (US
centimeter) n centimetro; **centipede**
['sɛntɪpiːd] n centopiedi m inv
central ['sɛntrəl] adj centrale; **Central**
America n America centrale; **central**
heating n riscaldamento centrale;
central reservation n (BRIT Aut)
banchina f spartitraffico inv
centre ['sɛntəʳ] (US **center**) n centro
▷ vt centrare; **centre-forward** n (Sport)
centroavanti m inv; **centre-half** n (Sport)
centromediano
century ['sɛntjurɪ] n secolo; **twentieth ~**

ventesimo secolo

CEO n abbr = **chief executive officer**

ceramic [sɪ'ræmɪk] adj ceramico(-a)

cereal ['si:rɪəl] n cereale m

ceremony ['sɛrɪmənɪ] n cerimonia; **to stand on ~** fare complimenti

certain ['sə:tən] adj certo(-a); **to make ~ of** assicurarsi di; **for ~** per certo, di sicuro; **certainly** adv certamente, certo; **certainty** n certezza

certificate [sə'tɪfɪkɪt] n certificato; diploma m

certify ['sə:tɪfaɪ] vt certificare; (award diploma to) conferire un diploma a; (declare insane) dichiarare pazzo(-a)

cf. abbr (= compare) cfr.

CFC n (= chlorofluorocarbon) CFC m inv

chain [tʃeɪn] n catena (also: **~ up**) incatenare; **chain-smoke** vi fumare una sigaretta dopo l'altra

chair [tʃɛəʳ] n sedia; (armchair) poltrona; (of university) cattedra; (of meeting) presidenza ▷ vt (meeting) presiedere; **chairlift** n seggiovia; **chairman** (irreg) n presidente m; **chairperson** n presidente(-essa); **chairwoman** (irreg) n presidentessa

chalet ['ʃæleɪ] n chalet m inv

chalk [tʃɔ:k] n gesso; **chalkboard** (US) n lavagna

challenge ['tʃælɪndʒ] n sfida ▷ vt sfidare; (statement, right) mettere in dubbio; **to ~ sb to do** sfidare qn a fare; **challenging** adj (task) impegnativo(-a); (look) di sfida

chamber ['tʃeɪmbəʳ] n camera; **chambermaid** n cameriera

champagne [ʃæm'peɪn] n champagne m inv

champion ['tʃæmpɪən] n campione(-essa); **championship** n campionato

chance [tʃɑ:ns] n caso; (opportunity) occasione f; (likelihood) possibilità f inv ▷ vt **to ~ it** rischiare, provarci ▷ adj fortuito(-a); **to take a ~** rischiare; **by ~** per caso

chancellor ['tʃɑ:nsələʳ] n cancelliere m; **Chancellor of the Exchequer** [-ɪks'tʃɛkəʳ] (BRIT) n Cancelliere dello Scacchiere

chandelier [ʃændə'lɪəʳ] n lampadario

change [tʃeɪndʒ] vt cambiare; (transform): **to ~ sb into** trasformare qn in ▷ vi cambiare; (change one's clothes) cambiarsi; (be transformed): **to ~ into** trasformarsi in ▷ n cambiamento; (of clothes) cambio; (money returned) resto; (coins) spiccioli; **where can I ~ some money?** dove posso cambiare dei soldi?; **to ~ one's mind** cambiare idea; **keep the ~!** tenga pure il resto!; **sorry, I don't have any ~** mi dispiace, non ho spiccioli; **for a ~** tanto per

cambiare; **change over** vi (from sth to sth) passare; (players etc) scambiarsi (di posto o di campo) ▷ vt cambiare; **changeable** adj (weather) variabile; **change machine** n distributore automatico di monete; **changing room** n (BRIT: in shop) camerino; (: Sport) spogliatoio

channel ['tʃænl] n canale m; (of river, sea) alveo ▷ vt canalizzare; **Channel Tunnel** n **the Channel Tunnel** il tunnel sotto la Manica

chant [tʃɑ:nt] n canto; salmodia ▷ vt cantare; salmodiare

chaos ['keɪɔs] n caos m

chaotic [keɪ'ɔtɪk] adj caotico(-a)

chap [tʃæp] (BRIT: inf) n (man) tipo

chapel ['tʃæpəl] n cappella

chapped [tʃæpt] adj (skin, lips) screpolato(-a)

chapter ['tʃæptəʳ] n capitolo

character ['kærɪktəʳ] n carattere m; (in novel, film) personaggio; **characteristic** [-'rɪstɪk] adj caratteristico(-a) ▷ n caratteristica; **characterize** ['kærɪktəraɪz] vt caratterizzare; (describe): **to characterize (as)** descrivere (come)

charcoal ['tʃɑ:kəul] n carbone m di legna

charge [tʃɑ:dʒ] n accusa; (cost) prezzo; (responsibility) responsabilità ▷ vt (gun, battery, Mil: enemy) caricare; (customer) fare pagare a; (sum) fare pagare; (Law): **to ~ sb (with)** accusare qn (di) ▷ vi (gen with: up, along etc) lanciarsi; **charge card** n carta f clienti inv; **charger** n (also: **battery charger**) caricabatterie m inv; (old: warhorse) destriero

charismatic [kærɪz'mætɪk] adj carismatico(-a)

charity ['tʃærɪtɪ] n carità; (organization) opera pia; **charity shop** n (BRIT) negozi che vendono articoli di seconda mano e devolvono il ricavato in beneficenza

charm [tʃɑ:m] n fascino; (on bracelet) ciondolo ▷ vt affascinare, incantare; **charming** adj affascinante

chart [tʃɑ:t] n tabella; grafico; (map) carta nautica ▷ vt fare una carta nautica di; **~s** npl (Mus) hit parade f

charter ['tʃɑ:təʳ] vt (plane) noleggiare ▷ n (document) carta; **chartered accountant** ['tʃɑ:təd-] (BRIT) n ragioniere(-a) professionista; **charter flight** n volo m charter inv

chase [tʃeɪs] vt inseguire; (also: **~ away**) cacciare ▷ n caccia

chat [tʃæt] vi (also: **have a ~**) chiacchierare ▷ n chiacchierata; **chat up** vt (BRIT inf: girl) abbordare; **chat room** n (Internet) chat room f inv; **chat show** (BRIT) n talk show *m inv*

chatter ['tʃætə^r] *vi* (*person*) ciarlare; (*bird*) cinguettare; (*teeth*) battere ▷ *n* ciarle *fpl*; cinguettio

chauffeur ['ʃəufə^r] *n* autista *m*

chauvinist ['ʃəuvɪnɪst] *n* (*male chauvinist*) maschilista *m*; (*nationalist*) sciovinista *m/f*

cheap [tʃiːp] *adj* economico(-a); (*joke*) grossolano(-a); (*poor quality*) di cattiva qualità ▷ *adv* a buon mercato; **can you recommend a ~ hotel/restaurant, please?** potrebbe indicarmi un albergo/ristorante non troppo caro?; **cheap day return** *n* biglietto ridotto di andata e ritorno valido in giornata; **cheaply** *adv* a buon prezzo, a buon mercato

cheat [tʃiːt] *vi* imbrogliare; (*at school*) copiare ▷ *vt* ingannare ▷ *n* imbroglione *m*; **to ~ sb out of sth** defraudare qn di qc; **cheat on** *vt fus* (*husband, wife*) tradire

Chechnya [tʃɪtʃˈnjaː] *n* Cecenia

check [tʃɛk] *vt* verificare; (*passport, ticket*) controllare; (*halt*) fermare; (*restrain*) contenere ▷ *n* verifica; controllo; (*curb*) freno; (*US: bill*) conto; (*pattern: gen pl*) quadretti *mpl*; (*US*) = **cheque** ▷ *adj* (*pattern, cloth*) a quadretti; **check in** *vi* (*in hotel*) registrare; (*at airport*) presentarsi all'accettazione ▷ *vt* (*luggage*) depositare; **check off** *vt* segnare; **check out** *vi* (*in hotel*) saldare il conto; **check up** *vi* **to ~ up (on sth)** investigare (qc); **to ~ up on sb** informarsi sul conto di qn; **checkbook** (*US*) *n* = **chequebook**; **checked** *adj* a quadretti; **checkers** (*US*) *n* dama; **check-in** *n* (*also:* **check-in desk**: *at airport*) check-in *m inv*, accettazione *f* (bagagli *inv*); **checking account** (*US*) *n* conto corrente; **checklist** *n* lista di controllo; **checkmate** *n* scaccomatto; **checkout** *n* (*in supermarket*) cassa; **checkpoint** *n* posto di blocco; **checkroom** (*US*) *n* deposito *m* bagagli *inv*; **checkup** *n* (*Med*) controllo medico

cheddar ['tʃedə^r] *n* formaggio duro di latte di mucca di colore bianco o arancione

cheek [tʃiːk] *n* guancia; (*impudence*) faccia tosta; **cheekbone** *n* zigomo; **cheeky** *adj* sfacciato(-a)

cheer [tʃɪə^r] *vt* applaudire; (*gladden*) rallegrare ▷ *vi* applaudire ▷ *n* grido (di incoraggiamento); **cheer up** *vi* rallegrarsi, farsi animo ▷ *vt* rallegrare; **cheerful** *adj* allegro(-a)

cheerio ['tʃɪərɪˈəu] (*BRIT*) *excl* ciao!

cheerleader ['tʃɪəliːdə^r] *n* cheerleader *f inv*

cheese [tʃiːz] *n* formaggio; **cheeseburger** *n* cheeseburger *m inv*; **cheesecake** *n* specie di torta di ricotta, a volte con frutta

chef [ʃef] *n* capocuoco

chemical ['kemɪkəl] *adj* chimico(-a) ▷ *n* prodotto chimico

chemist ['kemɪst] *n* (*BRIT: pharmacist*) farmacista *m/f*; (*scientist*) chimico(-a); **chemistry** *n* chimica; **chemist's (shop)** (*BRIT*) *n* farmacia

cheque [tʃɛk] (*US* **check**) *n* assegno; **chequebook** *n* libretto degli assegni; **cheque card** *n* carta *f* assegni *inv*

cherry ['tʃerɪ] *n* ciliegia; (*also:* **~ tree**) ciliegio

chess [tʃes] *n* scacchi *mpl*

chest [tʃest] *n* petto; (*box*) cassa

chestnut ['tʃesnʌt] *n* castagna; (*also:* **~ tree**) castagno

chest of drawers *n* cassettone *m*

chew [tʃuː] *vt* masticare; **chewing gum** *n* chewing gum *m*

chic [ʃiːk] *adj* elegante

chick [tʃɪk] *n* pulcino; (*inf*) pollastrella

chicken ['tʃɪkɪn] *n* pollo; (*inf: coward*) coniglio; **chicken out** (*inf*) *vi* avere fifa; **chickenpox** *n* varicella

chickpea ['tʃɪkpiː] *n* cece *m*

chief [tʃiːf] *n* capo ▷ *adj* principale; **chief executive (officer)** *n* direttore *m* generale; **chiefly** *adv* per lo più, soprattutto

child [tʃaɪld] (*pl* **children**) *n* bambino(-a); **child abuse** *n* molestie *fpl* a minori; **child benefit** *n* (*BRIT*) ≈ assegni *mpl* familiari; **childbirth** *n* parto; **child-care** *n* il badare ai bambini; **childhood** *n* infanzia; **childish** *adj* puerile; **child minder** [-'maɪndə^r] (*BRIT*) *n* bambinaia; **children** ['tʃɪldrən] *npl of* **child**

Chile ['tʃɪlɪ] *n* Cile *m*

Chilean ['tʃɪlɪən] *adj, n* cileno(-a)

chill [tʃɪl] *n* freddo; (*Med*) infreddatura ▷ *vt* raffreddare; **chill out** (*esp US*) *vi* (*inf*) darsi una calmata

chil(l)i ['tʃɪlɪ] *n* peperoncino

chilly ['tʃɪlɪ] *adj* freddo(-a), fresco(-a); **to feel ~** sentirsi infreddolito(-a)

chimney ['tʃɪmnɪ] *n* camino

chimpanzee [tʃɪmpænˈziː] *n* scimpanzé *m inv*

chin [tʃɪn] *n* mento

China ['tʃaɪnə] *n* Cina

china ['tʃaɪnə] *n* porcellana

Chinese [tʃaɪˈniːz] *adj* cinese ▷ *n inv* cinese *m/f*; (*Ling*) cinese *m*

chip [tʃɪp] *n* (*gen pl: Culin*) patatina fritta; (*: US: also:* **potato ~**) patatina; (*of wood, glass, stone*) scheggia; (*also:* **micro~**) chip *m inv* ▷ *vt* (*cup, plate*) scheggiare; **chip**

shop n (BRIT) vedi nota nel riquadro

● **CHIP SHOP**
●
● I **chip shops**, anche chiamati "fish
● and chip shops", sono friggitorie che
● vendono principalmente filetti di pesce
● impanati e patatine fritte.

chiropodist [kɪ'rɔpədɪst] (BRIT) n pedicure
m/f inv
chisel ['tʃɪzl] n cesello
chives [tʃaɪvz] npl erba cipollina
chlorine ['klɔːriːn] n cloro
choc-ice ['tʃɔkaɪs] n (BRIT) gelato ricoperto
al cioccolato
chocolate ['tʃɔklɪt] ▷ n (substance)
cioccolato, cioccolata; (drink) cioccolata;
(a sweet) cioccolatino
choice [tʃɔɪs] n scelta ▷ adj scelto(-a)
choir ['kwaɪəʳ] n coro
choke [tʃəuk] vi soffocare ▷ vt soffocare;
(block): **to be ~d with** essere intasato(-a) di
▷ n (Aut) valvola dell'aria
cholesterol [kə'lɛstərɔl] n colesterolo
choose [tʃuːz] (pt **chose,**, pp **chosen**)
vt scegliere; **to ~ to do** decidere di fare;
preferire fare
chop [tʃɔp] vt (wood) spaccare; (Culin:
also: ~ **up**) tritare ▷ n (Culin) costoletta;
chop down vt (tree) abbattere; **chop off**
vt tagliare; **chopsticks** ['tʃɔpstɪks] npl
bastoncini mpl cinesi
chord [kɔːd] n (Mus) accordo
chore [tʃɔːʳ] n faccenda; **household ~s**
faccende fpl domestiche
chorus ['kɔːrəs] n coro; (repeated part of
song: also fig) ritornello
chose [tʃəuz] pt of **choose**
chosen ['tʃəuzn] pp of **choose**
Christ [kraɪst] n Cristo
christen ['krɪsn] vt battezzare;
christening n battesimo
Christian ['krɪstɪən] adj, n cristiano(-a);
Christianity [-'ænɪtɪ] n cristianesimo;
Christian name n nome m (di battesimo)
Christmas ['krɪsməs] n Natale m; **Merry
~!** Buon Natale!; **Christmas card** n
cartolina di Natale; **Christmas carol**
n canto natalizio; **Christmas Day** n il
giorno di Natale; **Christmas Eve** n la
vigilia di Natale; **Christmas pudding** n
(esp BRIT) specie di budino con frutta secca,
spezie e brandy; **Christmas tree** n albero
di Natale
chrome [krəum] n cromo
chronic ['krɔnɪk] adj cronico(-a)
chrysanthemum [krɪ'sænθəməm] n
crisantemo

chubby ['tʃʌbɪ] adj paffuto(-a)
chuck [tʃʌk] (inf) vt buttare, gettare; (BRIT:
also: ~ **up**) piantare; **chuck out** vt buttar
fuori
chuckle ['tʃʌkl] vi ridere sommessamente
chum [tʃʌm] n compagno(-a)
chunk [tʃʌŋk] n pezzo
church [tʃəːtʃ] n chiesa; **churchyard** n
sagrato
churn [tʃəːn] n (for butter) zangola; (for milk)
bidone m
chute [ʃuːt] n (also: **rubbish ~**) canale m di
scarico; (BRIT: children's slide) scivolo
chutney ['tʃʌtnɪ] n salsa piccante (di frutta,
zucchero e spezie)
CIA (US) n abbr (= Central Intelligence Agency)
CIA f
CID (BRIT) n abbr (= Criminal Investigation
Department) ≈ polizia giudiziaria
cider ['saɪdəʳ] n sidro
cigar [sɪ'gaːʳ] n sigaro
cigarette [sɪgə'rɛt] n sigaretta; **cigarette
lighter** n accendino
cinema ['sɪnəmə] n cinema m inv
cinnamon ['sɪnəmən] n cannella
circle ['səːkl] n cerchio; (of friends etc)
circolo; (in cinema) galleria ▷ vi girare in
circolo ▷ vt (surround) circondare; (move
round) girare intorno a
circuit ['səːkɪt] n circuito
circular ['səːkjuləʳ] adj circolare ▷ n
circolare f
circulate ['səːkjuleɪt] vi circolare ▷ vt
far circolare; **circulation** [-'leɪʃən] n
circolazione f; (of newspaper) tiratura
circumstances ['səːkəmstənsɪz] npl
circostanze fpl; (financial condition)
condizioni fpl finanziarie
circus ['səːkəs] n circo
cite [saɪt] vt citare
citizen ['sɪtɪzn] n (of country) cittadino(-a);
(of town) abitante m/f; **citizenship** n
cittadinanza
citrus fruits ['sɪtrəs-] npl agrumi mpl
city ['sɪtɪ] n città f inv; **the C~** la Città di
Londra (centro commerciale); **city centre**
n centro della città; **city technology
college** n (BRIT) istituto tecnico superiore
(finanziato dall'industria)
civic ['sɪvɪk] adj civico(-a)
civil ['sɪvɪl] adj civile; **civilian** [sɪ'vɪlɪən]
adj, n borghese m/f
civilization [sɪvɪlaɪ'zeɪʃən] n civiltà f inv
civilized ['sɪvɪlaɪzd] adj civilizzato(-a); (fig)
cortese
civil: civil law n codice m, civile; (study)
diritto civile; **civil rights** npl diritti mpl
civili; **civil servant** n impiegato(-a)
statale; **Civil Service** n amministrazione f

statale; **civil war** n guerra civile
CJD abbr (= Creutzfeld Jacob disease) malattia
di Creutzfeldt-Jacob
claim [kleɪm] vt (assert): **to ~ (that)/to be**
sostenere (che)/di essere; (credit, rights etc)
rivendicare; (damages) richiedere ▷ vi (for
insurance) fare una domanda d'indennizzo
▷ n pretesa; rivendicazione f; richiesta;
claim form n (gen) modulo di richiesta;
(for expenses) modulo di rimborso spese
clam [klæm] n vongola
clamp [klæmp] n pinza; morsa ▷ vt
stringere con una morsa; (Aut: wheel)
applicare i ceppi bloccaruote a
clan [klæn] n clan m inv
clap [klæp] vi applaudire
claret ['klærət] n vino di Bordeaux
clarify ['klærɪfaɪ] vt chiarificare, chiarire
clarinet [klærɪ'nɛt] n clarinetto
clarity ['klærɪtɪ] n clarità
clash [klæʃ] n frastuono; (fig) scontro ▷ vi
scontrarsi; cozzare
clasp [klɑːsp] n (hold) stretta; (of necklace,
bag) fermaglio, fibbia ▷ vt stringere
class [klɑːs] n classe f ▷ vt classificare
classic ['klæsɪk] adj classico(-a) ▷ n
classico; **classical** adj classico(-a)
classification [klæsɪfɪ'keɪʃən] n
classificazione f
classify ['klæsɪfaɪ] vt classificare
classmate ['klɑːsmeɪt] n compagno(-a)
di classe
classroom ['klɑːsrum] n aula
classy ['klɑːsɪ] adj (inf) chic inv, elegante
clatter ['klætəʳ] n tintinnio; scalpitio ▷ vi
tintinnare; scalpitare
clause [klɔːz] n clausola; (Ling)
proposizione f
claustrophobic [klɔːstrə'fəubɪk] adj
claustrofobico(-a)
claw [klɔː] n (of bird of prey) artiglio; (of
lobster) pinza
clay [kleɪ] n argilla
clean [kliːn] adj pulito(-a); (clear, smooth)
liscio(-a) ▷ vt pulire; **clean up** vt (also fig)
ripulire; **cleaner** n (person) donna delle
pulizie; **cleaner's** n (also: **dry cleaner's**)
tintoria; **cleaning** n pulizia
cleanser ['klɛnzəʳ] n detergente m
clear [klɪəʳ] adj chiaro(-a); (glass etc)
trasparente; (road, way) libero(-a);
(conscience) pulito(-a) ▷ vt sgombrare;
liberare; (table) sparecchiare; (cheque)
fare la compensazione di; (Law: suspect)
discolpare; (obstacle) superare ▷ vi
(weather) rasserenarsi; (fog) andarsene
▷ adv **~ of** distante da; **clear away** vt
(things, clothes etc) mettere a posto; **to ~**
away the dishes sparecchiare la tavola;

clear up vt mettere in ordine; (mystery)
risolvere; **clearance** n (removal) sgombro;
(permission) autorizzazione f, permesso;
clear-cut adj ben delineato(-a),
distinto(-a); **clearing** n radura; **clearly**
adv chiaramente; **clearway** (BRIT) n
strada con divieto di sosta
clench [klɛntʃ] vt stringere
clergy ['kləːdʒɪ] n clero
clerk [klɑːk, (US) kləːrk] n (BRIT)
impiegato(-a); (US) commesso(-a)
clever ['klɛvəʳ] adj (mentally) intelligente;
(deft, skilful) abile; (device, arrangement)
ingegnoso(-a)
cliché ['kliːʃeɪ] n cliché m inv
click [klɪk] vi scattare ▷ vt (heels etc)
battere; (tongue) far schioccare
client ['klaɪənt] n cliente m/f
cliff [klɪf] n scogliera scoscesa, rupe f
climate ['klaɪmɪt] n clima m
climax ['klaɪmæks] n culmine m; (sexual)
orgasmo
climb [klaɪm] vi salire; (clamber)
arrampicarsi ▷ vt salire; (Climbing) scalare
▷ n salita; arrampicata; scalata; **climb**
down vi scendere; (BRIT fig) far marcia
indietro; **climber** n rocciatore(-trice);
alpinista m/f; **climbing** n alpinismo
clinch [klɪntʃ] vt (deal) concludere
cling [klɪŋ] (pt, pp clung) vi **to ~ (to)**
aggrapparsi (a); (of clothes) aderire
strettamente (a)
Clingfilm® ['klɪŋfɪlm] n pellicola
trasparente (per alimenti)
clinic ['klɪnɪk] n clinica
clip [klɪp] n (for hair) forcina; (also: **paper**
~) graffetta; (TV, Cinema) sequenza ▷ vt
attaccare insieme; (hair, nails) tagliare;
(hedge) tosare; **clipping** n (from newspaper)
ritaglio
cloak [kləuk] n mantello ▷ vt avvolgere;
cloakroom n (for coats etc) guardaroba m
inv; (BRIT: W.C.) gabinetti mpl
clock [klɔk] n orologio; **clock in** or **on**
vi timbrare il cartellino (all'entrata);
clock off or **out** vi timbrare il cartellino
(all'uscita); **clockwise** adv in senso orario;
clockwork n movimento or meccanismo
a orologeria ▷ adj a molla
clog [klɔg] n zoccolo ▷ vt intasare ▷ vi
(also: **~ up**) intasarsi, bloccarsi
clone [kləun] n clone m
close¹ [kləus] adj **~ (to)** vicino(-a)
(a); (watch, link, relative) stretto(-a);
(examination) attento(-a); (contest)
combattuto(-a); (weather) afoso(-a) ▷ adv
vicino, dappresso; **~ to** vicino a; **~ by**, **~**
at hand a portata di mano; **a ~ friend**
un amico intimo; **to have a ~ shave** (fig)

scamparla bella

close² [kləʊz] vt chiudere ▷ vi (shop etc)
chiudere; (lid, door etc) chiudersi; (end) finire
▷ n (end) fine f; **what time do you ~?** a
che ora chiudete?; **close down** vi cessare
(definitivamente); **closed** adj chiuso(-a)

closely ['kləʊslɪ] adv (examine, watch) da
vicino; (related) strettamente

closet ['klɔzɪt] n (cupboard) armadio

close-up ['kləʊsʌp] n primo piano

closing time n orario di chiusura

closure ['kləʊʒəʳ] n chiusura

clot [klɔt] n (also: **blood ~**) coagulo; (inf:
idiot) scemo(-a) ▷ vi coagularsi

cloth [klɔθ] n (material) tessuto, stoffa;
(rag) strofinaccio

clothes [kləʊðz] npl abiti mpl, vestiti
mpl; **clothes line** n corda (per stendere il
bucato); **clothes peg** (US **clothes pin**) n
molletta

clothing ['kləʊðɪŋ] n = **clothes**

cloud [klaʊd] n nuvola; **cloud over** vi
rannuvolarsi; (fig) offuscarsi; **cloudy** adj
nuvoloso(-a); (liquid) torbido(-a)

clove [kləʊv] n chiodo di garofano; **clove
of garlic** n spicchio d'aglio

clown [klaʊn] n pagliaccio ▷ vi (also: ~
about, ~ around) fare il pagliaccio

club [klʌb] n (society) club m inv, circolo;
(weapon, Golf) mazza ▷ vt bastonare ▷ vi
to ~ together associarsi; **~s** npl (Cards)
fiori mpl; **club class** n (Aviat) classe f club
inv

clue [kluː] n indizio; (in crosswords)
definizione f; **I haven't a ~** non ho la
minima idea

clump [klʌmp] n (of flowers, trees) gruppo;
(of grass) ciuffo

clumsy ['klʌmzɪ] adj goffo(-a)

clung [klʌŋ] pt, pp of **cling**

cluster ['klʌstəʳ] n gruppo ▷ vi
raggrupparsi

clutch [klʌtʃ] n (grip, grasp) presa, stretta;
(Aut) frizione f ▷ vt afferrare, stringere
forte

cm abbr (= centimetre) cm

Co. abbr = **county**; **company**

c/o abbr (= care of) presso

coach [kəʊtʃ] n (bus) pullman m inv;
(horse-drawn, of train) carrozza; (Sport)
allenatore(-trice); (tutor) chi dà ripetizioni
▷ vt allenare; dare ripetizioni a; **coach
station** (BRIT) n stazione f delle corriere;
coach trip n viaggio in pullman

coal [kəʊl] n carbone m

coalition [kəʊə'lɪʃən] n coalizione f

coarse [kɔːs] adj (salt, sand etc) grosso(-a);
(cloth, person) rozzo(-a)

coast [kəʊst] n costa ▷ vi (with cycle

etc) scendere a ruota libera; **coastal** adj
costiero(-a); **coastguard** n guardia
costiera; **coastline** n linea costiera

coat [kəʊt] n cappotto; (of animal) pelo;
(of paint) mano f ▷ vt coprire; **coat
hanger** n attaccapanni m inv; **coating** n
rivestimento

coax [kəʊks] vt indurre (con moine)

cob [kɔb] n see **corn**

cobbled ['kɔbld] adj **~ street** strada
pavimentata a ciottoli

cobweb ['kɔbwɛb] n ragnatela

cocaine [kə'keɪn] n cocaina

cock [kɔk] n (rooster) gallo; (male bird)
maschio ▷ vt (gun) armare; **cockerel** n
galletto

cockney ['kɔknɪ] n cockney m/f inv
(abitante dei quartieri popolari dell'East End
di Londra)

cockpit ['kɔkpɪt] n abitacolo

cockroach ['kɔkrəʊtʃ] n blatta

cocktail ['kɔkteɪl] n cocktail m inv

cocoa ['kəʊkəʊ] n cacao

coconut ['kəʊkənʌt] n noce f di cocco

cod [kɔd] n merluzzo

C.O.D. abbr = **cash on delivery**

code [kəʊd] n codice m

coeducational ['kəʊɛdju'keɪʃənl] adj
misto(-a)

coffee ['kɔfɪ] n caffè m inv; **coffee bar**
(BRIT) n caffè m inv; **coffee bean** n grano
or chicco di caffè; **coffee break** n pausa
per il caffè; **coffee maker** n bollitore
m per il caffè; **coffeepot** n caffettiera;
coffee shop n ≈ caffè m inv; **coffee table**
n tavolino

coffin ['kɔfɪn] n bara

cog [kɔg] n dente m

cognac ['kɔnjæk] n cognac m inv

coherent [kəʊ'hɪərənt] adj coerente

coil [kɔɪl] n rotolo; (Elec) bobina;
(contraceptive) spirale f ▷ vt avvolgere

coin [kɔɪn] n moneta ▷ vt (word) coniare

coincide [kəʊɪn'saɪd] vi coincidere;
coincidence [kəʊ'ɪnsɪdəns] n
combinazione f

Coke® [kəʊk] n coca

coke [kəʊk] n coke m

colander ['kɔləndəʳ] n colino

cold [kəʊld] adj freddo(-a) ▷ n freddo;
(Med) raffreddore m; **it's ~** fa freddo; **to
be ~** (person) aver freddo; (object) essere
freddo(-a); **to catch ~** prendere freddo;
to catch a ~ prendere un raffreddore;
in ~ blood a sangue freddo; **cold sore** n
erpete m

coleslaw ['kəʊlslɔː] n insalata di cavolo
bianco

colic ['kɔlɪk] n colica

collaborate [kə'læbəreɪt] *vi* collaborare
collapse [kə'læps] *vi* crollare ▷ *n* crollo; (*Med*) collasso
collar ['kɔləʳ] *n* (*of coat, shirt*) colletto; (*of dog, cat*) collare *m*; **collarbone** *n* clavicola
colleague ['kɔliːg] *n* collega *m/f*
collect [kə'lɛkt] *vt* (*gen*) raccogliere; (*as a hobby*) fare collezione di; (*BRIT: call and pick up*) prendere; (*money owed, pension*) riscuotere; (*donations, subscriptions*) fare una colletta di ▷ *vi* adunarsi, riunirsi; ammucchiarsi; **to call ~** (*US Tel*) fare una chiamata a carico del destinatario; **collection** [kə'lɛkʃən] *n* raccolta; collezione *f*; (*for money*) colletta; **collective** *adj* collettivo(-a) ▷ *n* collettivo; **collector** [kə'lɛktəʳ] *n* collezionista *m/f*
college ['kɔlɪdʒ] *n* college *m inv*; (*of technology etc*) istituto superiore
collide [kə'laɪd] *vi* **to ~ with** scontrarsi (con)
collision [kə'lɪʒən] *n* collisione *f*, scontro
cologne [kə'ləun] *n* (*also: eau de ~*) acqua di colonia
Colombia [kə'lɔmbɪə] *n* Colombia; **Colombian** *adj, n* colombiano(-a)
colon ['kəulən] *n* (*sign*) due punti *mpl*; (*Med*) colon *m inv*
colonel ['kəːnl] *n* colonnello
colonial [kə'ləunɪəl] *adj* coloniale
colony ['kɔlənɪ] *n* colonia
colour *etc* ['kʌləʳ] (*US* **color**) *n* colore *m* ▷ *vt* colorare; (*tint, dye*) tingere; (*fig: affect*) influenzare ▷ *vi* (*blush*) arrossire; **colour in** *vt* colorare; **colour-blind** *adj* daltonico(-a); **coloured** *adj* (*photo*) a colori; (*person*) di colore; **colour film** *n* (*for camera*) pellicola a colori; **colourful** *adj* pieno(-a) di colore, a vivaci colori; (*personality*) colorato(-a); **colouring** *n* (*substance*) colorante *m*; (*complexion*) colorito; **colour television** *n* televisione *f* a colori
column ['kɔləm] *n* colonna
coma ['kəumə] *n* coma *m inv*
comb [kəum] *n* pettine *m* ▷ *vt* (*hair*) pettinare; (*area*) battere a tappeto
combination [kɔmbɪ'neɪʃən] *n* combinazione *f*
combine [*vb* kəm'baɪn, *n* 'kɔmbaɪn] *vt* **to ~ (with)** combinare (con); (*one quality with another*) unire (a) ▷ *vi* unirsi; (*Chem*) combinarsi ▷ *n* (*Econ*) associazione *f*
come [kʌm] (*pt* **came**, *pp* **come**) *vi* venire; arrivare; **to ~ to** (*decision etc*) raggiungere; **I've ~ to like him** ha cominciato a piacermi; **to ~ undone** slacciarsi; **to ~**

loose allentarsi; **come across** *vt fus* trovare per caso; **come along** *vi* (*pupil, work*) fare progressi; **~ along!** avanti!, andiamo!, forza!; **come back** *vi* ritornare; **come down** *vi* scendere; (*prices*) calare; (*buildings*) essere demolito(-a); **come from** *vt fus* venire da; provenire da; **come in** *vi* entrare; **come off** *vi* (*button*) staccarsi; (*stain*) andar via; (*attempt*) riuscire; **come on** *vi* (*pupil, work, project*) fare progressi; (*lights*) accendersi; (*electricity*) entrare in funzione; **~ on!** avanti!, andiamo!, forza!; **come out** *vi* uscire; (*stain*) andare via; **come round** *vi* (*after faint, operation*) riprendere conoscenza, rinvenire; **come to** *vi* rinvenire; **come up** *vi* (*sun*) salire; (*problem*) sorgere; (*event*) essere in arrivo; (*in conversation*) saltar fuori; **come up with** *vt fus* **he came up with an idea** venne fuori con un'idea
comeback ['kʌmbæk] *n* (*Theatre etc*) ritorno
comedian [kə'miːdɪən] *n* comico
comedy ['kɔmɪdɪ] *n* commedia
comet ['kɔmɪt] *n* cometa
comfort ['kʌmfət] *n* comodità *f inv*, benessere *m*; (*relief*) consolazione *f*, conforto ▷ *vt* consolare, confortare; **comfortable** *adj* comodo(-a); (*financially*) agiato(-a); **comfort station** (*US*) *n* gabinetti *mpl*
comic ['kɔmɪk] *adj* (*also: ~al*) comico(-a) ▷ *n* comico; (*BRIT: magazine*) giornaletto; **comic book** (*US*) *n* giornalino (a fumetti); **comic strip** *n* fumetto
comma ['kɔmə] *n* virgola
command [kə'mɑːnd] *n* ordine *m*, comando; (*Mil: authority*) comando; (*mastery*) padronanza ▷ *vt* comandare; **to ~ sb to do** ordinare a qn di fare; **commander** *n* capo; (*Mil*) comandante *m*
commemorate [kə'mɛməreɪt] *vt* commemorare
commence [kə'mɛns] *vt, vi* cominciare; **commencement** (*US*) *n* (*Univ*) cerimonia di consegna dei diplomi
commend [kə'mɛnd] *vt* lodare; raccomandare
comment ['kɔmɛnt] *n* commento ▷ *vi* **to ~ (on)** fare commenti (su); **commentary** ['kɔməntərɪ] *n* commentario; (*Sport*) radiocronaca; telecronaca; **commentator** ['kɔmənteɪtəʳ] *n* commentatore(-trice); radiocronista *m/f*; telecronista *m/f*
commerce ['kɔməːs] *n* commercio
commercial [kə'məːʃəl] *adj* commerciale ▷ *n* (*TV, Radio: advertisement*) pubblicità *f inv*; **commercial break** *n* intervallo pubblicitario

commission [kə'mɪʃən] *n* commissione
f ▷ *vt* (*work of art*) commissionare; **out
of ~** (*Naut*) in disarmo; **commissioner** *n*
(*Police*) questore *m*

commit [kə'mɪt] *vt* (*act*) commettere;
(*to sb's care*) affidare; **to ~ o.s. to do**
impegnarsi (a fare); **to ~ suicide** suicidarsi;
commitment *n* impegno; promessa

committee [kə'mɪtɪ] *n* comitato

commodity [kə'mɔdɪtɪ] *n* prodotto,
articolo

common ['kɔmən] *adj* comune; (*pej*)
volgare; (*usual*) normale ▷ *n* terreno
comune; **the C~s** (*BRIT*) ▷ *npl* la Camera
dei Comuni; **in ~** in comune; **commonly**
adv comunemente, usualmente;
commonplace *adj* banale, ordinario(-a);
Commons *npl* (*BRIT Pol*): **the (House
of) Commons** la Camera dei Comuni;
common sense *n* buon senso;
Commonwealth *n* **the Commonwealth**
il Commonwealth

● **COMMONWEALTH**
●
● Il **Commonwealth** è un'associazione
● di stati sovrani indipendenti e di
● alcuni territori annessi che facevano
● parte dell'antico Impero Britannico.
● Nel 1931 questi assunsero il nome
● di "Commonwealth of Nations",
● denominazione successivamente
● semplificata in "Commonwealth".
● Attualmente gli stati del
● "Commonwealth" riconoscono ancora il
● proprio capo di stato.

communal ['kɔmjuːnl] *adj* (*for common
use*) pubblico(-a)

commune [*n* 'kɔmjuːn, *vb* kə'mjuːn] *n*
(*group*) comune *f* ▷ *vi* **to ~ with** mettersi in
comunione con

communicate [kə'mjuːnɪkeɪt] *vt*
comunicare, trasmettere ▷ *vi* **to ~ with**
comunicare (con)

communication [kəmjuːnɪ'keɪʃən] *n*
comunicazione *f*

communion [kə'mjuːnɪən] *n* (*also*: **Holy
C~**) comunione *f*

communism ['kɔmjunɪzəm] *n*
comunismo; **communist** *adj*, *n*
comunista *m/f*

community [kə'mjuːnɪtɪ] *n* comunità *f
inv*; **community centre** (*US* **community
center**) *n* circolo ricreativo; **community
service** *n* (*BRIT*) ≈ lavoro sostitutivo

commute [kə'mjuːt] *vi* fare il pendolare
▷ *vt* (*Law*) commutare; **commuter** *n*
pendolare *m/f*

compact [*adj* kəm'pækt, *n* 'kɔmpækt]
adj compatto(-a) ▷ *n* (*also*: **powder
~**) portacipria *m inv*; **compact disc** *n*
compact disc *m inv*; **compact disc player**
n lettore *m* CD *inv*

companion [kəm'pænɪən] *n*
compagno(-a)

company ['kʌmpənɪ] *n* (*also Comm,
Mil, Theatre*) compagnia; **to keep sb ~**
tenere compagnia a qn; **company car**
n macchina (di proprietà) della ditta;
company director *n* amministratore *m*,
consigliere *m* di amministrazione

comparable ['kɔmpərəbl] *adj* simile

comparative [kəm'pærətɪv] *adj*
relativo(-a); (*adjective etc*) comparativo(-a);
comparatively *adv* relativamente

compare [kəm'pεər] *vt* **to ~ sth/sb
with/to** confrontare qc/qn con/a ▷ *vi*
to ~ (with) reggere il confronto (con);
comparison [-'pærɪsn] *n* confronto; **in
comparison (with)** in confronto (a)

compartment [kəm'pɑːtmənt] *n*
compartimento; (*Rail*) scompartimento; **a
non-smoking ~** uno scompartimento per
non-fumatori

compass ['kʌmpəs] *n* bussola; **~es** *npl*
(*Math*) compasso

compassion [kəm'pæʃən] *n* compassione
f

compatible [kəm'pætɪbl] *adj* compatibile

compel [kəm'pεl] *vt* costringere,
obbligare; **compelling** *adj* (*fig: argument*)
irresistibile

compensate ['kɔmpənseɪt] *vt* risarcire
▷ *vi* **to ~ for** compensare; **compensation**
[-'seɪʃən] *n* compensazione *f*; (*money*)
risarcimento

compete [kəm'piːt] *vi* (*take part*)
concorrere; (*vie*): **to ~ with** fare
concorrenza (a)

competent ['kɔmpɪtənt] *adj* competente

competition [kɔmpɪ'tɪʃən] *n* gara;
concorso; (*Econ*) concorrenza

competitive [kəm'pεtɪtɪv] *adj* (*Econ*)
concorrenziale; (*sport*) agonistico(-a);
(*person*) che ha spirito di competizione; che
ha spirito agonistico

competitor [kəm'pεtɪtər] *n* concorrente
m/f

complacent [kəm'pleɪsnt] *adj*
compiaciuto(-a) di sé

complain [kəm'pleɪn] *vi* lagnarsi,
lamentarsi; **complaint** *n* lamento; (*in
shop etc*) reclamo; (*Med*) malattia

complement [*n* 'kɔmplɪmənt, *vb*
'kɔmplɪmεnt] *n* complemento; (*especially
of ship's crew etc*) effettivo ▷ *vt* (*enhance*)
accompagnarsi bene a; **complementary**

[kɔmplɪ'mɛntərɪ] *adj* complementare
complete [kəm'pliːt] *adj* completo(-a)
▷ *vt* completare; *(a form)* riempire;
completely *adv* completamente;
completion *n* completamento
complex ['kɔmplɛks] *adj* complesso(-a)
▷ *n* (*Psych, of buildings etc*) complesso
complexion [kəm'plɛkʃən] *n* (*of face*)
carnagione *f*
compliance [kəm'plaɪəns] *n*
acquiescenza; **in ~ with** (*orders, wishes etc*)
in conformità con
complicate ['kɔmplɪkeɪt] *vt* complicare;
complicated *adj* complicato(-a);
complication [-'keɪʃən] *n* complicazione *f*
compliment [*n* 'kɔmplɪmənt, *vb*
'kɔmplɪmɛnt] *n* complimento ▷ *vt* fare
un complimento a; **complimentary**
[-'mɛntərɪ] *adj* complimentoso(-a),
elogiativo(-a); *(free)* in omaggio
comply [kəm'plaɪ] *vi* **to ~ with** assentire
a; conformarsi a
component [kəm'pəunənt] *adj*
componente ▷ *n* componente *m*
compose [kəm'pəuz] *vt* (*form*): **to be ~d
of** essere composto di; (*music, poem etc*)
comporre; **to ~ o.s.** ricomporsi; **composer**
n (*Mus*) compositore(-trice); **composition**
[kɔmpə'zɪʃən] *n* composizione *f*
composure [kəm'pəuʒə^r] *n* calma
compound ['kɔmpaund] *n* (*Chem, Ling*)
composto; (*enclosure*) recinto ▷ *adj*
composto(-a)
comprehension [kɔmprɪ'hɛnʃən] *n*
comprensione *f*
comprehensive [kɔmprɪ'hɛnsɪv] *adj*
completo(-a); **comprehensive (school)**
(BRIT) *n* scuola secondaria aperta a tutti
> Be careful not to translate
> **comprehensive** by the Italian word
> **comprensivo**.
compress [*vb* kəm'prɛs, *n* 'kɔmprɛs] *vt*
comprimere ▷ *n* (*Med*) compressa
comprise [kəm'praɪz] *vt* (*also*: **be ~d**)
comprendere
compromise ['kɔmprəmaɪz] *n*
compromesso ▷ *vt* compromettere ▷ *vi*
venire a un compromesso
compulsive [kəm'pʌlsɪv] *adj* (*liar, gambler*)
che non riesce a controllarsi; (*viewing,
reading*) cui non si può fare a meno
compulsory [kəm'pʌlsərɪ] *adj*
obbligatorio(-a)
computer [kəm'pjuːtə^r] *n* computer
m inv, elaboratore *m* elettronico;
computer game *n* gioco per computer;
computer-generated *adj* realizzato(-a)
al computer; **computerize** *vt*
computerizzare; **computer programmer**

n programmatore(-trice); **computer
programming** *n* programmazione
f di computer; **computer science** *n*
informatica; **computer studies** *npl*
informatica; **computing** *n* informatica
con [kɔn] (*inf*) *vt* truffare ▷ *n* truffa
conceal [kən'siːl] *vt* nascondere
concede [kən'siːd] *vt* ammettere
conceited [kən'siːtɪd] *adj*
presuntuoso(-a), vanitoso(-a)
conceive [kən'siːv] *vt* concepire ▷ *vi*
concepire un bambino
concentrate ['kɔnsəntreɪt] *vi*
concentrarsi ▷ *vt* concentrare
concentration [kɔnsən'treɪʃən] *n*
concentrazione *f*
concept ['kɔnsɛpt] *n* concetto
concern [kən'səːn] *n* affare *m*; (*Comm*)
azienda, ditta; (*anxiety*) preoccupazione
f ▷ *vt* riguardare; **to be ~ed (about)**
preoccuparsi (di); **concerning** *prep*
riguardo a, circa
concert ['kɔnsət] *n* concerto; **concert
hall** *n* sala da concerti
concerto [kən'tʃəːtəu] *n* concerto
concession [kən'sɛʃən] *n* concessione *f*
concise [kən'saɪs] *adj* conciso(-a)
conclude [kən'kluːd] *vt* concludere;
conclusion [-'kluːʒən] *n* conclusione *f*
concrete ['kɔnkriːt] *n* calcestruzzo ▷ *adj*
concreto(-a), di calcestruzzo
concussion [kən'kʌʃən] *n* commozione
f cerebrale
condemn [kən'dɛm] *vt* condannare;
(*building*) dichiarare pericoloso(-a)
condensation [kɔndɛn'seɪʃən] *n*
condensazione *f*
condense [kən'dɛns] *vi* condensarsi ▷ *vt*
condensare
condition [kən'dɪʃən] *n* condizione *f*;
(*Med*) malattia ▷ *vt* condizionare; **on ~
that** a condizione che + *sub*, a condizione
di; **conditional** *adj* condizionale; **to
be conditional upon** dipendere da;
conditioner *n* (*for hair*) balsamo; (*for
fabrics*) ammorbidente *m*
condo ['kɔndəu] (*US*) *n abbr* (*inf*)
= **condominium**
condom ['kɔndəm] *n* preservativo
condominium [kɔndə'mɪnɪəm] (*US*) *n*
condominio
condone [kən'dəun] *vt* condonare
conduct [*n* 'kɔndʌkt, *vb* kən'dʌkt]
n condotta ▷ *vt* condurre; (*manage*)
dirigere; amministrare; (*Mus*) dirigere;
to ~ o.s. comportarsi; **conducted tour**
[kən'dʌktɪd-] *n* gita accompagnata;
conductor *n* (*of orchestra*) direttore *m*
d'orchestra; (*on bus*) bigliettaio; (*US*: *on*

train) controllore *m*; (*Elec*) conduttore *m*
cone [kəun] *n* cono; (*Bot*) pigna; (*traffic cone*) birillo
confectionery [kən'fɛkʃənrɪ] *n* dolciumi *mpl*
confer [kən'fəːʳ] *vt* **to ~ sth on** conferire qc a ▷ *vi* conferire
conference ['kɔnfərns] *n* congresso
confess [kən'fɛs] *vt* confessare, ammettere ▷ *vi* confessare; **confession** [kən'fɛʃən] *n* confessione *f*
confide [kən'faɪd] *vi* **to ~ in** confidarsi con
confidence ['kɔnfɪdns] *n* confidenza; (*trust*) fiducia; (*self-assurance*) sicurezza di sé; **in ~** (*speak, write*) in confidenza, confidenzialmente; **confident** *adj* sicuro(-a), sicuro(-a) di sé; **confidential** [kɔnfɪ'dɛnʃəl] *adj* riservato(-a), confidenziale
confine [kən'faɪn] *vt* limitare; (*shut up*) rinchiudere; **confined** *adj* (*space*) ristretto(-a)
confirm [kən'fəːm] *vt* confermare; **confirmation** [kɔnfə'meɪʃən] *n* conferma; (*Rel*) cresima
confiscate ['kɔnfɪskeɪt] *vt* confiscare
conflict [*n* 'kɔnflɪkt, *vb* kən'flɪkt] *n* conflitto ▷ *vi* essere in conflitto
conform [kən'fɔːm] *vi* **to ~ to** conformarsi (a)
confront [kən'frʌnt] *vt* (*enemy, danger*) affrontare; **confrontation** [kɔnfrən'teɪʃən] *n* scontro
confuse [kən'fjuːz] *vt* (*one thing with another*) confondere; **confused** *adj* confuso(-a); **confusing** *adj* che fa confondere; **confusion** [-'fjuːʒən] *n* confusione *f*
congestion [kən'dʒɛstʃən] *n* congestione *f*
congratulate [kən'grætjuleɪt] *vt* **to ~ sb (on)** congratularsi con qn (per *or* di); **congratulations** [-'leɪʃənz] *npl* auguri *mpl*; (*on success*) complimenti *mpl*, congratulazioni *fpl*
congregation [kɔŋgrɪ'geɪʃən] *n* congregazione *f*
congress ['kɔŋgrɛs] *n* congresso; **congressman** (*irreg*: *us*) *n* membro del Congresso; **congresswoman** (*irreg*: *us*) *n* (donna) membro del Congresso
conifer ['kɔnɪfəʳ] *n* conifero
conjugate ['kɔndʒugeɪt] *vt* coniugare
conjugation [kɔndʒə'geɪʃən] *n* coniugazione *f*
conjunction [kən'dʒʌŋkʃən] *n* congiunzione *f*
conjure ['kʌndʒəʳ] *vi* fare giochi di prestigio

connect [kə'nɛkt] *vt* connettere, collegare; (*Elec, Tel*) collegare; (*fig*) associare ▷ *vi* (*train*): **to ~ with** essere in coincidenza con; **to be ~ed with** (*associated*) aver rapporti con; **connecting flight** *n* volo in coincidenza; **connection** [-ʃən] ▷ *n* relazione *f*, rapporto; (*Elec*) connessione *f*; (*train, plane*) coincidenza; (*Tel*) collegamento
conquer ['kɔŋkəʳ] *vt* conquistare; (*feelings*) vincere
conquest ['kɔŋkwɛst] *n* conquista
cons [kɔnz] *npl see* **convenience**; **pro**
conscience ['kɔnʃəns] *n* coscienza
conscientious [kɔnʃɪ'ɛnʃəs] *adj* coscienzioso(-a)
conscious ['kɔnʃəs] *adj* consapevole; (*Med*) cosciente; **consciousness** *n* consapevolezza; coscienza
consecutive [kən'sɛkjutɪv] *adj* consecutivo(-a); **on 3 ~ occasions** 3 volte di fila
consensus [kən'sɛnsəs] *n* consenso; **the ~ of opinion** l'opinione *f* unanime *or* comune
consent [kən'sɛnt] *n* consenso ▷ *vi* **to ~ (to)** acconsentire (a)
consequence ['kɔnsɪkwəns] *n* conseguenza, risultato; importanza
consequently ['kɔnsɪkwəntlɪ] *adv* di conseguenza, dunque
conservation [kɔnsə'veɪʃən] *n* conservazione *f*
conservative [kən'səːvətɪv] *adj* conservatore(-trice); (*cautious*) cauto(-a); **Conservative** (*BRIT*) *adj, n* (*Pol*) conservatore(-trice)
conservatory [kən'səːvətrɪ] *n* (*greenhouse*) serra; (*Mus*) conservatorio
consider [kən'sɪdəʳ] *vt* considerare; (*take into account*) tener conto di; **to ~ doing sth** considerare la possibilità di fare qc; **considerable** [kən'sɪdərəbl] *adj* considerevole, notevole; **considerably** *adv* notevolmente, decisamente; **considerate** [kən'sɪdərɪt] *adj* premuroso(-a); **consideration** [kənsɪdə'reɪʃən] *n* considerazione *f*; **considering** [kən'sɪdərɪŋ] *prep* in considerazione di
consignment [kən'saɪnmənt] *n* (*of goods*) consegna; spedizione *f*
consist [kən'sɪst] *vi* **to ~ of** constare di, essere composto(-a) di
consistency [kən'sɪstənsɪ] *n* consistenza; (*fig*) coerenza
consistent [kən'sɪstənt] *adj* coerente
consolation [kɔnsə'leɪʃən] *n* consolazione *f*
console¹ [kən'səul] *vt* consolare

console² ['kɔnsəul] n quadro di comando
consonant ['kɔnsənənt] n consonante f
conspicuous [kən'spɪkjuəs] adj
  cospicuo(-a)
conspiracy [kən'spɪrəsɪ] n congiura,
  cospirazione f
constable ['kʌnstəbl] (BRIT) n ≈ poliziotto,
  agente m di polizia; **chief ~** ≈ questore m
constant ['kɔnstənt] adj costante,
  continuo(-a); **constantly** adv
  costantemente; continuamente
constipated ['kɔnstɪpeɪtɪd] adj
  stitico(-a); **constipation** [kɔnstɪ'peɪʃən]
  n stitichezza
constituency [kən'stɪtjuənsɪ] n collegio
  elettorale
constitute ['kɔnstɪtjuːt] vt costituire
constitution [kɔnstɪ'tjuːʃən] n
  costituzione f
constraint [kən'streɪnt] n costrizione f
construct [kən'strʌkt] vt costruire;
  construction [-ʃən] n costruzione f;
  constructive adj costruttivo(-a)
consul ['kɔnsl] n console m; **consulate**
  ['kɔnsjulɪt] n consolato
consult [kən'sʌlt] vt consultare;
  consultant n (Med) consulente m medico;
  (other specialist) consulente; **consultation**
  [-'teɪʃən] n (Med) consulto; (discussion)
  consultazione f; **consulting room** [kə
  n'sʌltɪŋ-] (BRIT) n ambulatorio
consume [kən'sjuːm] vt consumare;
  consumer n consumatore(-trice)
consumption [kən'sʌmpʃən] n consumo
cont. abbr = **continued**
contact ['kɔntækt] n contatto; (person)
  conoscenza ▷ vt mettersi in contatto con;
  contact lenses npl lenti fpl a contatto
contagious [kən'teɪdʒəs] adj (also fig)
  contagioso(-a)
contain [kən'teɪn] vt contenere; **to ~ o.s.**
  contenersi; **container** n recipiente m; (for
  shipping etc) container m inv
contaminate [kən'tæmɪneɪt] vt
  contaminare
cont'd abbr = **continued**
contemplate ['kɔntəmpleɪt] vt
  contemplare; (consider) pensare a (or di)
contemporary [kən'tɛmpərərɪ] adj, n
  contemporaneo(-a)
contempt [kən'tɛmpt] n disprezzo; **~ of
  court** (Law) oltraggio alla Corte
contend [kən'tɛnd] vt **to ~ that** sostenere
  che ▷ vi **to ~ with** lottare contro
content¹ ['kɔntɛnt] n contenuto; **~s** npl
  (of box, case etc) contenuto; **(table of) ~s**
  indice m
content² [kən'tɛnt] adj contento(-a),
  soddisfatto(-a) ▷ vt contentare,

soddisfare; **contented** adj contento(-a),
  soddisfatto(-a)
contest [n 'kɔntɛst, vb kən'tɛst] n
  lotta; (competition) gara, concorso ▷ vt
  contestare; impugnare; (compete for)
  essere in lizza per; **contestant** [kə
  n'tɛstənt] n concorrente m/f; (in fight)
  avversario(-a)
context ['kɔntɛkst] n contesto
continent ['kɔntɪnənt] n continente
  m; **the C~** (BRIT) l'Europa continentale;
  continental [-'nɛntl] adj continentale;
  continental breakfast n colazione f
  all'europea (senza piatti caldi); **continental
  quilt** (BRIT) n piumino
continual [kən'tɪnjuəl] adj continuo(-a);
  continually adv di continuo
continue [kən'tɪnjuː] vi continuare ▷ vt
  continuare; (start again) riprendere
continuity [kɔntɪ'njuːɪtɪ] n continuità;
  (TV, Cinema) (ordine m della) sceneggiatura
continuous [kən'tɪnjuəs] adj
  continuo(-a), ininterrotto(-a); **continuous
  assessment** n (BRIT) valutazione f
  continua; **continuously** adv (repeatedly)
  continuamente; (uninterruptedly)
  ininterrottamente
contour ['kɔntuər] n contorno, profilo;
  (also: **~ line**) curva di livello
contraception [kɔntrə'sɛpʃən] n
  contraccezione f
contraceptive [kɔntrə'sɛptɪv] adj
  contraccettivo(-a) ▷ n contraccettivo
contract [n 'kɔntrækt, vb kən'trækt] n
  contratto ▷ vi (become smaller) contrarsi;
  (Comm): **to ~ to do sth** fare un contratto
  per fare qc ▷ vt (illness) contrarre;
  contractor n imprenditore m
contradict [kɔntrə'dɪkt] vt contraddire;
  contradiction [kɔntrə'dɪkʃən] n
  contraddizione f; **to be in contradiction
  with** discordare con
contrary¹ ['kɔntrərɪ] adj contrario(-a);
  (unfavourable) avverso(-a), contrario(-a)
  ▷ n contrario; **on the ~** al contrario;
  unless you hear to the ~ salvo
  contrordine
contrary² [kən'trɛərɪ] adj (perverse)
  bisbetico(-a)
contrast [n 'kɔntrɑːst, vb kən'trɑːst] n
  contrasto ▷ vt mettere in contrasto; **in ~
  to** contrariamente a
contribute [kən'trɪbjuːt] vi contribuire
  ▷ vt **to ~ £10/an article to** dare
  10 sterline/un articolo a; **to ~ to**
  contribuire a; (newspaper) scrivere
  per; **contribution** [kɔntrɪ'bjuːʃən] n
  contributo; **contributor** n (to newspaper)
  collaboratore(-trice)

control [kən'trəul] vt controllare; (firm, operation etc) dirigere ▷ n controllo; **~s** npl (of vehicle etc) comandi mpl; (governmental) controlli mpl; **under ~** sotto controllo; **to be in ~ of** avere il controllo di; **to go out of ~** (car) non rispondere ai comandi; (situation) sfuggire di mano; **control tower** n (Aviat) torre f di controllo

controversial [kɔntrə'və:ʃl] adj controverso(-a), polemico(-a)

controversy ['kɔntrəvə:sɪ] n controversia, polemica

convenience [kən'vi:nɪəns] n comodità f inv; **at your ~** a suo comodo; **all modern ~s** (BRIT), **all mod cons** tutte le comodità moderne

convenient [kən'vi:nɪənt] adj comodo(-a)

> Be careful not to translate convenient by the Italian word conveniente.

convent ['kɔnvənt] n convento

convention [kən'venʃən] n convenzione f; (meeting) convegno; **conventional** adj convenzionale

conversation [kɔnvə'seɪʃən] n conversazione f

conversely [kɔn'və:slɪ] adv al contrario, per contro

conversion [kən'və:ʃən] n conversione f; (BRIT: of house) trasformazione f, rimodernamento

convert [vb kən'və:t, n 'kɔnvə:t] vt (Comm, Rel) convertire; (alter) trasformare ▷ n convertito(-a); **convertible** n macchina decappottabile

convey [kən'veɪ] vt trasportare; (thanks) comunicare; (idea) dare; **conveyor belt** [kən'veɪər-] n nastro trasportatore

convict [vb kən'vɪkt, n 'kɔnvɪkt] vt dichiarare colpevole ▷ n carcerato(-a); **conviction** [-ʃən] n condanna; (belief) convinzione f

convince [kən'vɪns] vt convincere, persuadere; **convinced** adj **convinced of/that** convinto(-a) di/che; **convincing** adj convincente

convoy ['kɔnvɔɪ] n convoglio

cook [kuk] vt cucinare, cuocere ▷ vi cuocere; (person) cucinare ▷ n cuoco(-a); **cook book** n libro di cucina; **cooker** n fornello, cucina; **cookery** n cucina; **cookery book** (BRIT) n = **cook book**; **cookie** (US) n biscotto; **cooking** n cucina

cool [ku:l] adj fresco(-a); (not afraid, calm) calmo(-a); (unfriendly) freddo(-a) ▷ vt raffreddare; (room) rinfrescare ▷ vi (water) raffreddarsi; (air) rinfrescarsi; **cool down** vi raffreddarsi; (fig: person, situation) calmarsi; **cool off** vi (become calmer) calmarsi; (lose enthusiasm) perdere interesse

cop [kɔp] (inf) n sbirro

cope [kəup] vi **to ~ with** (problems) far fronte a

copper ['kɔpər] n rame m; (inf: policeman) sbirro

copy ['kɔpɪ] n copia ▷ vt copiare; **copyright** n diritto d'autore

coral ['kɔrəl] n corallo

cord [kɔ:d] n corda; (Elec) filo; **~s** npl (trousers) calzoni mpl (di velluto) a coste; **cordless** adj senza cavo

corduroy ['kɔ:dərɔɪ] n fustagno

core [kɔ:r] n (of fruit) torsolo; (of organization etc) cuore m ▷ vt estrarre il torsolo da

coriander [kɔrɪ'ændər] n coriandolo

cork [kɔ:k] n sughero; (of bottle) tappo; **corkscrew** n cavatappi m inv

corn [kɔ:n] n (BRIT: wheat) grano; (US: maize) granturco; (on foot) callo; **~ on the cob** (Culin) pannocchia cotta

corned beef ['kɔ:nd-] n carne f di manzo in scatola

corner ['kɔ:nər] n angolo; (Aut) curva ▷ vt intrappolare; mettere con le spalle al muro; (Comm: market) accaparrare ▷ vi prendere una curva

corner shop (BRIT) piccolo negozio di generi alimentari

cornflakes ['kɔ:nfleɪks] npl fiocchi mpl di granturco

cornflour ['kɔ:nflauər] (BRIT) n farina finissima di granturco

cornstarch ['kɔ:nstɑ:tʃ] (US) n = **cornflour**

Cornwall ['kɔ:nwəl] n Cornovaglia

coronary ['kɔrənərɪ] n **~ (thrombosis)** trombosi f coronaria

coronation [kɔrə'neɪʃən] n incoronazione f

coroner ['kɔrənər] n magistrato incaricato di indagare la causa di morte in circostanze sospette

corporal ['kɔ:pərl] n caporalmaggiore m ▷ adj **~ punishment** pena corporale

corporate ['kɔ:pərɪt] adj costituito(-a) (in corporazione), comune

corporation [kɔ:pə'reɪʃən] n (of town) consiglio comunale; (Comm) ente m

corps [kɔ:, pl kɔ:z] n inv corpo

corpse [kɔ:ps] n cadavere m

correct [kə'rɛkt] adj (accurate) corretto(-a), esatto(-a); (proper) corretto(-a) ▷ vt correggere; **correction** [-ʃən] n correzione f

correspond [kɔrɪs'pɔnd] vi corrispondere; **correspondence** n corrispondenza; **correspondent** n corrispondente m/f; **corresponding** adj corrispondente

corridor ['kɒrɪdɔːʳ] *n* corridoio
corrode [kə'rəud] *vt* corrodere ▷ *vi*
corrodersi
corrupt [kə'rʌpt] *adj* corrotto(-a); (*Comput*)
alterato(-a) ▷ *vt* corrompere; **corruption**
n corruzione *f*
Corsica ['kɔːsɪkə] *n* Corsica
cosmetic [kɔz'mɛtɪk] *n* cosmetico ▷ *adj*
(*fig: measure etc*) superficiale; **cosmetic
surgery** *n* chirurgia plastica
cosmopolitan [kɔzmə'pɒlɪtn] *adj*
cosmopolita
cost [kɔst] (*pt, pp* **cost**) *n* costo ▷ *vt*
costare; (*find out the cost of*) stabilire il
prezzo di; **~s** *npl* (*Comm, Law*) spese *fpl*;
how much does it ~? quanto costa?; **at all
~s** a ogni costo
co-star ['kəustɑːʳ] *n* attore/trice della stessa
importanza del protagonista
Costa Rica ['kɔstə'riːkə] *n* Costa Rica
costly ['kɔstlɪ] *adj* costoso(-a), caro(-a)
cost of living *adj* **~ allowance** indennità *f*
inv di contingenza
costume ['kɔstjuːm] *n* costume *m*; (*lady's
suit*) tailleur *m inv*; (*BRIT: also:* **swimming
~**) costume *m* da bagno
cosy ['kəuzɪ] (*US* **cozy**) *adj* intimo(-a); **I'm
very ~ here** sto proprio bene qui
cot [kɔt] *n* (*BRIT: child's*) lettino; (*US:
campbed*) brandina
cottage ['kɔtɪdʒ] *n* cottage *m inv*; **cottage
cheese** *n* fiocchi *mpl* di latte magro
cotton ['kɔtn] *n* cotone *m*; **cotton on** *vi*
(*inf*): **to ~ on (to sth)** afferrare (qc); **cotton
bud** *n* (*BRIT*) cotton fioc® *m inv*; **cotton
candy** (*US*) *n* zucchero filato; **cotton wool**
(*BRIT*) *n* cotone idrofilo
couch [kautʃ] *n* sofà *m inv*
cough [kɔf] *vi* tossire ▷ *n* tosse *f*; **I've got
a ~** ho la tosse; **cough mixture, cough
syrup** *n* sciroppo per la tosse
could [kud] *pt of* **can²**
couldn't = **could not**
council ['kaunsl] *n* consiglio; **city** or
town ~ consiglio comunale; **council
estate** (*BRIT*) *n* quartiere *m* di case
popolari; **council house** (*BRIT*) *n* casa
popolare; **councillor** (*US* **councilor**) *n*
consigliere(-a); **council tax** *n* (*BRIT*) *tassa
comunale sulla proprietà*
counsel ['kaunsl] *n* avvocato;
consultazione *f* ▷ *vt* consigliare;
counselling (*US* **counseling**) *n* (*Psych*)
assistenza psicologica; **counsellor**
(*US* **counselor**) *n* consigliere(-a); (*US*)
avvocato
count [kaunt] *vt, vi* contare ▷ *n* (*of votes etc*)
conteggio; (*of pollen etc*) livello; (*nobleman*)
conte *m*; **count in** (*inf*) *vt* includere; **~ me**

in ci sto anch'io; **count on** *vt fus* contare
su; **countdown** *n* conto alla rovescia
counter ['kauntəʳ] *n* banco ▷ *vt* opporsi
a ▷ *adv* **~ to** contro; in opposizione a;
counter clockwise
[-'klɒkwaɪz] (*US*) *adv* in senso antiorario
counterfeit ['kauntəfɪt] *n* contraffazione
f, falso ▷ *vt* contraffare, falsificare ▷ *adj*
falso(-a)
counterpart ['kauntəpɑːt] *n* (*of document
etc*) copia; (*of person*) corrispondente *m/f*
countess ['kauntɪs] *n* contessa
countless ['kauntlɪs] *adj* innumerevole
country ['kʌntrɪ] *n* paese *m*; (*native land*)
patria; (*as opposed to town*) campagna;
(*region*) regione *f*; **country and western
(music)** *n* musica country e western,
country *m*; **country house** *n* villa in
campagna; **countryside** *n* campagna
county ['kauntɪ] *n* contea
coup [kuː] (*pl* **coups**) *n* colpo; (*also:* **~
d'état**) colpo di Stato
couple ['kʌpl] *n* coppia; **a ~ of** un paio di
coupon ['kuːpɒn] *n* buono; (*detachable
form*) coupon *m inv*
courage ['kʌrɪdʒ] *n* coraggio; **courageous**
adj coraggioso(-a)
courgette [kuə'ʒɛt] (*BRIT*) *n* zucchina
courier ['kurɪəʳ] *n* corriere *m*; (*for tourists*)
guida
course [kɔːs] *n* corso; (*of ship*) rotta; (*for
golf*) campo; (*part of meal*) piatto; **of ~**
senz'altro, naturalmente; **~ of action**
modo d'agire; **a ~ of treatment** (*Med*)
una cura
court [kɔːt] *n* corte *f*; (*Tennis*) campo ▷ *vt*
(*woman*) fare la corte a; **to take to ~** citare
in tribunale
courtesy ['kəːtəsɪ] *n* cortesia; **(by) ~ of**
per gentile concessione di; **courtesy bus,
courtesy coach** *n* autobus *m inv* gratuito
(*di hotel, aeroporto*)
court: **court-house** (*US*) *n* palazzo di
giustizia; **courtroom** *n* tribunale *m*;
courtyard *n* cortile *m*
cousin ['kʌzn] *n* cugino(-a); **first ~** cugino
di primo grado
cover ['kʌvəʳ] *vt* coprire; (*book, table*)
rivestire; (*include*) comprendere; (*Press*)
fare un servizio su ▷ *n* (*of pan*) coperchio;
(*over furniture*) fodera; (*of bed*) copriletto;
(*of book*) copertina; (*shelter*) riparo; (*Comm,
Insurance, of spy*) copertura; **~s** *npl* (*on
bed*) lenzuola *fpl* e coperte *fpl*; **to take ~**
(*shelter*) ripararsi; **under ~** al riparo; **under
~ of darkness** protetto dall'oscurità;
under separate ~ (*Comm*) a parte, in
plico separato; **cover up** *vi* **to ~ up for
sb** coprire qn; **coverage** *n* (*Press, Radio,*

_TV_): **to give full coverage to sth** fare un ampio servizio su qc; **cover charge** _n_ coperto; **cover-up** _n_ occultamento (di informazioni)

cow [kau] _n_ vacca ▷ _vt_ (_person_) intimidire

coward ['kauəd] _n_ vigliacco(-a); **cowardly** _adj_ vigliacco(-a)

cowboy ['kaubɔɪ] _n_ cow-boy _m inv_

cozy ['kəuzɪ] (_US_) _adj_ = **cosy**

crab [kræb] _n_ granchio

crack [kræk] _n_ fessura, crepa; incrinatura; (_noise_) schiocco; (: _of gun_) scoppio; (_drug_) crack _m inv_ ▷ _vt_ spaccare; incrinare; (_whip_) schioccare; (_nut_) schiacciare; (_problem_) risolvere; (_code_) decifrare ▷ _adj_ (_troops_) fuori classe; **to ~ a joke** fare una battuta; **crack down on** _vt fus_ porre freno a; **cracked** _adj_ (_inf_) matto(-a); **cracker** _n_ cracker _m inv_; petardo

crackle ['krækl] _vi_ crepitare

cradle ['kreɪdl] _n_ culla

craft [krɑːft] _n_ mestiere _m_; (_cunning_) astuzia; (_boat_) naviglio; **craftsman** (_irreg_) _n_ artigiano; **craftsmanship** _n_ abilità

cram [kræm] _vt_ (_fill_): **to ~ sth with** riempire qc di; (_put_): **to ~ sth into** stipare qc in ▷ _vi_ (_for exams_) prepararsi (in gran fretta)

cramp [kræmp] _n_ crampo; **I've got ~ in my leg** ho un crampo alla gamba; **cramped** _adj_ ristretto(-a)

cranberry ['krænbərɪ] _n_ mirtillo

crane [kreɪn] _n_ gru _f inv_

crap [kræp] _n_ (_inf!_) fesserie _fpl_; **to have a ~** cacare (!)

crash [kræʃ] _n_ fragore _m_; (_of car_) incidente _m_; (_of plane_) caduta; (_of business etc_) crollo ▷ _vt_ fracassare ▷ _vi_ (_plane_) fracassarsi; (_car_) avere un incidente; (_two cars_) scontrarsi; (_business etc_) fallire, andare in rovina; **crash course** _n_ corso intensivo; **crash helmet** _n_ casco

crate [kreɪt] _n_ cassa

crave [kreɪv] _vt, vi_ **to ~ (for)** desiderare ardentemente

crawl [krɔːl] _vi_ strisciare carponi; (_vehicle_) avanzare lentamente ▷ _n_ (_Swimming_) crawl _m_

crayfish ['kreɪfɪʃ] _n inv_ (_freshwater_) gambero (d'acqua dolce); (_saltwater_) gambero

crayon ['kreɪən] _n_ matita colorata

craze [kreɪz] _n_ mania

crazy ['kreɪzɪ] _adj_ matto(-a); (_inf: keen_): **~ about sb** pazzo(-a) di qn; **~ about sth** matto(-a) per qc

creak [kriːk] _vi_ cigolare, scricchiolare

cream [kriːm] _n_ crema; (_fresh_) panna ▷ _adj_ (_colour_) color crema _inv_; **cream cheese** _n_ formaggio fresco; **creamy** _adj_ cremoso(-a)

crease [kriːs] _n_ grinza; (_deliberate_) piega ▷ _vt_ sgualcire ▷ _vi_ sgualcirsi

create [kriː'eɪt] _vt_ creare; **creation** [-ʃən] _n_ creazione _f_; **creative** _adj_ creativo(-a); **creator** _n_ creatore(-trice)

creature ['kriːtʃə˙] _n_ creatura

crèche [krɛʃ] _n_ asilo infantile

credentials [krɪ'dɛnʃlz] _npl_ credenziali _fpl_

credibility [krɛdɪ'bɪlɪtɪ] _n_ credibilità

credible ['krɛdɪbl] _adj_ credibile; (_witness, source_) attendibile

credit ['krɛdɪt] _n_ credito; onore _m_ ▷ _vt_ (_Comm_) accreditare; (_believe: also:_ **give ~ to**) credere, prestar fede a; **~s** _npl_ (_Cinema_) titoli _mpl_; **to ~ sb with** (_fig_) attribuire a qn; **to be in ~** (_person_) essere creditore(-trice); (_bank account_) essere coperto(-a); **credit card** _n_ carta di credito; **do you take credit cards?** accettate carte di credito?

creek [kriːk] _n_ insenatura; (_US_) piccolo fiume _m_

creep [kriːp] (_pt, pp_ **crept**) _vi_ avanzare furtivamente (_or_ pian piano)

cremate [krɪ'meɪt] _vt_ cremare

crematorium [krɛmə'tɔːrɪəm] (_pl_ **crematoria**) _n_ forno crematorio

crept [krɛpt] _pt, pp of_ **creep**

crescent ['krɛsnt] _n_ (_shape_) mezzaluna; (_street_) strada semicircolare

cress [krɛs] _n_ crescione _m_

crest [krɛst] _n_ cresta; (_of coat of arms_) cimiero

crew [kruː] _n_ equipaggio; **crew-neck** _n_ girocollo

crib [krɪb] _n_ culla ▷ _vt_ (_inf_) copiare

cricket ['krɪkɪt] _n_ (_insect_) grillo; (_game_) cricket _m_; **cricketer** _n_ giocatore _m_ di cricket

crime [kraɪm] _n_ crimine _m_; **criminal** ['krɪmɪnl] _adj, n_ criminale _m/f_

crimson ['krɪmzn] _adj_ color cremisi _inv_

cringe [krɪndʒ] _vi_ acquattarsi; (_in embarrassment_) sentirsi sprofondare

cripple ['krɪpl] _n_ zoppo(-a) ▷ _vt_ azzoppare

crisis ['kraɪsɪs] (_pl_ **crises**) _n_ crisi _f inv_

crisp [krɪsp] _adj_ croccante; (_fig_) frizzante; vivace; deciso(-a); **crispy** _adj_ croccante

criterion [kraɪ'tɪərɪən] (_pl_ **criteria**) _n_ criterio

critic ['krɪtɪk] _n_ critico; **critical** _adj_ critico(-a); **criticism** ['krɪtɪsɪzm] _n_ critica; **criticize** ['krɪtɪsaɪz] _vt_ criticare

Croat ['krəuæt] _adj, n_ = **Croatian**

Croatia [krəu'eɪʃə] _n_ Croazia; **Croatian** _adj_ croato(-a) ▷ _n_ croato(-a); (_Ling_) croato

crockery ['krɒkərɪ] _n_ vasellame _m_

crocodile ['krɒkədaɪl] _n_ coccodrillo

crocus ['krəukəs] n croco
croissant ['krwas] n brioche f inv, croissant m inv
crook [kruk] n truffatore m; (of shepherd) bastone m; **crooked** ['krukɪd] adj curvo(-a), storto(-a); (action) disonesto(-a)
crop [krɔp] n (produce) coltivazione f; (amount produced) raccolto; (riding crop) frustino ▷ vt (hair) rapare; **crop up** vi presentarsi
cross [krɔs] n croce f; (Biol) incrocio ▷ vt (street etc) attraversare; (arms, legs, Biol) incrociare; (cheque) sbarrare ▷ adj di cattivo umore; **cross off** vt cancellare (tirando una riga con la penna); **cross out** vt cancellare; **cross over** vi attraversare; **cross-Channel ferry** ['krɔs'tʃænl-] n traghetto che attraversa la Manica; **crosscountry (race)** n cross-country m inv; **crossing** n incrocio; (sea passage) traversata; (also: **pedestrian crossing**) passaggio pedonale; **how long does the crossing take?** quanto dura la traversata?; **crossing guard** (US) n dipendente comunale che aiuta i bambini ad attraversare la strada; **crossroads** n incrocio; **crosswalk** (US) n strisce fpl pedonali, passaggio pedonale; **crossword** n cruciverba m inv
crotch [krɔtʃ] n (Anat) inforcatura; (of garment) pattina
crouch [krautʃ] vi acquattarsi; rannicchiarsi
crouton ['kru:tɔn] n crostino
crow [krəu] n (bird) cornacchia; (of cock) canto del gallo ▷ vi (cock) cantare
crowd [kraud] n folla ▷ vt affollare, stipare ▷ vi **to ~ round/in** affollarsi intorno a/in; **crowded** adj affollato(-a); **crowded with** stipato(-a) di
crown [kraun] n corona; (of head) calotta cranica; (of hat) cocuzzolo; (of hill) cima ▷ vt incoronare; (fig: career) coronare; **crown jewels** npl gioielli mpl della Corona
crucial ['kru:ʃl] adj cruciale, decisivo(-a)
crucifix ['kru:sɪfɪks] n crocifisso
crude [kru:d] adj (materials) greggio(-a), non raffinato(-a); (fig: basic) crudo(-a), primitivo(-a); (: vulgar) rozzo(-a), grossolano(-a); **crude (oil)** n (petrolio) greggio
cruel ['kruəl] adj crudele; **cruelty** n crudeltà f inv
cruise [kru:z] n crociera ▷ vi andare a velocità di crociera; (taxi) circolare
crumb [krʌm] n briciola
crumble ['krʌmbl] vt sbriciolare ▷ vi sbriciolarsi; (plaster etc) sgretolarsi; (land, earth) franare; (building, fig) crollare
crumpet ['krʌmpɪt] n specie di frittella

crumple ['krʌmpl] vt raggrinzare, spiegazzare
crunch [krʌntʃ] vt sgranocchiare; (underfoot) scricchiolare ▷ n (fig) punto or momento cruciale; **crunchy** adj croccante
crush [krʌʃ] n folla; (love): **to have a ~ on sb** avere una cotta per qn; (drink): **lemon ~** spremuta di limone ▷ vt schiacciare; (crumple) sgualcire
crust [krʌst] n crosta; **crusty** adj (bread) croccante; (person) brontolone(-a); (remark) brusco(-a)
crutch [krʌtʃ] n gruccia
cry [kraɪ] vi piangere; (shout) urlare ▷ n urlo, grido; **cry out** vi, vt gridare
crystal ['krɪstl] n cristallo
cub [kʌb] n cucciolo; (also: ~ **scout**) lupetto
Cuba ['kju:bə] n Cuba
Cuban ['kju:bən] adj, n cubano(-a)
cube [kju:b] n cubo ▷ vt (Math) elevare al cubo; **cubic** adj cubico(-a); (metre, foot) cubo(-a)
cubicle ['kju:bɪkl] n scompartimento separato; cabina
cuckoo ['kuku:] n cucù m inv
cucumber ['kju:kʌmbəʳ] n cetriolo
cuddle ['kʌdl] vt abbracciare, coccolare ▷ vi abbracciarsi
cue [kju:] n (snooker cue) stecca; (Theatre etc) segnale m
cuff [kʌf] n (BRIT: of shirt, coat etc) polsino; (US: of trousers) risvolto; **off the ~** improvvisando; **cufflinks** npl gemelli mpl
cuisine [kwɪ'zi:n] n cucina
cul-de-sac ['kʌldəsæk] n vicolo cieco
cull [kʌl] vt (ideas etc) scegliere ▷ n (of animals) abbattimento selettivo
culminate ['kʌlmɪneɪt] vi **to ~ in** culminare con
culprit ['kʌlprɪt] n colpevole m/f
cult [kʌlt] n culto
cultivate ['kʌltɪveɪt] vt (also fig) coltivare
cultural ['kʌltʃərəl] adj culturale
culture ['kʌltʃəʳ] n (also fig) cultura
cumin ['kʌmɪn] n (spice) cumino
cunning ['kʌnɪŋ] n astuzia, furberia ▷ adj astuto(-a), furbo(-a)
cup [kʌp] n tazza; (prize, of bra) coppa
cupboard ['kʌbəd] n armadio
cup final n (BRIT Football) finale f di coppa
curator [kjuə'reɪtəʳ] n direttore m (di museo ecc)
curb [kə:b] vt tenere a freno ▷ n freno; (US) bordo del marciapiede
curdle ['kə:dl] vi cagliare
cure [kjuəʳ] vt guarire; (Culin) trattare; affumicare; essiccare ▷ n rimedio
curfew ['kə:fju:] n coprifuoco
curiosity [kjuərɪ'ɔsɪtɪ] n curiosità

curious ['kjʊərɪəs] *adj* curioso(-a)

curl [kə:l] *n* riccio ▷ *vt* ondulare; (*tightly*) arricciare ▷ *vi* arricciarsi; **curl up** *vi* rannicchiarsi; **curler** *n* bigodino; **curly** ['kə:lɪ] *adj* ricciuto(-a)

currant ['kʌrnt] *n* (*dried*) sultanina; (*bush, fruit*) ribes *m inv*

currency ['kʌrnsɪ] *n* moneta; **to gain ~** (*fig*) acquistare larga diffusione

current ['kʌrnt] *adj* corrente ▷ *n* corrente *f*; **current account** (BRIT) *n* conto corrente; **current affairs** *npl* attualità *fpl*; **currently** *adv* attualmente

curriculum [kə'rɪkjʊləm] (*pl* **curriculums** *or* **curricula**) *n* curriculum *m inv*; **curriculum vitae** [-'viːtaɪ] *n* curriculum vitae *m inv*

curry ['kʌrɪ] *n* curry *m inv* ▷ *vt* **to ~ favour with** cercare di attirarsi i favori di; **curry powder** *n* curry *m*

curse [kə:s] *vt* maledire ▷ *vi* bestemmiare ▷ *n* maledizione *f*; bestemmia

cursor ['kə:sər] *n* (*Comput*) cursore *m*

curt [kə:t] *adj* secco(-a)

curtain ['kə:tn] *n* tenda; (*Theatre*) sipario

curve [kə:v] *n* curva ▷ *vi* curvarsi; **curved** *adj* curvo(-a)

cushion ['kʊʃən] *n* cuscino ▷ *vt* (*shock*) fare da cuscinetto a

custard ['kʌstəd] *n* (*for pouring*) crema

custody ['kʌstədɪ] *n* (*of child*) tutela; **to take into ~** (*suspect*) mettere in detenzione preventiva

custom ['kʌstəm] *n* costume *m*, consuetudine *f*; (*Comm*) clientela

customer ['kʌstəmər] *n* cliente *m/f*

customized ['kʌstəmaɪzd] *adj* (*car etc*) fuoriserie *inv*

customs ['kʌstəmz] *npl* dogana; **customs officer** *n* doganiere *m*

cut [kʌt] (*pt, pp* **cut**) *vt* tagliare; (*shape, make*) intagliare; (*reduce*) ridurre ▷ *vi* tagliare ▷ *n* taglio; (*in salary etc*) riduzione *f*; **I've ~ myself** mi sono tagliato; **to ~ a tooth** mettere un dente; **cut back** *vt* (*plants*) tagliare; (*production, expenditure*) ridurre; **cut down** *vt* (*tree etc*) abbattere ▷ *vt fus* (*also:* **~ down on**) ridurre; **cut off** *vt* tagliare; (*fig*) isolare; **cut out** *vt* tagliare fuori; eliminare; ritagliare; **cut up** *vt* tagliare a pezzi; **cutback** *n* riduzione *f*

cute [kju:t] *adj* (*sweet*) carino(-a)

cutlery ['kʌtlərɪ] *n* posate *fpl*

cutlet ['kʌtlɪt] *n* costoletta; (*nut etc cutlet*) cotoletta vegetariana

cut: **cut-price** (BRIT) *adj* a prezzo ridotto; **cut-rate** (US) *adj* = **cut-price**; **cutting** ['kʌtɪŋ] *adj* tagliente ▷ *n* (*from newspaper*) ritaglio (di giornale); (*from plant*) talea

CV *n abbr* = **curriculum vitae**

cwt *abbr* = **hundredweight(s)**

cybercafé ['saɪbəkaefeɪ] *n* cybercaffè *m inv*

cyberspace ['saɪbəspeɪs] *n* ciberspazio

cycle ['saɪkl] *n* ciclo; (*bicycle*) bicicletta ▷ *vi* andare in bicicletta; **cycle hire** *n* noleggio *m* biciclette *inv*; **cycle lane** *n* pista ciclabile; **cycle path** *n* pista ciclabile; **cycling** ['saɪklɪŋ] *n* ciclismo; **cyclist** ['saɪklɪst] *n* ciclista *m/f*

cyclone ['saɪkləun] *n* ciclone *m*

cylinder ['sɪlɪndər] *n* cilindro

cymbal ['sɪmbl] *n* piatto

cynical ['sɪnɪkl] *adj* cinico(-a)

Cypriot ['sɪprɪət] *adj*, *n* cipriota (*m/f*)

Cyprus ['saɪprəs] *n* Cipro

cyst [sɪst] *n* cisti *f inv*; **cystitis** [sɪs'taɪtɪs] *n* cistite *f*

czar [zɑːr] *n* zar *m inv*

Czech [tʃɛk] *adj* ceco(-a) ▷ *n* ceco(-a); (*Ling*) ceco; **Czech Republic** *n* **the Czech Republic** la Repubblica Ceca

D [di:] *n* (*Mus*) re *m*

dab [dæb] *vt* (*eyes, wound*) tamponare; (*paint, cream*) applicare (con leggeri colpetti)

dad, daddy [dæd, 'dædɪ] *n* babbo, papà *m inv*

daffodil ['dæfədɪl] *n* trombone *m*, giunchiglia

daft [dɑːft] *adj* sciocco(-a)

dagger ['dægəʳ] *n* pugnale *m*

daily ['deɪlɪ] *adj* quotidiano(-a), giornaliero(-a) ▷ *n* quotidiano ▷ *adv* tutti i giorni

dairy ['dɛərɪ] *n* (*BRIT: shop*) latteria; (*on farm*) caseificio ▷ *adj* caseario(-a); **dairy produce** *npl* latticini *mpl*

daisy ['deɪzɪ] *n* margherita

dam [dæm] *n* diga ▷ *vt* sbarrare; costruire dighe su

damage ['dæmɪdʒ] *n* danno, danni *mpl*; (*fig*) danno ▷ *vt* danneggiare; **~s** *npl* (*Law*) danni

damn [dæm] *vt* condannare; (*curse*) maledire ▷ *n* (*inf*): **I don't give a ~** non me ne frega niente ▷ *adj* (*inf: also:* **~ed**): **this ~ ...** questo maledetto ...; **~ it !** accidenti!

damp [dæmp] *adj* umido(-a) ▷ *n* umidità, umido ▷ *vt* (*also:* **~en**: *cloth, rag*) inumidire, bagnare; (: *enthusiasm etc*) spegnere

dance [dɑːns] *n* danza, ballo; (*ball*) ballo ▷ *vi* ballare; **dance floor** *n* pista da ballo; **dancer** *n* danzatore(-trice); (*professional*) ballerino(-a); **dancing** ['dɑːnsɪŋ] *n* danza, ballo

dandelion ['dændɪlaɪən] *n* dente *m* di leone

dandruff ['dændrəf] *n* forfora

Dane [deɪn] *n* danese *m/f*

danger ['deɪndʒəʳ] *n* pericolo; **there is a ~ of fire** c'è pericolo di incendio; **in ~** in pericolo; **he was in ~ of falling** rischiava di cadere; **dangerous** *adj* pericoloso(-a)

dangle ['dæŋgl] *vt* dondolare; (*fig*) far balenare ▷ *vi* pendolare

Danish ['deɪnɪʃ] *adj* danese ▷ *n* (*Ling*) danese *m*

dare [dɛəʳ] *vt* **to ~ sb to do** sfidare qn a fare ▷ *vi* **to ~ to do sth** osare fare qc; **I ~ say** (*I suppose*) immagino (che); **daring** *adj* audace, ardito(-a) ▷ *n* audacia

dark [dɑːk] *adj* (*night, room*) buio(-a), scuro(-a); (*colour, complexion*) scuro(-a); (*fig*) cupo(-a), tetro(-a), nero(-a) ▷ *n* **in the ~** al buio; **in the ~ about** (*fig*) all'oscuro di; **after ~** a notte fatta; **darken** *vt* (*colour*) scurire ▷ *vi* (*sky, room*) oscurarsi; **darkness** *n* oscurità, buio; **darkroom** *n* camera oscura

darling ['dɑːlɪŋ] *adj* caro(-a) ▷ *n* tesoro

dart [dɑːt] *n* freccetta; (*Sewing*) pince *f inv* ▷ *vi* **to ~ towards** precipitarsi verso; **to ~ away/along** sfrecciare via/lungo; **dartboard** *n* bersaglio (per freccette); **darts** *n* tiro al bersaglio (con freccette)

dash [dæʃ] *n* (*sign*) lineetta; (*small quantity*) punta ▷ *vt* (*missile*) gettare; (*hopes*) infrangere ▷ *vi* **to ~ towards** precipitarsi verso

dashboard ['dæʃbɔːd] *n* (*Aut*) cruscotto

data ['deɪtə] *npl* dati *mpl*; **database** *n* base *f* di dati, data base *m inv*; **data processing** *n* elaborazione *f* (elettronica) dei dati

date [deɪt] *n* data; appuntamento; (*fruit*) dattero ▷ *vt* datare; (*person*) uscire con; **what's the ~ today?** quanti ne abbiamo oggi?; **~ of birth** data di nascita; **to ~** (*until now*) fino a oggi; **dated** *adj* passato(-a) di moda

daughter ['dɔːtəʳ] *n* figlia; **daughter-in-law** *n* nuora

daunting ['dɔːntɪŋ] *adj* non invidiabile

dawn [dɔːn] *n* alba ▷ *vi* (*day*) spuntare; (*fig*): **it ~ed on him that ...** gli è venuto in mente che ...

day [deɪ] *n* giorno; (*as duration*) giornata; (*period of time, age*) tempo, epoca; **the ~ before** il giorno avanti *or* prima; **the ~ after, the following ~** il giorno dopo or seguente; **the ~ after tomorrow** dopodomani; **the ~ before yester-** l'altroieri; **by ~** di giorno; **day-care centre** n scuola materna; **daydream** vi sognare a occhi aperti; **daylight** n luce f del giorno; **day return** (BRIT) n biglietto giornaliero di andata e ritorno; **daytime** n giorno; **day-to-day** adj (life, organization) quotidiano(-a), **day trip** n gita (di un giorno)

dazed [deɪzd] adj stordito(-a)

dazzle ['dæzl] vt abbagliare; **dazzling** adj (light) abbagliante; (colour) violento(-a); (smile) smagliante

DC abbr (= direct current) c.c.

dead [dɛd] adj morto(-a); (numb) intirizzito(-a); (telephone) muto(-a); (battery) scarico(-a) ▷ adv assolutamente, perfettamente ▷ npl **the ~** i morti; **he was shot ~** fu colpito a morte; **~ tired** stanco(-a) morto(-a); **to stop ~** fermarsi di colpo; **dead end** n vicolo cieco; **deadline** n scadenza; **deadly** adj mortale; (weapon, poison) micidiale; **Dead Sea** n **the Dead Sea** il mar Morto

deaf [dɛf] adj sordo(-a); **deafen** vt assordare; **deafening** adj fragoroso(-a), assordante

deal [di:l] (pt, pp **dealt**) n accordo; (business deal) affare m ▷ vt (blow, cards) dare; **a great ~ (of)** molto(-a); **deal with** vt fus (Comm) fare affari con, trattare con; (handle) occuparsi di; (be about: book etc) trattare di; **dealer** n commerciante m/f; **dealings** npl (Comm) relazioni fpl; (relations) rapporti mpl

dealt [dɛlt] pt, pp of **deal**

dean [di:n] n (Rel) decano; (Scol) preside m di facoltà (or di collegio)

dear [dɪə^r] adj caro(-a) ▷ n **my ~** caro mio/ cara mia ▷ excl **~ me!** Dio mio!; **D~ Sir/ Madam** (in letter) Egregio Signore/Egregia Signora; **D~ Mr/Mrs X** Gentile Signor/ Signora X; **dearly** adv (love) moltissimo; (pay) a caro prezzo

death [dɛθ] n morte f; (Admin) decesso; **death penalty** n pena di morte; **death sentence** n condanna a morte

debate [dɪ'beɪt] n dibattito ▷ vt dibattere; discutere

debit ['dɛbɪt] n debito ▷ vt **to ~ a sum to sb** or **to sb's account** addebitare una somma a qn; **debit card** n carta di debito

debris ['dɛbri:] n detriti mpl

debt [dɛt] n debito; **to be in ~** essere indebitato(-a)

debut ['deɪbju:] n debutto

Dec. abbr (= December) dic.

decade ['dɛkeɪd] n decennio

decaffeinated [dɪ'kæfɪneɪtɪd] adj decaffeinato(-a)

decay [dɪ'keɪ] n decadimento; (also: **tooth ~**) carie f ▷ vi (rot) imputridire

deceased [dɪ'si:st] n defunto(-a)

deceit [dɪ'si:t] n inganno; **deceive** [dɪ'si:v] vt ingannare

December [dɪ'sɛmbə^r] n dicembre m

decency ['di:sənsɪ] n decenza

decent ['di:sənt] adj decente; (respectable) per bene; (kind) gentile

deception [dɪ'sɛpʃən] n inganno

deceptive [dɪ'sɛptɪv] adj ingannevole

decide [dɪ'saɪd] vt (person) far prendere una decisione a; (question, argument) risolvere, decidere ▷ vi decidere, decidersi; **to ~ to do/that** decidere di fare/che; **to ~ on** decidere per

decimal ['dɛsɪməl] adj decimale ▷ n decimale m

decision [dɪ'sɪʒən] n decisione f

decisive [dɪ'saɪsɪv] adj decisivo(-a); (person) deciso(-a)

deck [dɛk] n (Naut) ponte m; (of bus): **top ~** imperiale m; (record deck) piatto; (of cards) mazzo; **deckchair** n sedia a sdraio

declaration [dɛklə'reɪʃən] n dichiarazione f

declare [dɪ'klɛə^r] vt dichiarare

decline [dɪ'klaɪn] n (decay) declino; (lessening) ribasso ▷ vt declinare; rifiutare ▷ vi declinare; diminuire

decorate ['dɛkəreɪt] vt (adorn, give a medal to) decorare; (paint and paper) tinteggiare e tappezzare; **decoration** [-'reɪʃən] n (medal etc, adornment) decorazione f; **decorator** n decoratore m

decrease [n 'di:kri:s, vb di:'kri:s] n diminuzione f ▷ vt, vi diminuire

decree [dɪ'kri:] n decreto

dedicate ['dɛdɪkeɪt] vt consacrare; (book etc) dedicare; **dedicated** adj coscienzioso(-a); (Comput) specializzato(-a), dedicato(-a); **dedication** [dɛdɪ'keɪʃən] n (devotion) dedizione f; (in book etc) dedica

deduce [dɪ'dju:s] vt dedurre

deduct [dɪ'dʌkt] vt **to ~ sth from** dedurre qc (da); **deduction** [dɪ'dʌkʃən] n deduzione f

deed [di:d] n azione f, atto; (Law) atto

deem [di:m] vt (formal) giudicare, ritenere; **to ~ it wise to do** ritenere prudente fare

deep [di:p] adj profondo(-a); **4 metres ~** profondo(-a) 4 metri ▷ adv **spectators stood 20 ~** c'erano 20 file di spettatori; **how ~ is the water?** quanto è profonda l'acqua?; **deep-fry** vt friggere in olio

abbondante; **deeply** adv profondamente
deer [dɪə[r]] n inv the ~ i cervidi; **(red)** ~
cervo; **(fallow)** ~ daino; **roe** ~ capriolo
default [dɪ'fɔːlt] n (Comput: also: ~ **value**)
default m inv; **by** ~ (Sport) per abbandono
defeat [dɪ'fiːt] n sconfitta ▷ vt (team,
opponents) sconfiggere
defect [n 'diːfɛkt, vb dɪ'fɛkt] n difetto ▷ vi
to ~ **to the enemy** passare al nemico;
defective [dɪ'fɛktɪv] adj difettoso(-a)
defence [dɪ'fɛns] (US **defense**) n difesa
defend [dɪ'fɛnd] vt difendere; **defendant**
n imputato(-a); **defender** n difensore(-a)
defense [dɪ'fɛns] (US) n = **defence**
defensive [dɪ'fɛnsɪv] adj difensivo(-a) ▷ n
on the ~ sulla difensiva
defer [dɪ'fəː[r]] vt (postpone) differire,
rinviare
defiance [dɪ'faɪəns] n sfida; **in** ~ **of**
a dispetto di; **defiant** [dɪ'faɪənt] adj
(attitude) di sfida; (person) ribelle
deficiency [dɪ'fɪʃənsɪ] n deficienza;
carenza; **deficient** adj deficiente;
insufficiente; **to be deficient in** mancare
di
deficit ['dɛfɪsɪt] n deficit m inv
define [dɪ'faɪn] vt definire
definite ['dɛfɪnɪt] adj (fixed) definito(-a),
preciso(-a); (clear, obvious) ben definito(-a),
esatto(-a); (Ling) determinativo(-a); **he
was** ~ **about it** ne era sicuro; **definitely**
adv indubbiamente
definition [dɛfɪ'nɪʃən] n definizione f
deflate [diː'fleɪt] vt sgonfiare
deflect [dɪ'flɛkt] vt deflettere, deviare
defraud [dɪ'frɔːd] vt defraudare
defrost [diː'frɔst] vt (fridge) disgelare
defuse [diː'fjuːz] vt disinnescare; (fig)
distendere
defy [dɪ'faɪ] vt sfidare; (efforts etc) resistere
a; **it defies description** supera ogni
descrizione
degree [dɪ'griː] n grado; (Scol) laurea
(universitaria); **a first** ~ **in maths** una
laurea in matematica; **by** ~**s** (gradually)
gradualmente, a poco a poco; **to some** ~
fino a un certo punto, in certa misura
dehydrated [diːhaɪ'dreɪtɪd] adj
disidratato(-a); (milk, eggs) in polvere
de-icer ['diː'aɪsə[r]] n sbrinatore m
delay [dɪ'leɪ] vt ritardare ▷ vi **to** ~ **(in
doing sth)** ritardare (a fare qc) ▷ n ritardo;
to be ~ed subire un ritardo; (person) essere
trattenuto(-a)
delegate [n 'dɛlɪgɪt, vb 'dɛlɪgeɪt] n
delegato(-a) ▷ vt delegare
delete [dɪ'liːt] vt cancellare
deli ['dɛlɪ] n = **delicatessen**
deliberate [adj dɪ'lɪbərɪt, vb dɪ'lɪbə

reɪt] adj (intentional) intenzionale;
(slow) misurato(-a) ▷ vi deliberare,
riflettere; **deliberately** adv (on purpose)
deliberatamente
delicacy ['dɛlɪkəsɪ] n delicatezza
delicate ['dɛlɪkɪt] adj delicato(-a)
delicatessen [dɛlɪkə'tɛsn] n ≈ salumeria
delicious [dɪ'lɪʃəs] adj delizioso(-a),
squisito(-a)
delight [dɪ'laɪt] n delizia, gran piacere m
▷ vt dilettare; **to take (a)** ~ **in** dilettarsi
in; **delighted** adj **delighted (at** or
with) contentissimo(-a) (di), felice (di);
delighted to do felice di fare; **delightful**
adj delizioso(-a), incantevole
delinquent [dɪ'lɪŋkwənt] adj, n
delinquente m/f
deliver [dɪ'lɪvə[r]] vt (mail) distribuire;
(goods) consegnare; (speech) pronunciare;
(Med) far partorire; **delivery** n
distribuzione f; consegna; (of speaker)
dizione f; (Med) parto
delusion [dɪ'luːʒən] n illusione f
de luxe [də'lʌks] adj di lusso
delve [dɛlv] vi **to** ~ **into** frugare in; (subject)
far ricerche in
demand [dɪ'mɑːnd] vt richiedere;
(rights) rivendicare ▷ n domanda; (claim)
rivendicazione f; **in** ~ ricercato(-a),
richiesto(-a); **on** ~ a richiesta;
demanding adj (boss) esigente; (work)
impegnativo(-a)
demise [dɪ'maɪz] n decesso
demo ['dɛməu] (inf) n abbr
(= demonstration) manifestazione f
democracy [dɪ'mɔkrəsɪ] n
democrazia; **democrat** ['dɛməkræt]
n democratico(-a); **democratic**
[dɛmə'krætɪk] adj democratico(-a)
demolish [dɪ'mɔlɪʃ] vt demolire
demolition [dɛmə'lɪʃən] n demolizione f
demon ['diːmən] n (also fig) demonio ▷ cpd
a ~ **squash player** un mago dello squash;
a ~ **driver** un guidatore folle
demonstrate ['dɛmənstreɪt] vt
dimostrare, provare ▷ vi dimostrare,
manifestare; **demonstration** [-'streɪʃə
n] n dimostrazione f; (Pol) dimostrazione,
manifestazione f; **demonstrator**
n (Pol) dimostrante m/f; (Comm)
dimostratore(-trice)
demote [dɪ'məut] vt far retrocedere
den [dɛn] n tana, covo; (room) buco
denial [dɪ'naɪəl] n diniego; rifiuto
denim ['dɛnɪm] n tessuto di cotone
ritorto; ~**s** npl (jeans) blue jeans mpl
Denmark ['dɛnmɑːk] n Danimarca
denomination [dɪnɔmɪ'neɪʃən] n (money)
valore m; (Rel) confessione f

denounce [dɪ'nauns] vt denunciare

dense [dɛns] adj fitto(-a); (smoke) denso(-a); (inf: person) ottuso(-a), duro(-a)

density ['dɛnsɪtɪ] n densità f inv

dent [dɛnt] n ammaccatura ▷ vt (also: **make a ~ in**) ammaccare

dental ['dɛntl] adj dentale; **dental floss** [-flɔs] n filo interdentale; **dental surgery** n ambulatorio del dentista

dentist ['dɛntɪst] n dentista m/f

dentures ['dɛntʃəz] npl dentiera

deny [dɪ'naɪ] vt negare; (refuse) rifiutare

deodorant [diː'əudərənt] n deodorante m

depart [dɪ'pɑːt] vi partire; **to ~ from** (fig) deviare da

department [dɪ'pɑːtmənt] n (Comm) reparto; (Scol) sezione f, dipartimento; (Pol) ministero; **department store** n grande magazzino

departure [dɪ'pɑːtʃər] n partenza; (fig): **~ from** deviazione f da; **a new ~** una svolta (decisiva); **departure lounge** n (at airport) sala d'attesa

depend [dɪ'pɛnd] vi **to ~ on** dipendere da; (rely on) contare su; **it ~s** dipende; **~ing on the result …** a seconda del risultato …; **dependant** n persona a carico; **dependent** adj **to be dependent on** dipendere da; (child, relative) essere a carico di ▷ n = **dependant**

depict [dɪ'pɪkt] vt (in picture) dipingere; (in words) descrivere

deport [dɪ'pɔːt] vt deportare; espellere

deposit [dɪ'pɔzɪt] n (Comm, Geo) deposito; (of ore, oil) giacimento; (Chem) sedimento; (part payment) acconto; (for hired goods etc) cauzione f ▷ vt depositare; dare in acconto; mettere or lasciare in deposito; **deposit account** n conto vincolato

depot ['dɛpəu] n deposito; (us) stazione f ferroviaria

depreciate [dɪ'priːʃɪeɪt] vi svalutarsi

depress [dɪ'prɛs] vt deprimere; (price, wages) abbassare; (press down) premere; **depressed** adj (person) depresso(-a), abbattuto(-a); (price) in ribasso; (industry) in crisi; **depressing** adj deprimente; **depression** [dɪ'prɛʃən] n depressione f

deprive [dɪ'praɪv] vt **to ~ sb of** privare qn di; **deprived** adj disgraziato(-a)

dept. abbr = **department**

depth [dɛpθ] n profondità f inv; **in the ~s of** nel profondo di; nel cuore di; **out of one's ~** (in water) dove non si tocca; (fig) a disagio

deputy ['dɛpjutɪ] adj **~ head** (BRIT Scol) vicepreside m/f ▷ n (assistant) vice m/f inv; (us: also: **~ sheriff**) vice-sceriffo

derail [dɪ'reɪl] vt **to be ~ed** deragliare

derelict ['dɛrɪlɪkt] adj abbandonato(-a)

derive [dɪ'raɪv] vt **to ~ sth from** derivare qc da; trarre qc da ▷ vi **to ~ from** derivare da

descend [dɪ'sɛnd] vt, vi discendere, scendere; **to ~ from** discendere da; **to ~ to** (lying, begging) abbassarsi a; **descendant** n discendente m/f; **descent** [dɪ'sɛnt] n discesa; (origin) discendenza, famiglia

describe [dɪs'kraɪb] vt descrivere; **description** [-'krɪpʃən] n descrizione f; (sort) genere m, specie f

desert [n 'dɛzət, vb dɪ'zəːt] n deserto ▷ vt lasciare, abbandonare ▷ vi (Mil) disertare; **deserted** [dɪ'zəːtɪd] adj deserto(-a)

deserve [dɪ'zəːv] vt meritare

design [dɪ'zaɪn] n (art, sketch) disegno; (layout, shape) linea; (pattern) fantasia; (intention) intenzione f ▷ vt disegnare; progettare

designate vt [vb 'dɛzɪgneɪt, adj 'dɛzɪgnɪt] designare ▷ adj designato(-a)

designer [dɪ'zaɪnər] n (Art, Tech) disegnatore(-trice); (of fashion) modellista m/f

desirable [dɪ'zaɪərəbl] adj desiderabile; **it is ~ that** è opportuno che + sub

desire [dɪ'zaɪər] n desiderio, voglia ▷ vt desiderare, volere

desk [dɛsk] n (in office) scrivania; (for pupil) banco; (BRIT: in shop, restaurant) cassa; (in hotel) ricevimento; (at airport) accettazione f; **desk-top publishing** n desktop publishing m

despair [dɪs'pɛər] n disperazione f ▷ vi **to ~ of** disperare di

despatch [dɪs'pætʃ] n, vt = **dispatch**

desperate ['dɛspərɪt] adj disperato(-a); (fugitive) capace di tutto; **to be ~ for sth/to do** volere disperatamente qc/fare; **desperately** adv disperatamente; (very) terribilmente, estremamente; **desperation** [dɛspə'reɪʃən] n disperazione f

despise [dɪs'paɪz] vt disprezzare, sdegnare

despite [dɪs'paɪt] prep malgrado, a dispetto di, nonostante

dessert [dɪ'zəːt] n dolce m; frutta; **dessertspoon** n cucchiaio da dolci

destination [dɛstɪ'neɪʃən] n destinazione f

destined ['dɛstɪnd] adj **to be ~ to do/for** essere destinato(-a) a fare/per

destiny ['dɛstɪnɪ] n destino

destroy [dɪs'trɔɪ] vt distruggere

destruction [dɪs'trʌkʃən] n distruzione f

destructive [dɪs'trʌktɪv] adj distruttivo(-a)

detach [dɪ'tætʃ] vt staccare, distaccare; **detached** adj (attitude) distante;

detached house n villa
detail ['di:teɪl] n particolare m, dettaglio
▷ vt dettagliare, particolareggiare;
in ~ nei particolari; **detailed** adj
particolareggiato(-a)
detain [dɪ'teɪn] vt trattenere; (in captivity)
detenere
detect [dɪ'tɛkt] vt scoprire, scorgere; (Med,
Police, Radar etc) individuare; **detection**
[dɪ'tɛkʃən] n scoperta; individuazione
f; **detective** n investigatore(-trice);
detective story n giallo
detention [dɪ'tɛnʃən] n detenzione f; (Scol)
permanenza forzata per punizione
deter [dɪ'tə:ʳ] vt dissuadere
detergent [dɪ'tə:dʒənt] n detersivo
deteriorate [dɪ'tɪərɪəreɪt] vi deteriorarsi
determination [dɪtə:mɪ'neɪʃən] n
determinazione f
determine [dɪ'tə:mɪn] vt determinare;
determined adj (person) risoluto(-a),
deciso(-a); **determined to do** deciso(-a)
a fare
deterrent [dɪ'tɛrənt] n deterrente m; **to
act as a ~** fungere da deterrente
detest [dɪ'tɛst] vt detestare
detour ['di:tuəʳ] n deviazione f
detract [dɪ'trækt] vi **to ~ from** detrarre da
detrimental [dɛtrɪ'mɛntl] adj **~ to**
dannoso(-a) a, nocivo(-a) a
devastating ['dɛvəsteɪtɪŋ] adj
devastatore(-trice), sconvolgente
develop [dɪ'vɛləp] vt sviluppare; (habit)
prendere (gradualmente) ▷ vi svilupparsi;
(facts, symptoms: appear) manifestarsi,
rivelarsi; **can you ~ this film?** può
sviluppare questo rullino?; **developing
country** n paese m in via di sviluppo;
development n sviluppo
device [dɪ'vaɪs] n (apparatus) congegno
devil ['dɛvl] n diavolo; demonio
devious ['di:vɪəs] adj (person) subdolo(-a)
devise [dɪ'vaɪz] vt escogitare, concepire
devote [dɪ'vəut] vt **to ~ sth to** dedicare qc
a; **devoted** adj devoto(-a); **to be devoted
to sb** essere molto affezionato(-a) a qn;
devotion [dɪ'vəuʃən] n devozione f,
attaccamento; (Rel) atto di devozione,
preghiera
devour [dɪ'vauəʳ] vt divorare
devout [dɪ'vaut] adj pio(-a), devoto(-a)
dew [dju:] n rugiada
diabetes [daɪə'bi:ti:z] n diabete m
diabetic [daɪə'bɛtɪk] adj, n diabetico(-a)
diagnose [daɪəg'nəuz] vt diagnosticare
diagnosis [daɪəg'nəusɪs] (pl **diagnoses**) n
diagnosi f inv
diagonal [daɪ'ægənl] adj diagonale ▷ n
diagonale f

diagram ['daɪəgræm] n diagramma m
dial ['daɪəl] n quadrante m; (on radio)
lancetta; (on telephone) disco combinatore
▷ vt (number) fare
dialect ['daɪəlɛkt] n dialetto
dialling code, (US **area code**) n prefisso;
what's the ~ for Paris? qual è il prefisso
telefonico di Parigi?
dialling tone ['daɪəlɪŋ-] (US **dial tone**) n
segnale m di linea libera
dialogue ['daɪəlɔg] (US **dialog**) n dialogo
diameter [daɪ'æmɪtəʳ] n diametro
diamond ['daɪəmənd] n diamante m;
(shape) rombo; **~s** npl (Cards) quadri mpl
diaper ['daɪəpəʳ] (US) n pannolino
diarrhoea [daɪə'ri:ə] (US **diarrhea**) n
diarrea
diary ['daɪərɪ] n (daily account) diario; (book)
agenda
dice [daɪs] n inv dado ▷ vt (Culin) tagliare
a dadini
dictate [dɪk'teɪt] vt dettare; **dictation**
[dɪk'teɪʃən] n dettatura; (Scol) dettato
dictator [dɪk'teɪtəʳ] n dittatore m
dictionary ['dɪkʃənrɪ] n dizionario
did [dɪd] pt of **do**
didn't [dɪdnt] = **did not**
die [daɪ] vi morire; **to be dying for sth/to
do sth** morire dalla voglia di qc/di fare
qc; **die down** vi abbassarsi; **die out** vi
estinguersi
diesel ['di:zəl] n (vehicle) diesel m inv
diet ['daɪət] n alimentazione f; (restricted
food) dieta ▷ vi (also: **be on a ~**) stare a
dieta
differ ['dɪfəʳ] vi **to ~ from sth** differire
da qc, essere diverso(-a) da qc; **to ~
from sb over sth** essere in disaccordo
con qn su qc; **difference** n differenza;
(disagreement) screzio; **different** adj
diverso(-a); **differentiate** [-'rɛnʃɪeɪt] vi
to differentiate between discriminare
or fare differenza fra; **differently** adv
diversamente
difficult ['dɪfɪkəlt] adj difficile; **difficulty** n
difficoltà f inv
dig [dɪg] (pt, pp **dug**) vt (hole) scavare;
(garden) vangare ▷ n (prod) gomitata;
(archaeological) scavo; (fig) frecciata; **dig
up** vt (tree etc) sradicare; (information)
scavare fuori
digest [vb daɪ'dʒɛst, n 'daɪdʒɛst] vt digerire
▷ n compendio; **digestion** [dɪ'dʒɛstʃən] n
digestione f
digit ['dɪdʒɪt] n cifra; (finger) dito; **digital**
adj digitale; **digital camera** n macchina
fotografica digitale; **digital TV** n
televisione f digitale
dignified ['dɪgnɪfaɪd] adj dignitoso(-a)

dignity ['dɪgnɪtɪ] n dignità
digs [dɪgz] (BRIT: inf) npl camera ammobiliata
dilemma [daɪ'lɛmə] n dilemma m
dill [dɪl] n aneto
dilute [daɪ'luːt] vt diluire; (with water) annacquare
dim [dɪm] adj (light) debole; (shape etc) vago(-a), (room) in penombra; (inf: person) tonto(-a) ▷ vt (light) abbassare
dime [daɪm] (US) n = 10 cents
dimension [daɪ'mɛnʃən] n dimensione f
diminish [dɪ'mɪnɪʃ] vt, vi diminuire
din [dɪn] n chiasso, fracasso
dine [daɪn] vi pranzare; **diner** n (person) cliente m/f; (US: place) tavola calda
dinghy ['dɪŋgɪ] n battello pneumatico; (also: **rubber ~**) gommone m
dingy ['dɪndʒɪ] adj grigio(-a)
dining car ['daɪnɪŋ-] (BRIT) n vagone m ristorante
dining room n sala da pranzo
dining table n tavolo da pranzo
dinner ['dɪnəʳ] n (lunch) pranzo; (evening meal) cena; (public) banchetto; **dinner jacket** n smoking m inv; **dinner party** n cena; **dinner time** n ora di pranzo (or cena)
dinosaur ['daɪnəsɔːʳ] n dinosauro
dip [dɪp] n discesa; (in sea) bagno; (Culin) salsetta ▷ vt immergere; bagnare; (BRIT Aut: lights) abbassare ▷ vi abbassarsi
diploma [dɪ'pləumə] n diploma m
diplomacy [dɪ'pləuməsɪ] n diplomazia
diplomat ['dɪpləmæt] n diplomatico; **diplomatic** [dɪplə'mætɪk] adj diplomatico(-a)
dipstick ['dɪpstɪk] n (Aut) indicatore m di livello dell'olio
dire [daɪəʳ] adj terribile; estremo(-a)
direct [daɪ'rɛkt] adj diretto(-a) ▷ vt dirigere; (order): **to ~ sb to do sth** dare direttive a qn di fare qc ▷ adv direttamente; **can you ~ me to ...?** mi può indicare la strada per ...?; **direct debit** n (Banking) addebito effettuato per ordine di un cliente di banca
direction [dɪ'rɛkʃən] n direzione f; **~s** npl (advice) chiarimenti mpl; **sense of ~** senso dell'orientamento; **~s for use** istruzioni fpl
directly [dɪ'rɛktlɪ] adv (in straight line) direttamente; (at once) subito
director [dɪ'rɛktəʳ] n direttore(-trice), amministratore(-trice); (Theatre, Cinema) regista m/f
directory [dɪ'rɛktərɪ] n elenco; **directory enquiries** (US **directory assistance**) n informazioni fpl elenco abbonati inv
dirt [dəːt] n sporcizia; immondizia; (earth)

terra; **dirty** adj sporco(-a) ▷ vt sporcare
disability [dɪsə'bɪlɪtɪ] n invalidità f inv; (Law) incapacità f inv
disabled [dɪs'eɪbld] adj invalido(-a); (mentally) ritardato(-a) ▷ npl **the ~** gli invalidi
disadvantage [dɪsəd'vɑːntɪdʒ] n svantaggio
disagree [dɪsə'griː] vi (differ) discordare; (be against, think otherwise): **to ~ (with)** essere in disaccordo (con), dissentire (da); **disagreeable** adj sgradevole; (person) antipatico(-a); **disagreement** n disaccordo; (argument) dissapore m
disappear [dɪsə'pɪəʳ] vi scomparire; **disappearance** n scomparsa
disappoint [dɪsə'pɔɪnt] vt deludere; **disappointed** adj deluso(-a); **disappointing** adj deludente; **disappointment** n delusione f
disapproval [dɪsə'pruːvəl] n disapprovazione f
disapprove [dɪsə'pruːv] vi **to ~ of** disapprovare
disarm [dɪs'ɑːm] vt disarmare; **disarmament** n disarmo
disaster [dɪ'zɑːstəʳ] n disastro; **disastrous** [dɪ'zɑːstrəs] adj disastroso(-a)
disbelief ['dɪsbə'liːf] n incredulità
disc [dɪsk] n disco; (Comput) = **disk**
discard [dɪs'kɑːd] vt (old things) scartare; (fig) abbandonare
discharge [vb dɪs'tʃɑːdʒ, n 'dɪstʃɑːdʒ] vt (duties) compiere; (Elec, waste etc) scaricare; (Med) emettere; (patient) dimettere; (employee) licenziare; (soldier) congedare; (defendant) liberare ▷ n (Elec) scarica; (Med) emissione f, (dismissal) licenziamento; congedo; liberazione f
discipline ['dɪsɪplɪn] n disciplina ▷ vt disciplinare; (punish) punire
disc jockey n disc jockey m inv
disclose [dɪs'kləuz] vt rivelare, svelare
disco ['dɪskəu] n abbr discoteca
discoloured [dɪs'kʌləd] (US **discolored**) adj scolorito(-a), ingiallito(-a)
discomfort [dɪs'kʌmfət] n disagio; (lack of comfort) scomodità f inv
disconnect [dɪskə'nɛkt] vt sconnettere, staccare; (Elec, Radio) staccare; (gas, water) chiudere
discontent [dɪskən'tɛnt] n scontentezza
discontinue [dɪskən'tɪnjuː] vt smettere, cessare; **"~d"** (Comm) "fuori produzione"
discount [n 'dɪskaunt, vb dɪs'kaunt] n sconto ▷ vt scontare; (idea) non badare a; **are there ~s for students?** ci sono sconti

per studenti?

discourage [dɪsˈkʌrɪdʒ] vt scoraggiare

discover [dɪsˈkʌvəʳ] vt scoprire; **discovery** n scoperta

discredit [dɪsˈkrɛdɪt] vt screditare; mettere in dubbio

discreet [dɪˈskriːt] adj discreto(-a)

discrepancy [dɪˈskrɛpənsɪ] n discrepanza

discretion [dɪˈskrɛʃən] n discrezione f; **use your own ~** giudichi lei

discriminate [dɪˈskrɪmɪneɪt] vi **to ~ between** distinguere tra; **to ~ against** discriminare contro; **discrimination** [-ˈneɪʃən] n discriminazione f; (judgment) discernimento

discuss [dɪˈskʌs] vt discutere; (debate) dibattere; **discussion** [dɪˈskʌʃən] n discussione f

disease [dɪˈziːz] n malattia

disembark [dɪsɪmˈbɑːk] vt, vi sbarcare

disgrace [dɪsˈgreɪs] n vergogna; (disfavour) disgrazia ▷ vt disonorare, far cadere in disgrazia; **disgraceful** adj scandaloso(-a), vergognoso(-a)

disgruntled [dɪsˈgrʌntld] adj scontento(-a), di cattivo umore

disguise [dɪsˈgaɪz] n travestimento ▷ vt **to ~ (as)** travestire (da); **in ~** travestito(-a)

disgust [dɪsˈgʌst] n disgusto, nausea ▷ vt disgustare, far schifo a; **disgusted** [dɪsˈgʌstɪd] adj indignato(-a); **disgusting** [dɪsˈgʌstɪŋ] adj disgustoso(-a), ripugnante

dish [dɪʃ] n piatto; **to do** or **wash the ~es** fare i piatti; **dishcloth** n strofinaccio

dishonest [dɪsˈɔnɪst] adj disonesto(-a)

dishtowel [ˈdɪʃtauəl] (US) n strofinaccio dei piatti

dishwasher [ˈdɪʃwɔʃəʳ] n lavastoviglie f inv

disillusion [dɪsɪˈluːʒən] vt disilludere, disingannare

disinfectant [dɪsɪnˈfɛktənt] n disinfettante m

disintegrate [dɪsˈɪntɪgreɪt] vi disintegrarsi

disk [dɪsk] n (Comput) disco; **single-/double-sided ~** disco a facciata singola/doppia; **disk drive** n lettore m; **diskette** (US) n =**disk**

dislike [dɪsˈlaɪk] n antipatia, avversione f; (gen pl) cosa che non piace ▷ vt **he ~s it** non gli piace

dislocate [ˈdɪsləkeɪt] vt slogare

disloyal [dɪsˈlɔɪəl] adj sleale

dismal [ˈdɪzml] adj triste, cupo(-a)

dismantle [dɪsˈmæntl] vt (machine) smontare

dismay [dɪsˈmeɪ] n costernazione f ▷ vt sgomentare

dismiss [dɪsˈmɪs] vt congedare; (employee) licenziare; (idea) scacciare; (Law) respingere; **dismissal** n congedo; licenziamento

disobedient [dɪsəˈbiːdɪənt] adj disubbidiente

disobey [dɪsəˈbeɪ] vt disubbidire a

disorder [dɪsˈɔːdəʳ] n disordine m; (rioting) tumulto; (Med) disturbo

disorganized [dɪsˈɔːgənaɪzd] adj (person, life) disorganizzato(-a); (system, meeting) male organizzato(-a)

disown [dɪsˈəun] vt rinnegare

dispatch [dɪsˈpætʃ] vt spedire, inviare ▷ n spedizione f, invio; (Mil, Press) dispaccio

dispel [dɪsˈpɛl] vt dissipare, scacciare

dispense [dɪsˈpɛns] vt distribuire, amministrare; **dispense with** vt fus fare a meno di; **dispenser** n (container) distributore m

disperse [dɪsˈpəːs] vt disperdere; (knowledge) disseminare ▷ vi disperdersi

display [dɪsˈpleɪ] n esposizione f; (of feeling etc) manifestazione f; (screen) schermo ▷ vt mostrare; (goods) esporre; (pej) ostentare

displease [dɪsˈpliːz] vt dispiacere a, scontentare; **~d with** scontento di

disposable [dɪsˈpəuzəbl] adj (pack etc) a perdere; (income) disponibile

disposal [dɪsˈpəuzl] n eliminazione f; (of property) cessione f; **at one's ~** alla sua disposizione

dispose [dɪsˈpəuz] vi **~ of** sbarazzarsi di; **disposition** [-ˈzɪʃən] n disposizione f; (temperament) carattere m

disproportionate [dɪsprəˈpɔːʃənət] adj sproporzionato(-a)

dispute [dɪsˈpjuːt] n disputa; (also: **industrial ~**) controversia (sindacale) ▷ vt contestare; (matter) discutere; (victory) disputare

disqualify [dɪsˈkwɔlɪfaɪ] vt (Sport) squalificare; **to ~ sb from sth/from doing** rendere qn incapace a qc/a fare; squalificare qn da qc/da fare; **to ~ sb from driving** ritirare la patente a qn

disregard [dɪsrɪˈgɑːd] vt non far caso a, non badare a

disrupt [dɪsˈrʌpt] vt disturbare; creare scompiglio in; **disruption** [dɪsˈrʌpʃən] n disordine m; interruzione f

dissatisfaction [dɪssætɪsˈfækʃən] n scontentezza, insoddisfazione f

dissatisfied [dɪsˈsætɪsfaɪd] adj **~ (with)** scontento(a) or insoddisfatto(a) (di)

dissect [dɪˈsɛkt] vt sezionare

dissent [dɪ'sɛnt] n dissenso

dissertation [dɪsə'teɪʃən] n tesi f inv, dissertazione f

dissolve [dɪ'zɔlv] vt dissolvere, sciogliere; (Pol, marriage etc) sciogliere ▷ vi dissolversi, sciogliersi

distance ['dɪstns] n distanza; **in the ~** in lontananza

distant ['dɪstnt] adj lontano(-a), distante; (manner) riservato(-a), freddo(-a)

distil [dɪs'tɪl] (US **distill**) vt distillare; **distillery** n distilleria

distinct [dɪs'tɪŋkt] adj distinto(-a); **as ~ from** a differenza di; **distinction** [dɪs'tɪŋkʃən] n distinzione f; (in exam) lode f; **distinctive** adj distintivo(-a)

distinguish [dɪs'tɪŋgwɪʃ] vt distinguere; discernere; **distinguished** adj (eminent) eminente

distort [dɪs'tɔːt] vt distorcere; (Tech) deformare

distract [dɪs'trækt] vt distrarre; **distracted** adj distratto(-a); **distraction** [dɪs'trækʃən] n distrazione f

distraught [dɪs'trɔːt] adj stravolto(-a)

distress [dɪs'trɛs] n angoscia ▷ vt affliggere; **distressing** adj doloroso(-a)

distribute [dɪs'trɪbjuːt] vt distribuire; **distribution** [-'bjuːʃən] n distribuzione f; **distributor** n distributore m

district ['dɪstrɪkt] n (of country) regione f; (of town) quartiere m; (Admin) distretto; **district attorney** (US) n ≈ sostituto procuratore m della Repubblica

distrust [dɪs'trʌst] n diffidenza, sfiducia ▷ vt non aver fiducia in

disturb [dɪs'təːb] vt disturbare; **disturbance** n disturbo; (political etc) disordini mpl; **disturbed** adj (worried, upset) turbato(-a); **emotionally disturbed** con turbe emotive; **disturbing** adj sconvolgente

ditch [dɪtʃ] n fossa ▷ vt (inf) piantare in asso

ditto ['dɪtəu] adv idem

dive [daɪv] n tuffo; (of submarine) immersione f ▷ vi tuffarsi; immergersi; **diver** n tuffatore(-trice), palombaro

diverse [daɪ'vəːs] adj vario(-a)

diversion [daɪ'vəːʃən] n (BRIT Aut) deviazione f; (distraction) divertimento

diversity [daɪ'vəːsɪtɪ] n diversità f inv, varietà f inv

divert [daɪ'vəːt] vt deviare

divide [dɪ'vaɪd] vt dividere; (separate) separare ▷ vi dividersi; **divided highway** (US) n strada a doppia carreggiata

divine [dɪ'vaɪn] adj divino(-a)

diving ['daɪvɪŋ] n tuffo; **diving board** n trampolino

division [dɪ'vɪʒən] n divisione f; separazione f; (esp Football) serie f

divorce [dɪ'vɔːs] n divorzio ▷ vt divorziare da; (dissociate) separare; **divorced** adj divorziato(-a); **divorcee** [-'siː] n divorziato(-a)

D.I.Y. (BRIT) n abbr = **do-it-yourself**

dizzy ['dɪzɪ] adj **to feel ~** avere il capogiro

DJ n abbr = **disc jockey**

DNA n abbr (= deoxyribonucleic acid) DNA m; **DNA test** n test m inv del DNA

 KEYWORD

do [duː] (pt **did**, pp **done**) n (inf: party etc) festa; **it was rather a grand do** è stato un ricevimento piuttosto importante ▷ vb **1** (in negative constructions: non tradotto): **I don't understand** non capisco

2 (to form questions: non tradotto): **didn't you know?** non lo sapevi?; **why didn't you come?** perché non sei venuto?

3 (for emphasis, in polite expressions): **she does seem rather late** sembra essere piuttosto in ritardo; **do sit down** si accomodi la prego, prego si sieda; **do take care!** mi raccomando, sta attento!

4 (used to avoid repeating vb): **she swims better than I do** lei nuota meglio di me; **do you agree? — yes, I do/no, I don't** sei d'accordo? — sì/no; **she lives in Glasgow — so do I** lei vive a Glasgow — anch'io; **he asked me to help him and I did** mi ha chiesto di aiutarlo ed io l'ho fatto

5 (in question tags): **you like him, don't you?** ti piace, vero?; **I don't know him, do I?** non lo conosco, vero?

▷ vt (gen, carry out, perform etc) fare; **what are you doing tonight?** che fa stasera?; **to do the cooking** cucinare; **to do the washing-up** fare i piatti; **to do one's teeth** lavarsi i denti; **to do one's hair/nails** farsi i capelli/le unghie; **the car was doing 100** la macchina faceva i 100 all'ora ▷ vi **1** (act, behave) fare; **do as I do** faccia come me, faccia come faccio io

2 (get on, fare) andare; **he's doing well/badly at school** va bene/male a scuola; **how do you do?** piacere!

3 (suit) andare bene; **this room will do** questa stanza va bene

4 (be sufficient) bastare; **will £10 do?** basteranno 10 sterline?; **that'll do** basta così; **that'll do!** (in annoyance) ora basta!; **to make do (with)** arrangiarsi (con)

do away with vt fus (kill) far fuori; (abolish) abolire

do up vt (laces) allacciare; (dress, buttons) abbottonare; (renovate: room, house) rimettere a nuovo, rifare

do with vt fus (need) aver bisogno di; (be connected): **what has it got to do with you?** e tu che c'entri?; **I won't have anything to do with it** non voglio avere niente a che farci; **it has to do with money** si tratta di soldi

do without vi fare senza ▷ vt fus fare a meno di

dock [dɔk] n (Naut) bacino; (Law) banco degli imputati ▷ vi entrare in bacino; (Space) agganciarsi; **~s** npl (Naut) dock m inv

doctor ['dɔktər] n medico(-a); (Ph.D. etc) dottore(-essa) ▷ vt (drink etc) adulterare; **call a ~!** chiamate un dottore!; **Doctor of Philosophy** n dottorato di ricerca; (person) titolare m/f di un dottorato di ricerca

document ['dɔkjumənt] n documento; **documentary** [-'mɛntərɪ] adj (evidence) documentato(-a) ▷ n documentario; **documentation** [dɔkjumən'teɪʃən] n documentazione f

dodge [dɔdʒ] n trucco; schivata ▷ vt schivare, eludere

dodgy ['dɔdʒɪ] adj (inf: uncertain) rischioso(-a); (untrustworthy) sospetto(-a)

does [dʌz] vb see **do**

doesn't ['dʌznt] = **does not**

dog [dɔg] n cane m ▷ vt (follow closely) pedinare; (fig: memory etc) perseguitare; **doggy bag** n sacchetto per gli avanzi (da portare a casa)

do-it-yourself ['duːɪtjɔː'sɛlf] n il far da sé

dole [dəul] (BRIT) n sussidio di disoccupazione; **to be on the ~** vivere del sussidio

doll [dɔl] n bambola

dollar ['dɔlər] n dollaro

dolphin ['dɔlfɪn] n delfino

dome [dəum] n cupola

domestic [də'mɛstɪk] adj (duty, happiness, animal) domestico(-a); (policy, affairs, flights) nazionale; **domestic appliance** n elettrodomestico

dominant ['dɔmɪnənt] adj dominante

dominate ['dɔmɪneɪt] vt dominare

domino ['dɔmɪnəu] (pl **dominoes**) n domino; **dominoes** n (game) gioco del domino

donate [də'neɪt] vt donare; **donation** [də'neɪʃən] n donazione f

done [dʌn] pp of **do**

donkey ['dɔŋkɪ] n asino

donor ['dəunər] n donatore(-trice); **donor card** n tessera di donatore di organi

don't [dəunt] = **do not**

donut ['dəunʌt] (US) n = **doughnut**

doodle ['duːdl] vi scarabocchiare

doom [duːm] n destino; rovina ▷ vt **to be ~ed (to failure)** essere predestinato(-a) (a fallire)

door [dɔːʳ] n porta; **doorbell** n campanello; **door handle** n maniglia; **doorknob** ['dɔːnɔb] n pomello, maniglia; **doorstep** n gradino della porta; **doorway** n porta

dope [dəup] n (inf: drugs) roba ▷ vt (horse etc) drogare

dormitory ['dɔːmɪtrɪ] n dormitorio; (US) casa dello studente

DOS [dɔs] n abbr (= disk operating system) DOS m

dosage ['dəusɪdʒ] n posologia

dose [dəus] n dose f; (bout) attacco

dot [dɔt] n punto; macchiolina ▷ vt **~ted with** punteggiato(-a) di; **on the ~** in punto; **dotted line** ['dɔtɪd-] n linea punteggiata

double ['dʌbl] adj doppio(-a) ▷ adv (twice): **to cost ~ sth** costare il doppio (di qc) ▷ n sosia m inv ▷ vt raddoppiare; (fold) piegare doppio or in due ▷ vi raddoppiarsi; **at the ~**, **on the ~** a passo di corsa; **double back** vi (person) tornare sui propri passi; **double bass** n contrabbasso; **double bed** n letto matrimoniale; **double-check** vt, vi ricontrollare; **double-click** vi (Comput) fare doppio click; **double-cross** vt fare il doppio gioco con; **doubledecker** n autobus m inv a due piani; **double glazing** (BRIT) n doppi vetri mpl; **double room** n camera matrimoniale; **doubles** n (Tennis) doppio; **double yellow lines** npl (BRIT: Aut) linea gialla doppia continua che segnala il divieto di sosta

doubt [daut] n dubbio ▷ vt dubitare di; **to ~ that** dubitare che + sub; **doubtful** adj dubbioso(-a), incerto(-a); (person) equivoco(-a); **doubtless** adv indubbiamente

dough [dəu] n pasta, impasto; **doughnut** (US **donut**) n bombolone m

dove [dʌv] n colombo(-a)

down [daun] n piume fpl ▷ adv giù, di sotto ▷ prep giù per ▷ vt (inf: drink) scolarsi; **~ with X!** abbasso X!; **down-and-out** n barbone m; **downfall** n caduta; rovina; **downhill** adv **to go downhill** andare in discesa; (fig) lasciarsi andare; andare a rotoli

Downing Street ['daʊnɪŋ-] n **lo ~** residenza del primo ministro inglese

● **DOWNING STREET**
●
● Al numero 10 di **Downing Street**, nel
● quartiere di Westminster a Londra, si
● trova la residenza del primo ministro
● inglese, al numero 11 quella del
● **Chancellor of the Exchequer**.

down: **download** vt (Comput) scaricare; **downright** adj franco(-a); (refusal) assoluto(-a)

Down's syndrome n sindrome f di Down

down: **downstairs** adv di sotto; al piano inferiore; **down-to-earth** adj pratico(-a); **downtown** adv in città; **down under** adv (Australia etc) agli antipodi; **downward** ['daʊnwəd] adj, adv in giù, in discesa; **downwards** ['daʊnwədz] adv = **downward**

doz. abbr = **dozen**

doze [dəʊz] vi sonnecchiare

dozen ['dʌzn] n dozzina; **a ~ books** una dozzina di libri; **~s of** decine fpl di

Dr. abbr (= doctor) dott.; (in street names) = **drive**

drab [dræb] adj tetro(-a), grigio(-a)

draft [drɑːft] n abbozzo; (Pol) bozza; (Comm) tratta; (us: call-up) leva ▷ vt abbozzare; see also **draught**

drag [dræg] vt trascinare; (river) dragare ▷ vi trascinarsi ▷ n (inf) noioso(-a); noia, fatica; (women's clothing): **in ~** travestito (da donna)

dragon ['drægən] n drago

dragonfly ['drægənflaɪ] n libellula

drain [dreɪn] n (for sewage) fogna; (on resources) salasso ▷ vt (land, marshes) prosciugare; (vegetables) scolare ▷ vi (water) defluire (via); **drainage** n prosciugamento; fognatura; **drainpipe** n tubo di scarico

drama ['drɑːmə] n (art) dramma m, teatro; (play) commedia; (event) dramma; **dramatic** [drə'mætɪk] adj drammatico(-a)

drank [dræŋk] pt of **drink**

drape [dreɪp] vt drappeggiare; **~s** (us) npl (curtains) tende fpl

drastic ['dræstɪk] adj drastico(-a)

draught [drɑːft] (us **draft**) n corrente f d'aria; (Naut) pescaggio; **on ~** (beer) alla spina; **draught beer** n birra alla spina; **draughts** (BRIT) n (gioco della) dama

draw [drɔː] (pt **drew**, pp **drawn**) vt tirare; (take out) estrarre; (attract) attirare; (picture) disegnare; (line, circle) tracciare;

(money) ritirare ▷ vi (Sport) pareggiare ▷ n pareggio; (in lottery) estrazione f; **to ~ near** avvicinarsi; **draw out** vi (lengthen) allungarsi ▷ vt (money) ritirare; **draw up** vi (stop) arrestarsi, fermarsi ▷ vt (chair) avvicinare; (document) compilare; **drawback** n svantaggio, inconveniente m

drawer [drɔːʳ] n cassetto

drawing ['drɔːɪŋ] n disegno; **drawing pin** (BRIT) n puntina da disegno; **drawing room** n salotto

drawn [drɔːn] pp of **draw**

dread [drɛd] n terrore m ▷ vt tremare all'idea di; **dreadful** adj terribile

dream [driːm] (pt, pp **dreamed** or **dreamt**) n sogno ▷ vt, vi sognare; **dreamer** n sognatore(-trice)

dreamt [drɛmt] pt, pp of **dream**

dreary ['drɪərɪ] adj tetro(-a); monotono(-a)

drench [drɛntʃ] vt inzuppare

dress [drɛs] n vestito; (no pl: clothing) abbigliamento ▷ vt vestire; (wound) fasciare ▷ vi vestirsi; **to get ~ed** vestirsi; **dress up** vi vestirsi a festa; (in fancy dress) vestirsi in costume; **dress circle** (BRIT) n prima galleria; **dresser** n (BRIT: cupboard) credenza; (us) cassettone m; **dressing** n (Med) benda; (Culin) condimento; **dressing gown** (BRIT) n vestaglia; **dressing room** n (Theatre) camerino; (Sport) spogliatoio; **dressing table** n toilette f inv; **dressmaker** n sarta

drew [druː] pt of **draw**

dribble ['drɪbl] vi (baby) sbavare ▷ vt (ball) dribblare

dried [draɪd] adj (fruit, beans) secco(-a); (eggs, milk) in polvere

drier ['draɪəʳ] n = **dryer**

drift [drɪft] n (of current etc) direzione f; forza; (of snow) cumulo; turbine m; (general meaning) senso ▷ vi (boat) essere trasportato(-a) dalla corrente; (sand, snow) ammucchiarsi

drill [drɪl] n trapano; (Mil) esercitazione f ▷ vt trapanare; (troops) addestrare ▷ vi (for oil) fare trivellazioni

drink [drɪŋk] (pt **drank**, pp **drunk**) n bevanda, bibita; (alcoholic drink) bicchierino; (sip) sorso ▷ vt, vi bere; **to have a ~** bere qualcosa; **would you like a ~?** vuoi qualcosa da bere?; **a ~ of water** un po' d'acqua; **drink-driving** n guida in stato di ebbrezza; **drinker** n bevitore(-trice); **drinking water** n acqua potabile

drip [drɪp] n goccia; gocciolamento; (Med) fleboclisi f inv ▷ vi gocciolare; (tap) sgocciolare

drive [draɪv] (pt **drove**, pp **driven**) n passeggiata or giro in macchina; (also: **~way**) viale m d'accesso; (energy) energia; (campaign) campagna; (also: **disk ~**) lettore m ▷ vt guidare; (nail) piantare; (push) cacciare, spingere; (Tech: motor) azionare; far funzionare ▷ vi (Aut: at controls) guidare; (: travel) andare in macchina; **left-/right-hand ~** guida a sinistra/destra; **to ~ sb mad** far impazzire qn; **drive out** vt (force out) cacciare, mandare via; **drive-in** (esp us) adj, n drive-in (m inv)

driven ['drɪvn] pp of **drive**

driver ['draɪvəʳ] n conducente m/f; (of taxi) tassista m; (chauffeur: of bus) autista m/f; **driver's license** (us) n patente f di guida

driveway ['draɪvweɪ] n viale m d'accesso

driving ['draɪvɪŋ] n guida; **driving instructor** n istruttore(-trice) di scuola guida; **driving lesson** n lezione f di guida; **driving licence** (BRIT) n patente f di guida; **driving test** n esame m di guida

drizzle ['drɪzl] n pioggerella

droop [druːp] vi (flower) appassire; (head, shoulders) chinarsi

drop [drɔp] n (of water) goccia; (lessening) diminuzione f; (fall) caduta ▷ vt lasciare cadere; (voice, eyes, price) abbassare; (set down from car) far scendere; (name from list) lasciare fuori ▷ vi cascare; (wind) abbassarsi; **drop in** vi (inf: visit): **to ~ in (on)** fare un salto (da), passare (da); **drop off** vi (sleep) addormentarsi ▷ vt (passenger) far scendere; **drop out** vi (withdraw) ritirarsi; (student etc) smettere di studiare

drought [draut] n siccità f inv

drove [drəuv] pt of **drive**

drown [draun] vt affogare; (fig: noise) soffocare ▷ vi affogare

drowsy ['drauzɪ] adj sonnolento(-a), assonnato(-a)

drug [drʌg] n farmaco; (narcotic) droga ▷ vt drogare; **to be on ~s** drogarsi; (Med) prendere medicinali; **hard/soft ~s** droghe pesanti/leggere; **drug addict** n tossicomane m/f; **drug dealer** n trafficante m/f di droga; **druggist** (us) n persona che gestisce un drugstore; **drugstore** (us) n drugstore m inv

drum [drʌm] n tamburo; (for oil, petrol) fusto ▷ vi tamburellare; **~s** npl (set of drums) batteria; **drummer** n batterista m/f

drunk [drʌŋk] pp of **drink** ▷ adj ubriaco(-a); ebbro(-a) ▷ n (also: **~ard**) ubriacone(-a); **drunken** adj ubriaco(-a); da ubriaco

dry [draɪ] adj secco(-a); (day, clothes) asciutto(-a) ▷ vt seccare; (clothes, hair, hands) asciugare ▷ vi asciugarsi; **dry off** vi asciugarsi ▷ vt asciugare; **dry up** vi seccarsi; **dry-cleaner's** n lavasecco m inv; **dry-cleaning** n pulitura a secco; **dryer** n (for hair) föhn m inv, asciugacapelli m inv; (for clothes) asciugabiancheria; (us: spin-dryer) centrifuga

DSS n abbr (= Department of Social Security) ministero della Previdenza sociale

DTP n abbr (= desk-top publishing) desktop publishing m inv

dual ['djuəl] adj doppio(-a); **dual carriageway** (BRIT) n strada a doppia carreggiata

dubious ['djuːbɪəs] adj dubbio(-a)

Dublin ['dʌblɪn] n Dublino f

duck [dʌk] n anatra ▷ vi abbassare la testa

due [djuː] adj dovuto(-a); (expected) atteso(-a); (fitting) giusto(-a) ▷ n dovuto ▷ adv **~ north** diritto verso nord

duel ['djuəl] n duello

duet [djuːˈɛt] n duetto

dug [dʌg] pt, pp of **dig**

duke [djuːk] n duca m

dull [dʌl] adj (light) debole; (boring) noioso(-a); (slow-witted) ottuso(-a); (sound, pain) sordo(-a); (weather, day) fosco(-a), scuro(-a) ▷ vt (pain, grief) attutire; (mind, senses) intorpidire

dumb [dʌm] adj muto(-a); (pej) stupido(-a)

dummy ['dʌmɪ] n (tailor's model) manichino; (Tech, Comm) riproduzione f; (BRIT: for baby) tettarella ▷ adj falso(-a), finto(-a)

dump [dʌmp] n (also: **rubbish ~**) discarica di rifiuti; (inf: place) buco ▷ vt (put down) scaricare; mettere giù; (get rid of) buttar via

dumpling ['dʌmplɪŋ] n specie di gnocco

dune [djuːn] n duna

dungarees [dʌŋɡəˈriːz] npl tuta

dungeon ['dʌndʒən] n prigione f sotterranea

duplex ['djuːplɛks] (us) n (house) casa con muro divisorio in comune con un'altra; (apartment) appartamento su due piani

duplicate [n 'djuːplɪkət, vb 'djuːplɪkeɪt] n doppio ▷ vt duplicare; **in ~** in doppia copia

durable ['djuərəbl] adj durevole; (clothes, metal) resistente

duration [djuəˈreɪʃən] n durata

during ['djuərɪŋ] prep durante, nel corso di

dusk [dʌsk] n crepuscolo

dust [dʌst] n polvere f ▷ vt (furniture) spolverare; (cake etc): **to ~ with** cospargere con; **dustbin** (BRIT) n pattumiera; **duster** n straccio per la polvere; **dustman** (irreg: BRIT) n netturbino; **dustpan** n pattumiera; **dusty** adj polveroso(-a)

Dutch [dʌtʃ] adj olandese ▷ n (Ling) olandese m; **the ~** npl gli Olandesi; **to go ~** (inf) fare alla romana; **Dutchman, Dutchwoman** (irreg) n olandese m/f

duty ['dju:tɪ] n dovere m; (tax) dazio, tassa; **on ~** di servizio; **off ~** libero(-a), fuori servizio; **duty-free** adj esente da dazio

duvet ['du:veɪ] (BRIT) n piumino, piumone m

DVD n abbr (= digital versatile or video disk) DVD m inv; **DVD player** n lettore m DVD

dwarf [dwɔːf] n nano(-a) ▷ vt far apparire piccolo

dwell [dwɛl] (pt, pp dwelt) vi dimorare; **dwell on** vt fus indugiare su

dwelt [dwɛlt] pt, pp of **dwell**

dwindle ['dwɪndl] vi diminuire

dye [daɪ] n tinta ▷ vt tingere

dying ['daɪɪŋ] adj morente, moribondo(-a)

dynamic [daɪ'næmɪk] adj dinamico(-a)

dynamite ['daɪnəmaɪt] n dinamite f

dyslexia [dɪs'lɛksɪə] n dislessia

dyslexic [dɪs'lɛksɪk] adj, n dislessico(-a)

E [iː] n (Mus) mi m

E111 n abbr (also: **form ~**) E111 (modulo CEE per rimborso spese mediche)

each [iːtʃ] adj ogni, ciascuno(-a) ▷ pron ciascuno(-a), ognuno(-a); **~ one** ognuno(-a); **~ other** si or ci etc; **they hate ~ other** si odiano (l'un l'altro); **you are jealous of ~ other** siete gelosi l'uno dell'altro; **they have 2 books ~** hanno 2 libri ciascuno

eager ['iːgəʳ] adj impaziente, desideroso(-a); ardente; **to be ~ for** essere desideroso di, aver gran voglia di

eagle ['iːgl] n aquila

ear [ɪəʳ] n orecchio; (of corn) pannocchia; **earache** n mal m d'orecchi; **eardrum** n timpano

earl [əːl] (BRIT) n conte m

earlier ['əːlɪəʳ] adj precedente ▷ adv prima

early ['əːlɪ] adv presto, di buon'ora; (ahead of time) in anticipo ▷ adj (near the beginning) primo(-a); (sooner than expected) prematuro(-a); (quick: reply) veloce; **at an ~ hour** di buon'ora; **to have an ~ night** andare a letto presto; **in the ~** or **~ in the spring/19th century** all'inizio della primavera/dell'Ottocento; **early retirement** n ritiro anticipato

earmark ['ɪəmɑːk] vt **to ~ sth for** destinare qc a

earn [əːn] vt guadagnare; (*rest, reward*) meritare

earnest ['əːnɪst] adj serio(-a); **in ~** sul serio

earnings ['əːnɪŋz] npl guadagni mpl; (*salary*) stipendio

ear: **earphones** ['ɪəfəʊnz] npl cuffia; **earplugs** npl tappi mpl per le orecchie; **earring** ['ɪərɪŋ] n orecchino

earth [əːθ] n terra ▷ vt (BRIT Elec) mettere a terra; **earthquake** n terremoto

ease [iːz] n agio, comodo ▷ vt (*soothe*) calmare; (*loosen*) allentare; **to ~ sth out/in** tirare fuori/infilare qc con delicatezza; facilitare l'uscita/l'entrata di qc; **at ~** a proprio agio; (*Mil*) a riposo

easily ['iːzɪlɪ] adv facilmente

east [iːst] n est m ▷ adj dell'est ▷ adv a oriente; **the E~** l'Oriente m; (*Pol*) l'Est; **eastbound** ['iːstbaʊnd] adj (*traffic*) diretto(-a) a est; (*carriageway*) che porta a est

Easter ['iːstər] n Pasqua; **Easter egg** n uovo di Pasqua

eastern ['iːstən] adj orientale, d'oriente; dell'est

Easter Sunday n domenica di Pasqua

easy ['iːzɪ] adj facile; (*manner*) disinvolto(-a) ▷ adv **to take it** or **things ~** prendersela con calma; **easy-going** adj accomodante

eat [iːt] (*pt* **ate**, *pp* **eaten**) vt, vi mangiare; **can we have something to ~?** possiamo mangiare qualcosa?; **eat out** vi mangiare fuori

eavesdrop ['iːvzdrɔp] vi **to ~ (on a conversation)** origliare (una conversazione)

e-book ['iːbuk] n libro elettronico

e-business ['iːbɪznɪs] n (*company*) azienda che opera in Internet; (*commerce*) commercio elettronico

EC n abbr (= *European Community*) CE f

eccentric [ɪk'sɛntrɪk] adj, n eccentrico(-a)

echo ['ɛkəʊ] (*pl* **echoes**) n eco m or f ▷ vt ripetere; fare eco a ▷ vi echeggiare; dare un eco

eclipse [ɪ'klɪps] n eclissi f inv

eco-friendly [iːkəʊ'frɛndlɪ] adj ecologico(-a)

ecological [iːkə'lɔdʒɪkəl] adj ecologico(-a)

ecology [ɪ'kɔlədʒɪ] n ecologia

e-commerce [iːkɔməːs] n commercio elettronico

economic [iːkə'nɔmɪk] adj economico(-a); **economical** adj economico(-a); (*person*) economo(-a); **economics** n economia ▷ npl lato finanziario

economist [ɪ'kɔnəmɪst] n economista m/f

economize [ɪ'kɔnəmaɪz] vi risparmiare, fare economia

economy [ɪ'kɔnəmɪ] n economia; **economy class** n (*Aviat*) classe f turistica; **economy class syndrome** n sindrome f della classe economica

ecstasy ['ɛkstəsɪ] n estasi f inv; **ecstatic** [ɛks'tætɪk] adj estatico(-a), in estasi

eczema ['ɛksɪmə] n eczema m

edge [ɛdʒ] n margine m; (*of table, plate, cup*) orlo; (*of knife etc*) taglio ▷ vt bordare; **on ~** (*fig*) = **edgy**; **to edge away from** sgattaiolare da

edgy ['ɛdʒɪ] adj nervoso(-a)

edible ['ɛdɪbl] adj commestibile; (*meal*) mangiabile

Edinburgh ['ɛdɪnbərə] n Edimburgo f

edit ['ɛdɪt] vt curare; **edition** [ɪ'dɪfən] n edizione f; **editor** n (*in newspaper*) redattore(-trice), redattore(-trice) capo; (*of sb's work*) curatore(-trice); **editorial** [-'tɔːrɪəl] adj redazionale, editoriale ▷ n editoriale m

Be careful not to translate *editor* by the Italian word *editore*.

educate ['ɛdjukeɪt] vt istruire; educare; **educated** adj istruito(-a)

education [ɛdju'keɪfən] n educazione f; (*schooling*) istruzione f; **educational** adj pedagogico(-a); scolastico(-a); istruttivo(-a)

eel [iːl] n anguilla

eerie ['ɪərɪ] adj che fa accapponare la pelle

effect [ɪ'fɛkt] n effetto ▷ vt effettuare; **to take ~** (*law*) entrare in vigore; (*drug*) fare effetto; **in ~** effettivamente; **~s** npl (*Theat*) effetti mpl scenici; (*property*) effetti mpl; **effective** adj efficace; (*actual*) effettivo(-a); **effectively** adv efficacemente; effettivamente

efficiency [ɪ'fɪfənsɪ] n efficienza; rendimento effettivo

efficient [ɪ'fɪfənt] adj efficiente; **efficiently** adv efficientemente; efficacemente

effort ['ɛfət] n sforzo; **effortless** adj senza sforzo, facile

e.g. adv abbr (= *exempli gratia*) per esempio, p.es.

egg [ɛg] n uovo; **hard-boiled/soft-boiled ~** uovo sodo/alla coque; **eggcup** n portauovo m inv; **eggplant** (*esp us*) n melanzana; **eggshell** n guscio d'uovo; **egg white** n albume m, bianco d'uovo; **egg yolk** n tuorlo, rosso (d'uovo)

ego ['iːgəʊ] n ego m inv

Egypt ['iːdʒɪpt] n Egitto; **Egyptian** [ɪ'dʒɪpfən] adj, n egiziano(-a)

eight [eɪt] num otto; **eighteen** num diciotto; **eighteenth** num diciottesimo(-a); **eighth** [eɪtθ] num

ottavo(-a); **eightieth** ['eɪtɪɪθ] *num*
ottantesimo(-a); **eighty** *num* ottanta
Eire ['ɛərə] *n* Repubblica d'Irlanda
either ['aɪðəʳ] *adj* l'uno(-a) o l'altro(-a);
(*both, each*) ciascuno(-a) ▷ *pron* ~ **(of
them)** (o) l'uno(-a) o l'altro(-a) ▷ *adv*
neanche ▷ *conj* ~ **good or bad** o buono o
cattivo; **on ~ side** su ciascun lato; **I don't
like** ~ non mi piace né l'uno né l'altro; **no, I
don't** ~ no, neanch'io
eject [ɪ'dʒɛkt] *vt* espellere; lanciare
elaborate [*adj* ɪ'læbərɪt, *vb* ɪ'læbəreɪt]
adj elaborato(-a), minuzioso(-a) ▷ *vt*
elaborare ▷ *vi* fornire i particolari
elastic [ɪ'læstɪk] *adj* elastico(-a) ▷ *n*
elastico; **elastic band** (*BRIT*) *n* elastico
elbow ['ɛlbəu] *n* gomito
elder ['ɛldəʳ] *adj* maggiore, più vecchio(-a)
▷ *n* (*tree*) sambuco; **one's ~s** i più anziani;
elderly *adj* anziano(-a) ▷ *npl* **the elderly**
gli anziani
eldest ['ɛldɪst] *adj, n* **the ~ (child)** il(la)
maggiore (dei bambini)
elect [ɪ'lɛkt] *vt* eleggere ▷ *adj* **the
president ~** il presidente designato; **to
~ to do** decidere di fare; **election** [ɪ'lɛkʃə
n] *n* elezione *f*; **electoral** [ɪ'lɛktərəl] *adj*
elettorale; **electorate** *n* elettorato
electric [ɪ'lɛktrɪk] *adj* elettrico(-a);
electrical *adj* elettrico(-a); **electric
blanket** *n* coperta elettrica; **electric fire**
n stufa elettrica; **electrician** [ɪlɛk'trɪʃən]
n elettricista *m*; **electricity** [ɪlɛk'trɪsɪtɪ]
n elettricità; **electric shock** *n* scossa
(elettrica); **electrify** [ɪ'lɛktrɪfaɪ] *vt* (*Rail*)
elettrificare; (*audience*) elettrizzare
electronic [ɪlɛk'trɔnɪk] *adj* elettronico(-a);
electronic mail *n* posta elettronica;
electronics *n* elettronica
elegance ['ɛlɪgəns] *n* eleganza
elegant ['ɛlɪgənt] *adj* elegante
element ['ɛlɪmənt] *n* elemento; (*of heater,
kettle etc*) resistenza
elementary [ɛlɪ'mɛntərɪ] *adj* elementare;
elementary school (*US*) *n* scuola
elementare
elephant ['ɛlɪfənt] *n* elefante(-essa)
elevate ['ɛlɪveɪt] *vt* elevare
elevator ['ɛlɪveɪtəʳ] *n* elevatore *m*; (*US: lift*)
ascensore *m*
eleven [ɪ'lɛvn] *num* undici; **eleventh** *adj*
undicesimo(-a)
eligible ['ɛlɪdʒəbl] *adj* eleggibile; (*for
membership*) che ha i requisiti
eliminate [ɪ'lɪmɪneɪt] *vt* eliminare
elm [ɛlm] *n* olmo
eloquent ['ɛləkwənt] *adj* eloquente
else [ɛls] *adv* altro; **something ~**
qualcos'altro; **somewhere ~** altrove;

everywhere ~ in qualsiasi altro luogo;
nobody ~ nessun altro; **where ~?** in quale
altro luogo?; **little ~** poco altro; **elsewhere**
adv altrove
elusive [ɪ'luːsɪv] *adj* elusivo(-a)
e-mail *n abbr* (= *electronic mail*) posta
elettronica ▷ *vt* mandare un messaggio
di posta elettronica a; **e-mail address** *n*
indirizzo di posta elettronica
embankment [ɪm'bæŋkmənt] *n* (*of road,
railway*) terrapieno
embargo [ɪm'bɑːgəu] *n* (*pl* **embargoes**)
(*Comm, Naut*) embargo ▷ *vt* mettere
l'embargo su; **to put an ~ on sth** mettere
l'embargo su qc
embark [ɪm'bɑːk] *vi* **to ~ (on)** imbarcarsi
(su) ▷ *vt* imbarcare; **to ~ on** (*fig*)
imbarcarsi in
embarrass [ɪm'bærəs] *vt* imbarazzare;
embarrassed *adj* imbarazzato(-a);
embarrassing *adj* imbarazzante;
embarrassment *n* imbarazzo
embassy ['ɛmbəsɪ] *n* ambasciata
embrace [ɪm'breɪs] *vt* abbracciare ▷ *vi*
abbracciarsi ▷ *n* abbraccio
embroider [ɪm'brɔɪdəʳ] *vt* ricamare;
embroidery *n* ricamo
embryo ['ɛmbrɪəu] *n* embrione *m*
emerald ['ɛmərəld] *n* smeraldo
emerge [ɪ'məːdʒ] *vi* emergere
emergency [ɪ'məːdʒənsɪ] *n* emergenza;
in an ~ in caso di emergenza; **emergency
brake** (*US*) *n* freno a mano; **emergency
exit** *n* uscita di sicurezza; **emergency
landing** *n* atterraggio forzato;
emergency room (*US: Med*) *n* pronto
soccorso; **emergency services** *npl* (*fire,
police, ambulance*) servizi *mpl* di pronto
intervento
emigrate ['ɛmɪgreɪt] *vi* emigrare;
emigration [ɛmɪ'greɪʃən] *n* emigrazione *f*
eminent ['ɛmɪnənt] *adj* eminente
emissions [ɪ'mɪʃənz] *npl* emissioni *fpl*
emit [ɪ'mɪt] *vt* emettere
emotion [ɪ'məuʃən] *n* emozione *f*;
emotional *adj* (*person*) emotivo(-a);
(*scene*) commovente; (*tone, speech*)
carico(-a) d'emozione
emperor ['ɛmpərəʳ] *n* imperatore *m*
emphasis ['ɛmfəsɪs] (*pl* **-ases**) *n* enfasi *f
inv*; importanza
emphasize ['ɛmfəsaɪz] *vt* (*word, point*)
sottolineare; (*feature*) mettere in evidenza
empire ['ɛmpaɪəʳ] *n* impero
employ [ɪm'plɔɪ] *vt* impiegare; **employee**
[-'iː] *n* impiegato(-a); **employer** *n*
principale *m/f*, datore *m* di lavoro;
employment *n* impiego; **employment
agency** *n* agenzia di collocamento

empower [ɪm'pauəʳ] *vt* **to ~ sb to do** concedere autorità a qn di fare

empress ['ɛmprɪs] *n* imperatrice *f*

emptiness ['ɛmptɪnɪs] *n* vuoto

empty ['ɛmptɪ] *adj* vuoto(-a); (*threat, promise*) vano(-a) ▷ *vt* vuotare ▷ *vi* vuotarsi; (*liquid*) scaricarsi; **empty-handed** *adj* a mani vuote

EMU *n abbr* (= *economic and monetary union*) unione *f* economica e monetaria

emulsion [ɪ'mʌlʃən] *n* emulsione *f*

enable [ɪ'neɪbl] *vt* **to ~ sb to do** permettere a qn di fare

enamel [ɪ'næməl] *n* smalto; (*also:* **~ paint**) vernice *f* a smalto

enchanting [ɪn'tʃɑ:ntɪŋ] *adj* incantevole, affascinante

encl. *abbr* (= *enclosed*) all.

enclose [ɪn'kləuz] *vt* (*land*) circondare, recingere; (*letter etc*) **to ~ (with)** allegare (con); **please find ~d** trovi qui accluso

enclosure [ɪn'kləuʒəʳ] *n* recinto

encore [ɔŋ'kɔ:ʳ] *excl* bis ▷ *n* bis *m inv*

encounter [ɪn'kauntəʳ] *n* incontro ▷ *vt* incontrare

encourage [ɪn'kʌrɪdʒ] *vt* incoraggiare; **encouragement** *n* incoraggiamento

encouraging [ɪn'kʌrɪdʒɪŋ] *adj* incoraggiante

encyclop(a)edia [ɛnsaɪkləu'pi:dɪə] *n* enciclopedia

end [ɛnd] *n* fine *f*; (*aim*) fine *m*; (*of table*) bordo estremo; (*of pointed object*) punta ▷ *vt* finire; (*also:* **bring to an ~, put an ~ to**) mettere fine a ▷ *vi* finire; **in the ~** alla fine; **on ~** (*object*) ritto(-a); **to stand on ~** (*hair*) rizzarsi; **for hours on ~** per ore ed ore; **end up** *vi* **to ~ up in** finire in

endanger [ɪn'deɪndʒəʳ] *vt* mettere in pericolo

endearing [ɪn'dɪərɪŋ] *adj* accattivante

endeavour [ɪn'dɛvəʳ] (*US* **endeavor**) *n* sforzo, tentativo ▷ *vi* **to ~ to do** cercare *or* sforzarsi di fare

ending ['ɛndɪŋ] *n* fine *f*, conclusione *f*; (*Ling*) desinenza

endless ['ɛndlɪs] *adj* senza fine

endorse [ɪn'dɔ:s] *vt* (*cheque*) girare; (*approve*) approvare, appoggiare; **endorsement** *n* approvazione *f*; (*on driving licence*) contravvenzione registrata sulla patente

endurance [ɪn'djuərəns] *n* resistenza; pazienza

endure [ɪn'djuəʳ] *vt* sopportare, resistere a ▷ *vi* durare

enemy ['ɛnəmɪ] *adj, n* nemico(-a)

energetic [ɛnə'dʒɛtɪk] *adj* energico(-a), attivo(-a)

energy ['ɛnədʒɪ] *n* energia

enforce [ɪn'fɔ:s] *vt* (*Law*) applicare, far osservare

engaged [ɪn'geɪdʒd] *adj* (*BRIT: busy, in use*) occupato(-a); (*betrothed*) fidanzato(-a); **the line's ~** la linea è occupata; **to get ~** fidanzarsi; **engaged tone** (*BRIT*) *n* (*Tel*) segnale *m* di occupato

engagement [ɪn'geɪdʒmənt] *n* impegno, obbligo; appuntamento; (*to marry*) fidanzamento; **engagement ring** *n* anello di fidanzamento

engaging [ɪn'geɪdʒɪŋ] *adj* attraente

engine ['ɛndʒɪn] *n* (*Aut*) motore *m*; (*Rail*) locomotiva

engineer [ɛndʒɪ'nɪəʳ] *n* ingegnere *m*; (*BRIT: for repairs*) tecnico; (*on ship: US: Rail*) macchinista *m*; **engineering** *n* ingegneria

England ['ɪŋglənd] *n* Inghilterra

English ['ɪŋglɪʃ] *adj* inglese ▷ *n* (*Ling*) inglese *m*; **the ~** *npl* gli Inglesi; **English Channel** *n* **the English Channel** la Manica; **Englishman** (*irreg*) *n* inglese *m*; **Englishwoman** (*irreg*) *n* inglese *f*

engrave [ɪn'greɪv] *vt* incidere

engraving [ɪn'greɪvɪŋ] *n* incisione *f*

enhance [ɪn'hɑ:ns] *vt* accrescere

enjoy [ɪn'dʒɔɪ] *vt* godere; (*have: success, fortune*) avere; **to ~ o.s.** godersela, divertirsi; **enjoyable** *adj* piacevole; **enjoyment** *n* piacere *m*, godimento

enlarge [ɪn'lɑ:dʒ] *vt* ingrandire ▷ *vi* **to ~ on** (*subject*) dilungarsi su; **enlargement** *n* (*Phot*) ingrandimento

enlist [ɪn'lɪst] *vt* arruolare; (*support*) procurare ▷ *vi* arruolarsi

enormous [ɪ'nɔ:məs] *adj* enorme

enough [ɪ'nʌf] *adj, n* **~ time/books** assai tempo/libri; **have you got ~?** ne ha abbastanza *or* a sufficienza? ▷ *adv* **big ~** abbastanza grande; **he has not worked ~** non ha lavorato abbastanza; **~!** basta!; **that's ~, thanks** basta così, grazie; **I've had ~ of him** ne ho abbastanza di lui; **... which, funnily** *or* **oddly ~** ... che, strano a dirsi

enquire [ɪn'kwaɪəʳ] *vt, vi* (*esp BRIT*) = **inquire**

enquiry [ɪn'kwaɪərɪ] *n* (*esp BRIT*) = **inquiry**

enrage [ɪn'reɪdʒ] *vt* fare arrabbiare

enrich [ɪn'rɪtʃ] *vt* arricchire

enrol [ɪn'rəul] (*US* **enroll**) *vt* iscrivere ▷ *vi* iscriversi; **enrolment** (*US* **enrollment**) *n* iscrizione *f*

en route [ɔn'ru:t] *adv* **~ for/from/to** in viaggio per/da/a

en suite [ɔn'swi:t] *adj* **room with ~**

bathroom camera con bagno
ensure [ɪnˈʃʊəʳ] vt assicurare; garantire
entail [ɪnˈteɪl] vt comportare
enter [ˈɛntəʳ] vt entrare in; (army)
arruolarsi in; (competition) partecipare a;
(sb for a competition) iscrivere; (write down)
registrare; (Comput) inserire ▷ vi entrare
enterprise [ˈɛntəpraɪz] n (undertaking,
company) impresa; (spirit) iniziativa;
free ~ liberalismo economico; **private
~** iniziativa privata; **enterprising** [ˈɛntə
praɪzɪŋ] adj intraprendente
entertain [ɛntəˈteɪn] vt divertire; (invite)
ricevere; (idea, plan) nutrire; **entertainer** n
comico(-a); **entertaining** adj divertente;
entertainment n (amusement)
divertimento; (show) spettacolo
enthusiasm [ɪnˈθuːzɪæzəm] n
entusiasmo
enthusiast [ɪnˈθuːzɪæst] n entusiasta m/
f; **enthusiastic** [-ˈæstɪk] adj entusiasta,
entusiastico(-a); **to be enthusiastic
about sth/sb** essere appassionato(-a) di
qc/entusiasta di qn
entire [ɪnˈtaɪəʳ] adj intero(-a); **entirely** adv
completamente, interamente
entitle [ɪnˈtaɪtl] vt (give right): **to ~ sb to
sth/to do** dare diritto a qn a qc/a fare;
entitled adj (book) che si intitola; **to be
entitled to do** avere il diritto di fare
entrance [n ˈɛntrns, vb ɪnˈtrɑːns] n
entrata, ingresso; (of person) entrata
▷ vt incantare, rapire; **where's the ~?**
dov'è l'entrata?; **to gain ~ to** (university
etc) essere ammesso a; **entrance
examination** n esame m di ammissione;
entrance fee n tassa d'iscrizione; (to
museum etc) prezzo d'ingresso; **entrance
ramp** (us) n (Aut) rampa di accesso;
entrant [ˈɛntrnt] n partecipante m/f;
concorrente m/f
entrepreneur [ɔntrəprəˈnəːʳ] n
imprenditore m
entrust [ɪnˈtrʌst] vt **to ~ sth to** affidare
qc a
entry [ˈɛntrɪ] n entrata; (way in) entrata,
ingresso; (item: on list) iscrizione f; (in
dictionary) voce f; **no ~** vietato l'ingresso;
(Aut) divieto di accesso; **entry phone** n
citofono
envelope [ˈɛnvələup] n busta
envious [ˈɛnvɪəs] adj invidioso(-a)
environment [ɪnˈvaɪrnmənt] n
ambiente m; **environmental** [-
ˈmɛntl] adj ecologico(-a); ambientale;
environmentally [ɪnvaɪərənˈmɛntəlɪ]
adv **environmentally sound/friendly**
che rispetta l'ambiente
envisage [ɪnˈvɪzɪdʒ] vt immaginare;

prevedere
envoy [ˈɛnvɔɪ] n inviato(-a)
envy [ˈɛnvɪ] n invidia ▷ vt invidiare; **to ~ sb
sth** invidiare qn per qc
epic [ˈɛpɪk] n poema m epico ▷ adj
epico(-a)
epidemic [ɛpɪˈdɛmɪk] n epidemia
epilepsy [ˈɛpɪlɛpsɪ] n epilessia
epileptic [ɛpɪˈlɛptɪk] adj, n epilettico(-a);
epileptic fit n attacco epilettico
episode [ˈɛpɪsəud] n episodio
equal [ˈiːkwl] adj uguale ▷ n pari m/f
inv ▷ vt uguagliare; **~ to** (task) all'altezza
di; **equality** [iːˈkwɔlɪtɪ] n uguaglianza;
equalize vi pareggiare; **equally** adv
ugualmente
equation [ɪˈkweɪʃən] n (Math) equazione f
equator [ɪˈkweɪtəʳ] n equatore m
equip [ɪˈkwɪp] vt equipaggiare, attrezzare;
to ~ sb/sth with fornire qn/qc di; **to
be well ~ped** (office etc) essere ben
attrezzato(-a); **he is well ~ped for the
job** ha i requisiti necessari per quel lavoro;
equipment n attrezzatura; (electrical etc)
apparecchiatura
equivalent [ɪˈkwɪvələnt] adj equivalente
▷ n equivalente m; **to be ~ to** equivalere a
ER abbr (BRIT) = **Elizabeth Regina** (US:
Med) = **emergency room**
era [ˈɪərə] n era, età f inv
erase [ɪˈreɪz] vt cancellare; **eraser** n
gomma
erect [ɪˈrɛkt] adj eretto(-a) ▷ vt costruire;
(assemble) montare; **erection** [ɪˈrɛkʃə
n] n costruzione f; montaggio; (Physiol)
erezione f
ERM n (= Exchange Rate Mechanism) ERM m
erode [ɪˈrəud] vt erodere; (metal)
corrodere
erosion [ɪˈrəuʒən] n erosione f
erotic [ɪˈrɔtɪk] adj erotico(-a)
errand [ˈɛrnd] n commissione f
erratic [ɪˈrætɪk] adj imprevedibile; (person,
mood) incostante
error [ˈɛrəʳ] n errore m
erupt [ɪˈrʌpt] vi (volcano) mettersi (or
essere) in eruzione; (war, crisis) scoppiare;
eruption [ɪˈrʌpʃən] n eruzione f; scoppio
escalate [ˈɛskəleɪt] vi intensificarsi
escalator [ˈɛskəleɪtəʳ] n scala mobile
escape [ɪˈskeɪp] n evasione f; fuga; (of gas
etc) fuga, fuoriuscita ▷ vi fuggire; (from
jail) evadere, scappare; (leak) uscire ▷ vt
sfuggire a; **to ~ from** (place) fuggire da;
(person) sfuggire a
escort [n ˈɛskɔːt, vb ɪˈskɔːt] n scorta; (male
companion) cavaliere m ▷ vt scortare;
accompagnare
especially [ɪˈspɛʃlɪ] adv specialmente;

soprattutto; espressamente
espionage ['ɛspɪɑnɑːʒ] n spionaggio
essay ['ɛseɪ] n (Scol) composizione f;
(Literature) saggio
essence ['ɛsns] n essenza
essential [ɪ'sɛnʃl] adj essenziale ▷ n
elemento essenziale; **essentially** adv
essenzialmente; **essentials** npl **the
essentials** l'essenziale msg
establish [ɪ'stæblɪʃ] vt stabilire; (business)
mettere su; (one's power etc) affermare;
establishment n stabilimento; **the
Establishment** la classe dirigente,
l'establishment m
estate [ɪ'steɪt] n proprietà f inv; beni
mpl, patrimonio; (BRIT: also: **housing ~**)
complesso edilizio; **estate agent** (BRIT) n
agente m immobiliare; **estate car** (BRIT) n
giardiniera
estimate [n 'ɛstɪmət, vb 'ɛstɪmeɪt] n
stima; (Comm) preventivo ▷ vt stimare,
valutare
etc abbr (= et cetera) etc., ecc.
eternal [ɪ'təːnl] adj eterno(-a)
eternity [ɪ'təːnɪtɪ] n eternità
ethical ['ɛθɪkl] adj etico(-a), morale;
ethics ['ɛθɪks] n etica ▷ npl morale f
Ethiopia [iːθɪ'əupɪə] n Etiopia
ethnic ['ɛθnɪk] adj etnico(-a); **ethnic
minority** n minoranza etnica
etiquette ['ɛtɪkɛt] n etichetta
EU n abbr (= European Union) UE f
euro ['juərəu] n (currency) euro m inv
Europe ['juərəp] n Europa; **European**
[-'piːən] adj, n europeo(-a); **European
Community** n Comunità Europea;
European Union n Unione f europea
Eurostar® ['juərəustɑːʳ] n Eurostar®
m inv
evacuate [ɪ'vækjueɪt] vt evacuare
evade [ɪ'veɪd] vt (tax) evadere; (duties etc)
sottrarsi a; (person) schivare
evaluate [ɪ'væljueɪt] vt valutare
evaporate [ɪ'væpəreɪt] vi evaporare
eve [iːv] n **on the ~ of** alla vigilia di
even ['iːvn] adj regolare; (number) pari
inv ▷ adv anche, perfino; **~ if, ~ though**
anche se; **~ more** ancora di più; **~ so** ciò
nonostante; **not ~** nemmeno; **to get ~
with sb** dare la pari a qn
evening ['iːvnɪŋ] n sera; (as duration,
event) serata; **in the ~** la sera; **evening
class** n corso serale; **evening dress**
n (woman's) abito da sera; **in evening
dress** (man) in abito scuro; (woman) in
abito lungo
event [ɪ'vɛnt] n avvenimento; (Sport)
gara; **in the ~ of** in caso di; **eventful** adj
denso(-a) di eventi

eventual [ɪ'vɛntʃuəl] adj finale
⬛ Be careful not to translate **eventual**
by the Italian word **eventuale**.
eventually [ɪ'vɛntʃuəlɪ] adv alla fine
⬛ Be careful not to translate **eventually**
by the Italian word **eventualmente**.
ever ['ɛvəʳ] adv mai; (at all times) sempre;
the best ~ il migliore che ci sia mai stato;
have you ~ seen it? l'ha mai visto?; **~
since** adv da allora ▷ conj sin da quando;
~ so pretty così bello(-a); **evergreen** n
sempreverde m
every ['ɛvrɪ] adj ogni; **~ day** tutti i
giorni, ogni giorno; **~ other/third day**
ogni due/tre giorni; **~ other car** una
macchina su due; **~ now and then** ogni
tanto, di quando in quando; **everybody**
pron = **everyone**; **everyday** adj
quotidiano(-a); di ogni giorno; **everyone**
pron ognuno, tutti pl; **everything** pron
tutto, ogni cosa; **everywhere** adv (gen)
dappertutto; (wherever) ovunque
evict [ɪ'vɪkt] vt sfrattare
evidence ['ɛvɪdns] n (proof) prova; (of
witness) testimonianza; (sign): **to show ~
of** dare segni di; **to give ~** deporre
evident ['ɛvɪdnt] adj evidente; **evidently**
adv evidentemente
evil ['iːvl] adj cattivo(-a), maligno(-a) ▷ n
male m
evoke [ɪ'vəuk] vt evocare
evolution [iːvə'luːʃən] n evoluzione f
evolve [ɪ'vɔlv] vt elaborare ▷ vi
svilupparsi, evolversi
ewe [juː] n pecora
ex (inf) [ɛks] n **my ex** il (la) mio(-a) ex
ex- [ɛks] prefix ex
exact [ɪg'zækt] adj esatto(-a) ▷ vt **to ~ sth
(from)** estorcere qc (da); esigere qc (da);
exactly adv esattamente
exaggerate [ɪg'zædʒəreɪt] vt, vi esagerare;
exaggeration [-'reɪʃən] n esagerazione f
exam [ɪg'zæm] n abbr (Scol)
= **examination**
examination [ɪgzæmɪ'neɪʃən] n (Scol)
esame m; (Med) controllo
examine [ɪg'zæmɪn] vt esaminare;
examiner n esaminatore(-trice)
example [ɪg'zɑːmpl] n esempio; **for ~** ad
or per esempio
exasperated [ɪg'zɑːspəreɪtɪd] adj
esasperato(-a)
excavate ['ɛkskəveɪt] vt scavare
exceed [ɪk'siːd] vt superare; (one's powers,
time limit) oltrepassare; **exceedingly** adv
eccessivamente
excel [ɪk'sɛl] vi eccellere ▷ vt sorpassare;
to ~ o.s (BRIT) superare se stesso
excellence ['ɛksələns] n eccellenza

excellent ['ɛksələnt] *adj* eccellente
except [ɪk'sɛpt] *prep* (*also:* ~ **for, ~ing**) salvo, all'infuori di, eccetto ▷ *vt* escludere; ~ **if/when** salvo se/quando; ~ **that** salvo che; **exception** [ɪk'sɛpʃən] *n* eccezione *f*; **to take exception to** trovare a ridire su; **exceptional** [ɪk'sɛpʃənl] *adj* eccezionale; **exceptionally** [ɪk'sɛpʃənəlɪ] *adv* eccezionalmente
excerpt ['ɛksəːpt] *n* estratto
excess [ɪk'sɛs] *n* eccesso; **excess baggage** *n* bagaglio in eccedenza; **excessive** *adj* eccessivo(-a)
exchange [ɪks'tʃeɪndʒ] *n* scambio; (*also:* **telephone ~**) centralino ▷ *vt* **to ~ (for)** scambiare (con); **could I ~ this, please?** posso cambiarlo, per favore?; **exchange rate** *n* tasso di cambio
excite [ɪk'saɪt] *vt* eccitare; **to get ~d** eccitarsi; **excited** *adj* **to get excited** essere elettrizzato(-a); **excitement** *n* eccitazione *f*; agitazione *f*; **exciting** *adj* avventuroso(-a); (*film, book*) appassionante
exclaim [ɪk'skleɪm] *vi* esclamare; **exclamation** [ɛksklə'meɪʃən] *n* esclamazione *f*; **exclamation mark** (*us* **exclamation point**) *n* punto esclamativo
exclude [ɪk'skluːd] *vt* escludere
excluding [ɪk'skluːdɪŋ] *prep* ~ **VAT** IVA esclusa
exclusion [ɪk'skluːʒən] *n* esclusione *f*; **to the ~ of** escludendo
exclusive [ɪk'skluːsɪv] *adj* esclusivo(-a); ~ **of VAT** I.V.A. esclusa; **exclusively** *adv* esclusivamente
excruciating [ɪk'skruːʃɪeɪtɪŋ] *adj* straziante, atroce
excursion [ɪk'skəːʃən] *n* escursione *f*, gita
excuse [*n* ɪk'skjuːs, *vb* ɪk'skjuːz] *n* scusa ▷ *vt* scusare; **to ~ sb from** (*activity*) dispensare qn da; ~ **me!** mi scusi!; **now, if you will ~ me …** ora, mi scusi ma …
ex-directory ['ɛksdɪ'rɛktərɪ] (*BRIT*) *adj* (*Tel*): **to be ~** non essere sull'elenco
execute ['ɛksɪkjuːt] *vt* (*prisoner*) giustiziare; (*plan etc*) eseguire; **execution** [ɛksɪ'kjuːʃən] *n* esecuzione *f*
executive [ɪg'zɛkjutɪv] *n* (*Comm*) dirigente *m*; (*Pol*) esecutivo ▷ *adj* esecutivo(-a)
exempt [ɪg'zɛmpt] *adj* esentato(-a) ▷ *vt* **to ~ sb from** esentare qn da
exercise ['ɛksəsaɪz] *n* (*keep fit*) moto; (*Scol, Mil etc*) esercizio ▷ *vt* esercitare; (*patience*) usare; (*dog*) portar fuori ▷ *vi* (*also:* **take ~**) fare del moto; **exercise book** *n* quaderno
exert [ɪg'zəːt] *vt* esercitare; **to ~ o.s.** sforzarsi; **exertion** [-ʃən] *n* sforzo
exhale [ɛks'heɪl] *vt, vi* espirare

exhaust [ɪg'zɔːst] *n* (*also:* ~ **fumes**) scappamento; (*also:* ~ **pipe**) tubo di scappamento ▷ *vt* esaurire; **exhausted** *adj* esaurito(-a); **exhaustion** [ɪg'zɔːstʃən] *n* esaurimento; **nervous exhaustion** sovraffaticamento mentale
exhibit [ɪg'zɪbɪt] *n* (*Art*) oggetto esposto; (*Law*) documento *or* oggetto esibito ▷ *vt* esporre; (*courage, skill*) dimostrare; **exhibition** [ɛksɪ'bɪʃən] *n* mostra, esposizione *f*
exhilarating [ɪg'zɪləreɪtɪŋ] *adj* esilarante; stimolante
exile ['ɛksaɪl] *n* esilio; (*person*) esiliato(-a) ▷ *vt* esiliare
exist [ɪg'zɪst] *vi* esistere; **existence** *n* esistenza; **existing** *adj* esistente
exit ['ɛksɪt] *n* uscita ▷ *vi* (*Theatre, Comput*) uscire; **where's the ~?** dov'è l'uscita?; **exit ramp** (*us*) *n* (*Aut*) rampa di uscita
exotic [ɪg'zɔtɪk] *adj* esotico(-a)
expand [ɪk'spænd] *vt* espandere; estendere; allargare ▷ *vi* (*business, gas*) espandersi; (*metal*) dilatarsi
expansion [ɪk'spænʃən] *n* (*gen*) espansione *f*; (*of town, economy*) sviluppo; (*of metal*) dilatazione *f*
expect [ɪk'spɛkt] *vt* (*anticipate*) prevedere, aspettarsi, prevedere *or* aspettarsi che + *sub*; (*require*) richiedere, esigere; (*suppose*) supporre; (*await, also baby*) aspettare ▷ *vi* **to be ~ing** essere in stato interessante; **to ~ sb to do** aspettarsi che qn faccia; **expectation** [ɛkspɛk'teɪʃən] *n* aspettativa; speranza
expedition [ɛkspə'dɪʃən] *n* spedizione *f*
expel [ɪk'spɛl] *vt* espellere
expenditure [ɪk'spɛndɪtʃə'] *n* spesa
expense [ɪk'spɛns] *n* spesa; (*high cost*) costo; **~s** *npl* (*Comm*) spese *fpl*, indennità *fpl*; **at the ~ of** a spese di; **expense account** *n* conto *m* spese *inv*
expensive [ɪk'spɛnsɪv] *adj* caro(-a), costoso(-a); **it's too ~** è troppo caro
experience [ɪk'spɪərɪəns] *n* esperienza ▷ *vt* (*pleasure*) provare; (*hardship*) soffrire; **experienced** *adj* esperto(-a)
experiment [*n* ɪk'spɛrɪmənt, *vb* ɪk'spɛrɪmɛnt] *n* esperimento, esperienza ▷ *vi* **to ~ (with/on)** fare esperimenti (con/su); **experimental** [ɪkspɛrɪ'mɛntl] *adj* sperimentale; **at the experimental stage** in via di sperimentazione
expert ['ɛkspəːt] *adj, n* esperto(-a); **expertise** [-'tiːz] *n* competenza
expire [ɪk'spaɪə'] *vi* (*period of time, licence*) scadere; **expiry** *n* scadenza; **expiry date** *n* (*of medicine, food item*) data di scadenza
explain [ɪk'spleɪn] *vt* spiegare;

explanation [ɛksplə'neɪʃən] *n* spiegazione *f*

explicit [ɪk'splɪsɪt] *adj* esplicito(-a)

explode [ɪk'spləud] *vi* esplodere

exploit [*n* 'ɛksplɔɪt, *vb* ɪk'splɔɪt] *n* impresa ▷ *vt* sfruttare; **exploitation** [-'teɪʃən] *n* sfruttamento

explore [ɪk'splɔː^r] *vt* esplorare; (*possibilities*) esaminare; **explorer** *n* esploratore(-trice)

explosion [ɪk'spləuʒən] *n* esplosione *f*; **explosive** [ɪk'spləusɪv] *adj* esplosivo(-a) ▷ *n* esplosivo

export [*vb* ɛk'spɔːt, *n* 'ɛkspɔːt] *vt* esportare ▷ *n* esportazione *f*; articolo di esportazione ▷ *cpd* d'esportazione; **exporter** *n* esportatore *m*

expose [ɪk'spəuz] *vt* esporre; (*unmask*) smascherare; (*position*) esposto(-a); **exposure** [ɪk'spəuʒə^r] *n* esposizione *f*; (*Phot*) posa; (*Med*) assideramento

express [ɪk'sprɛs] *adj* (*definite*) chiaro(-a), espresso(-a); (*BRIT: letter etc*) espresso *inv* ▷ *n* (*train*) espresso ▷ *vt* esprimere; **expression** [ɪk'sprɛʃən] *n* espressione *f*; **expressway** (*US*) *n* (*urban motorway*) autostrada che attraversa la città

exquisite [ɛk'skwɪzɪt] *adj* squisito(-a)

extend [ɪk'stɛnd] *vt* (*visit*) protrarre; (*road, deadline*) prolungare; (*building*) ampliare; (*offer*) offrire, porgere ▷ *vi* (*land, period*) estendersi; **extension** [ɪk'stɛnʃən] *n* (*of road, term*) prolungamento; (*of contract, deadline*) proroga; (*building*) annesso; (*to wire, table*) prolunga; (*telephone*) interno; (: *in private house*) apparecchio supplementare; **extension lead** *n* prolunga

extensive [ɪk'stɛnsɪv] *adj* esteso(-a), ampio(-a); (*damage*) su larga scala; (*coverage, discussion*) esauriente; (*use*) grande

extent [ɪk'stɛnt] *n* estensione *f*; **to some ~** fino a un certo punto; **to such ~ that ...** a un tal punto che ...; **to what ~?** fino a che punto?; **to the ~ of ...** fino al punto di ...

exterior [ɛk'stɪərɪə^r] *adj* esteriore, esterno(-a) ▷ *n* esteriore *m*, esterno; aspetto (esteriore)

external [ɛk'stəːnl] *adj* esterno(-a), esteriore

extinct [ɪk'stɪŋkt] *adj* estinto(-a); **extinction** [ɪk'stɪŋkʃən] *n* estinzione *f*

extinguish [ɪk'stɪŋgwɪʃ] *vt* estinguere

extra ['ɛkstrə] *adj* extra *inv*, supplementare ▷ *adv* (*in addition*) di più ▷ *n* extra *m inv*; (*surcharge*) supplemento; (*Cinema, Theatre*) comparsa

extract [*vb* ɪk'strækt, *n* 'ɛkstrækt] *vt* estrarre; (*money, promise*) strappare ▷ *n* estratto; (*passage*) brano

extradite ['ɛkstrədaɪt] *vt* estradare

extraordinary [ɪk'strɔːdnrɪ] *adj* straordinario(-a)

extravagance [ɪk'strævəgəns] *n* sperpero; stravaganza

extravagant [ɪk'strævəgənt] *adj* (*lavish*) prodigo(-a); (*wasteful*) dispendioso(-a)

▌Be careful not to translate *extravagant* by the Italian word *stravagante*.

extreme [ɪk'striːm] *adj* estremo(-a) ▷ *n* estremo; **extremely** *adv* estremamente

extremist [ɪk'striːmɪst] *adj*, *n* estremista (*m/f*)

extrovert ['ɛkstrəvəːt] *n* estroverso(-a)

eye [aɪ] *n* occhio; (*of needle*) cruna ▷ *vt* osservare; **to keep an ~ on** tenere d'occhio; **eyeball** *n* globo dell'occhio; **eyebrow** *n* sopracciglio; **eyedrops** *npl* gocce *fpl* oculari, collirio; **eyelash** *n* ciglio; **eyelid** *n* palpebra; **eyeliner** *n* eye-liner *m inv*; **eyeshadow** *n* ombretto; **eyesight** *n* vista; **eye witness** *n* testimone *m/f* oculare

F [ɛf] n (Mus) fa m

fabric ['fæbrɪk] n stoffa, tessuto

fabulous ['fæbjuləs] adj favoloso(-a); (super) favoloso(-a), fantastico(-a)

face [feɪs] n faccia, viso, volto; (expression) faccia; (of clock) quadrante m; (of building) facciata ▷ vt essere di fronte a; (facts, situation) affrontare; **~ down** a faccia in giù; **to make** or **pull a ~** fare una smorfia; **in the ~** (difficulties etc) di fronte a; **on the ~ of it** a prima vista; **~ to ~** faccia a faccia; **face up to** vt fus affrontare, far fronte a; **face cloth** (BRIT) n guanto di spugna; **face pack** n (BRIT) maschera di bellezza

facial ['feɪʃəl] adj del viso

facilitate [fə'sɪlɪteɪt] vt facilitare

facilities [fə'sɪlɪtɪz] npl attrezzature fpl; **credit ~** facilitazioni fpl di credito

fact [fækt] n fatto; **in ~** in effetti

faction ['fækʃən] n fazione f

factor ['fæktər] n fattore m; **I'd like a ~ 15 suntan lotion** vorrei una crema solare con fattore di protezione 15

factory ['fæktərɪ] n fabbrica, stabilimento
Be careful not to translate factory by the Italian word fattoria.

factual ['fæktjuəl] adj che si attiene ai fatti

faculty ['fækəltɪ] n facoltà f inv; (US) corpo insegnante

fad [fæd] n mania; capriccio

fade [feɪd] vi sbiadire, sbiadirsi; (light, sound, hope) attenuarsi, affievolirsi; (flower) appassire; **fade away** vi (sound) affievolirsi

fag [fæg] (BRIT: inf) n (cigarette) cicca

Fahrenheit ['fɑːrənhaɪt] n Fahrenheit m inv

fail [feɪl] vt (exam) non superare; (candidate) bocciare; (courage, memory) mancare a ▷ vi fallire; (student) essere respinto(-a); (eyesight, health, light) venire a mancare; **to ~ to do sth** (neglect) mancare di fare qc; (be unable) non riuscire a fare qc; **without ~** senza fallo; certamente; **failing** n difetto ▷ prep in mancanza di; **failure** ['feɪljər] n fallimento; (person) fallito(-a); (mechanical etc) guasto

faint [feɪnt] adj debole; (recollection) vago(-a); (mark) indistinto(-a) ▷ n (Med) svenimento ▷ vi svenire; **to feel ~** sentirsi svenire; **faintest** adj **I haven't the faintest idea** non ho la più pallida idea; **faintly** adv debolmente; vagamente

fair [fɛər] adj (person, decision) giusto(-a), equo(-a); (quite large, quite good) discreto(-a); (hair etc) biondo(-a); (skin, complexion) chiaro(-a); (weather) bello(-a), clemente ▷ adv (play) lealmente ▷ n fiera; (BRIT: funfair) luna park m inv; **fairground** n luna park m inv; **fair-haired** [fɛə'hɛəd] adj (person) biondo(-a); **fairly** adv equamente; (quite) abbastanza; **fairway** n (Golf) fairway m inv

fairy ['fɛərɪ] n fata; **fairy tale** n fiaba

faith [feɪθ] n fede f; (trust) fiducia; (sect) religione f, fede f; **faithful** adj fedele; **faithfully** adv fedelmente; **yours faithfully** (BRIT: in letters) distinti saluti

fake [feɪk] n imitazione f; (picture) falso; (person) impostore(-a) ▷ adj falso(-a) ▷ vt (accounts) falsificare; (illness) fingere; (painting) contraffare

falcon ['fɔːlkən] n falco, falcone m

fall [fɔːl] (pt fell, pp fallen) n caduta; (in temperature) abbassamento; (in price) ribasso; (US: autumn) autunno ▷ vi cadere; (temperature, price, night) scendere; **~s** npl (waterfall) cascate fpl; **to ~ flat** (on one's face) cadere bocconi; (joke) fare cilecca; (plan) fallire; **fall apart** vi cadere a pezzi; **fall down** vi (person) cadere; (building) crollare; **fall for** vt fus (person) prendere una cotta per; **to ~ for a trick** (or **a story** etc**)** cascarci; **fall off** vi cadere; (diminish) diminuire, abbassarsi; **fall out** vi (hair, teeth) cadere; (friends etc) litigare; **fall over** vi cadere; **fall through** vi (plan, project) fallire

fallen ['fɔːlən] *pp of* **fall**
fallout ['fɔːlaut] *n* fall-out *m*
false [fɔːls] *adj* falso(-a); **under ~
pretences** con l'inganno; **false alarm**
n falso allarme *m*; **false teeth** (*BRIT*) *npl*
denti *mpl* finti
fame [feɪm] *n* fama, celebrità
familiar [fə'mɪlɪəʳ] *adj* familiare; (*close*)
intimo(-a); **to be ~ with** (*subject*)
conoscere; **familiarize** [fə'mɪlɪəraɪz] *vt*
to familiarize o.s. with familiarizzare con
family ['fæmɪlɪ] *n* famiglia; **family doctor**
n medico di famiglia; **family planning** *n*
pianificazione *f* familiare
famine ['fæmɪn] *n* carestia
famous ['feɪməs] *adj* famoso(-a)
fan [fæn] *n* (*folding*) ventaglio; (*Elec*)
ventilatore *m*; (*person*) ammiratore(-trice),
tifoso(-a) ▷ *vt* far vento a; (*fire, quarrel*)
alimentare
fanatic [fə'nætɪk] *n* fanatico(-a)
fan belt *n* cinghia del ventilatore
fan club *n* fan club *m inv*
fancy ['fænsɪ] *n* immaginazione *f*,
fantasia; (*whim*) capriccio ▷ *adj* (*hat*)
stravagante; (*hotel, food*) speciale ▷ *vt* (*feel
like, want*) aver voglia di; (*imagine, think*)
immaginare; **to take a ~ to** incapricciarsi
di; **he fancies her** (*inf*) gli piace; **fancy
dress** *n* costume *m* (per maschera)
fan heater *n* (*BRIT*) stufa ad aria calda
fantasize ['fæntəsaɪz] *vi* fantasticare,
sognare
fantastic [fæn'tæstɪk] *adj* fantastico(-a)
fantasy ['fæntəsɪ] *n* fantasia,
immaginazione *f*; fantasticheria; chimera
fanzine ['fænziːn] *n* rivista specialistica
(*per appassionati*)
FAQs *abbr* (= *frequently asked questions*)
FAQ *fpl*
far [fɑːʳ] *adj* lontano(-a) ▷ *adv* lontano;
(*much, greatly*) molto; **is it ~ from here?**
è molto lontano da qui?; **how ~?** quanto
lontano?; (*referring to activity etc*) fino a
dove?; **how ~ is the town centre?** quanto
dista il centro da qui?; **~ away, ~ off**
lontano, distante; **~ better** assai migliore;
~ from lontano da; **by ~** di gran lunga; **go
as ~ as the farm** vada fino alla fattoria; **as
~ as I know** per quel che so
farce [fɑːs] *n* farsa
fare [fɛəʳ] *n* (*on trains, buses*) tariffa; (*in taxi*)
prezzo della corsa; (*food*) vitto, cibo; **half ~**
metà tariffa; **full ~** tariffa intera
Far East *n* **the ~** l'Estremo Oriente *m*
farewell [fɛə'wɛl] *excl, n* addio
farm [fɑːm] *n* fattoria, podere *m* ▷ *vt*
coltivare; **farmer** *n* coltivatore(-trice),
agricoltore(-trice); **farmhouse** *n* fattoria;

farming *n* (*gen*) agricoltura; (*of crops*)
coltivazione *f*; (*of animals*) allevamento;
farmyard *n* aia
far-reaching [fɑː'riːtʃɪŋ] *adj* di vasta
portata
fart [fɑːt] (*inf!*) *vi* scoreggiare (!)
farther ['fɑːðəʳ] *adv* più lontano ▷ *adj* più
lontano(-a)
farthest ['fɑːðɪst] *superl of* **far**
fascinate ['fæsɪneɪt] *vt* affascinare;
fascinated *adj* affascinato(-a);
fascinating *adj* affascinante;
fascination [-'neɪʃən] *n* fascino
fascist ['fæʃɪst] *adj, n* fascista (*m/f*)
fashion ['fæʃən] *n* moda; (*manner*)
maniera, modo ▷ *vt* foggiare, formare; **in
~** alla moda; **out of ~** passato(-a) di moda;
fashionable *adj* alla moda, di moda;
fashion show *n* sfilata di moda
fast [fɑːst] *adj* rapido(-a), svelto(-a),
veloce; (*clock*): **to be ~** andare avanti; (*dye,
colour*) solido(-a) ▷ *adv* rapidamente; (*stuck, held*) saldamente ▷ *n* digiuno ▷ *vi*
digiunare; **~ asleep** profondamente
addormentato
fasten ['fɑːsn] *vt* chiudere, fissare; (*coat*)
abbottonare, allacciare ▷ *vi* chiudersi,
fissarsi; abbottonarsi; allacciarsi
fast food *n* fast food *m*
fat [fæt] *adj* grasso(-a); (*book, profit etc*)
grosso(-a) ▷ *n* grasso
fatal ['feɪtl] *adj* fatale; mortale;
disastroso(-a); **fatality** [fə'tælɪtɪ] *n* (*road
death etc*) morto(-a), vittima; **fatally** *adv*
a morte
fate [feɪt] *n* destino; (*of person*) sorte *f*
father ['fɑːðəʳ] *n* padre *m*; **Father
Christmas** *n* Babbo Natale; **father-in-
law** *n* suocero
fatigue [fə'tiːg] *n* stanchezza
fattening ['fætnɪŋ] *adj* (*food*) che fa
ingrassare
fatty ['fætɪ] *adj* (*food*) grasso(-a) ▷ *n* (*inf*)
ciccione(-a)
faucet ['fɔːsɪt] (*US*) *n* rubinetto
fault [fɔːlt] *n* colpa; (*Tennis*) fallo; (*defect*)
difetto; (*Geo*) faglia ▷ *vt* criticare; **it's my ~**
è colpa mia; **to find ~ with** trovare da ridire
su; **at ~** in fallo; **faulty** *adj* difettoso(-a)
fauna ['fɔːnə] *n* fauna
favour *etc* ['feɪvəʳ] (*US* **favor**) *n* favore *m*
▷ *vt* (*proposition*) favorire, essere favorevole
a; (*pupil etc*) favorire; (*team, horse*) dare per
vincente; **to do sb a ~** fare un favore *or*
una cortesia a qn; **to find ~ with** (*person*)
entrare nelle buone grazie di; (: *suggestion*)
avere l'approvazione di; **in ~ of** in favore
di; **favourable** *adj* favorevole; **favourite**
[-rɪt] *adj, n* favorito(-a)

fawn [fɔːn] n daino ▷ adj (also: **~-coloured**) marrone chiaro inv ▷ vi **to ~ (up)on** adulare servilmente

fax [fæks] n (document) facsimile m inv, telecopia; (machine) telecopiatrice f ▷ vt telecopiare, trasmettere in facsimile

FBI (US) n abbr (= Federal Bureau of Investigation) F.B.I. f

fear [fɪəʳ] n paura, timore m ▷ vt aver paura di, temere; **for ~ of** per paura di; **fearful** adj pauroso(-a); (sight, noise) terribile, spaventoso(-a); **fearless** adj intrepido(-a), senza paura

feasible ['fiːzəbl] adj possibile, realizzabile

feast [fiːst] n festa, banchetto; (Rel: also: **~ day**) festa ▷ vi banchettare

feat [fiːt] n impresa, fatto insigne

feather ['fɛðəʳ] n penna

feature ['fiːtʃəʳ] n caratteristica; (Press, TV) articolo ▷ vt (film) avere come protagonista ▷ vi figurare; **~s** npl (of face) fisionomia; **feature film** n film m inv principale

Feb. [fɛb] abbr (= February) feb

February ['fɛbruərɪ] n febbraio

fed [fɛd] pt, pp of **feed**

federal ['fɛdərəl] adj federale

federation [fɛdə'reɪʃən] n federazione f

fed up adj **to be ~** essere stufo(-a)

fee [fiː] n pagamento; (of doctor, lawyer) onorario; (for examination) tassa d'esame; **school ~s** tasse fpl scolastiche

feeble ['fiːbl] adj debole

feed [fiːd] (pt, pp **fed**) n (of baby) pappa; (of animal) mangime m; (on printer) meccanismo di alimentazione ▷ vt nutrire; (baby) allattare; (horse etc) dare da mangiare a; (fire, machine) alimentare; (data, information): **to ~ into** inserire in; **feedback** n feed-back m

feel [fiːl] (pt, pp **felt**) n consistenza; (sense of touch) tatto ▷ vt toccare; palpare; tastare; (cold, pain, anger) sentire; (think, believe): **to ~ (that)** pensare che; **to ~ hungry/cold** aver fame/freddo; **to ~ lonely/better** sentirsi solo/meglio; **I don't ~ well** non mi sento bene; **it ~s soft** è morbido al tatto; **to ~ like** (want) aver voglia di; **to ~ about** or **around for** cercare a tastoni; **feeling** n sensazione f; (emotion) sentimento

feet [fiːt] npl of **foot**

fell [fɛl] pt of **fall** ▷ vt (tree) abbattere

fellow ['fɛləu] n individuo, tipo; compagno; (of learned society) membro cpd; **fellow citizen** n concittadino(-a); **fellow countryman** (irreg) n compatriota m; **fellow men** npl simili mpl; **fellowship** n associazione f; compagnia; specie di borsa di studio universitaria

felony ['fɛlənɪ] n reato, crimine m

felt [fɛlt] pt, pp of **feel** ▷ n feltro

female ['fiːmeɪl] n (Zool) femmina; (pej: woman) donna, femmina ▷ adj (Biol, Elec) femmina inv; (sex, character) femminile; (vote etc) di donne

feminine ['fɛmɪnɪn] adj femminile

feminist ['fɛmɪnɪst] n femminista m/f

fence [fɛns] n recinto ▷ vt (also: **~ in**) recingere ▷ vi (Sport) tirare di scherma; **fencing** n (Sport) scherma

fend [fɛnd] vi **to ~ for o.s.** arrangiarsi; **fend off** vt (attack, questions) respingere, difendersi da

fender ['fɛndəʳ] n parafuoco; (on boat) parabordo; (US) parafango; paraurti m inv

fennel ['fɛnl] n finocchio

ferment [vb fə'mɛnt, n 'fəːmɛnt] vi fermentare ▷ n (fig) agitazione f, eccitazione f

fern [fəːn] n felce f

ferocious [fə'rəuʃəs] adj feroce

ferret ['fɛrɪt] n furetto

ferry ['fɛrɪ] n (small) traghetto; (large: also: **~boat**) nave f traghetto inv ▷ vt traghettare

fertile ['fəːtaɪl] adj fertile; (Biol) fecondo(-a); **fertilize** ['fəːtɪlaɪz] vt fertilizzare; fecondare; **fertilizer** ['fəːtɪlaɪzə] n fertilizzante m

festival ['fɛstɪvəl] n (Rel) festa; (Art, Mus) festival m inv

festive ['fɛstɪv] adj di festa; **the ~ season** (BRIT: Christmas) il periodo delle feste

fetch [fɛtʃ] vt andare a prendere; (sell for) essere venduto(-a) per

fête [feɪt] n festa

fetus ['fiːtəs] (US) n = **foetus**

feud [fjuːd] n contesa, lotta

fever ['fiːvəʳ] n febbre f; **feverish** adj febbrile

few [fjuː] adj pochi(-e); **a ~** adj qualche inv ▷ pron alcuni(-e); **fewer** adj meno inv, meno numerosi(-e); **fewest** adj il minor numero di

fiancé [fɪ'ãːŋseɪ] n fidanzato; **fiancée** n fidanzata

fiasco [fɪ'æskəu] n fiasco

fib [fɪb] n piccola bugia

fibre ['faɪbəʳ] (US **fiber**) n fibra; **Fibreglass®** ['faɪbəglɑːs] (US **fiberglass**) n fibra di vetro

fickle ['fɪkl] adj incostante, capriccioso(-a)

fiction ['fɪkʃən] n narrativa, romanzi mpl; (sth made up) finzione f; **fictional** adj immaginario(-a)

fiddle ['fɪdl] n (Mus) violino; (cheating) imbroglio; truffa ▷ vt (BRIT: accounts) falsificare, falsare; **fiddle with** vt fus gingillarsi con

fidelity [fɪˈdɛlɪtɪ] n fedeltà; (*accuracy*) esattezza

field [fiːld] n campo; **field marshal** n feldmaresciallo

fierce [fɪəs] adj (*animal, person, fighting*) feroce; (*loyalty*) assoluto(-a); (*wind*) furioso(-a); (*heat*) intenso(-a)

fifteen [fɪfˈtiːn] num quindici; **fifteenth** num quindicesimo(-a)

fifth [fɪfθ] num quinto(-a)

fiftieth [ˈfɪftɪɪθ] num cinquantesimo(-a)

fifty [ˈfɪftɪ] num cinquanta; **fifty-fifty** adj **a fifty-fifty chance** una possibilità su due ▷ adv fifty-fifty, metà per ciascuno

fig [fɪg] n fico

fight [faɪt] (pt, pp **fought**) n zuffa, rissa; (*Mil*) battaglia, combattimento; (*against cancer etc*) lotta ▷ vt (*person*) azzuffarsi con; (*enemy: also Mil*) combattere; (*cancer, alcoholism, emotion*) lottare contro, combattere; (*election*) partecipare a ▷ vi combattere; **fight back** vi difendersi; (*Sport, after illness*) riprendersi ▷ vt (*tears*) ricacciare; **fight off** vt (*attack, attacker*) respingere; (*disease, sleep, urge*) lottare contro; **fighting** n combattimento

figure [ˈfɪgə'] n figura; (*number, cipher*) cifra ▷ vt (*think: esp US*) pensare ▷ vi (*appear*) figurare; **figure out** vt riuscire a capire; calcolare

file [faɪl] n (*tool*) lima; (*dossier*) incartamento; (*folder*) cartellina; (*Comput*) archivio; (*row*) fila ▷ vt (*nails, wood*) limare; (*papers*) archiviare; (*Law: claim*) presentare; passare agli atti; **filing cabinet** [ˈfaɪlɪŋ-] n casellario

Filipino [fɪlɪˈpiːnəʊ] n filippino(-a); (*Ling*) tagal m

fill [fɪl] vt riempire; (*job*) coprire ▷ n **to eat one's ~** mangiare a sazietà; **fill in** vt (*hole*) riempire; (*form*) compilare; **fill out** vt (*form, receipt*) riempire; **fill up** vt riempire; **~ it up, please** (*Aut*) il pieno, per favore

fillet [ˈfɪlɪt] n filetto; **fillet steak** n bistecca di filetto

filling [ˈfɪlɪŋ] n (*Culin*) impasto, ripieno; (*for tooth*) otturazione f; **filling station** n stazione f di rifornimento

film [fɪlm] n (*Cinema*) film m inv; (*Phot*) pellicola, rullino; (*of powder, liquid*) sottile strato ▷ vt, vi girare; **I'd like a 36-exposure ~** vorrei un rullino da 36 pose; **film star** n divo(-a) dello schermo

filter [ˈfɪltə'] n filtro ▷ vt filtrare; **filter lane** (BRIT) n (*Aut*) corsia di svincolo

filth [fɪlθ] n sporcizia; **filthy** adj lordo(-a), sozzo(-a); (*language*) osceno(-a)

fin [fɪn] n (*of fish*) pinna

final [ˈfaɪnl] adj finale, ultimo(-a); definitivo(-a) ▷ n (*Sport*) finale f; **~s** npl (*Scol*) esami mpl finali; **finale** [fɪˈnɑːlɪ] n finale m; **finalist** [ˈfaɪnəlɪst] n (*Sport*) finalista m/f; **finalize** [ˈfaɪnəlaɪz] vt mettere a punto; **finally** [ˈfaɪnəlɪ] adv (*lastly*) alla fine; (*eventually*) finalmente

finance [faɪˈnæns] n finanza; (*capital*) capitale m ▷ vt finanziare; **~s** npl (*funds*) finanze fpl; **financial** [faɪˈnænʃəl] adj finanziario(-a); **financial year** n anno finanziario, esercizio finanziario

find [faɪnd] (pt, pp **found**) vt trovare; (*lost object*) ritrovare ▷ n trovata, scoperta; **to ~ sb guilty** (*Law*) giudicare qn colpevole; **find out** vt (*truth, secret*) scoprire; (*person*) cogliere in fallo; **to ~ out about** informarsi su; (*by chance*) scoprire; **findings** npl (*Law*) sentenza, conclusioni fpl; (*of report*) conclusioni

fine [faɪn] adj bello(-a); ottimo(-a); (*thin, subtle*) fine ▷ adv (*well*) molto bene ▷ n (*Law*) multa ▷ vt (*Law*) multare; **to be ~** (*person*) stare bene; (*weather*) far bello; **fine arts** npl belle arti fpl

finger [ˈfɪŋgə'] n dito ▷ vt toccare, tastare; **little/index ~** mignolo/(dito) indice m; **fingernail** n unghia; **fingerprint** n impronta digitale; **fingertip** n punta del dito

finish [ˈfɪnɪʃ] n fine f; (*polish etc*) finitura ▷ vt, vi finire; **when does the show ~?** quando finisce lo spettacolo?; **to ~ doing sth** finire di fare qc; **to ~ third** arrivare terzo(-a); **finish off** vt compiere; (*kill*) uccidere; **finish up** vi, vt finire

Finland [ˈfɪnlənd] n Finlandia; **Finn** [fɪn] n finlandese m/f; **Finnish** adj finlandese ▷ n (*Ling*) finlandese m

fir [fəː'] n abete m

fire [faɪə'] n fuoco; (*destructive*) incendio; (*gas fire, electric fire*) stufa ▷ vt (*gun*) far fuoco con; (*arrow*) sparare; (*fig*) infiammare; (*inf: dismiss*) licenziare ▷ vi sparare, far fuoco; **~!** al fuoco!; **on ~** in fiamme; **fire alarm** n allarme m d'incendio; **firearm** n arma da fuoco; **fire brigade** [-brɪˈgeɪd] (US **fire department**) n (*corpo dei*) pompieri mpl; **fire engine** n autopompa; **fire escape** n scala di sicurezza; **fire exit** n uscita di sicurezza; **fire extinguisher** [-ɪkˈstɪŋgwɪʃə'] n estintore m; **fireman** (*irreg*) n pompiere m; **fireplace** n focolare m; **fire station** n caserma dei pompieri; **firetruck** (US) n =**fire engine**; **firewall** n (*Internet*) firewall m inv; **firewood** n legna; **fireworks** npl fuochi mpl d'artificio

firm [fəːm] adj fermo(-a) ▷ n ditta,

azienda; **firmly** adv fermamente

first [fə:st] adj primo(-a) ▷ adv (before others) il primo, la prima; (before other things) per primo; (when listing reasons etc) per prima cosa ▷ n (person: in race) primo(-a); (Aut) prima; **at ~** dapprima, all'inizio; **~ of all** prima di tutto; **first aid** n pronto soccorso; **first-aid kit** n cassetta pronto soccorso; **first-class** adj laurea con lode; (Aut) prima; **first-hand** adj di prima mano; **first lady** (us) n moglie f del presidente; **firstly** adv in primo luogo; **first name** n prenome m; **first-rate** adj di prima qualità, ottimo(-a)

fiscal ['fɪskəl] adj fiscale; **fiscal year** n anno fiscale

fish [fɪʃ] n inv pesce m ▷ vt (river, area) pescare in ▷ vi pescare; **to go ~ing** andare a pesca, **fish and chip shop** n see **chip shop**; **fisherman** (irreg) n pescatore m; **fish fingers** (brit) npl bastoncini mpl di pesce (surgelati); **fishing** n pesca; **fishing boat** n barca da pesca; **fishing line** n lenza; **fishmonger** n pescivendolo; **fishmonger's (shop)** n pescheria; **fish sticks** (us) npl = **fish fingers**; **fishy** (inf) adj (tale, story) sospetto(-a)

fist [fɪst] n pugno

fit [fɪt] adj (Med, Sport) in forma; (proper) adatto(-a), appropriato(-a); conveniente ▷ vt (clothes) stare bene a; (put in, attach) mettere; installare; (equip) fornire, equipaggiare ▷ vi (clothes) stare bene; (parts) andare bene, adattarsi; (in space, gap) entrare ▷ n (Med) accesso, attacco; **~ to** in grado di; **~ for** adatto(-a), degno(-a) di; **a ~ of anger** un accesso d'ira; **this dress is a good ~** questo vestito sta bene; **by ~s and starts** a sbalzi; **fit in** vi accordarsi; adattarsi; **fitness** n (Med) forma fisica; **fitted** adj **fitted cupboards** armadi mpl a muro; **fitted carpet** moquette f inv; **fitted kitchen** (brit) cucina componibile; **fitting** adj appropriato(-a) ▷ n (of dress) prova; (of piece of equipment) montaggio, aggiustaggio; **fitting room** n camerino; **fittings** npl (in building) impianti mpl

five [faɪv] num cinque; **fiver** (inf) n (brit) biglietto da cinque sterline; (us) biglietto da cinque dollari

fix [fɪks] vt fissare; (mend) riparare; (meal, drink) preparare ▷ n **to be in a ~** essere nei guai; **fix up** vt (meeting) fissare; **to ~ sb up with sth** procurare qc a qn; **fixed** [fɪkst] adj (prices etc) fisso(-a); **fixture** ['fɪkstʃər] n impianto (fisso); (Sport) incontro (del calendario sportivo)

fizzy ['fɪzɪ] adj frizzante; gassato(-a)

flag [flæg] n bandiera; (also: **~stone**) pietra da lastricare ▷ vi stancarsi; affievolirsi; **flagpole** ['flægpəʊl] n albero

flair [flɛər] n (for business etc) fiuto; (for languages etc) facilità; (style) stile m

flak [flæk] n (Mil) fuoco d'artiglieria; (inf: criticism) critiche fpl

flake [fleɪk] n (of rust, paint) scaglia; (of snow, soap powder) fiocco ▷ vi (also: **~ off**) sfaldarsi

flamboyant [flæm'bɔɪənt] adj sgargiante

flame [fleɪm] n fiamma

flamingo [flə'mɪŋgəʊ] n fenicottero, fiammingo

flammable ['flæməbl] adj infiammabile

flan [flæn] (brit) n flan m inv

flank [flæŋk] n fianco ▷ vt fiancheggiare

flannel ['flænl] n (brit: also: **face ~**) quanto di spugna; (fabric) flanella

flap [flæp] n (of pocket) patta; (of envelope) lembo ▷ vt (wings) battere ▷ vi (sail, flag) sbattere; (inf: also: **be in a ~**) essere in agitazione

flare [flɛər] n (of skirt etc) svasatura; **~s** (trousers) pantaloni mpl a zampa d'elefante; **flare up** vi andare in fiamme; (fig: person) infiammarsi di rabbia; (: revolt) scoppiare

flash [flæʃ] n vampata; (also: **news ~**) notizia f lampo inv; (Phot) flash m inv ▷ vt accendere e spegnere; (send: message) trasmettere; (: look, smile) lanciare ▷ vi brillare; (light on ambulance, eyes etc) lampeggiare; **in a ~** in un lampo; **to ~ one's headlights** lampeggiare; **he ~ed by** or **past** ci passò davanti come un lampo; **flashback** n flashback m inv; **flashbulb** n cubo m flash inv; **flashlight** n lampadina tascabile

flask [flɑːsk] n fiasco; (also: **vacuum ~**) Thermos® m inv

flat [flæt] adj piatto(-a); (tyre) sgonfio(-a), a terra; (battery) scarico(-a); (beer) svampito(-a); (denial) netto(-a); (Mus) bemolle inv; (: voice) stonato(-a); (rate, fee) unico(-a) ▷ n (brit: rooms) appartamento; (Aut) pneumatico sgonfio; (Mus) bemolle m; **to work ~ out** lavorare a più non posso; **flatten** vt (also: **flatten out**) appiattire; (building, city) spianare

flatter ['flætər] vt lusingare; **flattering** adj lusinghiero(-a); (dress) che dona

flaunt [flɔːnt] vt fare mostra di

flavour etc ['fleɪvər] (us **flavor**) n gusto ▷ vt insaporire, aggiungere sapore a; **what ~s do you have?** che gusti avete?; **strawberry-~ed** al gusto di fragola; **flavouring** n essenza (artificiale)

flaw [flɔː] n difetto; **flawless** adj senza difetti

flea [fliː] *n* pulce *f*; **flea market** *n* mercato delle pulci

flee [fliː] (*pt, pp* **fled**) *vt* fuggire da ▷ *vi* fuggire, scappare

fleece [fliːs] *n* vello ▷ *vt* (*inf*) pelare

fleet [fliːt] *n* flotta; (*of lorries etc*) convoglio; parco

fleeting ['fliːtɪŋ] *adj* fugace, fuggitivo(-a); (*visit*) volante

Flemish ['flɛmɪʃ] *adj* fiammingo(-a)

flesh [flɛʃ] *n* carne *f*; (*of fruit*) polpa

flew [fluː] *pt of* **fly**

flex [flɛks] *n* filo (flessibile) ▷ *vt* flettere; (*muscles*) contrarre; **flexibility** *n* flessibilità; **flexible** *adj* flessibile; **flexitime** ['flɛksɪtaɪm] *n* orario flessibile

flick [flɪk] *n* colpetto; scarto ▷ *vt* dare un colpetto a; **flick through** *vt fus* sfogliare

flicker ['flɪkər] *vi* tremolare

flies [flaɪz] *npl of* **fly**

flight [flaɪt] *n* volo; (*escape*) fuga; (*also:* **~ of steps**) scalinata; **flight attendant** (*US*) *n* steward *m inv*, hostess *f inv*

flimsy ['flɪmzɪ] *adj* (*shoes, clothes*) leggero(-a); (*building*) poco solido(-a); (*excuse*) che non regge

flinch [flɪntʃ] *vi* ritirarsi; **to ~ from** tirarsi indietro di fronte a

fling [flɪŋ] (*pt, pp* **flung**) *vt* lanciare, gettare

flint [flɪnt] *n* selce *f*; (*in lighter*) pietrina

flip [flɪp] *vt* (*switch*) far scattare; (*coin*) lanciare in aria

flip-flops ['flɪpflɒps] *npl* (*esp BRIT: sandals*) infradito *mpl*

flipper ['flɪpər] *n* pinna

flirt [fləːt] *vi* flirtare ▷ *n* civetta

float [fləʊt] *n* galleggiante *m*; (*in procession*) carro; (*money*) somma ▷ *vi* galleggiare

flock [flɒk] *n* (*of sheep, Rel*) gregge *m*; (*of birds*) stormo ▷ *vi* **to ~ to** accorrere in massa a

flood [flʌd] *n* alluvione *m*; (*of letters etc*) marea ▷ *vt* allagare; (*people*) invadere ▷ *vi* (*place*) allagarsi; (*people*): **to ~ into** riversarsi in; **flooding** *n* inondazione *f*; **floodlight** *n* riflettore *m* ▷ *vt* illuminare a giorno

floor [flɔːr] *n* pavimento; (*storey*) piano; (*of sea, valley*) fondo ▷ *vt* (*blow*) atterrare; (*: question*) ridurre al silenzio; **which ~ is it on?** a che piano si trova?; **ground ~** (*BRIT*), **first ~** (*US*) pianterreno; **first ~** (*BRIT*), **second ~** (*US*) primo piano; **floorboard** *n* tavellone *m* di legno; **flooring** *n* (*floor*) pavimento; (*material*) materiale *m* per pavimentazioni; **floor show** *n* spettacolo di varietà

flop [flɒp] *n* fiasco ▷ *vi* far fiasco; (*fall*)

lasciarsi cadere; **floppy** ['flɒpɪ] *adj* floscio(-a), molle

floral ['flɔːrl] *adj* floreale

Florence ['flɒrəns] *n* Firenze *f*

Florentine ['flɒrəntaɪn] *adj* fiorentino(-a)

florist ['flɒrɪst] *n* fioraio(-a); **florist's (shop)** *n* fioraio(-a)

flotation [fləʊˈteɪʃən] *n* (*Comm*) lancio

flour ['flaʊər] *n* farina

flourish ['flʌrɪʃ] *vi* fiorire ▷ *n* (*bold gesture*): **with a ~** con ostentazione

flow [fləʊ] *n* flusso; circolazione *f* ▷ *vi* fluire; (*traffic, blood in veins*) circolare; (*hair*) scendere

flower ['flaʊər] *n* fiore *m* ▷ *vi* fiorire; **flower bed** *n* aiuola; **flowerpot** *n* vaso da fiori

flown [fləʊn] *pp of* **fly**

fl. oz. *abbr* = **fluid ounce**

flu [fluː] *n* influenza

fluctuate ['flʌktjueɪt] *vi* fluttuare, oscillare

fluent ['fluːənt] *adj* (*speech*) facile, sciolto(-a); corrente; **he speaks ~ Italian, he's ~ in Italian** parla l'italiano correntemente

fluff [flʌf] *n* lanugine *f*; **fluffy** *adj* lanuginoso(-a); (*toy*) di peluche

fluid ['fluːɪd] *adj* fluido(-a) ▷ *n* fluido; **fluid ounce** *n* (*BRIT*) = 0.028 l; 0.05 pints

fluke [fluːk] (*inf*) *n* colpo di fortuna

flung [flʌŋ] *pt, pp of* **fling**

fluorescent [fluəˈrɛsnt] *adj* fluorescente

fluoride ['fluəraɪd] *n* fluoruro

flurry ['flʌrɪ] *n* (*of snow*) tempesta; **a ~ of activity** uno scoppio di attività

flush [flʌʃ] *n* rossore *m*; (*fig: of youth, beauty etc*) rigoglio, pieno vigore ▷ *vt* ripulire con un getto d'acqua ▷ *vi* arrossire ▷ *adj* **~ with** a livello di, pari a; **to ~ the toilet** tirare l'acqua

flute [fluːt] *n* flauto

flutter ['flʌtər] *n* agitazione *f*; (*of wings*) battito ▷ *vi* (*bird*) battere le ali

fly [flaɪ] (*pt* **flew**, *pp* **flown**) *n* (*insect*) mosca; (*on trousers: also:* **flies**) chiusura ▷ *vt* pilotare; (*passengers, cargo*) trasportare (in aereo); (*distances*) percorrere ▷ *vi* volare; (*passengers*) andare in aereo; (*escape*) fuggire; (*flag*) sventolare; **fly away** *vi* volar via; **fly-drive** *n* **fly-drive holiday** fly and drive *m inv*; **flying** *n* (*activity*) aviazione *f*; (*action*) volo ▷ *adj* **flying visit** visita volante; **with flying colours** con risultati brillanti; **flying saucer** *n* disco volante; **flyover** (*BRIT*) *n* (*bridge*) cavalcavia *m inv*

FM *abbr* (= *frequency modulation*) FM

foal [fəʊl] *n* puledro

foam [fəʊm] *n* schiuma; (*also:* **~ rubber**)

gommapiuma® ⊳ vi schiumare; (*soapy water*) fare la schiuma

focus ['fəukəs] (*pl* **focuses**) *n* fuoco; (*of interest*) centro ⊳ vt (*field glasses etc*) mettere a fuoco ⊳ vi **to ~ on** (*with camera*) mettere a fuoco; (*person*) fissare lo sguardo su; **in ~** a fuoco; **out of ~** sfocato(-a)

foetus ['fi:təs] (*us* **fetus**) *n* feto

fog [fɔg] *n* nebbia; **foggy** *adj* **it's foggy** c'è nebbia; **fog lamp** (*us* **fog light**) *n* (*Aut*) faro *m* antinebbia *inv*

foil [fɔɪl] *vt* confondere, frustrare ⊳ *n* lamina di metallo; (*kitchen foil*) foglio di alluminio; (*Fencing*) fioretto; **to act as a ~ to** (*fig*) far risaltare

fold [fəuld] *n* (*bend, crease*) piega; (*Agr*) ovile *m*; (*fig*) gregge *m* ⊳ vt piegare; (*arms*) incrociare; **fold up** vi (*map, bed, table*) piegarsi; (*business*) crollare ⊳ vt (*map etc*) piegare, ripiegare; **folder** *n* (*for papers*) cartella; cartellina; **folding** *adj* (*chair, bed*) pieghevole

foliage ['fəuliɪdʒ] *n* fogliame *m*

folk [fəuk] *npl* gente *f* ⊳ *adj* popolare; **~s** *npl* (*family*) famiglia; **folklore** ['fəuklɔːr] *n* folclore *m*; **folk music** *n* musica folk *inv*; **folk song** *n* canto popolare

follow ['fɔləu] *vt* seguire ⊳ vi seguire; (*result*) conseguire, risultare; **to ~ suit** fare lo stesso; **follow up** vt (*letter, offer*) fare seguito a; (*case*) seguire; **follower** *n* seguace *m/f*, discepolo(-a); **following** *adj* seguente ⊳ *n* seguito, discepoli *mpl*; **follow-up** *n* seguito

fond [fɔnd] *adj* (*memory, look*) tenero(-a), affettuoso(-a); **to be ~ of sb** volere bene a qn; **he's ~ of walking** gli piace fare camminate

food [fu:d] *n* cibo; **food mixer** *n* frullatore *m*; **food poisoning** *n* intossicazione *f*; **food processor** [-'prəusesə] *n* tritatutto *m inv* elettrico; **food stamp** (*us*) *n* buono alimentare dato agli indigenti

fool [fu:l] *n* sciocco(-a); (*Culin*) frullato ⊳ vt ingannare ⊳ vi (*gen: fool around*) fare lo sciocco; **fool about, fool around** vi (*waste time*) perdere tempo; **foolish** *adj* scemo(-a), stupido(-a); imprudente; **foolproof** *adj* (*plan etc*) sicurissimo(-a)

foot [fut] (*pl* **feet**) *n* piede *m*; (*measure*) piede (= 304 mm; 12 inches); (*of animal*) zampa ⊳ vt (*bill*) pagare; **on ~** a piedi; **footage** *n* (*Cinema: length*) ≈ metraggio; (*: material*) sequenza; **foot-and-mouth (disease)** [futənd'mauθ-] *n* afta epizootica; **football** *n* pallone *m*; (*sport*: *BRIT*) calcio; (*: us*) football *m* americano; **footballer** *n* (*BRIT*) = **football player**; **football match** *n* (*BRIT*) partita di calcio;

football player *n* (*BRIT: also:* **footballer**) calciatore *m*; (*us*) giocatore *m* di football americano; **footbridge** *n* passerella; **foothills** *npl* contrafforti *fpl*; **foothold** *n* punto d'appoggio; **footing** *n* (*fig*) posizione *f*; **to lose one's footing** mettere un piede in fallo; **footnote** *n* nota (a piè di pagina); **footpath** *n* sentiero; (*in street*) marciapiede *m*; **footprint** *n* orma, impronta; **footstep** *n* passo; (*footprint*) orma, impronta; **footwear** *n* calzatura

 KEYWORD

for [fɔːr] *prep* **1** (*indicating destination, intention, purpose*) per; **the train for London** il treno per Londra; **he went for the paper** è andato a prendere il giornale; **it's time for lunch** è ora di pranzo; **what's it for?** a che serve?; **what for?** (*why*) perché?

2 (*on behalf of, representing*) per; **to work for sb/sth** lavorare per qn/qc; **I'll ask him for you** glielo chiederò a nome tuo; **G for George** G come George

3 (*because of*) per, a causa di; **for this reason** per questo motivo

4 (*with regard to*) per; **it's cold for July** è freddo per luglio; **for everyone who voted yes, 50 voted no** per ogni voto a favore ce n'erano 50 contro

5 (*in exchange for*) per; **I sold it for £5** l'ho venduto per 5 sterline

6 (*in favour of*) per, a favore di; **are you for or against us?** è con noi o contro di noi?; **I'm all for it** sono completamente a favore

7 (*referring to distance, time*) per; **there are roadworks for 5 km** ci sono lavori in corso per 5 km; **he was away for 2 years** è stato via per 2 anni; **she will be away for a month** starà via un mese; **it hasn't rained for 3 weeks** non piove da 3 settimane; **can you do it for tomorrow?** può farlo per domani?

8 (*with infinitive clauses*): **it is not for me to decide** non sta a me decidere; **it would be best for you to leave** sarebbe meglio che lei se ne andasse; **there is still time for you to do it** ha ancora tempo per farlo; **for this to be possible ...** perché ciò sia possibile ...

9 (*in spite of*) nonostante; **for all his complaints, he's very fond of her** nonostante tutte le sue lamentele, le vuole molto bene

⊳ *conj* (*since, as: rather formal*) dal momento che, poiché

forbid [fə'bɪd] (*pt* **forbad(e)**, *pp* **forbidden**) *vt* vietare, interdire; **to ~ sb to do sth** proibire a qn di fare qc; **forbidden** *pt of* **forbid** ▷ *adj* (*food*) proibito(-a); (*area, territory*) vietato(-a); (*word, subject*) tabù *inv*

force [fɔːs] *n* forza ▷ *vt* forzare; **forced** *adj* forzato(-a); **forceful** *adj* forte, vigoroso(-a)

ford [fɔːd] *n* guado

fore [fɔːʳ] *n* **to come to the ~** mettersi in evidenza; **forearm** ['fɔːrɑːm] *n* avambraccio; **forecast** ['fɔːkɑːst] (*irreg: like* **cast**) *n* previsione *f* ▷ *vt* prevedere; **forecourt** ['fɔːkɔːt] *n* (*of garage*) corte *f* esterna; **forefinger** ['fɔːfɪŋgəʳ] *n* (*dito*) indice *m*; **forefront** ['fɔːfrʌnt] *n* **in the forefront of** all'avanguardia in; **foreground** ['fɔːgraund] *n* primo piano; **forehead** ['fɔrɪd] *n* fronte *f*

foreign ['fɔrɪn] *adj* straniero(-a); (*trade*) estero(-a); (*object, matter*) estraneo(-a); **foreign currency** *n* valuta estera; **foreigner** *n* straniero(-a); **foreign exchange** *n* cambio con l'estero; (*currency*) valuta estera; **Foreign Office** (BRIT) *n* Ministero degli Esteri; **Foreign Secretary** (BRIT) *n* ministro degli Affari esteri

fore: **foreman** ['fɔːmən] (*irreg*) *n* caposquadra *m*; **foremost** ['fɔːməust] *adj* principale; più in vista ▷ *adv* **first and foremost** innanzitutto; **forename** *n* nome *m* di battesimo

forensic [fə'rɛnsɪk] *adj* **~ medicine** medicina legale

foresee [fɔː'siː] (*irreg: like* **see**) *vt* prevedere; **foreseeable** *adj* prevedibile

forest ['fɔrɪst] *n* foresta; **forestry** ['fɔrɪstrɪ] *n* silvicoltura

forever [fə'rɛvəʳ] *adv* per sempre; (*endlessly*) sempre, di continuo

foreword ['fɔːwəːd] *n* prefazione *f*

forfeit ['fɔːfɪt] *vt* perdere; (*one's happiness, health*) giocarsi

forgave [fə'geɪv] *pt of* **forgive**

forge [fɔːdʒ] *n* fucina ▷ *vt* (*signature, money*) contraffare, falsificare; (*wrought iron*) fucinare, foggiare; **forger** *n* contraffattore *m*; **forgery** *n* falso; (*activity*) contraffazione *f*

forget [fə'gɛt] (*pt* **forgot**, *pp* **forgotten**) *vt, vi* dimenticare; **I've forgotten my key/passport** ho dimenticato la chiave/il passaporto; **forgetful** *adj* di corta memoria; **forgetful of** dimentico(-a) di

forgive [fə'gɪv] (*pt* **forgave**, *pp* **forgiven**) *vt* perdonare; **to ~ sb for sth** perdonare qc a qn

forgot [fə'gɔt] *pt of* **forget**

forgotten [fə'gɔtn] *pp of* **forget**

fork [fɔːk] *n* (*for eating*) forchetta; (*for gardening*) forca; (*of roads, rivers, railways*) biforcazione *f* ▷ *vi* (*road etc*) biforcarsi

forlorn [fə'lɔːn] *adj* (*person*) sconsolato(-a); (*place*) abbandonato(-a); (*attempt*) disperato(-a); (*hope*) vano(-a)

form [fɔːm] *n* forma; (*Scol*) classe *f*; (*questionnaire*) scheda ▷ *vt* formare; **in top ~** in gran forma

formal ['fɔːməl] *adj* formale; (*gardens*) simmetrico(-a), regolare; **formality** [fɔː'mælɪtɪ] *n* formalità *f inv*

format ['fɔːmæt] *n* formato ▷ *vt* (*Comput*) formattare

formation [fɔː'meɪʃən] *n* formazione *f*

former ['fɔːməʳ] *adj* vecchio(-a); (*before n*) ex *inv* (*before n*); **the ~ ... the latter** quello ... questo; **formerly** *adv* in passato

formidable ['fɔːmɪdəbl] *adj* formidabile

formula ['fɔːmjulə] *n* formula

fort [fɔːt] *n* forte *m*

forthcoming [fɔːθ'kʌmɪŋ] *adj* (*event*) prossimo(-a); (*help*) disponibile; (*character*) aperto(-a), comunicativo(-a)

fortieth ['fɔːtɪɪθ] *num* quarantesimo(-a)

fortify ['fɔːtɪfaɪ] *vt* (*city*) fortificare; (*person*) armare

fortnight ['fɔːtnaɪt] (BRIT) *n* quindici giorni *mpl*, due settimane *fpl*; **fortnightly** *adj* bimensile ▷ *adv* ogni quindici giorni

fortress ['fɔːtrɪs] *n* fortezza, rocca

fortunate ['fɔːtʃənɪt] *adj* fortunato(-a); **it is ~ that** è una fortuna che; **fortunately** *adv* fortunatamente

fortune ['fɔːtʃən] *n* fortuna; **fortune-teller** *n* indovino(-a)

forty ['fɔːtɪ] *num* quaranta

forum ['fɔːrəm] *n* foro

forward ['fɔːwəd] *adj* (*ahead of schedule*) in anticipo; (*movement, position*) in avanti; (*not shy*) aperto(-a), diretto(-a) ▷ *n* (*Sport*) avanti *m inv* ▷ *vt* (*letter*) inoltrare; (*parcel, goods*) spedire; (*career, plans*) promuovere, appoggiare; **to move ~** avanzare; **forwarding address** *n* nuovo recapito cui spedire la posta; **forward(s)** *adv* avanti; **forward slash** *n* barra obliqua

fossil ['fɔsl] *adj* fossile ▷ *n* fossile *m*

foster ['fɔstəʳ] *vt* incoraggiare, nutrire; (*child*) avere in affidamento; **foster child** *n* bambino(-a) preso(-a) in affidamento; **foster mother** *n* madre *f* affidataria

fought [fɔːt] *pt, pp of* **fight**

foul [faul] *adj* (*smell, food, temper etc*) cattivo(-a); (*weather*) brutto(-a); (*language*) osceno(-a) ▷ *n* (*Sport*) fallo ▷ *vt* sporcare; **foul play** *n* (*Law*): **the police suspect foul play** la polizia sospetta un atto criminale

found [faund] *pt, pp of* **find** ▷ *vt* (*establish*) fondare; **foundation** [-'deɪʃə n] *n* (*act*) fondazione *f*; (*base*) base *f*; (*also*: **foundation cream**) fondo tinta; **foundations** *npl* (*of building*) fondamenta *fpl*

founder ['faundəʳ] *n* fondatore(-trice) ▷ *vi* affondare

fountain ['fauntɪn] *n* fontana; **fountain pen** *n* penna stilografica

four [fɔːʳ] *num* quattro; **on all ~s** a carponi; **four-letter word** ['fɔːlɛtə-] *n* parolaccia; **four-poster** *n* (*also*: **four-poster bed**) letto a quattro colonne; **fourteen** *num* quattordici; **fourteenth** *num* quattordicesimo(-a); **fourth** *num* quarto(-a); **four-wheel drive** ['fɔːwiːl-] *n* (*Aut*) **with four-wheel drive** con quattro ruote motrici

fowl [faul] *n* pollame *m*; volatile *m*

fox [fɔks] *n* volpe *f* ▷ *vt* confondere

foyer ['fɔɪeɪ] *n* atrio; (*Theatre*) ridotto

fraction ['frækʃən] *n* frazione *f*

fracture ['fræktʃəʳ] *n* frattura

fragile ['frædʒaɪl] *adj* fragile

fragment ['frægmənt] *n* frammento

fragrance ['freɪgrəns] *n* fragranza, profumo

frail [freɪl] *adj* debole, delicato(-a)

frame [freɪm] *n* (*of building*) armatura; (*of human, animal*) ossatura, corpo; (*of picture*) cornice *f*; (*of door, window*) telaio; (*of spectacles*: *also*: **~s**) montatura ▷ *vt* (*picture*) incorniciare; **framework** *n* struttura

France [frɑːns] *n* Francia

franchise ['fræntʃaɪz] *n* (*Pol*) diritto di voto; (*Comm*) concessione *f*

frank [fræŋk] *adj* franco(-a), aperto(-a) ▷ *vt* (*letter*) affrancare; **frankly** *adv* francamente, sinceramente

frantic ['fræntɪk] *adj* frenetico(-a)

fraud [frɔːd] *n* truffa; (*Law*) frode *f*; (*person*) impostore *m*

fraught [frɔːt] *adj* **~ with** pieno(-a) di, intriso(-a) da

fray [freɪ] *vt* logorare ▷ *vi* logorarsi

freak [friːk] *n* fenomeno, mostro

freckle ['frɛkl] *n* lentiggine *f*

free [friː] *adj* libero(-a); (*gratis*) gratuito(-a) ▷ *vt* (*prisoner, jammed person*) liberare; (*jammed object*) districare; **is this seat ~?** è libero questo posto?; **~ of charge, for ~** gratuitamente; **freedom** ['friːdəm] *n* libertà; **Freefone®** *n* numero verde; **free gift** *n* regalo, omaggio; **free kick** *n* calcio libero; **freelance** *adj* indipendente; **freely** *adv* liberamente; (*liberally*)

liberalmente; **Freepost®** *n* affrancatura a carico del destinatario; **free-range** *adj* (*hen*) ruspante; (*eggs*) di gallina ruspante; **freeway** (*Us*) *n* superstrada; **free will** *n* libero arbitrio; **of one's own free will** di spontanea volontà

freeze [friːz] (*pt* **froze**, *pp* **frozen**) *vi* gelare ▷ *vt* gelare; (*food*) congelare; (*prices, salaries*) bloccare ▷ *n* gelo; blocco; **freezer** *n* congelatore *m*; **freezing** ['friːzɪŋ] *adj* (*wind, weather*) gelido(-a); **freezing point** *n* punto di congelamento; **3 degrees below freezing point** 3 gradi sotto zero

freight [freɪt] *n* (*goods*) merce *f*, merci *fpl*; (*money charged*) spese *fpl* di trasporto; **freight train** (*Us*) *n* treno *m* merci *inv*

French [frɛntʃ] *adj* francese ▷ *n* (*Ling*) francese *m*; **the ~** *npl* i Francesi; **French bean** *n* fagiolino; **French bread** *n* baguette *f inv*; **French dressing** *n* (*Culin*) condimento per insalata; **French fried potatoes** (*Us* **French fries**) *npl* patate *fpl* fritte; **Frenchman** (*irreg*) *n* francese *m*; **French stick** *n* baguette *f inv*; **French window** *n* portafinestra; **Frenchwoman** (*irreg*) *n* francese *f*

frenzy ['frɛnzɪ] *n* frenesia

frequency ['friːkwənsɪ] *n* frequenza

frequent [*adj* 'friːkwənt, *vb* frɪ'kwɛnt] *adj* frequente ▷ *vt* frequentare; **frequently** *adv* frequentemente, spesso

fresh [frɛʃ] *adj* fresco(-a); (*new*) nuovo(-a); (*cheeky*) sfacciato(-a); **freshen** *vi* (*wind, air*) rinfrescare; **freshen up** *vi* rinfrescarsi; **fresher** (*Brit*: *inf*) *n* (*Scol*) matricola; **freshly** *adv* di recente, di fresco; **freshman** (*irreg*: *Us*) *n* = **fresher**; **freshwater** *adj* (*fish*) d'acqua dolce

fret [frɛt] *vi* agitarsi, affliggersi

Fri. *abbr* (= *Friday*) ven.

friction ['frɪkʃən] *n* frizione *f*, attrito

Friday ['fraɪdɪ] *n* venerdì *m inv*

fridge [frɪdʒ] (*Brit*) *n* frigo, frigorifero

fried [fraɪd] *pt, pp of* **fry** ▷ *adj* fritto(-a)

friend [frɛnd] *n* amico(-a); **friendly** *adj* amichevole; **friendship** *n* amicizia

fries [fraɪz] (*esp Us*) *npl* patate *fpl* fritte

frigate ['frɪgɪt] *n* (*Naut*: *modern*) fregata

fright [fraɪt] *n* paura, spavento; **to take ~** spaventarsi; **frighten** *vt* spaventare, far paura a; **frightened** *adj* spaventato(-a); **frightening** *adj* spaventoso(-a), pauroso(-a); **frightful** *adj* orribile

frill [frɪl] *n* balza

fringe [frɪndʒ] *n* (*decoration*: *Brit*: *of hair*) frangia; (*edge*: *of forest etc*) margine *m*

Frisbee® ['frɪzbɪ] *n* frisbee® *m inv*

fritter ['frɪtəʳ] *n* frittella

frivolous ['frɪvələs] *adj* frivolo(-a)

fro [frəu] *see* **to**
frock [frɔk] *n* vestito
frog [frɔg] *n* rana; **frogman** (*irreg*) *n* uomo *m* rana *inv*

🔵 KEYWORD

from [frɔm] *prep* **1** (*indicating starting place, origin etc*) da; **where do you come from?**, **where are you from?** da dove viene?, di dov'è?; **from London to Glasgow** da Londra a Glasgow; **a letter from my sister** una lettera da mia sorella; **tell him from me that ...** gli dica da parte mia che ...
2 (*indicating time*) da; **from one o'clock to** *or* **until** *or* **till two** dall'una alle due; **from January (on)** da gennaio, a partire da gennaio
3 (*indicating distance*) da; **the hotel is 1 km from the beach** l'albergo è a 1 km dalla spiaggia
4 (*indicating price, number etc*) da; **prices range from £10 to £50** i prezzi vanno dalle 10 alle 50 sterline
5 (*indicating difference*) da; **he can't tell red from green** non sa distinguere il rosso dal verde
6 (*because of, on the basis of*): **from what he says** da quanto dice lui; **weak from hunger** debole per la fame

front [frʌnt] *n* (*of house, dress*) davanti *m inv*; (*of train*) testa; (*of book*) copertina; (*promenade: also:* **sea ~**) lungomare *m*; (*Mil, Pol, Meteor*) fronte *m*; (*fig: appearances*) fronte *f* ▷ *adj* primo(-a); anteriore, davanti *inv*; **in ~ of** davanti a; **front door** *n* porta d'entrata; (*of car*) sportello anteriore; **frontier** ['frʌntɪəʳ] *n* frontiera; **front page** *n* prima pagina; **front-wheel drive** ['frʌntwiːl-] *n* trasmissione *f* anteriore
frost [frɔst] *n* gelo; (*also:* **hoar~**) brina; **frostbite** *n* congelamento; **frosting** (*US*) *n* (*on cake*) glassa; **frosty** *adj* (*weather, look*) gelido(-a)
froth ['frɔθ] *n* spuma; schiuma
frown [fraun] *vi* accigliarsi
froze [frəuz] *pt of* **freeze**
frozen ['frəuzn] *pp of* **freeze**
fruit [fruːt] *n inv* (*also fig*) frutto; (*collectively*) frutta; **fruit juice** *n* succo di frutta; **fruit machine** (*BRIT*) *n* macchina *f* mangiasoldi *inv*; **fruit salad** *n* macedonia
frustrate [frʌsˈtreɪt] *vt* frustrare; **frustrated** *adj* frustrato(-a)
fry [fraɪ] (*pt, pp* **fried**) *vt* friggere; *see also* **small**; **frying pan** *n* padella
ft. *abbr* = **foot**; **feet**

fudge [fʌdʒ] *n* (*Culin*) specie di caramella a base di latte, burro e zucchero
fuel [fjuəl] *n* (*for heating*) combustibile *m*; (*for propelling*) carburante *m*; **fuel tank** *n* deposito *m* nafta *inv*; (*on vehicle*) serbatoio (della benzina)
fulfil [fulˈfɪl] *vt* (*function*) compiere; (*order*) eseguire; (*wish, desire*) soddisfare, appagare
full [ful] *adj* pieno(-a); (*details, skirt*) ampio(-a) ▷ *adv* **to know ~ well that** sapere benissimo che; **I'm ~ (up)** sono sazio; **a ~ two hours** due ore intere; **at ~ speed** a tutta velocità; **in ~** per intero; **full-length** *adj* (*film*) a lungometraggio; (*coat, novel*) lungo(-a); (*portrait*) in piedi; **full moon** *n* luna piena; **full-scale** *adj* (*attack, war*) su larga scala; (*model*) in grandezza naturale; **full stop** *n* punto; **full-time** *adj, adv* (*work*) a tempo pieno; **fully** *adv* interamente, pienamente, completamente; (*at least*) almeno
fumble ['fʌmbl] *vi*: **to ~ with sth** armeggiare con qc
fume [fjuːm] *vi* essere furioso(-a); **fumes** *npl* esalazioni *fpl*, vapori *mpl*
fun [fʌn] *n* divertimento, spasso; **to have ~** divertirsi; **for ~** per scherzo; **to make ~ of** prendersi gioco di
function ['fʌŋkʃən] *n* funzione *f*; cerimonia, ricevimento ▷ *vi* funzionare
fund [fʌnd] *n* fondo, cassa; (*source*) fondo; (*store*) riserva; **~s** *npl* (*money*) fondi *mpl*
fundamental [fʌndəˈmɛntl] *adj* fondamentale
funeral ['fjuːnərəl] *n* funerale *m*; **funeral director** *n* impresario di pompe funebri; **funeral parlour** [-ˈpɑːləʳ] *n* impresa di pompe funebri
funfair ['fʌnfɛəʳ] *n* luna park *m inv*
fungus ['fʌŋgəs] (*pl* **fungi**) *n* fungo; (*mould*) muffa
funnel ['fʌnl] *n* imbuto; (*of ship*) ciminiera
funny ['fʌnɪ] *adj* divertente, buffo(-a); (*strange*) strano(-a), bizzarro(-a)
fur [fəːʳ] *n* pelo; pelliccia; (*BRIT: in kettle etc*) deposito calcare; **fur coat** *n* pelliccia
furious ['fjuərɪəs] *adj* furioso(-a); (*effort*) accanito(-a)
furnish ['fəːnɪʃ] *vt* ammobiliare; (*supply*) fornire; **furnishings** *npl* mobili *mpl*, mobilia
furniture ['fəːnɪtʃəʳ] *n* mobili *mpl*; **piece of ~** mobile *m*
furry ['fəːrɪ] *adj* (*animal*) peloso(-a)
further ['fəːðəʳ] *adj* supplementare, altro(-a); nuovo(-a); più lontano(-a) ▷ *adv* più lontano; (*more*) di più; (*moreover*) inoltre ▷ *vt* favorire, promuovere; **further**

education *n* ≈ corsi *mpl* di formazione; **college of further education** istituto statale con corsi specializzati (di formazione professionale, aggiornamento professionale ecc); **furthermore** [fəːðəˈmɔːʳ] *adv* inoltre, per di più

furthest [ˈfəːðɪst] *superl of* **far**

fury [ˈfjuərɪ] *n* furore *m*

fuse [fjuːz] (*US* **fuze**) *n* fusibile *m*; (*for bomb etc*) miccia, spoletta ▷ *vt* fondere ▷ *vi* fondersi; **to ~ the lights** (*BRIT Elec*) far saltare i fusibili; **fuse box** *n* cassetta dei fusibili

fusion [ˈfjuːʒən] *n* fusione *f*

fuss [fʌs] *n* agitazione *f*; (*complaining*) storie *fpl*; **to make a ~** fare delle storie; **fussy** *adj* (*person*) puntiglioso(-a), esigente; che fa le storie; (*dress*) carico(-a) di fronzoli; (*style*) elaborato(-a)

future [ˈfjuːtʃəʳ] *adj* futuro(-a) ▷ *n* futuro, avvenire *m*; (*Ling*) futuro; **in ~** in futuro; **~s** *npl* (*Comm*) operazioni *fpl* a termine

fuze [fjuːz] (*US*) = **fuse**

fuzzy [ˈfʌzɪ] *adj* (*Phot*) indistinto(-a), sfocato(-a); (*hair*) crespo(-a)

G [dʒiː] *n* (*Mus*) sol *m*

g. *abbr* (= *gram, gravity*) g.

gadget [ˈgædʒɪt] *n* aggeggio

Gaelic [ˈgeɪlɪk] *adj* gaelico(-a) ▷ *n* (*Ling*) gaelico

gag [gæg] *n* bavaglio; (*joke*) facezia, scherzo ▷ *vt* imbavagliare

gain [geɪn] *n* guadagno, profitto ▷ *vt* guadagnare ▷ *vi* (*clock, watch*) andare avanti; (*benefit*): **to ~ (from)** trarre beneficio (da); **to ~ 3lbs (in weight)** aumentare di 3 libbre; **to ~ on sb** (*in race etc*) guadagnare su qn

gal. *abbr* = **gallon**

gala [ˈgɑːlə] *n* gala; **swimming ~** manifestazione *f* di nuoto

galaxy [ˈgæləksɪ] *n* galassia

gale [geɪl] *n* vento forte; burrasca

gall bladder [ˈgɔːl-] *n* cistifellea

gallery [ˈgælərɪ] *n* galleria

gallon [ˈgælən] *n* gallone *m* (= 8 pints; BRIT = 4.543l; US = 3.785l)

gallop [ˈgæləp] *n* galoppo ▷ *vi* galoppare

gallstone [ˈgɔːlstəun] *n* calcolo biliare

gamble [ˈgæmbl] *n* azzardo, rischio calcolato ▷ *vt, vi* giocare; **to ~ on** (*fig*) giocare su; **gambler** *n* giocatore(-trice) d'azzardo; **gambling** *n* gioco d'azzardo

game [geɪm] *n* gioco; (*event*) partita; (*Tennis*) game *m inv*; (*Culin, Hunting*)

selvaggina ▷ *adj* (*ready*): **to be ~ (for sth/
to do)** essere pronto(-a) (a qc/a fare); **big
~** selvaggina grossa; **~s** *npl* (*Scol*) attività
fpl sportive; **big ~** selvaggina grossa;
games console [geɪmz-] *n* console *f inv*
dei videogame; **game show** ['geɪmʃəʊ] *n*
gioco a premi

gammon ['gæmən] *n* (*bacon*) quarto di
maiale; (*ham*) prosciutto affumicato

gang [gæŋ] *n* banda, squadra ▷ *vi* **to ~ up
on sb** far combutta contro qn

gangster ['gæŋstər] *n* gangster *m inv*

gap [gæp] *n* (*space*) buco; (*in time*)
intervallo; (*difference*): **~ (between)** divario
(tra)

gape [geɪp] *vi* (*person*) restare a bocca
aperta; (*shirt, hole*) essere spalancato(-a)

gap year *n* (*Scol*) anno di pausa durante il
quale gli studenti viaggiono o lavorano

garage ['gæraːʒ] *n* garage *m inv*; **garage
sale** *n* vendita di oggetti usati nel garage di
un privato

garbage ['gɑːbɪdʒ] (*US*) *n* immondizie *fpl*,
rifiuti *mpl*; (*inf*) sciocchezze *fpl*; **garbage
can** (*US*) *n* bidone *m* della spazzatura;
garbage collector (*US*) *n* spazzino(-a)

garden ['gɑːdn] *n* giardino; **~s** *npl* (*public
park*) giardini pubblici; **garden centre**
n vivaio; **gardener** *n* giardiniere(-a);
gardening *n* giardinaggio

garlic ['gɑːlɪk] *n* aglio

garment ['gɑːmənt] *n* indumento

garnish ['gɑːnɪʃ] *vt* (*food*) guarnire

garrison ['gærɪsn] *n* guarnigione *f*

gas [gæs] *n* gas *m inv*; (*US: gasoline*) benzina
▷ *vt* asfissiare con il gas; **I can smell ~**
sento odore di gas; **gas cooker** (*BRIT*) *n*
cucina a gas; **gas cylinder** *n* bombola del
gas; **gas fire** (*BRIT*) *n* radiatore *m* a gas

gasket ['gæskɪt] *n* (*Aut*) guarnizione *f*

gasoline ['gæsəliːn] (*US*) *n* benzina

gasp [gɑːsp] *n* respiro affannoso, ansito
▷ *vi* ansare, ansimare; (*in surprise*) restare
senza fiato

gas: **gas pedal** (*esp US*) *n* pedale *m*
dell'acceleratore; **gas station** (*US*) *n*
distributore *m* di benzina; **gas tank** (*US*) *n*
(*Aut*) serbatoio (di benzina)

gate [geɪt] *n* cancello; (*at airport*) uscita

gateau ['gætəʊ, -z] (*pl* **gateaux**) *n* torta

gatecrash ['geɪtkræʃ] (*BRIT*) *vt* partecipare
senza invito a

gateway ['geɪtweɪ] *n* porta

gather ['gæðər] *vt* (*flowers, fruit*) cogliere;
(*pick up*) raccogliere; (*assemble*) radunare;
raccogliere; (*understand*) capire; (*Sewing*)
increspare ▷ *vi* (*assemble*) radunarsi; **to ~
speed** acquistare velocità; **gathering** *n*
adunanza

gauge [geɪdʒ] *n* (*instrument*) indicatore *m*
▷ *vt* misurare; (*fig*) valutare

gave [geɪv] *pt of* **give**

gay [geɪ] *adj* (*homosexual*) omosessuale;
(*cheerful*) gaio(-a), allegro(-a); (*colour*)
vivace, vivo(-a)

gaze [geɪz] *n* sguardo fisso ▷ *vi* **to ~ at**
guardare fisso

GB *abbr* = **Great Britain**

GCSE (*BRIT*) *n abbr* General Certificate of
Secondary Education

gear [gɪər] *n* attrezzi *mpl*,
equipaggiamento; (*Tech*) ingranaggio;
(*Aut*) marcia ▷ *vt* (*fig: adapt*): **to ~ sth to**
adattare qc a; **in top** *or* (*US*) **high/low ~** in
quarta (*or* quinta)/seconda; **in ~** in marcia;
gear up *vi* **to ~ up (to do)** prepararsi (a
fare); **gear box** *n* scatola del cambio; **gear
lever** *n* leva del cambio; **gear shift** (*US*),
gear stick (*BRIT*) *n* = **gear lever**

geese [giːs] *npl of* **goose**

gel [dʒɛl] *n* gel *m inv*

gem [dʒɛm] *n* gemma

Gemini ['dʒɛmɪnaɪ] *n* Gemelli *mpl*

gender ['dʒɛndər] *n* genere *m*

gene [dʒiːn] *n* (*Biol*) gene *m*

general ['dʒɛnərl] *n* generale *m* ▷ *adj*
generale; **in ~** in genere; **general
anaesthetic** (*US* **general anesthetic**)
n anestesia totale; **general election**
n elezioni *fpl* generali; **generalize**
vi generalizzare; **generally** *adv*
generalmente; **general practitioner**
n medico generico; **general store** *n*
emporio

generate ['dʒɛnəreɪt] *vt* generare

generation [dʒɛnə'reɪʃən] *n* generazione *f*

generator ['dʒɛnəreɪtər] *n*
generatore *m*

generosity [dʒɛnə'rɔsɪtɪ] *n* generosità

generous ['dʒɛnərəs] *adj* generoso(-a);
(*copious*) abbondante

genetic [dʒɪ'nɛtɪk] *adj* genetico(-a);
~ engineering ingegneria genetica;
genetically modified *adj* geneticamente
modificato(-a), transgenico(-a); **genetics**
n genetica

Geneva [dʒɪ'niːvə] *n* Ginevra

genitals ['dʒɛnɪtlz] *npl* genitali *mpl*

genius ['dʒiːnɪəs] *n* genio

Genoa ['dʒɛnəʊə] *n* Genova

gent [dʒɛnt] *n abbr* = **gentleman**

gentle ['dʒɛntl] *adj* delicato(-a); (*person*)
dolce

▌ Be careful not to translate *gentle* by
the Italian word *gentile*.

gentleman ['dʒɛntlmən] (*irreg*) *n* signore
m; (*well-bred man*) gentiluomo

gently ['dʒɛntlɪ] *adv* delicatamente

gents [dʒɛnts] n W.C. m (per signori)
genuine ['dʒɛnjuɪn] adj autentico(-a);
sincero(-a); **genuinely** adv genuinamente
geographic(al) [dʒɪə'græfɪk(l)] adj
geografico(-a)
geography [dʒɪ'ɔgrəfɪ] n geografia
geology [dʒɪ'ɔlədʒɪ] n geologia
geometry [dʒɪ'ɔmətrɪ] n geometria
geranium [dʒɪ'reɪnjəm] n geranio
geriatric [dʒɛrɪ'ætrɪk] adj geriatrico(-a)
germ [dʒə:m] n (Med) microbo; (Biol, fig)
germe m
German ['dʒə:mən] adj tedesco(-a) ▷ n
tedesco(-a); (Ling) tedesco; **German
measles** (BRIT) n rosolia
Germany ['dʒə:mənɪ] n Germania
gesture ['dʒɛstjə'] n gesto

○ **KEYWORD**

get [gɛt] (pt, pp **got**, (US) pp **gotten**) vi **1**
(become, be) diventare, farsi; **to get old**
invecchiare; **to get tired** stancarsi; **to get
drunk** ubriacarsi; **to get killed** venire or
rimanere ucciso(-a); **when do I get paid?**
quando mi pagate?; **it's getting late** si sta
facendo tardi
2 (go): **to get to/from** andare a/da; **to get
home** arrivare or tornare a casa; **how did
you get here?** come sei venuto?
3 (begin) mettersi a, cominciare a; **to get
to know sb** incominciare a conoscere qn;
let's get going or **started** muoviamoci
4 (modal aux vb): **you've got to do it** devi
farlo
▷ vt **1**: **to get sth done** (do) fare qc; (have
done) far fare qc; **to get one's hair cut** farsi
tagliare i capelli; **to get sb to do sth** far
fare qc a qn
2 (obtain: money, permission, results)
ottenere; (find: job, flat) trovare; (fetch:
person, doctor) chiamare; (: object)
prendere; **to get sth for sb** prendere
or procurare qc a qn; **get me Mr Jones,
please** (Tel) mi passi il signor Jones, per
favore; **can I get you a drink?** le posso
offrire da bere?
3 (receive: present, letter, prize) ricevere;
(acquire: reputation) farsi; **how much did
you get for the painting?** quanto le
hanno dato per il quadro?
4 (catch) prendere; (hit: target etc) colpire;
to get sb by the arm/throat afferrare
qn per un braccio/alla gola; **get him!**
prendetelo!
5 (take, move) portare; **to get sth to sb** far
avere qc a qn; **do you think we'll get it
through the door?** pensi che riusciremo a
farlo passare per la porta?

6 (catch, take: plane, bus etc) prendere;
where do we get the ferry to …? dove si
prende il traghetto per …?
7 (understand) afferrare; (hear) sentire; **I've
got it!** ci sono arrivato!, ci sono!; **I'm sorry,
I didn't get your name** scusi, non ho
capito (or sentito) il suo nome
8 (have, possess): **to have got** avere; **how
many have you got?** quanti ne ha?
get along vi (agree) andare d'accordo;
(depart) andarsene; (manage) = **get by**
get at vt fus (attack) prendersela con;
(reach) raggiungere, arrivare a
get away vi partire, andarsene; (escape)
scappare
get away with vt fus cavarsela; farla
franca
get back vi (return) ritornare, tornare ▷ vt
riottenere, riavere; **when do we get back?**
quando ritorniamo?
get by vi (pass) passare; (manage) farcela
get down vi, vt fus scendere ▷ vt far
scendere; (depress) buttare giù
get down to vt fus (work) mettersi a (fare)
get in vi entrare; (train) arrivare; (arrive
home) ritornare, tornare
get into vt fus entrare in; **to get into a
rage** incavolarsi
get off vi (from train etc) scendere; (depart:
person, car) andare via; (escape) cavarsela
▷ vt (remove: clothes, stain) levare ▷ vt fus
(train, bus) scendere da; **where do I get
off?** dove devo scendere?
get on vi (at exam etc) andare; (agree): **to
get on (with)** andare d'accordo (con) ▷ vt
fus montare in; (horse) montare su
get out vi uscire; (of vehicle) scendere ▷ vt
tirar fuori, far uscire
get out of vt fus uscire da; (duty etc)
evitare
get over vt fus (illness) riaversi da
get round vt fus aggirare; (fig: person)
rigirare
get through vi (Tel) avere la linea
get through to vt fus (Tel) parlare a
get together vi riunirsi ▷ vt raccogliere;
(people) adunare
get up vi (rise) alzarsi ▷ vt fus salire su per
get up to vt fus (reach) raggiungere; (prank
etc) fare

getaway ['gɛtəweɪ] n fuga
Ghana ['gɑːnə] n Ghana m
ghastly ['gɑːstlɪ] adj orribile, orrendo(-a);
(pale) spettrale
ghetto ['gɛtəu] n ghetto
ghost [gəust] n fantasma m, spettro
giant ['dʒaɪənt] n gigante m ▷ adj
gigantesco(-a), enorme

gift [gɪft] n regalo; (donation, ability) dono; **gifted** adj dotato(-a); **gift shop** (US **gift store**) n negozio di souvenir

gift token, gift voucher n buono m omaggio inv

gig [gɪg] n (inf: of musician) serata

gigabyte [gi:gəbaɪt] n gigabyte m inv

gigantic [dʒaɪˈgæntɪk] adj gigantesco(-a)

giggle [ˈgɪgl] vi ridere scioccamente

gills [gɪlz] npl (of fish) branchie fpl

gilt [gɪlt] n doratura ▷ adj dorato(-a)

gimmick [ˈgɪmɪk] n trucco

gin [dʒɪn] n (liquor) gin m inv

ginger [ˈdʒɪndʒər] n zenzero

gipsy [ˈdʒɪpsɪ] n zingaro(-a)

giraffe [dʒɪˈrɑːf] n giraffa

girl [gəːl] n ragazza; (young unmarried woman) signorina; (daughter) figlia, figliola; **girlfriend** n (of girl) amica; (of boy) ragazza; **Girl Scout** (US) n Giovane Esploratrice f

gist [dʒɪst] n succo

give [gɪv] (pt **gave**, pp **given**) vt dare ▷ vi cedere; **to ~ sb sth, ~ sth to sb** dare qc a qn; **I'll ~ you £5 for it** te lo pago 5 sterline; **to ~ a cry/sigh** emettere un grido/sospiro; **to ~ a speech** fare un discorso; **give away** vt dare via; (disclose) rivelare; (bride) condurre all'altare; **give back** vt rendere; **give in** vi cedere ▷ vt consegnare; **give out** vt distribuire; annunciare; **give up** vi rinunciare ▷ vt rinunciare a; **to ~ up smoking** smettere di fumare; **to ~ o.s. up** arrendersi

given [ˈgɪvn] pp of **give** ▷ adj (fixed: time, amount) dato(-a), determinato(-a) ▷ conj **~ (that)** ... dato che ...; **~ the circumstances** ... date le circostanze ...

glacier [ˈglæsɪər] n ghiacciaio

glad [glæd] adj lieto(-a), contento(-a); **gladly** [ˈglædlɪ] adv volentieri

glamorous [ˈglæmərəs] adj affascinante, seducente

glamour [ˈglæmər] (US **glamor**) n fascino

glance [glɑːns] n occhiata, sguardo ▷ vi **to ~ at** dare un'occhiata a; **to ~ off** (bullet) rimbalzare su

gland [glænd] n ghiandola

glare [glɛər] n (of anger) sguardo furioso; (of light) riverbero, luce f abbagliante; (of publicity) chiasso ▷ vi abbagliare; **to ~ at** guardare male; **glaring** adj (mistake) madornale

glass [glɑːs] n (substance) vetro; (tumbler) bicchiere m; **~es** npl (spectacles) occhiali mpl

glaze [gleɪz] vt (door) fornire di vetri; (pottery) smaltare ▷ n smalto

gleam [gliːm] vi luccicare

glen [glɛn] n valletta

glide [glaɪd] vi scivolare; (Aviat, birds) planare; **glider** n (Aviat) aliante m

glimmer [ˈglɪmər] n barlume m

glimpse [glɪmps] n impressione f fugace ▷ vt vedere al volo

glint [glɪnt] vi luccicare

glisten [ˈglɪsn] vi luccicare

glitter [ˈglɪtər] vi scintillare

global [ˈgləubl] adj globale; **global warming** n effetto m serra inv

globe [gləub] n globo, sfera

gloom [gluːm] n oscurità, buio; (sadness) tristezza, malinconia; **gloomy** adj scuro(-a), fosco(-a), triste

glorious [ˈgloːrɪəs] adj glorioso(-a), magnifico(-a)

glory [ˈgloːrɪ] n gloria; splendore m

gloss [glɔs] n (shine) lucentezza; (also: **~ paint**) vernice f a olio

glossary [ˈglɔsərɪ] n glossario

glossy [ˈglɔsɪ] adj lucente

glove [glʌv] n guanto; **glove compartment** n (Aut) vano portaoggetti

glow [gləu] vi ardere; (face) essere luminoso(-a)

glucose [ˈgluːkəus] n glucosio

glue [gluː] n colla ▷ vt incollare

GM adj abbr (= genetically modified) geneticamente modificato(-a)

gm abbr = **gram**

GMO n abbr (= genetically modified organism) OGM m inv

GMT abbr (= Greenwich Mean Time) T.M.G.

gnaw [nɔː] vt rodere

go [gəu] (pt **went**, pp **gone**) (pl **goes**) vi andare; (depart) partire, andarsene; (work) funzionare; (time) passare; (break etc) rompersi; (be sold): **to go for £10** essere venduto per 10 sterline; (fit, suit): **to go with** andare bene con; (become): **to go pale** diventare pallido(-a); **to go mouldy** ammuffire ▷ n **to have a go (at)** provare; **to be on the go** essere in moto; **whose go is it?** a chi tocca?; **he's going to do** sta per fare; **to go for a walk** andare a fare una passeggiata; **to go dancing/ shopping** andare a ballare/fare la spesa; **just then the bell went** proprio allora suonò il campanello; **how did it go?** com'è andato?; **to go round the back/by the shop** passare da dietro/davanti al negozio; **go ahead** vi andare avanti; **go away** vi partire, andarsene; **go back** vi tornare, ritornare; **go by** vi (years, time) scorrere ▷ vt fus attenersi a, seguire (alla lettera); prestar fede a; **go down** vi scendere; (ship) affondare; (sun) tramontare ▷ vt fus scendere; **go for** vt fus (fetch) andare a prendere; (*like*) andar matto(-a) per; (*attack*) attaccare; saltare addosso a; **go in** *vi* entrare; **go into** *vt fus* entrare in; (*investigate*) indagare, esaminare; (*embark on*) lanciarsi in; **go off** *vi* partire, andar via; (*food*) guastarsi; (*explode*) esplodere, scoppiare; (*event*) passare ▷ *vt fus* **I've ~ne off chocolate** la cioccolata non mi piace più; **the gun went off** il fucile si scaricò; **go on** *vi* continuare; (*happen*) succedere; **to ~ on doing** continuare a fare; **go out** *vi* uscire; (*couple*): **they went out for 3 years** sono stati insieme per 3 anni; (*fire, light*) spegnersi; **go over** *vi* ribaltarsi ▷ *vt fus* (*check*) esaminare; **go past** *vi* passare ▷ *vt fus* passare davanti a; **go round** *vi* (*circulate: news, rumour*) circolare; (*revolve*) girare; (*visit*): **to ~ round (to sb's)** passare (da qn); (*make a detour*): **to ~ round (by)** passare (per); (*suffice*) bastare (per tutti); **go through** *vt fus* (*town etc*) attraversare; (*files, papers*) passare in rassegna; (*examine: list etc*) leggere da cima a fondo; **go up** *vi* salire; **go with** *vt fus* (*accompany*) accompagnare; **go without** *vt fus* fare a meno di

go-ahead ['gəʊəhɛd] *adj* intraprendente ▷ *n* via *m*

goal [gəʊl] *n* (*Sport*) gol *m*, rete *f*; (: *place*) porta; (*fig: aim*) fine *m*, scopo; **goalkeeper** *n* portiere *m*; **goal-post** *n* palo (della porta)

goat [gəʊt] *n* capra

gobble ['gɔbl] *vt* (*also:* **~ down, ~ up**) ingoiare

god [gɔd] *n* dio; **G~** Dio; **godchild** *n* figlioccio(-a); **goddaughter** *n* figlioccia; **goddess** *n* dea; **godfather** *n* padrino; **godmother** *n* madrina; **godson** *n* figlioccio

goggles ['gɔglz] *npl* occhiali *mpl* (di protezione)

going ['gəʊɪŋ] *n* (*conditions*) andare *m*, stato del terreno ▷ *adj* **the ~ rate** la tariffa in vigore

gold [gəʊld] *n* oro ▷ *adj* d'oro; **golden** *adj* (*made of gold*) d'oro; (*gold in colour*) dorato(-a); **goldfish** *n* pesce *m* dorato or rosso; **goldmine** *n* (*also fig*) miniera d'oro; **gold-plated** *adj* placcato(-a) oro *inv*

golf [gɔlf] *n* golf *m*; **golf ball** *n* (*for game*) pallina da golf; (*on typewriter*) pallina; **golf club** *n* circolo di golf; (*stick*) bastone *m* or mazza da golf; **golf course** *n* campo di golf; **golfer** *n* giocatore(-trice) di golf

gone [gɔn] *pp of* **go** ▷ *adj* partito(-a)

gong [gɔŋ] *n* gong *m inv*

good [gʊd] *adj* buono(-a); (*kind*) buono(-a), gentile; (*child*) bravo(-a) ▷ *n* bene *m*; **~s** *npl* (*Comm etc*) beni *mpl*; merci *fpl*; **~!** bene!, ottimo!; **to be ~ at** essere bravo(-a) in; **to be ~ for** andare bene per; **it's ~ for you** fa bene; **would you be ~ enough to ...?** avrebbe la gentilezza di ...?; **a ~ deal (of)** molto(-a), una buona quantità (di); **a ~ many** molti(-e); **to make ~** (*loss, damage*) compensare; **it's no ~ complaining** brontolare non serve a niente; **for ~** per sempre, definitivamente; **~ morning!** buon giorno!; **~ afternoon/evening!** buona sera!; **~ night!** buona notte!; **goodbye** *excl* arrivederci!; **Good Friday** *n* Venerdì Santo; **good-looking** *adj* bello(-a); **good-natured** *adj* affabile; **goodness** *n* (*of person*) bontà; **for goodness sake!** per amor di Dio!; **goodness gracious!** santo cielo!, mamma mia!; **goods train** (*BRIT*) *n* treno *m* merci *inv*; **goodwill** *n* amicizia, benevolenza

goose [guːs] (*pl* **geese**) *n* oca

gooseberry ['gʊzbərɪ] *n* uva spina; **to play ~** (*BRIT*) tenere la candela

goose bumps, goose pimples *npl* pelle f d'oca

gorge [gɔːdʒ] *n* gola ▷ *vt* **to ~ o.s. (on)** ingozzarsi (di)

gorgeous ['gɔːdʒəs] *adj* magnifico(-a)

gorilla [gə'rɪlə] *n* gorilla *m inv*

gosh (*inf*) [gɔʃ] *excl* perdinci!

gospel ['gɔspl] *n* vangelo

gossip ['gɔsɪp] *n* chiacchiere *fpl*; pettegolezzi *mpl*; (*person*) pettegolo(-a) ▷ *vi* chiacchierare; **gossip column** *n* cronaca mondana

got [gɔt] *pt, pp of* **get**

gotten ['gɔtn] (*US*) *pp of* **get**

gourmet ['gʊəmeɪ] *n* buongustaio(-a)

govern ['gʌvən] *vt* governare; **government** ['gʌvnmənt] *n* governo; **governor** ['gʌvənər] *n* (*of state, bank*) governatore *m*; (*of school, hospital*) amministratore *m*; (*BRIT: of prison*) direttore(-trice)

gown [gaʊn] *n* vestito lungo; (*of teacher, BRIT: of judge*) toga

G.P. *n abbr* = **general practitioner**

grab [græb] *vt* afferrare, arraffare; (*property, power*) impadronirsi di ▷ *vi* **to ~ at** cercare di afferrare

grace [greɪs] *n* grazia ▷ *vt* onorare; **5 days' ~** dilazione *f* di 5 giorni; **graceful** *adj* elegante, aggraziato(-a); **gracious** ['greɪʃəs] *adj* grazioso(-a), misericordioso(-a)

grade [greɪd] *n* (*Comm*) qualità *f inv*; classe *f*; categoria; (*in hierarchy*) grado; (*Scol: mark*) voto; (*US: school class*) classe ▷ *vt* classificare; ordinare; graduare; **grade crossing** (*US*) *n* passaggio a livello; **grade**

school (US) n scuola elementare
gradient ['greɪdɪənt] n pendenza, inclinazione f
gradual ['grædjuəl] adj graduale; **gradually** adv man mano, a poco a poco
graduate [n 'grædjuɪt, vb 'grædjueɪt] n (of university) laureato(-a); (US: of high school) diplomato(-a) ▷ vi laurearsi; diplomarsi; **graduation** [-'eɪʃən] n (ceremony) consegna delle lauree (or dei diplomi)
graffiti [grə'fi:tɪ] npl graffiti mpl
graft [grɑ:ft] n (Agr, Med) innesto; (bribery) corruzione f; (BRIT: hard work): **it's hard ~** è un lavoraccio ▷ vt innestare
grain [greɪn] n grano; (of sand) granello; (of wood) venatura
gram [græm] n grammo
grammar ['græmə'] n grammatica; **grammar school** (BRIT) n ≈ liceo
gramme [græm] n = **gram**
gran (inf) [græn] n (BRIT) nonna
grand [grænd] adj grande, magnifico(-a); grandioso(-a); **grandad** (inf) n = **granddad**; **grandchild** (pl -**children**) n nipote m; **granddad** (inf) n nonno; **granddaughter** n nipote f; **grandfather** n nonno; **grandma** (inf) n nonna; **grandmother** n nonna; **grandpa** (inf) n = **granddad**; **grandparents** npl nonni mpl; **grand piano** n pianoforte m a coda; **Grand Prix** ['grɑ̃:'pri:] n (Aut) Gran Premio, Grand Prix m inv; **grandson** n nipote m
granite ['grænɪt] n granito
granny ['grænɪ] (inf) n nonna
grant [grɑ:nt] vt accordare; (a request) accogliere; (admit) ammettere, concedere ▷ n (Scol) borsa; (Admin) sussidio, sovvenzione f; **to take sth for ~ed** dare qc per scontato; **to take sb for ~ed** dare per scontata la presenza di qn
grape [greɪp] n chicco d'uva, acino
grapefruit ['greɪpfru:t] n pompelmo
graph [grɑ:f] n grafico; **graphic** adj grafico(-a); (vivid) vivido(-a); **graphics** n grafica ▷ npl illustrazioni fpl
grasp [grɑ:sp] vt afferrare ▷ n (grip) presa; (fig) potere m; comprensione f
grass [grɑ:s] n erba; **grasshopper** n cavalletta
grate [greɪt] n graticola (del focolare) ▷ vi cigolare, stridere ▷ vt (Culin) grattugiare
grateful ['greɪtful] adj grato(-a), riconoscente
grater ['greɪtə'] n grattugia
gratitude ['grætɪtju:d] n gratitudine f
grave [greɪv] n tomba ▷ adj grave, serio(-a)
gravel ['grævl] n ghiaia

gravestone ['greɪvstəun] n pietra tombale
graveyard ['greɪvjɑ:d] n cimitero
gravity ['grævɪtɪ] n (Physics) gravità; pesantezza; (seriousness) gravità, serietà
gravy ['greɪvɪ] n intingolo della carne; salsa
gray [greɪ] adj = **grey**
graze [greɪz] vi pascolare, pascere ▷ vt (touch lightly) sfiorare; (scrape) escoriare ▷ n (Med) escoriazione f
grease [gri:s] n (fat) grasso; (lubricant) lubrificante m ▷ vt ingrassare; lubrificare; **greasy** adj grasso(-a), untuoso(-a)
great [greɪt] adj grande; (inf) magnifico(-a), meraviglioso(-a); **Great Britain** n Gran Bretagna; **great-grandfather** n bisnonno; **great-grandmother** n bisnonna; **greatly** adv molto
Greece [gri:s] n Grecia
greed [gri:d] n (also: ~**iness**) avarizia; (for food) golosità, ghiottoneria; **greedy** adj avido(-a); goloso(-a), ghiotto(-a)
Greek [gri:k] adj greco(-a) ▷ n greco(-a); (Ling) greco
green [gri:n] adj verde; (inexperienced) inesperto(-a), ingenuo(-a) ▷ n verde m; (stretch of grass) prato; (on golf course) green m inv; ~**s** npl (vegetables) verdura; **green card** n (BRIT Aut) carta verde; (US Admin) permesso di soggiorno e di lavoro; **greengage** ['gri:ngeɪdʒ] n susina Regina Claudia; **greengrocer** (BRIT) n fruttivendolo(-a), erbivendolo(-a); **greenhouse** n serra; **greenhouse effect** n effetto serra
Greenland ['gri:nlənd] n Groenlandia
green salad n insalata verde
greet [gri:t] vt salutare; **greeting** n saluto; **greeting(s) card** n cartolina d'auguri
grew [gru:] pt of **grow**
grey [greɪ] (US **gray**) adj grigio(-a); **grey-haired** adj dai capelli grigi; **greyhound** n levriere m
grid [grɪd] n grata; (Elec) rete f; **gridlock** ['grɪdluk] n (traffic jam) paralisi f inv del traffico; **gridlocked** adj paralizzato(-a) dal traffico; (talks etc) in fase di stallo
grief [gri:f] n dolore m
grievance ['gri:vəns] n lagnanza
grieve [gri:v] vi addolorarsi; rattristarsi ▷ vt addolorare; **to ~ for sb** (dead person) piangere qn
grill [grɪl] n (on cooker) griglia; (also: **mixed ~**) grigliata mista ▷ vt (BRIT) cuocere ai ferri; (inf: question) interrogare senza sosta
grille [grɪl] n grata; (Aut) griglia
grim [grɪm] adj sinistro(-a), brutto(-a)

grime [graɪm] n sudiciume m
grin [grɪn] n sorriso smagliante ▷ vi fare un gran sorriso
grind [graɪnd] (pt, pp **ground**) vt macinare; (make sharp) arrotare ▷ n (work) sgobbata
grip [grɪp] n impugnatura; presa; (holdall) borsa da viaggio ▷ vt (object) afferrare; (attention) catturare; **to come to ~s with** affrontare; cercare di risolvere; **gripping** ['grɪpɪŋ] adj avvincente
grit [grɪt] n ghiaia; (courage) fegato ▷ vt (road) coprire di sabbia; **to ~ one's teeth** stringere i denti
grits [grɪts] (us) npl macinato grosso (di avena etc)
groan [grəun] n gemito ▷ vi gemere
grocer ['grəusər] n negoziante m di generi alimentari; **groceries** npl provviste fpl; **grocer's (shop)** n negozio di (generi) alimentari
grocery ['grəusərɪ] n (shop) (negozio di) alimentari
groin [grɔɪn] n inguine m
groom [gru:m] n palafreniere m; (also: **bride~**) sposo ▷ vt (horse) strigliare; (fig): **to ~ sb for** avviare qn a; **well-~ed** (person) curato(-a)
groove [gru:v] n scanalatura, solco
grope [grəup] vi **to ~ for** cercare a tastoni
gross [grəus] adj grossolano(-a); (Comm) lordo(-a); **grossly** adv (greatly) molto
grotesque [grəu'tɛsk] adj grottesco(-a)
ground [graund] pt, pp of **grind** ▷ n suolo, terra; (land) terreno; (Sport) campo; (reason: gen pl) ragione f; (us: also: **~ wire**) terra ▷ vt (plane) tenere a terra; (us Elec) mettere la presa a terra a; **~s** npl (of coffee etc) fondi mpl; (gardens etc) terreno, giardini mpl; **on/to the ~** per/a terra; **to gain/lose ~** guadagnare/perdere terreno; **ground floor** n pianterreno; **groundsheet** (Brit) n telone m impermeabile; **groundwork** n preparazione f
group [gru:p] n gruppo ▷ vt (also: **~ together**) raggruppare ▷ vi (also: **~ together**) raggrupparsi
grouse [graus] n inv (bird) tetraone m ▷ vi (complain) brontolare
grovel ['grɔvl] vi (fig): **to ~ (before)** strisciare (di fronte a)
grow [grəu] (pt **grew,**, pp **grown**) vi crescere; (increase) aumentare; (develop) svilupparsi; (become): **to ~ rich/weak** arricchirsi/indebolirsi ▷ vt coltivare, far crescere; **grow on** vt fus **that painting is ~ing on me** quel quadro più lo guardo più mi piace; **grow up** vi farsi grande, crescere
growl [graul] vi ringhiare
grown [grəun] pp of **grow**; **grown-up** n

adulto(-a), grande m/f
growth [grəuθ] n crescita, sviluppo; (what has grown) crescita; (Med) escrescenza, tumore m
grub [grʌb] n larva; (inf: food) roba (da mangiare)
grubby ['grʌbɪ] adj sporco(-a)
grudge [grʌdʒ] n rancore m ▷ vt **to ~ sb sth** dare qc a qn di malavoglia; invidiare qc a qn; **to bear sb a ~ (for)** serbar rancore a qn (per)
gruelling ['gruəlɪŋ] (us **grueling**) adj estenuante
gruesome ['gru:səm] adj orribile
grumble ['grʌmbl] vi brontolare, lagnarsi
grumpy ['grʌmpɪ] adj scorbutico(-a)
grunt [grʌnt] vi grugnire
guarantee [gærən'ti:] n garanzia ▷ vt garantire
guard [ga:d] n guardia; (one man) guardia, sentinella; (Brit Rail) capotreno; (on machine) schermo protettivo; (also: **fire~**) parafuoco ▷ vt fare la guardia a; (protect): **to ~ (against)** proteggere (da); **to be on one's ~** stare in guardia; **guardian** n custode m; (of minor) tutore(-trice)
guerrilla [gə'rɪlə] n guerrigliero
guess [gɛs] vi indovinare ▷ vt indovinare; (us) credere, pensare ▷ n **to take** or **have a ~** provare a indovinare
guest [gɛst] n ospite m/f; (in hotel) cliente m/f; **guest house** n pensione f; **guest room** n camera degli ospiti
guidance ['gaɪdəns] n guida, direzione f
guide [gaɪd] n (person, book etc) guida; (Brit: also: **girl ~**) giovane esploratrice f ▷ vt guidare; **is there an English-speaking ~?** c'è una guida che parla inglese?; **guidebook** n guida; **do you have a guidebook in English?** avete una guida in inglese?; **guide dog** n cane m guida inv; **guided tour** n visita guidata; **what time does the guided tour start?** a che ora comincia la visita guidata?; **guidelines** npl (fig) indicazioni fpl, linee fpl direttive
guild [gɪld] n arte f, corporazione f; associazione f
guilt [gɪlt] n colpevolezza; **guilty** adj colpevole
guinea pig ['gɪnɪ-] n cavia
guitar [gɪ'ta:r] n chitarra; **guitarist** n chitarrista m/f
gulf [gʌlf] n golfo; (abyss) abisso
gull [gʌl] n gabbiano
gulp [gʌlp] vi deglutire; (from emotion) avere il nodo in gola ▷ vt (also: **~ down**) tracannare, inghiottire
gum [gʌm] n (Anat) gengiva; (glue) colla;

g

(also: **~drop**) caramella gommosa; (also: **chewing ~**) chewing-gum *m inv* ▷ *vt* **to ~ (together)** incollare

gun [gʌn] *n* fucile *m*; (*small*) pistola, rivoltella; (*rifle*) carabina; (*shotgun*) fucile da caccia; (*cannon*) cannone *m*; **gunfire** *n* spari *mpl*; **gunman** (*irreg*) *n* bandito armato; **gunpoint** *n* **at gunpoint** sotto minaccia di fucile; **gunpowder** *n* polvere *f* da sparo; **gunshot** *n* sparo

gush [gʌʃ] *vi* sgorgare; (*fig*) abbandonarsi ad effusioni

gust [gʌst] *n* (*of wind*) raffica; (*of smoke*) buffata

gut [gʌt] *n* intestino, budello; **~s** *npl* (*Anat*) interiora *fpl*; (*courage*) fegato

gutter ['gʌtə'] *n* (*of roof*) grondaia; (*in street*) cunetta

guy [gaɪ] *n* (*inf: man*) tipo, elemento; (*also:* **~rope**) cavo *or* corda di fissaggio; (*figure*) *effigie di Guy Fawkes*

Guy Fawkes Night [-'fɔːks-] *n* (*BRIT*) vedi nota nel riquadro

gym [dʒɪm] *n* (*also:* **~nasium**) palestra; (*also:* **~nastics**) ginnastica; **gymnasium** [dʒɪm'neɪzɪəm] *n* palestra; **gymnast** ['dʒɪmnæst] *n* ginnasta *m/f*; **gymnastics** [-'næstɪks] *n, npl* ginnastica; **gym shoes** *npl* scarpe *fpl* da ginnastica

gynaecologist [gaɪnɪ'kɔlədʒɪst] (*US* **gynecologist**) *n* ginecologo(-a)

gypsy ['dʒɪpsɪ] *n* = **gipsy**

haberdashery ['hæbə'dæʃərɪ] (*BRIT*) *n* merceria

habit ['hæbɪt] *n* abitudine *f*; (*costume*) abito; (*Rel*) tonaca

habitat ['hæbɪtæt] *n* habitat *m inv*

hack [hæk] *vt* tagliare, fare a pezzi ▷ *n* (*pej: writer*) scribacchino(-a); **hacker** ['hækə'] *n* (*Comput*) pirata *m* informatico

had [hæd] *pt, pp of* **have**

haddock ['hædək] (*pl* **haddock** *or* **haddocks**) *n* eglefino

hadn't ['hædnt] = **had not**

haemorrhage ['hɛmərɪdʒ] (*US* **hemorrhage**) *n* emorragia

haemorrhoids ['hɛmərɔɪdz] (*US* **hemorrhoids**) *npl* emorroidi *fpl*

haggle ['hægl] *vi* mercanteggiare

Hague [heɪg] *n* **The ~** L'Aia

hail [heɪl] *n* grandine *f*; (*of criticism etc*) pioggia ▷ *vt* (*call*) chiamare; (*flag down: taxi*) fermare; (*greet*) salutare ▷ *vi* grandinare; **hailstone** *n* chicco di grandine

hair [hɛə'] *n* capelli *mpl*; (*single hair: on head*) capello; (: *on body*) pelo; **to do one's ~** pettinarsi; **hairband** ['hɛəbænd] *n* (*elastic*) fascia per i capelli; (*rigid*) cerchietto; **hairbrush** *n* spazzola per capelli; **haircut** *n* taglio di capelli; **hairdo** ['hɛəduː] *n* acconciatura, pettinatura;

hairdresser n parrucchiere(-a);
hairdresser's n parrucchiere(-a); **hair
dryer** n asciugacapelli m inv; **hair gel** n
gel m inv per capelli; **hair spray** n lacca
per capelli; **hairstyle** n pettinatura,
acconciatura; **hairy** adj irsuto(-a),
peloso(-a); (inf: frightening) spaventoso(-a)
hake [heɪk] (pl **hake** or **hakes**) n nasello
half [hɑːf] (pl **halves**) n mezzo, metà
f inv ▷ adj mezzo(-a) ▷ adv a mezzo, a
metà; **~ an hour** mezz'ora; **~ a dozen**
mezza dozzina; **~ a pound** mezza libbra;
two and a ~ due e mezzo; **a week and
a ~** una settimana e mezza; **~ (of it)** la
metà; **~ (of)** la metà di; **to cut sth in ~**
tagliare qc in due; **~ asleep** mezzo(-a)
addormentato(-a); **half board** (BRIT)
n mezza pensione; **half-brother** n
fratellastro; **half day** n mezza giornata;
half fare n tariffa a metà prezzo; **half-
hearted** adj tiepido(-a); **half-hour** n
mezz'ora; **half-price** adj, adv a metà
prezzo; **half term** (BRIT) n (Scol) vacanza
a or di metà trimestre; **half-time** n (Sport)
intervallo; **halfway** adv a metà strada
hall [hɔːl] n sala, salone m; (entrance way)
entrata
hallmark ['hɔːlmɑːk] n marchio di
garanzia; (fig) caratteristica
hallo [hə'ləu] excl = **hello**
hall of residence (BRIT) n casa dello
studente
Halloween [hæləu'iːn] n vigilia
d'Ognissanti

⬤ **HALLOWEEN**
⬤
⬤ Negli Stati Uniti e in Gran Bretagna il
⬤ 31 ottobre si festeggia **Halloween**, la
⬤ notte delle streghe e dei fantasmi. I
⬤ bambini, travestiti da fantasmi, streghe
⬤ o mostri, bussano alle porte e ricevono
⬤ dolci e piccoli doni.

hallucination [hۉluːsɪ'neɪʃən] n
allucinazione f
hallway ['hɔːlweɪ] n corridoio; (entrance)
ingresso
halo ['heɪləu] n (of saint etc) aureola
halt [hɔːlt] n fermata ▷ vt fermare ▷ vi
fermarsi
halve [hɑːv] vt (apple etc) dividere a metà;
(expense) ridurre di metà
halves [hɑːvz] npl of **half**
ham [hæm] n prosciutto
hamburger ['hæmbə:gə'] n hamburger
m inv
hamlet ['hæmlɪt] n paesetto
hammer ['hæmə'] n martello ▷ vt

martellare ▷ vi **to ~ on** or **at the door**
picchiare alla porta
hammock ['hæmək] n amaca
hamper ['hæmpə'] vt impedire ▷ n cesta
hamster ['hæmstə'] n criceto
hamstring ['hæmstrɪŋ] n (Anat) tendine
m del ginocchio
hand [hænd] n mano f, (of clock) lancetta;
(handwriting) scrittura; (at cards) mano;
(: game) partita; (worker) operaio(-a) ▷ vt
dare, passare; **to give sb a ~** dare una
mano a qn; **at ~** a portata di mano; **in
~** a disposizione; (work) in corso; **on ~**
(person) disponibile; (services) pronto(-a)
a intervenire; **to ~** (information etc) a
portata di mano; **on the one ~ ...,** **on
the other ~** da un lato ..., dall'altro;
hand down vt passare giù; (tradition,
heirloom) tramandare; (us: sentence, verdict)
emettere; **hand in** vt consegnare; **hand
out** vt distribuire; **hand over** vt passare;
cedere; **handbag** n borsetta; **hand
baggage** n bagaglio a mano; **handbook**
n manuale m; **handbrake** n freno a mano;
handcuffs npl manette fpl; **handful** n
manciata, pugno
handicap ['hændɪkæp] n handicap m inv
▷ vt handicappare; **to be physically ~ped**
essere handicappato(-a); **to be mentally
~ped** essere un(a) handicappato(-a)
mentale
handkerchief ['hæŋkətʃɪf] n fazzoletto
handle ['hændl] n (of door etc) maniglia; (of
cup etc) ansa; (of knife etc) impugnatura; (of
saucepan) manico; (for winding) manovella
▷ vt toccare, maneggiare; (deal with)
occuparsi di; (treat: people) trattare; **"~
with care"** "fragile"; **to fly off the ~** (fig)
perdere le staffe, uscire dai gangheri;
handlebar(s) n(pl) manubrio
hand: hand luggage n bagagli mpl a
mano; **handmade** adj fatto(-a) a mano;
handout n (money, food) elemosina;
(leaflet) volantino; (at lecture) prospetto
handsome ['hænsəm] adj bello(-a); (profit,
fortune) considerevole
handwriting ['hændraɪtɪŋ] n scrittura
handy ['hændɪ] adj (person) bravo(-a);
(close at hand) a portata di mano;
(convenient) comodo(-a)
hang [hæŋ] (pt, pp **hung**) vt appendere;
(criminal: pt, pp **hanged**) impiccare ▷ vi
(painting) essere appeso(-a); (hair)
scendere; (drapery) cadere; **to get the
~ of sth** (inf) capire come qc funziona;
hang about or **around** vi bighellonare,
ciondolare; **hang down** vi ricadere;
hang on vi (wait) aspettare; **hang out**
vt (washing) stendere (fuori); (inf: live)

stare ▷ vi penzolare, pendere; **hang round** vi = **hang around**; **hang up** vi (Tel) riattaccare ▷ vt appendere

hanger ['hæŋəʳ] n gruccia

hang-gliding ['-glaɪdɪŋ] n volo col deltaplano

hangover ['hæŋəuvəʳ] n (after drinking) postumi mpl di sbornia

hankie ['hæŋkɪ] n abbr = **handkerchief**

happen ['hæpən] vi accadere, succedere; (chance): **to ~ to do sth** fare qc per caso; **what ~ed?** cos'è successo?; **as it ~s** guarda caso

happily ['hæpɪlɪ] adv felicemente; fortunatamente

happiness ['hæpɪnɪs] n felicità, contentezza

happy ['hæpɪ] adj felice, contento(-a); **~ with** (arrangements etc) soddisfatto(-a) di; **to be ~ to do** (willing) fare volentieri; **~ birthday!** buon compleanno!

harass ['hærəs] vt molestare; **harassment** n molestia

harbour ['hɑːbəʳ] (us **harbor**) n porto ▷ vt (hope, fear) nutrire; (criminal) dare rifugio a

hard [hɑːd] adj duro(-a) ▷ adv (work) sodo; (think, try) bene; **to look ~ at** guardare fissamente; esaminare attentamente; **no ~ feelings!** senza rancore!; **to be ~ of hearing** essere duro(-a) d'orecchio; **to be ~ done by** essere trattato(-a) ingiustamente; **hardback** n libro rilegato; **hardboard** n legno precompresso; **hard disk** n (Comput) disco rigido; **harden** vt, vi indurire

hardly ['hɑːdlɪ] adv (scarcely) appena; **it's ~ the case** non è proprio il caso; **~ anyone/ anywhere** quasi nessuno/da nessuna parte; **~ ever** quasi mai

hard: **hardship** ['hɑːdʃɪp] n avversità f inv; privazioni fpl; **hard shoulder** (BRIT) n (Aut) corsia d'emergenza; **hard-up** (inf) adj al verde; **hardware** ['hɑːdwɛəʳ] n ferramenta fpl; (Comput) hardware m; (Mil) armamenti mpl; **hardware shop** (us **hardware store**) n (negozio di) ferramenta fpl; **hard-working** [-'wəːkɪŋ] adj lavoratore(-trice)

hardy ['hɑːdɪ] adj robusto(-a); (plant) resistente al gelo

hare [hɛəʳ] n lepre f

harm [hɑːm] n male m; (wrong) danno ▷ vt (person) fare male a; (thing) danneggiare; **out of ~'s way** al sicuro; **harmful** adj dannoso(-a); **harmless** adj innocuo(-a), inoffensivo(-a)

harmony ['hɑːmənɪ] n armonia

harness ['hɑːnɪs] n (for horse) bardatura, finimenti mpl; (for child) briglie fpl; (safety harness) imbracatura ▷ vt (horse) bardare; (resources) sfruttare

harp [hɑːp] n arpa ▷ vi **to ~ on about** insistere tediosamente su

harsh [hɑːʃ] adj (life, winter) duro(-a); (judge, criticism) severo(-a); (sound) rauco(-a); (light) violento(-a)

harvest ['hɑːvɪst] n raccolto; (of grapes) vendemmia ▷ vt fare il raccolto di, raccogliere; vendemmiare

has [hæz] vb see **have**

hasn't ['hæznt] = **has not**

hassle ['hæsl] (inf) n sacco di problemi

haste [heɪst] n fretta; precipitazione f; **hasten** ['heɪsn] vt affrettare ▷ vi **to hasten (to)** affrettarsi (a); **hastily** adv in fretta; precipitosamente; **hasty** adj affrettato(-a), precipitoso(-a)

hat [hæt] n cappello

hatch [hætʃ] n (Naut: also: **~way**) boccaporto; (also: **service ~**) portello di servizio ▷ vi (bird) uscire dal guscio; (egg) schiudersi

hatchback ['hætʃbæk] n (Aut) tre (or cinque) porte f inv

hate [heɪt] vt odiare, detestare ▷ n odio; **hatred** ['heɪtrɪd] n odio

haul [hɔːl] vt trascinare, tirare ▷ n (of fish) pescata; (of stolen goods etc) bottino

haunt [hɔːnt] vt (fear) pervadere; (person) frequentare ▷ n rifugio; **this house is ~ed** questa casa è abitata da un fantasma; **haunted** adj (castle etc) abitato(-a) dai fantasmi or dagli spiriti; (look) ossessionato(-a), tormentato(-a)

○ **KEYWORD**

have [hæv] (pt, pp **had**) aux vb **1** (gen) avere; essere; **to have arrived/gone** essere arrivato(-a)/andato(-a); **to have eaten/slept** avere mangiato/dormito; **he has been kind/promoted** è stato gentile/promosso; **having finished** or **when he had finished, he left** dopo aver finito, se n'è andato

2 (in tag questions): **you've done it, haven't you?** l'ha fatto, (non è) vero?; **he hasn't done it, has he?** non l'ha fatto, vero?

3 (in short answers and questions): **you've made a mistake — no I haven't/so I have** ha fatto un errore — ma no, niente affatto/sì, è vero; **we haven't paid — yes we have!** non abbiamo pagato — ma sì che abbiamo pagato!; **I've been there before, have you?** ci sono già stato, e lei?
▷ modal aux vb (be obliged): **to have (got) to do sth** dover fare qc; **I haven't got**

or **I don't have to wear glasses** non ho
bisogno di portare gli occhiali
▷ vt **1** (*possess, obtain*) avere; **he has (got)
blue eyes/dark hair** ha gli occhi azzurri/i
capelli scuri; **do you have** or **have you got
a car/phone?** ha la macchina/il telefono?;
may I have your address? potrebbe
darmi il suo indirizzo?; **you can have it for
£5** te lo lascio per 5 sterline
2 (+ *noun: take, hold etc*): **to have
breakfast/a swim/a bath** fare
colazione/una nuotata/un bagno; **to
have lunch** pranzare; **to have dinner**
cenare; **to have a drink** bere qualcosa; **to
have a cigarette** fumare una sigaretta
3: **to have sth done** far fare qc; **to have
one's hair cut** farsi tagliare i capelli; **to
have sb do sth** far fare qc a qn
4 (*experience, suffer*) avere; **to have a
cold/flu** avere il raffreddore/l'influenza;
she had her bag stolen le hanno rubato
la borsa
5 (*inf: dupe*): **you've been had!** ci sei
cascato!
　have out vt **to have it out with sb** (*settle
a problem etc*) mettere le cose in chiaro
con qn

haven ['heɪvn] n porto; (*fig*) rifugio
haven't ['hævnt] = **have not**
havoc ['hævək] n caos m
Hawaii [hə'waɪ:] n le Hawaii
hawk [hɔ:k] n falco
hawthorn ['hɔ:θɔ:n] n biancospino
hay [heɪ] n fieno; **hay fever** n febbre f da
fieno; **haystack** n pagliaio
hazard ['hæzəd] n azzardo, ventura;
pericolo, rischio ▷ vt (*guess etc*) azzardare;
hazardous adj pericoloso(-a); **hazard
warning lights** npl (*Aut*) luci fpl di
emergenza
haze [heɪz] n foschia
hazel ['heɪzl] n (*tree*) nocciolo ▷ adj (*eyes*)
(color) nocciola inv; **hazelnut** ['heɪzlnʌt]
n nocciola
hazy ['heɪzɪ] adj fosco(-a); (*idea*) vago(-a)
he [hi:] pron lui, egli; **it is he who ...** è lui
che ...
head [hɛd] n testa; (*leader*) capo; (*of
school*) preside m/f ▷ vt (*list*) essere in
testa a; (*group*) essere a capo di; **~s or
tails** testa (o croce), pari (o dispari); **~
first** a capofitto, di testa; **~ over heels
in love** pazzamente innamorato(-a);
to ~ the ball colpire una palla di testa;
head for vt fus dirigersi verso; **head off**
vt (*threat, danger*) sventare; **headache**
n mal m di testa; **heading** n titolo;
intestazione f; **headlamp** (*BRIT*) n

= **headlight**; **headlight** n fanale m;
headline n titolo; **head office** n sede
f (centrale); **headphones** npl cuffia;
headquarters npl ufficio centrale; (*Mil*)
quartiere m generale; **headroom** n (*in
car*) altezza dell'abitacolo; (*under bridge*)
altezza limite; **headscarf** n foulard m inv;
headset n = **headphones**; **headteacher**
n (*of primary school*) direttore(-trice); (*of
secondary school*) preside; **head waiter** n
capocameriere m
heal [hi:l] vt, vi guarire
health [hɛlθ] n salute f; **health care** n
assistenza sanitaria; **health centre** (*BRIT*)
n poliambulatorio; **health food** n cibo
macrobiotico; **Health Service** (*BRIT*) n
the Health Service ≈ il Servizio Sanitario
Statale; **healthy** adj (*person*) sano(-a), in
buona salute; (*climate*) salubre; (*appetite,
economy etc*) sano(-a)
heap [hi:p] n mucchio ▷ vt (*stones, sand*):
to ~ (up) ammucchiare; (*plate, sink*): **to
~ sth with** riempire qc di; **~s of** (*inf*) un
mucchio di
hear [hɪər] (*pt, pp* **heard**) vt sentire; (*news*)
ascoltare ▷ vi sentire; **to ~ about** avere
notizie di; sentire parlare di; **to ~ from sb**
ricevere notizie da qn
hearing ['hɪərɪŋ] n (*sense*) udito; (*of
witnesses*) audizione f; (*of a case*) udienza;
hearing aid n apparecchio acustico
hearse [hə:s] n carro funebre
heart [hɑ:t] n cuore m; **~s** npl (*Cards*) cuori
mpl; **to lose ~** scoraggiarsi; **to take ~** farsi
coraggio; **at ~** in fondo; **by ~** (*learn, know*)
a memoria; **heart attack** n attacco di
cuore; **heartbeat** n battito del cuore;
heartbroken adj **to be heartbroken**
avere il cuore spezzato; **heartburn** n
bruciore m di stomaco; **heart disease** n
malattia di cuore
hearth [hɑ:θ] n focolare m
heartless ['hɑ:tlɪs] adj senza cuore
hearty ['hɑ:tɪ] adj caloroso(-a);
robusto(-a), sano(-a); vigoroso(-a)
heat [hi:t] n calore m; (*fig*) ardore m;
fuoco; (*Sport: also:* **qualifying ~**) prova
eliminatoria ▷ vt scaldare; **heat up** vi
(*liquids*) scaldarsi; (*room*) riscaldarsi ▷ vt
riscaldare; **heated** adj riscaldato(-a);
(*argument*) acceso(-a); **heater** n radiatore
m; (*stove*) stufa
heather ['hɛðər] n erica
heating ['hi:tɪŋ] n riscaldamento
heatwave ['hi:tweɪv] n ondata di caldo
heaven ['hɛvn] n paradiso, cielo;
heavenly adj divino(-a), celeste
heavily ['hɛvɪlɪ] adv pesantemente; (*drink,
smoke*) molto

heavy ['hɛvɪ] *adj* pesante; (*sea*) grosso(-a); (*rain, blow*) forte; (*weather*) afoso(-a); (*drinker, smoker*) gran (*before noun*); **it's too ~** è troppo pesante

Hebrew ['hiːbruː] *adj* ebreo(-a) ▷ *n* (*Ling*) ebraico

hectare ['hɛktaːʳ] *n* (*BRIT*) ettaro

hectic ['hɛktɪk] *adj* movimentato(-a)

he'd [hiːd] = **he would**; **he had**

hedge [hɛdʒ] *n* siepe *f* ▷ *vi* essere elusivo(-a); **to ~ one's bets** (*fig*) coprirsi dai rischi

hedgehog ['hɛdʒhɔg] *n* riccio

heed [hiːd] *vt* (*also:* **take ~ of**) badare a, far conto di

heel [hiːl] *n* (*Anat*) calcagno; (*of shoe*) tacco ▷ *vt* (*shoe*) rifare i tacchi a

hefty ['hɛftɪ] *adj* (*person*) robusto(-a); (*parcel*) pesante; (*profit*) grosso(-a)

height [haɪt] *n* altezza; (*high ground*) altura; (*fig: of glory*) apice *m*; (: *of stupidity*) colmo; **heighten** *vt* (*fig*) accrescere

heir [ɛəʳ] *n* erede *m*; **heiress** *n* erede *f*

held [hɛld] *pt, pp of* **hold**

helicopter ['hɛlɪkɔptəʳ] *n* elicottero

hell [hɛl] *n* inferno; **~!** (*inf*) porca miseria!, accidenti!

he'll [hiːl] = **he will**; **he shall**

hello [həˈləu] *excl* buon giorno!; ciao! (*to sb one addresses as "tu"*); (*surprise*) ma guarda!

helmet ['hɛlmɪt] *n* casco

help [hɛlp] *n* aiuto; (*charwoman*) donna di servizio ▷ *vt* aiutare; **~!** aiuto!; **can you ~ me?** può aiutarmi?; **~ yourself (to bread)** si serva (del pane); **he can't ~ it** non ci può far niente; **help out** *vi* aiutare ▷ *vt* **to ~ sb out** aiutare qn; **helper** *n* aiutante *m/f*, assistente *m/f*; **helpful** *adj* di grande aiuto; (*useful*) utile; **helping** *n* porzione *f*; **helpless** *adj* impotente; debole; **helpline** *n* ≈ telefono amico; (*Comm*) servizio *m* informazioni *inv* (*a pagamento*)

hem [hɛm] *n* orlo ▷ *vt* fare l'orlo a

hemisphere ['hɛmɪsfɪəʳ] *n* emisfero

hemorrhage ['hɛmərɪdʒ] (*US*) *n* = **haemorrhage**

hemorrhoids ['hɛmərɔɪdz] (*US*) *npl* = **haemorrhoids**

hen [hɛn] *n* gallina; (*female bird*) femmina

hence [hɛns] *adv* (*therefore*) dunque; **2 years ~** di qui a 2 anni

hen night *n* (*inf*) addio al nubilato

hepatitis [hɛpəˈtaɪtɪs] *n* epatite *f*

her [həːʳ] *pron* (*direct*) la, l' + *vowel*; (*indirect*) le; (*stressed, after prep*) lei ▷ *adj* il (la) suo(-a), i (le) suoi (sue); *see also* **me**; **my**

herb [həːb] *n* erba; **herbal** *adj* di erbe; **herbal tea** *n* tisana

herd [həːd] *n* mandria

here [hɪəʳ] *adv* qui, qua ▷ *excl* ehi!; **~!** (*at roll call*) presente!; **~ is/are** ecco; **~ he/she is** eccolo/eccola

hereditary [hɪˈrɛdɪtrɪ] *adj* ereditario(-a)

heritage ['hɛrɪtɪdʒ] *n* eredità; (*fig*) retaggio

hernia ['həːnɪə] *n* ernia

hero ['hɪərəu] (*pl* **heroes**) *n* eroe *m*; **heroic** [hɪˈrəuɪk] *adj* eroico(-a)

heroin ['hɛrəuɪn] *n* eroina

heroine ['hɛrəuɪn] *n* eroina

heron ['hɛrən] *n* airone *m*

herring ['hɛrɪŋ] *n* aringa

hers [həːz] *pron* il (la) suo(-a), i (le) suoi (sue); *see also* **mine¹**

herself [həːˈsɛlf] *pron* (*reflexive*) si; (*emphatic*) lei stessa; (*after prep*) se stessa, sé; *see also* **oneself**

he's [hiːz] = **he is**; **he has**

hesitant ['hɛzɪtənt] *adj* esitante, indeciso(-a)

hesitate ['hɛzɪteɪt] *vi* **to ~ (about/to do)** esitare (su/a fare); **hesitation** [-'teɪʃən] *n* esitazione *f*

heterosexual ['hɛtərəu'sɛksjuəl] *adj, n* eterosessuale *m/f*

hexagon ['hɛksəgən] *n* esagono

hey [heɪ] *excl* ehi!

heyday ['heɪdeɪ] *n* **the ~ of** i bei giorni di, l'età d'oro di

HGV *n abbr* = **heavy goods vehicle**

hi [haɪ] *excl* ciao!

hibernate ['haɪbəneɪt] *vi* ibernare

hiccough ['hɪkʌp] *vi* singhiozzare

hiccup ['hɪkʌp] = **hiccough**

hid [hɪd] *pt of* **hide**

hidden ['hɪdn] *pp of* **hide**

hide [haɪd] (*pt* **hid**, *pp* **hidden**) *n* (*skin*) pelle *f* ▷ *vt* **to ~ sth (from sb)** nascondere qc (a qn) ▷ *vi* **to ~ (from sb)** nascondersi (da qn)

hideous ['hɪdɪəs] *adj* laido(-a); orribile

hiding ['haɪdɪŋ] *n* (*beating*) bastonata; **to be in ~** (*concealed*) tenersi nascosto(-a)

hi-fi ['haɪfaɪ] *n* stereo ▷ *adj* ad alta fedeltà, hi-fi *inv*

high [haɪ] *adj* alto(-a); (*speed, respect, number*) grande; (*wind*) forte; (*voice*) acuto(-a) ▷ *adv* alto, in alto; **20m ~** alto(-a) 20m; **highchair** *n* seggiolone *m*; **high-class** *adj* (*neighbourhood*) elegante; (*hotel*) di prim'ordine; (*person*) di gran classe; (*food*) raffinato(-a); **higher education** *n* studi *mpl* superiori; **high heels** *npl* (*heels*) tacchi *mpl* alti; (*shoes*) scarpe *fpl* con i tacchi alti; **high jump** *n* (*Sport*) salto in alto; **highlands** *npl* zona montuosa; **the Highlands** le Highlands scozzesi; **highlight** *n* (*fig: of event*) momento culminante; (*in hair*) colpo di sole ▷ *vt* mettere in evidenza; **highlights** *npl* (*in hair*) colpi *mpl* di sole; **highlighter** *n* (*pen*) evidenziatore *m*; **highly** *adv* molto; **to speak highly of** parlare molto bene di; **highness** *n* **Her Highness** Sua Altezza; **high-rise** *n* (*also:* **high-rise block, high-rise building**) palazzone *m*; **high school** *n* scuola secondaria; (*US*) istituto superiore d'istruzione; **high season** (*BRIT*) *n* alta stagione; **high street** (*BRIT*) *n* strada principale; **high-tech** (*inf*) *adj* high-tech *inv*; **highway** ['haɪweɪ] *n* strada maestra; **Highway Code** (*BRIT*) *n* codice *m* della strada

hijack ['haɪdʒæk] *vt* dirottare; **hijacker** *n* dirottatore(-trice)

hike [haɪk] *vi* fare un'escursione a piedi ▷ *n* escursione *f* a piedi; **hiker** *n* escursionista *m/f*; **hiking** *n* escursioni *fpl* a piedi

hilarious [hɪ'lɛərɪəs] *adj* (*behaviour, event*) spassosissimo(-a)

hill [hɪl] *n* collina, colle *m*; (*fairly high*) montagna; (*on road*) salita; **hillside** *n* fianco della collina; **hill walking** *n* escursioni *fpl* in collina; **hilly** *adj* collinoso(-a); montagnoso(-a)

him [hɪm] *pron* (*direct*) lo, l' + *vowel*; (*indirect*) gli; (*stressed, after prep*) lui; *see also* **me**; **himself** *pron* (*reflexive*) si; (*emphatic*) lui stesso; (*after prep*) se stesso, sé; *see also* **oneself**

hind [haɪnd] *adj* posteriore ▷ *n* cerva

hinder ['hɪndər] *vt* ostacolare

hindsight ['haɪndsaɪt] *n* **with ~** con il senno di poi

Hindu ['hɪnduː] *n* indù *m/f inv*; **Hinduism** *n* (*Rel*) induismo

hinge [hɪndʒ] *n* cardine *m* ▷ *vi* (*fig*): **to ~ on** dipendere da

hint [hɪnt] *n* (*suggestion*) allusione *f*; (*advice*) consiglio; (*sign*) accenno ▷ *vt* **to ~ that** lasciar capire che ▷ *vi* **to ~ at** alludere a

hip [hɪp] *n* anca, fianco

hippie ['hɪpɪ] *n* hippy *m/f inv*

hippo ['hɪpəu] (*pl* **hippos**) *n* ippopotamo

hippopotamus [hɪpə'pɔtəməs] (*pl* **hippopotamuses** *or* **hippopotami**) *n* ippopotamo

hippy ['hɪpɪ] *n* = **hippie**

hire ['haɪər] *vt* (*BRIT: car, equipment*) noleggiare; (*worker*) assumere, dare lavoro a ▷ *n* nolo, noleggio; **for ~** da nolo; (*taxi*) libero(-a); **I'd like to ~ a car** vorrei noleggiare una macchina; **hire(d) car** (*BRIT*) *n* macchina a nolo; **hire purchase** (*BRIT*) *n* acquisto (*or* vendita) rateale

his [hɪz] *adj, pron* il (la) suo (sua), i (le) suoi (sue); *see also* **my**; **mine¹**

Hispanic [hɪs'pænɪk] *adj* ispanico(-a)

hiss [hɪs] *vi* fischiare; (*cat, snake*) sibilare

historian [hɪ'stɔːrɪən] *n* storico(-a)

historic(al) [hɪ'stɔrɪk(l)] *adj* storico(-a)

history ['hɪstərɪ] *n* storia

hit [hɪt] (*pt, pp* **hit**) *vt* colpire, picchiare; (*knock against*) battere; (*reach: target*) raggiungere; (*collide with: car*) urtare contro; (*fig: affect*) colpire; (*find: problem etc*) incontrare ▷ *n* colpo; (*success, song*) successo; **to ~ it off with sb** andare molto d'accordo con qn; **hit back** *vi* **to ~ back at sb** restituire il colpo a qn

hitch [hɪtʃ] *vt* (*fasten*) attaccare; (*also:* **~ up**) tirare su ▷ *n* (*difficulty*) intoppo, difficoltà *f inv*; **to ~ a lift** fare l'autostop; **hitch-hike** *vi* fare l'autostop; **hitch-hiker** *n* autostoppista *m/f*; **hitch-hiking** *n* autostop *m*

hi-tech ['haɪtɛk] *adj* high-tech *inv*

hitman ['hɪtmæn] (*irreg*) *n* (*inf*) sicario

HIV *abbr* **~-negative/-positive** *adj* sieronegativo(-a)/sieropositivo(-a)

hive [haɪv] *n* alveare *m*

hoard [hɔːd] *n* (*of food*) provviste *fpl*; (*of money*) gruzzolo ▷ *vt* ammassare

hoarse [hɔːs] *adj* rauco(-a)

hoax [həuks] *n* scherzo; falso allarme

hob [hɔb] *n* piastra (con fornelli)

hobble ['hɔbl] *vi* zoppicare

hobby ['hɔbɪ] *n* hobby *m inv*, passatempo

hobo ['həubəu] (*US*) *n* vagabondo

hockey ['hɔkɪ] *n* hockey *m*; **hockey stick** *n* bastone *m* da hockey

hog [hɔg] *n* maiale *m* ▷ *vt* (*fig*) arraffare; **to go the whole ~** farlo fino in fondo

Hogmanay [hɔgmə'neɪ] *n* (*Scottish*) ≈ San Silvestro

hoist [hɔɪst] *n* paranco ▷ *vt* issare

hold [həuld] (*pt, pp* **held**) *vt* tenere; (*contain*) contenere; (*keep back*) trattenere; (*believe*) mantenere; considerare; (*possess*) avere, possedere; detenere ▷ *vi* (*withstand pressure*) tenere; (*be valid*) essere valido(-a) ▷ *n* presa; (*control*): **to have a ~ over** avere controllo su; (*Naut*) stiva; **~ the line!** (*Tel*) resti in linea!; **to ~ one's own** (*fig*) difendersi bene; **to catch** *or* **get (a) ~ of** afferrare; **hold back** *vt* trattenere; (*secret*) tenere celato(-a); **hold on** *vi* tener fermo; (*wait*) aspettare; **~ on!** (*Tel*) resti in linea!; **hold out** *vt* offrire ▷ *vi* (*resist*) resistere; **hold up** *vt* (*raise*) alzare; (*support*) sostenere; (*delay*) ritardare; (*rob*) assaltare; **holdall** (*BRIT*) *n* borsone *m*; **holder** *n* (*container*) contenitore *m*; (*of ticket, title*) possessore/posseditrice; (*of office etc*) incaricato/a; (*of record*) detentore(-trice)

hole [həul] *n* buco, buca

holiday ['hɔlədɪ] n vacanza; (day off)
giorno di vacanza; (public) giorno festivo;
on ~ in vacanza; **I'm on ~ here** sono qui
in vacanza; **holiday camp** (BRIT) n (also:
holiday centre) ≈ villaggio (di vacanze);
holiday job n (BRIT) ≈ lavoro estivo;
holiday-maker (BRIT) n villeggiante m/f;
holiday resort n luogo di villeggiatura
Holland ['hɔlənd] n Olanda
hollow ['hɔləu] adj cavo(-a); (container,
claim) vuoto(-a); (laugh, sound) cupo(-a) ▷ n
cavità f inv; (in land) valletta, depressione f
▷ vt **to ~ out** scavare
holly ['hɔlɪ] n agrifoglio
Hollywood ['hɔlɪwud] n Hollywood f
holocaust ['hɔləkɔːst] n olocausto
holy ['həulɪ] adj santo(-a); (bread, ground)
benedetto(-a), consacrato(-a)
home [həum] n casa; (country) patria;
(institution) casa, ricovero ▷ cpd familiare;
(cooking etc) casalingo(-a); (Econ, Pol)
nazionale, interno(-a); (Sport) di casa ▷ adv
a casa; in patria; (right in: nail etc) fino in
fondo; **at ~** a casa; (in situation) a proprio
agio; **to go** or **come ~** tornare a casa (or
in patria); **make yourself at ~** si metta
a suo agio; **home address** n indirizzo
di casa; **homeland** n patria; **homeless**
adj senza tetto; spatriato(-a); **homely**
adj semplice, alla buona; accogliente;
home-made adj casalingo(-a); **home
match** n partita in casa; **Home Office**
(BRIT) n ministero degli Interni; **home
owner** n proprietario(-a) di casa; **home
page** n (Comput) home page f inv; **Home
Secretary** (BRIT) n ministro degli Interni;
homesick adj **to be homesick** avere la
nostalgia; **home town** n città f inv natale;
homework n compiti mpl (per casa)
homicide ['hɔmɪsaɪd] (US) n omicidio
homoeopathic [həumɪə'pæθɪk] (US
homeopathic) adj omeopatico(-a)
homoeopathy [həumɪ'ɔpəθɪ] (US
homeopathy) n omeopatia
homosexual [hɔməu'sɛksjuəl] adj, n
omosessuale m/f
honest ['ɔnɪst] adj onesto(-a);
sincero(-a); **honestly** adv onestamente,
sinceramente; **honesty** n onestà
honey ['hʌnɪ] n miele m; **honeymoon**
n luna di miele, viaggio di nozze; **we're
on honeymoon** siamo in luna di miele;
honeysuckle n (Bot) caprifoglio
Hong Kong ['hɔŋ'kɔŋ] n Hong Kong f
honorary ['ɔnərərɪ] adj onorario(-a); (duty,
title) onorifico(-a)
honour ['ɔnəʳ] (US **honor**) vt onorare ▷ n
onore m; **honourable** (US **honorable**) adj
onorevole; **honours degree** n (Scol) laurea

specializzata
hood [hud] n cappuccio; (on cooker) cappa;
(BRIT Aut) capote f; (US Aut) cofano
hoof [huːf] (pl **hooves**) n zoccolo
hook [huk] n gancio; (for fishing) amo ▷ vt
uncinare; (dress) agganciare
hooligan ['huːlɪgən] n giovinastro,
teppista m
hoop [huːp] n cerchio
hooray [huː'reɪ] excl = **hurray**
hoot [huːt] vi (Aut) suonare il clacson;
(siren) ululare; (owl) gufare
Hoover® ['huːvəʳ] (BRIT) n aspirapolvere m
inv ▷ vt **hoover** pulire con l'aspirapolvere
hooves [huːvz] npl of **hoof**
hop [hɔp] vi saltellare, saltare; (on one foot)
saltare su una gamba
hope [həup] vt **to ~ that/to do** sperare
che/di fare ▷ vi sperare ▷ n speranza;
I ~ so/not spero di sì/no; **hopeful** adj
(person) pieno(-a) di speranza; (situation)
promettente; **hopefully** adv con
speranza; **hopefully he will recover**
speriamo che si riprenda; **hopeless** adj
senza speranza, disperato(-a); (useless)
inutile
hops [hɔps] npl luppoli mpl
horizon [hə'raɪzn] n orizzonte m;
horizontal [hɔrɪ'zɔntl] adj orizzontale
hormone ['hɔːməun] n ormone m
horn [hɔːn] n (Zool, Mus) corno; (Aut)
clacson m inv
horoscope ['hɔrəskəup] n oroscopo
horrendous [hə'rɛndəs] adj orrendo(-a)
horrible ['hɔrɪbl] adj orribile, tremendo(-a)
horrid ['hɔrɪd] adj orrido(-a); (person)
odioso(-a)
horrific [hɔ'rɪfɪk] adj (accident)
spaventoso(-a); (film) orripilante
horrifying ['hɔrɪfaɪɪŋ] adj terrificante
horror ['hɔrəʳ] n orrore m; **horror film** n
film m inv dell'orrore
hors d'œuvre [ɔː'dəːvrə] n antipasto
horse [hɔːs] n cavallo; **horseback: on
horseback** adj, adv a cavallo; **horse
chestnut** n ippocastano; **horsepower** n
cavallo (vapore); **horse-racing** n ippica;
horseradish n rafano; **horse riding** n
(BRIT) equitazione f
hose [həuz] n (also: **~pipe**) tubo; (also:
garden ~) tubo per annaffiare
hospital ['hɔspɪtl] n ospedale m; **where's
the nearest ~?** dov'è l'ospedale più vicino?
hospitality [hɔspɪ'tælɪtɪ] n ospitalità
host [həust] n ospite m; (Rel) ostia; (large
number): **a ~ of** una schiera di
hostage ['hɔstɪdʒ] n ostaggio(-a)
hostel ['hɔstl] n ostello; (also: **youth ~**)
ostello della gioventù

hostess ['həustɪs] n ospite f; (BRIT: air hostess) hostess f inv

hostile ['hɔstaɪl] adj ostile

hostility [hɔ'stɪlɪtɪ] n ostilità f inv

hot [hɔt] adj caldo(-a); (as opposed to only warm) molto caldo(-a); (spicy) piccante; (fig) accanito(-a); ardente; violento(-a), focoso(-a); **to be ~** (person) aver caldo; (object) essere caldo(-a); (weather) far caldo; **hot dog** n hot dog m inv

hotel [həu'tɛl] n albergo

hot-water bottle [hɔt'wɔːtə-] n borsa dell'acqua calda

hound [haund] vt perseguitare ▷ n segugio

hour ['auər] n ora; **hourly** adj all'ora

house [n haus, pl 'hauzɪz] [vb hauz] n (also: firm) casa; (Pol) camera; (Theatre) sala; pubblico; spettacolo; (dynasty) casata ▷ vt (person) ospitare, alloggiare; **on the ~** (fig) offerto(-a) dalla casa; **household** n famiglia; casa; **householder** n padrone(-a) di casa; (head of house) capofamiglia m/f; **housekeeper** n governante f; **housekeeping** n (work) governo della casa; (money) soldi mpl per le spese di casa; **housewife** (irreg) n massaia, casalinga; **house wine** n vino della casa; **housework** n faccende fpl domestiche

housing ['hauzɪŋ] n alloggio; **housing development** (BRIT), **housing estate** n zona residenziale con case popolari e/o private

hover ['hɔvər] vi (bird) librarsi; **hovercraft** n hovercraft m inv

how [hau] adv come; **~ are you?** come sta?; **~ do you do?** piacere!; **~ far is it to the river?** quanto è lontano il fiume?; **~ long have you been here?** da quando è qui?; **~ lovely!/awful!** che bello!/orrore!; **~ many?** quanti(-e)?; **~ much?** quanto(-a)?; **~ much milk?** quanto latte?; **~ many people?** quante persone?; **~ old are you?** quanti anni ha?

however [hau'ɛvər] adv in qualsiasi modo or maniera che; (+ adjective) per quanto + sub; (in questions) come ▷ conj comunque, però

howl [haul] vi ululare; (baby, person) urlare

H.P. abbr = **hire purchase; horsepower**

h.p. n abbr = **H.P**

HQ n, abbr = **headquarters**

hr(s) abbr (= hour(s)) h

HTML abbr (= hypertext markup language) HTML m inv

hubcap ['hʌbkæp] n coprimozzo

huddle ['hʌdl] vi **to ~ together** rannicchiarsi l'uno contro l'altro

huff [hʌf] n **in a ~** stizzito(-a)

hug [hʌg] vt abbracciare; (shore, kerb) stringere

huge [hjuːdʒ] adj enorme, immenso(-a)

hull [hʌl] n (of ship) scafo

hum [hʌm] vt (tune) canticchiare ▷ vi canticchiare; (insect, plane, tool) ronzare

human ['hjuːmən] (irreg) adj umano(-a) ▷ n essere m umano

humane [hjuː'meɪn] adj umanitario(-a)

humanitarian [hjuːmænɪ'tɛərɪən] adj umanitario(-a)

humanity [hjuː'mænɪtɪ] n umanità

human rights npl diritti mpl dell'uomo

humble ['hʌmbl] adj umile, modesto(-a) ▷ vt umiliare

humid ['hjuːmɪd] adj umido(-a); **humidity** [hjuː'mɪdɪtɪ] n umidità

humiliate [hjuː'mɪlɪeɪt] vt umiliare; **humiliating** adj umiliante; **humiliation** [-'eɪʃən] n umiliazione f

hummus ['huməs] n purè di ceci

humorous ['hjuːmərəs] adj umoristico(-a); (person) buffo(-a)

humour ['hjuːmər] (US **humor**) n umore m ▷ vt accontentare

hump [hʌmp] n gobba

hunch [hʌntʃ] n (premonition) intuizione f

hundred ['hʌndrəd] num cento; **~s of** centinaia fpl di; **hundredth** [-ɪdθ] num centesimo(-a)

hung [hʌŋ] pt, pp of **hang**

Hungarian [hʌŋ'gɛərɪən] adj ungherese ▷ n ungherese m/f; (Ling) ungherese m

Hungary ['hʌŋgərɪ] n Ungheria

hunger ['hʌŋgər] n fame f ▷ vi **to ~ for** desiderare ardentemente

hungry ['hʌŋgrɪ] adj affamato(-a); **to be ~** aver fame

hunt [hʌnt] vt (seek) cercare; (Sport) cacciare ▷ vi **to ~ (for)** andare a caccia (di) ▷ n caccia; **hunter** n cacciatore m; **hunting** n caccia

hurdle ['həːdl] n (Sport, fig) ostacolo

hurl [həːl] vt lanciare con violenza

hurrah [hu'rɑː] excl = **hurray**

hurray [hu'reɪ] excl urra!, evviva!

hurricane ['hʌrɪkən] n uragano

hurry ['hʌrɪ] n fretta ▷ vi (also: **~ up**) affrettarsi ▷ vt (also: **~ up**: person) affrettare; (work) far in fretta; **to be in a ~** aver fretta; **hurry up** vi sbrigarsi

hurt [həːt] (pt, pp **hurt**) vt (cause pain to) far male a; (injure, fig) ferire ▷ vi far male

husband ['hʌzbənd] n marito

hush [hʌʃ] n silenzio, calma ▷ vt zittire

husky ['hʌskɪ] adj roco(-a) ▷ n cane m eschimese

hut [hʌt] n rifugio; (shed) ripostiglio

hyacinth ['haɪəsɪnθ] n giacinto

h

hydrangea [haɪ'dreɪnʒə] *n* ortensia
hydrofoil ['haɪdrəufɔɪl] *n* aliscafo
hydrogen ['haɪdrədʒən] *n* idrogeno
hygiene ['haɪdʒiːn] *n* igiene *f*; **hygienic**
  [haɪ'dʒiːnɪk] *adj* igienico(-a)
hymn [hɪm] *n* inno; cantica
hype [haɪp] (*inf*) *n* campagna pubblicitaria
hyphen ['haɪfn] *n* trattino
hypnotize ['hɪpnətaɪz] *vt* ipnotizzare
hypocrite ['hɪpəkrɪt] *n* ipocrita *m/f*
hypocritical [hɪpə'krɪtɪkl] *adj* ipocrita
hypothesis [haɪ'pɔθɪsɪs] (*pl* **hypotheses**)
  n ipotesi *f inv*
hysterical [hɪ'stɛrɪkl] *adj* isterico(-a)
hysterics [hɪ'stɛrɪks] *npl* accesso di
  isteria; (*laughter*) attacco di riso

I [aɪ] *pron* io
ice [aɪs] *n* ghiaccio; (*on road*) gelo; (*ice
  cream*) gelato ▷ *vt* (*cake*) glassare ▷ *vi*
  (*also:* **~ over**) ghiacciare; (*also:* **~ up**)
  gelare; **iceberg** *n* iceberg *m inv*; **ice
  cream** *n* gelato; **ice cube** *n* cubetto
  di ghiaccio; **ice hockey** *n* hockey *m* su
  ghiaccio
Iceland ['aɪslənd] *n* Islanda; **Icelander** *n*
  islandese *m/f*; **Icelandic** [aɪs'lændɪk] *adj*
  islandese ▷ *n* (*Ling*) islandese *m*
ice: **ice lolly** (*BRIT*) *n* ghiacciolo; **ice rink**
  n pista di pattinaggio; **ice skating** *n*
  pattinaggio sul ghiaccio
icing ['aɪsɪŋ] *n* (*Culin*) glassa; **icing sugar**
  (*BRIT*) *n* zucchero a velo
icon ['aɪkɔn] *n* icona
icy ['aɪsɪ] *adj* ghiacciato(-a); (*weather,
  temperature*) gelido(-a)
I'd [aɪd] = **I would**; **I had**
ID card *n* = **identity card**
idea [aɪ'dɪə] *n* idea
ideal [aɪ'dɪəl] *adj* ideale ▷ *n* ideale *m*;
  ideally [aɪ'dɪəlɪ] *adv* perfettamente,
  assolutamente; **ideally the book
  should have ...** l'ideale sarebbe che il
  libro avesse ...
identical [aɪ'dɛntɪkl] *adj* identico(-a)
identification [aɪdɛntɪfɪ'keɪʃən] *n*
  identificazione *f*; **(means of) ~** carta

d'identità

identify [aɪ'dɛntɪfaɪ] vt identificare

identity [aɪ'dɛntɪtɪ] n identità f inv; **identity card** n carta d'identità

ideology [aɪdɪ'ɔlədʒɪ] n ideologia

idiom ['ɪdɪəm] n idioma m; (phrase) espressione f idiomatica

idiot ['ɪdɪət] n idiota m/f

idle ['aɪdl] adj inattivo(-a); (lazy) pigro(-a), ozioso(-a); (unemployed) disoccupato(-a); (question, pleasures) ozioso(-a) ▷ vi (engine) girare al minimo

idol ['aɪdl] n idolo

idyllic [ɪ'dɪlɪk] adj idillico(-a)

i.e. adv abbr (= that is) cioè

if [ɪf] conj se; **if I were you ...** se fossi in te ..., io al tuo posto ...; **if so** se è così; **if not** se no; **if only** se solo or soltanto

ignite [ɪg'naɪt] vt accendere ▷ vi accendersi

ignition [ɪg'nɪʃən] n (Aut) accensione f; **to switch on/off the ~** accendere/spegnere il motore

ignorance ['ɪgnərəns] n ignoranza; **to keep sb in ~ of sth** tenere qn all'oscuro di qc

ignorant ['ɪgnərənt] adj ignorante; **to be ~ of** (subject) essere ignorante in; (events) essere ignaro(-a) di

ignore [ɪg'nɔːʳ] vt non tener conto di; (person, fact) ignorare

I'll [aɪl] = **I will**; **I shall**

ill [ɪl] adj (sick) malato(-a); (bad) cattivo(-a) ▷ n male m ▷ adv **to speak** etc **~ of sb** parlare etc male di qn; **to take** or **be taken ~** ammalarsi

illegal [ɪ'liːgl] adj illegale

illegible [ɪ'lɛdʒɪbl] adj illeggibile

illegitimate [ɪlɪ'dʒɪtɪmət] adj illegittimo(-a)

ill health n problemi mpl di salute

illiterate [ɪ'lɪtərət] adj analfabeta, illetterato(-a); (letter) scorretto(-a)

illness ['ɪlnɪs] n malattia

illuminate [ɪ'luːmɪneɪt] vt illuminare

illusion [ɪ'luːʒən] n illusione f

illustrate ['ɪləstreɪt] vt illustrare

illustration [ɪlə'streɪʃən] n illustrazione f

I'm [aɪm] = **I am**

image ['ɪmɪdʒ] n immagine f; (public face) immagine (pubblica)

imaginary [ɪ'mædʒɪnərɪ] adj immaginario(-a)

imagination [ɪmædʒɪ'neɪʃən] n immaginazione f, fantasia

imaginative [ɪ'mædʒɪnətɪv] adj immaginoso(-a)

imagine [ɪ'mædʒɪn] vt immaginare

imbalance [ɪm'bæləns] n squilibrio

imitate ['ɪmɪteɪt] vt imitare; **imitation** [-'teɪʃən] n imitazione f

immaculate [ɪ'mækjulət] adj immacolato(-a); (dress, appearance) impeccabile

immature [ɪmə'tjuəʳ] adj immaturo(-a)

immediate [ɪ'miːdɪət] adj immediato(-a); **immediately** adv (at once) subito, immediatamente; **immediately next to** proprio accanto a

immense [ɪ'mɛns] adj immenso(-a); enorme; **immensely** adv immensamente

immerse [ɪ'məːs] vt immergere

immigrant ['ɪmɪgrənt] n immigrante m/f; immigrato(-a); **immigration** [ɪmɪ'greɪʃən] n immigrazione f

imminent ['ɪmɪnənt] adj imminente

immoral [ɪ'mɔrl] adj immorale

immortal [ɪ'mɔːtl] adj, n immortale m/f

immune [ɪ'mjuːn] adj **~ (to)** immune (da); **immune system** n sistema m immunitario

immunize ['ɪmjunaɪz] vt immunizzare

impact ['ɪmpækt] n impatto

impair [ɪm'pɛəʳ] vt danneggiare

impartial [ɪm'pɑːʃl] adj imparziale

impatience [ɪm'peɪʃəns] n impazienza

impatient [ɪm'peɪʃənt] adj impaziente; **to get** or **grow ~** perdere la pazienza

impeccable [ɪm'pɛkəbl] adj impeccabile

impending [ɪm'pɛndɪŋ] adj imminente

imperative [ɪm'pɛrətɪv] adj imperativo(-a); necessario(-a), urgente; (voice) imperioso(-a)

imperfect [ɪm'pəːfɪkt] adj imperfetto(-a); (goods etc) difettoso(-a) ▷ n (Ling: also: **~ tense**) imperfetto

imperial [ɪm'pɪərɪəl] adj imperiale; (measure) legale

impersonal [ɪm'pəːsənl] adj impersonale

impersonate [ɪm'pəːsəneɪt] vt impersonare; (Theatre) fare la mimica di

impetus ['ɪmpətəs] n impeto

implant [ɪm'plɑːnt] vt (Med) innestare; (fig: idea, principle) inculcare

implement [n 'ɪmplɪmənt, vb 'ɪmplɪmɛnt] n attrezzo; (for cooking) utensile m ▷ vt effettuare

implicate ['ɪmplɪkeɪt] vt implicare

implication [ɪmplɪ'keɪʃən] n implicazione f; **by ~** implicitamente

implicit [ɪm'plɪsɪt] adj implicito(-a); (complete) completo(-a)

imply [ɪm'plaɪ] vt insinuare; suggerire

impolite [ɪmpə'laɪt] adj scortese

import [vb ɪm'pɔːt, n 'ɪmpɔːt] vt importare ▷ n (Comm) importazione f

importance [ɪm'pɔːtns] n importanza
important [ɪm'pɔːtnt] adj importante;
  it's not ~ non ha importanza
importer [ɪm'pɔːtəʳ] n
  importatore(-trice)
impose [ɪm'pəuz] vt imporre ▷ vi **to ~
  on sb** sfruttare la bontà di qn; **imposing**
  [ɪm'pəuzɪŋ] adj imponente
impossible [ɪm'pɔsɪbl] adj impossibile
impotent ['ɪmpətnt] adj impotente
impoverished [ɪm'pɔvərɪʃt] adj
  impoverito(-a)
impractical [ɪm'præktɪkl] adj non
  pratico(-a)
impress [ɪm'prɛs] vt impressionare; (mark)
  imprimere, stampare; **to ~ sth on sb** far
  capire qc a qn
impression [ɪm'prɛʃən] n impressione
  f; **to be under the ~ that** avere
  l'impressione che
impressive [ɪm'prɛsɪv] adj notevole
imprison [ɪm'prɪzn] vt imprigionare;
  imprisonment n imprigionamento
improbable [ɪm'prɔbəbl] adj improbabile;
  (excuse) inverosimile
improper [ɪm'prɔpəʳ] adj scorretto(-a);
  (unsuitable) inadatto(-a), improprio(-a);
  sconveniente, indecente
improve [ɪm'pruːv] vt migliorare ▷ vi
  migliorare; (pupil etc) fare progressi;
  improvement n miglioramento;
  progresso
improvise ['ɪmprəvaɪz] vt, vi improvvisare
impulse ['ɪmpʌls] n impulso; **on ~**
  d'impulso, impulsivamente; **impulsive**
  [ɪm'pʌlsɪv] adj impulsivo(-a)

 KEYWORD

in [ɪn] prep **1** (indicating place, position) in;
  in the house/garden in casa/giardino;
  in the box nella scatola; **in the fridge**
  nel frigorifero; **I have it in my hand** ce
  l'ho in mano; **in town/the country** in
  città/campagna; **in school** a scuola; **in
  here/there** qui/lì dentro
  2 (with place names: of town, region,
  country): **in London** a Londra; **in England**
  in Inghilterra; **in the United States** negli
  Stati Uniti; **in Yorkshire** nello Yorkshire
  3 (indicating time: during, in the space of) in;
  in spring/summer in primavera/estate;
  in 1988 nel 1988; **in May** in or a maggio; **I'll
  see you in July** ci vediamo a luglio; **in the
  afternoon** nel pomeriggio; **at 4 o'clock
  in the afternoon** alle 4 del pomeriggio;
  I did it in 3 hours/days l'ho fatto in 3
  ore/giorni; **I'll see you in 2 weeks** or **in 2
  weeks' time** ci vediamo tra 2 settimane

4 (indicating manner etc) a; **in a loud/soft
  voice** a voce alta/bassa; **in pencil** a
  matita; **in English/French** in inglese/
  francese; **the boy in the blue shirt** il
  ragazzo con la camicia blu
  5 (indicating circumstances): **in the sun**
  al sole; **in the shade** all'ombra; **in the
  rain** sotto la pioggia; **a rise in prices** un
  aumento dei prezzi
  6 (indicating mood, state): **in tears** in
  lacrime; **in anger** per la rabbia; **in
  despair** disperato(-a); **in good condition**
  in buono stato, in buone condizioni; **to
  live in luxury** vivere nel lusso
  7 (with ratios, numbers): **1 in 10** 1 su 10;
  20 pence in the pound 20 pence per
  sterlina; **they lined up in twos** si misero
  in fila a due a due
  8 (referring to people, works) in; **the
  disease is common in children** la
  malattia è comune nei bambini; **in (the
  works of) Dickens** in Dickens
  9 (indicating profession etc) in; **to be in
  teaching** fare l'insegnante, insegnare; **to
  be in publishing** essere nell'editoria
  10 (after superlative) di; **the best in the
  class** il migliore della classe
  11 (with present participle): **in saying this**
  dicendo questo, nel dire questo
  ▷ adv **to be in** (person: at home, work)
  esserci; (train, ship, plane) essere
  arrivato(-a); (in fashion) essere di moda; **to
  ask sb in** invitare qn ad entrare; **to run/
  limp** etc **in** entrare di corsa/zoppicando
  etc
  ▷ n **the ins and outs of the problem**
  tutti i particolari del problema

inability [ɪnə'bɪlɪtɪ] n **~ (to do)** incapacità
  (di fare)
inaccurate [ɪn'ækjurət] adj inesatto(-a),
  impreciso(-a)
inadequate [ɪn'ædɪkwət] adj
  insufficiente
inadvertently [ɪnəd'vəːtntlɪ] adv senza
  volerlo
inappropriate [ɪnə'prəuprɪət] adj
  non adatto(-a); (word, expression)
  improprio(-a)
inaugurate [ɪ'nɔːgjureɪt] vt inaugurare;
  (president, official) insediare
Inc. (us) abbr (= incorporated) S.A.
incapable [ɪn'keɪpəbl] adj incapace
incense [n 'ɪnsɛns, vb ɪn'sɛns] n incenso
  ▷ vt (anger) infuriare
incentive [ɪn'sɛntɪv] n incentivo
inch [ɪntʃ] n pollice m (25 mm, 12 in a foot);
  within an ~ of a un pelo da; **he didn't give
  an ~** non ha ceduto di un millimetro

incidence [ˈɪnsɪdns] *n* (*of crime, disease*)
incidenza

incident [ˈɪnsɪdnt] *n* incidente *m*; (*in book*)
episodio

incidentally [ɪnsɪˈdɛntəlɪ] *adv* (*by the way*)
a proposito

inclination [ɪnklɪˈneɪʃən] *n* inclinazione *f*

incline [*n* ˈɪnklaɪn, *vb* ɪnˈklaɪn] *n*
pendenza, pendio ▷ *vt* inclinare ▷ *vi*
(*surface*) essere inclinato(-a); **to be ~d to
do** tendere a fare; essere propenso(-a) a
fare

include [ɪnˈkluːd] *vt* includere,
comprendere; **is service ~d?** il servizio è
compreso?; **including** *prep* compreso(-a),
incluso(-a); **inclusion** [ɪnˈkluːʒən] *n*
inclusione *f*; **inclusive** [ɪnˈkluːsɪv] *adj*
incluso(-a), compreso(-a); **inclusive of
tax** *etc* tasse *etc* comprese

income [ˈɪnkʌm] *n* reddito; **income
support** *n* (*BRIT*) sussidio di indigenza
or povertà; **income tax** *n* imposta sul
reddito

incoming [ˈɪnkʌmɪŋ] *adj* (*flight, mail*) in
arrivo; (*government*) subentrante; (*tide*)
montante

incompatible [ɪnkəmˈpætɪbl] *adj*
incompatibile

incompetence [ɪnˈkɔmpɪtns] *n*
incompetenza, incapacità

incompetent [ɪnˈkɔmpɪtnt] *adj*
incompetente, incapace

incomplete [ɪnkəmˈpliːt] *adj*
incompleto(-a)

inconsistent [ɪnkənˈsɪstənt] *adj*
incoerente; **~ with** non coerente con

inconvenience [ɪnkənˈviːnjəns] *n*
inconveniente *m*; (*trouble*) disturbo ▷ *vt*
disturbare

inconvenient [ɪnkənˈviːnjənt] *adj*
scomodo(-a)

incorporate [ɪnˈkɔːpəreɪt] *vt* incorporare;
(*contain*) contenere

incorrect [ɪnkəˈrɛkt] *adj* scorretto(-a);
(*statement*) inesatto(-a)

increase [*n* ˈɪnkriːs, *vb* ɪnˈkriːs] *n* aumento
▷ *vi, vt* aumentare; **increasingly** *adv*
sempre più

incredible [ɪnˈkrɛdɪbl] *adj* incredibile;
incredibly *adv* incredibilmente

incur [ɪnˈkəːʳ] *vt* (*expenses*) incorrere;
(*anger, risk*) esporsi a; (*debt*) contrarre;
(*loss*) subire

indecent [ɪnˈdiːsnt] *adj* indecente

indeed [ɪnˈdiːd] *adv* infatti; veramente;
yes ~! certamente!

indefinitely [ɪnˈdɛfɪnɪtlɪ] *adv* (*wait*)
indefinitamente

independence [ɪndɪˈpɛndns] *n*

indipendenza; **Independence Day** (*US*) *n*
vedi nota nel riquadro

⬤ **INDEPENDENCE DAY**
⬤
⬤ Negli Stati Uniti il 4 luglio si festeggia
⬤ **l'Independence Day**, giorno in
⬤ cui, nel 1776, 13 colonie britanniche
⬤ proclamarono la propria indipendenza
⬤ dalla Gran Bretagna ed entrarono
⬤ ufficialmente a far parte degli Stati Uniti
⬤ d'America.

independent [ɪndɪˈpɛndnt] *adj*
indipendente; **independent school** *n*
(*BRIT*) istituto scolastico indipendente che si
autofinanzia

index [ˈɪndɛks] (*pl* **indexes**) *n* (*in book*)
indice *m*; (: *in library etc*) catalogo; (*pl
indices: ratio, sign*) indice *m*

India [ˈɪndɪə] *n* India; **Indian** *adj, n*
indiano(-a)

indicate [ˈɪndɪkeɪt] *vt* indicare; **indication**
[-ˈkeɪʃən] *n* indicazione *f*, segno;
indicative [ɪnˈdɪkətɪv] *adj* **indicative of**
indicativo(-a) di; **indicator** [ˈɪndɪkeɪtəʳ] *n*
indicatore *m*; (*Aut*) freccia

indices [ˈɪndɪsiːz] *npl of* **index**

indict [ɪnˈdaɪt] *vt* accusare; **indictment**
[ɪnˈdaɪtmənt] *n* accusa

indifference [ɪnˈdɪfrəns] *n* indifferenza

indifferent [ɪnˈdɪfrənt] *adj* indifferente;
(*poor*) mediocre

indigenous [ɪnˈdɪdʒɪnəs] *adj* indigeno(-a)

indigestion [ɪndɪˈdʒɛstʃən] *n*
indigestione *f*

indignant [ɪnˈdɪgnənt] *adj* **~ (at sth/with
sb)** indignato(-a) (per qc/contro qn)

indirect [ɪndɪˈrɛkt] *adj* indiretto(-a)

indispensable [ɪndɪˈspɛnsəbl] *adj*
indispensabile

individual [ɪndɪˈvɪdjuəl] *n* individuo
▷ *adj* individuale; (*characteristic*)
particolare, originale; **individually** *adv*
singolarmente, uno(-a) per uno(-a)

Indonesia [ɪndəˈniːzɪə] *n* Indonesia

indoor [ˈɪndɔːʳ] *adj* da interno; (*plant*)
d'appartamento; (*swimming pool*)
coperto(-a); (*sport, games*) fatto(-a) al
coperto; **indoors** [ɪnˈdɔːz] *adv* all'interno

induce [ɪnˈdjuːs] *vt* persuadere; (*bring
about, Med*) provocare

indulge [ɪnˈdʌldʒ] *vt* (*whim*) compiacere,
soddisfare; (*child*) viziare ▷ *vi* **to ~ in
sth** concedersi qc; abbandonarsi a qc;
indulgent *adj* indulgente

industrial [ɪnˈdʌstrɪəl] *adj* industriale;
(*injury*) sul lavoro; **industrial estate**
(*BRIT*) *n* zona industriale; **Industrialist**

[ɪn'dʌstrɪəlɪst] *n* industriale *m*; **industrial park** (*US*) *n* = **industrial estate**
industry ['ɪndəstrɪ] *n* industria; (*diligence*) operosità
inefficient [ɪnɪ'fɪʃənt] *adj* inefficiente
inequality [ɪnɪ'kwɔlɪtɪ] *n* ineguaglianza
inevitable [ɪn'ɛvɪtəbl] *adj* inevitabile; **inevitably** *adv* inevitabilmente
inexpensive [ɪnɪk'spɛnsɪv] *adj* poco costoso(-a)
inexperienced [ɪnɪks'pɪərɪənst] *adj* inesperto(-a), senza esperienza
inexplicable [ɪnɪk'splɪkəbl] *adj* inesplicabile
infamous ['ɪnfəməs] *adj* infame
infant ['ɪnfənt] *n* bambino(-a)
infantry ['ɪnfəntrɪ] *n* fanteria
infant school *n* (*BRIT*) scuola elementare (*per bambini dall'età di 5 a 7 anni*)
infect [ɪn'fɛkt] *vt* infettare; **infection** [ɪn'fɛkʃən] *n* infezione *f*; **infectious** [ɪn'fɛkʃəs] *adj* (*disease*) infettivo(-a), contagioso(-a); (*person: fig: enthusiasm*) contagioso(-a)
infer [ɪn'fəːʳ] *vt* inferire, dedurre
inferior [ɪn'fɪərɪəʳ] *adj* inferiore; (*goods*) di qualità scadente ▷ *n* inferiore *m/f*; (*in rank*) subalterno(-a)
infertile [ɪn'fəːtaɪl] *adj* sterile
infertility [ɪnfəː'tɪlɪtɪ] *n* sterilità
infested [ɪn'fɛstɪd] *adj* ~ **(with)** infestato(-a) (di)
infinite ['ɪnfɪnɪt] *adj* infinito(-a); **infinitely** *adv* infinitamente
infirmary [ɪn'fəːmərɪ] *n* ospedale *m*; (*in school, factory*) infermeria
inflamed [ɪn'fleɪmd] *adj* infiammato(-a)
inflammation [ɪnflə'meɪʃən] *n* infiammazione *f*
inflatable [ɪn'fleɪtəbl] *adj* gonfiabile
inflate [ɪn'fleɪt] *vt* (*tyre, balloon*) gonfiare; (*fig*) esagerare; gonfiare; **inflation** [ɪn'fleɪʃən] *n* (*Econ*) inflazione *f*
inflexible [ɪn'flɛksɪbl] *adj* inflessibile, rigido(-a)
inflict [ɪn'flɪkt] *vt* **to ~ on** infliggere a
influence ['ɪnfluəns] *n* influenza ▷ *vt* influenzare; **under the ~ of alcohol** sotto l'effetto dell'alcool; **influential** [ɪnflu'ɛnʃl] *adj* influente
influx ['ɪnflʌks] *n* afflusso
info (*inf*) ['ɪnfəu] *n* = **information**
inform [ɪn'fɔːm] *vt* **to ~ sb (of)** informare qn (di) ▷ *vi* **to ~ on sb** denunciare qn
informal [ɪn'fɔːml] *adj* informale; (*announcement, invitation*) non ufficiale
information [ɪnfə'meɪʃən] *n* informazioni *fpl*; particolari *mpl*; **a piece of ~** un'informazione; **information office** *n*

ufficio *m* informazioni *inv*; **information technology** *n* informatica
informative [ɪn'fɔːmətɪv] *adj* istruttivo(-a)
infra-red [ɪnfrə'rɛd] *adj* infrarosso(-a)
infrastructure ['ɪnfrəstrʌktʃəʳ] *n* infrastruttura
infrequent [ɪn'friːkwənt] *adj* infrequente, raro(-a)
infuriate [ɪn'fjuərɪeɪt] *vt* rendere furioso(-a)
infuriating [ɪn'fjuərɪeɪtɪŋ] *adj* molto irritante
ingenious [ɪn'dʒiːnjəs] *adj* ingegnoso(-a)
ingredient [ɪn'griːdɪənt] *n* ingrediente *m*; elemento
inhabit [ɪn'hæbɪt] *vt* abitare; **inhabitant** [ɪn'hæbɪtnt] *n* abitante *m/f*
inhale [ɪn'heɪl] *vt* inalare ▷ *vi* (*in smoking*) aspirare; **inhaler** *n* inalatore *m*
inherent [ɪn'hɪərənt] *adj* ~ **(in** *or* **to)** inerente (a)
inherit [ɪn'hɛrɪt] *vt* ereditare; **inheritance** *n* eredità
inhibit [ɪn'hɪbɪt] *vt* (*Psych*) inibire; **inhibition** [-'bɪʃən] *n* inibizione *f*
initial [ɪ'nɪʃl] *adj* iniziale ▷ *n* iniziale *f* ▷ *vt* siglare; **~s** *npl* (*of name*) iniziali *fpl*; (*as signature*) sigla; **initially** *adv* inizialmente, all'inizio
initiate [ɪ'nɪʃɪeɪt] *vt* (*start*) avviare; intraprendere; iniziare; (*person*) iniziare; **to ~ sb into a secret** mettere qn a parte di un segreto; **to ~ proceedings against sb** (*Law*) intentare causa contro qn
initiative [ɪ'nɪʃətɪv] *n* iniziativa
inject [ɪn'dʒɛkt] *vt* (*liquid*) iniettare; (*patient*): **to ~ sb with sth** fare a qn un'iniezione di qc; (*funds*) immettere; **injection** [ɪn'dʒɛkʃən] *n* iniezione *f*, puntura
injure ['ɪndʒəʳ] *vt* ferire; (*damage: reputation etc*) nuocere a; **injured** *adj* ferito(-a); **injury** ['ɪndʒərɪ] *n* ferita
injustice [ɪn'dʒʌstɪs] *n* ingiustizia
ink [ɪŋk] *n* inchiostro; **ink-jet printer** ['ɪŋkdʒɛt-] *n* stampante *f* a getto d'inchiostro
inland [*adj* 'ɪnlənd, *adv* ɪn'lænd] *adj* interno(-a) ▷ *adv* all'interno; **Inland Revenue** (*BRIT*) *n* Fisco
in-laws ['ɪnlɔːz] *npl* suoceri *mpl*; famiglia del marito (*or* della moglie)
inmate ['ɪnmeɪt] *n* (*in prison*) carcerato(-a); (*in asylum*) ricoverato(-a)
inn [ɪn] *n* locanda
inner ['ɪnəʳ] *adj* interno(-a), interiore; **inner-city** *n* centro di una zona urbana
inning ['ɪnɪŋ] *n* (*US: Baseball*) ripresa; **~s**

(Cricket) turno di battuta
innocence ['ɪnəsns] n innocenza
innocent ['ɪnəsnt] adj innocente
innovation [ɪnəu'veɪʃən] n innovazione f
innovative ['ɪnəu'veɪtɪv] adj innovativo(-a)
in-patient ['ɪnpeɪʃənt] n ricoverato(-a)
input ['ɪnput] n Input m
inquest ['ɪnkwɛst] n inchiesta
inquire [ɪn'kwaɪər] vi informarsi ▷ vt domandare, informarsi su; **inquiry** n domanda; (Law) indagine f, investigazione f; **"inquiries"** "informazioni"
ins. abbr = **inches**
insane [ɪn'seɪn] adj matto(-a), pazzo(-a); (Med) alienato(-a)
insanity [ɪn'sænɪtɪ] n follia; (Med) alienazione f mentale
insect ['ɪnsɛkt] n insetto; **insect repellent** n insettifugo
insecure [ɪnsɪ'kjuər] adj malsicuro(-a); (person) insicuro(-a)
insecurity [ɪnsɪ'kjuərɪtɪ] n mancanza di sicurezza
insensitive [ɪn'sɛnsɪtɪv] adj insensibile
insert [ɪn'səːt] vt inserire, introdurre
inside ['ɪn'saɪd] n interno, parte f interiore ▷ adj interno(-a), interiore ▷ adv dentro, all'interno ▷ prep dentro, all'interno di; (of time): **~ 10 minutes** entro 10 minuti; **inside lane** n (Aut) corsia di marcia; **inside out** adv (turn) a rovescio; (know) in fondo
insight ['ɪnsaɪt] n acume m, perspicacia; (glimpse, idea) percezione f
insignificant [ɪnsɪg'nɪfɪknt] adj insignificante
insincere [ɪnsɪn'sɪər] adj insincero(-a)
insist [ɪn'sɪst] vi insistere; **to ~ on doing** insistere per fare; **to ~ that** insistere perché + sub; (claim) sostenere che; **insistent** adj insistente
insomnia [ɪn'sɔmnɪə] n insonnia
inspect [ɪn'spɛkt] vt ispezionare; (BRIT: ticket) controllare; **inspection** [ɪn'spɛkʃən] n ispezione f; controllo; **inspector** n ispettore(-trice); (BRIT: on buses, trains) controllore m
inspiration [ɪnspə'reɪʃən] n ispirazione f; **inspire** [ɪn'spaɪər] vt ispirare; **inspiring** adj stimolante
instability [ɪnstə'bɪlɪtɪ] n instabilità
install [ɪn'stɔːl] (US **instal**) vt installare; **installation** [ɪnstə'leɪʃən] n installazione f
instalment [ɪn'stɔːlmənt] (US **installment**) n rata; (of TV serial etc) puntata; **in ~s** (pay) a rate; (receive) una parte per volta; (: publication) a fascicoli
instance ['ɪnstəns] n esempio, caso; **for ~**

per or ad esempio; **in the first ~** in primo luogo
instant ['ɪnstənt] n istante m, attimo ▷ adj immediato(-a); urgente; (coffee, food) in polvere; **instantly** adv immediatamente, subito
instead [ɪn'stɛd] adv invece; **~ of** invece di
instinct ['ɪnstɪŋkt] n istinto; **instinctive** adj istintivo(-a)
institute ['ɪnstɪtjuːt] n istituto ▷ vt istituire, stabilire; (inquiry) avviare; (proceedings) iniziare
institution [ɪnstɪ'tjuːʃən] n istituzione f; (educational institution, mental institution) istituto
instruct [ɪn'strʌkt] vt **to ~ sb in sth** insegnare qc a qn; **to ~ sb to do** dare ordini a qn di fare; **instruction** [ɪn'strʌkʃən] n istruzione f; **instructions (for use)** istruzioni per l'uso; **instructor** n istruttore(-trice); (for skiing) maestro(-a)
instrument ['ɪnstrəmənt] n strumento; **instrumental** [-'mɛntl] adj (Mus) strumentale; **to be instrumental in** essere d'aiuto in
insufficient [ɪnsə'fɪʃənt] adj insufficiente
insulate ['ɪnsjuleɪt] vt isolare; **insulation** [-'leɪʃən] n isolamento
insulin ['ɪnsjulɪn] n insulina
insult [n 'ɪnsʌlt, vb ɪn'sʌlt] n insulto, affronto ▷ vt insultare; **insulting** adj offensivo(-a), ingiurioso(-a)
insurance [ɪn'ʃuərəns] n assicurazione f; **fire/life ~** assicurazione contro gli incendi/sulla vita; **insurance company** n società di assicurazioni; **insurance policy** n polizza d'assicurazione
insure [ɪn'ʃuər] vt assicurare
intact [ɪn'tækt] adj intatto(-a)
intake ['ɪnteɪk] n (Tech) immissione f; (of food) consumo; (BRIT: of pupils etc) afflusso
integral ['ɪntɪgrəl] adj integrale; (part) integrante
integrate ['ɪntɪgreɪt] vt integrare ▷ vi integrarsi
integrity [ɪn'tɛgrɪtɪ] n integrità
intellect ['ɪntəlɛkt] n intelletto; **intellectual** [-'lɛktjuəl] adj, n intellettuale m/f
intelligence [ɪn'tɛlɪdʒəns] n intelligenza; (Mil etc) informazioni fpl
intelligent [ɪn'tɛlɪdʒənt] adj intelligente
intend [ɪn'tɛnd] vt (gift etc): **to ~ sth for** destinare qc a; **to ~ to do** aver l'intenzione di fare
intense [ɪn'tɛns] adj intenso(-a); (person) di forti sentimenti
intensify [ɪn'tɛnsɪfaɪ] vt intensificare
intensity [ɪn'tɛnsɪtɪ] n intensità

intensive [ɪn'tɛnsɪv] *adj* intensivo(-a);
intensive care *n* terapia intensiva;
intensive care unit (ICU) *n* reparto
terapia intensiva

intent [ɪn'tɛnt] *n* intenzione *f* ▷ *adj* ~ **(on)**
intento(-a) (a), immerso(-a) (in); **to all ~s
and purposes** a tutti gli effetti; **to be ~ on
doing sth** essere deciso a fare qc

intention [ɪn'tɛnʃən] *n* intenzione
f; **intentional** *adj* intenzionale,
deliberato(-a)

interact [ɪntər'ækt] *vi* interagire;
interaction [ɪntər'ækʃən] *n* azione *f*
reciproca, interazione *f*; **interactive** *adj*
(*Comput*) interattivo(-a)

intercept [ɪntə'sɛpt] *vt* intercettare;
(*person*) fermare

interchange ['ɪntətʃeɪndʒ] *n* (*exchange*)
scambio; (*on motorway*) incrocio
pluridirezionale

intercourse ['ɪntəkɔːs] *n* rapporti *mpl*

interest ['ɪntrɪst] *n* interesse *m*; (*Comm*:
stake, share) interessi *mpl* ▷ *vt* interessare;
interested *adj* interessato(-a); **to be
interested in** interessarsi di; **interesting**
adj interessante; **interest rate** *n* tasso di
interesse

interface ['ɪntəfeɪs] *n* (*Comput*) interfaccia

interfere [ɪntə'fɪər] *vi* **to ~ in** (*quarrel*,
other people's business) immischiarsi in;
to ~ with (*object*) toccare; (*plans, duty*)
interferire con; **interference** [ɪntə'fɪərə
ns] *n* interferenza

interim ['ɪntərɪm] *adj* provvisorio(-a) ▷ *n*
in the ~ nel frattempo

interior [ɪn'tɪərɪər] *n* interno; (*of
country*) entroterra ▷ *adj* interno(-a);
(*minister*) degli Interni; **interior design** *n*
architettura d'interni

intermediate [ɪntə'miːdɪət] *adj*
intermedio(-a)

intermission [ɪntə'mɪʃən] *n* pausa;
(*Theatre, Cinema*) intermissione *f*, intervallo

intern [*vb* ɪn'tə:n, *n* 'ɪntə:n] *vt* internare
▷ *n* (*us*) medico interno

internal [ɪn'tə:nl] *adj* interno(-a); **Internal
Revenue Service** (*us*) *n* Fisco

international [ɪntə'næʃənl] *adj*
internazionale ▷ *n* (*BRIT Sport*) incontro
internazionale

Internet ['ɪntənɛt] *n* **the ~** Internet *f*;
Internet café *n* cybercaffè *m inv*; **Internet
Service Provider** *n* Provider *m inv*;
Internet user *n* utente *m/f* Internet

interpret [ɪn'tə:prɪt] *vt* interpretare
▷ *vi* fare da interprete; **interpretation**
[ɪntə:prɪ'teɪʃən] *n* interpretazione *f*;
interpreter *n* interprete *m/f*; **could you
act as an interpreter for us?** ci potrebbe

fare da interprete?

interrogate [ɪn'tɛrəugeɪt] *vt* interrogare;
interrogation [-'geɪʃən] *n* interrogazione
f; (*of suspect etc*) interrogatorio

interrogative [ɪntə'rɔgətɪv] *adj*
interrogativo(-a) ▷ *n* (*Ling*) interrogativo

interrupt [ɪntə'rʌpt] *vt, vi* interrompere;
interruption [-'rʌpʃən] *n* interruzione *f*

intersection [ɪntə'sɛkʃən] *n* intersezione
f; (*of roads*) incrocio

interstate ['ɪntəsteɪt] (*us*) *n* fra stati

interval ['ɪntəvl] *n* intervallo; **at ~s** a
intervalli

intervene [ɪntə'viːn] *vi* (*time*) intercorrere;
(*event, person*) intervenire

interview ['ɪntəvjuː] *n* (*Radio, TV
etc*) intervista; (*for job*) colloquio ▷ *vt*
intervistare; avere un colloquio con;
interviewer *n* intervistatore(-trice)

intimate [*adj* 'ɪntɪmət, *vb* 'ɪntɪmeɪt] *adj*
intimo(-a); (*knowledge*) profondo(-a) ▷ *vt*
lasciar capire

intimidate [ɪn'tɪmɪdeɪt] *vt* intimidire,
intimorire

intimidating [ɪn'tɪmɪdeɪtɪŋ] *adj* (*sight*)
spaventoso(-a); (*appearance, figure*)
minaccioso(-a)

into ['ɪntuː] *prep* dentro, in; **come ~ the
house** entra in casa; **he worked late ~ the
night** lavorò fino a tarda notte; **~ Italian**
in italiano

intolerant [ɪn'tɔlərnt] *adj* **~ of**
intollerante di

intranet ['ɪntrənɛt] *n* intranet *f*

intransitive [ɪn'trænsɪtɪv] *adj*
intransitivo(-a)

intricate ['ɪntrɪkət] *adj* intricato(-a),
complicato(-a)

intrigue [ɪn'triːg] *n* intrigo ▷ *vt*
affascinare; **intriguing** *adj* affascinante

introduce [ɪntrə'djuːs] *vt* introdurre;
to ~ sb (to sb) presentare qn (a qn); **to
~ sb to** (*pastime, technique*) iniziare qn a;
introduction [-'dʌkʃən] *n* introduzione
f; (*of person*) presentazione *f*; (*to new
experience*) iniziazione *f*; **introductory** *adj*
introduttivo(-a)

intrude [ɪn'truːd] *vi* (*person*): **to ~ (on)**
intromettersi (in); **intruder** *n* intruso(-a)

intuition [ɪntjuː'ɪʃən] *n* intuizione *f*

inundate ['ɪnʌndeɪt] *vt* **to ~ with**
inondare di

invade [ɪn'veɪd] *vt* invadere

invalid [*n* 'ɪnvəlɪd, *adj* ɪn'vælɪd] *n*
malato(-a); (*with disability*) invalido(-a)
▷ *adj* (*not valid*) invalido(-a), non valido(-a)

invaluable [ɪn'væljuəbl] *adj* prezioso(-a);
inestimabile

invariably [ɪn'vɛərɪəblɪ] *adv*

invariabilmente; sempre

invasion [ɪn'veɪʒən] n invasione f

invent [ɪn'vɛnt] vt inventare; **invention** [ɪn'vɛnʃən] n invenzione f; **inventor** n inventore m

inventory ['ɪnvəntrɪ] n inventario

inverted commas [ɪn'vəːtɪd-] (BRIT) npl virgolette fpl

invest [ɪn'vɛst] vt investire ▷ vi **to ~ (in)** investire (in)

investigate [ɪn'vɛstɪgeɪt] vt investigare, indagare; (crime) fare indagini su; **investigation** [-'geɪʃən] n investigazione f; (of crime) indagine f

investigator [ɪn'vɛstɪgeɪtəʳ] n investigatore(-trice); **a private ~** un investigatore privato, un detective

investment [ɪn'vɛstmənt] n investimento

investor [ɪn'vɛstəʳ] n investitore(-trice); azionista m/f

invisible [ɪn'vɪzɪbl] adj invisibile

invitation [ɪnvɪ'teɪʃən] n invito

invite [ɪn'vaɪt] vt invitare; (opinions etc) sollecitare; **inviting** adj invitante, attraente

invoice ['ɪnvɔɪs] n fattura ▷ vt fatturare

involve [ɪn'vɔlv] vt (entail) richiedere, comportare; (associate): **to ~ sb (in)** implicare qn (in); coinvolgere qn (in); **involved** adj involuto(-a), complesso(-a); **to be involved in** essere coinvolto(-a) in; **involvement** n implicazione f; coinvolgimento

inward ['ɪnwəd] adj (movement) verso l'interno; (thought, feeling) interiore, intimo(-a); **inward(s)** adv verso l'interno

IQ n abbr (= intelligence quotient) quoziente m d'intelligenza

IRA n abbr (= Irish Republican Army) IRA f

Iran [ɪ'rɑːn] n Iran m; **Iranian** adj, n iraniano(-a)

Iraq [ɪ'rɑːk] n Iraq m; **Iraqi** adj, n iracheno(-a)

Ireland ['aɪələnd] n Irlanda

iris ['aɪrɪs] (pl **irises**) n iride f; (Bot) giaggiolo, iride

Irish ['aɪrɪʃ] adj irlandese ▷ npl **the ~** gli Irlandesi; **Irishman** (irreg) n irlandese m; **Irish Sea** n Mar m d'Irlanda; **Irishwoman** (irreg) n irlandese f

iron ['aɪən] n ferro; (for clothes) ferro da stiro ▷ adj di or in ferro ▷ vt (clothes) stirare

ironic(al) [aɪ'rɔnɪk(l)] adj ironico(-a); **ironically** adv ironicamente

ironing ['aɪənɪŋ] n (act) stirare m; (clothes) roba da stirare; **ironing board** n asse f da stiro

irony ['aɪrənɪ] n ironia

irrational [ɪ'ræʃənl] adj irrazionale

irregular [ɪ'rɛgjuləʳ] adj irregolare

irrelevant [ɪ'rɛləvənt] adj non pertinente

irresistible [ɪrɪ'zɪstɪbl] adj irresistibile

irresponsible [ɪrɪ'spɔnsɪbl] adj irresponsabile

irrigation [ɪrɪ'geɪʃən] n irrigazione f

irritable ['ɪrɪtəbl] adj irritabile

irritate ['ɪrɪteɪt] vt irritare; **irritating** adj (person, sound etc) irritante; **irritation** [-'teɪʃən] n irritazione f

IRS (US) n abbr = **Internal Revenue Service**

is [ɪz] vb see **be**

ISDN n abbr (= Integrated Services Digital Network) I.S.D.N. f

Islam ['ɪzlɑːm] n Islam m; **Islamic** [ɪz'læmɪk] adj islamico(-a)

island ['aɪlənd] n isola; **islander** n isolano(-a)

isle [aɪl] n isola

isn't ['ɪznt] = **is not**

isolated ['aɪsəleɪtɪd] adj isolato(-a)

isolation [aɪsə'leɪʃən] n isolamento

ISP n abbr (= Internet Service Provider) provider m inv

Israel ['ɪzreɪl] n Israele m; **Israeli** [ɪz'reɪlɪ] adj, n israeliano(-a)

issue ['ɪʃjuː] n questione f, problema m; (of banknotes etc) emissione f; (of newspaper etc) numero ▷ vt (statement) rilasciare; (rations, equipment) distribuire; (book) pubblicare; (banknotes, cheques, stamps) emettere; **at ~** in gioco, in discussione; **to take ~ with sb (over sth)** prendere posizione contro qn (riguardo a qc); **to make an ~ of sth** fare un problema di qc

KEYWORD

it [ɪt] pron **1** (specific: subject) esso(-a); (: direct object) lo (la), l'; (: indirect object) gli (le); **where's my book? — it's on the table** dov'è il mio libro? — è sulla tavola; **I can't find it** non lo (or la) trovo; **give it to me** dammelo (or dammela); **about/from/ of it** ne; **I spoke to him about it** gliene ho parlato; **what did you learn from it?** quale insegnamento ne hai tratto?; **I'm proud of it** ne sono fiero; **did you go to it?** ci sei andato?; **put the book in it** mettici il libro

2 (impers): **it's raining** piove; **it's Friday tomorrow** domani è venerdì; **it's 6 o'clock** sono le 6; **who is it? — it's me** chi è? — sono io

IT n abbr see **information technology**

Italian [ɪ'tæljən] adj italiano(-a) ▷ n

italiano(-a); (*Ling*) italiano; **the ~s** gli
Italiani; **what's the ~ (word) for ...?** come
si dice in italiano ...?

italics [ɪ'tælɪks] *npl* corsivo

Italy ['ɪtəlɪ] *n* Italia

itch [ɪtʃ] *n* prurito ▷ *vi* (*person*) avere il
prurito; (*part of body*) prudere; **to ~ to do
sth** aver una gran voglia di fare qc; **itchy**
adj che prude; **to be itchy** = **to itch**

it'd ['ɪtd] = **it would**; **it had**

item ['aɪtəm] *n* articolo; (*on agenda*) punto;
(*also:* **news ~**) notizia

itinerary [aɪ'tɪnərərɪ] *n* itinerario

it'll ['ɪtl] = **it will**; **it shall**

its [ɪts] *adj* il (la) suo(-a), i (le) suoi (sue)

it's [ɪts] = **it is**; **it has**

itself [ɪt'sɛlf] *pron* (*emphatic*) esso(-a)
stesso(-a); (*reflexive*) si

ITV (BRIT) *n abbr* (= *Independent Television*)
rete televisiva in concorrenza con la BBC

I've [aɪv] = **I have**

ivory ['aɪvərɪ] *n* avorio

ivy ['aɪvɪ] *n* edera

jab [dʒæb] *vt* dare colpetti a ▷ *n* (*Med:
inf*) puntura; **to ~ sth into** affondare *or*
piantare qc dentro

jack [dʒæk] *n* (*Aut*) cricco; (*Cards*) fante *m*

jacket ['dʒækɪt] *n* giacca; (*of book*)
copertura; **jacket potato** *n* *patata cotta al
forno con la buccia*

jackpot ['dʒækpɔt] *n* primo premio (in
denaro)

Jacuzzi® [dʒə'kuːzɪ] *n* vasca per
idromassaggio Jacuzzi®

jagged ['dʒægɪd] *adj* seghettato(-a); (*cliffs
etc*) frastagliato(-a)

jail [dʒeɪl] *n* prigione *f* ▷ *vt* mandare in
prigione; **jail sentence** *n* condanna al
carcere

jam [dʒæm] *n* marmellata; (*also:* **traffic
~**) ingorgo; (*inf*) pasticcio ▷ *vt* (*passage
etc*) ingombrare, ostacolare; (*mechanism,
drawer etc*) bloccare; (*Radio*) disturbare con
interferenze ▷ *vi* incepparsi; **to ~ sth into**
forzare qc dentro; infilare qc a forza dentro

Jamaica [dʒə'meɪkə] *n* Giamaica

jammed [dʒæmd] *adj* (*door*) bloccato(-a);
(*rifle, printer*) inceppato(-a)

Jan. *abbr* (= *January*) gen., genn.

janitor ['dʒænɪtəʳ] *n* (*caretaker*) portiere *m*;
(: *Scol*) bidello

January ['dʒænjuərɪ] *n* gennaio

Japan [dʒə'pæn] *n* Giappone *m*; **Japanese**

[dʒæpə'niːz] *adj* giapponese ▷ *n inv*
giapponese *m/f*; *(Ling)* giapponese *m*
jar [dʒɑːʳ] *n (glass)* barattolo, vasetto ▷ *vi*
(sound) stridere; *(colours etc)* stonare
jargon ['dʒɑːgən] *n* gergo
javelin ['dʒævlɪn] *n* giavellotto
jaw [dʒɔː] *n* mascella
jazz [dʒæz] *n* Jazz *m*
jealous ['dʒɛləs] *adj* geloso(-a); **jealousy**
n gelosia
jeans [dʒiːnz] *npl* (blue-)jeans *mpl*
Jello® ['dʒɛləʊ] *(us) n* gelatina di frutta
jelly ['dʒɛlɪ] *n* gelatina; **jellyfish** *n* medusa
jeopardize ['dʒɛpədaɪz] *vt* mettere in
pericolo
jerk [dʒəːk] *n* sobbalzo, scossa; sussulto;
(inf: idiot) tonto(-a) ▷ *vt* dare una scossa a
▷ *vi (vehicles)* sobbalzare
Jersey ['dʒəːzɪ] *n* Jersey *m*
jersey ['dʒəːzɪ] *n* maglia; *(fabric)* jersey *m*
Jesus ['dʒiːzəs] *n* Gesù *m*
jet [dʒɛt] *n (of gas, liquid)* getto; *(Aviat)*
aviogetto; **jet lag** *n* (problemi *mpl*
dovuti allo) sbalzo dei fusi orari; **jet-ski** *vi*
acquascooter *m inv*
jetty ['dʒɛtɪ] *n* molo
Jew [dʒuː] *n* ebreo
jewel ['dʒuːəl] *n* gioiello; **jeweller** *(us*
jeweler) *n* orefice *m*, gioielliere(-a);
jeweller's (shop) *(us* **jewelry store)**
n oreficeria, gioielleria; **jewellery** *(us*
jewelry) *n* gioielli *mpl*
Jewish ['dʒuːɪʃ] *adj* ebreo(-a), ebraico(-a)
jigsaw ['dʒɪgsɔː] *n (also: ~ puzzle)* puzzle
m inv
job [dʒɔb] *n* lavoro; *(employment)* impiego,
posto; **it's not my ~** *(duty)* non è compito
mio; **it's a good ~ that ...** meno male
che ...; **just the ~!** proprio quello che
ci vuole; **job centre** *(brit) n* ufficio di
collocamento; **jobless** *adj* senza lavoro,
disoccupato(-a)
jockey ['dʒɔkɪ] *n* fantino, jockey *m inv*
▷ *vi* **to ~ for position** manovrare per una
posizione di vantaggio
jog [dʒɔg] *vt* urtare ▷ *vi (Sport)* fare footing,
fare jogging; **to ~ sb's memory** rinfrescare
la memoria a qn; **to ~ along** trottare; *(fig)*
andare avanti piano piano; **jogging** *n*
footing *m*, jogging *m*
join [dʒɔɪn] *vt* unire, congiungere; *(become
member of)* iscriversi a; *(meet)* raggiungere;
riunirsi a ▷ *vi (roads, rivers)* confluire ▷ *n*
giuntura; **join in** *vi* partecipare ▷ *vt
fus* unirsi a; **join up** *vi* incontrarsi; *(Mil)*
arruolarsi
joiner ['dʒɔɪnəʳ] *(brit) n* falegname *m*
joint [dʒɔɪnt] *n (Tech)* giuntura; giunto;
(Anat) articolazione *f*, giuntura; *(brit Culin)*

arrosto; *(inf: place)* locale *m*; *(: of cannabis)*
spinello ▷ *adj* comune; **joint account** *n*
(at bank etc) conto in partecipazione, conto
comune; **jointly** *adv* in comune, insieme
joke [dʒəʊk] *n* scherzo; *(funny story)*
barzelletta; *(also:* **practical ~)** beffa ▷ *vi*
scherzare; **to play a ~ on sb** fare uno
scherzo a qn; **joker** *n (Cards)* matta, jolly
m inv
jolly ['dʒɔlɪ] *adj* allegro(-a), gioioso(-a)
▷ *adv (brit: inf)* veramente, proprio
jolt [dʒəʊlt] *n* scossa, sobbalzo ▷ *vt* urtare
Jordan ['dʒɔːdən] *n (country)* Giordania;
(river) Giordano
journal ['dʒəːnl] *n* giornale *m*; rivista;
diario; **journalism** *n* giornalismo;
journalist *n* giornalista *m/f*
journey ['dʒəːnɪ] *n* viaggio; *(distance
covered)* tragitto; **how was your ~?** com'è
andato il viaggio?; **the ~ takes two hours**
il viaggio dura due ore
joy [dʒɔɪ] *n* gioia; **joyrider** *n* chi ruba
un'auto per farvi un giro; **joy stick** *n (Aviat)*
barra di comando; *(Comput)* joystick *m inv*
Jr *abbr* =**junior**
judge [dʒʌdʒ] *n* giudice *m/f* ▷ *vt* giudicare
judo ['dʒuːdəu] *n* judo
jug [dʒʌg] *n* brocca, bricco
juggle ['dʒʌgl] *vi* fare giochi di destrezza;
juggler *n* giocoliere(-a)
juice [dʒuːs] *n* succo; **juicy** ['dʒuːsɪ] *adj*
succoso(-a)
Jul. *abbr* (=July) lug., lu.
July [dʒuː'laɪ] *n* luglio
jumble ['dʒʌmbl] *n* miscuglio ▷ *vt (also:*
~ up) mischiare; **jumble sale** *(brit) n*
vendita di beneficenza

⬤ **JUMBLE SALE**
⬤
⬤ Una **jumble sale** è un mercatino di
⬤ oggetti di seconda mano organizzato
⬤ in chiese, scuole o in circoli ricreativi,
⬤ i cui proventi vengono devoluti in
⬤ beneficenza.

jumbo ['dʒʌmbəu] *adj* **~ jet** jumbo-jet *m
inv*; **~ size** formato gigante
jump [dʒʌmp] *vi* saltare, balzare; *(start)*
sobbalzare; *(increase)* rincarare ▷ *vt* saltare
▷ *n* salto, balzo; sobbalzo
jumper ['dʒʌmpəʳ] *n (brit: pullover)*
maglione *m*, pullover *m inv*; *(us: dress)*
scamiciato
jumper cables *(us) npl* =**jump leads**
jump leads *(brit) npl* cavi *mpl* per batteria
Jun. *abbr* =**junior**
junction ['dʒʌŋkʃən] *n (brit: of roads)*
incrocio; *(of rails)* nodo ferroviario

June [dʒuːn] *n* giugno

jungle ['dʒʌŋgl] *n* giungla

junior ['dʒuːnɪəʳ] *adj, n* **he's ~ to me by 2 years, he's my ~ by 2 years** è più giovane di me (di 2 anni); **he's ~ to me** (*seniority*) è al di sotto di me, ho più anzianità di lui; **junior high school** (*us*) *n* scuola media (*da 12 a 15 anni*); **junior school** (*BRIT*) *n* scuola elementare (*da 8 a 11 anni*)

junk [dʒʌŋk] *n* cianfrusaglie *fpl*; (*cheap goods*) robaccia; **junk food** *n* porcherie *fpl*

junkie ['dʒʌŋkɪ] (*inf*) *n* drogato(-a)

junk mail *n* stampe *fpl* pubblicitarie

Jupiter ['dʒuːpɪtəʳ] *n* (*planet*) Giove *m*

jurisdiction [dʒuərɪs'dɪkʃən] *n* giurisdizione *f*; **it falls** *or* **comes within/outside our ~** è/non è di nostra competenza

jury ['dʒuərɪ] *n* giuria

just [dʒʌst] *adj* giusto(-a) ▷ *adv* **he's ~ done it/left** lo ha appena fatto/è appena partito; **~ right** proprio giusto; **~ 2 o'clock** le 2 precise; **she's ~ as clever as you** è in gamba proprio quanto te; **it's ~ as well that …** meno male che …; **~ as I arrived** proprio mentre arrivavo; **it was ~ before/ enough/here** era poco prima/appena assai/proprio qui; **it's ~ me** sono solo io; **~ missed/caught** appena perso/preso; **~ listen to this!** senta un po' questo!

justice ['dʒʌstɪs] *n* giustizia

justification [dʒʌstɪfɪ'keɪʃən] *n* giustificazione *f*; (*Typ*) giustezza

justify ['dʒʌstɪfaɪ] *vt* giustificare

jut [dʒʌt] *vi* (*also*: **~ out**) sporgersi

juvenile ['dʒuːvənaɪl] *adj* giovane, giovanile; (*court*) dei minorenni; (*books*) per ragazzi ▷ *n* giovane *m/f*, minorenne *m/f*

K *abbr* (= *one thousand*) mille; (= *kilobyte*) K

kangaroo [kæŋgə'ruː] *n* canguro

karaoke [kɑːrə'əukɪ] *n* karaoke *m inv*

karate [kə'rɑːtɪ] *n* karatè *m*

kebab [kə'bæb] *n* spiedino

keel [kiːl] *n* chiglia; **on an even ~** (*fig*) in uno stato normale

keen [kiːn] *adj* (*interest, desire*) vivo(-a); (*eye, intelligence*) acuto(-a); (*competition*) serrato(-a); (*edge*) affilato(-a); (*eager*) entusiasta; **to be ~ to do** *or* **on doing sth** avere una gran voglia di fare qc; **to be ~ on sth** essere appassionato(-a) di qc; **to be ~ on sb** avere un debole per qn

keep [kiːp] (*pt, pp* **kept**) *vt* tenere; (*hold back*) trattenere; (*feed: one's family etc*) mantenere, sostenere; (*a promise*) mantenere; (*chickens, bees, pigs etc*) allevare ▷ *vi* (*food*) mantenersi; (*remain: in a certain state or place*) restare ▷ *n* (*of castle*) maschio; (*food etc*): **enough for his ~** abbastanza per vitto e alloggio; (*inf*): **for ~s** per sempre; **to ~ doing sth** continuare a fare qc; fare qc di continuo; **to ~ sb from doing** impedire a qn di fare; **to ~ sb busy/a place tidy** tenere qn occupato(-a)/un luogo in ordine; **to ~ sth to o.s.** tenere qc per sé; **to ~ sth (back) from sb** celare qc a qn; **to ~ time** (*clock*) andar bene; **keep away** *vt* **to ~ sth/sb away from sb**

tenere qc/qn lontano da qn ▷ vi **to ~ away (from)** stare lontano (da); **keep back** vt (crowds, tears, money) trattenere ▷ vi tenersi indietro; **keep off** vt (dog, person) tenere lontano da ▷ vi stare alla larga; **~ your hands off!** non toccare!, giù le mani!; **"~ off the grass"** "non calpestare l'erba"; **keep on** vi **to ~ on doing** continuare a fare; **to ~ on (about sth)** continuare a insistere (su qc); **keep out** vt tener fuori; **"~ out"** "vietato l'accesso"; **keep up** vt continuare, mantenere ▷ vi **to ~ up with** tener dietro a, andare di pari passo con; (work etc) farcela a seguire; **keeper** n custode m/f, guardiano(-a); **keeping** n (care) custodia; **in keeping with** in armonia con; in accordo con

kennel ['kɛnl] n canile m; **~s** npl canile m; **to put a dog in ~s** mettere un cane al canile

Kenya ['kɛnjə] n Kenia m

kept [kɛpt] pt, pp of **keep**

kerb [kə:b] (BRIT) n orlo del marciapiede

kerosene ['kɛrəsi:n] n cherosene m

ketchup ['kɛtʃəp] n ketchup m inv

kettle ['kɛtl] n bollitore m

key [ki:] n (gen, Mus) chiave f; (of piano, typewriter) tasto ▷ adj chiave inv ▷ vt (also: **~ in**) digitare; **can I have my ~?** posso avere la mia chiave?; **keyboard** n tastiera; **keyhole** n buco della serratura; **keyring** n portachiavi m inv

kg abbr (= kilogram) Kg

khaki ['kɑ:ki] adj cachi ▷ n cachi m

kick [kɪk] vt calciare, dare calci a; (inf: habit etc) liberarsi di ▷ vi (of horse) tirar calci ▷ n calcio; (thrill): **he does it for ~s** lo fa giusto per il piacere di farlo; **kick off** vi (Sport) dare il primo calcio; **kick-off** n (Sport) calcio d'inizio

kid [kɪd] n (inf: child) ragazzino(-a); (animal, leather) capretto ▷ vi (inf) scherzare

kidnap ['kɪdnæp] vt rapire, sequestrare; **kidnapping** n sequestro (di persona)

kidney ['kɪdnɪ] n (Anat) rene m; (Culin) rognone m; **kidney bean** n fagiolo borlotto

kill [kɪl] vt uccidere, ammazzare ▷ n uccisione f; **killer** n uccisore m, killer m inv; assassino(-a); **killing** n assassinio; **to make a killing** (inf) fare un bel colpo

kiln [kɪln] n forno

kilo ['ki:ləu] n chilo; **kilobyte** n (Comput) kilobyte m inv; **kilogram(me)** ['kɪlə ugræm] n chilogrammo; **kilometre** ['kɪlə mi:tər] (us **kilometer**) n chilometro; **kilowatt** ['kɪləuwɔt] n chilowatt m inv

kilt [kɪlt] n gonnellino scozzese

kin [kɪn] n see **next**; **kith**

kind [kaɪnd] adj gentile, buono(-a) ▷ n sorta, specie f; (species) genere m; **what ~ of ...?** che tipo di ...?; **to be two of a ~** essere molto simili; **in ~** (Comm) in natura

kindergarten ['kɪndəgɑ:tn] n giardino d'infanzia

kindly ['kaɪndlɪ] adj pieno(-a) di bontà, benevolo(-a) ▷ adv con bontà, gentilmente; **will you ~ ...** vuole ... per favore

kindness ['kaɪndnɪs] n bontà, gentilezza

king [kɪŋ] n re m inv; **kingdom** n regno, reame m; **kingfisher** n martin m inv pescatore; **king-size(d) bed** n letto king-size

kiosk ['ki:ɔsk] n edicola, chiosco; (BRIT Tel) cabina (telefonica)

kipper ['kɪpər] n aringa affumicata

kiss [kɪs] n bacio ▷ vt baciare; **to ~ (each other)** baciarsi; **kiss of life** n respirazione f bocca a bocca

kit [kɪt] n equipaggiamento, corredo; (set of tools etc) attrezzi mpl; (for assembly) scatola di montaggio

kitchen ['kɪtʃɪn] n cucina

kite [kaɪt] n (toy) aquilone m

kitten ['kɪtn] n gattino(-a), micino(-a)

kiwi ['ki:wi:] n (also: **~ fruit**) kiwi m inv

km abbr (= kilometre) km

km/h abbr (= kilometres per hour) km/h

knack [næk] n **to have the ~ of** avere l'abilità di

knee [ni:] n ginocchio; **kneecap** n rotula

kneel [ni:l] (pt, pp knelt) vi (also: **~ down**) inginocchiarsi

knelt [nɛlt] pt, pp of **kneel**

knew [nju:] pt of **know**

knickers ['nɪkəz] (BRIT) npl mutandine fpl

knife [naɪf] (pl **knives**) n coltello ▷ vt accoltellare, dare una coltellata a

knight [naɪt] n cavaliere m; (Chess) cavallo

knit [nɪt] vt fare a maglia ▷ vi lavorare a maglia; (broken bones) saldarsi; **to ~ one's brows** aggrottare le sopracciglia; **knitting** n lavoro a maglia; **knitting needle** n ferro (da calza); **knitwear** n maglieria

knives [naɪvz] npl of **knife**

knob [nɔb] n bottone m; manopola

knock [nɔk] vt colpire; urtare; (fig: inf) criticare ▷ vi (at door etc): **to ~ at/on** bussare a ▷ n bussata; colpo, botta; **knock down** vt abbattere; **knock off** vi (inf: finish) smettere (di lavorare) ▷ vt (from price) far abbassare; (inf: steal) sgraffignare; **knock out** vt stendere; (Boxing) mettere K.O.; (defeat) battere; **knock over** vt (person) investire; (object) far cadere; **knockout** n (Boxing) knock out m inv ▷ cpd a eliminazione

knot [nɔt] *n* nodo ▷ *vt* annodare
know [nəu] (*pt* **knew**, *pp* **known**) *vt*
sapere; (*person, author, place*) conoscere;
I don't ~ non lo so; **do you ~ where
I can …?** sa dove posso …?; **to ~ how
to do** sapere fare; **to ~ about** *or* **of
sth/sb** conoscere qc/qn; **know-
all** *n* sapientone(-a); **know-how** *n*
tecnica; pratica; **knowing** *adj* (*look etc*)
d'intesa; **knowingly** *adv* (*purposely*)
consapevolmente; (*smile, look*) con aria
d'intesa; **know-it-all** (*US*) *n* = **know-all**
knowledge ['nɔlɪdʒ] *n* consapevolezza;
(*learning*) conoscenza, sapere *m*;
knowledgeable *adj* ben informato(-a)
known [nəun] *pp of* **know**
knuckle ['nʌkl] *n* nocca
koala [kəu'ɑːlə] *n* (*also:* **~ bear**) koala *m inv*
Koran [kɔ'rɑːn] *n* Corano
Korea [kə'rɪə] *n* Corea; **Korean** *adj, n*
coreano(-a)
kosher ['kəuʃəʳ] *adj* kasher *inv*
Kosovar, Kosovan ['kɔsəvaʳ, 'kɔsəvən]
adj kosovaro(-a)
Kosovo ['kusəvəu] *n* Kosovo
Kremlin ['krɛmlɪn] *n* **the ~** il Cremlino
Kuwait [ku'weɪt] *n* Kuwait *m*

L (*BRIT*) *abbr* = **learner driver**
l. *abbr* (= *litre*) l
lab [læb] *n abbr* (= *laboratory*) laboratorio
label ['leɪbl] *n* etichetta, cartellino; (*brand:
of record*) casa ▷ *vt* etichettare
labor *etc* ['leɪbəʳ] (*US*) = **labour** *etc*
laboratory [lə'bɔrətərɪ] *n* laboratorio
Labor Day (*US*) *n* festa del lavoro

⬤ **LABOR DAY**
⬤
⬤ Negli Stati Uniti e nel Canada il **Labor
⬤ Day**, la festa del lavoro, cade il primo
⬤ lunedì di settembre, contrariamente a
⬤ quanto accade nella maggior parte dei
⬤ paesi europei dove tale celebrazione ha
⬤ luogo il primo maggio.

labor union (*US*) *n* sindacato
labour ['leɪbəʳ] (*US* **labor**) *n* (*task*) lavoro;
(*workmen*) manodopera; (*Med*): **to be in
~** avere le doglie ▷ *vi* **to ~ (at)** lavorare
duro (a); **L~, the L~ party** (*BRIT*) il partito
laburista, i laburisti; **hard ~** lavori *mpl*
forzati; **labourer** *n* manovale *m*; **farm
labourer** lavoratore *m* agricolo
lace [leɪs] *n* merletto, pizzo; (*of shoe etc*)
laccio ▷ *vt* (*shoe: also:* **~ up**) allacciare
lack [læk] *n* mancanza ▷ *vt* mancare di;
through *or* **for ~ of** per mancanza di; **to be**

~ing mancare; **to be ~ing in** mancare di

lacquer ['lækə'] n lacca

lacy ['leɪsɪ] adj (like lace) che sembra un pizzo

lad [læd] n ragazzo, giovanotto

ladder ['lædə'] n scala; (BRIT: in tights) smagliatura

ladle ['leɪdl] n mestolo

lady ['leɪdɪ] n signora; dama; **L~ Smith** lady Smith; **the ladies' (room)** i gabinetti per signore; **ladybird** (US **ladybug**) n coccinella

lag [læg] n (of time) lasso, intervallo ▷ vi (also: **~ behind**) trascinarsi ▷ vt (pipes) rivestire di materiale isolante

lager ['lɑːgə'] n lager m inv

lagoon [lə'guːn] n laguna

laid [leɪd] pt, pp of **lay**; **laid back** (inf) adj rilassato(-a), tranquillo(-a)

lain [leɪn] pp of **lie**

lake [leɪk] n lago

lamb [læm] n agnello

lame [leɪm] adj zoppo(-a); (excuse etc) zoppicante

lament [lə'mɛnt] n lamento ▷ vt lamentare, piangere

lamp [læmp] n lampada; **lamppost** ['læmppəust] (BRIT) n lampione m; **lampshade** ['læmpʃeɪd] n paralume m

land [lænd] n (as opposed to sea) terra (ferma); (country) paese m; (soil) terreno; suolo; (estate) terreni mpl, terre fpl ▷ vi (from ship) sbarcare; (Aviat) atterrare; (fig: fall) cadere ▷ vt (passengers) sbarcare; (goods) scaricare; **to ~ sb with sth** affibbiare qc a qn; **landing** n atterraggio; (of staircase) pianerottolo; **landing card** n carta di sbarco; **landlady** n padrona or proprietaria di casa; **landlord** n padrone m or proprietario di casa; (of pub etc) padrone m; **landmark** n punto di riferimento; (fig) pietra miliare; **landowner** n proprietario(-a) terriero(-a); **landscape** n paesaggio; **landslide** n (Geo) frana; (fig: Pol) valanga

lane [leɪn] n stradina; (Aut, in race) corsia; **"get in ~"** "immettersi in corsia"

language ['læŋgwɪdʒ] n lingua; (way one speaks) linguaggio; **what ~s do you speak?** che lingue parla?; **bad ~** linguaggio volgare; **language laboratory** n laboratorio linguistico

lantern ['læntn] n lanterna

lap [læp] n (of track) giro; (of body): **in** or **on one's ~** in grembo ▷ vt (also: **~ up**) papparsi, leccare ▷ vi (waves) sciabordare

lapel [lə'pɛl] n risvolto

lapse [læps] n lapsus m inv; (longer) caduta ▷ vi (law) cadere; (membership, contract)

scadere; **to ~ into bad habits** pigliare cattive abitudini; **~ of time** spazio di tempo

laptop (computer) ['læptɔp-] n laptop m inv

lard [lɑːd] n lardo

larder ['lɑːdə'] n dispensa

large [lɑːdʒ] adj grande; (person, animal) grosso(-a); **at ~** (free) in libertà; (generally) in generale; nell'insieme; **largely** adv in gran parte; **large-scale** adj (map, drawing etc) in grande scala; (reforms, business activities) su vasta scala

lark [lɑːk] n (bird) allodola; (joke) scherzo, gioco

laryngitis [lærɪn'dʒaɪtɪs] n laringite f

lasagne [lə'zænjə] n lasagne fpl

laser ['leɪzə'] n laser m; **laser printer** n stampante f laser inv

lash [læʃ] n frustata; (also: **eye~**) ciglio ▷ vt frustare; (tie): **to ~ to/together** legare a insieme; **lash out** vi **to ~ out (at** or **against sb)** attaccare violentemente (qn)

lass [læs] n ragazza

last [lɑːst] adj ultimo(-a); (week, month, year) scorso(-a), passato(-a) ▷ adv per ultimo ▷ vi durare; **~ week** la settimana scorsa; **~ night** ieri sera, la notte scorsa; **at ~** finalmente, alla fine; **~ but one** penultimo(-a); **lastly** adv infine, per finire; **last-minute** adj fatto(-a) (or preso(-a) etc) all'ultimo momento

latch [lætʃ] n chiavistello; **latch onto** vt fus (cling to: person) attaccarsi a, appiccicarsi a; (: idea) afferrare, capire

late [leɪt] adj (not on time) in ritardo; (far on in day etc) tardi inv; tardo(-a); (former) ex; (dead) defunto(-a) ▷ adv tardi; (behind time, schedule) in ritardo; **sorry I'm ~** scusi il ritardo; **the flight is two hours ~** il volo ha due ore di ritardo; **it's too ~** è troppo tardi; **of ~** di recente; **in the ~ afternoon** nel tardo pomeriggio; **in ~ May** verso la fine di maggio; **latecomer** n ritardatario(-a); **lately** adv recentemente; **later** ['leɪtə'] adj (date etc) posteriore; (version etc) successivo(-a) ▷ adv più tardi; **later on** più avanti; **latest** ['leɪtɪst] adj ultimo(-a), più recente; **at the latest** al più tardi

lather ['lɑːðə'] n schiuma di sapone ▷ vt insaponare

Latin ['lætɪn] n latino ▷ adj latino(-a); **Latin America** n America Latina; **Latin American** adj sudamericano(-a)

latitude ['lætɪtjuːd] n latitudine f; (fig) libertà d'azione

latter ['lætə'] adj secondo(-a), più recente ▷ n **the ~** quest'ultimo, il secondo

laugh [lɑːf] n risata ▷ vi ridere; **laugh at**

vt fus (misfortune etc) ridere di; **laughter** *n* riso; risate *fpl*

launch [lɔ:ntʃ] *n (of rocket, Comm)* lancio; *(of new ship)* varo; *(also: **motor ~**)* lancia ▷ *vt (rocket, Comm)* lanciare; *(ship, plan)* varare; **launch into** *vt fus* lanciarsi in

launder ['lɔ:ndə'] *vt* lavare e stirare

Launderette® [lɔ:n'drɛt] *(BRIT) n* lavanderia (automatica)

Laundromat® ['lɔ:ndrəmæt] *(US) n* lavanderia automatica

laundry ['lɔ:ndrɪ] *n* lavanderia; *(clothes)* biancheria; *(: dirty)* panni *mpl* da lavare

lava ['lɑ:və] *n* lava

lavatory ['lævətərɪ] *n* gabinetto

lavender ['lævəndə'] *n* lavanda

lavish ['lævɪʃ] *adj* copioso(-a), abbondante; *(giving freely):* **~ with** prodigo(-a) di, largo(-a) in ▷ *vt* **to ~ sth on sb** colmare qn di qc

law [lɔ:] *n* legge *f*; **civil/criminal ~** diritto civile/penale; **lawful** *adj* legale, lecito(-a); **lawless** *adj* che non conosce nessuna legge

lawn [lɔ:n] *n* tappeto erboso; **lawnmower** *n* tosaerba *m or f inv*

lawsuit ['lɔ:su:t] *n* processo, causa

lawyer ['lɔ:jə'] *n (for sales, wills etc)* ≈ notaio; *(partner, in court)* ≈ avvocato(-essa)

lax [læks] *adj* rilassato(-a), negligente

laxative ['læksətɪv] *n* lassativo

lay [leɪ] *(pt, pp laid) pt of lie* ▷ *adj* laico(-a); *(not expert)* profano(-a) ▷ *vt* posare, mettere; *(eggs)* fare; *(trap)* tendere; *(plans)* fare, elaborare; **to ~ the table** apparecchiare la tavola; **lay down** *vt* mettere giù; *(rules etc)* formulare, fissare; **to ~ down the law** dettar legge; **to ~ down one's life** dare la propria vita; **lay off** *vt (workers)* licenziare; **lay on** *vt (provide)* fornire; **lay out** *vt (display)* presentare, disporre; **lay-by** *(BRIT) n* piazzola (di sosta)

layer ['leɪə'] *n* strato

layman ['leɪmən] *(irreg) n* laico; profano

layout ['leɪaut] *n* lay-out *m inv*, disposizione *f*; *(Press)* impaginazione *f*

lazy ['leɪzɪ] *adj* pigro(-a)

lb. *abbr* = **pound** *(weight)*

lead¹ [li:d] *(pt, pp led) n (front position)* posizione *f* di testa; *(distance, time ahead)* vantaggio; *(clue)* indizio; *(Elec)* filo (elettrico); *(for dog)* guinzaglio; *(Theatre)* parte *f* principale ▷ *vt* guidare, condurre; *(induce)* indurre; *(be leader of)* essere a capo di ▷ *vi* condurre; *(Sport)* essere in testa; **in the ~** in testa; **to ~ the way** fare strada; **lead up to** *vt fus* portare a

lead² [lɛd] *n (metal)* piombo; *(in pencil)* mina

leader ['li:də'] *n* capo; leader *m inv*; *(in newspaper)* articolo di fondo; *(Sport)* chi è in testa; **leadership** *n* direzione *f*; capacità di comando

lead-free ['lɛdfri:] *adj* senza piombo

leading ['li:dɪŋ] *adj* primo(-a), principale

lead singer *n* cantante alla testa di un gruppo

leaf [li:f] *(pl leaves) n* foglia ▷ *vi* **to ~ through sth** sfogliare qc; **to turn over a new ~** cambiar vita

leaflet ['li:flɪt] *n* dépliant *m inv*; *(Pol, Rel)* volantino

league [li:g] *n* lega; *(Football)* campionato; **to be in ~ with** essere in lega con

leak [li:k] *n (out)* fuga; *(in)* infiltrazione *f*; *(security leak)* fuga d'informazioni ▷ *vi (roof, bucket)* perdere; *(liquid)* uscire; *(shoes)* lasciar passare l'acqua ▷ *vt (information)* divulgare

lean [li:n] *(pt, pp leaned or leant) adj* magro(-a) ▷ *vt* **to ~ sth on sth** appoggiare qc su qc ▷ *vi (slope)* pendere; *(rest):* **to ~ against** appoggiarsi contro; essere appoggiato(-a) a; **to ~ on** appoggiarsi a; **lean forward** *vi* sporgersi in avanti; **lean over** *vi* inclinarsi; **leaning** *n* **leaning (towards)** propensione *f* (per)

leant [lɛnt] *pt, pp of* **lean**

leap [li:p] *(pt, pp leaped or leapt) n* salto, balzo ▷ *vi* saltare, balzare

leapt [lɛpt] *pt, pp of* **leap**

leap year *n* anno bisestile

learn [lə:n] *(pt, pp learned or learnt) vt, vi* imparare; **to ~ about sth** *(hear, read)* apprendere qc; **to ~ to do sth** imparare a fare qc; **learner** *n* principiante *m/f*; apprendista *m/f*; *(BRIT: also: **learner driver**)* guidatore(-a) principiante; **learning** *n* erudizione *f*, sapienza

learnt [lə:nt] *pt, pp of* **learn**

lease [li:s] *n* contratto d'affitto ▷ *vt* affittare

leash [li:ʃ] *n* guinzaglio

least [li:st] *adj* **the ~** *(+ noun)* il (la) più piccolo(-a), il (la) minimo(-a); *(smallest amount of)* il (la) meno ▷ *adv (+ verb)* meno; **the ~** *(+ adjective):* **the ~ beautiful girl** la ragazza meno bella; **the ~ possible effort** il minimo sforzo possibile; **I have the ~ money** ho meno denaro di tutti; **at ~** almeno; **not in the ~** affatto, per nulla

leather ['lɛðə'] *n* cuoio

leave [li:v] *(pt, pp left) vt* lasciare; *(go away from)* partire da ▷ *vi* partire, andarsene; *(bus, train)* partire ▷ *n (time off)* congedo; *(Mil, consent)* licenza; **what time does the train/bus ~?** a che ora parte il treno/

l'autobus?; **to be left** rimanere; **there's some milk left over** c'è rimasto del latte; **on ~** in congedo; **leave behind** vt (person, object) lasciare; (: forget) dimenticare; **leave out** vt omettere, tralasciare

leaves [li:vz] npl of **leaf**

Lebanon ['lɛbənən] n Libano

lecture ['lɛktʃəʳ] n conferenza; (Scol) lezione f ▷ vi fare conferenze; fare lezioni ▷ vt (scold): **to ~ sb on** or **about sth** rimproverare qn or fare una ramanzina a qn per qc; **to give a ~ on** tenere una conferenza su; **lecture hall** n aula magna; **lecturer** ['lɛktʃərəʳ] (BRIT) n (at university) professore(-essa), docente m/f; **lecture theatre** n = **lecture hall**

led [lɛd] pt, pp of **lead**

ledge [lɛdʒ] n (of window) davanzale m; (on wall etc) sporgenza; (of mountain) cornice f, cengia

leek [li:k] n porro

left [lɛft] pt, pp of **leave** ▷ adj sinistro(-a) ▷ adv a sinistra ▷ n sinistra; **on the ~, to the ~** a sinistra; **the L~** (Pol) la sinistra; **left-hand** adj **the left-hand side** il lato sinistro; **left-hand drive** adj guida a sinistra; **left-handed** adj mancino(-a); **left-luggage locker** n armadietto per deposito bagagli; **left-luggage (office)** (BRIT) n deposito m bagagli inv; **left-overs** npl avanzi mpl, resti mpl; **left-wing** adj (Pol) di sinistra

leg [lɛg] n gamba; (of animal) zampa; (of furniture) piede m; (Culin: of chicken) coscia; (of journey) tappa; **1st/2nd ~** (Sport) partita di andata/ritorno

legacy ['lɛgəsɪ] n eredità f inv

legal ['li:gl] adj legale; **legal holiday** (US) n giorno festivo, festa nazionale; **legalize** vt legalizzare; **legally** adv legalmente; **legally binding** legalmente vincolante

legend ['lɛdʒənd] n leggenda; **legendary** ['lɛdʒəndərɪ] adj leggendario(-a)

leggings ['lɛgɪŋz] npl ghette fpl

legible ['lɛdʒəbl] adj leggibile

legislation [lɛdʒɪsˈleɪʃən] n legislazione f

legislative ['lɛdʒɪslətɪv] adj legislativo(-a)

legitimate [lɪˈdʒɪtɪmət] adj legittimo(-a)

leisure ['lɛʒəʳ] n agio, tempo libero; ricreazioni fpl; **at ~** con comodo; **leisure centre** n centro di ricreazione; **leisurely** adj tranquillo(-a), fatto(-a) con comodo or senza fretta

lemon ['lɛmən] n limone m; **lemonade** [-'neɪd] n limonata; **lemon tea** n tè m inv al limone

lend [lɛnd] (pt, pp lent) vt **to ~ sth (to sb)** prestare qc (a qn); **could you ~ me some money?** mi può prestare dei soldi?

length [lɛŋθ] n lunghezza; (distance) distanza; (section: of road, pipe etc) pezzo, tratto; (of time) periodo; **at ~** (at last) finalmente, alla fine; (lengthily) a lungo; **lengthen** vt allungare, prolungare ▷ vi allungarsi; **lengthways** adv per il lungo; **lengthy** adj molto lungo(a)

lens [lɛnz] n lente f; (of camera) obiettivo

Lent [lɛnt] n Quaresima

lent [lɛnt] pt, pp of **lend**

lentil ['lɛntl] n lenticchia

Leo ['li:əu] n Leone m

leopard ['lɛpəd] n leopardo

leotard ['li:ətɑːd] n calzamaglia

leprosy ['lɛprəsɪ] n lebbra

lesbian ['lɛzbɪən] n lesbica

less [lɛs] adj, pron, adv meno ▷ prep ~ **tax/10% discount** meno tasse/il 10% di sconto; ~ **than ever** meno che mai; ~ **than half** meno della metà; ~ **and ~** sempre meno; **the ~ he works ...** meno lavora ...; **lessen** ['lɛsn] vi diminuire, attenuarsi ▷ vt diminuire, ridurre; **lesser** ['lɛsəʳ] adj minore, più piccolo(-a); **to a lesser extent** in grado or misura minore

lesson ['lɛsn] n lezione f; **to teach sb a ~** dare una lezione a qn

let [lɛt] (pt, pp let) vt lasciare; (BRIT: lease) dare in affitto; **to ~ sb do sth** lasciar fare qc a qn, lasciare che qn faccia qc; **to ~ sb know sth** far sapere qc a qn; **~'s go** andiamo; **~ him come** lo lasci venire; **"to ~"** "affittasi"; **let down** vt (lower) abbassare; (dress) allungare; (hair) sciogliere; (tyre) sgonfiare; (disappoint) deludere; **let in** vt lasciare entrare; (visitor etc) far entrare; **let off** vt (allow to go) lasciare andare; (firework etc) far partire; **let out** vt lasciare uscire; (scream) emettere

lethal ['li:θl] adj letale, mortale

letter ['lɛtəʳ] n lettera; **letterbox** (BRIT) n buca delle lettere

lettuce ['lɛtɪs] n lattuga, insalata

leukaemia [lu:ˈki:mɪə] (US **leukemia**) n leucemia

level ['lɛvl] adj piatto(-a), piano(-a); orizzontale ▷ adv **to draw ~ with** mettersi alla pari di ▷ n livello ▷ vt livellare, spianare; **to be ~ with** essere alla pari di; **level crossing** (BRIT) n passaggio a livello

lever ['li:vəʳ] n leva; **leverage** n **leverage (on** or **with)** forza (su); (fig) ascendente m (su)

levy ['lɛvɪ] n tassa, imposta ▷ vt imporre

liability [laɪəˈbɪlətɪ] n responsabilità f inv; (handicap) peso

liable ['laɪəbl] adj (subject): ~ **to**

soggetto(-a) a; passibile di; *(responsible)*: ~ **for** responsabile (di); *(likely)*: ~ **to do** propenso(-a) a fare
liaise [liː'eɪz] *vi* **to ~ (with)** mantenere i contatti (con)
liar ['laɪəʳ] *n* bugiardo(-a)
liberal ['lɪbərl] *adj* liberale; *(generous)*: **to be ~ with** distribuire liberalmente; **Liberal Democrat** *n* liberaldemocratico(-a)
liberate ['lɪbəreɪt] *vt* liberare
liberation [lɪbə'reɪʃən] *n* liberazione *f*
liberty ['lɪbətɪ] *n* libertà *f* inv; **at ~** *(criminal)* in libertà; **at ~ to do** libero(-a) di fare
Libra ['liːbrə] *n* Bilancia
librarian [laɪ'brɛərɪən] *n* bibliotecario(-a)
library ['laɪbrərɪ] *n* biblioteca
Libya ['lɪbɪə] *n* Libia
lice [laɪs] *npl of* **louse**
licence ['laɪsns] *(US* **license***)* *n* autorizzazione *f*, permesso; *(Comm)* licenza; *(Radio, TV)* canone *m*, abbonamento; *(also:* **driving ~**: *US: also:* **driver's license***)* patente *f* di guida; *(excessive freedom)* licenza
license ['laɪsns] *n (US)* = **licence** ▷ *vt* dare una licenza a; **licensed** *adj (for alcohol)* che ha la licenza di vendere bibite alcoliche; **license plate** *(esp US)* *n (Aut)* targa (automobilistica); **licensing hours** *(BRIT)* *npl* orario d'apertura *(di un pub)*
lick [lɪk] *vt* leccare; *(inf: defeat)* stracciare; **to ~ one's lips** *(fig)* leccarsi i baffi
lid [lɪd] *n* coperchio; *(eyelid)* palpebra
lie [laɪ] *(pt* **lay***, pp* **lain***)* *vi (rest)* giacere, star disteso(-a); *(of object: be situated)* trovarsi, essere; *(tell lies: pt, pp* **lied***)* mentire, dire bugie ▷ *n* bugia, menzogna; **to ~ low** *(fig)* latitare; **lie about** *or* **around** *vi (things)* essere in giro; *(person)* bighellonare; **lie down** *vi* stendersi, sdraiarsi
Liechtenstein ['lɪktənstaɪn] *n* Liechtenstein *m*
lie-in ['laɪɪn] *(BRIT)* *n* **to have a ~** rimanere a letto
lieutenant [lɛf'tɛnənt, *(US)* luː'tɛnənt] *n* tenente *m*
life [laɪf] *(pl* **lives***)* *n* vita ▷ *cpd* di vita; della vita; a vita; **to come to ~** rianimarsi; **life assurance** *(BRIT)* *n* = **life insurance**; **lifeboat** *n* scialuppa di salvataggio; **lifeguard** *n* bagnino; **life insurance** *n* assicurazione *f* sulla vita; **life jacket** *n* giubbotto di salvataggio; **lifelike** *adj* verosimile; rassomigliante; **life preserver** [-prɪ'zə:vəʳ] *(US)* *n* salvagente *m*; giubbotto di salvataggio; **life sentence** *n* ergastolo; **lifestyle** *n* stile *m* di vita; **lifetime** *n* **in his lifetime** durante

la sua vita; **once in a lifetime** una volta nella vita
lift [lɪft] *vt* sollevare; *(ban, rule)* levare ▷ *vi (fog)* alzarsi ▷ *n (BRIT: elevator)* ascensore *m*; **to give sb a ~** *(BRIT)* dare un passaggio a qn; **can you give me a ~ to the station?** può darmi un passaggio fino alla stazione?; **lift up** *vt* sollevare, alzare; **lift-off** *n* decollo
light [laɪt] *(pt, pp* **lighted** *or* **lit***)* *n* luce *f*, lume *m*; *(daylight)* luce *f*, giorno; *(lamp)* lampada; *(Aut: rear light)* luce *f* di posizione; *(: headlamp)* fanale *m*; *(for cigarette etc)*: **have you got a ~?** ha da accendere?; **~s** *npl (Aut: traffic lights)* semaforo *vt (candle, cigarette, fire)* accendere; *(room)*: **to be lit by** essere illuminato(-a) da *adj (room, colour)* chiaro(-a); *(not heavy, also fig)* leggero(-a); **to come to ~** venire alla luce, emergere; **light up** *vi* illuminarsi ▷ *vt* illuminare; **light bulb** *n* lampadina; **lighten** *vt (make less heavy)* alleggerire; **lighter** *n (also:* **cigarette lighter***)* accendino; **light-hearted** *adj* gioioso(-a), gaio(-a); **lighthouse** *n* faro; **lighting** *n* illuminazione *f*; **lightly** *adv* leggermente; **to get off lightly** cavarsela a buon mercato
lightning ['laɪtnɪŋ] *n* lampo, fulmine *m*
lightweight ['laɪtweɪt] *adj (suit)* leggero(-a) ▷ *n (Boxing)* peso leggero
like [laɪk] *vt (person)* volere bene a; *(activity, object, food)*: **I ~ swimming/ that book/chocolate** mi piace nuotare/quel libro/il cioccolato ▷ *prep* come ▷ *adj* simile, uguale ▷ *n* **the ~** uno(-a) uguale; **his ~s and dis~s** i suoi gusti; **I would ~, I'd ~** mi piacerebbe, vorrei; **would you ~ a coffee?** gradirebbe un caffè?; **to be/look ~ sb/sth** somigliare a qn/qc; **what does it look/taste ~?** che aspetto/gusto ha?; **what does it sound ~?** come fa?; **that's just ~ him** è proprio da lui; **do it ~ this** fallo così; **it is nothing ~ ...** non è affatto come ...; **likeable** *adj* simpatico(-a)
likelihood ['laɪklɪhud] *n* probabilità
likely ['laɪklɪ] *adj* probabile; plausibile; **he's ~ to leave** probabilmente partirà, è probabile che parta; **not ~!** neanche per sogno!
likewise ['laɪkwaɪz] *adv* similmente, nello stesso modo
liking ['laɪkɪŋ] *n* **~ (for)** debole *m* (per); **to be to sb's ~** piacere a qn
lilac ['laɪlək] *n* lilla *m inv*
Lilo® ['laɪləu] *n* materassino gonfiabile
lily ['lɪlɪ] *n* giglio
limb [lɪm] *n* arto

limbo ['lɪmbəʊ] *n* **to be in ~** (*fig*) essere lasciato(-a) nel dimenticatoio

lime [laɪm] *n* (*tree*) tiglio; (*fruit*) limetta; (*Geo*) calce *f*

limelight ['laɪmlaɪt] *n* **in the ~** (*fig*) alla ribalta, in vista

limestone ['laɪmstəʊn] *n* pietra calcarea; (*Geo*) calcare *m*

limit ['lɪmɪt] *n* limite *m* ▷ *vt* limitare; **limited** *adj* limitato(-a), ristretto(-a); **to be limited to** limitarsi a

limousine ['lɪməzi:n] *n* limousine *f inv*

limp [lɪmp] *n* **to have a ~** zoppicare ▷ *vi* zoppicare ▷ *adj* floscio(-a), flaccido(-a)

line [laɪn] *n* linea; (*rope*) corda; (*for fishing*) lenza; (*wire*) filo; (*of poem*) verso; (*row, series*) fila, riga; coda; (*on face*) ruga ▷ *vt* (*clothes*): **to ~ (with)** foderare (di); (*box*): **to ~ (with)** rivestire *or* foderare (di); (*trees, crowd*) fiancheggiare; **~ of business** settore *m or* ramo d'attività; **in ~ with** in linea con; **line up** *vi* allinearsi, mettersi in fila ▷ *vt* mettere in fila; (*event, celebration*) preparare

linear ['lɪnɪəʳ] *adj* lineare

linen ['lɪnɪn] *n* biancheria, panni *mpl*; (*cloth*) tela di lino

liner ['laɪnəʳ] *n* nave *f* di linea; (*for bin*) sacchetto

line-up ['laɪnʌp] *n* allineamento, fila; (*Sport*) formazione *f* di gioco

linger ['lɪŋgəʳ] *vi* attardarsi; indugiare; (*smell, tradition*) persistere

lingerie ['lænʒəri:] *n* biancheria intima femminile

linguist ['lɪŋgwɪst] *n* linguista *m/f*; poliglotta *m/f*; **linguistic** *adj* linguistico(-a)

lining ['laɪnɪŋ] *n* fodera

link [lɪŋk] *n* (*of a chain*) anello; (*relationship*) legame *m*; (*connection*) collegamento ▷ *vt* collegare, unire, congiungere; (*associate*): **to ~ with** *or* **to** collegare a; **~s** *npl* (*Golf*) pista *or* terreno da golf; **link up** *vt* collegare, unire ▷ *vi* riunirsi; associarsi

lion ['laɪən] *n* leone *m*; **lioness** *n* leonessa

lip [lɪp] *n* labbro; (*of cup etc*) orlo; **lip-read** *vi* leggere sulle labbra; **lip salve** [-sælv] *n* burro di cacao; **lipstick** *n* rossetto

liqueur [lɪ'kjʊəʳ] *n* liquore *m*

liquid ['lɪkwɪd] *n* liquido ▷ *adj* liquido(-a); **liquidizer** *n* frullatore *m* (a brocca)

liquor ['lɪkəʳ] *n* alcool *m*; **liquor store** (*us*) *n* negozio di liquori

Lisbon ['lɪzbən] *n* Lisbona

lisp [lɪsp] *n* pronuncia blesa della "s"

list [lɪst] *n* lista, elenco ▷ *vt* (*write down*) mettere in lista; fare una lista di; (*enumerate*) elencare

listen ['lɪsn] *vi* ascoltare; **to ~ to** ascoltare; **listener** *n* ascoltatore(-trice)

lit [lɪt] *pt, pp of* **light**

liter ['li:təʳ] (*us*) *n* = **litre**

literacy ['lɪtərəsɪ] *n* il sapere leggere e scrivere

literal ['lɪtərl] *adj* letterale, **literally** *adv* alla lettera, letteralmente

literary ['lɪtərərɪ] *adj* letterario(-a)

literate ['lɪtərət] *adj* che sa leggere e scrivere

literature ['lɪtərɪtʃəʳ] *n* letteratura; (*brochures etc*) materiale *m*

litre ['li:təʳ] (*us* **liter**) *n* litro

litter ['lɪtəʳ] *n* (*rubbish*) rifiuti *mpl*; (*young animals*) figliata; **litter bin** (*BRIT*) *n* cestino per rifiuti; **littered** *adj* **littered with** coperto(-a) di

little ['lɪtl] *adj* (*small*) piccolo(-a); (*not much*) poco(-a) ▷ *adv* poco; **a ~** un po' (di); **a ~ bit** un pochino; **~ by ~** a poco a poco; **little finger** *n* mignolo

live¹ [lɪv] *vi* vivere; (*reside*) vivere, abitare; **where do you ~?** dove abita?; **live together** *vi* vivere insieme, convivere; **live up to** *vt fus* tener fede a, non venir meno a

live² [laɪv] *adj* (*animal*) vivo(-a); (*wire*) sotto tensione; (*bullet, missile*) inesploso(-a); (*broadcast*) diretto(-a); (*performance*) dal vivo

livelihood ['laɪvlɪhud] *n* mezzi *mpl* di sostentamento

lively ['laɪvlɪ] *adj* vivace, vivo(-a)

liven up ['laɪvn'ʌp] *vt* (*discussion, evening*) animare ▷ *vi* ravvivarsi

liver ['lɪvəʳ] *n* fegato

lives [laɪvz] *npl of* **life**

livestock ['laɪvstɔk] *n* bestiame *m*

living ['lɪvɪŋ] *adj* vivo(-a), vivente ▷ *n* **to earn** *or* **make a ~** guadagnarsi la vita; **living room** *n* soggiorno

lizard ['lɪzəd] *n* lucertola

load [ləʊd] *n* (*weight*) peso; (*thing carried*) carico ▷ *vt* (*also:* **~ up**): **to ~ (with)** (*lorry, ship*) caricare (di); (*gun, camera, Comput*) caricare (con); **a ~ of, ~s of** (*fig*) un sacco di; **loaded** *adj* (*vehicle*): **loaded (with)** carico(-a) (di); (*question*) capzioso(-a); (*inf: rich*) carico(-a) di soldi

loaf [ləʊf] (*pl* **loaves**) *n* pane *m*, pagnotta

loan [ləʊn] *n* prestito ▷ *vt* dare in prestito; **on ~** in prestito

loathe [ləʊð] *vt* detestare, aborrire

loaves [ləʊvz] *npl of* **loaf**

lobby ['lɔbɪ] *n* atrio, vestibolo; (*Pol: pressure group*) gruppo di pressione ▷ *vt* fare pressione su

lobster ['lɔbstə^r] n aragosta
local ['ləukl] adj locale ▷ n (BRIT: pub)
≈ bar m inv all'angolo; **the ~s** npl (local
inhabitants) la gente della zona; **local
anaesthetic** n anestesia locale; **local
authority** n ente m locale; **local
government** n amministrazione f locale;
locally ['ləukəlɪ] adv da queste parti; nel
vicinato
locate [ləu'keɪt] vt (find) trovare; (situate)
collocare; situare
location [ləu'keɪʃən] n posizione f; **on ~**
(Cinema) all'esterno
loch [lɔx] n lago
lock [lɔk] n (of door, box) serratura; (of
canal) chiusa; (of hair) ciocca, riccio ▷ vt
(with key) chiudere a chiave ▷ vi (door etc)
chiudersi; (wheels) bloccarsi, incepparsi;
lock in vt chiudere dentro (a chiave);
lock out vt chiudere fuori; **lock up** vt
(criminal, mental patient) rinchiudere;
(house) chiudere (a chiave) ▷ vi chiudere
tutto (a chiave)
locker ['lɔkə^r] n armadietto; **locker-room**
(US) n (Sport) spogliatoio
locksmith ['lɔksmɪθ] n magnano
locomotive [ləukə'məutɪv] n
locomotiva
lodge [lɔdʒ] n casetta, portineria; (hunting
lodge) casino di caccia ▷ vi (person): **to
~ (with)** essere a pensione (presso or
da); (bullet etc) conficcarsi ▷ vt (appeal
etc) presentare, fare; **to ~ a complaint**
presentare un reclamo; **lodger** n
affittuario(-a); (with room and meals)
pensionante m/f
lodging ['lɔdʒɪŋ] n alloggio; see also
board
loft [lɔft] n solaio, soffitta
log [lɔg] n (of wood) ceppo; (also: **~book**:
Naut, Aviat) diario di bordo; (Aut) libretto
di circolazione ▷ vt registrare; **log in** vi
(Comput) aprire una sessione (con codice
di riconoscimento); **log off** vi (Comput)
terminare una sessione
logic ['lɔdʒɪk] n logica; **logical** adj
logico(-a)
logo ['ləugəu] n logo m inv
lollipop ['lɔlɪpɔp] n lecca lecca m inv
lolly ['lɔlɪ] (inf) n lecca lecca m inv; (also: **ice
~**) ghiacciolo; (money) grana
London ['lʌndən] n Londra; **Londoner** n
londinese m/f
lone [ləun] adj solitario(-a)
loneliness ['ləunlɪnɪs] n solitudine f,
isolamento
lonely ['ləunlɪ] adj solo(-a); solitario(-a),
isolato(-a)
long [lɔŋ] adj lungo(-a) ▷ adv a lungo,

per molto tempo ▷ vi **to ~ for sth/to do**
desiderare qc/di fare, non veder l'ora di
aver qc/di fare; **so** or **as ~ as** (while) finché;
(provided that) sempre che + sub; **don't be
~!** fai presto!; **how ~ is this river/course?**
quanto è lungo questo fiume/corso?;
6 metres ~ lungo 6 metri; **6 months ~**
che dura 6 mesi, di 6 mesi; **all night ~**
tutta la notte; **he no ~er comes** non
viene più; **~ before** molto tempo prima;
before ~ (+ future) presto, fra poco; (+ past)
poco tempo dopo; **at ~ last** finalmente;
long-distance adj (race) di fondo; (call)
interurbano(-a); **long-haul** ['lɔŋ,hɔːl] adj
(flight) a lunga percorrenza inv; **longing** n
desiderio, voglia, brama
longitude ['lɔŋgɪtjuːd] n longitudine f
long: long jump n salto in lungo; **long-
life** adj (milk) a lunga conservazione;
(batteries) di lunga durata; **long-sighted**
adj presbite; **long-standing** adj di
vecchia data; **long-term** adj a lungo
termine
loo [luː] (BRIT: inf) n W.C. m inv, cesso
look [luk] vi guardare; (seem) sembrare,
parere; (building etc): **to ~ south/on
to the sea** dare a sud/sul mare ▷ n
sguardo; (appearance) aspetto, aria;
~s npl (good looks) bellezza; **look after**
vt fus occuparsi di, prendere cura di;
(keep an eye on) guardare, badare a; **look
around** vi guardarsi intorno; **look at** vt
fus guardare; **look back** vi **to ~ back on**
(event etc) ripensare a; **look down on** vt
fus (fig) guardare dall'alto, disprezzare;
look for vt fus cercare; **we're ~ing for a
hotel/restaurant** stiamo cercando un
albergo/ristorante; **look forward to** vt fus
non veder l'ora di; (in letters): **we ~ forward
to hearing from you** in attesa di una
vostra gentile risposta; **look into** vt fus
esaminare; **look out** vi (beware): **to ~ out
(for)** stare in guardia (per); **look out for** vt
fus cercare; **look round** vi (turn) girarsi,
voltarsi; (in shop) dare un'occhiata; **look
through** vt fus (papers, book) scorrere;
(telescope) guardare attraverso; **look up**
vi alzare gli occhi; (improve) migliorare
▷ vt (word) cercare; (friend) andare a
trovare; **look up to** vt fus avere rispetto
per; **lookout** n posto d'osservazione;
guardia; **to be on the lookout (for)** stare
in guardia (per)
loom [luːm] n telaio ▷ vi (also: **~ up**)
apparire minaccioso(-a); (event) essere
imminente
loony ['luːnɪ] (inf) n pazzo(-a)
loop [luːp] n cappio ▷ vt **to ~ sth round
sth** passare qc intorno a qc; **loophole** n

via d'uscita; scappatoia

loose [lu:s] *adj* (*knot*) sciolto(-a); (*screw*) allentato(-a); (*stone*) cadente; (*clothes*) ampio(-a), largo(-a); (*animal*) in libertà, scappato(-a); (*life, morals*) dissoluto(-a) ▷ *n* **to be on the ~** essere in libertà; **loosely** *adv* senza stringere; approssimativamente; **loosen** *vt* sciogliere; (*belt etc*) allentare

loot [lu:t] *n* bottino ▷ *vt* saccheggiare

lop-sided ['lɔp'saɪdɪd] *adj* non equilibrato(-a), asimmetrico(-a)

lord [lɔ:d] *n* signore *m*; **L~ Smith** lord Smith; **the L~** il Signore; **good L~!** buon Dio!; **the (House of) L~s** (BRIT) la Camera dei Lord

lorry ['lɔrɪ] (BRIT) *n* camion *m inv*; **lorry driver** (BRIT) *n* camionista *m*

lose [lu:z] (*pt, pp* **lost**) *vt* perdere ▷ *vi* perdere; **I've lost my wallet/passport** ho perso il portafoglio/passaporto; **to ~ (time)** (*clock*) ritardare; **lose out** *vi* rimetterci; **loser** *n* perdente *m/f*

loss [lɔs] *n* perdita; **to be at a ~** essere perplesso(-a)

lost [lɔst] *pt, pp of* **lose** ▷ *adj* perduto(-a); **I'm ~** mi sono perso; **lost property** (US **lost and found**) *n* oggetti *mpl* smarriti

lot [lɔt] *n* (*at auctions*) lotto; (*destiny*) destino, sorte *f*; **the ~** tutto(-a) quanto(-a); tutti(-e) quanti(-e); **a ~** molto; **a ~ of** una gran quantità di, un sacco di; **~s of** molto(-a); **to draw ~s (for sth)** tirare a sorte (per qc)

lotion ['ləʊʃən] *n* lozione *f*

lottery ['lɔtərɪ] *n* lotteria

loud [laʊd] *adj* forte, alto(-a); (*gaudy*) vistoso(-a), sgargiante ▷ *adv* (*speak etc*) forte; **out ~** (*read etc*) ad alta voce; **loudly** *adv* fortemente, ad alta voce; **loudspeaker** *n* altoparlante *m*

lounge [laʊndʒ] *n* salotto, soggiorno; (*at airport, station*) sala d'attesa; (BRIT: also: **~ bar**) bar *m inv* con servizio a tavolino ▷ *vi* oziare

louse [laʊs] (*pl* **lice**) *n* pidocchio

lousy ['laʊzɪ] (*inf*) *adj* orrendo(-a), schifoso(-a); **to feel ~** stare da cani

love [lʌv] *n* amore *m* ▷ *vt* amare; voler bene a; **to ~ to do: I ~ to do** mi piace fare; **to be/fall in ~ with** essere innamorato(-a)/innamorarsi di; **to make ~** fare l'amore; **"15 ~"** (*Tennis*) "15 a zero"; **love affair** *n* relazione *f*; **love life** *n* vita sentimentale

lovely ['lʌvlɪ] *adj* bello(-a); (*delicious: smell, meal*) buono(-a)

lover ['lʌvə^r] *n* amante *m/f*; (*person in love*) innamorato(-a); (*amateur*): **a ~ of** un(-un')

amante di; un(-un') appassionato(-a) di

loving ['lʌvɪŋ] *adj* affettuoso(-a)

low [ləʊ] *adj* basso(-a) ▷ *adv* in basso ▷ *n* (*Meteor*) depressione *f*; **to be ~ on** (*supplies etc*) avere scarsità di; **to feel ~** sentirsi giù; **low-alcohol** *adj* a basso contenuto alcolico; **low-calorie** *adj* a basso contenuto calorico

lower ['ləʊə^r] *adj* (*bottom: of 2 things*) più basso; (*less important*) meno importante ▷ *vt* calare; (*prices, eyes, voice*) abbassare

low-fat ['ləʊ'fæt] *adj* magro(-a)

loyal ['lɔɪəl] *adj* fedele, leale; **loyalty** *n* fedeltà, lealtà; **loyalty card** *n* carta che offre sconti a clienti abituali

L.P. *n abbr* = **long-playing record**

L-plates ['ɛlpleɪts] (BRIT) *npl* contrassegno P principiante

Lt *abbr* (= *lieutenant*) Ten.

Ltd *abbr* (= *limited*) ≈ S.r.l.

luck [lʌk] *n* fortuna, sorte *f*; **bad ~** sfortuna, mala sorte; **good ~!** buona fortuna!; **luckily** *adv* fortunatamente, per fortuna; **lucky** *adj* fortunato(-a); (*number etc*) che porta fortuna

lucrative ['lu:krətɪv] *adj* lucrativo(-a), lucroso(-a), profittevole

ludicrous ['lu:dɪkrəs] *adj* ridicolo(-a)

luggage ['lʌgɪdʒ] *n* bagagli *mpl*; **our ~ hasn't arrived** i nostri bagagli non sono arrivati; **luggage rack** *n* portabagagli *m inv*

lukewarm ['lu:kwɔ:m] *adj* tiepido(-a)

lull [lʌl] *n* intervallo di calma ▷ *vt* **to ~ sb to sleep** cullare qn finché si addormenta

lullaby ['lʌləbaɪ] *n* ninnananna

lumber ['lʌmbə^r] *n* (*wood*) legname *m*; (*junk*) roba vecchia

luminous ['lu:mɪnəs] *adj* luminoso(-a)

lump [lʌmp] *n* pezzo; (*in sauce*) grumo; (*swelling*) gonfiore *m*; (*also:* **sugar ~**) zolletta ▷ *vt* (*also:* **~ together**) riunire, mettere insieme; **lump sum** *n* somma globale; **lumpy** *adj* (*sauce*) pieno(-a) di grumi; (*bed*) bitorzoluto(-a)

lunatic ['lu:nətɪk] *adj* pazzo(-a), matto(-a)

lunch [lʌntʃ] *n* pranzo, colazione *f*; **lunch break** *n* intervallo del pranzo; **lunch time** *n* ora di pranzo

lung [lʌŋ] *n* polmone *m*

lure [luə^r] *n* richiamo; lusinga ▷ *vt* attirare (con l'inganno)

lurk [lə:k] *vi* stare in agguato

lush [lʌʃ] *adj* lussureggiante

lust [lʌst] *n* lussuria; cupidigia; desiderio; (*fig*): **~ for** sete *f* di

Luxembourg ['lʌksəmbə:g] *n* (*state*) Lussemburgo *m*; (*city*) Lussemburgo *f*

luxurious [lʌgˈzjuərɪəs] *adj* sontuoso(-a), di lusso
luxury [ˈlʌkʃərɪ] *n* lusso ▷ *cpd* di lusso
Be careful not to translate *luxury* by the Italian word *lussuria*.
Lycra® [ˈlaɪkrə] *n* lycra® *f inv*
lying [ˈlaɪɪŋ] *n* bugie *fpl*, menzogne *fpl* ▷ *adj* bugiardo(-a)
lyrics [ˈlɪrɪks] *npl* (*of song*) parole *fpl*

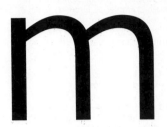

m. *abbr* = **metre; mile; million**
M.A. *abbr* = **Master of Arts**
ma (*inf*) [mɑː] *n* mamma
mac [mæk] (*BRIT*) *n* impermeabile *m*
macaroni [mækəˈrəunɪ] *n* maccheroni *mpl*
Macedonia [mæsɪˈdəunɪə] *n* Macedonia; **Macedonian** [mæsɪˈdəunɪən] *adj* macedone ▷ *n* macedone *m/f*; (*Ling*) macedone *m*
machine [məˈʃiːn] *n* macchina ▷ *vt* (*Tech*) lavorare a macchina; (*dress etc*) cucire a macchina; **machine gun** *n* mitragliatrice *f*; **machinery** *n* macchinario, macchine *fpl*; (*fig*) macchina; **machine washable** *adj* lavabile in lavatrice
macho [ˈmætʃəu] *adj* macho *inv*
mackerel [ˈmækrl] *n inv* sgombro
mackintosh [ˈmækɪntɔʃ] (*BRIT*) *n* impermeabile *m*
mad [mæd] *adj* matto(-a), pazzo(-a); (*foolish*) sciocco(-a); (*angry*) furioso(-a); **to be ~ about** (*keen*) andare pazzo(-a) per
Madagascar [mædəˈgæskəʳ] *n* Madagascar *m*
madam [ˈmædəm] *n* signora
mad cow disease *n* encefalite *f* bovina spongiforme
made [meɪd] *pt, pp of* **make**; **made-to-measure** (*BRIT*) *adj* fatto(-a) su

misura; **made-up** ['meɪdʌp] *adj* (*story*) inventato(-a)

madly ['mædlɪ] *adv* follemente

madman ['mædmən] (*irreg*) *n* pazzo, alienato

madness ['mædnɪs] *n* pazzia

Madrid [mə'drɪd] *n* Madrid *f*

Mafia ['mæfɪə] *n* mafia *f*

mag [mæg] *n abbr* (BRIT *inf*) = **magazine** (*Press*)

magazine [mægə'zi:n] *n* (*Press*) rivista; (*Radio, TV*) rubrica

> Be careful not to translate *magazine* by the Italian word *magazzino*.

maggot ['mægət] *n* baco, verme *m*

magic ['mædʒɪk] *n* magia ▷ *adj* magico(-a); **magical** *adj* magico(-a); **magician** [mə'dʒɪʃən] *n* mago(-a)

magistrate ['mædʒɪstreɪt] *n* magistrato; giudice *m/f*

magnet ['mægnɪt] *n* magnete *m*, calamita; **magnetic** [-'nɛtɪk] *adj* magnetico(-a)

magnificent [mæg'nɪfɪsnt] *adj* magnifico(-a)

magnify ['mægnɪfaɪ] *vt* ingrandire; **magnifying glass** *n* lente *f* d'ingrandimento

magpie ['mægpaɪ] *n* gazza

mahogany [mə'hɔgənɪ] *n* mogano

maid [meɪd] *n* domestica; (*in hotel*) cameriera

maiden name ['meɪdn-] *n* nome *m* da nubile *or* da ragazza

mail [meɪl] *n* posta ▷ *vt* spedire (per posta); **mailbox** (US) *n* cassetta delle lettere; **mailing list** *n* elenco d'indirizzi; **mailman** (*irreg*: US) *n* portalettere *m inv*, postino; **mail-order** *n* vendita (*or* acquisto) per corrispondenza

main [meɪn] *adj* principale ▷ *n* (*pipe*) conduttura principale; **main course** *n* (*Culin*) piatto principale, piatto forte; **mainland** [meɪnlənd] *n* continente *m*; **mainly** *adv* principalmente, soprattutto; **main road** *n* strada principale; **mainstream** *n* (*fig*) corrente *f* principale; **main street** *n* strada principale

maintain [meɪn'teɪn] *vt* mantenere; (*affirm*) sostenere; **maintenance** ['meɪntənəns] *n* manutenzione *f*; (*alimony*) alimenti *mpl*

maisonette [meɪzə'nɛt] *n* (BRIT) appartamento a due piani

maize [meɪz] *n* granturco, mais *m*

majesty ['mædʒɪstɪ] *n* maestà *f inv*

major ['meɪdʒə'] *n* (*Mil*) maggiore *m* ▷ *adj* (*greater, Mus*) maggiore; (*in importance*) principale, importante

Majorca [mə'jɔ:kə] *n* Maiorca

majority [mə'dʒɔrɪtɪ] *n* maggioranza

make [meɪk] (*pt, pp* **made**) *vt* fare; (*manufacture*) fare, fabbricare; (*cause to be*): **to ~ sb sad** *etc* rendere qn triste *etc*; (*force*): **to ~ sb do sth** costringere qn a fare qc, far fare qc a qn; (*equal*): **2 and 2 ~ 4** 2 più 2 fa 4 ▷ *n* fabbricazione *f*; (*brand*) marca; **to ~ a fool of sb** far fare a qn la figura dello scemo; **to ~ a profit** realizzare un profitto; **to ~ a loss** subire una perdita; **to ~ it** (*arrive*) arrivare; (*achieve sth*) farcela; **what time do you ~ it?** che ora fai?; **to ~ do with** arrangiarsi con; **make off** *vi* svignarsela; **make out** *vt* (*write out*) scrivere; (*: cheque*) emettere; (*understand*) capire; (*see*) distinguere; (*: numbers*) decifrare; **make up** *vt* (*constitute*) formare; (*invent*) inventare; (*parcel*) fare ▷ *vi* conciliarsi; (*with cosmetics*) truccarsi; **make up for** *vt fus* compensare; ricuperare; **makeover** ['meɪkəuvə'] *n* (*change of image*) cambiamento di immagine; (*of room, house*) trasformazione *f*; **maker** *n* (*of programme etc*) creatore(-trice); (*manufacturer*) fabbricante *m*; **makeshift** *adj* improvvisato(-a); **make-up** *n* trucco

making ['meɪkɪŋ] *n* (*fig*): **in the ~** in formazione; **to have the ~s of** (*actor, athlete etc*) avere la stoffa di

malaria [mə'lɛərɪə] *n* malaria

Malaysia [mə'leɪzɪə] *n* Malaysia

male [meɪl] *n* (*Biol*) maschio ▷ *adj* maschile; maschio(-a)

malicious [mə'lɪʃəs] *adj* malevolo(-a); (*Law*) doloso(-a)

malignant [mə'lɪgnənt] *adj* (*Med*) maligno(-a)

mall [mɔ:l] *n* (*also*: **shopping ~**) centro commerciale

mallet ['mælɪt] *n* maglio

malnutrition [mælnju:'trɪʃən] *n* denutrizione *f*

malpractice [mæl'præktɪs] *n* prevaricazione *f*; negligenza

malt [mɔ:lt] *n* malto

Malta ['mɔ:ltə] *n* Malta; **Maltese** [mɔ:l'ti:z] *adj, n* (*pl inv*) maltese (*m/f*); (*Ling*) maltese *m*

mammal ['mæml] *n* mammifero

mammoth ['mæməθ] *adj* enorme, gigantesco(-a)

man [mæn] (*pl* **men**) *n* uomo ▷ *vt* fornire d'uomini; stare a; **an old ~** un vecchio; **~ and wife** marito e moglie

manage ['mænɪdʒ] *vi* farcela ▷ *vt* (*be in charge of*) occuparsi di; gestire; **to ~ to do sth** riuscire a far qc; **manageable** *adj* maneggevole; fattibile; **management** *n*

m

amministrazione f, direzione f; **manager**
n direttore m; (of shop, restaurant)
gerente m; (of artist, Sport) manager m
inv; **manageress** [-ə'rɛs] n direttrice
f; gerente f; **managerial** [-ə'dʒɪərɪəl]
adj dirigenziale; **managing director** n
amministratore m delegato

mandarin ['mændərɪn] n (person, fruit)
mandarino

mandate ['mændeɪt] n mandato

mandatory ['mændətərɪ] adj
obbligatorio(-a), ingiuntivo(-a)

mane [meɪn] n criniera

mangetout ['mɔnʒ'tuː] n pisello dolce,
taccola

mango ['mæŋgəu] (pl **mangoes**) n mango

man: **manhole** ['mænhəul] n botola
stradale; **manhood** ['mænhud] n età
virile; virilità

mania ['meɪnɪə] n mania; **maniac**
['meɪnɪæk] n maniaco(-a)

manic ['mænɪk] adj (behaviour, activity)
maniacale

manicure ['mænɪkjuər] n manicure f inv

manifest ['mænɪfɛst] vt manifestare ▷ adj
manifesto(-a), palese

manifesto [mænɪ'fɛstəu] n manifesto

manipulate [mə'nɪpjuleɪt] vt manipolare

man: **mankind** [mæn'kaɪnd] n umanità,
genere m umano; **manly** ['mænlɪ] adj
virile; coraggioso(-a); **man-made** adj
sintetico(-a); artificiale

manner ['mænər] n maniera, modo;
(behaviour) modo di fare; (type, sort):
all ~ of things ogni genere di cosa;
~s npl (conduct) maniere fpl; **bad ~s**
maleducazione f

manoeuvre [mə'nuːvər] (US **maneuver**)
vt manovrare ▷ vi far manovre ▷ n
manovra

manpower ['mænpauər] n manodopera

mansion ['mænʃən] n casa signorile

manslaughter ['mænslɔːtər] n omicidio
preterintenzionale

mantelpiece ['mæntlpiːs] n mensola del
caminetto

manual ['mænjuəl] adj manuale ▷ n
manuale m

manufacture [mænju'fæktʃər] vt fabbricare ▷ n fabbricazione
f, manifattura; **manufacturer** n
fabbricante m

manure [mə'njuər] n concime m

manuscript ['mænjuskrɪpt] n
manoscritto

many ['mɛnɪ] adj molti(-e) ▷ pron
molti(-e); **a great ~** moltissimi(-e), un gran
numero (di); **~ a time** molte volte

map [mæp] n carta (geografica); (of city)

cartina; **can you show it to me on the ~?**
può indicarmelo sulla cartina?

maple ['meɪpl] n acero

mar [maːr] vt sciupare

Mar. abbr (= March) mar.

marathon ['mærəθən] n maratona

marble ['maːbl] n marmo; (toy) pallina,
bilia

March [maːtʃ] n marzo

march [maːtʃ] vi marciare; sfilare ▷ n
marcia

mare [mɛər] n giumenta

margarine [maːdʒə'riːn] n margarina

margin ['maːdʒɪn] n margine m; **marginal**
adj marginale; **marginal seat** (Pol)
seggio elettorale ottenuto con una stretta
maggioranza; **marginally** adv (bigger,
better) lievemente, di poco; (different) un po'

marigold ['mærɪgəuld] n calendola

marijuana [mærɪ'waːnə] n marijuana

marina [mə'riːnə] n marina

marinade n [mærɪ'neɪd] marinata ▷ vt
['mærɪneɪd] = **marinate**

marinate ['mærɪneɪt] vt marinare

marine [mə'riːn] adj (animal, plant)
marino(-a); (forces, engineering)
marittimo(-a) ▷ n (BRIT) fante m di marina;
(US) marine m inv

marital ['mærɪtl] adj maritale, coniugale;
marital status n stato civile

maritime ['mærɪtaɪm] adj marittimo(-a)

marjoram ['maːdʒərəm] n maggiorana

mark [maːk] n segno; (stain) macchia; (of
skid etc) traccia; (BRIT Scol) voto; (Sport)
bersaglio; (currency) marco ▷ vt segnare;
(stain) macchiare; (indicate) indicare; (BRIT
Scol) dare un voto a; correggere; **to ~ time**
segnare il passo; **marked** adj spiccato(-a),
chiaro(-a); **marker** n (sign) segno;
(bookmark) segnalibro

market ['maːkɪt] n mercato ▷ vt (Comm)
mettere in vendita; **marketing** n
marketing m; **marketplace** n (piazza del)
mercato; (world of trade) piazza, mercato;
market research n indagine f or ricerca
di mercato

marmalade ['maːməleɪd] n marmellata
d'arance

maroon [mə'ruːn] vt (also fig): **to be ~ed
(in or at)** essere abbandonato(-a) (in) ▷ adj
bordeaux inv

marquee [maː'kiː] n padiglione m

marriage ['mærɪdʒ] n matrimonio;
marriage certificate n certificato di
matrimonio

married ['mærɪd] adj sposato(-a); (life,
love) coniugale, matrimoniale

marrow ['mærəu] n midollo; (vegetable)
zucca

marry ['mærɪ] *vt* sposare, sposarsi con; (*vicar, priest etc*) dare in matrimonio ▷ *vi* (*also*: **get married**) sposarsi

Mars [mɑːz] *n* (*planet*) Marte *m*

marsh [mɑːʃ] *n* palude *f*

marshal ['mɑːʃl] *n* maresciallo; (*us*: *fire*) capo; (: *police*) capitano ▷ *vt* (*thoughts, support*) ordinare; (*soldiers*) adunare

martyr ['mɑːtə^r] *n* martire *m/f*

marvel ['mɑːvl] *n* meraviglia ▷ *vi* **to ~ (at)** meravigliarsi (di); **marvellous** (*us* **marvelous**) *adj* meraviglioso(-a)

Marxism ['mɑːksɪzəm] *n* marxismo

Marxist ['mɑːksɪst] *adj, n* marxista *m/f*

marzipan ['mɑːzɪpæn] *n* marzapane *m*

mascara [mæs'kɑːrə] *n* mascara *m*

mascot ['mæskət] *n* mascotte *f inv*

masculine ['mæskjulɪn] *adj* maschile; (*woman*) mascolino(-a)

mash [mæʃ] *vt* passare, schiacciare; **mashed potatoes** *npl* purè *m* di patate

mask [mɑːsk] *n* maschera ▷ *vt* mascherare

mason ['meɪsn] *n* (*also*: **stone~**) scalpellino; (*also*: **free~**) massone *m*; **masonry** *n* muratura

mass [mæs] *n* moltitudine *f*, massa; (*Physics*) massa; (*Rel*) messa ▷ *cpd* di massa ▷ *vi* ammassarsi; **the ~es** *npl* (*ordinary people*) le masse; **~es of** (*inf*) una montagna di

massacre ['mæsəkə^r] *n* massacro

massage ['mæsɑːʒ] *n* massaggio

massive ['mæsɪv] *adj* enorme, massiccio(-a)

mass media *npl* mass media *mpl*

mass-produce ['mæsprə'djuːs] *vt* produrre in serie

mast [mɑːst] *n* albero

master ['mɑːstə^r] *n* padrone *m*; (*Art etc, teacher: in primary school*) maestro; (: *in secondary school*) professore *m*; (*title for boys*): **M~ X** Signorino X ▷ *vt* domare; (*learn*) imparare a fondo; (*understand*) conoscere a fondo; **mastermind** *n* mente *f* superiore ▷ *vt* essere il cervello di; **Master of Arts/Science** *n* Master *m inv* in lettere/scienze; **masterpiece** *n* capolavoro

masturbate ['mæstəbeɪt] *vi* masturbare

mat [mæt] *n* stuoia; (*also*: **door~**) stoino, zerbino; (*also*: **table ~**) sottopiatto ▷ *adj* = **matt**

match [mætʃ] *n* fiammifero; (*game*) partita, incontro; (*fig*) uguale *m/f*; matrimonio; partito ▷ *vt* intonare; (*go well with*) andare benissimo con; (*equal*) uguagliare; (*correspond to*) corrispondere a; (*pair: also*: **~ up**) accoppiare ▷ *vi*

combaciare; **to be a good ~** andare bene; **matchbox** *n* scatola per fiammiferi; **matching** *adj* ben assortito(-a)

mate [meɪt] *n* compagno(-a) di lavoro; (*inf*: *friend*) amico(-a); (*animal*) compagno(-a); (*in merchant navy*) secondo ▷ *vi* accoppiarsi

material [mə'tɪərɪəl] *n* (*substance*) materiale *m*, materia; (*cloth*) stoffa ▷ *adj* materiale; **~s** *npl* (*equipment*) materiali *mpl*

materialize [mə'tɪərɪəlaɪz] *vi* materializzarsi, realizzarsi

maternal [mə'təːnl] *adj* materno(-a)

maternity [mə'təːnɪtɪ] *n* maternità; **maternity hospital** *n* ≈ clinica ostetrica; **maternity leave** *n* congedo di maternità

math [mæθ] (*us*) *n* = **maths**

mathematical [mæθə'mætɪkl] *adj* matematico(-a)

mathematician [mæθəmə'tɪʃən] *n* matematico(-a)

mathematics [mæθə'mætɪks] *n* matematica

maths [mæθs] (*us* **math**) *n* matematica

matinée ['mætɪneɪ] *n* matinée *f inv*

matron ['meɪtrən] *n* (*in hospital*) capoinfermiera; (*in school*) infermiera

matt [mæt] *adj* opaco(-a)

matter ['mætə^r] *n* questione *f*; (*Physics*) materia, sostanza; (*content*) contenuto; (*Med: pus*) pus *m* ▷ *vi* importare; **it doesn't ~** non importa; (*I don't mind*) non fa niente; **what's the ~?** che cosa c'è?; **no ~ what** qualsiasi cosa accada; **as a ~ of course** come cosa naturale; **as a ~ of fact** in verità; **~s** *npl* (*affairs*) questioni

mattress ['mætrɪs] *n* materasso

mature [mə'tjuə^r] *adj* maturo(-a); (*cheese*) stagionato(-a) ▷ *vi* maturare; stagionare; **mature student** *n* studente universitario che ha più di 25 anni; **maturity** *n* maturità

maul [mɔːl] *vt* lacerare

mauve [məuv] *adj* malva *inv*

max *abbr* = **maximum**

maximize ['mæksɪmaɪz] *vt* (*profits etc*) massimizzare; (*chances*) aumentare al massimo

maximum ['mæksɪməm] (*pl* **maxima**) *adj* massimo(-a) ▷ *n* massimo

May [meɪ] *n* maggio

may [meɪ] (*conditional* **might**) *vi* (*indicating possibility*): **he ~ come** può darsi che venga; (*be allowed to*): **~ I smoke?** posso fumare?; (*wishes*): **~ God bless you!** Dio la benedica!; **you ~ as well go** tanto vale che tu te ne vada

maybe ['meɪbiː] *adv* forse, può darsi; **~ he'll ...** può darsi che lui ... + *sub*, forse lui ...

May Day *n* il primo maggio

mayhem ['meɪhɛm] *n* cagnara

mayonnaise [meɪə'neɪz] *n* maionese *f*
mayor [mɛəʳ] *n* sindaco; **mayoress** *n* sindaco (*donna*); moglie *f* del sindaco
maze [meɪz] *n* labirinto, dedalo
MD *n abbr* (= *Doctor of Medicine*) titolo di studio; (*Comm*) *see* **managing director**
me [mi:] *pron* mi, m' + *vowel or silent "h"*; (*stressed, after prep*) me; **he heard me** mi ha *or* m'ha sentito; **give me a book** dammi (*or* mi dia*) un libro; **it's me** sono io; **with me** con me; **without me** senza di me
meadow ['mɛdəʊ] *n* prato
meagre ['mi:gəʳ] (*us* **meager**) *adj* magro(-a)
meal [mi:l] *n* pasto; (*flour*) farina; **mealtime** *n* l'ora di mangiare
mean [mi:n] (*pt, pp* **meant**) *adj* (*with money*) avaro(-a), gretto(-a); (*unkind*) meschino(-a), maligno(-a); (*shabby*) misero(-a); (*average*) medio(-a) ▷ *vt* (*signify*) significare, voler dire; (*intend*): **to ~ to do** aver l'intenzione di fare ▷ *n* mezzo; (*Math*) media; **~s** *npl* (*way, money*) mezzi *mpl*; **by ~s of** per mezzo di; **by all ~s** ma certo, prego; **to be ~t for** essere destinato(-a) a; **do you ~ it?** dice sul serio?; **what do you ~?** che cosa vuol dire?
meaning ['mi:nɪŋ] *n* significato, senso; **meaningful** *adj* significativo(-a); **meaningless** *adj* senza senso
meant [mɛnt] *pt, pp of* **mean**
meantime ['mi:ntaɪm] *adv* (*also*: **in the ~**) nel frattempo
meanwhile ['mi:nwaɪl] *adv* nel frattempo
measles ['mi:zlz] *n* morbillo
measure ['mɛʒəʳ] *vt, vi* misurare ▷ *n* misura; (*also*: **tape ~**) metro
measurement ['mɛʒəmənt] *n* (*act*) misurazione *f*; (*measure*) misura; **chest/ hip ~** giro petto/fianchi; **to take sb's ~s** prendere le misure di qn
meat [mi:t] *n* carne *f*; **I don't eat ~** non mangio carne; **cold ~** affettato; **meatball** *n* polpetta di carne
Mecca ['mɛkə] *n* (*also fig*) la Mecca
mechanic [mɪ'kænɪk] *n* meccanico; **can you send a ~?** può mandare un meccanico?; **mechanical** *adj* meccanico(-a)
mechanism ['mɛkənɪzəm] *n* meccanismo
medal ['mɛdl] *n* medaglia; **medallist** (*us* **medalist**) *n* (*Sport*): **to be a gold medallist** essere medaglia d'oro
meddle ['mɛdl] *vi* **to ~ in** immischiarsi in, mettere le mani in; **to ~ with** toccare
media ['mi:dɪə] *npl* media *mpl*
mediaeval [mɛdɪ'i:vl] *adj* = **medieval**
mediate ['mi:dɪeɪt] *vi* fare da mediatore(-trice)

medical ['mɛdɪkl] *adj* medico(-a) ▷ *n* visita medica; **medical certificate** *n* certificato medico
medicated ['mɛdɪkeɪtɪd] *adj* medicato(-a)
medication [mɛdɪ'keɪʃən] *n* medicinali *mpl*, farmaci *mpl*
medicine ['mɛdsɪn] *n* medicina
medieval [mɛdɪ'i:vl] *adj* medievale
mediocre [mi:dɪ'əʊkəʳ] *adj* mediocre
meditate ['mɛdɪteɪt] *vi* **to ~ (on)** meditare (su)
meditation [mɛdɪ'teɪʃən] *n* meditazione *f*
Mediterranean [mɛdɪtə'reɪnɪən] *adj* mediterraneo(-a); **the ~ (Sea)** il (mare) Mediterraneo
medium ['mi:dɪəm] (*pl* **media**) *adj* medio(-a) ▷ *n* (*means*) mezzo; (*pl* **mediums**: *person*) medium *m inv*; **medium-sized** *adj* (*tin etc*) di grandezza media; (*clothes*) di taglia media; **medium wave** *n* onde *fpl* medie
meek [mi:k] *adj* dolce, umile
meet [mi:t] (*pt, pp* **met**) *vt* incontrare; (*for the first time*) fare la conoscenza di; (*go and fetch*) andare a prendere; (*fig*) affrontare; soddisfare; raggiungere ▷ *vi* incontrarsi; (*in session*) riunirsi; (*join: objects*) unirsi; **nice to ~ you** piacere (di conoscerla); **meet up** *vi* **to ~ up with sb** incontrare qn; **meet with** *vt fus* incontrare; **meeting** *n* incontro; (*session: of club etc*) riunione *f*; (*interview*) intervista; **she's at a meeting** (*Comm*) è in riunione; **meeting place** *n* luogo d'incontro
megabyte ['mɛgəbaɪt] *n* (*Comput*) megabyte *m inv*
megaphone ['mɛgəfəʊn] *n* megafono
melancholy ['mɛlənkəlɪ] *n* malinconia ▷ *adj* malinconico(-a)
melody ['mɛlədɪ] *n* melodia
melon ['mɛlən] *n* melone *m*
melt [mɛlt] *vi* (*gen*) sciogliersi, struggersi; (*metals*) fondersi ▷ *vt* sciogliere, struggere; fondere
member ['mɛmbəʳ] *n* membro; **Member of Congress** (*us*) *n* membro del Congresso; **Member of Parliament** (*BRIT*) *n* deputato(-a); **Member of the European Parliament** (*BRIT*) *n* eurodeputato(-a); **Member of the Scottish Parliament** (*BRIT*) *n* deputato(-a) del Parlamento scozzese; **membership** *n* iscrizione *f*, (numero d')iscritti *mpl*, membri *mpl*; **membership card** *n* tessera (di iscrizione)
memento [mə'mɛntəʊ] *n* ricordo, souvenir *m inv*
memo ['mɛməʊ] *n* appunto; (*Comm etc*) comunicazione *f* di servizio
memorable ['mɛmərəbl] *adj* memorabile

memorandum [mɛmə'rændəm] (*pl* **memoranda**) *n* appunto; (*Comm etc*) comunicazione *f* di servizio

memorial [mɪ'mɔːrɪəl] *n* monumento commemorativo ▷ *adj* commemorativo(-a)

memorize ['mɛməraɪz] *vt* memorizzare

memory ['mɛmərɪ] *n* (*also Comput*) memoria; (*recollection*) ricordo

men [mɛn] *npl of* **man**

menace ['mɛnəs] *n* minaccia ▷ *vt* minacciare

mend [mɛnd] *vt* aggiustare, riparare; (*darn*) rammendare ▷ *n* **on the ~** in via di guarigione

meningitis [mɛnɪn'dʒaɪtɪs] *n* meningite *f*

menopause ['mɛnəupɔːz] *n* menopausa

men's room *n* **the men's room** (*esp us*) la toilette degli uomini

menstruation [mɛnstru'eɪʃən] *n* mestruazione *f*

menswear ['mɛnzwɛər] *n* abbigliamento maschile

mental ['mɛntl] *adj* mentale; **mental hospital** *n* ospedale *m* psichiatrico; **mentality** [mɛn'tælɪtɪ] *n* mentalità *f inv*; **mentally** *adv* **to be mentally handicapped** essere minorato psichico

menthol ['mɛnθɔl] *n* mentolo

mention ['mɛnʃən] *n* menzione *f* ▷ *vt* menzionare, far menzione di; **don't ~ it!** non c'è di che!, prego!

menu ['mɛnjuː] *n* (*set menu, Comput*) menù *m inv*; (*printed*) carta; **could we see the ~?** ci può portare il menù?

MEP *n abbr* = **Member of the European Parliament**

mercenary ['məːsɪnərɪ] *adj* venale ▷ *n* mercenario

merchandise ['məːtʃəndaɪz] *n* merci *fpl*

merchant ['məːtʃənt] *n* mercante *m*, commerciante *m*; **merchant navy** (*us* **merchant marine**) *n* marina mercantile

merciless ['məːsɪlɪs] *adj* spietato(-a)

mercury ['məːkjurɪ] *n* mercurio

mercy ['məːsɪ] *n* pietà; (*Rel*) misericordia; **at the ~ of** alla mercè di

mere [mɪər] *adj* semplice; **by a ~ chance** per mero caso; **merely** *adv* semplicemente, non … che

merge [məːdʒ] *vt* unire ▷ *vi* fondersi, unirsi; (*Comm*) fondersi; **merger** *n* (*Comm*) fusione *f*

meringue [mə'ræŋ] *n* meringa

merit ['mɛrɪt] *n* merito, valore *m* ▷ *vt* meritare

mermaid ['məːmeɪd] *n* sirena

merry ['mɛrɪ] *adj* gaio(-a), allegro(-a); **M~ Christmas!** Buon Natale!; **merry-go-round** *n* carosello

mesh [mɛʃ] *n* maglia; rete *f*

mess [mɛs] *n* confusione *f*, disordine *m*; (*fig*) pasticcio; (*dirt*) sporcizia; (*Mil*) mensa; **mess about** *or* **around** (*inf*) *vi* trastullarsi; **mess with** (*inf*) *vt fus* (*challenge, confront*) litigare con; (*drugs, drinks*) abusare di; **mess up** *vt* sporcare; fare un pasticcio di; rovinare

message ['mɛsɪdʒ] *n* messaggio; **can I leave a ~?** posso lasciare un messaggio?; **are there any ~s for me?** ci sono messaggi per me?

messenger ['mɛsɪndʒər] *n* messaggero(-a)

Messrs ['mɛsəz] *abbr* (*on letters*) Spett.

messy ['mɛsɪ] *adj* sporco(-a), disordinato(-a)

met [mɛt] *pt, pp of* **meet**

metabolism [mɛ'tæbəlɪzəm] *n* metabolismo

metal ['mɛtl] *n* metallo; **metallic** [-'tælɪk] *adj* metallico(-a)

metaphor ['mɛtəfər] *n* metafora

meteor ['miːtɪər] *n* meteora; **meteorite** ['miːtɪəraɪt] *n* meteorite *m*

meteorology [miːtɪə'rɔlədʒɪ] *n* meteorologia

meter ['miːtər] *n* (*instrument*) contatore *m*; (*parking meter*) parchimetro; (*us: unit*) = **metre**

method ['mɛθəd] *n* metodo; **methodical** [mɪ'θɔdɪkl] *adj* metodico(-a)

meths [mɛθs] (*BRIT*) *n* alcool *m* denaturato

meticulous [mɛ'tɪkjuləs] *adj* meticoloso(-a)

metre ['miːtər] (*us* **meter**) *n* metro

metric ['mɛtrɪk] *adj* metrico(-a)

metro ['mɛtrəu] *n* metro *m inv*

metropolitan [mɛtrə'pɔlɪtən] *adj* metropolitano(-a)

Mexican ['mɛksɪkən] *adj, n* messicano(-a)

Mexico ['mɛksɪkəu] *n* Messico

mg *abbr* (= *milligram*) mg

mice [maɪs] *npl of* **mouse**

micro... ['maɪkrəu] *prefix* micro...; **microchip** *n* microcircuito integrato; **microphone** *n* microfono; **microscope** *n* microscopio; **microwave** *n* (*also:* **microwave oven**) forno a microonde

mid [mɪd] *adj* **~ May** metà maggio; **~ afternoon** metà pomeriggio; **in ~ air** a mezz'aria; **midday** *n* mezzogiorno

middle ['mɪdl] *n* mezzo; centro; (*waist*) vita ▷ *adj* di mezzo; **in the ~ of the night** nel bel mezzo della notte; **middle-aged** *adj* di mezza età; **Middle Ages** *npl* **the Middle Ages** il Medioevo; **middle-class** *adj* ≈ borghese; **Middle East** *n* Medio

m

Oriente *m*; **middle name** *n* secondo nome *m*; **middle school** *n* (*US*) scuola media per ragazzi dagli 11 ai 14 anni; (*BRIT*) scuola media per ragazzi dagli 8 o 9 ai 12 o 13 anni

midge [mɪdʒ] *n* moscerino

midget ['mɪdʒɪt] *n* nano(-a)

midnight ['mɪdnaɪt] *n* mezzanotte *f*

midst [mɪdst] *n* **in the ~ of** in mezzo a

midsummer [mɪd'sʌmər] *n* mezza or piena estate *f*

midway [mɪd'weɪ] *adj, adv* **~ (between)** a mezza strada (fra); **~ (through)** a metà (di)

midweek [mɪd'wiːk] *adv* a metà settimana

midwife ['mɪdwaɪf] (*pl* **midwives**) *n* levatrice *f*

midwinter [mɪd'wɪntər] *n* pieno inverno

might [maɪt] *vb see* **may** ▷ *n* potere *m*, forza; **mighty** *adj* forte, potente

migraine ['miːgreɪn] *n* emicrania

migrant ['maɪgrənt] *adj* (*bird*) migratore(-trice); (*worker*) emigrato(-a)

migrate [maɪ'greɪt] *vi* (*bird*) migrare; (*person*) emigrare

migration [maɪ'greɪʃən] *n* migrazione *f*

mike [maɪk] *n abbr* (= *microphone*) microfono

Milan [mɪ'læn] *n* Milano *f*

mild [maɪld] *adj* mite; (*person, voice*) dolce; (*flavour*) delicato(-a); (*illness*) leggero(-a); (*interest*) blando(-a) ▷ *n* (*beer*) birra leggera; **mildly** ['maɪldlɪ] *adv* mitemente; dolcemente; delicatamente; leggermente; blandamente; **to put it mildly** a dire poco

mile [maɪl] *n* miglio; **mileage** *n* distanza in miglia, ≈ chilometraggio; **mileometer** [maɪ'lɔmɪtər] *n* ≈ contachilometri *m inv*; **milestone** ['maɪlstəun] *n* pietra miliare

military ['mɪlɪtərɪ] *adj* militare

militia [mɪ'lɪʃə] *n* milizia

milk [mɪlk] *n* latte *m* ▷ *vt* (*cow*) mungere; (*fig*) sfruttare; **milk chocolate** *n* cioccolato al latte; **milkman** (*irreg*) *n* lattaio; **milky** *adj* lattiginoso(-a); (*colour*) latteo(-a)

mill [mɪl] *n* mulino; (*small: for coffee, pepper etc*) macinino; (*factory*) fabbrica; (*spinning mill*) filatura ▷ *vt* macinare ▷ *vi* (*also:* **~ about**) brulicare

millennium [mɪ'lɛnɪəm] (*pl* **millenniums** *or* **millennia**) *n* millennio

milli... ['mɪlɪ] *prefix*: **milligram(me)** *n* milligrammo; **millilitre** ['mɪlɪliːtər] (*US* **milliliter**) *n* millilitro; **millimetre** (*US* **millimeter**) *n* millimetro

million ['mɪljən] *num* milione *m*; **millionaire** *n* milionario, ≈ miliardario; **millionth** *num* milionesimo(-a)

milometer [maɪ'lɔmɪtər] *n* = **mileometer**

mime [maɪm] *n* mimo ▷ *vt, vi* mimare

mimic ['mɪmɪk] *n* imitatore(-trice) ▷ *vt* fare la mimica di

min. *abbr* = **minute(s)**; **minimum**

mince [mɪns] *vt* tritare, macinare ▷ *n* (*BRIT Culin*) carne *f* tritata or macinata; **mincemeat** *n* frutta secca tritata per uso in pasticceria; (*US*) carne *f* tritata or macinata; **mince pie** *n* specie di torta con frutta secca

mind [maɪnd] *n* mente *f* ▷ *vt* (*attend to, look after*) badare a, occuparsi di; (*be careful*) fare attenzione a, stare attento(-a) a; (*object to*): **I don't ~ the noise** il rumore non mi dà alcun fastidio; **I don't ~** non m'importa; **do you ~ if ...?** le dispiace se...?; **it is on my ~** mi preoccupa; **to my ~** secondo me, a mio parere; **to be out of one's ~** essere uscito(-a) di mente; **to keep** *or* **bear sth in ~** non dimenticare qc; **to make up one's ~** decidersi; **~ you, ...** sì, però va detto che ...; **never ~** non importa, non fa niente; (*don't worry*) non preoccuparti; **"~ the step"** "attenzione allo scalino"; **mindless** *adj* idiota

mine¹ [maɪn] *pron* il (la) mio(-a); (*pl*) i (le) miei (mei); **that book is ~** quel libro è mio; **yours is red, ~ is green** il tuo è rosso, il mio è verde; **a friend of ~** un mio amico

mine² [maɪn] *n* miniera; (*explosive*) mina ▷ *vt* (*coal*) estrarre; (*ship, beach*) minare; **minefield** *n* (*also fig*) campo minato; **miner** ['maɪnər] *n* minatore *m*

mineral ['mɪnərəl] *adj* minerale ▷ *n* minerale *m*; **mineral water** *n* acqua minerale

mingle ['mɪŋgl] *vi* **to ~ with** mescolarsi a, mischiarsi con

miniature ['mɪnətʃər] *adj* in miniatura ▷ *n* miniatura

minibar ['mɪnɪbɑːr] *n* minibar *m inv*

minibus ['mɪnɪbʌs] *n* minibus *m inv*

minicab ['mɪnɪkæb] *n* (*BRIT*) ≈ taxi *m inv*

minimal ['mɪnɪml] *adj* minimo(-a)

minimize ['mɪnɪmaɪz] *vt* minimizzare

minimum ['mɪnɪməm] (*pl* **minima**) *n* minimo ▷ *adj* minimo(-a)

mining ['maɪnɪŋ] *n* industria mineraria

miniskirt ['mɪnɪskəːt] *n* minigonna

minister ['mɪnɪstər] *n* (*BRIT Pol*) ministro; (*Rel*) pastore *m*

ministry ['mɪnɪstrɪ] *n* ministero

minor ['maɪnər] *adj* minore, di poca importanza; (*Mus*) minore ▷ *n* (*Law*) minorenne *m/f*

Minorca [mɪ'nɔːkə] *n* Minorca

minority [maɪ'nɔrɪtɪ] *n* minoranza

mint [mɪnt] *n* (*plant*) menta; (*sweet*) pasticca di menta ▷ *vt* (*coins*) battere; **the (Royal) M~** (*BRIT*), **the (US) M~** (*US*) la Zecca; **in ~ condition** come nuovo(-a) di zecca

minus ['maɪnəs] n (also: **~ sign**) segno meno ▷ prep meno

minute [adj maɪ'njuːt, n 'mɪnɪt] adj minuscolo(-a); (detail) minuzioso(-a) ▷ n minuto; **~s** npl (of meeting) verbale m

miracle ['mɪrəkl] n miracolo

miraculous [mɪ'rækjuləs] adj miracoloso(-a)

mirage ['mɪrɑːʒ] n miraggio

mirror ['mɪrər] n specchio; (in car) specchietto

misbehave [mɪsbɪ'heɪv] vi comportarsi male

misc. abbr = **miscellaneous**; **miscarriage** ['mɪskærɪdʒ] n (Med) aborto spontaneo; **miscarriage of justice** errore m giudiziario

miscellaneous [mɪsɪ'leɪnɪəs] adj (items) vario(-a); (selection) misto(-a)

mischief ['mɪstʃɪf] n (naughtiness) birichineria; (maliciousness) malizia; **mischievous** adj birichino(-a)

misconception ['mɪskən'sɛpʃən] n idea sbagliata

misconduct [mɪs'kɔndʌkt] n cattiva condotta; **professional ~** reato professionale

miser ['maɪzər] n avaro

miserable ['mɪzərəbl] adj infelice; (wretched) miserabile; (weather) deprimente; (offer, failure) misero(-a)

misery ['mɪzərɪ] n (unhappiness) tristezza; (wretchedness) miseria

misfortune [mɪs'fɔːtʃən] n sfortuna

misgiving [mɪs'gɪvɪŋ] n apprensione f; **to have ~s about** avere dei dubbi per quanto riguarda

misguided [mɪs'gaɪdɪd] adj sbagliato(-a), poco giudizioso(-a)

mishap ['mɪshæp] n disgrazia

misinterpret [mɪsɪn'tə:prɪt] vt interpretare male

misjudge [mɪs'dʒʌdʒ] vt giudicare male

mislay [mɪs'leɪ] (irreg) vt smarrire

mislead [mɪs'liːd] (irreg) vt sviare; **misleading** adj ingannevole

misplace [mɪs'pleɪs] vt smarrire

misprint ['mɪsprɪnt] n errore m di stampa

misrepresent [mɪsrɛprɪ'zɛnt] vt travisare

Miss [mɪs] n Signorina

miss [mɪs] vt (fail to get) perdere; (fail to hit) mancare; (fail to see): **you can't ~ it** non puoi non vederlo; (regret the absence of): **I ~ him** sento la sua mancanza ▷ vi mancare ▷ n (shot) colpo mancato; **we ~ed our train** abbiamo perso il treno; **miss out** (BRIT) vt omettere; **miss out on**

vt fus (fun, party) perdersi; (chance, bargain) lasciarsi sfuggire

missile ['mɪsaɪl] n (Mil) missile m; (object thrown) proiettile m

missing ['mɪsɪŋ] adj perso(-a), smarrito(-a); (person) scomparso(-a); (: after disaster, Mil) disperso(-a); (removed) mancante; **to be ~** mancare

mission ['mɪʃən] n missione f; **missionary** n missionario(-a)

misspell [mɪs'spɛl] vt (irreg: like **spell**) sbagliare l'ortografia di

mist [mɪst] n nebbia, foschia ▷ vi (also: **~ over, ~ up**) annebbiarsi; (: BRIT: windows) appannarsi

mistake [mɪs'teɪk] (irreg: like **take**) n sbaglio, errore m ▷ vt sbagliarsi di; fraintendere; **to make a ~** fare uno sbaglio, sbagliare; **there must be some ~** ci dev'essere un errore; **by ~** per sbaglio; **to ~ for** prendere per; **mistaken** pp of **mistake** ▷ adj (idea etc) sbagliato(-a); **to be mistaken** sbagliarsi

mister ['mɪstər] (inf) n signore m; see **Mr**

mistletoe ['mɪsltəu] n vischio

mistook [mɪs'tuk] pt of **mistake**

mistress ['mɪstrɪs] n padrona; (lover) amante f; (BRIT Scol) insegnante f

mistrust [mɪs'trʌst] vt diffidare di

misty ['mɪstɪ] adj nebbioso(-a), brumoso(-a)

misunderstand [mɪsʌndə'stænd] (irreg) vt, vi capire male, fraintendere; **misunderstanding** n malinteso, equivoco; **there's been a misunderstanding** c'è stato un malinteso

misunderstood [mɪsʌndə'stud] pt, pp of **misunderstand**

misuse [n mɪs'juːs, vb mɪs'juːz] n cattivo uso; (of power) abuso ▷ vt far cattivo uso di; abusare di

mitt(en) ['mɪt(n)] n mezzo guanto; manopola

mix [mɪks] vt mescolare ▷ vi (people): **to ~ with** avere a che fare con ▷ n mescolanza; preparato; **mix up** vt mescolare; (confuse) confondere; **mixed** adj misto(-a); **mixed grill** n (BRIT) misto alla griglia; **mixed salad** n insalata mista; **mixed-up** adj (confused) confuso(-a); **mixer** n (for food: electric) frullatore m; (: hand) frullino; (person): **he is a good mixer** è molto socievole; **mixture** n mescolanza; (blend: of tobacco etc) miscela; (Med) sciroppo; **mix-up** n confusione f

ml abbr (= millilitre(s)) ml

mm abbr (= millimetre) mm

moan [məun] n gemito ▷ vi (inf: complain): **to ~ (about)** lamentarsi (di)

moat [məʊt] n fossato
mob [mɔb] n calca ▷ vt accalcarsi intorno a
mobile ['məʊbaɪl] adj mobile ▷ n
 (decoration) mobile m; **mobile home** n
 grande roulotte f inv (utilizzata come
 domicilio); **mobile phone** n telefono
 portatile, telefonino
mobility [məʊ'bɪlɪtɪ] n mobilità; (of
 applicant) disponibilità a viaggiare
mobilize ['məʊbɪlaɪz] vt mobilitare ▷ vi
 mobilitarsi
mock [mɔk] vt deridere, burlarsi di ▷ adj
 falso(-a); **~s** npl (BRIT: Scol: inf) simulazione
 f degli esami; **mockery** n derisione f; **to
 make a mockery of** burlarsi di; (exam)
 rendere una farsa
mod cons ['mɔd'kɔnz] npl abbr
 (BRIT) = **modern conveniences**; see
 convenience
mode [məʊd] n modo
model ['mɔdl] n modello; (person: for
 fashion) indossatore(-trice); (: for artist)
 modello(-a) ▷ adj (small-scale: railway etc)
 in miniatura; (child, factory) modello inv
 ▷ vt modellare ▷ vi fare l'indossatore (or
 l'indossatrice); **to ~ clothes** presentare
 degli abiti
modem ['məʊdɛm] n modem m inv
moderate [adj 'mɔdərət, vb 'mɔdəreɪt] adj
 moderato(-a) ▷ vi moderarsi, placarsi ▷ vt
 moderare
moderation [mɔdə'reɪʃən] n
 moderazione f, misura; **in ~** in quantità
 moderata, con moderazione
modern ['mɔdən] adj moderno(-a); **mod
 cons** comodità fpl moderne; **modernize**
 vt modernizzare; **modern languages** npl
 lingue fpl moderne
modest ['mɔdɪst] adj modesto(-a);
 modesty n modestia
modification [mɔdɪfɪ'keɪʃən] n
 modificazione f; **to make ~s** fare or
 apportare delle modifiche
modify ['mɔdɪfaɪ] vt modificare
module ['mɔdju:l] n modulo
mohair ['məʊheəʳ] n mohair m
Mohammed [məʊ'hæmɪd] n
 Maometto
moist [mɔɪst] adj umido(-a); **moisture**
 ['mɔɪstʃəʳ] n umidità; (on glass) goccioline
 fpl di vapore; **moisturizer** ['mɔɪstʃəraɪzə
ʳ] n idratante f
mold etc [məʊld] (US) n, vt = **mould**
mole [məʊl] n (animal, fig) talpa; (spot) neo
molecule ['mɔlɪkju:l] n molecola
molest [məʊ'lɛst] vt molestare
molten ['məʊltən] adj fuso(-a)
mom [mɔm] (US) n = **mum**
moment ['məʊmənt] n momento,
istante m; **at that ~** in quel momento; **at
 the ~** al momento, in questo momento;
momentarily ['məʊməntərɪlɪ] adv
 per un momento; (US: very soon) da un
 momento all'altro; **momentary** adj
 momentaneo(-a), passeggero(-a);
momentous [-'mɛntəs] adj di grande
 importanza
momentum [məʊ'mɛntəm] n (Physics)
 momento; (fig) impeto; **to gather ~**
 aumentare di velocità
mommy ['mɔmɪ] (US) n = **mummy**
Mon. abbr (= Monday) lun.
Monaco ['mɔnəkəʊ] n Principato di
 Monaco
monarch ['mɔnək] n monarca m;
 monarchy n monarchia
monastery ['mɔnəstərɪ] n monastero
Monday ['mʌndɪ] n lunedì m inv
monetary ['mʌnɪtərɪ] adj monetario(-a)
money ['mʌnɪ] n denaro, soldi mpl; **I
 haven't got any ~** non ho soldi; **money
 belt** n marsupio (per soldi); **money order**
 n vaglia m inv
mongrel ['mʌŋgrəl] n (dog) cane m
 bastardo
monitor ['mɔnɪtəʳ] n (TV, Comput) monitor
 m inv ▷ vt controllare
monk [mʌŋk] n monaco
monkey ['mʌŋkɪ] n scimmia
monologue ['mɔnəlɔg] n monologo
monopoly [mə'nɔpəlɪ] n monopolio
monosodium glutamate [mɔnə'səʊdɪə
 m'glu:təmeɪt] n glutammato di sodio
monotonous [mə'nɔtənəs] adj
 monotono(-a)
monsoon [mɔn'su:n] n monsone m
monster ['mɔnstəʳ] n mostro
month [mʌnθ] n mese m; **monthly** adj
 mensile ▷ adv al mese; ogni mese
monument ['mɔnjumənt] n monumento
mood [mu:d] n umore m; **to be in a good/
 bad ~** essere di buon/cattivo umore;
 moody adj (variable) capriccioso(-a),
 lunatico(-a); (sullen) imbronciato(-a)
moon [mu:n] n luna; **moonlight** n chiaro
 di luna
moor [mʊəʳ] n brughiera ▷ vt (ship)
 ormeggiare ▷ vi ormeggiarsi
moose [mu:s] n inv alce m
mop [mɔp] n lavapavimenti m inv; (also: ~
 of hair) zazzera ▷ vt lavare con lo straccio;
 (face) asciugare; **mop up** vt asciugare con
 uno straccio
mope [məʊp] vi fare il broncio
moped ['məʊpɛd] n (BRIT) ciclomotore m
moral ['mɔrl] adj morale ▷ n morale f; **~s**
 npl (principles) moralità
morale [mɔ'rɑ:l] n morale m

morality [mə'ræliti] n moralità
morbid ['mɔ:bid] adj morboso(-a)

 KEYWORD

more [mɔ:ʳ] adj **1** (greater in number etc)
più; **more people/letters than we
expected** più persone/lettere di quante
ne aspettavamo; **I have more wine/
money than you** ho più vino/soldi di te;
I have more wine than beer ho più vino
che birra
2 (additional) altro(-a), ancora; **do you
want (some) more tea?** vuole dell'altro
tè?, vuole ancora del tè?; **I have no** or **I
don't have any more money** non ho
più soldi
▷ pron **1** (greater amount) più; **more than 10**
più di 10; **it cost more than we expected**
ha costato più di quanto ci aspettavamo
2 (further or additional amount) ancora;
is there any more? ce n'è ancora?;
there's no more non ce n'è più; **a little
more** ancora un po'; **many/much more**
molti(-e)/molto(-a) di più
▷ adv **more dangerous/easily (than)**
più pericoloso/facilmente (di); **more and
more** sempre di più; **more and more
difficult** sempre più difficile; **more or less**
più o meno; **more than ever** più che mai

moreover [mɔ:'rəuvəʳ] adv inoltre, di più
morgue [mɔ:g] n obitorio
morning ['mɔ:niŋ] n mattina, mattino;
(duration) mattinata ▷ cpd del mattino;
in the ~ la mattina; **7 o'clock in the ~** le 7
di or della mattina; **morning sickness** n
nausee fpl mattutine
Moroccan [mə'rɔkən] adj, n
marocchino(-a)
Morocco [mə'rɔkəu] n Marocco
moron ['mɔ:rɔn] (inf) n deficiente m/f
morphine ['mɔ:fi:n] n morfina
morris dancing n vedi nota nel riquadro

● **MORRIS DANCING**
●
● Il **morris dancing** è una danza
● folcloristica inglese tradizionalmente
● riservata agli uomini. Vestiti di bianco
● e con dei campanelli attaccati alle
● caviglie, i ballerini eseguono una danza
● tenendo in mano dei fazzoletti bianchi
● e lunghi bastoni. Questa danza è molto
● popolare nelle feste paesane.

Morse [mɔ:s] n (also: **~ code**) alfabeto
Morse
mortal ['mɔ:tl] adj mortale ▷ n mortale m

mortar ['mɔ:təʳ] n (Constr) malta; (dish)
mortaio
mortgage ['mɔ:gidʒ] n ipoteca; (loan)
prestito ipotecario ▷ vt ipotecare
mortician [mɔ:'tiʃən] (US) n impresario di
pompe funebri
mortified ['mɔ:tifaid] adj umiliato(-a)
mortuary ['mɔ:tjuəri] n camera
mortuaria; obitorio
mosaic [məu'zeiik] n mosaico
Moscow ['mɔskəu] n Mosca
Moslem ['mɔzləm] adj, n = **Muslim**
mosque [mɔsk] n moschea
mosquito [mɔs'ki:təu] (pl **mosquitoes**)
n zanzara
moss [mɔs] n muschio
most [məust] adj (almost all) la maggior
parte di; (largest, greatest): **who has (the)
~ money?** chi ha più soldi di tutti? ▷ pron
la maggior parte ▷ adv più; (work, sleep
etc) di più; (very) molto, estremamente;
the ~ (also: **+ adjective**) il(-la) più; **~ of** la
maggior parte di; **~ of them** quasi tutti; **I
saw (the) ~** ho visto più io; **at the (very)
~** al massimo; **to make the ~ of** trarre il
massimo vantaggio da; **a ~ interesting
book** un libro estremamente interessante;
mostly adv per lo più
MOT (BRIT) n abbr = **Ministry of
Transport**; **the ~ (test)** revisione annuale
obbligatoria degli autoveicoli
motel [məu'tel] n motel m inv
moth [mɔθ] n farfalla notturna; tarma
mother ['mʌðəʳ] n madre f ▷ vt (care
for) fare da madre a; **motherhood** n
maternità; **mother-in-law** n suocera;
mother-of-pearl [mʌðərəv'pə:l] n
madreperla; **Mother's Day** n la festa della
mamma; **mother-to-be** [mʌðətə'bi:]
n futura mamma; **mother tongue** n
madrelingua
motif [məu'ti:f] n motivo
motion ['məuʃən] n movimento, moto;
(gesture) gesto; (at meeting) mozione f ▷ vt,
vi **to ~ (to) sb to do** fare cenno a qn di
fare; **motionless** adj immobile; **motion
picture** n film m inv
motivate ['məutiveit] vt (act, decision)
dare origine a, motivare; (person) spingere
motivation [məuti'veiʃən] n motivazione
f
motive ['məutiv] n motivo
motor ['məutəʳ] n motore m;
(BRIT: inf: vehicle) macchina ▷ cpd
automobilistico(-a); **motorbike** n moto f
inv; **motorboat** n motoscafo; **motorcar**
(BRIT) n automobile f; **motorcycle**
n motocicletta; **motorcyclist** n
motociclista m/f; **motoring** (BRIT) n

m

turismo automobilistico; **motorist** n automobilista m/f; **motor racing** (BRIT) n corse fpl automobilistiche; **motorway** (BRIT) n autostrada

motto ['mɔtəu] (pl **mottoes**) n motto

mould [məuld] (US **mold**) n forma, stampo; (mildew) muffa ▷ vt formare; (fig) foggiare; **mouldy** adj ammuffito(-a); (smell) di muffa

mound [maund] n rialzo, collinetta; (heap) mucchio

mount [maunt] n (Geo) monte m ▷ vt montare; (horse) montare a ▷ vi (increase) aumentare; **mount up** vi (build up) accumularsi

mountain ['mauntɪn] n montagna ▷ cpd di montagna; **mountain bike** n mountain bike f inv; **mountaineer** [-'nɪə ʳ] n alpinista m/f; **mountaineering** [-'nɪə rɪŋ] n alpinismo; **mountainous** adj montagnoso(-a); **mountain range** n catena montuosa

mourn [mɔːn] vt piangere, lamentare ▷ vi **to ~ (for sb)** piangere (la morte di qn); **mourner** n parente m/f or amico(-a) del defunto; **mourning** n lutto; **in mourning** in lutto

mouse [maus] (pl **mice**) n topo; (Comput) mouse m inv; **mouse mat, mouse pad** n (Comput) tappetino del mouse

moussaka [mu'sɑːkə] n moussaka

mousse [muːs] n mousse f inv

moustache [məs'tɑːʃ] (US **mustache**) n baffi mpl

mouth [mauθ, pl mauðz] n bocca; (of river) bocca, foce f; (opening) orifizio; **mouthful** n boccata; **mouth organ** n armonica; **mouthpiece** n (Mus) imboccatura, bocchino; (spokesman) portavoce m/f inv; **mouthwash** n collutorio

move [muːv] n (movement) movimento; (in game) mossa; (: turn to play) turno; (change: of house) trasloco; (: of job) cambiamento ▷ vt muovere; (change position of) spostare; (emotionally) commuovere; (Pol: resolution etc) proporre ▷ vi (gen) muoversi, spostarsi; (also: ~ house) cambiar casa, traslocare; **to get a ~ on** affrettarsi, sbrigarsi; **can you ~ your car, please?** può spostare la macchina, per favore?; **to ~ sb to do sth** indurre or spingere qn a fare qc; **to ~ towards** andare verso; **move back** vi (return) ritornare; **move in** vi (to a house) entrare (in una nuova casa); (police etc) intervenire; **move off** vi partire; **move on** vi riprendere la strada; **move out** vi (of house) sgombrare; **move over** vi spostarsi; **move up** vi avanzare; **movement** ['muːvmənt] n (gen)

movimento; (gesture) gesto; (of stars, water, physical) moto

movie ['muːvɪ] n film m inv; **the ~s** il cinema; **movie theater** (US) n cinema m inv

moving ['muːvɪŋ] adj mobile; (causing emotion) commovente

mow [məu] (pt **mowed**, pp **mowed** or **mown**) vt (grass) tagliare; (corn) mietere; **mower** n (also: **lawnmower**) tagliaerba m inv

Mozambique [məuzəm'biːk] n Mozambico

MP n abbr = **Member of Parliament**

MP3 n abbr M3; **MP3 player** n lettore m MP3

mpg n abbr = **miles per gallon** (30 mpg = 9.4 l. per 100 km)

m.p.h. n abbr = **miles per hour** (60 m.p.h = 96 km/h)

Mr ['mɪstəʳ] (US **Mr.**) n **Mr X** Signor X, Sig. X

Mrs ['mɪsɪz] (US **Mrs.**) n **Mrs X** Signora X, Sig.ra X

Ms [mɪz] (US **Ms.**) n = **Miss or Mrs**; **Ms X** ≈ Signora X, ≈ Sig.ra X

- **Ms**
-
- In inglese si usa **Ms** al posto di "Mrs"
- (Signora) o "Miss" (Signorina) per evitare
- la distinzione tradizionale tra le donne
- sposate e quelle nubili.

MSP n abbr = **Member of the Scottish Parliament**

Mt abbr (Geo: = mount) M.

 KEYWORD

much [mʌtʃ] adj, pron molto(-a); **he's done so much work** ha lavorato così tanto; **I have as much money as you** ho tanti soldi quanti ne hai tu; **how much is it?** quant'è?; **it costs too much** costa troppo; **as much as you want** quanto vuoi ▷ adv **1** (greatly) molto, tanto; **thank you very much** molte grazie; **he's very much the gentleman** è il vero gentiluomo; **I read as much as I can** leggo quanto posso; **as much as you** tanto quanto te **2** (by far) molto; **it's much the biggest company in Europe** è di gran lunga la più grossa società in Europa **3** (almost) grossomodo, praticamente; **they're much the same** sono praticamente uguali

muck [mʌk] n (dirt) sporcizia; **muck up** (inf) vt (ruin) rovinare; **mucky** adj (dirty)

sporco(-a), lordo(-a)
mucus ['mju:kəs] n muco
mud [mʌd] n fango
muddle ['mʌdl] n confusione f, disordine m; pasticcio ▷ vt (also: **~ up**) confondere
muddy ['mʌdɪ] adj fangoso(-a)
mudguard ['mʌdgɑːd] n parafango
muesli ['mju:zlɪ] n muesli m
muffin ['mʌfɪn] n specie di pasticcino soffice da tè
muffled ['mʌfld] adj smorzato(-a), attutito(-a)
muffler ['mʌflə'] (us) n (Aut) marmitta; (: on motorbike) silenziatore m
mug [mʌg] n (cup) tazzone m; (for beer) boccale m; (inf: face) muso; (: fool) scemo(-a) ▷ vt (assault) assalire; **mugger** ['mʌgə'] n aggressore m, **mugging** n assalto
muggy ['mʌgɪ] adj afoso(-a)
mule [mju:l] n mulo
multicoloured ['mʌltɪkʌləd] (us **multicolored**) adj multicolore, variopinto(-a)
multimedia ['mʌltɪ'mi:dɪə] adj multimedia inv
multinational [mʌltɪ'næʃənl] adj, n multinazionale (f)
multiple ['mʌltɪpl] adj multiplo(-a), molteplice ▷ n multiplo; **multiple choice (test)** n esercizi mpl a scelta multipla; **multiple sclerosis** [-sklɪ'rəusɪs] n sclerosi f a placche
multiplex cinema ['mʌltɪplɛks-] n cinema m inv multisala inv
multiplication [mʌltɪplɪ'keɪʃən] n moltiplicazione f
multiply ['mʌltɪplaɪ] vt moltiplicare ▷ vi moltiplicarsi
multistorey ['mʌltɪ'stɔːrɪ] (BRIT) adj (building, car park) a più piani
mum [mʌm] (BRIT: inf) n mamma ▷ adj **to keep ~** non aprire bocca
mumble ['mʌmbl] vt, vi borbottare
mummy ['mʌmɪ] n (BRIT: mother) mamma; (embalmed) mummia
mumps [mʌmps] n orecchioni mpl
munch [mʌntʃ] vt, vi sgranocchiare
municipal [mju:'nɪsɪpl] adj municipale
mural ['mjuərl] n dipinto murale
murder ['mə:də'] n assassinio, omicidio ▷ vt assassinare; **murderer** n omicida m, assassino
murky ['mə:kɪ] adj tenebroso(-a)
murmur ['mə:mə'] n mormorio ▷ vt, vi mormorare
muscle ['mʌsl] n muscolo; (fig) forza; **muscular** ['mʌskjulə'] adj muscolare; (person, arm) muscoloso(-a)

museum [mju:'zɪəm] n museo
mushroom ['mʌʃrum] n fungo ▷ vi crescere in fretta
music ['mju:zɪk] n musica; **musical** adj musicale; (person) portato(-a) per la musica ▷ n (show) commedia musicale; **musical instrument** n strumento musicale; **musician** [-'zɪʃən] n musicista m/f
Muslim ['mʌzlɪm] adj, n musulmano(-a)
muslin ['mʌzlɪn] n mussola
mussel ['mʌsl] n cozza
must [mʌst] aux vb (obligation): **I ~ do it** devo farlo; (probability): **he ~ be there by now** dovrebbe essere arrivato ormai; **I ~ have made a mistake** devo essermi sbagliato ▷ n **it's a ~** è d'obbligo
mustache ['mʌstæʃ] (us) n = **moustache**
mustard ['mʌstəd] n senape f, mostarda
mustn't ['mʌsnt] = **must not**
mute [mju:t] adj, n muto(-a)
mutilate ['mju:tɪleɪt] vt mutilare
mutiny ['mju:tɪnɪ] n ammutinamento
mutter ['mʌtə'] vt, vi borbottare, brontolare
mutton ['mʌtn] n carne f di montone
mutual ['mju:tʃuəl] adj mutuo(-a), reciproco(-a)
muzzle ['mʌzl] n muso; (protective device) museruola; (of gun) bocca ▷ vt mettere la museruola a
my [maɪ] adj il (la) mio(-a); (pl) i (le) miei (mie); **my house** la mia casa; **my books** i miei libri; **my brother** mio fratello; **I've washed my hair/cut my finger** mi sono lavato i capelli/tagliato il dito
myself [maɪ'sɛlf] pron (reflexive) mi; (emphatic) io stesso(-a); (after prep) me; see also **oneself**
mysterious [mɪs'tɪərɪəs] adj misterioso(-a)
mystery ['mɪstərɪ] n mistero
mystical ['mɪstɪkəl] adj mistico(-a)
mystify ['mɪstɪfaɪ] vt mistificare; (puzzle) confondere
myth [mɪθ] n mito; **mythology** [mɪ'θɒlədʒɪ] n mitologia

n

narrative ['nærətɪv] n narrativa
narrator [nə'reɪtəʳ] n narratore(-trice)
narrow ['nærəʊ] adj stretto(-a); (fig)
   limitato(-a), ristretto(-a) ▷ vi restringersi;
   to have a ~ escape farcela per un pelo;
   narrow down vt (search, investigation,
   possibilities) restringere; (list) ridurre;
   narrowly adv per un pelo; (time) per poco;
   narrow-minded adj meschino(-a)
nasal ['neɪzl] adj nasale
nasty ['nɑːstɪ] adj (person, remark:
   unpleasant) cattivo(-a); (: rude) villano(-a);
   (smell, wound, situation) brutto(-a)
nation ['neɪʃən] n nazione f
national ['næʃənl] adj nazionale ▷ n
   cittadino(-a); **national anthem** n inno
   nazionale; **national dress** n costume
   m nazionale; **National Health Service**
   (BRIT) n servizio nazionale di assistenza
   sanitaria, ≈ S.S.N. m; **National Insurance**
   (BRIT) n ≈ Previdenza Sociale; **nationalist**
   adj, n nazionalista (m/f); **nationality**
   [-'nælɪtɪ] n nazionalità f inv; **nationalize**
   vt nazionalizzare; **national park** n
   parco nazionale; **National Trust** n
   sovrintendenza ai beni culturali e ambientali

● **NATIONAL TRUST**
●
● Fondato nel 1895, il **National Trust** è
● un'organizzazione che si occupa della
● tutela e della salvaguardia di luoghi
● di interesse storico o ambientale nel
● Regno Unito.

nationwide ['neɪʃənwaɪd] adj diffuso(-a)
   in tutto il paese ▷ adv in tutto il paese
native ['neɪtɪv] n abitante m/f del paese
   ▷ adj indigeno(-a); (country) natio(-a);
   (ability) innato(-a); **a ~ of Russia** un nativo
   della Russia; **a ~ speaker of French** una
   persona di madrelingua francese; **Native
   American** n discendente di tribù dell'America
   settentrionale
NATO ['neɪtəʊ] n abbr (= North Atlantic
   Treaty Organization) N.A.T.O. f
natural ['nætʃrəl] adj naturale; (ability)
   innato(-a); (manner) semplice; **natural gas**
   n gas m metano; **natural history** n storia
   naturale; **naturally** adv naturalmente;
   (by nature: gifted) di natura; **natural
   resources** npl risorse fpl naturali
nature ['neɪtʃəʳ] n natura; (character)
   natura, indole f; **by ~** di natura; **nature
   reserve** n (BRIT) parco naturale
naughty ['nɔːtɪ] adj (child) birichino(-a),
   cattivello(-a); (story, film) spinto(-a)
nausea ['nɔːsɪə] n (Med) nausea; (fig:
   disgust) schifo

n/a abbr = **not applicable**
nag [næg] vt tormentare ▷ vi brontolare in
   continuazione
nail [neɪl] n (human) unghia; (metal) chiodo
   ▷ vt inchiodare; **to ~ sb down to (doing)
   sth** costringere qn a (fare) qc; **nailbrush**
   n spazzolino da or per unghie; **nailfile** n
   lima da or per unghie; **nail polish** n smalto
   da or per unghie; **nail polish remover** n
   acetone m, solvente m; **nail scissors** npl
   forbici fpl da or per unghie; **nail varnish**
   (BRIT) n = **nail polish**
naïve [naɪ'iːv] adj ingenuo(-a)
naked ['neɪkɪd] adj nudo(-a)
name [neɪm] n nome m; (reputation) nome,
   reputazione f ▷ vt (baby etc) chiamare;
   (plant, illness) nominare; (person, object)
   identificare; (price, date) fissare; **what's
   your ~?** come si chiama?; **by ~** di nome;
   she knows them all by ~ li conosce tutti
   per nome; **namely** adv cioè
nanny ['nænɪ] n bambinaia
nap [næp] n (sleep) pisolino; (of cloth)
   peluria; **to be caught ~ping** essere preso
   alla sprovvista
napkin ['næpkɪn] n (also: **table ~**)
   tovagliolo
nappy ['næpɪ] n (BRIT) pannolino
narcotics [nɑː'kɒtɪkz] npl (drugs)
   narcotici, stupefacenti mpl

naval ['neɪvl] *adj* navale

navel ['neɪvl] *n* ombelico

navigate ['nævɪgeɪt] *vt* percorrere navigando ▷ *vi* navigare; (*Aut*) fare da navigatore; **navigation** [-'geɪʃən] *n* navigazione *f*

navy ['neɪvɪ] *n* marina

Nazi ['nɑːtsɪ] *n* nazista *m/f*

NB *abbr* (= *nota bene*) N.B.

near [nɪər] *adj* vicino(-a); (*relation*) prossimo(-a) ▷ *adv* vicino ▷ *prep* (*also*: **~ to**) vicino a, presso; (: *time*) verso ▷ *vt* avvicinarsi a; **nearby** [nɪə'baɪ] *adj* vicino(-a) ▷ *adv* vicino; **is there a bank nearby?** c'è una banca qui vicino?; **nearly** *adv* quasi; **I nearly fell** per poco non sono caduto; **near-sighted** [nɪə'saɪtɪd] *adj* miope

neat [niːt] *adj* (*person, room*) ordinato(-a); (*work*) pulito(-a); (*solution, plan*) ben indovinato(-a), azzeccato(-a); (*spirits*) liscio(-a); **neatly** *adv* con ordine; (*skilfully*) abilmente

necessarily ['nɛsɪsrɪlɪ] *adv* necessariamente

necessary ['nɛsɪsrɪ] *adj* necessario(-a)

necessity [nɪ'sɛsɪtɪ] *n* necessità *f inv*

neck [nɛk] *n* collo; (*of garment*) colletto ▷ *vi* (*inf*) pomiciare, sbaciucchiarsi; **~ and ~** testa a testa; **necklace** ['nɛklɪs] *n* collana; **necktie** ['nɛktaɪ] *n* cravatta

nectarine ['nɛktərɪn] *n* nocepesca

need [niːd] *n* bisogno ▷ *vt* aver bisogno di; **do you ~ anything?** ha bisogno di qualcosa?; **to ~ to do** dover fare; aver bisogno di fare; **you don't ~ to go** non devi andare, non c'è bisogno che tu vada

needle ['niːdl] *n* ago; (*on record player*) puntina ▷ *vt* punzecchiare

needless ['niːdlɪs] *adj* inutile

needlework ['niːdlwəːk] *n* cucito

needn't ['niːdnt] = **need not**

needy ['niːdɪ] *adj* bisognoso(-a)

negative ['nɛgətɪv] *n* (*Ling*) negazione *f*; (*Phot*) negativo ▷ *adj* negativo(-a)

neglect [nɪ'glɛkt] *vt* trascurare ▷ *n* (*of person, duty*) negligenza; (*of child, house etc*) scarsa cura; **state of ~** stato di abbandono

negotiate [nɪ'gəuʃɪeɪt] *vi* **to ~ (with)** negoziare (con) ▷ *vt* (*Comm*) negoziare; (*obstacle*) superare; **negotiations** [nɪgə uʃɪ'eɪʃənz] *pl n* trattative *fpl*, negoziati *mpl*

negotiator [nɪ'gəuʃɪeɪtər] *n* negoziatore(-trice)

neighbour ['neɪbər] (*us* **neighbor**) *n* vicino(-a); **neighbourhood** *n* vicinato; **neighbouring** *adj* vicino(-a)

neither ['naɪðər] *adj, pron* né l'uno(-a) né l'altro(-a), nessuno(-a) dei (delle) due ▷ *conj* neanche, nemmeno, neppure ▷ *adv* **~ good nor bad** né buono né cattivo; **I didn't move and ~ did Claude** io non mi mossi e nemmeno Claude; **..., ~ did I refuse** ..., ma non ho nemmeno rifiutato

neon ['niːɔn] *n* neon *m*

Nepal [nɪ'pɔːl] *n* Nepal *m*

nephew ['nɛvjuː] *n* nipote *m*

nerve [nəːv] *n* nervo; (*fig*) coraggio; (*impudence*) faccia tosta; **~s** (*nervousness*) nervoso; **a fit of ~s** una crisi di nervi

nervous ['nəːvəs] *adj* nervoso(-a); (*anxious*) agitato(-a), in apprensione; **nervous breakdown** *n* esaurimento nervoso

nest [nɛst] *n* nido ▷ *vi* fare il nido, nidificare

net [nɛt] *n* rete *f* ▷ *adj* netto(-a) ▷ *vt* (*fish etc*) prendere con la rete; (*profit*) ricavare un utile netto di; **the N~** (*Internet*) Internet *f*; **netball** *n* specie di pallacanestro

Netherlands ['nɛðələndz] *npl* **the ~** i Paesi Bassi

nett [nɛt] *adj* = **net**

nettle ['nɛtl] *n* ortica

network ['nɛtwəːk] *n* rete *f*

neurotic [njuə'rɔtɪk] *adj, n* nevrotico(-a)

neuter ['njuːtər] *adj* neutro(-a) ▷ *vt* (*cat etc*) castrare

neutral ['njuːtrəl] *adj* neutro(-a); (*person, nation*) neutrale ▷ *n* (*Aut*): **in ~** in folle

never ['nɛvər] *adv* (*non...*) mai; **I've ~ been to Spain** non sono mai stato in Spagna; **~ again** mai più; **I'll ~ go there again** non ci vado più; **~ in my life** mai in vita mia; *see also* **mind**; **never-ending** *adj* interminabile; **nevertheless** [nɛvə ðə'lɛs] *adv* tuttavia, ciò nonostante, ciò nondimeno

new [njuː] *adj* nuovo(-a); (*brand new*) nuovo(-a) di zecca; **New Age** *n* New Age *f inv*; **newborn** *adj* neonato(-a); **newcomer** ['njuːkʌmər] *n* nuovo(-a) venuto(-a); **newly** *adv* di recente

news [njuːz] *n* notizie *fpl*; (*Radio*) giornale *m* radio; (*TV*) telegiornale *m*; **a piece of ~** una notizia; **news agency** *n* agenzia di stampa; **newsagent** (*BRIT*) *n* giornalaio; **newscaster** *n* (*Radio, TV*) annunciatore(-trice); **news dealer** (*US*) *n* = **newsagent**; **newsletter** *n* bollettino; **newspaper** *n* giornale *m*; **newsreader** *n* = **newscaster**

newt [njuːt] *n* tritone *m*

New Year *n* Anno Nuovo; **New Year's Day** *n* il Capodanno; **New Year's Eve** *n* la vigilia di Capodanno

New York [-'jɔ:k] n New York f
New Zealand [-'zi:lənd] n Nuova Zelanda;
 New Zealander n neozelandese m/f
next [nɛkst] adj prossimo(-a) ▷ adv
 accanto; (in time) dopo; **the ~ day** il giorno
 dopo, l'indomani; **~ time** la prossima
 volta; **~ year** l'anno prossimo; **when do
 we meet ~?** quando ci rincontriamo?; **~
 to** accanto a; **~ to nothing** quasi niente;
 ~ please! (avanti) il prossimo!; **next door**
 adv, adj accanto inv; **next-of-kin** n parente
 m/f prossimo(-a)
NHS n abbr = **National Health Service**
nibble ['nɪbl] vt mordicchiare
nice [naɪs] adj (holiday, trip) piacevole; (flat,
 picture) bello(-a); (person) simpatico(-a),
 gentile; **nicely** adv bene
niche [ni:ʃ] n (Archit) nicchia
nick [nɪk] n taglietto; tacca ▷ vt (inf)
 rubare; **in the ~ of time** appena in tempo
nickel ['nɪkl] n nichel m; (US) moneta da
 cinque centesimi di dollaro
nickname ['nɪkneɪm] n
 soprannome m
nicotine ['nɪkəti:n] n nicotina
niece [ni:s] n nipote f
Nigeria [naɪ'dʒɪərɪə] n Nigeria
night [naɪt] n notte f; (evening) sera; **at
 ~** la sera; **by ~** di notte; **the ~ before
 last** l'altro ieri notte (or sera); **night
 club** n locale m notturno; **nightdress**
 n camicia da notte; **nightie** ['naɪtɪ] n
 = **nightdress**; **nightlife** ['naɪtlaɪf] n vita
 notturna; **nightly** ['naɪtlɪ] adj di ogni
 notte or sera; (by night) notturno(-a)
 ▷ adv ogni notte or sera; **nightmare**
 ['naɪtmɛəʳ] n incubo
night: **night school** n scuola serale; **night
 shift** n turno di notte; **night-time** n
 notte f
nil [nɪl] n nulla m; (BRIT Sport) zero
nine [naɪn] num nove; **nineteen** num
 diciannove; **nineteenth** [naɪn'ti:nθ] num
 diciannovesimo(-a); **ninetieth** ['naɪntɪɪθ]
 num novantesimo(-a); **ninety** num
 novanta; **ninth** [naɪnθ] num nono(-a)
nip [nɪp] vt pizzicare; (bite) mordere
nipple ['nɪpl] n (Anat) capezzolo
nitrogen ['naɪtrədʒən] n azoto

○ **KEYWORD**

no [nəʊ] (pl **noes**) adv (opposite of "yes") no;
 are you coming? — no (I'm not) viene?
 — no (non vengo); **would you like some
 more? — no thank you** ne vuole ancora
 un po'? — no, grazie
 ▷ adj (not any) nessuno(-a); **I have no
 money/time/books** non ho soldi/

tempo/libri; **no student would have
 done it** nessuno studente lo avrebbe
 fatto; **"no parking"** "divieto di sosta"; **"no
 smoking"** "vietato fumare"
 ▷ n no m inv

nobility [nəʊ'bɪlɪtɪ] n nobiltà
noble ['nəʊbl] adj nobile
nobody ['nəʊbədɪ] pron nessuno
nod [nɔd] vi accennare col capo, fare un
 cenno; (in agreement) annuire con un cenno
 del capo; (sleep) sonnecchiare ▷ vt **to ~
 one's head** fare di sì col capo ▷ n cenno;
 nod off vi assopirsi
noise [nɔɪz] n rumore m; (din, racket)
 chiasso; **I can't sleep for the ~** non riesco
 a dormire a causa del rumore; **noisy**
 adj (street, car) rumoroso(-a); (person)
 chiassoso(-a)
nominal ['nɔmɪnl] adj nominale; (rent)
 simbolico(-a)
nominate ['nɔmɪneɪt] vt (propose)
 proporre come candidato; (elect)
 nominare; **nomination** [nɔmɪ'neɪʃə
 n] n nomina; candidatura; **nominee**
 [nɔmɪ'ni:] n persona nominata,
 candidato(-a)
none [nʌn] pron (not one thing) niente;
 (not one person) nessuno(-a); **~ of you**
 nessuno(-a) di voi; **I've ~ left** non ne ho
 più; **he's ~ the worse for it** non ne ha
 risentito
nonetheless [nʌnðə'lɛs] adv
 nondimeno
non-fiction [nɔn'fɪkʃən] n saggistica
nonsense ['nɔnsəns] n sciocchezze fpl
non: **non-smoker** n non fumatore(-trice);
 non-smoking adj (person) che non fuma;
 (area, section) per non fumatori; **non-stick**
 adj antiaderente, antiadesivo(-a)
noodles ['nu:dlz] npl taglierini mpl
noon [nu:n] n mezzogiorno
no-one ['nəʊwʌn] pron = **nobody**
nor [nɔ:ʳ] conj = **neither** ▷ adv see **neither**
norm [nɔ:m] n norma
normal ['nɔ:ml] adj normale; **normally**
 adv normalmente
north [nɔ:θ] n nord m, settentrione m
 ▷ adj nord inv, del nord, settentrionale
 ▷ adv verso nord; **North America** n
 America del Nord; **North American**
 adj, n nordamericano(-a); **northbound**
 ['nɔ:θbaʊnd] adj (traffic) diretto(-a)
 a nord; (carriageway) nord inv; **north-
 east** n nord-est m; **northeastern** adj
 nordorientale; **northern** ['nɔ:ðən] adj del
 nord, settentrionale; **Northern Ireland**
 n Irlanda del Nord; **North Korea** n Corea
 del Nord; **North Pole** n Polo Nord; **North**

Sea *n* Mare *m* del Nord; **north-west**
n nord-ovest *m*; **northwestern** *adj*
nordoccidentale

Norway ['nɔ:weɪ] *n* Norvegia; **Norwegian**
[nɔ:'wi:dʒən] *adj* norvegese ▷ *n*
norvegese *m/f*; (*Ling*) norvegese *m*

nose [nəuz] *n* naso; (*of animal*) muso
▷ *vi* **to ~ about** aggirarsi; **nosebleed** *n*
emorragia nasale; **nosey** (*inf*) *adj* = **nosy**

nostalgia [nɔs'tældʒɪə] *n* nostalgia

nostalgic [nɔs'tældʒɪk] *adj*
nostalgico(-a)

nostril ['nɔstrɪl] *n* narice *f*; (*of horse*)
frogia

nosy ['nəuzɪ] (*inf*) *adj* curioso(-a)

not [nɔt] *adv* non; **he is ~ or isn't here** non
è qui, non c'è; **you must ~ or you mustn't
do that** non devi fare quello; **it's too late,
isn't it or is it ~?** è troppo tardi, vero?, **~
that I don't like him** non che (lui) non mi
piaccia; **~ yet/now** non ancora/ora; *see
also* **all**; **only**

notable ['nəutəbl] *adj* notevole; **notably**
['nəutəblɪ] *adv* (*markedly*) notevolmente;
(*particularly*) in particolare

notch [nɔtʃ] *n* tacca; (*in saw*) dente *m*

note [nəut] *n* nota; (*letter, banknote*)
biglietto ▷ *vt* (*also:* **~ down**) prendere
nota di; **to take ~s** prendere appunti;
notebook *n* taccuino; **noted** ['nəutɪd]
adj celebre; **notepad** *n* bloc-notes *m inv*;
notepaper *n* carta da lettere

nothing ['nʌθɪŋ] *n* nulla *m*, niente *m*;
(*zero*) zero; **he does ~** non fa niente; **~
new/much** *etc* niente di nuovo/speciale
etc; **for ~** per niente

notice ['nəutɪs] *n* avviso; (*of leaving*)
preavviso ▷ *vt* notare, accorgersi di; **to
take ~ of** fare attenzione a; **to bring sth
to sb's ~** far notare qc a qn; **at short ~**
con un breve preavviso; **until further ~**
fino a nuovo avviso; **to hand in one's ~**
licenziarsi; **noticeable** *adj* evidente

notify ['nəutɪfaɪ] *vt* **to ~ sth to sb** far
sapere qc a qn; **to ~ sb of sth** avvisare qn
di qc

notion ['nəuʃən] *n* idea; (*concept*) nozione
f; **~s** *npl* (*US: haberdashery*) merceria

notorious [nəu'tɔ:rɪəs] *adj*
famigerato(-a)

notwithstanding [nɔtwɪθ'stændɪŋ] *adv*
nondimeno ▷ *prep* nonostante, malgrado

nought [nɔ:t] *n* zero

noun [naun] *n* nome *m*, sostantivo

nourish ['nʌrɪʃ] *vt* nutrire; **nourishment**
n nutrimento

Nov. *abbr* (= *November*) nov.

novel ['nɔvl] *n* romanzo ▷ *adj* nuovo(-a);
novelist *n* romanziere(-a); **novelty** *n*

novità *f inv*

November [nəu'vɛmbəʳ] *n* novembre *m*

novice ['nɔvɪs] *n* principiante *m/f*; (*Rel*)
novizio/a

now [nau] *adv* ora, adesso ▷ *conj* **~
(that)** adesso che, ora che; **by ~** ormai;
just ~ proprio ora; **right ~** subito,
immediatamente; **~ and then, ~ and
again** ogni tanto; **from ~ on** da ora in poi;
nowadays ['nauədeɪz] *adv* oggidì

nowhere ['nəuwɛəʳ] *adv* in nessun luogo,
da nessuna parte

nozzle ['nɔzl] *n* (*of hose etc*) boccaglio; (*of
fire extinguisher*) lancia

nr *abbr* (BRIT) = **near**

nuclear ['nju:klɪəʳ] *adj* nucleare

nucleus ['nju:klɪəs] (*pl* **nuclei**) *n* nucleo

nude [nju:d] *adj* nudo(-a) ▷ *n* (*Art*) nudo;
in the ~ tutto(-a) nudo(-a)

nudge [nʌdʒ] *vt* dare una gomitata a

nudist ['nju:dɪst] *n* nudista *m/f*

nudity ['nju:dɪtɪ] *n* nudità

nuisance ['nju:sns] *n* **it's a ~** è una
seccatura; **he's a ~** è uno scocciatore

numb [nʌm] *adj* **~ (with)** intorpidito(-a)
(da); (*with fear*) impietrito(-a) (da); **~ with
cold** intirizzito(-a) (dal freddo)

number ['nʌmbəʳ] *n* numero ▷ *vt*
numerare; (*include*) contare; **a ~ of** un
certo numero di; **to be ~ed among** venire
annoverato(-a) tra; **they were 10 in ~**
erano in tutto 10; **number plate** (BRIT)
n (*Aut*) targa; **Number Ten** *n* (BRIT: = 10
Downing Street) residenza del Primo Ministro
del Regno Unito

numerical [nju:'mɛrɪkl] *adj*
numerico(-a)

numerous ['nju:mərəs] *adj*
numeroso(-a)

nun [nʌn] *n* suora, monaca

nurse [nə:s] *n* infermiere(-a); (*also:*
~maid) bambinaia ▷ *vt* (*patient, cold*)
curare; (*baby:* BRIT) cullare; (: *US*) allattare,
dare il latte a

nursery ['nə:sərɪ] *n* (*room*) camera dei
bambini; (*institution*) asilo; (*for plants*)
vivaio; **nursery rhyme** *n* filastrocca;
nursery school *n* scuola materna;
nursery slope (BRIT) *n* (*Ski*) pista per
principianti

nursing ['nə:sɪŋ] *n* (*profession*)
professione *f* di infermiere (*or* di
infermiera); (*care*) cura; **nursing home** *n*
casa di cura

nurture ['nə:tʃəʳ] *vt* allevare; nutrire

nut [nʌt] *n* (*of metal*) dado; (*fruit*) noce *f*

nutmeg ['nʌtmɛg] *n* noce *f* moscata

nutrient ['nju:trɪənt] *adj* nutriente ▷ *n*
sostanza nutritiva

nutrition [njuːˈtrɪʃən] *n* nutrizione *f*
nutritious [njuːˈtrɪʃəs] *adj* nutriente
nuts [nʌts] (*inf*) *adj* matto(-a)
NVQ *n abbr* (BRIT) = **National Vocational Qualification**
nylon [ˈnaɪlɔn] *n* nailon *m* ▷ *adj* di nailon

oak [əuk] *n* quercia ▷ *adj* di quercia
O.A.P. (BRIT) *n, abbr* = **old age pensioner**
oar [ɔːʳ] *n* remo
oasis [əuˈeɪsɪs] (*pl* **oases**) *n* oasi *f inv*
oath [əuθ] *n* giuramento; (*swear word*) bestemmia
oatmeal [ˈəutmiːl] *n* farina d'avena
oats [əuts] *npl* avena
obedience [əˈbiːdɪəns] *n* ubbidienza
obedient [əˈbiːdɪənt] *adj* ubbidiente
obese [əuˈbiːs] *adj* obeso(-a)
obesity [əuˈbiːsɪtɪ] *n* obesità
obey [əˈbeɪ] *vt* ubbidire a; (*instructions, regulations*) osservare
obituary [əˈbɪtjuərɪ] *n* necrologia
object [*n* ˈɔbdʒɪkt, *vb* əbˈdʒɛkt] *n* oggetto; (*purpose*) scopo, intento; (*Ling*) complemento oggetto ▷ *vi* **to ~ to** (*attitude*) disapprovare; (*proposal*) protestare contro, sollevare delle obiezioni contro; **expense is no ~** non si bada a spese; **to ~ that** obiettare che; **objection** [əbˈdʒɛkʃən] *n* obiezione *f*; **objective** *n* obiettivo
obligation [ɔblɪˈgeɪʃən] *n* obbligo, dovere *m*; **without ~** senza impegno
obligatory [əˈblɪgətərɪ] *adj* obbligatorio(-a)
oblige [əˈblaɪdʒ] *vt* (*force*): **to ~ sb to do** costringere qn a fare; (*do a favour*) fare una

cortesia a; **to be ~d to sb for sth** essere
grato a qn per qc
oblique [ə'bli:k] *adj* obliquo(-a); (*allusion*)
indiretto(-a)
obliterate [ə'blɪtəreɪt] *vt* cancellare
oblivious [ə'blɪvɪəs] *adj* **~ of** incurante di;
inconscio(-a) di
oblong ['ɔblɔŋ] *adj* oblungo(-a) ▷ *n*
rettangolo
obnoxious [əb'nɔkʃəs] *adj* odioso(-a);
(*smell*) disgustoso(-a), ripugnante
oboe ['əubəu] *n* oboe *m*
obscene [əb'si:n] *adj* osceno(-a)
obscure [əb'skjuəʳ] *adj* oscuro(-a) ▷ *vt*
oscurare; (*hide: sun*) nascondere
observant [əb'zə:vnt] *adj* attento(-a)

> Be careful not to translate *observant*
> by the Italian word *osservante*.

observation [ɔbzə'veɪʃən] *n* osservazione
f; (*by police etc*) sorveglianza
observatory [əb'zə:vətrɪ] *n*
osservatorio
observe [əb'zə:v] *vt* osservare;
(*remark*) fare osservare; **observer** *n*
osservatore(-trice)
obsess [əb'sɛs] *vt* ossessionare; **obsession**
[əb'sɛʃən] *n* ossessione *f*; **obsessive** *adj*
ossessivo(-a)
obsolete ['ɔbsəli:t] *adj* obsoleto(-a)
obstacle ['ɔbstəkl] *n* ostacolo
obstinate ['ɔbstɪnɪt] *adj* ostinato(-a)
obstruct [əb'strʌkt] *vt* (*block*) ostruire,
ostacolare; (*halt*) fermare; (*hinder*)
impedire; **obstruction** [əb'strʌkʃən] *n*
ostruzione *f*; ostacolo
obtain [əb'teɪn] *vt* ottenere
obvious ['ɔbvɪəs] *adj* ovvio(-a), evidente;
obviously *adv* ovviamente; certo
occasion [ə'keɪʒən] *n* occasione *f*;
(*event*) avvenimento; **occasional** *adj*
occasionale; **occasionally** *adv* ogni
tanto
occult [ɔ'kʌlt] *adj* occulto(-a) ▷ *n* **the ~**
l'occulto
occupant ['ɔkjupənt] *n* occupante *m/f*; (*of
boat, car etc*) persona a bordo
occupation [ɔkju'peɪʃən] *n* occupazione *f*;
(*job*) mestiere *m*, professione *f*
occupy ['ɔkjupaɪ] *vt* occupare; **to ~ o.s. in
doing** occuparsi a fare
occur [ə'kə:ʳ] *vi* succedere, capitare; **to ~
to sb** venire in mente a qn; **occurrence** *n*
caso, fatto; presenza

> Be careful not to translate *occur* by
> the Italian word *occorrere*.

ocean ['əuʃən] *n* oceano
o'clock [ə'klɔk] *adv* **it is 5 o'clock** sono le 5
Oct. *abbr* (= *October*) ott.
October [ɔk'təubəʳ] *n* ottobre *m*

octopus ['ɔktəpəs] *n* polpo, piovra
odd [ɔd] *adj* (*strange*) strano(-a),
bizzarro(-a); (*number*) dispari *inv*; (*not of a
set*) spaiato(-a); **60-~** 60 e oltre; **at ~ times**
di tanto in tanto; **the ~ one out** l'eccezione
f; **oddly** *adv* stranamente; **odds** *npl* (*in
betting*) quota
odometer [ɔ'dɔmɪtəʳ] *n* odometro
odour ['əudəʳ] (*us* **odor**) *n* odore *m*;
(*unpleasant*) cattivo odore

 KEYWORD

of [ɔv, əv] *prep* **1** (*gen*) di; **a boy of 10** un
ragazzo di 10 anni; **a friend of ours** un
nostro amico; **that was kind of you** è
stato molto gentile da parte sua
2 (*expressing quantity, amount, dates etc*)
di; **a kilo of flour** un chilo di farina; **how
much of this do you need?** quanto gliene
serve?; **there were 3 of them** (*people*)
erano in 3; (*objects*) ce n'erano 3; **3 of us
went** 3 di noi sono andati; **the 5th of July**
il 5 luglio
3 (*from, out of*) di, in; **of made of wood**
(fatto) di *or* in legno

KEYWORD

off [ɔf] *adv* **1** (*distance, time*): **it's a long way
off** è lontano; **the game is 3 days off** la
partita è tra 3 giorni
2 (*departure, removal*) via; **to go off to
Paris** andarsene a Parigi; **I must be off**
devo andare via; **to take off one's coat**
togliersi il cappotto; **the button came off**
il bottone è venuto via *or* si è staccato; **10%
off** con lo sconto del 10%
3 (*not at work*): **to have a day off** avere un
giorno libero; **to be off sick** essere assente
per malattia
▷ *adj* (*engine*) spento(-a); (*tap*) chiuso(-a);
(*cancelled*) sospeso(-a); (BRIT: *food*)
andato(-a) a male; **on the off chance**
nel caso; **to have an off day** non essere
in forma
▷ *prep* **1** (*motion, removal etc*) da; (*distant
from*) a poca distanza da; **a street off the
square** una strada che parte dalla piazza
2: **to be off meat** non mangiare più la
carne

offence [ə'fɛns] (*us* **offense**) *n* (*Law*)
contravvenzione *f*; (: *more serious*) reato; **to
take ~ at** offendersi per
offend [ə'fɛnd] *vt* (*person*) offendere;
offender *n* delinquente *m/f*; (*against
regulations*) contravventore(-trice)
offense [ə'fɛns] (*us*) *n* = **offence**

offensive [əˈfɛnsɪv] adj offensivo(-a); (smell etc) sgradevole, ripugnante ▷ n (Mil) offensiva

offer [ˈɔfəʳ] n offerta, proposta ▷ vt offrire; **"on ~"** (Comm) "in offerta speciale"

offhand [ɔfˈhænd] adj disinvolto(-a), noncurante ▷ adv su due piedi

office [ˈɔfɪs] n (place) ufficio; (position) carica; **doctor's ~** (US) studio; **to take ~** entrare in carica; **office block** (US **office building**) n complesso di uffici; **office hours** npl orario d'ufficio; (US Med) orario di visite

officer [ˈɔfɪsəʳ] n (Mil etc) ufficiale m; (also: **police ~**) agente m di polizia; (of organization) funzionario

office worker n impiegato(-a) d'ufficio

official [əˈfɪʃl] adj (authorized) ufficiale ▷ n ufficiale m; (civil servant) impiegato(-a) statale; funzionario

off: **off-licence** (BRIT) n (shop) spaccio di bevande alcoliche; **off-line** adj, adv (Comput) off-line inv, fuori linea; (: switched off) spento(-a); **off-peak** adj (ticket, heating etc) a tariffa ridotta; (time) non di punta; **off-putting** (BRIT) adj sgradevole, antipatico(-a); **off-season** adj, adv fuori stagione; **offset** [ˈɔfsɛt] (irreg) vt (counteract) controbilanciare, compensare; **offshore** [ɔfˈʃɔːʳ] adj (breeze) di terra; (island) vicino alla costa; (fishing) costiero(-a); **offside** [ˈɔfsaɪd] adj (Sport) fuori gioco; (Aut: in Britain) destro(-a); (: in Italy etc) sinistro(-a); **offspring** [ˈɔfsprɪŋ] n inv prole f, discendenza

often [ˈɔfn] adv spesso; **how ~ do you go?** quanto spesso ci vai?

oh [əu] excl oh!

oil [ɔɪl] n olio; (petroleum) petrolio; (for central heating) nafta ▷ vt (machine) lubrificare; **oil filter** n (Aut) filtro dell'olio; **oil painting** n quadro a olio; **oil refinery** n raffineria di petrolio; **oil rig** n derrick m inv; (at sea) piattaforma per trivellazioni subacquee; **oil slick** n chiazza d'olio; **oil tanker** n (ship) petroliera; (truck) autocisterna per petrolio; **oil well** n pozzo petrolifero; **oily** adj unto(-a), oleoso(-a); (food) grasso(-a)

ointment [ˈɔɪntmənt] n unguento

O.K. [ˈəuˈkeɪ] excl d'accordo! ▷ adj non male inv ▷ vt approvare; **is it O.K.?, are you O.K.?** tutto bene?

old [əuld] adj vecchio(-a); (ancient) antico(-a), vecchio(-a); (person) vecchio(-a), anziano(-a); **how ~ are you?** quanti anni ha?; **he's 10 years ~** ha 10 anni; **~er brother** fratello maggiore; **old age** n

vecchiaia; **old-age pension** [ˈəuldeɪdʒ-] n (BRIT) pensione f di vecchiaia; **old-age pensioner** (BRIT) n pensionato(-a); **old-fashioned** adj antiquato(-a), fuori moda; (person) all'antica; **old people's home** n ricovero per anziani

olive [ˈɔlɪv] n (fruit) oliva; (tree) olivo ▷ adj (also: **~-green**) verde oliva inv; **olive oil** n olio d'oliva

Olympic [əuˈlɪmpɪk] adj olimpico(-a); **the ~ Games, the ~s** i giochi olimpici, le Olimpiadi

omelet(te) [ˈɔmlɪt] n omelette f inv

omen [ˈəumən] n presagio, augurio

ominous [ˈɔmɪnəs] adj minaccioso(-a); (event) di malaugurio

omit [əuˈmɪt] vt omettere

 KEYWORD

on [ɔn] prep **1** (indicating position) su; **on the wall** sulla parete; **on the left** a or sulla sinistra

2 (indicating means, method, condition etc): **on foot** a piedi; **on the train/plane** in treno/aereo; **on the telephone** al telefono; **on the radio/television** alla radio/televisione; **to be on drugs** drogarsi; **on holiday** in vacanza

3 (of time): **on Friday** venerdì; **on Fridays** il or di venerdì; **on June 20th** il 20 giugno; **on Friday, June 20th** venerdì, 20 giugno; **a week on Friday** venerdì a otto; **on his arrival** al suo arrivo; **on seeing this** vedendo ciò

4 (about, concerning) su, di; **information on train services** informazioni sui collegamenti ferroviari; **a book on Goldoni/physics** un libro su Goldoni/di or sulla fisica

▷ adv **1** (referring to dress, covering): **to have one's coat on** avere indosso il cappotto; **to put one's coat on** mettersi il cappotto; **what's she got on?** cosa indossa?; **she put her boots/gloves/hat on** si mise gli stivali/i guanti/il cappello; **screw the lid on tightly** avvita bene il coperchio

2 (further, continuously): **to walk on, go on** etc continuare, proseguire etc; **to read on** continuare a leggere; **on and off** ogni tanto

▷ adj **1** (in operation: machine, TV, light) acceso(-a); (: tap) aperto(-a); (: brake) inserito(-a); **is the meeting still on?** (in progress) la riunione è ancora in corso?; (not cancelled) è confermato l'incontro?; **there's a good film on at the cinema** danno un buon film al cinema

2 (*inf*): **that's not on!** (*not acceptable*) non si fa così!; (*not possible*) non se ne parla neanche!

once [wʌns] *adv* una volta ▷ *conj* non appena, quando; **~ he had left/it was done** dopo che se n'era andato/fu fatto; **at ~** subito; (*simultaneously*) a un tempo; **~ a week** una volta per settimana; **~ more** ancora una volta; **~ and for all** una volta per sempre; **~ upon a time** c'era una volta

oncoming ['ɒnkʌmɪŋ] *adj* (*traffic*) che viene in senso opposto

 KEYWORD

one [wʌn] *num* uno(-a); **one hundred and fifty** centocinquanta; **one day** un giorno ▷ *adj* **1** (*sole*) unico(-a), **the one book which** l'unico libro che; **the one man who** l'unico che

2 (*same*) stesso(-a); **they came in the one car** sono venuti nella stessa macchina ▷ *pron* **1**: **this one** questo(-a); **that one** quello(-a); **I've already got one/a red one** ne ho già uno/uno rosso; **one by one** uno per uno

2: **one another** l'un l'altro; **to look at one another** guardarsi; **to help one another** auitarsi l'un l'altro *or* a vicenda

3 (*impersonal*) si; **one never knows** non si sa mai; **to cut one's finger** tagliarsi un dito; **one needs to eat** bisogna mangiare

one: **one-off** (*BRIT*: *inf*) *n* fatto eccezionale
oneself [wʌn'sɛlf] *pron* (*reflexive*) si; (*after prep*) se stesso(-a), sé; **to do sth (by) ~** fare qc da sé; **to hurt ~** farsi male; **to keep sth for ~** tenere qc per sé; **to talk to ~** parlare da solo
one: **one-shot** [wʌn'ʃɒt] (*US*) *n* = **one-off**; **one-sided** *adj* (*argument*) unilaterale; **one-to-one** *adj* (*relationship*) univoco(-a); **one-way** *adj* (*street, traffic*) a senso unico
ongoing ['ɒngəʊɪŋ] *adj* in corso; in attuazione
onion ['ʌnjən] *n* cipolla
on-line ['ɒnlaɪn] *adj, adv* (*Comput*) on-line *inv*
onlooker ['ɒnlʊkə^r] *n* spettatore(-trice)
only ['əʊnlɪ] *adv* solo, soltanto ▷ *adj* solo(-a), unico(-a) ▷ *conj* solo che, ma; **an ~ child** un figlio unico; **not ~ ... but also** non solo ... ma anche
on-screen [ɒn'skri:n] *adj* sullo schermo *inv*
onset ['ɒnsɛt] *n* inizio
onto ['ɒntu] *prep* = **on to**
onward(s) ['ɒnwəd(z)] *adv* (*move*) in avanti; **from that time onward(s)** da

quella volta in poi
oops [ʊps] *excl* ops! (*esprime rincrescimento per un piccolo contrattempo*); **~-a-daisy!** oplà!
ooze [u:z] *vi* stillare
opaque [əʊ'peɪk] *adj* opaco(-a)
open ['əʊpn] *adj* aperto(-a); (*road*) libero(-a); (*meeting*) pubblico(-a) ▷ *vt* aprire ▷ *vi* (*eyes, door, debate*) aprirsi; (*flower*) sbocciare; (*shop, bank, museum*) aprire; (*book etc*: *commence*) cominciare; **is it ~ to the public?** è aperto al pubblico?; **in the ~ (air)** all'aperto; **what time do you ~?** a che ora aprite?; **open up** *vt* aprire; (*blocked road*) sgombrare ▷ *vi* (*shop, business*) aprire; **open-air** *adj* all'aperto; **opening** *adj* (*speech*) di apertura ▷ *n* apertura; (*opportunity*) occasione *f*, opportunità *f inv*; sbocco; **opening hours** *npl* orario d'apertura; **open learning** *n* sistema educativo secondo il quale lo studente ha maggior controllo e gestione delle modalità di apprendimento; **openly** *adv* apertamente; **open-minded** *adj* che ha la mente aperta; **open-necked** *adj* col collo slacciato; **open-plan** *adj* senza pareti divisorie; **Open University** *n* (*BRIT*) vedi nota nel riquadro

● **OPEN UNIVERSITY**

La **Open University**, fondata in Gran
Bretagna nel 1969, organizza corsi
di laurea per corrispondenza o via
Internet. Alcune lezioni possono venir
seguite per radio o alla televisione e
vengono organizzati regolari corsi
estivi.

opera ['ɒpərə] *n* opera; **opera house** *n* opera; **opera singer** *n* cantante *m/f* d'opera *or* lirico(-a)
operate ['ɒpəreɪt] *vt* (*machine*) azionare, far funzionare; (*system*) usare ▷ *vi* funzionare; (*drug*) essere efficace; **to ~ on sb (for)** (*Med*) operare qn (di)
operating room (*US*) *n* = **operating theatre**
operating theatre *n* (*Med*) sala operatoria
operation [ɒpə'reɪʃən] *n* operazione *f*; **to be in ~** (*machine*) essere in azione *or* funzionamento; (*system*) essere in vigore; **to have an ~** (*Med*) subire un'operazione; **operational** *adj* in funzione; d'esercizio
operative ['ɒpərətɪv] *adj* (*measure*) operativo(-a)
operator ['ɒpəreɪtə^r] *n* (*of machine*) operatore(-trice); (*Tel*) centralinista *m/f*

opinion [ə'pɪnɪən] *n* opinione *f*, parere *m*;
in my ~ secondo me, a mio avviso; **opinion
poll** *n* sondaggio di opinioni

opponent [ə'pəunənt] *n* avversario(-a)

opportunity [ɔpə'tjuːnɪtɪ] *n* opportunità
f inv, occasione *f*; **to take the ~ of doing**
cogliere l'occasione per fare

oppose [ə'pəuz] *vt* opporsi a; **~d to**
contrario(-a) a; **as ~d to** in contrasto con

opposite ['ɔpəzɪt] *adj* opposto(-a); (*house
etc*) di fronte ▷ *adv* di fronte, dirimpetto
▷ *prep* di fronte a ▷ *n* **the ~** il contrario,
l'opposto; **the ~ sex** l'altro sesso

opposition [ɔpə'zɪʃən] *n* opposizione *f*

oppress [ə'prɛs] *vt* opprimere

opt [ɔpt] *vi* **to ~ for** optare per; **to ~ to do**
scegliere di fare; **opt out** *vi* **to ~ out of**
ritirarsi da

optician [ɔp'tɪʃən] *n* ottico

optimism ['ɔptɪmɪzəm] *n* ottimismo

optimist ['ɔptɪmɪst] *n* ottimista *m/f*;
optimistic [-'mɪstɪk] *adj* ottimistico(-a)

optimum ['ɔptɪməm] *adj* ottimale

option ['ɔpʃən] *n* scelta; (*Scol*) materia
facoltativa; (*Comm*) opzione *f*; **optional**
adj facoltativo(-a); (*Comm*) a scelta

or [ɔːʳ] *conj* o, oppure; (*with negative*): **he
hasn't seen or heard anything** non
ha visto né sentito niente; **or else** se no,
altrimenti; oppure

oral ['ɔːrəl] *adj* orale ▷ *n* esame *m* orale

orange ['ɔrɪndʒ] *n* (*fruit*) arancia ▷ *adj*
arancione; **orange juice** *n* succo
d'arancia; **orange squash** *n* succo
d'arancia (*da diluire con l'acqua*)

orbit ['ɔːbɪt] *n* orbita ▷ *vt* orbitare intorno
a

orchard ['ɔːtʃəd] *n* frutteto

orchestra ['ɔːkɪstrə] *n* orchestra; (*us:
seating*) platea

orchid ['ɔːkɪd] *n* orchidea

ordeal [ɔː'diːl] *n* prova, travaglio

order ['ɔːdəʳ] *n* ordine *m*; (*Comm*)
ordinazione *f* ▷ *vt* ordinare; **can I ~ now,
please?** posso ordinare, per favore?; **in
~** in ordine; (*of document*) in regola; **in
(working) ~** funzionante; **in ~ to do** per
fare; **in ~ that** affinché + *sub*; **on ~** (*Comm*)
in ordinazione; **out of ~** non in ordine; (*not
working*) guasto; **to ~ sb to do** ordinare
a qn di fare; **order form** *n* modulo
d'ordinazione; **orderly** *n* (*Mil*) attendente
m; (*Med*) inserviente *m* ▷ *adj* (*room*) in
ordine; (*mind*) metodico(-a); (*person*)
ordinato(-a), metodico(-a)

ordinary ['ɔːdnrɪ] *adj* normale, comune;
(*pej*) mediocre; **out of the ~** diverso dal
solito, fuori dell'ordinario

ore [ɔːʳ] *n* minerale *m* grezzo

oregano [ɔrɪ'gɑːnəu] *n* origano

organ ['ɔːgən] *n* organo; **organic**
[ɔː'gænɪk] *adj* organico(-a); (*of food*)
biologico(-a); **organism** *n* organismo

organization [ɔːgənaɪ'zeɪʃən] *n*
organizzazione *f*

organize ['ɔːgənaɪz] *vt* organizzare; **to
get ~d** organizzarsi; **organized** ['ɔːgə
naɪzd] *adj* organizzato(-a); **organizer** *n*
organizzatore(-trice)

orgasm ['ɔːgæzəm] *n* orgasmo

orgy ['ɔːdʒɪ] *n* orgia

oriental [ɔːrɪ'ɛntl] *adj*, *n* orientale *m/f*

orientation [ɔːrɪɛn'teɪʃən] *n*
orientamento

origin ['ɔrɪdʒɪn] *n* origine *f*

original [ə'rɪdʒɪnl] *adj* originale; (*earliest*)
originario(-a) ▷ *n* originale *m*; **originally**
adv (*at first*) all'inizio

originate [ə'rɪdʒɪneɪt] *vi* **to ~ from** essere
originario(-a) di; (*suggestion*) provenire da;
to ~ in avere origine in

Orkneys ['ɔːknɪz] *npl* **the ~** (*also:* **the
Orkney Islands**) le Orcadi

ornament ['ɔːnəmənt] *n* ornamento;
(*trinket*) ninnolo; **ornamental** [-'mɛntl]
adj ornamentale

ornate [ɔː'neɪt] *adj* molto ornato(-a)

orphan ['ɔːfn] *n* orfano(-a)

orthodox ['ɔːθədɔks] *adj* ortodosso(-a)

orthopaedic [ɔːθə'piːdɪk] (*us* **orthopedic**)
adj ortopedico(-a)

osteopath ['ɔstɪəpæθ] *n* specialista *m/f* di
osteopatia

ostrich ['ɔstrɪtʃ] *n* struzzo

other ['ʌðəʳ] *adj* altro(-a) ▷ *pron* **the ~
(one)** l'altro(-a); **~s** (*other people*) altri *mpl*;
~ than altro che; a parte; **otherwise** *adv*,
conj altrimenti

otter ['ɔtəʳ] *n* lontra

ouch [autʃ] *excl* ohi!, ahi!

ought [ɔːt] (*pt* **ought**) *aux vb* **I ~ to do
it** dovrei farlo; **this ~ to have been
corrected** questo avrebbe dovuto essere
corretto; **he ~ to win** dovrebbe vincere

ounce [auns] *n* oncia (= 28.35 *g*, 16 *in a
pound*)

our ['auəʳ] *adj* il (la) nostro(-a); (*pl*) i (le)
nostri(-e); *see also* **my**; **ours** *pron* il (la)
nostro(-a); (*pl*) i (le) nostri(-e); *see also*
mine; **ourselves** *pron pl* (*reflexive*) ci; (*after
preposition*) noi; (*emphatic*) noi stessi(-e);
see also **oneself**

oust [aust] *vt* cacciare, espellere

out [aut] *adv* (*gen*) fuori; **~ here/there**
qui/là fuori; **to speak ~ loud** parlare
forte; **to have a night ~** uscire una sera;
the boat was 10 km ~ la barca era a 10
km dalla costa; **3 days ~ from Plym~h** a 3

giorni da Plymouth; **~ of** (*outside*) fuori di; (*because of*) per; **~ of 10** su 10; **~ of petrol** senza benzina; **outback** ['autbæk] *n* (*in Australia*) interno, entroterra; **outbound** *adj* **outbound (for** *or* **da)** in partenza (per *or* da); **outbreak** ['autbreɪk] *n* scoppio; epidemia; **outburst** ['autbə:st] *n* scoppio; **outcast** ['autkɑ:st] *n* esule *m/f*; (*socially*) paria *m inv*; **outcome** ['autkʌm] *n* esito, risultato; **outcry** ['autkraɪ] *n* protesta, clamore *m*; **outdated** [aut'deɪtɪd] *adj* (*custom, clothes*) fuori moda; (*idea*) sorpassato(-a); **outdoor** [aut'dɔ:ʳ] *adj* all'aperto; **outdoors** *adv* fuori; all'aria aperta

outer ['autəʳ] *adj* esteriore; **outer space** *n* spazio cosmico

outfit ['autfɪt] *n* (*clothes*) completo; (*: for sport*) tenuta

out: **outgoing** ['autgəuɪŋ] *adj* (*character*) socievole; **outgoings** (BRIT) *npl* (*expenses*) spese *fpl*, uscite *fpl*; **outhouse** ['authaus] *n* costruzione *f* annessa

outing ['autɪŋ] *n* gita; escursione *f*

out: **outlaw** ['autlɔ:] *n* fuorilegge *m/f* ▷ *vt* bandire; **outlay** ['autleɪ] *n* spese *fpl*; (*investment*) sborsa, spesa; **outlet** ['autlɛt] *n* (*for liquid etc*) sbocco, scarico; (US Elec) presa di corrente; (*also*: **retail outlet**) punto di vendita; **outline** ['autlaɪn] *n* contorno, profilo; (*summary*) abbozzo, grandi linee *fpl* ▷ *vt* (*fig*) descrivere a grandi linee; **outlook** ['autluk] *n* prospettiva, vista; **outnumber** [aut'nʌmbəʳ] *vt* superare in numero; **out-of-date** *adj* (*passport*) scaduto(-a); (*clothes*) fuori moda *inv*; **out-of-doors** [autəv'dɔ:z] *adv* all'aperto; **out-of-the-way** *adj* (*place*) fuori mano *inv*; **out-of-town** [autəv'taun] *adj* (*shopping centre etc*) fuori città; **outpatient** ['autpeɪʃənt] *n* paziente *m/f* esterno(-a); **outpost** ['autpəust] *n* avamposto; **output** ['autput] *n* produzione *f*; (Comput) output *m inv*

outrage ['autreɪdʒ] *n* oltraggio; scandalo ▷ *vt* oltraggiare; **outrageous** [-'reɪdʒəs] *adj* oltraggioso(-a), scandaloso(-a)

outright [*adv* aut'raɪt, *adj* 'autraɪt] *adv* completamente; schiettamente; apertamente; sul colpo ▷ *adj* completo(-a), schietto(-a) e netto(-a)

outset ['autsɛt] *n* inizio

outside [aut'saɪd] *n* esterno, esteriore *m* ▷ *adj* esterno(-a), esteriore ▷ *adv* fuori, all'esterno ▷ *prep* fuori di, all'esterno di; **at the ~** (*fig*) al massimo; **outside lane** *n* (Aut) corsia di sorpasso; **outside line** *n* (Tel) linea esterna; **outsider** *n* (*in race etc*) outsider *m inv*; (*stranger*) estraneo(-a)

out: **outsize** ['autsaɪz] *adj* (*clothes*) per taglie forti; **outskirts** ['autskə:ts] *npl* sobborghi *mpl*; **outspoken** [aut'spəukən] *adj* molto franco(-a); **outstanding** [aut'stændɪŋ] *adj* eccezionale, di rilievo; (*unfinished*) non completo(-a); non evaso(-a); non regolato(-a)

outward ['autwəd] *adj* (*sign, appearances*) esteriore; (*journey*) d'andata; **outwards** ['autwədz] *adv* (*esp* BRIT) = **outward**

outweigh [aut'weɪ] *vt* avere maggior peso di

oval ['əuvl] *adj* ovale ▷ *n* ovale *m*

ovary ['əuvərɪ] *n* ovaia

oven ['ʌvn] *n* forno; **oven glove** *n* guanto da forno; **ovenproof** *adj* da forno; **oven-ready** *adj* pronto(-a) da infornare

over ['əuvəʳ] *adv* al di sopra ▷ *adj* (*or adv*) (*finished*) finito(-a), terminato(-a); (*too*) troppo; (*remaining*) che avanza ▷ *prep* su; sopra; (*above*) al di sopra di; (*on the other side of*) di là di; (*more than*) più di; (*during*) durante; **~ here** qui; **~ there** là; **all ~** (*everywhere*) dappertutto; (*finished*) tutto(-a) finito(-a); **~ and ~ (again)** più e più volte; **~ and above** oltre (a); **to ask sb ~** invitare qn (a passare)

overall [*adj, n* 'əuvərɔ:l, *adv* əuvər'ɔ:l] *adj* totale ▷ *n* (BRIT) grembiule *m* ▷ *adv* nell'insieme, complessivamente; **~s** *npl* (*worker's overalls*) tuta (da lavoro)

overboard ['əuvəbɔ:d] *adv* (Naut) fuori bordo, in mare

overcame [əuvə'keɪm] *pt of* **overcome**

overcast ['əuvəkɑ:st] *adj* (*sky*) coperto(-a)

overcharge [əuvə'tʃɑ:dʒ] *vt* **to ~ sb for sth** far pagare troppo caro a qn per qc

overcoat ['əuvəkəut] *n* soprabito, cappotto

overcome [əuvə'kʌm] (*irreg*) *vt* superare; sopraffare

over: **overcrowded** [əuvə'kraudɪd] *adj* sovraffollato(-a); **overdo** [əuvə'du:] (*irreg*) *vt* esagerare; (*overcook*) cuocere troppo; **overdone** [əuvə'dʌn] *adj* troppo cotto(-a); **overdose** ['əuvədəus] *n* dose *f* eccessiva; **overdraft** ['əuvədrɑ:ft] *n* scoperto (di conto); **overdrawn** [əuvə'drɔ:n] *adj* (*account*) scoperto(-a); **overdue** [əuvə'dju:] *adj* in ritardo; **overestimate** [əuvər'ɛstɪmeɪt] *vt* sopravvalutare

overflow [*vb* əuvə'fləu, *n* 'əuvəfləu] *vi* traboccare ▷ *n* (*also*: **~ pipe**) troppopieno

overgrown [əuvə'grəun] *adj* (*garden*) ricoperto(-a) di vegetazione

overhaul [*vb* əuvə'hɔ:l, *n* 'əuvəhɔ:l] *vt* revisionare ▷ *n* revisione *f*

overhead [*adv* əuvə'hɛd, *adj, n* 'əuvəhɛd] *adv* di sopra ▷ *adj* aereo(-a); (*lighting*)

verticale ▷ n (US) = **overheads**;
overhead projector n lavagna luminosa;
overheads npl spese fpl generali
over: **overhear** [əuvə'hɪəʳ] (irreg) vt sentire
(per caso); **overheat** [əuvə'hi:t] vi (engine)
surriscaldare; **overland** adj, adv per via di
terra; **overlap** [əuvə'læp] vi sovrapporsi;
overleaf [əuvə'li:f] adv a tergo; **overload**
[əuvə'ləud] vt sovraccaricare; **overlook**
[əuvə'luk] vt (have view of) dare su; (miss)
trascurare; (forgive) passare sopra a
overnight [əuvə'naɪt] adv (happen)
durante la notte; (fig) tutto ad un tratto
▷ adj di notte; **he stayed there ~** ci ha
passato la notte; **overnight bag** n borsa
da viaggio
overpass ['əuvəpɑ:s] n cavalcavia m inv
overpower [əuvə'pauəʳ] vt sopraffare;
overpowering adj irresistibile; (heat,
stench) soffocante
over: **overreact** [əuvəri:'ækt] vi reagire
in modo esagerato; **overrule** [əuvə'ru:l]
vt (decision) annullare; (claim) respingere;
overrun [əuvə'rʌn] (irreg: like **run**) vt
(country) invadere; (time limit) superare
overseas [əuvə'si:z] adv oltremare;
(abroad) all'estero ▷ adj (trade) estero(-a);
(visitor) straniero(-a)
oversee [əuvə'si:] vt irreg sorvegliare
overshadow [əuvə'ʃædəu] vt far ombra
su; (fig) eclissare
oversight ['əuvəsaɪt] n omissione f, svista
oversleep [əuvə'sli:p] (irreg) vt dormire
troppo a lungo
overspend [əuvə'spɛnd] vi irreg spendere
troppo; **we have overspent by 5000
dollars** abbiamo speso 5000 dollari di
troppo
overt [əu'və:t] adj palese
overtake [əuvə'teɪk] (irreg) vt sorpassare
over: **overthrow** [əuvə'θrəu] (irreg) vt
(government) rovesciare; **overtime** ['əuvə
taɪm] n (lavoro) straordinario
overtook [əuvə'tuk] pt of **overtake**
over: **overturn** [əuvə'tə:n] vt rovesciare
▷ vi rovesciarsi; **overweight** [əuvə'weɪt]
adj (person) troppo grasso(-a); **overwhelm**
[əuvə'wɛlm] vt sopraffare; sommergere;
schiacciare; **overwhelming** adj (victory,
defeat) schiacciante; (heat, desire)
intenso(-a)
ow [au] excl ahi!
owe [əu] vt **to ~ sb sth, to ~ sth to sb**
dovere qc a qn; **how much do I ~ you?**
quanto le devo?; **owing to** prep a causa di
owl [aul] n gufo
own [əun] vt possedere ▷ adj proprio(-a);
a room of my ~ la mia propria camera; **to
get one's ~ back** vendicarsi; **on one's ~**

tutto(-a) solo(-a); **own up** vi confessare;
owner n proprietario(-a); **ownership** n
possesso
ox [ɔks] (pl **oxen**) n bue m
Oxbridge ['ɔksbrɪdʒ] n le università di
Oxford e/o Cambridge
oxen ['ɔksn] npl of **ox**
oxygen ['ɔksɪdʒən] n ossigeno
oyster ['ɔɪstəʳ] n ostrica
oz. abbr = **ounce(s)**
ozone ['əuzəun] n ozono; **ozone friendly**
adj che non danneggia l'ozono; **ozone
layer** n fascia d'ozono

P

p [pi:] *abbr* = **penny**; **pence**

P.A. *n abbr* = **personal assistant**; **public address system**

p.a. *abbr* = **per annum**

pace [peɪs] *n* passo; (*speed*) passo; velocità ▷ *vi* **to ~ up and down** camminare su e giù; **to keep ~ with** camminare di pari passo a; (*events*) tenersi al corrente di; **pacemaker** *n* (*Med*) segnapasso; (*Sport: also:* **pace setter**) battistrada *m inv*

Pacific [pə'sɪfɪk] *n* **the ~ (Ocean)** il Pacifico, l'Oceano Pacifico

pacifier ['pæsɪfaɪəʳ] (*US*) *n* (*dummy*) succhiotto, ciuccio (*col*)

pack [pæk] *n* pacco; (*US: of cigarettes*) pacchetto; (*backpack*) zaino; (*of hounds*) muta; (*of thieves etc*) banda; (*of cards*) mazzo ▷ *vt* (*in suitcase etc*) mettere; (*box*) riempire; (*cram*) stipare, pigiare; **to ~ (one's bags)** fare la valigia; **to ~ sb off** spedire via qn; **~ it in!** (*inf*) dacci un taglio!; **pack in** (*BRIT inf*) *vi* (*watch, car*) guastarsi ▷ *vt* mollare, piantare; **~ it in!** piantala!; **pack up** *vi* (*BRIT inf: machine*) guastarsi; (: *person*) far fagotto ▷ *vt* (*belongings, clothes*) mettere in una valigia; (*goods, presents*) imballare

package ['pækɪdʒ] *n* pacco; balla; (*also:* **~ deal**) pacchetto; forfait *m inv*; **package holiday** *n* vacanza organizzata; **package tour** *n* viaggio organizzato

packaging ['pækɪdʒɪŋ] *n* confezione *f*, imballo

packed [pækt] *adj* (*crowded*) affollato(-a); **packed lunch** *n* pranzo al sacco

packet ['pækɪt] *n* pacchetto

packing ['pækɪŋ] *n* imballaggio

pact [pækt] *n* patto, accordo; trattato

pad [pæd] *n* blocco; (*to prevent friction*) cuscinetto; (*inf: flat*) appartamentino ▷ *vt* imbottire; **padded** *adj* imbottito(-a)

paddle ['pædl] *n* (*oar*) pagaia; (*US: for table tennis*) racchetta da ping-pong ▷ *vi* sguazzare ▷ *vt* **to ~ a canoe** *etc* vogare con la pagaia; **paddling pool** (*BRIT*) *n* piscina per bambini

paddock ['pædək] *n* prato recintato; (*at racecourse*) paddock *m inv*

padlock ['pædlɔk] *n* lucchetto

paedophile ['pi:dəufaɪl] (*US* **pedophile**) *adj, n* pedofilo(-a)

page [peɪdʒ] *n* pagina; (*also:* **~ boy**) paggio ▷ *vt* (*in hotel etc*) (far) chiamare

pager ['peɪdʒəʳ] *n* (*Tel*) cercapersone *m inv*

paid [peɪd] *pt, pp of* **pay** ▷ *adj* (*work, official*) rimunerato(-a); **to put ~ to** (*BRIT*) mettere fine a

pain [peɪn] *n* dolore *m*; **to be in ~** soffrire, aver male; **to take ~s to do** mettercela tutta per fare; **painful** *adj* doloroso(-a), che fa male; difficile, penoso(-a); **painkiller** *n* antalgico, antidolorifico; **painstaking** ['peɪnzteɪkɪŋ] *adj* (*person*) sollecito(-a); (*work*) accurato(-a)

paint [peɪnt] *n* vernice *f*, colore *m* ▷ *vt* dipingere; (*walls, door etc*) verniciare; **to ~ the door blue** verniciare la porta di azzurro; **paintbrush** *n* pennello; **painter** *n* (*artist*) pittore *m*; (*decorator*) imbianchino; **painting** *n* pittura; verniciatura; (*picture*) dipinto, quadro

pair [pɛəʳ] *n* (*of shoes, gloves etc*) paio; (*of people*) coppia; duo *m inv*; **a ~ of scissors/ trousers** un paio di forbici/pantaloni

pajamas [pɪ'dʒɑːməz] (*US*) *npl* pigiama *m*

Pakistan [pɑːkɪ'stɑːn] *n* Pakistan *m*; **Pakistani** *adj, n* pakistano(-a)

pal [pæl] (*inf*) *n* amico(-a), compagno(-a)

palace ['pæləs] *n* palazzo

pale [peɪl] *adj* pallido(-a) ▷ *n* **to be beyond the ~** aver oltrepassato ogni limite

Palestine ['pælɪstaɪn] *n* Palestina; **Palestinian** [-'tɪnɪən] *adj, n* palestinese *m/f*

palm [pɑːm] *n* (*Anat*) palma, palmo; (*also:* **~ tree**) palma ▷ *vt* **to ~ sth off on sb** (*inf*) rifilare qc a qn

pamper ['pæmpəʳ] *vt* viziare, coccolare

pamphlet ['pæmflət] *n* dépliant *m inv*

pan [pæn] *n* (*also*: **sauce~**) casseruola; (*also*: **frying ~**) padella

pancake ['pænkeɪk] *n* frittella

panda ['pændə] *n* panda *m inv*

pane [peɪn] *n* vetro

panel ['pænl] *n* (*of wood, cloth etc*) pannello; (*Radio, TV*) giuria

panhandler ['pænhændlər] (*US*) *n* (*inf*) accattone(-a)

panic ['pænɪk] *n* panico ▷ *vi* perdere il sangue freddo

panorama [pænə'rɑːmə] *n* panorama *m*

pansy ['pænzɪ] *n* (*Bot*) viola del pensiero, pensée *f inv*; (*inf*: *pej*) femminuccia

pant [pænt] *vi* ansare

panther ['pænθər] *n* pantera

panties ['pæntɪz] *npl* slip *m*, mutandine *fpl*

pantomime ['pæntəmaɪm] (*BRIT*) *n* pantomima

● **PANTOMIME**
●
● In Gran Bretagna la **pantomime** è una
● sorta di libera interpretazione delle
● favole più conosciute, che vengono
● messe in scena a teatro durante il
● periodo natalizio. È uno spettacolo
● per tutta la famiglia che prevede la
● partecipazione del pubblico.

pants [pænts] *npl* mutande *fpl*, slip *m*; (*US*: *trousers*) pantaloni *mpl*

paper ['peɪpər] *n* carta; (*also*: **wall~**) carta da parati, tappezzeria; (*also*: **news~**) giornale *m*; (*study, article*) saggio; (*exam*) prova scritta ▷ *adj* di carta ▷ *vt* tappezzare; **~s** *npl* (*also*: **identity ~s**) carte *fpl*, documenti *mpl*; **paperback** *n* tascabile *m*; edizione *f* economica; **paper bag** *n* sacchetto di carta; **paper clip** *n* graffetta, clip *f inv*; **paper shop** *n* (*BRIT*) giornalaio (*negozio*); **paperwork** *n* lavoro amministrativo

paprika ['pæprɪkə] *n* paprica

par [pɑːr] *n* parità, pari *f*; (*Golf*) norma; **on a ~ with** alla pari con

paracetamol [pærə'siːtəmɔl] (*BRIT*) *n* paracetamolo

parachute ['pærəʃuːt] *n* paracadute *m inv*

parade [pə'reɪd] *n* parata ▷ *vt* (*fig*) fare sfoggio di ▷ *vi* sfilare in parata

paradise ['pærədaɪs] *n* paradiso

paradox ['pærədɔks] *n* paradosso

paraffin ['pærəfɪn] (*BRIT*) *n* **~ (oil)** paraffina

paragraph ['pærəgrɑːf] *n* paragrafo

parallel ['pærəlɛl] *adj* parallelo(-a); (*fig*) analogo(-a) ▷ *n* (*line*) parallela; (*fig, Geo*) parallelo

paralysed ['pærəlaɪzd] *adj* paralizzato(-a)

paralysis [pə'rælɪsɪs] *n* paralisi *f inv*

paramedic [pærə'mɛdɪk] *n* paramedico

paranoid ['pærənɔɪd] *adj* paranoico(-a)

parasite ['pærəsaɪt] *n* parassita *m*

parcel ['pɑːsl] *n* pacco, pacchetto ▷ *vt* (*also*: **~ up**) impaccare

pardon ['pɑːdn] *n* perdono; grazia ▷ *vt* perdonare; (*Law*) graziare; **~ me!** mi scusi!; **I beg your ~!** scusi!; **I beg your ~?** (*BRIT*), **~ me?** (*US*) prego?

parent ['pɛərənt] *n* genitore *m*; **~s** *npl* (*mother and father*) genitori *mpl*; **parental** [pə'rɛntl] *adj* dei genitori

█ Be careful not to translate **parent** by the Italian word **parente**.

Paris ['pærɪs] *n* Parigi *f*

parish ['pærɪʃ] *n* parrocchia; (*BRIT*: *civil*) ≈ municipio

Parisian [pə'rɪzɪən] *adj, n* parigino(-a)

park [pɑːk] *n* parco ▷ *vt, vi* parcheggiare; **can I ~ here?** posso parcheggiare qui?

parking ['pɑːkɪŋ] *n* parcheggio; **"no ~"** "sosta vietata"; **parking lot** (*US*) *n* posteggio, parcheggio; **parking meter** *n* parchimetro; **parking ticket** *n* multa per sosta vietata

parkway ['pɑːkweɪ] (*US*) *n* viale *m*

parliament ['pɑːləmənt] *n* parlamento; **parliamentary** [pɑːlə'mɛntərɪ] *adj* parlamentare

Parmesan [pɑːmɪ'zæn] *n* (*also*: **~ cheese**) parmigiano

parole [pə'rəul] *n* **on ~** in libertà per buona condotta

parrot ['pærət] *n* pappagallo

parsley ['pɑːslɪ] *n* prezzemolo

parsnip ['pɑːsnɪp] *n* pastinaca

parson ['pɑːsn] *n* prete *m*; (*Church of England*) parroco

part [pɑːt] *n* parte *f*; (*of machine*) pezzo; (*US*: *in hair*) scriminatura ▷ *adj* in parte ▷ *adv* = **partly** ▷ *vt* separare ▷ *vi* (*people*) separarsi; **to take ~ in** prendere parte a; **for my ~** per parte mia; **to take sth in góod ~** prendere bene qc; **to take sb's ~** parteggiare per *or* prendere le parti di qn; **for the most ~** in generale; nella maggior parte dei casi; **part with** *vt fus* separarsi da; rinunciare a

partial ['pɑːʃl] *adj* parziale; **to be ~ to** avere un debole per

participant [pɑː'tɪsɪpənt] *n* **~ (in)** partecipante *m/f* (a)

participate [pɑː'tɪsɪpeɪt] *vi* **to ~ (in)** prendere parte (a), partecipare (a)

particle ['pɑːtɪkl] *n* particella

particular [pə'tɪkjulər] *adj* particolare;

speciale; (*fussy*) difficile; meticoloso(-a);
in ~ in particolare, particolarmente;
particularly *adv* particolarmente; in
particolare; **particulars** *npl* particolari
mpl, dettagli *mpl*; (*information*)
informazioni *fpl*

parting ['pɑ:tɪŋ] *n* separazione *f*; (BRIT: *in
hair*) scriminatura ▷ *adj* d'addio

partition [pɑ:'tɪʃən] *n* (*Pol*) partizione *f*;
(*wall*) tramezzo

partly ['pɑ:tlɪ] *adv* parzialmente; in parte

partner ['pɑ:tnər] *n* (*Comm*) socio(-a);
(*wife, husband etc, Sport*) compagno(-a);
(*at dance*) cavaliere/dama; **partnership** *n*
associazione *f*; (*Comm*) società *f inv*

part of speech *n* parte *f* del discorso

partridge ['pɑ:trɪdʒ] *n* pernice *f*

part-time ['pɑ:t'taɪm] *adj*, *adv* a orario
ridotto

party ['pɑ:tɪ] *n* (*Pol*) partito; (*group*)
gruppo; (*Law*) parte *f*; (*celebration*)
ricevimento; serata; festa ▷ *cpd* (*Pol*) del
partito, di partito

pass [pɑ:s] *vt* (*gen*) passare; (*place*) passare
davanti a; (*exam*) passare, superare;
(*candidate*) promuovere; (*overtake, surpass*)
sorpassare, superare; (*approve*) approvare
▷ *vi* passare ▷ *n* (*permit*) lasciapassare
m inv; permesso; (*in mountains*) passo,
gola; (*Sport*) passaggio; (*Scol*): **to get a ~**
prendere la sufficienza; **could you ~ the
salt/oil, please?** mi passa il sale/l'olio,
per favore?; **to ~ sth through a hole** *etc*
far passare qc attraverso un buco *etc*; **to
make a ~ at sb** (*inf*) fare delle proposte *or*
delle avances a qn; **pass away** *vi* morire;
pass by *vi* passare ▷ *vt* trascurare; **pass
on** *vt* passare; **pass out** *vi* svenire; **pass
over** *vi* (*die*) spirare ▷ *vt* lasciare da parte;
pass up *vt* (*opportunity*) lasciarsi sfuggire,
perdere; **passable** *adj* (*road*) praticabile;
(*work*) accettabile

passage ['pæsɪdʒ] *n* (*gen*) passaggio; (*also:*
~way) corridoio; (*in book*) brano, passo; (*by
boat*) traversata

passenger ['pæsɪndʒər] *n* passeggero(-a)

passer-by [pɑ:sə'baɪ] *n* passante *m/f*

passing place *n* (*Aut*) piazzola di sosta

passion ['pæʃən] *n* passione *f*; amore
m; **passionate** *adj* appassionato(-a);
passion fruit *n* frutto della passione

passive ['pæsɪv] *adj* (*also Ling*) passivo(-a)

passport ['pɑ:spɔ:t] *n* passaporto;
passport control *n* controllo *m*
passaporti *inv*; **passport office** *n* ufficio
m, passaporti *inv*

password ['pɑ:swə:d] *n* parola d'ordine

past [pɑ:st] *prep* (*further than*) oltre, di là di;
dopo; (*later than*) dopo ▷ *adj* passato(-a);
(*president etc*) ex *inv* ▷ *n* passato; **he's ~
forty** ha più di quarant'anni; **ten ~ eight** le
otto e dieci; **for the ~ few days** da qualche
giorno; in questi ultimi giorni; **to run ~**
passare di corsa

pasta ['pæstə] *n* pasta

paste [peɪst] *n* (*glue*) colla; (*Culin*) pâté *m
inv*; pasta ▷ *vt* collare

pastel ['pæstl] *adj* pastello *inv*

pasteurized ['pæstəraɪzd] *adj*
pastorizzato(-a)

pastime ['pɑ:staɪm] *n* passatempo

pastor ['pɑ:stər] *n* pastore *m*

past participle [-'pɑ:tɪsɪpl] *n* (*Ling*)
participio passato

pastry ['peɪstrɪ] *n* pasta

pasture ['pɑ:stʃər] *n* pascolo

pasty¹ ['pæstɪ] *n* pasticcio di carne

pasty² ['peɪstɪ] *adj* (*face etc*) smorto(-a)

pat [pæt] *vt* accarezzare, dare un colpetto
(affettuoso) a

patch [pætʃ] *n* (*of material, on tyre*) toppa;
(*eye patch*) benda; (*spot*) macchia ▷ *vt*
(*clothes*) rattoppare; **(to go through) a
bad ~** (attraversare) un brutto periodo;
patchy *adj* irregolare

pâté ['pæteɪ] *n* pâté *m inv*

patent ['peɪtnt] *n* brevetto ▷ *vt* brevettare
▷ *adj* patente, manifesto(-a)

paternal [pə'tə:nl] *adj* paterno(-a)

paternity leave [pə'tə:nɪtɪ-] *n* congedo
di paternità

path [pɑ:θ] *n* sentiero, viottolo; viale
m; (*fig*) via, strada; (*of planet, missile*)
traiettoria

pathetic [pə'θetɪk] *adj* (*pitiful*)
patetico(-a); (*very bad*) penoso(-a)

pathway ['pɑ:θweɪ] *n* sentiero

patience ['peɪʃns] *n* pazienza; (BRIT *Cards*)
solitario

patient ['peɪʃnt] *n* paziente *m/f*,
malato(-a) ▷ *adj* paziente

patio ['pætɪəu] *n* terrazza

patriotic [pætrɪ'ɔtɪk] *adj* patriottico(-a)

patrol [pə'trəul] *n* pattuglia ▷ *vt*
pattugliare; **patrol car** *n* autoradio *f inv*
(della polizia)

patron ['peɪtrən] *n* (*in shop*) cliente *m/f*; (*of
charity*) benefattore(-trice); **~ of the arts**
mecenate *m/f*

patronizing ['pætrənaɪzɪŋ] *adj*
condiscendente

pattern ['pætən] *n* modello; (*design*)
disegno, motivo; **patterned** *adj* a disegni,
a motivi; (*material*) fantasia *inv*

pause [pɔ:z] *n* pausa ▷ *vi* fare una pausa,
arrestarsi

pave [peɪv] *vt* pavimentare; **to ~ the way
for** aprire la via a

P

pavement ['peɪvmənt] (BRIT) n
marciapiede m

> Be careful not to translate *pavement* by the Italian word *pavimento*.

pavilion [pə'vɪlɪən] n (Sport) edificio annesso a campo sportivo

paving ['peɪvɪŋ] n pavimentazione f

paw [pɔ:] n zampa

pawn [pɔ:n] n (Chess) pedone m; (fig) pedina ▷ vt dare in pegno; **pawn broker** n prestatore m su pegno

pay [peɪ] (pt, pp **paid**) n stipendio; paga ▷ vt pagare ▷ vi (be profitable) rendere; **can I ~ by credit card?** posso pagare con la carta di credito?; **to ~ attention (to)** fare attenzione (a); **to ~ sb a visit** far visita a qn; **to ~ one's respects to sb** porgere i propri rispetti a qn; **pay back** vt rimborsare; **pay for** vt fus pagare; **pay in** vt versare; **pay off** vt (debt) saldare; (person) pagare; (employee) pagare e licenziare ▷ vi (scheme, decision) dare dei frutti; **pay out** vt (money) sborsare, tirar fuori; (rope) far allentare; **pay up** vt saldare; **payable** adj pagabile; **pay day** n giorno di paga; **pay envelope** (US) n = **pay packet**; **payment** n pagamento; versamento; saldo; **payout** n pagamento; (in competition) premio; **pay packet** (BRIT) n busta f paga inv; **pay phone** n cabina telefonica; **payroll** n ruolo (organico); **pay slip** n foglio m paga inv; **pay television** n televisione f a pagamento, pay-tv f inv

PC n abbr = **personal computer** ▷ adv abbr = **politically correct**

p.c. abbr = **per cent**

PDA n abbr (= personal digital assistant) PDA m inv

PE n abbr (= physical education) ed. fisica

pea [pi:] n pisello

peace [pi:s] n pace f; **peaceful** adj pacifico(-a), calmo(-a)

peach [pi:tʃ] n pesca

peacock ['pi:kɔk] n pavone m

peak [pi:k] n (of mountain) cima, vetta; (mountain itself) picco; (of cap) visiera; (fig) apice m, culmine m; **peak hours** npl ore fpl di punta

peanut ['pi:nʌt] n arachide f, nocciolina americana; **peanut butter** n burro di arachidi

pear [pɛəʳ] n pera

pearl [pə:l] n perla

peasant ['pɛznt] n contadino(-a)

peat [pi:t] n torba

pebble ['pɛbl] n ciottolo

peck [pɛk] vt (also: ~ **at**) beccare ▷ n colpo di becco; (kiss) bacetto; **peckish** (BRIT: inf) adj **I feel peckish** ho un languorino

peculiar [pɪ'kju:lɪəʳ] adj strano(-a), bizzarro(-a); peculiare; ~ **to** peculiare di

pedal ['pɛdl] n pedale m ▷ vi pedalare

pedalo ['pɛdələu] n pedalò m inv

pedestal ['pɛdəstl] n piedestallo

pedestrian [pɪ'dɛstrɪən] n pedone(-a) ▷ adj pedonale; (fig) prosaico(-a), pedestre; **pedestrian crossing** (BRIT) n passaggio pedonale; **pedestrianized** adj **a pedestrianized street** una zona pedonalizzata; **pedestrian precinct** (BRIT), **pedestrian zone** (US) n zona pedonale

pedigree ['pɛdɪgri:] n (of animal) pedigree m inv; (fig) background m inv ▷ cpd (animal) di razza

pedophile ['pi:dəufaɪl] (US) n = **paedophile**

pee [pi:] (inf) vi pisciare

peek [pi:k] vi guardare furtivamente

peel [pi:l] n buccia; (of orange, lemon) scorza ▷ vt sbucciare ▷ vi (paint etc) staccarsi

peep [pi:p] n (BRIT: look) sguardo furtivo, sbirciata; (sound) pigolio ▷ vi (BRIT) guardare furtivamente

peer [pɪəʳ] vi **to ~ at** scrutare ▷ n (noble) pari m inv; (equal) pari m/f inv, uguale m/f; (contemporary) contemporaneo(-a)

peg [pɛg] n caviglia; (for coat etc) attaccapanni m inv; (BRIT: also: **clothes ~**) molletta

pelican ['pɛlɪkən] n pellicano; **pelican crossing** (BRIT) n (Aut) attraversamento pedonale con semaforo a controllo manuale

pelt [pɛlt] vt **to ~ sb (with)** bombardare qn (con) ▷ vi (rain) piovere a dirotto; (inf: run) filare ▷ n pelle f

pelvis ['pɛlvɪs] n pelvi f inv, bacino

pen [pɛn] n penna; (for sheep) recinto

penalty ['pɛnltɪ] n penalità f inv; sanzione f penale; (fine) ammenda; (Sport) penalizzazione f

pence [pɛns] (BRIT) npl of **penny**

pencil ['pɛnsl] n matita; **pencil in** vt scrivere a matita; **pencil case** n astuccio per matite; **pencil sharpener** n temperamatite m inv

pendant ['pɛndnt] n pendaglio

pending ['pɛndɪŋ] prep in attesa di ▷ adj in sospeso

penetrate ['pɛnɪtreɪt] vt penetrare

penfriend ['pɛnfrɛnd] (BRIT) n corrispondente m/f

penguin ['pɛngwɪn] n pinguino

penicillin [pɛnɪ'sɪlɪn] n penicillina

peninsula [pə'nɪnsjulə] n penisola

penis ['pi:nɪs] n pene m

penitentiary [pɛnɪ'tɛnʃərɪ] (US) n carcere m

penknife ['pɛnnaɪf] n temperino
penniless ['pɛnɪlɪs] adj senza un soldo
penny ['pɛnɪ] (pl **pennies** or **pence**) (BRIT)
n penny m; (US) centesimo
penpal ['pɛnpæl] n corrispondente m/f
pension ['pɛnʃən] n pensione f; **pensioner**
(BRIT) n pensionato(-a)
pentagon ['pɛntəgən] n pentagono; **the**
P~ (US Pol) il Pentagono
penthouse ['pɛnthaus] n appartamento
(di lusso) nell'attico
penultimate [pɪ'nʌltɪmət] adj
penultimo(-a)
people ['piːpl] npl gente f; persone fpl;
(citizens) popolo ▷ n (nation, race) popolo;
4/several ~ came 4/parecchie persone
sono venute; **~ say that ...** si dice che ...
pepper ['pɛpər] n pepe m; (vegetable)
peperone m ▷ vt (fig): **to ~ with** spruzzare
di; **peppermint** n (sweet) pasticca di
menta
per [pəːr] prep per; a; **~ hour** all'ora; **~ kilo**
etc il chilo etc; **~ day** al giorno
perceive [pə'siːv] vt percepire; (notice)
accorgersi di
per cent adv per cento
percentage [pə'sɛntɪdʒ] n percentuale f
perception [pə'sɛpʃən] n percezione f;
sensibilità; perspicacia
perch [pəːtʃ] n (fish) pesce m persico; (for
bird) sostegno, ramo ▷ vi appollaiarsi
percussion [pə'kʌʃən] n percussione f;
(Mus) strumenti mpl a percussione
perfect [adj, n 'pəːfɪkt, vb pə'fɛkt] adj
perfetto(-a) ▷ n (also: **~ tense**) perfetto,
passato prossimo ▷ vt perfezionare;
mettere a punto; **perfection** [pə'fɛkʃə
n] n perfezione f; **perfectly** adv
perfettamente, alla perfezione
perform [pə'fɔːm] vt (carry out) eseguire,
fare; (symphony) suonare; (play, ballet)
dare; (opera) fare ▷ vi suonare; recitare;
performance n esecuzione f; (at theatre
etc) rappresentazione f, spettacolo; (of
an artist) interpretazione f; (of player etc)
performance f; (of car, engine) prestazione f;
performer n artista m/f
perfume ['pəːfjuːm] n profumo
perhaps [pə'hæps] adv forse
perimeter [pə'rɪmɪtər] n perimetro
period ['pɪərɪəd] n periodo; (History) epoca;
(Scol) lezione f; (full stop) punto; (Med)
mestruazioni fpl ▷ adj (costume, furniture)
d'epoca; **periodical** [-'ɔdɪkl] n periodico;
periodically adv periodicamente
perish ['pɛrɪʃ] vi perire, morire; (decay)
deteriorarsi
perjury ['pəːdʒərɪ] n spergiuro
perk [pəːk] (inf) n vantaggio

perm [pəːm] n (for hair) permanente f
permanent ['pəːmənənt] adj
permanente; **permanently** adv
definitivamente
permission [pə'mɪʃən] n permesso
permit [n 'pəːmɪt, vb pə'mɪt] n permesso
▷ vt permettere; **to ~ sb to do** permettere
a qn di fare
perplex [pə'plɛks] vt lasciare perplesso(-a)
persecute ['pəːsɪkjuːt] vt perseguitare
persecution [pəːsɪ'kjuːʃən] n
persecuzione f
persevere [pəːsɪ'vɪər] vi perseverare
Persian ['pəːʃən] adj persiano(-a) ▷ n (Ling)
persiano; **the (~) Gulf** n il Golfo Persico
persist [pə'sɪst] vi **to ~ (in doing)**
persistere (nel fare); ostinarsi (a fare);
persistent adj persistente; ostinato(-a)
person ['pəːsn] n persona; **in ~** di or in
persona, personalmente; **personal**
adj personale; individuale; **personal**
assistant n segretaria personale;
personal computer n personal computer
m inv; **personality** [-'nælɪtɪ] n personalità
f inv; **personally** adv personalmente; **to**
take sth personally prendere qc come
una critica personale; **personal organizer**
n (Filofax®) Fulltime®; (electronic)
agenda elettronica; **personal stereo** n
Walkman® m inv
personnel [pəːsə'nɛl] n personale m
perspective [pə'spɛktɪv] n prospettiva
perspiration [pəːspɪ'reɪʃən] n
traspirazione f, sudore m
persuade [pə'sweɪd] vt **to ~ sb to do sth**
persuadere qn a fare qc
persuasion [pə'sweɪʒən] n persuasione f;
(creed) convinzione f, credo
persuasive [pə'sweɪsɪv] adj persuasivo(-a)
perverse [pə'vəːs] adj perverso(-a)
pervert [n 'pəːvəːt, vb pə'vəːt] n
pervertito(-a) ▷ vt pervertire
pessimism ['pɛsɪmɪzəm] n pessimismo
pessimist ['pɛsɪmɪst] n pessimista
m/f; **pessimistic** [-'mɪstɪk] adj
pessimistico(-a)
pest [pɛst] n animale m (or insetto)
pestifero; (fig) peste f
pester ['pɛstər] vt tormentare, molestare
pesticide ['pɛstɪsaɪd] n pesticida m
pet [pɛt] n animale m domestico ▷ cpd
favorito(-a) ▷ vt accarezzare; **teacher's ~**
favorito(-a) del maestro
petal ['pɛtl] n petalo
petite [pə'tiːt] adj piccolo(-a) e
aggraziato(-a)
petition [pə'tɪʃən] n petizione f
petrified ['pɛtrɪfaɪd] adj (fig) morto(-a)
di paura

p

petrol ['pɛtrəl] (BRIT) n benzina; **two/four-star ~** = benzina normale/super; **I've run out of ~** sono rimasto senza benzina

▮ Be careful not to translate *petrol* by the Italian word *petrolio*.

petroleum [pə'trəuliəm] n petrolio
petrol: **petrol pump** (BRIT) n (*in car, at garage*) pompa di benzina; **petrol station** (BRIT) n stazione f di rifornimento; **petrol tank** (BRIT) n serbatoio della benzina
petticoat ['pɛtɪkəut] n sottana
petty ['pɛtɪ] adj (*mean*) meschino(-a); (*unimportant*) insignificante
pew [pju:] n panca (di chiesa)
pewter ['pju:tə'] n peltro
phantom ['fæntəm] n fantasma m
pharmacist ['fɑ:məsɪst] n farmacista m/f
pharmacy ['fɑ:məsɪ] n farmacia
phase [feɪz] n fase f, periodo; **phase in** vt introdurre gradualmente; **phase out** vt (*machinery*) eliminare gradualmente; (*product*) ritirare gradualmente; (*job, subsidy*) abolire gradualmente
Ph.D. n abbr = **Doctor of Philosophy**
pheasant ['fɛznt] n fagiano
phenomena [fə'nɔmɪnə] npl of **phenomenon**
phenomenal [fɪ'nɔmɪnl] adj fenomenale
phenomenon [fə'nɔmɪnən] (pl **phenomena**) n fenomeno
Philippines ['fɪlɪpi:nz] npl **the ~** le Filippine
philosopher [fɪ'lɔsəfə'] n filosofo(-a)
philosophical [fɪlə'sɔfɪkl] adj filosofico(-a)
philosophy [fɪ'lɔsəfɪ] n filosofia
phlegm [flɛm] n flemma
phobia ['fəubjə] n fobia
phone [fəun] n telefono ▷ vt telefonare; **to be on the ~** avere il telefono; (*be calling*) essere al telefono; **phone back** vt, vi richiamare; **phone up** vt telefonare a ▷ vi telefonare; **phone book** n guida del telefono, elenco telefonico; **phone booth** n = **phone box**; **phone box** n cabina telefonica; **phone call** n telefonata; **phonecard** n scheda telefonica; **phone number** n numero di telefono
phonetics [fə'nɛtɪks] n fonetica
phoney ['fəunɪ] adj falso(-a), fasullo(-a)
photo ['fəutəu] n foto f inv
photo... ['fəutəu] prefix: **photo album** n (*new*) album m inv per fotografie; (*containing photos*) album m inv delle fotografie; **photocopier** n fotocopiatrice f; **photocopy** n fotocopia ▷ vt fotocopiare
photograph ['fəutəgræf] n fotografia ▷ vt fotografare; **photographer** [fə'tɔgrəfə]

'] n fotografo; **photography** [fə'tɔgrəfɪ] n fotografia
phrase [freɪz] n espressione f; (*Ling*) locuzione f; (*Mus*) frase f ▷ vt esprimere; **phrase book** n vocabolarietto
physical ['fɪzɪkl] adj fisico(-a); **physical education** n educazione f fisica; **physically** adv fisicamente
physician [fɪ'zɪʃən] n medico
physicist ['fɪzɪsɪst] n fisico
physics ['fɪzɪks] n fisica
physiotherapist [fɪzɪəu'θɛrəpɪst] n fisioterapista m/f
physiotherapy [fɪzɪəu'θɛrəpɪ] n fisioterapia
physique [fɪ'zi:k] n fisico; costituzione f
pianist ['pi:ənɪst] n pianista m/f
piano [pɪ'ænəu] n pianoforte m
pick [pɪk] n (*tool: also:* **~-axe**) piccone m ▷ vt scegliere; (*gather*) cogliere; (*remove*) togliere; (*lock*) far scattare; **take your ~** scelga; **the ~ of** il fior fiore di; **to ~ one's nose** mettersi le dita nel naso; **to ~ one's teeth** pulirsi i denti con lo stuzzicadenti; **to ~ a quarrel** attaccar briga; **pick on** vt fus (*person*) avercela con; **pick out** vt scegliere; (*distinguish*) distinguere; **pick up** vi (*improve*) migliorarsi ▷ vt raccogliere; (*Police, Radio*) prendere; (*collect*) passare a prendere; (*Aut: give lift to*) far salire; (*person: for sexual encounter*) rimorchiare; (*learn*) imparare; **to ~ up speed** acquistare velocità; **to ~ o.s. up** rialzarsi
pickle ['pɪkl] n (*also:* **~s**: *as condiment*) sottaceti mpl; (*fig: mess*) pasticcio ▷ vt mettere sottaceto; mettere in salamoia
pickpocket ['pɪkpɔkɪt] n borsaiolo
pick-up ['pɪkʌp] n (BRIT: *on record player*) pick-up m inv; (*small truck: also:* **~ truck, ~ van**) camioncino
picnic ['pɪknɪk] n picnic m inv; **picnic area** n area per il picnic
picture ['pɪktʃə'] n quadro; (*painting*) pittura; (*photograph*) foto(grafia); (*drawing*) disegno; (*film*) film m inv ▷ vt raffigurarsi; **~s** (BRIT) npl (*cinema*): **the ~s** il cinema; **would you take a ~ of us, please?** può farci una foto, per favore?; **picture frame** n cornice m inv; **picture messaging** n picture messaging m, invio di messaggini con disegni
picturesque [pɪktʃə'rɛsk] adj pittoresco(-a)
pie [paɪ] n torta; (*of meat*) pasticcio
piece [pi:s] n pezzo; (*of land*) appezzamento; (*item*): **a ~ of furniture/advice** un mobile/consiglio ▷ vt **to ~ together** mettere insieme; **to take to ~s** smontare

pie chart n grafico a torta

pier [pɪəʳ] n molo; (of bridge etc) pila

pierce [pɪəs] vt forare; (with arrow etc) trafiggere; **pierced** adj **I've got pierced ears** ho i buchi per gli orecchini

pig [pɪg] n maiale m, porco

pigeon ['pɪdʒən] n piccione m

piggy bank ['pɪgɪ-] n salvadanaio

pigsty ['pɪgstaɪ] n porcile m

pigtail ['pɪgteɪl] n treccina

pike [paɪk] n (fish) luccio

pilchard ['pɪltʃəd] n specie di sardina

pile [paɪl] n (pillar, of books) pila; (heap) mucchio; (of carpet) pelo; **to ~ into** (car) stiparsi or ammucchiarsi in; **pile up** vt ammucchiare ▷ vi ammucchiarsi; **piles** [paɪlz] npl emorroidi fpl; **pile-up** ['paɪlʌp] n (Aut) tamponamento a catena

pilgrimage ['pɪlgrɪmɪdʒ] n pellegrinaggio

pill [pɪl] n pillola; **the ~** la pillola

pillar ['pɪləʳ] n colonna

pillow ['pɪləu] n guanciale m; **pillowcase** n federa

pilot ['paɪlət] n pilota m/f ▷ cpd (scheme etc) pilota inv ▷ vt pilotare; **pilot light** n fiamma pilota

pimple ['pɪmpl] n foruncolo

pin [pɪn] n spillo; (Tech) perno ▷ vt attaccare con uno spillo; **~s and needles** formicolio; **to ~ sb down** (fig) obbligare qn a pronunziarsi; **to ~ sth on sb** (fig) addossare la colpa di qc a qn

PIN n abbr (= personal identification number) codice m segreto

pinafore ['pɪnəfɔːʳ] n (also: **~ dress**) grembiule m (senza maniche)

pinch [pɪntʃ] n pizzicotto, pizzico ▷ vt pizzicare; (inf: steal) grattare; **at a ~** in caso di bisogno

pine [paɪn] n (also: **~ tree**) pino ▷ vi **to ~ for** struggersi dal desiderio di

pineapple ['paɪnæpl] n ananas m inv

ping [pɪŋ] n (noise) tintinnio; **ping-pong®** n ping-pong® m

pink [pɪŋk] adj rosa inv ▷ n (colour) rosa m inv; (Bot) garofano

pinpoint ['pɪnpɔɪnt] vt indicare con precisione

pint [paɪnt] n pinta (BRIT = 0.57l; US = 0.47l); (BRIT: inf) ≈ birra da mezzo

pioneer [paɪə'nɪəʳ] n pioniere(-a)

pious ['paɪəs] adj pio(-a)

pip [pɪp] n (seed) seme m; (BRIT: time signal on radio) segnale m orario

pipe [paɪp] n tubo; (for smoking) pipa ▷ vt portare per mezzo di tubazione; **pipeline** n conduttura; (for oil) oleodotto; **piper** n piffero; suonatore(-trice) di cornamusa

pirate ['paɪərət] n pirata m ▷ vt riprodurre abusivamente

Pisces ['paɪsiːz] n Pesci mpl

piss [pɪs] (inf) vi pisciare; **pissed** (inf) adj (drunk) ubriaco(-a) fradicio(-a)

pistol ['pɪstl] n pistola

piston ['pɪstən] n pistone m

pit [pɪt] n buca, fossa; (also: **coal ~**) miniera, (quarry) cava ▷ vt **to ~ sb against sb** opporre qn a qn

pitch [pɪtʃ] n (BRIT Sport) campo; (Mus) tono; (tar) pece f; (fig) grado, punto ▷ vt (throw) lanciare ▷ vi (fall) cascare; **to ~ a tent** piantare una tenda; **pitch-black** adj nero(-a) come la pece

pitfall ['pɪtfɔːl] n trappola

pith [pɪθ] n (of plant) midollo; (of orange) parte f interna della scorza; (fig) essenza, succo; vigore m

pitiful ['pɪtɪful] adj (touching) pietoso(-a)

pity ['pɪtɪ] n pietà ▷ vt aver pietà di; **what a ~!** che peccato!

pizza ['piːtsə] n pizza

placard ['plækɑːd] n affisso

place [pleɪs] n posto, luogo; (proper position, rank, seat) posto; (house) casa, alloggio; (home): **at/to his ~** a casa sua ▷ vt (object) posare, mettere; (identify) riconoscere; individuare; **to take ~** aver luogo; succedere; **to change ~s with sb** scambiare il posto con qn; **out of ~** (not suitable) inopportuno(-a); **in the first ~** in primo luogo; **to ~ an order** dare un'ordinazione; **to be ~d** (in race, exam) classificarsi; **place mat** n sottopiatto; (in linen etc) tovaglietta; **placement** n collocamento; (job) lavoro

placid ['plæsɪd] adj placido(-a), calmo(-a)

plague [pleɪg] n peste f ▷ vt tormentare

plaice [pleɪs] n inv pianuzza

plain [pleɪn] adj (clear) chiaro(-a), palese; (simple) semplice; (frank) franco(-a), aperto(-a); (not handsome) bruttino(-a); (without seasoning etc) scondito(-a); naturale; (in one colour) tinta unita inv ▷ adv francamente, chiaramente ▷ n pianura; **plain chocolate** n cioccolato fondente; **plainly** adv chiaramente; (frankly) francamente

plaintiff ['pleɪntɪf] n attore(-trice)

plait [plæt] n treccia

plan [plæn] n pianta; (scheme) progetto, piano ▷ vt (think in advance) progettare; (prepare) organizzare ▷ vi far piani or progetti; **to ~ to do** progettare di fare

plane [pleɪn] n (Aviat) aereo; (tree) platano; (tool) pialla; (Art, Math etc) piano ▷ adj piano(-a), piatto(-a) ▷ vt (with tool) piallare

planet ['plænɪt] n pianeta m

plank [plæŋk] n tavola, asse f

p

planning ['plænɪŋ] n progettazione f; **family ~** pianificazione f delle nascite

plant [plɑːnt] n pianta; (machinery) impianto; (factory) fabbrica ▷ vt piantare; (bomb) mettere

plantation [plæn'teɪʃən] n piantagione f

plaque [plæk] n placca

plaster ['plɑːstəʳ] n intonaco; (also: ~ of Paris) gesso; (BRIT: also: **sticking ~**) cerotto ▷ vt intonacare; ingessare; (cover): **to ~ with** coprire di; **plaster cast** n (Med) ingessatura, gesso; (model, statue) modello in gesso

plastic ['plæstɪk] n plastica ▷ adj (made of plastic) di or in plastica; **plastic bag** n sacchetto di plastica; **plastic surgery** n chirurgia plastica

plate [pleɪt] n (dish) piatto; (in book) tavola; (dental plate) dentiera; **gold/silver ~** vasellame m d'oro/d'argento

plateau ['plætəu] (pl **plateaus** or **plateaux**) n altipiano

platform ['plætfɔːm] n (stage, at meeting) palco; (Rail) marciapiede m; (BRIT: of bus) piattaforma; **which ~ does the train for Rome go from?** da che binario parte il treno per Roma?

platinum ['plætɪnəm] n platino

platoon [plə'tuːn] n plotone m

platter ['plætəʳ] n piatto

plausible ['plɔːzɪbl] adj plausibile, credibile; (person) convincente

play [pleɪ] n gioco; (Theatre) commedia ▷ vt (game) giocare a; (team, opponent) giocare contro; (instrument, piece of music) suonare; (record, tape) ascoltare; (role, part) interpretare ▷ vi giocare; suonare; recitare; **to ~ safe** giocare sul sicuro; **play back** vt riascoltare, risentire; **play up** vi (cause trouble) fare i capricci; **player** n giocatore(-trice); (Theatre) attore(-trice); (Mus) musicista m/f; **playful** adj giocoso(-a); **playground** n (in school) cortile m per la ricreazione; (in park) parco m giochi inv; **playgroup** n giardino d'infanzia; **playing card** n carta da gioco; **playing field** n campo sportivo; **playschool** n = **playgroup**; **playtime** n (Scol) ricreazione f; **playwright** n drammaturgo(-a)

plc abbr (= public limited company) società per azioni a responsabilità limitata quotata in borsa

plea [pliː] n (request) preghiera, domanda; (Law) (argomento di) difesa

plead [pliːd] vt patrocinare; (give as excuse) addurre a pretesto ▷ vi (Law) perorare la causa; (beg): **to ~ with sb** implorare qn

pleasant ['plɛznt] adj piacevole, gradevole

please [pliːz] excl per piacere!, per favore!; (acceptance): **yes, ~** sì, grazie ▷ vt piacere a ▷ vi piacere; (think fit): **do as you ~** faccia come le pare; **~ yourself!** come ti (or le) pare!; **pleased** adj **pleased (with)** contento(-a) (di); **pleased to meet you!** piacere!

pleasure ['plɛʒəʳ] n piacere m; **"it's a ~"** "prego"

pleat [pliːt] n piega

pledge [plɛdʒ] n pegno; (promise) promessa ▷ vt impegnare; promettere

plentiful ['plɛntɪful] adj abbondante, copioso(-a)

plenty ['plɛntɪ] n **~ of** tanto(-a), molto(-a); un'abbondanza di

pliers ['plaɪəz] npl pinza

plight [plaɪt] n situazione f critica

plod [plɔd] vi camminare a stento; (fig) sgobbare

plonk [plɔŋk] (inf) n (BRIT: wine) vino da poco ▷ vt **to ~ sth down** buttare giù qc bruscamente

plot [plɔt] n congiura, cospirazione f; (of story, play) trama; (of land) lotto ▷ vt (mark out) fare la pianta di; rilevare; (: diagram etc) tracciare; (conspire) congiurare, cospirare ▷ vi congiurare

plough [plau] (US **plow**) n aratro ▷ vt (earth) arare; **to ~ money into** (company etc) investire danaro in; **ploughman's lunch** ['plaumənz-] (BRIT) n pasto a base di pane, formaggio e birra

plow [plau] (US) = **plough**

ploy [plɔɪ] n stratagemma m

pluck [plʌk] vt (fruit) cogliere; (musical instrument) pizzicare; (bird) spennare; (hairs) togliere ▷ n coraggio, fegato; **to ~ up courage** farsi coraggio

plug [plʌg] n tappo; (Elec) spina; (Aut: also: **spark(ing) ~**) candela ▷ vt (hole) tappare; (inf: advertise) spingere; **plug in** vt (Elec) attaccare a una presa; **plughole** n (BRIT) scarico

plum [plʌm] n (fruit) susina

plumber ['plʌməʳ] n idraulico

plumbing ['plʌmɪŋ] n (trade) lavoro di idraulico; (piping) tubature fpl

plummet ['plʌmɪt] vi **to ~ (down)** cadere a piombo

plump [plʌmp] adj grassoccio(-a) ▷ vi **to ~ for** (inf: choose) decidersi per

plunge [plʌndʒ] n tuffo; (fig) caduta ▷ vt immergere ▷ vi (fall) cadere, precipitare; (dive) tuffarsi; **to take the ~** saltare il fosso

plural ['pluərl] adj plurale ▷ n plurale m

plus [plʌs] n (also: **~ sign**) segno più ▷ prep più; **ten/twenty ~** più di dieci/venti

ply [plaɪ] vt (a trade) esercitare ▷ vi (ship)

fare il servizio ▷ n (of wool, rope) capo; **to ~ sb with drink** dare di bere continuamente a qn; **plywood** n legno compensato

P.M. n abbr = **prime minister**

p.m. adv abbr (= post meridiem) del pomeriggio

PMS n abbr (= premenstrual syndrome) sindrome f premestruale

PMT n abbr (= premenstrual tension) sindrome f premestruale

pneumatic drill [nju:'mætɪk-] n martello pneumatico

pneumonia [nju:'məunɪə] n polmonite f

poach [pəutʃ] vt (cook: egg) affogare; (: fish) cuocere in bianco; (steal) cacciare (or pescare) di frodo ▷ vi fare il bracconiere; **poached** adj (egg) affogato(-a)

P.O. Box n abbr = **Post Office Box**

pocket ['pɔkɪt] n tasca ▷ vt intascare; **to be out of ~** (BRIT) rimetterci; **pocketbook** (US) n (wallet) portafoglio; **pocket money** n paghetta, settimana

pod [pɔd] n guscio

podiatrist [pɔ'di:ətrɪst] (US) n callista m/f, pedicure m/f

podium ['pəudɪəm] n podio

poem ['pəuɪm] n poesia

poet ['pəuɪt] n poeta/essa; **poetic** [-'ɛtɪk] adj poetico(-a); **poetry** n poesia

poignant ['pɔɪnjənt] adj struggente

point [pɔɪnt] n (gen) punto; (tip: of needle etc) punta; (in time) punto, momento; (Scol) voto; (main idea, important part) nocciolo; (Elec) presa (di corrente); (also: **decimal ~**): **2 ~ 3 (2.3)** 2 virgola 3 (2,3) ▷ vt (show) indicare; (gun etc): **to ~ sth at** puntare qc contro ▷ vi **to ~ at** mostrare a dito; **~s** npl (Aut) puntine fpl; (Rail) scambio; **to be on the ~ of doing sth** essere sul punto di or stare per fare qc; **to make a ~** fare un'osservazione; **to get/miss the ~** capire/non capire; **to come to the ~** venire al fatto; **there's no ~ in doing** è inutile (fare); **point out** vt far notare; **point-blank** adv (also: **at point-blank range**) a bruciapelo; (fig) categoricamente; **pointed** adj (shape) aguzzo(-a), appuntito(-a); (remark) specifico(-a); **pointer** n (needle) lancetta; (fig) indicazione f, consiglio; **pointless** adj inutile, vano(-a); **point of view** n punto di vista

poison ['pɔɪzn] n veleno ▷ vt avvelenare; **poisonous** adj velenoso(-a)

poke [pəuk] vt (fire) attizzare; (jab with finger, stick etc) punzecchiare; (put): **to ~ sth in(to)** spingere qc dentro; **poke about** or **around** vi frugare; **poke out** vi (stick out) sporgere fuori

poker ['pəukə'] n attizzatoio; (Cards) poker m

Poland ['pəulənd] n Polonia

polar ['pəulə'] adj polare; **polar bear** n orso bianco

Pole [pəul] n polacco(-a)

pole [pəul] n (of wood) palo; (Elec, Geo) polo; **pole bean** (US) n (runner bean) fagiolino; **pole vault** n salto con l'asta

police [pə'li:s] n polizia ▷ vt mantenere l'ordine in; **police car** n macchina della polizia; **police constable** (BRIT) n agente m di polizia; **police force** n corpo di polizia, polizia; **policeman** (irreg) n poliziotto, agente m di polizia; **police officer** n = **police constable**; **police station** n posto di polizia; **policewoman** (irreg) n donna f poliziotto inv

policy ['pɔlɪsɪ] n politica; (also: **insurance ~**) polizza (d'assicurazione)

polio ['pəulɪəu] n polio f

Polish ['pəulɪʃ] adj polacco(-a) ▷ n (Ling) polacco

polish ['pɔlɪʃ] n (for shoes) lucido; (for floor) cera; (for nails) smalto; (shine) lucentezza, lustro; (fig: refinement) raffinatezza ▷ vt lucidare; (fig: improve) raffinare; **polish off** vt (food) mangiarsi; **polished** adj (fig) raffinato(-a)

polite [pə'laɪt] adj cortese; **politeness** n cortesia

political [pə'lɪtɪkl] adj politico(-a); **politically** adv politicamente; **politically correct** politicamente corretto(-a)

politician [pɔlɪ'tɪʃən] n politico

politics ['pɔlɪtɪks] n politica ▷ npl (views, policies) idee fpl politiche

poll [pəul] n scrutinio; (votes cast) voti mpl; (also: **opinion ~**) sondaggio (d'opinioni) ▷ vt ottenere

pollen ['pɔlən] n polline m

polling station ['pəulɪŋ-] (BRIT) n sezione f elettorale

pollute [pə'lu:t] vt inquinare

pollution [pə'lu:ʃən] n inquinamento

polo ['pəuləu] n polo; **polo-neck** n collo alto; (also: **polo-neck sweater**) dolcevita ▷ adj a collo alto; **polo shirt** n polo f inv

polyester [pɔlɪ'ɛstə'] n poliestere m

polystyrene [pɔlɪ'staɪri:n] n polistirolo

polythene ['pɔlɪθi:n] n politene m; **polythene bag** n sacco di plastica

pomegranate ['pɔmɪgrænɪt] n melagrana

pompous ['pɔmpəs] adj pomposo(-a)

pond [pɔnd] n pozza; stagno

ponder ['pɔndə'] vt ponderare, riflettere su

pony ['pəunɪ] n pony m inv; **ponytail** n coda di cavallo; **pony trekking**

[-trɛkɪŋ] (BRIT) n escursione f a cavallo
poodle ['puːdl] n barboncino, barbone m
pool [puːl] n (puddle) pozza; (pond) stagno;
(also: **swimming ~**) piscina; (fig: of light)
cerchio; (billiards) specie di biliardo a buca
▷ vt mettere in comune; **~s** npl (football
pools) ≈ totocalcio; **typing ~** servizio
comune di dattilografia
poor [puə**r**] adj povero(-a); (mediocre)
mediocre, cattivo(-a) ▷ npl **the ~** i poveri; **~
in** povero(-a) di; **poorly** adv poveramente;
male ▷ adj indisposto(-a), malato(-a)
pop [pɒp] n (noise) schiocco; (Mus) musica
pop; (drink) bibita gasata; (US: inf: father)
babbo ▷ vt (put) mettere (in fretta) ▷ vi
scoppiare; (cork) schioccare; **pop in** vi
passare; **pop out** vi fare un salto fuori;
popcorn n pop-corn m
poplar ['pɒplə**r**] n pioppo
popper ['pɒpə**r**] n bottone m a pressione
poppy ['pɒpɪ] n papavero
Popsicle® ['pɒpsɪkl] (US) n (ice lolly)
ghiacciolo
pop star n pop star f inv
popular ['pɒpjulə**r**] adj popolare;
(fashionable) in voga; **popularity** [-'lærɪtɪ]
n popolarità
population [pɒpju'leɪʃən] n popolazione f
porcelain ['pɔːslɪn] n porcellana
porch [pɔːtʃ] n veranda
pore [pɔː**r**] n poro ▷ vi **to ~ over** essere
immerso(-a) in
pork [pɔːk] n carne f di maiale; **pork chop**
n braciola or costoletta di maiale; **pork pie**
n (BRIT: Culin) pasticcio di maiale in crosta
porn [pɔːn] (inf) n pornografia ▷ adj
porno inv; **pornographic** [pɔːnə'græfɪk]
adj pornografico(-a); **pornography**
[pɔː'nɔgrəfɪ] n pornografia
porridge ['pɒrɪdʒ] n porridge m
port [pɔːt] n (gen, wine) porto; (Naut: left
side) babordo
portable ['pɔːtəbl] adj portatile
porter ['pɔːtə**r**] n (for luggage) facchino,
portabagagli m inv; (doorkeeper) portiere
m, portinaio
portfolio [pɔːt'fəʊlɪəʊ] n (case) cartella;
(Pol, Finance) portafoglio; (of artist) raccolta
dei propri lavori
portion ['pɔːʃən] n porzione f
port of call n (porto di) scalo
portrait ['pɔːtreɪt] n ritratto
portray [pɔː'treɪ] vt fare il ritratto di;
(character on stage) rappresentare; (in
writing) ritrarre
Portugal ['pɔːtjʊgl] n Portogallo
Portuguese [pɔːtjuː'giːz] adj portoghese
▷ n inv portoghese m/f; (Ling) portoghese
m

pose [pəʊz] n posa ▷ vi posare; (pretend):
to ~ as atteggiarsi a, posare a ▷ vt porre
posh [pɒʃ] (inf) adj elegante; (family) per
bene
position [pə'zɪʃən] n posizione f; (job)
posto ▷ vt sistemare
positive ['pɒzɪtɪv] adj positivo(-a); (certain)
sicuro(-a), certo(-a); (definite) preciso(-a),
definitivo(-a); **positively** adv (affirmatively,
enthusiastically) positivamente; (decisively)
decisamente; (really) assolutamente
possess [pə'zɛs] vt possedere; **possession**
[pə'zɛʃən] n possesso; **possessions** npl
(belongings) beni mpl; **possessive** adj
possessivo(-a)
possibility [pɒsɪ'bɪlɪtɪ] n possibilità f inv
possible ['pɒsɪbl] adj possibile; **as big as ~**
il più grande possibile; **possibly** ['pɒsɪblɪ]
adv (perhaps) forse; **if you possibly can**
se le è possibile; **I cannot possibly come**
proprio non posso venire
post [pəʊst] n (BRIT) posta; (: collection)
levata; (job, situation) posto; (Mil)
postazione f; (pole) palo ▷ vt (BRIT:
send by post) imbucare; (: appoint): **to ~
to** assegnare a; **where can I ~ these
cards?** dove posso imbucare queste
cartoline?; **postage** n affrancatura;
postal adj postale; **postal order** n vaglia
m inv postale; **postbox** (BRIT) n cassetta
postale; **postcard** n cartolina; **postcode**
n (BRIT) codice m (di avviamento) postale
poster ['pəʊstə**r**] n manifesto, affisso
postgraduate ['pəʊst'grædjuət] n
laureato/a che continua gli studi
postman ['pəʊstmən] (irreg) n postino
postmark ['pəʊstmɑːk] n bollo or timbro
postale
post-mortem [-'mɔːtəm] n autopsia
post office n (building) ufficio postale;
(organization): **the Post Office** ≈ le Poste e
Telecomunicazioni
postpone [pəs'pəʊn] vt rinviare
posture ['pɒstʃə**r**] n portamento; (pose)
posa, atteggiamento
postwoman ['pəʊstwʊmən] (BRIT: irreg)
n postina
pot [pɒt] n (for cooking) pentola; casseruola;
(teapot) teiera; (coffeepot) caffettiera; (for
plants, jam) vaso; (inf: marijuana) erba
▷ vt (plant) piantare in vaso; **a ~ of tea
for two** tè per due; **to go to ~** (inf: work,
performance) andare in malora
potato [pə'teɪtəʊ] (pl **potatoes**) n patata;
potato peeler n sbucciapatate m inv
potent ['pəʊtnt] adj potente, forte
potential [pə'tɛnʃl] adj potenziale ▷ n
possibilità fpl
pothole ['pɒthəʊl] n (in road) buca; (BRIT:

underground) caverna

pot plant n pianta in vaso

potter ['pɒtə'] n vasaio ▷ vi **to ~ around, ~ about** (BRIT) lavoracchiare; **pottery** n ceramiche fpl; (factory) fabbrica di ceramiche

potty ['pɒtɪ] adj (inf: mad) tocco(-a) ▷ n (child's) vasino

pouch [pautʃ] n borsa; (Zool) marsupio

poultry ['pəultrɪ] n pollame m

pounce [pauns] vi **to ~ (on)** piombare (su)

pound [paund] n (weight) libbra; (money) (lira) sterlina ▷ vt (beat) battere; (crush) pestare, polverizzare ▷ vi (beat) battere, martellare; **pound sterling** n sterlina (inglese)

pour [pɔː'] vt versare ▷ vi riversarsi; (rain) piovere a dirotto; **pour in** vi affluire in gran quantità; **pour out** vi (people) uscire a fiumi ▷ vt vuotare; versare; (fig) sfogare; **pouring** adj **pouring rain** pioggia torrenziale

pout [paut] vi sporgere le labbra; fare il broncio

poverty ['pɒvətɪ] n povertà, miseria

powder ['paudə'] n polvere f ▷ vt **to ~ one's face** incipriarsi il viso; **powdered milk** n latte m in polvere

power ['pauə'] n (strength) potenza, forza; (ability, Pol: of party, leader) potere m; (Elec) corrente f; **to be in ~** (Pol etc) essere al potere; **power cut** (BRIT) n interruzione f or mancanza di corrente; **power failure** n interruzione f della corrente elettrica; **powerful** adj potente, forte; **powerless** adj impotente; **powerless to do** impossibilitato(-a) a fare; **power point** (BRIT) n presa di corrente; **power station** n centrale f elettrica

p.p. abbr **= per procurationem; p.p. J. Smith** per J. Smith; (= pages) p.p.

PR abbr **= public relations**

practical ['præktɪkl] adj pratico(-a); **practical joke** n beffa; **practically** adv praticamente

practice ['præktɪs] n pratica; (of profession) esercizio; (at football etc) allenamento; (business) gabinetto; clientela ▷ vt, vi (US) **= practise; in ~** (in reality) in pratica; **out of ~** fuori esercizio

practise ['præktɪs] (US **practice**) vt (work at: piano, one's backhand etc) esercitarsi a; (train for: skiing, running etc) allenarsi a; (a sport, religion) praticare; (method) usare; (profession) esercitare ▷ vi esercitarsi; (train) allenarsi; (lawyer, doctor) esercitare; **practising** adj (Christian etc) praticante; (lawyer) che esercita la professione

practitioner [præk'tɪʃənə'] n

professionista m/f

pragmatic [præg'mætɪk] adj pragmatico(-a)

prairie ['prɛərɪ] n prateria

praise [preɪz] n elogio, lode f ▷ vt elogiare, lodare

pram [præm] (BRIT) n carrozzina

prank [præŋk] n burla

prawn [prɔːn] n gamberetto; **prawn cocktail** n cocktail m inv di gamberetti

pray [preɪ] vi pregare; **prayer** [prɛə'] n preghiera

preach [priːtʃ] vt, vi predicare; **preacher** n predicatore(-trice); (US: minister) pastore m

precarious [prɪ'kɛərɪəs] adj precario(-a)

precaution [prɪ'kɔːʃən] n precauzione f

precede [prɪ'siːd] vt precedere; **precedent** ['prɛsɪdənt] n precedente m; **preceding** [prɪ'siːdɪŋ] adj precedente

precinct ['priːsɪŋkt] (US) n circoscrizione f

precious ['prɛʃəs] adj prezioso(-a)

precise [prɪ'saɪs] adj preciso(-a); **precisely** adv precisamente

precision [prɪ'sɪʒən] n precisione f

predator ['prɛdətə'] n predatore m

predecessor ['priːdɪsɛsə'] n predecessore(-a)

predicament [prɪ'dɪkəmənt] n situazione f difficile

predict [prɪ'dɪkt] vt predire; **predictable** adj prevedibile; **prediction** [prɪ'dɪkʃən] n predizione f

predominantly [prɪ'dɒmɪnəntlɪ] adv in maggior parte; soprattutto

preface ['prɛfəs] n prefazione f

prefect ['priːfɛkt] n (BRIT: in school) studente(-essa) con funzioni disciplinari; (French etc, Admin) prefetto

prefer [prɪ'fəː'] vt preferire; **to ~ doing** or **to do** preferire fare; **preferable** ['prɛfrəbl] adj preferibile; **preferably** ['prɛfrəblɪ] adv preferibilmente; **preference** ['prɛfrəns] n preferenza

prefix ['priːfɪks] n prefisso

pregnancy ['prɛgnənsɪ] n gravidanza

pregnant ['prɛgnənt] adj incinta ag

prehistoric ['priːhɪs'tɔrɪk] adj preistorico(-a)

prejudice ['prɛdʒudɪs] n pregiudizio; (harm) torto, danno; **prejudiced** adj **prejudiced (against)** prevenuto(-a) (contro); **prejudiced (in favour of)** ben disposto(-a) (verso)

preliminary [prɪ'lɪmɪnərɪ] adj preliminare

prelude ['prɛljuːd] n preludio

premature ['prɛmətʃuə'] adj prematuro(-a)

premier ['prɛmɪə'] adj primo(-a) ▷ n (Pol) primo ministro

P

première ['prɛmıɛəʳ] n prima
Premier League n ≈ serie A
premises ['prɛmısız] npl locale m; **on the
~** sul posto; **business ~** locali commerciali
premium ['pri:mıəm] n premio; **to be at a
~** essere ricercatissimo
premonition [prɛmə'nıʃən] n
premonizione f
preoccupied [pri:'ɔkjupaıd] adj
preoccupato(-a)
prepaid [pri:'peıd] adj pagato(-a) in
anticipo
preparation [prɛpə'reıʃən] n
preparazione f; **~s** npl (for trip, war)
preparativi mpl
preparatory school [prı'pærətərı-] n
scuola elementare privata
prepare [prı'pɛəʳ] vt preparare ▷ vi **to ~
for** prepararsi a; **~d to** pronto(-a) a
preposition [prɛpə'zıʃən] n preposizione f
prep school n = **preparatory school**
prerequisite [pri:'rɛkwızıt] n requisito
indispensabile
preschool ['pri:'sku:l] adj (age)
prescolastico(-a); (child) in età
prescolastica
prescribe [prı'skraıb] vt (Med) prescrivere
prescription [prı'skrıpʃən] n prescrizione
f; (Med) ricetta; **could you write me a ~?**
mi può fare una ricetta medica?
presence ['prɛzns] n presenza; **~ of mind**
presenza di spirito
present [adj, n 'prɛznt, vb prı'zɛnt] adj
presente; (wife, residence, job) attuale ▷ n
(actuality): **the ~** il presente; (gift) regalo
▷ vt presentare; (give): **to ~ sb with sth**
offrire qc a qn; **to give sb a ~** fare un regalo
a qn; **at ~** al momento; **presentable**
[prı'zɛntəbl] adj presentabile;
presentation [-'teıʃən] n presentazione f;
(ceremony) consegna ufficiale; **present-
day** adj attuale, d'oggigiorno; **presenter**
n (Radio, TV) presentatore(-trice);
presently adv (soon) fra poco, presto; (at
present) al momento; **present participle**
n participio presente
preservation [prɛzə'veıʃən] n
preservazione f, conservazione f
preservative [prı'zə:vətıv] n conservante
m
preserve [prı'zə:v] vt (keep safe)
preservare, proteggere; (maintain)
conservare; (food) mettere in conserva ▷ n
(often pl: jam) marmellata; (: fruit) frutta
sciroppata
preside [prı'zaıd] vi **to ~ (over)** presiedere
(a)
president ['prɛzıdənt] n presidente m;
presidential [-'dɛnʃl] adj presidenziale

press [prɛs] n (newspapers etc): **the P~** la
stampa; (tool, machine) pressa; (for wine)
torchio ▷ vt (push) premere, pigiare;
(squeeze) spremere; (: hand) stringere;
(clothes: iron) stirare; (pursue) incalzare;
(insist): **to ~ sth on sb** far accettare qc da
qn ▷ vi premere; accalcare; **we are ~ed
for time** ci manca il tempo; **to ~ for sth**
insistere per avere qc; **press conference**
n conferenza f stampa inv; **pressing** adj
urgente; **press stud** (BRIT) n bottone m
a pressione; **press-up** (BRIT) n flessione f
sulle braccia
pressure ['prɛʃəʳ] n pressione f; **to put ~
on sb (to do)** mettere qn sotto pressione
(affinché faccia); **pressure cooker** n
pentola a pressione; **pressure group** n
gruppo di pressione
prestige [prɛs'ti:ʒ] n prestigio
prestigious [prɛs'tıdʒəs] adj
prestigioso(-a)
presumably [prı'zju:məblı] adv
presumibilmente
presume [prı'zju:m] vt supporre
pretence [prı'tɛns] (US **pretense**) n (claim)
pretesa; **to make a ~ of doing** far finta di
fare; **under false ~s** con l'inganno
pretend [prı'tɛnd] vt (feign) fingere ▷ vi far
finta; **to ~ to do** far finta di fare
pretense [prı'tɛns] (US) n = **pretence**
pretentious [prı'tɛnʃəs] adj
pretenzioso(-a)
pretext ['pri:tɛkst] n pretesto
pretty ['prıtı] adj grazioso(-a), carino(-a)
▷ adv abbastanza, assai
prevail [prı'veıl] vi (win, be usual)
prevalere; (persuade): **to ~ (up)on sb to
do** persuadere qn a fare; **prevailing** adj
dominante
prevalent ['prɛvələnt] adj (belief)
predominante; (customs) diffuso(-a);
(fashion) corrente; (disease) comune
prevent [prı'vɛnt] vt **to ~ sb from doing**
impedire a qn di fare; **to ~ sth from
happening** impedire che qc succeda;
prevention [-'vɛnʃən] n prevenzione f;
preventive adj preventivo(-a)
preview ['pri:vju:] n (of film) anteprima
previous ['pri:vıəs] adj precedente;
anteriore; **previously** adv prima
prey [preı] n preda ▷ vi **to ~ on** far preda
di; **it was ~ing on his mind** lo stava
ossessionando
price [praıs] n prezzo ▷ vt (goods) fissare
il prezzo di; valutare; **priceless** adj
inapprezzabile; **price list** n listino (dei)
prezzi
prick [prık] n puntura ▷ vt pungere; **to ~
up one's ears** drizzare gli orecchi

prickly ['prɪklɪ] *adj* spinoso(-a)
pride [praɪd] *n* orgoglio; superbia ▷ *vt* **to ~
o.s. on** essere orgoglioso(-a) di, vantarsi di
priest [priːst] *n* prete *m*, sacerdote *m*
primarily ['praɪmərɪlɪ] *adv*
principalmente, essenzialmente
primary ['praɪmərɪ] *adj* primario(-a); (*first
in importance*) primo(-a) ▷ *n* (*US: election*)
primarie *fpl*; **primary school** (*BRIT*) *n*
scuola elementare
prime [praɪm] *adj* primario(-a),
fondamentale; (*excellent*) di prima qualità
▷ *vt* (*wood*) preparare; (*fig*) mettere al
corrente ▷ *n* **in the ~ of life** nel fiore della
vita; **Prime Minister** *n* primo ministro
primitive ['prɪmɪtɪv] *adj* primitivo(-a)
primrose ['prɪmrəʊz] *n* primavera
prince [prɪns] *n* principe *m*
princess [prɪn'sɛs] *n* principessa
principal ['prɪnsɪpl] *adj* principale ▷ *n*
(*headmaster*) preside *m*; **principally** *adv*
principalmente
principle ['prɪnsɪpl] *n* principio; **in ~** in
linea di principio; **on ~** per principio
print [prɪnt] *n* (*mark*) impronta; (*letters*)
caratteri *mpl*; (*fabric*) tessuto stampato;
(*Art, Phot*) stampa ▷ *vt* imprimere;
(*publish*) stampare, pubblicare; (*write
in capitals*) scrivere in stampatello; **out
of ~** esaurito(-a); **print out** *vt* (*Comput*)
stampare; **printer** *n* tipografo; (*machine*)
stampante *f*; **printout** *n* tabulato
prior ['praɪər] *adj* precedente; (*claim etc*) più
importante; **~ to doing** prima di fare
priority [praɪ'ɒrɪtɪ] *n* priorità *f inv*;
precedenza
prison ['prɪzn] *n* prigione *f* ▷ *cpd* (*system*)
carcerario(-a); (*conditions, food*) nelle *or*
delle prigioni; **prisoner** *n* prigioniero(-a);
prisoner-of-war *n* prigioniero(-a) di
guerra
pristine ['prɪstiːn] *adj* immacolato(-a)
privacy ['prɪvəsɪ] *n* solitudine *f*, intimità
private ['praɪvɪt] *adj* privato(-a); personale
▷ *n* soldato semplice; **"~"** (*on envelope*)
"riservata"; (*on door*) "privato"; **in ~** in
privato; **privately** *adv* in privato; (*within
oneself*) dentro di sé; **private property**
n proprietà privata; **private school** *n*
scuola privata
privatize ['praɪvɪtaɪz] *vt* privatizzare
privilege ['prɪvɪlɪdʒ] *n* privilegio
prize [praɪz] *n* premio ▷ *adj* (*example, idiot*)
perfetto(-a); (*bull, novel*) premiato(-a)
▷ *vt* apprezzare, pregiare; **prize-
giving** *n* premiazione *f*; **prizewinner** *n*
premiato(-a)
pro [prəʊ] *n* (*Sport*) professionista
m/f ▷ *prep* pro; **the ~s and cons** il pro e il

contro
probability [prɒbə'bɪlɪtɪ] *n* probabilità *f
inv*; **in all ~** con tutta probabilità
probable ['prɒbəbl] *adj* probabile
probably ['prɒbəblɪ] *adv* probabilmente
probation [prə'beɪʃən] *n* **on ~** (*employee*) in
prova; (*Law*) in libertà vigilata
probe [prəʊb] *n* (*Med, Space*) sonda;
(*enquiry*) indagine *f*, investigazione *f* ▷ *vt*
sondare, esplorare; indagare
problem ['prɒbləm] *n* problema *m*
procedure [prə'siːdʒər] *n* (*Admin,
Law*) procedura; (*method*) metodo,
procedimento
proceed [prə'siːd] *vi* (*go forward*) avanzare,
andare avanti; (*go about it*) procedere;
(*continue*): **to ~ (with)** continuare; **to ~ to**
andare a; passare a; **to ~ to do** mettersi
a fare; **proceedings** *npl* misure *fpl*; (*Law*)
procedimento; (*meeting*) riunione *f*;
(*records*) rendiconti *mpl*; atti *mpl*; **proceeds**
['prəʊsiːdz] *npl* profitto, incasso
process ['prəʊsɛs] *n* processo; (*method*)
metodo, sistema *m* ▷ *vt* trattare;
(*information*) elaborare
procession [prə'sɛʃən] *n* processione *f*,
corteo; **funeral ~** corteo funebre
proclaim [prə'kleɪm] *vt* proclamare,
dichiarare
prod [prɒd] *vt* dare un colpetto a;
pungolare ▷ *n* colpetto
produce [*n* 'prɒdjuːs, *vb* prə'djuːs] *n* (*Agr*)
prodotto, prodotti *mpl* ▷ *vt* produrre;
(*show*) esibire, mostrare; (*cause*) cagionare,
causare; **producer** *n* (*Theatre*) regista *m/f*;
(*Agr, Cinema*) produttore *m*
product ['prɒdʌkt] *n* prodotto;
production [prə'dʌkʃən] *n* produzione
f; **productive** [prə'dʌktɪv] *adj*
produttivo(-a); **productivity**
[prɒdʌk'tɪvɪtɪ] *n* produttività
Prof. *abbr* (= *professor*) Prof.
profession [prə'fɛʃən] *n* professione *f*;
professional *n* professionista *m/f* ▷ *adj*
professionale; (*work*) da professionista
professor [prə'fɛsər] *n* professore
m (*titolare di una cattedra*); (*US*)
professore(-essa)
profile ['prəʊfaɪl] *n* profilo
profit ['prɒfɪt] *n* profitto; beneficio ▷ *vi* **to
~ (by *or* from)** approfittare (di); **profitable**
adj redditizio(-a)
profound [prə'faʊnd] *adj* profondo(-a)
programme ['prəʊgræm] (*US* **program**)
n programma *m* ▷ *vt* programmare;
programmer (*US* **programer**) *n*
programmatore(-trice); **programming**
(*US* **programing**) *n* programmazione *f*
progress [*n* 'prəʊgrɛs, *vb* prə'grɛs] *n*

P

progresso ▷ *vi* avanzare, procedere;
in ~ in corso; **to make ~** far progressi;
progressive [-'grɛsɪv] *adj* progressivo(-a);
(*person*) progressista
prohibit [prə'hɪbɪt] *vt* proibire, vietare
project [*n* 'prɒdʒɛkt, *vb* prə'dʒɛkt] *n* (*plan*)
piano; (*venture*) progetto; (*Scol*) studio
▷ *vt* proiettare ▷ *vi* (*stick out*) sporgere;
projection [prə'dʒɛkʃən] *n* proiezione
f; sporgenza; **projector** [prə'dʒɛktər] *n*
proiettore *m*
prolific [prə'lɪfɪk] *adj* (*artist etc*)
fecondo(-a)
prolong [prə'lɒŋ] *vt* prolungare
prom [prɒm] *n abbr* = **promenade**; (*us:
ball*) ballo studentesco

● **PROM**
●
● In Gran Bretagna i **Proms**, o
● "promenade concerts", sono concerti di
● musica classica, i più noti dei quali sono
● eseguiti nella prestigiosa **Royal Albert
● Hall** a Londra. Si chiamano così perché
● un tempo il pubblico seguiva i concerti
● in piedi, passeggiando (in inglese
● "promenade" voleva dire, appunto,
● passeggiata). Negli Stati Uniti, invece,
● con **prom**, si intende l'annuale ballo
● studentesco di un'università o di una
● scuola secondaria.

promenade [prɒmə'nɑːd] *n* (*by sea*)
lungomare *m*
prominent ['prɒmɪnənt] *adj*
(*standing out*) prominente; (*important*)
importante
promiscuous [prə'mɪskjuəs] *adj* (*sexually*)
di facili costumi
promise ['prɒmɪs] *n* promessa ▷ *vt*,
vi promettere; **to ~ sb sth, ~ sth to sb**
promettere qc a qn; **to ~ (sb) that/to
do sth** promettere (a qn) che/di fare qc;
promising *adj* promettente
promote [prə'məut] *vt* promuovere;
(*venture, event*) organizzare; **promotion**
[-'məuʃən] *n* promozione *f*
prompt [prɒmpt] *adj* rapido(-a),
svelto(-a); puntuale; (*reply*) sollecito(-a)
▷ *adv* (*punctually*) in punto ▷ *n* (*Comput*)
prompt *m* ▷ *vt* incitare, provocare;
(*Theatre*) suggerire a; **to ~ sb to do** incitare
qn a fare; **promptly** *adv* prontamente;
puntualmente
prone [prəun] *adj* (*lying*) prono(-a); **~ to**
propenso(-a) a, incline a
prong [prɒŋ] *n* rebbio, punta
pronoun ['prəunaun] *n* pronome *m*
pronounce [prə'nauns] *vt* pronunciare;

how do you ~ it? come si pronuncia?
pronunciation [prənʌnsɪ'eɪʃən] *n*
pronuncia
proof [pruːf] *n* prova; (*of book*) bozza; (*Phot*)
provino ▷ *adj* **~ against** a prova di
prop [prɒp] *n* sostegno, appoggio ▷ *vt*
(*also: ~ up*) sostenere, appoggiare; (*lean*):
to ~ sth against appoggiare qc contro
or a; **~s** oggetti *m inv* di scena; **prop up** *vt*
sostenere, appoggiare
propaganda [prɒpə'gændə] *n*
propaganda
propeller [prə'pɛlər] *n* elica
proper ['prɒpər] *adj* (*suited, right*)
adatto(-a), appropriato(-a); (*seemly*)
decente; (*authentic*) vero(-a); (*inf: real:
noun*) + vero(-a) e proprio(-a); **properly**
['prɒpəlɪ] *adv* (*eat, study*) bene; (*behave*)
come si deve; **proper noun** *n* nome *m*
proprio
property ['prɒpətɪ] *n* (*things owned*) beni
mpl; (*land, building*) proprietà *f inv*; (*Chem
etc: quality*) proprietà
prophecy ['prɒfɪsɪ] *n* profezia
prophet ['prɒfɪt] *n* profeta *m*
proportion [prə'pɔːʃən] *n* proporzione *f*;
(*share*) parte *f*; **~s** *npl* (*size*) proporzioni *fpl*;
proportional *adj* proporzionale
proposal [prə'pəuzl] *n* proposta; (*plan*)
progetto; (*of marriage*) proposta di
matrimonio
propose [prə'pəuz] *vt* proporre, suggerire
▷ *vi* fare una proposta di matrimonio; **to
~ to do** proporsi di fare, aver l'intenzione
di fare
proposition [prɒpə'zɪʃən] *n* proposizione
f; (*offer*) proposta
proprietor [prə'praɪətər] *n*
proprietario(-a)
prose [prəuz] *n* prosa
prosecute ['prɒsɪkjuːt] *vt* processare;
prosecution [-'kjuːʃən] *n* processo;
(*accusing side*) accusa; **prosecutor** *n* (*also:
public prosecutor) ≈ procuratore *m* della
Repubblica
prospect [*n* 'prɒspɛkt, *vb* prə'spɛkt] *n*
prospettiva; (*hope*) speranza ▷ *vi* **to ~ for**
cercare; **~s** *npl* (*for work etc*) prospettive
fpl; **prospective** [-'spɛktɪv] *adj* possibile;
futuro(-a)
prospectus [prə'spɛktəs] *n* prospetto,
programma *m*
prosper ['prɒspər] *vi* prosperare;
prosperity [prɒ'spɛrɪtɪ] *n* prosperità;
prosperous *adj* prospero(-a)
prostitute ['prɒstɪtjuːt] *n* prostituta;
male ~ uomo che si prostituisce
protect [prə'tɛkt] *vt* proteggere,
salvaguardare; **protection** *n* protezione *f*;

protective *adj* protettivo(-a)
protein ['prəuti:n] *n* proteina
protest [*n* 'prəutɛst, *vb* prə'tɛst] *n* protesta
▷ *vt, vi* protestare
Protestant ['prɔtɪstənt] *adj, n* protestante
m/f
protester [prə'tɛstər] *n* dimostrante *m/f*
protractor [prə'træktər] *n* (Geom)
goniometro
proud [praud] *adj* fiero(-a), orgoglioso(-a);
(pej) superbo(-a)
prove [pru:v] *vt* provare, dimostrare ▷ *vi*
to ~ (to be) correct *etc* risultare vero(-a)
etc; **to ~ o.s.** mostrare le proprie capacità
proverb ['prɔvə:b] *n* proverbio
provide [prə'vaid] *vt* fornire, provvedere;
to ~ sb with sth fornire *or* provvedere qn di
qc; **provide for** *vt fus* provvedere a; (future
event) prevedere; **provided** *conj* **provided
(that)** purché + *sub*, a condizione che +
sub; **providing** [prə'vaidiŋ] *conj* purché
+*sub*, a condizione che +*sub*
province ['prɔvins] *n* provincia;
provincial [prə'vinʃəl] *adj* provinciale
provision [prə'viʒən] *n* (supply) riserva;
(supplying) provvista; rifornimento;
(stipulation) condizione *f*; **~s** *npl*
(food) provviste *fpl*; **provisional** *adj*
provvisorio(-a)
provocative [prə'vɔkətiv] *adj* (aggressive)
provocatorio(-a); (thought-provoking)
stimolante; (seductive) provocante
provoke [prə'vəuk] *vt* provocare; incitare
prowl [praul] *vi* (also: **~ about, ~ around**)
aggirarsi ▷ *n* **to be on the ~** aggirarsi
proximity [prɔk'simiti] *n* prossimità
proxy ['prɔksi] *n* **by ~** per procura
prudent ['pru:dnt] *adj* prudente
prune [pru:n] *n* prugna secca ▷ *vt* potare
pry [prai] *vi* **to ~ into** ficcare il naso in
PS *abbr* (= postscript) P.S.
pseudonym ['sju:dənim] *n* pseudonimo
psychiatric [saiki'ætrik] *adj*
psichiatrico(-a)
psychiatrist [sai'kaiətrist] *n* psichiatra
m/f
psychic ['saikik] *adj* (also: **~al**) psichico(-a);
(person) dotato(-a) di qualità telepatiche
psychoanalysis [saikəuə'nælisis, -si:z] *n*
(pl **-ses**) *n* psicanalisi *f inv*
psychological [saikə'lɔdʒikl] *adj*
psicologico(-a)
psychologist [sai'kɔlədʒist] *n*
psicologo(-a)
psychology [sai'kɔlədʒi] *n* psicologia
psychotherapy [saikəu'θɛrəpi] *n*
psicoterapia
pt *abbr* (= pint; point) pt.
PTO *abbr* (= please turn over) v.r.

pub [pʌb] *n abbr* (= public house) pub *m inv*
puberty ['pju:bəti] *n* pubertà
public ['pʌblik] *adj* pubblico(-a) ▷ *n*
pubblico; **in ~** in pubblico
publication [pʌbli'keiʃən] *n*
pubblicazione *f*
public: **public company** *n* società *f inv*
per azioni (costituita tramite pubblica
sottoscrizione); **public convenience** (BRIT)
n gabinetti *mpl*; **public holiday** *n* giorno
festivo, festa nazionale; **public house**
(BRIT) *n* pub *m inv*
publicity [pʌb'lisiti] *n* pubblicità
publicize ['pʌblisaiz] *vt* rendere
pubblico(-a)
public: **public limited company** *n*
≈ società per azioni a responsabilità
limitata (quotata in Borsa); **publicly**
['pʌblikli] *adv* pubblicamente; **public
opinion** *n* opinione *f* pubblica; **public
relations** *n* pubbliche relazioni *fpl*; **public
school** *n* (BRIT) scuola privata; (US) scuola
statale; **public transport** *n* mezzi *mpl*
pubblici
publish ['pʌbliʃ] *vt* pubblicare; **publisher** *n*
editore *m*; **publishing** *n* (industry) editoria;
(of a book) pubblicazione *f*
pub lunch *n* pranzo semplice ed economico
servito nei pub
pudding ['pudiŋ] *n* budino; (BRIT:
dessert) dolce *m*; **black ~**, (US) **blood ~**
sanguinaccio
puddle ['pʌdl] *n* pozza, pozzanghera
Puerto Rico ['pwə:təu'ri:kəu] *n* Portorico
puff [pʌf] *n* sbuffo ▷ *vt* **to ~ one's pipe**
tirare sboccate di fumo ▷ *vi* (pant) ansare;
puff pastry *n* pasta sfoglia
pull [pul] *n* (tug). **to give sth a ~** tirare su
qc ▷ *vt* tirare; (muscle) strappare; (trigger)
premere ▷ *vi* tirare; **to ~ to pieces** fare
a pezzi; **to ~ one's punches** (Boxing)
risparmiare l'avversario; **to ~ one's
weight** dare il proprio contributo; **to ~
o.s. together** ricomporsi, riprendersi;
to ~ sb's leg prendere in giro qn; **pull
apart** *vt* (break) fare a pezzi; **pull away** *vi*
(move off: vehicle) muoversi, partire; (boat)
staccarsi dal molo, salpare; (draw back:
person) indietreggiare; **pull back** *vt* (lever
etc) tirare indietro; (curtains) aprire ▷ *vi*
(from confrontation etc) tirarsi indietro; (Mil:
withdraw) ritirarsi; **pull down** *vt* (house)
demolire; (tree) abbattere; **pull in** *vi* (Aut:
at the kerb) accostarsi; (Rail) entrare in
stazione; **pull off** *vt* (clothes) togliere;
(deal etc) portare a compimento; **pull out**
vi partire; (Aut: come out of line) spostarsi
sulla mezzeria ▷ *vt* staccare; far uscire;
(withdraw) ritirare; **pull over** *vi* (Aut)

accostare; **pull up** vi (stop) fermarsi ▷ vt
(raise) sollevare; (uproot) sradicare
pulley ['pʊlɪ] n puleggia, carrucola
pullover ['pʊləʊvəʳ] n pullover m inv
pulp [pʌlp] n (of fruit) polpa
pulpit ['pʊlpɪt] n pulpito
pulse [pʌls] n polso; (Bot) legume m; **~s** npl
(Culin) legumi mpl
puma ['pju:mə] n puma m inv
pump [pʌmp] n pompa; (shoe) scarpetta
▷ vt pompare; **pump up** vt gonfiare
pumpkin ['pʌmpkɪn] n zucca
pun [pʌn] n gioco di parole
punch [pʌntʃ] n (blow) pugno; (tool)
punzone m; (drink) ponce m ▷ vt (hit): **to ~
sb/sth** dare un pugno a qn/qc; **punch-up**
(BRIT: inf) n rissa
punctual ['pʌŋktjuəl] adj puntuale
punctuation [pʌŋktjuˈeɪʃən] n
interpunzione f, punteggiatura
puncture ['pʌŋktʃəʳ] n foratura ▷ vt forare
> Be careful not to translate *puncture*
> by the Italian word *puntura*.

punish ['pʌnɪʃ] vt punire; **punishment** n
punizione f
punk [pʌŋk] n (also: **~ rocker**) punk m/f inv;
(also: **~ rock**) musica punk, punk rock m;
(US: inf: hoodlum) teppista m
pup [pʌp] n cucciolo(-a)
pupil ['pju:pl] n allievo(-a); (Anat) pupilla
puppet ['pʌpɪt] n burattino
puppy ['pʌpɪ] n cucciolo(-a), cagnolino(-a)
purchase ['pə:tʃɪs] n acquisto, compera
▷ vt comprare
pure [pjuəʳ] adj puro(-a); **purely** ['pjuəlɪ]
adv puramente
purify ['pjuərɪfaɪ] vt purificare
purity ['pjuərɪtɪ] n purezza
purple ['pə:pl] adj di porpora; viola inv
purpose ['pə:pəs] n intenzione f, scopo;
on ~ apposta
purr [pə:ʳ] vi fare le fusa
purse [pə:s] n (BRIT) borsellino; (US)
borsetta ▷ vt contrarre
pursue [pə'sju:] vt inseguire; (fig: activity
etc) continuare con; (: aim etc) perseguire
pursuit [pə'sju:t] n inseguimento m (fig)
ricerca; (pastime) passatempo
pus [pʌs] n pus m
push [pʊʃ] n spinta; (effort) grande
sforzo; (drive) energia ▷ vt spingere;
(button) premere; (thrust): **to ~ sth (into)**
ficcare qc (in); (fig) fare pubblicità a ▷ vi
spingere; premere; **to ~ for** (fig) insistere
per; **push in** vi introdursi a forza; **push
off** (inf) vi filare; **push on** vi (continue)
continuare; **push over** vt far cadere; **push
through** vi farsi largo spingendo ▷ vt
(measure) far approvare; **pushchair** (BRIT)

n passeggino; **pusher** n (drug pusher)
spacciatore(-trice); **push-up** (US) n (press-
up) flessione f sulle braccia
pussy(-cat) ['pʊsɪ(-)] (inf) n micio
put [pʊt] (pt, pp **put**) vt mettere, porre;
(say) dire, esprimere; (a question) fare;
(estimate) stimare; **put away** vt (return)
mettere a posto; **put back** vt (replace)
rimettere (a posto); (postpone) rinviare;
(delay) ritardare; **put by** vt (money)
mettere da parte; **put down** vt (parcel
etc) posare, mettere giù; (pay) versare;
(in writing) mettere per iscritto; (revolt,
animal) sopprimere; (attribute) attribuire;
put forward vt (ideas) avanzare,
proporre; **put in** vt (application, complaint)
presentare; (time, effort) mettere; **put
off** vt (postpone) rimandare, rinviare;
(discourage) dissuadere; **put on** vt (clothes,
lipstick etc) mettere; (light etc) accendere;
(play etc) mettere in scena; (food, meal)
mettere su; (brake) mettere; **to ~ on
weight** ingrassare; **to ~ on airs** darsi
delle arie; **put out** vt mettere fuori; (one's
hand) porgere; (light etc) spegnere; (person:
inconvenience) scomodare; **put through**
vt (Tel: call) passare; (: person) mettere in
comunicazione; (plan) far approvare; **put
up** vt (raise) sollevare, alzare; (: umbrella)
aprire; (: tent) montare; (pin up) affiggere;
(hang) appendere; (build) costruire, erigere;
(increase) aumentare; (accommodate)
alloggiare; **put aside** vt (lay down: book
etc) mettere da una parte, posare; (save)
mettere da parte; (in shop) tenere da
parte; **put together** vt mettere insieme,
riunire; (assemble: furniture) montare; (:
meal) improvvisare; **put up with** vt fus
sopportare
putt [pʌt] n colpo leggero; **putting green**
n green m inv; campo da putting
puzzle ['pʌzl] n enigma m, mistero;
(jigsaw) puzzle m; (also: **crossword ~**)
parole fpl incrociate, cruciverba m inv ▷ vt
confondere, rendere perplesso(-a) ▷ vi
scervellarsi; **puzzled** adj perplesso(-a);
puzzling adj (question) poco chiaro(-a);
(attitude, set of instructions) incomprensibile
pyjamas [pɪ'dʒɑ:məz] (BRIT) npl pigiama m
pylon ['paɪlən] n pilone m
pyramid ['pɪrəmɪd] n piramide f
Pyrenees [pɪrɪ'ni:z] npl **the ~** i Pirenei

quack [kwæk] *n* (*of duck*) qua qua *m inv*; (*pej: doctor*) dottoruccio(-a)

quadruple [kwɔ'drupl] *vt* quadruplicare ▷ *vi* quadruplicarsi

quail [kweɪl] *n* (*Zool*) quaglia ▷ *vi* (*person*): **to ~ at** *or* **before** perdersi d'animo davanti a

quaint [kweɪnt] *adj* bizzarro(-a); (*old-fashioned*) antiquato(-a); grazioso(-a), pittoresco(-a)

quake [kweɪk] *vi* tremare ▷ *n abbr* = **earthquake**

qualification [kwɔlɪfɪ'keɪʃən] *n* (*degree etc*) qualifica, titolo; (*ability*) competenza, qualificazione *f*; (*limitation*) riserva, restrizione *f*

qualified ['kwɔlɪfaɪd] *adj* qualificato(-a); (*able*): **~ to** competente in, qualificato(-a) a; (*limited*) condizionato(-a)

qualify ['kwɔlɪfaɪ] *vt* abilitare; (*limit: statement*) modificare, precisare ▷ *vi* **to ~ (as)** qualificarsi (come); **to ~ (for)** acquistare i requisiti necessari (per); (*Sport*) qualificarsi (per *or* a)

quality ['kwɔlɪtɪ] *n* qualità *f inv*

qualm [kwɑːm] *n* dubbio; scrupolo

quantify ['kwɔntɪfaɪ] *vt* quantificare

quantity ['kwɔntɪtɪ] *n* quantità *f inv*

quarantine ['kwɔrntiːn] *n* quarantena

quarrel ['kwɔrl] *n* lite *f*, disputa ▷ *vi* litigare

quarry ['kwɔrɪ] *n* (*for stone*) cava; (*animal*) preda

quart [kwɔːt] *n* ≈ litro

quarter ['kwɔːtəʳ] *n* quarto; (*us: coin*) quarto di dollaro; (*of year*) trimestre *m*; (*district*) quartiere *m* ▷ *vt* dividere in quattro; (*Mil*) alloggiare; **~s** *npl* (*living quarters*) alloggio; (*Mil*) alloggi *mpl*, quadrato; **a ~ of an hour** un quarto d'ora; **quarter final** *n* quarto di finale; **quarterly** *adj* trimestrale ▷ *adv* trimestralmente

quartet(te) [kwɔː'tɛt] *n* quartetto

quartz [kwɔːts] *n* quarzo

quay [kiː] *n* (*also: ~side*) banchina

queasy ['kwiːzɪ] *adj* (*stomach*) delicato(-a); **to feel ~** aver la nausea

queen [kwiːn] *n* (*gen*) regina; (*Cards etc*) regina, donna

queer [kwɪəʳ] *adj* strano(-a), curioso(-a) ▷ *n* (*inf*) finocchio

quench [kwɛntʃ] *vt* **to ~ one's thirst** dissetarsi

query ['kwɪərɪ] *n* domanda, questione *f* ▷ *vt* mettere in questione

quest [kwɛst] *n* cerca, ricerca

question ['kwɛstʃən] *n* domanda, questione *f* ▷ *vt* (*person*) interrogare; (*plan, idea*) mettere in questione *or* in dubbio; **it's a ~ of doing** si tratta di fare; **beyond ~** fuori di dubbio; **out of the ~** fuori discussione, impossibile; **questionable** *adj* discutibile; **question mark** *n* punto interrogativo; **questionnaire** [kwɛstʃə'nɛəʳ] *n* questionario

queue [kjuː] (*BRIT*) *n* coda, fila ▷ *vi* fare la coda

quiche [kiːʃ] *n* torta salata a base di uova, formaggio, prosciutto o altro

quick [kwɪk] *adj* rapido(-a), veloce; (*reply*) pronto(-a); (*mind*) pronto(-a), acuto(-a) ▷ *n* **cut to the ~** (*fig*) toccato(-a) sul vivo; **be ~!** fa presto!; **quickly** *adv* rapidamente, velocemente

quid [kwɪd] (*BRIT: inf*) *n inv* sterlina

quiet ['kwaɪət] *adj* tranquillo(-a), quieto(-a); (*ceremony*) semplice ▷ *n* tranquillità, calma ▷ *vt, vi* (*US*) = **quieten**; **keep ~!** sta zitto!; **quieten** (*also: quieten down*) *vi* calmarsi, chetarsi ▷ *vt* calmare, chetare; **quietly** *adv* tranquillamente, calmamente; sommessamente

quilt [kwɪlt] *n* trapunta; (*continental quilt*) piumino

quirky ['kwəːkɪ] *adj* stravagante

quit [kwɪt] (*pt, pp* **quit** *or* **quitted**) *vt* mollare; (*premises*) lasciare, partire da ▷ *vi* (*give up*) mollare; (*resign*) dimettersi

quite [kwaɪt] *adv* (*rather*) assai; (*entirely*) completamente, del tutto; **I ~ understand** capisco perfettamente; **that's not ~ big enough** non è proprio sufficiente; **~ a few of them** non pochi di loro; **~ (so)!** esatto!

quits [kwɪts] *adj* **~ (with)** pari (con); **let's call it ~** adesso siamo pari

quiver ['kwɪvə^r] *vi* tremare, fremere

quiz [kwɪz] *n* (*game*) quiz *m inv*; indovinello ▷ *vt* interrogare

quota ['kwəʊtə] *n* quota

quotation [kwəʊ'teɪʃən] *n* citazione *f*; (*of shares etc*) quotazione *f*; (*estimate*) preventivo; **quotation marks** *npl* virgolette *fpl*

quote [kwəʊt] *n* citazione *f* ▷ *vt* (*sentence*) citare; (*price*) dare, fissare; (*shares*) quotare ▷ *vi* **to ~ from** citare; **~s** *npl* = **quotation marks**

rabbi ['ræbaɪ] *n* rabbino

rabbit ['ræbɪt] *n* coniglio

rabies ['reɪbiːz] *n* rabbia

RAC (BRIT) *n abbr* = **Royal Automobile Club**

rac(c)oon [rə'kuːn] *n* procione *m*

race [reɪs] *n* razza; (*competition, rush*) corsa ▷ *vt* (*horse*) far correre ▷ *vi* correre; (*engine*) imballarsi; **race car** (US) *n* = **racing car**; **racecourse** *n* campo di corse, ippodromo; **racehorse** *n* cavallo da corsa; **racetrack** *n* pista

racial ['reɪʃl] *adj* razziale

racing ['reɪsɪŋ] *n* corsa; **racing car** (BRIT) *n* macchina da corsa; **racing driver** (BRIT) *n* corridore *m* automobilista

racism ['reɪsɪzəm] *n* razzismo; **racist** *adj*, *n* razzista *m/f*

rack [ræk] *n* rastrelliera; (*also:* **luggage ~**) rete *f*, portabagagli *m inv*; (*also:* **roof ~**) portabagagli; (*dish rack*) scolapiatti *m inv* ▷ *vt* **~ed by** torturato(-a) da; **to ~ one's brains** scervellarsi

racket ['rækɪt] *n* (*for tennis*) racchetta; (*noise*) fracasso; baccano; (*swindle*) imbroglio, truffa; (*organized crime*) racket *m inv*

racquet ['rækɪt] *n* racchetta

radar ['reɪdɑː^r] *n* radar *m*

radiation [reɪdɪ'eɪʃən] *n* irradiamento;

(*radioactive*) radiazione *f*
radiator ['reɪdɪeɪtər] *n* radiatore *m*
radical ['rædɪkl] *adj* radicale
radio ['reɪdɪəu] *n* radio *f inv*; **on the ~** alla radio; **radioactive** [reɪdɪəu'æktɪv] *adj* radioattivo(-a); **radio station** *n* stazione *f* radio *inv*
radish ['rædɪʃ] *n* ravanello
RAF *n abbr* = **Royal Air Force**
raffle ['ræfl] *n* lotteria
raft [rɑːft] *n* zattera; (*also*: **life ~**) zattera di salvataggio
rag [ræg] *n* straccio, cencio; (*pej: newspaper*) giornalaccio, bandiera; (*for charity*) iniziativa studentesca a scopo benefico; **~s** (*torn clothes*) stracci *mpl*, brandelli *mpl*
rage [reɪdʒ] *n* (*fury*) collera, furia ▷ *vi* (*person*) andare su tutte le furie; (*storm*) infuriare; **it's all the ~** fa furore
ragged ['rægɪd] *adj* (*edge*) irregolare; (*clothes*) logoro(-a); (*appearance*) pezzente
raid [reɪd] *n* (*Mil*) incursione *f*; (*criminal*) rapina; (*by police*) irruzione *f* ▷ *vt* fare un'incursione in; rapinare; fare irruzione in
rail [reɪl] *n* (*on stair*) ringhiera; (*on bridge, balcony*) parapetto; (*of ship*) battagliola; **railcard** (*BRIT*) tessera di riduzione ferroviaria; **railing(s)** *n(pl)* ringhiere *fpl*; **railroad** (*US*) *n* = **railway**; **railway** (*BRIT*: *irreg*) *n* ferrovia; **railway line** (*BRIT*) *n* linea ferroviaria; **railway station** (*BRIT*) *n* stazione *f* ferroviaria
rain [reɪn] *n* pioggia ▷ *vi* piovere; **in the ~** sotto la pioggia; **it's ~ing** piove; **rainbow** *n* arcobaleno; **raincoat** *n* impermeabile *m*; **raindrop** *n* goccia di pioggia; **rainfall** *n* pioggia; (*measurement*) piovosità; **rainforest** *n* foresta pluviale; **rainy** *adj* piovoso(-a)
raise [reɪz] *n* aumento ▷ *vt* (*lift*) alzare; sollevare; (*increase*) aumentare; (*a protest, doubt, question*) sollevare; (*cattle, family*) allevare; (*crop*) coltivare; (*army, funds*) raccogliere; (*loan*) ottenere; **to ~ one's voice** alzare la voce
raisin ['reɪzn] *n* uva secca
rake [reɪk] *n* (*tool*) rastrello ▷ *vt* (*garden*) rastrellare
rally ['rælɪ] *n* (*Pol etc*) riunione *f*; (*Aut*) rally *m inv*; (*Tennis*) scambio ▷ *vt* riunire, radunare ▷ *vi* (*sick person, Stock Exchange*) riprendersi
RAM [ræm] *n abbr* (= *random access memory*) memoria ad accesso casuale
ram [ræm] *n* montone *m*, ariete *m* ▷ *vt* conficcare; (*crash into*) cozzare, sbattere contro; percuotere; speronare
Ramadan [ræmə'dæn] *n* Ramadan *m inv*

ramble ['ræmbl] *n* escursione *f* ▷ *vi* (*pej: also*: **~ on**) divagare; **rambler** *n* escursionista *m/f*; (*Bot*) rosa rampicante; **rambling** *adj* (*speech*) sconnesso(-a); (*house*) tutto(-a) a nicchie e corridoi; (*Bot*) rampicante
ramp [ræmp] *n* rampa; **on/off ~** (*US Aut*) raccordo di entrata/uscita
rampage [ræm'peɪdʒ] *n* **to go on the ~** scatenarsi in modo violento
ran [ræn] *pt of* **run**
ranch [rɑːntʃ] *n* ranch *m inv*
random ['rændəm] *adj* fatto(-a) or detto(-a) per caso; (*Comput, Math*) casuale ▷ *n* **at ~** a casaccio
rang [ræŋ] *pt of* **ring**
range [reɪndʒ] *n* (*of mountains*) catena; (*of missile, voice*) portata; (*of proposals, products*) gamma; (*Mil: also*: **shooting ~**) campo di tiro; (*also*: **kitchen ~**) fornello, cucina economica ▷ *vt* disporre ▷ *vi* **to ~ over** coprire; **to ~ from ... to** andare da ... a
ranger ['reɪndʒər] *n* guardia forestale
rank [ræŋk] *n* fila; (*status, Mil*) grado; (*BRIT: also*: **taxi ~**) posteggio di taxi ▷ *vi* **to ~ among** essere tra ▷ *adj* puzzolente; vero(-a) e proprio(-a); **the ~ and file** (*fig*) la gran massa
ransom ['rænsəm] *n* riscatto; **to hold sb to ~** (*fig*) esercitare pressione su qn
rant [rænt] *vi* vociare
rap [ræp] *vt* bussare a; picchiare su ▷ *n* (*music*) rap *m inv*
rape [reɪp] *n* violenza carnale, stupro; (*Bot*) ravizzone *m* ▷ *vt* violentare
rapid ['ræpɪd] *adj* rapido(-a); **rapidly** *adv* rapidamente; **rapids** *npl* (*Geo*) rapida
rapist ['reɪpɪst] *n* violentatore *m*
rapport [ræ'pɔːr] *n* rapporto *m*
rare [rɛər] *adj* raro(-a); (*Culin: steak*) al sangue; **rarely** ['rɛəlɪ] *adv* raramente
rash [ræʃ] *adj* imprudente, sconsiderato(-a) ▷ *n* (*Med*) eruzione *f*; (*of events etc*) scoppio
rasher ['ræʃər] *n* fetta sottile (di lardo or prosciutto)
raspberry ['rɑːzbərɪ] *n* lampone *m*
rat [ræt] *n* ratto
rate [reɪt] *n* (*proportion*) tasso, percentuale *f*; (*speed*) velocità *f inv*; (*price*) tariffa ▷ *vt* giudicare; stimare; **~s** *npl* (*BRIT: property tax*) imposte *fpl* comunali; (*fees*) tariffe *fpl*; **to ~ sb/sth as** valutare qn/qc come
rather ['rɑːðər] *adv* piuttosto; **it's ~ expensive** è piuttosto caro; (*too*) è un po' caro; **there's ~ a lot** ce n'è parecchio; **I would** *or* **I'd ~ go** preferirei andare
rating ['reɪtɪŋ] *n* (*assessment*) valutazione *f*; (*score*) punteggio di merito; **~s** *npl* (*Radio,*

TV) indice m di ascolto
ratio ['reɪʃɪəu] n proporzione f, rapporto
ration ['ræʃən] n (gen pl) razioni fpl ▷ vt
razionare; **~s** npl razioni fpl
rational ['ræʃənl] adj razionale,
ragionevole; (solution, reasoning)
logico(-a)
rattle ['rætl] n tintinnio; (louder) strepito;
(for baby) sonaglino ▷ vi risuonare,
tintinnare; fare un rumore di ferraglia ▷ vt
scuotere (con strepito)
rave [reɪv] vi (in anger) infuriarsi; (with
enthusiasm) andare in estasi; (Med) delirare
▷ n (BRIT: inf: party) rave m inv
raven ['reɪvən] n corvo
ravine [rə'vi:n] n burrone m
raw [rɔ:] adj (uncooked) crudo(-a); (not
processed) greggio(-a); (sore) vivo(-a);
(inexperienced) inesperto(-a); (weather, day)
gelido(-a)
ray [reɪ] n raggio; **a ~ of hope** un barlume
di speranza
razor ['reɪzər] n rasoio; **razor blade** n lama
di rasoio
Rd abbr = **road**
re [ri:] prep con riferimento a
RE n abbr (BRIT Mil: = Royal Engineers) ≈ G.
M. (Genio Militare); (BRIT) = **religious
education**
reach [ri:tʃ] n portata; (of river etc) tratto
▷ vt raggiungere; arrivare a ▷ vi stendersi;
out of/within ~ fuori/a portata di mano;
within ~ of the shops/station vicino ai
negozi/alla stazione; **reach out** vt (hand)
allungare ▷ vi **to ~ out for** stendere la
mano per prendere
react [ri:'ækt] vi reagire; **reaction** [-'ækʃə
n] n reazione f; **reactor** [ri:'æktər] n
reattore m
read [ri:d, pt, pp red] (pt, pp **read**) vi leggere
▷ vt leggere; (understand) intendere,
interpretare; (study) studiare; **read
out** vt leggere ad alta voce; **reader** n
lettore(-trice); (BRIT: at university) professore
con funzioni preminenti di ricerca
readily ['rɛdɪlɪ] adv volentieri; (easily)
facilmente; (quickly) prontamente
reading ['ri:dɪŋ] n lettura; (understanding)
interpretazione f; (on instrument)
indicazione f
ready ['rɛdɪ] adj pronto(-a); (willing)
pronto(-a), disposto(-a); (available)
disponibile ▷ n **at the ~** (Mil) pronto a
sparare; **when will my photos be ~?**
quando saranno pronte le mie foto?; **to
get ~** vi prepararsi ▷ vt preparare; **ready-
made** adj prefabbricato(-a); (clothes)
confezionato(-a)
real [rɪəl] adj reale; vero(-a); **in ~ terms**

in realtà; **real ale** n birra ad effervescenza
naturale; **real estate** n beni mpl immobili;
realistic [-'lɪstɪk] adj realistico(-a);
reality [ri:'ælɪtɪ] n realtà f inv
realization [rɪəlaɪ'zeɪʃən] n presa di
coscienza; realizzazione f
realize ['rɪəlaɪz] vt (understand) rendersi
conto di
really ['rɪəlɪ] adv veramente, davvero; **~!**
(indicating annoyance) oh, insomma!
realm [rɛlm] n reame m, regno
Realtor® ['rɪəltɔːr] (US) n agente m
immobiliare
reappear [ri:ə'pɪər] vi ricomparire,
riapparire
rear [rɪər] adj di dietro; (Aut: wheel etc)
posteriore ▷ n didietro, parte f posteriore
▷ vt (cattle, family) allevare ▷ vi (also: **~ up**:
animal) impennarsi
rearrange [ri:ə'reɪndʒ] vt riordinare
rear: **rear-view mirror** ['rɪəvju:-] n (Aut)
specchio retrovisore; **rear-wheel drive** n
trazione fpl posteriore
reason ['ri:zn] n ragione f; (cause, motive)
ragione, motivo ▷ vi **to ~ with sb** far
ragionare qn; **it stands to ~ that** è
ovvio che; **reasonable** adj ragionevole;
(not bad) accettabile; **reasonably**
adv ragionevolmente; **reasoning** n
ragionamento
reassurance [ri:ə'ʃuərəns] n
rassicurazione f
reassure [ri:ə'ʃuər] vt rassicurare; **to ~ sb
of** rassicurare qn di or su
rebate ['ri:beɪt] n (on tax etc) sgravio
rebel [n 'rɛbl, vb ri'bɛl] n ribelle m/f
▷ vi ribellarsi; **rebellion** n ribellione f;
rebellious adj ribelle
rebuild [ri:'bɪld] vt irreg ricostruire
recall [ri'kɔ:l] vt richiamare; (remember)
ricordare, richiamare alla mente ▷ n
richiamo
rec'd abbr = **received**
receipt [ri'si:t] n (document) ricevuta; (act
of receiving) ricevimento; **~s** npl (Comm)
introiti mpl; **can I have a ~, please?** posso
avere una ricevuta, per favore?
receive [ri'si:v] vt ricevere; (guest)
ricevere, accogliere; **receiver** [ri'si:
vər] n (Tel) ricevitore m; (Radio, TV)
apparecchio ricevente; (of stolen goods)
ricettatore(-trice); (Comm) curatore m
fallimentare
recent ['ri:snt] adj recente; **recently** adv
recentemente
reception [ri'sɛpʃən] n ricevimento;
(welcome) accoglienza; (TV etc) ricezione
f; **reception desk** n (in hotel) reception f
inv; (in hospital, at doctor's) accettazione f;

(in offices etc) portineria; **receptionist** n receptionist m/f inv

recession [rɪ'sɛʃən] n recessione f

recharge [riː'tʃɑːdʒ] vt (battery) ricaricare

recipe ['rɛsɪpɪ] n ricetta

recipient [rɪ'sɪpɪənt] n beneficiario(-a); (of letter) destinatario(-a)

recital [rɪ'saɪtl] n recital m inv

recite [rɪ'saɪt] vt (poem) recitare

reckless ['rɛkləs] adj (driver etc) spericolato(-a); (spending) folle

reckon ['rɛkən] vt (count) calcolare; (think): **I ~ that …** penso che …

reclaim [rɪ'kleɪm] vt (demand back) richiedere, reclamare; (land) bonificare; (materials) recuperare

recline [rɪ'klaɪn] vi stare sdraiato(-a)

recognition [rɛkəg'nɪʃən] n riconoscimento, **transformed beyond ~** irriconoscibile

recognize ['rɛkəgnaɪz] vt **to ~ (by/as)** riconoscere (a or da/come)

recollection [rɛkə'lɛkʃən] n ricordo

recommend [rɛkə'mɛnd] vt raccomandare; (advise) consigliare; **can you ~ a good restaurant?** mi può consigliare un buon ristorante?; **recommendation** [rɛkəmən'deɪʃən] n raccomandazione f; consiglio

reconcile ['rɛkənsaɪl] vt (two people) riconciliare; (two facts) conciliare, quadrare; **to ~ o.s. to** rassegnarsi a

reconsider [riːkən'sɪdər] vt riconsiderare

reconstruct [riːkən'strʌkt] vt ricostruire

record [n 'rɛkɔːd, vb rɪ'kɔːd] n ricordo, documento; (of meeting etc) nota, verbale m; (register) registro; (file) pratica, dossier m inv; (Comput) record m inv; (also: **criminal ~**) fedina penale sporca; (Mus: disc) disco; (Sport) record m inv, primato ▷ vt (set down) prendere nota di, registrare; (Mus: song etc) registrare; **in ~ time** a tempo di record; **off the ~** adj ufficioso(-a) ▷ adv ufficiosamente; **recorded delivery** (BRIT) n (Post): **recorded delivery letter** etc lettera etc raccomandata; **recorder** n (Mus) flauto diritto; **recording** n (Mus) registrazione f; **record player** n giradischi m inv

recount [rɪ'kaunt] vt raccontare, narrare

recover [rɪ'kʌvər] vt ricuperare ▷ vi **to ~ (from)** riprendersi (da); **recovery** [rɪ'kʌvərɪ] n ricupero; ristabilimento; ripresa

▪ Be careful not to translate recover by the Italian word ricoverare.

recreate [riːkrɪ'eɪt] vt ricreare

recreation [rɛkrɪ'eɪʃən] n ricreazione f; svago; **recreational drug** [rɛkrɪ'eɪʃənl-] n sostanza stupefacente usata a scopo ricreativo;

recreational vehicle (US) n camper m inv

recruit [rɪ'kruːt] n recluta; (in company) nuovo(-a) assunto(-a) ▷ vt reclutare; **recruitment** n reclutamento

rectangle ['rɛktæŋgl] n rettangolo; **rectangular** [-'tæŋgjulər] adj rettangolare

rectify ['rɛktɪfaɪ] vt (error) rettificare; (omission) riparare

rector ['rɛktər] n (Rel) parroco (anglicano)

recur [rɪ'kəːr] vi riaccadere; (symptoms) ripresentarsi; **recurring** adj (Math) periodico(-a)

recyclable [riː'saɪkləbl] adj riciclabile

recycle [riː'saɪkl] vt riciclare

recycling [riː'saɪklɪŋ] n riciclaggio

red [rɛd] n rosso; (Pol: pej) rosso(-a) ▷ adj rosso(-a); **in the ~** (account) scoperto; (business) in deficit; **Red Cross** n Croce f Rossa; **redcurrant** n ribes m inv

redeem [rɪ'diːm] vt (debt) riscattare; (sth in pawn) ritirare; (fig, also Rel) redimere

red: red-haired [-'hɛəd] adj dai capelli rossi; **redhead** ['rɛdhɛd] n rosso(-a); **red-hot** adj arroventato(-a); **red light** n **to go through a red light** (Aut) passare col rosso; **red-light district** ['rɛdlaɪt-] n quartiere m a luci rosse; **red meat** n carne f rossa

reduce [rɪ'djuːs] vt ridurre; (lower) ridurre, abbassare; **"~ speed now"** (Aut) "rallentare"; **at a ~d price** scontato(-a); **reduced** adj (decreased) ridotto(-a); **at a reduced price** a prezzo ribassato or ridotto; **"greatly reduced prices"** "grandi ribassi"; **reduction** [rɪ'dʌkʃən] n riduzione f; (of price) ribasso; (discount) sconto; **is there a reduction for children/ students?** ci sono riduzioni per i bambini/ gli studenti?

redundancy [rɪ'dʌndənsɪ] n licenziamento

redundant [rɪ'dʌndnt] adj (worker) licenziato(-a); (detail, object) superfluo(-a); **to be made ~** essere licenziato (per eccesso di personale)

reed [riːd] n (Bot) canna; (Mus: of clarinet etc) ancia

reef [riːf] n (at sea) scogliera

reel [riːl] n bobina, rocchetto; (Fishing) mulinello; (Cinema) rotolo; (dance) danza veloce scozzese ▷ vi (sway) barcollare

ref [rɛf] (inf) n abbr (= referee) arbitro

refectory [rɪ'fɛktərɪ] n refettorio

refer [rɪ'fəːr] vt **to ~ sth to** (dispute, decision) deferire qc a; **to ~ sb to** (inquirer, Med: patient) indirizzare qn a; (reader: to text) rimandare qn a ▷ vi **~ to** (allude to) accennare a; (consult) rivolgersi a

referee [rɛfə'riː] *n* arbitro; (BRIT: *for job application*) referenza ▷ *vt* arbitrare

reference ['rɛfrəns] *n* riferimento; (*mention*) menzione *f*, allusione *f*; (*for job application*) referenza; **with ~ to** (*Comm: in letter*) in or con riferimento a; **reference number** *n* numero di riferimento

refill [*vb* riː'fɪl, *n* 'riːfɪl] *vt* riempire di nuovo; (*pen, lighter etc*) ricaricare ▷ *n* (*for pen etc*) ricambio

refine [rɪ'faɪn] *vt* raffinare; **refined** *adj* (*person, taste*) raffinato(-a); **refinery** *n* raffineria

reflect [rɪ'flɛkt] *vt* (*light, image*) riflettere; (*fig*) rispecchiare ▷ *vi* (*think*) riflettere, considerare; **it ~s badly/well on him** si ripercuote su di lui in senso negativo/positivo; **reflection** [-'flɛkʃən] *n* riflessione *f*; (*image*) riflesso; (*criticism*): **reflection on** giudizio su; attacco a; **on reflection** pensandoci sopra

reflex ['riːflɛks] *adj* riflesso(-a) ▷ *n* riflesso

reform [rɪ'fɔːm] *n* (*of sinner etc*) correzione *f*; (*of law etc*) riforma ▷ *vt* correggere; riformare

refrain [rɪ'freɪn] *vi* **to ~ from doing** trattenersi dal fare ▷ *n* ritornello

refresh [rɪ'frɛʃ] *vt* rinfrescare; (*food, sleep*) ristorare; **refreshing** *adj* (*drink*) rinfrescante; (*sleep*) riposante, ristoratore(-trice); **refreshments** *npl* rinfreschi *mpl*

refrigerator [rɪ'frɪdʒəreɪtəʳ] *n* frigorifero

refuel [riː'fjuəl] *vi* far rifornimento (di carburante)

refuge ['rɛfjuːdʒ] *n* rifugio; **to take ~ in** rifugiarsi in; **refugee** [rɛfju'dʒiː] *n* rifugiato(-a), profugo(-a)

refund [*n* 'riːfʌnd, *vb* rɪ'fʌnd] *n* rimborso ▷ *vt* rimborsare

refurbish [riː'fəːbɪʃ] *vt* rimettere a nuovo

refusal [rɪ'fjuːzəl] *n* rifiuto; **to have first ~ on** avere il diritto d'opzione su

refuse [*n* 'rɛfjuːs, *vb* rɪ'fjuːz] *n* rifiuti *mpl* ▷ *vt, vi* rifiutare; **to ~ to do** rifiutare di fare

regain [rɪ'geɪn] *vt* riguadagnare; riacquistare, ricuperare

regard [rɪ'gɑːd] *n* riguardo, stima ▷ *vt* considerare, stimare; **to give one's ~s to** porgere i suoi saluti a; **"with kindest ~s"** "cordiali saluti"; **regarding** *prep* riguardo a, per quanto riguarda; **regardless** *adv* lo stesso; **regardless of** a dispetto di, nonostante

regenerate [rɪ'dʒɛnəreɪt] *vt* rigenerare

reggae ['rɛgeɪ] *n* reggae *m*

regiment ['rɛdʒɪmənt] *n* reggimento

region ['riːdʒən] *n* regione *f*; **in the ~ of** (*fig*) all'incirca di; **regional** *adj* regionale

register ['rɛdʒɪstəʳ] *n* registro; (*also*: **electoral ~**) lista elettorale ▷ *vt* registrare; (*vehicle*) immatricolare; (*letter*) assicurare; (*instrument*) segnare ▷ *vi* iscriversi; (*at hotel*) firmare il registro; (*make impression*) entrare in testa; **registered** (BRIT) *adj* (*letter*) assicurato(-a)

registrar ['rɛdʒɪstrɑːʳ] *n* ufficiale *m* di stato civile; segretario

registration [rɛdʒɪs'treɪʃən] *n* (*act*) registrazione *f*; iscrizione *f*; (*Aut: also:* **~ number**) numero di targa

registry office (BRIT) *n* anagrafe *f*; **to get married in a ~** ≈ sposarsi in municipio

regret [rɪ'grɛt] *n* rimpianto, rincrescimento ▷ *vt* rimpiangere; **regrettable** *adj* deplorevole

regular ['rɛgjuləʳ] *adj* regolare; (*usual*) abituale, normale; (*soldier*) dell'esercito regolare ▷ *n* (*client etc*) cliente *m/f* abituale; **regularly** *adv* regolarmente

regulate ['rɛgjuleɪt] *vt* regolare; **regulation** [-'leɪʃən] *n* regolazione *f*; (*rule*) regola, regolamento

rehabilitation ['riːhəbɪlɪ'teɪʃən] *n* (*of offender*) riabilitazione *f*; (*of disabled*) riadattamento

rehearsal [rɪ'həːsəl] *n* prova

rehearse [rɪ'həːs] *vt* provare

reign [reɪn] *n* regno ▷ *vi* regnare

reimburse [riːɪm'bəːs] *vt* rimborsare

rein [reɪn] *n* (*for horse*) briglia

reincarnation [riːɪnkɑː'neɪʃən] *n* reincarnazione *f*

reindeer ['reɪndɪəʳ] *n inv* renna

reinforce [riːɪn'fɔːs] *vt* rinforzare; **reinforcements** *npl* (*Mil*) rinforzi *mpl*

reinstate [riːɪn'steɪt] *vt* reintegrare

reject [*n* 'riːdʒɛkt, *vb* rɪ'dʒɛkt] *n* (*Comm*) scarto ▷ *vt* rifiutare, respingere; (*Comm: goods*) scartare; **rejection** [rɪ'dʒɛkʃən] *n* rifiuto

rejoice [rɪ'dʒɔɪs] *vi* **to ~ (at** or **over)** provare diletto in

relate [rɪ'leɪt] *vt* (*tell*) raccontare; (*connect*) collegare ▷ *vi* **to ~ to** (*connect*) riferirsi a; (*get on with*) stabilire un rapporto con; **relating to** che riguarda, rispetto a; **related** *adj* **related (to)** imparentato(-a) (con); collegato(-a) or connesso(-a) (a)

relation [rɪ'leɪʃən] *n* (*person*) parente *m/f*; (*link*) rapporto, relazione *f*; **~s** *npl* (*relatives*) parenti *mpl*; **relationship** *n* rapporto; (*personal ties*) rapporti *mpl*, relazioni *fpl*; (*also:* **family relationship**) legami *mpl* di parentela

relative ['rɛlətɪv] *n* parente *m/f* ▷ *adj* relativo(-a); (*respective*) rispettivo(-a); **relatively** *adv* relativamente; (*fairly,* *rather*) abbastanza

relax [rɪ'læks] *vi* rilasciarsi; (*person: unwind*) rilassarsi ▷ *vt* rilasciare; (*mind, person*) rilassare; **relaxation** [riːlæk'seɪʃə n] *n* rilasciamento; rilassamento; (*entertainment*) ricreazione *f*, svago; **relaxed** *adj* rilassato(-a); **relaxing** *adj* rilassante

relay ['riːleɪ] *n* (*Sport*) corsa a staffetta ▷ *vt* (*message*) trasmettere

release [rɪ'liːs] *n* (*from prison*) rilascio; (*from obligation*) liberazione *f*; (*of gas etc*) emissione *f*; (*of film etc*) distribuzione *f*; (*record*) disco; (*device*) disinnesto ▷ *vt* (*prisoner*) rilasciare; (*from obligation, wreckage etc*) liberare; (*book, film*) fare uscire; (*news*) rendere pubblico(-a); (*gas etc*) emettere; (*Tech: catch, spring etc*) disinnestare

relegate ['rɛləgeɪt] *vt* relegare; (BRIT *Sport*): **to be ~d** essere retrocesso(-a)

relent [rɪ'lɛnt] *vi* cedere; **relentless** *adj* implacabile

relevant ['rɛləvənt] *adj* pertinente; (*chapter*) in questione; **~ to** pertinente a

> Be careful not to translate *relevant* by the Italian word *rilevante*.

reliable [rɪ'laɪəbl] *adj* (*person, firm*) fidato(-a), che dà affidamento; (*method*) sicuro(-a); (*machine*) affidabile

relic ['rɛlɪk] *n* (*Rel*) reliquia; (*of the past*) resto

relief [rɪ'liːf] *n* (*from pain, anxiety*) sollievo; (*help, supplies*) soccorsi *mpl*; (*Art, Geo*) rilievo

relieve [rɪ'liːv] *vt* (*pain, patient*) sollevare; (*bring help*) soccorrere; (*take over from: gen*) sostituire; (: *guard*) rilevare; **to ~ sb of sth** (*load*) alleggerire qn di qc; **to ~ o.s.** fare i propri bisogni; **relieved** *adj* sollevato(-a); **to be relieved that ...** essere sollevato(-a) (dal fatto) che ...; **I'm relieved to hear it** mi hai tolto un peso con questa notizia

religion [rɪ'lɪdʒən] *n* religione *f*

religious [rɪ'lɪdʒəs] *adj* religioso(-a); **religious education** *n* religione *f*

relish ['rɛlɪʃ] *n* (*Culin*) condimento; (*enjoyment*) gran piacere *m* ▷ *vt* (*food etc*) godere; **to ~ doing** adorare fare

relocate ['riːləʊ'keɪt] *vt* trasferire ▷ *vi* trasferirsi

reluctance [rɪ'lʌktəns] *n* riluttanza

reluctant [rɪ'lʌktənt] *adj* riluttante, mal disposto(-a); **reluctantly** *adv* di mala voglia, a malincuore

rely [rɪ'laɪ]: **to ~ on** *vt fus* contare su; (*be dependent*) dipendere da

remain [rɪ'meɪn] *vi* restare, rimanere; **remainder** *n* resto; (*Comm*) rimanenza; **remaining** *adj* che rimane; **remains** *npl*

resti *mpl*

remand [rɪ'mɑːnd] *n* **on ~** in detenzione preventiva ▷ *vt* **to ~ in custody** rinviare in carcere; trattenere a disposizione della legge

remark [rɪ'mɑːk] *n* osservazione *f* ▷ *vt* osservare, dire; **remarkable** *adj* notevole; eccezionale

remarry [riː'mærɪ] *vi* risposarsi

remedy ['rɛmədɪ] *n* **~ (for)** rimedio (per) ▷ *vt* rimediare a

remember [rɪ'mɛmbər] *vt* ricordare, ricordarsi di; **~ me to him** salutalo da parte mia; **Remembrance Day** [rɪ'mɛmbrəns-] *n* 11 novembre, giorno della commemorazione dei caduti in guerra

● **REMEMBRANCE DAY**
●
● In Gran Bretagna, il **Remembrance**
● **Day** è un giorno di commemorazione
● dei caduti in guerra. Si celebra ogni anno
● la domenica più vicina all'11 novembre,
● anniversario della firma dell'armistizio
● con la Germania nel 1918.

remind [rɪ'maɪnd] *vt* **to ~ sb of sth** ricordare qc a qn; **to ~ sb to do** ricordare a qn di fare; **reminder** *n* richiamo; (*note etc*) promemoria *m*

reminiscent [rɛmɪ'nɪsnt] *adj* **~ of** che fa pensare a, che richiama

remnant ['rɛmnənt] *n* resto, avanzo

remorse [rɪ'mɔːs] *n* rimorso

remote [rɪ'məʊt] *adj* remoto(-a), lontano(-a); (*person*) distaccato(-a); **remote control** *n* telecomando; **remotely** *adv* remotamente; (*slightly*) vagamente

removal [rɪ'muːvəl] *n* (*taking away*) rimozione *f*; soppressione *f*; (BRIT: *from house*) trasloco; (*from office: dismissal*) destituzione *f*; (*Med*) ablazione *f*; **removal man** (*irreg*) *n* (BRIT) addetto ai traslochi; **removal van** (BRIT) *n* furgone *m* per traslochi

remove [rɪ'muːv] *vt* togliere, rimuovere; (*employee*) destituire; (*stain*) far sparire; (*doubt, abuse*) sopprimere, eliminare

Renaissance [rɪ'neɪsɑːns] *n* **the ~** il Rinascimento

rename [riː'neɪm] *vt* ribattezzare

render ['rɛndər] *vt* rendere

rendezvous ['rɒndɪvuː] *n* appuntamento; (*place*) luogo d'incontro; (*meeting*) incontro

renew [rɪ'njuː] *vt* rinnovare; (*negotiations*) riprendere

renovate ['rɛnəveɪt] *vt* rinnovare; (*art work*) restaurare

renowned [rɪ'naund] *adj* rinomato(-a)

rent [rɛnt] *n* affitto ▷ *vt* (*take for rent*) prendere in affitto; (*also*: **~ out**) dare in affitto; **rental** *n* (*for television, car*) fitto

reorganize [riː'ɔːgənaɪz] *vt* riorganizzare

rep [rɛp] *n abbr* (*Comm*: = *representative*) rappresentante *m/f*; (*Theatre*: = *repertory*) teatro di repertorio

repair [rɪ'pɛəʳ] *n* riparazione *f* ▷ *vt* riparare; **in good/bad ~** in buone/cattive condizioni; **where can I get this ~ed?** dove lo posso far riparare?; **repair kit** *n* corredo per riparazioni

repay [riː'peɪ] (*irreg*) *vt* (*money, creditor*) rimborsare, ripagare; (*sb's efforts*) ricompensare; (*favour*) ricambiare; **repayment** *n* pagamento; rimborso

repeat [rɪ'piːt] *n* (*Radio, TV*) replica ▷ *vt* ripetere; (*pattern*) riprodurre; (*promise, attack, also Comm*: *order*) rinnovare ▷ *vi* ripetere; **can you ~ that, please?** può ripetere, per favore?; **repeatedly** *adv* ripetutamente, spesso; **repeat prescription** *n* (*BRIT*) ricetta ripetibile

repellent [rɪ'pɛlənt] *adj* repellente ▷ *n* **insect ~** prodotto *m* anti-insetti *inv*

repercussions [riːpə'kʌʃənz] *npl* ripercussioni *fpl*

repetition [rɛpɪ'tɪʃən] *n* ripetizione *f*

repetitive [rɪ'pɛtɪtɪv] *adj* (*movement*) che si ripete; (*work*) monotono(-a); (*speech*) pieno(-a) di ripetizioni

replace [rɪ'pleɪs] *vt* (*put back*) rimettere a posto; (*take the place of*) sostituire; **replacement** *n* rimessa; sostituzione *f*; (*person*) sostituto(-a)

replay ['riːpleɪ] *n* (*of match*) partita ripetuta; (*of tape, film*) replay *m inv*

replica ['rɛplɪkə] *n* replica, copia

reply [rɪ'plaɪ] *n* risposta ▷ *vi* rispondere

report [rɪ'pɔːt] *n* rapporto; (*Press etc*) cronaca; (*BRIT*: *also*: **school ~**) pagella; (*of gun*) sparo ▷ *vt* riportare; (*Press etc*) fare una cronaca di; (*bring to notice*: *occurrence*) segnalare; (*: person*) denunciare ▷ *vi* (*make a report*) fare un rapporto (*or* una cronaca); (*present o.s.*): **to ~ (to sb)** presentarsi (a qn); **I'd like to ~ a theft** vorrei denunciare un furto; **report card** (*US, Scottish*) *n* pagella; **reportedly** *adv* stando a quanto si dice; **he reportedly told them to ...** avrebbe detto loro di ...; **reporter** *n* reporter *m inv*

represent [rɛprɪ'zɛnt] *vt* rappresentare; **representation** [-'teɪʃən] *n* rappresentazione *f*; (*petition*) rappresentanza; **representative** *n* rappresentante *m/f*; (*US Pol*) deputato(-a) ▷ *adj* rappresentativo(-a)

repress [rɪ'prɛs] *vt* reprimere; **repression** [-'prɛʃən] *n* repressione *f*

reprimand ['rɛprɪmɑːnd] *n* rimprovero ▷ *vt* rimproverare

reproduce [riːprə'djuːs] *vt* riprodurre ▷ *vi* riprodursi; **reproduction** [-'dʌkʃən] *n* riproduzione *f*

reptile ['rɛptaɪl] *n* rettile *m*

republic [rɪ'pʌblɪk] *n* repubblica; **republican** *adj, n* repubblicano(-a)

reputable ['rɛpjutəbl] *adj* di buona reputazione; (*occupation*) rispettabile

reputation [rɛpju'teɪʃən] *n* reputazione *f*

request [rɪ'kwɛst] *n* domanda; (*formal*) richiesta ▷ *vt* **to ~ (of** *or* **from sb)** chiedere (a qn); **request stop** (*BRIT*) *n* (*for bus*) fermata facoltativa *or* a richiesta

require [rɪ'kwaɪəʳ] *vt* (*need*: *person*) aver bisogno di; (*: thing, situation*) richiedere; (*want*) volere; esigere; (*order*): **to ~ sb to do sth** ordinare a qn di fare qc; **requirement** *n* esigenza; bisogno; requisito

resat [riː'sæt] *pt, pp of* **resit**

rescue ['rɛskjuː] *n* salvataggio; (*help*) soccorso ▷ *vt* salvare

research [rɪ'sɜːtʃ] *n* ricerca, ricerche *fpl* ▷ *vt* fare ricerche su

resemblance [rɪ'zɛmbləns] *n* somiglianza

resemble [rɪ'zɛmbl] *vt* assomigliare a

resent [rɪ'zɛnt] *vt* risentirsi di; **resentful** *adj* pieno(-a) di risentimento; **resentment** *n* risentimento

reservation [rɛzə'veɪʃən] *n* (*booking*) prenotazione *f*; (*doubt*) dubbio; (*protected area*) riserva; (*BRIT*: *on road*: *also*: **central ~**) spartitraffico *m inv*; **reservation desk** (*US*) *n* (*in hotel*) reception *f inv*

reserve [rɪ'zəːv] *n* riserva ▷ *vt* (*seats etc*) prenotare; **reserved** *adj* (*shy*) riservato(-a)

reservoir ['rɛzəvwɑːʳ] *n* serbatoio

residence ['rɛzɪdəns] *n* residenza; **residence permit** (*BRIT*) *n* permesso di soggiorno

resident ['rɛzɪdənt] *n* residente *m/f*; (*in hotel*) cliente *m/f* fisso(-a) ▷ *adj* residente; (*doctor*) fisso(-a); (*course, college*) a tempo pieno con pernottamento; **residential** [-'dɛnʃəl] *adj* di residenza; (*area*) residenziale

residue ['rɛzɪdjuː] *n* resto; (*Chem, Physics*) residuo

resign [rɪ'zaɪn] *vt* (*one's post*) dimettersi da ▷ *vi* dimettersi; **to ~ o.s. to** rassegnarsi a; **resignation** [rɛzɪg'neɪʃən] *n* dimissioni *fpl*; rassegnazione *f*

resin ['rɛzɪn] *n* resina

resist [rɪ'zɪst] *vt* resistere a; **resistance** *n* resistenza

resit ['riːsɪt] (*BRIT*) (*pt, pp* **resat**) *vt* (*exam*) ripresentarsi a; (*subject*) ridare l'esame di

▷ *n* **he's got his French ~ on Friday** deve ridare l'esame di francese venerdì

resolution [rɛzə'luːʃən] *n* risoluzione *f*

resolve [rɪ'zɔlv] *n* risoluzione *f* ▷ *vi (decide):* **to ~ to do** decidere di fare ▷ *vt (problem)* risolvere

resort [rɪ'zɔːt] *n (town)* stazione *f*; *(recourse)* ricorso ▷ *vi* **to ~ to** aver ricorso a; **in the last ~** come ultima risorsa

resource [rɪ'sɔːs] *n* risorsa; **resourceful** *adj* pieno(-a) di risorse, intraprendente

respect [rɪs'pɛkt] *n* rispetto ▷ *vt* rispettare; **respectable** *adj* rispettabile; **respectful** *adj* rispettoso(-a); **respective** [rɪs'pɛktɪv] *adj* rispettivo(-a); **respectively** *adv* rispettivamente

respite ['rɛspaɪt] *n* respiro, tregua

respond [rɪs'pɔnd] *vi* rispondere; **response** [rɪs'pɔns] *n* risposta

responsibility [rɪspɔnsɪ'bɪlɪtɪ] *n* responsabilità *f inv*

responsible [rɪs'pɔnsɪbl] *adj (trustworthy)* fidato(-a); *(job)* di (grande) responsabilità; **~ (for)** responsabile (di); **responsibly** *adv* responsabilmente

responsive [rɪs'pɔnsɪv] *adj* che reagisce

rest [rɛst] *n* riposo; *(stop)* sosta, pausa; *(Mus)* pausa; *(object: to support sth)* appoggio, sostegno; *(remainder)* resto, avanzi *mpl* ▷ *vi* riposarsi; *(remain)* rimanere, restare; *(be supported):* **to ~ on** appoggiarsi su ▷ *vt* (far) riposare; *(lean):* **to ~ sth on/against** appoggiare qc su/ contro; **the ~ of them** gli altri; **it ~s with him to decide** sta a lui decidere

restaurant ['rɛstərɔŋ] *n* ristorante *m*; **restaurant car** *(BRIT)* *n* vagone *m* ristorante

restless ['rɛstlɪs] *adj* agitato(-a), irrequieto(-a)

restoration [rɛstə'reɪʃən] *n* restauro; restituzione *f*

restore [rɪ'stɔːʳ] *vt (building, to power)* restaurare; *(sth stolen)* restituire; *(peace, health)* ristorare

restrain [rɪs'treɪn] *vt (feeling, growth)* contenere, frenare; *(person):* **to ~ (from doing)** trattenere (dal fare); **restraint** *n (restriction)* limitazione *f*; *(moderation)* ritegno; *(of style)* contenutezza

restrict [rɪs'trɪkt] *vt* restringere, limitare; **restriction** [-kʃən] *n* **restriction (on)** restrizione *f* (di), limitazione *f*

rest room *(US)* *n* toletta

restructure [riː'strʌktʃəʳ] *vt* ristrutturare

result [rɪ'zʌlt] *n* risultato ▷ *vi* **to ~ in** avere per risultato; **as a ~ of** in or di conseguenza a, in seguito a

resume [rɪ'zjuːm] *vt, vi (work, journey)* riprendere

résumé ['reɪzjumeɪ] *n* riassunto; *(US)* curriculum *m inv* vitae

resuscitate [rɪ'sʌsɪteɪt] *vt (Med)* risuscitare

retail ['riːteɪl] *adj, adv* al minuto ▷ *vt* vendere al minuto; **retailer** *n* commerciante *m/f* al minuto, dettagliante *m/f*

retain [rɪ'teɪn] *vt (keep)* tenere, serbare

retaliation [rɪtælɪ'eɪʃən] *n* rappresaglie *fpl*

retarded [rɪ'tɑːdɪd] *adj* ritardato(-a)

retire [rɪ'taɪəʳ] *vi (give up work)* andare in pensione; *(withdraw)* ritirarsi, andarsene; *(go to bed)* andare a letto, ritirarsi; **retired** *adj (person)* pensionato(-a); **retirement** *n* pensione *f*; *(act)* pensionamento

retort [rɪ'tɔːt] *vi* rimbeccare

retreat [rɪ'triːt] *n* ritirata; *(place)* rifugio ▷ *vi* battere in ritirata

retrieve [rɪ'triːv] *vt (sth lost)* ricuperare, ritrovare; *(situation, honour)* salvare; *(error, loss)* rimediare a

retrospect ['rɛtrəspɛkt] *n* **in ~** guardando indietro; **retrospective** [-'spɛktɪv] *adj* retrospettivo(-a); *(law)* retroattivo(-a)

return [rɪ'təːn] *n (going or coming back)* ritorno; *(of sth stolen etc)* restituzione *f*; *(Finance: from land, shares)* profitto, reddito ▷ *cpd (journey, match)* di ritorno; *(BRIT: ticket)* di andata e ritorno ▷ *vi* tornare, ritornare ▷ *vt* rendere, restituire; *(bring back)* riportare; *(send back)* mandare indietro; *(put back)* rimettere; *(Pol: candidate)* eleggere; **~s** *npl (Comm)* incassi *mpl*; profitti *mpl*; **in ~ (for)** in cambio (di); **by ~ of post** a stretto giro di posta; **many happy ~s (of the day)!** cento di questi giorni!; **return ticket** *n (esp BRIT)* biglietto di andata e ritorno

reunion [riː'juːnɪən] *n* riunione *f*

reunite [riːjuː'naɪt] *vt* riunire

revamp ['riː'væmp] *vt (firm)* riorganizzare

reveal [rɪ'viːl] *vt (make known)* rivelare, svelare; *(display)* rivelare, mostrare; **revealing** *adj* rivelatore(-trice); *(dress)* scollato(-a)

revel ['rɛvl] *vi* **to ~ in sth/in doing** dilettarsi di qc/a fare

revelation [rɛvə'leɪʃən] *n* rivelazione *f*

revenge [rɪ'vɛndʒ] *n* vendetta ▷ *vt* vendicare; **to take ~ on** vendicarsi di

revenue ['rɛvənjuː] *n* reddito

Reverend ['rɛvərənd] *adj (in titles)* reverendo(-a)

reversal [rɪ'vəːsl] *n* capovolgimento

reverse [rɪ'vəːs] *n* contrario, opposto; *(back, defeat)* rovescio; *(Aut: also: ~ gear)* marcia indietro ▷ *adj (order, direction)*

contrario(-a), opposto(-a) ▷ vt (turn)
invertire, rivoltare; (change) capovolgere,
rovesciare; (Law: judgment) cassare; (car)
fare marcia indietro con ▷ vi (BRITAut,
person etc) fare marcia indietro; **reverse-
charge call** [rɪ'vəːstʃɑːdʒ-] (BRIT) n (Tel)
telefonata con addebito al ricevente;
reversing lights (BRIT) npl (Aut) luci fpl per
la retromarcia
revert [rɪ'vəːt] vi **to ~ to** tornare a
review [rɪ'vjuː] n rivista; (of book, film)
recensione f; (of situation) esame m ▷ vt
passare in rivista; fare la recensione di; fare
il punto di
revise [rɪ'vaɪz] vt (manuscript) rivedere,
correggere; (opinion) emendare,
modificare; (study: subject, notes) ripassare;
revision [rɪ'vɪʒən] n revisione f; ripasso
revival [rɪ'vaɪvəl] n ripresa; ristabilimento;
(of faith) risveglio
revive [rɪ'vaɪv] vt (person) rianimare;
(custom) far rivivere; (hope, courage,
economy) ravvivare; (play, fashion)
riesumare ▷ vi (person) rianimarsi; (hope)
ravvivarsi; (activity) riprendersi
revolt [rɪ'vəult] n rivolta, ribellione f ▷ vi
rivoltarsi, ribellarsi ▷ vt (far) rivoltare;
revolting adj ripugnante
revolution [rɛvə'luːʃən] n rivoluzione f; (of
wheel etc) rivoluzione, giro; **revolutionary**
adj, n rivoluzionario(-a)
revolve [rɪ'vɔlv] vi girare
revolver [rɪ'vɔlvər] n rivoltella
reward [rɪ'wɔːd] n ricompensa, premio
▷ vt **to ~ (for)** ricompensare (per);
rewarding adj (fig) gratificante
rewind [riː'waɪnd] (irreg) vt (watch)
ricaricare; (ribbon etc) riavvolgere
rewrite [riː'raɪt] vt irreg riscrivere
rheumatism ['ruːmətɪzəm] n
reumatismo
rhinoceros [raɪ'nɔsərəs] n rinoceronte m
rhubarb ['ruːbɑːb] n rabarbaro
rhyme [raɪm] n rima; (verse) poesia
rhythm ['rɪðm] n ritmo
rib [rɪb] n (Anat) costola ▷ vt (tease)
punzecchiare
ribbon ['rɪbən] n nastro; **in ~s** (torn) a
brandelli
rice [raɪs] n riso; **rice pudding** n budino
di riso
rich [rɪtʃ] adj ricco(-a); (clothes)
sontuoso(-a); (abundant): **~ in** ricco(-a) di
rid [rɪd] (pt, pp **rid**) vt **to ~ sb of** sbarazzare
or liberare qn di; **to get ~ of** sbarazzarsi di
riddle ['rɪdl] n (puzzle) indovinello ▷ vt **to
be ~d with** (holes) essere crivellato(-a) di;
(doubts) essere pieno(-a) di
ride [raɪd] (pt **rode**, pp **ridden**) n (on horse)

cavalcata; (outing) passeggiata; (distance
covered) cavalcata; corsa ▷ vi (as sport)
cavalcare; (go somewhere: on horse, bicycle)
andare (a cavallo or in bicicletta etc);
(journey: on bicycle, motorcycle, bus) andare,
viaggiare ▷ vt (a horse) montare, cavalcare;
to take sb for a ~ (fig) prendere in giro qn;
fregare qn; **to ~ a horse/bicycle/camel**
montare a cavallo/in bicicletta/in groppa a
un cammello; **rider** n cavalcatore(-trice);
(in race) fantino; (on bicycle) ciclista m/f; (on
motorcycle) motociclista m/f
ridge [rɪdʒ] n (of hill) cresta; (of roof) colmo;
(on object) riga (in rilievo)
ridicule ['rɪdɪkjuːl] n ridicolo; scherno ▷ vt
mettere in ridicolo; **ridiculous** [rɪ'dɪkjulə
s] adj ridicolo(-a)
riding ['raɪdɪŋ] n equitazione f; **riding
school** n scuola d'equitazione
rife [raɪf] adj diffuso(-a); **to be ~ with**
abbondare di
rifle ['raɪfl] n carabina ▷ vt vuotare
rift [rɪft] n fessura, crepatura; (fig:
disagreement) incrinatura, disaccordo
rig [rɪg] n (also: **oil ~**: on land) derrick m inv;
(: at sea) piattaforma di trivellazione ▷ vt
(election etc) truccare
right [raɪt] adj giusto(-a); (suitable)
appropriato(-a); (not left) destro(-a)
▷ n giusto; (title, claim) diritto; (not left)
destra ▷ adv (answer) correttamente;
(not on the left) a destra ▷ vt raddrizzare;
(fig) riparare ▷ excl bene!; **to be ~** (person)
aver ragione; (answer) essere giusto(-a) or
corretto(-a); **by ~s** di diritto; **on the ~** a
destra; **to be in the ~** aver ragione, essere
nel giusto; **~ now** proprio adesso; subito;
~ away subito; **right angle** n angolo
retto; **rightful** adj (heir) legittimo(-a);
right-hand adj **right-hand drive** guida
a destra; **the right-hand side** il lato
destro; **right-handed** adj (person) che
adopera la mano destra; **rightly** adv bene,
correttamente; (with reason) a ragione;
right of way n diritto di passaggio; (Aut)
precedenza; **right-wing** adj (Pol) di destra
rigid ['rɪdʒɪd] adj rigido(-a); (principle)
rigoroso(-a)
rigorous ['rɪgərəs] adj rigoroso(-a)
rim [rɪm] n orlo; (of spectacles) montatura;
(of wheel) cerchione m
rind [raɪnd] n (of bacon) cotenna; (of lemon
etc) scorza
ring [rɪŋ] (pt **rang**, pp **rung**) n anello; (of
people, objects) cerchio; (of spies) giro;
(of smoke etc) spirale m; (arena) pista,
arena; (for boxing) ring m inv; (sound of bell)
scampanio ▷ vi (person, bell, telephone)
suonare; (also: **~ out**: voice, words)

risuonare; (*Tel*) telefonare; (*ears*) fischiare ▷ *vt* (*BRIT Tel*) telefonare a; (: *bell, doorbell*) suonare; **to give sb a ~** (*BRIT Tel*) dare un colpo di telefono a qn; **ring back** *vt, vi* (*Tel*) richiamare; **ring off** (*BRIT*) *vi* (*Tel*) mettere giù, riattaccare; **ring up** (*BRIT*) *vt* (*Tel*) telefonare a; **ringing tone** (*BRIT*) *n* (*Tel*) segnale *m* di libero; **ringleader** *n* (*of gang*) capobanda *m*, **ring road** (*BRIT*) *n* raccordo anulare

ring tone *n* suoneria

rink [rɪŋk] *n* (*also:* **ice ~**) pista di pattinaggio

rinse [rɪns] *n* risciacquatura; (*hair tint*) cachet *m inv* ▷ *vt* sciacquare

riot ['raɪət] *n* sommossa, tumulto; (*of colours*) orgia ▷ *vi* tumultuare; **to run ~** creare disordine

rip [rɪp] *n* strappo ▷ *vt* strappare ▷ *vi* strapparsi; **rip off** *vt* (*inf: cheat*) fregare; **rip up** *vt* stracciare

ripe [raɪp] *adj* (*fruit, grain*) maturo(-a); (*cheese*) stagionato(-a)

rip-off ['rɪpɔf] *n* (*inf*): **it's a ~!** è un furto!

ripple ['rɪpl] *n* increspamento, ondulazione *f*; mormorio ▷ *vi* incresparsi

rise [raɪz] (*pt* **rose**, *pp* **risen**) *n* (*slope*) salita, pendio; (*hill*) altura; (*increase: in wages: BRIT*) aumento; (: *in prices, temperature*) rialzo, aumento; (*fig: to power etc*) ascesa ▷ *vi* alzarsi, levarsi; (*prices*) aumentare; (*waters, river*) crescere; (*sun, wind, person: from chair, bed*) levarsi; (*also:* **~ up**: *building*) ergersi; (: *rebel*) insorgere; ribellarsi; (*in rank*) salire; **to give ~ to** provocare, dare origine a; **to ~ to the occasion** essere all'altezza; **risen** ['rɪzn] *pp of* **rise**; **rising** *adj* (*increasing: number*) sempre crescente; (: *prices*) in aumento; (*tide*) montante; (*sun, moon*) nascente, che sorge

risk [rɪsk] *n* rischio; pericolo ▷ *vt* rischiare; **to take** *or* **run the ~ of doing** correre il rischio di fare; **at ~** in pericolo; **at one's own ~** a proprio rischio e pericolo; **risky** *adj* rischioso(-a)

rite [raɪt] *n* rito; **last ~s** l'estrema unzione

ritual ['rɪtjuəl] *adj* rituale ▷ *n* rituale *m*

rival ['raɪvl] *n* rivale *m/f*; (*in business*) concorrente *m/f* ▷ *adj* rivale; che fa concorrenza ▷ *vt* essere in concorrenza con; **to ~ sb/sth in** competere con qn/qc in; **rivalry** *n* rivalità; concorrenza

river ['rɪvə^r] *n* fiume *m* ▷ *cpd* (*port, traffic*) fluviale; **up/down ~** a monte/valle; **riverbank** *n* argine *m*

rivet ['rɪvɪt] *n* ribattino, rivetto ▷ *vt* (*fig*) concentrare, fissare

Riviera [rɪvɪ'ɛərə] *n* **the (French) ~** la Costa Azzurra; **the Italian ~** la Riviera

road [rəud] *n* strada; (*small*) cammino; (*in town*) via ▷ *cpd* stradale; **major/minor ~** strada con/senza diritto di precedenza; **which ~ do I take for …?** che strada devo prendere per andare a…?; **roadblock** *n* blocco stradale; **road map** *n* carta stradale; **road rage** *n* comportamento aggressivo al volante; **road safety** *n* sicurezza sulle strade; **roadside** *n* margine *m* della strada; **roadsign** *n* cartello stradale; **road tax** *n* (*BRIT*) tassa di circolazione; **roadworks** *npl* lavori *mpl* stradali

roam [rəum] *vi* errare, vagabondare

roar [rɔː^r] *n* ruggito; (*of crowd*) tumulto; (*of thunder, storm*) muggito; (*of laughter*) scoppio ▷ *vi* ruggire; tumultuare; muggire; **to ~ with laughter** scoppiare dalle risa; **to do a ~ing trade** fare affari d'oro

roast [rəust] *n* arrosto ▷ *vt* arrostire; (*coffee*) tostare, torrefare; **roast beef** *n* arrosto di manzo

rob [rɔb] *vt* (*person*) rubare; (*bank*) svaligiare; **to ~ sb of sth** derubare qn di qc; (*fig: deprive*) privare qn di qc; **robber** *n* ladro; (*armed*) rapinatore *m*; **robbery** *n* furto; rapina

robe [rəub] *n* (*for ceremony etc*) abito; (*also:* **bath ~**) accappatoio; (*US: also:* **lap ~**) coperta

robin ['rɔbɪn] *n* pettirosso

robot ['rəubɔt] *n* robot *m inv*

robust [rəu'bʌst] *adj* robusto(-a); (*economy*) solido(-a)

rock [rɔk] *n* (*substance*) roccia; (*boulder*) masso; roccia; (*in sea*) scoglio; (*US: pebble*) ciottolo; (*BRIT: sweet*) zucchero candito ▷ *vt* (*swing gently: cradle*) dondolare; (: *child*) cullare; (*shake*) scrollare, far tremare ▷ *vi* dondolarsi; scrollarsi, tremare; **on the ~s** (*drink*) col ghiaccio; (*marriage etc*) in crisi; **rock and roll** *n* rock and roll *m*; **rock climbing** *n* roccia

rocket ['rɔkɪt] *n* razzo

rocking chair *n* sedia a dondolo

rocky ['rɔkɪ] *adj* (*hill*) roccioso(-a); (*path*) sassoso(-a); (*marriage etc*) instabile

rod [rɔd] *n* (*metallic, Tech*) asta; (*wooden*) bacchetta; (*also:* **fishing ~**) canna da pesca

rode [rəud] *pt of* **ride**

rodent ['rəudnt] *n* roditore *m*

rogue [rəug] *n* mascalzone *m*

role [rəul] *n* ruolo; **role-model** *n* modello (di comportamento)

roll [rəul] *n* rotolo; (*of banknotes*) mazzo; (*also:* **bread ~**) panino; (*register*) lista; (*sound: of drums etc*) rullo ▷ *vt* rotolare; (*also:* **~ up**: *string*) aggomitolare; (: *sleeves*)

rimboccare; (*cigarettes*) arrotolare; (*eyes*)
roteare; (*also:* **~ out**: *pastry*) stendere;
(*lawn, road etc*) spianare ▷ *vi* rotolare;
(*wheel*) girare; (*drum*) rullare; (*vehicle:
also:* **~ along**) avanzare; (*ship*) rollare; **roll
over** *vi* rivoltarsi; **roll up** (*inf*) *vi* (*arrive*)
arrivare ▷ *vt* (*carpet*) arrotolare; **roller** *n*
rullo; (*wheel*) rotella; (*for hair*) bigodino;
Rollerblades® *npl* pattini *mpl* in linea;
roller coaster [-'kəʊstəʳ] *n* montagne
fpl russe; **roller skates** *npl* pattini *mpl*
a rotelle; **roller-skating** *n* pattinaggio
a rotelle; **to go roller-skating** andare a
pattinare (*con i pattini a rotelle*); **rolling pin**
n matterello
ROM [rɔm] *n abbr* (= *read only memory*)
memoria di sola lettura
Roman ['rəʊmən] *adj, n* romano(-a);
Roman Catholic *adj, n* cattolico(-a)
romance [rə'mæns] *n* storia (*or* avventura
or film *m inv*) romantico(-a); (*charm*) poesia;
(*love affair*) idillio
Romania [rəʊ'meɪnɪə] *n* Romania
Romanian [rəʊ'meɪnɪən] *adj* romeno(-a)
▷ *n* romeno; (*Ling*) romeno
Roman numeral *n* numero romano
romantic [rə'mæntɪk] *adj* romantico(-a);
sentimentale
Rome [rəʊm] *n* Roma
roof [ruːf] *n* tetto; (*of tunnel, cave*) volta ▷ *vt*
coprire (con un tetto); **~ of the mouth**
palato; **roof rack** *n* (*Aut*) portabagagli
m inv
rook [ruk] *n* (*bird*) corvo nero; (*Chess*) torre *f*
room [ruːm] *n* (*in house*) stanza; (*bedroom,
in hotel*) camera; (*in school etc*) sala;
(*space*) posto, spazio; **roommate** *n*
compagno(-a) di stanza; **room service**
n servizio da camera; **roomy** *adj*
spazioso(-a); (*garment*) ampio(-a)
rooster ['ruːstəʳ] *n* gallo
root [ruːt] *n* radice *f* ▷ *vi* (*plant, belief*)
attecchire
rope [rəʊp] *n* corda, fune *f*; (*Naut*) cavo ▷ *vt*
(*box*) legare; (*climbers*) legare in cordata;
(*area: also:* **~ off**) isolare cingendo con
cordoni; **to know the ~s** (*fig*) conoscere i
trucchi del mestiere
rose [rəʊz] *pt of* **rise** ▷ *n* rosa; (*also:* **~ bush**)
rosaio; (*on watering can*) rosetta
rosé ['rəʊzeɪ] *n* vino rosato
rosemary ['rəʊzmərɪ] *n* rosmarino
rosy ['rəʊzɪ] *adj* roseo(-a)
rot [rɔt] *n* (*decay*) putrefazione *f*; (*inf:
nonsense*) stupidaggini *fpl* ▷ *vt, vi*
imputridire, marcire
rota ['rəʊtə] *n* tabella dei turni
rotate [rəʊ'teɪt] *vt* (*revolve*) far girare;
(*change round: jobs*) fare a turno ▷ *vi*
(*revolve*) girare
rotten ['rɔtn] *adj* (*decayed*) putrido(-a),
marcio(-a); (*dishonest*) corrotto(-a); (*inf:
bad*) brutto(-a); (: *action*) vigliacco(-a); **to
feel ~** (*ill*) sentirsi da cani
rough [rʌf] *adj* (*skin, surface*) ruvido(-a);
(*terrain, road*) accidentato(-a); (*voice*)
rauco(-a); (*person, manner: coarse*)
rozzo(-a), aspro(-a); (: *violent*) brutale;
(*district*) malfamato(-a); (*weather*)
cattivo(-a); (*sea*) mosso(-a); (*plan*)
abbozzato(-a); (*guess*) approssimativo(-a)
▷ *n* (*Golf*) macchia; **to ~ it** far vita dura;
to sleep ~ (BRIT) dormire all'addiaccio;
roughly *adv* (*handle*) rudemente,
brutalmente; (*make*) grossolanamente;
(*speak*) bruscamente; (*approximately*)
approssimativamente
roulette [ruː'lɛt] *n* roulette *f*
round [raund] *adj* rotondo(-a); (*figures*)
tondo(-a) ▷ *n* (BRIT: *of toast*) fetta; (*duty:
of policeman, milkman etc*) giro; (: *of doctor*)
visite *fpl*; (*game: of cards, golf, in competition*)
partita; (*of ammunition*) cartuccia; (*Boxing*)
round *m inv*; (*of talks*) serie *f inv* ▷ *vt* (*corner*)
girare; (*bend*) prendere ▷ *prep* intorno a
▷ *adv* **all ~** tutt'attorno; **to go the long
way ~** fare il giro più lungo; **all the year
~** tutto l'anno; **it's just ~ the corner**
(*also fig*) è dietro l'angolo; **~ the clock**
ininterrottamente; **to go ~ to sb's house**
andare da qn; **go ~ the back** passi dietro;
enough to go ~ abbastanza per tutti; **~ of
applause** applausi *mpl*; **~ of drinks** giro di
bibite; **~ of sandwiches** sandwich *m inv*;
round off *vt* (*speech etc*) finire; **round up**
vt radunare; (*criminals*) fare una retata di;
(*prices*) arrotondare; **roundabout** *n* (BRIT
Aut) rotatoria; (: *at fair*) giostra ▷ *adj* (*route,
means*) indiretto(-a); **round trip** *n* (viaggio
di) andata e ritorno; **roundup** *n* raduno;
(*of criminals*) retata
rouse [rauz] *vt* (*wake up*) svegliare; (*stir up*)
destare; provocare; risvegliare
route [ruːt] *n* itinerario; (*of bus*) percorso
routine [ruː'tiːn] *adj* (*work*) corrente,
abituale; (*procedure*) solito(-a) ▷ *n* (*pej*)
routine *f*, tran tran *m*; (*Theatre*) numero
row[1] [rəu] *n* (*line*) riga, fila; (*Knitting*) ferro;
(*behind one another: of cars, people*) fila; (*in
boat*) remata ▷ *vi* (*in boat*) remare; (*as
sport*) vogare ▷ *vt* (*boat*) manovrare a remi;
in a ~ (*fig*) di fila
row[2] [rau] *n* (*racket*) baccano, chiasso;
(*dispute*) lite *f*; (*scolding*) sgridata ▷ *vi*
(*argue*) litigare
rowboat ['rəʊbəʊt] (US) *n* barca a remi
rowing ['rəʊɪŋ] *n* canottaggio; **rowing
boat** (BRIT) *n* barca a remi

royal ['rɔɪəl] *adj* reale; **royalty** ['rɔɪə ltɪ] *n* (*royal persons*) (membri *mpl* della) famiglia reale; (*payment: to author*) diritti *mpl* d'autore

rpm *abbr* (= *revolutions per minute*) giri/min.

R.S.V.P. *abbr* (= *répondez s'il vous plaît*) R.S.V.P.

Rt. Hon. (BRIT) *abbr* (= *Right Honourable*) ≈ Onorevole

rub [rʌb] *n* **to give sth a ~** strofinare qc; (*sore place*) massaggiare qc ▷ *vt* strofinare; massaggiare; (*hands: also:* **~ together**) sfregarsi; **to ~ sb up** (BRIT) or **~ sb the wrong way** (US) lisciare qn contro pelo; **rub in** *vt* (*ointment*) far penetrare (massaggiando or frizionando); **rub off** *vi* andare via; **rub out** *vt* cancellare

rubber ['rʌbəʳ] *n* gomma; **rubber band** *n* elastico; **rubber gloves** *npl* guanti *mpl* di gomma

rubbish ['rʌbɪʃ] *n* (*from household*) immondizie *fpl*, rifiuti *mpl*; (*fig, pej*) cose *fpl* senza valore; robaccia; sciocchezze *fpl*; **rubbish bin** (BRIT) *n* pattumiera; **rubbish dump** *n* (*in town*) immondezzaio

rubble ['rʌbl] *n* macerie *fpl*; (*smaller*) pietrisco

ruby ['ruːbɪ] *n* rubino

rucksack ['rʌksæk] *n* zaino

rudder ['rʌdəʳ] *n* timone *m*

rude [ruːd] *adj* (*impolite: person*) scortese, rozzo(-a); (*: word, manners*) grossolano(-a), rozzo(-a); (*shocking*) indecente

ruffle ['rʌfl] *vt* (*hair*) scompigliare; (*clothes, water*) increspare; (*fig: person*) turbare

rug [rʌg] *n* tappeto; (BRIT: *for knees*) coperta

rugby ['rʌgbɪ] *n* (*also:* **~ football**) rugby *m*

rugged ['rʌgɪd] *adj* (*landscape*) aspro(-a); (*features, determination*) duro(-a); (*character*) brusco(-a)

ruin ['ruːɪn] *n* rovina ▷ *vt* rovinare; **~s** *npl* (*of building, castle etc*) rovine *fpl*, ruderi *mpl*

rule [ruːl] *n* regola; (*regulation*) regolamento, regola; (*government*) governo; (*ruler*) riga ▷ *vt* (*country*) governare; (*person*) dominare ▷ *vi* regnare; decidere; (*Law*) dichiarare; **as a ~** normalmente; **rule out** *vt* escludere; **ruler** *n* (*sovereign*) sovrano(-a); (*for measuring*) regolo, riga; **ruling** *adj* (*party*) al potere; (*class*) dirigente ▷ *n* (*Law*) decisione *f*

rum [rʌm] *n* rum *m*

Rumania *etc* [ruːˈmeɪnɪə] *n* = **Romania** *etc*

rumble ['rʌmbl] *n* rimbombo; brontolio ▷ *vi* rimbombare; (*stomach, pipe*) brontolare

rumour ['ruːməʳ] (US **rumor**) *n* voce *f* ▷ *vt*

it is ~ed that corre voce che

▮ Be careful not to translate *rumour* by the Italian word *rumore*.

rump steak [rʌmp-] *n* bistecca di girello

run [rʌn] (*pt* **ran**, *pp* **run**) *n* corsa; (*outing*) gita (in macchina); (*distance travelled*) percorso, tragitto; (*Ski*) pista; (*Cricket, Baseball*) meta; (*series*) serie *f*; (*Theatre*) periodo di rappresentazione; (*in tights, stockings*) smagliatura ▷ *vt* (*distance*) correre; (*operate: business*) gestire, dirigere; (*: competition, course*) organizzare; (*: hotel*) gestire; (*: house*) governare; (*Comput*) eseguire; (*water, bath*) far scorrere; (*force through: rope, pipe*) **to ~ sth through** far passare qc attraverso; (*pass: hand, finger*) **to ~ sth over** passare qc su; (*Press: feature*) presentare ▷ *vi* correre; (*flee*) scappare; (*pass: road etc*) passare; (*work: machine, factory*) funzionare, andare; (*bus, train: operate*) far servizio; (*: travel*) circolare; (*continue: play, contract*) durare; (*slide: drawer/flow: river, bath*) scorrere; (*colours, washing*) stemperarsi; (*in election*) presentarsi candidato; (*nose*) colare; **there was a ~ on ...** c'era una corsa a ...; **in the long ~** a lungo andare; **on the ~** in fuga; **to ~ a race** partecipare ad una gara; **I'll ~ you to the station** la porto alla stazione; **to ~ a risk** correre un rischio; **run after** *vt fus* (*to catch up*) rincorrere; (*chase*) correre dietro a; **run away** *vi* fuggire; **run down** *vt* (*production*) ridurre gradualmente; (*factory*) rallentare l'attività di; (*Aut*) investire; (*criticize*) criticare; **to be ~ down** (*person: tired*) essere esausto(-a); **run into** *vt fus* (*meet: person*) incontrare per caso; (*: trouble*) incontrare, trovare; (*collide with*) andare a sbattere contro; **run off** *vi* fuggire ▷ *vt* (*water*) far scolare; (*copies*) fare; **run out** *vi* (*person*) uscire di corsa; (*liquid*) colare; (*lease*) scadere; (*money*) esaurirsi; **run out of** *vt fus* rimanere a corto di; **run over** *vt* (*Aut*) investire, mettere sotto ▷ *vt fus* (*revise*) rivedere; **run through** *vt fus* (*instructions*) dare una scorsa a; (*rehearse: play*) riprovare, ripetere; **run up** *vt* (*debt*) lasciar accumulare; **to ~ up against** (*difficulties*) incontrare; **runaway** *adj* (*person*) fuggiasco(-a); (*horse*) in libertà; (*truck*) fuori controllo

rung [rʌŋ] *pp of* **ring** ▷ *n* (*of ladder*) piolo

runner ['rʌnəʳ] *n* (*in race*) corridore *m*; (*: horse*) partente *m/f*; (*on sledge*) pattino; (*for drawer etc*) guida; **runner bean** (BRIT) *n* fagiolo rampicante; **runner-up** *n* secondo(-a) arrivato(-a)

running ['rʌnɪŋ] *n* corsa; direzione *f*; organizzazione *f*; funzionamento

r

▷ *adj* (*water*) corrente; (*commentary*)
simultaneo(-a); **to be in/out of the ~ for**
sth essere/non essere più in lizza per qc; **6**
days ~ 6 giorni di seguito
runny ['rʌnɪ] *adj* che cola
run-up ['rʌnʌp] *n* **~ to** (*election etc*) periodo
che precede
runway ['rʌnweɪ] *n* (*Aviat*) pista (di
decollo)
rupture ['rʌptʃər] *n* (*Med*) ernia
rural ['rʊrəl] *adj* rurale
rush [rʌʃ] *n* corsa precipitosa; (*hurry*)
furia, fretta; (*sudden demand*): **~ for** corsa
a; (*current*) flusso; (*of emotion*) impeto;
(*Bot*) giunco ▷ *vt* mandare *or* spedire
velocemente; (*attack: town etc*) prendere
d'assalto ▷ *vi* precipitarsi; **rush hour** *n*
ora di punta
Russia ['rʌʃə] *n* Russia; **Russian** *adj*
russo(-a) ▷ *n* russo(-a); (*Ling*) russo
rust [rʌst] *n* ruggine *f* ▷ *vi* arrugginirsi
rusty ['rʌstɪ] *adj* arrugginito(-a)
ruthless ['ruːθlɪs] *adj* spietato(-a)
RV *abbr* (= *revised version*) versione riveduta
della Bibbia ▷ *n abbr* (*US*) *see* **recreational**
vehicle
rye [raɪ] *n* segale *f*

S

Sabbath ['sæbəθ] *n* (*Jewish*) sabato;
(*Christian*) domenica
sabotage ['sæbətɑːʒ] *n* sabotaggio ▷ *vt*
sabotare
saccharin(e) ['sækərɪn] *n* saccarina
sachet ['sæʃeɪ] *n* bustina
sack [sæk] *n* (*bag*) sacco ▷ *vt* (*dismiss*)
licenziare, mandare a spasso; (*plunder*)
saccheggiare; **to get the ~** essere
mandato a spasso
sacred ['seɪkrɪd] *adj* sacro(-a)
sacrifice ['sækrɪfaɪs] *n* sacrificio ▷ *vt*
sacrificare
sad [sæd] *adj* triste
saddle ['sædl] *n* sella ▷ *vt* (*horse*) sellare; **to**
be ~d with sth (*inf*) avere qc sulle spalle
sadistic [sə'dɪstɪk] *adj* sadico(-a)
sadly ['sædlɪ] *adv* tristemente; (*regrettably*)
sfortunatamente; **~ lacking in**
penosamente privo di
sadness ['sædnɪs] *n* tristezza
s.a.e. *n abbr* (= *stamped addressed envelope*)
busta affrancata e con indirizzo
safari [sə'fɑːrɪ] *n* safari *m inv*
safe [seɪf] *adj* sicuro(-a); (*out of danger*)
salvo(-a), al sicuro; (*cautious*) prudente
▷ *n* cassaforte *f*; **~ from** al sicuro da; **~**
and sound sano(-a) e salvo(-a); **(just) to**
be on the ~ side per non correre rischi;
could you put this in the ~, please? lo

potrebbe mettere nella cassaforte, per favore?; **safely** adv sicuramente; sano(-a) e salvo(-a); prudentemente; **safe sex** n sesso sicuro

safety ['seɪftɪ] n sicurezza; **safety belt** n cintura di sicurezza; **safety pin** n spilla di sicurezza

saffron ['sæfrən] n zafferano

sag [sæg] vi incurvarsi; afflosciarsi

sage [seɪdʒ] n (herb) salvia; (man) saggio

Sagittarius [sædʒɪ'teərɪəs] n Sagittario

Sahara [sə'hɑːrə] n **the ~ (Desert)** il (deserto del) Sahara

said [sɛd] pt, pp of **say**

sail [seɪl] n (on boat) vela; (trip): **to go for a ~** fare un giro in barca a vela ▷ vt (boat) condurre, governare ▷ vi (travel: ship) navigare; (: passenger) viaggiare per mare; (set off) salpare; (sport) fare della vela; **they ~ed into Genoa** entrarono nel porto di Genova; **sailboat** (US) n barca a vela; **sailing** n (sport) vela; **to go sailing** fare della vela; **sailing boat** n barca a vela; **sailor** n marinaio

saint [seɪnt] n santo(-a)

sake [seɪk] n **for the ~ of** per, per amore di

salad ['sæləd] n insalata; **salad cream** (BRIT) n (tipo di) maionese f; **salad dressing** n condimento per insalata

salami [sə'lɑːmɪ] n salame m

salary ['sælərɪ] n stipendio

sale [seɪl] n vendita; (at reduced prices) svendita, liquidazione f; (auction) vendita all'asta; **"for ~"** "in vendita"; **on ~** in vendita; **on ~ or return** da vendere o rimandare; **~s** npl (total amount sold) vendite fpl; **sales assistant** (US **sales clerk**) n commesso(-a); **salesman/woman** (irreg) n commesso(-a); (representative) rappresentante m/f; **salesperson** (irreg) n (in shop) commesso; (representative) rappresentante m/f di commercio; **sales rep** n rappresentante m/f di commercio

saline ['seɪlaɪn] adj salino(-a)

saliva [sə'laɪvə] n saliva

salmon ['sæmən] n inv salmone m

salon ['sælɔn] n (hairdressing salon) parrucchiere(-a); (beauty salon) salone m di bellezza

saloon [sə'luːn] n (US) saloon m inv, bar m inv; (BRIT: Aut) berlina; (ship's lounge) salone m

salt [sɔlt] n sale m ▷ vt salare; **saltwater** adj di mare; **salty** adj salato(-a)

salute [sə'luːt] n saluto ▷ vt salutare

salvage ['sælvɪdʒ] n (saving) salvataggio; (things saved) beni mpl salvati or recuperati ▷ vt salvare, mettere in salvo

Salvation Army [sæl'veɪʃən-] n Esercito della Salvezza

same [seɪm] adj stesso(-a), medesimo(-a) ▷ pron **the ~** lo (la) stesso(-a), gli (le) stessi(-e); **the ~ book as** lo stesso libro di (o che); **at the ~ time** allo stesso tempo; **all** or **just the ~** tuttavia; **to do the ~ as sb** fare come qn; **the ~ to you!** altrettanto a te!

sample ['sɑːmpl] n campione m ▷ vt (food) assaggiare; (wine) degustare

sanction ['sæŋkʃən] n sanzione f ▷ vt sancire, sanzionare; **~s** npl (Pol) sanzioni fpl

sanctuary ['sæŋktjuərɪ] n (holy place) santuario; (refuge) rifugio; (for wildlife) riserva

sand [sænd] n sabbia ▷ vt (also: **~ down**) cartavetrare

sandal ['sændl] n sandalo

sand: sandbox ['sændbɔks] (US) n = **sandpit**; **sandcastle** ['sændkɑːsl] n castello di sabbia; **sand dune** n duna di sabbia; **sandpaper** ['sændpeɪpə'] n carta vetrata; **sandpit** ['sændpɪt] n (for children) buca di sabbia; **sands** npl spiaggia; **sandstone** ['sændstəun] n arenaria

sandwich ['sændwɪtʃ] n tramezzino, panino, sandwich m inv ▷ vt **~ed between** incastrato(-a) fra; **cheese/ham ~** sandwich al formaggio/prosciutto

sandy ['sændɪ] adj sabbioso(-a); (colour) color sabbia inv; biondo(-a) rossiccio(-a)

sane [seɪn] adj (person) sano(-a) di mente; (outlook) sensato(-a)

sang [sæŋ] pt of **sing**

sanitary towel ['sænɪtərɪ-] (US **sanitary napkin**) n assorbente m (igienico)

sanity ['sænɪtɪ] n sanità mentale; (common sense) buon senso

sank [sæŋk] pt of **sink**

Santa Claus [sæntə'klɔːz] n Babbo Natale

sap [sæp] n (of plants) linfa ▷ vt (strength) fiaccare

sapphire ['sæfaɪə'] n zaffiro

sarcasm ['sɑːkæzm] n sarcasmo

sarcastic [sɑː'kæstɪk] adj sarcastico(-a); **to be ~** fare del sarcasmo

sardine [sɑː'diːn] n sardina

Sardinia [sɑː'dɪnɪə] n Sardegna

SASE (US) n abbr (= self-addressed stamped envelope) busta affrancata e con indirizzo

sat [sæt] pt, pp of **sit**

Sat. abbr (= Saturday) sab.

satchel ['sætʃl] n cartella

satellite ['sætəlaɪt] adj satellite ▷ n satellite m; **satellite dish** n antenna parabolica; **satellite television** n televisione f via satellite

s

satin ['sætɪn] *n* raso ▷ *adj* di raso
satire ['sætaɪəʳ] *n* satira
satisfaction [sætɪs'fækʃən] *n*
soddisfazione *f*
satisfactory [sætɪs'fæktərɪ] *adj*
soddisfacente
satisfied ['sætɪsfaɪd] *adj* (*customer*)
soddisfatto(-a); **to be ~ (with sth)** essere
soddisfatto(-a) (di qc)
satisfy ['sætɪsfaɪ] *vt* soddisfare; (*convince*)
convincere
Saturday ['sætədɪ] *n* sabato
sauce [sɔːs] *n* salsa; (*containing meat, fish*)
sugo; **saucepan** *n* casseruola
saucer ['sɔːsəʳ] *n* sottocoppa *m*, piattino
Saudi Arabia ['saudɪ-] *n* Arabia Saudita
sauna ['sɔːnə] *n* sauna
sausage ['sɔsɪdʒ] *n* salsiccia; **sausage roll**
n rotolo di pasta sfoglia ripieno di salsiccia
sautéed ['səuteɪd] *adj* saltato(-a)
savage ['sævɪdʒ] *adj* (*cruel, fierce*)
selvaggio(-a), feroce; (*primitive*)
primitivo(-a) ▷ *n* selvaggio(-a) ▷ *vt*
attaccare selvaggiamente
save [seɪv] *vt* (*person, belongings, Comput*)
salvare; (*money*) risparmiare, mettere
da parte; (*time*) risparmiare; (*food*)
conservare; (*avoid: trouble*) evitare; (*Sport*)
parare ▷ *vi* (*also: ~ up*) economizzare ▷ *n*
(*Sport*) parata ▷ *prep* salvo, a eccezione di
savings ['seɪvɪŋz] *npl* (*money*) risparmi *mpl*;
savings account *n* libretto di risparmio;
savings and loan association (*us*) *n*
≈ società di credito immobiliare
savoury ['seɪvərɪ] (*us* **savory**) *adj* (*dish: not
sweet*) salato(-a)
saw [sɔː] (*pt* **sawed**, *pp* **sawed** *or* **sawn**) *pt*
of **see** ▷ *n* (*tool*) sega ▷ *vt* segare; **sawdust**
n segatura
sawn [sɔːn] *pp of* **saw**
saxophone ['sæksəfəun] *n* sassofono
say [seɪ] (*pt, pp* **said**) *n* **to have one's ~**
fare sentire il proprio parere; **to have
a** *or* **some ~** avere voce in capitolo ▷ *vt*
dire; **could you ~ that again?** potrebbe
ripeterlo?; **that goes without ~ing** va da
sé; **saying** *n* proverbio, detto
scab [skæb] *n* crosta; (*pej*) crumiro(-a)
scaffolding ['skæfəldɪŋ] *n* impalcatura
scald [skɔːld] *n* scottatura ▷ *vt* scottare
scale [skeɪl] *n* scala; (*of fish*) squama ▷ *vt*
(*mountain*) scalare; **~s** *npl* (*for weighing*)
bilancia; **on a large ~** su vasta scala; **~ of
charges** tariffa
scallion ['skæljən] *n* cipolla; (*us: shallot*)
scalogna; (: *leek*) porro
scallop ['skɔləp] *n* (*Zool*) pettine *m*;
(*Sewing*) smerlo
scalp [skælp] *n* cuoio capelluto ▷ *vt*

scotennare
scalpel ['skælpl] *n* bisturi *m inv*
scam [skæm] *n* (*inf*) truffa
scampi ['skæmpɪ] *npl* scampi *mpl*
scan [skæn] *vt* scrutare; (*glance at
quickly*) scorrere, dare un'occhiata a; (*TV*)
analizzare; (*Radar*) esplorare ▷ *n* (*Med*)
ecografia
scandal ['skændl] *n* scandalo; (*gossip*)
pettegolezzi *mpl*
Scandinavia [skændɪ'neɪvɪə] *n*
Scandinavia; **Scandinavian** *adj, n*
scandinavo(-a)
scanner ['skænəʳ] *n* (*Radar, Med*) scanner
m inv
scapegoat ['skeɪpɡəut] *n* capro espiatorio
scar [skɑː] *n* cicatrice *f* ▷ *vt* sfregiare
scarce [skɛəs] *adj* scarso(-a); (*copy, edition*)
raro(-a); **to make o.s. ~** (*inf*) squagliarsela;
scarcely *adv* appena
scare [skɛəʳ] *n* spavento; panico ▷ *vt*
spaventare, atterrire; **there was a bomb ~
at the bank** hanno evacuato la banca per
paura di un attentato dinamitardo; **to ~ sb
stiff** spaventare a morte qn; **scarecrow** *n*
spaventapasseri *m inv*; **scared** *adj* **to be
scared** aver paura
scarf [skɑːf] (*pl* **scarves** *or* **scarfs**) *n* (*long*)
sciarpa; (*square*) fazzoletto da testa,
foulard *m inv*
scarlet ['skɑːlɪt] *adj* scarlatto(-a)
scarves [skɑːvz] *npl of* **scarf**
scary ['skɛərɪ] *adj* che spaventa
scatter ['skætəʳ] *vt* spargere; (*crowd*)
disperdere ▷ *vi* disperdersi
scenario [sɪ'nɑːrɪəu] *n* (*Theatre, Cinema*)
copione *m*; (*fig*) situazione *f*
scene [siːn] *n* (*Theatre, fig etc*) scena;
(*of crime, accident*) scena, luogo; (*sight,
view*) vista, veduta; **scenery** *n* (*Theatre*)
scenario; (*landscape*) panorama *m*; **scenic**
adj scenico(-a); panoramico(-a)
scent [sɛnt] *n* profumo; (*sense of smell*)
olfatto, odorato; (*fig: track*) pista
sceptical ['skɛptɪkəl] (*us* **skeptical**) *adj*
scettico(-a)
schedule ['ʃɛdjuːl, (*us*) 'skɛdjuːl] *n*
programma *m*, piano; (*of trains*) orario; (*of
prices etc*) lista, tabella ▷ *vt* fissare; **on ~** in
orario; **to be ahead of/behind ~** essere in
anticipo/ritardo sul previsto; **scheduled
flight** *n* volo di linea
scheme [skiːm] *n* piano, progetto;
(*method*) sistema *m*; (*dishonest plan, plot*)
intrigo, trama; (*arrangement*) disposizione
f, sistemazione *f*; (*pension scheme etc*)
programma *m* ▷ *vi* fare progetti; (*intrigue*)
complottare
schizophrenic [skɪtsə'frɛnɪk] *adj, n*

schizofrenico(-a)

scholar ['skɔlə^r] n (expert) studioso(-a);
scholarship n erudizione f; (grant) borsa
di studio

school [sku:l] n (primary, secondary)
scuola; (university: US) università f
inv ▷ cpd scolare, scolastico(-a) ▷ vt
(animal) addestrare; **schoolbook** n libro
scolastico; **schoolboy** n scolaro; **school
children** npl scolari mpl; **schoolgirl**
n scolara; **schooling** n istruzione f;
schoolteacher n insegnante m/f,
docente m/f; (primary) maestro(-a)

science ['saɪəns] n scienza; **science
fiction** n fantascienza; **scientific**
[-'tɪfɪk] adj scientifico(-a); **scientist** n
scienziato(-a)

sci-fi ['saɪfaɪ] n abbr (inf) = **science fiction**

scissors ['sɪzəz] npl forbici fpl

scold [skəuld] vt rimproverare

scone [skɔn] n focaccina da tè

scoop [sku:p] n mestolo; (for ice cream)
cucchiaio dosatore; (Press) colpo
giornalistico, notizia (in) esclusiva

scooter ['sku:tə^r] n (motor cycle)
motoretta, scooter m inv; (toy)
monopattino

scope [skəup] n (capacity: of plan,
undertaking) portata; (: of person) capacità
fpl; (opportunity) possibilità fpl

scorching ['skɔ:tʃɪŋ] adj cocente,
scottante

score [skɔ:^r] n punti mpl, punteggio;
(Mus) partitura, spartito; (twenty) venti
▷ vt (goal, point) segnare, fare; (success)
ottenere ▷ vi segnare; (Football) fare un
goal; (keep score) segnare i punti; **~s of**
(very many) un sacco di; **on that ~** a questo
riguardo; **to ~ 6 out of 10** prendere 6 su
10; **score out** vt cancellare con un segno;
scoreboard n tabellone m segnapunti;
scorer n marcatore(-trice); (keeping score)
segnapunti m inv

scorn [skɔ:n] n disprezzo ▷ vt
disprezzare

Scorpio ['skɔ:pɪəu] n Scorpione m

scorpion ['skɔ:pɪən] n scorpione m

Scot [skɔt] n scozzese m/f

Scotch tape® n scotch® m

Scotland ['skɔtlənd] n Scozia

Scots [skɔts] adj scozzese; **Scotsman**
(irreg) n scozzese m; **Scotswoman** (irreg) n
scozzese f; **Scottish** ['skɔtɪʃ] adj scozzese;
Scottish Parliament n Parlamento
scozzese

scout [skaut] n (Mil) esploratore m; (also:
boy ~) giovane esploratore, scout m inv

scowl [skaul] vi accigliarsi, aggrottare le
sopracciglia; **to ~ at** guardare torvo

scramble ['skræmbl] n arrampicata ▷ vi
inerpicarsi; **to ~ out** etc uscire etc in fretta;
to ~ for azzuffarsi per; **scrambled eggs**
npl uova fpl strapazzate

scrap [skræp] n pezzo, pezzetto; (fight)
zuffa; (also: **~ iron**) rottami mpl di ferro,
ferraglia ▷ vt demolire; (fig) scartare ▷ vi
to ~ (with sb) fare a botte (con qn); **~s** npl
(waste) scarti mpl; **scrapbook** n album m
inv di ritagli

scrape [skreɪp] vt, vi raschiare, grattare ▷ n
to get into a ~ cacciarsi in un guaio

scrap paper n cartaccia

scratch [skrætʃ] n graffio ▷ cpd **~ team**
squadra raccogliticcia ▷ vt graffiare,
rigare ▷ vi grattare; (paint, car) graffiare;
to start from ~ cominciare or partire
da zero; **to be up to ~** essere all'altezza;
scratch card n (BRIT) cartolina f gratta
e vinci

scream [skri:m] n grido, urlo ▷ vi urlare,
gridare

screen [skri:n] n schermo; (fig) muro,
cortina, velo ▷ vt schermare, fare schermo
a; (from the wind etc) riparare; (film)
proiettare; (book) adattare per lo schermo;
(candidates etc) selezionare; **screening**
n (Med) dépistage m inv; **screenplay** n
sceneggiatura; **screen saver** n (Comput)
screen saver m inv

screw [skru:] n vite f ▷ vt avvitare; **screw
up** vt (paper etc) spiegazzare; (inf: ruin)
rovinare; **to ~ up one's eyes** strizzare gli
occhi; **screwdriver** n cacciavite m

scribble ['skrɪbl] n scarabocchio ▷ vt
scribacchiare in fretta ▷ vi scarabocchiare

script [skrɪpt] n (Cinema etc) copione m; (in
exam) elaborato or compito d'esame

scroll [skrəul] n rotolo di carta

scrub [skrʌb] n (land) boscaglia ▷ vt pulire
strofinando; (reject) annullare

scruffy ['skrʌfɪ] adj sciatto(-a)

scrum(mage) ['skrʌm(ɪdʒ)] n mischia

scrutiny ['skru:tɪnɪ] n esame m accurato

scuba diving ['sku:bə-] n immersioni fpl
subacquee

sculptor ['skʌlptə^r] n scultore m

sculpture ['skʌlptʃə^r] n scultura

scum [skʌm] n schiuma; (pej: people) feccia

scurry ['skʌrɪ] vi sgambare, affrettarsi

sea [si:] n mare m ▷ cpd marino(-a), del
mare; (bird, fish) di mare; (route, transport)
marittimo(-a); **by ~** (travel) per mare; **on
the ~** (boat) in mare; (town) di mare; **to be
all at ~** (fig) non sapere che pesci pigliare;
out to ~ al largo; **(out) at ~** in mare;
seafood n frutti mpl di mare; **sea front** n
lungomare m; **seagull** n gabbiano

seal [si:l] n (animal) foca; (stamp) sigillo;

(impression) impronta del sigillo ▷ *vt* sigillare; **seal off** *vt* (*close*) sigillare; (*forbid entry to*) bloccare l'accesso a

sea level *n* livello del mare

seam [siːm] *n* cucitura; (*of coal*) filone *m*

search [səːtʃ] *n* ricerca; (*Law: at sb's home*) perquisizione *f* ▷ *vt* frugare ▷ *vi* **to ~ for** ricercare; **in ~ of** alla ricerca di; **search engine** *n* (*Comput*) motore *m* di ricerca; **search party** *n* squadra di soccorso

sea: **seashore** ['siːʃɔːʳ] *n* spiaggia; **seasick** ['siːsɪk] *adj* che soffre il mal di mare; **seaside** ['siːsaɪd] *n* spiaggia; **seaside resort** *n* stazione *f* balneare

season ['siːzn] *n* stagione *f* ▷ *vt* condire, insaporire; **seasonal** *adj* stagionale; **seasoning** *n* condimento; **season ticket** *n* abbonamento

seat [siːt] *n* sedile *m*; (*in bus, train: place*) posto; (*Parliament*) seggio; (*buttocks*) didietro; (*of trousers*) fondo ▷ *vt* far sedere; (*have room for*) avere *or* essere fornito(-a) di posti a sedere per; **I'd like to book two ~s** vorrei prenotare due posti; **to be ~ed** essere seduto(-a); **seat belt** *n* cintura di sicurezza; **seating** *n* posti *mpl* a sedere

sea: **sea water** *n* acqua di mare; **seaweed** ['siːwiːd] *n* alghe *fpl*

sec. *abbr* = **second(s)**

secluded [sɪ'kluːdɪd] *adj* isolato(-a), appartato(-a)

second ['sɛkənd] *num* secondo(-a) ▷ *adv* (*in race etc*) al secondo posto ▷ *n* (*unit of time*) secondo; (*Aut: also: ~ gear*) seconda; (*Comm: imperfect*) scarto; (*BRIT: Scol: degree*) laurea con punteggio discreto ▷ *vt* (*motion*) appoggiare; **secondary** *adj* secondario(-a); **secondary school** *n* scuola secondaria; **second-class** *adj* di seconda classe ▷ *adv* in seconda classe; **secondhand** *adj* di seconda mano, usato(-a); **secondly** *adv* in secondo luogo; **second-rate** *adj* scadente; **second thoughts** *npl* ripensamenti *mpl*; **on second thoughts** (*BRIT*) *or* **thought** (*US*) ripensandoci bene

secrecy ['siːkrəsɪ] *n* segretezza

secret ['siːkrɪt] *adj* segreto(-a) ▷ *n* segreto; **in ~** in segreto

secretary ['sɛkrətrɪ] *n* segretario(-a); **S~ of State (for)** (*BRIT: Pol*) ministro (di)

secretive ['siːkrətɪv] *adj* riservato(-a)

secret service *n* servizi *mpl* segreti

sect [sɛkt] *n* setta

section ['sɛkʃən] *n* sezione *f*

sector ['sɛktəʳ] *n* settore *m*

secular ['sɛkjuləʳ] *adj* secolare

secure [sɪ'kjuəʳ] *adj* sicuro(-a); (*firmly fixed*) assicurato(-a), ben fermato(-a); (*in safe place*) al sicuro ▷ *vt* (*fix*) fissare, assicurare; (*get*) ottenere, assicurarsi; **securities** *npl* (*Stock Exchange*) titoli *mpl*

security [sɪ'kjuərɪtɪ] *n* sicurezza; (*for loan*) garanzia; **security guard** *n* guardia giurata

sedan [sə'dæn] (*US*) *n* (*Aut*) berlina

sedate [sɪ'deɪt] *adj* posato(-a), calmo(-a) ▷ *vt* calmare

sedative ['sɛdɪtɪv] *n* sedativo, calmante *m*

seduce [sɪ'djuːs] *vt* sedurre; **seductive** [-'dʌktɪv] *adj* seducente

see [siː] (*pt* **saw**, *pp* **seen**) *vt* vedere; (*accompany*): **to ~ sb to the door** accompagnare qn alla porta ▷ *vi* vedere; (*understand*) capire ▷ *n* sede *f* vescovile; **to ~ that** (*ensure*) badare che + *sub*, fare in modo che + *sub*; **~ you soon!** a presto!; **see off** *vt* salutare alla partenza; **see out** *vt* (*take to the door*) accompagnare alla porta; **see through** *vt* portare a termine ▷ *vt fus* non lasciarsi ingannare da; **see to** *vt fus* occuparsi di

seed [siːd] *n* seme *m*; (*fig*) germe *m*; (*Tennis etc*) testa di serie; **to go to ~** fare seme; (*fig*) scadere

seeing ['siːɪŋ] *conj* **~ (that)** visto che

seek [siːk] (*pt, pp* **sought**) *vt* cercare

seem [siːm] *vi* sembrare, parere; **there ~s to be ...** sembra che ci sia ...; **seemingly** *adv* apparentemente

seen [siːn] *pp of* **see**

seesaw ['siːsɔː] *n* altalena a bilico

segment ['sɛgmənt] *n* segmento

segregate ['sɛgrɪgeɪt] *vt* segregare, isolare

seize [siːz] *vt* (*grasp*) afferrare; (*take possession of*) impadronirsi di; (*Law*) sequestrare

seizure ['siːʒəʳ] *n* (*Med*) attacco; (*Law*) confisca, sequestro

seldom ['sɛldəm] *adv* raramente

select [sɪ'lɛkt] *adj* scelto(-a) ▷ *vt* scegliere, selezionare; **selection** [-'lɛkʃən] *n* selezione *f*, scelta; **selective** *adj* selettivo(-a)

self [sɛlf] *n* **the ~** l'io *m* ▷ *prefix* auto...; **self-assured** *adj* sicuro(-a) di sé; **self-catering** (*BRIT*) *adj* in cui ci si cucina da sé; **self-centred** (*US* **self-centered**) *adj* egocentrico(-a); **self-confidence** *n* sicurezza di sé; **self-confident** *adj* sicuro(-a) di sé; **self-conscious** *adj* timido(-a); **self-contained** (*BRIT*) (*flat*) indipendente; **self-control** *n* autocontrollo; **self-defence** (*US* **self-defense**) *n* autodifesa; (*Law*) legittima difesa; **self-drive** *adj* (*BRIT: rented car*) senza autista; **self-employed** adj che lavora in proprio; **self-esteem** n amor proprio m; **self-indulgent** adj indulgente verso se stesso(-a); **self-interest** n interesse m personale; **selfish** adj egoista; **self-pity** n autocommiserazione f; **self-raising** (US **self-rising**) adj **self-raising flour** miscela di farina e lievito; **self-respect** n rispetto di sé, amor proprio; **self-service** n autoservizio, self-service m

sell [sɛl] (pt, pp **sold**) vt vendere ▷ vi vendersi; **to ~ at** or **for 1000 euros** essere in vendita a 1000 euro; **sell off** vt svendere, liquidare; **sell out** vi **to ~ out (of sth)** esaurire (qc); **the tickets are all sold out** i biglietti sono esauriti; **sell-by date** ['sɛlbaɪ-] n data di scadenza; **seller** n venditore(-trice)

Sellotape® ['sɛləʊteɪp] (BRIT) n nastro adesivo, scotch® m

selves [sɛlvz] npl of **self**

semester [sɪ'mɛstər] (US) n semestre m

semi... ['sɛmɪ] prefix semi...; **semicircle** n semicerchio; **semidetached (house)** [sɛmɪdɪ'tætʃt-] (BRIT) n casa gemella; **semi-final** n semifinale f

seminar ['sɛmɪnɑːr] n seminario

semi-skimmed ['sɛmɪ'skɪmd] adj (milk) parzialmente scremato(-a)

senate ['sɛnɪt] n senato; **senator** n senatore(-trice)

send [sɛnd] (pt, pp **sent**) vt mandare; **send back** vt rimandare; **send for** vt fus mandare a chiamare, far venire; **send in** vt (report, application, resignation) presentare; **send off** vt (goods) spedire; (BRIT: Sport: player) espellere; **send on** vt (BRIT: letter) inoltrare; (luggage etc: in advance) spedire in anticipo; **send out** vt (invitation) diramare; **send up** vt (person, price) far salire; (BRIT: parody) mettere in ridicolo; **sender** n mittente m/f; **send-off** n **to give sb a good send-off** festeggiare la partenza di qn

senile ['siːnaɪl] adj senile

senior ['siːnɪər] adj (older) più vecchio(-a); (of higher rank) di grado più elevato; **senior citizen** n persona anziana; **senior high school** (US) n ≈ liceo

sensation [sɛn'seɪʃən] n sensazione f; **sensational** adj sensazionale; (marvellous) eccezionale

sense [sɛns] n senso; (feeling) sensazione f, senso; (meaning) senso, significato; (wisdom) buonsenso ▷ vt sentire, percepire; **it makes ~** ha senso; **senseless** adj sciocco(-a); (unconscious) privo(-a) di sensi; **sense of humour** (BRIT) n senso dell'umorismo

sensible ['sɛnsɪbl] adj sensato(-a), ragionevole

◾ Be careful not to translate **sensible** by the Italian word **sensibile**.

sensitive ['sɛnsɪtɪv] adj sensibile; (skin, question) delicato(-a)

sensual ['sɛnsjuəl] adj sensuale

sensuous ['sɛnsjuəs] adj sensuale

sent [sɛnt] pt, pp of **send**

sentence ['sɛntns] n (Ling) frase f; (Law: judgment) sentenza; (: punishment) condanna ▷ vt **to ~ sb to death/to 5 years** condannare qn a morte/a 5 anni

sentiment ['sɛntɪmənt] n sentimento; (opinion) opinione f; **sentimental** [-'mɛntl] adj sentimentale

Sep. abbr (= September) Sett.

separate [adj 'sɛprɪt, vb 'sɛpəreɪt] adj separato(-a) ▷ vt separare ▷ vi separarsi; **separately** adv separatamente; **separates** npl (clothes) coordinati mpl; **separation** [-'reɪʃən] n separazione f

September [sɛp'tɛmbər] n settembre m

septic ['sɛptɪk] adj settico(-a); (wound) infettato(-a); **septic tank** n fossa settica

sequel ['siːkwl] n conseguenza; (of story) seguito; (of film) sequenza

sequence ['siːkwəns] n (series) serie f; (order) ordine m

sequin ['siːkwɪn] n lustrino, paillette f inv

Serb [səːb] adj, n = **Serbian**

Serbia ['səːbɪə] n Serbia

Serbian ['səːbɪən] adj serbo(-a) ▷ n serbo(-a); (Ling) serbo

sergeant ['sɑːdʒənt] n sergente m; (Police) brigadiere m

serial ['sɪərɪəl] n (Press) romanzo a puntate; (Radio, TV) trasmissione f a puntate, serial m inv; **serial killer** n serial-killer m/f inv; **serial number** n numero di serie

series ['sɪəriːz] n inv serie f inv; (Publishing) collana

serious ['sɪərɪəs] adj serio(-a), grave; **seriously** adv seriamente

sermon ['səːmən] n sermone m

servant ['səːvənt] n domestico(-a)

serve [səːv] vt (employer etc) servire, essere a servizio di; (purpose) servire a; (customer, food, meal) servire; (apprenticeship) fare; (prison term) scontare ▷ vi (also Tennis) servire; (be useful): **to ~ as/for/to do** servire da/per/per fare ▷ n (Tennis) servizio; **it ~s him right** ben gli sta, se l'è meritata; **server** n (Comput) server m inv

service ['səːvɪs] n servizio; (Aut: maintenance) assistenza, revisione f ▷ vt (car, washing machine) revisionare; **to be of ~ to sb** essere d'aiuto a qn; **~ included/**

not included servizio compreso/escluso; **~s** (_BRIT: on motorway_) stazione _f_ di servizio; (_Mil_): **the S-~s** le Forze Armate; **service area** _n_ (_on motorway_) area di servizio; **service charge** (_BRIT_) _n_ servizio; **serviceman** (_irreg_) _n_ militare _m_; **service station** _n_ stazione _f_ di servizio

serviette [sə:vɪ'ɛt] (_BRIT_) _n_ tovagliolo

session ['sɛʃən] _n_ (_sitting_) seduta, sessione _f_; (_Scol_) anno scolastico (_or_ accademico)

set [sɛt] (_pt, pp_ **set**) _n_ serie _f_ inv; (_of cutlery etc_) servizio; (_Radio, TV_) apparecchio; (_Tennis_) set _m_ inv; (_group of people_) mondo, ambiente _m_; (_Cinema_) scenario; (_Theatre: stage_) scene _fpl_; (_: scenery_) scenario; (_Math_) insieme _m_; (_Hairdressing_) messa in piega ▷ _adj_ (_fixed_) stabilito(-a), determinato(-a); (_ready_) pronto(-a) ▷ _vt_ (_place_) posare, mettere; (_arrange_) sistemare; (_fix_) fissare; (_adjust_) regolare; (_decide: rules etc_) stabilire, fissare ▷ _vi_ (_sun_) tramontare; (_jam, jelly_) rapprendersi; (_concrete_) fare presa; **to be ~ on doing** essere deciso a fare; **to ~ to music** mettere in musica; **to ~ on fire** dare fuoco a; **to ~ free** liberare; **to ~ sth going** mettere in moto qc; **to ~ sail** prendere il mare; **set aside** _vt_ mettere da parte; **set down** _vt_ (_bus, train_) lasciare; **set in** _vi_ (_infection_) svilupparsi; (_complications_) intervenire; **the rain has ~ in for the day** ormai pioverà tutto il giorno; **set off** _vi_ partire ▷ _vt_ (_bomb_) far scoppiare; (_cause to start_) mettere in moto; (_show up well_) dare risalto a; **set out** _vi_ partire ▷ _vt_ (_arrange_) disporre; (_state_) esporre, presentare; **to ~ out to do** proporsi di fare; **set up** _vt_ (_organization_) fondare, costituire; **setback** _n_ (_hitch_) contrattempo, inconveniente _m_; **set menu** _n_ menù _m_ inv fisso

settee [sɛ'ti:] _n_ divano, sofà _m_ inv

setting ['sɛtɪŋ] _n_ (_background_) ambiente _m_; (_of controls_) posizione _f_; (_of sun_) tramonto; (_of jewel_) montatura

settle ['sɛtl] _vt_ (_argument, matter_) appianare; (_accounts_) regolare; (_Med: calm_) calmare ▷ _vi_ (_bird, dust etc_) posarsi; (_sediment_) depositarsi; **to ~ for sth** accontentarsi di qc; **to ~ on sth** decidersi per qc; **settle down** _vi_ (_get comfortable_) sistemarsi; (_calm down_) calmarsi; (_get back to normal: situation_) tornare alla normalità; **settle in** _vi_ sistemarsi; **settle up** _vi_ **to ~ up with sb** regolare i conti con qn; **settlement** _n_ (_payment_) pagamento, saldo; (_agreement_) accordo; (_colony_) colonia; (_village etc_) villaggio, comunità _f_ inv

setup ['sɛtʌp] _n_ (_arrangement_) sistemazione _f_; (_situation_) situazione _f_

seven ['sɛvn] _num_ sette; **seventeen** _num_ diciassette; **seventeenth** [sɛvn'ti:nθ] _num_ diciassettesimo(-a); **seventh** _num_ settimo(-a); **seventieth** ['sɛvntɪɪθ] _num_ settantesimo(-a); **seventy** _num_ settanta

sever ['sɛvər] _vt_ recidere, tagliare; (_relations_) troncare

several ['sɛvərl] _adj, pron_ alcuni(-e), diversi(-e); **~ of us** alcuni di noi

severe [sɪ'vɪər] _adj_ severo(-a); (_serious_) serio(-a), grave; (_hard_) duro(-a); (_plain_) semplice, sobrio(-a)

sew [səu] (_pt_ **sewed**, _pp_ **sewn**) _vt, vi_ cucire

sewage ['su:ɪdʒ] _n_ acque _fpl_ di scolo

sewer ['su:ər] _n_ fogna

sewing ['səuɪŋ] _n_ cucitura; cucito; **sewing machine** _n_ macchina da cucire

sewn [səun] _pp_ of **sew**

sex [sɛks] _n_ sesso; **to have ~ with** avere rapporti sessuali con; **sexism** ['sɛksɪzəm] _n_ sessismo; **sexist** _adj, n_ sessista _m/f_; **sexual** ['sɛksjuəl] _adj_ sessuale; **sexual intercourse** _n_ rapporti _mpl_ sessuali; **sexuality** [sɛksju'ælɪtɪ] _n_ sessualità; **sexy** ['sɛksɪ] _adj_ provocante, sexy _inv_

shabby ['ʃæbɪ] _adj_ malandato(-a); (_behaviour_) vergognoso(-a)

shack [ʃæk] _n_ baracca, capanna

shade [ʃeɪd] _n_ ombra; (_for lamp_) paralume _m_; (_of colour_) tonalità _f_ inv; (_small quantity_): **a ~ (more/too large)** un po' (di più/ troppo grande) ▷ _vt_ ombreggiare, fare ombra a; **in the ~** all'ombra; **~s** (_US_) _npl_ (_sunglasses_) occhiali _mpl_ da sole

shadow ['ʃædəu] _n_ ombra ▷ _vt_ (_follow_) pedinare; **shadow cabinet** (_BRIT_) _n_ (_Pol_) governo _m_ ombra _inv_

shady ['ʃeɪdɪ] _adj_ ombroso(-a); (_fig: dishonest_) losco(-a), equivoco(-a)

shaft [ʃɑ:ft] _n_ (_of arrow, spear_) asta; (_Aut, Tech_) albero; (_of mine_) pozzo; (_of lift_) tromba; (_of light_) raggio

shake [ʃeɪk] (_pt_ **shook**, _pp_ **shaken**) _vt_ scuotere; (_bottle, cocktail_) agitare ▷ _vi_ tremare; **to ~ one's head** (_in refusal, dismay_) scuotere la testa; **to ~ hands with sb** stringere _or_ dare la mano a qn; **shake off** _vt_ scrollare (via); (_fig_) sbarazzarsi di; **shake up** _vt_ scuotere; **shaky** _adj_ (_hand, voice_) tremante; (_building_) traballante

shall [ʃæl] _aux vb_ **I ~ go** andrò; **~ I open the door?** apro io la porta?; **I'll get some, ~ I?** ne prendo un po', va bene?

shallow ['ʃæləu] _adj_ poco profondo(-a); (_fig_) superficiale

sham [ʃæm] _n_ finzione _f_, messinscena; (_jewellery, furniture_) imitazione _f_

shambles ['ʃæmblz] _n_ confusione _f_, baraonda, scompiglio

shame [ʃeɪm] n vergogna ▷ vt far vergognare; **it is a ~ (that/to do)** è un peccato (che + sub/fare); **what a ~!** che peccato!; **shameful** adj vergognoso(-a); **shameless** adj sfrontato(-a); (immodest) spudorato(-a)

shampoo [ʃæm'pu:] n shampoo m inv ▷ vt fare lo shampoo a

shandy ['ʃændɪ] n birra con gassosa

shan't [ʃɑ:nt] = **shall not**

shape [ʃeɪp] n forma ▷ vt formare; (statement) formulare; (sb's ideas) condizionare; **to take ~** prendere forma

share [ʃeəʳ] n (thing received, contribution) parte f; (Comm) azione f ▷ vt dividere; (have in common) condividere, avere in comune; **shareholder** n azionista m/f

shark [ʃɑ:k] n squalo, pescecane m

sharp [ʃɑ:p] adj (razor, knife) affilato(-a), (point) acuto(-a), acuminato(-a); (nose, chin) aguzzo(-a); (outline, contrast) netto(-a); (cold, pain) pungente; (voice) stridulo(-a); (person: quick-witted) sveglio(-a); (: unscrupulous) disonesto(-a); (Mus): **C ~** do diesis ▷ n (Mus) diesis m inv ▷ adv **at 2 o'clock ~** alle due in punto; **sharpen** vt affilare; (pencil) fare la punta a; (fig) acuire; **sharpener** n (also: **pencil sharpener**) temperamatite m inv; **sharply** adv (turn, stop) bruscamente; (stand out, contrast) nettamente; (criticize, retort) duramente, aspramente

shatter ['ʃætəʳ] vt mandare in frantumi, frantumare; (fig: upset) distruggere; (: ruin) rovinare ▷ vi frantumarsi, andare in pezzi; **shattered** adj (grief-stricken) sconvolto(-a); (exhausted) a pezzi, distrutto(-a)

shave [ʃeɪv] vt radere, rasare ▷ vi radersi, farsi la barba ▷ n **to have a ~** farsi la barba; **shaver** n (also: **electric shaver**) rasoio elettrico

shaving cream n crema da barba

shaving foam n = **shaving cream**

shavings ['ʃeɪvɪŋz] npl (of wood etc) trucioli mpl

shawl [ʃɔ:l] n scialle m

she [ʃi:] pron ella, lei; **~-cat** gatta; **~-elephant** elefantessa

sheath [ʃi:θ] n fodero, guaina; (contraceptive) preservativo

shed [ʃɛd] (pt, pp **shed**) n capannone m ▷ vt (leaves, fur etc) perdere; (tears, blood) versare; (workers) liberarsi di

she'd [ʃi:d] = **she had**; **she would**

sheep [ʃi:p] n inv pecora; **sheepdog** n cane m da pastore; **sheepskin** n pelle f di pecora

sheer [ʃɪəʳ] adj (utter) vero(-a)

(e proprio(-a)); (steep) a picco, perpendicolare; (almost transparent) sottile ▷ adv a picco

sheet [ʃi:t] n (on bed) lenzuolo; (of paper) foglio; (of glass, ice) lastra; (of metal) foglio, lamina

sheik(h) [ʃeɪk] n sceicco

shelf [ʃɛlf] (pl **shelves**) n scaffale m, mensola

shell [ʃɛl] n (on beach) conchiglia; (of egg, nut etc) guscio; (explosive) granata; (of building) scheletro ▷ vt (peas) sgranare; (Mil) bombardare

she'll [ʃi:l] = **she will**; **she shall**

shellfish ['ʃɛlfɪʃ] n inv (crab etc) crostaceo; (scallop etc) mollusco; (as food) crostacei; molluschi

shelter ['ʃɛltəʳ] n riparo, rifugio ▷ vt riparare, proteggere; (give lodging to) dare rifugio or asilo a ▷ vi ripararsi, mettersi al riparo; **sheltered** adj riparato(-a)

shelves ['ʃɛlvz] npl of **shelf**

shelving ['ʃɛlvɪŋ] n scaffalature fpl

shepherd ['ʃɛpəd] n pastore m ▷ vt (guide) guidare; **shepherd's pie** (BRIT) n timballo di carne macinata e purè di patate

sheriff ['ʃɛrɪf] n sceriffo

sherry ['ʃɛrɪ] n sherry m inv

she's [ʃi:z] = **she is**; **she has**

Shetland ['ʃɛtlənd] n (also: **the ~s, the ~ Isles**) le isole Shetland, le Shetland

shield [ʃi:ld] n scudo; (trophy) scudetto; (protection) schermo ▷ vt **to ~ (from)** riparare (da), proteggere (da or contro)

shift [ʃɪft] n (change) cambiamento; (of workers) turno ▷ vt spostare, muovere; (remove) rimuovere ▷ vi spostarsi, muoversi

shin [ʃɪn] n tibia

shine [ʃaɪn] (pt, pp **shone**) n splendore m, lucentezza ▷ vi (ri)splendere, brillare ▷ vt far brillare, far risplendere; (torch): **to ~ sth on** puntare qc verso

shingles ['ʃɪŋglz] n (Med) herpes zoster m

shiny ['ʃaɪnɪ] adj lucente, lucido(-a)

ship [ʃɪp] n nave f ▷ vt trasportare (via mare); (send) spedire (via mare); **shipment** n carico; **shipping** n (ships) naviglio; (traffic) navigazione f; **shipwreck** n relitto; (event) naufragio ▷ vt **to be shipwrecked** naufragare, fare naufragio; **shipyard** n cantiere m navale

shirt [ʃə:t] n camicia; **in ~ sleeves** in maniche di camicia

shit [ʃɪt] (inf!) excl merda (!)

shiver ['ʃɪvəʳ] n brivido ▷ vi rabbrividire, tremare

shock [ʃɔk] n (impact) urto, colpo; (Elec) scossa; (emotional) colpo, shock m inv;

s

(*Med*) shock ▷ *vt* colpire, scioccare; scandalizzare; **shocking** *adj* scioccante, traumatizzante; scandaloso(-a)

shoe [ʃuː] (*pt, pp* **shod**) *n* scarpa; (*also*: **horse~**) ferro di cavallo ▷ *vt* (*horse*) ferrare; **shoelace** *n* stringa; **shoe polish** *n* lucido per scarpe; **shoeshop** *n* calzoleria

shone [ʃɔn] *pt, pp of* **shine**

shook [ʃuk] *pt of* **shake**

shoot [ʃuːt] (*pt, pp* **shot**) *n* (*on branch, seedling*) germoglio ▷ *vt* (*game*) cacciare, andare a caccia di; (*person*) sparare a; (*execute*) fucilare; (*film*) girare ▷ *vi* (*with gun*): **to ~ (at)** fare fuoco (su); (*with bow*): **to ~ (at)** tirare (su); (*Football*) sparare, tirare (forte); **shoot down** *vt* (*plane*) abbattere; **shoot up** *vi* (*fig*) salire alle stelle; **shooting** *n* (*shots*) sparatoria; (*Hunting*) caccia

shop [ʃɔp] *n* negozio; (*workshop*) officina ▷ *vi* (*also*: **go ~ping**) fare spese; **shop assistant** (*BRIT*) *n* commesso(-a); **shopkeeper** *n* negoziante *m/f*, bottegaio(-a); **shoplifting** *n* taccheggio; **shopping** *n* (*goods*) spesa, acquisti *mpl*; **shopping bag** *n* borsa per la spesa; **shopping centre** (*US* **shopping center**) *n* centro commerciale; **shopping mall** *n* centro commerciale; **shopping trolley** *n* (*BRIT*) carrello del supermercato; **shop window** *n* vetrina

shore [ʃɔːʳ] *n* (*of sea*) riva, spiaggia; (*of lake*) riva ▷ *vt* **to ~ (up)** puntellare; **on ~** a riva

short [ʃɔːt] *adj* (*not long*) corto(-a); (*soon finished*) breve; (*person*) basso(-a); (*curt*) brusco(-a), secco(-a); (*insufficient*) insufficiente ▷ *n* (*also*: **~ film**) cortometraggio; **to be ~ of sth** essere a corto di *or* mancare di qc; **in ~** in breve; **~ of doing** a meno che non si faccia; **everything ~ of** tutto fuorché; **it is ~ for** è l'abbreviazione *or* il diminutivo di; **to cut ~** (*speech, visit*) accorciare, abbreviare; **to fall ~ of** venir meno a; non soddisfare; **to run ~ of** rimanere senza; **to stop ~** fermarsi di colpo; **to stop ~ of** non arrivare fino a; **shortage** *n* scarsezza, carenza; **shortbread** *n* biscotto di pasta frolla; **shortcoming** *n* difetto; **short(crust) pastry** (*BRIT*) *n* pasta frolla; **shortcut** *n* scorciatoia; **shorten** *vt* accorciare, ridurre; **shortfall** *n* deficit *m*; **shorthand** (*BRIT*) *n* stenografia; **short-lived** *adj* di breve durata; **shortly** *adv* fra poco; **shorts** *npl* (*also*: **a pair of shorts**) i calzoncini; **short-sighted** (*BRIT*) *adj* miope; **short-sleeved** [ˈʃɔːtsliːvd] *adj* a maniche corte; **short story** *n* racconto, novella; **short-tempered** *adj* irascibile;

short-term *adj* (*effect*) di *or* a breve durata; (*borrowing*) a breve scadenza

shot [ʃɔt] *pt, pp of* **shoot** ▷ *n* sparo, colpo; (*try*) prova; (*Football*) tiro; (*injection*) iniezione *f*; (*Phot*) foto *f inv*; **like a ~** come un razzo; (*very readily*) immediatamente; **shotgun** *n* fucile *m* da caccia

should [ʃud] *aux vb* **I ~ go now** dovrei andare ora; **he ~ be there now** dovrebbe essere arrivato ora; **I ~ go if I were you** se fossi in te andrei; **I ~ like to** mi piacerebbe

shoulder [ˈʃəuldəʳ] *n* spalla; (*BRIT*: *of road*): **hard ~** banchina ▷ *vt* (*fig*) addossarsi, prendere sulle proprie spalle; **shoulder blade** *n* scapola

shouldn't [ˈʃudnt] = **should not**

shout [ʃaut] *n* urlo, grido ▷ *vt* gridare ▷ *vi* (*also*: **~ out**) urlare, gridare

shove [ʃʌv] *vt* spingere; (*inf*: *put*): **to ~ sth in** ficcare qc in

shovel [ˈʃʌvl] *n* pala ▷ *vt* spalare

show [ʃəu] (*pt* **showed**, *pp* **shown**) *n* (*of emotion*) dimostrazione *f*, manifestazione *f*; (*semblance*) apparenza; (*exhibition*) mostra, esposizione *f*; (*Theatre, Cinema*) spettacolo ▷ *vt* far vedere, mostrare; (*courage etc*) dimostrare, dar prova di; (*exhibit*) esporre ▷ *vi* vedersi, essere visibile; **for ~** per fare scena; **on ~** (*exhibits etc*) esposto(-a); **can you ~ me where it is, please?** può mostrarmi dov'è, per favore?; **show in** *vt* (*person*) far entrare; **show off** *vi* (*pej*) esibirsi, mettersi in mostra ▷ *vt* (*display*) mettere in risalto; (*pej*) mettere in mostra; **show out** *vt* (*person*) accompagnare alla porta; **show up** *vi* (*stand out*) essere ben visibile; (*inf*: *turn up*) farsi vedere ▷ *vt* mettere in risalto; **show business** *n* industria dello spettacolo

shower [ˈʃauəʳ] *n* (*rain*) acquazzone *m*; (*of stones etc*) pioggia; (*also*: **~bath**) doccia ▷ *vi* fare la doccia ▷ *vt* **to ~ sb with** (*gifts, abuse etc*) coprire qn di; (*missiles*) lanciare contro qn una pioggia di; **to have a ~** fare la doccia; **shower cap** *n* cuffia da doccia; **shower gel** *n* gel *m* doccia *inv*

showing [ˈʃəuɪŋ] *n* (*of film*) proiezione *f*

show jumping *n* concorso ippico (di salto ad ostacoli)

shown [ʃəun] *pp of* **show**

show: **show-off** (*inf*) *n* (*person*) esibizionista *m/f*; **showroom** *n* sala d'esposizione

shrank [ʃræŋk] *pt of* **shrink**

shred [ʃrɛd] *n* (*gen pl*) brandello ▷ *vt* fare a brandelli; (*Culin*) sminuzzare, tagliuzzare

shrewd [ʃruːd] *adj* astuto(-a), scaltro(-a)

shriek [ʃriːk] *n* strillo ▷ *vi* strillare

shrimp [ʃrɪmp] *n* gamberetto

shrine [ʃraɪn] n reliquario; (place) santuario
shrink [ʃrɪŋk] (pt **shrank**, pp **shrunk**) vi restringersi; (fig) ridursi; (also: ~ **away**) ritrarsi ▷ vt (wool) far restringere ▷ n (inf: pej) psicanalista m/f; **to ~ from doing sth** rifuggire dal fare qc
shrivel ['ʃrɪvl] (also: ~ **up**) vt raggrinzare, avvizzire ▷ vi raggrinzirsi, avvizzire
shroud [ʃraʊd] n lenzuolo funebre ▷ vt **~ed in mystery** avvolto(-a) nel mistero
Shrove Tuesday ['ʃrəʊv-] n martedì m grasso
shrub [ʃrʌb] n arbusto
shrug [ʃrʌg] n scrollata di spalle ▷ vt, vi **to ~ (one's shoulders)** alzare le spalle, fare spallucce; **shrug off** vt passare sopra a
shrunk [ʃrʌŋk] pp of **shrink**
shudder ['ʃʌdəʳ] n brivido ▷ vi rabbrividire
shuffle ['ʃʌfl] vt (cards) mescolare; **to ~ (one's feet)** strascicare i piedi
shun [ʃʌn] vt sfuggire, evitare
shut [ʃʌt] (pt, pp **shut**) vt chiudere ▷ vi chiudersi, chiudere; **shut down** vt, vi chiudere definitivamente; **shut up** vi (inf: keep quiet) stare zitto(-a), fare silenzio ▷ vt (close) chiudere; (silence) far tacere; **shutter** n imposta; (Phot) otturatore m
shuttle ['ʃʌtl] n spola, navetta; (space shuttle) navetta (spaziale); (also: ~ **service**) servizio m navetta inv; **shuttlecock** ['ʃʌtlkɔk] n volano
shy [ʃaɪ] adj timido(-a)
sibling ['sɪblɪŋ] n (formal) fratello/sorella
Sicily ['sɪsɪlɪ] n Sicilia
sick [sɪk] adj (ill) malato(-a); (vomiting): **to be ~** vomitare; (humour) macabro(-a); **to feel ~** avere la nausea; **to be ~ of** (fig) averne abbastanza di; **sickening** adj (fig) disgustoso(-a), rivoltante; **sick leave** n congedo per malattia; **sickly** adj malaticcio(-a); (causing nausea) nauseante; **sickness** n malattia; (vomiting) vomito
side [saɪd] n lato; (of lake) riva; (team) squadra ▷ cpd (door, entrance) laterale ▷ vi **to ~ with sb** parteggiare per qn, prendere le parti di qn; **by the ~ of** a fianco di; (road) sul ciglio di; **~ by ~** fianco a fianco; **from ~ to ~** da una parte all'altra; **to take ~s (with)** schierarsi (con); **sideboard** n credenza; **sideboards** (BRIT), **sideburns** ['saɪdbə:nz] npl (whiskers) basette fpl; **sidelight** n (Aut) luce f di posizione; **sideline** n (Sport) linea laterale; (fig) attività secondaria; **side order** n contorno (pietanza); **side road** n strada secondaria; **side street** n traversa; **sidetrack** vt (fig) distrarre; **sidewalk** (US) n marciapiede m; **sideways** adv (move) di lato, di fianco

siege [si:dʒ] n assedio
sieve [sɪv] n setaccio ▷ vt setacciare
sift [sɪft] vt passare al crivello; (fig) vagliare
sigh [saɪ] n sospiro ▷ vi sospirare
sight [saɪt] n (faculty) vista; (spectacle) spettacolo; (on gun) mira ▷ vt avvistare; **in ~** in vista; **on ~** a vista; **out of ~** non visibile; **sightseeing** n giro turistico; **to go sightseeing** visitare una località
sign [saɪn] n segno; (with hand etc) segno, gesto; (notice) insegna, cartello ▷ vt firmare; (player) ingaggiare; **where do I ~?** dove devo firmare?; **sign for** vt fus (item) firmare per l'accettazione di; **sign in** vi firmare il registro (all'arrivo); **sign on** vi (Mil) arruolarsi; (as unemployed) iscriversi sulla lista (dell'ufficio di collocamento) ▷ vt (Mil) arruolare; (employee) assumere; **sign up** vi (Mil) arruolarsi; (for course) iscriversi ▷ vt (player) ingaggiare; (recruits) reclutare
signal ['sɪgnl] n segnale m ▷ vi (Aut) segnalare, mettere la freccia ▷ vt (person) fare segno a; (message) comunicare per mezzo di segnali
signature ['sɪgnətʃəʳ] n firma
significance [sɪg'nɪfɪkəns] n significato; importanza
significant [sɪg'nɪfɪkənt] adj significativo(-a)
signify ['sɪgnɪfaɪ] vt significare
sign language n linguaggio dei muti
signpost ['saɪnpəʊst] n cartello indicatore
Sikh [si:k] adj, n sikh (m/f) inv
silence ['saɪlns] n silenzio ▷ vt far tacere, ridurre al silenzio
silent ['saɪlnt] adj silenzioso(-a); (film) muto(-a); **to remain ~** tacere, stare zitto
silhouette [sɪlu:'ɛt] n silhouette f inv
silicon chip ['sɪlɪkən-] n piastrina di silicio
silk [sɪlk] n seta ▷ adj di seta
silly ['sɪlɪ] adj stupido(-a), sciocco(-a)
silver ['sɪlvəʳ] n argento; (money) monete da 5, 10, 20 or 50 pence; (also: ~**ware**) argenteria ▷ adj d'argento; **silver-plated** adj argentato(-a)
similar ['sɪmɪləʳ] adj **~ (to)** simile (a); **similarity** [sɪmɪ'lærɪtɪ] n somiglianza, rassomiglianza; **similarly** adv allo stesso modo; così pure
simmer ['sɪməʳ] vi cuocere a fuoco lento
simple ['sɪmpl] adj semplice; **simplicity** [-'plɪsɪtɪ] n semplicità; **simplify** vt semplificare; **simply** adv semplicemente
simulate ['sɪmjuleɪt] vt fingere, simulare
simultaneous [sɪməl'teɪnɪəs] adj simultaneo(-a); **simultaneously** adv simultaneamente, contemporaneamente
sin [sɪn] n peccato ▷ vi peccare
since [sɪns] adv da allora ▷ prep da ▷ conj

(*time*) da quando; (*because*) poiché, dato che; **~ then, ever ~** da allora

sincere [sɪnˈsɪəʳ] *adj* sincero(-a); **sincerely** *adv* **yours sincerely** (*in letters*) distinti saluti

sing [sɪŋ] (*pt* **sang**, *pp* **sung**) *vt*, *vi* cantare

Singapore [sɪŋgəˈpɔːʳ] *n* Singapore *f*

singer [ˈsɪŋəʳ] *n* cantante *m/f*

singing [ˈsɪŋɪŋ] *n* canto

single [ˈsɪŋgl] *adj* solo(-a), unico(-a); (*unmarried: man*) celibe; (: *woman*) nubile; (*not double*) semplice ▷ *n* (BRIT: *also:* **~ ticket**) biglietto de (sola) andata; (*record*) 45 giri *m*; **~s** *n* (*Tennis*) singolo; **single out** *vt* scegliere; (*distinguish*) distinguere; **single bed** *n* letto singolo; **single file** *n* **in single file** in fila indiana; **single-handed** *adv* senza aiuto, da solo(-a); **single-minded** *adj* tenace, risoluto(-a); **single parent** *n* (*mother*) ragazza *f* madre *inv*; (*father*) ragazzo *m* padre *inv*; **single-parent family** famiglia monoparentale; **single room** *n* camera singola

singular [ˈsɪŋgjuləʳ] *adj* (*exceptional*, Ling) singolare ▷ *n* (*Ling*) singolare *m*

sinister [ˈsɪnɪstəʳ] *adj* sinistro(-a)

sink [sɪŋk] (*pt* **sank**, *pp* **sunk**) *n* lavandino, acquaio ▷ *vt* (*ship*) (fare) affondare, colare a picco; (*foundations*) scavare; (*piles etc*): **to ~ sth into** conficcare qc in ▷ *vi* affondare, andare a fondo; (*ground etc*) cedere, avvallarsi; **my heart sank** mi sentii venir meno; **sink in** *vi* penetrare

sinus [ˈsaɪnəs] *n* (*Anat*) seno

sip [sɪp] *n* sorso ▷ *vt* sorseggiare

sir [səʳ] *n* signore *m*; **S~ John Smith** Sir John Smith; **yes ~** sì, signore

siren [ˈsaɪərn] *n* sirena

sirloin [ˈsəːlɔɪn] *n* controfiletto

sister [ˈsɪstəʳ] *n* sorella; (*nun*) suora; (BRIT: *nurse*) infermiera *f* caposala *inv*; **sister-in-law** *n* cognata

sit [sɪt] (*pt*, *pp* **sat**) *vi* sedere, sedersi; (*assembly*) essere in seduta; (*for painter*) posare ▷ *vt* (*exam*) sostenere, dare; **sit back** *vi* (*in seat*) appoggiarsi allo schienale; **sit down** *vi* sedersi; **sit on** *vt fus* (*jury*, *committee*) far parte di; **sit up** *vi* tirarsi su a sedere; (*not go to bed*) stare alzato(-a) fino a tardi

sitcom [ˈsɪtkɔm] *n abbr* (= *situation comedy*) commedia di situazione; (*TV*) telefilm *m inv* comico d'interni

site [saɪt] *n* posto; (*also:* **building ~**) cantiere *m* ▷ *vt* situare

sitting [ˈsɪtɪŋ] *n* (*of assembly etc*) seduta; (*in canteen*) turno; **sitting room** *n* soggiorno

situated [ˈsɪtjueɪtɪd] *adj* situato(-a)

situation [sɪtjuˈeɪʃən] *n* situazione *f*; (*job*) lavoro; (*location*) posizione *f*; **"~s vacant"** (BRIT) "offerte *fpl* di impiego"

six [sɪks] *num* sei; **sixteen** *num* sedici; **sixteenth** [sɪksˈtiːnθ] *num* sedicesimo(-a); **sixth** *num* sesto(-a); **sixth form** *n* (BRIT) ultimo biennio delle scuole superiori; **sixth-form college** *n* istituto che offre corsi di preparazione all'esame di maturità per ragazzi dai 16 ai 18 anni; **sixtieth** [ˈsɪkstɪɪθ] *num* sessantesimo(-a) ▷ *pron* (*in series*) sessantesimo(-a); (*fraction*) sessantesimo; **sixty** *num* sessanta

size [saɪz] *n* dimensioni *fpl*; (*of clothing*) taglia, misura; (*of shoes*) numero; (*glue*) colla; **sizeable** *adj* considerevole

sizzle [ˈsɪzl] *vi* sfrigolare

skate [skeɪt] *n* pattino; (*fish: pl inv*) razza ▷ *vi* pattinare; **skateboard** *n* skateboard *m inv*; **skateboarding** *n* skateboard *m inv*; **skater** *n* pattinatore(-trice); **skating** *n* pattinaggio; **skating rink** *n* pista di pattinaggio

skeleton [ˈskɛlɪtn] *n* scheletro

skeptical [ˈskɛptɪkl] (US) *adj* = **sceptical**

sketch [skɛtʃ] *n* (*drawing*) schizzo, abbozzo; (*Theatre*) scenetta comica, sketch *m inv* ▷ *vt* abbozzare, schizzare

skewer [ˈskjuːəʳ] *n* spiedo

ski [skiː] *n* sci *m inv* ▷ *vi* sciare; **ski boot** *n* scarpone *m* da sci

skid [skɪd] *n* slittamento ▷ *vi* slittare

ski: **skier** [ˈskiːəʳ] *n* sciatore(-trice); **skiing** [ˈskiːɪŋ] *n* sci *m*

skilful [ˈskɪlful] (US **skillful**) *adj* abile

ski lift *n* sciovia

skill [skɪl] *n* abilità *f inv*, capacità *f inv*; **skilled** *adj* esperto(-a); (*worker*) qualificato(-a), specializzato(-a)

skim [skɪm] *vt* (*milk*) scremare; (*glide over*) sfiorare ▷ *vi* **to ~ through** (*fig*) scorrere, dare una scorsa a; **skimmed milk** (US **skim milk**) *n* latte *m* scremato

skin [skɪn] *n* pelle *f* ▷ *vt* (*fruit etc*) sbucciare; (*animal*) scuoiare, spellare; **skinhead** *n* skinhead *m/f inv*; **skinny** *adj* molto magro(-a), pelle e ossa *inv*

skip [skɪp] *n* saltello, balzo; (BRIT: *container*) benna ▷ *vi* saltare; (*with rope*) saltare la corda ▷ *vt* saltare

ski: **ski pass** *n* ski pass *m*; **ski pole** *n* racchetta (da sci)

skipper [ˈskɪpəʳ] *n* (*Naut*, *Sport*) capitano

skipping rope [ˈskɪpɪŋ-] (US **skip rope**) *n* corda per saltare

skirt [skəːt] *n* gonna, sottana ▷ *vt* fiancheggiare, costeggiare

skirting board (BRIT) *n* zoccolo

ski slope *n* pista da sci

ski suit *n* tuta da sci

skull [skʌl] n cranio, teschio

skunk [skʌŋk] n moffetta

sky [skaɪ] n cielo; **skyscraper** n grattacielo

slab [slæb] n lastra; (of cake, cheese) fetta

slack [slæk] adj (loose) allentato(-a); (slow) lento(-a); (careless) negligente; **slacks** npl (trousers) pantaloni mpl

slain [sleɪn] pp of **slay**

slam [slæm] vt (door) sbattere; (throw) scaraventare; (criticize) stroncare ▷ vi sbattere

slander ['slɑːndər] n calunnia; diffamazione f

slang [slæŋ] n gergo, slang m

slant [slɑːnt] n pendenza, inclinazione f; (fig) angolatura f, punto di vista

slap [slæp] n manata, pacca; (on face) schiaffo ▷ vt dare una manata a; schiaffeggiare ▷ adv (directly) in pieno; **~ a coat of paint on it** dagli una mano di vernice

slash [slæʃ] vt tagliare; (face) sfregiare; (fig: prices) ridurre drasticamente, tagliare

slate [sleɪt] n ardesia; (piece) lastra di ardesia ▷ vt (fig: criticize) stroncare, distruggere

slaughter ['slɔːtər] n strage f, massacro ▷ vt (animal) macellare; (people) trucidare, massacrare; **slaughterhouse** n macello, mattatoio

Slav [slɑːv] adj, n slavo(-a)

slave [sleɪv] n schiavo(-a) ▷ vi (also: **~ away**) lavorare come uno schiavo; **slavery** n schiavitù f

slay [sleɪ] (pt **slew**, pp **slain**) vt (formal) uccidere

sleazy ['sliːzɪ] adj trasandato(-a)

sled [slɛd] (US) = **sledge**

sledge [slɛdʒ] n slitta

sleek [sliːk] adj (hair, fur) lucido(-a), lucente; (car, boat) slanciato(-a), affusolato(-a)

sleep [sliːp] (pt, pp **slept**) n sonno ▷ vi dormire; **to go to ~** addormentarsi; **sleep in** vi (oversleep) dormire fino a tardi; **sleep together** vi (have sex) andare a letto insieme; **sleeper** (BRIT) n (Rail: on track) traversina; (: train) treno di vagoni letto; **sleeping bag** n sacco a pelo; **sleeping car** n vagone m letto inv, carrozza f letto inv; **sleeping pill** n sonnifero; **sleepover** n notte f che un ragazzino passa da amici; **sleepwalk** vi camminare nel sonno; (as a habit) essere sonnambulo(-a); **sleepy** adj assonnato(-a), sonnolento(-a); (fig) addormentato(-a)

sleet [sliːt] n nevischio

sleeve [sliːv] n manica; (of record) copertina; **sleeveless** adj (garment) senza maniche

sleigh [sleɪ] n slitta

slender ['slɛndər] adj snello(-a), sottile; (not enough) scarso(-a), esiguo(-a)

slept [slɛpt] pt, pp of **sleep**

slew [sluː] pt of **slay** ▷ vi (BRIT) girare

slice [slaɪs] n fetta ▷ vt affettare, tagliare a fette

slick [slɪk] adj (skilful) brillante; (clever) furbo(-a) ▷ n (also: **oil ~**) chiazza di petrolio

slide [slaɪd] (pt, pp **slid**) n scivolone m; (in playground) scivolo; (Phot) diapositiva; (BRIT: also: **hair ~**) fermaglio (per capelli) ▷ vt far scivolare ▷ vi scivolare; **sliding** adj (door) scorrevole

slight [slaɪt] adj (slim) snello(-a), sottile; (frail) delicato(-a), fragile; (trivial) insignificante; (small) piccolo(-a) ▷ n offesa, affronto; **not in the ~est** affatto, neppure per sogno; **slightly** adv lievemente, un po'

slim [slɪm] adj magro(-a), snello(-a) ▷ vi dimagrire; fare (or seguire) una dieta dimagrante; **slimming** ['slɪmɪŋ] adj (diet) dimagrante; (food) ipocalorico(-a)

slimy ['slaɪmɪ] adj (also fig: person) viscido(-a), (covered with mud) melmoso(-a)

sling [slɪŋ] (pt, pp **slung**) n (Med) fascia al collo; (for baby) marsupio ▷ vt lanciare, tirare

slip [slɪp] n scivolata, scivolone m; (mistake) errore m, sbaglio; (underskirt) sottoveste f; (of paper) striscia di carta; tagliando, scontrino ▷ vt (slide) far scivolare ▷ vi (slide) scivolare; (move smoothly): **to ~ into/out of** scivolare in/fuori da; (decline) declinare; **to ~ sth on/off** infilarsi/ togliersi qc; **to give sb the ~** sfuggire qn; **a ~ of the tongue** un lapsus linguae; **slip up** vi sbagliarsi

slipper ['slɪpər] n pantofola

slippery ['slɪpərɪ] adj scivoloso(-a)

slip road (BRIT) n (to motorway) rampa di accesso

slit [slɪt] (pt, pp **slit**) n fessura, fenditura; (cut) taglio ▷ vt fendere; tagliare

slog [slɔg] (BRIT) n faticata ▷ vi lavorare con accanimento, sgobbare

slogan ['sləʊgən] n motto, slogan m inv

slope [sləʊp] n pendio; (side of mountain) versante m; (ski slope) pista; (of roof) pendenza; (of floor) inclinazione f ▷ vi **to ~ down** declinare; **to ~ up** essere in salita; **sloping** adj inclinato(-a)

sloppy ['slɔpɪ] adj (work) tirato(-a) via; (appearance) sciatto(-a)

slot [slɔt] n fessura ▷ vt **to ~ sth into** infilare qc in; **slot machine** n

(BRIT: *vending machine*) distributore *m*
automatico; (*for gambling*) slot-machine
f inv

Slovakia [sləʊ'vækɪə] *n* Slovacchia
Slovene ['sləʊviːn] *adj* sloveno(-a) ▷ *n*
sloveno(-a); (*Ling*) sloveno
Slovenia [sləʊ'viːnɪə] *n* Slovenia;
Slovenian *adj, n* = **Slovene**
slow [sləʊ] *adj* lento(-a); (*watch*): **to be ~**
essere indietro ▷ *adv* lentamente ▷ *vt, vi*
(*also:* **~ down, ~ up**) rallentare; **"~"** (*road
sign*) "rallentare"; **slow down** *vi* rallentare;
slowly *adv* lentamente; **slow motion** *n*
in slow motion al rallentatore

slug [slʌɡ] *n* lumaca; (*bullet*) pallottola;
sluggish *adj* lento(-a); (*trading*) stagnante
slum [slʌm] *n* catapecchia
slump [slʌmp] *n* crollo, caduta; (*economic*)
depressione *f*, crisi *f inv* ▷ *vi* crollare
slung [slʌŋ] *pt, pp of* **sling**
slur [sləːʳ] *n* (*fig*): **~ (on)** calunnia (su) ▷ *vt*
pronunciare in modo indistinto
sly [slaɪ] *adj* (*smile, remark*) sornione(-a);
(*person*) furbo(-a)
smack [smæk] *n* (*slap*) pacca; (*on face*)
schiaffo ▷ *vt* schiaffeggiare; (*child*)
picchiare ▷ *vi* **to ~ of** puzzare di
small [smɔːl] *adj* piccolo(-a); **small ads**
(BRIT) *npl* piccola pubblicità; **small
change** *n* moneta, spiccioli *mpl*
smart [smɑːt] *adj* elegante; (*fashionable*)
alla moda; (*clever*) intelligente; (*quick*)
sveglio(-a) ▷ *vi* bruciare; **smartcard**
['smɑːtkɑːd] *n* smartcard *f inv*, carta
intelligente
smash [smæʃ] *n* (*also:* **~-up**) scontro,
collisione *f*; (*smash hit*) successone *m* ▷ *vt*
frantumare, fracassare; (*Sport: record*)
battere ▷ *vi* frantumarsi, andare in
pezzi; **smashing** (*inf*) *adj* favoloso(-a),
formidabile
smear [smɪəʳ] *n* macchia; (*Med*) striscio
▷ *vt* spalmare; (*make dirty*) sporcare;
smear test *n* (BRIT *Med*) Pap-test *m inv*
smell [smɛl] (*pt smelt or smelled*) *n* odore
m; (*sense*) olfatto, odorato ▷ *vt* sentire
(l')odore di ▷ *vi* (*food etc*): **to ~ (of)** avere
odore (di); (*pej*) puzzare, avere un cattivo
odore; **smelly** *adj* puzzolente
smelt [smɛlt] *pt, pp of* **smell** ▷ *vt* (*ore*)
fondere
smile [smaɪl] *n* sorriso ▷ *vi* sorridere
smirk [sməːk] *n* sorriso furbo; sorriso
compiaciuto
smog [smɔɡ] *n* smog *m*
smoke [sməʊk] *n* fumo ▷ *vt, vi* fumare;
do you mind if I ~? le dà fastidio se fumo?;
smoke alarm *n* rivelatore *f* di fumo;
smoked *adj* (*bacon, glass*) affumicato(-a);

smoker *n* (*person*) fumatore(-trice);
(*Rail*) carrozza per fumatori; **smoking**
n fumo; **"no smoking"** (*sign*) "vietato
fumare"; **smoky** *adj* fumoso(-a); (*taste*)
affumicato(-a)
smooth [smuːð] *adj* liscio(-a); (*sauce*)
omogeneo(-a); (*flavour, whisky*) amabile;
(*movement*) regolare; (*person*) mellifluo(-a)
▷ *vt* (*also:* **~ out**) lisciare, spianare; (:
difficulties) appianare
smother ['smʌðəʳ] *vt* soffocare
SMS *abbr* (= *short message service*) SMS; **SMS
message** *n* SMS *m inv*, messaggino
smudge [smʌdʒ] *n* macchia; sbavatura
▷ *vt* imbrattare, sporcare
smug [smʌɡ] *adj* soddisfatto(-a),
compiaciuto(-a)
smuggle ['smʌɡl] *vt* contrabbandare;
smuggling *n* contrabbando
snack [snæk] *n* spuntino; **snack bar** *n*
tavola calda, snack bar *m inv*
snag [snæɡ] *n* intoppo, ostacolo
imprevisto
snail [sneɪl] *n* chiocciola
snake [sneɪk] *n* serpente *m*
snap [snæp] *n* (*sound*) schianto, colpo
secco; (*photograph*) istantanea ▷ *adj*
improvviso(-a) ▷ *vt* (far) schioccare; (*break*)
spezzare di netto ▷ *vi* spezzarsi con un
rumore secco; (*fig: person*) parlare con tono
secco; **to ~ shut** chiudersi di scatto; **snap
at** *vt fus* (*dog*) cercare di mordere; **snap up**
vt afferrare; **snapshot** *n* istantanea
snarl [snɑːl] *vi* ringhiare
snatch [snætʃ] *n* (*small amount*)
frammento ▷ *vt* strappare (con violenza);
(*fig*) rubare
sneak [sniːk] (*pt* (US) **snuck**) *vi* **to ~ in/out**
entrare/uscire di nascosto ▷ *n* spione(-a);
to ~ up on sb avvicinarsi quatto quatto a
qn; **sneakers** *npl* scarpe *fpl* da ginnastica
sneer [snɪəʳ] *vi* sogghignare; **to ~ at** farsi
beffe di
sneeze [sniːz] *n* starnuto ▷ *vi* starnutire
sniff [snɪf] *n* fiutata, annusata ▷ *vi* tirare
su col naso ▷ *vt* fiutare, annusare
snigger ['snɪɡəʳ] *vi* ridacchiare, ridere
sotto i baffi
snip [snɪp] *n* pezzetto; (*bargain*) (buon)
affare *m*, occasione *f* ▷ *vt* tagliare
sniper ['snaɪpəʳ] *n* (*marksman*) franco
tiratore *m*, cecchino
snob [snɔb] *n* snob *m/f inv*
snooker ['snuːkəʳ] *n* tipo di gioco del biliardo
snoop ['snuːp] *vi* **to ~ about** curiosare
snooze [snuːz] *n* sonnellino, pisolino ▷ *vi*
fare un sonnellino
snore [snɔːʳ] *vi* russare
snorkel ['snɔːkl] *n* (*of swimmer*) respiratore

m a tubo

snort [snɔːt] *n* sbuffo ▷ *vi* sbuffare

snow [snəu] *n* neve *f* ▷ *vi* nevicare;
snowball *n* palla di neve ▷ *vi* (*fig*) crescere
a vista d'occhio; **snowstorm** *n* tormenta

snub [snʌb] *vt* snobbare ▷ *n* offesa,
affronto

snug [snʌg] *adj* comodo(-a); (*room, house*)
accogliente, comodo(-a)

 KEYWORD

so [səu] *adv* **1** (*thus, likewise*) così; **if so** se è
così, quand'è così; **I didn't do it — you did
so!** non l'ho fatto io — sì che l'hai fatto!;
so do I, so am I *etc* anch'io; **it's 5 o'clock
— so it is!** sono le 5 — davvero!; **I hope
so** lo spero; **I think so** penso di sì; **so far**
finora, fin qui; (*in past*) fino ad allora
2 (*in comparisons etc: to such a degree*) così;
so big (that) così grande (che); **she's not
so clever as her brother** lei non è (così)
intelligente come suo fratello
3: **so much** *adj* tanto(-a)
▷ *adv* tanto; **I've got so much work/
money** ho tanto lavoro/tanti soldi; **I love
you so much** ti amo tanto; **so many**
tanti(-e)
4 (*phrases*): **10 or so** circa 10; **so long!** (*inf:
goodbye*) ciao!, ci vediamo!
▷ *conj* **1** (*expressing purpose*): **so as to do**
in modo *or* così da fare; **we hurried so as
not to be late** ci affrettammo per non fare
tardi; **so (that)** affinché + *sub*, perché + *sub*
2 (*expressing result*): **he didn't arrive so I
left** non è venuto così me ne sono andata;
so you see, I could have gone vedi, sarei
potuto andare

soak [səuk] *vt* inzuppare; (*clothes*) mettere
a mollo ▷ *vi* (*clothes etc*) essere a mollo;
soak up *vt* assorbire; **soaking** *adj* (*also:*
soaking wet) fradicio(-a)

so-and-so ['səuənsəu] *n* (*somebody*) un
tale; **Mr/Mrs ~** signor/signora tal dei tali

soap [səup] *n* sapone *m*; **soap opera** *n*
soap opera *f inv*; **soap powder** *n* detersivo

soar [sɔːʳ] *vi* volare in alto; (*price etc*) salire
alle stelle; (*building*) ergersi

sob [sɔb] *n* singhiozzo ▷ *vi* singhiozzare

sober ['səubəʳ] *adj* sobrio(-a); (*not drunk*)
non ubriaco(-a); (*moderate*) moderato(-a);
sober up *vt* far passare la sbornia a ▷ *vi*
farsi passare la sbornia

so-called ['səu'kɔːld] *adj* cosiddetto(-a)

soccer ['sɔkəʳ] *n* calcio

sociable ['səuʃəbl] *adj* socievole

social ['səuʃl] *adj* sociale ▷ *n* festa, serata;
socialism *n* socialismo; **socialist** *adj, n*

socialista *m/f*; **socialize** *vi* **to socialize
(with)** socializzare (con); **social life** *n*
vita sociale; **socially** *adv* socialmente,
in società; **social security** (*BRIT*) *n*
previdenza sociale; **social services** *npl*
servizi *mpl* sociali; **social work** *n* servizio
sociale; **social worker** *n* assistente *m/f*
sociale

society [sə'saɪətɪ] *n* società *f inv*; (*club*)
società, associazione *f*; (*also:* **high ~**) alta
società

sociology [səusɪ'ɔlədʒɪ] *n* sociologia

sock [sɔk] *n* calzino

socket ['sɔkɪt] *n* cavità *f inv*; (*of eye*) orbita;
(*BRIT: Elec: also:* **wall ~**) presa di corrente

soda ['səudə] *n* (*Chem*) soda; (*also:* **~
water**) acqua di seltz; (*US: also:* **~ pop**)
gassosa

sodium ['səudɪəm] *n* sodio

sofa ['səufə] *n* sofà *m inv*; **sofa bed** *n*
divano *m* letto *inv*

soft [sɔft] *adj* (*not rough*) morbido(-a); (*not
hard*) soffice; (*not loud*) sommesso(-a); (*not
bright*) tenue; (*kind*) gentile; **soft drink**
n analcolico; **soft drugs** *npl* droghe *fpl*
leggere; **soften** ['sɔfn] *vt* ammorbidire;
addolcire; attenuare ▷ *vi* ammorbidirsi;
addolcirsi; attenuarsi; **softly** *adv*
dolcemente; morbidamente; **software**
['sɔftwɛəʳ] *n* (*Comput*) software *m*

soggy ['sɔgɪ] *adj* inzuppato(-a)

soil [sɔɪl] *n* terreno ▷ *vt* sporcare

solar ['səuləʳ] *adj* solare; **solar power** *n*
energie solare; **solar system** *n* sistema
m solare

sold [səuld] *pt, pp of* **sell**

soldier ['səuldʒəʳ] *n* soldato, militare *m*

sold out *adj* (*Comm*) esaurito(-a)

sole [səul] *n* (*of foot*) pianta (del piede);
(*of shoe*) suola; (*fish: pl* **sole**) sogliola
▷ *adj* solo(-a), unico(-a); **solely** *adv*
solamente, unicamente; **I will hold you
solely responsible** la considererò il solo
responsabile

solemn ['sɔləm] *adj* solenne

solicitor [sə'lɪsɪtəʳ] (*BRIT*) *n* (*for wills etc*)
≈ notaio; (*in court*) ≈ avvocato

solid ['sɔlɪd] *adj* solido(-a); (*not hollow*)
pieno(-a); (*meal*) sostanzioso(-a) ▷ *n*
solido

solitary ['sɔlɪtərɪ] *adj* solitario(-a)

solitude ['sɔlɪtjuːd] *n* solitudine *f*

solo ['səuləu] *n* assolo; **soloist** *n* solista
m/f

soluble ['sɔljubl] *adj* solubile

solution [sə'luːʃən] *n* soluzione *f*

solve [sɔlv] *vt* risolvere

solvent ['sɔlvənt] *adj* (*Comm*) solvibile ▷ *n*
(*Chem*) solvente *m*

s

sombre ['sɔmbə'] (*us* **somber**) *adj*
scuro(-a); (*mood, person*) triste

 KEYWORD

some [sʌm] *adj* **1** (*a certain amount or number
of*): **some tea/water/cream** del tè/
dell'acqua/della panna; **some children/
apples** dei bambini/delle mele
2 (*certain: in contrasts*) certo(-a); **some
people say that ...** alcuni dicono che ...,
certa gente dice che ...
3 (*unspecified*) un(a) certo(-a), qualche;
some woman was asking for you una
tale chiedeva di lei; **some day** un giorno,
some day next week un giorno della
prossima settimana
 ▷ *pron* **1** (*a certain number*) alcuni(-e),
certi(-e); **I've got some** (*books etc*) ne ho
alcuni; **some (of them) have been sold**
alcuni sono stati venduti
2 (*a certain amount*) un po'; **I've got some**
(*money, milk*) ne ho un po'; **I've read some
of the book** ho letto parte del libro
 ▷ *adv* **some 10 people** circa 10 persone

some: **somebody** ['sʌmbədɪ] *pron*
= **someone**; **somehow** ['sʌmhau] *adv*
in un modo o nell'altro, in qualche modo;
(*for some reason*) per qualche ragione;
someone ['sʌmwʌn] *pron* qualcuno;
someplace ['sʌmpleɪs] (*us*) *adv*
= **somewhere**; **something** ['sʌmθɪŋ]
pron qualcosa, qualche cosa; **something
nice** qualcosa di bello; **something to do**
qualcosa da fare; **sometime** ['sʌmtaɪm]
adv (*in future*) una volta o l'altra; (*in past*):
sometime last month durante il mese
scorso; **sometimes** ['sʌmtaɪmz] *adv*
qualche volta; **somewhat** ['sʌmwɔt] *adv*
piuttosto; **somewhere** ['sʌmwɛə'] *adv* in
or da qualche parte
son [sʌn] *n* figlio
song [sɔŋ] *n* canzone *f*
son-in-law ['sʌnɪnlɔ:] *n* genero
soon [su:n] *adv* presto, fra poco; (*early, a
short time after*) presto; **~ afterwards** poco
dopo; *see also* **as**; **sooner** *adv* (*time*) prima;
(*preference*): **I would sooner do** preferirei
fare; **sooner or later** prima o poi
soothe [su:ð] *vt* calmare
sophisticated [sə'fɪstɪkeɪtɪd]
adj sofisticato(-a); raffinato(-a);
complesso(-a)
sophomore ['sɔfəmɔː'] (*us*) *n*
studente(-essa) del secondo anno
soprano [sə'prɑːnəu] *n* (*voice*) soprano *m*;
(*singer*) soprano *m/f*
sorbet ['sɔːbeɪ] *n* sorbetto

sordid ['sɔːdɪd] *adj* sordido(-a)
sore [sɔː'] *adj* (*painful*) dolorante ▷ *n* piaga
sorrow ['sɔrəu] *n* dolore *m*
sorry ['sɔrɪ] *adj* spiacente; (*condition,
excuse*) misero(-a); **~!** scusa! (*or* scusi! *or*
scusate!); **to feel ~ for sb** rincrescersi
per qn
sort [sɔːt] *n* specie *f*, genere *m*; **sort out** *vt*
(*papers*) classificare; ordinare; (*: letters etc*)
smistare; (*: problems*) risolvere; (*Comput*)
ordinare
SOS *n abbr* (= *save our souls*) S.O.S. *m inv*
so-so ['səusəu] *adv* così così
sought [sɔːt] *pt, pp of* **seek**
soul [səul] *n* anima
sound [saund] *adj* (*healthy*) sano(-a); (*safe,
not damaged*) solido(-a), in buono stato;
(*reliable, not superficial*) solido(-a); (*sensible*)
giudizioso(-a), di buon senso ▷ *adv* **~
asleep** profondamente addormentato
 ▷ *n* suono; (*noise*) rumore *m*; (*Geo*) stretto
 ▷ *vt* (*alarm*) suonare ▷ *vi* suonare; (*fig:
seem*) sembrare; **to ~ like** rassomigliare a;
soundtrack *n* (*of film*) colonna sonora
soup [su:p] *n* minestra; brodo; zuppa
sour ['sauə'] *adj* aspro(-a); (*fruit*)
acerbo(-a); (*milk*) acido(-a); (*fig*)
arcigno(-a); acido(-a); **it's ~ grapes** è
soltanto invidia
source [sɔːs] *n* fonte *f*, sorgente *f*; (*fig*)
fonte
south [sauθ] *n* sud *m*, meridione *m*,
mezzogiorno ▷ *adj* del sud, sud *inv*,
meridionale ▷ *adv* verso sud; **South
Africa** *n* Sudafrica *m*; **South African**
adj, n sudafricano(-a); **South America** *n*
Sudamerica *m*, America del sud; **South
American** *adj, n* sudamericano(-a);
southbound ['sauθbaund] *adj* (*gen*)
diretto(-a) a sud; (*carriageway*) sud
inv; **southeastern** [sauθ'i:stən] *adj*
sudorientale; **southern** ['sʌðən] *adj*
del sud, meridionale; esposto(-a) a sud;
South Korea *n* Corea *f* del Sud; **South
Pole** *n* Polo Sud; **southward(s)** *adv*
verso sud; **south-west** *n* sud-ovest
m; **southwestern** [sauθ'westən] *adj*
sudoccidentale
souvenir [su:və'nɪə'] *n* ricordo, souvenir
m inv
sovereign ['sɔvrɪn] *adj, n* sovrano(-a)
sow¹ [səu] (*pt* **sowed**, *pp* **sown**) *vt*
seminare
sow² [sau] *n* scrofa
soya ['sɔɪə] (*us* **soy**) *n* **~ bean** *n* seme *m* di
soia; **soya sauce** *n* salsa di soia
spa [spɑː] *n* (*resort*) stazione *f* termale; (*us:
also*: **health ~**) centro di cure estetiche
space [speɪs] *n* spazio; (*room*) posto;

spazio; (*length of time*) intervallo ▷ *cpd*
spaziale ▷ *vt* (*also*: **~ out**) distanziare;
spacecraft *n inv* veicolo spaziale;
spaceship *n* = **spacecraft**
spacious ['speɪʃəs] *adj* spazioso(-a),
ampio(-a)
spade [speɪd] *n* (*tool*) vanga; pala; (*child's*)
paletta; **~s** *npl* (*Cards*) picche *fpl*
spaghetti [spə'gɛtɪ] *n* spaghetti *mpl*
Spain [speɪn] *n* Spagna
spam [spæm] (*Comput*) *n* spamming ▷ *vt*
to ~ sb inviare a qn messaggi pubblicitari
non richiesti via email
span [spæn] *n* (*of bird, plane*) apertura
alare; (*of arch*) campata; (*in time*) periodo;
durata ▷ *vt* attraversare; (*fig*) abbracciare
Spaniard ['spænjəd] *n* spagnolo(-a)
Spanish ['spænɪʃ] *adj* spagnolo(-a) ▷ *n*
(*Ling*) spagnolo, **the ~** *npl* gli Spagnoli
spank [spæŋk] *vt* sculacciare
spanner ['spænə'] (*BRIT*) *n* chiave *f* inglese
spare [spɛə'] *adj* di riserva, di scorta;
(*surplus*) in più, d'avanzo ▷ *n* (*part*) pezzo
di ricambio ▷ *vt* (*do without*) fare a meno
di; (*afford to give*) concedere; (*refrain from
hurting, using*) risparmiare; **to ~** (*surplus*)
d'avanzo; **spare part** *n* pezzo di ricambio;
spare room *n* stanza degli ospiti; **spare
time** *n* tempo libero; **spare tyre** (*US* **spare
tire**) *n* (*Aut*) gomma di scorta; **spare
wheel** *n* (*Aut*) ruota di scorta
spark [spɑːk] *n* scintilla; **spark(ing) plug**
n candela
sparkle ['spɑːkl] *n* scintillio, sfavillio ▷ *vi*
scintillare, sfavillare
sparrow ['spærəʊ] *n* passero
sparse [spɑːs] *adj* sparso(-a), rado(-a)
spasm ['spæzəm] *n* (*Med*) spasmo; (*fig*)
accesso, attacco
spat [spæt] *pt, pp of* **spit**
spate [speɪt] *n* (*fig*): **~ of** diluvio *or* fiume
m di
spatula ['spætjʊlə] *n* spatola
speak [spiːk] (*pt* **spoke**, *pp* **spoken**) *vt*
(*language*) parlare; (*truth*) dire ▷ *vi* parlare;
I don't ~ Italian non parlo italiano; **do you
~ English?** parla inglese?; **to ~ to sb/of** *or*
about sth parlare a qn/di qc; **can I ~ to ...?**
posso parlare con...?; **~ up!** parla più forte!;
speaker *n* (*in public*) oratore(-trice);
(*also*: **loudspeaker**) altoparlante *m*; (*Pol*):
the Speaker *il presidente della Camera dei
Comuni* (*BRIT*) *or dei Rappresentanti* (*US*)
spear [spɪə'] *n* lancia ▷ *vt* infilzare
special ['spɛʃl] *adj* speciale; **special
delivery** *n* (*Post*): **by special delivery**
per espresso; **special effects** *npl*
(*Cine*) effetti *mpl* speciali; **specialist** *n*
specialista *m/f*; **speciality** [spɛʃɪ'ælɪtɪ]

n specialità *f inv*; **I'd like to try a local
speciality** vorrei assaggiare una specialità
del posto; **specialize** *vi* **to specialize
(in)** specializzarsi (in); **specially** *adv*
specialmente, particolarmente;
special needs *adj* **special needs
children** bambini *mpl* con difficoltà di
apprendimento; **special offer** *n* (*Comm*)
offerta speciale; **special school** *n* (*BRIT*)
scuola speciale (*per portatori di handicap*);
specialty (*US*) = **speciality**
species ['spiːʃiːz] *n inv* specie *f inv*
specific [spə'sɪfɪk] *adj* specifico(-a);
preciso(-a); **specifically** *adv*
esplicitamente; (*especially*) appositamente
specify ['spɛsɪfaɪ] *vt* specificare, precisare;
unless otherwise specified salvo
indicazioni contrarie
specimen ['spɛsɪmən] *n* esemplare *m*,
modello; (*Med*) campione *m*
speck [spɛk] *n* puntino, macchiolina;
(*particle*) granello
spectacle ['spɛktəkl] *n* spettacolo; **~s**
npl (*glasses*) occhiali *mpl*; **spectacular**
[-'tækjʊlə'] *adj* spettacolare
spectator [spɛk'teɪtə'] *n* spettatore *m*
spectrum ['spɛktrəm] (*pl* **spectra**) *n*
spettro
speculate ['spɛkjʊleɪt] *vi* speculare; (*try to
guess*): **to ~ about** fare ipotesi su
sped [spɛd] *pt, pp of* **speed**
speech [spiːtʃ] *n* (*faculty*) parola; (*talk,
Theatre*) discorso; (*manner of speaking*)
parlata; **speechless** *adj* ammutolito(-a),
muto(-a)
speed [spiːd] *n* velocità *f inv*; (*promptness*)
prontezza; **at full** *or* **top ~** a tutta velocità;
speed up *vi, vt* accelerare; **speedboat** *n*
motoscafo; **speeding** *n* (*Aut*) eccesso
di velocità; **speed limit** *n* limite *m* di
velocità; **speedometer** [spɪ'dɔmɪtə'] *n*
tachimetro; **speedy** *adj* veloce, rapido(-a),
pronto(-a)
spell [spɛl] (*pt, pp* **spelt** (*BRIT*) *or* **spelled**) *n*
(*also*: **magic ~**) incantesimo; (*period of time*)
(*breve*) periodo ▷ *vt* (*in writing*) scrivere
(lettera per lettera); (*aloud*) dire lettera per
lettera; (*fig*) significare; **to cast a ~ on sb**
fare un incantesimo a qn; **he can't ~** fa
errori di ortografia; **spell out** *vt* (*letter by
letter*) dettare lettera per lettera; (*explain*):
to ~ sth out for sb spiegare qc a qn per
filo e per segno; **spellchecker** ['spɛltʃɛkə
'] *n* correttore *m* ortografico; **spelling** *n*
ortografia
spelt [spɛlt] (*BRIT*) *pt, pp of* **spell**
spend [spɛnd] (*pt, pp* **spent**) *vt* (*money*)
spendere; (*time, life*) passare; **spending** *n*
government spending spesa pubblica

s

spent [spɛnt] *pt, pp of* **spend**

sperm [spə:m] *n* sperma *m*

sphere [sfɪəʳ] *n* sfera

spice [spaɪs] *n* spezia ▷ *vt* aromatizzare

spicy ['spaɪsɪ] *adj* piccante

spider ['spaɪdəʳ] *n* ragno

spike [spaɪk] *n* punta

spill [spɪl] (*pt, pp* **spilt** *or* **spilled**) *vt* versare, rovesciare ▷ *vi* versarsi, rovesciarsi

spin [spɪn] (*pt, pp* **spun**) *n* (*revolution of wheel*) rotazione *f*; (*Aviat*) avvitamento; (*trip in car*) giretto ▷ *vt* (*wool etc*) filare; (*wheel*) far girare ▷ *vi* girare

spinach ['spɪnɪtʃ] *n* spinacio; (*as food*) spinaci *mpl*

spinal ['spaɪnl] *adj* spinale

spin doctor (*inf*) *n* esperto di comunicazioni responsabile dell'immagine di un partito politico

spin-dryer [spɪn'draɪəʳ] (*BRIT*) *n* centrifuga

spine [spaɪn] *n* spina dorsale; (*thorn*) spina

spiral ['spaɪərl] *n* spirale *f* ▷ *vi* (*fig*) salire a spirale

spire ['spaɪəʳ] *n* guglia

spirit ['spɪrɪt] *n* spirito; (*ghost*) spirito, fantasma *m*; (*mood*) stato d'animo, umore *m*; (*courage*) coraggio; **~s** *npl* (*drink*) alcolici *mpl*; **in good ~s** di buon umore

spiritual ['spɪrɪtjuəl] *adj* spirituale

spit [spɪt] (*pt, pp* **spat**) *n* (*for roasting*) spiedo; (*saliva*) sputo; saliva ▷ *vi* sputare; (*fire, fat*) scoppiettare

spite [spaɪt] *n* dispetto ▷ *vt* contrariare, far dispetto a; **in ~ of** nonostante, malgrado; **spiteful** *adj* dispettoso(-a)

splash [splæʃ] *n* spruzzo; (*sound*) splash *m inv*; (*of colour*) schizzo ▷ *vt* spruzzare ▷ *vi* (*also*: **~ about**) sguazzare; **splash out** (*inf*) *vi* (*BRIT*) fare spese folli

splendid ['splɛndɪd] *adj* splendido(-a), magnifico(-a)

splinter ['splɪntəʳ] *n* scheggia ▷ *vi* scheggiarsi

split [splɪt] (*pt, pp* **split**) *n* spaccatura; (*fig: division, quarrel*) scissione *f* ▷ *vt* spaccare; (*party*) dividere; (*work, profits*) spartire, ripartire ▷ *vi* (*divide*) dividersi; **split up** *vi* (*couple*) separarsi, rompere; (*meeting*) sciogliersi

spoil [spɔɪl] (*pt, pp* **spoilt** *or* **spoiled**) *vt* (*damage*) rovinare, guastare; (*mar*) sciupare; (*child*) viziare

spoilt [spɔɪlt] *pt, pp of* **spoil**

spoke [spəuk] *pt of* **speak** ▷ *n* raggio

spoken ['spəukn] *pp of* **speak**

spokesman ['spəuksmən] (*irreg*) *n* portavoce *m inv*

spokesperson ['spəukspə:sn] *n* portavoce *m/f*

spokeswoman ['spəukswumən] (*irreg*) *n* portavoce *f inv*

sponge [spʌndʒ] *n* spugna; (*also*: **~ cake**) pan *m* di spagna ▷ *vt* spugnare, pulire con una spugna ▷ *vi* **to ~ off** *or* **on** scroccare a; **sponge bag** (*BRIT*) *n* nécessaire *m inv*

sponsor ['spɔnsəʳ] *n* (*Radio, TV, Sport etc*) sponsor *m inv*; (*Pol: of bill*) promotore(-trice) ▷ *vt* sponsorizzare; (*bill*) presentare; **sponsorship** *n* sponsorizzazione *f*

spontaneous [spɔn'teɪnɪəs] *adj* spontaneo(-a)

spooky ['spu:kɪ] (*inf*) *adj* che fa accapponare la pelle

spoon [spu:n] *n* cucchiaio; **spoonful** *n* cucchiaiata

sport [spɔ:t] *n* sport *m inv*; (*person*) persona di spirito ▷ *vt* sfoggiare; **sport jacket** (*US*) *n* = **sports jacket**; **sports car** *n* automobile *f* sportiva; **sports centre** (*BRIT*) *n* centro sportivo; **sports jacket** (*BRIT*) *n* giacca sportiva; **sportsman** (*irreg*) *n* sportivo; **sportswear** *n* abiti *mpl* sportivi; **sportswoman** (*irreg*) *n* sportiva; **sporty** *adj* sportivo(-a)

spot [spɔt] *n* punto; (*mark*) macchia; (*dot: on pattern*) pallino; (*pimple*) foruncolo; (*place*) posto; (*Radio, TV*) spot *m inv*; (*small amount*): **a ~ of** un po' di ▷ *vt* (*notice*) individuare, distinguere; **on the ~** sul posto; (*immediately*) su due piedi; (*in difficulty*) nei guai; **spotless** *adj* immacolato(-a); **spotlight** *n* proiettore *m*; (*Aut*) faro ausiliario

spouse [spauz] *n* sposo(-a)

sprain [spreɪn] *n* storta, distorsione *f* ▷ *vt* **to ~ one's ankle** storcersi una caviglia

sprang [spræŋ] *pt of* **spring**

sprawl [sprɔ:l] *vi* sdraiarsi (in modo scomposto); (*place*) estendersi (disordinatamente)

spray [spreɪ] *n* spruzzo; (*container*) nebulizzatore *m*, spray *m inv*; (*of flowers*) mazzetto ▷ *vt* spruzzare; (*crops*) irrorare

spread [sprɛd] (*pt, pp* **spread**) *n* diffusione *f*; (*distribution*) distribuzione *f*; (*Culin*) pasta (da spalmare); (*inf: food*) banchetto ▷ *vt* (*cloth*) stendere, distendere; (*butter etc*) spalmare; (*disease, knowledge*) propagare, diffondere ▷ *vi* stendersi, distendersi; spalmarsi; propagarsi, diffondersi; **spread out** *vi* (*move apart*) separarsi; **spreadsheet** *n* foglio elettronico ad espansione

spree [spri:] *n* **to go on a ~** fare baldoria

spring [sprɪŋ] (*pt* **sprang**, *pp* **sprung**) *n* (*leap*) salto, balzo; (*coiled metal*) molla;

(*season*) primavera; (*of water*) sorgente
f ▷ vi saltare, balzare; **spring up** vi
(*problem*) presentarsi; **spring onion** n
(BRIT) cipollina

sprinkle ['sprɪŋkl] vt spruzzare; spargere;
to ~ water etc **on, ~ with water** etc
spruzzare dell'acqua etc su

sprint [sprɪnt] n scatto ▷ vi scattare

sprung [sprʌŋ] pp of **spring**

spun [spʌn] pt, pp of **spin**

spur [spə:ʳ] n sperone m; (*fig*) sprone m,
incentivo ▷ vt (*also*: **~ on**) spronare; **on the
~ of the moment** lì per lì

spurt [spə:t] n (*of water*) getto; (*of energy*)
scatto ▷ vi sgorgare

spy [spaɪ] n spia ▷ vi **to ~ on** spiare ▷ vt
(*see*) scorgere

sq. abbr = **square**

squabble ['skwɔbl] vi bisticciarsi

squad [skwɔd] n (*Mil*) plotone m; (*Police*)
squadra

squadron ['skwɔdrn] n (*Mil*) squadrone m;
(*Aviat, Naut*) squadriglia

squander ['skwɔndəʳ] vt dissipare

square [skwɛəʳ] n quadrato; (*in town*)
piazza ▷ adj quadrato(-a); (*inf*: *ideas,
person*) di vecchio stampo ▷ vt (*arrange*)
regolare; (*Math*) elevare al quadrato;
(*reconcile*) conciliare; **all ~** pari; **a ~ meal** un
pasto abbondante; **2 metres ~** di 2 metri
per 2; **1 ~ metre** 1 metro quadrato; **square
root** n radice f quadrata

squash [skwɔʃ] n (*Sport*) squash m; (BRIT:
drink): **lemon/orange ~** sciroppo di
limone/arancia; (*US*) zucca; (*Sport*) squash
m ▷ vt schiacciare

squat [skwɔt] adj tarchiato(-a), tozzo(-a)
▷ vi (*also*: **~ down**) accovacciarsi; **squatter**
n occupante m/f abusivo(-a)

squeak [skwi:k] vi squittire

squeal [skwi:l] vi strillare

squeeze [skwi:z] n pressione f; (*also Econ*)
stretta ▷ vt premere; (*hand, arm*) stringere

squid [skwɪd] n calamaro

squint [skwɪnt] vi essere strabico(-a) ▷ n
he has a ~ è strabico

squirm [skwə:m] vi contorcersi

squirrel ['skwɪrəl] n scoiattolo

squirt [skwə:t] vi schizzare; zampillare
▷ vt spruzzare

Sr abbr = **senior**

Sri Lanka [srɪ'læŋkə] n Sri Lanka m

St abbr = **saint**; **street**

stab [stæb] n (*with knife etc*) pugnalata; (*of
pain*) fitta; (*inf*: *try*): **to have a ~ at (doing)
sth** provare (a fare) qc ▷ vt pugnalare

stability [stə'bɪlɪtɪ] n stabilità

stable ['steɪbl] n (*for horses*) scuderia; (*for
cattle*) stalla ▷ adj stabile

stack [stæk] n catasta, pila ▷ vt
accatastare, ammucchiare

stadium ['steɪdɪəm] n stadio

staff [stɑ:f] n (*work force*: *gen*) personale
m; (: BRIT: *Scol*) personale insegnante ▷ vt
fornire di personale

stag [stæg] n cervo

stage [steɪdʒ] n palcoscenico; (*profession*):
the ~ il teatro, la scena; (*point*) punto;
(*platform*) palco ▷ vt (*play*) allestire,
mettere in scena; (*demonstration*)
organizzare; **in ~s** per gradi; a tappe

stagger ['stægəʳ] vi barcollare ▷ vt (*person*)
sbalordire; (*hours, holidays*) scaglionare;
staggering adj (*amazing*) sbalorditivo(-a)

stagnant ['stægnənt] adj stagnante

stag night, stag party n festa di addio
al celibato

stain [steɪn] n macchia; (*colouring*)
colorante m ▷ vt macchiare; (*wood*)
tingere; **stained glass** [steɪnd'glɑ:s] n
vetro colorato; **stainless steel** n acciaio
inossidabile

staircase ['stɛəkeɪs] n scale fpl, scala

stairs [stɛəz] npl (*flight of stairs*) scale fpl,
scala

stairway ['stɛəweɪ] n = **staircase**

stake [steɪk] n palo, piolo; (*Comm*)
interesse m; (*Betting*) puntata, scommessa
▷ vt (*bet*) scommettere; (*risk*) rischiare; **to
be at ~** essere in gioco

stale [steɪl] adj (*bread*) raffermo(-a);
(*food*) stantio(-a); (*air*) viziato(-a); (*beer*)
svaporato(-a); (*smell*) di chiuso

stalk [stɔ:k] n gambo, stelo ▷ vt inseguire

stall [stɔ:l] n bancarella; (*in stable*) box m
inv di stalla ▷ vt (*Aut*) far spegnere; (*fig*)
bloccare ▷ vi (*Aut*) spegnersi, fermarsi; (*fig*)
temporeggiare

stamina ['stæmɪnə] n vigore m, resistenza

stammer ['stæməʳ] n balbuzie f ▷ vi
balbettare

stamp [stæmp] n (*postage stamp*)
francobollo; (*implement*) timbro; (*mark,
also fig*) marchio, impronta; (*on document*)
bollo; timbro ▷ vi (*also*: **~ one's foot**)
battere il piede ▷ vt battere; (*letter*)
affrancare; (*mark with a stamp*) timbrare;
stamp out vt (*fire*) estinguere; (*crime*)
eliminare; (*opposition*) soffocare; **stamped
addressed envelope** n (BRIT) busta
affrancata e indirizzata

Be careful not to translate *stamp* the
Italian word by *stampa*.

stampede [stæm'pi:d] n fuggi fuggi m inv

stance [stæns] n posizione f

stand [stænd] (pt, pp **stood**) n (*position*)
posizione f; (*for taxis*) posteggio; (*structure*)
supporto, sostegno; (*at exhibition*)

stand *m inv*; (*in shop*) banco; (*at market*) bancarella; (*booth*) chiosco; (*Sport*) tribuna ▷ *vi* stare in piedi; (*rise*) alzarsi in piedi; (*be placed*) trovarsi ▷ *vt* (*place*) mettere, porre; (*tolerate, withstand*) resistere, sopportare; (*treat*) offrire; **to make a ~** prendere posizione; **to ~ for parliament** (*BRIT*) presentarsi come candidato (per il parlamento); **stand back** *vi* prendere le distanze; **stand by** *vi* (*be ready*) tenersi pronto(-a) ▷ *vt fus* (*opinion*) sostenere; **stand down** *vi* (*withdraw*) ritirarsi; **stand for** *vt fus* (*signify*) rappresentare, significare; (*tolerate*) sopportare, tollerare; **stand in for** *vt fus* sostituire; **stand out** *vi* (*be prominent*) spiccare; **stand up** *vi* (*rise*) alzarsi in piedi; **stand up for** *vt fus* difendere; **stand up to** *vt fus* tener testa a, resistere a

standard ['stændəd] *n* modello, standard *m inv*; (*level*) livello; (*flag*) stendardo ▷ *adj* (*size etc*) normale, standard *inv*; **~s** *npl* (*morals*) principi *mpl*, valori *mpl*; **standard of living** *n* livello di vita

stand-by ['stændbaɪ] *n* riserva, sostituto; **to be on ~** (*gen*) tenersi pronto(-a); (*doctor*) essere di guardia; **stand-by ticket** *n* (*Aviat*) biglietto senza garanzia

standing ['stændɪŋ] *adj* diritto(-a), in piedi; (*permanent*) permanente ▷ *n* rango, condizione *f*, posizione *f*; **of many years' ~** che esiste da molti anni; **standing order** (*BRIT*) *n* (*at bank*) ordine *m* di pagamento (permanente)

stand: **standpoint** ['stændpɔɪnt] *n* punto di vista; **standstill** ['stændstɪl] *n* **at a standstill** fermo(-a); (*fig*) a un punto morto; **to come to a standstill** fermarsi; giungere a un punto morto

stank [stæŋk] *pt of* **stink**

staple ['steɪpl] *n* (*for papers*) graffetta ▷ *adj* (*food etc*) di base ▷ *vt* cucire

star [stɑːʳ] *n* stella; (*celebrity*) divo(-a) ▷ *vi* **to ~ (in)** essere il (*or* la) protagonista (di) ▷ *vt* (*Cinema*) essere interpretato(-a) da; **the ~s** *npl* (*Astrology*) le stelle

starboard ['stɑːbəd] *n* dritta

starch [stɑːtʃ] *n* amido

stardom ['stɑːdəm] *n* celebrità

stare [stɛəʳ] *n* sguardo fisso ▷ *vi* **to ~ at** fissare

stark [stɑːk] *adj* (*bleak*) desolato(-a) ▷ *adv* **~ naked** completamente nudo(-a)

start [stɑːt] *n* inizio; (*of race*) partenza; (*sudden movement*) sobbalzo; (*advantage*) vantaggio ▷ *vt* cominciare, iniziare; (*car*) mettere in moto ▷ *vi* cominciare; (*on journey*) partire, mettersi in viaggio; (*jump*) sobbalzare; **when does the film ~?**

a che ora comincia il film?; **to ~ doing** *or* **to do sth** (in)cominciare a fare qc; **start off** *vi* cominciare; (*leave*) partire; **start out** *vi* (*begin*) cominciare; (*set out*) partire; **start up** *vi* cominciare; (*car*) avviarsi ▷ *vt* iniziare; (*car*) avviare; **starter** *n* (*Aut*) motorino d'avviamento; (*Sport*: *official*) starter *m inv*; (*BRIT*: *Culin*) primo piatto; **starting point** *n* punto di partenza

startle ['stɑːtl] *vt* far trasalire; **startling** *adj* sorprendente

starvation [stɑːˈveɪʃən] *n* fame *f*, inedia

starve [stɑːv] *vi* morire di fame; soffrire la fame ▷ *vt* far morire di fame, affamare

state [steɪt] *n* stato ▷ *vt* dichiarare, affermare; annunciare; **the S~s** (*USA*) gli Stati Uniti; **to be in a ~** essere agitato(-a); **statement** *n* dichiarazione *f*; **state school** *n* scuola statale; **statesman** (*irreg*) *n* statista *m*

static ['stætɪk] *n* (*Radio*) scariche *fpl* ▷ *adj* statico(-a)

station ['steɪʃən] *n* stazione *f* ▷ *vt* collocare, disporre

stationary ['steɪʃənərɪ] *adj* fermo(-a), immobile

stationer's (shop) *n* cartoleria

stationery ['steɪʃnərɪ] *n* articoli *mpl* di cancelleria

station wagon (*US*) *n* giardinetta

statistic [stəˈtɪstɪk] *n* statistica; **statistics** *n* (*science*) statistica

statue ['stætjuː] *n* statua

stature ['stætʃəʳ] *n* statura

status ['steɪtəs] *n* posizione *f*, condizione *f* sociale; prestigio; stato; **status quo** [-ˈkwəʊ] *n* **the status quo** lo statu quo

statutory ['stætjutrɪ] *adj* stabilito(-a) dalla legge, statutario(-a)

staunch [stɔːntʃ] *adj* fidato(-a), leale

stay [steɪ] *n* (*period of time*) soggiorno, permanenza ▷ *vi* rimanere; (*reside*) alloggiare, stare; (*spend some time*) trattenersi, soggiornare; **to ~ put** non muoversi; **to ~ the night** fermarsi per la notte; **stay away** *vi* (*from person, building*) stare lontano (*from event*) non andare; **stay behind** *vi* restare indietro; **stay in** *vi* (*at home*) stare in casa; **stay on** *vi* restare, rimanere; **stay out** *vi* (*of house*) rimanere fuori (di casa); **stay up** *vi* (*at night*) rimanere alzato(-a)

steadily ['stedɪlɪ] *adv* (*firmly*) saldamente; (*constantly*) continuamente; (*fixedly*) fisso; (*walk*) con passo sicuro

steady ['stedɪ] *adj* (*not wobbling*) fermo(-a); (*regular*) costante; (*person, character*) serio(-a); (: *calm*) calmo(-a), tranquillo(-a) ▷ *vt* stabilizzare; calmare

steak [steɪk] n (meat) bistecca; (fish) trancia

steal [sti:l] (pt **stole**, pp **stolen**) vt rubare ▷ vi rubare; (move) muoversi furtivamente; **my wallet has been stolen** mi hanno rubato il portafoglio

steam [sti:m] n vapore m ▷ vt (Culin) cuocere a vapore ▷ vi fumare; **steam up** vi (window) appannarsi; **to get ~ed up about sth** (fig) andare in bestia per qc; **steamy** adj (room) pieno(-a) di vapore; (window) appannato(-a)

steel [sti:l] n acciaio ▷ adj di acciaio

steep [sti:p] adj ripido(-a), scosceso(-a); (price) eccessivo(-a) ▷ vt inzuppare; (washing) mettere a mollo

steeple ['sti:pl] n campanile m

steer [stɪə^r] vt guidare ▷ vi (Naut: person) governare; (car) guidarsi; **steering** n (Aut) sterzo; **steering wheel** n volante m

stem [stɛm] n (of flower, plant) stelo; (of tree) fusto; (of glass) gambo; (of fruit, leaf) picciolo ▷ vt contenere, arginare

step [stɛp] n passo; (stair) gradino, scalino; (action) mossa, azione f ▷ vi **to ~ forward/back** fare un passo avanti/indietro; **~s** npl (BRIT) = **stepladder**; **to be in/out of ~ (with)** stare/non stare al passo (con); **step down** vi (fig) ritirarsi; **step in** vi fare il proprio ingresso; **step up** vt aumentare; intensificare; **stepbrother** n fratellastro; **stepchild** n figliastro(-a); **stepdaughter** n figliastra; **stepfather** n patrigno; **stepladder** n scala a libretto; **stepmother** n matrigna; **stepsister** n sorellastra; **stepson** n figliastro

stereo ['stɛrɪəu] n (system) sistema m stereofonico; (record player) stereo m inv ▷ adj (also: **~phonic**) stereofonico(-a)

stereotype ['stɪərɪətaɪp] n stereotipo

sterile ['stɛraɪl] adj sterile; **sterilize** ['stɛrɪlaɪz] vt sterilizzare

sterling ['stə:lɪŋ] adj (gold, silver) di buona lega ▷ n (Econ) (lira) sterlina; **a pound ~** una lira sterlina

stern [stə:n] adj severo(-a) ▷ n (Naut) poppa

steroid ['stɛrɔɪd] n steroide m

stew [stju:] n stufato ▷ vt cuocere in umido

steward ['stju:əd] n (Aviat, Naut, Rail) steward m inv; (in club etc) dispensiere m; **stewardess** n assistente f di volo, hostess f inv

stick [stɪk] (pt, pp **stuck**) n bastone m; (of rhubarb, celery) gambo; (of dynamite) candelotto ▷ vt (glue) attaccare; (thrust): **to ~ sth into** conficcare or piantare or infiggere qc in; (inf: put) ficcare; (inf: tolerate) sopportare ▷ vi attaccarsi; (remain) restare, rimanere; **stick out** vi sporgere, spuntare; **stick up** vi sporgere, spuntare; **stick up for** vt fus difendere; **sticker** n cartellino adesivo; **sticking plaster** n cerotto adesivo; **stick shift** (US) n (Aut) cambio manuale

sticky ['stɪkɪ] adj attaccaticcio(-a), vischioso(-a); (label) adesivo(-a); (fig: situation) difficile

stiff [stɪf] adj rigido(-a), duro(-a); (muscle) legato(-a), indolenzito(-a); (difficult) difficile, arduo(-a); (cold) freddo(-a), formale; (strong) forte; (high: price) molto alto(-a) ▷ adv **bored ~** annoiato(-a) a morte

stifling ['staɪflɪŋ] adj (heat) soffocante

stigma ['stɪgmə] n (fig) stigma m

stiletto [stɪ'lɛtəu] (BRIT) n (also: **~ heel**) tacco a spillo

still [stɪl] adj fermo(-a); silenzioso(-a) ▷ adv (up to this time, even) ancora; (nonetheless) tuttavia, ciò nonostante

stimulate ['stɪmjuleɪt] vt stimolare

stimulus ['stɪmjuləs] (pl **stimuli**) n stimolo

sting [stɪŋ] (pt, pp **stung**) n puntura; (organ) pungiglione m ▷ vt pungere

stink [stɪŋk] (pt **stank**, pp **stunk**) n fetore m, puzzo ▷ vi puzzare

stir [stə:^r] n agitazione f, clamore m ▷ vt mescolare; (fig) risvegliare ▷ vi muoversi; **stir up** vt provocare, suscitare; **stir-fry** vt saltare in padella ▷ n pietanza al salto

stitch [stɪtʃ] n (Sewing) punto; (Knitting) maglia; (Med) punto (di sutura); (pain) fitta ▷ vt cucire, attaccare; suturare

stock [stɔk] n riserva, provvista; (Comm) giacenza, stock m inv; (Agr) bestiame m; (Culin) brodo; (descent) stirpe f; (Finance) titoli mpl; azioni fpl ▷ adj (fig: reply etc) consueto(-a); classico(-a) ▷ vt (have in stock) avere, vendere; **~s and shares** valori mpl di borsa; **in ~** in magazzino; **out of ~** esaurito(-a); **stockbroker** ['stɔkbrəukə^r] n agente m di cambio; **stock cube** (BRIT) n dado; **stock exchange** n Borsa (valori); **stockholder** ['stɔkhəuldə^r] n (Finance) azionista m/f

stocking ['stɔkɪŋ] n calza

stock market n Borsa, mercato finanziario

stole [stəul] pt of **steal** ▷ n stola

stolen ['stəuln] pp of **steal**

stomach ['stʌmək] n stomaco; (belly) pancia ▷ vt sopportare, digerire; **stomachache** n mal m di stomaco

stone [stəun] n pietra; (pebble) sasso, ciottolo; (in fruit) nocciolo; (Med) calcolo;

(BRIT: *weight*) = 6.348 kg; 14 *libbre* ▷ *adj*
di pietra ▷ *vt* lapidare; (*fruit*) togliere il
nocciolo a

stood [stʊd] *pt, pp of* **stand**

stool [stuːl] *n* sgabello

stoop [stuːp] *vi* (*also:* **have a ~**) avere una
curvatura; (*also:* **~ down**) chinarsi, curvarsi

stop [stɔp] *n* arresto; (*stopping place*)
fermata; (*in punctuation*) punto
▷ *vt* arrestare, fermare; (*break off*)
interrompere; (*also:* **put a ~ to**) porre fine
a ▷ *vi* fermarsi; (*rain, noise etc*) cessare,
finire; **to ~ doing sth** cessare or finire di
fare qc; **could you ~ here/at the corner?**
può fermarsi qui/all'angolo?; **to ~ dead**
fermarsi di colpo; **stop by** *vi* passare, fare
un salto; **stop off** *vi* sostare brevemente;
stopover *n* breve sosta; (*Aviat*) scalo;
stoppage ['stɔpɪdʒ] *n* arresto, fermata;
(*of pay*) trattenuta; (*strike*) interruzione *f*
del lavoro

storage ['stɔːrɪdʒ] *n* immagazzinamento

store [stɔːʳ] *n* provvista, riserva; (*depot*)
deposito; (BRIT: *department store*) grande
magazzino; (US: *shop*) negozio ▷ *vt*
immagazzinare; **~s** *npl* (*provisions*)
rifornimenti *mpl*, scorte *fpl*; **in ~** di riserva;
in serbo; **storekeeper** (US) *n* negoziante
m/f

storey ['stɔːrɪ] (US **story**) *n* piano

storm [stɔːm] *n* tempesta, temporale
m, burrasca; uragano ▷ *vi* (*fig*) infuriarsi
▷ *vt* prendere d'assalto; **stormy** *adj*
tempestoso(-a), burrascoso(-a)

story ['stɔːrɪ] *n* storia; favola; racconto;
(US) = **storey**

stout [staʊt] *adj* solido(-a), robusto(-a);
(*friend, supporter*) tenace; (*fat*)
corpulento(-a), grasso(-a) ▷ *n* birra scura

stove [stəʊv] *n* (*for cooking*) fornello; (:
small) fornelletto; (*for heating*) stufa

straight [streɪt] *adj* dritto(-a); (*frank*)
onesto(-a), franco(-a); (*simple*) semplice
▷ *adv* diritto; (*drink*) liscio; **to put** or **get**
~ mettere in ordine, mettere ordine in; **~**
away, ~ off (*at once*) immediatamente;
straighten *vt* (*also:* **straighten out**)
raddrizzare; **straightforward** *adj*
semplice; onesto(-a), franco(-a)

strain [streɪn] *n* (*Tech*) sollecitazione
f; (*physical*) sforzo; (*mental*) tensione *f*;
(*Med*) strappo; distorsione *f*; (*streak, trace*)
tendenza; elemento ▷ *vt* tendere; (*muscle*)
sforzare; (*ankle*) storcere; (*resources*) pesare
su; (*food*) colare; passare; **strained** *adj*
(*muscle*) stirato(-a); (*laugh etc*) forzato(-a);
(*relations*) teso(-a); **strainer** *n* passino,
colino

strait [streɪt] *n* (*Geo*) stretto; **~s** *npl* **to be**

in dire ~s (*fig*) essere nei guai

strand [strænd] *n* (*of thread*) filo; **stranded**
adj nei guai; senza mezzi di trasporto

strange [streɪndʒ] *adj* (*not known*)
sconosciuto(-a); (*odd*) strano(-a),
bizzarro(-a); **strangely** *adv* stranamente;
stranger *n* sconosciuto(-a); estraneo(-a)

strangle ['stræŋgl] *vt* strangolare

strap [stræp] *n* cinghia; (*of slip, dress*)
spallina, bretella

strategic [strə'tiːdʒɪk] *adj* strategico(-a)

strategy ['strætɪdʒɪ] *n* strategia

straw [strɔː] *n* paglia; (*drinking straw*)
cannuccia; **that's the last ~!** è la goccia
che fa traboccare il vaso!

strawberry ['strɔːbərɪ] *n* fragola

stray [streɪ] *adj* (*animal*) randagio(-a);
(*bullet*) vagante; (*scattered*) sparso(-a) ▷ *vi*
perdersi

streak [striːk] *n* striscia; (*of hair*) mèche
f inv ▷ *vt* striare, screziare ▷ *vi* **to ~ past**
passare come un fulmine

stream [striːm] *n* ruscello; corrente *f*;
(*of people, smoke etc*) fiume *m* ▷ *vt* (*Scol*)
dividere in livelli di rendimento ▷ *vi*
scorrere; **to ~ in/out** entrare/uscire a fiotti

street [striːt] *n* strada, via; **streetcar** (US)
n tram *m inv*; **street light** *n* lampione *m*;
street map *n* pianta (di una città)

street plan *n* pianta (di una città)

strength [strɛŋθ] *n* forza; **strengthen** *vt*
rinforzare; fortificare; consolidare

strenuous ['strɛnjʊəs] *adj* vigoroso(-a),
energico(-a); (*tiring*) duro(-a), pesante

stress [strɛs] *n* (*force, pressure*) pressione *f*;
(*mental strain*) tensione *f*; (*accent*) accento
▷ *vt* insistere su, sottolineare; accentare;
stressed *adj* (*tense: person*) stressato(-a);
(*Ling, Poetry: syllable*) accentato(-a);
stressful *adj* (*job*) difficile, stressante

stretch [strɛtʃ] *n* (*of sand etc*) distesa
▷ *vi* stirarsi; (*extend*): **to ~ to** or **as far as**
estendersi fino a ▷ *vt* tendere, allungare;
(*spread*) distendere; (*fig*) spingere (al
massimo); **stretch out** *vi* allungarsi,
estendersi ▷ *vt* (*arm etc*) allungare,
tendere; (*to spread*) distendere

stretcher ['strɛtʃəʳ] *n* barella, lettiga

strict [strɪkt] *adj* (*severe*) rigido(-a),
severo(-a); (*precise*) preciso(-a), stretto(-a);
strictly *adv* severamente; rigorosamente;
strettamente

stride [straɪd] (*pt* **strode**, *pp* **stridden**) *n*
passo lungo ▷ *vi* camminare a grandi passi

strike [straɪk] (*pt, pp* **struck**) *n* sciopero;
(*of oil etc*) scoperta; (*attack*) attacco
▷ *vt* colpire; (*oil etc*) scoprire, trovare;
(*bargain*) fare; (*fig*): **the thought** or **it**
~s me that ... mi viene in mente che ...

▷ *vi* scioperare; (*attack*) attaccare; (*clock*) suonare; **on ~** (*workers*) in sciopero; **to ~ a match** accendere un fiammifero; **striker** *n* scioperante *m/f*; (*Sport*) attaccante *m*; **striking** *adj* che colpisce

string [strɪŋ] (*pt, pp* **strung**) *n* spago; (*row*) fila; sequenza; catena; (*Mus*) corda ▷ *vt* **to ~ out** disporre di fianco; **to ~ together** (*words, ideas*) mettere insieme; **the ~s** *npl* (*Mus*) gli archi; **to pull ~s for sb** (*fig*) raccomandare qn

strip [strɪp] *n* striscia ▷ *vt* spogliare; (*paint*) togliere; (*also:* **~ down**: *machine*) smontare ▷ *vi* spogliarsi; **strip off** *vt* (*paint etc*) staccare ▷ *vi* (*person*) spogliarsi

stripe [straɪp] *n* striscia, riga; (*Mil, Police*) gallone *m*; **striped** *adj* a strisce *or* righe

stripper ['strɪpə^r] *n* spogliarellista *m/f*

strip-search ['strɪpsəːtʃ] *vt* **to ~ sb** perquisire qn facendolo(-a) spogliare ▷ *n* perquisizione (*facendo spogliare il perquisto*)

strive [straɪv] (*pt* **strove**, *pp* **striven**) *vi* **to ~ to do** sforzarsi di fare

strode [strəud] *pt of* **stride**

stroke [strəuk] *n* colpo; (*Swimming*) bracciata; (*: style*) stile *m*; (*Med*) colpo apoplettico ▷ *vt* accarezzare; **at a ~** in un attimo

stroll [strəul] *n* giretto, passeggiatina ▷ *vi* andare a spasso; **stroller** (*US*) *n* passeggino

strong [strɔŋ] *adj* (*gen*) forte; (*sturdy: table, fabric etc*) robusto(-a); **they are 50 ~** sono in 50; **stronghold** *n* (*also fig*) roccaforte *f*; **strongly** *adv* fortemente, con forza; energicamente; vivamente

strove [strəuv] *pt of* **strive**

struck [strʌk] *pt, pp of* **strike**

structure ['strʌktʃə^r] *n* struttura; (*building*) costruzione *f*, fabbricato

struggle ['strʌgl] *n* lotta ▷ *vi* lottare

strung [strʌŋ] *pt, pp of* **string**

stub [stʌb] *n* mozzicone *m*; (*of ticket etc*) matrice *f*, talloncino ▷ *vt* **to ~ one's toe** urtare *or* sbattere il dito del piede; **stub out** *vt* schiacciare

stubble ['stʌbl] *n* stoppia; (*on chin*) barba ispida

stubborn ['stʌbən] *adj* testardo(-a), ostinato(-a)

stuck [stʌk] *pt, pp of* **stick** ▷ *adj* (*jammed*) bloccato(-a)

stud [stʌd] *n* bottoncino; borchia; (*also:* **~ earring**) orecchino a pressione; (*also:* **~ farm**) scuderia, allevamento di cavalli; (*also:* **~ horse**) stallone *m* ▷ *vt* (*fig*): **~ded with** tempestato(-a) di

student ['stjuːdənt] *n* studente(-essa) ▷ *cpd* studentesco(-a); universitario(-a);

degli studenti; **student driver** (*US*) conducente *m/f* principiante; **students' union** *n* (*BRIT: association*) circolo universitario; (*: building*) sede *f* del circolo universitario

studio ['stjuːdɪəu] *n* studio; **studio flat** (*US* **studio apartment**) *n* monolocale *m*

study ['stʌdɪ] *n* studio ▷ *vt* studiare; esaminare ▷ *vi* studiare

stuff [stʌf] *n* roba; (*substance*) sostanza, materiale *m* ▷ *vt* imbottire; (*Culin*) farcire; (*dead animal*) impagliare; (*inf: push*) ficcare; **stuffing** *n* imbottitura; (*Culin*) ripieno; **stuffy** *adj* (*room*) mal ventilato(-a), senz'aria; (*ideas*) antiquato(-a)

stumble ['stʌmbl] *vi* inciampare; **to ~ across** (*fig*) imbattersi in

stump [stʌmp] *n* ceppo; (*of limb*) moncone *m* ▷ *vt* **to be ~ed** essere sconcertato(-a)

stun [stʌn] *vt* stordire; (*amaze*) sbalordire

stung [stʌŋ] *pt, pp of* **sting**

stunk [stʌŋk] *pp of* **stink**

stunned [stʌnd] *adj* (*from blow*) stordito(-a); (*amazed, shocked*) sbalordito(-a)

stunning ['stʌnɪŋ] *adj* sbalorditivo(-a); (*girl etc*) fantastico(-a)

stunt [stʌnt] *n* bravata; trucco pubblicitario

stupid ['stjuːpɪd] *adj* stupido(-a); **stupidity** [-'pɪdɪtɪ] *n* stupidità *f inv*, stupidaggine *f*

sturdy ['stəːdɪ] *adj* robusto(-a), vigoroso(-a); solido(-a)

stutter ['stʌtə^r] *n* balbuzie *f* ▷ *vi* balbettare

style [staɪl] *n* stile *m*; (*distinction*) eleganza, classe *f*; **stylish** *adj* elegante; **stylist** *n* **hair stylist** parrucchiere(-a)

sub... [sʌb] *prefix* sub..., sotto...; **subconscious** *adj* subcosciente ▷ *n* subcosciente *m*

subdued [səb'djuːd] *adj* pacato(-a); (*light*) attenuato(-a)

subject [*n* 'sʌbdʒɪkt, *vb* səb'dʒɛkt] *n* soggetto; (*citizen etc*) cittadino(-a); (*Scol*) materia ▷ *vt* **to ~ to** sottomettere a; esporre a; **to be ~ to** (*law*) essere sottomesso(-a) a; (*disease*) essere soggetto(-a) a; **subjective** [-'dʒɛktɪv] *adj* soggettivo(-a); **subject matter** *n* argomento; contenuto

subjunctive [səb'dʒʌŋktɪv] *adj* congiuntivo(-a) ▷ *n* congiuntivo

submarine [sʌbmə'riːn] *n* sommergibile *m*

submission [səb'mɪʃən] *n* sottomissione *f*; (*claim*) richiesta

submit [səb'mɪt] *vt* sottomettere ▷ *vi* sottomettersi

subordinate [sə'bɔːdɪnət] *adj, n*
subordinato(-a)

subscribe [səb'skraɪb] *vi* contribuire; **to ~ to** (*opinion*) approvare, condividere; (*fund*) sottoscrivere a; (*newspaper*) abbonarsi a; essere abbonato(-a) a

subscription [səb'skrɪpʃən] *n* sottoscrizione *f*; abbonamento

subsequent ['sʌbsɪkwənt] *adj* successivo(-a), seguente; conseguente; **subsequently** *adv* in seguito, successivamente

subside [səb'saɪd] *vi* cedere, abbassarsi; (*flood*) decrescere; (*wind*) calmarsi

subsidiary [səb'sɪdɪərɪ] *adj* sussidiario(-a); accessorio(-a) ▷ *n* filiale *f*

subsidize ['sʌbsɪdaɪz] *vt* sovvenzionare

subsidy ['sʌbsɪdɪ] *n* sovvenzione *f*

substance ['sʌbstəns] *n* sostanza

substantial [səb'stænʃl] *adj* solido(-a); (*amount, progress etc*) notevole; (*meal*) sostanzioso(-a)

substitute ['sʌbstɪtjuːt] *n* (*person*) sostituto(-a), (*thing*) succedaneo, surrogato ▷ *vt* **to ~ sth/sb for** sostituire qc/qn a; **substitution** [sʌbstɪ'tjuːʃən] *n* sostituzione *f*

subtle ['sʌtl] *adj* sottile

subtract [səb'trækt] *vt* sottrarre

suburb ['sʌbəːb] *n* sobborgo; **the ~s** la periferia; **suburban** [sə'bəːbən] *adj* suburbano(-a)

subway ['sʌbweɪ] *n* (*US: underground*) metropolitana; (*BRIT: underpass*) sottopassaggio

succeed [sək'siːd] *vi* riuscire; avere successo ▷ *vt* succedere a; **to ~ in doing** riuscire a fare

success [sək'sɛs] *n* successo; **successful** *adj* (*venture*) coronato(-a) da successo, riuscito(-a); **to be successful (in doing)** riuscire (a fare); **successfully** *adv* con successo

succession [sək'sɛʃən] *n* successione *f*

successive [sək'sɛsɪv] *adj* successivo(-a); consecutivo(-a)

successor [sək'sɛsəʳ] *n* successore *m*

succumb [sə'kʌm] *vi* soccombere

such [sʌtʃ] *adj* (*of that kind*): **~ a book** un tale libro, un libro del genere; **~ books** tali libri, libri del genere; (*so much*): **~ courage** tanto coraggio ▷ *adv* talmente, così; **~ a long trip** un viaggio così lungo; **~ a lot of** talmente *or* così tanto(-a); **~ as** (*like*) come; **as ~** come *or* in quanto tale; **such-and-such** *adj* tale (*after noun*)

suck [sʌk] *vt* succhiare; (*breast, bottle*) poppare

Sudan [suː'dɑːn] *n* Sudan *m*

sudden ['sʌdn] *adj* improvviso(-a); **all of a ~** improvvisamente, all'improvviso; **suddenly** *adv* bruscamente, improvvisamente, di colpo

sue [suː] *vt* citare in giudizio

suede [sweɪd] *n* pelle *f* scamosciata

suffer ['sʌfəʳ] *vt* soffrire, patire; (*bear*) sopportare, tollerare ▷ *vi* soffrire; **to ~ from** soffrire di; **suffering** *n* sofferenza

suffice [sə'faɪs] *vi* essere sufficiente, bastare

sufficient [sə'fɪʃənt] *adj* sufficiente; **~ money** abbastanza soldi

suffocate ['sʌfəkeɪt] *vi* (*have difficulty breathing*) soffocare; (*die through lack of air*) asfissiare

sugar ['ʃugəʳ] *n* zucchero ▷ *vt* zuccherare

suggest [sə'dʒɛst] *vt* proporre, suggerire; indicare; **suggestion** [-'dʒɛstʃən] *n* suggerimento, proposta; indicazione *f*

suicide ['suɪsaɪd] *n* (*person*) suicida *m/f*; (*act*) suicidio; *see also* **commit**; **suicide bombing** *n* attentato suicida

suit [suːt] *n* (*man's*) vestito; (*woman's*) completo, tailleur *m inv*; (*Law*) causa; (*Cards*) seme *m*, colore *m* ▷ *vt* andar bene a *or* per; essere adatto(-a) a *or* per; (*adapt*): **to ~ sth to** adattare qc a; **well ~ed** ben assortito(-a); **suitable** *adj* adatto(-a); appropriato(-a); **suitcase** ['suːtkeɪs] *n* valigia

suite [swiːt] *n* (*of rooms*) appartamento; (*Mus*) suite *f inv*; (*furniture*): **bedroom/ dining room ~** arredo *or* mobilia per la camera da letto/sala da pranzo

sulfur ['sʌlfəʳ] (*US*) *n* = **sulphur**

sulk [sʌlk] *vi* fare il broncio

sulphur ['sʌlfəʳ] (*US* **sulfur**) *n* zolfo

sultana [sʌl'tɑːnə] *n* (*fruit*) uva (secca) sultanina

sum [sʌm] *n* somma; (*Scol etc*) addizione *f*; **sum up** *vt, vi* riassumere

summarize ['sʌməraɪz] *vt* riassumere, riepilogare

summary ['sʌmərɪ] *n* riassunto

summer ['sʌməʳ] *n* estate *f* ▷ *cpd* d'estate, estivo(-a); **summer holidays** *npl* vacanze *fpl* estive; **summertime** *n* (*season*) estate *f*

summit ['sʌmɪt] *n* cima, sommità; (*Pol*) vertice *m*

summon ['sʌmən] *vt* chiamare, convocare

Sun. *abbr* (= *Sunday*) dom.

sun [sʌn] *n* sole *m*; **sunbathe** *vi* prendere un bagno di sole; **sunbed** *n* lettino solare; **sunblock** *n* protezione *f* solare totale; **sunburn** *n* (*painful*) scottatura; **sunburned, sunburnt** *adj* abbronzato(-a); (*painfully*) scottato(-a)

Sunday ['sʌndɪ] *n* domenica

Sunday paper n giornale m della domenica

sunflower ['sʌnflauə'] n girasole m
sung [sʌŋ] pp of **sing**
sunglasses ['sʌnglɑ:sɪz] npl occhiali mpl da sole
sunk [sʌŋk] pp of **sink**
sun: sunlight n (luce f del) sole m; **sun lounger** n sedia a sdraio; **sunny** adj assolato(-a), soleggiato(-a); (fig) allegro(-a), felice; **sunrise** n levata del sole, alba; **sun roof** n (Aut) tetto apribile; **sunscreen** n (cream) crema solare protettiva; **sunset** n tramonto; **sunshade** n parasole m; **sunshine** n luce f (del) sole m; **sunstroke** n insolazione f, colpo di sole; **suntan** n abbronzatura; **suntan lotion** n lozione f solare; **suntan oil** n olio solare
super ['su:pə'] (inf) adj fantastico(-a)
superb [su:'pə:b] adj magnifico(-a)
superficial [su:pə'fɪʃəl] adj superficiale
superintendent [su:pərɪn'tendənt] n direttore(-trice); (Police) ≈ commissario (capo)
superior [su'pɪərɪə'] adj, n superiore m/f
superlative [su'pə:lətɪv] adj superlativo(-a), supremo(-a) ▷ n (Ling) superlativo
supermarket ['su:pəmɑ:kɪt] n supermercato
supernatural [su:pə'nætʃərəl] adj soprannaturale ▷ n soprannaturale m
superpower ['su:pəpauə'] n (Pol) superpotenza
superstition [su:pə'stɪʃən] n superstizione f
superstitious [su:pə'stɪʃəs] adj superstizioso(-a)
superstore ['su:pəstɔ:'] n (BRIT) grande supermercato
supervise ['su:pəvaɪz] vt (person etc) sorvegliare; (organization) soprintendere a; **supervision** [-'vɪʒən] n sorveglianza; supervisione f; **supervisor** n sorvegliante m/f; soprintendente m/f; (in shop) capocommesso(-a)
supper ['sʌpə'] n cena
supple ['sʌpl] adj flessibile; agile
supplement [n 'sʌplɪmənt, vb sʌplɪ'mɛnt] n supplemento ▷ vt completare, integrare
supplier [sə'plaɪə'] n fornitore m
supply [sə'plaɪ] vt (provide) fornire; (equip): **to ~ (with)** approvvigionare (di), attrezzare (con) ▷ n riserva, provvista; (supplying) approvvigionamento; (Tech) alimentazione f; **supplies** npl (food) viveri mpl; (Mil) sussistenza
support [sə'pɔ:t] n (moral, financial etc) sostegno, appoggio; (Tech) supporto ▷ vt sostenere; (financially) mantenere; (uphold) sostenere, difendere; **supporter** n (Pol etc) sostenitore(-trice), fautore(-trice); (Sport) tifoso(-a)

> Be careful not to translate **support** by the Italian word **sopportare**.

suppose [sə'pəuz] vt supporre; immaginare; **to be ~d to do** essere tenuto(-a) a fare; **supposedly** [sə'pə uzɪdlɪ] adv presumibilmente; **supposing** conj se, ammesso che + sub
suppress [sə'prɛs] vt reprimere; sopprimere; occultare
supreme [su'pri:m] adj supremo(-a)
surcharge ['sə:tʃɑ:dʒ] n supplemento
sure [ʃuə'] adj sicuro(-a); (definite, convinced) sicuro(-a), certo(-a); **~!** (of course) senz'altro!, certo!; **~ enough** infatti; **to make ~ of sth/that** assicurarsi di qc/che; **surely** adv sicuramente; certamente
surf [sə:f] n (waves) cavalloni mpl; (foam) spuma
surface ['sə:fɪs] n superficie f ▷ vt (road) asfaltare ▷ vi risalire alla superficie; (fig: news, feeling) venire a galla
surfboard ['sə:fbɔ:d] n tavola per surfing
surfing ['sə:fɪŋ] n surfing m
surge [sə:dʒ] n (strong movement) ondata; (of feeling) impeto ▷ vi gonfiarsi; (people) riversarsi
surgeon ['sə:dʒən] n chirurgo
surgery ['sə:dʒərɪ] n chirurgia; (BRIT: room) studio or gabinetto medico, ambulatorio; (: also: **~ hours**) orario delle visite or di consultazione; **to undergo ~** subire un intervento chirurgico
surname ['sə:neɪm] n cognome m
surpass [sə:'pɑ:s] vt superare
surplus ['sə:pləs] n eccedenza; (Econ) surplus m inv ▷ adj eccedente, d'avanzo
surprise [sə'praɪz] n sorpresa; (astonishment) stupore m ▷ vt sorprendere; stupire; **surprised** [sə'praɪzd] adj (look, smile) sorpreso(-a); **to be surprised** essere sorpreso, sorprendersi; **surprising** adj sorprendente, stupefacente; **surprisingly** adv (easy, helpful) sorprendentemente
surrender [sə'rɛndə'] n resa, capitolazione f ▷ vi arrendersi

s

surround [sə'raund] vt circondare;
(Mil etc) accerchiare; **surrounding** adj
circostante; **surroundings** npl dintorni
mpl; (fig) ambiente m
surveillance [sə:'veɪləns] n sorveglianza,
controllo
survey [n 'sə:veɪ, vb sə:'veɪ] n quadro
generale; (study) esame m; (in housebuying
etc) perizia; (of land) rilevamento, rilievo
topografico ▷ vt osservare; esaminare;
valutare; rilevare; **surveyor** n perito;
geometra m; (of land) agrimensore m
survival [sə'vaɪvl] n sopravvivenza; (relic)
reliquia, vestigio
survive [sə'vaɪv] vi sopravvivere ▷ vt
sopravvivere a; **survivor** n superstite m/f,
sopravvissuto(-a)
suspect [adj, n 'sʌspɛkt, vb səs'pɛkt] adj
sospetto(-a) ▷ n persona sospetta ▷ vt
sospettare; (think likely) supporre; (doubt)
dubitare
suspend [səs'pɛnd] vt sospendere;
suspended sentence n condanna con
la condizionale; **suspenders** npl (BRIT)
giarrettiere fpl; (US) bretelle fpl
suspense [səs'pɛns] n apprensione f; (in
film etc) suspense m; **to keep sb in ~** tenere
qn in sospeso
suspension [səs'pɛnʃən] n (gen Aut)
sospensione f; (of driving licence) ritiro
temporaneo; **suspension bridge** n ponte
m sospeso
suspicion [səs'pɪʃən] n sospetto;
suspicious [səs'pɪʃəs] adj (suspecting)
sospettoso(-a); (causing suspicion)
sospetto(-a)
sustain [səs'teɪn] vt sostenere;
sopportare; (Law: charge) confermare;
(suffer) subire
swallow ['swɔləu] n (bird) rondine f ▷ vt
inghiottire; (fig: story) bere
swam [swæm] pt of **swim**
swamp [swɔmp] n palude f ▷ vt
sommergere
swan [swɔn] n cigno
swap [swɔp] vt **to ~ (for)** scambiare (con)
swarm [swɔ:m] n sciame m ▷ vi (bees)
sciamare; (people) brulicare; (place): **to be
~ing with** brulicare di
sway [sweɪ] vi (tree) ondeggiare; (person)
barcollare ▷ vt (influence) influenzare,
dominare
swear [swɛəʳ] (pt **swore**, pp **sworn**) vi
(curse) bestemmiare, imprecare ▷ vt
(promise) giurare; **swear in** vt prestare
giuramento a; **swearword** n parolaccia
sweat [swɛt] n sudore m, traspirazione f
▷ vi sudare
sweater ['swɛtəʳ] n maglione m

sweatshirt ['swɛtʃə:t] n felpa
sweaty ['swɛtɪ] adj sudato(-a),
bagnato(-a) di sudore
Swede [swi:d] n svedese m/f
swede [swi:d] (BRIT) n rapa svedese
Sweden ['swi:dn] n Svezia; **Swedish** ['swi:
dɪʃ] adj svedese ▷ n (Ling) svedese m
sweep [swi:p] (pt, pp **swept**) n spazzata;
(also: **chimney ~**) spazzacamino ▷ vt
spazzare, scopare; (current) spazzare ▷ vi
(hand) muoversi con gesto ampio; (wind)
infuriare
sweet [swi:t] n (BRIT: pudding) dolce m;
(candy) caramella ▷ adj dolce; (fresh)
fresco(-a); (fig) piacevole; delicato(-a),
grazioso(-a); gentile; **sweetcorn** n
granturco dolce; **sweetener** ['swi:tnə
ʳ] n (Culin) dolcificante m; **sweetheart**
n innamorato(-a); **sweetshop** n (BRIT)
≈ pasticceria
swell [swɛl] (pt **swelled**, pp **swollen**,
swelled) n (of sea) mare m lungo ▷ adj (US:
inf: excellent) favoloso(-a) ▷ vt gonfiare,
ingrossare; aumentare ▷ vi gonfiarsi,
ingrossarsi; (sound) crescere; (also: **~ up**)
gonfiarsi; **swelling** n (Med) tumefazione
f, gonfiore m
swept [swɛpt] pt, pp of **sweep**
swerve [swə:v] vi deviare; (driver) sterzare;
(boxer) scartare
swift [swɪft] n (bird) rondone m ▷ adj
rapido(-a), veloce
swim [swɪm] (pt **swam**, pp **swum**) n **to
go for a ~** andare a fare una nuotata ▷ vi
nuotare; (Sport) fare del nuoto; (head, room)
girare ▷ vt (river, channel) attraversare
or percorrere a nuoto; (length) nuotare;
swimmer n nuotatore(-trice); **swimming**
n nuoto; **swimming costume** (BRIT) n
costume m da bagno; **swimming pool** n
piscina; **swimming trunks** npl costume
m da bagno (da uomo); **swimsuit** n
costume m da bagno
swing [swɪŋ] (pt, pp **swung**) n altalena;
(movement) oscillazione f; (Mus) ritmo;
swing m ▷ vt dondolare, far oscillare;
(also: **~ round**) far girare ▷ vi oscillare,
dondolare; (also: **~ round**: object) roteare;
(: person) girarsi, voltarsi; **to be in full ~**
(activity) essere in piena attività; (party etc)
essere nel pieno
swipe card n tessera magnetica
swirl [swə:l] vi turbinare, far mulinello
Swiss [swɪs] adj, n inv svizzero(-a)
switch [swɪtʃ] n (for light, radio etc)
interruttore m; (change) cambiamento
▷ vt (change) cambiare; scambiare; **switch
off** vt spegnere; **could you ~ off the
light?** puoi spegnere la luce?; **switch on**

vt accendere; (*engine, machine*) mettere in moto, avviare; **switchboard** *n* (*Tel*) centralino

Switzerland ['swɪtsələnd] *n* Svizzera

swivel ['swɪvl] *vi* (*also:* **~ round**) girare

swollen ['swəulən] *pp of* **swell**

swoop [swu:p] *n* incursione *f* ▷ *vi* (*also:* **~ down**) scendere in picchiata, piombare

swop [swɔp] *n, vt* = **swap**

sword [sɔ:d] *n* spada; **swordfish** *n* pesce *m* spada *inv*

swore [swɔ:ʳ] *pt of* **swear**

sworn [swɔ:n] *pp of* **swear** ▷ *adj* giurato(-a)

swum [swʌm] *pp of* **swim**

swung [swʌŋ] *pt, pp of* **swing**

syllable ['sɪləbl] *n* sillaba

syllabus ['sɪləbəs] *n* programma *m*

symbol ['sɪmbl] *n* simbolo; **symbolic(al)** [sɪm'bɔlɪk(l)] *adj* simbolico(-a); **to be symbolic(al) of sth** simboleggiare qc

symmetrical [sɪ'mɛtrɪkl] *adj* simmetrico(-a)

symmetry ['sɪmɪtrɪ] *n* simmetria

sympathetic [sɪmpə'θɛtɪk] *adj* (*showing pity*) compassionevole; (*kind*) comprensivo(-a); **~ towards** ben disposto(-a) verso

> Be careful not to translate *sympathetic* by the Italian word *simpatico*.

sympathize ['sɪmpəθaɪz] *vi* **to ~ with** (*person*) compatire; partecipare al dolore di; (*cause*) simpatizzare per

sympathy ['sɪmpəθɪ] *n* compassione *f*

symphony ['sɪmfənɪ] *n* sinfonia

symptom ['sɪmptəm] *n* sintomo; indizio

synagogue ['sɪnəgɔg] *n* sinagoga

syndicate ['sɪndɪkɪt] *n* sindacato

syndrome ['sɪndrəum] *n* sindrome *f*

synonym ['sɪnənɪm] *n* sinonimo

synthetic [sɪn'θɛtɪk] *adj* sintetico(-a)

Syria ['sɪrɪə] *n* Siria

syringe [sɪ'rɪndʒ] *n* siringa

syrup ['sɪrəp] *n* sciroppo; (*also:* **golden ~**) melassa raffinata

system ['sɪstəm] *n* sistema *m*; (*order*) metodo; (*Anat*) organismo; **systematic** [-'mætɪk] *adj* sistematico(-a); metodico(-a); **systems analyst** *n* analista *m* di sistemi

ta [tɑ:] (*BRIT: inf*) *excl* grazie!

tab [tæb] *n* (*loop on coat etc*) laccetto; (*label*) etichetta; **to keep ~s on** (*fig*) tenere d'occhio

table ['teɪbl] *n* tavolo, tavola; (*Math, Chem etc*) tavola ▷ *vt* (*BRIT: motion etc*) presentare; **a ~ for 4, please** un tavolo per 4, per favore; **to lay** *or* **set the ~** apparecchiare *or* preparare la tavola; **tablecloth** *n* tovaglia; **table d'hôte** [tɑ:bl'dəut] *adj* (*meal*) a prezzo fisso; **table lamp** *n* lampada da tavolo; **tablemat** *n* sottopiatto; **tablespoon** *n* cucchiaio da tavola; (*also:* **tablespoonful:** *as measurement*) cucchiaiata

tablet ['tæblɪt] *n* (*Med*) compressa; (*of stone*) targa

table tennis *n* tennis *m* da tavolo, ping-pong® *m*

tabloid ['tæblɔɪd] *n* (*newspaper*) tabloid *m inv* (*giornale illustrato di formato ridotto*); **the ~s, the ~ press** i giornali popolari

taboo [tə'bu:] *adj, n* tabù *m inv*

tack [tæk] *n* (*nail*) bulletta; (*fig*) approccio ▷ *vt* imbullettare; imbastire ▷ *vi* bordeggiare

tackle ['tækl] *n* attrezzatura, equipaggiamento; (*for lifting*) paranco; (*Football*) contrasto; (*Rugby*) placcaggio ▷ *vt* (*difficulty*) affrontare; (*Football*) contrastare; (*Rugby*) placcare

tacky ['tækɪ] *adj* appiccicaticcio(-a); (*pej*) scadente

tact [tækt] *n* tatto: **tactful** *adj* delicato(-a), discreto(-a)

tactics ['tæktɪks] *n, npl* tattica

tactless ['tæktlɪs] *adj* che manca di tatto

tadpole ['tædpəul] *n* girino

taffy ['tæfɪ] (*us*) *n* caramella *f* mou *inv*

tag [tæg] *n* etichetta

tail [teɪl] *n* coda; (*of shirt*) falda ▷ *vt* (*follow*) seguire, pedinare; **~s** *npl* (*formal suit*) frac *m inv*

tailor ['teɪlə^r] *n* sarto

Taiwan [taɪ'wɑːn] *n* Taiwan *m*; **Taiwanese** [taɪwə'niːz] *adj, n* taiwanese

take [teɪk] (*pt* **took**, *pp* **taken**) *vt* prendere; (*gain: prize*) ottenere, vincere; (*require: effort, courage*) occorrere, volerci; (*tolerate*) accettare, sopportare; (*hold: passengers etc*) contenere; (*accompany*) accompagnare; (*bring, carry*) portare; (*exam*) sostenere, presentarsi a; **to ~ a photo/a shower** fare una fotografia/una doccia; **I ~ it that** suppongo che; **take after** *vt fus* assomigliare a; **take apart** *vt* smontare; **take away** *vt* portare via; togliere; **take back** *vt* (*return*) restituire; riportare; (*one's words*) ritirare; **take down** *vt* (*building*) demolire; (*letter etc*) scrivere; **take in** *vt* (*deceive*) imbrogliare, abbindolare; (*understand*) capire; (*include*) comprendere, includere; (*lodger*) prendere, ospitare; **take off** *vi* (*Aviat*) decollare; (*go away*) andarsene ▷ *vt* (*remove*) togliere; **take on** *vt* (*work*) accettare, intraprendere; (*employee*) assumere; (*opponent*) sfidare, affrontare; **take out** *vt* portare fuori; (*remove*) togliere; (*licence*) prendere, ottenere; **to ~ sth out of sth** (*drawer, pocket etc*) tirare qc fuori da qc; estrarre qc da qc; **take over** *vt* (*business*) rilevare ▷ *vi* **to ~ over from sb** prendere le consegne or il controllo da qn; **take up** *vt* (*dress*) accorciare; (*occupy: time, space*) occupare; (*engage in: hobby etc*) mettersi a; **to ~ sb up on sth** accettare qc da qn; **takeaway** (*BRIT*) *n* (*shop etc*) ≈ rosticceria; (*food*) pasto per asporto; **taken** *pp of* **take**; **takeoff** *n* (*Aviat*) decollo; **takeout** (*us*) *n* = **takeaway**; **takeover** *n* (*Comm*) assorbimento; **takings** ['teɪkɪŋz] *npl* (*Comm*) incasso

talc [tælk] *n* (*also*: **~um powder**) talco

tale [teɪl] *n* racconto, storia; **to tell ~s** (*fig: to teacher, parent etc*) fare la spia

talent ['tælnt] *n* talento; **talented** *adj* di talento

talk [tɔːk] *n* discorso; (*gossip*) chiacchiere *fpl*; (*conversation*) conversazione *f*; (*interview*) discussione *f* ▷ *vi* parlare; **~s** *npl* (*Pol etc*) colloqui *mpl*; **to ~ about** parlare di; **to ~ sb out of/into doing** dissuadere qn da/convincere qn a fare; **to ~ shop** parlare di lavoro *or* di affari; **talk over** *vt* discutere; **talk show** *n* conversazione *f* televisiva, talk show *m inv*

tall [tɔːl] *adj* alto(-a); **to be 6 feet ~** ≈ essere alto 1 metro e 80

tambourine [tæmbə'riːn] *n* tamburello

tame [teɪm] *adj* addomesticato(-a); (*fig: story, style*) insipido(-a), scialbo(-a)

tamper ['tæmpə^r] *vi* **to ~ with** manomettere

tampon ['tæmpɔn] *n* tampone *m*

tan [tæn] *n* (*also*: **sun~**) abbronzatura ▷ *vi* abbronzarsi ▷ *adj* (*colour*) marrone rossiccio *inv*

tandem ['tændəm] *n* tandem *m inv*

tangerine [tændʒə'riːn] *n* mandarino

tangle ['tæŋgl] *n* groviglio; **to get into a ~** aggrovigliarsi; (*fig*) combinare un pasticcio

tank [tæŋk] *n* serbatoio; (*for fish*) acquario; (*Mil*) carro armato

tanker ['tæŋkə^r] *n* (*ship*) nave *f* cisterna *inv*; (*truck*) autobotte *f*, autocisterna

tanned [tænd] *adj* abbronzato(-a)

tantrum ['tæntrəm] *n* accesso di collera

Tanzania [tænzə'nɪə] *n* Tanzania

tap [tæp] *n* (*on sink etc*) rubinetto; (*gentle blow*) colpetto ▷ *vt* dare un colpetto a; (*resources*) sfruttare, utilizzare; (*telephone*) mettere sotto controllo; **on ~** (*fig: resources*) a disposizione; **tap dancing** *n* tip tap *m*

tape [teɪp] *n* nastro; (*also*: **magnetic ~**) nastro (magnetico); (*sticky tape*) nastro adesivo ▷ *vt* (*record*) registrare (su nastro); (*stick*) attaccare con nastro adesivo; **tape measure** *n* metro a nastro; **tape recorder** *n* registratore *m* (a nastro)

tapestry ['tæpɪstrɪ] *n* arazzo; tappezzeria

tar [tɑː^r] *n* catrame *m*

target ['tɑːgɪt] *n* bersaglio; (*fig: objective*) obiettivo

tariff ['tærɪf] *n* tariffa

tarmac ['tɑːmæk] *n* (*BRIT: on road*) macadam *m* al catrame; (*Aviat*) pista di decollo

tarpaulin [tɑː'pɔːlɪn] *n* tela incatramata

tarragon ['tærəgən] *n* dragoncello

tart [tɑːt] *n* (*Culin*) crostata; (*BRIT: inf: pej: woman*) sgualdrina ▷ *adj* (*flavour*) aspro(-a), agro(-a)

tartan ['tɑːtn] *n* tartan *m inv*

tartar(e) sauce *n* salsa tartara

task [tɑːsk] *n* compito; **to take to ~** rimproverare

taste [teɪst] n gusto; (flavour) sapore m, gusto; (sample) assaggio; (fig: glimpse, idea) idea ▷ vt gustare; (sample) assaggiare ▷ vi **to ~ of** or **like** (fish etc) sapere or avere sapore di; **in good/bad ~** di buon/cattivo gusto; **can I have a ~?** posso assaggiarlo?; **you can ~ the garlic (in it)** (ci) si sente il sapore dell'aglio; **tasteful** adj di buon gusto; **tasteless** adj (food) insipido(-a); (remark) di cattivo gusto; **tasty** adj saporito(-a), gustoso(-a)

tatters ['tætəz] npl **in ~** a brandelli

tattoo [tə'tu:] n tatuaggio; (spectacle) parata militare ▷ vt tatuare

taught [tɔ:t] pt, pp of **teach**

taunt [tɔ:nt] n scherno ▷ vt schernire

Taurus ['tɔ:rəs] n Toro

taut [tɔ:t] adj teso(-a)

tax [tæks] n (on goods) imposta; (on services) tassa; (on income) imposte fpl, tasse fpl ▷ vt tassare; (fig: strain: patience etc) mettere alla prova; **tax-free** adj esente da imposte

taxi ['tæksɪ] n taxi m inv ▷ vi (Aviat) rullare; **can you call me a ~, please?** può chiamarmi un taxi, per favore?; **taxi driver** n tassista m/f; **taxi rank** (BRIT) n = **taxi stand**; **taxi stand** n posteggio dei taxi

tax payer n contribuente m/f

TB n abbr = **tuberculosis**

tea [ti:] n tè m inv; (BRIT: snack: for children) merenda; **high ~** (BRIT) cena leggera (presa nel tardo pomeriggio); **tea bag** n bustina di tè; **tea break** (BRIT) n intervallo per il tè

teach [ti:tʃ] (pt, pp **taught**) vt **to ~ sb sth, ~ sth to sb** insegnare qc a qn ▷ vi insegnare; **teacher** n insegnante m/f; (in secondary school) professore(-essa); (in primary school) maestro(-a); **teaching** n insegnamento

tea: **tea cloth** n (for dishes) strofinaccio; (BRIT: for trolley) tovaglietta da tè; **teacup** ['ti:kʌp] n tazza da tè

tea leaves npl foglie fpl di tè

team [ti:m] n squadra; (of animals) tiro; **team up** vi **to ~ up (with)** mettersi insieme (a)

teapot ['ti:pɔt] n teiera

tear¹ [tɛəʳ] (pt **tore**, pp **torn**) n strappo ▷ vt strappare ▷ vi strapparsi; **tear apart** vt (also fig) distruggere; **tear down** vt +adv (building, statue) demolire; (poster, flag) tirare giù; **tear off** vt (sheet of paper etc) strappare; (one's clothes) togliersi di dosso; **tear up** vt (sheet of paper etc) strappare

tear² [tɪəʳ] n lacrima; **in ~s** in lacrime; **tearful** ['tɪəful] adj piangente, lacrimoso(-a); **tear gas** n gas m lacrimogeno

tearoom ['ti:ru:m] n sala da tè

tease [ti:z] vt canzonare; (unkindly) tormentare

tea: **teaspoon** n cucchiaino da tè; (also: **teaspoonful**: as measurement) cucchiaino; **teatime** n ora del tè; **tea towel** (BRIT) n strofinaccio (per i piatti)

technical ['tɛknɪkl] adj tecnico(-a)

technician [tɛk'nɪʃən] n tecnico(-a)

technique [tɛk'ni:k] n tecnica

technology [tɛk'nɔlədʒɪ] n tecnologia

teddy (bear) ['tɛdɪ-] n orsacchiotto

tedious ['ti:dɪəs] adj noioso(-a), tedioso(-a)

tee [ti:] n (Golf) tee m inv

teen [ti:n] adj = **teenage** ▷ n (US) = **teenager**

teenage ['ti:neɪdʒ] adj (fashions etc) per giovani, per adolescenti; **teenager** n adolescente m/f

teens [ti:nz] npl **to be in one's ~** essere adolescente

teeth [ti:θ] npl of **tooth**

teetotal [ti:'təutl] adj astemio(-a)

telecommunications ['tɛlɪkəmju:-nɪ'keɪʃənz] n telecomunicazioni fpl

telegram ['tɛlɪgræm] n telegramma m

telegraph pole n palo del telegrafo

telephone ['tɛlɪfəun] n telefono ▷ vt (person) telefonare a; (message) comunicare per telefono; **telephone book** n elenco telefonico; **telephone booth** (BRIT), **telephone box** n cabina telefonica; **telephone call** n telefonata; **telephone directory** n elenco telefonico; **telephone number** n numero di telefono

telesales ['tɛlɪseɪlz] n vendita per telefono

telescope ['tɛlɪskəup] n telescopio

televise ['tɛlɪvaɪz] vt teletrasmettere

television ['tɛlɪvɪʒən] n televisione f; **on ~** alla televisione; **television programme** n programma m televisivo

tell [tɛl] (pt, pp **told**) vt dire; (relate: story) raccontare; (distinguish): **to ~ sth from** distinguere qc da ▷ vi (talk): **to ~ (of)** parlare (di); (have effect) farsi sentire, avere effetto; **to ~ sb to do** dire a qn di fare; **tell off** vt rimproverare, sgridare; **teller** n (in bank) cassiere(-a)

telly ['tɛlɪ] (BRIT: inf) n abbr (= television) tivù f inv

temp [tɛmp] n abbr (= temporary) segretaria temporanea

temper ['tɛmpəʳ] n (nature) carattere m; (mood) umore m; (fit of anger) collera ▷ vt (moderate) moderare; **to be in a ~** essere in collera; **to lose one's ~** andare in collera

temperament ['tɛmprəmənt] n (nature) temperamento; **temperamental** [-'mɛntl] adj capriccioso(-a)

temperature ['tɛmprətʃəʳ] n

temperatura; **to have** *or* **run a ~** avere la febbre

temple ['tɛmpl] *n* (*building*) tempio; (*Anat*) tempia

temporary ['tɛmpərərɪ] *adj* temporaneo(-a); (*job, worker*) avventizio(-a), temporaneo(-a)

tempt [tɛmpt] *vt* tentare; **to ~ sb into doing** indurre qn a fare; **temptation** [-'teɪʃən] *n* tentazione *f*; **tempting** *adj* allettante

ten [tɛn] *num* dieci

tenant ['tɛnənt] *n* inquilino(-a)

tend [tɛnd] *vt* badare a, occuparsi di ▷ *vi* **to ~ to do** tendere a fare; **tendency** ['tɛndənsɪ] *n* tendenza

tender ['tɛndə^r] *adj* tenero(-a); (*sore*) dolorante ▷ *n* (*Comm: offer*) offerta; (*money*): **legal ~** moneta in corso legale ▷ *vt* offrire

tendon ['tɛndən] *n* tendine *m*

tenner ['tɛnə^r] *n* (BRIT *inf*) (banconota da) dieci sterline *fpl*

tennis ['tɛnɪs] *n* tennis *m*; **tennis ball** *n* palla da tennis; **tennis court** *n* campo da tennis; **tennis match** *n* partita di tennis; **tennis player** *n* tennista *m/f*; **tennis racket** *n* racchetta da tennis

tenor ['tɛnə^r] *n* (*Mus*) tenore *m*

tenpin bowling ['tɛnpɪn-] *n* bowling *m*

tense [tɛns] *adj* teso(-a) ▷ *n* (*Ling*) tempo

tension ['tɛnʃən] *n* tensione *f*

tent [tɛnt] *n* tenda

tentative ['tɛntətɪv] *adj* esitante, incerto(-a); (*conclusion*) provvisorio(-a)

tenth [tɛnθ] *num* decimo(-a)

tent: **tent peg** *n* picchetto da tenda; **tent pole** *n* palo da tenda, montante *m*

tepid ['tɛpɪd] *adj* tiepido(-a)

term [tə:m] *n* termine *m*; (*Scol*) trimestre *m*; (*Law*) sessione *f* ▷ *vt* chiamare, definire; **~s** *npl* (*conditions*) condizioni *fpl*; (*Comm*) prezzi *mpl*, tariffe *fpl*; **in the short/long ~** a breve/lunga scadenza; **to be on good ~s with sb** essere in buoni rapporti con qn; **to come to ~s with** (*problem*) affrontare

terminal ['tə:mɪnl] *adj* finale, terminale; (*disease*) terminale ▷ *n* (*Elec*) morsetto; (*Comput*) terminale *m*; (*Aviat, for oil, ore etc*) terminal *m inv*; (BRIT: *also:* **coach ~**) capolinea *m*

terminate ['tə:mɪneɪt] *vt* mettere fine a

termini ['tə:mɪnaɪ] *npl of* **terminus**

terminology [tə:mɪ'nɔlədʒɪ] *n* terminologia

terminus ['tə:mɪnəs] (*pl* **termini**) *n* (*for buses*) capolinea *m*; (*for trains*) stazione *f* terminale

terrace ['tɛrəs] *n* terrazza; (BRIT: *row of*

houses) fila di case a schiera; **terraced** *adj* (*garden*) a terrazze

terrain [tɛ'reɪn] *n* terreno

terrestrial [tɪ'rɛstrɪəl] *adj* (*life*) terrestre; (BRIT: *channel*) terrestre

terrible ['tɛrɪbl] *adj* terribile; **terribly** *adv* terribilmente; (*very badly*) malissimo

terrier ['tɛrɪə^r] *n* terrier *m inv*

terrific [tə'rɪfɪk] *adj* incredibile, fantastico(-a); (*wonderful*) formidabile, eccezionale

terrified ['tɛrɪfaɪd] *adj* atterrito(-a)

terrify ['tɛrɪfaɪ] *vt* terrorizzare; **terrifying** *adj* terrificante

territorial [tɛrɪ'tɔ:rɪəl] *adj* territoriale

territory ['tɛrɪtərɪ] *n* territorio

terror ['tɛrə^r] *n* terrore *m*; **terrorism** *n* terrorismo; **terrorist** *n* terrorista *m/f*

test [tɛst] *n* (*trial, check: of courage etc*) prova; (*Med*) esame *m*; (*Chem*) analisi *f inv*; (*exam: of intelligence etc*) test *m inv*; (: *in school*) compito in classe; (*also:* **driving ~**) esame *m* di guida ▷ *vt* provare; esaminare; analizzare; sottoporre ad esame; **to ~ sb in history** esaminare qn in storia

testicle ['tɛstɪkl] *n* testicolo

testify ['tɛstɪfaɪ] *vi* (*Law*) testimoniare, deporre; **to ~ to sth** (*Law*) testimoniare qc; (*gen*) comprovare *or* dimostrare qc

testimony ['tɛstɪmənɪ] *n* (*Law*) testimonianza, deposizione *f*

test: **test match** *n* (*Cricket, Rugby*) partita internazionale; **test tube** *n* provetta

tetanus ['tɛtənəs] *n* tetano

text [tɛkst] *n* testo; (*on mobile phone*) SMS *m inv*, messaggino ▷ *vt* **to ~ sb** (*inf*) mandare un SMS a qn; **textbook** *n* libro di testo

textile ['tɛkstaɪl] *n* tessile *m*

text message *n* (*Tel*) SMS *m inv*, messaggino

text messaging [-'mɛsɪdʒɪŋ] *n* il mandarsi SMS

texture ['tɛkstʃə^r] *n* tessitura; (*of skin, paper etc*) struttura

Thai [taɪ] *adj* tailandese ▷ *n* tailandese *m/f*; (*Ling*) tailandese *m*

Thailand ['taɪlænd] *n* Tailandia

Thames [tɛmz] *n* **the ~** il Tamigi

than [ðæn, ðən] *conj* (*in comparisons*) che; (*with numerals, pronouns, proper names*) di; **more ~ 10/once** più di 10/una volta; **I have more/less ~ you** ne ho più/meno di te; **I have more pens ~ pencils** ho più penne che matite; **she is older ~ you think** è più vecchia di quanto tu (non) pensi

thank [θæŋk] *vt* ringraziare; **~ you (very much)** grazie (tante); **~s** *npl* ringraziamenti *mpl*, grazie *fpl excl* grazie!;

~s to grazie a; **thankfully** adv con riconoscenza; con sollievo; **thankfully there were few victims** grazie al cielo ci sono state poche vittime; **Thanksgiving (Day)** n giorno del ringraziamento

◉ **THANKSGIVING (DAY)**
◉
◉ Negli Stati Uniti il quarto giovedì di
◉ novembre ricorre il **Thanksgiving**
◉ **(Day)**, festa che rievoca la celebrazione
◉ con cui i Padri Pellegrini, fondatori della
◉ colonia di Plymouth in Massachusetts,
◉ ringraziarono Dio del buon raccolto
◉ del 1621.

 KEYWORD

that [ðæt] (pl **those**) adj (demonstrative) quel (quell', quello) m; quella (quell') f; **that man/woman/book** quell'uomo/quella donna/quel libro; (not "this") quell'uomo/ quella donna/quel libro là; **that one** quello(-a) là
▷ pron **1** (demonstrative) ciò; (not "this one") quello(-a); **who's that?** chi è?; **what's that?** cos'è quello?; **is that you?** sei tu?; **I prefer this to that** preferisco questo a quello; **that's what he said** questo è ciò che ha detto; **what happened after that?** che è successo dopo?; **that is (to say)** cioè **2** (relative: direct) che; (: indirect) cui; **the book (that) I read** il libro che ho letto; **the box (that) I put it in** la scatola in cui l'ho messo; **the people (that) I spoke to** le persone con cui or con le quali ho parlato **3** (relative: of time) in cui; **the day (that) he came** il giorno in cui è venuto
▷ conj che; **he thought that I was ill** pensava che io fossi malato
▷ adv (demonstrative) così; **I can't work that much** non posso lavorare (così) tanto; **that high** così alto; **the wall's about that high and that thick** il muro è alto circa così e spesso circa così

thatched [θætʃt] adj (roof) di paglia
thaw [θɔː] n disgelo ▷ vi (ice) sciogliersi; (food) scongelarsi ▷ vt (food: also: **~ out**) (fare) scongelare

 KEYWORD

the [ðiː, ðə] def art **1** (gen) il (lo, l') m; la (l') f; i (gli) mpl; le fpl; **the boy/girl/ink** il ragazzo/la ragazza/l'inchiostro; **the books/pencils** i libri/le matite; **the history of the world** la storia del mondo; **give it to the postman** dallo al postino;

I haven't the time/money non ho tempo/soldi; **the rich and the poor** i ricchi e i poveri
2 (in titles): **Elizabeth the First** Elisabetta prima; **Peter the Great** Pietro il grande
3 (in comparisons): **the more he works, the more he earns** più lavora più quadagna

theatre ['θɪətə'] (US **theater**) n teatro; (also: **lecture ~**) aula magna; (also: **operating ~**) sala operatoria
theft [θɛft] n furto
their [ðɛə'] adj il (la) loro; (pl) i (le) loro; **theirs** pron il (la) loro; (pl) i (le) loro; see also **my**; **mine**
them [ðɛm, ðəm] pron (direct) li (le); (indirect) gli (loro (after vb)); (stressed, after prep: people) loro; (: people, things) essi(-e); see also **me**
theme [θiːm] n tema m; **theme park** n parco di divertimenti (intorno a un tema centrale)
themselves [ðəm'sɛlvz] pl pron (reflexive) si; (emphatic) loro stessi(-e); (after prep) se stessi(-e)
then [ðɛn] adv (at that time) allora; (next) poi, dopo; (and also) e poi ▷ conj (therefore) perciò, dunque, quindi ▷ adj **the ~ president** il presidente di allora; **by ~** allora; **from ~ on** da allora in poi
theology [θɪ'ɒlədʒɪ] n teologia
theory ['θɪərɪ] n teoria
therapist ['θɛrəpɪst] n terapista m/f
therapy ['θɛrəpɪ] n terapia

 KEYWORD

there [ðɛə'] adv **1**: **there is, there are** c'è, ci sono; **there are 3 of them** (people) sono in 3; (things) ce ne sono 3; **there is no-one here** non c'è nessuno qui; **there has been an accident** c'è stato un incidente
2 (referring to place) là, lì; **up/in/down there** lassù/là dentro/laggiù; **he went there on Friday** ci è andato venerdì; **I want that book there** voglio quel libro là or lì; **there he is!** eccolo!
3: **there, there** (esp to child) su, su

there: **thereabouts** [ðɛərə'bauts] adv (place) nei pressi, da quelle parti; (amount) giù di lì, all'incirca; **thereafter** [ðɛər'ɑːftə'] adv da allora in poi; **thereby** [ðɛə'baɪ] adv con ciò; **therefore** ['ðɛəfɔː'] adv perciò, quindi; **there's** [ðɛəz] = **there is**; **there has**
thermal ['θəːml] adj termico(-a)
thermometer [θə'mɒmɪtə'] n

termometro
thermostat ['θə:məstæt] n termostato
these [ði:z] pl pron, adj questi(-e)
thesis ['θi:sɪs] (pl **theses**) n tesi f inv
they [ðeɪ] pl pron essi (esse); (people only)
loro; **~ say that ...** (it is said that) si dice
che ...; **they'd** = **they had**; **they would**;
they'll = **they shall**; **they will**; **they're**
= **they are**; **they've** = **they have**
thick [θɪk] adj spesso(-a); (crowd)
compatto(-a); (stupid) ottuso(-a), lento(-a)
▷ n **in the ~ of** nel folto di; **it's 20 cm ~**
ha uno spessore di 20 cm; **thicken** vi
ispessire ▷ vt (sauce etc) ispessire, rendere
più denso(-a); **thickness** n spessore m
thief [θi:f] (pl **thieves**) n ladro(-a)
thigh [θaɪ] n coscia
thin [θɪn] adj sottile; (person) magro(-a);
(soup) poco denso(-a) ▷ vt **to ~ (down)**
(sauce, paint) diluire
thing [θɪŋ] n cosa; (object) oggetto;
(mania): **to have a ~ about** essere
fissato(-a) con; **~s** npl (belongings) cose fpl;
poor ~ poverino(-a); **the best ~ would be
to** la cosa migliore sarebbe di; **how are ~s?**
come va?
think [θɪŋk] (pt, pp **thought**) vi pensare,
riflettere ▷ vt pensare, credere; (imagine)
immaginare; **to ~ of** pensare a; **what did
you ~ of them?** cosa ne ha pensato?; **to
~ about sth/sb** pensare a qc/qn; **I'll ~
about it** ci penserò; **to ~ of doing** pensare
di fare; **I ~ so/not** penso di sì/no; **to ~ well
of** avere una buona opinione di; **think
over** vt riflettere su; **think up** vt ideare
third [θə:d] num terzo(-a) ▷ n terzo(-a);
(fraction) terzo, terza parte f; (Aut) terza;
(BRIT: Scol: degree) laurea col minimo dei voti;
thirdly adv in terzo luogo; **third party
insurance** (BRIT) n assicurazione f contro
terzi; **Third World** n **the Third World** il
Terzo Mondo
thirst [θə:st] n sete f; **thirsty** adj (person)
assetato(-a), che ha sete
thirteen [θə:'ti:n] num tredici; **thirteenth**
[-'ti:nθ] num tredicesimo(-a)
thirtieth ['θə:tɪɪθ] num trentesimo(-a)
thirty ['θə:tɪ] num trenta

KEYWORD

this [ðɪs] (pl **these**) adj (demonstrative)
questo(-a); **this man/woman/book**
quest'uomo/questa donna/questo libro;
(not "that") quest'uomo/questa donna/
questo libro qui; **this one** questo(-a) qui
▷ pron (demonstrative) questo(-a); (not "that
one") questo(-a) qui; **who/what is this?**
chi è/che cos'è questo?; **I prefer this to**

that preferisco questo a quello; **this is
where I live** io abito qui; **this is what he
said** questo è ciò che ha detto; **this is Mr
Brown** (in introductions, photo) questo è il
signor Brown; (on telephone) sono il signor
Brown
▷ adv (demonstrative): **this high/long** etc
alto/lungo etc così; **I didn't know things
were this bad** non sapevo andasse così
male

thistle ['θɪsl] n cardo
thorn [θɔ:n] n spina
thorough ['θʌrə] adj (search)
minuzioso(-a); (knowledge, research)
approfondito(-a), profondo(-a);
(person) coscienzioso(-a); (cleaning)
a fondo; **thoroughly** adv (search)
minuziosamente; (wash, study) a fondo;
(very) assolutamente
those [ðəuz] pl pron quelli(-e) ▷ pl adj quei
(quegli) mpl; quelle fpl
though [ðəu] conj benché, sebbene ▷ adv
comunque
thought [θɔ:t] pt, pp of **think** ▷ n pensiero;
(opinion) opinione f; **thoughtful** adj
pensieroso(-a), pensoso(-a); (considerate)
premuroso(-a); **thoughtless** adj
sconsiderato(-a); (behaviour) scortese
thousand ['θauzənd] num mille; **one ~**
mille; **~s of** migliaia di; **thousandth** num
millesimo(-a)
thrash [θræʃ] vt picchiare; bastonare;
(defeat) battere
thread [θrɛd] n filo; (of screw) filetto ▷ vt
(needle) infilare
threat [θrɛt] n minaccia; **threaten** vi
(storm) minacciare ▷ vt **to threaten sb
with/to do** minacciare qn con/di fare;
threatening adj minaccioso(-a)
three [θri:] num tre; **three-
dimensional** adj tridimensionale; (film)
stereoscopico(-a); **three-piece suite**
['θri:pi:s-] n salotto comprendente un
divano e due poltrone; **three-quarters**
npl tre quarti mpl; **three-quarters full**
pieno per tre quarti
threshold ['θrɛʃhəuld] n soglia
threw [θru:] pt of **throw**
thrill [θrɪl] n brivido ▷ vt (audience)
elettrizzare; **to be ~ed** (with gift etc) essere
elettrizzato(-a); **thrilled** adj **I was thrilled
to get your letter** la tua lettera mi ha
fatto veramente piacere; **thriller** n thriller
m inv; **thrilling** adj (book) pieno(-a) di
suspense; (news, discovery) elettrizzante
thriving ['θraɪvɪŋ] adj fiorente
throat [θrəut] n gola; **to have a sore ~**
avere (un or il) mal di gola

throb [θrɔb] *vi* palpitare; pulsare; vibrare

throne [θrəun] *n* trono

through [θru:] *prep* attraverso; (*time*) per, durante; (*by means of*) per mezzo di; (*owing to*) a causa di ▷ *adj* (*ticket, train, passage*) diretto(-a) ▷ *adv* attraverso; **to put sb ~ to sb** (*Tel*) passare qn a qn; **to be ~** (*Tel*) ottenere la comunicazione; (*have finished*) essere finito(-a); **"no ~ road"** (*BRIT*) "strada senza sbocco"; **throughout** *prep* (*place*) dappertutto in; (*time*) per *or* durante tutto(-a) ▷ *adv* dappertutto; sempre

throw [θrəu] (*pt* **threw**, *pp* **thrown**) *n* (*Sport*) lancio, tiro ▷ *vt* tirare, gettare; (*Sport*) lanciare, tirare; (*rider*) disarcionare; (*fig*) confondere; **to ~ a party** dare una festa; **throw away** *vt* gettare *or* buttare via; **throw in** *vt* (*Sport: ball*) rimettere in gioco, (*include*) aggiungere; **throw off** *vt* sbarazzarsi di; **throw out** *vt* buttare fuori; (*reject*) respingere; **throw up** *vi* vomitare

thru [θru:] (*US*) *prep, adj, adv* = **through**

thrush [θrʌʃ] *n* tordo

thrust [θrʌst] (*pt, pp* **thrust**) *vt* spingere con forza; (*push in*) conficcare

thud [θʌd] *n* tonfo

thug [θʌg] *n* delinquente *m*

thumb [θʌm] *n* (*Anat*) pollice *m*; **to ~ a lift** fare l'autostop; **thumbtack** (*US*) *n* puntina da disegno

thump [θʌmp] *n* colpo forte; (*sound*) tonfo ▷ *vt* (*person*) picchiare; (*object*) battere su ▷ *vi* picchiare; battere

thunder ['θʌndəʳ] *n* tuono ▷ *vi* tuonare; (*train etc*) **to ~ past** passare con un rombo; **thunderstorm** *n* temporale *m*

Thur(s). *abbr* (= *Thursday*) gio.

Thursday ['θəːzdɪ] *n* giovedì *m inv*

thus [ðʌs] *adv* così

thwart [θwɔːt] *vt* contrastare

thyme [taɪm] *n* timo

Tiber ['taɪbəʳ] *n* **the ~** il Tevere

Tibet [tɪ'bɛt] *n* Tibet *m*

tick [tɪk] *n* (*sound: of clock*) tic tac *m inv*; (*mark*) segno; spunta; (*Zool*) zecca; (*BRIT: inf*): **in a ~** in un attimo ▷ *vi* fare tic tac ▷ *vt* spuntare; **tick off** *vt* spuntare; (*person*) sgridare

ticket ['tɪkɪt] *n* biglietto; (*in shop: on goods*) etichetta; (*parking ticket*) multa; (*for library*) scheda; **a single/return ~ to ...** un biglietto di sola andata/di andata e ritorno per...; **ticket barrier** *n* (*BRIT: Rail*) cancelletto d'ingresso; **ticket collector** *n* bigliettaio; **ticket inspector** *n* controllore *m*; **ticket machine** *n* distributore *m* di biglietti; **ticket office** *n* biglietteria

tickle ['tɪkl] *vt* fare il solletico a; (*fig*) solleticare ▷ *vi* **it ~s** mi (*or* gli *etc*) fa il solletico; **ticklish** [-lɪʃ] *adj* che soffre il solletico; (*problem*) delicato(-a)

tide [taɪd] *n* marea; (*fig: of events*) corso; **high/low ~** alta/bassa marea

tidy ['taɪdɪ] *adj* (*room*) ordinato(-a), lindo(-a); (*dress, work*) curato(-a), in ordine; (*person*) ordinato(-a) ▷ *vt* (*also: ~ up*) riordinare, mettere in ordine

tie [taɪ] *n* (*string etc*) legaccio; (*BRIT: also: neck~*) cravatta; (*fig: link*) legame *m*; (*Sport: draw*) pareggio ▷ *vt* (*parcel*) legare; (*ribbon*) annodare ▷ *vi* (*Sport*) pareggiare; **to ~ sth in a bow** annodare qc; **to ~ a knot in sth** fare un nodo a qc; **tie down** *vt* legare; (*to price etc*) costringere ad accettare; **tie up** *vt* (*parcel, dog*) legare; (*boat*) ormeggiare; (*arrangements*) concludere; **to be ~d up** (*busy*) essere occupato(-a) *or* preso(-a)

tier [tɪəʳ] *n* fila; (*of cake*) piano, strato

tiger ['taɪgəʳ] *n* tigre *f*

tight [taɪt] *adj* (*rope*) teso(-a), tirato(-a); (*money*) poco(-a); (*clothes, budget, bend etc*) stretto(-a); (*control*) severo(-a), fermo(-a); (*inf: drunk*) sbronzo(-a) ▷ *adv* (*squeeze*) fortemente; (*shut*) ermeticamente; **tighten** *vt* (*rope*) tendere; (*screw*) stringere; (*control*) rinforzare ▷ *vi* tendersi; stringersi; **tightly** *adv* (*grasp*) bene, saldamente; **tights** (*BRIT*) *npl* collant *m inv*

tile [taɪl] *n* (*on roof*) tegola; (*on wall or floor*) piastrella, mattonella

till [tɪl] *n* registratore *m* di cassa ▷ *vt* (*land*) coltivare ▷ *prep, conj* = **until**

tilt [tɪlt] *vt* inclinare, far pendere ▷ *vi* inclinarsi, pendere

timber ['tɪmbəʳ] *n* (*material*) legname *m*

time [taɪm] *n* tempo; (*epoch: often pl*) epoca, tempo; (*by clock*) ora; (*moment*) momento; (*occasion*) volta; (*Mus*) tempo ▷ *vt* (*race*) cronometrare; (*programme*) calcolare la durata di; (*fix moment for*) programmare; (*remark etc*) dire (*or* fare) al momento giusto; **a long ~** molto tempo; **what ~ does the museum/shop open?** a che ora apre il museo/negozio?; **for the ~ being** per il momento; **4 at a ~** 4 per *or* alla volta; **from ~ to ~** ogni tanto; **at ~s** a volte; **in ~** (*soon enough*) in tempo; (*after some time*) col tempo; (*Mus*) a tempo; **in a week's ~** fra una settimana; **in no ~** in un attimo; **any ~** in qualsiasi momento; **on ~** puntualmente; **5 ~s 5** 5 volte 5, 5 per 5; **what ~ is it?** che ora è?, che ore sono?; **to have a good ~** divertirsi; **time limit** *n* limite *m* di tempo; **timely** *adj* opportuno(-a); **timer** *n* (*time switch*) temporizzatore *m*; (*in kitchen*) contaminuti *m inv*; **time-share** *adj* **time-share apartment/villa** appartamento/villa in multiproprietà; **timetable** n orario; **time zone** n fuso orario

timid ['tɪmɪd] adj timido(-a); (easily scared) pauroso(-a)

timing ['taɪmɪŋ] n (Sport) cronometraggio; (fig) scelta del momento opportuno

tin [tɪn] n stagno; (also: ~ **plate**) latta; (container) scatola; (BRIT: can) barattolo (di latta), lattina; **tinfoil** n stagnola

tingle ['tɪŋgl] vi pizzicare

tinker ['tɪŋkəʳ]: ~ **with** vt fus armeggiare intorno a; cercare di riparare

tinned [tɪnd] (BRIT) adj (food) in scatola

tin opener ['-əupnəʳ] (BRIT) n apriscatole m inv

tint [tɪnt] n tinta; **tinted** adj (hair) tinto(-a); (spectacles, glass) colorato(-a)

tiny ['taɪnɪ] adj minuscolo(-a)

tip [tɪp] n (end) punta; (gratuity) mancia; (BRIT: for rubbish) immondezzaio; (advice) suggerimento ▷ vt (waiter) dare la mancia a; (tilt) inclinare; (overturn: also: ~ **over**) capovolgere; (empty: also: ~ **out**) scaricare; **how much should I ~?** quanto devo lasciare di mancia?; **tip off** vt fare una soffiata a

tiptoe ['tɪptəu] n **on ~** in punta di piedi

tire ['taɪəʳ] n (US) = **tyre** ▷ vt stancare ▷ vi stancarsi; **tired** adj stanco(-a); **to be tired of** essere stanco or stufo di; **tire pressure** (US) n = **tyre pressure**; **tiring** adj faticoso(-a)

tissue ['tɪʃuː] n tessuto; (paper handkerchief) fazzoletto di carta; **tissue paper** n carta velina

tit [tɪt] n (bird) cinciallegra; **to give ~ for tat** rendere pan per focaccia

title ['taɪtl] n titolo

T-junction ['tiː'dʒʌŋkʃən] n incrocio a T

TM abbr = **trademark**

 KEYWORD

to [tuː, tə] prep **1** (direction) a; **to go to France/London/school** andare in Francia/a Londra/a scuola; **to go to Paul's/the doctor's** andare da Paul/dal dottore; **the road to Edinburgh** la strada per Edimburgo; **to the left/right** a sinistra/destra

2 (as far as) (fino) a; **from here to London** da qui a Londra; **to count to 10** contare fino a 10; **from 40 to 50 people** da 40 a 50 persone

3 (with expressions of time): **a quarter to 5** le 5 meno un quarto; **it's twenty to 3** sono le 3 meno venti

4 (for, of): **the key to the front door** la chiave della porta d'ingresso; **a letter to his wife** una lettera per la moglie

5 (expressing indirect object) a; **to give sth to sb** dare qc a qn; **to talk to sb** parlare a qn; **to be a danger to sb/sth** rappresentare un pericolo per qn/qc

6 (in relation to) a; **3 goals to 2** 3 goal a 2; **30 miles to the gallon** ≈ 11 chilometri con un litro

7 (purpose, result): **to come to sb's aid** venire in aiuto a qn; **to sentence sb to death** condannare a morte qn; **to my surprise** con mia sorpresa

▷ with vb **1** (simple infinitive): **to go/eat** etc andare/mangiare etc

2 (following another vb): **to want/try/start to do** volere/cercare di/cominciare a fare

3 (with vb omitted): **I don't want to** non voglio (farlo); **you ought to** devi (farlo)

4 (purpose, result) per; **I did it to help you** l'ho fatto per aiutarti

5 (equivalent to relative clause): **I have things to do** ho da fare; **the main thing is to try** la cosa più importante è provare

6 (after adjective etc): **ready to go** pronto a partire; **too old/young to ...** troppo vecchio/giovane per ...

▷ adv **to push the door to** accostare la porta

toad [təud] n rospo; **toadstool** n fungo (velenoso)

toast [təust] n (Culin) pane m tostato; (drink, speech) brindisi m inv ▷ vt (Culin) tostare; (drink to) brindare a; **a piece** or **slice of ~** una fetta di pane tostato; **toaster** n tostapane m inv

tobacco [tə'bækəu] n tabacco

toboggan [tə'bɔgən] n toboga m inv

today [tə'deɪ] adv oggi ▷ n (also fig) oggi m

toddler ['tɔdləʳ] n bambino(-a) che impara a camminare

toe [təu] n dito del piede; (of shoe) punta; **to ~ the line** (fig) stare in riga, conformarsi; **toenail** n unghia del piede

toffee ['tɔfɪ] n caramella

together [tə'gɛðəʳ] adv insieme; (at same time) allo stesso tempo; ~ **with** insieme a

toilet ['tɔɪlət] n (BRIT: lavatory) gabinetto ▷ cpd (bag, soap etc) da toletta; **where's the ~?** dov'è il bagno?; **toilet bag** n (BRIT) nécessaire m inv da toletta; **toilet paper** n carta igienica; **toiletries** npl articoli mpl da toletta; **toilet roll** n rotolo di carta igienica

token ['təukən] n (sign) segno; (substitute coin) gettone m; **book/record/gift ~** (BRIT) buono-libro/disco/regalo

Tokyo ['təukjəu] n Tokyo f

told [təuld] *pt, pp of* **tell**

tolerant ['tɔlərnt] *adj* **~ (of)** tollerante (nei confronti di)

tolerate ['tɔləreɪt] *vt* sopportare; (*Med, Tech*) tollerare

toll [təul] *n* (*tax, charge*) pedaggio ▷ *vi* (*bell*) suonare; **the accident ~ on the roads** il numero delle vittime della strada; **toll call** (*us*) *n* (*Tel*) (telefonata) interurbana; **toll-free** (*us*) *adj* senza addebito, gratuito(-a) ▷ *adv* gratuitamente; **toll-free number** ≈ numero verde

tomato [tə'mɑːtəu] (*pl* **tomatoes**) *n* pomodoro; **tomato sauce** *n* salsa di pomodoro

tomb [tuːm] *n* tomba; **tombstone** ['tuːmstəun] *n* pietra tombale

tomorrow [tə'mɔrəu] *adv* domani ▷ *n* (*also fig*) domani *m inv*; **the day after ~** dopodomani; **~ morning** domani mattina

ton [tʌn] *n* tonnellata; (*BRIT: 1016 kg: us: 907 kg: metric 1000 kg*); **~s of** (*inf*) un mucchio *or* sacco di

tone [təun] *n* tono ▷ *vi* (*also: ~ in*) intonarsi; **tone down** *vt* (*colour, criticism, sound*) attenuare

tongs [tɔŋz] *npl* (*for nails*) tenaglie *fpl*; (*for coal*) molle *fpl*; (*for hair*) arricciacapelli *m inv*

tongue [tʌŋ] *n* lingua; **~ in cheek** (*say, speak*) ironicamente

tonic ['tɔnɪk] *n* (*Med*) tonico; (*also: ~ water*) acqua tonica

tonight [tə'naɪt] *adv* stanotte; (*this evening*) stasera ▷ *n* questa notte; questa sera

tonne [tʌn] *n* (*BRIT: metric ton*) tonnellata

tonsil ['tɔnsl] *n* tonsilla; **tonsillitis** [-'laɪtɪs] *n* tonsillite *f*

too [tuː] *adv* (*excessively*) troppo; (*also*) anche; (*also: ~ much*) ▷ *adv* troppo ▷ *adj* troppo(-a); **~ many** troppi(-e)

took [tuk] *pt of* **take**

tool [tuːl] *n* utensile *m*, attrezzo; **tool box** *n* cassetta *f* portautensili; **tool kit** *n* cassetta di attrezzi

tooth [tuːθ] (*pl* **teeth**) *n* (*Anat, Tech*) dente *m*; **toothache** *n* mal *m* di denti; **toothbrush** *n* spazzolino da denti; **toothpaste** *n* dentifricio; **toothpick** *n* stuzzicadenti *m inv*

top [tɔp] *n* (*of mountain, page, ladder*) cima; (*of box, cupboard, table*) sopra *m inv*, parte *f* superiore; (*lid: of box, jar*) coperchio; (: *of bottle*) tappo; (*blouse etc*) sopra *m inv*; (*toy*) trottola ▷ *adj* più alto(-a); (*in rank*) primo(-a); (*best*) migliore ▷ *vt* (*exceed*) superare; (*be first in*) essere in testa a; **on ~ of** sopra, in cima a; (*in addition to*) oltre a; **from ~ to bottom** da cima a fondo;

top up (*us* **top off**) *vt* riempire; (*salary*) integrare; **top floor** *n* ultimo piano; **top hat** *n* cilindro

topic ['tɔpɪk] *n* argomento; **topical** *adj* d'attualità

topless ['tɔplɪs] *adj* (*bather etc*) col seno scoperto

topping ['tɔpɪŋ] *n* (*Culin*) guarnizione *f*

topple ['tɔpl] *vt* rovesciare, far cadere ▷ *vi* cadere; traballare

torch [tɔːtʃ] *n* torcia; (*BRIT: electric*) lampadina tascabile

tore [tɔːʳ] *pt of* **tear¹**

torment [*n* 'tɔːmɛnt, *vb* tɔː'mɛnt] *n* tormento ▷ *vt* tormentare

torn [tɔːn] *pp of* **tear¹**

tornado [tɔː'neɪdəu] (*pl* **tornadoes**) *n* tornado

torpedo [tɔː'piːdəu] (*pl* **torpedoes**) *n* siluro

torrent ['tɔrnt] *n* torrente *m*; **torrential** [tɔ'rɛnʃl] *adj* torrenziale

tortoise ['tɔːtəs] *n* tartaruga

torture ['tɔːtʃəʳ] *n* tortura ▷ *vt* torturare

Tory ['tɔːrɪ] (*BRIT: Pol*) *adj* dei tories, conservatore(-trice) ▷ *n* tory *m/f inv*, conservatore(-trice)

toss [tɔs] *vt* gettare, lanciare; (*one's head*) scuotere; **to ~ a coin** fare a testa o croce; **to ~ up for sth** fare a testa o croce per qc; **to ~ and turn** (*in bed*) girarsi e rigirarsi

total ['təutl] *adj* totale ▷ *n* totale *m* ▷ *vt* (*add up*) sommare; (*amount to*) ammontare a

totalitarian [təutælɪ'tɛərɪən] *adj* totalitario(-a)

totally ['təutəlɪ] *adv* completamente

touch [tʌtʃ] *n* tocco; (*sense*) tatto; (*contact*) contatto ▷ *vt* toccare; **a ~ of** (*fig*) un tocco di; un pizzico di; **to get in ~ with** mettersi in contatto con; **to lose ~** (*friends*) perdersi di vista; **touch down** *vi* (*on land*) atterrare; **touchdown** *n* atterraggio; (*on sea*) ammaraggio; (*us: Football*) meta; **touched** *adj* commosso(-a); **touching** *adj* commovente; **touchline** *n* (*Sport*) linea laterale; **touch-sensitive** *adj* sensibile al tatto

tough [tʌf] *adj* duro(-a); (*resistant*) resistente

tour ['tuəʳ] *n* viaggio; (*also:* **package ~**) viaggio organizzato *or* tutto compreso; (*of town, museum*) visita; (*by artist*) tournée *f inv* ▷ *vt* visitare; **tour guide** *n* guida turistica

tourism ['tuərɪzəm] *n* turismo

tourist ['tuərɪst] *n* turista *m/f* ▷ *adv* (*travel*) in classe turistica ▷ *cpd* turistico(-a); **tourist office** *n* pro loco *f inv*

t

tournament ['tuənəmənt] n torneo
tour operator n (BRIT) operatore m
turistico
tow [təu] vt rimorchiare; **"on ~"** (BRIT), **"in
~"** (US) "veicolo rimorchiato"; **tow away** vt
rimorchiare
toward(s) [tə'wɔːd(z)] prep verso; (of
attitude) nei confronti di; (of purpose) per
towel ['tauəl] n asciugamano; (also:
tea ~) strofinaccio; **towelling** n (fabric)
spugna
tower ['tauəʳ] n torre f; **tower block** (BRIT)
n palazzone m
town [taun] n città f inv; **to go to ~** andare
in città; (fig) mettercela tutta; **town
centre** n centro (città); **town hall** n
≈ municipio
tow truck (US) n carro m, attrezzi inv
toxic ['tɔksɪk] adj tossico(-a)
toy [tɔɪ] n giocattolo; **toy with** vt
fus giocare con; (idea) accarezzare,
trastullarsi con; **toyshop** n negozio di
giocattoli
trace [treɪs] n traccia ▷ vt (draw) tracciare;
(follow) seguire; (locate) rintracciare
track [træk] n (of person, animal) traccia;
(on tape, Sport, path: gen) pista; (: of bullet
etc) traiettoria; (: of suspect, animal) pista,
tracce fpl; (Rail) binario, rotaie fpl ▷ vt
seguire le tracce di; **to keep ~ of** seguire;
track down vt (prey) scovare; snidare;
(sth lost) rintracciare; **tracksuit** n tuta
sportiva
tractor ['træktəʳ] n trattore m
trade [treɪd] n commercio; (skill, job)
mestiere m ▷ vi commerciare ▷ vt **to ~
sth (for sth)** barattare qc (con qc); **to
~ with/in** commerciare con/in; **trade
in** vt (old car etc) dare come pagamento
parziale; **trademark** n marchio di
fabbrica; **trader** n commerciante
m/f; **tradesman** (irreg) n fornitore m;
(shopkeeper) negoziante m; **trade union**
n sindacato
trading ['treɪdɪŋ] n commercio
tradition [trə'dɪʃən] n tradizione f;
traditional adj tradizionale
traffic ['træfɪk] n traffico ▷ vi **to ~ in** (pej:
liquor, drugs) trafficare in; **traffic circle**
(US) n isola rotatoria; **traffic island** n
salvagente m, isola f, spartitraffico inv;
traffic jam n ingorgo (del traffico); **traffic
lights** npl semaforo; **traffic warden** n
addetto(-a) al controllo del traffico e del
parcheggio
tragedy ['trædʒədɪ] n tragedia
tragic ['trædʒɪk] adj tragico(-a)
trail [treɪl] n (tracks) tracce fpl, pista; (path)
sentiero; (of smoke etc) scia ▷ vt trascinare,

strascicare; (follow) seguire ▷ vi essere
al traino; (dress etc) strusciare; (plant)
arrampicarsi; strisciare; (in game) essere
in svantaggio; **trailer** n (Aut) rimorchio;
(US) roulotte f inv; (Cinema) prossimamente
m inv
train [treɪn] n treno; (of dress) coda,
strascico ▷ vt (apprentice, doctor etc)
formare; (sportsman) allenare; (dog)
addestrare; (memory) esercitare; (point:
gun etc): **to ~ sth on** puntare qc contro
▷ vi formarsi; allenarsi; **what time
does the ~ from Rome get in?** a che
ora arriva il treno da Roma?; **is this the
~ for …?** è questo il treno per…?; **one's
~ of thought** il filo dei propri pensieri;
trainee [treɪ'niː] n (in trade) apprendista
m/f; **trainer** n (Sport) allenatore(-trice);
(: shoe) scarpa da ginnastica; (of dogs
etc) addestratore(-trice); **trainers**
npl (shoes) scarpe fpl da ginnastica;
training n formazione f; allenamento;
addestramento; **in training** (Sport) in
allenamento; **training course** n corso di
formazione professionale; **training shoes**
npl scarpe fpl da ginnastica
trait [treɪt] n tratto
traitor ['treɪtəʳ] n traditore m
tram [træm] (BRIT) n (also: **~car**) tram
m inv
tramp [træmp] n (person) vagabondo(-a);
(inf: pej: woman) sgualdrina
trample ['træmpl] vt **to ~ (underfoot)**
calpestare
trampoline ['træmpəliːn] n trampolino
tranquil ['træŋkwɪl] adj tranquillo(-a);
tranquillizer (US **tranquilizer**) n (Med)
tranquillante m
transaction [træn'zækʃən] n
transazione f
transatlantic ['trænzət'læntɪk] adj
transatlantico(-a)
transcript ['trænskrɪpt] n trascrizione f
transfer [n 'trænsfəʳ, vb træns'fəːʳ] n (gen:
also Sport) trasferimento; (Pol: of power)
passaggio; (picture, design) decalcomania;
(: stick-on) autoadesivo ▷ vt trasferire;
passare; **to ~ the charges** (BRIT: Tel) fare
una chiamata a carico del destinatario
transform [træns'fɔːm] vt trasformare;
transformation n trasformazione f
transfusion [træns'fjuːʒən] n
trasfusione f
transit ['trænzɪt] n **in ~** in transito
transition [træn'zɪʃən] n passaggio,
transizione f
transitive ['trænzɪtɪv] adj (Ling)
transitivo(-a)
translate [trænz'leɪt] vt tradurre; **can**

you ~ this for me? me lo può tradurre?;
translation [-'leɪʃən] n traduzione f;
translator n traduttore(-trice)
transmission [trænz'mɪʃən] n
trasmissione f
transmit [trænz'mɪt] vt trasmettere;
transmitter n trasmettitore m
transparent [træns'pærnt] adj
trasparente
transplant [vb træns'plɑːnt, n
'trænsplɑːnt] vt trapiantare ▷ n (Med)
trapianto
transport [n 'trænspɔːt, vb træns'pɔː
t] n trasporto ▷ vt trasportare;
transportation [-'teɪʃən] n (mezzo di)
trasporto
transvestite [trænz'vɛstaɪt] n
travestito(-a)
trap [træp] n (snare, trick) trappola,
(carriage) calesse m ▷ vt prendere in
trappola, intrappolare
trash [træʃ] (pej) n (goods) ciarpame m;
(nonsense) sciocchezze fpl; **trash can** (US) n
secchio della spazzatura
trauma ['trɔːmə] n trauma m; **traumatic**
[-'mætɪk] adj traumatico(-a)
travel ['trævl] n viaggio; viaggi mpl ▷ vi
viaggiare ▷ vt (distance) percorrere;
travel agency n agenzia (di) viaggi;
travel agent n agente m di viaggio;
travel insurance n assicurazione f
di viaggio; **traveller** (US **traveler**) n
viaggiatore(-trice); **traveller's cheque**
(US **traveler's check**) n assegno turistico;
travelling (US **traveling**) n viaggi mpl;
travel-sick adj **to get travel-sick** (in
vehicle) soffrire di mal d'auto; (in aeroplane)
soffrire di mal d'aria; (in boat) soffrire di mal
di mare; **travel sickness** n mal m d'auto
(or di mare or d'aria)
tray [treɪ] n (for carrying) vassoio; (on desk)
vaschetta
treacherous ['trɛtʃərəs] adj infido(-a)
treacle ['triːkl] n melassa
tread [trɛd] (pt **trod**, pp **trodden**) n passo;
(sound) rumore m di passi; (of stairs) pedata;
(of tyre) battistrada m inv ▷ vi camminare;
tread on vt fus calpestare
treasure ['trɛʒəʳ] n tesoro ▷ vt (value)
tenere in gran conto, apprezzare molto;
(store) custodire gelosamente; **treasurer**
['trɛʒərəʳ] n tesoriere(-a)
treasury ['trɛʒərɪ] n **the T~** (BRIT), **the T~
Department** (US) il ministero del Tesoro
treat [triːt] n regalo ▷ vt trattare; (Med)
curare; **to ~ sb to sth** offrire qc a qn;
treatment ['triːtmənt] n trattamento
treaty ['triːtɪ] n patto, trattato
treble ['trɛbl] adj triplo(-a), triplice ▷ vt

triplicare ▷ vi triplicarsi
tree [triː] n albero
trek [trɛk] n escursione f a piedi;
escursione f in macchina; (tiring walk)
camminata sfiancante ▷ vi (as holiday) fare
dell'escursionismo
tremble ['trɛmbl] vi tremare
tremendous [trɪ'mɛndəs] adj (enormous)
enorme; (excellent) fantastico(-a),
strepitoso(-a)

> Be careful not to translate
> **tremendous** by the Italian word
> **tremendo**.

trench [trɛntʃ] n trincea
trend [trɛnd] n (tendency) tendenza; (of
events) corso; (fashion) moda; **trendy** adj
(idea) di moda; (clothes) all'ultima moda
trespass ['trɛspəs] vi **to ~ on** entrare
abusivamente in; **"no ~ing"** "proprietà
privata", "vietato l'accesso"
trial ['traɪəl] n (Law) processo; (test: of
machine etc) collaudo; **on ~** (Law) sotto
processo; **trial period** n periodo di prova
triangle ['traɪæŋgl] n (Math, Mus)
triangolo
triangular [traɪ'æŋgjʊləʳ] adj triangolare
tribe [traɪb] n tribù f inv
tribunal [traɪ'bjuːnl] n tribunale m
tribute ['trɪbjuːt] n tributo, omaggio; **to
pay ~ to** rendere omaggio a
trick [trɪk] n trucco; (joke) tiro; (Cards) presa
▷ vt imbrogliare, ingannare; **to play a ~
on sb** giocare un tiro a qn; **that should do
the ~** vedrai che funziona
trickle ['trɪkl] n (of water etc) rivolo;
gocciolio ▷ vi gocciolare
tricky ['trɪkɪ] adj difficile, delicato(-a)
tricycle ['traɪsɪkl] n triciclo
trifle ['traɪfl] n sciocchezza; (BRIT: Culin)
≈ zuppa inglese ▷ adv **a ~ long** un po'
lungo
trigger ['trɪgəʳ] n (of gun) grilletto
trim [trɪm] adj (house, garden) ben
tenuto(-a); (figure) snello(-a) ▷ n (haircut
etc) spuntata, regolata; (embellishment)
finiture fpl; (on car) guarnizioni fpl ▷ vt
spuntare; (decorate): **to ~ (with)** decorare
(con); (Naut: a sail) orientare
trio ['triːəʊ] n trio
trip [trɪp] n viaggio; (excursion) gita,
escursione f; (stumble) passo falso ▷ vi
inciampare; (go lightly) camminare con
passo leggero; **on a ~** in viaggio; **trip up** vi
inciampare ▷ vt fare lo sgambetto a
triple ['trɪpl] adj triplo(-a)
triplets ['trɪplɪts] npl bambini(-e)
trigemini(-e)
tripod ['traɪpɒd] n treppiede m
triumph ['traɪʌmf] n trionfo ▷ vi **to**

~ (over) trionfare (su); **triumphant**
[traɪˈʌmfənt] adj trionfante
trivial [ˈtrɪvɪəl] adj insignificante;
(*commonplace*) banale

> Be careful not to translate *trivial* by
> the Italian word *triviale*.

trod [trɒd] pt of **tread**
trodden [ˈtrɒdn] pp of **tread**
trolley [ˈtrɒlɪ] n carrello
trombone [trɒmˈbəʊn] n trombone m
troop [truːp] n gruppo; (*Mil*) squadrone m;
~s npl (*Mil*) truppe fpl
trophy [ˈtrəʊfɪ] n trofeo
tropical [ˈtrɒpɪkl] adj tropicale
trot [trɒt] n trotto ▷ vi trottare; **on the ~**
(*BRIT: fig*) di fila, uno(-a) dopo l'altro(-a)
trouble [ˈtrʌbl] n difficoltà f inv, problema
m; difficoltà fpl, problemi; (*worry*)
preoccupazione f; (*bother, effort*) sforzo;
(*Pol*) conflitti mpl, disordine m; (*Med*):
stomach etc **~** disturbi mpl gastrici etc
▷ vt disturbare; (*worry*) preoccupare ▷ vi
to ~ to do disturbarsi a fare; **~s** npl (*Pol*
etc) disordini mpl; **to be in ~** avere dei
problemi; **it's no ~!** di niente!; **what's the
~?** cosa c'è che non va?; **I'm sorry to ~ you**
scusi il disturbo; **troubled** adj (*person*)
preoccupato(-a), inquieto(-a); (*epoch, life*)
agitato(-a), difficile; **troublemaker** n
elemento disturbatore, agitatore(-trice);
(*child*) disloco(-a); **troublesome** adj
fastidioso(-a), seccante
trough [trɒf] n (*drinking trough*)
abbeveratoio; (*also:* **feeding ~**) trogolo,
mangiatoia; (*channel*) canale m
trousers [ˈtraʊzəz] npl pantaloni mpl,
calzoni mpl; **short ~** calzoncini mpl
trout [traʊt] n inv trota
trowel [ˈtraʊəl] n cazzuola
truant [ˈtruənt] (*BRIT*) n **to play ~**
marinare la scuola
truce [truːs] n tregua
truck [trʌk] n autocarro, camion m inv;
(*Rail*) carro merci aperto; (*for luggage*)
carrello m portabagagli inv; **truck driver** n
camionista m/f
true [truː] adj vero(-a); (*accurate*)
accurato(-a), esatto(-a); (*genuine*) reale;
(*faithful*) fedele; **to come ~** avverarsi
truly [ˈtruːlɪ] adv veramente; (*truthfully*)
sinceramente; (*faithfully*): **yours ~** (*in letter*)
distinti saluti
trumpet [ˈtrʌmpɪt] n tromba
trunk [trʌŋk] n (*of tree, person*) tronco; (*of
elephant*) proboscide f; (*case*) baule m; (*us:
Aut*) bagagliaio; **~s** (*also:* **swimming ~s**)
calzoncini mpl da bagno
trust [trʌst] n fiducia; (*Law*)
amministrazione f fiduciaria; (*Comm*)

trust m inv ▷ vt (*rely on*) contare su; (*hope*)
sperare; (*entrust*): **to ~ sth to sb** affidare qc
a qn; **trusted** adj fidato(-a); **trustworthy**
adj fidato(-a), degno(-a) di fiducia
truth [truːθ, pl truːðz] n verità f inv;
truthful adj (*person*) sincero(-a);
(*description*) veritiero(-a), esatto(-a)
try [traɪ] n prova, tentativo; (*Rugby*) meta
▷ vt (*Law*) giudicare; (*test: also:* **~ out**)
provare; (*strain*) mettere alla prova ▷ vi
provare; **to have a ~** fare un tentativo;
to ~ to do (*seek*) cercare di fare; **try on**
vt (*clothes*) provare; **trying** adj (*day,
experience*) logorante, pesante; (*child*)
difficile, insopportabile
T-shirt [ˈtiːʃəːt] n maglietta
tub [tʌb] n tinozza; mastello; (*bath*)
bagno
tube [tjuːb] n tubo; (*BRIT: underground*)
metropolitana, metrò m inv; (*for tyre*)
camera d'aria
tuberculosis [tjubəːkjuˈləʊsɪs] n
tubercolosi f inv
tube station (*BRIT*) n stazione f della
metropolitana
tuck [tʌk] vt (*put*) mettere; **tuck away** vt
riporre; (*building*): **to be ~ed away** essere
in un luogo isolato; **tuck in** vt mettere
dentro; (*child*) rimboccare ▷ vi (*eat*)
mangiare di buon appetito; abbuffarsi;
tuck shop n negozio di pasticceria (*in una
scuola*)
Tue(s). abbr (= *Tuesday*) mar.
Tuesday [ˈtjuːzdɪ] n martedì m inv
tug [tʌg] n (*ship*) rimorchiatore m ▷ vt
tirare con forza
tuition [tjuːˈɪʃən] n (*BRIT*) lezioni fpl; (:
private tuition) lezioni fpl private; (*us: school
fees*) tasse fpl scolastiche
tulip [ˈtjuːlɪp] n tulipano
tumble [ˈtʌmbl] n (*fall*) capitombolo ▷ vi
capitombolare, ruzzolare; **to ~ to sth**
(*inf*) realizzare qc; **tumble dryer** (*BRIT*) n
asciugatrice f
tumbler [ˈtʌmblər] n bicchiere m (senza
stelo)
tummy [ˈtʌmɪ] (*inf*) n pancia
tumour [ˈtjuːmər] (*us* **tumor**) n tumore m
tuna [ˈtjuːnə] n inv (*also:* **~ fish**) tonno
tune [tjuːn] n (*melody*) melodia, aria
▷ vt (*Mus*) accordare; (*Radio, TV, Aut*)
regolare, mettere a punto; **to be in/out
of ~** (*instrument*) essere accordato(-a)/
scordato(-a); (*singer*) essere intonato(-a)/
stonato(-a); **tune in** vi **to ~ in (to)**
(*Radio, TV*) sintonizzarsi (su); **tune up** vi
(*musician*) accordare lo strumento
tunic [ˈtjuːnɪk] n tunica
Tunisia [tjuːˈnɪzɪə] n Tunisia

tunnel ['tʌnl] n galleria ▷ vi scavare una galleria

turbulence ['tə:bjuləns] n (Aviat) turbolenza

turf [tə:f] n terreno erboso; (clod) zolla ▷ vt coprire di zolle erbose

Turin [tjuə'rɪn] n Torino f

Turk [tə:k] n turco(-a)

Turkey ['tə:kɪ] n Turchia

turkey ['tə:kɪ] n tacchino

Turkish ['tə:kɪʃ] adj turco(-a) ▷ n (Ling) turco

turmoil ['tə:mɔɪl] n confusione f, tumulto

turn [tə:n] n giro; (change) cambiamento; (in road) curva; (tendency: of mind, events) tendenza; (performance) numero; (chance) turno; (Med) crisi f inv, attacco ▷ vt girare, voltare; (change): **to ~ sth into** trasformare qc in ▷ vi girare; (person: look back) girarsi, voltarsi; (reverse direction) girare; (change) cambiare; (milk) andare a male; (become) diventare; **a good ~** un buon servizio; **it gave me quite a ~** mi ha fatto prendere un bello spavento; **"no left ~"** (Aut) "divieto di svolta a sinistra"; **it's your ~** tocca a lei; **in ~** a sua volta; a turno; **to ~s (at sth)** fare (qc) a turno; **~ left/right at the next junction** al prossimo incrocio, giri a sinistra/destra; **turn around** vi (person) girarsi; (rotate) girare ▷ vt (object) girare; **turn away** vi girarsi (dall'altra parte) ▷ vt mandare via; **turn back** vi ritornare, tornare indietro ▷ vt far tornare indietro; (clock) spostare indietro; **turn down** vt (refuse) rifiutare; (reduce) abbassare; (fold) ripiegare; **turn in** vi (inf: go to bed) andare a letto ▷ vt (fold) voltare in dentro; **turn off** vi (from road) girare, voltare ▷ vt (light, radio, engine etc) spegnere; **I can't ~ the heating off** non riesco a spegnere il riscaldamento; **turn on** vt (light, radio etc) accendere; **I can't ~ the heating on** non riesco ad accendere il riscaldamento; **turn out** vt (light, gas) chiudere; spegnere ▷ vi (voters) presentarsi; **to ~ out to be ...** rivelarsi ..., risultare ...; **turn over** vi (person) girarsi ▷ vt girare; **turn round** vi girare; (person) girarsi; **turn to** vt fus **to ~ to sb** girarsi verso qn; **to ~ to sb for help** rivolgersi a qn per aiuto; **turn up** vi (person) arrivare, presentarsi; (lost object) saltar fuori ▷ vt (collar, sound) alzare; **turning** n (in road) curva; **turning point** n (fig) svolta decisiva

turnip ['tə:nɪp] n rapa

turn: turnout ['tə:naut] n presenza, affluenza; **turnover** ['tə:nəuvə'] n (Comm) turnover m inv, (Culin): **apple** etc **turnover** sfogliatella alle mele ecc; **turnstile** ['tə:nstaɪl] n tornella; **turn-up** (BRIT) n (on trousers) risvolto

turquoise ['tə:kwɔɪz] n turchese m ▷ adj turchese

turtle ['tə:tl] n testuggine f; **turtleneck (sweater)** ['tə:tlnɛk-] n maglione m con il collo alto

Tuscany ['tʌskənɪ] n Toscana

tusk [tʌsk] n zanna

tutor ['tju:tə'] n (in college) docente m/f (responsabile di un gruppo di studenti); (private teacher) precettore m; **tutorial** [-'tɔ:rɪəl] n (Scol) lezione f con discussione (a un gruppo limitato)

tuxedo [tʌk'si:dəu] (US) n smoking m inv

TV [ti:'vi:] n abbr (= television) tivù f inv

tweed [twi:d] n tweed m inv

tweezers ['twi:zəz] npl pinzette fpl

twelfth [twɛlfθ] num dodicesimo(-a)

twelve [twɛlv] num dodici; **at ~ o'clock** alle dodici, a mezzogiorno; (midnight) a mezzanotte

twentieth ['twɛntɪɪθ] num ventesimo(-a)

twenty ['twɛntɪ] num venti

twice [twaɪs] adv due volte; **~ as much** due volte tanto; **~ a week** due volte alla settimana

twig [twɪg] n ramoscello ▷ vt, vi (inf) capire

twilight ['twaɪlaɪt] n crepuscolo

twin [twɪn] adj, n gemello(-a) ▷ vt **to ~ one town with another** fare il gemellaggio di una città con un'altra; **twin(-bedded) room** n stanza con letti gemelli; **twin beds** npl letti mpl gemelli

twinkle ['twɪŋkl] vi scintillare; (eyes) brillare

twist [twɪst] n torsione f; (in wire, flex) piega; (in road) curva; (in story) colpo di scena ▷ vt attorcigliare; (ankle) slogare; (weave) intrecciare; (roll around) arrotolare; (fig) distorcere ▷ vi (road) serpeggiare

twit [twɪt] (inf) n cretino(-a)

twitch [twɪtʃ] n tiratina; (nervous) tic m inv ▷ vi contrarsi

two [tu:] num due; **to put ~ and ~ together** (fig) fare uno più uno

type [taɪp] n (category) genere m; (model) modello; (example) tipo; (Typ) tipo, carattere m ▷ vt battere (a macchina), dattilografare; **typewriter** n macchina da scrivere

typhoid ['taɪfɔɪd] n tifoidea

typhoon [taɪ'fu:n] n tifone m

typical ['tɪpɪkl] adj tipico(-a); **typically** adv tipicamente; **typically, he arrived**

late come al solito è arrivato tardi
typing ['taɪpɪŋ] *n* dattilografia
typist ['taɪpɪst] *n* dattilografo(-a)
tyre ['taɪər] (*US* **tire**) *n* pneumatico, gomma; **I've got a flat ~** ho una gomma a terra; **tyre pressure** *n* pressione *f* (delle gomme)

UFO ['juːfəu] *n abbr* (= *unidentified flying object*) UFO *m inv*
Uganda [juː'gændə] *n* Uganda
ugly ['ʌglɪ] *adj* brutto(-a)
UHT *abbr* (= *ultra heat treated*) UHT *inv*, a lunga conservazione
UK *n abbr* = **United Kingdom**
ulcer ['ʌlsər] *n* ulcera; (*also*: **mouth ~**) afta
ultimate ['ʌltɪmət] *adj* ultimo(-a), finale; (*authority*) massimo(-a), supremo(-a); **ultimately** *adv* alla fine; in definitiva, in fin dei conti
ultimatum [ʌltɪ'meɪtəm, -tə] (*pl* **ultimatums** *or* **ultimata**) *n* ultimatum *m inv*
ultrasound [ʌltrə'saund] *n* (*Med*) ultrasuono
ultraviolet ['ʌltrə'vaɪəlɪt] *adj* ultravioletto(-a)
umbrella [ʌm'brɛlə] *n* ombrello
umpire ['ʌmpaɪər] *n* arbitro
UN *n abbr* (= *United Nations*) ONU *f*
unable [ʌn'eɪbl] *adj* **to be ~ to** non potere, essere nell'impossibilità di; essere incapace di
unacceptable [ʌnək'sɛptəbl] *adj* (*proposal, behaviour*) inaccettabile; (*price*) impossibile
unanimous [juː'nænɪməs] *adj* unanime
unarmed [ʌn'ɑːmd] *adj* (*without a weapon*)

disarmato(-a); (*combat*) senz'armi

unattended [ʌnə'tɛndɪd] *adj* (*car, child, luggage*) incustodito(-a)

unattractive [ʌnə'træktɪv] *adj* poco attraente

unavailable [ʌnə'veɪləbl] *adj* (*article, room, book*) non disponibile; (*person*) impegnato(-a)

unavoidable [ʌnə'vɔɪdəbl] *adj* inevitabile

unaware [ʌnə'wɛəʳ] *adj* **to be ~ of** non sapere, ignorare; **unawares** *adv* di sorpresa, alla sprovvista

unbearable [ʌn'bɛərəbl] *adj* insopportabile

unbeatable [ʌn'biːtəbl] *adj* imbattibile

unbelievable [ʌnbɪ'liːvəbl] *adj* incredibile

unborn [ʌn'bɔːn] *adj* non ancora nato(-a)

unbutton [ʌn'bʌtn] *vt* sbottonare

uncalled-for [ʌn'kɔːldfɔːʳ] *adj* (*remark*) fuori luogo *inv*; (*action*) ingiustificato(-a)

uncanny [ʌn'kænɪ] *adj* misterioso(-a), strano(-a)

uncertain [ʌn'səːtn] *adj* incerto(-a); dubbio(-a); **uncertainty** *n* incertezza

unchanged [ʌn'tʃeɪndʒd] *adj* invariato(-a)

uncle ['ʌŋkl] *n* zio

unclear [ʌn'klɪəʳ] *adj* non chiaro(-a); **I'm still ~ about what I'm supposed to do** non ho ancora ben capito cosa dovrei fare

uncomfortable [ʌn'kʌmfətəbl] *adj* scomodo(-a); (*uneasy*) a disagio, agitato(-a); (*unpleasant*) fastidioso(-a)

uncommon [ʌn'kɔmən] *adj* raro(-a), insolito(-a), non comune

unconditional [ʌnkən'dɪʃənl] *adj* incondizionato(-a), senza condizioni

unconscious [ʌn'kɔnʃəs] *adj* privo(-a) di sensi, svenuto(-a); (*unaware*) inconsapevole, inconscio(-a) ▷ *n* **the ~** l'inconscio

uncontrollable [ʌnkən'trəuləbl] *adj* incontrollabile; indisciplinato(-a)

unconventional [ʌnkən'vɛnʃənl] *adj* poco convenzionale

uncover [ʌn'kʌvəʳ] *vt* scoprire

undecided [ʌndɪ'saɪdɪd] *adj* indeciso(-a)

undeniable [ʌndɪ'naɪəbl] *adj* innegabile, indiscutibile

under ['ʌndəʳ] *prep* sotto; (*less than*) meno di; al disotto di; (*according to*) secondo, in conformità a ▷ *adv* (al) disotto; **~ there** là sotto; **~ repair** in riparazione; **undercover** *adj* segreto(-a), clandestino(-a);

underdone *adj* (*Culin*) al sangue; (*pej*) poco cotto(-a); **underestimate** *vt* sottovalutare; **undergo** *vt* (*irreg*) subire; (*treatment*) sottoporsi a; **undergraduate** *n* studente(-essa) universitario(-a); **underground** *n* (*BRIT:*

railway) metropolitana; (*Pol*) movimento clandestino ▷ *adj* sotterraneo(-a); (*fig*) clandestino(-a) ▷ *adv* sottoterra; **to go underground** (*fig*) darsi alla macchia; **undergrowth** *n* sottobosco; **underline** *vt* sottolineare; **undermine** *vt* minare; **underneath** [ʌndə'niːθ] *adv* sotto, disotto ▷ *prep* sotto, al di sotto di; **underpants** *npl* mutande *fpl*, slip *m inv*; **underpass** (*BRIT*) *n* sottopassaggio; **underprivileged** *adj* non abbiente; meno favorito(-a); **underscore** *vt* sottolineare; **undershirt** (*US*) *n* maglietta; **underskirt** (*BRIT*) *n* sottoveste *f*

understand [ʌndə'stænd] (*irreg: like* **stand**) *vt, vi* capire, comprendere; **I don't ~** non capisco; **I ~ that ...** sento che ...; credo di capire che ...; **understandable** *adj* comprensibile; **understanding** *adj* comprensivo(-a) ▷ *n* comprensione *f*; (*agreement*) accordo

understatement [ʌndə'steɪtmənt] *n* **that's an ~!** a dire poco!

understood [ʌndə'stud] *pt, pp of* **understand** ▷ *adj* inteso(-a); (*implied*) sottinteso(-a)

undertake [ʌndə'teɪk] (*irreg: like* **take**) *vt* intraprendere; **to ~ to do sth** impegnarsi a fare qc

undertaker ['ʌndəteɪkəʳ] *n* impresario di pompe funebri

undertaking [ʌndə'teɪkɪŋ] *n* impresa; (*promise*) promessa

under: **underwater** [ʌndə'wɔːtəʳ] *adv* sott'acqua ▷ *adj* subacqueo(-a); **underway** [ʌndə'weɪ] *adj* **to be underway** essere in corso; **underwear** ['ʌndəwɛəʳ] *n* biancheria (intima); **underwent** [ʌndə'wɛnt] *vb see* **undergo**; **underworld** ['ʌndəwəːld] *n* (*of crime*) malavita

undesirable [ʌndɪ'zaɪərəbl] *adj* sgradevole

undisputed [ʌndɪs'pjuːtɪd] *adj* indiscusso(-a)

undo [ʌn'duː] *vt* (*irreg*) disfare

undone [ʌn'dʌn] *pp of* **undo**; **to come ~** slacciarsi

undoubtedly [ʌn'dautɪdlɪ] *adv* senza alcun dubbio

undress [ʌn'drɛs] *vi* spogliarsi

unearth [ʌn'əːθ] *vt* dissotterrare; (*fig*) scoprire

uneasy [ʌn'iːzɪ] *adj* a disagio; (*worried*) preoccupato(-a); (*peace*) precario(-a)

unemployed [ʌnɪm'plɔɪd] *adj* disoccupato(-a) ▷ *npl* **the ~** i disoccupati

unemployment [ʌnɪm'plɔɪmənt] *n* disoccupazione *f*; **unemployment**

u

benefit (us **unemployment compensation**) n sussidio di disoccupazione

unequal [ʌnˈiːkwəl] adj (length, objects) disuguale; (amounts) diverso(-a); (division of labour) ineguale

uneven [ʌnˈiːvn] adj ineguale; irregolare

unexpected [ʌnɪkˈspɛktɪd] adj inatteso(-a), imprevisto(-a); **unexpectedly** adv inaspettatamente

unfair [ʌnˈfɛəʳ] adj ~ (to) ingiusto(-a) (nei confronti di)

unfaithful [ʌnˈfeɪθful] adj infedele

unfamiliar [ʌnfəˈmɪlɪəʳ] adj sconosciuto(-a), strano(-a); **to be ~ with** non avere familiarità con

unfashionable [ʌnˈfæʃnəbl] adj (clothes) fuori moda; (district) non alla moda

unfasten [ʌnˈfɑːsn] vt slacciare; sciogliere

unfavourable [ʌnˈfeɪvərəbl] (us **unfavorable**) adj sfavorevole

unfinished [ʌnˈfɪnɪʃt] adj incompleto(-a)

unfit [ʌnˈfɪt] adj (ill) malato(-a), in cattiva salute; (incompetent): ~ **(for)** incompetente (in); (: work, Mil) inabile (a)

unfold [ʌnˈfəuld] vt spiegare ▷ vi (story, plot) svelarsi

unforgettable [ʌnfəˈgɛtəbl] adj indimenticabile

unfortunate [ʌnˈfɔːtʃnət] adj sfortunato(-a); (event, remark) infelice; **unfortunately** adv sfortunatamente, purtroppo

unfriendly [ʌnˈfrɛndlɪ] adj poco amichevole, freddo(-a)

unfurnished [ʌnˈfəːnɪʃt] adj non ammobiliato(-a)

unhappiness [ʌnˈhæpɪnɪs] n infelicità

unhappy [ʌnˈhæpɪ] adj infelice; ~ **about/ with** (arrangements etc) insoddisfatto(-a) di

unhealthy [ʌnˈhɛlθɪ] adj (gen) malsano(-a); (person) malaticcio(-a)

unheard-of [ʌnˈhəːdɔv] adj inaudito(-a), senza precedenti

unhelpful [ʌnˈhɛlpful] adj poco disponibile

unhurt [ʌnˈhəːt] adj illeso(-a)

unidentified [ʌnaɪˈdɛntɪfaɪd] adj non identificato(-a)

uniform [ˈjuːnɪfɔːm] n uniforme f, divisa ▷ adj uniforme

unify [ˈjuːnɪfaɪ] vt unificare

unimportant [ʌnɪmˈpɔːtənt] adj senza importanza, di scarsa importanza

uninhabited [ʌnɪnˈhæbɪtɪd] adj disabitato(-a)

unintentional [ʌnɪnˈtɛnʃənəl] adj involontario(-a)

union [ˈjuːnjən] n unione f; (also: **trade ~**)

sindacato ▷ cpd sindacale, dei sindacati; **Union Jack** n bandiera nazionale britannica

unique [juːˈniːk] adj unico(-a)

unisex [ˈjuːnɪsɛks] adj unisex inv

unit [ˈjuːnɪt] n unità f inv; (section: of furniture etc) elemento; (team, squad) reparto, squadra

unite [juːˈnaɪt] vt unire ▷ vi unirsi; **united** adj unito(-a); unificato(-a); (efforts) congiunto(-a); **United Kingdom** n Regno Unito; **United Nations (Organization)** n (Organizzazione f delle) Nazioni Unite; **United States (of America)** n Stati mpl Uniti (d'America)

unity [ˈjuːnɪtɪ] n unità

universal [juːnɪˈvəːsl] adj universale

universe [ˈjuːnɪvəːs] n universo

university [juːnɪˈvəːsɪtɪ] n università f inv

unjust [ʌnˈdʒʌst] adj ingiusto(-a)

unkind [ʌnˈkaɪnd] adj scortese; crudele

unknown [ʌnˈnəun] adj sconosciuto(-a)

unlawful [ʌnˈlɔːful] adj illecito(-a), illegale

unleaded [ʌnˈlɛdɪd] adj (petrol, fuel) verde, senza piombo

unleash [ʌnˈliːʃ] vt (fig) scatenare

unless [ʌnˈlɛs] conj a meno che (non) + sub

unlike [ʌnˈlaɪk] adj diverso(-a) ▷ prep a differenza di, contrariamente a

unlikely [ʌnˈlaɪklɪ] adj improbabile

unlimited [ʌnˈlɪmɪtɪd] adj illimitato(-a)

unlisted [ʌnˈlɪstɪd] (us) adj (Tel): **to be ~** non essere sull'elenco

unload [ʌnˈləud] vt scaricare

unlock [ʌnˈlɔk] vt aprire

unlucky [ʌnˈlʌkɪ] adj sfortunato(-a); (object, number) che porta sfortuna

unmarried [ʌnˈmærɪd] adj non sposato(-a); (man only) scapolo, celibe; (woman only) nubile

unmistak(e)able [ʌnmɪsˈteɪkəbl] adj inconfondibile

unnatural [ʌnˈnætʃrəl] adj innaturale; contro natura

unnecessary [ʌnˈnɛsəsərɪ] adj inutile, superfluo(-a)

UNO [ˈjuːnəu] n abbr (= United Nations Organization) ONU f

unofficial [ʌnəˈfɪʃl] adj non ufficiale; (strike) non dichiarato(-a) dal sindacato

unpack [ʌnˈpæk] vi disfare la valigia (or le valigie) ▷ vt disfare

unpaid [ʌnˈpeɪd] adj (holiday) non pagato(-a); (work) non retribuito(-a); (bill, debt) da pagare

unpleasant [ʌnˈplɛznt] adj spiacevole

unplug [ʌnˈplʌg] vt staccare

unpopular [ʌnˈpɔpjuləʳ] adj impopolare

unprecedented [ʌnˈprɛsɪdəntɪd] adj senza precedenti

unpredictable [ʌnprɪ'dɪktəbl] *adj* imprevedibile

unprotected ['ʌnprə'tɛktɪd] *adj* (*sex*) non protetto(-a)

unqualified [ʌn'kwɔlɪfaɪd] *adj* (*teacher*) non abilitato(-a); (*success*) assoluto(-a), senza riserve

unravel [ʌn'rævl] *vt* dipanare, districare

unreal [ʌn'rɪəl] *adj* irreale

unrealistic [ʌnrɪə'lɪstɪk] *adj* non realistico(-a)

unreasonable [ʌn'riːznəbl] *adj* irragionevole

unrelated [ʌnrɪ'leɪtɪd] *adj* ~ **(to)** senza rapporto (con); non imparentato(-a) (con)

unreliable [ʌnrɪ'laɪəbl] *adj* (*person, machine*) che non dà affidamento; (*news, source of information*) inattendibile

unrest [ʌn'rɛst] *n* agitazione *f*

unroll [ʌn'rəʊl] *vt* srotolare

unruly [ʌn'ruːlɪ] *adj* indisciplinato(-a)

unsafe [ʌn'seɪf] *adj* pericoloso(-a), rischioso(-a)

unsatisfactory ['ʌnsætɪs'fæktərɪ] *adj* che lascia a desiderare, insufficiente

unscrew [ʌn'skruː] *vt* svitare

unsettled [ʌn'sɛtld] *adj* (*person*) turbato(-a); indeciso(-a); (*weather*) instabile

unsettling [ʌn'sɛtlɪŋ] *adj* inquietante

unsightly [ʌn'saɪtlɪ] *adj* brutto(-a), sgradevole a vedersi

unskilled [ʌn'skɪld] *adj* non specializzato(-a)

unspoiled ['ʌn'spɔɪld], **unspoilt** ['ʌn'spɔɪlt] *adj* (*place*) non deturpato(-a)

unstable [ʌn'steɪbl] *adj* (*gen*) instabile; (*mentally*) squilibrato(-a)

unsteady [ʌn'stɛdɪ] *adj* instabile, malsicuro(-a)

unsuccessful [ʌnsək'sɛsful] *adj* (*writer, proposal*) che non ha successo; (*marriage, attempt*) mal riuscito(-a), fallito(-a); **to be** ~ (*in attempting sth*) non avere successo

unsuitable [ʌn'suːtəbl] *adj* inadatto(-a); inopportuno(-a); sconveniente

unsure [ʌn'ʃuə] *adj* incerto(-a); **to be** ~ **of o.s** essere insicuro(-a)

untidy [ʌn'taɪdɪ] *adj* (*room*) in disordine; (*appearance*) trascurato(-a); (*person*) disordinato(-a)

untie [ʌn'taɪ] *vt* (*knot, parcel*) disfare; (*prisoner, dog*) slegare

until [ʌn'tɪl] *prep* fino a; (*after negative*) prima di ▷ *conj* finché, fino a quando; (*in past, after negative*) prima che + *sub*, prima di + *infinitive*; ~ **he comes** finché *or* fino a quando non arriva; ~ **now** finora; ~ **then** fino ad allora

untrue [ʌn'truː] *adj* (*statement*) falso(-a), non vero(-a)

unused [ʌn'juːzd] *adj* nuovo(-a)

unusual [ʌn'juːʒuəl] *adj* insolito(-a), eccezionale, raro(-a); **unusually** *adv* insolitamente

unveil [ʌn'veɪl] *vt* scoprire; svelare

unwanted [ʌn'wɔntɪd] *adj* (*clothing*) smesso(-a); (*child*) non desiderato(-a)

unwell [ʌn'wɛl] *adj* indisposto(-a); **to feel** ~ non sentirsi bene

unwilling [ʌn'wɪlɪŋ] *adj* **to be** ~ **to do** non voler fare

unwind [ʌn'waɪnd] (*irreg: like* **wind¹**) *vt* svolgere, srotolare ▷ *vi* (*relax*) rilassarsi

unwise [ʌn'waɪz] *adj* poco saggio(-a)

unwittingly [ʌn'wɪtɪŋlɪ] *adv* senza volerlo

unwrap [ʌn'ræp] *vt* disfare; aprire

unzip [ʌn'zɪp] *vt* aprire (la chiusura lampo di); (*Comput*) dezippare

---

 KEYWORD

up [ʌp] *prep* **he went up the stairs/the hill** è salito su per le scale/sulla collina; **the cat was up a tree** il gatto era su un albero; **they live further up the street** vivono un po' più su nella stessa strada

▷ *adv* **1** (*upwards, higher*) su, in alto; **up in the sky/the mountains** su nel cielo/in montagna; **up there** lassù; **up above** su in alto

2: **to be up** (*out of bed*) essere alzato(-a); (*prices, level*) essere salito(-a)

3: **up to** (*as far as*) fino a; **up to now** finora

4: **to be up to** (*depending on*): **it's up to you** sta a lei, dipende da lei; (*equal to*): **he's not up to it** (*job, task etc*) non ne è all'altezza; (*inf: be doing*): **what is he up to?** cosa sta combinando?

▷ *n* **ups and downs** alti e bassi *mpl*

up-and-coming ['ʌpənd'kʌmɪŋ] *adj* pieno(-a) di promesse, promettente

upbringing ['ʌpbrɪŋɪŋ] *n* educazione *f*

update [ʌp'deɪt] *vt* aggiornare

upfront [ʌp'frʌnt] *adj* (*inf*) franco(-a), aperto(-a) ▷ *adv* (*pay*) subito

upgrade [ʌp'greɪd] *vt* (*house, job*) migliorare; (*employee*) avanzare di grado

upheaval [ʌp'hiːvl] *n* sconvolgimento; tumulto

uphill [ʌp'hɪl] *adj* in salita; (*fig: task*) difficile ▷ *adv* **to go** ~ andare in salita, salire

upholstery [ʌp'həʊlstərɪ] *n* tappezzeria

upmarket [ʌp'mɑːkɪt] *adj* (*product*) che si rivolge ad una fascia di mercato superiore

upon [ə'pɔn] *prep* su

upper ['ʌpə'] *adj* superiore ▷ *n* (*of shoe*)

u

tomaia; **upper-class** adj dell'alta borghesia

upright ['ʌpraɪt] adj diritto(-a); verticale; (fig) diritto(-a), onesto(-a)

uprising ['ʌpraɪzɪŋ] n insurrezione f, rivolta

uproar ['ʌprɔːʳ] n tumulto, clamore m

upset [n 'ʌpsɛt, vb, adj ʌp'sɛt] (irreg: like **set**) n (to plan etc) contrattempo; (stomach upset) disturbo ▷ vt (glass etc) rovesciare; (plan, stomach) scombussolare; (person: offend) contrariare; (: grieve) addolorare; sconvolgere ▷ adj contrariato(-a), addolorato(-a); (stomach) scombussolato(-a)

upside-down [ʌpsaɪd'daun] adv sottosopra

upstairs [ʌp'stɛəz] adv, adj di sopra, al piano superiore ▷ n piano di sopra

up-to-date ['ʌptə'deɪt] adj moderno(-a); aggiornato(-a)

uptown ['ʌptaun] (US) adv verso i quartieri residenziali ▷ adj dei quartieri residenziali

upward ['ʌpwəd] adj ascendente; verso l'alto; **upward(s)** adv in su, verso l'alto

uranium [juə'reɪnɪəm] n uranio

Uranus [juə'reɪnəs] n (planet) Urano

urban ['ɜːbən] adj urbano(-a)

urge [ɜːdʒ] n impulso; stimolo; forte desiderio ▷ vt **to ~ sb to do** esortare qn a fare, spingere qn a fare; raccomandare a qn di fare

urgency ['ɜːdʒənsɪ] n urgenza; (of tone) insistenza

urgent ['ɜːdʒənt] adj urgente; (voice) insistente

urinal ['juərɪnl] n (BRIT: building) vespasiano; (: vessel) orinale m, pappagallo

urinate ['juərɪneɪt] vi orinare

urine ['juərɪn] n orina

us [ʌs] pron ci; (stressed, after prep) noi; see also **me**

US(A) n abbr (= United States (of America)) USA mpl

use [n juːs, vb juːz] n uso; impiego, utilizzazione f ▷ vt usare, utilizzare, servirsi di; **in ~** in uso; **out of ~** fuori uso; **to be of ~** essere utile, servire; **it's no ~** non serve, è inutile; **she ~d to do it** lo faceva (una volta), era solita farlo; **to be ~d to** avere l'abitudine di; **use up** vt consumare; esaurire; **used** adj (object, car) usato(-a); **useful** adj utile; **useless** adj inutile; (person) inetto(-a); **user** n utente m/f; **user-friendly** adj (computer) di facile uso

usual ['juːʒuəl] adj solito(-a); **as ~** come al solito, come d'abitudine; **usually** adv di solito

utensil [juː'tɛnsl] n utensile m; **kitchen ~s** utensili da cucina

utility [juː'tɪlɪtɪ] n utilità; (also: **public ~**) servizio pubblico

utilize ['juːtɪlaɪz] vt utilizzare; sfruttare

utmost ['ʌtməust] adj estremo(-a) ▷ n **to do one's ~** fare il possibile or di tutto

utter ['ʌtəʳ] adj assoluto(-a), totale ▷ vt pronunciare, proferire; emettere; **utterly** adv completamente, del tutto

U-turn ['juː'tɜːn] n inversione f a U

V

v. *abbr* = **verse**; **versus**; **volt**; (= *vide*) vedi, vedere

vacancy ['veɪkənsɪ] *n* (BRIT: *job*) posto libero; (*room*) stanza libera; **"no vacancies"** "completo"

> Be careful not to translate *vacancy* by the Italian word *vacanza*.

vacant ['veɪkənt] *adj* (*job, seat etc*) libero(-a); (*expression*) assente

vacate [və'keɪt] *vt* lasciare libero(-a)

vacation [və'keɪʃən] (*esp US*) *n* vacanze *fpl*; **vacationer** (*US* **vacationist**) *n* vacanziere(-a)

vaccination [væksɪ'neɪʃən] *n* vaccinazione *f*

vaccine ['væksiːn] *n* vaccino

vacuum ['vækjum] *n* vuoto; **vacuum cleaner** *n* aspirapolvere *m inv*

vagina [və'dʒaɪnə] *n* vagina

vague [veɪg] *adj* vago(-a); (*blurred: photo, memory*) sfocato(-a)

vain [veɪn] *adj* (*useless*) inutile, vano(-a); (*conceited*) vanitoso(-a); **in ~** inutilmente, invano

Valentine's Day ['væləntaɪnzdeɪ] *n* San Valentino *m*

valid ['vælɪd] *adj* valido(-a), valevole; (*excuse*) valido(-a)

valley ['vælɪ] *n* valle *f*

valuable ['væljuəbl] *adj* (*jewel*) di (grande) valore; (*time, help*) prezioso(-a); **valuables** *npl* oggetti *mpl* di valore

value ['væljuː] *n* valore *m* ▷ *vt* (*fix price*) valutare, dare un prezzo a; (*cherish*) apprezzare, tenere a; **~s** *npl* (*principles*) valori *mpl*

valve [vælv] *n* valvola

vampire ['væmpaɪə'] *n* vampiro

van [væn] *n* (*Aut*) furgone *m*; (BRIT: *Rail*) vagone *m*

vandal ['vændl] *n* vandalo(-a); **vandalism** *n* vandalismo; **vandalize** *vt* vandalizzare

vanilla [və'nɪlə] *n* vaniglia ▷ *cpd* (*ice cream*) alla vaniglia

vanish ['vænɪʃ] *vi* svanire, scomparire

vanity ['vænɪtɪ] *n* vanità

vapour ['veɪpə'] (*US* **vapor**) *n* vapore *m*

variable ['vɛərɪəbl] *adj* variabile; (*mood*) mutevole

variant ['vɛərɪənt] *n* variante *f*

variation [vɛərɪ'eɪʃən] *n* variazione *f*; (*in opinion*) cambiamento

varied ['vɛərɪd] *adj* vario(-a), diverso(-a)

variety [və'raɪətɪ] *n* varietà *f inv*; (*quantity*) quantità, numero

various ['vɛərɪəs] *adj* vario(-a), diverso(-a); (*several*) parecchi(-e), molti(-e)

varnish ['vɑːnɪʃ] *n* vernice *f*; (*nail varnish*) smalto ▷ *vt* verniciare; mettere lo smalto su

vary ['vɛərɪ] *vt, vi* variare, mutare

vase [vɑːz] *n* vaso

Vaseline® ['væsɪliːn] *n* vaselina

vast [vɑːst] *adj* vasto(-a); (*amount, success*) enorme

VAT [væt] *n abbr* (= *value added tax*) I.V.A. *f*

Vatican ['vætɪkən] *n* **the ~** il Vaticano

vault [vɔːlt] *n* (*of roof*) volta; (*tomb*) tomba; (*in bank*) camera blindata ▷ *vt* (*also:* **~ over**) saltare (d'un balzo)

VCR *n abbr* = **video cassette recorder**

VDU *n abbr* = **visual display unit**

veal [viːl] *n* vitello

veer [vɪə'] *vi* girare; virare

vegan ['viːgən] *n* vegetaliano(-a)

vegetable ['vɛdʒtəbl] *n* verdura, ortaggio ▷ *adj* vegetale

vegetarian [vɛdʒɪ'tɛərɪən] *adj, n* vegetariano(-a); **do you have any ~ dishes?** avete piatti vegetariani?

vegetation [vɛdʒɪ'teɪʃən] *n* vegetazione *f*

vehicle ['viːɪkl] *n* veicolo

veil [veɪl] *n* velo

vein [veɪn] *n* vena; (*on leaf*) nervatura

Velcro® ['vɛlkrəu] *n* velcro® *m inv*

velvet ['vɛlvɪt] *n* velluto ▷ *adj* di velluto

vending machine ['vɛndɪŋ-] *n* distributore *m* automatico

vendor ['vɛndə'] *n* venditore(-trice)

vengeance ['vɛndʒəns] n vendetta; **with a ~** (fig) davvero; furiosamente
Venice ['vɛnɪs] n Venezia
venison ['vɛnɪsn] n carne f di cervo
venom ['vɛnəm] n veleno
vent [vɛnt] n foro, apertura; (in dress, jacket) spacco ▷ vt (fig: one's feelings) sfogare, dare sfogo a
ventilation [vɛntɪ'leɪʃən] n ventilazione f
venture ['vɛntʃər] n impresa (rischiosa) ▷ vt rischiare, azzardare ▷ vi avventurarsi; **business ~** iniziativa commerciale
venue ['vɛnjuː] n luogo (designato) per l'incontro
Venus ['viːnəs] n (planet) Venere m
verb [vəːb] n verbo; **verbal** adj verbale; (translation) orale
verdict ['vəːdɪkt] n verdetto
verge [vəːdʒ] (BRIT) n bordo, orlo; **"soft ~s"** (BRIT: Aut) banchine fpl cedevoli; **on the ~ of doing** sul punto di fare
verify ['vɛrɪfaɪ] vt verificare; (prove the truth of) confermare
versatile ['vəːsətaɪl] adj (person) versatile; (machine, tool etc) (che si presta) a molti usi
verse [vəːs] n versi mpl; (stanza) stanza, strofa; (in bible) versetto
version ['vəːʃən] n versione f
versus ['vəːsəs] prep contro
vertical ['vəːtɪkl] adj verticale ▷ n verticale m
very ['vɛrɪ] adv molto ▷ adj **the ~ book which** proprio il libro che; **the ~ last** proprio l'ultimo; **at the ~ least** almeno; **~ much** moltissimo
vessel ['vɛsl] n (Anat) vaso; (Naut) nave f; (container) recipiente m
vest [vɛst] n (BRIT) maglia; (: sleeveless) canottiera; (US: waistcoat) gilè m inv
vet [vɛt] n abbr (BRIT: = veterinary surgeon) veterinario ▷ vt esaminare minuziosamente
veteran ['vɛtərn] n (also: **war ~**) veterano
veterinary surgeon ['vɛtrɪnərɪ-] (US **veterinarian**) n veterinario
veto ['viːtəu] (pl **vetoes**) n veto ▷ vt opporre il veto a
via ['vaɪə] prep (by way of) via; (by means of) tramite
viable ['vaɪəbl] adj attuabile; vitale
vibrate [vaɪ'breɪt] vi **to ~ (with)** vibrare (di); (resound) risonare (di)
vibration [vaɪ'breɪʃən] n vibrazione f
vicar ['vɪkər] n pastore m
vice [vaɪs] n (evil) vizio; (Tech) morsa; **vice-chairman** (irreg) n vicepresidente m
vice versa ['vaɪsɪ'vəːsə] adv viceversa
vicinity [vɪ'sɪnɪtɪ] n vicinanze fpl
vicious ['vɪʃəs] adj (remark, dog) cattivo(-a);

(blow) violento(-a)
victim ['vɪktɪm] n vittima
victor ['vɪktər] n vincitore m
Victorian [vɪk'tɔːrɪən] adj vittoriano(-a)
victorious [vɪk'tɔːrɪəs] adj vittorioso(-a)
victory ['vɪktərɪ] n vittoria
video ['vɪdɪəu] cpd video... ▷ n (video film) video m inv; (also: **~ cassette**) videocassetta; (also: **~ cassette recorder**) videoregistratore m; **video camera** n videocamera; **video (cassette) recorder** n videoregistratore m; **video game** n videogioco; **video shop** n videonoleggio; **video tape** n videotape m inv; **video wall** n schermo m multivideo inv
vie [vaɪ] vi **to ~ with** competere con, rivaleggiare con
Vienna [vɪ'ɛnə] n Vienna
Vietnam [vjɛt'næm] n Vietnam m; **Vietnamese** adj, n inv vietnamita m/f
view [vjuː] n vista, veduta; (opinion) opinione f ▷ vt (look at: also fig) considerare; (house) visitare; **on ~** (in museum etc) esposto(-a); **in full ~ of** sotto gli occhi di; **in ~ of the weather/the fact that** considerato il tempo/che; **in my ~** a mio parere; **viewer** n spettatore(-trice); **viewpoint** n punto di vista; (place) posizione f
vigilant ['vɪdʒɪlənt] adj vigile
vigorous ['vɪgərəs] adj vigoroso(-a)
vile [vaɪl] adj (action) vile; (smell) disgustoso(-a), nauseante; (temper) pessimo(-a)
villa ['vɪlə] n villa
village ['vɪlɪdʒ] n villaggio; **villager** n abitante m/f di villaggio
villain ['vɪlən] n (scoundrel) canaglia; (BRIT: criminal) criminale m; (in novel etc) cattivo
vinaigrette [vɪneɪ'grɛt] n vinaigrette f inv
vine [vaɪn] n vite f; (climbing plant) rampicante m
vinegar ['vɪnɪgər] n aceto
vineyard ['vɪnjɑːd] n vigna, vigneto
vintage ['vɪntɪdʒ] n (year) annata, produzione f ▷ cpd d'annata
vinyl ['vaɪnl] n vinile m
viola [vɪ'əulə] n viola
violate ['vaɪəleɪt] vt violare
violation [vaɪə'leɪʃən] n violazione f; **in ~ of sth** violando qc
violence ['vaɪələns] n violenza
violent ['vaɪələnt] adj violento(-a)
violet ['vaɪələt] adj (colour) viola inv, violetto(-a) ▷ n (plant) violetta; (colour) violetto
violin [vaɪə'lɪn] n violino
VIP n abbr (= very important person) V.I.P. m/f inv

virgin ['və:dʒɪn] n vergine f ▷ adj vergine inv

Virgo ['və:gəu] n (sign) Vergine f

virtual ['və:tjuəl] adj effettivo(-a), vero(-a); (Comput, Physics) virtuale; (in effect): **it's a ~ impossibility** è praticamente impossibile; **the ~ leader** il capo all'atto pratico; **virtually** ['və:tjuəlɪ] adv (almost) praticamente; **virtual reality** n (Comput) realtà virtuale

virtue ['və:tju:] n virtù f inv; (advantage) pregio, vantaggio; **by ~ of** grazie a

virus ['vaɪərəs] n (also Comput) virus m inv

visa ['vi:zə] n visto

vise [vaɪs] n (US) (Tech) = **vice**

visibility [vɪzɪ'bɪlɪtɪ] n visibilità

visible ['vɪzəbl] adj visibile

vision ['vɪʒən] n (sight) vista; (foresight, in dream) visione f

visit ['vɪzɪt] n visita; (stay) soggiorno ▷ vt (person: US: also: ~ **with**) andare a trovare; (place) visitare; **visiting hours** npl (in hospital etc) orario delle visite; **visitor** n visitatore(-trice); (guest) ospite m/f; **visitor centre** (US **visitor center**) n centro informazioni per visitatori di museo, zoo, parco ecc

visual ['vɪzjuəl] adj visivo(-a); visuale; ottico(-a); **visualize** ['vɪzjuəlaɪz] vt immaginare, figurarsi; (foresee) prevedere

vital ['vaɪtl] adj vitale

vitality [vaɪ'tælɪtɪ] n vitalità

vitamin ['vɪtəmɪn] n vitamina

vivid ['vɪvɪd] adj vivido(-a)

V-neck ['vi:nɛk] n maglione m con lo scollo a V

vocabulary [vəu'kæbjulərɪ] n vocabolario

vocal ['vəukl] adj (Mus) vocale; (communication) verbale

vocational [vəu'keɪʃənl] adj professionale

vodka ['vɔdkə] n vodka f inv

vogue [vəug] n moda; (popularity) popolarità, voga

voice [vɔɪs] n voce f ▷ vt (opinion) esprimere; **voice mail** n servizio di segreteria telefonica

void [vɔɪd] n vuoto ▷ adj (invalid) nullo(-a); (empty): ~ **of** privo(-a) di

volatile ['vɔlətaɪl] adj volatile; (fig) volubile

volcano [vɔl'keɪnəu] (pl **volcanoes**) n vulcano

volleyball ['vɔlɪbɔ:l] n pallavolo f

volt [vəult] n volt m inv; **voltage** n tensione f, voltaggio

volume ['vɔlju:m] n volume m

voluntarily ['vɔləntrɪlɪ] adv volontariamente; gratuitamente

voluntary ['vɔləntərɪ] adj volontario(-a); (unpaid) gratuito(-a), non retribuito(-a)

volunteer [vɔlən'tɪər] n volontario(-a) ▷ vt offrire volontariamente ▷ vi (Mil) arruolarsi volontario; **to ~ to do** offrire (volontariamente) di fare

vomit ['vɔmɪt] n vomito ▷ vt, vi vomitare

vote [vəut] n voto, suffragio; (cast) voto; (franchise) diritto di voto ▷ vt **to be ~d chairman** etc venir eletto presidente etc; (propose): **to ~ that** approvare la proposta che ▷ vi votare; **~ of thanks** discorso di ringraziamento; **voter** n elettore(-trice); **voting** n scrutinio

voucher ['vautʃər] n (for meal, petrol etc) buono

vow [vau] n voto, promessa solenne ▷ vt **to ~ to do/that** giurare di fare/che

vowel ['vauəl] n vocale f

voyage ['vɔɪdʒ] n viaggio per mare, traversata

vulgar ['vʌlgər] adj volgare

vulnerable ['vʌlnərəbl] adj vulnerabile

vulture ['vʌltʃər] n avvoltoio

V

waddle ['wɒdl] *vi* camminare come una papera

wade [weɪd] *vi* **to ~ through** camminare a stento in; (*fig: book*) leggere con fatica

wafer ['weɪfə^r] *n* (*Culin*) cialda

waffle ['wɒfl] *n* (*Culin*) cialda; (*inf*) ciance *fpl* ▷ *vi* cianciare

wag [wæg] *vt* agitare, muovere ▷ *vi* agitarsi

wage [weɪdʒ] *n* (*also:* **~s**) salario, paga ▷ *vt* **to ~ war** fare la guerra

wag(g)on ['wægən] *n* (*horse-drawn*) carro; (*BRIT: Rail*) vagone *m* (merci)

wail [weɪl] *n* gemito; (*of siren*) urlo ▷ *vi* gemere; urlare

waist [weɪst] *n* vita, cintola; **waistcoat** (*BRIT*) *n* panciotto, gilè *m inv*

wait [weɪt] *n* attesa ▷ *vi* aspettare, attendere; **to ~ for** aspettare; **~ for me, please** aspettami, per favore; **I can't ~ to** (*fig*) non vedo l'ora di; **wait on** *vt fus* servire; **waiter** *n* cameriere *m*; **waiting list** *n* lista di attesa; **waiting room** *n* sala d'aspetto *or* d'attesa; **waitress** *n* cameriera

waive [weɪv] *vt* rinunciare a, abbandonare

wake [weɪk] (*pt* **woke, waked**, *pp* **woken, waked**) *vt* (*also:* **~ up**) svegliare ▷ *vi* (*also:* **~ up**) svegliarsi ▷ *n* (*for dead person*) veglia funebre; (*Naut*) scia

Wales [weɪlz] *n* Galles *m*

walk [wɔːk] *n* passeggiata; (*short*) giretto; (*gait*) passo, andatura; (*path*) sentiero; (*in park etc*) sentiero, vialetto ▷ *vi* camminare; (*for pleasure, exercise*) passeggiare ▷ *vt* (*distance*) fare *or* percorrere a piedi; (*dog*) accompagnare, portare a passeggiare; **10 minutes' ~ from** 10 minuti di cammino *or* a piedi da; **from all ~s of life** di tutte le condizioni sociali; **walk out** *vi* (*audience*) andarsene; (*workers*) scendere in sciopero; **walker** *n* (*person*) camminatore(-trice); **walkie-talkie** ['wɔːkɪ'tɔːkɪ] *n* walkie-talkie *m inv*; **walking** *n* camminare *m*; **walking shoes** *npl* pedule *fpl*; **walking stick** *n* bastone *m* da passeggio; **Walkman®** ['wɔːkmən] *n* Walkman® *m inv*; **walkway** *n* passaggio pedonale

wall [wɔːl] *n* muro; (*internal, of tunnel, cave*) parete *f*

wallet ['wɒlɪt] *n* portafoglio; **I can't find my ~** non trovo il portafoglio

wallpaper ['wɔːlpeɪpə^r] *n* carta da parati ▷ *vt* (*room*) mettere la carta da parati in

walnut ['wɔːlnʌt] *n* noce *f*; (*tree, wood*) noce *m*

walrus ['wɔːlrəs] (*pl* **walrus** *or* **walruses**) *n* tricheco

waltz [wɔːlts] *n* valzer *m inv* ▷ *vi* ballare il valzer

wand [wɒnd] *n* (*also:* **magic ~**) bacchetta (magica)

wander ['wɒndə^r] *vi* (*person*) girare senza meta, girovagare; (*thoughts*) vagare ▷ *vt* girovagare per

want [wɒnt] *vt* volere; (*need*) aver bisogno di ▷ *n* **for ~ of** per mancanza di; **wanted** *adj* (*criminal*) ricercato(-a); **"wanted"** (*in adverts*) "cercasi"

war [wɔː^r] *n* guerra; **to make ~ (on)** far guerra (a)

ward [wɔːd] *n* (*in hospital: room*) corsia; (:*section*) reparto; (*Pol*) circoscrizione *f*; (*Law: child: also:* **~ of court**) pupillo(-a)

warden ['wɔːdn] *n* (*of park, game reserve, youth hostel*) guardiano(-a); (*BRIT: of institution*) direttore(-trice); (*BRIT: also:* **traffic ~**) addetto(-a) al controllo del traffico e del parcheggio

wardrobe ['wɔːdrəub] *n* (*cupboard*) guardaroba *m inv*, armadio; (*clothes*) guardaroba; (*Cinema, Theatre*) costumi *mpl*

warehouse ['wɛəhaus] *n* magazzino

warfare ['wɔːfɛə^r] *n* guerra

warhead ['wɔːhɛd] *n* (*Mil*) testata

warm [wɔːm] *adj* caldo(-a); (*thanks, welcome, applause*) caloroso(-a); (*person*) cordiale; **it's ~** fa caldo; **I'm ~** ho caldo; **warm up** *vi* scaldarsi, riscaldarsi

▷ vt scaldare, riscaldare; (*engine*) far scaldare; **warmly** adv (*applaud, welcome*) calorosamente; (*dress*) con abiti pesanti; **warmth** n calore m

warn [wɔːn] vt **to ~ sb that/(not) to do/of** avvertire or avvisare qn che/di (non) fare/di; **warning** n avvertimento; (*notice*) avviso; (*signal*) segnalazione f; **warning light** n spia luminosa

warrant ['wɔrnt] n (*voucher*) buono; (*Law: to arrest*) mandato di cattura; (: *to search*) mandato di perquisizione

warranty ['wɔrəntɪ] n garanzia

warrior ['wɔrɪəʳ] n guerriero(-a)

Warsaw ['wɔːsɔː] n Varsavia

warship ['wɔːʃɪp] n nave f da guerra

wart [wɔːt] n verruca

wartime ['wɔːtaɪm] n **in ~** in tempo di guerra

wary ['wɛərɪ] adj prudente

was [wɔz] pt of **be**

wash [wɔʃ] vt lavare ▷ vi lavarsi; (*sea*): **to ~ over/against sth** infrangersi su/contro qc ▷ n lavaggio; (*of ship*) scia; **to give sth a ~** lavare qc, dare una lavata a qc; **to have a ~** lavarsi; **wash up** vi (BRIT) lavare i piatti; (US) darsi una lavata; **washbasin** (US **washbowl**) n lavabo; **wash cloth** (US) n pezzuola (per lavarsi); **washer** n (*Tech*) rondella; **washing** n (*linen etc*) bucato; **washing line** n (BRIT) corda del bucato; **washing machine** n lavatrice f; **washing powder** (BRIT) n detersivo (in polvere)

Washington ['wɔʃɪŋtən] n Washington f

wash: **washing-up** n rigovernatura, lavatura dei piatti; **washing-up liquid** n detersivo liquido (per stoviglie); **washroom** n gabinetto

wasn't ['wɔznt] = **was not**

wasp [wɔsp] n vespa

waste [weɪst] n spreco; (*of time*) perdita; (*rubbish*) rifiuti mpl; (*also: **household ~***) immondizie fpl ▷ adj (*material*) di scarto; (*food*) avanzato(-a); (*land*) incolto(-a) ▷ vt sprecare; **waste ground** (BRIT) n terreno incolto or abbandonato; **wastepaper basket** ['weɪstpeɪpə-] n cestino per la carta straccia

watch [wɔtʃ] n (*also: **wrist ~***) orologio (da polso); (*act of watching, vigilance*) sorveglianza; (*guard: Mil, Naut*) guardia; (*Naut: spell of duty*) quarto ▷ vt (*look at*) osservare; (: *match, programme*) guardare; (*spy on, guard*) sorvegliare, tenere d'occhio; (*be careful of*) fare attenzione a ▷ vi osservare, guardare; (*keep guard*) fare or montare la guardia; **watch out** vi fare attenzione; **watchdog** n (*also fig*) cane m da guardia; **watch strap** n cinturino da

orologio

water ['wɔːtəʳ] n acqua ▷ vt (*plant*) annaffiare ▷ vi (*eyes*) lacrimare; (*mouth*): **to make sb's mouth ~** far venire l'acquolina in bocca a qn; **in British ~s** nelle acque territoriali britanniche; **water down** vt (*milk*) diluire; (*fig: story*) edulcorare; **watercolour** (US **watercolor**) n acquerello; **watercress** n crescione m; **waterfall** n cascata; **watering can** n annaffiatoio; **watermelon** n anguria, cocomero; **waterproof** adj impermeabile; **water-skiing** n sci m acquatico

watt [wɔt] n watt m inv

wave [weɪv] n onda; (*of hand*) gesto, segno; (*in hair*) ondulazione f; (*fig: surge*) ondata ▷ vi fare un cenno con la mano; (*branches, grass*) ondeggiare; (*flag*) sventolare ▷ vt (*hand*) fare un gesto con; (*handkerchief*) sventolare; (*stick*) brandire; **wavelength** n lunghezza d'onda

waver ['weɪvəʳ] vi esitare; (*voice*) tremolare

wavy ['weɪvɪ] adj ondulato(-a); ondeggiante

wax [wæks] n cera ▷ vt dare la cera a; (*car*) lucidare ▷ vi (*moon*) crescere

way [weɪ] n via, strada; (*path, access*) passaggio; (*distance*) distanza; (*direction*) parte f, direzione f; (*manner*) modo, stile m; (*habit*) abitudine f; **which ~? — this ~** da che parte or in quale direzione? — da questa parte or per di qua; **on the ~** (*en route*) per strada; **to be on one's ~** essere in cammino or sulla strada; **to be in the ~** bloccare il passaggio; (*fig*) essere tra i piedi or d'impiccio; **to go out of one's ~ to do** (*fig*) mettercela tutta or fare di tutto per fare; **under ~** (*project*) in corso; **to lose one's ~** perdere la strada; **in a ~** in un certo senso; **in some ~s** sotto certi aspetti; **no ~!** (*inf*) neanche per idea!; **by the ~ ...** a proposito ...; **"~ in"** (BRIT) "entrata", "ingresso"; **"~ out"** (BRIT) "uscita"; **the ~ back** la strada del ritorno; **"give ~"** (BRIT: *Aut*) "dare la precedenza"

W.C. ['dʌblju:'si:] (BRIT) n W.C. m inv, gabinetto

we [wiː] pl pron noi

weak [wiːk] adj debole; (*health*) precario(-a); (*beam etc*) fragile; (*tea*) leggero(-a); **weaken** vi indebolirsi ▷ vt indebolire; **weakness** n debolezza; (*fault*) punto debole, difetto; **to have a weakness for** avere un debole per

wealth [welθ] n (*money, resources*) ricchezza, ricchezze fpl; (*of details*) abbondanza, profusione f; **wealthy** adj ricco(-a)

weapon ['wɛpən] n arma; **~s of mass**

w

destruction armi *mpl* di distruzione di massa

wear [wɛəʳ] (*pt* **wore**, *pp* **worn**) *n* (*use*) uso; (*damage through use*) logorio, usura; (*clothing*): **sports/baby ~** abbigliamento sportivo/per neonati ▷ *vt* (*clothes*) portare; (*put on*) mettersi; (*damage: through use*) consumare ▷ *vi* (*last*) durare; (*rub etc through*) consumarsi; **evening ~** abiti *mpl* or tenuta da sera; **wear off** *vi* sparire lentamente; **wear out** *vt* consumare; (*person, strength*) esaurire

weary ['wɪərɪ] *adj* stanco(-a) ▷ *vi* **to ~ of** stancarsi di

weasel ['wiːzl] *n* (*Zool*) donnola

weather ['wɛðəʳ] *n* tempo ▷ *vt* (*storm, crisis*) superare; **What's the ~ like?** che tempo fa?; **under the ~** (*fig: ill*) poco bene; **weather forecast** *n* previsioni *fpl* del tempo, bollettino meteorologico

weave [wiːv] (*pt* **wove**, *pp* **woven**) *vt* (*cloth*) tessere; (*basket*) intrecciare

web [wɛb] *n* (*of spider*) ragnatela; (*on foot*) palma; (*fabric, also fig*) tessuto; **the (World Wide) W~** la Rete; **web page** *n* (*Comput*) pagina *f* web *inv*; **website** *n* (*Comput*) sito (Internet)

wed [wɛd] (*pt, pp* **wedded**) *vt* sposare ▷ *vi* sposarsi

we'd [wiːd] = **we had; we would**

Wed. *abbr* (= *Wednesday*) mer.

wedding ['wɛdɪŋ] *n* matrimonio; **wedding anniversary** *n* anniversario di matrimonio; **wedding day** *n* giorno delle nozze *or* del matrimonio; **wedding dress** *n* abito nuziale; **wedding ring** *n* fede *f*

wedge [wɛdʒ] *n* (*of wood etc*) zeppa; (*of cake*) fetta ▷ *vt* (*fix*) fissare con zeppe; (*pack tightly*) incastrare

Wednesday ['wɛdnzdɪ] *n* mercoledì *m inv*

wee [wiː] (*Scottish*) *adj* piccolo(-a)

weed [wiːd] *n* erbaccia ▷ *vt* diserbare; **weedkiller** *n* diserbante *m*

week [wiːk] *n* settimana; **a ~ today/on Friday** oggi/venerdì a otto; **weekday** *n* giorno feriale; (*Comm*) giornata lavorativa; **weekend** *n* fine settimana *m or f inv*, weekend *m inv*; **weekly** *adv* ogni settimana, settimanalmente ▷ *adj* settimanale ▷ *n* settimanale *m*

weep [wiːp] (*pt, pp* **wept**) *vi* (*person*) piangere

weigh [weɪ] *vt, vi* pesare; **to ~ anchor** salpare l'ancora; **weigh up** *vt* valutare

weight [weɪt] *n* peso; **to lose/put on ~** dimagrire/ingrassare; **weightlifting** *n* sollevamento pesi

weir [wɪəʳ] *n* diga

weird [wɪəd] *adj* strano(-a), bizzarro(-a); (*eerie*) soprannaturale

welcome ['wɛlkəm] *adj* benvenuto(-a) ▷ *n* accoglienza, benvenuto ▷ *vt* dare il benvenuto a; (*be glad of*) rallegrarsi di; **thank you — you're ~!** grazie — prego!

weld [wɛld] *n* saldatura ▷ *vt* saldare

welfare ['wɛlfɛəʳ] *n* benessere *m*; **welfare state** *n* stato assistenziale

well [wɛl] *n* pozzo ▷ *adv* bene ▷ *adj* **to be ~** (*person*) stare bene ▷ *excl* allora!; ma!; ebbene!; **as ~** anche; **as ~ as** così come; oltre a; **~ done!** bravo(-a)!; **get ~ soon!** guarisci presto!; **to do ~** andare bene

we'll [wiːl] = **we will; we shall**

well: **well-behaved** *adj* ubbidiente; **well-built** *adj* (*person*) ben fatto(-a); **well-dressed** *adj* ben vestito(-a), vestito(-a) bene

wellies (*inf*) ['wɛlɪz] *npl* (BRIT) stivali *mpl* di gomma

well: **well-known** *adj* noto(-a), famoso(-a); **well-off** *adj* benestante, danaroso(-a); **well-paid** [wɛl'peɪd] *adj* ben pagato(-a)

Welsh [wɛlʃ] *adj* gallese ▷ *n* (*Ling*) gallese *m*; **Welshman** (*irreg*) *n* gallese *m*; **Welshwoman** (*irreg*) *n* gallese *f*

went [wɛnt] *pt* of **go**

wept [wɛpt] *pt, pp* of **weep**

were [wəːʳ] *pt* of **be**

we're [wɪəʳ] = **we are**

weren't [wəːnt] = **were not**

west [wɛst] *n* ovest *m*, occidente *m*, ponente *m* ▷ *adj* (a) ovest *inv*, occidentale ▷ *adv* verso ovest; **the W~** l'Occidente *m*; **westbound** ['wɛstbaund] *adj* (*traffic*) diretto(-a) a ovest; (*carriageway*) ovest *inv*; **western** *adj* occidentale, dell'ovest ▷ *n* (*Cinema*) western *m inv*; **West Indian** *adj* delle Indie Occidentali ▷ *n* abitante *m/f* delle Indie Occidentali; **West Indies** [-'ɪndɪz] *npl* Indie *fpl* Occidentali

wet [wɛt] *adj* umido(-a), bagnato(-a); (*soaked*) fradicio(-a); (*rainy*) piovoso(-a) ▷ *n* (BRIT: *Pol*) politico moderato; **to get ~** bagnarsi; **"~ paint"** "vernice fresca"; **wetsuit** *n* tuta da sub

we've [wiːv] = **we have**

whack [wæk] *vt* picchiare, battere

whale [weɪl] *n* (*Zool*) balena

wharf [wɔːf] (*pl* **wharves**) *n* banchina

 KEYWORD

what [wɔt] *adj* **1** (*in direct/indirect questions*) che; quale; **what size is it?** che taglia è?; **what colour is it?** di che colore è?; **what books do you want?** quali *or* che libri vuole?

2 (*in exclamations*) che; **what a mess!** che

disordine!
▷ pron **1** (*interrogative*) che cosa, cosa, che; **what are you doing?** che *or* (che) cosa fai?; **what are you talking about?** di che cosa parli?; **what is it called?** come si chiama?; **what about me?** e io?; **what about doing ...?** e se facessimo ...?
2 (*relative*) ciò che, quello che; **I saw what you did/was on the table** ho visto quello che hai fatto/quello che era sul tavolo
3 (*indirect use*) (che) cosa; **he asked me what she had said** mi ha chiesto che cosa avesse detto; **tell me what you're thinking about** dimmi a cosa stai pensando
▷ excl (*disbelieving*) cosa!, come!

whatever [wɔtˈɛvə] adj **~ book** qualunque *or* qualsiasi libro + *sub* ▷ pron **do ~ is necessary/you want** faccia qualunque *or* qualsiasi cosa sia necessaria/lei voglia; **~ happens** qualunque cosa accada; **no reason ~** *or* **whatsoever** nessuna ragione affatto *or* al mondo; **nothing ~** proprio niente
whatsoever [wɔtsəuˈɛvə] adj = **whatever**
wheat [wiːt] n grano, frumento
wheel [wiːl] n ruota; (*Aut: also*: **steering ~**) volante m; (*Naut*) (ruota del) timone m ▷ vt spingere ▷ vi (*birds*) roteare; (*also*: **~ round**) girare; **wheelbarrow** n carriola; **wheelchair** n sedia a rotelle; **wheel clamp** n (*Aut*) morsa che blocca la ruota di una vettura in sosta vietata
wheeze [wiːz] vi ansimare

 KEYWORD

when [wɛn] adv quando; **when did it happen?** quando è successo?
▷ conj **1** (*at, during, after the time that*) quando; **she was reading when I came in** quando sono entrato lei leggeva; **that was when I needed you** era allora che avevo bisogno di te
2 (*on, at which*): **on the day when I met him** il giorno in cui l'ho incontrato; **one day when it was raining** un giorno che pioveva
3 (*whereas*) quando, mentre; **you said I was wrong when in fact I was right** mi hai detto che avevo torto, quando in realtà avevo ragione

whenever [wɛnˈɛvə] adv quando mai ▷ conj quando; (*every time that*) ogni volta che
where [wɛəʳ] adv, conj dove; **this is ~** è qui che; **whereabouts** adv dove ▷ n **sb's**

whereabouts luogo dove qn si trova; **whereas** conj mentre; **whereby** pron per cui; **wherever** [-ˈɛvəʳ] conj dovunque + sub; (*interrogative*) dove mai
whether [ˈwɛðəʳ] conj se; **I don't know ~ to accept or not** non so se accettare o no; **it's doubtful ~** è poco probabile che; **~ you go or not** che lei vada o no

 KEYWORD

which [wɪtʃ] adj **1** (*interrogative: direct, indirect*) quale; **which picture do you want?** quale quadro vuole?; **which one?** quale?; **which one of you did it?** chi di voi lo ha fatto?
2: **in which case** nel qual caso
▷ pron **1** (*interrogative*) quale; **which (of these) are yours?** quali di questi sono suoi?; **which of you are coming?** chi di voi viene?
2 (*relative*) che; (: *indirect*) cui, il (la) quale; **the apple which you ate/which is on the table** la mela che hai mangiato/che è sul tavolo; **the chair on which you are sitting** la sedia sulla quale *or* su cui sei seduto; **he said he knew, which is true** ha detto che lo sapeva, il che è vero; **after which** dopo di che

whichever [wɪtʃˈɛvə] adj **take ~ book you prefer** prenda qualsiasi libro che preferisce; **~ book you take** qualsiasi libro prenda
while [waɪl] n momento ▷ conj mentre; (*as long as*) finché; (*although*) sebbene + sub; per quanto + sub; **for a ~** per un po'
whilst [waɪlst] conj = **while**
whim [wɪm] n capriccio
whine [waɪn] n gemito ▷ vi gemere; uggiolare; piagnucolare
whip [wɪp] n frusta; (*for riding*) frustino; (*Pol: person*) capogruppo (*che sovrintende alla disciplina dei colleghi di partito*) ▷ vt frustare; (*cream, eggs*) sbattere; **whipped cream** n panna montata
whirl [wəːl] vt (*far*) girare rapidamente, (*far*) turbinare ▷ vi (*dancers*) volteggiare; (*leaves, water*) sollevarsi in vortice
whisk [wɪsk] n (*Culin*) frusta; frullino ▷ vt sbattere, frullare; **to ~ sb away** *or* **off** portar via qn a tutta velocità
whiskers [ˈwɪskəz] npl (*of animal*) baffi mpl; (*of man*) favoriti mpl
whisky [ˈwɪskɪ] (*us, Ireland* **whiskey**) n whisky m inv
whisper [ˈwɪspəʳ] n sussurro ▷ vt, vi sussurrare
whistle [ˈwɪsl] n (*sound*) fischio; (*object*)

w

fischietto ▷ *vi* fischiare

white [waɪt] *adj* bianco(-a); (*with fear*) pallido(-a) ▷ *n* bianco; (*person*) bianco(-a); **White House** *n* Casa Bianca; **whitewash** *n* (*paint*) bianco di calce ▷ *vt* imbiancare; (*fig*) coprire

whiting ['waɪtɪŋ] *n inv* (*fish*) merlango

Whitsun ['wɪtsn] *n* Pentecoste *f*

whittle ['wɪtl] *vt* **to ~ away, ~ down** ridurre, tagliare

whizz [wɪz] *vi* **to ~ past** *or* **by** passare sfrecciando

⊙ **KEYWORD**

who [hu:] *pron* **1** (*interrogative*) chi; **who is it?, who's there?** chi è?
2 (*relative*) che; **the man who spoke to me** l'uomo che ha parlato con me; **those who can swim** quelli che sanno nuotare

whoever [hu:ˈɛvə] *pron* **~ finds it** chiunque lo trovi; **ask ~ you like** lo chieda a chiunque vuole; **~ she marries** chiunque sposerà, non importa chi sposerà; **~ told you that?** chi mai gliel'ha detto?

whole [həul] *adj* (*complete*) tutto(-a), completo(-a); (*not broken*) intero(-a), intatto(-a) ▷ *n* (*all*): **the ~ of** tutto(-a) il (la); (*entire unit*) tutto; (*not broken*) tutto; **the ~ of the town** tutta la città, la città intera; **on the ~, as a ~** nel complesso, nell'insieme; **wholefood(s)** *n(pl)* cibo integrale; **wholeheartedly** [həulˈhɑːtɪdlɪ] *adv* sentitamente, di tutto cuore; **wholemeal** *adj* (*bread, flour*) integrale; **wholesale** *n* commercio *or* vendita all'ingrosso ▷ *adj* all'ingrosso; (*destruction*) totale; **wholewheat** *adj* = **wholemeal**; **wholly** *adv* completamente, del tutto

⊙ **KEYWORD**

whom [hu:m] *pron* **1** (*interrogative*) chi; **whom did you see?** chi hai visto?; **to whom did you give it?** a chi lo hai dato?
2 (*relative*) che, *prep* + il (la) quale (*check syntax of Italian verb used*); **the man whom I saw/to whom I spoke** l'uomo che ho visto/al quale ho parlato

whore [hɔ:] (*inf: pej*) *n* puttana

⊙ **KEYWORD**

whose [hu:z] *adj* **1** (*possessive: interrogative*) di chi; **whose book is this?, whose is this book?** di chi è questo libro?; **whose daughter are you?** di chi sei figlia?

2 (*possessive: relative*): **the man whose son you rescued** l'uomo il cui figlio hai salvato; **the girl whose sister you were speaking to** la ragazza alla cui sorella stavi parlando
▷ *pron* di chi; **whose is this?** di chi è questo?; **I know whose it is** so di chi è

⊙ **KEYWORD**

why [waɪ] *adv* perché; **why not?** perché no?; **why not do it now?** perché non farlo adesso?
▷ *conj* **I wonder why he said that** mi chiedo perché l'abbia detto; **that's not why I'm here** non è questo il motivo per cui sono qui; **the reason why** il motivo per cui
▷ *excl* (*surprise*) ma guarda un po'!; (*remonstrating*) ma (via)!; (*explaining*) ebbene!

wicked ['wɪkɪd] *adj* cattivo(-a), malvagio(-a); maligno(-a); perfido(-a)

wicket ['wɪkɪt] *n* (*Cricket*) porta; area tra le due porte

wide [waɪd] *adj* largo(-a); (*area, knowledge*) vasto(-a); (*choice*) ampio(-a) ▷ *adv* **to open ~** spalancare; **to shoot ~** tirare a vuoto *or* fuori bersaglio; **widely** *adv* (*differing*) molto, completamente; (*travelled, spaced*) molto; (*believed*) generalmente; **widen** *vt* allargare, ampliare; **wide open** *adj* spalancato(-a); **widespread** *adj* (*belief etc*) molto *or* assai diffuso(-a)

widow ['wɪdəu] *n* vedova; **widower** *n* vedovo

width [wɪdθ] *n* larghezza

wield [wi:ld] *vt* (*sword*) maneggiare; (*power*) esercitare

wife [waɪf] (*pl* **wives**) *n* moglie *f*

wig [wɪg] *n* parrucca

wild [waɪld] *adj* selvatico(-a); selvaggio(-a); (*sea, weather*) tempestoso(-a); (*idea, life*) folle; stravagante; (*applause*) frenetico(-a); **wilderness** ['wɪldənɪs] *n* deserto; **wildlife** *n* natura; **wildly** *adv* selvaggiamente; (*applaud*) freneticamente; (*hit, guess*) a casaccio; (*happy*) follemente

⊙ **KEYWORD**

will [wɪl] (*pt, pp* **willed**) *aux vb* **1** (*forming future tense*): **I will finish it tomorrow** lo finirò domani; **I will have finished it by tomorrow** lo finirò entro domani; **will you do it? — yes I will/no I won't** lo farai? — sì

(lo farò)/no (non lo farò)
2 (*in conjectures, predictions*): **he will** or
he'll be there by now dovrebbe essere
arrivato ora; **that will be the postman**
sarà il postino
3 (*in commands, requests, offers*): **will you
be quiet!** vuoi stare zitto?; **will you come?**
vieni anche tu?; **will you help me?** mi
aiuti?, mi puoi aiutare?; **will you have a
cup of tea?** vorrebbe una tazza di tè?; **I
won't put up with it!** non lo accetterò!
▷ *vt* **to will sb to do** volere che qn faccia;
he willed himself to go on continuò
grazie a un grande sforzo di volontà
▷ *n* volontà; testamento

willing ['wɪlɪŋ] *adj* volonteroso(-a); **~
to do** disposto(-a) a fare; **willingly** *adv*
volentieri
willow ['wɪləu] *n* salice *m*
willpower ['wɪlpauəʳ] *n* forza di volontà
wilt [wɪlt] *vi* appassire
win [wɪn] (*pt, pp* **won**) *n* (*in sports etc*)
vittoria ▷ *vt* (*battle, prize, money*) vincere;
(*popularity*) conquistare ▷ *vi* vincere; **win
over** *vt* convincere
wince [wɪns] *vi* trasalire
wind¹ [waɪnd] (*pt, pp* **wound**) *vt*
attorcigliare; (*wrap*) avvolgere; (*clock, toy*)
caricare ▷ *vi* (*road, river*) serpeggiare; **wind
down** *vt* (*car window*) abbassare; (*fig:
production, business*) diminuire; **wind up** *vt*
(*clock*) caricare; (*debate*) concludere
wind² [wɪnd] *n* vento; (*Med*) flatulenza;
(*breath*) respiro, fiato ▷ *vt* (*take breath
away*) far restare senza fiato; **~ power**
energia eolica
windfall ['wɪndfɔːl] *n* (*money*) guadagno
insperato
winding ['waɪndɪŋ] *adj* (*road*)
serpeggiante; (*staircase*) a chiocciola
windmill ['wɪndmɪl] *n* mulino a vento
window ['wɪndəu] *n* finestra; (*in car, train,
plane*) finestrino; (*in shop etc*) vetrina; (*also:
~ pane*) vetro; **I'd like a ~ seat** vorrei un
posto vicino al finestrino; **window box**
n cassetta da fiori; **window cleaner** *n*
(*person*) pulitore *m* di finestre; **window
pane** *n* vetro; **window seat** *n* posto
finestrino; **windowsill** *n* davanzale *m*
windscreen ['wɪndskriːn] (*us*
windshield) *n* parabrezza *m inv*;
windscreen wiper (*us* **windshield wiper**)
n tergicristallo
windsurfing ['wɪndsəːfɪŋ] *n* windsurf
m inv
windy ['wɪndɪ] *adj* ventoso(-a); **it's ~** c'è
vento
wine [waɪn] *n* vino; **wine bar** *n* enoteca

(*per degustazione*); **wine glass** *n* bicchiere
m da vino; **wine list** *n* lista dei vini; **wine
tasting** *n* degustazione *f* dei vini
wing [wɪŋ] *n* ala; (*Aut*) fiancata; **wing
mirror** *n* (*BRIT*) specchietto retrovisore
esterno
wink [wɪŋk] *n* ammiccamento ▷ *vi*
ammiccare, fare l'occhiolino; (*light*)
baluginare
winner ['wɪnəʳ] *n* vincitore(-trice)
winning ['wɪnɪŋ] *adj* (*team, goal*) vincente;
(*smile*) affascinante
winter ['wɪntəʳ] *n* inverno; **winter sports**
npl sport *mpl* invernali; **wintertime** *n*
inverno, stagione *f* invernale
wipe [waɪp] *n* pulita, passata ▷ *vt* pulire
(*strofinando*); (*erase: tape*) cancellare; **wipe
out** *vt* (*debt*) pagare, liquidare; (*memory*)
cancellare; (*destroy*) annientare; **wipe up**
vt asciugare
wire ['waɪəʳ] *n* filo; (*Elec*) filo elettrico; (*Tel*)
telegramma *m* ▷ *vt* (*house*) fare l'impianto
elettrico di; (*also:* **~ up**) collegare,
allacciare; (*person*) telegrafare a
wiring ['waɪərɪŋ] *n* impianto elettrico
wisdom ['wɪzdəm] *n* saggezza; (*of action*)
prudenza; **wisdom tooth** *n* dente *m* del
giudizio
wise [waɪz] *adj* saggio(-a); prudente;
giudizioso(-a)
wish [wɪʃ] *n* (*desire*) desiderio; (*specific
desire*) richiesta ▷ *vt* desiderare, volere;
best ~es (*on birthday etc*) i migliori auguri;
with best ~es (*in letter*) cordiali saluti,
con i migliori saluti; **to ~ sb goodbye**
dire arrivederci a qn; **he ~ed me well** mi
augurò di riuscire; **to ~ to do/sb to do**
desiderare *or* volere fare/che qn faccia; **to
~ for** desiderare
wistful ['wɪstful] *adj* malinconico(-a)
wit [wɪt] *n* (*also:* **~s**) intelligenza; presenza
di spirito; (*wittiness*) spirito, arguzia;
(*person*) bello spirito
witch [wɪtʃ] *n* strega

 KEYWORD

with [wɪð, wɪθ] *prep* **1** (*in the company
of*) con; **I was with him** ero con lui; **we
stayed with friends** siamo stati da amici;
I'll be with you in a minute vengo subito
2 (*descriptive*) con; **a room with a view**
una stanza con vista sul mare (*or* sulle
montagne etc*); **the man with the grey
hat/blue eyes** l'uomo con il cappello
grigio/gli occhi blu
3 (*indicating manner, means, cause*): **with
tears in her eyes** con le lacrime agli occhi;
red with anger rosso dalla rabbia; **to**

w

shake with fear tremare di paura
4: **I'm with you** (*I understand*) la seguo; **to be with it** (*inf: up-to-date*) essere alla moda; (: *alert*) essere sveglio(-a)

withdraw [wɪθ'drɔː] (*irreg: like* **draw**) *vt* ritirare; (*money from bank*) ritirare; prelevare ▷ *vi* ritirarsi; **withdrawal** *n* ritiro; prelievo; (*of army*) ritirata; **withdrawal symptoms** *n* (*Med*) crisi *f* di astinenza; **withdrawn** *adj* (*person*) distaccato(-a)
withdrew [wɪθ'druː] *pt of* **withdraw**
wither ['wɪðəʳ] *vi* appassire
withhold [wɪθ'həuld] (*irreg: like* **hold**) *vt* (*money*) trattenere; (*permission*): **to ~ (from)** rifiutare (a); (*information*): **to ~ (from)** nascondere (a)
within [wɪð'ɪn] *prep* all'interno; (*in time, distances*) entro ▷ *adv* all'interno, dentro; **~ reach (of)** alla portata (di); **~ sight (of)** in vista (di); **~ a mile of** entro un miglio da; **~ the week** prima della fine della settimana
without [wɪð'aut] *prep* senza; **to go ~ sth** fare a meno di qc
withstand [wɪθ'stænd] (*irreg: like* **stand**) *vt* resistere a
witness ['wɪtnɪs] *n* (*person, also Law*) testimone *m/f* ▷ *vt* (*event*) essere testimone di; (*document*) attestare l'autenticità di
witty ['wɪtɪ] *adj* spiritoso(-a)
wives [waɪvz] *npl of* **wife**
wizard ['wɪzəd] *n* mago
wk *abbr* = **week**
wobble ['wɔbl] *vi* tremare; (*chair*) traballare
woe [wəu] *n* dolore *m*; disgrazia
woke [wəuk] *pt of* **wake**
woken ['wəukn] *pp of* **wake**
wolf [wulf] (*pl* **wolves**) *n* lupo
woman ['wumən] (*pl* **women**) *n* donna
womb [wuːm] *n* (*Anat*) utero
women ['wɪmɪn] *npl of* **woman**
won [wʌn] *pt, pp of* **win**
wonder ['wʌndəʳ] *n* meraviglia ▷ *vi* **to ~ whether/why** domandarsi se/perché; **to ~ at** essere sorpreso(-a) di; meravigliarsi di; **to ~ about** domandarsi di; pensare a; **it's no ~ that** c'è poco or non c'è da meravigliarsi che + *sub*; **wonderful** *adj* meraviglioso(-a)
won't [wəunt] = **will not**
wood [wud] *n* legno; (*timber*) legname *m*; (*forest*) bosco; **wooden** *adj* di legno; (*fig*) rigido(-a); inespressivo(-a); **woodwind** *npl* (*Mus*): **the woodwind** i legni; **woodwork** *n* (*craft, subject*) falegnameria
wool [wul] *n* lana; **to pull the ~ over sb's eyes** (*fig*) imbrogliare qn; **woollen** (*us*

woolen) *adj* di lana; (*industry*) laniero(-a); **woolly** (*us* **wooly**) *adj* di lana; (*fig: ideas*) confuso(-a)
word [wəːd] *n* parola; (*news*) notizie *fpl* ▷ *vt* esprimere, formulare; **in other ~s** in altre parole; **to break/keep one's ~** non mantenere/mantenere la propria parola; **to have ~s with sb** avere un diverbio con qn; **wording** *n* formulazione *f*; **word processing** *n* elaborazione *f* di testi, word processing *m*; **word processor** *n* word processor *m inv*
wore [wɔːʳ] *pt of* **wear**
work [wəːk] *n* lavoro; (*Art, Literature*) opera ▷ *vi* lavorare; (*mechanism, plan etc*) funzionare; (*medicine*) essere efficace ▷ *vt* (*clay, wood etc*) lavorare; (*mine etc*) sfruttare; (*machine*) far funzionare; (*cause: effect, miracle*) fare; **to be out of ~** essere disoccupato(-a); **~s** *n* (*BRIT: factory*) fabbrica *npl* (*of clock, machine*) meccanismo; **how does this ~?** come funziona?; **the TV isn't ~ing** la TV non funziona; **to ~ loose** allentarsi; **work out** *vi* (*plans etc*) riuscire, andare bene ▷ *vt* (*problem*) risolvere; (*plan*) elaborare; **it ~s out at £100** fa 100 sterline; **worker** *n* lavoratore(-trice), operaio(-a); **work experience** *n* (*previous jobs*) esperienze *fpl* lavorative; (*student training placement*) tirocinio; **workforce** *n* forza lavoro; **working class** *n* classe *f* operaia; **working week** *n* settimana lavorativa; **workman** (*irreg*) *n* operaio; **work of art** *n* opera d'arte; **workout** *n* (*Sport*) allenamento; **work permit** *n* permesso di lavoro; **workplace** *n* posto di lavoro; **workshop** *n* officina; (*practical session*) gruppo di lavoro; **work station** *n* stazione *f* di lavoro; **work surface** *n* piano di lavoro; **worktop** *n* piano di lavoro
world [wəːld] *n* mondo ▷ *cpd* (*champion*) del mondo; (*power, war*) mondiale; **to think the ~ of sb** (*fig*) pensare un gran bene di qn; **World Cup** *n* (*Football*) Coppa del Mondo; **world-wide** *adj* universale; **World-Wide Web** *n* World Wide Web *m*
worm [wəːm] *n* (*also: earth~*) verme *m*
worn [wɔːn] *pp of* **wear** ▷ *adj* usato(-a); **worn-out** *adj* (*object*) consumato(-a), logoro(-a); (*person*) sfinito(-a)
worried ['wʌrɪd] *adj* preoccupato(-a)
worry ['wʌrɪ] *n* preoccupazione *f* ▷ *vt* preoccupare ▷ *vi* preoccuparsi; **worrying** *adj* preoccupante
worse [wəːs] *adj* peggiore ▷ *adv, n* peggio; **a change for the ~** un peggioramento; **worsen** *vt, vi* peggiorare; **worse off** *adj* in condizioni (economiche) peggiori

worship ['wə:ʃɪp] n culto ▷ vt (God) adorare, venerare; (person) adorare; **Your W~** (BRIT: to mayor) signor sindaco; (: to judge) signor giudice

worst [wə:st] adj il (la) peggiore ▷ adv, n peggio; **at ~** al peggio, per male che vada

worth [wə:θ] n valore m ▷ adj **to be ~** valere; **it's ~ it** ne vale la pena; **it is ~ one's while (to do)** vale la pena (fare); **worthless** adj di nessun valore; **worthwhile** adj (activity) utile; (cause) lodevole

worthy ['wə:ðɪ] adj (person) degno(-a); (motive) lodevole; **~ of** degno di

 KEYWORD

would [wʊd] aux vb **1** (conditional tense): **if you asked him he would do it** se glielo chiedesse lo farebbe; **if you had asked him he would have done it** se glielo avesse chiesto lo avrebbe fatto
2 (in offers, invitations, requests): **would you like a biscuit?** vorrebbe or vuole un biscotto?; **would you ask him to come in?** lo faccia entrare, per cortesia; **would you open the window please?** apra la finestra, per favore
3 (in indirect speech): **I said I would do it** ho detto che l'avrei fatto
4 (emphatic): **it WOULD have to snow today!** doveva proprio nevicare oggi!
5 (insistence): **she wouldn't do it** non ha voluto farlo
6 (conjecture): **it would have been midnight** sarà stato mezzanotte; **it would seem so** sembrerebbe proprio di sì
7 (indicating habit): **he would go there on Mondays** andava lì ogni lunedì

wouldn't ['wʊdnt] = **would not**
wound¹ [waʊnd] pt, pp of **wind¹**
wound² [wu:nd] n ferita ▷ vt ferire
wove [wəʊv] pt of **weave**
woven ['wəʊvn] pp of **weave**
wrap [ræp] vt avvolgere; (pack: also: ~ up) incartare; **wrapper** n (on chocolate) carta; (BRIT: of book) copertina; **wrapping** ['ræpɪŋ] n carta; **wrapping paper** n carta da pacchi; (for gift) carta da regali
wreath [ri:θ, pl ri:ðz] n corona
wreck [rɛk] n (sea disaster) naufragio; (ship) relitto; (pej: person) rottame m ▷ vt demolire; (ship) far naufragare; (fig) rovinare; **wreckage** n rottami mpl; (of building) macerie fpl; (of ship) relitti mpl
wren [rɛn] n (Zool) scricciolo
wrench [rɛntʃ] n (Tech) chiave f; (tug) torsione f brusca; (fig) strazio ▷ vt

strappare; storcere; **to ~ sth from** strappare qc a or da
wrestle ['rɛsl] vi **to ~ (with sb)** lottare (con qn); **wrestler** n lottatore(-trice); **wrestling** n lotta
wretched ['rɛtʃɪd] adj disgraziato(-a); (inf: weather, holiday) orrendo(-a), orribile; (: child, dog) pestifero(-a)
wriggle ['rɪgl] vi (also: ~ about) dimenarsi; (: snake, worm) serpeggiare, muoversi serpeggiando
wring [rɪŋ] (pt, pp **wrung**) vt torcere; (wet clothes) strizzare; (fig) **to ~ sth out of** strappare qc a
wrinkle ['rɪŋkl] n (on skin) ruga; (on paper etc) grinza ▷ vt (nose) torcere; (forehead) corrugare ▷ vi (skin, paint) raggrinzirsi
wrist [rɪst] n polso
write [raɪt] (pt **wrote**, pp **written**) vt, vi scrivere; **write down** vt annotare; (put in writing) mettere per iscritto; **write off** vt (debt, plan) cancellare; **write out** vt mettere per iscritto; (cheque, receipt) scrivere; **write-off** n perdita completa; **writer** n autore(-trice), scrittore(-trice)
writing ['raɪtɪŋ] n scrittura; (of author) scritto, opera; **in ~** per iscritto; **writing paper** n carta da lettere
written ['rɪtn] pp of **write**
wrong [rɒŋ] adj sbagliato(-a); (not suitable) inadatto(-a); (wicked) cattivo(-a); (unfair) ingiusto(-a) ▷ adv in modo sbagliato, erroneamente ▷ n (injustice) torto ▷ vt fare torto a; **I took a ~ turning** ho sbagliato strada; **you are ~ to do it** ha torto a farlo; **you are ~ about that, you've got it ~** si sbaglia; **to be in the ~** avere torto; **what's ~?** cosa c'è che non va?; **to go ~** (person) sbagliarsi; (plan) fallire, non riuscire; (machine) guastarsi; **wrongly** adv (incorrectly, by mistake) in modo sbagliato; **wrong number** n (Tel): **you've got the wrong number** ha sbagliato numero
wrote [rəʊt] pt of **write**
wrung [rʌŋ] pt, pp of **wring**
WWW n abbr = **World Wide Web**; **the ~** la Rete

w

XL *abbr* = **extra large**

Xmas [ˈɛksməs] *n abbr* = **Christmas**

X-ray [ˈɛksreɪ] *n* raggio X; (*photograph*) radiografia ▷ *vt* radiografare

xylophone [ˈzaɪləfəun] *n* xilofono

yacht [jɔt] *n* panfilo, yacht *m inv*; **yachting** *n* yachting *m*, sport *m* della vela

yard [jɑːd] *n* (*of house etc*) cortile *m*; (*measure*) iarda (= *914 mm; 3 feet*); **yard sale** (US) *n* vendita di oggetti usati nel cortile di una casa privata

yarn [jɑːn] *n* filato; (*tale*) lunga storia

yawn [jɔːn] *n* sbadiglio ▷ *vi* sbadigliare

yd. *abbr* = **yard(s)**

yeah [jɛə] (*inf*) *adv* sì

year [jɪəʳ] *n* anno; (*referring to harvest, wine etc*) annata; **he is 8 ~s old** ha 8 anni; **an eight-~-old child** un(a) bambino(-a) di otto anni; **yearly** *adj* annuale ▷ *adv* annualmente

yearn [jəːn] *vi* **to ~ for sth/to do** desiderare ardentemente qc/di fare

yeast [jiːst] *n* lievito

yell [jɛl] *n* urlo ▷ *vi* urlare

yellow [ˈjɛləu] *adj* giallo(-a); **Yellow Pages®** *npl* pagine *fpl* gialle

yes [jɛs] *adv* sì ▷ *n* sì *m inv*; **to say/answer ~** dire/rispondere di sì

yesterday [ˈjɛstədɪ] *adv* ieri ▷ *n* ieri *m inv*; **~ morning/evening** ieri mattina/sera; **all day ~** ieri per tutta la giornata

yet [jɛt] *adv* ancora; già ▷ *conj* ma, tuttavia; **it is not finished ~** non è ancora finito; **the best ~** finora il

migliore; **as ~** finora
yew [ju:] *n* tasso (*albero*)
Yiddish ['jɪdɪʃ] *n* yiddish *m*
yield [ji:ld] *n* produzione *f*, resa; reddito
▷ *vt* produrre, rendere; (*surrender*)
cedere ▷ *vi* cedere; (US: *Aut*) dare la
precedenza
yob(bo) ['jɔb(əu)] *n* (BRIT *inf*) bullo
yoga ['jəugə] *n* yoga *m*
yog(h)urt ['jəugət] *n* iogurt *m inv*
yolk [jəuk] *n* tuorlo, rosso d'uovo

 KEYWORD

you [ju:] *pron* **1** (*subject*) tu; (: *polite form*) lei;
(: *pl*) voi; (: *very formal*) loro; **you Italians
enjoy your food** a voi Italiani piace
mangiare bene; **you and I will go** tu ed io
or lei ed io andiamo
2 (*object: direct*) ti; la; vi; loro (*after vb*); (:
indirect) ti; le; vi; loro (*after vb*); **I know you**
ti *or* la *or* vi conosco; **I gave it to you** te
l'ho dato; gliel'ho dato; ve l'ho dato; l'ho
dato loro
3 (*stressed, after prep, in comparisons*) te; lei;
voi; loro; **I told you to do it** ho detto a TE
(*or a* LEI *etc*) di farlo; **she's younger than
you** è più giovane di te (*or* lei *etc*)
4 (*impers: one*) si; **fresh air does you good**
l'aria fresca fa bene; **you never know** non
si sa mai

you'd [ju:d] = **you had**; **you would**
you'll [ju:l] = **you will**; **you shall**
young [jʌŋ] *adj* giovane ▷ *npl* (*of animal*)
piccoli *mpl*; (*people*): **the ~** i giovani, la
gioventù; **youngster** *n* giovanotto,
ragazzo; (*child*) bambino(-a)
your [jɔːʳ] *adj* il (la) tuo(-a) *pl*, i (le) tuoi
(tue); il (la) suo(-a); (*pl*) i (le) suoi (sue); il
(la) vostro(-a); (*pl*) i (le) vostri(-e); il (la)
loro; (*pl*) i (le) loro; *see also* **my**
you're [juəʳ] = **you are**
yours [jɔːz] *pron* il (la) tuo(-a); (*pl*) i (le)
tuoi (tue); (*polite form*) il (la) suo(-a); (*pl*)
i (le) suoi (sue); il (la) vostro(-a); (*pl*)
i (le) vostri(-e); (: *very formal*) il (la) loro;
(*pl*) i (le) loro; *see also* **mine**; **faithfully**;
sincerely
yourself [jɔːˈsɛlf] *pron* (*reflexive*) ti;
si; (*after prep*) te; sé; (*emphatic*) tu
stesso(-a); lei stesso(-a); **yourselves** *pl*
pron (*reflexive*) vi; si; (*after prep*) voi; loro;
(*emphatic*) voi stessi(-e); loro stessi(-e); *see
also* **oneself**
youth [ju:θ, *pl* ju:ðz] *n* gioventù *f*; (*young
man*) giovane *m*, ragazzo; **youth club** *n*
centro giovanile; **youthful** *adj* giovane;
da giovane; giovanile; **youth hostel** *n*

ostello della gioventù
you've [ju:v] = **you have**
Yugoslavia ['ju:gəuˈslɑːvɪə] *n* (*Hist*)
Jugoslavia

Z

zeal [ziːl] *n* zelo; entusiasmo
zebra [ˈziːbrə] *n* zebra; **zebra crossing**
  (BRIT) *n* (passaggio pedonale a) strisce *fpl*,
  zebre *fpl*
zero [ˈzɪərəu] *n* zero
zest [zɛst] *n* gusto; (*Culin*) buccia
zigzag [ˈzɪgzæg] *n* zigzag *m inv* ▷ *vi*
  zigzagare
Zimbabwe [zɪmˈbɑːbwɪ] *n* Zimbabwe *m*
zinc [zɪŋk] *n* zinco
zip [zɪp] *n* (*also:* ~ **fastener**, (US) **zipper**)
  chiusura *f or* cerniera *f* lampo *inv* ▷ *vt* (*also:*
  ~ **up**) chiudere con una cerniera lampo;
   zip code (US) *n* codice *m* di avviamento
  postale; **zipper** (US) *n* cerniera *f* lampo *inv*
zit [zɪt] *n* brufolo
zodiac [ˈzəudɪæk] *n* zodiaco
zone [zəun] *n* (*also Mil*) zona
zoo [zuː] *n* zoo *m inv*
zoology [zuːˈɔlədʒɪ] *n* zoologia
zoom [zuːm] *vi* **to ~ past** sfrecciare; **zoom
  lens** *n* zoom *m inv*, obiettivo a focale
  variabile
zucchini [zuːˈkiːnɪ] (US) *npl* (*courgettes*)
  zucchine *fpl*